A Canadian Indian Bibliography 1960–1970

THOMAS S. ABLER, SALLY M. WEAVER

with CLAIRE C. VEILLETTE
IRIS V. YUZDEPSKI

and William R. Courtade, Danielle Desmarais,
Aaron D. Gresson, John S. Long,
H. Claudine VanEvery, Dennis G. Willms

with the assistance of Lydia Forbes, S. Lynne Primrose,
Mary E. Schmieder, David Burkett

including

CASE LAW DIGEST prepared by
DOUGLAS E. SANDERS
with Paul C. Taylor

A Canadian Indian Bibliography 1960–1970

University of Toronto Press

© 1974 University of Toronto Press
Toronto and Buffalo
ISBN 0-8020-2092-5
Printed in Canada

INTRODUCTION TO THE BIBLIOGRAPHY

This annotated bibliography lists material of scholarly interest published between 1960 and 1970 on the Canadian Indian and Metis. The Case Law Digest that is part of it, however, covers the period 1867-1972. Although no bibliography can claim to be absolutely comprehensive, we have attempted to include a maximum number of sources, and the work, having been prepared by anthropologists and lawyers, is fairly multi-disciplinary in its scope. Because of time limitations, the survey of Indian-Metis literature has been limited to cultural material, to the exclusion of works on physical anthropology, bio-medical reports, and archeological and linguistic studies. Both French- and English-language materials have been consulted, although all abstracts are in English. Material published bilingually has been so indicated.

The bibliography covers Indian cultures within the political boundaries of Canada. With respect to such tribes as the Blackfoot, Ojibwa, and Iroquois which live on both sides of the Canadian-American border, only materials relating to the Canadian communities have been included. The reader is cautioned that there is much literature on the American components of these tribes which is not cited here, and for guidance to this literature he should consult the bibliographies listed in the first section of this work. Eskimo materials have been entered only if they form an integral part of a discussion of or comparison with Indian cultures. For references to Eskimos, as well as Sub-Arctic Indians, the reader should consult the *Arctic Bibliography*.

Two maps have been provided in the bibliography. The culture area and tribal map is a composite of those in G.P. Murdock's *An Ethnographic Bibliography of North America* (1963) and W. Duff's *The Indian History of British Columbia* (1964). The linguistic map is taken from *Canada Showing Location of Indian Bands with Linguistic Affiliations* (1965) published by the Indian Affairs Branch of the Department of Citizenship and Immigration. For the location of specific reserves the reader is referred to the *Atlas of Indian Reserves and Settlements in Canada* (1971) published by the Department of Indian Affairs and Northern Development.

The types of material searched included books and monographs, journals, theses, unpublished papers and reports, publications by Indians (indicated in the index by "author-Indian" when known), and federal and provincial government documents. Newspapers and popular magazines were omitted. Indian publications, particularly local serials and newspapers, were extremely difficult to obtain. The reader is advised to contact the office of the National Indian Brotherhood in Ottawa for a full listing.

Unpublished material was included only if a copy could be obtained by our research team to read and abstract. The availability of such writing is indicated following the bibliographic entry: if the entry reads "available at," the material must be obtained in person by the researcher at that institution; if the entry reads "available from," correspondence with that institution and payment for duplicating costs will allow the reader to obtain a copy of the work.

Unpublished material collected by the Canadian Indian Bibliography Project have been deposited according to the author's preference either in the manuscript division of the Bibliothèque nationale du Québec, Montréal, or in the reference branch of the National Library of Canada, Ottawa.

In addition to normal bibliographic searching, graduate departments known to have produced, or thought likely to have produced, theses that fell within the scope of this book were requested to forward the proper bibliographic information. Unless otherwise indicated, a thesis is available from the university which granted the degree. Theses which we were unable to obtain because of time limitations have been listed in the bibliography without annotation.

Federal government statutes, bills, committee reports, and the published and unpublished materials of the Department of Indian Affairs and Northern Development received the greatest attention. Certain federal departmental libraries, however, known to contain relevant materials, were not searched: National Health and Welfare, Regional Economic Expansion, Secretary of State, Manpower and Immigration, and Labour. Provincial government documents received less coverage than federal documents, these governments having traditionally less jurisdiction over the Indian. The most recently revised statutes of each province, however, if produced between 1960 and 1970, and acts passed during the same decade subsequent to this compilation have been searched and abstracted.

THOMAS S. ABLER
SALLY M. WEAVER
University of Waterloo

INTRODUCTION TO THE CASE LAW DIGEST (pp. 306–62)

This digest represents an attempt to bring together all case law relating to Indian legal questions decided since 1 July 1867.

For the purpose of consistency of terminology, the term "Indian" is always employed to mean an Indian as defined by the Indian Act. Terms such as "Treaty

Indian" and "Unenfranchised Indian," common particularly in the early cases, are not employed. All criminal cases are described as "R v ...." "R" stands for Rex or Regina, the Crown which is prosecuting the individual. In the law reports the description may be reversed: " ...... v R." In the law reports terms such as Rex, Regina, The King, or Attorney General may be employed instead of "R." When the index refers to sections of the Indian Act, they are always references to the numbers as found in the 1970 Revised Statutes of Canada.

The reported cases in this digest are drawn from a wide range of law reports. The citations are the standard ones employed for Canadian law reports. The major reports drawn upon are the following: Appeal Cases (A.C.), British Columbia Reports (B.C.R.), Dominion Law Reports (D.L.R.), Exchequer Court Reports (Ex. C.R.), Federal Court Reports (F.C.), Ontario Reports (O.R.), Ontario Law Reports (O.L.R.), Supreme Court Reports (S.C.R.), Western Weekly Reports (W.W.R.), Canadian Criminal Cases (C.C.C.), and Criminal Reports (C.R.). The bulk of the cases digested in this work will be available at any law library in Canada.

Since completing the case law bibliography in the spring of 1972, certain additional (and unindexed herein) cases have come to my attention:

Ontario Provincial Court (Nipissing), Judge Kenrick.
1969, R. v. Potts, unreported. FACTS: Potts, an Indian, was charged with possession of a gill net, taking trout in closed season, and taking fish other than by angling, all contrary to the Game and Fisheries Act of Ontario. HELD: There was no exemption for treaty Indians from the provincial legislation. Potts was convicted and minimum penalties imposed.

Ontario District Court (Parry Sound), Judge Little.
1971, R. v. Pawis (1972) 2 O.R. 516. FACTS: Pawis, an Indian, was charged under the Liquor Control Act of Ontario with possession of liquor. Pawis had the liquor on a reserve. HELD: Because the Indian Act liquor sections apply on this reserve, Provincial liquor laws cannot apply.

Saskatchewan District Court, Judge Bendas.
1972, R. v. Pritchard, unreported. FACTS: Pritchard testified that he was not registered as an Indian persuant to the Indian Act but was entitled to be so registered. HELD: The Indian Act, section 2, states that the term Indian includes a person entitled to be registered as an Indian. Therefore Pritchard was an Indian and had the benefits of the Natural Resources Transfer Agreement. Provincial laws could not be applied to prevent him from hunting for food.

Manitoba Court of Appeal, Judge Dickson.
1972, Canard v. Attorney General of Canada, unreported. FACTS: Different

administrators for the estate of Alexander Canard, a deceased Indian, were appointed under the Indian Act and under the laws of the province of Manitoba. HELD: The Indian Act sections on estates denied the Widow the right to administer the estate of her deceased husband and therefore denied her equality before the law. The sections of the Indian Act are inoperative because discrimination on the basis of race and therefore contrary to the Bill of Rights. (This case has been appealed to the Supreme Court of Canada.)

Ontario County Court (Brant), Judge Fanjoy.
1972, In re David Froman, unreported. FACTS: The registration of an illegitimate child of a status Indian woman was challenged persuant to section 12(2) of the Indian Act. It was argued that section 12(2) was inoperative because offensive to the Bill of Rights on the basis that the illegitimate child of a male Indian cannot be so challenged. HELD: Section 11(1)(c) of the Indian Act does not permit the registration of illegitimate children of male Indians. The different treatment of illegitimate children, depending upon the sex of the Indian parent, reflects biological differences between men and women and does not offend the Bill of Rights. (This case is being appealed.)

Manitoba Court of Appeal, Judge Monnin.
1966, R. v. Roulette, unreported. FACTS: This case is identical to R. v. Francis (Supreme Court of Canada, appealed from Manitoba Court of Appeal). HELD: For this case, one of seven similar cases, a conviction was upheld for the reasons expressed in the Manitoba Court of Appeal judgment in R. v. Daniels.

I would like to express thanks to the lawyers who have supplied me with copies of unreported judgments. I would like also to thank the Faculty of Law of the University of Windsor for their encouragement during the preparation of this digest. The vagueness and complexity of Indian Law has been a buttress for paternalism in Canada. The goal of this project has been to make Indian law accessible in the hope that it could be clarified and developed into a consistent and rational body of law.

DOUGLAS SANDERS
Native Law Centre
Carleton University
Ottawa

ACKNOWLEDGMENTS

We wish to thank the following institutions for financially supporting the Canadian Indian Bibliography Project: the Canada Council; the Government of Ontario, Provincial Secretary and Citizenship Department and the Department of Social and Family Services; University of Waterloo; and the Department of Indian Affairs and Northern Development.

In addition we wish to extend our gratitude to the following individuals and institutions who have assisted our research team throughout the duration of the project:

Mr. Donat Savoie, Northern Science Research Group, DIAND

Mr. Russell Moses, Special Assistant to the Minister, DIAND

National Indian Brotherhood, Mrs. M. Deacey

National Library of Canada, Miss H. Rogers, Mrs. W.E. Strong, Mrs. A. Pendlebury, Mrs. H.L. Piedra, Mr. L.F. MacRae, Dr. I. Wees, Mrs. F. Rose, J. Quellette, J. Chandonnet, B. Witham, C. Turnbull, Y. Ranger, D. Monroe, C. Ashley, M. Moore, A. Schwartz

University of Victoria, Dr. Robert Lane

Vancouver City College, George A. Mintz

McMaster University, Dr. Richard Preston

Canadian Research Centre for Anthropology, St. Paul University, Ottawa, Mr. J. Lotz

Carleton University, Mrs. G. Roxburgh, Miss D. Honeywell

Department of Citizenship and Immigration, Miss M. Clowes

National Museum of Man, Dr. Gordon Day, Miss A. Dawe, Mrs. A. Knight, Mrs. K. Kelland

Indian-Eskimo Association of Canada, Toronto Office, Ms. S. Cheda

Library, University of Waterloo, Miss J. Boettger, Miss M. Carter, Miss D. Wilkins, Mrs. M. Banks

Philip E. Smith, Computing Consultant, Arts Faculty, University of Waterloo

Computing Centre, University of Waterloo, Roger Watt, Allison Smith

Department of Regional Economic Expansion, Miss V. Cooper, Dr. K.B. Cooke, Dr. D. Whiteside

Department of Indian Affairs and Northern Development

Mr. W.A. Gryba, Mr. L.J. Nevin, Mr. A.J. Kerr, Miss E. Whetung, Mr. P. Bakker, Mr. A. Petch, Mr. W. Sendlove, Mrs. C. Walker, Miss N. Smith, Mrs. F.C. Pace, Mrs. J. Darby, Mrs. R. Thompson, Mr. G. Healey, Mr. M. Nolet, Mrs. M.R. Watson, Mr. E. Gamble, Mr. G. Parsons, Mr. P. Usher, Miss E.F. Noel, Miss R. Quinlan, Miss M.H. Lovelock, Mr. J.P.R. Boyer, Mr. G. Higgins

Centre d'Etudes Nordiques, Université Laval, Louis-Edmond Hamelin, Jacqueline Bouchard

Bibliothèque nationale du Québec, Roland Auger, Georges Cartier
Gouvernement du Québec, Ministère des Affaires Culturelles, Camil Guy
Département d'Anthropologie, Université Laval, Michel Audet, Paul Charest
Département d'Anthropologie, Université de Montréal, Frank Auger
Laboratoire d'Anthropologie Amérindienne, Montréal, Remi Savard, Sylvie Vincent
Government of Saskatchewan, Department of Welfare, Mrs. F. Driedger
Manitoba Indian Brotherhood, Miss D. Body
University of British Columbia
Victoria Provincial Museum
Victoria Public Archives
University of Alberta
Alberta Provincial Museum and Archives Library
Boreal Institute, University of Alberta
University of Saskatchewan (Saskatoon and Regina)
Edmonton Public Library
University of Manitoba
University of Winnipeg
Centre for Settlement Studies, University of Manitoba
University of Toronto
Royal Ontario Museum
University of New Brunswick
Indian and Northern Curriculum Resources Centre, University of Saskatchewan, Saskatoon
University of Prince Edward Island
Ontario Institute for Studies in Education
Toronto Central Library
Dalhousie University
Memorial University
Institute of Social and Economic Research, Memorial University of Newfoundland
University of Victoria Library
Government of Manitoba, Department of Health and Social Development
Frank E. Price and Associates, Winnipeg

We hope no one has been omitted from this list – there were so many people across the country consulted by the sixteen of us that it is possible; if so, we apologize.

This bibliography is the product also of much labour from each of the sixteen people named on the title page. We worked as a team and must collectively receive credit or blame for the merits and faults of this compilation.

T.S.A. & S.M.W.

CONTENTS

Maps

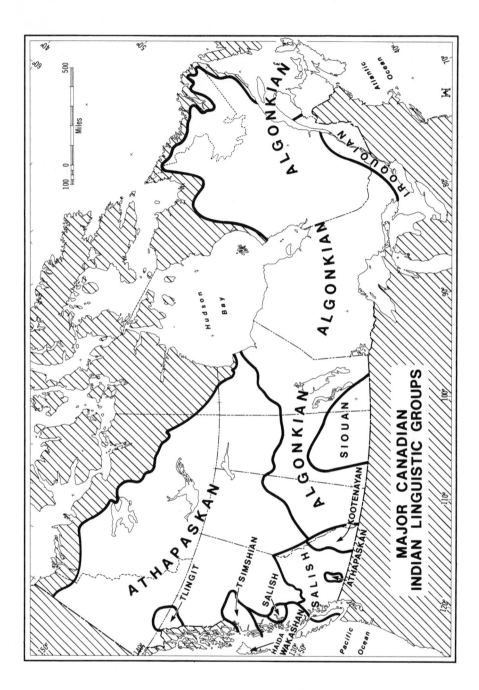

MAJOR CANADIAN
INDIAN LINGUISTIC GROUPS

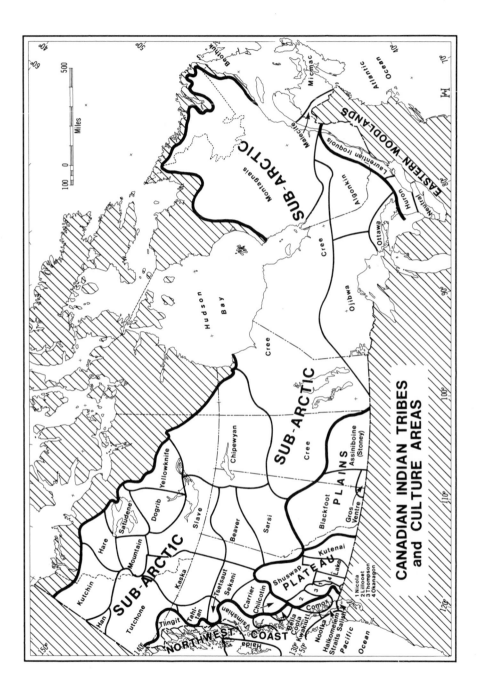

CANADIAN INDIAN TRIBES
and CULTURE AREAS

A Canadian Indian Bibliography 1960–1970

BIBLIOGRAPHIES

1   **1967-**
BIBLIOGRAPHIE: SECTION 1: LES CIVILISATIONS AMERINDIENNES ET LES
PREMIERES DECOUVERTES. Revue d'Histoire de l'Amerique Francaise 21-.
Quarterly.   SLP

2   **1969**
CHIPPEWA AND DAKOTA INDIANS: A SUBJECT CATALOG OF BOOKS,
PAMPHLETS, PERIODICAL ARTICLES, AND MANUSCRIPTS IN THE
MINNESOTA HISTORICAL SOCIETY. St. Paul: Minnesota Historical Society.
Unpaged.   SLP

3   **ARCTIC INSTITUTE OF NORTH AMERICA. Library.**
1968
CATALOGUE OF THE LIBRARY OF THE ARCTIC INSTITUTE OF NORTH
AMERICA. Boston: Hall. 4 vols.

The "First Supplement"was published in 1971.   SLP

4   **BRITISH COLUMBIA. Provincial Museum. Department of Recreation and
Conservation.**
1970
A SELECTED LIST OF PUBLICATIONS ON THE INDIANS OF BRITISH
COLUMBIA. Revised Edition. British Columbia: Queen's Printer. 31 pp.

Previous editions were published in 1961 and 1963.   IVY

5   **CANADA. Department of Indian Affairs and Northern Development.**
1970
FILMS ON THE INDIAN PEOPLE OF CANADA. Ottawa: Information Canada. 15
pp.   Also in French.

A catalog of 42 films of Indians gives a short description of each film.   JSL

6   **CHEDA   SHERRILL**
1970
BIBLIOGRAPHY: INDIANS AND EDUCATION. Unpublished paper. Available
from Indian-Eskimo Association. 4 pp.   SLP

7   **CHEDA   SHERRILL**
1970
THE FIRST AMERICANS: A READING GUIDE. Ontario Library Review 54:2 23-
229.   SLP

8   **COOKE   ALAN,   FABIEN   CARON,   comps.**
1968
BIBLIOGRAPHY OF THE QUEBEC-LABRADOR PENINSULA. Boston: Hall. 2
vols.   SLP

9   **DALHOUSIE UNIVERSITY. Library.**
1970
CANADIAN INDIANS: REPRESENTATIVE SOURCES. Dalhousie University
Library Bibliographies. Halifax: n.p. 27 pp.   SLP

10   **DARTMOUTH COLLEGE. Library.**
1967
DICTIONARY CATALOGUE OF THE STEFANSSON COLLECTION ON THE
POLAR REGIONS IN THE DARTMOUTH COLLEGE LIBRARY. Boston: Hall. 8
vols.   SLP

11   **EWERS   JOHN C**
1960
SELECTED REFERENCES ON THE PLAINS INDIANS. Smithsonian
Anthropological Bibliographies 1. Washington: Smithsonian Institution.   36 pp.   SLP

12   **FREEMAN   JOHN F, comp., SMITH MURPHY D, ed.**
1966
A GUIDE TO MANUSCRIPTS RELATING TO THE AMERICAN INDIAN IN THE
LIBRARY OF THE AMERICAN PHILOSOPHICAL SOCIETY. American
Philosophical Society Memoir 65. Philadelphia: American Philosophical Society. 491
pp.   TSA

13   **GREEN   VICKI**
1970
ANNOTATED BIBLIOGRAPHY ON INDIAN EDUCATION. Vancouver: Indian
Education Resources Center, University of British Columbia. 36 pp.   CCV

14   **GUTHE   ALFRED K, KELLY   PATRICIA B**
1963
AN ANTHROPOLOGICAL BIBLIOGRAPHY OF THE EASTERN SEABORD,
VOLUME II. Eastern States Archaeological Federation Research Publication No. 2.
Trenton, NJ: Eastern States Archaeological Federation. 82 pp.

The 1st volume was published in 1947.   SLP

15   **HARVARD UNIVERSITY. Peabody Museum. Library.**
1963
CATALOGUE OF THE LIBRARY OF THE PEABODY MUSEUM OF
ARCHAEOLOGY AND ETHNOLOGY: AUTHORS. Boston: Hall. 26 vols.

The "First Supplement"(6 volumes) and "Second Supplement"(2 volumes) were published in 1970 and 1971 respectively.   SLP

16   **HARVARD UNIVERSITY. Peabody Museum. Library.**
1963
CATALOGUE OF THE LIBRARY OF THE PEABODY MUSEUM OF
ARCHAEOLOGY AND ETHNOLOGY: SUBJECTS. Boston: Hall. 27 vols.

The "First Supplement' (6 volumes) and the "Second Supplement"(3 volumes) were published in 1970 and 1971 respectively.   SLP

17   **HAYWOOD   CHARLES**
1961
A BIBLIOGRAPHY OF NORTH AMERICAN FOLKLORE AND FOLKSONG.
VOLUME II: THE AMERICAN INDIANS NORTH OF MEXICO, INCLUDING
THE ESKIMOS. 2nd Revised Edition. New York: Dover. Volume 2 of 2 vols.   CCV

18   **HONIGMANN   JOHN J, HELM   JUNE**
1968
ETHNOGRAPHIC BIBLIOGRAPHY OF NORTHERN NORTH AMERICA AND
GREENLAND. WITH ADDENDA (1969) PREPARED BY JUNE HELM.
Unpublished paper. Available from National Library of Canada. 23 pp.   SLP

19   **INDIAN-ESKIMO ASSOCIATION OF CANADA**
1968-
PUBLICATIONS LIST. Toronto: Indian-Eskimo Association. Irregular.   SLP

20   **JONES   MARY JANE**
1969
MACKENZIE DELTA BIBLIOGRAPHY. Mackenzie Delta Research Project 6.
Ottawa: Queen's Printer. 119 pp.   CCV

21   **KEEPER   CYRIL**
1969
A SURVEY OF COMMISSIONS OF INQUIRY AND INVESTIGATION
RELATING TO LAND CLAIMS OF PEOPLE OF NATIVE ANCESTRY IN
CANADA. Unpublished paper. Available from Library, Department of the Secretary of
State, Ottawa. 18 pp.   MES

22   **KIDD   KENNETH E, ROGERS   EDWARD S**
1964
BRIEF BIBLIOGRAPHY OF ONTARIO ANTHROPOLOGY. Royal Ontario
Museum Art and Archaeology Occasional Paper 7. Toronto: Royal Ontario Museum;
University of Toronto. 20 pp.   SLP

23   **KNAUSS   PIERRE**
1966
MIKMAK TRIBAL BIBLIOGRAPHY. Terra Ameriga 2(2):24-26.   IVY

24   **LOWTHER   BARBARA J**
1968
A BIBLIOGRAPHY OF BRITISH COLUMBIA: LAYING THE FOUNDATIONS
1849-1899. Victoria, B.C.: University of Victoria. 328 pp.   SLP

25   **MALYCKY   ALEXANDER**
1970
UNIVERSITY RESEARCH ON CANADA'S INDIANS AND METIS: A
PRELIMINARY CHECK LIST. Canadian Ethnic Studies/Etudes Ethniques du
Canada 2(1):95-107.   IVY

26   **MCDIARMID   G L, ed.**
1967
CULTURE CONTACT, WITH SPECIAL REFERENCE TO THE INDIANS OF
NORTH AMERICA: AN ANNOTATED BIBLIOGRAPHY. Collected by Larry J.
Orton. Toronto: Ontario Institute for Studies in Education. 24 pp.   SLP

27   **MCILWRAITH   T F**
1956-1967
BIBLIOGRAPHY OF CANADIAN ANTHROPOLOGY. In National Museum Of
Canada Bulletins 142, 147, 162, 167, 173, 190, 194, 204. Ottawa: Queen's Printer.
Irregular.

In Bulletin 162, the title is "Bibliography of Anthropological Literature."   SLP

28   **MURDOCK   GEORGE PETER**
1960
ETHNOGRAPHIC BIBLIOGRAPHY OF NORTH AMERICA. 3rd Edition. New
Haven, CT: Human Relations Area Files. 393 pp.   SLP

29   **NEWBERRY LIBRARY**
1961
DICTIONARY CATALOG OF THE EDWARD E. AYER COLLECTION OF
AMERICANA AND THE AMERICAN INDIANS. Boston: Hall. 16 vols.   SLP

30   **OGLE   ROBERT W,   MALYCKY   ALEXANDER**
1970
PERIODICAL PUBLICATIONS OF CANADA'S INDIANS AND METIS: A
PRELIMINARY CHECK LIST. Canadian Ethnic Studies/Etudes Ethniques du
Canada 2(1):109-115.   IVY

31   **ONTARIO. Department of Education.**
1969
MULTI-MEDIA RESOURCE LIST ESKIMOS AND INDIANS. Toronto:
Department of Education. 50 pp.   IVY

32   **ONTARIO. Department of Education.**
1970
MULTI-MEDIA RESOURCE LIST ESKIMOS AND INDIANS: 1970
SUPPLEMENT. Toronto: Department of Education. 16 pp.   IVY

33   **PRESTON   R J,   GEHRET   K L**
1970

BOREAL FOREST ALGONKIAN ETHNOGRAPHIC BIBLIOGRAPHY.
Unpublished paper. Available from National Museum of Man, Ethnology Division,
Ottawa. 103 pp.   SLP

34   **RENAUD   ANDRE, ed.**
1967
ONE HUNDRED BOOKS FOR INDIAN SCHOOL TEACHERS. Ottawa: Oblate
Fathers Indian and Eskimo Welfare Commission. 105 pp.   IVY

35   **SANDERS   DOUGLAS**
1969
BIBLIOGRAPHY OF LANDS AND TREATIES. Unpublished paper. Available from
Library, University of Waterloo. 11 pp.   SLP

36   **SELBY   SUZANNE R**
1968
(BIBLIOGRAPHY). The Musk-Ox 4:1-103.   IVY

37   **SPENCER   LORAINE,   HOLLAND   SUSAN**
1968
NORTHERN ONTARIO: A BIBLIOGRAPHY. Toronto: University of Toronto Press.
121 pp.   SLP

38   **TREMBLAY   MARC ADELARD**
1970
BIBLIOGRAPHIE SUR L'ADMINISTRATION DES INDIENS DU CANADA ET
DES ETATS-UNIS. Unpublished paper. Available from Bibliotheque Nationale du
Quebec. 77 pp.   DD

39   **ULLOM   JUDITH C**
1969
FOLKLORE OF THE NORTH AMERICAN INDIANS: AN ANNOTATED
BIBLIOGRAPHY. Washington: Library of Congress. 126 pp.   SLP

40   **UNIVERSITY OF MANITOBA. Center for Settlement Studies.**
1969-1970
BIBLIOGRAPHY - RESOURCE FRONTIER COMMUNITIES. Series 3:
Bibliography and Information Nos. 1-3. Winnipeg: Center for Settlement Studies,
University of Manitoba. 3 vols.   SLP

41   **UNIVERSITY OF SASKATCHEWAN. Indian and Northern Curriculum
Resources Centre.**
1970
TEACHER'S GUIDE TO RESOURCE MATERIALS IN CROSS-CULTURAL
EDUCATION: PART ONE: INDIANS, ESKIMOS AND EARLY EXPLORERS.
Saskatoon: Indian and Northern Curriculum Resources Centre, University of
Saskatchewan. Various paging.   SLP

42   **WARDWELL   ALLEN,   LEBOV   LOIS**
1970
ANNOTATED BIBLIOGRAPHY OF NORTHWEST COAST INDIAN ART.
Primitive Art Bibliographies No. 8. New York: Library, Museum of Primitive Art. 25
pp.   SLP

43   **WEINMAN   PAUL L**
1969
A BIBLIOGRAPHY OF THE IROQUOIAN LITERATURE. New York State Museum
and Science Service Bulletin 411. Albany, NY: University of the State of New York. 254
pp.   IVY

GENERAL AND COMPARATIVE STUDIES

44   **n.d.**
COMMUNITY DEVELOPMENT - THE PAS. Unpublished paper. Available from
Library, Department of Health and Social Development, Winnipeg, Man. 9 pp.

A summary of the activities of Community Development in The Pas, Manitoba, is
given.   IVY

45   **n.d.**
COMMUNITY DEVELOPMENT AS A WAY OF LIFE. Unpublished paper.
Available from Library, Department of Health and Social Development, Winnipeg,
Man. 5 pp.

Community development in Manitoba is considered under 5 aspects - as a philosophy, as
a program, as a process, as a method, and as a movement.   IVY

46   **n.d.**
DEPARTMENT OF MANPOWER AND IMMIGRATION. Unpublished paper.
Available from Indian-Eskimo Association. 4 pp.

Programs and services of the Department of Manpower and Immigration are described.   IVY

47   **n.d.**
INDIAN AND ESKIMO CHILDREN: CANADIAN CONFERENCE ON
CHILDREN. Unpublished paper. Available from Department of Health Services and
Hospital Insurance, Health Branch, Educational Services, Victoria. 8 pp.

A general statement on Indian children (4 pages) and a 2 page report of the 1959 British
Columbia Federal-Provincial Committee on Indians is included in this report.   IVY

48   **1961**
THE PEOPLE OF INDIAN ANCESTRY IN MANITOBA. Unpublished paper
delivered to Short Course for Rural Municipalities, June, 1969. Available from Library,
Department of Health and Social Development, Winnipeg, Man. 9 pp.

Addressed to officials of rural municipalities, this report discusses the definition and
status of Indians and Metis, population and distribution of people of Indian descent in

Manitoba, and the problems of fringe communities. The Community Development program is described.   IVY

49   **1964**

LEADERSHIP DEVELOPMENT AMONG INDIANS. Citizen 10(3):23-27.

Several Indian projects involving government and Indian sponsorship are described for the Blood of Alberta and the Ojibwa of Ontario.   ADG

50   **1964**

SPECIAL HELP TO NORTHERN NATIVES: ALBERTA'S NEW COMMUNITY DEVELOPMENT BRANCH DEVISES AN IMAGINATIVE APPROACH TOWARD HELPING INDIANS AND METIS IMPROVE THEIR SKILLS. INCOME. Western Business and Industry 38(November):54-55.

Alberta's community development program is briefly described.   IVY

51   **1965**

CITIZENSHIP PROJECTS: INDIAN STUDY PROGRAM - B.C. COUNCIL OF WOMEN. Citizen 11(3):27-29.

With the assistance of the University of British Columbia Extension Department, the British Columbia Council of Women designed a project to introduce non-Indians to the history, culture, and development of British Columbia Indians. The project's origin, development, and impact are discussed.   ADG

52   **1965**

INDIAN STUDY PROGRAM - B.C. COUNCIL OF WOMEN. Citizen 11(3):27-29.

In 1961, the B.C. Council of Women launched, with the assistance of the University of British Columbia Extension Department, an Indian study program. This 3-year study is briefly discussed.   IVY

53   **1966**

ALCOHOL AND THE NORTH AMERICAN INDIAN: IMPLICATIONS FOR THE MANAGEMENT OF PROBLEMS. Unpublished paper prepared for North American Association of Alcoholism Programs. Albuquerque, NM, 1966. Available from Alcoholism and Drug Addiction Research Foundation, Toronto. 11 pp.

Both the underlying motivation and patterns of consumption contribute to the existence of alcohol as a major problem for the Indian. This problem, moreover, does not seem amenable to current theories of alcoholism and its treatment. The solution is to educate the Indian to use alcohol moderately.   ADG

54   **1967**

CANADIAN INDIAN WORKSHOP 1966. Citizen 13(1):27-29.

Discussed are the origin, program, and evaluation of the first Canadian Indian workshop held at the University of Manitoba, July 12-August 12, 1966.   IVY

55   **1967**

ROUND TABLE CONFERENCE OF JOB OPPORTUNITIES & VOCATIONAL TRAINING. Proposed Alberta Native Federation and Alberta Committee, Indian-Eskimo Association of Canada. Edmonton, May 5-6, 1967. Available from Indian-Eskimo Association, 47 pp.

Various aspects of the Manpower training program and its services are discussed. An effective liaison should be obtained between the Indians and the specialists who have access to jobs. Counseling services in placement centers should be improved. There should be a clear-cut jurisdiction between federal and provincial governments with regard to Indian people. Also discussed are: the Indian stereotype, job discrimination, relocation, vocational education and training, financial assistance, housing, and recreation. Appendix C (pages 31-36) is an address by Mr. Roy Piepenburg, Superintendent of Schools, Indian Affairs.   IVY

56   **1968**

THE CANADIAN INDIAN IN ONTARIO SCHOOL TEXTS: A STUDY OF SOCIAL STUDIES TEXTBOOKS GRADES 1 THROUGH 8. Unpublished paper prepared for University Women's Club of Port Credit. Available from Indian-Eskimo Association. 41 pp.

Using 3 guides, the original culture of the Canadian Indian, the history of culture contact between Indians and non-Indians, and the situation of the Canadian Indian today, this report examines social studies texts used in Ontario schools for content and accuracy of material presented on the Canadian Indian.   HCV

57   **1969**

PUBLIC LIBRARY SERVICES FOR CANADIAN INDIANS. American Library Associations. A.L.A. Bulletin 63:1243-1244.

The experiences of librarians serving Canadian reserve Indians are described in the context of federal-provincial library services to the Indian. Past failure of librarians to adequately assess and meet Indian reading needs and interests has been corrected. Some of the parallels between serving Canadian Indians and American ghetto dwellers are noted.   ADG

58   **1970**

CHRISTMAS AMONG THE INDIANS: EXTRACTS FROM PIONEER MISSIONARY JOURNALS. The United Church Observer N.S. 33(6):12-14,37.

Presented are extracts from the journals of Robert Brocking, Oxford House, Manitoba, 1856; James Evans, Cumberland House, Saskatchewan, 1840; C. M. Tate, Bella Bella, British Columbia, 1882; Alfred E. Green, Nass River, British Columbia, 1881; and Thomas Crosby, Port Simpson, British Columbia, 1874.   IVY

59   **1970**

EARLY CANADIAN INDIAN WRITING SYSTEMS. Tawow 1(2):26-33.

Early attempts in writing Indian languages are illustrated.   IVY

60   **1970**
FIRST ALL CANADA INDIAN CULTURAL CONFERENCE. Tawow 1(2):10-15.

A report is given on the Indian Cultural Conference attended by 30 delegates from across Canada. Discussed are programs to ensure cultural retention and development including the importance of maintaining Indian languages.   IVY

61   **1970**
INDIANS, ESKIMOS AND LABOUR. Canadian Labour 15(2):16-17,36.

The need for positive programs by the federal government to assist Canada's native people follows a brief history of Indians and Eskimos in Canada.   IVY

62   **1970**
THE SILENT MINORITY: CANADA'S INDIANS - AND WHAT THE UNIONS ARE DOING TO HELP THEM BUILD A BETTER FUTURE. Free Labour World 1970(June):18-20.

The Canadian Labour Congress set up its own action programs emphasizing the training of native leaders. One such program was initiated in the Kenora, Ontario, district.   IVY

63   **ADAMS   IAN**
1970
THE POVERTY WALL. Toronto: McClelland and Stewart. 154 pp.

Manifestations of poverty and factors contributing to it in Canada are examined. Chapter 2 is devoted to the story of Charlie Wenjack, the 12 year old Ojibwa boy who died of exposure in 1966 while trying to walk 400 miles from the residential school in Kenora to his home on a northern Ontario reserve. Details of the inquest into his death and the recommendations pertaining to Indian education made by the jury are reported. In the discussion (chapter 7) of legislation serving to maintain the status quo, 2 pages are devoted to the topic of Indian administration.   CCV

64   **ADAMSON   EDITH**
1969
PUBLIC LIBRARY SERVICE TO THE INDIANS OF CANADA. Canadian Library 26:48-53.

The growth and development of library services to Indian bands is outlined. Libraries now operating on reserves are described.   IVY

65   **ALBERTA NATIVE COMMUNICATIONS SOCIETY**
1970
EXECUTIVE DIRECTOR'S REPORT: STATEMENT OF PROGRESS. Unpublished paper. Available from National Library of Canada. 10 pp.

This is a brief report on the structure of the Alberta Native Communications Society with a description of operations which include radio programs both in the native and English languages, audio and video-taped programs, and the Society's monthly newspaper.   HCV

66   **ALBERTA NATIVE WOMEN'S SOCIETY**
1968
REPORT OF THE FIRST ALBERTA NATIVE WOMEN'S CONFERENCE:
THEME: PAST, PRESENT AND FUTURE. Edmonton, March 12-15, 1968. Available
from Indian-Eskimo Association. 52 pp.

Concerns and mutual interests of the Alberta Native Women's Society are expressed at
their first conference. Comments, discussion, and recommendations are made on the subjects of education, employment, welfare, housing, alcohol, loans, community organization and development, native people in the city, legal rights, health, youth and recreation, the Alberta Metis, self-government, federal and provincial governments, women's
rights, and the proposed women's conference in 1969. Of special concern was the Department of National Health and Welfare's intention to curtail health services to Treaty
Indians starting May 1, 1968. Communications from Premier Manning concerning the
health issue are included in the appendices.   DGW

67   **ALBERTA. Department of Culture, Youth and Recreation.**
n.d.
PROGRAMS AND SERVICES AVAILABLE FOR INDIANS AND METIS.
Unpublished paper. Available from National Library of Canada. 12 pp.

A list of programs available on reserves is provided which includes leadership training
courses, 4-H, Junior Forest Wardens, and the Alberta Service Corps for young people 18
years of age and over. Other programs are mentioned that can involve and assist the Indian and Metis youth and their communities.   HCV

68   **ANDRAS   ROBERT**
1969
NOTES FOR AN ADDRESS BY THE HONORABLE ROBERT ANDRAS, P.C., M.P.
GRENVILLE-CARLETON ANNUAL MEETING. Speech delivered to Grenville-
Carleton Annual Meeting. Ottawa, April 19, 1969. Available from Information Services,
Records and Research, Department of Indian Affairs and Northern Development
(Speech #3-695). 10 pp.

The importance of self-determination for Indians, with listening, responding, and stepping aside as 3 steps to its realization, is proposed in a discussion of Indian struggles for
identity and recognition.   CCV

69   **ANELL   BENGT**
1964
ANIMAL HUNTING DISGUISES AMONG THE NORTH AMERICAN INDIANS.
Studia Ethnographica Upsaliensia 21:1-34.

Throughout most of America north of Mexico (with the Northeast an exception), Indians utilized animal disguises to approach or to lure the game they were hunting. The ethnographic literature and historic sources are examined to show the nature and distribution of this practice. In Canada it was found among the Eskimo, the Northern Athabascan tribes, the Nootka, the Coast Salish, the Plateau tribes, and the Plains tribes.

Animals imitated include caribou, deer, antelope, buffalo, and wolf. The world distribution of the trait suggests that it was introduced into America by late Paleolithic hunters who settled in the Great Basin.   TSA

70   **ANELL   BENGT**
1969
RUNNING DOWN AND DRIVING OF GAME IN NORTH AMERICA. Studia Ethnographica Upsaliensia 30. Uppsala: Uppsala Universitet. 129 pp.

An overview and comparison of various methods utilized by North American Indians in driving and running down game are presented.   Biological and ecological factors as well as cultural development and economic specialization are decisive in determination of method. Running down, the oldest, appears to have been of limited importance although this technique on snowshoes is widely reported. Driving falls into 3 categories. The first, involving no special aids, is potentially practicable anywhere. The methods in the second category exploit topographical features and/or utilize additional equipment. Finally there are drives utilizing aids which in themselves could function as traps. Within each category numerous variations are possible and practiced. Discussion of the game sought and methods used, including tribal variations and adaptations, is conducted by region and includes all of Canada's culture areas with variation in coverage corresponding to the availability of sources. It is demonstrated that the use of fire and dogs featured far less than previously believed.   CCV

71   **ARNOLD   A J**
1968
HUMAN RIGHTS AND SOCIAL WELFARE EXPERIENCE IN WESTERN CANADA. Unpublished paper. Available from Library, Department of Health and Social Development, Winnipeg, Man. 24 pp.

Human rights legislation of British Columbia, Alberta, and Saskatchewan is discussed with reference to Indian arrests and the law.   IVY

72   **BAGNELL   KENNETH**
1963
AN INDIAN CHIEF'S DAUGHTER SAYS WE HELPED DIG THE RUT IN WHICH INDIANS LIE. The United Church Observer N.S. 25(17):21.

Gloria Webster, university graduate and professional worker at Vancouver's YWCA, discussed how the dependency of the Indian is a direct result of government and church administrators who have traditionally made the Indian's decisions for him.   IVY

73   **BAILEY   RICHARD W**
1968
HOUSING FOR INDIANS AND METIS IN NORTHERN SASKATCHEWAN. Habitat 11(4):18-23.

In 1965 the federal and provincial governments initiated a 12-year housing program in the Northern Affairs Region of Saskatchewan for Metis and enfranchised Indians of low income. The financial arrangements between the governments and the homeowner are discussed.   IVY

74   **BAILEY   S J**
1964
SOCIAL PROGRAMS IN THE INDIAN AFFAIRS BRANCH. In Proceedings. Indian
Study Conference. Provincial Council of Women of British Columbia. Unpublished
paper. Available from Department of Extension. University of British Columbia.
Appendix 'B'. 9 pp.

The federal policy towards welfare and community development is outlined. Welfare
services should be provided by the province rather than by the Indian Affairs Branch.
The Community Development program is to be developed over the next 3 years.   IVY

75   **BALDWIN   GORDON C**
1969
GAMES OF THE AMERICAN INDIAN. New York: W.W. Norton. 150 pp.

American Indian recreational activities are surveyed with special attention to regional
and tribal variations including Canadian groups. Children's rattles, dolls, tops, whistles,
and other toys are described as are games like tag, hide-and-seek, and tug-of-war which
have European counterparts. Play with miniature weapons and household articles is discussed along with mock warfare and other imitative activities which develop essential
skills and function to prepare the children for adult roles in their culture. Adult activities
described include gambling, games of guessing, chance, skill, and varieties of ball games.
String figures and storytelling are treated briefly. Numerous illustrations and photographs demonstrate variations in toys and game equipment.   CCV

76   **BANNER   STEPHEN**
1969
THE INTEGRATION OF THE CANADIAN INDIAN: A STUDY OF NON-
ASSIMILATION. Unpublished paper. Available from National Library of Canada. 21
pp.

This study concerns the Indian's unwillingness to participate in the political and social
life that surrounds him. This is a preliminary attempt to discover which are the more
important variables in determining the Canadian Indian's isolationism.   HCV

77   **BARBEAU   MARIUS**
1960
INDIAN DAYS ON THE WESTERN PRAIRIES. National Museum of Canada
Bulletin 163. Ottawa: Queen's Printer. 234 pp.

The Indians of the western prairies of Canada - Assiniboine, Blackfoot, Plains Cree,
Kutenai, Salish, Sarsi, Beaver, Carrier, and Sekani - are discussed. The history of Indian-
White relations since 1800 is summarized. Over 80 Indian legends, collected around
1926, are included, along with 165 illustrations.   JSL

78   **BARBEAU   MARIUS**
1960
LEGEND AND HISTORY IN THE OLDEST GEOGRAPHICAL NAMES OF THE
ST. LAWRENCE. Canadian Geographical Journal 61:2-9.

Indian words which became place names in Eastern Canada are listed and defined.   IVY

79   **BARBEAU   MARIUS**
1966
COMMENT ON DECOUVRIT L'AMERIQUE. Montreal: Librairie Beauchemin. 119 pp.

The source of human occupation of North America is subjected to a general examination by culture area. Certain culture traits having parallels in other parts of the globe are mentioned and explanatory notes or related hypotheses are suggested.   CCV

80   **BARNOUW   VICTOR**
1963
CULTURE AND PERSONALITY. Homewood, IL: Dorsey. 410 pp.

Canadian examples feature strongly in this synthesis of cross-cultural data on the relationship between culture and personality.   Benedict's analysis of Kwakiutl culture is evaluated. Chapter 9 is devoted to the Ontario and Wisconsin Ojibwa, particularly the ethnographic material of Landes, Hallowell, Barnouw, James, Friedl, and Boggs. Analyses of life histories, dreams, and symbolism are presented. Data from projective tests from Rorschach tests administered to the Tuscarora, Kaska and Ojibwa are examined briefly. A brief discussion of culturally patterned mental disorders mentions Ojibwa, Cree, and Naskapi-Montagnais examples.   CCV

81   **BATTISTE   C A,   BARBER   S H**
n.d.
NORTHERN SASKATCHEWAN SURVEY. Unpublished paper. Available from The Saskatchewan Indian and Metis Department, Regina. 9 pp.

This report summarizes and defines the major problem areas in northern Saskatchewan as education, training, health, and employment and income.   IVY

82   **BIRD   PERCY I**
1964
MANITOBA INDIAN BROTHERHOOD CONFERENCE. Unpublished minutes of Manitoba Indian Brotherhood Conference, South Central Manitoba.   Winnipeg, October 22, 1964. Available from National Library of Canada. 6 pp.

Issues affecting Indians on reserves including claims and the claims commission; housing; land shortages; assistance to widows, unmarried mothers, and men over 50; treaty payments; and Fairford Dam are aired at the Manitoba Indian Brotherhood Conference.   CCV

83   **BOROVOY   ALAN A**
1966
INDIAN POVERTY IN CANADA. Canadian Labour 11(12):13-15.

Mass pressures and collective bargaining are 2 skills the Indian peoples must utilize to acquire power. With guidance from the Human Rights Committee of the Ontario Federation of Labour, the demonstration of Indian peoples at Kenora in November, 1965, substantiates this.   IVY

84   **BOYS J V**
1966
INDIAN MANPOWER IN RESOURCE DEVELOPMENT. In Manpower for
Resource Development. D. B. Turner and D. J. Robinson, eds. British Columbia Natural
Resources Conference Transactions 16:105-108.

Industry is asked to provide information on marketable skills in order that Indians may
acquire such training and gain employment.   IVY

85   **BRITISH COLUMBIA ASSOCIATION OF NON STATUS INDIANS**
n.d.
THE B.C. ASSOCIATION OF NON STATUS INDIANS. Unpublished paper.
Available from British Columbia Association of Non Status Indians, Vancouver, B.C. 3
pp.

The 3 page report presents the policies of the British Columbia Association of Non Status
Indians.   IVY

86   **BUCKSAR RICHARD G**
1970
SQUATTERS IN CANADA'S NORTHLAND: AN APPRAISAL. The Northian 6(4):
15-21.

This broad discussion of squatters in parts of Ontario and the Northwest Territories pays
brief attention to Indian squatters, their backgrounds, and encounters with the towns-
people around them.   ADG

87   **CANADA. Advisory Commission on the Development of Government in the
Northwest Territories.**
1965
VERBATIM REPORT OF PUBLIC HEARINGS. Ottawa: Queen's Printer. 6 vols.

Volumes 1 to 4, and 6 contain verbatim accounts of public hearings held in 44 communities in the Northwest Territories. Volume 5 contains a verbatim account of the meeting
held in Ottawa. The meetings, briefs, and submissions are abstracted in published books.
JSL

88   **CANADA. Advisory Commission on the Development of Government in the
Northwest Territories.**
1966
REPORT OF THE ADVISORY COMMISSION ON THE DEVELOPMENT OF
GOVERNMENT IN THE NORTHWEST TERRITORIES. Ottawa: Department of
Indian Affairs and Northern Development. 2 vols.

Volume 1 (214 pages) contains the report of the Advisory Committee which is organized
into 7 parts: introduction, evolution of the present government, a review of government
today in the Northwest Territories, non-governmental factors, alternatives, postulates,
and recommendations. Volume 2 (203 pages) contains 8 appendices. Appendix A discusses the travel and hearings. Appendix B contains a table and index to briefs. Appendix
C contains a table and index to submissions. Appendix D contains indexes to the verbatim report. Appendix E lists the introductory remarks and questions. Appendix F is a list

of persons at the Ottawa hearings. Appendix G is a map showing the Commission's travel route. Appendix H contains acknowledgements.   JSL

89   **CANADA. Advisory Commission on the Development of Government in the Northwest Territories.**
1966
SETTLEMENTS OF THE NORTHWEST TERRITORIES: DESCRIPTIONS PREPARED FOR THE ADVISORY COMMISSION ON THE DEVELOPMENT OF GOVERNMENT IN THE NORTHWEST TERRITORIES (NORTHERN SETTLEMENTS). Ottawa: Department of Northern Affairs and National Resources. 4 vols.

Descriptions of Northwest Territories' settlements in 1965 and early 1966 were compiled for the Advisory Commission. Department of Northern Affairs and National Resources files and library materials were used to describe 51 settlements. Within each description, 22 topics are discussed: name, location, geology and physiography, access, climate, population, religious facilities, postal facilities, administrative facilities, police facilities, education facilities, recreational facilities, medical facilities, telecommunication facilities, commercial enterprises, history and remarks, economic activities, acknowledgements and references, community organization and leaders, photographs, and maps. The descriptions are arranged alphabetically by name of the settlement. Volume 1 describes settlements from Aklavik to Eskimo Point. Volume 2 describes Fort Franklin to Hall Beach. Volume 3 discusses Hay River to Pond Inlet. Volume 4 discusses Rae to Yellowknife.   JSL

90   **CANADA. Advisory Commission on the Development of Government in the Northwest Territories.**
1966
SUMMARY REPORT OF THE ADVISORY COMMISSION ON THE DEVELOPMENT OF GOVERNMENT IN THE NORTHWEST TERRITORIES. Ottawa: Department of Northern Affairs and National Resources. 19 pp.   Also in French.

A short summary of the report was prepared. There is 1 native version, in alphabetic and syllabic text.   JSL

91   **CANADA. Department of Citizenship and Immigration. Indian Affairs Branch.**
n.d.
INDIANS OF QUEBEC AND THE MARITIME PROVINCES. Ottawa: Department of Citizenship and Immigration. 55 pp.   Also in French.

An historical introduction to the Indians of Quebec, Nova Scotia, New Brunswick, Prince Edward Island, and Newfoundland was prepared. Discussed are the Cree, Micmac, Malecite, Beothuk, Montagnais, Naskapi, Algonkin, and the Laurentian Iroquois. Attention is given to the area's exploration, colonization, administration, missions, and contemporary life.   JSL

92   **CANADA. Department of Citizenship and Immigration. Indian Affairs Branch.**
1960
INDIANS OF BRITISH COLUMBIA: AN HISTORICAL REVIEW. Ottawa: Department of Citizenship and Immigration. 16 pp.

An historical sketch of the Indians of British Columbia is presented. Discussed are the Coast Salish, Nootka, Kwakiutl, Bella Coola, Haida, Tsimshian, Interior Salish, Kootenay, Chilcotin, Carrier, Tsetsaut, Tahtlan, and Sekani cultures. Attention is given to exploration and trade, colonization, administration, and the contemporary scene.   JSL

93   **CANADA. Department of Citizenship and Immigration. Indian Affairs Branch.**
1961
THE CANADIAN INDIAN: A REFERENCE PAPER. Ottawa: Department of Citizenship and Immigration. 20 pp.

Survey coverage is given to all aspects of the field of Indian affairs in this revision of the 1959 edition. This publication is revised in succeeding years (1962, 1963, 1964) and published under the same title.   JSL

94   **CANADA. Department of Citizenship and Immigration. Indian Affairs Branch.**
1961
INDIANS OF THE PRAIRIE PROVINCES: AN HISTORICAL REVIEW. Ottawa: Department of Citizenship and Immigration. 25 pp.

An historical description of the Metis and Indians of Alberta, Saskatchewan, and Manitoba is given. Discussed are the Blackfoot, Assiniboine, Sarcee, Gros Ventre, Kootenay, Slave, Beaver, Chipewyan, Cree, and Ojibwa. Attention is given to the explorers and traders, treaties, missions, the North-west rebellion, transition, and the contemporary scene.   JSL

95   **CANADA. Department of Citizenship and Immigration. Indian Affairs Branch.**
1962
INDIANS OF ONTARIO: AN HISTORICAL REVIEW. Ottawa: Department of Citizenship and Immigration. 44 pp.

Iroquoian and Algonkian groups are discussed in this introduction to the cultures and history of the Indians of Ontario. Also examined are the fur trade; British colonization; and mission activities of the Roman Catholic, Methodist, and Moravian churches as well as the Church of England. For the post-Confederation era, attention is given to Indian administration, legislation, treaties, 20th-century social and economic conditions, education, and population.   JSL

96   **CANADA. Department of Citizenship and Immigration. Indian Affairs Branch.**
1964
INDIANS OF BRITISH COLUMBIA: AN HISTORICAL REVIEW. Ottawa: Department of Citizenship and Immigration. 19 pp.

A revision of the 1960 edition.   JSL

97   **CANADA. Department of Citizenship and Immigration. Indian Affairs Branch.**
1964
INDIANS OF THE PRAIRIE PROVINCES: AN HISTORICAL REVIEW. Ottawa: Department of Citizenship and Immigration. 32 pp.

A revision of the 1961 edition.   JSL

98   **CANADA. Department of Citizenship and Immigration. Indian Affairs Branch.**
1964
SCHEDULE OF INDIAN RESERVES AND SETTLEMENTS PART I: PRINCE
EDWARD ISLAND, NOVA SCOTIA, NEW BRUNSWICK, QUEBEC, ONTARIO,
MANITOBA, SASKATCHEWAN, ALBERTA, YUKON AND NORTHWEST
TERRITORIES. Ottawa: Department of Citizenship and Immigration. 82 pp.

A revised schedule of Indian reserves and settlements in Canada, excluding British Columbia, was produced. Information is provided as to the reserves' number, province,
band, agency, and location.   JSL

99   **CANADA. Department of Citizenship and Immigration. Indian Affairs Branch.**
1964
TRADITIONAL LINGUISTIC AND CULTURAL AFFILIATIONS OF
CANADIAN INDIAN BANDS. Ottawa: Department of Citizenship and Immigration.
49 pp.   Also in French.

An explanation of Canadian Indian culture areas and linguistic groups is given. A table
of bands gives linguistic group, language, culture area, and population for each
band. JSL

100   **CANADA. Department of Indian Affairs and Northern Development.**
1967
PAVILION TELLS INDIANS' STORY. Ottawa: Department of Indian Affairs and
Northern Development. 8 pp.   Also in French.

The Canadian Indians' pavilion at Expo '67 is described and explained with photos and a
brief introduction to the Indian hostesses.   CCV

101   **CANADA. Department of Indian Affairs and Northern Development.**
1969
INDIAN SUMMER. Ottawa: Queen's Printer. 28 pp.

A story of the meaning of summer to Indians is presented. Mentioned are Indian dances,
songs, and costumes. Life in an Indian community is described. Photographs, some in
color, accompany the text.   JSL

102   **CANADA. Department of Indian Affairs and Northern Development. Indian Affairs**
Branch.
n.d.
INDIAN AFFAIRS FACTS AND FIGURES: LATEST FIGURES TO DEC. 31, 1968.
Ottawa: Department of Indian Affairs and Northern Development. 17 cards.

Figures are given for Indian population, number of bands and reserves, acreage, residence pattern, and enfranchisement. Other topics include the health services budget, staff
of the Indian and Eskimo Affairs programs, historical background of the Indians, community planning, Indian and Eskimo economic development, education, vital statistics,

budget, forecast expenditures, estimates, community development, grants to bands, leadership training, homemakers' clubs, cultural development, local development, and friendship centers.   JSL

103   **CANADA. Department of Indian Affairs and Northern Development. Indian Affairs Branch.**
1966
THE CANADIAN INDIAN: A REFERENCE PAPER. Ottawa: Queen's Printer. 13 pp.   Also in French.

An overview of the Indian linguistic groups found in Canada, the Indian treaties and government obligations, Indian status, education, welfare, and economic development is presented.   CCV

104   **CANADA. Department of Indian Affairs and Northern Development. Indian Affairs Branch.**
1967
INDIANS OF BRITISH COLUMBIA: AN HISTORICAL REVIEW. Ottawa: Queen's Printer. 16 pp.

A minor revision of the 1964 edition.   JSL

105   **CANADA. Department of Indian Affairs and Northern Development. Indian Affairs Branch.**
1967
INDIANS OF ONTARIO: AN HISTORICAL REVIEW. Ottawa: Queen's Printer. 40 pp.

A minor revision of the 1962 edition.   JSL

106   **CANADA. Department of Indian Affairs and Northern Development. Indian Affairs Branch.**
1967
INDIANS OF QUEBEC AND THE MARITIME PROVINCES: AN HISTORICAL REVIEW. Ottawa: Queen's Printer. 36 pp.   Also in French.

The Department's brief description of the native people of Quebec and the Maritimes and their history was slightly revised.   JSL

107   **CANADA. Department of Indian Affairs and Northern Development. Indian Affairs Branch.**
1967
INDIANS OF THE PRAIRIE PROVINCES: AN HISTORICAL REVIEW. Ottawa: Queen's Printer. 26 pp.

A minor revision of the 1964 edition.   JSL

108   **CANADA. Department of Indian Affairs and Northern Development. Indian Affairs Branch.**
1967

LINGUISTIC AND CULTURAL AFFILIATIONS OF CANADIAN INDIAN
BANDS. Ottawa: Queen's Printer. 26 pp.

The culture areas and linguistic groups of Canadian Indians are explained. A table of
Indian bands gives each band's population, linguistic group, language, and culture area.
This is a slight revision of the 1964 edition.   JSL

109   **CANADA. Department of Indian Affairs and Northern Development. Indian Affairs
Branch.**
1967
SASKATCHEWAN REGION INDIAN LABOUR FORCE SURVEY JULY 1967.
Ottawa: Department of Indian Affairs and Northern Development. 20 pp.

Data on the Saskatchewan region Indian labor force are presented by agency. Education
level for males and females and the age characteristics of the labor force at each agency
are provided.   CCV

110   **CANADA. Department of Indian Affairs and Northern Development. Indian Affairs
Branch.**
1969
INDIANS OF BRITISH COLUMBIA: AN HISTORICAL REVIEW. Ottawa: Queen's
Printer. 16 pp.

A minor revision of the 1967 edition.   JSL

111   **CANADA. Department of Indian Affairs and Northern Development. Indian Affairs
Branch.**
1969
INDIANS OF ONTARIO: AN HISTORICAL REVIEW. Ottawa: Queen's Printer. 40
pp.

A minor revision of the 1967 edition.   JSL

112   **CANADA. Department of Indian Affairs and Northern Development. Indian Affairs
Branch.**
1970
LINGUISTIC AND CULTURAL AFFILIATION OF CANADIAN INDIAN
BANDS. Ottawa: Queen's Printer. 42 pp.

The 1967 version was slightly revised, with the addition of 9 maps. The maps indicate
population, linguistic group, and language for each band in the region.   JSL

113   **CANADA. Department of Indian Affairs and Northern Development. Regional
Office, Winnipeg, Manitoba.**
1970
DIRECTORY OF SERVICES TO TREATY INDIAN PEOPLE OF MANITOBA.
Winnipeg: Department of Indian Affairs and Northern Development. 155 pp.

This directory, compiled by the Community Affairs Section, Regional Office of the Department of Indian Affairs and Northern Development, Winnipeg, Manitoba, provides a
basic description and specific information to guide the reader to those persons or offices
which render major services to the Indian people of Manitoba.   IVY

114   **CANADA. Department of Northern Affairs and National Resources and Department of Citizenship and Immigration.**
1960
INDIAN AND ESKIMO CHILDREN. Toronto: Canadian Conference on Children. 10 pp.

A document, prepared jointly by the 2 federal departments, is submitted to the 1st Canadian Conference on Children. Government programs and the problems in the acculturation of Indian and Eskimo children are discussed briefly.   CCV

115   **CANADA. Department of Northern Affairs and National Resources.**
1965
THE NORTHWEST TERRITORIES TODAY: A REFERENCE PAPER FOR THE ADVISORY COMMISSION ON THE DEVELOPMENT OF GOVERNMENT IN THE NORTHWEST TERRITORIES. Ottawa: Department of Northern Affairs and National Resources. 136 pp.   Also in French.

A brief survey of the Northwest Territories discusses the economic base, social aspects and governmental services, and political development. The survey concludes that the main social problem involves the natives - Indian, Metis, and Eskimo. Because natives have an extremely low cash income, relative to Whites, training and education are needed to enable them to enter skilled and semi-skilled occupations.   JSL

116   **CANADA. Department of the Secretary of State. Canadian Citizenship Branch.**
1967
THE CANADIAN FAMILY TREE. Ottawa: Queen's Printer. 354 pp.

Pages 167-175 discuss Canadian Indians. Pages 229-235 discuss Canadian Metis. Indian linguistic and cultural groups, contact with Europeans, self-government, advisory councils, occupations, organizations, newspapers, and recreation are outlined. The historical background and activities of the Metis are presented. Each section concludes with an evaluation of the ethnic group's contributions to Canadian life.   JSL

117   **CANADA. Royal Commission on the Status of Women in Canada.**
1970
REPORT OF THE ROYAL COMMISSION ON THE STATUS OF WOMEN IN CANADA. Florence Bird, chairman. Ottawa: Information Canada. 488 pp.   Also in French.

Pages 210-217 of this report are devoted to a review of findings and recommendations related to native women in the North. Special emphasis is directed to education, housing, adult education and vocational training, employment, and participation of native women in decision making. Brief allusions to Indian women occur in the sections on poverty, law, and employment.   CCV

118   **CANADA. Senate. 28 Parliament, 2-3 Session. Special Committee on Poverty.**
1969-1970.
PROCEEDINGS OF THE SPECIAL SENATE COMMITTEE ON POVERTY. Nos. 1-70 and 1-12.   Also in French.

Numerous references to the situation and problems of the Indians of Canada are found in the proceedings of the Special Senate Committee on Poverty.   CCV

119   **CANADIAN FEDERATION OF UNIVERSITY WOMEN**
1970
PROGRAM REPORT. 18th Triennial Conference. Toronto, August 16-21, 1970.
Available from National Library of Canada. 37 pp.

Education, economic development, land and treaty rights, and friendship centers were aspects of the topic "Disadvantaged Canadians - Indians"discussed at this conference.   IVY

120   **CANADIAN LABOUR CONGRESS**
1964
RESOLUTION 331 - INDIANS, ESKIMOS AND METIS. 5th Constitutional
Convention of the Canada Labour Congress. Montreal, April 20-24, 1964. pp. 21-23,28.

Attention is called by the Convention to the special position and needs of the Canadians of Indian, Eskimo, and Metis extraction. After discussion the resolution was adopted.   IVY

121   **CARNEGIE   HENRY,   MEANS   JOHN E**
1967
EQUALITY OF OPPORTUNITY AND PLURALISM IN A FEDERAL SYSTEM:
THE CANADIAN EXPERIMENT. International Labour Review 95:381-416.

In this study of discrimination in Canada, the situation of Indians and Eskimos, one of the minority groups considered, is reviewed. Developments in federal policy concerning the administration of Indian Affairs since 1958 are mentioned.   IVY

122   **CHALMERS   J W,   ECCLES W J, et al.**
1966
PHILIPS' HISTORICAL ATLAS OF CANADA. Toronto: Vilas Industries. 48 pp.

Included in this historical atlas of Canada are maps of: the Riel rebellions, Indian linguistic groups (pre-conquest), Indian and Eskimo population distribution, missions, fur trade posts, fur trade routes and portages, and historic trails.   CCV

123   **CHRETIEN   JEAN**
1968-1970
SPEECHES BY THE HONORABLE JEAN CHRETIEN ON THE NORTH 1968,
1969, 1970. Unpublished collection of speeches. Available from Library, Department of Indian Affairs and Northern Development, Ottawa. 220 pp.

Nineteen speeches on the North delivered by Jean Chretien as Minister of Indian Affairs and Northern Development are compiled and bound. In addition to government projects and policies for resource development in the North, the significance of this development for Canada's native peoples and their roles in its realization are considered.   CCV

124   **CLARK   ALLAN**
1970
REPORT OF THE EXECUTIVE DIRECTOR. Unpublished paper delivered to 11th Annual Meeting of Members, Indian-Eskimo Association of Canada. Ottawa, June, 1970. Available from Indian-Eskimo Association. 33 pp.

This report of the Executive Director touches on the overall developments of the Indian-Eskimo Association from 1966 to 1970. Included in the discussion are the growth of native organizations, the new Indian policy, the non-status Indian, and some thoughts on a national Eskimo organization. The appendices include a list of native publications, financial statistics for the Association, and statistics for both native population and education.   HCV

125   **CLARK   BERTHA**
1969
THE ASPIRATIONS AND ROLE OF THE METIS WOMEN. In Voice of Alberta Native Women's Society: Alberta Native Women's Second Annual Conference. Edmonton, March 3-6, 1969. pp. 29-31.

Native women of today should have many roles: as mothers, wives, and participating members of a community. The responsibility entailed in each role is discussed.   IVY

126   **CLOUGH   W G**
1968
INDIAN LEADERSHIP CONFERENCE. Okanagan Historical Society Report 32:105-108.

The Indian Leadership Conference on community held at Naramata, British Columbia, from November 19 to 24, 1967, was suggested, organized, and paid for by Indians. A summary of the events and key notes of the speeches are given.   IVY

127   **COMMUNITY WELFARE PLANNING COUNCIL, MANITOBA INDIAN BROTHERHOOD**
1964
MINUTES OF THE COMMUNITY WELFARE PLANNING COUNCIL AND MANITOBA INDIAN BROTHERHOOD CONFERENCE. The Pas, Man., August 25-26, 1964. Available from National Library of Canada. 13 pp.

Delegates from regions and areas report local problems which include school dropouts and absenteeism, inadequate medical services, lack of employment opportunities, housing, and poor communications with Indian Affairs representatives.   CCV

128   **COMPTON   F H**
1967
COMMUNITY DEVELOPMENT AND MANPOWER DEVELOPMENT. Unpublished paper delivered to Canada Manpower Counsellors, April 7, 1967. Available from Library, Department of Health and Social Development, Winnipeg, Man. 14 pp.

The aims and objectives of Vocational Opportunity Services, a facet of Community Development Services in Manitoba, are discussed.   IVY

129   **CONFEDERATION OF NATIVE INDIANS OF BRITISH COLUMBIA**
1966
INDIAN ORGANIZATIONAL MEETING ON UNITY. Unpublished paper. Available from Provincial Museum, Victoria, B.C. 18 pp.

Minutes of the meeting held in Vancouver, March 19, 1966, which established the Confederation of Native Indians of British Columbia are presented. Included is a 3 page brief resulting from this meeting which states the objectives and policies of the organization.   IVY

130   **CONNOR   JUDITH**
1969
POVERTY IN CANADA: A BIBLIOGRAPHIC STUDY OF THE LITERATURE ON POVERTY IN THE UNITED STATES AND CANADA. M.S.W. Thesis. School of Social Work. University of Toronto. 342 pp.

A review of the literature on poverty in Canada is presented accompanied by an annotated bibliography of Canadian newspaper clippings, September, 1965-February, 1966. Discussion of poverty includes references to the life style, health, education, employment, and housing conditions as experienced by the Canadian Indian.   CCV

131   **COOPER   P F JR**
1968
APPLICATIONS OF MODERN TECHNOLOGY IN AN ARCTIC ENVIRONMENT. Polar Record 14:141-163.

Amenities available to the native inhabitants of the Mackenzie Delta in 1967 are reviewed and proposals for future study given.   IVY

132   **COURCHENE   DAVE**
1970
STATEMENT TO THE MANITOBA NORTHERN TASK FORCE. In An Interim Report from the Citizens of Northern Manitoba to the Manitoba Legislature. Compiled by the Northern Task Force. Winnipeg: Queen's Printer. Appendix pp. 1-5.

Concern is expressed that negotiations or consultations between the federal and the provincial government not be undertaken without the prior knowledge, consent, and participation of the Indian people of Manitoba. Recommendations in the areas of hunting and fishing rights, communication and transportation, education, housing, economic development, and provincial assistance in the funding of the Manitoba Indian Economic Development Fund are presented.   IVY

133   **CURRIE   WALTER**
1966
PROGRESS TOWARD EQUAL OPPORTUNITY. Unpublished paper delivered to 7th Annual Meeting of Members, Indian-Eskimo Association of Canada. Vancouver, B.C., December 2, 1966. Available from Indian-Eskimo Association. 5 pp.

Progress is reported in the areas of economics, education, friendship centers, and leadership but it is far too gradual. Much more needs to be done by federal and provincial authorities, and the native peoples.   IVY

134   **CUTHAND   DOUG**
1967
100 YEARS OF DISCRIMINATION. The Peak (Simon Fraser University) 5(15):10.

A century of discrimination against the Indian has brought the possibility of full scale race riots.   TSA

135   **DAHM   MARY**
1969
THE CULTURAL ENCOUNTER BETWEEN INDIAN AND WHITE. World Order 4(1):31-40.

The traditional culture of the natives of Canada is described pointing out cultural differences between Indians and non-Indian peoples. Injustices caused by ignorance and deliberate exploitation are briefly illustrated.   IVY

136   **DALLYN   F JOHN G,   EARLE   FRAZER G**
1965
A STUDY OF ATTITUDES TOWARDS INDIANS AND PEOPLE OF INDIAN DESCENT: THE PAS, MANITOBA. Winnipeg: Canadian Council of Christians and Jews. 34 pp.

The purpose of this survey, executed in the Pas, Manitoba, in 1961, is to study the attitudes of people towards Indians or persons of direct Indian descent. Based on the stereotype of Indians, the survey was structured so as to determine if there is prejudice directed towards Indians by the White community, the extent of this prejudice, and to infer what stereotypes have been accepted as the norm.   DGW

137   **DAVIS   ARTHUR K, ed.**
1970
CONFRONTATIONS: PLENARY SESSION I. In Canadian Confrontations: Hinterlands vs. Metropolis. Arthur K. Davis, ed. Edited Proceedings of the Eleventh Annual Meeting of the Western Association of Sociology and Anthropology, Banff, Alberta, December 28-30, 1969. Edmonton: University of Alberta Printing Service. pp. 1-32.

Present and past injustices and prospects for the future were discussed by several Indian and Metis speakers in a session chaired by Stan Daniels, President, Metis Association of Alberta. Recent violence committed against native people was recalled by Tony Antoine, President of the Native Alliance for Red Power. The racist nature of Canadian society and the fact that its native people are a colonized people were pointed out by Dr. Howard Adams, President of the Metis Society of Saskatchewan. He urged that sociologists and anthropologists study the revolution among Indians and half-breeds. Harold Cardinal, President of the Indian Association of Alberta touched upon the White Paper, religious suppression, achievements of other non-White peoples, and Indian identity. Also speaking in the session was Roy Atkinson, President of the National Farmers Union. These speeches are printed essentially as given.   TSA

138   **DE BRETAGNE G**
n.d.
A CONDENSATION OF HAWTHORN'S SURVEY OF THE CONTEMPORARY INDIAN OF CANADA. Unpublished paper. Available from Indian and Northern Curriculum Resource Centre, University of Saskatchewan. 12 pp.

The findings and recommendations of Part 1 of the Hawthorn report are summarized.   IVY

139   **DELISLE   ANDREW**
1968
HUMAN RIGHTS AND INDIANS. In Discussion on Human Rights. Noel A. Kinsella, chairman. Fredericton, N.B.: Human Rights Commission. pp. 119-123.

The past, present and future conditions of the Canadian Indian are dealt with in this paper presented at the Provincial Conference on Human Rights, Fredericton, New Brunswick, March 25 and 26, 1968.   IVY

140   **DICK   H B**
1969
THE JOHN HOWARD SOCIETY OF VANCOUVER ISLAND INDIAN COUNSELLOR-IN-TRAINING PROJECT. Unpublished paper. Available from National Library of Canada.

Endorsing the recommendations contained in the Canadian Corrections Association report, the Board of Directors of the John Howard Society initiated the Indian Counsellor-in-Training Project. A special committee has proposed to hire a native Indian, resident on Vancouver Island, to undergo on-the-job training for 3 years to enable him to assist Indians recently released from prison. An outline of the project costs is given, as well as a recommendation that the federal and provincial governments be approached to provide financial assistance to cover the cost of the Indian Counsellor-in-Training Project.   IVY

141   **DINSDALE   WALTER**
n.d.
SPEECHES BY WALTER DINSDALE. Unpublished collection of speeches. Available from Library, Department of Indian Affairs and Northern Development, Ottawa. 211 pp.

Twenty-two speeches of Walter Dinsdale delivered as Minister of the Department of Northern Affairs and National Resources are compiled and bound. Frequent references to resource conservation and development education and tourism appear as well as occasional reference to Canada's native people.   CCV

142   **DRIVER   HAROLD E**
1961
INDIANS OF NORTH AMERICA. Chicago: University of Chicago Press. 667 pp.

A comprehensive description is provided of North American Indian cultures at the height of their history before important interference from European culture. The time span varies from the 16th to the 19th century. The material is treated under topic headings within which culture areas form sub-divisions. Theory is included with particular attention to culture change by diffusion. Canadian references are located in the index under tribe or culture area. Numerous trait distribution maps are placed in the appendix.   CCV

143   **DRIVER   HAROLD E**
1969

INDIANS OF NORTH AMERICA. 2nd Edition Revised. Chicago: University of Chicago Press. 632 pp.

This revision includes additional material on ethnohistory and culture change after 1492 A.D. with particular emphasis on the 20th century. The form and content of the chapters on archaeology, horticulture, and music have been altered and expanded. Pages 532-546 are devoted entirely to a review of Canadian Indian ethnohistory and the current scene.   CCV

144   **DUNNING   R W**
n.d.
A WORKING PAPER ON CANADIAN INDIAN RESEARCH. Unpublished paper. Available from National Museum of Man, Ethnology Division, Ottawa, with permission of the author. 20 pp.

Offered are some suggestions concerning the factors which have inhibited social research and analysis of present Indian status in society. A limited ethnocentric approach to reserve society must be foregone for a more complex and holistic view, for integral parts of the reserve system are external to that system.   DGW

145   **DUNSTAN   WILLIAM**
1963
CANADIAN INDIANS TODAY. Canadian Geographical Journal 67:182-193.

General information on the programs and policies of the Indian Affairs Branch is provided. Accomplishments of individual Indians in modern Canada are noted.   IVY

146   **D'ASTOUS   JULES**
1964
ADDRESS. In Proceedings. Indian Study Conference. Provincial Council of Women of British Columbia. Available from Department of Extension, University of British Columbia. Appendix 'C'. 13 pp.

The objectives, aims, and outlook of the Indian Affairs Branch is briefly reviewed.   IVY

147   **ELEEN   JOHN**
1965
THE POVERTY OF CANADIAN INDIANS. Canadian Labour 10(7,8):25.

Examples of poverty among Indians are given.   IVY

148   **ERSKINE   J S**
1970
THE INDIAN DILEMMA. Dalhousie Review 50:34-39.

Problems discussed include the question of rights, discrimination, and retention of Indian culture. Economic and moral aspects of the traditional hunting society, with specific reference to the Micmac of Nova Scotia, have disappeared but the behavior pattern remains to hinder adaptation to an industrial society.   IVY

149   **FARB   PETER**
1969
MAN'S RISE TO CIVILIZATION AS SHOWN BY THE INDIANS OF NORTH
AMERICA FROM PRIMEVAL TIMES TO THE COMING OF THE INDUSTRIAL
STATE. London: Secker and Warburg. 332 pp.

A cultural evolutionary perspective is used to describe the social organization of North
American Indians who range from simple hunting and gathering bands through tribes
and chiefdoms to highly complex societies. The composite band among several Sub-Arctic groups is described with details of hunting territory, social sanctions, supernatural
concepts, and totemism. Discussions of Iroquois government and of Plains Indians in
reference to culture contact and change are included in the section on the tribal level. In
relation to the chiefdom, Northwest Coast society is examined in terms of status and
wealth. The Ghost Dance and millenarian movements are treated in the final section.   CCV

150   **FIDLER   DICK**
1970
RED POWER IN CANADA. Toronto: Vanguard. 15 pp.

The status of the Canadian Indian, the growing pan-Indian movement, and Indian peoples' basic demands are outlined in materials originally published in Labor Challenge.   CCV

151   **FIEDLER   LESLIE A**
1968
THE RETURN OF THE VANISHING AMERICAN. New York: Stein and Day. 192
pp.

An examination of the myths contributing to the character of American life, particularly
the West, is presented as literary anthropology. Implications and contradictions in the
image of the Indian portrayed in literature are discussed.   CCV

152   **FREEMAN   E G,   MORTON   DESMOND**
1966
INDIANS: DO WE CARE? Toronto: The New Democratic Party of Ontario. 9 pp.

A commentary of the contemporary Indian situation is given with a critical analysis of
present Indian policy.   IVY

153   **FURLONG   D B**
1968
TASK FORCE ON INDIAN OPPORTUNITY: POWER SUPPLY TO INDIAN
PEOPLE. Unpublished paper delivered to Task Force on Indian Opportunity,
Government of Saskatchewan. Regina, August 9, 1968. Available from Indian and
Metis Department, Regina. 7 pp.

The Saskatchewan Power Corporation provides electric service to 54 reserves. The federal government and, in some cases, band councils, contributed substantially to rapidly
electrify reserves since 1964. Costs to electrify northern isolated communities are prohib-
itive without financial assistance. A conclusion reached from a study of SPC problems on

Indian reserves is to involve band councils or residents more directly in collection services.   IVY

154   **GABER   A**
1966
PEOPLE OF INDIAN ANCESTRY IN THE INTERLAKE DEVELOPMENT
REGION: COMMUNITY DEVELOPMENT SERVICES STUDY. Unpublished
paper. Available from Indian and Northern Resource Center, University of
Saskatchewan. 64 pp.

A Community Development Officer was appointed to assist people of Indian ancestry participate in, and take advantage of, the extensive long-term redevelopment scheme for the Interlake. From September, 1965, the Officer investigated which communities were ready to participate in and take advantage of rural development schemes under ARDA as well as the Community Education Officer Programme. The study provides brief community profiles on the following: Peguis Reserve, Jackhead Reserve, Fairford Reserve, Fairford Metis, Little Saskatchewan, Lake St. Martin, Dauphin River Area, Pine Dock, Matheson Island, Riverton, Eriksdale Area, Lake Manitoba Reserve, and Vogar. The primary concern expressed is need for improved education, training programs for adults, leadership courses, and counseling services.   IVY

155   **GAGNE   RAYMOND C**
1969-1970
AMERINDIAN CULTURAL SURVIVAL: A DILEMMA. Folk 11-12:201-208.

Indians should be aware of the sociological forces at work in the perpetuation of cultural identity and should benefit from this knowledge. Based on this thesis, abstractions such as culture, language, personality, structuralism, sociodynamics, and survival, along with their interrelationships are discussed.   IVY

156   **GAMBILL   JERRY**
1968
ON THE ART OF STEALING HUMAN RIGHTS. Unpublished paper delivered to
New Brunswick Conference on Human Rights. Tobique Indian Reserve, N.B., August,
1968. Available from National Library of Canada. 3 pp.

The author lists various methods whereby human rights can be denied Indians.   HCV

157   **GEORGE   DAN**
1970
MY VERY GOOD DEAR FRIENDS. In The Only Good Indian: Essays by Canadian
Indians. Waubageshig, ed. Toronto: New Press. pp. 184-188.

A plea for respect and understanding is addressed to the White man on behalf of all Indians with particular emphasis on the problems of integration by Chief Dan George.   CCV

158   **GIBBS   MARY**
1970
SARAIN STUMP. Tawow 1(2):34-35.

A brief glimpse of the artist and poet, Sarain Stump, is given.   IVY

159   **GLADSTONE   JAMES**
1965
INDIANS AND ESKIMOS SEEK A PLACE IN CANADA'S FUTURE. In The
Decisive Years. S. M. Philip, ed. Toronto: Townley. pp. 28-31.

Discussing the present situation of Canada's Indians, achievements of various Indian
groups are pointed out and recent activities of voluntary and government agencies are
mentioned.   IVY

160   **GONICK   C W**
1969
THE TRAGEDY OF SOUTH INDIAN LAKE. Canadian Dimension 5(8):9-10.

Manitoba Hydro's decision to flood South Indian Lake is presented. This necessitated
relocation of 600 Indian and Metis and destroyed a viable trapping and fishing economy.   IVY

161   **GRANT   BRUCE**
1960
AMERICAN INDIANS YESTERDAY AND TODAY. New York: Dutton. 351 pp.

A revised encyclopedia of the American Indian is presented. Included are entries of great
leaders, wars, and culture heroes revealing details of Indian legends, beliefs, customs,
and characteristics as well as their influences on the White man, on history, and on place
names and language.   CCV

162   **GRIDLEY   MARION E**
1960
INDIANS OF TODAY. 3rd Edition. Chicago: Indian Council Fire. 232 pp.

Included among the biographies of prominent North American Indians are sketches of
Peter Kelly, Paul Mercer, Frank Calder, Gilbert Monture, Ethel Monture, James Gladstone, George Clutesi, Jay Silverheels, Jean-Paul Nolet, Ellen Newman Neel, Gerald T.
Feathers, Adam Cuthand, Elmer Jamieson, and Edward Abenahew. Education, general
activities, and tribal affiliation are presented for each.   CCV

163   **GUINARD   JOSEPH E**
1960
LES NOMS INDIENS DE MON PAYS: LEUR SIGNIFICATION, LEUR
HISTOIRE. Montreal: Rayonnement. 197 pp.

A list of Canadian Indian names is compiled with history and significance of each name,
its root, and tribal derivation noted.   CCV

164   **HANDLEY   JOSEPH**
1969
INDIANS AND METIS OF SASKATCHEWAN. Reference paper No. 2. Education
Committee Workshop, Saskatchewan Task Force on Indian-Metis Employment. Dr.

Howard Nixon, Chairman. Saskatoon, May 5-7, 1969. Available from National Library of Canada. 9 pp.

A brief review of the Saskatchewan Indian and Metis population is presented in terms of population growth, welfare and employment, child care, the law, and community services. CCV

165   **HARDING   JIM**
n.d.
CANADA'S INDIANS: A POWERLESS MINORITY. The Student Union for Peace Action. Unpublished paper. Available from Social Science Research, Victoria, B.C. 11 pp.

In this paper originally prepared in January of 1965, statistics on income, employment, housing and health, education, and administration of justice indicate problems facing people of Indian ancestry. The dilemma faced by many people of Indian ancestry is related to the discussion of stratification and the power structure in Canada. With an historical perspective, it is possible to view Canadian people of Indian ancestry as a colonial people. Some federal policies support this argument. To understand the nature of the problems of a member of a minority it is necessary to analyze the total society, in particular the dominant values which are inconsistent with his life chances.   IVY

166   **HARRINGTON   ROBERT F**
1967
EULACHON AND THE GREASE TRAILS OF BRITISH COLUMBIA. Canadian Geographical Journal 74:28-31.

Eulachon, "candlefish,"spawn 14 miles from the mouth of the Nass River, British Columbia. Its historical importance and the trails traversing the northwest interior of the province are discussed.   IVY

167   **HAWTHORN   HARRY B**
1960
RESEARCH AND THE INDIANS OF CANADA. Unpublished paper. Available from Indian-Eskimo Association. 21 pp.

Topics relating largely to social and welfare aspects which require further research are listed. Discussed are differences between welfare research and scientific research, qualities and types of research workers, and techniques for arriving at valid conclusions. IVY

168   **HAWTHORN   HARRY BERTRAM**
1967
EPILOGUE: THE INDIAN DECIDES. In Northern Dilemma: Reference Papers. Arthur K. Davis, Vernon C. Serl, et al., eds. Volume 2. Bellingham, WA: Western Washington State College. pp. 578-585.

The general problems of orienting programs directed toward Canadian Indians are discussed with focus on the needs to be fulfilled and the difficulties involved. The implications in the fields of education and economics are described.   CCV

169   **HAWTHORN   HARRY BERTRAM, ed.**
1966
A SURVEY OF THE CONTEMPORARY INDIANS OF CANADA: A REPORT ON
ECONOMIC, POLITICAL, EDUCATIONAL NEEDS AND POLICIES. VOLUME I.
Ottawa: Queen's Printer. 409 pp. Vol. 1 of 2 vols.

A survey of the contemporary Indians of Canada was commissioned by the Department
of Citizenship and Immigration in 1964. Over 40 scholars contributed to the study. The 3
major sources of data were: the 1964 resources questionnaire circulated to Indian agencies by the Department; Indian Affairs files and other information; and observation and
interviews on visits to reserves. The data collection lasted two and one-half years. Part 1
deals with economic, political, and administrative matters. Ninety-one recommendations
are made in the first volume. These deal with the Indians' general situation, their economic development, federal-provincial relations, politics, welfare, and local government.   JSL

170   **HAWTHORN   HARRY BERTRAM, ed.**
1967
A SURVEY OF THE CONTEMPORARY INDIANS OF CANADA: ECONOMIC,
POLITICAL, EDUCATIONAL NEEDS AND POLICIES. VOLUME II. OTTAWA:
Queen's Printer. 251 pp. Vol. 2 of 2 vols.

Part 2 of the survey deals with the education, band councils, band council elections, and
local decision-making. A total of 60 recommendations are put forth.   CCV

171   **HIRABAYASHI   GORDON K**
1963
APATHY AS A MODE OF ADJUSTMENT: A HYPOTHESIS. In The Metis in Alberta
Society: With Special Reference to Social, Economic and Cultural Factors Associated
with Persistently High Tuberculosis Incidence. B. Y. Card, G. K. Hirabayashi, et al., eds.
University of Alberta Committee for Social Research: A Report on Project A.
Edmonton: University of Alberta. pp. 375-384.

Indian and Metis attitudes, aspirations, and cultural values are discussed briefly in relation to a review of the literature.   CCV

172   **HIRANO   KEIICHI**
1962
THE ABORIGENE IN CANADIAN LITERATURE: NOTES BY A JAPANESE.
Canadian Literature 14:43-52.

Studying the works of the poets D. C. Scott and W. H. Robb, the author suggests that
lack of genuine Indian poetry of high quality rests not with the poet but the subject matter. Traditional Indian legends, though not without charm, are neither profound nor
rich. Considering the level of the Indian world view it cannot be expected to make a
strong impact on Canadian literature.   IVY

173   **HLADY   WALTER M**
1964
INDIAN IMMIGRATIONS IN MANITOBA AND THE WEST. Historical and
Scientific Society of Manitoba Papers (Series 3) 17:24-53.

A general picture of population movements of Indian tribes who live, or have lived, in Manitoba is presented. Considered in detail are the Cree, Assiniboine, Ojibwa, Chipewyan, Sioux, Blackfoot, Sarcees, Hidatsa, and Gros Ventres.   IVY

174   **HOBART   CHARLES W**
1964
NON-WHITES IN CANADA: INDIANS, ESKIMOS, NEGROES. In Social
Problems: A Canadian Profile. Richard Laskin, ed. New York: McGraw Hill. pp. 85-90.

A brief review of Indian-White relations and a summary of the problems facing Indians in Canadian society are included in this discussion of Canadian problems of race relations.   CCV

175   **HOLLOWAY   ROBERT**
1966
DRINKING AMONG INDIAN YOUTH: A STUDY OF THE DRINKING
BEHAVIOR, ATTITUDES AND BELIEFS OF INDIAN AND METIS YOUNG
PEOPLE IN MANITOBA. Winnipeg: Alcohol Education Service (Manitoba). 124 pp.

The objectives of this study have been to analyse the drinking habits of Indian and Metis youth, to compare these habits with those of the general adolescent population, and to gather some impressions of the degree and prevalence of dysfunctional alcohol use among this ethnic group. The primary data for this study were collected by means of questionnaires administered to 888 Indian and Metis young people between the ages of 14 and 19. It is concluded that Indian and Metis youth have a poor understanding of alcohol, are tolerant toward drinking by adults, and reflect excessive drinking patterns of adults.   IVY

176   **HOMEWOOD   E L**
1960
NOOSKIMIASK AND HIS BELLA COOLAS. The United Church Observer N.S.
22(6):8-10,24,33.

Dr. Watt, superintendent of the Home Mission hospital, reports on the activities of the church and hospital in Bella Coola, a segregated community of Indian and White villagers.   IVY

177   **HOMEWOOD   E L**
1960
THE OBSERVER GOES TO A NATIVE BANQUET. The United Church Observer
N.S. 21(22):8-11.

The Prince Rupert Presbytery held their 3-day meeting at Bella Coola. A photostory of a native banquet commemorating this event is presented.   IVY

178   **HOMEWOOD   E L**
1965
THE INDIAN AND THE RESERVE: SECOND OF A SERIES ON THE PLIGHT OF
CANADA'S INDIANS. The United Church Observer N.S. 27(2):19-21,45.

The question as to whether reserves should be maintained or abolished is explored by both Indian leaders and Whites.   IVY

179   **HOMEWOOD   E L**
1965
THE PLIGHT OF CANADA'S INDIANS: FIRST OF A SERIES. The United Church Observer N.S. 27(1):12-14,32.

An overview of the current situation of Canada's Indians is presented. Discussed are poverty, housing conditions, delinquency, and crime.   IVY

180   **HONIGMANN   JOHN J**
1961
NORTH AMERICA. In Psychological Anthropology: Approaches to Culture and Personality. Francis L. K. Hsu, ed. Homewood, IL: Dorsey. pp. 93-134.

Included in a review and evaluation of culture and personality research conducted in native North America are frequent references to accomplishment regarding Canadian groups. Hallowell's discussion of the Kwakiutl and the Ojibwa, and Honigmann's on the Kaska are briefly examined. Suggestions for further study are presented.   CCV

181   **HORN   KAHN-TINETA**
1963
INDIANS SEEK TO REGAIN THEIR RIGHTFUL STATUS. Human Relations (Ontario Human Rights Commission) 4(8):4.

The Indian is considered a second class citizen by many Whites and is blocked socially, economically and educationally. To overcome the obstacles in his way, the Indian must achieve professional status. Additional grants and scholarships will be needed to obtain this goal. An authentic and permanent market for Indian handicrafts is also to be sought. Self-help is essential if the Indian is to retain his heritage.   ADG

182   **HOWARD   JAMES H**
1965
TRUE PARTNERSHIP HERE IN OUR LAND. Unpublished paper delivered to 11th Indian-Metis Conference. Winnipeg, February 7, 1965. Available from National Library of Canada. 7 pp.

A general history of the North American Indian is presented. Four goals desired by Indians are: (1) more and better job opportunities, (2) more and better education, (3) better health conditions, and (4) the right to retain their identity as Indians. On-the-job training and relocation are suggested to increase employment. Special texts and courses are needed, and integrated schools with a full course of study are required to improve education.   IVY

183   **HOWLETT   JOYCE**
1965
POTATOES FOR CROSS LAKE INDIANS. The United Church Observer N.S. 27(1):23-24.

The Sunday school and young people of Toronto's Rosedale United Church helped to finance a potato farm at Cross Lake, Manitoba.   IVY

184   **HUI   SINCHEUNG CYNTHIA**
1965
RESPONSE ACQUISITION OF INDIAN AND NON-INDIAN JAIL INMATES.
M.A. Thesis. Department of Psyhcology. University of Saskatchewan. 70 pp.

Thirty-nine Indian and Metis and 38 non-Indian male inmate volunteers of a Saskatchewan provincial jail were administered a questionnaire and performance tests to evaluate response acquisition of Indian relative to non-Indian respondents. Attitudes towards work, education, family, money, sharing with others, ethnic association, self-assertion, and institutional and social controls were focused on by the tests. Ability to learn and recall urban and rural paired associates was compared as was responsivity to positive and negative verbal reinforcement. Little intergroup difference was revealed by data analyses supporting the hypothesis that behavior is comparable when environment or socio-economic factors are comparable.   CCV

185   **INDIAN AND NORTHERN CURRICULUM RESOURCES CENTRE**
n.d.
INDIAN, METIS AND ESKIMO LEADERS IN CONTEMPORARY CANADA.
Saskatoon, Sask.: Indian and Northern Curriculum Resources Centre, University of Saskatchewan. 33 pp.

A collection of biographies is presented on the following contemporary Canadian Indian, Eskimo, and Metis people: Allen Sapp, Dr. Gilbert Monture, Simonie Michael, Chief Dan George, David Courchene, Dr. Howard Adams, Jim Neilson, Annee Meekitjuk, Harold Cardinal, Mary Cousins, and Senator James Gladstone.   IVY

186   **INDIAN-ESKIMO ASSOCIATION OF CANADA**
1966
CONFERENCE ON CONCERNS OF INDIANS IN BRITISH COLUMBIA:
THEME: "EQUAL OPPORTUNITY IN OUR LAND."Sponsored by British Columbia Interim Committee of the Indian-Eskimo Association of Canada. Vancouver, December 2-4, 1966. Available from Indian-Eskimo Association. 40 pp.

Using the theme "Equal Opportunity In Our Land,"the British Columbia Interim Committee of the Indian-Eskimo Association of Canada sponsored this conference on the following Indian problems: law, housing, education, health, welfare, communication, industry, development, and employment. Special addresses were given by the Honourable Mr. Daniel R. J. Campbell, Minister of the Department of Municipal Affairs of the Government of British Columbia, and Mr. Alfred Scow, Crown Prosecutor of the city of New Westminster, British Columbia.   HCV

187   **INDIAN-ESKIMO ASSOCIATION. Ontario Division.**
1969
REPORT AND MINUTES OF THE FOURTH ANNUAL MEETING OF
MEMBERS. Unpublished paper. Available from Indian-Eskimo Assocation. 8 pp.

The duplication of programs and resources by the Union of Ontario Indians and the Ontario Division of the Indian-Eskimo Association of Canada is reported. Discussion of the reconstruction of the Ontario Division of the Indian-Eskimo Association occurred, from which it was suggested that it form a standing resource committee to assist the Union of Ontario Indians.   HCV

188   **JARVIS   ALLAN,   BAND   CHARLES S,   et al.**
1965
PANEL DISCUSSION BASED ON THE POINTS ARISING FROM AGENCY REPORTS AND THEME ADDRESS. In Norec Conference: The Development of Indian and Eskimo Art and Crafts in the Far North. Northern Regional Committee, Indian-Eskimo Association of Canada. Toronto, May 3, 1965. Available from Indian-Eskimo Association. pp. 25-37.

Members of the panel include: Alan Jarvis, Charles S. Band, Victor Vokes, Dr. Ivan H. Crowell, R. A. J. Phillips, and Eric Gourdeau. Personal viewpoints are expressed on the theme of the conference.   IVY

189   **JENNESS   DIAMOND**
1962
CANADA'S DEBT TO THE INDIANS. Canadian Geographical Journal 65:112-117.

Aboriginal contributions in foodstuffs, drugs, textiles, methods of transportation, and sports are described. The Indian's role in the exploration of Canada and in Canada's political history is also presented.   IVY

190   **JOBLIN   E E M**
1967
THE INDIANS OF CANADA. Toronto: United Church of Canada,Board of Home Missions. 10 pp.

Work of The United Church of Canada in Indian communities and urban centers is described. Quoting Indians and other interested parties, the contemporary situation is assessed.   IVY

191   **JOBLIN   E E M**
1970
INDIAN WORK 1969. Annual Report to The Board of Home Missions, The United Church of Canada. Available from National Library of Canada. 4 pp.

Highlights of the year's work are reported including conference co-ordinators, residences and residential schools, summer students serving in Indian communities, and publications concerning Indians.   IVY

192   **JORGENSEN   JOSEPH G**
1969
SALISH LANGUAGE AND CULTURE: A STATISTICAL ANALYSIS OF INTERNAL RELATIONSHIPS,HISTORY, AND EVOLUTION. Indiana University Publications Language Science Series 3. Bloomington: Indiana University. 173 pp.

Relationships among the various Salish speaking peoples of British Columbia, Washington, Oregon, Idaho, and Montana are analyzed from a linguistic viewpoint and from an examination of 285 attributes of the cultures of these groups. The technology, social organization, and religion are utilized to test an evolutionary hypothesis of culture growth and culture lag. The relationship between language change and culture change is explored.   IVY

193   **JOSEPHY   ALVIN M**
1968
THE INDIAN HERITAGE OF AMERICA. New York: Knopf. 384 pp.

An overview of aboriginal and traditional Indian cultures of the Americas is presented by culture area. The Subarctic, Northwest Pacific Coast, Northwest Woodlands, Plains, and Plateau Indians are discussed in Chapters 8, 9, 10, 12, and 14. Linguistic groups are indicated and aboriginal culture as deduced from archaeological finds is summarized. The American and Canadian conquests of the Indians including the fur trade, land disputes, treaties and principal battles are examined in Chapter 26. Pages 361-2 comprise a description of Canadian Indian Affairs organization and administration.   CCV

194   **KEEPER   J I**
1964
COMMUNITY DEVELOPMENT METHODS. Unpublished paper. Available from Library, Department of Health and Social Development, Winnipeg, Man. 4 pp.

The status and role of a White Community Development Officer is discussed.   IVY

195   **KEMPLING   F EDWIN**
1969
INDIAN CANADIANS. Toronto: United Church of Canada, Committee on Education for Mission and Stewardship, Division of Congregational Life and Work. 5 pp.

A minister (missionary and teacher) discusses the contemporary Indian situation, underlines the chief areas of tension and misunderstanding, and lists specific suggestions concerning the role of Christians in assisting the Indian.   IVY

196   **KENNEDY   ANTHONY A**
1968
HOUSING STUDY FOR ISOLATED COMMUNITIES. Ekistics 25:361-367.

A report prepared by Kennedy Smith Associates published in 1967 is abstracted. In its preparation 44 isolated communities and Indian reserves in Manitoba, Saskatchewan, and Alberta were visited and analyzed. The major physical distinguishing features of housing conditions are identified under the following categories: access and transportation, housing density and grouping, location and type of community facilities, and topography and vegetation. Using these factors 4 basic types of communities are established: isolated northern native communities, resource-based northern towns, mixed fringe communities, and southern agricultural communities. Housing groups are based mainly on technical considerations and 3 types are discussed and diagrammed.   IVY

197   **KENNEDY   ANTHONY A,   SIMONSEN   OVE C**
1968
CANADA'S COUNTRY GHETTOS. Architecture Canada 45(9):52-59.

Based on a housing report surveying 50 communities and reserves in the prairie provinces, proposals for further development and prototype testing are presented. Four basic types of communities were established: (1) isolated northern native communities, (2) resource-based towns, (3) mixed fringe communities, and (4) reserve agricultural communities. Three types of housing groups and some dwelling units are discussed and diagrammed. IVY

198 **KENNEDY SMITH ASSOCIATES**
1967
HOUSING STUDY ISOLATED COMMUNITIES AND INDIAN RESERVES PRAIRIE PROVINCES FIRST STAGE REPORT AUGUST, 1967. Unpublished paper. Available from Library, University of British Columbia. 139 pp.

Prepared under a grant from Central Mortgage and Housing Corporation the purpose of the report is to identify problems of housing in isolated communities and reserves and suggest means of raising the standards of housing. Data were obtained from a physical survey of approximately 45 communities in the 3 prairie provinces, each visit lasting from one-half day to 2 days. Divided into 4 major sections this report discusses the communities, the housing group, the dwelling unit, and its proposals. Part 1 describes the various community types: (1) the isolated northern community, (2) the mixed fringe community, (3) the resource based northern town, and (4) the agricultural community. Part 2 presents the factors affecting the size and physical disposition of the housing group and suggests varying forms and prototypes. Part 3, concerned with the family, sets forth a range of housing types. Part 4 contains the proposals for a continuation of the study and an outline for stages 2 and 3. Maps, diagrams and photographs accompany the text. IVY

199 **KIMBALL YEFFE, ANDERSON JEAN**
1965
THE ART OF AMERICAN INDIAN COOKING. Garden City, N.Y.: Doubleday. 215 pp.

A collection of North American Indian recipes is presented with attention to regional and cultural variation. The Plains, Northwest Coast, and Eastern Woodlands are treated individually with each chapter introduced by a discussion of food resources, cooking techniques, and other pertinent cultural details. CCV

200 **KIRSTIANSEN HILDA**
1960
INTEGRATION OF INDIANS. Canadian Home and School 19(5):24.

A half-page report lists committees and organizations in British Columbia concerned with Indian participation. IVY

201 **KNIGHT PETER**
1970
THE INDIANS OF TODAY. The Northian Newsletter (13):1-2.

Reserve life can be a good experience, especially if you have grown up on the reserve. It can, however, stifle ambition, the motive for learning. For this reason, social workers, as well as teachers, must be present in the schools where they can encourage the Indian child to achieve and persevere. Many Indians are unaware of racial discrimination. Indian

Affairs should encourage the Indians to make new projects and to expand existing ones such as co-op farming.   ADG

202   **KNOCKWOOD   NOEL**
1970
LEADERSHIP PROGRAM NEEDED. Tawow 1(2):2-5,38.

Community development programs must encourage native leadership. To this end, specific training in leadership for Indian youth should be given.   IVY

203   **KNOWLES   D W**
1968
PERSONAL CONTROL OF DECISIONS MADE BY INDIAN YOUTH.
Unpublished paper delivered to Counselors' Workshop. Victoria, B.C., 1968. Available from National Library of Canada. pp. 49-55.

Factors relating to decision-making are examined, particularly variables influencing decision-making by Indian youth. The unfamiliar settings encountered, differential cultural values, self-evaluation, and sense of responsibility are discussed in relation to the development of decision-making abilities.   CCV

204   **LAGASSE   JEAN H**
n.d.
ADDRESS. Unpublished paper delivered to Summer Festival of Saskatchewan House, Regina, Sask. Available from Library, Department of Health and Social Development, Winnipeg, Man. 10 pp.

For both employment and education, the socio-economic conditions under which people of Indian background were living were detrimental to their successful integration. If their culture is to be changed, then plans to alter the environment must be considered. The concept of community development is presented as a means of achieving this aim. IVY

205   **LAGASSE   JEAN H**
n.d.
PROBLEMS OF INDIAN-METIS-WHITE RELATIONSHIPS. Unpublished paper. Available from Library, Department of Health and Social Development, Winnipeg, Man. 16 pp.

General background information on the Indian and Metis of Manitoba is presented. IVY

206   **LAGASSE   JEAN H**
1961
A ROAD REACHES TOWN. Unpublished paper delivered to Third Annual Short Course of Northern Community Development, Saskatoon, April 13, 1961. Available from Library, Department of Health and Social Development, Winnipeg, Man. 8 pp.

This paper discusses changes in economics, social life, and culture which might take place as a result of a road going into a community.   IVY

207   **LAGASSE   JEAN H**
1962
A COMMUNITY DEVELOPMENT PROGRAM FOR MANITOBA. Unpublished
paper. Available from Legislative Library, Winnipeg, Man. 5 pp.

In 1960, Manitoba began a rehabilitation program for peoples of Indian ancestry based
on the Community Development experiences gained by the United Nations and the British Colonial Office. The community approach, starting with what the local people want,
is heavily dependent upon the recruitment of qualified personnel.   IVY

208   **LAGASSE   JEAN H**
1966
INDIANS OF CANADA. America Indigena 26:387-394.

Population figures from 1965, geographic and linguistic distributions, occupations, and
Indian legislation are outlined in general for the Indians and Metis of Canada. Included
are information on Eskimo population and occupations, and a list of organizations working among Indians.   WRC

209   **LAGASSE JEAN H,   MANITOBA. Department of Health and Public Welfare.
Community Development Service.**
1962
HOW TO SOLVE COMMUNITY PROBLEMS. Ottawa: Northern Co-ordination and
Research Centre, Department of Northern Affairs and National Resources. 9 pp.

A sequence for problem-solving at the community level is derived from the 7th Annual
Indian and Metis Conference "Local Administration"discussion group.   CCV

210   **LAING   ARTHUR**
n.d.
SPEECHES BY ARTHUR LAING 1964-1966. Unpublished collection of speeches.
Available from Library, Department of Indian Affairs and Northern Development,
Ottawa. 285 pp.

Twenty-two speeches delivered by Arthur Laing as Minister of Northern Affairs and
National Resources are compiled and bound. Resource development and conservation
are central themes although occasional brief references to Canada's native peoples are
included.   CCV

211   **LAING   ARTHUR**
1967-1968
SPEECHES BY THE HONORABLE ARTHUR LAING ON THE NORTH, 1967,
1968. Unpublished collection of speeches. Available from Library, Department of
Indian Affairs and Northern Development, Ottawa. 165 pp.

Fifteen speeches on the North by the Minister of Indian Affairs and Northern Development, Arthur Laing, are compiled and bound.   Resource and community development
are emphasized with frequent reference to government efforts to improve education and
employment opportunities for Canadian Indians and Eskimos. A discussion of the Elliot
Lake pilot project is included.   CCV

212   **LAVALLEE   MARY ANN**
1969
NATIVE WOMEN AS A WHOLE. In Voice of Alberta Native Women's Society:
Alberta Native Women's Second Annual Conference. Edmonton, March 3-6, 1969. pp.
17-18.

The role of the contemporary Indian woman and her commitment to her people are discussed.   IVY

213   **LAVALLEE   MARY ANN**
1970
YESTERDAY'S INDIAN WOMEN. Tawow 1(1):7.

An Indian grandmother is portrayed.   IVY

214   **LEACH   F**
n.d.
INDIANS OF THE PRAIRIES AND OLD INDIAN REMEDIES. Unpublished paper.
Available from National Library of Canada. 26 pp.

A general overview of the Indians of Manitoba, Saskatchewan, and Alberta is provided.
Discussed are migration, material culture, political organization, religion, and world
view. The final 13 pages list herbal medicines, noting designation by common name,
Saulteaux name, and Latin name, symptoms, type of medication, the part of the plant
used, and method.   IVY

215   **LEACH   F**
1968
A TRIP WITH THE TREATY PARTY. Moccasin Telegraph 27(2):1-3.

A brief account of a trip to make Treaty payments in Manitoba is given. General comparisons to past treaty parties are given.   IVY

216   **LEBERG   NATALIE**
1968
A STUDY OF THE MOTIVATION OF CANADIAN INDIAN MIGRANT
AGRICULTURAL WORKERS. M.A. Thesis. Department of Anthropology.
University of Washington.

The title has been verified, but a copy was not obtained in time to abstract it.   SLP

217   **LEECHMAN   DOUGLAS**
1960
THE MEETING OF THE WAYS. The Beaver 291(Summer):4-11.

A general description of Canadian Indian history since White contact is presented.   IVY

218   **LEFEBVRE   GEORGE W**
1968

THE SOCIAL AND PHYSICAL HEALTH EFFECTS OF PUBLIC HOUSING ON INDIAN RESERVES. M.S.W. Thesis. School of Social Work. University of Manitoba.

The title has been verified, but a copy was not obtained in time to abstract it.   SLP

219   **LENTON   LLOYD**
1960
INDIANS OF CANADA. America Indigena: 15-24.

A brief description of the Indians and Metis of Canada is given. Census data from 1956, geographical distribution, government attitudes, and social and economic problems are outlined. Included is a list of organizations working among Indians.   WRC

220   **LINKLATER   CLIVE**
n.d.
INTEGRATION OR INTERSOCIATION. Unpublished paper. Available from Indian and Northern Curriculum Resources Centre, University of Saskatchewan. 6 pp.

The meanings of the terms integration, assimilation, and intersociation are discussed.   IVY

221   **LIPS   EVA**
1970
SOME REMARKS ON THE PRESENT STATUS OF NORTH AMERICAN INDIANS. Verhandlungen des XXXVIII. Internationalen Amerikanistenkongresses. Vol. 2, pp. 255-260.

General information is provided on the Indians of North America (excluding Mexico).   IVY

222   **LLOYD   ANTONY JOHN**
1967
COMMUNITY DEVELOPMENT IN CANADA. Ottawa: Canadian Research Centre for Anthropology, Saint Paul University. 98 pp.

Community development in Canada is reviewed with attention to its significance for Indian and Metis communities. The federal and provincial involvement and the types of projects and programs are examined for each province. Problem areas are discussed as well as an overview of projects attempted in other countries.   CCV

223   **LOTZ   JIM**
1967
HUMAN RIGHTS OF INDIANS AND ESKIMOS. Canadian Labour 12(12): 12-13,33.

Indian and Eskimo peoples must be accepted as equals in Canadian society with their cultures as a valuable contribution to the Canadian identity. Employment opportunities must offer parity with Whites in terms of training, level of skills, status, and income.   IVY

224   **LOTZ   JIM**
1968
EDUCATION, AUTOMATION AND THE INVISIBLE CANADIANS. The Nova
University Journal 2:28-36.

A total environmental approach is suggested for learning about Indian and Eskimo traditional cultures. This shared process of learning involving the traditional peoples as both
teachers and students may be the most inexpensive and humane approach to human development in Canada's North.   IVY

225   **LOVEKIN   J P**
1969
FOCUS ON INDIAN EDUCATION. OTF Reporter 15:5-8.

Aspects of the present Indian situation include poverty, cultural identity, education, and
treaties.   IVY

226   **MALCHELOSSE   GERARD**
1963
PEUPLES SAUVAGES DE LA NOUVELLE-FRANCE (1600-1670). Cahiers des Dix
28:63-92.

This is an enumeration of all the Canadian Indian tribes and those American tribes on
the border with their precise geographic location. The tribes are divided according to
their linguistic affiliation to the Algonkian or to the Iroquois-Huron family. The second
part of the article consists of a chronology of the most important events in the history of
Indian wars between tribes and against the Europeans.   DD

227   **MANITOBA INDIAN BROTHERHOOD**
1967
REPORT MANITOBA INDIAN BROTHERHOOD MEETING DEC. 5-8, 1967.
Unpublished paper. Available from National Library of Canada. 49 pp.

A meeting of the provisional executive of the Manitoba Indian Brotherhood was held to
outline organization and reorganization. Desire for full participation of Indian people of
Manitoba and consideration of available leadership were basic considerations of structural organization and objectives encompassing self-determination and treaty rights. The
proposed constitution is appended to the report of the meeting.   CCV

228   **MANITOBA. Department of Health and Public Welfare. Bureau of Health and
Welfare Education.**
1961
HOW TO SOLVE COMMUNITY PROBLEMS. Winnipeg: Bureau of Health and
Welfare Education. 6 pp.

The material reproduced in this booklet was prepared by a study group which met during
the 7th annual Indian and Metis Conference sponsored by the Welfare Council of
Greater Winnipeg, February 21-24, 1961. It outlines in a step-by-step manner the method
that can be used to solve community problems in Indian and Metis communities.   IVY

229   **MANITOBA. Department of Welfare. Community Development Services.**
1964

COMMUNITY DEVELOPMENT SERVICES VOCATIONAL GUIDANCE AND
JOB PLACEMENT PROGRAM. Unpublished paper. Available from Library,
Department of Health and Social Development, Winnipeg, Man. 7 pp.

The program of vocational guidance and job placement, part of Community Development Services in Manitoba, is explained.   IVY

230   **MANITOBA. Department of Welfare. Community Development Services.**
1965
COORDINATION OF GOVERNMENT SERVICES IN AREAS SERVED BY
COMMUNITY DEVELOPMENT OFFICERS. Unpublished paper. Available from
Library, Department of Health and Social Development, Winnipeg, Man. 3 pp.

The role of the Community Development Officer and the function of his office are discussed.   IVY

231   **MANITOBA. Department of Welfare. Community Development Services.**
1965
PROCEEDINGS OF THE SUMMER STAFF CONFERENCE HELD AT CLEAR
LAKE, MANITOBA: AUGUST 23-27, 1965. Unpublished paper. Available from
Library, Department of Health and Social Development, Winnipeg, Man. 129 pp.

Community development is explained and the roles and functions of its personnel (including their wives) defined. Reports are given for the following areas: Churchill, The
Pas, Camperville-Duck Bay, Moose Lake, Oak River, Norway House, Pine Falls, Easterville, and Grand Rapids. The conference was evaluated by the participants.   IVY

232   **MANITOBA. Department of Welfare. Community Development Services.**
1965
VILLAGE LEVEL WORKER SERVICE FOR INDIAN AND METIS
COMMUNITIES IN MANITOBA: A PILOT PROJECT. Unpublished paper. Available
from Library, Department of Health and Social Development, Winnipeg, Man. 6 pp.

A pilot project is described in which native leaders, chosen by their communities, are
trained in the process, methods, and techniques of community development,and in the
science and art of its application.   IVY

233   **MANITOBA. Department of Welfare. Community Development Services.**
1968
PRESENTATION: INTRA-DEPARTMENTAL MEETING: MAY 22 & 23, 1968.
Unpublished paper. Available from Library, Department of Health and Social
Development, Winnipeg, Man. 46 pp.

Community development is explained and the roles and functions of its personnel defined. Descriptions of programs are given in the following areas: Interlake Region, Roseau River, Camperville-Duck Bay-Pine Creek-Swan River, Oak River, Portage, Winnipeg, The Pas, Easterville-Grand Rapids, Churchill, Norway House, Moose Lake, Berens
River, Bay Line, Garden Hill, Pukutawagan, Nelson House, and Cross Lake.   IVY

234   **MANITOBA. Northern Task Force.**
1970

AN INTERIM REPORT FROM THE CITIZENS OF NORTHERN MANITOBA TO
THE MANITOBA LEGISLATURE, COMPILED BY THE NORTHERN TASK
FORCE. Winnipeg. 64 pp.

The Special Committee of the Legislature on Northern Affairs, established on October
10, 1969, resolved itself into the Northern Task Force at its first meeting October 30,
1969. The Task Force visited 4 communities in northern Manitoba to hear from the people themselves what they saw as their problems and what they suggested as solutions.
This report lists the communities visited, summarizes and consolidates the problems and
solutions of the people, and submits 49 recommendations based on the information received during the public hearings. A statement to the Manitoba Northern Task Force by
Dave Courchene, President of the Manitoba Indian Brotherhood and member of the
Manitoba Northern Task Force, concludes the report. Concern is expressed that negotiations or consultations between the federal government and the provincial government
not be undertaken without the prior knowledge, consent, and participation of the Indian
people. Recommendations in the areas of hunting and fishing rights, communication and
transportation, education, economic development, housing, and provincial assistance in
the funding of the Manitoba Indian Economic Development Fund are presented.   IVY

235   **MANITOBA. Northern Task Force.**
1970
SUMMARY OF MINUTES OF PUBLIC HEARINGS. Winnipeg, Man. 2 vols.

The Special Committee of the Legislature on Northern Affairs, established on October
10, 1969, resolved itself into the Northern Task Force at its first meeting October 30,
1969. The Task Force visited 41 northern communities to hear from the people themselves what they perceived as problems and solutions to their problems. These communities received assistance from representatives of the Manitoba Indian Brotherhood, the
Manitoba Metis Federation, and community development officers of the provincial government. These summary minutes of the public hearings include the 97 written briefs
and those persons giving verbal presentations who identified themselves. The problems
and solutions related to specific matters in each community.   IVY

236   **MANITOBA. The Community Welfare Planning Council.**
1968
MAP OF MANITOBA SHOWING AREAS POPULATED BY INDIANS AND
METIS. Winnipeg: The Community Welfare Planning Council. 1 p.

A map of Manitoba shows Indian reserves and communities, Metis communities, roads
and railways. Other information includes Indian population by reserve or community
and Metis population by community.   IVY

237   **MANUEL   GEORGE**
1967
A NEW ERA. The Peak (Simon Fraser University) 5(15):9.

Indians desire to be both full participants and a distinct segment of Canadian society.   TSA

238   **MANUEL   GEORGE**
1970

STATEMENT. In The Only Good Indian: Essays by Canadian Indians. Waubageshig, ed. Toronto: New Press. pp. 2-3.

It is deemed necessary that if Indians are to achieve social, economic, and political independence, a vast program for socio-economic change must be initiated. And, if Indians continue to be flouted in their attempts to solve problems on a collaboration basis, a violent reaction to the bureaucratic structure is foreseen.   DGW

239   **MARJORIBANKS   ROBERT**
1968
INDIANS OF CANADA PAVILION - EXPO 67. Ottawa: Queen's Printer. 17 pp.
Also in French.

Indian views are presented to visitors to Expo 67. The booklet discusses creation, White men, Christianity, the government, reserves, work, education, and the future.   JSL

240   **MCDONALD   MARGARET,   WALKER   HARRY W,   et al.**
1968
PUSHING BACK THE NORTHERN FRONTIER. Canadian Geographical Journal 77:142-153.

CBC Northern Service has 29 stations and broadcasts in English, French, Indian languages, and Eskimo. Various programs, including those prepared by Indians and Eskimos in their own languages, are described.   IVY

241   **MCEWEN   E R**
1964
REPORT OF THE EXECUTIVE DIRECTOR. Unpublished paper delivered to 5th Annual Meeting, Indian-Eskimo Association of Canada. London, Ont., November 21, 1964. Available from Indian-Eskimo Association. 18 pp.

This report mentions many problematic factors and specific roles of the Indian-Eskimo Association of Canada in native affairs for the year 1964.   HCV

242   **MCEWEN   E R**
1965
EDUCATION OR ECONOMIC DEVELOPMENT - WHICH COMES FIRST?
Unpublished paper delivered to North Bay Conference. North Bay, Ont., November 21, 1965. Available from Indian-Eskimo Association. 5 pp.

A member of the Canadian delegation to the World Congress to Eradicate Illiteracy, sponsored by UNESCO, reports on this conference and the progress of the literacy program in Iran. From this experience, parallels are noted in education and economic development between Indian and Eskimo communities and underdeveloped countries.   IVY

243   **MCEWEN   E R**
1965
REPORT OF THE EXECUTIVE DIRECTOR. Unpublished paper delivered to 6th Annual Meeting, Indian-Eskimo Association of Canada. Toronto, October 21, 1965. Available from Indian-Eskimo Association. 13 pp.

The executive director's report presents the background and basic structure of the Indian-Eskimo Association. Work programs for the year 1964-65 are (1) the preparation of special studies and reports to be presented to the government, (2) committee activities, (3) friendship centers, (4) northern radio, (5) Indian-Eskimo Association publications, and (6) the project of famous Canadian Indians.   HCV

244   **MCEWEN   E R**
1966
REPORT OF THE EXECUTIVE DIRECTOR. Unpublished paper delivered to 7th Annual Meeting, Indian-Eskimo Association. Vancouver, December 2, 1966. Available from Indian-Eskimo Association. 14 pp.

This report gives an account of the Association's work and some background information on the range and depth of problems and obstacles native citizens face. This report also focuses on the national and provincial profile of the Association in such areas as hunting, fishing, population, health, education, and delinquency.   HCV

245   **MCEWEN   E R**
1967
REPORT OF THE EXECUTIVE DIRECTOR. Unpublished paper delivered to 8th Annual Meeting, Indian-Eskimo Association. Calgary, September 30, 1967. Available from Indian-Eskimo Association. 31 pp.

This report, in addition to giving an account of the Indian-Eskimo Association's activities, presents the role of Canadians in achieving the cause of the native Canadians. Included in this report is a profile of native Canadians, their population, housing, poverty, education, health, and delinquency, and a summary of the Indian-Eskimo Association's work at the national and provincial level.   HCV

246   **MCEWEN   E R**
1968
REPORT OF THE EXECUTIVE DIRECTOR. Unpublished paper delivered to 9th Annual Meeting, Indian-Eskimo Association. Toronto, September 28, 1968. Available from Indian-Eskimo Association. 32 pp.

This report presents the situation of the Indian-Eskimo Association in 1968, touching on aspects of Indian, Eskimo and Metis problems such as population, economy, housing, education, treaties and the Indian Act. The report also gives an account of the activities at the national and provincial level.   HCV

247   **MCEWEN   E R**
1969
REPORT OF THE EXECUTIVE DIRECTOR. Unpublished paper delivered to 10th Annual Member's Meeting, Indian-Eskimo Association of Canada. Winnipeg, June 13, 1969. Available from Indian-Eskimo Association. 24 pp.

This reports the development of the Indian-Eskimo Association of Canada from June, 1968, to June, 1969, showing its structure, resources, and major activities. It presents a summary of native education and the financial report of the Association for the year ending March 31, 1969.   HCV

248   **MENARIK   ELIJAH**
1966
PROGRESS TOWARD EQUAL OPPORTUNITY. Unpublished paper delivered to
Annual Meeting of Members, Indian-Eskimo Association of Canada. Vancouver, B.C.,
December 2, 1966. Available from Indian-Eskimo Association. 2 pp.

Local people must be involved to ensure progress toward equal opportunity. Eskimo and
Indian initiative must be supported and encouraged.   IVY

249   **MICHEA   JEAN**
1968
VIE ET MOEURS DES PEAUX-ROUGES. Paris: Societe Continentale d'Editions
Modernes Illustrees. 370 pp.

American Indian traditional life style and customs are reviewed regionally. Given extensive treatment are the Iroquois, the Northwest Coast, and the Plains. A chapter on the
contemporary scene discusses conditions in both Canada and the United States and includes an examination of the acculturation of the Carrier Indians of British
Columbia.   CCV

250   **MILORD   JAMES E**
1970
GENOCIDE IN CANADA: "WE CALL IT INTEGRATION."The United Church
Observer N.S. 33(2):24-26.

An Indian school teacher briefly discusses the uniqueness of various Indian cultures and
the Indians' contributions to society.   The suggestion that Indians develop aggressive
behavioral traits is believed tantamount to cultural genocide. What is needed is not services but friendship - with no strings attached.   IVY

251   **MORIN   LEOPOLD**
1970
MOOSONEE INDIANS' INTEGRATION. Kerygma 4(1):23-27.

Integration must be a slow and gradual process. Cultural changes deemed necessary for
integration are (1) acquisition of a foreign language (English or French), (2) adjustment
of new cultural values, (3) learning of new trades, and (4) adjustment to new social con-
ventions.   IVY

252   **MORLEY   JOHN**
1969
THE REAL PEOPLE. Monday Morning 3(9):25-26.

Natives of North America prefer to refer to themselves as the Original or Real People.
The Committee of Social Action for Indians of the Americas suggests that the Real People of North America be called North Americans. The original peoples, as exemplified by
the Long House People of the Iroquois, wish to preserve their traditional way of
life.   IVY

253   **MORLOCK   B H**
1965

THE BOY SCOUTS OF CANADA. In Norec Conference: The Development of Indian and Eskimo Art and Crafts in the Far North, Northern Regional Committee, Indian-Eskimo Association of Canada. Toronto, May 3, 1965. Unpublished paper. Available from Indian-Eskimo Association. pp. 7-8.

The Boy Scouts program of expansion in northern Canada is briefly outlined.   IVY

254   **MORRISON   O M**
1967
THESE PEOPLE WE CALL 'INDIANS.' The Educational Courier 38(2):21.

Canadians need to know more about Canada's aboriginal peoples. Some general information and references are provided.   IVY

255   **MORTIMORE   GEORGE**
1967
THE INDIANS ARE LOSING ANOTHER WAR. Continuous Learning 6:61-66.

The power struggle between superintendents and community development officers in Canada is a direct result of conflict in role definitions.   IVY

256   **MURDOCK   GEORGE PETER**
1967
ETHNOGRAPHIC ATLAS. Pittsburgh, PA: University of Pittsburgh Press. 128 pp.

A series of tables code data on the cultures of the world including the following culture clusters from Canada: Cree-Montagnais, Maritime Algonkians, Ojibwa, Northeastern Athapaskans, Carrier-Nahani, Upper Yukon, Tlingit-Haida, Tsimshian-Haisla, Kwakiutl-Bellacoola, Nootka-Quileute, Coast Salish, Interior Salish, Northern Plateau, Kutenai, Northwest Plains, Northeast Plains, Central Algonkians, Iroquois, and Middle Atlantic Algonkians. Data presented include 41 variables relating to subsistence, social organization, settlement pattern, religion, material culture, and linguistic affiliation. This volume is a summary of the first 21 installments of the "Ethnographic Atlas"to appear in the journal Ethnology. The "Ethnographic Atlas"continues in that journal, but has not been separately entered in this bibliography.   IVY

257   **NATIONAL INDIAN BROTHERHOOD OF CANADA, CANADIAN METIS SOCIETY, et al.**
1968
REPORT OF A JOINT MEETING OF THE BOARDS OF DIRECTORS OF THE ABOVE ORGANIZATIONS FOR THE PURPOSE OF REVIEWING AND RE-DIRECTING THE ROLE OF THE INDIAN-ESKIMO ASSOCIATION. Unpublished paper. Available from Indian-Eskimo Association. 56 pp.

This report contains discussions and conclusions in redirecting the role of the Indian-Eskimo Association of Canada with particular reference to other national Indian organizations. It is stated that native groups desire support from the Indian-Eskimo Association, but do not desire the latter to exercise power over them.   HCV

258   **NATIONAL INDIAN BROTHERHOOD OF CANADA, CANADIAN METIS SOCIETY, et al.**

1969
APPENDIX "D"TO THE BRIEF PRESENTED TO THE SPECIAL SENATE
COMMITTEE ON MASS MEDIA - DECEMBER, 1969: BACKGROUND: THE
PRESENT CONDITION OF NATIVE CANADIANS. Unpublished paper. Available
from Indian-Eskimo Association. 1 p.

Seven facts are presented on population, poverty, unemployment, income, mortality rate,
life expectancy, and education.   IVY

259   **NATIONAL INDIAN BROTHERHOOD OF CANADA, CANADIAN METIS
SOCIETY, et al.**
1969
APPENDIX "E"TO THE BRIEF PRESENTED TO THE SPECIAL SENATE
COMMITTEE ON MASS MEDIA - DECEMBER, 1969: RADIO, TELEVISION AND
FILMS AS A MEANS OF PRODUCING SOCIAL CHANGE. Unpublished paper.
Available from Indian-Eskimo Association. 3 pp.

Programs of the CBC and the National Film Board are discussed in terms of promoting
social change.   IVY

260   **NATIONAL INDIAN BROTHERHOOD OF CANADA, CANADIAN METIS
SOCIETY, et al.**
1969
APPENDIX "G"TO THE BRIEF PRESENTED TO THE SPECIAL SENATE
COMMITTEE ON MASS MEDIA - DECEMBER, 1969: PRESENT BROADCASTS
FOR NATIVE PEOPLES IN CANADA. Unpublished paper. Available from Indian-
Eskimo Association. 7 pp.

Current radio programs for native peoples in the Northwest Territories, Alberta, British
Columbia, and northern Ontario are discussed.   IVY

261   **NATIONAL INDIAN COUNCIL OF CANADA**
1965
MINUTES. NATIONAL INDIAN COUNCIL OF CANADA 5th ANNUAL
CONVENTION. Regina, August 9-11, 1965. Unpublished paper. Available from
National Library of Canada. 22 pp.

The minutes of the 5th annual convention of the National Indian Council of Canada are
compiled. An address by the Director, Indian and Metis Branch, Saskatchewan Government, outlines the activities of his department, particularly in employment and service programs. Community development programs are discussed by an official of the Indian Affairs Branch. Reports of the committees on crafts, Indian dancing, Claims Bill
123, education, Indian organization, constitution, and Indian press club are included.   CCV

262   **NATIONAL SPIRITUAL ASSEMBLY OF THE BAHA'IS OF CANADA**
1968
A PRESENTATION BY THE CANADIAN BAHA'I COMMUNITY. Unpublished
paper delivered to Canadian Conference on Human Rights. Ottawa, December 1-3,
1968. Available from National Library of Canada. 32 pp.

This paper is presented by the Baha'i Community with particular references to the Canadian native concerning human rights such as equality before the law, economic security, protection of minorities, and the right to and the nurturing of an identity.   HCV

263   **NICHOLAS   ANDREW**
1968
RESPONSE TO PAPER PRESENTED BY ANDREW DELISLE. In Discussion on Human Rights. Noel A. Kinsella, chairman. Fredericton, N.B.:   Human Rights Commission. pp. 125-131.

This paper responds to that presented by Andrew Delisle at the Provincial Conference on Human Rights, Fredericton, New Brunswick, March 25 and 16, 1968, and projects concern about the human rights of the Indians of New Brunswick.   IVY

264   **OLIVER   JESSIE**
1969
INDIANS OF CANADA: PROGRAM SUGGESTIONS. Toronto: United Church of Canada, Committee on Education for Missions and Stewardship, Division of Congregational Life and Work. 11 pp.

A list of suggestions to non-Indian leaders and Program Committees regarding projects involving Indians is given. Aimed at the appreciation of Indian people and the problems they face, these projects should be planned with the Indians and with their support.   IVY

265   **OPEKOKEW   DELIA**
1970
INDIAN PRINCESS CANADA PAGEANT. Tawow 1(3):32-35.

A report of the National Pageant held at Yellowknife, N.W.T., is given.   IVY

266   **OSWALT   WENDELL H**
1966
THIS LAND WAS THEIRS: A STUDY OF THE NORTH AMERICAN INDIAN.
New York: John Wiley and Sons. 560 pp.

Presented is a description of representative tribes from different cultural and biotic areas of North America. Chapters 1, 2, 7, and 9 deal with the Chipewyan, Beothuk, Tlingit, and Iroquois respectively. The cultural traits of each tribe are traced from historic times to its extinction or modern phase. In the introduction, the lifeways of the aboriginal Americans are discussed in a comparative context with a delineation of the major characteristics of each cultural area. The final chapter attempts to summarize the contemporary position of the Canadian and American Indian.   DGW

267   **O'CONNELL   MARTIN**
1964
BREAKING THE CYCLE OF POVERTY IN INDIAN RESERVE COMMUNITIES.
Unpublished paper delivered to Ontario Conference, Indian-Eskimo Association of Canada. London, Ont., November 21, 1964. Available from Indian-Eskimo Association. 9 pp.

A sound economic base is essential for the success of programs in improved housing, welfare, health, and general community development on Indian reserves. An Economic Development Agency with substantial capital funds is outlined which would supply loans, grants, technical services, and research of a development nature. The need of housing programs is emphasized throughout the report. To break the cycle of poverty, citizen initiative is needed.   IVY

268   O'CONNELL   MARTIN
1964
SUDBURY WORKSHOP, JUNE 25-27, 1964: REPORT OF RESOLUTIONS APPROVED AT THE NORTHEASTERN REGIONAL WORKSHOP OF THE INDIAN-ESKIMO ASSOCIATION OF CANADA IN CO-OPERATION WITH THE SUDBURY CITIZEN'S COMMITTEE IN SUDBURY, JUNE 25-27, 1964.
Unpublished paper. Available from Indian-Eskimo Association. 2 pp.

The Northeastern Regional Workshop of the Indian-Eskimo Association in co-operation with the Sudbury Citizen's Committee was held June 25-27, 1964. Passed in a session under the chairmanship of Mr. Wilfred Pelletier, resolutions concern education, Chief and Councillor seminars, conference facilities, recreation, Department of Health and Welfare facilities and regulations, band managers, and a Native Peoples Economic Development Agency.   IVY

269   **PELLETIER   WILFRED**
1967
SOME THOUGHTS ABOUT ORGANIZATION & LEADERSHIP. Unpublished paper. Available from National Library of Canada. 8 pp.

The author begins this paper with a story that he feels justifies the rejection of the establishment and the values of White society by the Indian and non-Indian young people. The paper relates the conflict of Indian and White values and attitudes toward organization, leadership, socialization, communication, and education.   HCV

270   **PENNEY   R J**
1965
THE FEDERATED WOMEN'S INSTITUTES OF CANADA. In Norec Conference: The Development of Indian and Eskimo Art and Crafts in the Far North, Northern Regional Committee, Indian-Eskimo Association of Canada. Toronto, May 3, 1965. Unpublished paper. Available from Indian-Eskimo Association. pp. 11-12.

Craft work is a major project of northern Women's Institutes. Activities in this area are briefly described.   IVY

271   **PINAY   ED**
1969
HUMAN AND NATURAL RESOURCES. Unpublished paper delivered to Mid-Canada Development Corridor Conference, Thunder Bay, August 18-22, 1969. Available from Center for Settlement Studies, University of Manitoba. 5 pp.

Economic development in Canada's mid-corridor must involve the native populations. The only successful approach is mutual dialogue, not paternalism.   IVY

272   **PINNEY   ROY**
      1968
      VANISHING TRIBES. New York: Thomas Y. Crowell. 272 pp.

      Brief treatments are given the Indians of the Northeast, the Plains, and the Pacific coast
      in this introduction to the cultures of primitive peoples.   TSA

273   **POOLE   D G**
      n.d.
      INTEGRATION. Unpublished paper. Available from Indian-Eskimo Association. 22
      pp.

      By comparing and contrasting the basic White and Indian cultures, the author defines
      integration and makes suggestions for its functions within both societies.   HCV

274   **POOLE   D G**
      1965
      A DISCUSSION OF INDIAN OBJECTIVES AND SOME PRACTICAL
      CONSIDERATIONS TOWARD THE REALIZATION OF THESE. Unpublished
      paper. Available from National Library of Canada. 27 pp.

      To achieve respect for and restoration of traditional practices, individual Indian popula-
      tions must unite racially, politically, economically, and geographically. Conflicting value
      orientations of Indian and White cultures concerning land, land ownership, and religion
      are discussed. Christian churches should be asked to terminate their present efforts as
      missionaries and leave reserves. Indians must set up their own educational system and
      have recourse to their total resources. Suggestions to this effect are offered.   IVY

275   **PORTEOUS   G F**
      1966
      CO-OPERATIVE INDIAN RESERVES. Unpublished paper. Available from National
      Library of Canada. 4 pp.

      This paper is a summary on how to organize and operate a co-operative and keep it func-
      tioning. Several examples of Indian co-operatives in Saskatchewan are provided.   HCV

276   **PROVINCIAL COUNCIL OF WOMEN OF BRITISH COLUMBIA**
      1964
      PROCEEDINGS. Indian Study Conference. Department of Extension, U.B.C., and
      Provincial Council of Women. Vancouver, November 18, 1964. Available from
      Department of Extension, University of British Columbia. 5 pp.

      A summary of the proceedings of the Indian Study Conference is given. Appended are
      the addresses (full text) of Mrs. J. E. Sowerby, Mr. S. J. Bailey, and Mr. Jules
      D'Astous. IVY

277   **QUINN   DAVID B,   ROUSSEAU   JACQUES**
      1966
      LES TOPONYMES AMERINDIENS DU CANADA CHEZ LES VOYAGEURS
      ANGLAIS, 1591-1602. Cahiers de Geographie de Quebec 10:263-277.

Eastern Canadian place names of Indian origin are discussed in 2 sections. Those arising from English sources are noted by David Quinn with an historical review. The 2nd portion of the analysis, by Jacques Rousseau, attacks the problem of tribal or linguistic origin. CCV

278 **RAYBURN J A**
1967
GEOGRAPHICAL NAMES OF AMERINDIAN ORIGIN IN CANADA: PART 1
INTRODUCTION. Names 15:203-215.

Place names originating from Amerindian languages in the Maritime Provinces and Quebec are presented. The main source of information is the records of the Canadian Permanent Committee on Geographical Names supplemented by the Committee's large reference collection of Indian dictionaries. IVY

279 **RAYBURN J A**
1969
GEOGRAPHICAL NAMES OF AMERINDIAN ORIGIN IN CANADA: PART 2.
Names 17:149-158.

Place names originating from Amerindian languages in Ontario, Manitoba, Saskatchewan, Alberta, British Columbia, the Northwest Territories, and the Yukon are presented. Probable meanings are given on 450 discrete geographical names in Parts 1 and 2. IVY

280 **REES MORRISS**
1967
AN EXCLAMATION. The Peak (Simon Fraser University) 5(15):10.

A former school teacher censures the behavior of Whites toward Indians in British Columbia towns. TSA

281 **REID D C S**
1962
NORM-SETTING AND NORM-VIOLATING BEHAVIOUR IN THE INDIAN OR HIS DESCENDANT. Unpublished paper prepared for Staff Conference of the John Howard Society of Alberta. Available from National Library of Canada. 4 pp.

Based on observations of the Indian prisoner and the cultural factors which lead to his personality development, the report is designed to give the after-care worker a better perspective and understanding of the native person. HCV

282 **REILLY FRANCIS J**
1967
A COMPARATIVE STUDY OF INDIAN AND NON-INDIAN PAROLE APPLICANTS IN ALBERTA: A COMPARATIVE ANALYSIS OF TWENTY INDIAN PAROLE APPLICANTS AND TWENTY NON-INDIAN PAROLE APPLICANTS INCARCERATED IN THE BOWDEN INSTITUTION DURING 1966 IN TERMS OF THE FOCI OF FAMILY, WORK, CRIME AND REHABILITATION. M.S.W. Thesis. Saint Patrick's College. University of Ottawa. 105 pp. Available from Library, School of Social Work, Carleton University.

Data were drawn from examination of case records of 20 Indian and 20 non-Indian applicants for parole from Bowden Institution and Nordegg Prison Camp during the period March 4, 1964, to July 1, 1966. The findings were classified and compared under family, work, crime, and rehabilitation. The non-Indian is classed as anti-social as a result of this study. He is observed to lack personal control and to rebel against the social controls of the culture. Because the Indian lacks personal controls and his culture lacks social controls, he is classed as asocial. The implications for treatment are noted.   CCV

283   **RENAUD   ANDRE**
1960
INDIANS OF CANADA AS AN ETHNIC MINORITY. Unpublished paper delivered to Research Seminar on Indian Matters, Annual Meeting of the Learned Societies of Canada. Kingston, Ont., June 12-15, 1960. Available from National Library of Canada. 9 pp.

Rather than assimilation another approach is offered; that of considering Indians an ethnic group in Canada and secondly, as an ethnic minority group. Describing characteristics, functions, and status of ethnic groupings and minority groups in Canada, it is shown that Indian populations in Canada fulfill in every respect the description of ethnic minority groups.   IVY

284   **RENAUD   ANDRE**
1961
INDIAN AND METIS AND POSSIBLE DEVELOPMENT AS ETHNIC GROUPS. Unpublished paper delivered to 3rd Annual Short Course on Northern Community Development. Saskatoon, April 14, 1961. Available from National Library of Canada. 10 pp.

Comparing Indian and Metis settlements to non-Indian ethnic communities and groups, it is evident that the Indian has been denied the right to persevere as an ethnic group. Recognizing the value of ethnic groups and the injustice of the present situation, support and encouragement should be given the Indians in their efforts to group themselves regionally and nationally.   IVY

285   **RENAUD   ANDRE**
1963
COMMUNAUTES ETHNIQUES ET COLLECTIVITES INDIENNES AU CANADA. Recherches Sociographiques 4(1):91-105.

The Indian collectivity is discussed as an ethnic group and its role in Canadian society is compared to that of other ethnic communities. The concentrated efforts to have the Indian abandon his culture is contrasted with the recognition of the cultural contributions of other ethnic groups. The fact that the Indian, faced with this policy, tends to withdraw is underlined. The implications of a revised approach to education which would emphasize positive aspects of Indian culture are indicated.   CCV

286   **RENAUD   ANDRE**
1965
INDIAN HAS AS MUCH TO OFFER WHITE MAN AS WHITE MAN HAS TO OFFER INDIAN, SAYS PROFESSOR-PRIEST. Canadian School Journal 43(9):7-8.

To industrial man, the Indian can offer an integrated personality and his knowledge that the joy of life is in human relationships. Through his ignorance and need to classify and categorize others, industrial man has created the Indian problem as it is called and reduced it to an economic issue, which theoretically should be eliminated by raising the Indians' standard of living. No one asked, however, whether or not the Indian might have something better. Thus, integration has become a means of assimilation rather than cultural sharing. Different views regarding matters such as work have led to many of the Indian-White conflicts. And if the Indian is to become a part of industrialized society, some way must be derived to show him the end product of his work. Similarly, school curricula must be made alive and relevant to the Indian child.   ADG

287   **RITZENTHALER   ROBERT E**
1969
AMERICAN INDIAN TRIBAL NAMES. Lore 19:66-68.

The ways in which tribal names were acquired are explored. These include the Haida, Tlingit, Ottawa, Flathead, Blackfoot, Iroquois, and Montagnais.   IVY

288   **ROBERT LAWRENCE PRODUCTIONS**
1969
THE INDIAN REVOLUTION: TRANSCRIPT OF THE PIERRE BERTON SHOW: PARTS 1-5. Available from National Library of Canada. 64 pp.

Transcripts are presented of the Pierre Berton shows: The Indian Revolution - Why the Indians Are Angry, Hollywood Indians - Textbook Indians, The Rape of the Language, Red Power, and Justifying the White Way. Indians across Canada are interviewed, many of them presenting opposing viewpoints, on the subjects of pan-Indianism, acculturation, integration, cultural values, education, Indian-White relations, and the "Indian problem."The programs were originally broadcast from Toronto, February 2-6, 1969.   CCV

289   **ROBERTSON   HEATHER**
1970
RESERVATIONS ARE FOR INDIANS. Toronto: James Lewis and Samuel. 303 pp.

Presented is a description and analysis of life on reserves and in Indian communities in Canada. The author, a journalist, spent 8 months (May 1966 to April 1967) travelling in western and northern Canada gathering first-hand information on reservation culture. The squalid physical conditions and psychological paralysis of many reserve dwellers are attributed to the structure and attitudes of Canadian society. Indians merely act as consumers of White institutions whose only function is to provide services for Indians, whether it is the hospital, school, the Bay store, the welfare department, or Indian Affairs. By presenting the study against the historical background of the government's Indian policy, it is shown that attempts at solving the Indian problem have failed merely because the Indian has not been treated as a human being.   DGW

290   **ROBERTSON   R G**
1967
THE COMING CRISIS IN THE NORTH. Journal of Canadian Studies 2(1):3-11.

A section of this paper relates to the critical human problem of the North. A total program of education for the next generation is proposed.   IVY

291   **ROGERS   E S**
1968
WITHIN TWO WORLDS. Rotunda 1(1):15-21.

The Ontario Indian is in transition, caught between the world of his forefathers and that of the White man. Although many of the Indian's problems are due to mismanagement by the Euro-Canadian, some are due to personal experiences. A partial answer to the latter may be effective counselling.   ADG

292   **ROGERS   EDWARD S**
1965
INDIAN TIME. Ontario Fish and Wildlife Review 4(4):23-26.

Examples from fieldwork observation in 1953 and 1954 with the Mistassini Cree of central Quebec illustrate the Indians' concept of time.   IVY

293   **ROGERS   EDWARD S**
1966
THE INDIAN CONCEPT OF PROPERTY. Ontario Fish and Wildlife Review 5(1):21-25.

The Indians' concept of property is illustrated by examples from fieldwork observation in 1953 and 1954 with the Mistassini Cree of central Quebec.   IVY

294   **ROGERS   EDWARD S**
1966
THE NATIVE PEOPLES OF CANADA. Unpublished paper. Available from Royal Ontario Museum, Toronto. 19 pp.

Environment, material culture, religious orientation, subsistence activities, warfare, and social organization are described for the 6 aboriginal culture areas of Canada.   IVY

295   **ROGERS   EDWARD S**
1970
THE INDIANS OF CANADA: A SURVEY. Toronto: Royal Ontario Museum. 20 pp.

A brief review of Canadian culture areas is presented touching on social organization, subsistence activities, and technology at the time of contact with Europeans.   CCV

296   **ROUSSEAU   JACQUES**
1960
LES PREMIERS CANADIENS. Cahiers des Dix 25:9-64.

This is a general review of the variety of Canadian Indian tribes as it was described by historians of the 19th century. Further information is given on Canadian Indian history from tribal origins to the contemporary problems of acculturation.   DD

297   **ROXBOROUGH   HENRY**
1966
ONE HUNDRED - NOT OUT: THE STORY OF NINETEENTH CENTURY
SPORT. Toronto: Ryerson. 252 pp.

Canadian 19th-century games, sports activities, and competitions locally evolved and
bearing foreign influence are reviewed. Chapter 2 is devoted to activities derived from
the Indians and includes brief accounts of competitions as does Chapter 3 which deals
with early settlers.   CCV

298   **SAPIR   EDWARD**
1967
ANTHROPOLOGIE. Paris: Editions de Minuit. 2 vols.

Twenty of Edward Sapir's works are compiled in 2 volumes and published in French.
The 1st volume is largely devoted to Sapir's theoretical contribution to the study of
behavior. The 2nd volume is devoted to a discussion of culture. The means of establishing chronological sequences in culture history are classified. The value of linguistic indicators is emphasized with frequent reference to North American Indian groups. The fundamental importance of hereditary privileges, the shift from the community village to
the clan, the origin of the emblematic system as compared to other totems, and the development of the notion of a hierarchy of individuals and privileges are emphasized in a
monograph on the social organization of the West Coast.   CCV

299   **SASKATCHEWAN**
1964
CONFERENCE BETWEEN THE PROVINCE OF SASKATCHEWAN AND THE
PEOPLE OF INDIAN ANCESTRY. Unpublished paper. Available from Library,
Department of Public Health, Regina, Sask. 115 pp.

Background information and actions of a conference held September 22 to 24, 1964, in
Regina are presented. Part 1 explains arrangements and lists authorized delegates, observers, and conference staff. Part 2 provides information about present provincial programs. Part 3 contains speeches made by W. Ross Thatcher and the Ministers of Natural
Resources, Agriculture, Cooperation and Cooperative Development, Public Health,
Municipal Affairs, and Social Welfare and Rehabilitation. These present the government's policy and objectives. Part 4 includes the resolutions and requests made during the
conference. These are requests for action in the areas of education; libraries; power and
telephone service; medicine; housing; economic development in agriculture, timber,
fishing, and tourism; farming research; construction; employment; co-operative matters;
and welfare.   IVY

300   **SASKATCHEWAN. Department of Welfare.**
n.d.
AIM: ADOPT INDIAN METIS. Regina: Department of Welfare. 1 p.

A 1 page pamphlet outlines the requirements for adoption of an Indian or Metis
child.   IVY

301   **SASKATCHEWAN. Department of Welfare. Program Division.**
n.d.
AIM: AN INTERIM INVENTORY: APRIL 1, 1967 TO FEBRUARY 1, 1969.

REPORT NO. 5. Unpublished paper. Available from National Library of Canada. 35 pp.

AIM is a program in operation designed to make the public more aware of the need for adoption homes, rather than foster homes, for Indian and Metis children. This program has advertised its objectives through the media of newspapers, slide series, and television.   HCV

302   **SASKATCHEWAN. Department of Welfare. Program Division.**
1969
CARLYLE WHITEBEAR RESERVE. REPORT NO. 11. Unpublished paper. Available from National Library of Canada. 14 pp.

Prepared in response to a request from the Associate Minister of the Department of Welfare that an investigation be conducted into the problems in the Carlyle area and recommendations be formulated as to the role a Department of Welfare worker might play, interviews were conducted with a small number of key people who had concerns with the community.   HCV

303   **SAUVE   CLAYTON**
1969
THEORETICAL CONSIDERATIONS FOR SOCIO-ECOLOGICAL
DEVELOPMENT AMONG NATIVE PEOPLE IN THE LESSER SLAVE LAKE
AREA. In Perspectives on Regions and Regionalism and Other Papers. B. Y. Card, ed. Proceedings of the Tenth Annual Meeting of the Western Association of Sociology and Anthropology, Held at Banff, Alberta, December 28, 29 and 30, 1968. Edmonton: University of Alberta Printing Service. pp. 201-209.

Research on North American Indians in the following areas is summarized: values, need for achievement, achievement orientation, acculturation, alienation, and ecological distance.   TSA

304   **SAUVE   CLAYTON**
1969
THEORETICAL CONSIDERATIONS FOR SOCIO-ECONOMIC DEVELOPMENT AMONG NATIVE PEOPLE. Unpublished paper. Available from National Library of Canada. 33 pp.

Because of social and economic underdevelopment among native people, the Research and Planning Division of the Alberta government undertook this study to isolate social and economic variables and to suggest how measurement of these variables may help in designing and carrying out native development programs. The appendix (pages 17-33) includes Gue's Value Orientation Questionnaire, Rosen's Achievement Orientation Test, Kuhn's Twenty Statements Test, and the Dean Alienation Scale.   IVY

305   **SAVARD   REMI**
1970
ET LES AUTRES QUEBECOIS.... Interpretation 4(3):117-131.

This is a plea to arouse the public conscience in favor of the Indian and Eskimo of Quebec. French Canadian anthropology has not been aware of the dominating posture of

Canadian society towards its native minority. The author suggests that French Canadians should understand the important differences between Indian culture and their own, and accept the Quebec Indians' new quest for cultural identity.   DD

306   **SCHMITT   N,   BARCLAY   W S**
1962
ACCIDENTAL DEATHS AMONG WEST COAST INDIANS. Canadian Journal of Public Health 53:409-412.

In 1959 accidents were the leading cause of death among registered Indians in British Columbia, and contributed a substantial percentage of the total accident mortality of the province.   IVY

307   **SHEFFE   NORMAN, ed.**
1970
ISSUES FOR THE SEVENTIES: CANADA'S INDIANS. Toronto: McGraw-Hill. 86 pp.

A collection of articles by or concerning Indians, from 1968 and 1969 periodicals and newspapers, is presented to demonstrate the current status of the Canadian Indian, difficulties involved in acculturation and education, existing relations with provincial and federal governments, and proposals for change.   CCV

308   **SINGER   MILTON**
1961
A SURVEY OF CULTURE AND PERSONALITY AND RESEARCH. In Studying Personality Cross-Culturally. Bert Kaplan, ed. New York: Harper and Row. pp. 9-90.

Included in this critical review of major theoretical and empirical works in the culture and personality field are brief references to Benedict's work on the Kwakiutl, Wallace on the Tuscarora, and Wallace and Hallowell on the Ojibwa.   CCV

309   **SMITH   ARTHUR J**
1965
THE ENVIRONMENT OF THE CANADIAN INDIAN. Habitat 8(4):2-9.

A survey of housing conditions in 18 Indian communities from northwest Ontario through British Columbia concludes that there is a very high proportion of overcrowded, inadequate, substandard housing and a real lack of community services. Photographs accompany text.   IVY

310   **SMITHERAM   H A**
1968
BACKGROUND INFORMATION AND COUNSELLING IMPLICATIONS FOR NATIVE INDIANS IN THE PACIFIC REGION: COUNSELLORS HANDBOOK. Unpublished paper. Available from Department of Manpower and Immigration, Vancouver, B.C. 35 pp.

The purpose of this report is to provide Manpower counselors with background knowledge of the Canadian Indian. Terms used in discussing Indian Affairs are defined. Statistical information on Canada's and British Columbia's native populations, some speeches and addresses, and a listing of agencies and services available to Indians of British Columbia are also included.   IVY

311   **SOCIAL SERVICE AUDIT INCORPORATED**
1969
SOCIAL SERVICE AUDIT REPORT, WINNIPEG, 1969. Unpublished paper. Available from Library, Department of Health and Social Development, Winnipeg, Man. 175 pp.

This report summarizes the present situation of social services in Metropolitan Winnipeg, assesses current problems and limitations, and recommends improved ways of getting services to people. Pages 93-95 specifically concern services for native peoples.   IVY

312   **SOCIAL SERVICE AUDIT INCORPORATED. Child Welfare Technical Committee.**
1968
REPORT. Unpublished paper. Available from Library, Department of Health and Social Development, Winnipeg, Man. 48 pp.

This report is an assessment of all phases of child welfare in Metropolitan Winnipeg. Pages 24-27 specifically concern the Indian and Metis child. The committee recommends: (1) an urban orientation program, (2) a head start program for pre-school children, (3) placement services, (4) subsidized rents, (5) special courses for those working with the Indians, (6) an adequate staff in areas with a large Indian or Metis population, (7) planning and administrative services to Indian and Metis taking place on a regional basis under provincial auspices, and (8) the establishment of a civil rights organization with special attention to Indians and Metis.   IVY

313   **SOWERBY   J E**
1964
ADDRESS: LOCAL INITIATIVE IN FURTHERING INTEGRATION. In Proceedings. Indian Study Conference. Provincial Council of Women of British Columbia. Available from Department of Extension, University of British Columbia. Appendix 'A'. 7 pp.

The programs, clubs, and projects in Kamloops which provide opportunities for integration are discussed.   IVY

314   **SPENCER   ROBERT F,   JOHNSON   ELDEN**
1968
ATLAS FOR ANTHROPOLOGY. 2nd Edition. Dubuque, IA: Wm. C. Brown. 61 pp.

Geographical locations are given in this atlas to tribes and ethnic groups commonly mentioned in anthropological textbooks. Maps locate world culture areas, tribal groups, and language families, case studies in the New and Old World, paleolithic sites, Near Eastern mesolithic-neolithic sites, North and South American prehistory, fossil man locations, and racial distributions of man.   DGW

315   **STAPLES   R S**
1965
THE COOPERATIVE UNION OF CANADA. In Norec Conference: The

Development of Indian and Eskimo Art and Crafts in the Far North, Northern Regional Committee, Indian-Eskimo Association of Canada. Toronto, May 3, 1965. Unpublished paper. Available from Indian-Eskimo Association. pp. 10-11.

Co-Ever, Co-operatives Everywhere, is designed to assist the people of Eskimo and Indian communities in Canada and the people in the West Indies to help themselves by organizing cooperatives. A project in Fort Resolution, Mackenzie district, is briefly outlined.   IVY

316   **STORY   NORAH**
1967
THE OXFORD COMPANION TO CANADIAN HISTORY AND LITERATURE.
Toronto: Oxford University Press. 935 pp.

A collection of articles is compiled to provide a source of reference to Canadian English and French historical and literary works. Biographies, political issues and parties, places, explorations, historic events, armed conflicts, regions and provinces, fiction, bibliographies, and Indian groups are included.   CCV

317   **STOUTENBURGH   JOHN L**
1960
DICTIONARY OF THE AMERICAN INDIAN. New York: Philosophical Library.
459 pp.

Tribal terms, concepts, locations, and culture traits relating to the North American Indian are defined.   DGW

318   **STRYNADKA   ARNOLD**
1970
ONE NATIVE PERSON'S COMMENTS ON THE FIELD OF ANTHROPOLOGY.
The Western Canadian Journal of Anthropology 1(3):32-36.

The merit of non-native anthropologists studying Indian cultures is questionned. Natives, regardless of their educational background, should be trained as field workers for ethnographic studies. In order that research programs be relevant to the contemporary scene, it is suggested that anthropologists work under the auspices of a native organization.   IVY

319   **SULLIVAN   MICHAEL**
1960
THE CAPITAL OF THE NORTH. Habitat 3(3):7-10.

The growth of Fort Smith is presented and its resident population is briefly described.   IVY

320   **SYMOR   NOLA**
n.d.
HISTORY, FILM AND COMMUNITY DEVELOPMENT: A POINT OF VIEW
ABOUT NATIVE-WHITE RELATIONS IN WESTERN CANADA. M.A. Thesis.
Interdisciplinary Program in Community Development. University of Alberta. n.p.

The title has been verified, but a copy was not obtained in time to abstract it.   SLP

321   **TAILFEATHERS   NELLIE**
1969
TREATY WOMEN AND HEALTH. In Voice of Alberta Native Women's Society:
Alberta Native Women's Second Annual Conference. Edmonton, March 3-6, 1969. pp.
20-21.

The contemporary Indian woman as part of the community and society must be aware of
her responsibility and the need to develop in this fast changing world.   IVY

322   **TAIT   MRS GEORGE E**
1965
THE I.O.D.E. In Norec Conference: The Development of Indian and Eskimo Art and
Crafts in the Far North, Northern Regional Committee, Indian-Eskimo Association of
Canada. Toronto, May 3, 1965. Unpublished paper. Available from Indian-Eskimo
Association. pp. 14-15.

The northern program of the Imperial Order of the Daughters of the Empire, concerned
largely with schools and hostels, is engaged in the encouragement of arts and crafts. Its
activities in this area are briefly described.   IVY

323   **TAYLOR   E L H**
1959-1960
FOUR YEARS INSIDE A YUKON DOG COLLAR. Queen's Quarterly 66:664-676.

An Anglican missionary among the Yukon Indians (in Champagne and Teslin) describes
his experiences.   IVY

324   **TEXTOR   ROBERT B**
1967
A CROSS-CULTURAL SUMMARY. New Haven, CT: Human Relations Area Files
Press. 744 pp.

This book is intended as a reference tool in the field of cross-cultural statistical inquiry
and contains 20,000 statistically significant correlations indicating what classes of culture
co-occur or overlap with other classes. Classes of culture are arranged dichotomously,
and utilize, selectively, all available sources of coded cross-cultural data (38 all told) for
the 400 culture samples developed by Murdock. Three statistical measures appear below
each table in the printout: (1) chi-square value, (2) the phi coefficient of strength and association, and (3) the probability value. Methodology, the format of printout, and how
to use it are discussed in pages 1-208, and the appendix of 536 pages contains the tables.   IVY

325   **TILL   RICHARD J**
1966
INDIAN AND NON-INDIAN VALUES: A STUDY COMPARING THE SOCIO-
ECONOMIC ASPIRATIONS OF A GROUP OF INDIAN CHILDREN TO THOSE
OF A GROUP OF NON-INDIAN CHILDREN. M.S.W. Thesis. School of Social
Work. St. Patrick's College. University of Ottawa. 52 pp. Available from Library, School
of Social Work, Carleton University.

A questionnaire was administered to 31 grade 7 and 8 students in a southern Saskatchewan Indian high school and 40 grade 7 and 8 White students in a rural southern Saskatchewan non-Indian high school. Minimal differences in the Indian and non-Indian aspirations are indicated by the study. Indian children are prepared to use the same means to achieve goals as White children.   CCV

326   **TROYER   WARNER**
1967
THE ONLY GOOD INDIAN IS A QUIET INDIAN. Quest 5(1):13-14,38.

The sharp contrast between the affluence of White Canadians and the poverty of Indians accounts for White Canada's insistence that the Indian be quiet. Despite the statistics on Indian poverty, government officials and parliamentarians are failing to fight for the Indians' need for funds and better services. It is suggested that centennial year is the proper time for a total commitment to action on behalf of the Indian.   ADG

327   **TURNER   ALLAN REAMAN**
1960
INDIAN PORTRAITS OF EDMUND MORRIS. Unpublished paper. Available from Archives of Saskatchewan, Regina. 4 pp.

Brief personal sketches are provided of the artist, Edmund Morris, and the 15 Indian men from Saskatchewan whose portraits make up the Saskatchewan Collection.   IVY

328   **UNION OF BRITISH COLUMBIA INDIAN CHIEFS**
1969
CONFERENCE: INDIAN CHIEFS OF BRITISH COLUMBIA NOVEMBER 17-22, 1969. KAMLOOPS, B.C. Unpublished paper. Available from Union of British Columbia Indian Chiefs, Vancouver, B.C. 125 pp.

Edited minutes of the first All-Chiefs' Conference, held in British Columbia, are presented. Mr. Harold Cardinal was the main speaker.   IVY

329   **UNIVERSITY OF SASKATCHEWAN**
1962
TRIBAL STUDIES. Ottawa: Indianescom Inc. 36 pp.

During a 6 week summer course (Education S-357) in 1962 at the University of Saskatchewan, data were compiled on the cultures of the 4 main tribes of Saskatchewan to the time of contact.   IVY

330   **VALLEE   FRANK G**
1966
INDIANS AND ESKIMOS OF CANADA - AN OVERVIEW OF STUDIES OF RELEVANCE TO THE ROYAL COMMISSION ON BILINGUALISM AND BICULTURALISM. Report No. 23, Vol. 1, Div:3-B. 309 pp.

A summary of studies related to Indians and Eskimos of Canada in the areas of population, economic and educational patterns, cultural values, and problems related to initiation and maintenance of voluntary organizations on a regional or national basis is presented. Pages 288-309 contain an annotated bibliography of these works.   CCV

331   **VANCOUVER INDIAN CENTRE SOCIETY**
1964
FIRST ANNUAL MEETING OF THE VANCOUVER INDIAN CENTRE .
SOCIETY. Available from Provincial Library, Victoria, B.C. 12 pp.

The first annual meeting of the Vancouver Indian Centre Society includes the president's, executive director's, committees', first vice-president's and chartered accountant's reports. It presents the development of a native organization whose aim is to assist Indians in making an adjustment to living in an urban setting.   IVY

332   **VELLATHOTTAM   THOMAS GEORGE**
1968
A HISTORY OF LACROSSE IN CANADA PRIOR TO 1914. M.À. Thesis. Faculty of Physical Education. University of Alberta. 111 pp.

The history of lacrosse in Canada is traced to 1914. The origins and tribal variations of the game are examined and its significance in native social organization is noted. White men began to play lacrosse in 1840, and on July 1, 1867, it was declared Canada's national game. The rise and fall of the game among White athletes are reviewed briefly.   CCV

333   **VOGET   FRED W**
1963
AMERICAN INDIAN REFORMATIONS AND ACCULTURATION. In Contributions to Anthropology, 1960. Part II. National Museum of Canada Bulletin 190. Ottawa: Queen's Printer. pp. 1-13.

The Iroquois Great Message of Handsome Lake, Peyotism, and the Shaker Church are discussed to assess the probable effects of reformative movements for acculturation.   JSL

334   **VOICE OF ALBERTA NATIVE WOMEN'S SOCIETY**
1969
RESOLUTIONS. In Voice of Alberta Native Women's Society: Alberta Native Women's Second Annual Conference. Edmonton, March 3-6, 1969. pp. 41-43.

Twelve resolutions were carried pertaining to education, the Voice of Alberta Native Women's Society, law, Team Products, and the conditions that exist in Conklin.   IVY

335   **WACKO   WILLIAM J**
n.d.
A CHALLENGE TO THE ALBERTA INDIAN PEOPLE, THE INDIAN AFFAIRS BRANCH STAFF AND THE INTERESTED PUBLIC. Unpublished paper. Available from National Library of Canada. 3 pp.

Food for thought on assisting and understanding Indian people is directed towards these 3 groups.   IVY

336   **WACKO   WILLIAM J**
n.d.
COMMUNITY DEVELOPMENT AND WHAT IT MEANS TO OUR PEOPLE.

Unpublished paper delivered to 10th Annual Indian Community and
Economic Development Conference. Available from National Library of Canada. 7 pp.

What Community Development is, and what it is not, are discussed in this paper.   IVY

337   **WACKO   WILLIAM J**
1967
SOME PERSONAL THOUGHTS AND IMPRESSIONS ABOUT COMMUNITY
DEVELOPMENT IN INDIAN AFFAIRS BRANCH. Unpublished paper. Available
from National Library of Canada. 29 pp.

Following visits with Community Development Officers, Regional Office staff, and Indian people across Canada, observations about Community Development are discussed
from 3 points of view: the administration (Indian Affairs Branch and its Regional and
Agency Offices), the Community Development Officer (field worker), and the Indian people themselves. Varying opinions are expressed on the success of the community development approach and its future development. Appendix A (10 pages) lists series of
quotes supporting or paralleling the observations made in the text. Appendix B - a memorandum dated January 19, 1967 - is a statement by Staff regarding their feelings towards
Community Development in Indian Affairs Branch.   IVY

338   **WARBURTON   CELIA**
1960
SASKATCHEWAN TRAPPERS' CONVENTION. Canadian Geographical Journal
61:52-57.

A report of the annual conference held at Prince Albert is given. Northern trappers met
with federal and provincial officials to discuss the development of the trapping industry.   IVY

339   **WHITFORD   J R**
1965
COMMUNITY DEVELOPMENT IN ALBERTA. Unpublished paper. Available from
Library, Department of Health and Social Development, Winnipeg, Man. 7 pp.

Community development and its objectives in Alberta are defined.   IVY

340   **WILLIAMSON   LLOYD PAUL**
1969
THE IMAGE OF INDIANS, FRENCH CANADIANS, AND AMERICANS IN
AUTHORIZED ONTARIO HIGH SCHOOL TEXTBOOKS: 1890-1930. M.A. Thesis.
Institute of Canadian Studies. Carleton University. 129 pp.

The images of Indians, French Canadians, and Americans portrayed in secondary school
history textbooks authorized for use in Ontario high schools in the period 1890-1930 are
examined and found biased. The Indian was presented as filthy, child-like, cruel, and
constantly at war. The native religion was pictured as somewhat amusing and Indian
women were associated with drudgery. The language was slanted. Indian behavior, with
its positive characteristics ignored, was contrasted with that of the "civilized"White. Indians were treated as a race rather than as individuals.   CCV

341   **WILLIE   ERNEST**
1970
ADDRESS TO GENERAL SYNOD BY REV. ERNEST WILLIE. In Bulletin 201:
Recent Statements by the Indians of Canada, General Synod Action 1969, Some
Government Responses, Suggested Resources. Anglican Church of Canada, Action Unit.
Toronto: Anglican Church of Canada. p. 19.

An address to the 1969 General synod of the Anglican Church is presented stressing the
need for understanding and co-operation between Indians and non-Indians in an era
when Indians are seeking recognition.   CCV

342   **WINNIPEG COMMUNITY WELFARE PLANNING COUNCIL**
1967
A SURVEY OF WELFARE SERVICES FOR INDIAN AND METIS PEOPLE IN
MANITOBA. Unpublished paper prepared for the Health and Welfare Subcommittee,
Indian and Metis Conference Committee of Manitoba. Available from Library,
Department of Health and Social Development, Winnipeg. 22 pp.

Information and problems encountered by workers in providing public assistance (or relief) services and child welfare services to Indians and Metis of Manitoba was secured
through questionnaires distributed to municipalities, child welfare agencies, and
churches. Data were collected in 1964 and 1965. Response came from 41 of 76 churches
approached, 8 child welfare agencies, and 32 of 190 municipalities. Eighteen recommendations are presented.   IVY

343   **WITTKOWER   E D,   WINTROB   R**
1969
DEVELOPMENT IN CANADIAN TRANSCULTURAL PSYCHIATRY. Canada's
Mental Health 17(3-4):21-27.

This article is an introduction to transcultural psychiatry. Among the various transcultural studies conducted to date, several have focused on the Indian: (1) The Cree Devel-
opment-Change Project (1964-1968) at McGill has conducted a series of studies on the
social, cultural, economic, psychological, ecological and political changes affecting 1500
Cree Indians of Mistassini, Waswanipi and Nemiscau bands. Among other things, these
studies have examined the psychological implications of cultural interruptions experienced by Cree children in White urban schools in southern Quebec and southern Ontario.
The identity conflict of Cree youth attending integrated schools has also received some
attention. (2) Faculty at the University of Saskatchewan have studied the urbanization
of Indians in the Saskatoon region, paying particular attention to the psychological adaptation of Indian females who move from their reserves to urban environments. (3) At the
University of British Columbia current research includes an investigation of the impact
of socio-cultural change on the mental health of Indians in British Columbia. This particular study has involved psychologists and cultural anthropologists in order to correlate
data on Indians hospitalized for mental illness in the Vancouver region with field research carried out in the home settings of the specific patients. (4) McGill University is
the center for an interdisciplinary study of the psycho-educational functioning of Indian
pupils on a reserve near Montreal.   ADG

344   **WORD   KATHLEEN**
1969

PAUL KANE SKETCHES. Rotunda 2(1):4-15.

Several of Paul Kane's field sketches are reproduced, accompanied by an account of Kane's work among the Indians.   ADG

345   **WUTTUNEE   WILLIAM I**
1960
RENAISSANCE OF THE INDIANS. The Beaver 291(Summer):46-47.

The barriers to integration are discussed. To speed up the process of natural integration, it must be carefully planned and assisted but never forced.   IVY

346   **WUTTUNEE   WILLIAM I**
1968
INTEGRATION - THE BEST SOLUTION. The Manitoba Teacher 46(5):6-8.

Indian organizations, both strong and weak, have tried without success, to influence legislation. The Indian's situation is similar to, or worse than that of other poor immigrants or developing nations. The struggle for independence is difficult for an Indian because of (1) a handicapping cultural environment, (2) ill health and low life expectancy, (3) language barriers, and (4) the need for Indians to be better than Whites in order to succeed. Adjustment of life outside the reserve includes both language and standard of conduct. Despite its limitations the reserve does provide some security for the Indian. Changes in international trade and economic relations are vital if a truly Canadian identity, which can include the Indian, is to be found.   ADG

347   **YELLOWFEET   ROSE**
1969
ALCOHOLISM. In Voice of Alberta Native Women's Society: Alberta Native Women's Second Annual Conference. Edmonton, March 3-6, 1969. pp. 25-26.

An alcoholic relates past experiences with alcoholism and her subsequent recovery through Alcoholics Anonymous.   IVY

348   **YUKON NATIVE BROTHERHOOD**
1970
BRIEF. Unpublished paper delivered to Special Senate Committee on Poverty. Whitehorse, Yukon, July 23, 1970. Available from National Library of Canada. 13 pp.

This brief summarizes the poverty situation in the Yukon using 7 specific topics - land, housing, education, employment, economic development, and the price of food to the native consumer. Recommendations are made to help rectify the poverty situation.   HCV

349   **ZENTNER   HENRY**
1970
THE IMPENDING IDENTITY CRISIS AMONG NATIVE PEOPLES. In Prairie Perspectives: Papers of the Western Canadian Studies Conference. David P. Gagan, ed. Toronto: Holt, Rinehart and Winston. pp. 78-89.

The threat to Indian identity posed by recent government policy statements is explored. Traditional Indian temporal orientation and values in the social, political, and economic spheres are in opposition to those held by the dominant society. These values, essential to self-determination and participation, were not developed when government held decision-making powers. Even if native peoples acquired overnight the motivations and skills requisite to management of their own affairs it would be at the expense of their unique identity.   CCV

LEGISLATION (BILLS AND ACTS)

350   **ALBERTA. Statutes. 14 Legislature, 1 Session.**
1960
THE STATUTES CORRECTION ACT, 1960. Statutes of the Province of Alberta, Chapter 99. An Act to Correct Errors of Revision, References, and Otherwise in the Statutes. Assented to April 11, 1960.

Section 4 amends Sections 12 and 13 of the Metis Betterment Act by striking out the words "The Public Lands Act"and by substituting the words "The Forests Act."   IVY

351   **ALBERTA. Statutes. 14 Legislature, 3 Session.**
1962
AN ACT TO AMEND THE BRAND ACT. Statutes of the Province of Alberta, Chapter 5. Assented to March 30, 1962.

Section 2 amends Section 10 of The Brand Act (being Chapter 30 of the Revised Statutes) by striking out subsection (3) which states that the allotting of a brand to an Indian on a reserve must be approved by the Regional Supervisor of the Indian Agency for the Province of Alberta.   IVY

352   **ALBERTA. Statutes. 15 Legislature, 1 Session.**
1964
THE MENTAL HEALTH ACT. Statutes of the Province of Alberta, Chapter 54. An Act Respecting Mentally Disordered Persons. Assented to April 15, 1964.

Section 39(1) repeals The Mental Diseases Act being Chapter 200 of the Revised Statutes. The Mental Diseases Act had barred removal to a hospital of Treaty Indians unless their expenses were guaranteed by the Superintendent General of Indian Affairs (Section 27).   IVY

353   **ALBERTA. Statutes. 15 Legislature, 2 Session.**
1965
AN ACT TO AMEND THE ELECTION ACT. Statutes of the Province of Alberta, Chapter 23. Assented to April 12, 1965.

Section 2 strikes out the clause (Section 16(b)) in The Election Act (1956, c. 15) which prohibited Indians from voting. Section 3 amends Form 31 and Form 33 of oaths by striking out the words "that you are not an Indian within the meaning of The Election Act."   IVY

354   **ALBERTA. Statutes. 15 Legislature, 2 Session.**
1965
THE MARRIAGE ACT. Statutes of the Province of Alberta, Chapter 52. An Act Respecting the Solemnization of Marriage. Assented to April 12, 1965.

Section 29(e and f) authorizes Indian agents and Supervisors of Metis Colonies to act ex officio as issuers of marriage licences to persons under their jurisdiction.   IVY

355   **ALBERTA. Statutes. 15 Legislature, 3 Session.**
1966
THE PUBLIC LANDS ACT, 1966. Statutes of the Province of Alberta, Chapter 80. An Act Respecting Public Lands. Assented to April 15, 1966.

Section 126 amends The Metis Betterment Act. Section 6 of that Act designates for settlement by members of settlement associations public lands under the administration of the Minister. Lands no longer suitable or required for this purpose transfer to the administration of the Minister of Lands and Forests. Section 22 of the Metis Betterment Act is amended to allow the creation of reserved areas for game rehabilitation in public lands under the administration of the Minister of Lands and Forests. Section 130(a) repeals The Public Lands Act being Chapter 259 of the Revised Statutes. While this new Act (Section 10) provides for the transfer of lands to the Government of Canada, it does not specifically mention such transfer to fulfill treaty obligations with Indians as did Section 119(c) of the Act it replaces.   IVY

356   **ALBERTA. Statutes. 16 Legislature, 2 Session.**
1969
THE DEPARTMENT OF SOCIAL DEVELOPMENT ACT. Statutes of the Province of Alberta, Chapter 101. An Act Respecting the Department of Social Development. Assented to May 7, 1969.

Section 6 amends Section 4(3) of The Metis Betterment Act by striking out the words "Minister of Public Welfare" and substituting the words "Minister of Social Development," and by striking out the words "Department of Public Welfare" and substituting the words "Department of Social Development."   IVY

357   **ALBERTA. Statutes. 16 Legislature, 2 Session.**
1969
THE NATIVE CO-OPERATIVE GUARANTEE ACT. Statutes of the Province of Alberta, Chapter 80. An Act Respecting Guarantees for Indians and Metis Co-operative Associations. Assented to May 7, 1969.

On the recommendation of the Minister, an association may borrow money for a period not exceeding 20 years. Repayment of the whole or part of the money and interest is guaranteed by the government who may take as security any real or personal property. During the period of the guarantee, the association shall not make any distribution of its earnings or profits among its members without the consent of the Provincial Treasurer, and at the request of the Minister the association shall submit to a full audit.   IVY

358   **ALBERTA. Statutes. 16 Legislature, 3 Session.**
1970
THE WILDLIFE ACT. Statutes of the Province of Alberta, Chapter 113. An Act for the Protection of Wildlife. Assented to April 15, 1970.

Section 119 repeals The Game Act being Chapter 126 of the Revised Statutes. The provisions respecting Indians which were found in the Game Act (Sections 84 and 142) are not found in The Wildlife Act. Section 62 of The Wildlife Act prohibits the holder of a trapping licence from hunting or trapping on Indian reserves and Metis areas. Section 121(3) strikes out the words "The Game Act"wherever they occur and substitutes the words "The Wildlife Act"in Sections 7 and 22 of The Metis Betterment Act.   IVY

359   **BRITISH COLUMBIA. Revised Statutes.**
1960
GAME ACT. Province of British Columbia Revised Statutes, Chapter 160.

Section 8 allows Indians to hunt male deer (other than wapiti) over a year of age for food. In defined areas they must first obtain a permit to do this. Section 15 denies non-resident Indians the privilege of hunting or acting as guides in the province.   Section 32(4) exempts Indians from taking out hunting licences. Section 34(4) allows an Indian to trap after the end of the open season upon purchase of a licence. Section 38(4) exempts Indians from the necessity of obtaining angling licences. Section 69(c) permits the Lieutenant Governor in Council to exempt Indians of the northern and north-easterly portions of the province from the provisions of this Act.   IVY

360   **BRITISH COLUMBIA. Revised Statutes.**
1960
GOVERNMENT LIQUOR ACT. Province of British Columbia Revised Statutes, Chapter 166.

Section 75 makes it illegal for a person prohibited from buying liquor under the Indian Act (Canada) to enter a government liquor store.   IVY

361   **BRITISH COLUMBIA. Revised Statutes.**
1960
INDIAN ADVISORY ACT. Province of British Columbia Revised Statutes, Chapter 186.

The Indian Advisory Committee is established to advise the Minister of Labour on all matters regarding the status and rights of Indians.   IVY

362   **BRITISH COLUMBIA. Revised Statutes.**
1960
INDIAN RESERVES MINERAL RESOURCES ACT. Province of British Columbia Revised Statutes, Chapter 187.

The Memorandum of Agreement dated January 26, 1943, between the governments of Canada and British Columbia is ratified.   IVY

363   **BRITISH COLUMBIA. Revised Statutes.**
1960
LAND ACT. Province of British Columbia Revised Statutes, Chapter 206.

Section 88(2) permits the Lieutenant Governor in Council to dispose of the provincial interest in any Indian reserve but a return of any alienations must be submitted to the Legislature at its next sitting.   IVY

364   **BRITISH COLUMBIA. Revised Statutes.**
1960

PUBLIC SCHOOLS ACT. Province of British Columbia Revised Statutes, Chapter 319.

Section 18(g) empowers the Council of Public Instruction to enter into agreements with the Government of Canada for the education of Indian children. Section 160(1d) empowers boards of school districts with the approval of the Minister to enter into similar agreements.   IVY

365   **BRITISH COLUMBIA. Revised Statutes.**
1960
VITAL STATISTICS ACT. Province of British Columbia Revised Statutes, Chapter 402.

Section 3 provides that with respect to the birth, death, or marriage of any Indian, the Indian Agent be ex officio District Registrar for such Indians.   IVY

366   **BRITISH COLUMBIA. Statutes. 26 Legislature, 1 Session.**
1961
STATUTE LAW AMENDMENT ACT. Province of British Columbia Statutes, Chapter 59. An Act to Amend and Repeal Certain Provisions of the Statute Law. Assented to March 27, 1961.

Section 12 amends The Government Liquor Act (Chapter 166, The Revised Statutes of British Columbia, 1960) to permit exemption by proclamation of Indians in a specific area from any disability in the right to purchase, possess, and consume liquor.   IVY

367   **BRITISH COLUMBIA. Statutes. 26 Legislature, 2 Session.**
1962
INDIAN ADVISORY ACT AMENDMENT ACT, 1962. Province of British Columbia Statutes, Chapter 28. An Act to Amend the Indian Advisory Act. Assented to March 29, 1962.

Section 2 of the Indian Advisory Act is amended by substituting the definition of Minister to mean Provincial Secretary.   IVY

368   **BRITISH COLUMBIA. Statutes. 27 Legislature, 3 Session.**
1966
WILDLIFE ACT. Province of British Columbia Statutes, Chapter 55. An Act to Provide for the Conservation of Wildlife. Assented to April 1, 1966.

Section 81 repeals The Game Act being Chapter 160 of the Revised Statutes, 1960. Section 3 exempts Indians from licence requirements for hunting, trapping, and angling.   IVY

369   **BRITISH COLUMBIA. Statutes. 29 Legislature, 1 Session.**
1970
LAND ACT. Province of British Columbia Statutes, Chapter 17. Assented to April 3, 1970.

Section 106 repeals The Land Act being Chapter 206 of the Revised Statutes, 1960.   IVY

370   **CANADA. House of Commons. 24 Parliament, 3 Session.**
1960
AN ACT TO AMEND THE CANADA ELECTIONS ACT. Bill C-3. As passed March
10, 1960.   Also in French.

The Bill would repeal paragraph (e) of subsection (2), and subsection (4), of Section 14
of the Canada Elections Act. The purpose of the amendment is to provide an unrestricted
Dominion franchise to Indians.   JSL

371   **CANADA. House of Commons. 24 Parliament, 3 Session.**
1960
AN ACT TO AMEND THE CANADA ELECTIONS ACT. Bill C-3. 1 Reading,
January 18, 1960.   Also in French.

The bill would repeal paragraph (e) of subsection (2), and subsection (4), of Section 14
of the Canada Elections Act. The purpose of the amendment is to provide an unrestricted
Dominion franchise to Indians.   JSL

372   **CANADA. House of Commons. 24 Parliament, 3 Session.**
1960
AN ACT TO AMEND THE INDIAN ACT (SECTION 112 REPEALED). Bill C-85. 1
Reading, July 18, 1960.   Also in French.

The proposed Bill would remove Section 112 of the Indian Act, whereby the Governor in
Council can enfranchise Indians or bands without their consent. Provisions are to be
made for the Minister to appoint a committee of inquiry where a band applies for enfranchisement and has submitted a plan for the disposal of band funds and land. The
committee is to be composed of 1 Departmental officer, a judge or retired judge, and 1
band delegate.   JSL

373   **CANADA. House of Commons. 24 Parliament, 3 Session.**
1960
AN ACT TO AMEND THE INDIAN ACT. Bill C-2. As passed March 10, 1960.   Also
in French.

Bill C-2 would repeal subsection (2) of Section 86 of the Indian Act. The Bill would ensure that tax exemption of Indian income, property, and estates was not incompatible
with the Dominion franchise.   JSL

374   **CANADA. House of Commons. 24 Parliament, 3 Session.**
1960
AN ACT TO AMEND THE INDIAN ACT. Bill C-2. 1 Reading, January 18, 1960.
Also in French.

Bill C-2 would repeal subsection (2) of Section 86 of the Indian Act. The Bill would ensure that tax exemption of Indian income, property, and estates was no longer incompatible with the Dominion franchise.   JSL

375   **CANADA. House of Commons. 24 Parliament, 4 Session.**
1960

AN ACT TO AMEND THE INDIAN ACT (SECTION 112 REPEALED). Bill C-85. 1 Reading, November 21, 1960.   Also in French.

The proposed bill would repeal Section 112 of the Indian Act, whereby the Governor in Council can enfranchise Indians or bands without their consent. Provisions are to be made for the Minister to appoint a committee of inquiry where a band applies for enfranchisement and has submitted a plan for the disposal of band funds and land. The committee is to be composed of 1 Departmental officer, a judge or retired judge, and 1 band delegate.   JSL

376   **CANADA. House of Commons. 24 Parliament, 4 Session.**
1961
AN ACT TO AMEND THE INDIAN ACT. Bill C-124. 1 Reading, September 11, 1961. Also in French.

The proposed bill would repeal Secions 93 through 96A of the Indian Act. Provisions would be made for band referendums to determine if possession of intoxicants on the reserve was an offense under the Indian Act or subject to provincial laws.   JSL

377   **CANADA. House of Commons. 24 Parliament, 4 Session.**
1961
AN ACT TO AMEND THE INDIAN ACT. Bill C-61. As passed February 14, 1961. Also in French.

Section 112 of the Indian Act would be repealed. Provisions would be made for the Minister to appoint a committee of inquiry where a band applies for enfranchisement, provided the band has submitted a plan for the disposal of band funds and land. The committee is to be composed of 1 Departmental officer, a judge or retired judge, and 1 band delegate.   JSL

378   **CANADA. House of Commons. 24 Parliament, 4 Session.**
1961
AN ACT TO AMEND THE INDIAN ACT. Bill C-61. 1 Reading, January 25, 1961. Also in French.

Bill C-61 would repeal Section 112 of the Indian Act and provide for a committee of inquiry to be established when a band applies for enfranchisement.   JSL

379   **CANADA. House of Commons. 24 Parliament, 5 Session.**
1962
AN ACT TO AMEND THE INDIAN ACT (LIQUOR RIGHTS). Bill C-26. 1 Reading, January 22, 1962.   Also in French.

The proposed bill would repeal Sections 93, 94, 95, 96 and 96A of the Indian Act. Provision would be made for local referendums to determine if alcohol possession on the reserve would be an offense under the Indian Act or subject to provincial law.   JSL

380   **CANADA. House of Commons. 24 Parliament, 5 Session.**
1962
CANADA COURT OF INDIAN CLAIMS ACT. Bill C-81. 1 Reading, April 2, 1962. Also in French.

Provision is proposed for a Canada Court of Indian Claims. Claims may be submitted by Parliament (regarding British Columbia and Oka), the Governor in Council, or Indians (via petition). The proposed jurisdiction and procedure of such a Court are outlined. Appeal to the Supreme Court of Canada is to be made possible.   JSL

381   **CANADA. House of Commons. 25 Parliament, 1 Session.**
1962
AN ACT TO AMEND THE AGRICULTURAL REHABILITATION AND DEVELOPMENT ACT (INDIAN RESERVES). Bill C-22. 1 Reading, October 1, 1962.
Also in French.

The purpose of this bill is to extend the benefits of the Agricultural Rehabilitation and Development Act (ARDA) to Indians and reserve lands.   JSL

382   **CANADA. House of Commons. 25 Parliament, 1 Session.**
1962
AN ACT TO AMEND THE INDIAN ACT (LIQUOR RIGHTS). Bill C-31. 1 Reading, October 1, 1962.   Also in French.

It is suggested that Sections 93, 94, 95, 96 and 96A of the Indian Act be repealed. Provision is to be made for local referendums to decide whether possession of intoxicants would be an offense under the Indian Act, or comes under provincial law.   JSL

383   **CANADA. House of Commons. 25 Parliament, 1 Session.**
1962
THE CANADA COURT OF INDIAN CLAIMS ACT. Bill C-19. 1 Reading, October 1, 1962.   Also in French.

It is proposed to establish a Court of Indian Claims. Claims made by Parliament (regarding Oka Reserve, and British Columbia), and by Indians (via petition) could be heard. The proposed jurisdiction and procedure of the Court are outlined. Appeals to the Supreme Court of Canada are to be made possible.   JSL

384   **CANADA. House of Commons. 25 Parliament, 1 Session.**
1962
INDIAN ACT. Bill C-14. 1 Reading, October 1, 1962.   Also in French.

It is proposed to consolidate the Indian Act and its various ammendments into 1 statute. The Indian Act of 1952 would be repealed.   JSL

385   **CANADA. House of Commons. 26 Parliament, 1 Session.**
1963
AN ACT TO AMEND THE AGRICULTURAL REHABILITATION AND DEVELOPMENT ACT (INDIAN RESERVES). Bill C-46. 1 Reading, May 20, 1963.
Also in French.

Provision is to be made for the benefits of the Agricultural Rehabilitation and Development Act (ARDA) to be extended to Indians and Indian reserves.   JSL

386   **CANADA. House of Commons. 26 Parliament, 1 Session.**
1963

AN ACT TO AMEND THE INDIAN ACT (LIQUOR RIGHTS). Bill C-34. 1 Reading, May 20, 1963.   Also in French.

Provision is to be made to repeal Sections 93, 94, 95, 96 and 96A of the Indian Act. Local referendums can decide whether possession of toxicants on the reserve would be subject to the Indian Act regulations or Provincial law.   JSL

387   **CANADA. House of Commons. 26 Parliament, 1 Session.**
1963
CANADA COURT OF INDIAN CLAIMS ACT. Bill C-67. 1 Reading, May 31, 1963. Also in French.

It is suggested that a Canada Court of Indian Claims be established. Claims from Parliament (regarding Oka Reserve and British Columbia), the Governor in Council, and Indians (via petition) may be received. The proposed jurisdiction and procedure of the Court are discussed. Appeals are to be made to the Supreme Court of Canada.   JSL

388   **CANADA. House of Commons. 26 Parliament, 1 Session.**
1963
INDIAN ACT. Bill C-71. 1 Reading, June 7, 1963.   Also in French.

A consolidation of the Indian Act and its various amendments is suggested. The 1952 Indian Act is to be repealed.   JSL

389   **CANADA. House of Commons. 26 Parliament, 1 Session.**
1963
INDIAN CLAIMS ACT. Bill C-130. 1 Reading, December 14, 1963.   Also in French.

Provision is to be made to establish an Indian Claims Commission. Discussed are the proposed duties of the Commission and who may be a claimant. The proposed powers of the Commission are outlined. An Indian Claims Appeal Court would hear appeals.   JSL

390   **CANADA. House of Commons. 26 Parliament, 2 Session.**
1964
AN ACT TO AMEND THE AGRICULTURAL REHABILITATION AND DEVELOPMENT ACT (INDIAN RESERVES). Bill C-4. 1 Reading, February 20, 1964.   Also in French.

Provision is to be made to extend the Agricultural Rehabilitation and Development Act (ARDA) to Indian reserves.   JSL

391   **CANADA. House of Commons. 26 Parliament, 2 Session.**
1964
AN ACT TO AMEND THE INDIAN ACT (LIQUOR RIGHTS). Bill C-6. 1 Reading, February 20, 1964.   Also in French.

It is suggested that Sections 93, 94, 95, 96 and 96A of the Indian Act be repealed. Local referendums could decide whether the individual band preferred to have possession of intoxicants treated as an offense under the Indian Act or as subject to provincial law. JSL

392   **CANADA. House of Commons. 26 Parliament, 3 Session.**
1965
AN ACT TO AMEND THE INDIAN ACT (LIQUOR RIGHTS). Bill C-91. 1 Reading,
April 28, 1965.   Also in French.

Provision is to be made to replace Sections 93 through 96A of the Indian Act, and provide measures for a local liquor referendum. Majority vote would decide whether possession of intoxicants on the reserve would be an offense under the Indian Act or subject to
provincial law.   JSL

393   **CANADA. House of Commons. 26 Parliament, 3 Session.**
1965
AN ACT TO AMEND THE INDIAN ACT (LIQUOR RIGHTS). Bill C-91. 1 Reading,
April 8, 1965.   Also in French.

Provision is to be made to replace Sections 93 through 96A of the Indian Act with measures allowing for a local referendum. A majority vote would decide whether possession
of intoxicants on the reserve was an offense under the Indian Act or subject to provincial
law.   JSL

394   **CANADA. House of Commons. 26 Parliament, 3 Session.**
1965
INDIAN CLAIMS ACT. Bill C-123. 1 Reading, June 21, 1965.   Also in French.

It is proposed that an Indian Claims Commission be created. Discussed are the proposed
duties of the Commission, qualifications of claimants, and powers of the Commission.
An Indian Claims Appeal Court would be established.   JSL

395   **CANADA. House of Commons. 26 Parliament, 3 Session.**
1965
NATIVE INDIAN AND ESKIMO ARTS AND CRAFTS ACT. Bill C-4. 1 Reading,
April 8, 1965.   Also in French.

It is suggested that the Native Cultural Council of Canada be created to preserve and
promote Indian and Eskimo arts and crafts.   The proposed membership and powers of
that body are discussed. The Council could regulate and certify the importation of native
goods.   JSL

396   **CANADA. House of Commons. 27 Parliament, 1 Session.**
1966
AN ACT TO AMEND THE INDIAN ACT. Bill C-203. 1 Reading, June 20, 1966.
Also in French.

Repeal of Sections 93 through 99 of the Indian Act is urged, to remove descriminatory
restrictions on the sale of intoxicants to Indians, possession of intoxicants by Indians off
or on reserves, and similar offenses.   JSL

397   **CANADA. House of Commons. 27 Parliament, 1 Session.**
1966
AN ACT TO REPEAL THE BRITISH COLUMBIA INDIAN RESERVES MINERAL
RESOURCES ACT. Bill C-8. 1 Reading, January 24, 1966.   Also in French.

Repeal of the British Columbia Indian Reserves Mineral Resources Act (1943) was proposed. The Bill provides for provincial control of mineral resources. Any revenues derived are to be divided between federal and provincial governments, provided Indian rights are ceded.   JSL

398   **CANADA. House of Commons. 27 Parliament, 1 Session.**
1966
CANADA COURT OF INDIAN CLAIMS ACT. Bill C-28. 1 Reading, January 24, 1966.   Also in French.

It is suggested that the Canada Court of Indian Claims be created. Claims made by Parliament (regarding British Columbia and Oka), the Governor in Council, and Indians (by petition) could be heard. Discussed are the jurisdiction and procedure of the Court. Appeal to the Supreme Court of Canada would be possible.   JSL

399   **CANADA. House of Commons. 27 Parliament, 1 Session.**
1966
INDIAN DAY ACT. Bill C-78. 1 Reading, January 24, 1966.   Also in French.

It is proposed that the first Saturday in August be declared as National Indian Day.   JSL

400   **CANADA. House of Commons. 27 Parliament, 1 Session.**
1966
NATIVE INDIAN AND ESKIMO ARTS AND CRAFTS ACT. Bill C-103. 1 Reading, January 24, 1966.   Also in French.

It is proposed that the Native Cultural Council of Canada be created to preserve and promote Indian and Eskimo arts and crafts.   The proposed powers and membership of the Council are outlined. The Council could regulate and certify imported native arts and crafts.   JSL

401   **CANADA. House of Commons. 27 Parliament, 2 Session.**
1967
AN ACT TO AMEND THE INDIAN ACT (RIGHTS GUARANTEED BY TREATIES). Bill C-120. 1 Reading, May 29, 1967.   Also in French.

An amendment of Section 87 of the Indian Act is proposed, to provide that treaty rights and privileges may not be taken away by federal statute unless specifically so declared in the statute.   JSL

402   **CANADA. House of Commons. 27 Parliament, 2 Session.**
1967
NATIONAL INDIAN DAY ACT. Bill C-45. 1 Reading, May 11, 1967.   Also in French.

It is suggested that the first Saturday in August be designated as National Indian Day.   JSL

403   **CANADA. House of Commons. 27 Parliament, 2 Session.**
1967

NATIVE INDIAN AND ESKIMO ARTS AND CRAFTS ACT. Bill C-76. 1 Reading, May 11, 1967.   Also in French.

The creation of a Native Cultural Council of Canada is suggested, to preserve and promote Indian and Eskimo arts and crafts. The proposed powers and membership of the Council are outlined. The Council could regulate and certify the importation of native arts and crafts.   JSL

404   **CANADA. House of Commons. 27 Parliament, 2 Session.**
1968
AN ACT TO REPEAL THE BRITISH COLUMBIA INDIAN RESERVES MINERAL RESOURCES ACT. Bill C-198. 1 Reading, January 29, 1968.   Also in French.

Repeal of the British Columbia Indian Reserves Mineral Resources Act (1943) was suggested. The Act had provided for provincial control of such resources, and revenues were divided between federal and provincial governments. Prior Indian surrender of mineral rights had been required.   JSL

405   **CANADA. House of Commons. 28 Parliament, 1 Session.**
1968
AN ACT TO AMEND THE FARM CREDIT ACT. Bill C-110. As passed October 31, 1968.   Also in French.

The Farm Credit Corporation would be able to make loans under the Farm Credit Act to Indians and Indian bands without the necessity of obtaining a first mortgage on farm lands. A maximum of $100,000 could be loaned to any 1 band.   JSL

406   **CANADA. House of Commons. 28 Parliament, 1 Session.**
1968
AN ACT TO AMEND THE FARM CREDIT ACT. Bill C-110. 1 Reading, October 1, 1968.   Also in French.

One of the amendments would enable the Farm Credit Corporation to make loans under the Farm Credit Act to Indians and Indian bands without the necessity of obtaining a first mortgage on farm lands as security. A maximum of $100,000 could be loaned to any 1 band.   JSL

407   **CANADA. House of Commons. 28 Parliament, 1 Session.**
1968
AN ACT TO AMEND THE MIGRATORY BIRDS CONVENTION ACT. Bill C-36. 1 Reading, September 20, 1968.   Also in French.

It is suggested that Indians be exempt from provisions of the Migratory Birds Convention Act under certain conditions. When birds are needed for food, treaty hunting rights could be restored.   JSL

408   **CANADA. House of Commons. 28 Parliament, 1 Session.**
1968
AN ACT TO REPEAL THE BRITISH COLUMBIA INDIAN RESERVES MINERAL RESOURCES ACT. Bill C-7. 1 Reading, September 20, 1968.   Also in French.

The repeal of the British Columbia Indian Reserves Mineral Resources Act (1943) was suggested. Under this Act, the province controls Indian mineral resources. Provided Indian rights were ceded, revenues would be divided between provincial and federal governments.   JSL

409   **CANADA. House of Commons. 28 Parliament, 1 Session.**
1968
BRITISH COLUMBIA INDIAN LAND QUESTION ACT. Bill C-121. 1 Reading, October 18, 1968.   Also in French.

The bill proposes recognition of aboriginal title in British Columbia. This title was never extinguished with the exception of that of lands ceded in Treaty Number 8. Provisions are to be made to negotiate for settlement by the Governor in Council.   JSL

410   **CANADA. House of Commons. 28 Parliament, 1 Session.**
1968
NATIVE INDIAN AND ESKIMO ARTS AND CRAFTS ACT. Bill C-30. 1 Reading, September 20, 1968.   Also in French.

It is proposed that a Native Cultural Council of Canada be established to preserve and promote Indian and Eskimo arts and crafts. The proposed membership and powers of such a Council are discussed. The Council could regulate and certify the importation of native arts and crafts.   JSL

411   **CANADA. House of Commons. 28 Parliament, 1 Session.**
1969
AN ACT TO AMEND THE INDIAN ACT (RIGHTS OF INDIAN WOMAN UPON MARRIAGE). Bill C-193. 1 Reading, May 15, 1969.   Also in French.

It is proposed to repeal paragraph (b) of subsection (1) of Section 12, and subsection (2) of Section 108 of the Indian Act. Section 14 would be changed to enable an Indian woman marrying the member of another band to become a member of her husband's band. These amendments would allow an Indian woman to marry a non-Indian without losing her Indian rights.   JSL

412   **CANADA. House of Commons. 28 Parliament, 2 Session.**
1969
AN ACT RESPECTING THE HUNTING AND FISHING RIGHTS OF INDIAN CANADIANS. Bill C-124. 1 Reading, October 30. 1969.   Also in French.

The purpose of this bill is to recognize and declare that the right of Canadian Indians to hunt and fish for food cannot be restricted or denied by federal or provincial law.   JSL

413   **CANADA. House of Commons. 28 Parliament, 2 Session.**
1969
AN ACT TO AMEND THE INDIAN ACT (RIGHTS OF INDIAN WOMAN UPON MARRIAGE). Bill C-84. 1 Reading, October 30. 1969.   Also in French.

It is proposed to repeal paragraph (b) of subsection (1) of Section 12, and subsection (2) of Section 108 of the Indian Act. Section 14 would be changed to enable an Indian woman marrying a member of another band to become a member of her husband's band. The amendments would allow an Indian woman to marry a non-Indian without losing her Indian rights.   JSL

414   **CANADA. House of Commons. 28 Parliament, 2 Session.**
1969
AN ACT TO REPEAL THE BRITISH COLUMBIA INDIAN RESERVES MINERAL RESOURCES ACT. Bill C-44. 1 Reading, October 30, 1969.   Also in French.

The repeal of the British Columbia Indian Resources Act is suggested. The province controls Indian minerals. Provided Indian rights are ceded, revenues from mineral exploitation are divided between provincial and federal governments.   JSL

415   **CANADA. House of Commons. 28 Parliament, 2 Session.**
1969
BRITISH COLUMBIA INDIAN LAND QUESTION ACT. Bill C-50. 1 Reading, October 20, 1969.   Also in French.

The bill proposes recognition of aboriginal title in British Columbia. This title was never extinguished, with the exception of that of lands ceded in Treaty Number 8. Provisions are to be made to negotiate for settlement by the Governor in Council.   JSL

416   **CANADA. House of Commons. 28 Parliament, 2 Session.**
1969
NATIVE INDIAN AND ESKIMO ARTS AND CRAFTS ACT. Bill C-28. 1 Reading, October 30, 1969.   Also in French.

It is proposed that a Native Cultural Council of Canada be created to preserve and promote Indian and Eskimo arts and crafts. The proposed membership and powers of the Council are discussed. The Council could control and certify imported native arts and crafts.   JSL

417   **CANADA. House of Commons. 28 Parliament, 3 Session.**
1970
AN ACT RESPECTING THE HUNTING AND FISHING RIGHTS OF INDIAN CANADIANS. Bill C-108. 1 Reading, October 20, 1970.   Also in French.

It is proposed that the rights of Canadian Indians to hunt and fish for food be recognized and that such rights not be restricted by any federal or provincial law.   JSL

418   **CANADA. House of Commons. 28 Parliament, 3 Session.**
1970
AN ACT TO AMEND THE INDIAN ACT (RIGHTS OF INDIAN WOMAN UPON MARRIAGE). Bill C-77. 1 Reading, October 20, 1970.   Also in French.

It is suggested that paragraph (b) of subsection (1) of Section 12, and subsection (2) of Section 108 of the Indian Act be repealed. Section 14 would be changed to allow Indian women marrying a member of another band to become a member of her husband's band. The amendments would allow an Indian woman to marry a non-Indian without losing her Indian rights.   JSL

419   **CANADA. Revised Statutes.**
1970
INDIAN ACT. Revised Statutes of Canada, 1970, Chapter I-6.   Also in French.

The new Act contains minor changes in legal language, but is basically unchanged. This is the first revision since 1963.   JSL

420   **CANADA. Statutes.**
1963
OFFICE CONSOLIDATION OF THE INDIAN ACT. 1952. Chapter 149 as amended by 1952-53, c. 41; 1956, c. 40; 1958, c. 19; 1960, c. 8; 1960-61, c. 9.   Also in French.

The Indian Act was revised to incorporate the amendments of 1960 and 1961.   JSL

421   **CANADA. Statutes. 24 Parliament, 3 Session.**
1960
AN ACT TO AMEND THE CANADA ELECTIONS ACT. Acts of the Parliament of Canada, Chapter 7. Assented to March 31, 1960.   Also in French.

Paragraph (e) of subsection (2) of the Canada Elections Act was repealed. Subsection (4) of Section 14 of the Act was also repealed. By these actions, all Indians were given the Dominion franchise.   JSL

422   **CANADA. Statutes. 24 Parliament, 3 Session.**
1960
AN ACT TO AMEND THE INDIAN ACT. Acts of the Parliament of Canada, Chapter 8. Assented to March 31, 1960.   Also in French.

Subsection (2) of Section 86 of the Indian Act was repealed. Tax exemption of Indian income, property, and estates was no longer incompatible with the Dominion franchise, and no provision was needed to waive this exemption.   JSL

423   **CANADA. Statutes. 24 Parliament, 4 Session.**
1961
AN ACT TO AMEND THE INDIAN ACT. Acts of the Parliament of Canada, Chapter 9. Assented to March 9, 1961.   Also in French.

Section 112 of the Indian Act was repealed. Provisions were made to establish a committee of inquiry for bands wishing to enfranchise.   JSL

424   **MANITOBA. Revised Statutes.**
1970
THE CROWN LANDS ACT. Revised Statutes of Manitoba, Chapter C340. An Act Respecting Crown Lands.

Section 7(1)(c) provides that out of the unoccupied Crown lands transferred to the province, some areas may be set aside to enable Canada to fulfill its obligations under the treaties.   IVY

425   **MANITOBA. Revised Statutes.**
1970

THE ELECTORAL DIVISIONS ACT. Revised Statutes of Manitoba, Chapter E40. An Act to Provide for the Division of the Province into Electoral Divisions.

Section 5 includes the portions of territory laid out in Indian reserves, not surveyed into townships or sections, within the respective electoral divisions.   IVY

426   **MANITOBA. Revised Statutes.**
1970
THE LIQUOR CONTROL ACT. Revised Statutes of Manitoba, Chapter L160. An Act to Provide for the Control, Purchase, and Sale of Liquor.

Section 52(5) provides that liquor and beer may be sold to any Indian and that any Indian may have and consume liquor in a residence on a reserve.   IVY

427   **MANITOBA. Revised Statutes.**
1970
THE MENTAL HEALTH ACT. Revised Statutes of Manitoba, Chapter M110. An Act Respecting the Care and Treatment of Mentally Disordered Persons and the Custody and Control of Their Estates.

Sections 19(1) and 50(1) provide that Indians and Eskimos may be refused admission to a hospital and an institution unless expense of their maintenance and other charges are guaranteed.   IVY

428   **MANITOBA. Revised Statutes.**
1970
THE UNCONDITIONAL GRANTS ACT. Revised Statutes of Manitoba, Chapter U10. An Act to Provide for the Making of Certain Grants to Municipalities and on Behalf of Persons in Unorganized Territory.

Sections 4(1), 4(2), and 5(1) provide that for purposes of this Act, the population of a municipality does not include persons residing on an Indian reserve. Section 7(1) permits the Minister, if authorized by an order of the Lieutenant Governor in Council, to make grants or payments of behalf of persons resident on Indian reserves.   IVY

429   **MANITOBA. Revised Statutes.**
1970
THE VITAL STATISTICS ACT. Revised Statutes of Manitoba, Chapter V60. An Act Respecting the Registration of Births, Marriages, Deaths and Other Vital Events.

Sections 53(n) and 53(o) permit the Lieutenant Governor in Council to make regulations prescribing special forms for registration in respect to Indians and authorizing Indian agents to act, ex officio, as division registrar.   IVY

430   **MANITOBA. Revised Statutes.**
1970
THE WILDLIFE ACT. Revised Statutes of Manitoba, Chapter W140. An Act Respecting the Administration and Conservation of Wildlife in the Province.

Section 46 provides that while Indians may take game under paragraph 13 of the Memorandum of Agreement approved under The Manitoba Natural Resources Act, if they sell any part or give it to a non-Indian they are guilty of an offense under this Act, as is the person who receives it. Section 47 makes it an offense to enter into a contract with an unlicensed Indian to trap or hunt. Section 48 allows an Indian who has killed a fur-bearing animal for food to use the pelt only for himself or his family. Section 49 defines certain lands to which Indians do not have right of access.   IVY

431   **NEW BRUNSWICK. Statutes. 43 Legislature, 4 Session.**
1960
SOCIAL ASSISTANCE ACT. Acts of the Legislature of New Brunswick, Chapter 9. Assented to April 14, 1960.

Section 11(e) denies payment of assistance to Indian mothers and foster mothers of dependent children.   IVY

432   **NEW BRUNSWICK. Statutes. 44 Legislature, 3 Session.**
1963
AN ACT TO AMEND THE ELECTIONS ACT. Acts of the Legislature of the Province of New Brunswick, Chapter 7. Assented to March 12, 1963.

Subsection (2) of Section 34 of the Elections Act, Chapter 70, of the Revised Statutes, 1952, is amended by striking out clause (d) which disqualified Indians ordinarily resident on an Indian reservation from voting. This did not apply to Indians who had served or are serving in Her Majesty's armed forces.   IVY

433   **NEWFOUNDLAND. Statutes.**
1963
THE ALCOHOLIC LIQUORS (INDIAN AND ESQUIMAUX) (AMENDMENT) ACT, 1963. Statutes of Newfoundland, No. 80. An Act Further to Amend the Alcoholic Liquors Act. Assented to June 20, 1963.

The Alcoholic Liquors Act, Chapter 93 of The Revised Statutes of Newfoundland, 1952, is amended. The Lieutenant-Governor may by proclamation designate areas of Labrador where an Indian or Esquimaux may buy or receive alcoholic liquor. During the period fixed in the proclamation, Indians and Esquimaux shall have the same rights in respect of the purchase, possession, and use of alcoholic liquors as any other person. Persons having a license who refuse to sell to Indians or Esquimaux are liable to a penalty.   IVY

434   **NOVA SCOTIA. Revised Statutes.**
1967
VITAL STATISTICS ACT. Revised Statutes of Nova Scotia, Chapter 330.

Section 45(l and m) authorizes the prescription of special forms for the registration of Indians and authorizes the Indian agent to act as ex officio division registrar for the Indians under his jurisdiction.   IVY

435   **ONTARIO. Revised Statutes.**
1970
THE ASSESSMENT ACT. Revised Statutes of Ontario, Chapter 32.

Section 3(2) provides that property exempt from taxation is that held in trust for a band or body of Indians, but not if occupied by a person who is not a member of a band or body of Indians. Section 26(2) provides for assessment of this land if the tenant is not a member of such band or body where rent or any valuable consideration is paid.   IVY

436   **ONTARIO. Revised Statutes.**
1970
THE COMMUNITY CENTRES ACT. Revised Statutes of Ontario, Chapter 73.

Section 10(2) permits the Minister to make grants to a band council to provide for the establishment of a community center on its reserve.   IVY

437   **ONTARIO. Revised Statutes.**
1970
THE DISTRICT WELFARE ADMINISTRATION BOARDS ACT. Revised Statutes of Ontario, Chapter 132.

Section 2(2) permits a band with the approval of the district welfare administration board and the director of the General Welfare Assistance Branch to become a municipality to which this Act applies. Section 8 provides that the amount required by the district welfare administration board for the provision of welfare services to the band shall be paid by the band council in accordance with a written agreement approved by the Minister between the board and the band council.   IVY

438   **ONTARIO. Revised Statutes.**
1970
THE GENERAL WELFARE ASSISTANCE ACT. Revised Statutes of Ontario, Chapter 192.

Section 12 presents options, procedures, and obligations for band councils desiring to come under this Act.   IVY

439   **ONTARIO. Revised Statutes.**
1970
THE HOMEMAKERS AND NURSES SERVICES ACT. Revised Statutes of Ontario, Chapter 203.

Section 3(2) allows a band council with the approval of the Minister to appoint a band member as welfare administrator of the band. Sections 5-9 permit the band to employ homemakers and nurses. Persons needing such service shall apply to the welfare administrator of the band and shall pay fees for such service to the extent that their financial circumstances permit.   IVY

440   **ONTARIO. Revised Statutes.**
1970
THE HOMES FOR THE AGED AND REST HOMES ACT. Revised Statutes of Ontario, Chapter 206.

Section 5 permits band councils to establish homes. Section 9 provides the structure and powers of the Board of Management of such homes, the Board to be appointed by the Lieutenant Governor in Council.   IVY

441   **ONTARIO. Revised Statutes.**
1970
THE INDIAN WELFARE SERVICES ACT. Revised Statutes of Ontario, Chapter 218.

Indian residents of Ontario are entitled to benefits under The Blind Persons' Allowances Act, The Disabled Persons' Allowances Act, and The Family Benefits Act. The Minister may make arrangements with Canada for compensation to bodies providing services to Indians.   IVY

442   **ONTARIO. Revised Statutes.**
1970
THE MARRIAGE ACT. Revised Statutes of Ontario, Chapter 261.

Section 30(2) permits the Lieutenant Governor in Council to appoint as issuer of marriage licences a member of a band upon recommendation of a council of the band. Section 39(1) provides that where both parties are Indians and wish to avail themselves of the provisions of this Act, one of the parties shall make an affidavit in Form 9 and no fee shall be paid for such licence. Form 9 (Section 39), the Affidavit by Indian, is reproduced.   IVY

443   **ONTARIO. Revised Statutes.**
1970
PROVINCIAL LAND TAX ACT. Revised Statutes of Ontario, Chapter 370.

Section 3(1)(2) exempts from taxation property held in trust for a band or body of Indians, but not if occupied by a person who is not a member of a band or body of Indians. Section 22(3) provides that Indian land be assessed where rent or any valuable consideration is paid if the tenant is not a member of such band or body.   IVY

444   **ONTARIO. Revised Statutes.**
1970
THE VITAL STATISTICS ACT. Revised Statutes of Ontario, Chapter 483.

Section 54(r) and 54(s) provide that the Lieutenant Governor in Council may make regulations providing for separate Indian registration and authorizing superintendents of Indian agencies to act ex officio as division registrar.   IVY

445   **PRINCE EDWARD ISLAND. Statutes. 50 General Assembly, 1 Session.**
1963
THE ELECTION ACT, 1963. The Acts of the General Assembly of Prince Edward Island, Chapter 11. The Prince Edward Island Election Act 1963. Assented to April 23, 1963.

Section 170 repeals Chapter 48 of the Revised Statutes of Prince Edward Island, 1951. Section 9 of that statute disqualified Indians ordinarily resident on an Indian reservation from voting.   IVY

446   **QUEBEC. Revised Statutes.**
1964
COLONIZATION LAND SALES ACT. Revised Statutes of the Province of Quebec, Chapter 102.   Also in French.

Section 16 permits settlers who hold land on disappropriated Indian reserves and who have title to this land from the federal government to receive letters patent from the Lieutenant-Governor in Council.   IVY

447   **QUEBEC. Revised Statutes.**
1964
ELECTION ACT. Revised Statutes of the Province of Quebec, Chapter 7.   Also in French.

Section 48(c) disqualifies Indians domiciled on land reserved for Indians or held in trust for them from voting.   IVY

448   **QUEBEC. Revised Statutes.**
1964
GAME ACT. Revised Statutes of the Province of Quebec, Chapter 202.   Also In French.

Section 6(4) permits Indians, subject to the conditions determined by the Lieutenant-Governor in Council, to hunt beaver in certain parts of the province indicated by him. Section 65(7) allows the Lieutenant-Governor in Council to create certain game reserves within which only Indians may hunt fur-bearing animals whenever he may deem it proper and on the conditions which he shall determine.   IVY

449   **QUEBEC. Revised Statutes.**
1964
LANDS AND FORESTS ACT. Revised Statutes of the Province of Quebec, Chapter 92.   Also in French.

Section 65 allows the Lieutenant-Governor in Council to set apart for the use of Indian bands the usufruct of public lands. Limits are placed in Section 66 on the acreage which may be set aside. Section 67 provides that the usufruct passes to the Government of Canada, to be held in trust for the Indians. This usufruct is inalienable, but returns to the province if the Indians cease to occupy these lands. Mining rights are not included. These lands may not be taken from territories under license to cut timber without the consent of the license-holder.   IVY

450   **QUEBEC. Statutes. 28 Legislature, 4 Session.**
1969
AN ACT TO AMEND THE ELECTION ACT. Statutes of the Province of Quebec, Chapter 13. Assented to May 2, 1969.   Also in French.

Section 1 amends Section 48 of the Election Act (Revised Statutes, 1964, Chapter 7) by striking out paragraph (c) which disqualified Indians domiciled on reserves from voting.   IVY

451   **QUEBEC. Statutes. 28 Legislature, 4 Session.**
1969
WILD-LIFE CONSERVATION ACT. Statutes of the Province of Quebec, Chapter 58. Assented to December 12, 1969.   Also in French.

This Act replaces the Game Act (Revised Statutes, 1964, Chapter 202).   IVY

452   **SASKATCHEWAN. Revised Statutes.**
1965
THE FUR ACT. The Revised Statutes of Saskatchewan, Chapter 357. An Act for the
Protection, Preservation and Production of Fur Animals.

Sections 8(1) and 8(2) provide that Indians may hunt fur animals for food at all seasons
of the year on all unoccupied Crown lands and on any other lands to which those Indians
have the right of access. School lands and the lands within game preserves, provincial
forests, provincial parks, registered traplines, and fur conservation areas shall be deemed
not to be unoccupied Crown land or lands to which Indians have right of access. Section
93 provides that if a fur animal is taken by an Indian for food during the closed season,
the pelt shall be the property of the Crown.   IVY

453   **SASKATCHEWAN. Revised Statutes.**
1965
THE GAME ACT. The Revised Statutes of Saskatchewan, Chapter 356. An Act for the
Protection of Game.

Section 15(1) and 15(2) provide that Indians within the province may hunt for food at all
seasons of the year on all unoccupied Crown lands and on any other lands to which the
said Indians may have right of access. School lands and lands within the game preserves,
provincial parks, registered traplines, or fur conservation areas shall be deemed not to be
unoccupied Crown land or lands to which Indians have a right of access.   IVY

454   **SASKATCHEWAN. Revised Statutes.**
1965
THE LIQUOR ACT. The Revised Statutes of Saskatchewan, Chapter 382. An Act to
Provide for the Regulation and Sale of Alcoholic Liquors.

Section 223(2) provides that liquor may be sold to an Indian off a reserve at any store established under this Act or at any premises licensed under the Liquor Licensing
Act.   IVY

455   **SASKATCHEWAN. Revised Statutes.**
1965
THE NORTHERN ADMINISTRATION ACT. The Revised Statutes of Saskatchewan,
Chapter 412. An Act to Provide for the Administration and Development of the
Northern Part of Saskatchewan.

Section 16(2) includes Indian reserves in the delineated district. Section 16(3)(7) provides
that a road allowance adjoining an Indian reserve shall be deemed to be in the district.
Section 50(3) provides that all lands held by or in trust for the use of any tribe of Indians
are exempt from taxation.   IVY

456   **SASKATCHEWAN. Revised Statutes.**
1965
THE VITAL STATISTICS ACT. The Revised Statutes of Saskatchewan, Chapter 47.
An Act Respecting the Registration of Births, Marriages, Deaths and Other Vital Events.

Sections 26(3) and 30(4) authorize each Indian superintendent to act ex officio as division registrar and entitle him to a fee of 25 cents for each registration of a birth, death, or still birth.   IVY

457   **SASKATCHEWAN. Statutes. 15 Legislature, 4 Session.**
1967
THE GAME ACT, 1967. Statutes of the Province of Saskatchewan, Chapter 78. An Act for the Protection of Game. Assented to April 1, 1967.

Section 8 of this act guarantees the right of Indians within the province of Saskatchewan to hunt for food at all seasons on lands to which they have access.   IVY

458   **SASKATCHEWAN. Statutes. 16 Legislature, 2 Session.**
1969
THE SASKATCHEWAN INDIAN AND METIS DEPARTMENT ACT, 1969.
Statutes of the Province of Saskatchewan, Chapter 54. An Act to Establish the Saskatchewan and Metis Department. Assented to March 31, 1969.

This act establishes the Saskatchewan Indian and Metis Department to assist people of Indian ancestry. Inquiries and collation of data and statistics relating to the general welfare of people of Indian ancestry shall be instituted. Programs shall be established to promote employment and to provide financial and technical assistance, in which specialists or consultants may be engaged. This act came into force on April 1, 1969.   IVY

INDIAN ADMINISTRATION AND GOVERNMENT POLICY

459   **1960**
INDIANS OF QUEBEC HOLD A FOLK SCHOOL. Citizen 6(4):11-14.

Twenty-eight Indian delegates from 5 tribes (Abnaki, Algonkin, Huron, Iroquois and Montagnais) attended a conference on leadership development among Indians and social action and community development on the reserve. One of the principal speakers was Rev. Andre Renaud who gave a lecture on change in Indian culture.   ADG

460   **1961**
INDIANS PARTICIPATE IN LEADERSHIP TRAINING CONFERENCE. Citizen 7(4):36-38.

Twenty-seven Indian men and women studied principles of effective leadership in a week-long training institute at Quetico, Ontario.   ADG

461   **1962**
COMMUNITY LEADERS OF SADDLE LAKE INDIAN AGENCY MEET IN TRAINING COURSES. Citizen 8(1):25-28.

Twenty-one representatives of 5 bands of the Saddle Lake Agency met at St. Paul, Alberta for a week-long course in leadership.   ADG

462   **1962**
INTEREST GROWS IN INDIANS AND ESKIMOS. Citizen 8(3):13-19.

Although it has had a short history, the Indian-Eskimo Association has developed rapidly and is presently engaged in numerous programs and projects. Leadership training for Indian, Metis and Eskimo people and urban projects such as the Indian and Metis Friendship Centre are major Association projects.   ADG

463   **1963**
FIRST INDIAN FOLK SCHOOL IN ONTARIO. Citizen 9(3):35-37.

In 1963, 27 delegates including 6 Indian chiefs met for the first Indian folk school in Ontario. Sponsored by the Ontario Folk School Council with the co-operation of the Indian Affairs Branch, this workshop focused on changes in home and community life and leadership skills for Indian leaders. These leaders noted that they would like to preserve the following aspects of Indian life: (1) dialect, (2) crafts and other skills, (3) band traditions, (4) dances, (5) Indian identity, and (6) the reserve system.   ADG

464   **1969**
THE DIVINE RIGHT TO BE HUMAN. The Labour Gazette 69:66-71.

Among the participants at the Conference of Human Rights, held in Ottawa in December 1968, were several Indian leaders and spokesmen protesting the inequality suffered by the Indian. Harold Cardinal called upon the Canadian government to respect Indian treaties, abolish the Indian Affairs Branch, and include aboriginal rights in the new Canadian Constitution.   ADG

465   **1969**
THE NEW POLICY FOR CANADA'S INDIANS. The Labour Gazette 69:513.

The policy statement on Indians issued by the federal government in June 1969 is reviewed. The government wishes to eliminate federal paternalism and permit Indians to manage their own affairs as do other citizens. For this reason, the Indian Act must be repealed and new legislation enacted which will permit Indians to acquire title to and control of their lands. It is also proposed that the provincial governments assume responsibility as they do for other citizens.   ADG

466   **1970**
THE INDIAN AND METIS IN SASKATCHEWAN. Unpublished paper. Available from Indian and Metis Department, Regina. 26 pp.

Following an account of Indians and Metis history in Saskatchewan, the government programs, mainly provincial, are outlined to show specifically the assistance that is available to people of Indian ancestry, emphasizing employment, education, financial assistance and housing.   IVY

467   **ANGLICAN CHURCH OF CANADA**
1960
BRIEF. In Minutes of Proceedings and Evidence. No. 9. June 2, 1960. Joint Committee of the Senate and the House of Commons on Indian Affairs. Canada. 24 Parliament, 3 Session. Ottawa: Queen's Printer. pp. 794-809.

Thirty-nine recommendations were offered in this extensive brief. Discussed are Indian administration, education, economic development, social services and citizenship.   JSL

468   ANGLICAN CHURCH OF CANADA
1970
GENERAL SYNOD RESOLUTIONS. In Bulletin 201: Recent Statements by the
Indians of Canada, General Synod Action 1969, Some Government Responses,
Suggested Resources. Anglican Church of Canada, Action Unit. Toronto: Anglican
Church of Canada. pp. 21-22.

The 1969 General Synod resolutions on the Hendry report are approved. Directions are
given for the establishment, in consultation with native people, other churches, and governments, of a program of development following the recommendations. Provision
is made for the establishment of a fund to support these activities. It is resolved to support National Indian Brotherhood demands for consultation with native people in policy-making and in funding research on aboriginal and other rights.   CCV

469   ARMSTRONG   TERENCE
1966
THE ADMINISTRATION OF NORTHERN PEOPLES: THE U.S.S.R. In The Arctic
Frontier. R. St. J. Macdonald, ed. Toronto: University of Toronto Press. pp. 57-88.

The Soviet treatment of minority peoples in the North is the focus of attention. On pages
86-88, possible lessons for Canadian administration of northern peoples in the area of
education and integration are discussed.   DGW

470   ASSOCIATION OF QUEBEC INDIANS
1970
BRIEF ABOUT THE TERRITORIAL RIGHTS OF THE INDIANS OF THE
PROVINCE OF QUEBEC, JANUARY 7, 1969. In Bulletin 202: Extracts from "Native
Rights of Canada". Toronto: Anglican Church of Canada. p. 39.

Presented are 9 statements by the executive of the Association of Quebec Indians. It is
claimed that native rights in Quebec have never been recognized. Five billion dollars is
considered the required compensation for disregarding these rights.   DGW

471   BATTLE   R F
1960
REPORT ON MARITIMES TRIP. Unpublished paper. Available at Development
Services Division, Department of Indian Affairs and Northern Development, Ottawa. 8
pp.

A trip to Maritime reserves is reported indicating observations on housing and living conditions, employment, and potential for economic development.   CCV

472   BATTLE   R F
1966
AN HISTORICAL REVIEW OF INDIAN AFFAIRS POLICIES AND NEW
DIRECTIONS FOR THE FUTURE. Address delivered to Trinity College Conference
on the Canadian Indian. Toronto, January 22, 1966. Available from Information
Services, Research and Records, Department of Indian Affairs and Northern
Development, Ottawa. 9 pp.

Indian Affairs policies and problems past and present are reviewed and presented with a discussion of current departmental expenditures and proposals by the Assistant Deputy Minister of the Indian Affairs Branch.   CCV

473   **BATTLE   R F**
1968
AN ADDRESS BY R. F. BATTLE ASSISTANT DEPUTY MINISTER, INDIAN AFFAIRS BRANCH, DEPARTMENT OF INDIAN AFFAIRS AND NORTHERN DEVELOPMENT. Speech delivered to National Association of Principals and Administrators of Indian Residences. Vancouver, March 11, 1968. Available from Information Services, Records and Research, Department of Indian Affairs and Northern Development, Ottawa (Speech #3-6747). 4 pp.

Current needs in education, government policies, and expenditures as well as the roles of schools, churches, Indian leaders, and other citizens in meeting demands are reviewed by the Assistant Deputy Minister of the Indian Affairs Branch.   CCV

474   **BATTLE   ROBERT F**
1969
A SPEECH BY MR. ROBERT F. BATTLE ASSISTANT DEPUTY MINISTER, SOCIAL AFFAIRS, DEPARTMENT OF INDIAN AFFAIRS AND NORTHERN DEVELOPMENT. Speech delivered to Manitoba and North Dakota International Symposium on the Legal Rights of Indians. Grand Forks, ND, March 6-7, 1969. Available from Information Services, Records and Research, Department of Indian Affairs and Northern Development, Ottawa (Speech #3-6818). 20 pp.

Underlined are needs to interpret treaty rights into meaningful legislation, to consult with Indian peoples, to standardize services, to implement Indian self-determination, and to protect land and hunting rights.   CCV

475   **BLACKNED-WATT   GERTRUDE**
1966
THIS LAND WAS OUR LAND. Human Relations (Ontario Human Rights Commission) 7(13):5.

This speech by an Indian student illustrates the government's failure to effectively coordinate its services for Indians. Indians should be placed in government agencies functioning on the Indian's behalf. Residential schools have made the Indian child unfit for either the Indian or White society.   ADG

476   **BOYD   ERIC E**
1968
THE INDIAN PEOPLE AND THE NEXT ONE HUNDRED YEARS. Speech delivered to Teach-In on the Canadian Indian at St. Francis Xavier University. Antigonish, N.S., January 27, 1968. Available from Information Services, Records and Research, Department of Indian Affairs and Northern Development, Ottawa (Speech #3-6741). 8 pp.

New Indian Affairs policies and what they hope to attain in the fields of education, employment, housing, and medical services are reviewed by the Executive Assistant to the Assistant Deputy Minister of Indian Affairs.   CCV

477   **BOYD   ERIC E**
1968
THE INDIAN PEOPLE AND THE ROLE OF GOVERNMENT. Speech delivered to
Glendon College Indian Forum. Toronto, October 10, 1968. Available from
Information Services, Records and Research, Department of Indian Affairs and
Northern Development, Ottawa (Speech #3-6807). 12 pp.

The role of government administration in Indian Affairs as well as specific trends to extension of provincial services to Indians, involvement of Indians in decision-making, and
provision of special facilities to facilitate adaptation are outlined by the chief of the Indian-Eskimo Bureau.   CCV

478   **BRITISH COLUMBIA INDIAN ARTS AND WELFARE SOCIETY**
1960
A BRIEF FOR PRESENTATION TO THE PARLIAMENTARY COMMITTEE ON
INDIAN AFFAIRS. In Minutes of Proceedings and Evidence. No. 7. May 26-27, 1960.
Joint Committee of the Senate and the House of Commons on Indian Affairs. 24
Parliament, 3 Session. Ottawa: Queen's Printer. pp. 696-701.

Discussed are proposals on federal voting, community services, economic development,
credit, co-operatives, credit unions, social welfare, adult education, age of school-leaving,
courses in Indain culture, liqour laws, adoption of children, and Indian craft development.   JSL

479   **BRITISH COLUMBIA. Department of Social Welfare.**
1960
SUBMISSION OF THE DEPARTMENT OF SOCIAL WELFARE TO THE JOINT
COMMITTEE OF THE SENATE AND THE HOUSE OF COMMONS APPOINTED
TO EXAMINE AND CONSIDER THE INDIAN ACT, AS WELL AS INDIAN
ADMINISTRATION IN GENERAL AND, IN PARTICULAR, THE SOCIAL AND
ECONOMIC STATUS OF THE INDIANS. In Minutes of Proceedings and Evidence.
No. 7. May 26-27, 1960. Joint Committee of the Senate and the House of Commons on
Indian Affairs. 24 Parliament, 3 Session. Ottawa: Queen's Printer. pp. 676-696.

Included in this extensive brief are observations on the socio-economic status of Indians
in British Columbia and suggested recommendations for solutions to the economic problems.   JSL

480   **BRITISH COLUMBIA. Department of the Provincial Secretary. British Columbia
Advisory Committee.**
n.d.
BULLETIN. Victoria, B.C.: Queen's Printer. 3 pp.

A 3-page pamphlet outlines the aims of the Advisory Committee and presents the topics
discussed at the meeting at Kamloops in 1964. Members of the Indian Advisory Committee are listed.   IVY

481   **BRITISH COLUMBIA. Department of the Provincial Secretary. British Columbia
Advisory Committee.**
1964
INDIAN ADVISORY COMMITTEE NEWSLETTER.

The stated function of the Indian Advisory Newsletter is to provide a communication link between the provincial government and the Indian community. Information considered of interest to the Indians of British Columbia is presented.   IVY

482   **BRITISH COLUMBIA. Department of the Provincial Secretary. British Columbia Indian Advisory Committee and the Director, Indian Advisory Act.**
1960-69.
ANNUAL REPORTS (ELEVENTH TO TWENTIETH): BRITISH COLUMBIA INDIAN ADVISORY COMMITTEE AND THE DIRECTOR, INDIAN ADVISORY ACT. British Columbia: Queen's Printer. 9 vols.

Provincial and federal legislation concerning Indians of British Columbia is reviewed. Meetings and conferences of native organizations are discussed. A summary of provincial and federal services, private organizations, and native associations is presented.   IVY

483   **CALUMET INDIAN CLUB**
1960
BRIEF OF CALUMET INDIAN CLUB. In Minutes of Proceedings and Evidence. No. 3. May 11-13, 1960. Joint Committee of the Senate and the House of Commons on Indian Affairs. Canada. 24 Parliament, 3 Session. Ottawa: Queen's Printer. pp. 297-299.

A short brief was submitted. Included are 10 resolutions.   JSL

484   **CAMPBELL   DAN**
1970
FIRST CITIZEN'S FUND. Victoria, B.C.: Queen's Printer. 3 pp.

Established to contribute support to projects involved with the advancement and expansion of the culture, education, economic circumstances, and positions of persons of native ancestry, the general and projected policies of the First Citizen's Fund are outlined.   IVY

485   **CANADA. Department of Citizenship and Immigration.**
1960
REPORT OF THE DEPARTMENT OF CITIZENSHIP AND IMMIGRATION 1959-60. Ottawa: Queen's Printer. 98 pp.   Also in French.

The annual report of the Indian Affairs Branch is given on pages 45 to 98. Discussed are band councils, employment placement, employment opportunities, wildlife and fisheries, revolving fund loans, agricultural assistance, handicrafts, public assistance, community organization, child care, social allowances, rehabilitation, housing and reserve development. The following aspects of education are discussed: enrolment, teaching staff, facilities and supplies, pupil transportation, vocational training, guidance, post-elementary education, teacher training, school supervision, statistical reports, curriculum, liason activities, joint schools, Indian school committees, adult education, and construction. Also discussed are reserves and land register, land sales and leases, petroleum and gas, mining, forestry, membership, estates, individual land holding register, band funds, savings, non-band accounts, annuities, enfranchisement, engineering and construction, and field administration. Included are the names and addresses of regional offices and agencies.

An extended treatment of each province is followed by statistical tables. Brief mention of Indians is made in the report of the Canadian Citizenship Branch.   JSL

486   **CANADA. Department of Citizenship and Immigration.**
1962
REPORT OF THE DEPARTMENT OF CITIZENSHIP AND IMMIGRATION 1960-61. Ottawa: Queen's Printer. 108 pp.   Also in French.

The annual report of the Indian Affairs Branch is given on pages 45 to 108. A resume of the year's activities is followed by consideration of specific programs. Among these are band councils, employment placement, employment opportunities, wildlife and fisheries, agricultural assistance, research and surveys, handicrafts, revolving fund loans, public assistance, winter employment, community organization, child care, social allowances, rehabilitation, housing and reserve development. In the education field, the following are mentioned: enrolment, teaching staff, Indian status teachers, salaries and qualifications, accomodation, turnover, supplies, libraries, furniture, recreation, transportation, practical arts, vocational training, extra-curricular activities, guidance, educational assistance, teacher training, supervision, statistical report, curriculum, liason activities, joint schools, school committees, adult education, and construction. Also discussed are new reserves, land sales, leases, petroleum and gas, mining, forestry, estates, individual land holdings registry, reserves land register, land surveys, membership, Indian trust funds, savings, transfer of control to bands, annuities, winter works, enfranchisement, engineering and construction, and field administration. Included is a list of the names and locations of regional offices and agencies. An extended picture is given for each province. Statistical tables provide further information. Brief mention of Indians is made in the report of the Canadian Citizenship Branch.   JSL

487   **CANADA. Department of Citizenship and Immigration.**
1962
REPORT OF THE DEPARTMENT OF CITIZENSHIP AND IMMIGRATION 1961-62. Ottawa: Queen's Printer. 79 pp.   Also in French.

The annual report of the Indian Affairs Branch is given on pages 25 to 45. A brief resume of the year's activities is presented. Further discussion deals with band councils, integrated classrooms, educational assistance, guidance, extra-curricular activities, curriculum, attendance, adult education, teaching staff, teacher training, supervision, residential schools, off-reserve welfare, housing, public assistance, provincial agreements, provincial welfare services, special joint services, Manitoba community development, winter works' programs, and employment placement. Also of concern to the Branch are research and surveys, wildlife and fisheries, agriculture, handicrafts, revolving fund loans, Indian veteran grants, petroleum and gas, land sales, leases, mining, forestry, estates, individual land holdings, membership, reserves, Indian trust funds, savings, annuities, engineering and construction, and field administration. Included is a list of the names and locations of regional offices and agencies. Statistical tables on pages 62 to 79 provide supplementary information. Brief mention of Indians is made in the report of the Canadian Citizenship Branch.   JSL

488   **CANADA. Department of Citizenship and Immigration.**
1963
REPORT OF THE DEPARTMENT OF CITIZENSHIP AND IMMIGRATION 1962-1963. Ottawa: Queen's Printer. 66 pp.   Also in French.

Pages 21 to 36 report on the activities of the Indian Affairs Branch. Following a brief resume of the year, individual programs are discussed. Among these are scholarships, curricula, supervision, adult education, residential schools, in-service training, extra-curricular activities, construction, development, research and surveys, trusts and land grants, reserve lands and resources, wildlife and fisheries, handicrafts, employment placement, winter works programs, public assistance, provincial welfare services, leadership training and community organizations, housing, field administration, band councils, membership, estates, individual land holdings, and engineering and construction. Included is a list of the names and locations of regional offices and agencies. Pages 57 to 66 provide statistical information. Brief mention of Indians exists in the report of the Canadian Citizenship Branch.   JSL

489   **CANADA. Department of Citizenship and Immigration.**
1965
REPORT OF THE DEPARTMENT OF CITIZENSHIP AND IMMIGRATION 1963-1964. Ottawa: Queen's Printer. 66 pp.   Also in French.

The annual report for 1963-1964 of the Indian Affairs Branch is given on pages 21 to 38. A brief resume of the year's activities is presented. Discussed are residential schools, curricula, supervision, teacher qualifications, teaching staff, adult education, vocational training, scholarships, construction, economic development, research and surveys, trusts and annuities, band property insurance, band loans, personal savings, revolving loan funds, re-establishment of Indian veterans, reserve lands, oil, gas, and minerals, forestry, agriculture, industrial development, handicrafts, wildlife and fisheries, employment placement, community employment program, welfare services, community services, field administration, housing, band councils, membership, enfranchisement, estates, individual land holdings, and engineering and construction. Included is a list of the names and locations of regional offices and agencies. Statistical tables are given in pages 59 to 66. Brief mention of Indians is made in the annual report of the Canadian Citizenship Branch.   JSL

490   **CANADA. Department of Citizenship and Immigration.**
1966
REPORT OF THE DEPARTMENT OF CITIZENSHIP AND IMMIGRATION 1964-1965. Ottawa: Queen's Printer. 73 pp.   Also in French.

Pages 25 to 43 contain the annual report of the Indian Affairs Branch. Following a resume of activities, the following programs are discussed: welfare services, community services, provincial agreements, cultural affairs, industrial development, employment placement, winter employment programs, agriculture, forestry, wildlife and fisheries, handicrafts, mineral resources, economic surveys and research, engineering and construction, housing, fire protection, reserve utilities, education curricula, supervision, adult education, vocational training, scholarships, school committees, residential schools, teaching staff, teacher qualifications, estates, enfranchisement, adoptions, protests, band re-organization, land transactions, management of land, leasing, land surveys and titles, band property insurance, band loans, personal savings, annuities, band council administration, field administration, and staff training. Included is a list of regional offices and Indian agencies. Statistical tables are presented on pages 65 to 73. Brief mention of Indians is made in the report of the Canadian Citizenship Branch.   JSL

491   **CANADA. Department of Citizenship and Immigration.**
1967
REPORT OF THE DEPARTMENT OF CITIZENSHIP AND IMMIGRATION 1965-
1966. Ottawa: Queen's Printer. 101 pp.   Also in French.

Under Order in Council P.C. 1965-2285 the transfer of the Indian Affairs Branch to the
Department of Northern Affairs and National Resources was authorized. A brief resume
of the period from April 1, 1965, to December 31, 1965, is presented. Statistical tables
present further information. The report on the balance of this fiscal year was presented
by the Department of National Affairs and Northern Resources which, with the addition
of the Branch, became the Department of Indian Affairs and Northern Development in
the next fiscal year.   JSL

492   **CANADA. Department of Citizenship and Immigration. Indian Affairs Branch.**
n.d.
DISCUSSION NOTES ON THE INDIAN ACT. Ottawa: Department of Citizenship
and Immigration. 31 pp.

A booklet was prepared for the Regional Indian Advisory Councils discussing the Indian
Act and its various sections. The booklet was reprinted in 1968 by the Department of
Indian Affairs and Northern Development.   JSL

493   **CANADA. Department of Citizenship and Immigration. Indian Affairs Branch.**
1960
A COMMENTARY ON THE INDIAN ACT PREPARED FOR THE MEMBERS OF
THE JOINT COMMITTEE OF THE SENATE AND THE HOUSE OF COMMONS
ON INDIAN AFFAIRS. Ottawa: Department of Citizenship and Immigration. 41 pp.
Also in French.

Each section of the Indian Act is explained, to assist the members of the Joint Committee.   JSL

494   **CANADA. Department of Citizenship and Immigration. Indian Affairs Branch.**
1961
BRIEF. In Minutes of Proceedings and Evidence. No. 1. May 11, 1961. Joint Committee
of the Senate and the House of Commons on Indian Affairs. Canada. 24 Parliament, 4
Session. Ottawa: Queen's Printer. pp. 417-435.

A brief was presented by the supervisor of fur and wildlife of the Branch. Discussed are
treaties, treaty rights, and legal factors in connection with wildlife and fisheries resources. Included as references are copies of treaties, proclamations, and legal judgments.   JSL

495   **CANADA. Department of Citizenship and Immigration. Indian Affairs Branch.**
1961
BRIEF. In Minutes of Proceedings and Evidence. No. 8 May 2-3, 1961. Joint Committee
of the Senate and the House of Commons on Indian Affairs. Canada. 24 Parliament, 4
Session. Ottawa: Queen's Printer. pp. 275-279.

A review of Branch activities and an outline of Branch organizations are provided.   JSL

496   **CANADA. Department of Citizenship and Immigration. Indian Affairs Branch.**
1961
BRIEF. In Minutes of Proceedings and Evidence. No. 14. May 23, 1961. Joint
Committee of the Senate and the House of Commons on Indian Affairs. Canada. 24
Parliament, 4 Session. Ottawa: Queen's Printer. pp. 537-542.

The Director's special assistant presented a brief on enfranchisement. Discussed are the
provisions in the Indian Act for individual and band enfranchisement, marriage to
Whites, Indian grievances, historical background of the concept of enfranchisement, reasons for non-acceptance, advantages and disadvantages of enfranchisement, and projections for the future.   JSL

497   **CANADA. Department of Citizenship and Immigration. Indian Affairs Branch.**
1961
BRIEF. In Minutes of Proceedings and Evidence. No. 15. May 24-25, 1961. Joint
Committee of the Senate and the House of Commons on Indian Affairs. Canada. 24
Parliament, 4 Session. Ottawa: Queen's Printer. pp. 566-569.

A brief was presented by the Director's special assistant, concerning the British Columbia
land issue. Discussed are the claims, the early historical background, and the post-confederation history. Special attention is directed to the 1912 Royal Commission, the 1926
Special Joint Committee findings, and the $100,000 special fund.   JSL

498   **CANADA. Department of Citizenship and Immigration. Indian Affairs Branch.**
1961
A HANDBOOK FOR INDIAN BAND CHIEFS AND COUNCILLORS. Ottawa:
Department of Citizenship and Immigration. 17 pp.   Also in French.

A handbook was prepared to provide chiefs and councilors with information necessary
for the efficient execution of their tasks.   The composition and election of band councils,
their terms of office, powers and duties, and meeting procedures are outlined. In addition, 9 questions arising from special legal status are explained.   JSL

499   **CANADA. Department of Citizenship and Immigration. Indian Affairs Branch.**
1962
THE INDIAN IN TRANSITION: INDIAN EDUCATION. Ottawa: Queen's Printer.
24 pp.   Also in French.

An outline of Indian education was compiled. Discussed are federal responsibilities, implementation of the 1948 recommendations of the Joint Committee, problems, schools,
curriculum, courses, financial aid, adult education, the role of parents, school committees,
and the role of the non-Indian.   JSL

500   **CANADA. Department of Citizenship and Immigration. Indian Affairs Branch.**
1962
THE INDIAN IN TRANSITION: THE INDIAN TODAY. Ottawa: Queen's Printer.
28 pp.   Also in French.

The contemporary Canadian Indians are discussed. Included are outlines of administration, Indian problems, education, employment, placement programs, economic activities, health, social welfare, the local community (housing, community life, homemakers' clubs), and local self-government.   JSL

501   **CANADA. Department of Citizenship and Immigration. Indian Affairs Branch.**
1963
INDIAN AFFAIRS FACTS AND FIGURES. Ottawa: Department of Citizenship and Immigration. 22 pp.

The statistical data published by the Department earlier in the year (April) were slightly revised and updated. This material was published in September of 1963. Subject headings remain unchanged.   JSL

502   **CANADA. Department of Citizenship and Immigration. Indian Affairs Branch.**
1963
INDIAN AFFAIRS FACTS AND FIGURES. Ottawa: Department of Citizenship and Immigration. 23 pp.

Statistical tables and numerical and financial data are given for Indian bands and reserves, branch expenditures, Indian population, staff statistics, band councils, band by-laws, band fund administration, bands under the Ontario Welfare Act, public assistance, homemakers' clubs, leadership training, construction programs, housing, revolving fund loans, leases and permits, forest production, handicraft production, employment placement programs, education, and enfranchisement. The material was published in April, 1963.   JSL

503   **CANADA. Department of Citizenship and Immigration. Indian Affairs Branch.**
1964
THE ADMINISTRATION OF INDIAN AFFAIRS: PREPARED FOR 1964
FEDERAL-PROVINCIAL CONFERENCE ON INDIAN AFFAIRS. Available from Library, Department of Indian Affairs and Northern Development, Ottawa. 107 pp.

This book was prepared to give provincial authorities information on the details and extent of Indian Affairs administration. Discussed are the purpose, aims, objectives, program areas, policies, expenditures, and future plans of the Indian Affairs Branch.   JSL

504   **CANADA. Department of Citizenship and Immigration. Indian Affairs Branch.**
1965
A HANDBOOK FOR INDIAN BAND CHIEFS AND COUNCILLORS. Ottawa: Department of Citizenship and Immigration. 24 pp.   Also in French.

The 1961 handbook was revised.   JSL

505   **CANADA. Department of Citizenship and Immigration. Indian Affairs Branch. Administration Division.**
1961
BRIEF. In Minutes of Proceedings and Evidence. No. 9. May 4, 1961. Joint Committee of the Senate and the House of Commons on Indian Affairs. Canada. 24 Parliament, 4 Session. Ottawa: Queen's Printer. pp. 323-330.

A review of activities in the Administrative Division is given. Discussed are band councils and elections, bylaws, liquor, law enforcement, crime and corrections, and public relations.   JSL

506   **CANADA. Department of Citizenship and Immigration. Indian Affairs Branch. Administration Division.**
1964
FACTS AND FIGURES. Ottawa: Department of Citizenship and Immigration. 49 pp.

Statistical information on Indians was published in September of 1964. Data are given for bands and reserves, population, enfranchisements, branch expenditures, staff, band councils, by-laws, band fund administration, bands in the Ontario Welfare Assistance Act, liquor privileges, construction, housing, public assistance, homemakers' clubs, leadership training, handicraft production, agriculture, land registry, survey of reserves, estates, individual land holdings, trust funds, revolving fund loans, leases and permits, Veterans Land Act, and education.   JSL

507   **CANADA. Department of Citizenship and Immigration. Indian Affairs Branch. Agencies Division.**
1961
BRIEF. In Minutes of Proceedings and Evidence. No. 8. May 2-3, 1961. Joint Committee of the Senate and the House of Commons on Indian Affairs. Canada. 24 Parliament, 4 Session. Ottawa: Queen's Printer. pp. 299-302.

The chief of the Branch's Agencies Division presented a brief on activities and duties of the Division.   JSL

508   **CANADA. Department of Citizenship and Immigration. Indian Affairs Branch. Economic Development Division.**
1961
BRIEF. In Minutes of Proceedings and Evidence. No. 10. May 9-10, 1961. Joint Committee of the Senate and the House of Commons on Indian Affairs. Canada. 24 Parliament, 4 Session. Ottawa: Queen's Printer. pp. 373-386.

A review of activities in the Economic Development Division is presented. Discussed are agriculture, wildlife and fisheries, fur rehabilitation, game management, fishing, sawmills, crafts, freezers, cooperatives, credit and finance, and research and surveys. The 2 major concerns of the Division are economic development and community development.   JSL

509   **CANADA. Department of Citizenship and Immigration. Indian Affairs Branch. Education Division.**
1960
STATISTICAL REPORT. Ottawa: Department of Citizenship and Immigration. 129 pp.

The statistical report of the Education Division for the school year 1959-1960 consists of 3 parts. In the first section, 19 tables summarize the promotions, non-promotions, and attendance of Indian pupils from kindergarten to grade 9 in Indian schools. The second section deals with the distribution of pupils in Indian schools by age, grade, and sex, and contains 71 tables. The third section, reporting on the destinations of pupils withdrawing from Indian schools, contains 36 tables. The reports are arranged according to administrative region, and separate figures given for day schools and residential schools.   JSL

510   **CANADA. Department of Citizenship and Immigration. Indian Affairs Branch. Education Division.**
1961
BRIEF. In Minutes of Proceedings and Evidence. No. 13. May 18, 1961. Joint Committee of the Senate and the House of Commons on Indian Affairs. Canada. 24 Parliament, 4 Session. Ottawa: Queen's Printer. pp. 492-495.

A supplementary brief was presented by the Education Division to complement their 1959 brief.   JSL

511   **CANADA. Department of Citizenship and Immigration. Indian Affairs Branch. Education Division.**
1961
STATISTICAL REPORT. Ottawa: Department of Citizenship and Immigration. 129 pp.

A statistical report for the school year 1960-1961 was issued by the Education Division. The format is identical to that of the 1960 report.   JSL

512   **CANADA. Department of Citizenship and Immigration. Indian Affairs Branch. Education Division.**
1962
STATISTICAL REPORT. Ottawa: Department of Citizenship and Immigration. 129 pp.

The Education Division's annual statistical report was compiled. The format is similar to the 1960 report.   JSL

513   **CANADA. Department of Citizenship and Immigration. Indian Affairs Branch. Education Division.**
1964
TEACH IN MANITOBA'S INDIAN SCHOOLS: A HANDBOOK FOR PROSPECTIVE TEACHERS IN INDIAN SCHOOLS. Winnipeg: Department of Citizenship and Immigration. 99 pp.

Text and photographs were compiled to serve as a guide and introduction for prospective teachers of Indians in Manitoba. Included is a map locating Indian schools in the province. Discussed are salaries, benefits, application, expenses, costs, housing, medical services, and school supplies and maintenance. A description is given for each of 44 schools. For 17 of the schools, pictures are appended.   JSL

514   **CANADA. Department of Citizenship and Immigration. Indian Affairs Branch. Engineering and Construction Division.**
1961
BRIEF. In Minutes of Proceedings and Evidence. No. 14. May 23, 1961. Joint Committee of the Senate and the House of Commons on Indian Affairs. Canada. 24 Parliament, 4 Session. Ottawa: Queen's Printer. pp. 515-517.

Discussed are construction of houses, schools, roads, bridges, and other buildings, utilities, mechanical equipment, maintenance, and repair.   JSL

515   **CANADA. Department of Citizenship and Immigration. Indian Affairs Branch. Reserves and Trusts Division.**
1961
BRIEF. In Minutes of Proceedings and Evidence. No. 12. May 16, 1961. Joint Committee of the Senate and the House of Commons on Indian Affairs. Canada. 24 Parliament, 4 Session. Ottawa: Queen's Printer. pp. 461-465.

The chief of the Reserves and Trusts Division presented a review of activities. The Division administers land and resource management, band funds, and membership. Discussed are land sales, leases, allotments, oil and gas, mining, timber, band funds, transfer of control to bands, and the reserve system.   JSL

516   **CANADA. Department of Citizenship and Immigration. Indian Affairs Branch. Welfare Division.**
1961
BRIEF. In Minutes of Proceedings and Evidence. No. 10. May 9-10, 1961. Joint Committee of the Senate and the House of Commons on Indian Affairs. Canada. 24 Parliament, 4 Session. Ottawa: Queen's Printer. pp. 353-360.

The chief of the Branch's Welfare Division presented a review of activities. The extension of welfare benefits and housing were discussed.   JSL

517   **CANADA. Department of Indian Affairs and Northern Development.**
n.d.
THE INDIAN PEOPLE IN PROFESSIONS, INDUSTRY, BUSINESS, TRADES.
Ottawa: Department of Indian Affairs and Northern Development. 18 pp.

Business opportunities for Indians are listed; some of the requirements for assistance, and the type of assistance available are included in a brochure prepared for distribution among Indians.   CCV

518   **CANADA. Department of Indian Affairs and Northern Development.**
1967
ANNUAL REPORT FISCAL YEAR 1966-67. Ottawa: Queen's Printer. 136 pp.   Also in French.

By Order in Council the Indian Affairs Branch was transferred from the Department of Citizenship and Immigration to the Department of Northern Affairs and National Resources. This is the first annual report of the resultant Department of Indian Affairs and Northern Development. Pages 45 to 69 contain the annual report of the Indian Affairs Branch. A resume of the year's activities is followed by discussion of education, community services, cultural affairs, welfare services, agriculture, craft industries, small businesses and cooperatives, tourist development, land use, mineral resources, wild crops, wildlife, tourist outfitting and guiding, fisheries, forestry, planned communities, estates, membership, surveys and titles, reserve lands, trusts and annuities, band loans, personal savings, annuities, federal-provincial relations, Indian consultation, and personnel. Included is a list of the names and locations of regional offices and agencies. Pages 121 to 129 contain statistical tables.   JSL

519   **CANADA. Department of Indian Affairs and Northern Development.**
1968
ANNUAL REPORT FISCAL YEAR 1967-68. Ottawa: Queen's Printer. 153 pp.   Also
in French.

Pages 61 to 101 deal with the Indian Affairs Branch. Discussed are federal-provincial relations, Indian consultation, estates, membership, land administration, land surveys and
titles, community development, band grants, homemakers' clubs, cultural affairs, welfare
services, school enrolment, teacher recruitment and training, school libraries, pre-school
classes, federal school construction, pupil transportation, vocational and professional
training, adult education, employment and relocation, planned communities, water and
sanitation services, electrification, design and construction of houses, roads, community
employment, personnel, land use, agriculture, tourist development, forestry, petroleum,
mining, craft industries, small businesses and cooperatives, fisheries, wildlife, wild crops,
outfitting and guiding, policy and planning. Included is a list of the names and locations
of regional and district offices, and Indian agencies. Statistical tables and charts provide
supplementary information.   JSL

520   **CANADA. Department of Indian Affairs and Northern Development.**
1968
REPORT OF THE INDIAN ACT CONSULTATION MEETING. CHILLIWACK,
BRITISH COLUMBIA. NOVEMBER 18, 19, 20, 21, 22, 1968. Ottawa: Department of
Indian Affairs and Northern Development. 142 pp.

Representatives from 42 British Columbia bands, the North American Indian Brotherhood, the Vancouver Indian Centre, and the Homemakers' Club met with Robert Andras, Walter Dieter, and Indian Affairs officials to discuss the Indian Act and Indian
rights.   JSL

521   **CANADA. Department of Indian Affairs and Northern Development.**
1968
REPORT OF THE INDIAN ACT CONSULTATION MEETING. EDMONTON,
ALBERTA. DECEMBER 12 AND 13, 1968. Ottawa: Department of Indian Affairs
and Northern Development. 95 pp.

Delegates from 41 Alberta bands, the Indian Association of Alberta, the Regional Advisory Council, and the Edmonton Native Friendship Centre, along with Senator Gladstone, met with Robert Andras, Walter Dieter, and Indian Affairs officials to discuss treaties, rights, and the Indian Act.   JSL

522   **CANADA. Department of Indian Affairs and Northern Development.**
1968
REPORT OF THE INDIAN ACT CONSULTATION MEETING. FORT WILLIAM,
ONTARIO. AUGUST 16, 17, 18, AND 19, 1968. Ottawa: Department of Indian
Affairs and Northern Development. 74 pp.

Spokesmen from 45 Ontario bands, the Regional Advisory Councils, the Kenora Friendship Centre, the Lakehead Friendship Centre, and Grand Council of Treaty Number
Three met with Robert Andras, Indian Affairs personnel, and Walter Dieter. Proposed
changes in the Indian Act, rights, and treaties were discussed.   JSL

523   **CANADA. Department of Indian Affairs and Northern Development.**
1968
REPORT OF THE INDIAN ACT CONSULTATION MEETING. KELOWNA,
BRITISH COLUMBIA. NOVEMBER 12, 13, 14, 15, 16, 1968. Ottawa: Department of
Indian Affairs and Northern Development. 115 pp.

Delegates from 28 British Columbia bands met with Jean Chretien, Walter Dieter, and
Indian Affairs officials to discuss the Indian Act and Indian rights.   JSL

524   **CANADA. Department of Indian Affairs and Northern Development.**
1968
REPORT OF THE INDIAN ACT CONSULTATION MEETING. MONCTON,
NEW BRUNSWICK. JULY 29, 30, AND 31, 1968. Ottawa: Department of Indian
Affairs and Northern Development. 100 pp.

Representatives of 28 bands from the Maritimes, 10 Regional Advisory Council members, and the Union of New Brunswick Indians met with Jean Chretien, other Indian
Affairs officers, and Walter Dieter. Discussed were suggested changes in the Indian Act,
rights, and treaties. The Union of New Brunswick Indians submitted a brief. It was decided that non-Indian chairmen would inhibit discussion of rights and treaties. For the
duration of the consultation meetings, only Indians chaired the discussions.   JSL

525   **CANADA. Department of Indian Affairs and Northern Development.**
1968
REPORT OF THE INDIAN ACT CONSULTATION MEETING. NANAIMO,
BRITISH COLUMBIA. OCTOBER 30, 31 AND NOVEMBER 1, 1968. Ottawa:
Department of Indian Affairs and Northern Development. 77 pp.

Delegates from 33 British Columbia bands and the Southern Vancouver Island Tribal
Federation met with Robert Andras, Walter Dieter, and Indian Affairs officers. One brief
concerning the Indian Act was submitted by all the delegates. Also discussed were Indian
rights - land, fishing, and hunting.   JSL

526   **CANADA. Department of Indian Affairs and Northern Development.**
1968
REPORT OF THE INDIAN ACT CONSULTATION MEETING. PRINCE
GEORGE, BRITISH COLUMBIA. OCTOBER 14, 15, 16, 17, 18, 1968. Ottawa:
Department of Indian Affairs and Northern Development. 113 pp.

Delegates from 30 British Columbia bands met with Walter Dieter and Indian Affairs
officers. The discussion focused on the Indian Act, rights, and treaties.   JSL

527   **CANADA. Department of Indian Affairs and Northern Development.**
1968
REPORT OF THE INDIAN ACT CONSULTATION MEETING. QUEBEC CITY,
QUEBEC. SEPTEMBER 30 AND OCTOBER 1, 2, 3 AND 4, 1968. Ottawa:
Department of Indian Affairs and Northern Development. 112 pp.

Spokesmen from 34 Quebec bands and the Indian Association of Quebec met with Jean
Chretien, Robert Andras, Walter Dieter, and Indian Affairs officers. The delegates discussed the Indian Act and Indian rights.   JSL

528   **CANADA. Department of Indian Affairs and Northern Development.**
1968
REPORT OF THE INDIAN ACT CONSULTATION MEETING. REGINA,
SASKATCHEWAN. SEPTEMBER 16, 17, 18, 19, AND 20, 1968. Ottawa: Department
of Indian Affairs and Northern Development. 111 pp.

Representatives from 66 Saskatchewan bands and 4 Indian and Metis Friendship Centres (Regina, Saskatoon, Prince Albert, and Battleford) met with Robert Andras, Walter Dieter, and Indian Affairs officers. Mr. Dieter was president of both the National Indian Brotherhood and the Federation of Saskatchewan Indians. The matters discussed were the Indian Act, rights, and treaties.   JSL

529   **CANADA. Department of Indian Affairs and Northern Development.**
1968
REPORT OF THE INDIAN ACT CONSULTATION MEETING. SUDBURY,
ONTARIO. AUGUST 21, 22, AND 23, 1968. Ottawa: Department of Indian Affairs
and Northern Development. 75 pp.

Representatives from 39 Ontario bands, Regional Advisory Councils, and the Northern Ontario Homemakers met with Jean Chretien, Robert Andras, Walter Dieter, and Indian Affairs officers. The items discussed included the Indian Act, rights and treaties.   JSL

530   **CANADA. Department of Indian Affairs and Northern Development.**
1968
REPORT OF THE INDIAN ACT CONSULTATION MEETING. TERRACE,
BRITISH COLUMBIA. OCTOBER 24, 25, 26 AND 28, 1968. Ottawa: Department of
Indian Affairs and Northern Development. 72 pp.

Delegates from 24 British Columbia bands and the Indian Benevolent Association (Prince Rupert) met with Walter Dieter and Indian Affairs officials to discuss the Indian Act and rights.   JSL

531   **CANADA. Department of Indian Affairs and Northern Development.**
1968
REPORT OF THE INDIAN ACT CONSULTATION MEETING. TORONTO,
ONTARIO. AUGUST 12, 13 AND 14, 1968. Ottawa: Department of Indian Affairs
and Northern Development. 51 pp.

Spokesmen from 28 Ontario bands, 2 Regional Advisory members, the Southern Ontario Homemakers' Club, Union of Ontario Indians, and the Toronto Indian Centre met with Robert Andras, Indian Affairs officers, and Walter Dieter. Discussed were proposed changes in the Indian Act, rights, and treaties.   JSL

532   **CANADA. Department of Indian Affairs and Northern Development.**
1968
REPORT OF THE INDIAN ACT CONSULTATION MEETING. WHITEHORSE,
YUKON TERRITORY. OCTOBER 21, 22 AND 23, 1968. Ottawa: Department of
Indian Affairs and Northern Development. 53 pp.

Delegates from 13 Yukon bands and the Yukon Native Brotherhood met with Jean Chretien, Walter Dieter, and Indian Affairs officers. The discussion focused on the Indian Act, rights, and treaties.   JSL

533   **CANADA. Department of Indian Affairs and Northern Development.**
1968
REPORT OF THE INDIAN ACT CONSULTATION MEETING. WINNIPEG,
MANITOBA. DECEMBER 18, 19 AND 20, 1968. Ottawa: Department of Indian
Affairs and Northern Development. 52 pp.

Representatives from 42 Manitoba Indian bands and the Manitoba Indian Brotherhood
met with Jean Chretien, Walter Dieter, and Indian Affairs officers. A brief was presented
by the Manitoba Indian Brotherhood discussing rights and treaties, and the Indian
Act.   JSL

534   **CANADA. Department of Indian Affairs and Northern Development.**
1968
REPORT OF THE INDIAN ACT CONSULTATION MEETING. YELLOWKNIFE,
NORTHWEST TERRITORIES. JULY 25, 26, AND 27, 1968. Ottawa: Department of
Indian Affairs and Northern Development. 3 pp.

The first Indian Act consultation was held at Yellowknife, Northwest Territories. Delegates from 16 bands and 8 Regional Advisory Council representatives from the Northwest Territories met with Robert Andras, Indian Affairs officials, and Walter Dieter
(President of the National Indian Brotherhood). Discussed were proposed changes in the
Indian Act, land rights, Treaties 8 and 11, hunting rights, fishing rights, trapping rights,
and the allocation of reserves.   JSL

535   **CANADA. Department of Indian Affairs and Northern Development.**
1969
THE MANITOBA PROJECT: A PARTNERSHIP UNDERTAKING BETWEEN
THE MANITOBA INDIAN BROTHERHOOD AND THE DEPARTMENT OF
INDIAN AFFAIRS AND NORTHERN DEVELOPMENT. Unpublished paper.
Available at Indian-Eskimo Economic Development Branch, Development Services
Division, Department of Indian Affairs and Northern Development. 20 pp.

Conclusions and recommendations arising from a Winnipeg meeting of departmental
and Manitoba Indian Brotherhood representatives January 20 to 22, 1969, are reported.
This meeting was a result of a brief submitted to Jean Chretien by the Manitoba Indian
Brotherhood requesting participation in and responsibility for determination of objectives, goals, and planning and for a decentralization of financial and program authority
corresponding to an increased band participation. Clarification of the role of the Manitoba Indian Brotherhood and long and short-term program objectives were achieved and
are reported.   CCV

536   **CANADA. Department of Indian Affairs and Northern Development.**
1969
RAPPORTEUR'S ACCOUNT OF NATIONAL CONFERENCE ON INDIAN ACT.
National Conference on Indian Act, Ottawa, April 28-May 2, 1969. Ottawa:
Department of Indian Affairs and Northern Development. 140 pp.

The rapporteur's account of the National Conference on the Indian Act is presented including talks by Mr. Chretien, Mr. Andras, and representations made by provincial dele-
gations. The Indian Act and national unity as well as Indian participation in decision-
making processes are discussed.   CCV

537   **CANADA. Department of Indian Affairs and Northern Development.**
1969
REPORT OF THE INDIAN ACT CONSULTATION MEETING. TERRACE,
BRITISH COLUMBIA. JANUARY 27 AND 28, 1969. Ottawa: Department of Indian
Affairs and Northern Development. 57 pp.

The last of the regional consultations was held in Terrace, B.C. Delegates from 20 bands,
the Native Brotherhood of British Columbia, and the Indian Benevolent Association
(Prince Rupert) met Jean Chretien, Walter Dieter, and Indian Affairs officers. The Indian delegates discussed the Indian Act and Indian rights.   JSL

538   **CANADA. Department of Indian Affairs and Northern Development.**
1969
REPORT OF THE INDIAN ACT CONSULTATION MEETING. TORONTO,
ONTARIO. JANUARY 10-14, 1969. Ottawa: Department of Indian Affairs and
Northern Development. 88 pp.

Delegates from 29 southern Ontario and 10 northern Ontario bands, the Regional Indian Advisory Council, Union of Ontario Indians, the Canadian Indian Centre of Toronto, and the Parry Sound Indian Friendship Centre met with Jean Chretien, Robert
Andras, Indian Affairs officials, representatives of the Department of National Health
and Welfare, and 3 Ontario government departments (Social and Family Services, Municipal Affairs, and Lands and Forests). The delegates discussed the Indian Act, treaties,
and rights. Appended is a report entitled "The Agricultural Potential of Land on Indian
Reserves"(1968) by the Agricultural Institute of Canada and the Department of Indian
Affairs and Northern Development.   JSL

539   **CANADA. Department of Indian Affairs and Northern Development.**
1969
STATEMENT OF THE GOVERNMENT OF CANADA ON INDIAN POLICY, 1969
(THE WHITE PAPER). Ottawa: Queen's Printer. 13 pp.   Also in French. Also in Cree.

Based on the government's explicit goal of social and cultural equality for Indians, this
proposal involves 6 basic ideas: removal of legal discrimination, recognition of Indian
culture, provision of services through regular government agencies, priority in help for
those who are furthest behind, recognition of lawful obligations, and transferance of the
control of Indian lands to Indians. Operationally, this would involve the repeal of the
Indian Act, provision for Indian control of their lands, elimination of the Indian
bureaucracy, transfer to provinces of responsibility for Indians, substantial funds for
economic development, and appointment of a Claims Commissioner.   JSL

540   **CANADA. Department of Indian Affairs and Northern Development.**
1969
SUMMARY OF SHARED-COST AGREEMENTS AND SERVICE CONTRACTS
WITH THE PROVINCES AND VOLUNTARY AGENCIES. Unpublished paper.
Available at Indian-Eskimo Economic Development Branch, Department of Indian
Affairs and Northern Development, Ottawa. 22 pp.

Shared costs agreements and service contracts held between the Department of Indian
Affairs and Northern Development and the provinces and voluntary agencies are reviewed. Agreements concerning education, medical care, roads, law enforcement, forest

fire prevention, conservation, management of fur resources, handicrafts, co-operatives, library services, welfare, and community development are listed.   CCV

541   **CANADA. Department of Indian Affairs and Northern Development.**
1970
ANNUAL REPORT FISCAL YEAR 1968-1969. Ottawa: Queen's Printer. 156 pp.
Also in French.

Among the aspects of Indian administration discussed in the Annual Report are the Indian-Eskimo Development Branch, Indian-Eskimo Bureau, education, and federal-provincial relations. The first-mentioned Department was established to deal with matters relating to lands, agriculture, commercial recreation, fisheries, forestry, tourist outfitting and guiding, the wildlife program, industrial development, and Indian loan funds. The Indian-Eskimo Bureau is concerned with correspondence and parliamentary questions, consultation, treaty activity and research, policy development, membership, social services, social development, cultural affairs, leadership training, human resources development program, housing and community improvement, water and sanitation services, electrification, road systems, trust funds, treaty obligations, and grants to bands. Discussed under education are school attendance, federal school construction, pupil transportation, professional training and development, research, vocational education, adult education, program highlights, pupil accomodation, scholarships, and estates. Statistical tables accompany each resume.   JSL

542   **CANADA. Department of Indian Affairs and Northern Development.**
1970
ANNUAL REPORT FISCAL YEAR 1969-1970. Ottawa: Queen's Printer. 196 pp.
Also in French.

Pages 105 to 167 deal with Indian-Eskimo Affairs, and the Indian Consultation and Negotiation Group. Discussed under the latter heading are the government policy proposals of 1969, Indian associations, per capita grants to the associations, consultation meetings and related funds. A list of regional and field offices is included. Discussed under the Indian-Eskimo Affairs heading are the activities of the Community Affairs Branch, Education Branch, and the Indian-Eskimo Economic Development Branch. The Education Branch discusses school attendance, federal school construction, pupil transportation, research, community libraries, professional training, student residences, boarding home program, scholarships, and post school program highlights. Among the interests of Community Affairs Branch are housing, water and sanitation, electrification, road systems, social services, cultural development, branch re-organization, leadership training, homemakers' clubs and other Indian women's organizations, youth activities, the inter-departmental committee, band government, band grants, and membership. Concerns of the 3rd Branch include land management and administration, land use, estates, Indian minerals program, oil and gas, mining, arts and crafts program, business and credit services, cooperatives, agriculture, fisheries, forestry, tourism and recreation development, tourist outfitting and guiding, wildlife and industrial, commercial and real estate development. Included with the remarks of the last 2 Branches are statistical tables.   JSL

543   **CANADA. Department of Indian Affairs and Northern Development.**
Administration Branch.
1960-1968

INDIAN AFFAIRS BRANCH FIELD MANUAL. Ottawa: Department of Indian Affairs and Northern Development.

Administrative policies and amendments in policy are contained in a field manual for Indian Affairs Branch officials. Included are sections on history, organization, Indian Acts, Indian status, band councils, lands and resources, education, economic development, welfare, and enfranchisement.   CCV

544   **CANADA. Department of Indian Affairs and Northern Development. Advisory Committee on Northern Development.**
1967
GOVERNMENT ACTIVITIES IN THE NORTH - 1966. Ottawa: Department of Indian Affairs and Northern Development. 255 pp.

The annual review of government activities in the Yukon and Northwest Territories was prepared for 1966.   JSL

545   **CANADA. Department of Indian Affairs and Northern Development. Advisory Committee on Northern Development.**
1968
GOVERNMENT ACTIVITIES IN THE NORTH: 1967 REPORT AND 1968 PLANS. Ottawa: Department of Indian Affairs and Northern Development. 258 pp.

The annual review of government activities in the Yukon and Northwest Territories was prepared for 1967.   JSL

546   **CANADA. Department of Indian Affairs and Northern Development. Advisory Committee on Northern Development.**
1969
GOVERNMENT ACTIVITIES IN THE NORTH: 1968 REPORT AND 1969 PLANS. Ottawa: Queen's Printer. 299 pp.   Also in French.

The annual review of government activities in the Yukon and Northwest Territories was prepared for 1968.   JSL

547   **CANADA. Department of Indian Affairs and Northern Development. Advisory Committee on Northern Development.**
1970
GOVERNMENT ACTIVITIES IN THE NORTH: 1969 REPORT AND 1970 PLANS. Ottawa: Information Canada. 332 pp.   Also in French.

The annual review of government activities in the Yukon and Northwest Territories was prepared for 1969.   JSL

548   **CANADA. Department of Indian Affairs and Northern Development. Indian Affairs Branch.**
n.d.
INDIAN RESERVE LANDS 361-0044-E1. Ottawa: Department of Indian Affairs and Northern Development. 5 pp.

The status of Indian reserve lands is reviewed with attention to problems of administration, transfer, and federal and provincial jurisdiction.   CCV

549   **CANADA. Department of Indian Affairs and Northern Development. Indian Affairs Branch.**
1966
STATEMENT FOR FEDERAL-PROVINCIAL CONFERENCE ON POVERTY.
Ottawa: Department of Indian Affairs and Northern Development. 15 pp.   Also in French.

A statement is submitted to the federal-provincial conference on poverty outlining the basic objectives of federal Indian administration. Data on the current situation in employment, housing, health, social assistance, co-ordination of activities between Indian and non-Indian groups, and federal and provincial programs, are provided.   CCV

550   **CANADA. Department of Indian Affairs and Northern Development. Indian Affairs Branch.**
1968
CHOOSING A PATH: A DISCUSSION HANDBOOK FOR THE INDIAN PEOPLE.
Ottawa: Queen's Printer. 22 pp.   Also in French.

A booklet was prepared to provide a basis for consultations with Indian spokesmen. The objectives of the government are outlined, and indicate a desire for social and cultural equality. An outline of the proposed new Indian Act raises 34 questions.   JSL

551   **CANADA. Department of Indian Affairs and Northern Development. Indian Affairs Branch.**
1968
CONSULTATIONS WITH INDIAN PEOPLE. Ottawa: Department of Indian Affairs and Northern Development. 41 pp.

Papers providing background information, explaining certain provisions of the Indian Act, and offering some alternatives to certain provisions are prepared for circulation among spokesmen, chiefs, councilors, and officials of Indian organizations prior to meetings with Indian Affairs officials. The need for an Indian Act, its provisions in terms of land use and transfer, band membership, Indian status, estates and property, Canada and Quebec pension plans, liquor regulations, band funds, and band representation are among the discussed topics.   CCV

552   **CANADA. Department of Indian Affairs and Northern Development. Indian Affairs Branch.**
1968
PUBLIC LIBRARY SERVICE TO INDIAN BANDS: CIRCULAR NO. 8. Ottawa: Department of Indian Affairs and Northern Development. 3 pp.

Government procedure for the establishment and maintenance of public library services for Indian bands in co-operation with provincial public library systems is outlined.   CCV

553   **CANADA. Department of Indian Affairs and Northern Development. Indian Affairs Branch.**
1969
HISTORY OF GOVERNMENT: INDIAN POLICY 361-0045-E1. Ottawa: Department of Indian Affairs and Northern Development. 6 pp.

The history of governing of the Canadian Indian is reviewed from contact to the present. European assumption of sovereignty over the Indians as well as responsibility for spiritual and material welfare are noted. From emphasis on trade and military alliances in the earlier periods attention was shifted to settlement and acculturation resulting in a new direction of policy in the 19th century. Reserves were created to protect the Indian from undesirable aspects of White culture. Today the inadequacies of policies inherited from earlier periods must be considered.   CCV

554   **CANADA. Department of Indian Affairs and Northern Development. Indian Affairs Branch.**
1969
INDIAN HOUSING PROGRAMS. Ottawa: Department of Indian Affairs and Northern Development. 21 pp.

Indian housing programs are reviewed with attention to subsidy housing programs, band-administered programs, off-reserve programs, Canadian Mortgage and Housing Corporation loans for on-reserve housing, and the interrelationships between all programs. Criteria for loans and establishment of priorities are included as well as statistical data.   CCV

555   **CANADA. Department of Indian Affairs and Northern Development. Indian Affairs Branch.**
1970
HOUSING AND COMMUNITY IMPROVEMENT. Ottawa: Department of Indian Affairs and Northern Development. 19 pp.   Also in French.

Programs of housing and services for Indians on reserves are reviewed in a letter to chiefs, Indian band councils, regional directors, agency superintendents, and district supervisors. Conditions and stipulations for assistance are outlined.   CCV

556   **CANADA. Department of Indian Affairs and Northern Development. Indian Affairs Branch. Indian-Eskimo Bureau.**
1970
STATEMENT BY THE PRIME MINISTER AT A MEETING WITH THE INDIAN ASSOCIATION OF ALBERTA AND THE NATIONAL INDIAN BROTHERHOOD. Ottawa: Department of Indian Affairs and Northern Development. 7 pp.

Prime Minister Trudeau's statement to the Indian Association of Alberta and the National Indian Brotherhood in Ottawa, June 4, 1970 is reported. Discussed are Indian reactions to the 1969 White Paper, Indian-government dialogue, Indian attitudes toward government policy-making, and possible solutions to problems.   CCV

557   **CANADA. Department of Indian Affairs and Northern Development. Information Services.**
1966-1967
PRESS RELEASES. No. 1-66163, 1-66152, 1-66147, 1-66144, 1-66119, 1-66118, 1-66117, 1-66116, 1-66108, 1-66106. October 1966 to March 1967. Available from Information Services, Records and Research, Department of Indian Affairs and Northern Development.   Also in French.

Indian Affairs communiques relating to education policies and facilities, housing programs, living conditions on reserves, grants to band councils, community development, and Expo '67 are included in the collection for the fiscal year 1966-1967.   CCV

558   **CANADA. Department of Indian Affairs and Northern Development. Information Services.**
1967-1968
PRESS RELEASES. No. 1-67155, 1-67148, 1-67129, 1-67122, 1-67115, 1-67112, 1-67107, 1-6793, 1-6792, 1-6778, 1-6776, 1-6775, 1-6756, 1-6754, 1-6738, 1-6732, 1-6731, 1-6723, 1-6711, 1-6710. April 7, 1967 to March 28, 1968. Available from Information Services, Records and Research, Department of Indian Affairs and Northern Development.   Also in French.

Included in the Department of Indian Affairs' communiques for the 1967-1968 fiscal year are several relating to Canadian Indians. Education and housing grants, community development, Indian Act consultations, band council activities, Expo '67, education programs, and recognition of prominent Indians, past and present, receive mention.   CCV

559   **CANADA. Department of Indian Affairs and Northern Development. Information Services.**
1968-69
PRESS RELEASES. April 3, 1968 to March 18, 1969. Available from Information Services, Records and Research, Department of Indian Affairs and Northern Development.   Also in French.

Ninety-four communiques relating to Canadian Indians are included in the Department of Indian Affairs' collection for the fiscal year 1968-69. Discussed in particular are government policies concerning housing, education, Indian Act consultations, land and hunting rights as well as grants in the fields of reserve improvement, housing, and Indian enterprise, and expanded educational facilities resulting from extension of provincial services to Indians.   CCV

560   **CANADA. Department of Indian Affairs and Northern Development. Information Services.**
1969-1970
PRESS RELEASES. April 2, 1969 to March 31, 1970. Available from Information Services, Records and Research, Department of Indian Affairs and Northern Development.   Also in French.

Forty-nine communiques relating to government grants and policies aimed at extending education and housing services and promoting Indian group and individual initiative are included in the Department of Indian Affairs 1969-70 fiscal year collection of communiques.   CCV

561   **CANADA. Department of Indian Affairs and Northern Development. Information Services.**
1970
PRESS RELEASES. April 15, 1970 to December 8, 1970. Available from Information Services, Records and Research, Department of Indian Affairs and Northern Development.

Fourteen communiques relating to Indian lands, increased education facilities and grants, community development, housing and construction projects, and recognition of Indian scholars and writers are included in the Department of Indian Affairs collection for 1970.   CCV

562   **CANADA. Department of Indian Affairs and Northern Development. Office of the Public Information Adviser.**
1966
RE-ORGANIZATION OF THE DEPARTMENT OF INDIAN AFFAIRS AND NORTHERN DEVELOPMENT. Ottawa: Department of Indian Affairs and Northern Development. 30 pp.   Also in French.

A plan for re-organization of the Indian Affairs Branch to standardize policies and provide mechanisms to cope with increased and divergent programs on the occasion of its entry into the department in 1966 is presented for the information of employees. The structure and allocation of responsibilities is reviewed briefly.   CCV

563   **CANADA. Department of National Health and Welfare.**
1960
ANNUAL REPORT FOR THE FISCAL YEAR ENDED MARCH 31, 1960. Ottawa: Queen's Printer. 162 pp.   Also in French.

Pages 24 to 32 contain the annual report of the Indian and Northern Health Services Directorate for 1959-1960. The Directorate provides necessary medical treatment for registered Indians and Eskimos, and administers territorial health programs. Discussed are the administrative organization, personnel, fiscal management, facilities, food service supervision, management, staff improvement, cooperation with other agencies, public health and treatment services, maternal and child health programs, tuberculosis control, treatment services, and research. Tables and graphs provide demographic statistics. Mention is made of the inevitable integration of health resources with the provinces.   JSL

564   **CANADA. Department of National Health and Welfare.**
1961
ANNUAL REPORT FOR THE FISCAL YEAR ENDED MARCH 31, 1961. Ottawa: Queen's Printer. 154 pp.   Also in French.

Pages 19 to 26 concern the Indian and Northern Services Directorate for 1960-1961. Discussed are the populations served, organization, and extended services. Tables provide demographic statistics. The government assumes no legal obligations for medical and health services of Indians. Ultimately the Department hopes for complete integration into provincial patterns.   JSL

565   **CANADA. Department of National Health and Welfare.**
1961
BRIEF. In Minutes of Proceedings and Evidence. No 15. May 24-25, 1961. Joint Committee of the Senate and the House of Commons on Indian Affairs. Canada. 24 Parliament, 4 Session. Ottawa: Queen's Printer. pp. 549-552.

The review of activities and outline of present programs contains information on the public health services, treatment programs, inter-governmental relationships, native attitudes, and recommendations.   JSL

566   **CANADA. Department of National Health and Welfare.**
1962
ANNUAL REPORT FOR THE FISCAL YEAR ENDED MARCH 31, 1962. Ottawa:
Queen's Printer. 159 pp.   Also in French.

Pages 92 to 99 of the Health Branch's report concern Indian and Northern health services for 1961-1962. Discussed are services, training programs, and demography and
health. Statistical tables are included. Stressed are negotiations with provincial health
authorities.   JSL

567   **CANADA. Department of National Health and Welfare.**
1966
ANNUAL REPORT FOR THE FISCAL YEAR ENDED MARCH 31, 1965. Ottawa:
Queen's Printer. 176 pp.   Also in French.

Pages 86 to 89 of the Medical Services Branch report give details concerning Indian and
northern health services. Indians are now insured under provincial or territorial hospital
plans. The health and demographic picture is presented. It is stressed that moral, not legal, obligations are assumed by the government.   JSL

568   **CANADA. Department of National Health and Welfare.**
1966
ANNUAL REPORT. MEDICAL SERVICES. 1965. Ottawa: Department of National
Health and Welfare. 195 pp.

A reprint of the Health Services section of the Department's annual report for the fiscal
year ending March, 1966, is followed by new materials. Pages 52 to 61 contain statistical
tables on Indian birth rate, life expectation, mortality rate, births, fertility rates, deaths,
and infant mortality. Annual reports for each region contain some Indian information
on demography, health, and training programs.   JSL

569   **CANADA. Department of National Health and Welfare.**
1967
ANNUAL REPORT FOR THE FISCAL YEAR ENDED MARCH 31, 1966. Ottawa:
Queen's Printer. 190 pp.   Also in French.

Pages 95 to 103 of the Medical Services section of the report deal with Indian and northern health services. Discussed are treatment , public health, and dental services, and demographic trends.   JSL

570   **CANADA. Department of National Health and Welfare.**
1968
ANNUAL REPORT FOR THE FISCAL YEAR ENDED MARCH 31, 1967. Ottawa:
Queen's Printer. 261 pp.   Also in French.

Pages 125 to 129 of the Medical Services section of the report concern Indian and northern health. Demographic trends and treatment services are discussed. Mention is made
of continuing negotiations for provincial services.   JSL

571   **CANADA. Department of National Health and Welfare.**
1969

ANNUAL REPORT FOR THE FISCAL YEAR ENDED MARCH 31, 1968. Ottawa: Queen's Printer. 214 pp.   Also in French.

Pages 99 to 103 of the Medical Services section provided details on Indian health services for 1967-1968. Discussed are dental services, Indian health status, and northern health. Information on birth rates, health, and life expectancy is given. It is stressed that humanitarian, not legal, obligations are assumed by the government.   JSL

572   **CANADA. Department of Northern Affairs and National Resources.**
1960
ANNUAL REPORT. FISCAL YEAR 1959-1960. Ottawa: Queen's Printer. 116 pp. Also in French.

Pages 22-27 contain the annual report of the Northern Administration Branch. Pages 96-98 contain statistics.   JSL

573   **CANADA. Department of Northern Affairs and National Resources.**
1962
ANNUAL REPORT. FISCAL YEAR 1960-1961. Ottawa: Queen's Printer. 101 pp. Also in French.

Pages 25-27 contain the annual report of the Northern Administration Branch. Pages 86-89 contain statistics.   JSL

574   **CANADA. Department of Northern Affairs and National Resources.**
1962
ANNUAL REPORT. FISCAL YEAR 1961-1962. Ottawa: Queen's Printer. 104 pp. Also in French.

Pages 18-44 contain the annual report of the Northern Administration Branch. Pages 85-89 contain statistics.   JSL

575   **CANADA. Department of Northern Affairs and National Resources.**
1962
PRESS RELEASES. No. 5320, 5310, 5298, 5266, 5256, 5255. Available from Information Services, Records and Research, Department of Indian Affairs and Northern Development.   Also in French.

References to Canadian Indians occur in 6 of the communiques issued by the Department of Northern Affairs and National Resources in 1962. Subjects include formation of the Indian Claims Commission, research projects, and promotion of Indian arts and crafts and cultural tradition.   CCV

576   **CANADA. Department of Northern Affairs and National Resources.**
1963
PRESS RELEASES. No. 5516, 5478, 5474, 5473, 5468, 5461, 5477. Available from Information Services, Records and Research, Department of Indian Affairs and Northern Development.   Also in French.

Seven Department of Northern Affairs and National Resources communiques for 1963 concern research projects relating to Canadian Indians and another refers to an exposition of Northwest Coast art.   CCV

577   **CANADA. Department of Northern Affairs and National Resources.**
1964
ANNUAL REPORT. FISCAL YEAR 1962-1963. Ottawa: Queen's Printer. 43 pp.
Also in French.

Pages 7-12 and 29-34 contain the annual report of the Northern Administration
Branch.   JSL

578   **CANADA. Department of Northern Affairs and National Resources.**
1965
ANNUAL REPORT. FISCAL YEAR 1963-1964. Ottawa: Queen's Printer. 53 pp.
Also in French.

Pages 9-22 and 36-44 contain the annual report of the Northern Administration
Branch.   JSL

579   **CANADA. Department of Northern Affairs and National Resources.**
1965
ANNUAL REPORT. FISCAL YEAR 1964-1965. Ottawa: Queen's Printer. 82 pp.
Also in French.

Pages 7-30 and 62-72 contain the annual report of the Northern Administration
Branch.   JSL

580   **CANADA. Department of Northern Affairs and National Resources.**
1966
ANNUAL REPORT FISCAL YEAR 1965-1966. Ottawa: Queen's Printer. 134 pp.
Also in French.

Pages 39 to 71 pertain to the Indian Affairs Branch. By Order in Council January 1, 1966,
the Indian Affairs Branch was transferred to the Department of Northern Affairs and
National Resources. Previously, the Branch had been part of the Department of Citizenship and Immigration. The annual report for the fiscal year 1965-1966 summarizes the
re-organization of the Branch. A resume of the year's programs is followed by discussions of individual topics. Among the topics are federal-provincial relations, Indian consultation, community development, cultural affairs, welfare services, employment and
relocation, wildlife and fisheries, forestry, craft industries, industrial and business development, mineral resources, agriculture, Indian housing and community improvement,
education, estates, enfranchisements, adoptions, protests, band re-organization, reserve
lands, trusts and annuities, band property insurance, band loans, personal savings, annuities, and staff development. A list of the names and locations of regional offices and Indian agencies is included. Pages 115 to 126 provide further statistical information in the
form of charts and tables.   JSL

581   **CANADA. Department of Northern Affairs and National Resources.**
1966
PRESS RELEASES. No. 1-66106, 1-66105. 1-6699. 1-6694, 1-6681, 1-6650, 1-6618,
1-65203, 1-65197, 1-65190, 1-65188, 1-65187. Available from Information Services,
Records and Research, Department of Indian Affairs and Northern Development.
Also in French.

Twelve communiques relating to Indian people are included in the Department of Northern Affairs and National Resources' collection for 1966. Changes in administration and plans for Expo '67 are featured as well as new policy proposals.   CCV

582   **CANADA. Department of Northern Affairs and National Resources. Advisory Committee on Northern Development.**
1960
GOVERNMENT ACTIVITIES IN THE NORTH - 1959. Ottawa: Department of Northern Affairs and National Resources. 128 pp.

The annual review of government activities in the Yukon and Northwest Territories was prepared for 1959. The information is presented separately for each department, agency, or Crown corporation.   JSL

583   **CANADA. Department of Northern Affairs and National Resources. Advisory Committee on Northern Development.**
1961
GOVERNMENT ACTIVITIES IN THE NORTH - 1960. Ottawa: Department of Northern Affairs and National Resources. 138 pp.   Also in French.

The annual review of government activities in the Yukon and Northwest Territories was prepared for 1960.   JSL

584   **CANADA. Department of Northern Affairs and National Resources. Advisory Committee on Northern Development.**
1962
GOVERNMENT ACTIVITIES IN THE NORTH - 1961. Ottawa: Department of Northern Affairs and National Resources. 166 pp.

The annual review of government activities in the Yukon and Northwest Territories was prepared for 1961.   JSL

585   **CANADA. Department of Northern Affairs and National Resources. Advisory Committee on Northern Development.**
1963
GOVERNMENT ACTIVITIES IN THE NORTH - 1962. Ottawa: Department of Northern Affairs and National Resources. 254 pp.

The annual review of government activities in the Yukon and Northwest Territories was prepared for 1962.   JSL

586   **CANADA. Department of Northern Affairs and National Resources. Advisory Committee on Northern Development.**
1964
GOVERNMENT ACTIVITIES IN THE NORTH - 1963. Ottawa: Department of Northern Affairs and National Resources. 202 pp.

The annual review of government activities in the Yukon and Northwest Territories was prepared for 1963.   JSL

587   **CANADA. Department of Northern Affairs and National Resources. Advisory Committee on Northern Development.**
1965
GOVERNMENT ACTIVITIES IN THE NORTH - 1964. Ottawa: Department of Northern Affairs and National Resources. 228 pp.

The annual review of government activities in the Yukon and Northwest Territories was prepared for 1964.   JSL

588   **CANADA. Department of Northern Affairs and National Resources. Advisory Committee on Northern Development.**
1966
GOVERNMENT ACTIVITIES IN THE NORTH - 1965. Ottawa: Department of Northern Affairs and National Resources. 229 pp.

The annual review of government activities in the Yukon and Northwest Territories was prepared for 1965.   JSL

589   **CANADA. Department of Northern Affairs and National Resources. Northern Administration Branch. Education Division.**
n.d.
NORTHERN EDUCATION: TEN YEARS OF PROGRESS. Ottawa: Department of Northern Affairs and National Resources. 14 pp.

This reviews educational activities in the Northwest Territories for the decade 1949-1959.   JSL

590   **CANADA. Department of Northern Affairs and National Resources. Northern Administration Branch. Welfare Division.**
n.d.
NORTHERN WELFARE '62: A SYMPOSIUM ON NORTHERN SOCIAL WORK. Ottawa: Department of Northern Affairs and National Resources. 71 pp.

Impressions of 21 persons associated with social work in Arctic Quebec and the Northwest Territories were collected. The symposium was not concerned with academic analysis, but with providing a glimpse of the people and the country.   JSL

591   **CANADA. Department of Northern Affairs and National Resources. Northern Administration Branch. Welfare Division.**
n.d.
NORTHERN WELFARE '64: A SYMPOSIUM ON NORTHERN SOCIAL WORK. Ottawa: Department of Northern Affairs and National Resources. 73 pp.

Contributions from 21 persons provide a glimpse of social welfare services in the Northwest Territories and Arctic Quebec.   JSL

592   **CANADA. Department of the Secretary of State.**
n.d.
REPORT OF THE SECRETARY OF STATE OF CANADA FOR THE YEAR ENDING MARCH 31, 1968. Ottawa: Queen's Printer. 61 pp.   Also in French.

Pages 11 and 12 concern the Indian participation program of the Citizenship Branch. Among the Branch's activities are support of native associations and encouragement of native participation in Canadian society.   JSL

593   **CANADA. Department of the Secretary of State.**
1968
REPORT OF THE SECRETARY OF STATE OF CANADA FOR THE YEAR ENDED MARCH 31, 1967. Ottawa: Queen's Printer. 29 pp.

On page 8 an outline of the Citizenship Branch's activities relating to Indians is given. The Branch's interests include urban adjustment, native associations and friendship centers.   JSL

594   **CANADA. Federal-Provincial Conference of Ministers of Finance and Provincial Treasurers.**
1968
FEDERAL-PROVINCIAL CONFERENCE OF MINISTERS OF FINANCE AND PROVINCIAL TREASURERS. Ottawa, November 4-5, 1968. Ottawa: Queen's Printer. 91 pp.   Also in French.

Brief references to responsibility for services to Indians occur on pages 44, 63, and 87 of the report of statements made by delegates to this 1968 Federal-Provincial Conference of Ministers of Finance and Provincial Treasurers. Discussed are turnover to provincial governments of responsibility for services, shared-cost work and welfare projects, and Indian health costs.   CCV

595   **CANADA. Federal-Provincial Conference on Indian Affairs.**
1964
REPORT OF PROCEEDINGS. Report prepared by Department of Citizenship and Immigration, Indian Affairs Branch. Ottawa. October 29-30, 1964. Available from Library, Department of Indian Affairs and Northern Development, Ottawa. 112 pp.

A 53-page report of proceedings is followed by 14 appendices. These are: the federal statement; 5 provincial statements (Ontario, Quebec, Manitoba, Saskatchewan, Alberta); the agenda; a communique of the conference; a list of provincial delegates; a brief on legal jurisdiction over Indian Affairs; details of the Regional Indian Advisory Committees; terms of reference of the Saskatchewan Federal-Provincial Coordinating Committee; financing of Indian Affairs; and a list of recent (1964) research and surveys in Indian Affairs.   JSL

596   **CANADA. House of Commons. 27 Parliament, 1 Session. Standing Committee on Indian Affairs, Human Rights and Citizenship and Immigration.**
1966-1967
MINUTES OF PROCEEDINGS AND EVIDENCE. Nos. 1-9. March 3, 1966 - April 26, 1967.   Also in French.

References to education needs, employment opportunities, educational personnel, community and industrial development, self-determination, claims, the Indian Act, treaty and civil rights, and law enforcement problems are found.   CCV

597   **CANADA. House of Commons. 27 Parliament, 1 Session. Standing Committee on Northern Affairs and National Resources.**
1966-1967
MINUTES OF PROCEEDINGS AND EVIDENCE. Nos. 1-26. March 3, 1966 - April 26, 1967.   Also in French.

Frequent references occur to the native peoples of Canada.   CCV

598   **CANADA. House of Commons. 28 Parliament, 1-2 Session. Standing Committee on Fisheries and Forestry.**
1968-1970
MINUTES OF PROCEEDINGS AND EVIDENCE. October 17, 1968 - June 5, 1969; January 27, 1970 - May 12, 1970.   Also in French.

The minutes and proceedings of the Standing Committee on Fisheries and Forestry include references to Canadian Indians in relation to licensing, fishing rights, financial assistance and aid programs, and salmon fishing in British Columbia.   CCV

599   **CANADA. House of Commons. 28 Parliament, 1-3 Session. Standing Committee on Indian Affairs and Northern Development.**
1968-1971
MINUTES OF PROCEEDINGS AND EVIDENCE. October 22, 1968 - June 10, 1969; November 20, 1969 - October 7, 1970; November 26, 1970 - December 2, 1971.   Also in French.

References to Canadian Indian administration are frequent and include references to educational personnel, schools, health, and public services as well as native organizations, land use, land rights, and community development.   CCV

600   **CANADA. Indian Superintendents' National Conference.**
1961
CONFERENCE REPORT: INDIAN SUPERINTENDENTS' NATIONAL CONFERENCE. Indian Affairs Branch report. Harrison Hot Springs, B.C., September 17-22, 1961. Ottawa: Department of Citizenship and Immigration. Available at Indian-Eskimo Bureau, Department of Indian Affairs and Northern Development. 118 pp.

Included with the reports from the chiefs of the welfare, economic development, agencies, education, reserves and trusts, and administrative divisions are the reports and recommendations from the parliamentary Joint Committee on Indian Affairs. Topics reviewed, discussed, and mentioned in recommendations include: Indian status and band membership, reserve resources, band councils, human resources, health and welfare, housing and community planning, employment, agency and band council workloads, education programs, community development, law enforcement, provision of utilities for reserves, and leadership training.   CCV

601   **CANADA. National Conference on Indian Act.**
1969
VERBATIM REPORT OF NATIONAL CONFERENCE ON INDIAN ACT. George Manuel, chairman. Ottawa, April 28-May 2, 1969. Ottawa: Department of Indian Affairs and Northern Development. 384 pp.

The verbatim report of the 1969 National Conference on the Indian Act presents discussion of the Indian Act, Indian participation in decision-making processes, and requests for clarification of government policy.   CCV

602   **CANADA. Senate and House of Commons. Joint Committee of the Senate and the House of Commons On Indian Affairs.**
1961
SECOND AND FINAL REPORT. In Minutes of Proceedings and Evidence. No. 16. May 30-July 7, 1961. Joint Committee of the Senate and the House of Commons on Indian Affairs. Canada. 24 Parliament, 4 Session. Ottawa: Queen's Printer. pp. 605-619.

The final report of the Joint Committee is tabled. Important changes are reported among Indians. Non-Indians are becoming more aware of, and concerned about, the needs and problems of Indians. It is suggested that Indians may soon be willing to assume the responsibilities and benefits of full citizenship. Less government control, and more individual and band responsibility are needed. Advancement of Indians should not prejudice their traditional cultural, historical, and economic benefits. More specific recommendations deal with Indian status and band membership, reserve resources, election and authority of band councils, band funds, education and human resources, health and welfare, taxation and legal rights, Indian Affairs administration, and an Indian Claims Commission.   JSL

603   **CANADA. Senate and House of Commons. 24 Parliament, 3 Session. Joint Committee of the Senate and the House of Commons on Indian Affairs.**
1960
MINUTES OF PROCEEDINGS AND EVIDENCE. NO. 1. April 1 and May 4, 1960. Also in French.

The Joint Committee created by a House resolution of April 29, 1959, continued into 1960 and 1961. Its duties were to examine the Indian Act and make suggestions for change. Included in the text are the names of Committee members, orders of reference, and reports. The meeting of April 1 was solely for organizational purposes. The witnesses present on May 4 represented the Dominion Abitibi Band, Amos, Quebec, and the Dominion Abitibi Band of La Sarre. The minutes of proceedings summarize the events of the day. The evidence includes a verbatim account of the meeting, band resolutions, and briefs. Appended is a list of Indian bands and organizations who requested a hearing. Also appended are briefs from 6 Quebec bands (Eastmain, Obedjiwan, Rupert House, Mistassini, Long Point, and Barriere Lake) and the Northern Citizens Guidance Association.   JSL

604   **CANADA. Senate and House of Commons. 24 Parliament, 3 Session. Joint Committee of the Senate and the House of Commons on Indian Affairs.**
1960
MINUTES OF PROCEEDINGS AND EVIDENCE. NO. 2. May 5, 1960.   Also in French.

Witnesses present on May 5 represented the Iroquois of St. Regis Band. Appended are briefs from 3 Quebec bands (Bersimis, Montagnais of Lake St. John, and Timiskaming).   JSL

605   **CANADA. Senate and House of Commons. 24 Parliament, 3 Session. Joint Committee of the Senate and the House of Commons on Indian Affairs.**
1960
MINUTES OF PROCEEDINGS AND EVIDENCE. NO. 3. May 11-13, 1960.   Also in French.

Witnesses represented the Indian Association of Alberta and the Blood Indian Reserve Protestant Group. The evidence includes a 44-page brief by the Indian Association of Alberta. Appended are briefs from the Friends of the Indians Society of Edmonton and the Calumet Indian Club.   JSL

606   **CANADA. Senate and House of Commons. 24 Parliament, 3 Session. Joint Committee of the Senate and the House of Commons on Indian Affairs.**
1960
MINUTES OF PROCEEDINGS AND EVIDENCE. NO. 4. May 18, 1960.   Also in French.

Witnesses present represented the Indian Advisory Committee and the Ontario Department of Public Welfare. Appended are briefs from 10 Ontario bands (Albany, Caribou Lake, Gull Bay, Martin Falls, Pays Plat, Chippewas of Rama, Saugeen, Timagami, Trout Lake, and Trout Lake Bearskin Group), Frontier College, the Indian Council Fire of Canada, and 3 religious bodies (Canadian Friends Service Committee, National Spiritual Assembly of the Baha'is of Canada, and the Unitarian Congregation of South Peel).   JSL

607   **CANADA. Senate and House of Commons. 24 Parliament, 3 Session. Joint Committee of the Senate and the House of Commons on Indian Affairs.**
1960
MINUTES OF PROCEEDINGS AND EVIDENCE. NO. 5. May 19, 1960.   Also in French.

Witnesses represented the Indian-Eskimo Association of Canada. The evidence includes a 28-page brief. Appended are briefs from 4 Nova Scotia bands (Annapolis Valley, Chapel Island, Eskasoni, and Middle River) and 2 from New Brunswick (Burnt Church and Oromocto).   JSL

608   **CANADA. Senate and House of Commons. 24 Parliament, 3 Session. Joint Committee of the Senate and the House of Commons on Indian Affairs.**
1960
MINUTES OF PROCEEDINGS AND EVIDENCE. NO. 6. May 25, 1960.   Also in French.

Witnesses represented the Federation of Saskatchewan Indians. Included in the evidence is an 81-page brief. Appended are briefs from 5 bands (Montreal Lake - William Charles, Moose Woods, Piapot, Peter Pond Lake, and Keesekoose).   JSL

609   **CANADA. Senate and House of Commons. 24 Parliament, 3 Session. Joint Committee of the Senate and the House of Commons on Indian Affairs.**
1960
MINUTES OF PROCEEDINGS AND EVIDENCE. NO. 7. May 26-27, 1960.   Also in French.

Witnesses represented the Nishga Tribal Council and the Interior Tribes of British Co-
lumbia (Aboriginal Native Rights Committee). The evidence includes briefs by both na-
tive associations, the Interior Tribes' brief being 30 pages. Appended are briefs from the
Province of British Columbia (21 pages), the British Columbia Indian Arts and Welfare
Society, the West Coast Allied Tribes, and 12 British Columbia bands (Anahim, Bella
Bella, Burrard, Comox, Omineca, Haida, Hartley Bay, Kanaka Bar, Sechelt, Soowahlie,
Stone, and Ulkatcho).   JSL

610   **CANADA. Senate and House of Commons. 24 Parliament, 3 Session. Joint
Committee of the Senate and the House of Commons on Indian Affairs.**
1960
MINUTES OF PROCEEDINGS AND EVIDENCE. NO. 8. June 1, 1960.   Also in
French.

Witnesses represented the Canadian Catholic Conference which submitted a 9-page
brief. Appended are briefs from the Province of Manitoba (11 pages) and the Presbyterian Church in Canada (10 pages).   JSL

611   **CANADA. Senate and House of Commons. 24 Parliament, 3 Session. Joint
Committee of the Senate and the House of Commons on Indian Affairs.**
1960
MINUTES OF PROCEEDINGS AND EVIDENCE. NO. 9. June 2, 1960.   Also in
French.

Witnesses represented the Anglican Church of Canada and the Co-operative Union of
Canada. The first witness presented a 16-page brief, the second witness read a 20-page
brief.   JSL

612   **CANADA. Senate and House of Commons. 24 Parliament, 3 Session. Joint
Committee of the Senate and the House of Commons on Indian Affairs.**
1960
MINUTES OF PROCEEDINGS AND EVIDENCE. NO. 10. June 8, 1960.   Also in
French.

Witnesses represented the United Church of Canada Board of Home Missions which
presented a 9-page brief. Appended are briefs from the Canadian Federation of Mayors
and Municipalities, the Canadian Home and School and Parent-Teacher Federation, the
Catholic Indians of Northern B.C. and the Yukon, 3 bands from Manitoba (God's Lake,
Shamattawa, and Waterhen Lake), and 2 Yukon bands (Carcross and Champagne).   JSL

613   **CANADA. Senate and House of Commons. 24 Parliament, 3 Session. Joint
Committee of the Senate and the House of Commons on Indian Affairs.**
1960
MINUTES OF PROCEEDINGS AND EVIDENCE. NO. 11. June 9-10, 1960.   Also
in French.

Witnesses represented 3 Alberta bands (Saddle Lake, Blackfoot, and Blood). Each pre-
sented a brief. Appended are briefs from the Catholic Indians of Blackfoot Reserve, the
Farm Women's Union of Alberta, and 6 Alberta bands (Hobbema Tall Cree and
Chipewyan Cree). Also appended are documents dealing with the Blood Indian reserve

and statistics on Indian social welfare benefits, both submitted by the Indian Affairs Branch.   JSL

614   **CANADA. Senate and House of Commons. 24 Parliament, 3 Session. Joint Committee of the Senate and the House of Commons on Indian Affairs.**
1960
MINUTES OF PROCEEDINGS AND EVIDENCE. NO. 12. June 16-17, 1960.   Also in French.

Witnesses represented the Province of Saskatchewan and the Centre for Community Studies (University of Saskatchewan). The evidence includes a 51-page brief from the Province.   JSL

615   **CANADA. Senate and House of Commons. 24 Parliament, 3 Session. Joint Committee of the Senate and the House of Commons on Indian Affairs.**
1960
MINUTES OF PROCEEDINGS AND EVIDENCE. NO. 13. June 22, 1960.   Also in French.

Witnesses represented the Six Nations Confederacy. Appended are 4 documents submitted by the Six Nations Confederacy in support of their claims (120 pp).   JSL

616   **CANADA. Senate and House of Commons. 24 Parliament, 3 Session. Joint Committee of the Senate and the House of Commons on Indian Affairs.**
1960
MINUTES OF PROCEEDINGS AND EVIDENCE. NO. 14. June 23-24, 1960.   Also in French.

Witnesses represented the Union of Ontario Indians which presented a 3-page brief as evidence. Appended are answers by the Indian Affairs Branch to questions raised by the Federation of Saskatchewan Indians, briefs from 3 bands in British Columbia (Osoyoos, Similkameen, and Okanagan), the Keesekoose band (Saskatchewan), the Elizabeth Fry Society (Toronto Branch), and the Commissioner of the Northwest Territories.   JSL

617   **CANADA. Senate and House of Commons. 24 Parliament, 4 Session. Joint Committee of the Senate and the House of Commons on Indian Affairs.**
1961
MINUTES OF PROCEEDINGS AND EVIDENCE. NO. 1. March 1 and March 14, 1961.   Also in French.

Witnesses represented the Oka Band of Quebec.   JSL

618   **CANADA. Senate and House of Commons. 24 Parliament, 4 Session. Joint Committee of the Senate and the House of Commons on Indian Affairs.**
1961
MINUTES OF PROCEEDINGS AND EVIDENCE. NO. 2. March 15, 1961.   Also in French.

Witnesses represented the Presbyterian Church in Canada.   JSL

619   **CANADA. Senate and House of Commons. 24 Parliament, 4 Session. Joint Committee of the Senate and the House of Commons on Indian Affairs.**
1961
MINUTES OF PROCEEDINGS AND EVIDENCE. NO. 3. March 16, 1961.   Also in French.

Witnesses represented the Canadian Medical Association.   JSL

620   **CANADA. Senate and House of Commons. 24 Parliament, 4 Session. Joint Committee of the Senate and the House of Commons on Indian Affairs.**
1961
MINUTES OF PROCEEDINGS AND EVIDENCE. NO. 4. March 21, 1961.   Also in French.

Witnesses represented the Province of Newfoundland which presented a 7 page brief.   JSL

621   **CANADA. Senate and House of Commons. 24 Parliament, 4 Session. Joint Committee of the Senate and the House of Commons on Indian Affairs.**
1961
MINUTES OF PROCEEDINGS AND EVIDENCE. NO. 5. March 22, 1961.   Also in French.

Witnesses represented the Native Brotherhood of British Columbia and the Canadian Welfare Council, both of which presented short briefs.   JSL

622   **CANADA. Senate and House of Commons. 24 Parliament, 4 Session. Joint Committee of the Senate and the House of Commons on Indian Affairs.**
1961
MINUTES OF PROCEEDINGS AND EVIDENCE. NO. 6. March 23, 1961.   Also in French.

Witnesses represented the Manitoba Indian Brotherhood and the Greater Winnipeg Welfare Council (Indian and Metis Committee). Briefs were presented by the Brotherhood and by the Council.   JSL

623   **CANADA. Senate and House of Commons. 24 Parliament, 4 Session. Joint Committee of the Senate and the House of Commons on Indian Affairs.**
1961
MINUTES OF PROCEEDINGS AND EVIDENCE. NO. 7. April 26-27, 1961.   Also in French.

Witnesses represented the Queen Victoria Treaty Protective Association, the Thunderchild Band (Saskatchewan), and the Qu'Appelle Indian Advisory Council of Chiefs Independent. Briefs were presented by the first witness, the Thunderchild Band, and the third witness. Appended are documents submitted by the third witness, and briefs from the Catholic Indian League of Canada, the Western Archaelogical Council, 2 British Columbia bands (Squamish and Lower Similkameen), 1 Ontario band (Attawaspikat), and 1 Manitoba band (Barren Lands).   JSL

624 **CANADA. Senate and House of Commons. 24 Parliament, 4 Session. Joint Committee of the Senate and the House of Commons on Indian Affairs.**
1961
MINUTES OF PROCEEDINGS AND EVIDENCE. NO. 8. May 2-3, 1961. Also in French.

Evidence was presented by the Director of the Indian Affairs Branch and the Chief of its Agencies Division. Appended is a brief from the Oka Indians, Quebec. JSL

625 **CANADA. Senate and House of Commons. 24 Parliament, 4 Session. Joint Committee of the Senate and the House of Commons on Indian Affairs.**
1961
MINUTES OF PROCEEDINGS AND EVIDENCE. NO. 9. May 4, 1961. Also in French.

A 7-page brief was presented by the Administration Division, Indian Affairs Branch. JSL

626 **CANADA. Senate and House of Commons. 24 Parliament, 4 Session. Joint Committee of the Senate and the House of Commons on Indian Affairs.**
1961
MINUTES OF PROCEEDINGS AND EVIDENCE. NO. 10. May 9-10, 1961. Also in French.

Briefs were presented by the Welfare Division and Economic Development Division of the Indian Affairs Branch. JSL

627 **CANADA. Senate and House of Commons. 24 Parliament, 4 Session. Joint Committee of the Senate and the House of Commons on Indian Affairs.**
1961
MINUTES OF PROCEEDINGS AND EVIDENCE. NO. 11. May 11, 1961. Also in French.

A 19-page brief was presented by the Supervisor of Fur and Wildlife, Indian Affairs Branch. JSL

628 **CANADA. Senate and House of Commons. 24 Parliament, 4 Session. Joint Committee of the Senate and the House of Commons on Indian Affairs.**
1961
MINUTES OF PROCEEDINGS AND EVIDENCE. NO. 12. May 16, 1961. Also in French.

A brief was presented by the Reserves and Trusts Division, Indian Affairs Branch. JSL

629 **CANADA. Senate and House of Commons. 24 Parliament, 4 Session. Joint Committee of the Senate and the House of Commons on Indian Affairs.**
1961
MINUTES OF PROCEEDINGS AND EVIDENCE. NO. 13. May 18, 1961. Also in French.

A brief of 3 pages was presented by the Education Division, Indian Affairs Branch.   JSL

630   **CANADA. Senate and House of Commons. 24 Parliament, 4 Session. Joint Committee of the Senate and the House of Commons on Indian Affairs.**
1961
MINUTES OF PROCEEDINGS AND EVIDENCE. NO. 14. May 23, 1961.   Also in French.

Witnesses represented the Engineering and Construction Division and the Directorate of the Indian Affairs Branch. Both presented briefs.   JSL

631   **CANADA. Senate and House of Commons. 24 Parliament, 4 Session. Joint Committee of the Senate and the House of Commons on Indian Affairs.**
1961
MINUTES OF PROCEEDINGS AND EVIDENCE. NO. 15. May 24-25, 1961.   Also in French.

Witnesses represented the Department of National Health and Welfare and the Indian Affairs Branch. Both presented briefs. Appended is a submission by the North American Brotherhood.   JSL

632   **CANADA. Senate and House of Commons. 24 Parliament, 4 Session. Joint Committee of the Senate and the House of Commons on Indian Affairs.**
1961
MINUTES OF PROCEEDINGS NO. 16, INCLUDING SECOND AND FINAL REPORT TO PARLIAMENT, ALSO INDEX TO BRIEFS (1959-1960-1961). May 30-July 7, 1961.   Also in French.

Witnesses represented the Indian Affairs Branch. The second and final report of the Committee is presented. The Indian Act was discussed. Appended is a brief from the Six Nations Iroquois Confederacy, Ontario. An index is provided for briefs submitted, 1959-61.   JSL

633   **CANADA. Special Planning Secretariat.**
1967
INDEX OF PROGRAMS FOR HUMAN DEVELOPMENT. Ottawa: Queen's Printer.
Unpaged.   Also in French.

Major federal programs directed toward the well-being and development of every citizen are listed by administering agency or department and by category. The 10 categories are: income support, pensions, and insurance; housing; community processes and institutions; extension or improvement of public services and service facilities; health, education, and social services; socio-economic integration and mobility; aids to productivity and industrial development; area development and land use; development of managerial and occupational skills; and employment incentives and labor standards. A list of regional offices is appended.   JSL

634   **CANADA. 28 Parliament, 2 Session. Special Joint Committee of the Senate and of the House of Commons on the Constitution of Canada.**
n.d.

MINUTES OF PROCEEDINGS AND EVIDENCE NOS. 1-18. March 3, 1970 - October 6, 1970.   Also in French.

References to native peoples in minutes of proceedings include discussion of civil rights, the Drybones case, Indian status, land and treaty rights, and submissions by native associations.   CCV

635   **CANADIAN CATHOLIC CONFERENCE**
1960
BRIEF. In Minutes of Proceedings and Evidence. No. 8. June 1, 1960. Joint Committee of the Senate and the House of Commons on Indian Affairs. Canada. 24 Parliament, 3 Session. Ottawa: Queen's Printer. pp. 724-732.

Twenty-two recommendations were suggested pertaining to economic development, education, community and family life, self-government, recognition of Indian cultures, and cultural integration.   JSL

636   **CANADIAN COUNCIL OF RESOURCE MINISTERS**
1964
AN INVENTORY OF JOINT PROGRAMS AND AGREEMENTS AFFECTING CANADA'S RENEWABLE RESOURCES TO MARCH 31, 1964. William E. Haviland, chairman. Report prepared by Canadian Council of Resource Ministers. Montreal: Canadian Council of Resource Ministers. 182 pp.   Also in French.

Joint programs affecting Canada's renewable resources are listed, summarized, and briefly described. Included on pages 64 to 67, and 111 to 116 are discussions of federal-provincial agreements concerning the construction of roads to Indian reserves, fur conservation, and registration of Indian traplines.   CCV

637   **CANADIAN FEDERATION OF MAYORS AND MUNICIPALITIES**
1960
BRIEF. In Minutes of Proceedings and Evidence. No. 10. June 8, 1960. Joint Committee of the Senate and the House of Commons on Indian Affairs. Canada. 24 Parliament, 3 Session. Ottawa: Queen's Printer. pp. 895-896.

Copies of 3 resolutions made by the Federation are brought to the attention of the Committee. These deal with the cost of municipal aid and hospitalization for treaty Indians, jail cost of Indian prisoners, and control of mosquito breeding areas on Indian reserves. JSL

638   **CANADIAN FRIENDS (QUAKERS) SERVICE COMMITTEE**
1960
BRIEF SUBMITTED BY CANADIAN FRIENDS (QUAKERS) SERVICE COMMITTEE TO THE PARLIAMENTARY COMMITTEE ON INDIAN AFFAIRS. In Minutes of Proceedings and Evidence. No. 4. May 18, 1960. Joint Committee of the Senate and the House of Commons on Indian Affairs. Canada. 24 Parliament, 3 Session. Ottawa: Queen's Printer. pp. 338-339.

Concern about the conditions of Indians prompted the Quakers to suggest a new direction in Indian Affairs administration which includes greater self-determination for the Indian.   JSL

639   **CANADIAN FRIENDS (QUAKERS) SERVICE COMMITTEE**
1969
BRIEF IN RESPONSE TO THE INDIAN POLICY STATEMENT OF THE
CANADIAN GOVERNMENT OF JUNE, 1969. Unpublished paper. Available from
National Library of Canada. 8 pp.

Criticisms made by native leaders of the consultation process involving the native people
and representatives of the federal government are examined and felt to be justified. Native organizations must be recognized by the government for purposes of consultation.
They should respond to the native concern about treaty and aboriginal claims and provide funds to the National Indian Brotherhood for legal research.   IVY

640   **CANADIAN HOME AND SCHOOL AND PARENT-TEACHER FEDERATION**
1960
BRIEF: INTEGRATION OF INDIAN AND WHITE CHILDREN. In Minutes of
Proceedings and Evidence. No. 10. June 8, 1960. Joint Committee of the Senate and the
House of Commons on Indian Affairs. Canada. 24 Parliament, 3 Session. Ottawa:
Queen's Printer. pp. 896-897.

The Federation re-affirms its policy to support integrated schools.   JSL

641   **CANADIAN MEDICAL ASSOCIATION**
1961
BRIEF. In Minutes of Proceedings and Evidence. No. 3. March 16, 1961. Joint
Committee of the Senate and the House of Commons on Indian Affairs. Canada. 24
Parliament, 4 Session. Ottawa: Queen's Printer. pp. 61-64.

This short brief discusses Indian health, and seeks to clarify the issue of federal responsibility to the Indian and to obtain a clear statement of government policy. Certain difficulties encountered by the medical profession are also discussed.   JSL

642   **CANADIAN WELFARE COUNCIL**
1961
BRIEF. In Minutes of Proceedings and Evidence. No. 5. March 22, 1961. Joint
Committee of the Senate and the House of Commons on Indian Affairs. Canada. 24
Parliament, 4 Session. Ottawa: Queen's Printer. pp. 95-103.

The Council cites inequities between Indian and White and discusses community development and the transition from rural to urban settings.   JSL

643   **CARDINAL   HAROLD**
1969
CANADIAN INDIANS AND THE FEDERAL GOVERNMENT. The Western
Canadian Journal of Anthropology 1(1):90-97.

The historical development of the Department of Indian Affairs and Northern Development is briefly reviewed. Present federal policy and reconstruction within the Department are disucssed. Several proposals are outlined to effect change in Indian-government
relationships.   IVY

644   **CARDINAL   HAROLD**
1969
THE UNJUST SOCIETY: THE TRAGEDY OF CANADA'S INDIANS. Edmonton:
Hurtig. 171 pp.

Recent negotiations between Indians and the government are reviewed and some of the
underlying causes for Indian dissatisfaction are explored in the fields of education, religion, employment, and in government policy and administration. The government's failure to consider and implement suggestions from Indian ranks and several proposals designed to increase Indian participation and improve their future are discussed.   CCV

645   **CATHOLIC INDIAN LEAGUE OF CANADA**
1961
MATTERS CONCERNING INDIANS OF ALBERTA: BRIEF TO BE PRESENTED
TO THE JOINT COMMITTEE OF THE SENATE AND THE HOUSE OF
COMMONS. In Minutes of Proceedings and Evidence. No. 7. April 26-27, 1961. Joint
Committee of the Senate and the House of Commons on Indian Affairs. Canada. 24
Parliament, 4 Session. Ottawa: Queen's Printer. pp. 250-262.

Urban adjustments and local educational problems are discussed in the resolutions presented by the league.   JSL

646   **CATHOLIC INDIANS OF NORTHERN B.C. AND THE YUKON**
1960
BRIEF OF THE CATHOLIC INDIANS OF NORTHERN B.C. AND THE YUKON
TO THE JOINT COMMITTEE OF THE SENATE AND THE HOUSE OF
COMMONS. In Minutes of Proceedings and Evidence. No. 10. June 8, 1960. Joint
Committee of the Senate and the House of Commons on Indian Affairs. Canada. 24
Parliament, 3 Session. Ottawa: Queen's Printer. pp. 898-900.

This short brief discusses education, hunting and fishing, employment, housing, self-government, health, liquor, and community improvements.   JSL

647   **CHRETIEN   JEAN**
1968-1970
SPEECHES BY THE HONOURABLE JEAN CHRETIEN ON INDIAN AFFAIRS,
1968, 1969, 1970. Unpublished collection of speeches. Available from Library,
Department of Indian Affairs and Northern Development, Ottawa. 120 pp.

Fourteen speeches on Indian Affairs delivered by Jean Chretien as Minister of Indian
Affairs and Northern Development are compiled and bound. Emphasis is on deficiencies
in the Indian Act, areas of improvement, and government policies for amelioration. Government desire to dialogue with Indian representatives and involve them in self-government is stressed.   CCV

648   **CHRETIEN   JEAN**
1969
INDIAN AFFAIRS MINISTER SPEAKS ON EQUAL OPPORTUNITIES. The
Labour Gazette 69:75.

At the 1968 meeting of the Save the Children Fund in Ottawa, Jean Chretien discussed government policies and actions regarding the Indian. Stress was placed upon the government's desire to consult with Indians before acting on their behalf, since failure to do so has been 1 of the government's major problems. He also commented on the possible role an Indian Claims Commission could play in fostering trust between the Indian and White man.   ADG

649   **CHRETIEN   JEAN**
1970
INDIAN POLICY: A REPLY. The Canadian Forum 49:279-280.

The government's proposed policy regarding Indians has resulted in some misunderstandings among concerned leaders. Realizing the unsuitability of overnight change or continued segregation of the Indians and Whites, the government decided to continue its policy of gradual transition, with some modifications. The government has no intention of terminating its responsibilities to the Indian; however it does recognize the failings of its past policy, as well as the penalty contained therein for the Indian. The proposal for change has been inspired by the Indian's demand for something more than monetary increases. The opposition now evident among many Canadians is the result of the fear change creates. Those persons who accuse the government of termination are doing the Indian a disservice. Many of the Indian leaders realize some of the positive aspects of the new policy and want their people to benefit from these.   ADG

650   **CHRETIEN   JEAN**
1970
REPLY FROM THE MINISTER OF INDIAN AFFAIRS AND NORTHERN DEVELOPMENT. In Bulletin 201: Recent Statements by the Indians of Canada, General Synod Action 1969, Some Government Responses, Suggested Resources. Toronto: Anglican Church of Canada. p. 24.

The government's position regarding treaty rights and native participation in policy-making is presented by Jean Chretien in his letter replying to the official stand of the Anglican Church of Canada.   CCV

651   **CLARK   HOWARD H**
1970
PRIMATE'S LETTER. In Bulletin 201: Recent Statements by the Indians of Canada, General Synod Action 1969, Some Government Responses, Suggested Resources. Toronto: Anglican Church of Canada. p. 23.

The resolutions of the 1969 General Synod of the Anglican Church regarding government policy-making and Canadian Indians are presented in the primate's letter to Prime Minister Pierre Trudeau. The position of the Anglican Church is support of the native in seeking justice through enforcement of treaties.   CCV

652   **CO-OPERATIVE UNION OF CANADA**
1960
BRIEF. In Minutes of Proceedings and Evidence. No. 9. June 2, 1960. Joint Committee of the Senate and the House of Commons on Indian Affairs. Canada. 24 Parliament, 3 Session. Ottawa: Queen's Printer. pp. 829-848.

Community development through self-government, best achieved by credit unions and cooperatives, is proposed as a solution to the Indian problem. JSL

653 **COTE E A**
1967
AN ADDRESS BY MR. E. A. COTE DEPUTY MINISTER DEPARTMENT OF INDIAN AFFAIRS AND NORTHERN DEVELOPMENT. Speech delivered to Law Club of the University of Alberta. Edmonton, November 2, 1967. Available from Information Services, Records and Research, Department of Indian Affairs and Northern Development, Ottawa (Speech #3-6735). 11 pp.

Some problems encountered by Canadian Indian people over the last century are outlined as well as some proposals to meet modern needs, particularly in housing, education, employment, and integration. CCV

654 **COURCHENE DAVE**
1969
PRESS RELEASE: WINNIPEG, JUNE 26, 1969. Unpublished paper. Available from National Library of Canada. 3 pp.

This is a press release by the president of the Manitoba Indian Brotherhood after the public presentation of the federal government's proposed Indian policy in 1969. Particular reference is made to racial and ethnic equality, the transfer of governmental service available to Indians from the federal level to the provincial, the dropping of the Indian Claims Commission, and changes in the Indian Act. HCV

655 **COURCHENE DAVE**
1970
ADDRESS TO GENERAL SYNOD. In Bulletin 201: Recent Statements by the Indians of Canada, General Synod Action 1969, Some Government Responses, Suggested Resources. Toronto: Anglican Church of Canada. pp. 7-14.

Comments are made on the future prospects of the Canadian Indian in regard to the recent federal white paper on Indian policy. In reaction to the lack of consultation and negotiation of the federal government with the Indians, the author foresees a division in the Indian ranks between those groups willing to seek solutions by peaceful means and those who will be aggravated into a militant violence. The author asks all churches regardless of denomination to assist the Indians in their request for a redefinition of Indian policy. DGW

656 **CURRIE WALTER**
1968
THE HIDDEN WORLD OF LEGISLATED DISCRIMINATION. The Northian 5(3):24-26.

One of the worst forms of discrimination against the Indian is that contained in the Indian Act. Because of the various components of this statute, many blood Indians are not legal Indians, the reserve does not really belong to the Indians, Indians cannot engage in free enterprise, wills are under control of the Minister of Indian Affairs, and parents have no legal voice in the education of their children. Several important changes must be

made: (1) Indians must be given responsibility for their destinies, (2) provincial governments must acknowledge and expedite the full citizenship of the Indian, and (3) the Indian Act must be revised, but the Indian people must have a say in its content.   ADG

657   **CURRIE   WALTER**
1969
TOO IMPATIENT? TOO UNCONCERNED? The Labour Gazette 69:646-650.

Walter Currie, an Ojibwa and president of the Indian-Eskimo Association of Canada,
addressed the Mid-Canada Development Corridor Conference at Lakehead University
on August 20, 1969. His speech constituted a review of the traditional Indian's patience
with and generosity towards early White settlers, and a plea that contemporary White
society be fair in repaying this patience and generosity.   ADG

658   **CUTHAND   ADAM**
1970
PREFACE. In Bulletin 201: Recent Statements by the Indians of Canada, General
Synod Action 1969, Some Government Responses, Suggested Resources. Toronto:
Anglican Church of Canada. pp. 5-6.

The President of the Manitoba Metis Federation requests political assistance from
churches in the attempt by Indian organizations to change government Indian policy.
Motions passed by the General Synod of the Anglican Church of Canada authorizing the
implementation of the Hendry Report should provide an example to other churches for
their involvement in Indian, Eskimo and Metis affairs.   DGW

659   **DAVEY   R F**
1965
THE ESTABLISHMENT AND GROWTH OF INDIAN SCHOOL
ADMINISTRATION WITH COMMENT BY CLARE C. BRANT. In The Education
of Indian Children in Canada: A Symposium Written by Members of Indian Affairs
Education Division with Comments by the Indian Peoples. L. G. P. Waller, ed. The
Canadian Superintendent 1965. Toronto: Ryerson Press. pp. 1-10.

Examining legislation from 1763 regarding the education of Indian children, an ebb and
flow of authority from provincial to federal governments is evident. This review provides
an insight into the present legal position and the administrative organization of the Indian Affairs Branch of the Department of Citizenship and Immigration. Clare C. Brant
of the Tyendinaga Band, Ontario, comments.   IVY

660   **DUNNING   R W**
1962
SOME ASPECTS OF GOVERNMENTAL INDIAN POLICY AND
ADMINISTRATION. Anthropologica N.S. 4:209-231.

The dependency of Indians upon the federal government is analyzed through examination of legislation and administration. Since administration hinges upon the superintend-
ency and the agency system, focus is centered upon the role and function of the
agent, who by his presence and power perpetuates this dependency. It is suggested that

(1) the position of agent be removed and jurisdiction be placed with the provincial government (treaty payments and other economic affairs excepted); (2) with regard to reserve populations in rural areas, law and order be established and maintained; (3) the quality of teachers be improved; and (4) the process of integration into the lower class strata be bypassed and an experimental project of voluntary and selective integration into the urban middle class be initiated.   IVY

661   **DUNNING   R W**
1969
INDIAN POLICY - A PROPOSAL FOR AUTONOMY. The Canadian Forum 49:206-207.

The government appears to be opting for termination of its responsibilities to the Indians. The government proposals could lead to the loss of land, requiring integration of Indian communities with the provinces as tax levying municipalities. This could hasten the loss of everything for those many Indians living at subsistence level, including their ethnic identity. Recommendations include: (1) government return of control of reserve land to Indians, (2) a capital development grant of $500 million over 10 years, (3) continuance of government services with a gradual abandoning of the agent system of supervision, (4) government encouragement to registered and non-registered Indians to seek justice for their grievances through the courts, and (5) government recognition of Indian organizations which represent wide segments of the population. Implementation of these proposals might result in 2 models of Indian community - bands which become municipalities and those who accept the capital development funds but refuse to incorporate with the provinces.   ADG

662   **DURAN   JAMES A JR**
1968
COMMENTING ON THE FEDERAL GOVERNMENT'S PROPOSED NEW POLICY ON INDIAN AFFAIRS: COST OF LAND SETTLEMENTS WITH THE INDIANS OF THE UNITED STATES. Unpublished paper. Available from Indian-Eskimo Association. 3 pp.

The establishment of the American Indian Claims Commission points out the difference between the policies of the United States and Canada toward aboriginal property rights.   IVY

663   **DURAN   JAMES A JR**
1968
COMMENTING ON THE FEDERAL GOVERNMENT'S PROPOSED NEW POLICY ON INDIAN AFFAIRS: DIFFERENT LEGAL STATUS OF U.S. AND CANADIAN INDIANS. Unpublished paper. Available from Indian-Eskimo Association. 4 pp.

The divergence of legal development respecting the treatment of Indian rights in the United States and Canada is examined. Compared are aboriginal claims, jurisdiction of tribal authorities, and hunting and fishing rights.   IVY

664   **DURAN   JAMES A JR**
1969-70

THE NEW INDIAN POLICY: LESSONS FROM THE U.S. Canadian Dimension 6(6):21-23.

Comments on the new Indian policy of the Government of Canada announced on June 24, 1969, are given with direct reference to the termination policy of the American government rescinded in 1959.   IVY

665   **DYEK   NOEL E**
1970
THE ADMINISTRATION OF FEDERAL INDIAN AID IN THE NORTH-WEST TERRITORIES, 1879-1885. M.A. Thesis. Department of History. University of Saskatchewan, Saskatoon. 103 pp.

Indian living conditions in the Canadian Northwest and government policies are described for the period from 1879-1885. In an attempt to make Indians self-supporting when the buffalo disappeared as a food resource, the reserve agricultural program was introduced. The initial partial success of the program and the roles of Indian leaders in seeking conditions which would facilitate transition to a family life style are noted. Government preoccupation with administrative economy is examined as a factor contributing to the failure of the program, a sense of dissatisfaction, and a growing Indian political movement. Indian participation in the Northwest Rebellion, although limited, resulted in adoption of a policy of repression and further decline in support for the agriculture program.   CCV

666   **ELIZABETH FRY SOCIETY**
1960
BRIEF. In Minutes of Proceedings and Evidence. No. 14. June 23-24, 1960. Joint Committee of the Senate and the House of Commons on Indian Affairs. Canada. 24 Parliament, 3 Session. Ottawa: Queen's Printer. pp. 1407-1408.

The high incidence of female Indians in Ontario's correctional institutions drew the Society's attention to the need for counselling on employment, housing, education, health, and community services. The brief contains proposals for community services, personnel, judicial services, and a pre-release program.   JSL

667   **ESTEY   C L**
1968
REMARKS. Delivered to Meeting of Task Force on Indian Opportunity. Government of Saskatchewan. Regina, August 9, 1968. Available from Indian and Metis Department, Regina. 7 pp.

Low rental housing in urban centres is available to people of Indian ancestry. In addition, houses built for people of Indian ancestry in northern Saskatchewan may be purchased for $5,000 with a grant of $500 being made toward the purchase by the province. Credit for his labor in the construction is applied to the purchase price. The occupant becomes owner after 15 years regardless of the amount of monthly payments which are scaled to his income. Houses have been purchased in large urban centres for transient families in which the head is receiving training or is beginning to work in one of these centres.   IVY

668   **FAIRCLOUGH   ELLEN L**
1961
INDIAN AFFAIRS IN 1960: A PROGRESS REPORT ON THE GOVERNMENT'S
PLACEMENT PROGRAM AND OTHER ASSISTANCE. The Monetary Times
Annual National Review 1961:36,38,40-41.

The Placement Program was initiated in 1957 to prepare Indians for industry. Selected
youth are counselled and encouraged to take regular, full-time employment in factories,
offices, and other businesses. Job opportunities for Indians living in rural and frontier
areas have been developed. One such project has been the Grand Rapids hydroelectric
development. Educational and home improvements have also been attempted. Through
the success of these programs business stereotypes of Indians are breaking down and
slowly employers are beginning to appreciate the potential value of Indian workers. Reserves are beginning to show greater interest and success in their own business enterprises.   ADG

669   **FAIRCLOUGH   ELLEN L**
1962
A 1961 REPORT ON THE WORK OF THE INDIAN AFFAIRS BRANCH. The
Monetary Times Annual National Review 1962:36,38.

If the Indian is to compete and survive in White society, he must learn the skills and technical knowledge of the White man. Indian Affairs educational objectives are equal education and opportunity for Indian and non-Indian youth, the provision of adult education facilities and opportunities, and the encouragement of integration between Indian
and non-Indian. Integration is, however, something which the Indian must accept and
seek for himself. Several problems exist for the federal school system: (1) great differences among Indians in terms of sophistication, residence, occupation and life style, (2)
language differences between pupil and teacher, (3) poor living conditions for the pupils,
and (4) a non-White value system.   ADG

670   **FARM WOMEN'S UNION OF ALBERTA**
1960
BRIEF. In Minutes of Proceedings and Evidence. No. 11. June 9-10, 1960. Joint
Committee of the Senate and the House of Commons on Indian Affairs. Canada. 24
Parliament, 3 Session. Ottawa: Queen's Printer. pp. 1019-1023.

Discussed in this brief are education of Indians, economic development, treaties, delinquency, free legal advice, and the importance of consultation. A self-help policy is urged.
Included are 15 resolutions by the Union.   JSL

671   **FEDERATION OF SASKATCHEWAN INDIANS**
1960
BRIEF OF THE FEDERATION OF SASKATCHEWAN INDIANS. In Minutes of
Proceedings and Evidence. No. 6. May 25, 1960. Joint Committee of the Senate and the
House of Commons on Indian Affairs. Canada. 24 Parliament, 3 Session. Ottawa:
Queen's Printer. pp. 439-519.

An extensive brief was presented which includes a discussion of the Indian Act, proposed
changes in the Act, resolutions pertaining to revisions of the Indian Act arising from the
1959 Saskatchewan Chiefs and Councillors Conference, and a model Indian Act.   JSL

672   **FLANAGAN   R T**
1963
A HISTORY OF THE DEPARTMENT OF NORTHERN AFFAIRS AND
NATIONAL RESOURCES IN ITS VARIOUS MANIFESTATIONS SINCE 1867
WITH SPECIAL REFERENCE TO ITS ROLE IN THE EXISTING NORTHWEST
TERRITORIES. Ottawa: Department of Northern Affairs and National Resources. 95
pp.

Annual reports and newspaper accounts were utilized to compile a history of departments responsible for the Northwest Territories since 1867. Appended is a chart of Departmental responsibilities and lists of Ministers, Deputy Ministers, Commissioners of Yukon Territory, Commissioners of Northwest Territories, Council Members, and expenditures.   JSL

673   **FREESTONE   AL**
1968
ENVIRONMENTAL SANITATION ON INDIAN RESERVES. Canadian Journal of
Public Health 59:25-27.

A regional public health inspector discusses the accomplishments in public health on Indian reserves in Saskatchewan (1961-1967). Sanitation workshops and the Community Health Worker Program are also reported.   IVY

674   **FRIENDS OF THE INDIANS SOCIETY OF EDMONTON**
1960
BRIEF OF THE FRIENDS OF THE INDIANS SOCIETY OF EDMONTON. In
Minutes of Proceedings and Evidence. No. 3. May 11-13, 1960. Joint Committee of the
Senate and the House of Commons on Indian Affairs. Canada. 24 Parliament, 3 Session.
Ottawa: Queen's Printer. pp. 292-297.

A brief was submitted which endorsed the resolutions of the Indian Association of Alberta, and added 27 recommendations of its own.   JSL

675   **FRONTIER COLLEGE**
1960
THE FRONTIER COLLEGE BRIEF TO THE JOINT COMMITTEE OF THE
SENATE AND THE HOUSE OF COMMONS ON INDIAN AFFAIRS. In Minutes of
Proceedings and Evidence. No. 4. May 18, 1960. Joint Committee of the Senate and the
House of Commons on Indian Affairs. Canada. 24 Parliament, 3 Session. Ottawa:
Queen's Printer. pp. 340-342.

Observations are made on the 416 Indian workers in the college. Recommendations include support of specialized adult education programs.   JSL

676   **FRY   ALAN**
1970
HOW A PEOPLE DIE. Toronto: Doubleday. 167 pp.

Derived from the author's experience as Indian Agent in British Columbia, a dramatized account is presented of an Indian Agent's and a law enforcement officer's attempts to administer a Northwest Coast Indian community.   CCV

677   **GIBBARD H J, KING PHYLLIS**
1967
HISTORY OF TRAPLINE MANAGEMENT IN ONTARIO. Ontario Fish and
Wildlife Review 6(1-2):2-6

A summation of legislation directed toward fur managment in Ontario is given.   IVY

678   **GREATER WINNIPEG WELFARE COUNCIL**
1961
BRIEF. In Minutes of Proceedings and Evidence. No. 6. March 23, 1961. Joint
Committee of the Senate and the House of Commons on Indian Affairs. Canada. 24
Parliament, 4 Session. Ottawa: Queen's Printer. pp. 144-159.

Community development and education are presented as partial solutions to the social
and economic problems of the Indians.   JSL

679   **GREEN   L C**
1969
CANADA'S INDIANS - FEDERAL POLICY, INTERNATIONAL AND
CONSTITUTIONAL LAW. n.p. Available from National Library of Canada. 36 pp.

The position of Canadian Indians is examined in light of policies followed by other nations toward minorities, declarations passed by the United Nations, and court cases both
within and outside Canada. A critical stance is taken toward the 1969 federal policy
statement.   CCV

680   **HELSON   DAVE**
n.d.
THE INDIAN AND THE LAW. Unpublished paper. Available from National Library
of Canada. 26 pp.

Some aspects of the legal status of the Canadian Indian are investigated to determine the
legal rights and obligations common to all Canadians and those which tend to restrict
the Indian's rights as an individual. Treaties; land title, use, and transfer; self-government; inheritance; personal and property rights; hunting and fishing rights; and alcohol
use are discussed with respect to the Indian Act, the areas of provincial jurisdiction, and
law enforcement. The results of specific cases and rulings are cited. It is maintained that
the contemporary Indian's social condition is a reflection of the laws intended for this
protection.   CCV

681   **HOLMES   ALVIN ISHMAEL**
1961
THE SOCIAL WELFARE ASPECTS AND IMPLICATIONS OF THE INDIAN ACT.
M.S.W. Thesis. School of Social Work. University of British Columbia. 111 pp.

The welfare implications of the Indian Act in Canada are examined. The historical background of Indian administration is reviewed briefly and relative aspects of property
rights, citizenship status, social assistance and child welfare, education, health, and housing are discussed. In each case the implications of present policy are noted. It is indicated
that Indians do not have equitable civic rights or welfare services. Much of their life is
carried on in isolation from other citizens. They are stereotyped negatively. Paternalistic

services are both inadequate for needs and detrimental to morale. Discussion is extended to ways and means of improving services and achieving equal status for Indians.   CCV

682   **HUTTON   ELIZABETH ANN**
1963
INDIAN AFFAIRS IN NOVA SCOTIA, 1760-1834. Nova Scotia Historical Society Collections 34:33-54.

During the late 18th and early 19th centuries the government moved toward a policy of establishing reserves for the Indians of Nova Scotia. Concern with Indians was manifested in 1760 in the touchhouse scheme which provided for fixed centers of trade and an agent to oversee this commerce. This was abolished in 1764 with a Superintendent of Indian Affairs replacing the agent. In 1768 the colonies were given the burden of managing Indian Affairs with its financial strain of providing relief. The first decade of the 19th century saw the establishment of 12 Indian districts with a resident correspondent in each. By 1834 the scheme of Indian reserves was operative in Nova Scotia.   IVY

683   **INDIAN ASSOCIATION OF ALBERTA**
1960
BRIEF. In Minutes of Proceedings and Evidence. No. 3. May 11-13, 1960. Joint Committee of the Senate and the House of Commons on Indian Affairs. Canada. 24 Parliament, 3 Session. Ottawa: Queen's Printer. pp. 125-168.

Following a preamble, topics discussed include history, treaty rights, self-government, education, health, welfare, employment, hunting, fishing, and trapping. Following the conclusion of the brief are appendices on allotment policy in the United States, and tables compiled for each Alberta agency on the above topics.   JSL

684   **INDIAN COUNCIL FIRE OF CANADA**
1960
MY NOTES AND RECOMMENDATIONS (By Big White Owl). In Minutes of Proceedings and Evidence. No. 4. May 18, 1960. Joint Committee of the Senate and the House of Commons on Indian Affairs. Canada. 24 Parliament, 3 Session. Ottawa: Queen's Printer. pp. 343-346.

This 4 point brief recommends urban integration centers, creation of a Canadian Indian Day, a Canadian Indian calendar, and the establishment of a Canadian Indian Office in Ottawa, separate from the Department of Indian Affairs.   JSL

685   **INDIAN-ESKIMO ASSOCIATION OF CANADA**
1960
BRIEF TO THE PARLIAMENTARY COMMITTEE ON INDIAN AFFAIRS. In Minutes of Proceedings and Evidence. No. 5. May 19, 1960. Joint Committee of the Senate and the House of Commons on Indian Affairs. Canada. 24 Parliament, 3 Session. Ottawa: Queen's Printer. pp. 363-395.

An extensive brief was submitted dealing with all aspects of the Indian Act and Indian status. Many recommendations are made which would promote Indian advancement.   JSL

686   **INDIAN-ESKIMO ASSOCIATION OF CANADA. Alberta Division.**
1969
ANNUAL REPORT AND REPORT OF THE PRESIDENT: ALBERTA DIVISION:
1968-69. Unpublished paper delivered to Annual Meeting, Indian-Eskimo Association
of Canada. Winnipeg, June 13, 1969. Available from Indian-Eskimo Association. 17 pp.

Lloyd Auger, President of the Alberta Division, discusses decentralization of the Indian-
Eskimo Association. Major activities of the Alberta Division reported include: (1) helping native organizations raise funds, (2) supporting initiatives and stands taken by native
organizations, and (3) creating public awareness of concerns and aspirations of the native people.   IVY

687   **INTERIOR TRIBES OF BRITISH COLUMBIA. ABORIGINAL NATIVE
RIGHTS REGIONAL COMMITTEE.**
1960
BRIEF PREPARED BY THE ABORIGINAL NATIVE RIGHTS REGIONAL
COMMITTEE OF THE INTERIOR TRIBES OF BRITISH COLUMBIA. In Minutes of
Proceedings and Evidence. No. 7. May 26-27, 1960. Joint Committee of the Senate and
the House of Commons on Indian Affairs. Canada. 24 Parliament, 3 Session. Ottawa:
Queen's Printer. pp. 592-621.

Extensive in coverage, this brief discusses the land question, non-treaty lands, allocation
of reserves, agriculture, alcohol, education, housing, fishing, federal voting privileges,
health services, social welfare, law enforcement and courts, credit, estates, administration, placement services, and self-government. Also discussed are a separate British Columbia Indian Act, a separate Indian Department, liason with interior Indians, and the
Indian Act. Pages 616-621 provide a supplementary brief, containing more specific demands from the agency level of the Department of Indian Affairs.   JSL

688   **JACK   HENRY**
1970
NATIVE ALLIANCE FOR RED POWER. In The Only Good Indian: Essays by
Canadian Indians. Waubageshig, ed. Toronto: New Press. pp. 162-180.

The original and revised aims and objectives of NARP are outlined and discussed by a
founding member. In addition the organization's history and activities are reviewed
briefly.   CCV

689   **JUDD   DAVID**
1969
CANADA'S NORTHERN POLICY: RETROSPECT AND PROSPECT. Polar Record
14:593-602.

Federal policies (political, economic, social) concerning the Canadian Arctic regions
(Northwest Territories, Arctic Quebec, and the Yukon) are discussed.   IVY

690   **JUDD   DAVID**
1969
CANADA'S NORTHERN POLICY: RETROSPECT AND PROSPECT. Polar Record
14:593-602.

Federal policies (political, economic, social) concerning the Canadian Arctic regions (Northwest Territories, Arctic Quebec, and the Yukon) are discussed.   IVY

691   **KAISER   S W**
1965
FINANCING INDIAN EDUCATION WITH COMMENT BY STANLEY CUTHAND. In The Education of Indian Children in Canada: A Symposium Written by Members of Indian Affairs Education Division with Comments by the Indian Peoples. L. G. P. Waller, ed. The Canadian Superintendent 1965. Toronto: Ryerson Press. pp. 28-35.

A discussion on federal expenditures for Indian education is presented. Reverend Stanley Cuthand of the Little Pine Band, Saskatchewan, comments.   IVY

692   **KASSIRER   EVE**
1970
PROGRAMS OF INTEREST TO INDIANS AND METIS ADMINISTERED BY THE DEPARTMENT OF REGIONAL ECONOMIC EXPANSION. Ottawa: Department of Regional Economic Expansion. 31 pp.

An inventory of the Department's projects utilized by Indians and Metis discusses 5 programs: the Agricultural and Rural Development Act (ARDA), the Prairie Farm Rehabilitation Administration (PFRA), NewStart, Fund for Rural Economic Development (FRED), and the Regional Development Incentives Act (RDIA). Each program is described and specific projects are tabulated according to type, province, band, departmental contribution, project number, and completion date. Projects initiated prior to June, 1970, are included. The materials are organized by region - Western, Central, and Eastern.   JSL

693   **KERR   ROBERT WILLIAM**
1969
LEGISLATION AGAINST DISCRIMINATION IN CANADA. Fredericton, N.B.: Human Rights Commission. 80 pp.

This paper includes all of the existing legislation in Canada at the federal, provincial and territorial levels which is directed against discrimination on grounds of race, color, religion, creed, nationality, ancestry, national or ethnic origin, place of origin, or age. It sets out the common law and civil law on discrimination in Canada and reviews the substantive legislative provisions that have been adopted to combat discrimination.   IVY

694   **LAFOREST   GERARD U**
1969
NATURAL RESOURCES AND PUBLIC PROPERTY UNDER THE CANADIAN CONSTITUTION. Toronto: University of Toronto Press. 230 pp.

A general survey of legislation concerning natural resources and public property within the framework of the Canadian constitution is presented with emphasis on the partition between the federal and provincial governments. Discussion of the Indian Act, hunting and fishing rights, Indian treaties, and jurisdiction over Indians is included. Indian administration and control of land is discussed in terms of title, surrender, compensation for land loss, and jurisdiction over Indian lands.   CCV

695   **LAGASSE   JEAN H**
1961
COMMUNITY DEVELOPMENT IN MANITOBA. Human Organization 20:233-237.

Based on census data up to 1961, the purposes and adaptation of the Manitoba Community Development program are reviewed. Directed toward the adjustment of Indian and Metis, the program is compared with previous concepts and applications of community development. It differed in the methods of operation with primary emphasis placed upon economic and social relationships within these small marginal groups and between them and the society at large. In order to deal effectively with the causes of problems, the foremost of which are cultural differences, greater determination by the serviced communities was urged. Due to its recent nature the program is not fully evaluated. However, the complexity of problems is noted with suggestions for the application of social science.   WRC

696   **LAING   ARTHUR**
1967-1968
SPEECHES BY THE HONORABLE ARTHUR LAING ON INDIAN AFFAIRS, 1967, 1968. Unpublished collection of speeches. Available from Library, Department of Indian Affairs and Northern Development, Ottawa. 162 pp.

Fourteen speeches on Indian Affairs delivered by Arthur Laing as Minister of Indian Affairs and Northern Development are compiled and bound. Some problem areas in Indian administration and major Indian dissatisfactions are discussed as well as existing and proposed remedial policies in education, employment, health, housing, self-government, and resource development. The necessity for assumption of responsibility and participation in ameliorative programs by Indian and non-Indian citizens is stressed.   CCV

697   **LESLIE   A G**
1967
NOTES FOR AN ADDRESS BY A. G. LESLIE, DIRECTOR OF DEVELOPMENT, INDIAN AFFAIRS BRANCH, TO THE DEPARTMENT OF SOCIOLOGY AND ANTHROPOLOGY AT THE UNIVERSITY OF CALGARY. Speech delivered to Department of Sociology and Anthropology, University of Calgary. Calgary, March 10, 1967. Available from Information Services, Records and Research, Department of Indian Affairs and Northern Development, Ottawa (Speech #3-6644). 14 pp.

Indian Affairs policies, programs, and projects in the fields of education, local self-government, and extension of provincial services to Indians as well as housing, utilities, community services, and economic development are explored.   CCV

698   **LYSYK   KENNETH**
1968
RESOURCE PAPER ON HUMAN RIGHTS AND CANADA'S NATIVE PEOPLE. Unpublished paper delivered to 9th Annual Meeting and Conference, Indian-Eskimo Association of Canada. Toronto, September 27, 1968. Available from Indian-Eskimo Association. 15 pp.

The relationship between the human rights of Indians and Eskimos and the law are explored. Referring to 4 articles in the Universal Declaration of Human Rights, it is shown that the human rights of native peoples have been violated, particularly in the area of aboriginal land rights and treaties.   IVY

699   **MACDONALD   JOHN A**
1968
QUEL EST L'AVENIR DES INDIENS: THE INDIAN AND HIS FUTURE. Speech delivered to Kiwanis Club. Ottawa, September 13, 1968. Available from Information Services, Records and Research, Department of Indian Affairs and Northern Development, Ottawa (Speech # 3-684). 11 pp.

The Deputy Minister of Indian Affairs outlines changing conditions under which legislation on Indians developed and surveys areas requiring reform. Difficulties facing contemporary Indian citizens and government efforts at consultation with Indian leaders in view of formulating new policies are discussed.   CCV

700   **MANITOBA**
1960
A BRIEF - SUBMITTED BY THE PROVINCE OF MANITOBA TO THE JOINT COMMITTEE OF THE SENATE AND THE HOUSE OF COMMONS ON INDIAN AFFAIRS.   In Minutes of Proceedings and Evidence. No. 8. June 1, 1960. Joint Committee of the Senate and the House of Commons on Indian Affairs. Canada. 24 Parliament, 3 Session. Ottawa: Queen's Printer. pp. 769-779.

Thirteen recommendations are submitted in this extensive brief. Discussed with reference to the Indians of Manitoba are federal-provincial responsibilities and coordination, rehabilitation programs, federal voting, liquor, enfranchisement, trespass, a simplified Indian Act, reserve lands, and adult education.   JSL

701   **MANITOBA INDIAN BROTHERHOOD**
1961
BRIEF. In Minutes of Proceedings and Evidence. No. 6. March 23, 1961. Joint Committee of the Senate and the House of Commons on Indian Affairs. Canada. 24 Parliament, 4 Session. Ottawa: Queen's Printer. pp. 121-126.

The Brotherhood discusses treaty rights in Manitoba, the Indian Act (especially Sections 32-33), employment, and relief. Extension of the federal franchise is urged.   JSL

702   **MARSHALL   BRIAN D**
1962
SOME PROBLEMS IN INDIAN AFFAIRS FIELD ADMINISTRATION. M.A. Thesis. School of Public Administration. Carleton University, Ottawa. 98 pp.

An interaction of social and cultural factors as well as operative difficulties are revealed by this examination of problems in Indian Affairs administration in Canada. Responsibilities and activities of Indian Affairs personnel and band councils, and obstacles in the fields of communication, education, acculturation, and community development are reviewed giving some indication of Indian problems generally. With reference to the literature recommendations are presented for improved organization.   CCV

703 MCCUE HARVEY see WAUBAGESHIG

704 MCEWEN ERNEST R
1970
COMMUNITY DEVELOPMENT SERVICES FOR CANADIAN INDIANS AND
METIS COMMUNITIES. Toronto: Indian-Eskimo Association of Canada. 52 pp.

Problems intrinsic to Canadian Indian and Metis community development programs are
described. In analyzing how these difficulties might be alleviated, the organization and
structure of successful community change programs in the Caribbean and Mexico were
studied. Five principles are considered essential to the success of a community change
program: (1) community development belonging to the people, (2) ready access to resources by the community, (3) complete and effective coordination of government services in regional settings, (4) employment of pilot undertakings to initiate the movement,
and (5) community development beginning within the culture and value system of the
people and moving forward from there. A series of recommendations on the basis of
these principles is put forward, including the proposed establishment of a Native Canadian Development Institute to serve all native communities.   DGW

705 MCGILP J
1965
THE SPECIAL CASE OF THE INDIAN RESERVE. In Rural Rehabilitation Policies:
An Exploration of Goals, Values, and Alternatives (A report on the first of three
symposiums on the problems of organization for rural development and rehabilitation).
Saskatoon: Center for Community Studies. pp. 77-80.

Part 1 of this paper reiterates the federal government's objective that the Indians of Canada should become increasingly independent self-supporting members of the general
community without having to lose their cultural identity. Part 2 outlines the principles
used by federal administrators in working with band councils.   IVY

706 MCGILP J G
1963
THE RELATIONS OF CANADIAN INDIANS AND CANADIAN
GOVERNMENTS. Canadian Public Administration 6:299-308.

This brief outline history of Indian Affairs Administration in Canada and Saskatchewan
sees the primary function of Indian Affairs as the administration of the interests and affairs of Indians in a manner which will enable them to become increasingly self-supporting and independent members of the community. The notion of wardship, according to
this article, is bad for the interests of the Indians for several reasons: (1) it affects the
child in his relations to others, (2) it impedes the progress of integration measures, (3) it
affects the attitudes of provincial and municipal officials toward Indians, and (4) it influences the entire outlook and motivation of Indians themselves. The article also criticizes
the myth surrounding the Indian as citizen. The author claims that the Indian is a citizen
of Canada as well as of a province. Nor does the Indian's citizenship stand or fall upon
his legal inability to consume liquor. He is, moreover, subject to all responsibilities and
penalties as are non-Indian citizens. This includes laws regarding law enforcement and
personal and real property.   ADG

707   **MCNICKLE   D'ARCY**
1961
PRIVATE INTERVENTION. Human Organization 20:208-215.

The development of private citizens' organizations for Indian welfare is described for Canada and the United States. A brief history of the respective governmental policies is reviewed beginning with the common English colonial experience. The subsequent similarities and disparities in the centralization of Indian affairs administration is noted between the 2 countries. The formation of Indian and non-Indian reform groups are considered as effective differential public reactions to inadequacies in these administrations. Included are brief lists of such organizations and their aims in Canada and the United States.   WRC

708   **MELLING   JOHN**
1962
RECENT INDIAN AFFAIRS IN CANADA. Continuous Learning 1:73-76.

Indians want to control their own destinies. It is not likely that the federal government will comply with this demand although it has encouraged the provinces to assume greater responsibility for the Indian. Certain parts of the Final Report of the Joint Parliamentary Committee on Indian Affairs will affect the political liberation of the Indians on reserves by fostering an effective Indian leadership. There are, however, a few problems: (1) some Indians cherish their traditional association with the British Crown because of its implications for Indian land, and (2) the federal government cannot disengage itself from responsibility for Indians and Indian land without an amendment to the British North America Act. If these difficulties can be overcome and the special rights of the Indian secured, provincial development of reserve land might create new jobs for the Indian.   ADG

709   **MELLING   JOHN**
1966
RECENT DEVELOPMENTS IN OFFICIAL POLICY TOWARDS CANADIAN INDIANS AND ESKIMOS. Race 7:379-399.

Analysis of the government's past and current relations with the Indian and Eskimo reveals a government more genuinely interested in the native people. But the government's policy of integration is presently unfeasible because of government and public neglect and misuse of the natives in the past. The reserve system, designed for administrative convenience, now presents the government with problems. Legal and constitutional ambiguities regarding the natives prevent the development of a uniform policy toward them. Indian communities must be revitalized and liberated, and then efforts must be made to remove the unfavorable attitudes and neglect of the Whites.   ADG

710   **MORTIMER   G E**
1967
THE INDIANS WERE HERE FIRST: TREAT THEM AS 'CITIZENS PLUS'. Human Relations (Ontario Human Rights Commission) 7(15):4-6.

This review of the Hawthorn-Tremblay Report places special emphasis on the report's sanctioning of the Indian's special status. It notes past federal and provincial government failures to accurately perceive and satisfy Indian needs. The present administrative task is to raise the Indian's level of living without taking anything away from him. Canada, especially through its Indian Affairs Branch, must provide the Indian with a number

of options to his present existence, and he must be free to choose his own way of life.
ADG

711   **MORTIMORE   GEORGE**
1969
TRANSCRIBED FROM TAPE FROM C.B.C. 'PREVIEW COMMENTARY'
BROADCAST JULY 2, 1969. Unpublished paper. Available from Indian-
Eskimo Association. 2 pp.

A free-lance commentator specializing in Indian Affairs comments on Chretien's White
Paper.   IVY

712   **MOSES   DONALD**
1969
FINAL REPORT: INDIAN CONSULTATION MEETINGS. Unpublished paper.
Available from Provincial Library and Archives, Victoria, B.C.   44 pp.

This report is based on meetings held with chiefs, councilors and band members
throughout British Columbia from July 24 to September 26, 1969. Part 1 lists suggestions
for projects using the monies of the First Citizens' Fund. Part 2 documents opinions of
band councils regarding the federal government's policy of 1969. Part 3 discusses the
necessity of having a British Columbia chiefs conference.   IVY

713   **MUNRO   DAVID A**
1969
THE INDIAN POLICY - A FLEXIBLE APPROACH. Speech delivered to Lethbridge
Chamber of Commerce. Lethbridge, November 19, 1969. Available from Information
Services, Records and Research, Department of Indian Affairs and Northern
Development, Ottawa (Speech # 3-6923). 12 pp.

Policy changes and problem areas are reviewed by the Assistant Deputy Minister (Indian
Consultation and Negotiation).   CCV

714   **NATIONAL INDIAN ADVISORY BOARD**
1966
MINUTES OF FIRST MEETING NATIONAL INDIAN ADVISORY BOARD.
Wilfred Bellegarde and R. F. Battle, chairmen. Ottawa, January 10-12, 1966. Ottawa:
Department of Indian Affairs and Northern Development. 80 pp.

The minutes of and speeches presented to the 1st meeting of the National Indian Advisory Board report discussion on education, resource conservation and development, employment and placement, clarification of federal and provincial areas of jurisdiction, welfare and community development, and the theme for the Indian pavilion at Expo
'67.   CCV

715   **NATIONAL INDIAN ADVISORY BOARD**
1966
MINUTES OF SECOND MEETING NATIONAL INDIAN ADVISORY BOARD.
Wilfred Bellegarde and R. F. Battle, chairmen. Ottawa, September 19-23, 1966. Ottawa:
Department of Indian Affairs and Northern Development. 66 pp.

Speeches and minutes of the 2nd meeting of the National Indian Advisory Board report discussion on the Indian Act, Indian Claims Commission, Migratory Birds Convention Act, and Canadian Youth Council. An address by R. A. W. Switzer, Dominion Fire Commissioner, to Indian chiefs and councilors on the subject of fire prevention on reservations is appended.   CCV

716   **NATIONAL INDIAN ADVISORY BOARD**
1966
MINUTES OF THIRD MEETING NATIONAL INDIAN ADVISORY BOARD. R. F. Battle and George Manuel, chairmen. Winnipeg, December 5-9, 1966. Ottawa: Department of Indian Affairs and Northern Development. 36 pp.

Speeches and minutes from the 3rd meeting of the National Indian Advisory Board report discussions on parts of the Indian Act, particularly enfranchisement, bands and band membership, administration of estates, administration of band funds, and the Canada Pension fund.   CCV

717   **NATIONAL INDIAN ADVISORY BOARD**
1967
MINTUES OF FOURTH MEETING NATIONAL INDIAN ADVISORY BOARD. R. F. Battle and George Manuel, chairmen. Ottawa, May 1-4 1967. Ottawa: Department of Indian Affairs and Northern Development. 101 pp.

Minutes of the 4th meeting of the National Indian Advisory Board report discussion of hunting rights, educational problems and proposals, standardization and promotion of Indian arts and crafts, enfranchisement, Indian health services, reservation lands, and housing. Appended are a list of discussion questions, proposals for revision of the Indian Act, information on Indian health services, and results of studies made on infant care and breast feeding including discussion and comparison of Indian and White populations.   CCV

718   **NATIONAL INDIAN ADVISORY BOARD**
1967
MINUTES OF FIFTH MEETING NATIONAL INDIAN ADVISORY BOARD. George Manuel and R. F. Battle, chairmen. Ottawa, August 2-4, 1967. Ottawa: Department of Indian Affairs and Northern Development. 73 pp.

The minutes of the 5th meeting of the National Indian Advisory Board report discussion of an Indian claims commission, the Migratory Birds Convention Act, and the role and value of regional Indian advisory councils.   CCV

719   **NATIONAL INDIAN BROTHERHOOD**
1969
STATEMENT ON THE PROPOSED NEW "INDIAN POLICY."Unpublished paper. Available from Indian-Eskimo Association. 6 pp.

Policy proposals put forward by the Minister of Indian Affairs will result in cultural genocide.   IVY

720   **NATIONAL SPIRITUAL ASSEMBLY OF THE BAHA'IS OF CANADA**
1960

SUBMISSION TO THE JOINT COMMITTEE OF THE SENATE AND THE HOUSE OF COMMONS ON INDIAN AFFAIRS. In Minutes of Proceedings and Evidence. No. 4. May 18, 1960. Joint Committee of the Senate and the House of Commons on Indian Affairs. Canada. 24 Parliament, 3 Session. Ottawa: Queen's Printer. pp. 349-352.

Observations and recommendations are made regarding Indian education.   JSL

721   **NICHOLAS   ANDREW**
1970
NEW BRUNSWICK INDIANS - CONSERVATIVE MILITANTS. In The Only Good Indian: Essays by Canadian Indians. Waubageshig, ed. Toronto: New Press. pp. 42-50.

Impressions of the socio-economic atmosphere on Malecite and Micmac Indian communities are conveyed. Discussed are problematic areas that are of stress to the Indians - areas where reform is long overdue. The structure of the Indian Affairs Branch, the new Indian policy (unanimously rejected by the Micmac and Malecite people in their submission to Prime Minister Trudeau in July 1970), discrimination inherent in the educational system, inadequate housing, health services, and the negotiation of aboriginal rights are all areas where Indians are determined to play a significant role in the process of change.   DGW

722   **NICHOLLS   JOHN   ENGLAND OSCAR**
1966
THE CAPACITY OF CANADIAN INDIANS FOR LOCAL GOVERNMENT ON THEIR RESERVES. M.A. Thesis. Department of Political Science. University of British Columbia. 142 pp.

Interviews conducted in 1965 with personnel of the Indian Affairs Branch and individuals concerned with municipal affairs in Ontario, Manitoba, Saskatchewan, Alberta, and British Columbia provide data for this study of the capacity of Canadian Indians for local government. The nature of government for Indians is examined in relation to the forms of local self-government operating for non-Indians. Evaluated is the capacity of Indians for similar administration of reserves in terms of legal competence, economic and administrative ability, and potential for future development. It is observed that federal controls and deficiencies of economic and administrative resources hamper growth of local government on reserves. Alternatives are advanced which are geared to facilitate assumption of responsibility for local government by Indians under the Indian Act. CCV

723   **NORTH AMERICAN INDIAN BROTHERHOOD**
1961
BRIEF. In Minutes of Proceedings and Evidence. No. 15. May 24-25, 1961. Joint Committee of the Senate and the House of Commons on Indian Affairs. Canada. 24 Parliament, 4 Session. Ottawa: Queen's Printer. pp. 579-601.

A brief was presented on behalf of the North American Indian Brotherhood's Grand Council and the Nova Scotia Council. Discussed are sections of the Indian Act, and local grievances. The latter include the British Columbia land question, and health services for Nova Scotia Micmacs.   JSL

724   **NORTHERN CITIZENS GUIDANCE ASSOCIATION**
1960
BRIEF. In Minutes of Proceedings and Evidence. No. 1. April 1 and May 4, 1960. Joint Committee of the Senate and the House of Commons on Indian Affairs. Canada. 24 Parliament, 3 Session. Ottawa: Queen's Printer. p. 74.

A short brief, expressing concern for the Indians of Northern Quebec, was submitted.   JSL

725   **NORTHWEST TERRITORIES**
1960
A BRIEF TO THE JOINT PARLIAMENTARY COMMITTEE ON INDIAN AFFAIRS. In Minutes of Proceedings and Evidence. No. 14. June 23-24, 1960. Joint Committee of the Senate and the House of Commons on Indian Affairs. Canada. 24 Parliament, 3 Session. Ottawa: Queen's Printer. pp. 1409-1411.

Discussed are the Indians of the Northwest Territories, legislation, education, economics, and social welfare services.   JSL

726   **ONTARIO HUMAN RIGHTS COMMISSION**
1964
SOCIAL JUSTICE FOR CANADA'S INDIANS. Human Relations (Ontario Human Rights Commission) 5(10):1.

It has been long known that Canada's Indians lacked full social justice, human dignity and equality of opportunity. This article describes some of the government and non-government agencies developed to cope with the legal and social barriers to full citizenship for the Indians.   ADG

727   **ONTARIO. Department of Public Welfare. Indian Advisory Committee.**
1960
BRIEF. In Minutes of Proceedings and Evidence. No. 4. May 18, 1960. Joint Committee of the Senate and the House of Commons on Indian Affairs. Canada. 24 Parliament, 3 Session. Ottawa: Queen's Printer. pp. 306-323.

A brief discussing the Indian Act was read into the evidence by the Indian Advisory Committee, Ontario Department of Public Welfare. Accompanying the brief is a commentary by the chairman, a Six Nations Indian.   JSL

728   **ONTARIO. Department of Social and Family Services.**
n.d.
INDIAN COMMUNITY DEVELOPMENT PROJECTS FOR FISCAL YEAR ENDING MARCH 31, 1970. Toronto: Department of Social and Family Services. 45 pp.

Grants totaling $1,000,000 were allotted to Indian Community Development projects, part of the 1969-1970 program of the Department of Social and Family Services with the people of Indian ancestry. Local involvement and Indian leadership were significant factors in the planning of these projects. A description of the 46 individual projects concerning housing, services, and social and cultural aspects is given as well as amount of the grant and the principals involved.   IVY

729   **PATTERSON   E PALMER**
1967
THE POET AND THE INDIAN: INDIAN THEMES IN THE POETRY OF
DUNCAN CAMPBELL SCOTT AND JOHN COLLIER. Ontario History 59:69-78.

The poetry of 2 former Indian administrators, Duncan Campbell Scott and John Collier,
concerned their Indian çlients. Although each man's poetry was romantic in its treatment
of the Indian, Scott's stress was on the savagery of the Indian and sought his assimilation
into White society. Collier saw the beauty and nobility of the Indian and opted for his
revitalization.   ADG

730   **PAYNE   MARGARET**
1962
INDIANS TRAIN FOR LEADERSHIP: A BRIEF REVIEW OF CURRENT
DEVELOPMENT. Citizen 8(3):20-23.

Leadership training courses offered in the different provinces are reviewed.   IVY

731   **PEARCE   TERRY**
1970
HUMAN PROBLEMS IN CANADA'S NORTH. The Labour Gazette 70:416-420.

Treatment of the arctic natives by Canada, the United States, and Denmark is compared
and contrasted by a Danish researcher. Canada's major problems in the North are seen as
human ones, with employment of the growing numbers of youth in the North being
cited.   ADG

732   **PRESBYTERIAN CHURCH IN CANADA**
1960
BRIEF TO THE PARLIAMENTARY COMMITTEE ON INDIAN AFFAIRS. In
Minutes of Proceedings and Evidence. No. 8. June 1, 1960. Joint Committee of the
Senate and the House of Commons on Indian Affairs. Canada. 24 Parliament, 3 Session.
Ottawa: Queen's Printer. pp. 781-790.

An extended brief was submitted, offering 15 recommendations. Discussed are community development, education, and off-reserve Indians.   JSL

733   **PROCTER   H A**
1964
SERVICES FOR THE ORIGINAL CANADIANS: PROGRESS REPORT ON THE
BUILDING OF HEALTH AND WELFARE SERVICES FOR CANADA'S INDIANS
AND ESKIMOS. Canada's Health and Welfare 19(3):2-3,7.

The associate director (Indian and Northern Health Services), Department of National
Health and Welfare, discusses health services for preschool children, school children,
and adults. The development of health insurance coverage for Indians is also briefly presented.   IVY

734   **PULFER   BETH**
n.d.
THE ADMINISTRATION OF BRITISH POLICY TO THE INDIANS IN THE

NORTHERN DISTRICT OF NORTH AMERICA, 1760-1783. M.A. Thesis. Department of History. University of Saskatchewan. Available with permission of the author, Beth Bilson.

The title has been verified, but a copy was not obtained in time to abstract it.   SLP

735   **QUEEN VICTORIA TREATY PROTECTIVE ASSOCIATION**
1961
BRIEF. In Minutes of Proceedings and Evidence. No. 7. April 26-27, 1961. Joint Committee of the Senate and the House of Commons on Indian Affairs. Canada. 24 Parliament, 4 Session. Ottawa: Queen's Printer. p. 182.

Unfulfilled treaty rights and promises are discussed by the Association.   JSL

736   **QU'APPELLE INDIAN ADVISORY COUNCIL OF CHIEFS INDEPENDENT**
1961
BRIEF. In Minutes of Proceedings and Evidence. No. 7. April 26-27, 1961. Joint Committee of the Senate and the House of Commons on Indian Affairs. Canada. 24 Parliament, 4 Session. Ottawa: Queen's Printer. pp. 214-226,246-247.

Unfulfilled treaty rights are discussed. Suggested changes in the Indian Act are proposed with reference to a separate Act for treaty Indians.   JSL

737   **RENAUD   ANDRE**
1965
ANIMATION CHEZ LES INDIENS. Bien-etre Social Canadien 17(2):43-48.

Community development programs geared to Indian communities are discussed with emphasis on the programs operating in Alberta and Manitoba, the operational aspects, and goals. Government Indian policy is examined, particularly education and the reasons for its lack of success. Some implications of a new orientation proposed in 1963 by Guy Favreau are explored.   CCV

738   **RICHINS   CLENWART PATRICK**
1964
ADMINISTRATIVE METHODS OF ACHIEVING PROGRAMME OBJECTIVES - AS ILLUSTRATED BY THE EDUCATION AND ECONOMIC DEVELOPMENT DIVISIONS OF INDIAN AFFAIRS BRANCH. M.A. Thesis. School of Public Administration. Carleton University. 152 pp.

The nature of administrative techniques utilized in the education and economic development divisions of Indian Affairs Branch is examined. The background of Indian Affairs and its general administrative orientation is summarized. Examined are internal administration methods in the economic development and education divisions as well as the coercive and persuasive external methods of each. Comparisons are drawn between the 2 divisions on the basis of the methods employed internally and externally and the nature of the programs being executed. It is generally concluded that methods vary with particular programs, that internal methods are subject to less variation than external methods, and that controlling, a method in itself, exerts a determining effect of selection of administrative means for achieving defined objectives.   CCV

739   **RIDDIOUGH   NORMAN**
1962
BETTER HOUSING FOR CANADA'S INDIANS. Ontario Housing 8(1):12-14.

Federal government policy towards housing for Indians is briefly presented.   IVY

740   **RODINE   H B**
1965
THE ADMINISTRATIVE STRUCTURE OF INDIAN EDUCATION, 1965 WITH
COMMENT BY EDWARD CROSS. In The Education of Indian Children in Canada:
A Symposium Written by Members of Indian Affairs Education Division with
Comments by the Indian Peoples. L. G. P. Waller, ed. The Canadian Superintendent
1965. Toronto: Ryerson Press. pp. 24-27.

Changes which have occurred in the administration of educational services within the
Branch since 1945 are briefly outlined. A table presents the 1964 reorganization of the
Education Division in Ontario. Edward Cross of the Caughnawaga Band adds a com-
ment.   IVY

741   **ROTH   O J**
1969
HEALTH SERVICES FOR INDIAN PEOPLE. In Voice of Alberta Native Women's
Society: Alberta Native Women's Second Annual Conference. Edmonton, March 3-6,
1969. pp. 22-23.

Duties of a Public Health Nurse are outlined.   IVY

742   **SALYZYN   VLADIMIR**
1966
GOALS IN INDIAN AFFAIRS. Canadian Welfare 42:79-81.

The circumstances commonly referred to as the Indian Problem can be best solved if they
are not grouped as such but are treated as individual Indian problems. Three distinct alternatives may be used in dealing with the problems of individual Indians: (1) complete
integration, (2) partial integration, and (3) complete segregation. The only solution to the
Indian problem in the long run is the integration of the Indians to such a degree that his
individual problems are no longer grouped automatically with those of other Indians. It
is important that whatever goals are recognized as desirable, they must be accompanied
by the appropriate kind of government program.   ADG

743   **SANDERS   DOUGLAS**
1970
A CRITICAL REVIEW OF THE NEW INDIAN POLICY AND NATIVE CLAIMS.
Unpublished paper. Available from Indian-Eskimo Association. 7 pp.

Two assertions of the new policy are discussed and criticized: (1) the division of powers
in the British North America Act which makes Indians a federal responsibility leads to
discrimination and inferior services and (2) the legal basis for special Indian claims is
untenable. As well the new policy is unimaginative, insensitive, and inaccurate. American
programs and policies should be studied and we should be innovating for our-
selves.   IVY

744   **SAPPIER   HAROLD**
1970
STATEMENT OF UNION OF NEW BRUNSWICK INDIANS BY HAROLD
SAPPIER, PRESIDENT, TO THE GOVERNMENT OF CANADA INDIAN
POLICY, 1969. In Bulletin 201: Recent Statements by the Indians of Canada, General
Synod Action 1969, Some Government Responses, Suggested Resources. Toronto:
Anglican Church of Canada. pp. 25-26.

The president of the Union of New Brunswick Indians presents that organization's position on the policy of the Department of Indian Affairs.   CCV

745   **SASKATCHEWAN**
1960
Brief. In Minutes of Proceedings and Evidence. No. 12. June 16-17, 1960. Joint
Committee of the Senate and the House of Commons on Indian Affairs. Canada. 24
Parliament, 3 Session. Ottawa: Queen's Printer. pp. 1029-1083.

Discussed in this extensive brief are the Indians of Saskatchewan, disabilities of Indian
status, economic problems, education, social services, policy, and administration of Indian Affairs. Included are 11 tables. Each discussion terminates with a summary and recommendations. It is concluded that off-reserve migration is inevitable and that the transition must be assisted by the government.   JSL

746   **SASKATCHEWAN. Department of National Resources. Indian and Metis Branch.**
n.d.
SASKATCHEWAN INDIAN AND METIS. Prince Albert: Herald Press. 1 p.

A 1 page pamphlet briefly summarizes programs initiated by the Indian and Metis
Branch from 1966 to 1970.   IVY

747   **SASKATCHEWAN. Indian and Metis Department.**
n.d.
TRAINING, PLACEMENT, ECONOMIC DEVELOPMENT. Saskatchewan: Indian
and Metis Department. 1 p.

A 1 page pamphlet states policy in regard to placement and training programs, and business loans for people of Indian ancestry.   IVY

748   **SASKATCHEWAN. Indian and Metis Department.**
1970
ANNUAL REPORT 1969-70: SASKATCHEWAN INDIAN & METIS
DEPARTMENT. Regina: Indian and Metis Department. 12 pp.

The powers, duties, and objectives of this department established April 1, 1969, are outlined, as well as those of its Administration, Placement and Training, and Economic
Development Branches.   IVY

749   **SASKATCHEWAN. Task Force on Indian Opportunity.**
1968

INAUGURAL MEETING AUGUST 9, 1968. Unpublished papers. Available from Indian and Metis Department, Regina. Various paging.

The principles and objectives of the Saskatchewan Task Force on Indian Opportunity are outlined at this meeting. The Task Force is composed of representatives from business, industry, the mining and petroleum industries, the University of Saskatchewan, the teaching profession, cooperatives, labor, and the churches, as well as representatives of the Indian and Metis people and provincial legislature. Five committees were set up: Public Sector, Private Sector, Selection, Housing, and Education.   IVY

750   **SASKATCHEWAN. Task Force on Indian Opportunity.**
1968
SECOND MEETING SEPTEMBER 13, 1968. Unpublished papers. Available from Indian and Metis Department, Regina. Various paging.

Briefs were submitted on employment, educational and training programs, housing, agriculture, wild rice production in the North, and the Molanosa Pulpwood Cooperative.   IVY

751   **SASKATCHEWAN. Task Force on Indian Opportunity.**
1969
(FOURTH MEETING) MARCH 28, 1969. Unpublished papers. Available from Indian and Metis Department, Regina. Various paging.

Reports were submitted on employment, a labor force survey of the Indian and Metis work force, education, provision of housing in urban centers, the recommendation that an inter-church committee be attached to the Task Force, a general survey of northern Saskatchewan, and the Cumberland House Project of Hunting and Fishing Resource Development.   IVY

752   **SASKATCHEWAN. Task Force on Indian Opportunity.**
1969
(SIXTH MEETING) DECEMBER 11, 1969. Unpublished papers. Available from Indian and Metis Department. Regina. Various paging.

Reports were submitted on employment, housing programs, agricultural programs, the progress of an outfitting industry established in the spring of 1969, education, and relocation projects.   IVY

753   **SASKATCHEWAN. Task Force on Indian Opportunity.**
1969
FIFTH MEETING JULY 3, 1969. Unpublished papers. Available from Indian and Metis Department, Regina. Various paging.

Briefs were presented on Indian Farming Opportunity and Related Education, the role of the church in urban centers, employment, housing, and the White Paper. An extensive brief, made up entirely of recommendations, was submitted by the education committee.   IVY

754   **SASKATCHEWAN. Task Force on Indian Opportunity.**
1969

THIRD MEETING DECEMBER 3, 1968. Unpublished papers. Available from Indian and Metis Department, Regina. Various paging.

Briefs were presented on special programs for people of Indian ancestry, ARDA programs assigned to assist Indians, vocational counseling for native people, employment, housing, and education and training.   IVY

755   **SERL   VERNON C**
1967
ACTION AND REACTION: AN OVERVIEW OF PROVINCIAL POLICIES AND PROGRAMS IN NORTHERN SASKATCHEWAN. In A Northern Dilemma: Reference Papers. Arthur K. Davis, Vernon C. Serl, et al., eds. Bellingham: Western Washington State College. pp. 8-68.

Historical background and provincial policies and programs in the development of northern Saskatchewan until 1962 are discussed.   Difficulties involved in economic expansion and assimilation in the area are described and related to the functioning of government programs. The economic problems are compounded by lack of educational skills and motivation among both Whites and Indians. Government programs tend to magnify Indian-White differences while perpetuating many of the problems they were designed to alleviate. There exists little potential for immediate large-scale development.   CCV

756   **SHIPLEY   NAN**
1968
TWILIGHT OF THE TREATIES. Queen's Quarterly 75:314-329.

Indian treaties and their implications for Whites and Indians are discussed.   IVY

757   **SOISETH   LEN**
1970
A COMMUNITY THAT CARES FOR CHILDREN. Canadian Welfare 46(3):8-10,26.

In 1968 a community controlled and supported child care center was opened in Sandy Bay to deal with the large number of unprotected children. This report traces the various stages of development and success of the project. It is concluded that the center has not only been relatively successful in protecting these neglected children, but it has also made it easier for the child who returns home to adjust there, aided the reduction of pressure that temporary absence from home can bring, and placed the child near his family, allowing the parent-child relationship to survive.   ADG

758   **SWANKEY   BEN**
1970
NATIONAL IDENTITY OR CULTURAL GENOCIDE? A REPLY TO OTTAWA'S NEW INDIAN POLICY. Toronto: Progress Books. 38 pp.

This pamphlet was written in protest to the Statement of the Government of Canada on Indian Policy 1969. It is considered that with this policy the federal government is attempting to accelerate the integration and cultural genocide of the Canadian Indian. It is felt that the struggle for social and economic equality parallels the struggle of labor in our society. United political action would increase their strength in the fight against big corporations and the government which represents them.   DGW

759   THATCHER   W ROSS
1968
OPENING REMARKS: MEETING OF THE INDIAN TASK FORCE. Unpublished paper delivered to initial meeting of the Task Force on Indian Opportunity, Government of Saskatchewan. Regina, August 9, 1968. Available from Indian and Metis Department, Regina. 7 pp.

This speech outlines the problems of unemployment, inadequate housing, and sub-normal educational standards faced by Indians and Metis. The Task Force is represented by business, industry, mining, the University of Saskatchewan, the teaching profession, cooperatives, labor, the churches, as well as representatives of the Indian and Metis people and the provincial legislature. The main objective is to find maximum employment for the native people.   IVY

760   THATCHER   W ROSS
1969
INDIAN AND METIS BILL: SPEECH OF THE HONOURABLE W. ROSS THATCHER, PREMIER OF SASKATCHEWAN. Regina: Queen's Printer. 8 pp.

In this speech to the members of the Saskatchewan Legislature, Premier Thatcher outlines the purpose, philosophy, and necessity of establishing a new department. It will coordinate all government programs, except agriculture, which are designed to assist people of Indian ancestry.   IVY

761   THOMPSON   P
1965
THE RESERVE TOMORROW. The Northian 2(3):11-15.

One day the Indian will decide he no longer needs the reserve. Indian culture has been replaced by a buckskin curtain which has cut it off from the outside world. Poverty and the loss of racial pride, self-autonomy, and self-respect are results of the reserve system. The dignity of the Indian must be re-defined and regained. Education is the only way of eliminating this culture of poverty. Indian parents must take responsibility for this recovery by directing their children's education. Integration is necessary as it means survival and providing for one's family. Jealousies and factional disputes must be avoided and the few available leaders must receive their people's support and encouragement.   ADG

762   TRUDEAU   PIERRE E
1970
REMARKS ON INDIAN ABORIGINAL AND TREATY RIGHTS: PART OF A SPEECH GIVEN AUGUST 8TH, 1969 IN VANCOUVER, BRITISH COLUMBIA. In Bulletin 202: Extracts from "Native Rights in Canada". The Anglican Church of Canada, ed. Toronto: Anglican Church of Canada. pp. 37-38.

Discussed is the position of the federal government in respect to its white paper policy on the Indian problem. This policy recognizes treaty rights but not aboriginal rights. The compensation for past injustices is considered redeemable by the practice of contemporary justice.   DGW

763   **UNION OF NOVA SCOTIA INDIANS**
1970
BRIEF. Delivered to Committee on the Constitution of Canada by Noel Doucette, President, Union of Nova Scotia Indians. Sydney, N.S., October 21, 1970. Available from National Library of Canada. 7 pp.

The federal government's responsibility under Section 91(24) of the British North America Act is discussed. Any procedure for review at that section must be decided by the Indian people.   IVY

764   **UNION OF ONTARIO INDIANS**
1960
BRIEF. In Minutes of Proceedings and Evidence. No. 14. June 23-24, 1960. Joint Committee of the Senate and the House of Commons on Indian Affairs. Canada. 24 Parliament, 3 Session. Ottawa: Queen's Printer. pp. 1325-1327.

Included in this short brief are 18 proposed amendments to the Indian Act.   JSL

765   **UNITARIAN CONGREGATION OF SOUTH PEEL**
1960
STATEMENT REGARDING INDIAN CANADIANS TO THE JOINT PARLIAMENTARY COMMITTEE ON INDIAN AFFAIRS. In Minutes of Proceedings and Evidence. No. 4. May 18, 1960. Joint Committee of the Senate and the House of Commons on Indian Affairs. Canada. 24 Parliament, 3 Session. Ottawa: Queen's Printer. pp. 359-360.

Suggestions deal with urban centers, integrated schools, correctional institutions, and Metis.   JSL

766   **UNITED CHURCH OF CANADA. BOARD OF HOME MISSIONS.**
1960
A BRIEF ON INDIAN AFFAIRS. In Minutes of Proceedings and Evidence. No. 10. June 8, 1960. Joint Committee of the Senate and the House of Commons on Indian Affairs. Canada. 24 Parliament, 3 Session. Ottawa: Queen's Printer. pp. 863-871.

Extensive coverage is given the role of the church, economic development, education, health services, administration, Indian involvement, and the Indian Act. A flexible approach with cooperation between Indian and White at all levels is stressed.   JSL

767   **WADDELL   K G**
1964
THE ROLE OF THE INDIAN AFFAIRS BRANCH IN THE MACKENZIE PAST, PRESENT AND FUTURE. Unpublished paper. Available from Library, Department of Indian Affairs and Northern Development, Ottawa. 45 pp.

The history of the role played by the Indian Affairs Branch in the Mackenzie is traced. The legislation and treaties which determine Indian hunting and fishing rights, land rights, and certain civil rights are reviewed. In addition the development of services for native peoples is outlined. The gradual shift to a western economy related to alterations in local ecology can also be noted.   CCV

768   **WAUBAGESHIG**
1970
THE COMFORTABLE CRISIS. In The Only Good Indian: Essays by Canadian Indians. Waubageshig, ed. Toronto: New Press. pp. 74-102.

Analyzed is Franz Fanon's theory of decolonization as it relates to the Canadian Indian experience. The relative stages of his model are examined as to how they result from a colonial dichotomy which determines social change. Indian-White relationships in Canada are viewed as being a colonial dichotomy maintained by the strictures of the Indian Act. Although Fanon's theory is partially applicable to the Canadian Indian situation, it is considered improbable that decolonization on a violent scale will be sought by the native population. For the effective means of perpetuating required changes, the Indians must recognize the Indian Act as being the main variable of the colonial situation, the strength of a united front, the imbalance of power which now exists, and the necessity for constructing an ideology.   DGW

769   **WAUBAGESHIG**
1970
INTRODUCTION. In The Only Good Indian: Essays by Canadian Indians. Waubageshig, ed. Toronto: New Press. pp. v-vii.

Remarks by the editor provide an introductory note for the contents of the publication. The purpose in compiling the articles was not to present a representative sample of native opinion, but rather, a representative description of Indian facts as they appear in Canada. A few of the opinions engendered by the editor are: (1) a system for native education is necessary, (2) the role of the Indian Affairs Branch must be surveyed, and (3) native communities must be prepared to offer long term plans and programs for financial assistance as well as guard against the abuse of funds.   DGW

770   **WEST COAST ALLIED TRIBES**
1960
BRIEF. In Minutes of Proceedings and Evidence. No. 7. May 26-27, 1960. Joint Committee of the Senate and the House of Commons on Indian Affairs. Canada. 24 Parliament, 3 Session. Ottawa: Queen's Printer. pp. 718-720.

Several specific revisions of the Indian Act are requested by the Association.   JSL

771   **WESTERN CANADIAN ARCHEOLOGICAL COUNCIL**
1961
RESOLUTIONS OF THE WESTERN ARCHEOLOGICAL COUNCIL. In Minutes of Proceedings and Evidence. No. 7. April 26-27, 1961. Joint Committee of the Senate and the House of Commons on Indian Affairs. Canada. 24 Parliament, 4 Session. Ottawa: Queen's Printer. pp. 266-268.

Regulations to protect archaeological sites on Indian reserves are urged.   JSL

HISTORY

772   **ANDREWS   RALPH W**
1962
CURTIS' WESTERN INDIANS. Seattle: Superior. 176 pp.

The work and life of photographer Edward S. Curtis (1868-1952) are reviewed revealing details of his contact with Indians of the American and Canadian west. His desire to record their traditional life style and his particular interest in religious beliefs are stressed. Curtis' life history is treated in the initial one-third of the book with the balance dealing with the tribes he studied. Photographs from Curtis' North American Indian include Canadian Plateau, Plains and Northwest Coast tribes. Ethnographic information recorded by Curtis accompanies each group of photographs.   CCV

773   **BAILEY   ALFRED GOLDSWORTHY**
1969
THE CONFLICT OF EUROPEAN AND EASTERN ALGONKIAN CULTURES: A STUDY IN CANADIAN CIVILIZATION. 2nd Edition. Toronto: University of Toronto Press. 206 pp.

Relying on historical and ethnographic data a reconstruction of the effects of European culture is presented for the Eastern Algonkian tribes in the 16th and 17th centuries. The second edition of the 1937 publication is prefaced by 13 pages of reappraisal of the origin of the Laurentian Iroquois and the discussion of family hunting territory.   CCV

774   **BARBEAU   MARIUS**
1966
FAMEUX PEAUX-ROUGES D'AMERIQUE DU NORD-EST AU NORD-OUEST. Montreal: Librairie Beauchemin. 284 pp.

General comments are presented on a number of famous American Indians. The collection is divided into East and West; Donnacona, Deganawida, Joseph Brant, Handsome Lake, Tchakta, Maquina, Legyerh, Mungo Martin, Sitka Jack, and Charles Edenshaw are among those included from Canadian tribes.   CCV

775   **BISHOP   MORRIS**
1961
WHITE MEN CAME TO THE ST. LAWRENCE: THE FRENCH AND THE LAND THEY FOUND. McGill University Beatty Memorial Lectures: 3 Series. Montreal: McGill University Press. 79 pp.

Some impressions of the country and the Indians encountered by the French upon their arrival in the St. Lawrence area in the 16th century are recounted. In particular the experiences of Sagard, Brule and Champlain are described.   CCV

776   **BREDIN   THOMAS**
1970
FROM SEA TO SEA: ALEXANDER MACKENZIE. Don Mills, Ont.: Longman. 117 pp.

Experiences of Alexander Mackenzie in reaching both the Arctic and Pacific Oceans via river routes, including constant encounters with Indians, are retold based on the "Voyages"published in 1801.   IVY

777   **BROWN   GEORGE W,   ROUSSEAU   JACQUES**
1965
THE INDIANS OF NORTHEASTERN NORTH AMERICA. In Dictionary of Canadian Biography: Volume I: 1000 to 1700. George W. Brown, Marcel Trudel, et al., eds. Toronto: University of Toronto Press. pp. 5-16.

The life histories of 65 Indians are included in this volume while Northeastern Indian culture from pre-contact until the 18th century is summarized briefly in this introductory article. Included is a description of the habitat, social organization and survival techniques of the rival Huron and Iroquois. The influences of the fur trade and missions as well as the Huron-Iroquois wars are reviewed.   CCV

778   **CHALMERS   JOHN W**
1960
FUR TRADE GOVERNOR: GOERGE SIMPSON 1820-1860. Edmonton: Institute of Applied Art. 190 pp.

Sir George Simpson's 40 years as governor of the Hudson's Bay Company in Canada are reconstructed from the Hudson's Bay Record Society and other sources. Description of Simpson's experiences reveals problems encountered in exploration, transportation, and survival. Attention is also directed to his family and includes details of common-law liasons between European men and Indian women.   CCV

779   **CHAMPAGNE   ANTONIO**
1964
GRAND RAPIDS: AN OLD HISTORICAL SPOT, 1727-1760. Historical and Scientific Society of Manitoba Papers (Series 3) 19:6-23.

La Verendrye and his sons, with Indians providing guides and information (maps), reach the region of the Grand Rapids (Lake Winnipeg and the surrounding country) in attempting to establish trading posts along the way.   IVY

780   **CHAPUT   DONALD**
1966
FROM INDIAN TO FRENCH: A FEMALE NAME CURIOSITY. Names 14:143-149.

Studying the naming patterns of female surnames of the Iroquoian, Siouan, and Algonkian linguistic groups of the Great Lakes regions, it was found that the tribe of origin was often used as the surname. Data are obtained from marriage contracts of Indian females and French males.   IVY

781   **CHURCHMAN   J W**
1967
TEXT OF SPEECH GIVEN BY J. W. CHURCHMAN, DIRECTOR, INDIAN AFFAIRS BRANCH, AT THE COMMEMORATION CEREMONY IN HONOUR OF CHIEF POUNDMAKER, AT CUT KNIFE, SASKATCHEWAN. Speech delivered

at Commemoration Ceremony in honour of Chief Poundmaker. Cut Knife, Sask., August 13, 1967. Available from Information Services, Records and Research, Department of Indian Affairs and Northern Development (Speech #3-6720). 3 pp.

Tribute is paid to Poundmaker, great chief and statesman of the Plains Indians, in a commemorative ceremony.   CCV

782   **CLUBB   SALLY**
1967
SILENT PARTNERS OF THE PLAINS. Arbos 4(2):9-16,39-43.

An historical outline of the Indians of Saskatchewan from earliest migration to present day is presented.   IVY

783   **DAILEY   R C**
1968
THE ROLE OF ALCOHOL AMONG NORTH AMERICAN INDIAN TRIBES AS REPORTED IN THE JESUIT RELATIONS. Anthropologica N.S. 10:45-59.

The similarities between intoxicated behavior and indigenous dreams and religious beliefs are considered in order to indicate that neither behavioral modification, other than economic dependence upon the White trader, nor initial moral aversion resulted from the use of alcohol among the Indians. The attitude of the Indian toward alcohol is thus contrasted with the Euro-Christian values of the Jesuit missionaries. Appended is an index of references to alcohol in the Jesuit Relations and Allied Documents.   WRC

784   **DAVIES   K G,   JOHNSON   ALICE M,   eds.**
1965
LETTERS FROM HUDSON BAY 1703-40. Hudson's Bay Record Society Publications 25. London: Hudson's Bay Record Society. 455 pp.

Letters from the Company men at the Albany, York, Churchill, and Moose trading posts draw attention to problems of defence, Indian relations, recruitment, supply, etc. Richard Glover's 68-page introduction provides background. Indian tribes mentioned include Blackfoot, Chipewyan, and Cree.   IVY

785   **DAY   GORDON M**
1962
ENGLISH-INDIAN CONTACTS IN NEW ENGLAND. Ethnohistory 9:24-40.

Attempts must be made to identify pre-contact ethnic units in order to profitably study the effect of European contact on New England Indian cultures.   IVY

786   **DEMPSEY   HUGH A**
1967
THE INDIANS OF ALBERTA. Alberta Historical Review 15(1):1-5.

The history of the Indian tribes of Alberta is briefly reviewed from their inception in the province to the period following World War II. Included are 3 photographs and 2 maps, indicating the distribution of tribes circa 1820 and the boundaries of treaties 6, 7, 8, and 9.   IVY

787   **DEMPSEY   HUGH A**
1969
INDIAN NAMES FOR ALBERTA COMMUNITIES. Glenbow-Alberta Institute
Occasional Paper No. 4. Calgary: Glenbow-Alberta Institute. 19 pp.

A list of Indian names for most Alberta communities presents translations and explanations, almost all of which were collected from native sources from 1960-1966.   IVY

788   **DESROSIERS   LEO-PAUL**
1960
IL Y A TROIS CENTS ANS. Cahiers des Dix 25:85-101.

A reconstruction is made of the events of 1660 in French Canada. Facts and hypotheses
present a picture of the psychological atmosphere prevalent in the colony and the war
tactics used by both the French and their Indian allies who were hard pressed by the Iroquois.   DD

789   **DESROSIERS   LEO-PAUL**
1961
LES ANNEES TERRIBLES. Cahiers des Dix 26:55-90.

Historical sources are utilized in a narration of the war between French Canada and the
Iroquois in 1661. The divergent interests of the Whites and Indians are emphasized.
Peace propositions and prisoner exchanges alternated with sudden battles and
heavy losses of human life.   DD

790   **DESROSIERS   LEO-PAUL**
1964
LA PAIX DE 1667. Cahiers des Dix 29:25-45.

This is an analysis of the events following the arrival in French Canada of the Carignan
regiment (1665) with a special interest in its influence on the French-Iroquois relationship. Several factors are discussed which bring the author to the conclusion that the 1667
peace treaty could not have lasted more than 20 years: the inferior French prices (compared with those at Albany) for furs, the proximity and growing power of the American
colonies who sought an alliance with the Iroquois, the hostility of the unsatisfied French-
allied tribes towards the Iroquois, and the trade of alcohol.   DD

791   **DRIMMER   FREDERICK, ed.**
1961
SCALPS AND TOMAHAWKS: NARRATIVES OF INDIAN CAPTIVITY. New
York: Coward-McCann. 378 pp.

Fifteen accounts of Indian captivity, 4 relating to Canada, are condensed and freely revised for this collection. These 18th and early 19th century narratives deal with treatment
received at the hands of Indian captors and subsequent life with the tribe.   Accounts include details of torture and massacre, servitude, and adoption experienced by captives.
Impressions of Indian survival tactics, warfare, socialization of children, kinship, and
adoption practices are recorded.   CCV

792   **DUFF   WILSON**
1964
THE INDIAN HISTORY OF BRITISH COLUMBIA: VOLUME I: THE IMPACT OF
THE WHITE MAN. British Columbia Provincial Museum of Natural History and
Anthropology. Anthropology in British Columbia Memoir 5. Victoria: Provincial
Museum of Natural History and Anthropology. 117 pp.

This historical study of the effects of White culture on the Indian cultures of British Columbia discerns 3 periods: the fur trade period (1774-1849), the colonial period (1849-
1871), and the period since Confederation. Two maps (pages 41 and 51) present population distribution in 1835 and 1963. A 20 page table, entitled British Columbia Tribes
and Bands - 1850-1963, denotes ethnic division and language, dialect, and regional
groups; tribes and bands (1850); names given by the Reserve Commission (1916); and
present band name and population (1963).   IVY

793   **ECCLES   W J**
1964
CANADA UNDER LOUIS XIV 1663-1701. Toronto: McClelland and Stewart. 275 pp.

Peace for New France could only be insured by crushing the Iroquois or by negotiating a
settlement with them. Various French policies in handling this situation are discussed.   IVY

794   **ECCLES   W J**
1969
THE CANADIAN FRONTIER 1534-1769. New York: Holt, Rinehart and Winston.
234 pp.

From extensive primary and secondary sources an analytical account of the French era of
Canadian history is presented with an appraisal of the spread of the fur trade and its effects on the colony and in Europe. The roles of many traditionally important figures are
re-evaluated and the significance of Indian diplomacy acquires a new perspective. Brief
reviews of Indian relations with missions, Indian spiritual beliefs, and warfare tactics are
included.   CCV

795   **FORBIS   RICHARD G**
1963
THE DIRECT HISTORICAL APPROACH IN THE PRAIRIE PROVINCES OF
CANADA. Great Plains Journal 3:9-16.

Because the direct historical approach has proved ineffectual on the Canadian prairies,
the direct ethnological approach and the inferential historical approach are 2 methods
reviewed and utilized in attempting to identify historic tribes with prehistoric remains.
IVY

796   **GLAZEBROOK   G P de T**
1968
LIFE IN ONTARIO: A SOCIAL HISTORY. Toronto: University of Toronto Press. 316
pp.

The description of the history of Ontario is introduced by a chapter on the fur trade and Indians which includes an overview of the inhabitants at contact.   CCV

797   **GOLDSTEIN   ROBERT ARNOLD**
1962
FRENCH-IROQUOIS DIPLOMATIC AND MILITARY RELATIONS, 1609-1701.
Ph.D. Thesis. Department of History. University of Minnesota. 325 pp. Available from University Microfilms.

French-Iroquois relations from 1609-1701 are examined to demonstrate the importance of the rivalry over fur trade in these relations, and to show the relationship of the conflict between French and Iroquois to the larger issue of Anglo-French imperial rivalry. A resume of the events prior to 1609 describes the intertribal warfare between the Iroquois and the Huron, Algonquin, and Montagnais. Although warfare ceased in 1701, the presence of the English in New York as allies of the Iroquois presented a fundamental economic conflict until the French were expelled in 1763.   JSL

798   **GREENING   WILLIAM EDWARD**
1961
THE OTTAWA. Toronto: McClelland and Stewart. 208 pp.

A summary of the major phases of the history of the Ottawa River region since the 17th century is presented. The first 2 chapters are devoted to description of the initial inhabitants of the area between the St. Lawrence and the Great Lakes; their subsistence activities; intertribal relations; contact with Brule, Champlain, and the missionaries; introduction of the fur trade; and warfare with the Iroquois.   CCV

799   **HAGAN   WILLIAM T**
1963
THE INDIAN IN AMERICAN HISTORY. New York: American Historical Association's Service Center for Teachers of History. 26 pp.

A pamphlet designed to aid teachers in comprehension of the cultural diversity of American Indians and to serve as a guideline in teaching and interpreting textbooks includes references to Canadian groups and principles applicable to Canada. A brief review of the roles of the fur trade, the French and the English in American history, Indian resistance to encroaching White settlement and culture, and stereotyping of the Indian are discussed. Publications for further reference are listed and the nature of their content described.   CCV

800   **HAINES   FRANCIS**
1970
THE BUFFALO. New York: Crowell. 242 pp.

Three chapters recount a brief history of the Canadian fur trade, the importance of the buffalo in the subsistence economy of the Metis and Indians of Saskatchewan and Manitoba, the rites used by the Plains Indians to attract buffalo, and the hunting methods devised by the Blackfoot.   DGW

801   **HALLOWELL   A IRVING**
1963

AMERICAN INDIANS, WHITE AND BLACK: THE PHENOMENON OF TRANSCULTURATION. Current Anthropology 4:519-531.

Based largely on early novels, the cultural assimilation of White men into North American Indian societies is examined historically. Fieldwork among the St. Francis Abnaki at Odanak, Quebec (1920's) provided 1 example of Indianization from the 18th century. This process of transculturization, contact which affects change solely in individuals, is distinguished from acculturation which affects change in socio-cultural systems. It is concluded that Indian social attitudes, values, and institutions (such as the adoption of Whites and Blacks) have proven more receptive to transculturites than White society which has no comparable pattern for acceptance and adjustment of newcomers. Consideration of other examples of transculturization from European and United States history cites the need for scholarly cross-cultural research.   WRC

802   **HOFFMAN   BERNARD G**
1961
CABOT TO CARTIER: SOURCES FOR A HISTORICAL ETHNOGRAPHY OF NORTHEASTERN NORTH AMERICA. Toronto: University of Toronto Press. 287 pp.

Many of the errors and contradictions revealed by an investigation of ethnographic documents relating to native groups of the Northeastern North American coast for the period 1497-1550 are summarized. Cartography and initial contacts with the Indians are emphasized in discussion.   CCV

803   **HOFFMAN   BERNARD G**
1961
THE CODEX CANADIENSIS: AN IMPORTANT DOCUMENT FOR GREAT LAKES ETHNOGRAPHY. Ethnohistory 8:382-400.

The Codex Canadiensis, also known as "Les Raret(es) des Indes,"depicts Indians, including Iroquois and Ottawa, and their material culture. It was likely produced around 1700.   IVY

804   **HORSMAN   REGINALD**
1964
MATTHEW ELLIOT, BRITISH INDIAN AGENT. Detroit: Wayne State University Press. 257 pp.

Part of Matthew Elliot's life history from the 1760's to his death in 1814 is reconstructed from historical and archival sources. Description of his position as Superintendent of Indian Affairs at Amherstburg and his activities in scouting and warfare during British-American conflict includes frequent reference to Indians. References are limited to mention of the Indian role in warfare, warfare tactics, demands, and difficulties involved in leading and controlling Indian warriors.   CCV

805   **INNIS   HAROLD A**
1962
AN INTRODUCTION TO CANADIAN ECONOMIC HISTORY. Revised Edition. Toronto: University of Toronto Press. 446 pp.

A reinterpretation of the fur trade in Canada dependent upon archival sources is presented with attention to the sequence of expansion and its economic implications. References to Indians include trading relations and desired goods, fur-bearing animals, care of furs, transportation, Indian-White relations, and tribes. CCV

806   **JAENEN   CORNELIUS J**
1970
THE MEETING OF THE FRENCH AND AMERINDIANS IN THE
SEVENTEENTH CENTURY. Unpublished paper presented at University of Western
Ontario. London, Ont., February 5, 1970. Available from National Library of Canada.
13 pp.

The French accommodated themselves to the Indian's ways, but also undermined the stability of indigenous culture. ADG

807   **JOHNSON   ALICE M, ed.**
1967
SASKATCHEWAN JOURNALS AND CORRESPONDENCE: EDMONTON
HOUSE 1795-1800, CHESTERFIELD HOUSE 1800-1802. Hudson's Bay Record
Society Publications 26. London: Hudson's Bay Record Society. 368 pp.

Seven volumes of journals and correspondence from 1795-1802 by fur traders and factors William Tomison, George Sutherland, James Bird, and Peter Fidler are presented. The 18th century advance westward of the Hudson's Bay Company along the southern and northern branches of the Saskatchewan River is the concern of this volume. Assiniboine, Blackfoot, Gros Ventre, Cree, Iroquois, Piegan, and Sarsi figure in the accounts. IVY

808   **JOSEPHY   ALVIN M JR**
1970
THE BOY ARTIST OF RED RIVER. American Heritage 21(2):3-49.

A brief biography of the artist Peter Rindisbacher is presented. In 1821 at age 15 he arrived in Canada and settled at Red River until the winter of 1825-1826 when his family moved south to the United States. While in Canada he painted Chippewa, Cree, Assiniboine, and Eastern Sioux. On pages 33-48 are reproductions of his paintings collected from varied sources including the museum of the United States Military Academy at West Point. IVY

809   **KENNEDY   JACQUELINE JUDITH**
1970
QU'APPELLE INDUSTRIAL SCHOOL: WHITE 'RITES' FOR THE INDIANS OF
THE OLD NORTH-WEST. M.A. Thesis. Institute of Canadian Studies. Carleton
University. 316 pp.

The history of the course of industrial school programs, particularly at Qu'Appelle, is examined as directed acculturation. A strong emphasis on Christian concepts and the arts and industries of European civilization is noted. It is felt that the Qu'Appelle school run by Oblate Father Hugonnard achieved relatively more success than similar school programs because the values and patterns emphasized did not differ greatly from traditional ones. Data on the school - the 1894 program of study, time-tables for 1886 and 1893, and a report on the status of discharged pupils up to June 30, 1893 - are appended.   CCV

810   **KERR D G G,   DAVIDSON R I K**
1966
CANADA: A VISUAL HISTORY. Toronto: Nelson. 170 pp.

A visual presentation of Canadian history from the time of early contact in America is given. Drawings, paintings, manuscripts, and photographs are adopted almost exclusively in compiling this edition.   DGW

811   **KERR DONALD GORDEN**
1961
A HISTORICAL ATLAS OF CANADA. Toronto: Nelson. 120 pp.

Canada's exploration and development are represented with maps accompanied by a brief text. Indian linguistic groups, explorations and fur trade, warfare, and Indian treaties are among those maps presented.   CCV

812   **KLINCK CARL F**
1961
TECUMSEH: FACT AND FICTION IN EARLY RECORDS. Englewood Cliffs, NJ: Prentice-Hall. 246 pp.

A collection of documents relating to Chief Tecumseh are presented with special emphasis on the strategies surrounding the War of 1812. Many of the sources are early Canadian records, and occasional references to Canadian tribes are included.   CCV

813   **KURATH GERTRUDE P**
1963
MODERN PAN-INDIAN DANCES AND SONGS. Folklorist 8:4-8.

Through visits and powwows, exchanges of dances and songs between American and Canadian Indians have resulted in a complex mixture of culture and arts. In addition there have been Euro-American modifications. New forms, all of them secular, have been developing.   IVY

814   **LAHONTAN BARON DE**
1965
A NEW BARON DE LAHONTAN MEMOIR ON NEW YORK AND THE GREAT LAKES BASIN. Edited with an introduction by Edward L. Towle and George A. Rawlyk. New York History 46:212-229.

A geo-political analysis written between 1710-1713 emphasizes the economic and strategic importance of the Great Lakes. A discussion of English-French relationships underlines the advantage enjoyed by the British through their alliance with the Iroquois.   IVY

815   **LANCTOT GUSTAVE**
1963
A HISTORY OF CANADA: VOLUME 1 - FROM ITS ORIGINS TO THE ROYAL

REGIME, 1663. Translation. Cambridge, MA: Harvard University Press. 393 pp.
Volume 1 of 3 vols.

The exploration and colonization of Canada until 1663 is recounted from historical and
archival sources. The Indians encountered by early explorers are described as well as initial missionary activities, Indian-White trade relations, warfare, and alliances.   CCV

816   **LANCTOT   GUSTAVE**
1964
A HISTORY OF CANADA: VOLUME 2 - FROM THE ROYAL REGIME TO THE
TREATY OF UTRECHT, 1663-1713. Cambridge, MA: Harvard University Press. 289
pp. Volume 2 of 3 vols.

The period from 1663 to 1713 during which colonization in New France was expanded
by emigration from France, establishment of missions, and far-reaching fur trade is reviewed. Relations between Indians and traders, colonists, and missionaries are described
as well as the Indian role in the French-English struggle for control.   CCV

817   **LANCTOT   GUSTAVE**
1965
A HISTORY OF CANADA: VOLUME 3: FROM THE TREATY OF UTRECHT TO
THE TREATY OF PARIS, 1713-1763. Cambridge, MA: Harvard University Press. 304
pp. Volume 3 of 3 vols.

The further expansion of the colonization of New France and its attainment of economic
significance during the 1713 to 1763 period is described. Brief mention of Indian-White
relations is included in reference to expanding settlement and French-English conflict.
CCV

818   **LARMOUR   JEAN   DRUMMOND   BERNICE**
1969
EDGAR DEWDNEY, COMMISSIONER OF INDIAN AFFAIRS AND
LIEUTENANT GOVERNOR OF THE NORTHWEST TERRITORIES, 1879-1888.
M.A. Thesis. Department of History. University of Saskatchewan. Regina, Sask. 290 pp.
Available from National Library of Canada.

Examined is the public career of Edgar Dewdney in the Northwest Territories from 1879
to 1888. The responsibilities he held as Commissioner of Indian Affairs and as Lieutenant Governor of the North West Territories are dealt with separately in this study.   Both
positions were held by Dewdney until 1888 when he was appointed Minister of the Interior.   DGW

819   **LENT   D GENEVA**
1963
WEST OF THE MOUNTAINS: JAMES SINCLAIR AND THE HUDSON'S BAY
COMPANY. Seattle: University of Washington Press. 334 pp.

In this biography of James Sinclair (1806-1856), a free trader from Rupert's Land of
Scotch and Indian ancestry, his part in championing the cause of free trade for the Red
River Metis is recorded.   IVY

820   **MACGREGOR   J G**
1966
PETER FIDLER: CANADA'S FORGOTTEN SURVEYOR 1769-1822. Toronto:
McClelland and Stewart. 265 pp.

During his 33 years in western Canada in the employ of the Hudson's Bay Company,
Peter Fidler travelled 48,000 miles and surveyed 7,300 miles, including many regions
which had been largely terra incognito. He had lived with and recorded the ways and
customs of the Plains, Woodland, and Barren Ground Indians. Based largely on his journals, his experiences and constant encounters with Indians have been recounted. Among
these are the Assiniboine, Beaver, Blackfoot, Blood, Chippewa, Chipewyan, Cree, Gros
Ventre, Iroquois, Kutenai, Piegan, Sarsi, Ojibwa, and Metis.   IVY

821   **MACKAY   DOUGLAS**
1966
THE HONOURABLE COMPANY: A HISTORY OF THE HUDSON'S BAY
COMPANY. Revised Edition. Toronto: McClelland and Stewart. 383 pp.

The history of the Hudson's Bay Company is studied from the time of its conception. In
the final revised chapter, the author mentions that the Company continues to be the
world's largest private trader. In 1965, $116,000,000 in fur alone was sold at its 3 auction
houses. The Company also leads as retailer in newly developing regions of Canada in its
continuing trade with Indians and Eskimos. Sales, excluding those of the Northern
Stores Department, have increased from $24,571,000 in 1936 to $243,029,000 in 1966.
A new member list of the Board of the Hudson's Bay Company in 1966 supplements the
appendices.   DGW

822   **MACKENZIE   ALEXANDER**
1967
ALEXANDER MACKENZIE'S VOYAGES TO THE PACIFIC OCEAN IN 1793.
New York: Citadel. 384 pp.

An edited version of Alexander Mackenzie's account of his second voyage, that from
Fort Chipewyan to the Pacific, is presented.   Mackenzie's impressions of his Indian
guides, Indians encountered en route, their clothing, dwellings, diet, and details of life
style are included verbatim.   CCV

823   **MAURICE   J**
1969-1970
DEMOGRAPHIC INFLUENCES AT YORK FORT 1714-1716. Historical and
Scientific Society of Manitoba Transactions (Series 3) 26:41-58.

Based on both French and English ethnohistorical materials, this historical account of
York Fort, Manitoba, from the time of its restoration to the English (1714), reveals the
complete dependence of the Indians on European trade goods for survival.   IVY

824   **MCCLELLAN   CATHARINE**
1964
CULTURE CONTACT IN THE EARLY HISTORIC PERIOD IN
NORTHWESTERN NORTH AMERICA. Arctic Anthropology 2(2):3-15.

Based partially on fieldwork conducted from 1948 to 1962 difficulties are noted in discerning the effects of culture contact among Indian peoples as well as between Indian and White. In order to understand the influence of the North Pacific Coast tribes, particularly the Tlingit, upon the social organization and trading patterns of the interior Athapaskans, the social units themselves rather than the oversimplified notion of the band must be determined. It is concluded that these units must also be established to examine the relation of Indian and White trade patterns.   WRC

825   **MCDONALD   T H, ed.**
1966
EXPLORING THE NORTHWEST TERRITORY: SIR ALEXANDER MACKENZIE'S JOURNAL OF A VOYAGE BY BARK CANOE FROM LAKE ATHABASKA TO THE PACIFIC OCEAN IN THE SUMMER OF 1789. Norman: University of Oklahoma Press. 133 pp.

An account of Alexander Mackenzie's canoe trip from Lake Athabaska to the Pacific is compiled from Mackenzie's own journal and other historical sources. Descriptive comments on the clothing, food, dwellings, and some social activities of the Indians Mackenzie observed are included.   CCV

826   **MCGUINESS   ROBERT**
1967
MISSIONARY JOURNEY OF FATHER DE SMET. Alberta Historical Review 15(2):12-19.

The Alberta portion of Father Pierre-Jean De Smet's peace mission from the Plateau tribes to the Blackfoot in 1844-1845 is described. An account of the Indians and missionaries he met en route is given, and a map, dated 1846, is included.   WRC

827   **MCKAY   W A**
1967
THE GREAT CANADIAN SKIN GAME. Toronto: MacMillan. 88 pp.

The history of the fur trade and its development in Canada is reconstructed. From 1534 into the 20th century, the author traces its evolution in relation to the exploration of the interior and the search for a northwest passage. Candid illustrations by Leo Rampen supplement the subtle humor and wit of the publication.   DGW

828   **MONTURE   ETHEL BRANT**
1960
CANADIAN PORTRAITS: BRANT, CROWFOOT, ORONHYATEKHA, FAMOUS INDIANS. Toronto: Clarke, Irwin. 160 pp.

The biographies of 3 Canadian Indians, Joseph Brant, Crowfoot, and Peter Martin, are given. Emphasis is placed upon the social context of their lives and their relationship to historical events. The description of the life of Joseph Brant includes his role in negotiations with the British and American governments and in the unification of the Six Nations and their migration from New York State to the Bay of Quinte and the Grand River. Crowfoot's life story (1821-1890) includes details of traditional Plains culture particularly buffalo hunting and the Sun dance. The gradual restriction of the Blackfoot to reservations and the difficulties of conversion from buffalo hunting to agriculture are described. The public service contributions of Peter Martin (1841-1907), particularly during 26 years as Supreme Chief Ranger of the Independent Order of Foresters, are recounted.   CCV

829   **MORSE   ERIC W**
1969
FUR TRADE CANOE ROUTES OF CANADA: THEN AND NOW. Ottawa: Queen's Printer. 125 pp.

From research in historical materials and personal exploration the Canadian fur trade canoe routes are described as they were developed and as they are at present. Information is provided concerning canoe construction, crews, and maneuvers as well as the Indian contribution to knowledge of routes and survival techniques.   CCV

830   **MORTON   DESMOND**
1970
DES CANADIENS ERRANTS: FRENCH CANADIAN TROOPS IN THE NORTH-WEST CAMPAIGN OF 1885. Journal of Canadian Studies 5(3):28-39.

French-Canadian contributions to the campaign, particularly those of the 65th battalion, are recounted.   IVY

831   **MORTON   W L**
1966
THE NORTHWEST COMPANY: PEDLARS EXTRAORDINARY. Minnesota History 40:157-165.

The role of the Indian and Metis in the fur trade is examined with a discussion of the rise and character of the North West Company.   IVY

832   **MORTON   W L**
1967
MANITOBA: A HISTORY. 2nd Edition. Toronto: University of Toronto Press. 547 pp.

Recounted is the history of Manitoba from the years 1612-1966. Its main concern is the agricultural settlement of the province to which all other themes are subordinated. Chapters relating to the Canadian Indian predominate with headings as follows: The Fur Trade of the Bay, 1612-1713; The Fur Trade of the Winnipeg Basin, 1714-1763; The River Lot and Buffalo Hunt, 1821-1856; and The Resistance of the Red River Metis, 1869-1871. Maps and plates supplement the content of the issue.   DGW

833   **MORTON   W L**
1970
THE HISTORIOGRAPHY OF THE GREAT WEST. The Canadian Historical Association Historical Papers 1970:46-59.

An analysis of the works of particular historians of the Great West (Canada from Ontario to the Pacific) is given. Those chosen have elaborated upon certain themes, one being the contact of cultures.   IVY

834   **NORTHLAND SCHOOL DIVISION NO. 61**
n.d.
INDIANS IN CANADA: PAST AND PRESENT - AN INTERIM RESOURCE UNIT
PREPARED FOR USE BY TEACHERS OF PUPILS OF INDIAN ANCESTRY IN
ALBERTA. Unpublished paper. Available from National Library of Canada. 72 pp.

Prepared for teachers, this booklet covers Indian history from Pre-Columbian times to
the present, using the traditional life style of the southern plains and the northern conif-
erous forest Indians as examples. The life of the contemporary Canadian Indian is discussed in the last chapter.   IVY

835   **O'MEARA   WALTER**
1960
THE SAVAGE COUNTRY. Boston: Houghton Mifflin. 308 pp.

Narrated is the story of the fur traders employed by the North West Company. Specifically, it outlines the adventures of the fur trader Alexander Henry the Younger during
the years 1799-1814. As an officer of the North West Company, his activities present a
perspective of life during the expansion of the fur trade into the West.   DGW

836   **O'MEARA   WALTER**
1968
DAUGHTERS OF THE COUNTRY: THE WOMEN OF THE FUR TRADERS AND
MOUNTAIN MEN. New York: Harcourt, Brace and World. 368 pp.

Discussed is the confrontation of Indian women and White men on the fur trade frontier, reporting events as documented in the fort journals and personal diaries of the traders themselves.   DGW

837   **PANNEKOEK   FRITS**
1970
PROTESTANT AGRICULTURAL MISSIONS IN THE CANADIAN WEST TO
1870. M.A. Thesis. Department of History. University of Alberta. 140 pp.

Attempts by Protestant missionaries to establish agricultural settlements on the prairies
in the 19th century met with failure.   Contributing to this were an initial opposition by
the Hudson's Bay Company and an ignorance of the realities of climate, geography, and
market on the part of the missionaries. A number of mission archives as well as the Hudson's Bay Company Archives serve as the basis of this study.   TSA

838   **PETTUS   TERRY**
1961
FROLIC AT FORT NISQUALLY. The Beaver 292:8-15.

The lighter side of life at the isolated fur trading posts in the Pacific Northwest in 1885
has been recorded by Edward Huggins.   IVY

839   **PHILLIPS   PAUL CHRISLER**
1961
THE FUR TRADE. With concluding chapters by J. W. Smurr. Norman, OK: University
of Oklahoma Press. 2 vols.

The relation of the fur trade to the struggle for dominance of more than half a continent is examined. Chapter 13, "The Iroquois and Anglo-French Imperialism," discusses the British-French rivalry and the important role of the Iroquois in this conflict. Scattered references to other tribes include the Huron, Abnaki, Assiniboine, Blackfoot, and Ottawa.   IVY

840   **PHILLIPS   R A J**
1967
CANADA'S NORTH. Toronto: Macmillan. 306 pp.

The native population receives mention in this narrative of the development of the Canadian Arctic and Sub-Arctic.   TSA

841   **POULIOT   LEON**
1966
DU JOURNAL DES JESUITES A LA RELATION: LA HARANGUE DE M. D'AILLEBOUST (1658). Revue d'Histoire de l'Amerique Francaise 20:345-348.

A discourse directed to the Huron and Algonkin in 1658 by D'Ailleboust, temporary governor, is reproduced. The Huron and Algonkin are reproached for treachery and threatened with war if better co-operation is not achieved.   CCV

842   **QUIMBY   GEORGE IRVING**
1960
INDIAN LIFE IN THE UPPER GREAT LAKES: 11,000 B.C. to A.D. 1800. Chicago: University of Chicago Press. 182 pp.

Reconstruction of the Upper Great Lakes Region prehistory and environment is described with reference to archaeological, geographical and botanical data. Chapters 11-13 deal with several aspects of the culture of the Huron, Ojibwa, Potawatomi, and Ottawa for the period 1600-1760. Chapter 16 is a brief description of the effects of contact with White men and the development of pan-Indian culture.   CCV

843   **RADISSON   PIERRE ESPRIT**
1961
THE EXPLORATIONS OF PIERRE ESPRIT RADISSON: FROM THE ORIGINAL MANUSCRIPT IN THE BODLEIAN LIBRARY AND THE BRITISH MUSEUM. Arthur T. Adams, ed. Minneapolis: Ross and Haines. 258 pp.

The written record of Pierre Esprit Radisson is presented with a foreword discussing the accuracy of his documents. Radisson and his brother-in-law, Sieur des Groseilliers, were French explorers and traders in the New World in the 17th century. In the spring of 1652, Radisson was captured by the Mohawks and was later adopted into one of their families. His experiences with the various Indian tribes as well as his relationship with the Hudson's Bay Company are recorded and commented on.   DGW

844   **RASKY   FRANK**
1967
THE TAMING OF THE CANADIAN WEST. Toronto: McClelland and Stewart. 271 pp.

This illustrated centennial edition recaptures the story of those explorers, adventurers, and seekers of fame and fortune who tamed the West. Wherever possible, the actual words of explorers and pioneers taken from their journals and diaries are recorded depicting the history of the West to the completion of the railroad across Canada in 1887. DGW

845   **ROE   FRANK GILBERT**
1960
BUFFALO TRAILS AND FUR POSTS. Queen's Quarterly 67:449-461.

The theory that trails made by buffalo determine the location of the historic fur posts is examined. IVY

846   **ROGERS   EDWARD S**
1969
INDIANS OF CANADA. Toronto: Clarke, Irwin. 5 pp.

A brief discussion of the Indians of Canada introduces 16 reproductions in portfolio plus 1 phonodisc. The contents of the folder are: an Ojibwa medicine scroll; a Jesuit map of the west, 1682; a speech of a chief at York Factory, 1743; a bill of lading for a trade canoe, ca. 1800; a map of Hearne's and Mackenzie's discoveries, 1796; a report of Treaty No. 7 with the Blackfoot, 1877; clippings on potlatch raids, 1922-23, and the Kenora march, 1965; an illustrated map of culture areas; and "Indian Voices"- song and protest on record. DGW

847   **ROSS   E D**
1961-1962
THE CANADIAN NORTHWEST IN 1811: A STUDY IN THE HISTORICAL GEOGRAPHY OF THE OLD NORTHWEST OF THE FUR TRADE ON THE EVE OF THE FIRST AGRICULTURAL SETTLEMENT. Ph.D. Thesis. Edinburgh University. Available with permission of the author.

The title has been verified, but a copy was not obtained in time to abstract it. SLP

848   **ROSS   ERIC**
1970
BEYOND THE RIVER AND THE BAY: SOME OBSERVATIONS ON THE STATE OF THE CANADIAN NORTHWEST IN 1811 WITH A VIEW TO PROVIDING THE INTENDING SETTLER WITH AN INTIMATE KNOWLEDGE OF THAT COUNTRY. Toronto: University of Toronto Press. 190 pp.

Presented in the form of an information guide for the intending settler, this study is approached in light of the historical geography of the old Northwest of the fur trade at the time of the arrival of the first Selkirk settlers. Discussed are relations of Indians with fur traders in 1811, and a description of the extent of the fur trade at that time. Information which would be of interest to an emigrating settler is given, for example, the ports of entry, a description of the East Winnipeg, Muskrat, English River, Red River, Saskatchewan, and Athabasca "countries," transportation and communication routes, and supporting enterprises in the region. Maps included are vegetation, fur traders' posts, regions

and countries of the Northwest, native population, principal fur trade routes, administrative departments and districts of the Northwest and Hudson's Bay Companys, and
part of Arrowsmith's 1811 map of North America.   DGW

849   **RUSSENHOLT   E S**
1965
SIDELIGHTS ON THE HISTORY OF ASSINIBOIA. Historical and Scientific Society
of Manitoba Papers (Series 3) 20:27-34.

Scattered references to the Metis and Sioux appear in this history of Assiniboia.   IVY

850   **RYERSON   STANLEY B**
1963
THE FOUNDING OF CANADA: BEGINNINGS TO 1815. 2nd Edition. Toronto:
Progress Books. 358 pp.

A reinterpretation of Canada's history from the earliest sources to 1815 is presented. The
conflicts and evolutionary progression resulting from the relationship of social organization to property are discussed. On pages 26-36 a description of the earliest forms of the
Athapaskan, Plains Indians, Algonkian, and Iroquoian cultures are viewed in the perspective of hunters, food-gatherers, and agriculturists. Chapter 5 discusses the evolution
on the Pacific Coast from communal society to slave ownership.   DGW

851   **SANDOZ   MARI**
1964
THE BEAVER MEN: SPEARHEADS OF EMPIRE. New York: Hastings House. 335
pp.

The historical importance of the beaver trade for foreign policy in America and Europe is
presented in this study of the period from circa 1630 to the mid-17th century.   DGW

852   **SAUM   LEWIS O**
1964
FRENCHMEN, ENGLISHMEN, AND THE INDIAN. The American West 1(4):4-
11,87-89.

The contention that the Frenchman was far superior to his English competitor in dealing
with the Indians is examined. A study of the literature of the fur trade reveals little evidence for such a generalization.   IVY

853   **SAUM   LEWIS O**
1965
THE FUR TRADER AND THE INDIAN. Seattle: University of Washington Press.
324 pp.

Analyzed from an historical perspective is the image of the North American Indian
which was created in the minds of the earliest traders and explorers. The presentation of
the fur traders' conception of the Indian is 1 dimension of this study's attempt at exploring frontier behavior and thinking.   DGW

854   **SHEPPE   WALTER**
1962
FIRST MAN WEST: ALEXANDER MACKENZIE'S JOURNAL OF HIS VOYAGE
TO THE PACIFIC COAST OF CANADA IN 1793. Berkeley: University of California
Press. 366 pp.

This historical study discusses Alexander Mackenzie's involvement in the fur trade and
his explorations in search of a trade route to the Pacific. Included is Mackenzie's own journal of the 1792-93 voyage which was originally published in London in 1801. Mackenzie's explorations were dependent upon the aid of the Indians who guided his party
and fed them when food shortages arose. In June and July of 1959 the author retraced as
far as possible Alexander Mackenzie's route. Appended are the chronology of Alexander
Mackenzie, his route of exploration, and notes on his original text.   DGW

855   **SKEELS   LYDIA   LOWNDES MAURY**
1968
LOCATION OF THE INDIAN TRIBES AT FIRST WHITE CONTACT IN
ALBERTA, CANADA. M.A. Thesis. Department of Archaeology. University of
Calgary. 113 pp. Available from National Library of Canada.

A survey of historic material culture is given for the tribes of Alberta. Tribal areas were
fluid during the 18th century. David Thompson's map of the area, based on a visit
between 1785 and 1812, is used to suggest archaeological sites. Historic locations of the
Cree, Assinbioine, Blackfoot, Piegan, Blood, Sarsi, Gros Ventre, Chipewyan, Slave, Beaver, Snake, Kootenay and Saleesh are given. Appended are excerpts from Thompson's
journals. JSL

856   **SMITH   DONALD BOYD**
1969
FRENCH CANADIAN HISTORIANS' IMAGES OF THE INDIAN IN THE
"HISTORIC PERIOD"OF NEW FRANCE, 1534-1663. M.A. Thesis. Department
of History. Laval University. 172 pp.

The evolution of the negative-positive image of the Indian in New France from the mid-
16th to the mid-17th centuries is traced in French Canadian historical works. Original
sources and secondary materials (19th and 20th centuries) are reviewed and related to
the social and political context in which the early authors (missionaries, traders, and explorers) and the more recent ones recorded their impressions. Individuals and groups
who have contributed to the projection of a positive image are noted. It is suggested that
the characterization of the Indian produced in the literature is related to the personality,
background, and experience of the author.   CCV

857   **SOSIN   JACK M**
1965
THE USE OF INDIANS IN THE WAR OF THE AMERICAN REVOLUTION: A
RE-ASSESSMENT OF RESPONSIBILITY. The Canadian Historical Review 46:101-
121.

Both sides share the blame for the introduction of Indians into the American Revolution. IVY

858   **SPRY   IRENE M, ed.**
1968
THE PAPERS OF THE PALLISER EXPEDITION 1857-1860. The Champlain Society
Publications 44. Toronto: Champlain Society. 694 pp.

An expedition of scientists, surveyors, and others led by Palliser intended to explore the
headwaters of the Assiniboine River to the foot of the Rocky Mountains and from the
northern branch of the Saskatchewan River to the 49th parallel. They had frequent contacts with the Cree, Blackfoot, Kutenai, Assiniboine, and Metis of the area.   IVY

859   **SURTEES   R J**
1969
THE DEVELOPMENT OF AN INDIAN RESERVE POLICY IN CANADA. Ontario
History 61:87-98.

The Indian reserve policy began in 1830, at which time the British Government replaced
its use of Indians as allies with a paternal program of gradually integrating them into
White society. Conflict between government agents and missionaries affected the success
of the policy, as did intra-departmental quarrels. The ultimate development of a benevolent reserve policy for Indians in Upper Canada was the result of missionary pressure on
the government to bring its services and policies more in line with missionary efforts.
ADG

860   **SYMINGTON   FRASER**
1969
THE CANADIAN INDIAN: THE ILLUSTRATED HISTORY OF THE GREAT
TRIBES OF CANADA. Toronto: McClelland and Stewart. 272 pp.

Presented is an illustrated history of the Canadian Indian from 1600 to the beginning of
the 20th century. It is the intent of the author to portray an abstracted view of Indian life
as it was or may have been at that time.   DGW

861   **TAYLOR   LEONARD JOHN**
1967
LAW AND ORDER AND THE MILITARY PROBLEM IN ASSINIBOIA 1821-69.
M.A.Thesis. Department of History. Carleton University. 137 pp.

Since Assiniboia came under the control of the Hudson's Bay Company and the Metis
population was a powerful majority, the relative infrequency of law breaking and disorder suggests satisfaction with the Company-appointed government. Those disruptions
which did occur were related to commercial rivalry and dissatisfaction rather than a
movement to change the existing government. The breakdown of effective government
in the 1860's was associated with a marked influx of Canadians. Also treated is intertribal warfare.   CCV

862   **THOMPSON   DAVID**
1962
DAVID THOMPSON'S NARRATIVE 1784-1812. Richard Glover, ed. New Edition.
The Champlain Society Publications 40. Toronto: Champlain Society. 410 pp.

David Thompson, working for both the Hudson's Bay and the North West Companies
explored and surveyed lands from Hudson Bay to the Pacific. Detailed descriptions of

the Cree, Plains Indians, and Piegan are given which include costume, material culture, subsistence activities, religion, and world view. Also mentioned are the Salish, Chippewa, Chipewyan, Kutenai, and Iroquois.   IVY

863   **TREMBLAY   VICTOR**
1964
LE TRAITRE DE 1603. Saguenayensia 6:27-29.

An historical account is given of the importance of the treaty signed by Champlain with the Iroquois, Algonkin, and Montagnais at the time of his first trip to Canada in 1603.   DD

864   **TREMBLAY   VICTOR**
1965
UNE EXPEDITION DES MONTAGNAIS EN 1609. Saguenayensia 7:122-125.

Comments are given on some of Samuel de Champlain's notes of a war expedition against the Iroquois in 1609. Champlain accompanied a Montagnais party on its journey and described its war preparations: the camp set-up, the ceremonial rites and the attack itself. DD

865   **TREMBLAY   VICTOR**
1966
DEUXIEME EXPEDITION DES MONTAGNAIS CONTRE LES IROQUOIS.
Saguenayensia 8:50-53.

This is the narration by Samuel de Champlain of a second expedition into Iroquois country undertaken in 1610 by the Algonkin and Montagnais. A brief presentation by the author points out the important parts of Champlain's narration which are the Montagnais war tactics and those suggested by Champlain himself to win the battle.   DD

866   **TREMBLAY   VICTOR**
1966
NEGOCIATIONS DE CHAMPLAIN - 1622. Saguenayensia 10:30-32.

Montagnais treaty negotiations with Champlain are related and the advantages of negotiation for both parts are presented. The importance of French influence on the Montagnais is stressed.   DD

867   **TRUDEL   MARCEL**
1968
INITIATION A LA NOUVELLE-FRANCE: HISTOIRE ET INSTITUTIONS.
Montreal: Holt, Rinehart and Winston. 323 pp.

Chapter 2 of this history of Canada under the French regime locates tribes and linguistic groups and presents brief notes on contact influences, aboriginal and Christian religions, and Indian contributions to Canadian culture. References to the Indian role in the history of New France are found throughout the text.   CCV

868   **TRUDEL   MARCEL, FREGAULT   GUY**
1963-

HISTOIRE DE LA NOUVELLE-FRANCE. Montreal: Editions Fides. Various paging. ·
II-vols.

Brief references to native peoples are found in this as yet incomplete history of New
France. The volumes published to date are Volume I, "Les Vaines Tenetatives 1524-
1603," and Volume II, "Le Comptoir 1604-1627."   SLP

869   **WASHBURN   WILCOMB E**
1964
THE INDIAN AND THE WHITE MAN. 2nd Edition. New York: New York
University Press. 480 pp.

This compilation of selected documents is meant to illuminate the most important aspects
of Indian-White relations. By presenting these it is hoped that the reader will recognize
some of the myths which have evolved out of historic events. The material itself is organized around 8 themes: first contact, personal relations, justification for dispossession,
the trade nexus, the missionary impulse, war, governmental relations, and literature and
the arts.   DGW

870   **WILLIAMS   GLYNDWR**
1969
ANDREW GRAHAM'S OBSERVATIONS ON HUDSON'S BAY 1767-91. Hudson's
Bay Record Society Publications 27. London: Hudson's Bay Record Society. 423 pp.

Andrew Graham served 15 years as Chief Factor at Severn York and Churchill settlements. In Chapter 7 (pages 143-212), physical appearance, material culture, religious
beliefs, subsistence activities, warfare, and mortuary rituals of the Cree are described.
Briefly mentioned in the same chapter are the Plains Cree, Assiniboine, Chipewyan, Gros
Ventre, and Ojibwa. References to Indians are scattered throughout the book.   IVY

871   **WRIGHT   GARY A**
1967
SOME ASPECTS OF EARLY AND MID-SEVENTEENTH CENTURY
EXCHANGE NETWORKS IN THE WESTERN GREAT LAKES. Michigan
Archaeologist 13:181-197.

Using historical documents, trade in the Western Great Lakes prior to the total disruption of the aboriginal exchange systems by the French fur trade (about 1660) is discussed. Three factors are considered: (1) ecology, (2) the social regulation of trade, and
(3) ceremony and status.   IVY

872   **ZOLTVANY   YVES F**
1964
THE PROBLEM OF WESTERN POLICY UNDER PHILIPPE DE RIGAUD DE
VAUDREUIL 1703-1725. Canadian Historical Association Report of the Annual
Meeting 1964. pp. 9-24.

French expansionism into the Great Lakes and Mississippi Valley regions in the early
18th century is examined. It is claimed that during the administration of Philippe de Rigaud de Vaudreuil the decision to hold the West against the English was taken and that
this position was essentially defensive in character. The use of Indian tribes by France
and England in the fur trade is discussed.   IVY

873   **ZOLTVANY   YVES F**
1967
THE FRONTIER POLICY OF PHILIPPE DE RIGAUD DE VAUDREUIL, 1713-1725. The Canadian Historical Review 48:227-250.

After 1713 it was considered urgent for New France to protect the Great Lakes country, the Mississippi Valley, and the New England border from English expansionist forces. The French policy consisted essentially of the formation of Indian alliances to resist the English advance. The strategy of this policy and role played by Philippe de Rigaud de Vaudreuil in shaping it are examined.   IVY

DEMOGRAPHY

874   **1966**
THE 1961 CENSUS IN THE NORTH. The Arctic Circular 16:47-60.

Comments on the 1961 Census figures are based on some notes written by J. R. Lotz. Indians are differentiated in 3 of 8 tables.   Areas include Northwest Territories (also specified Arctic islands), Yukon Territory, and New Quebec.   IVY

875   **CANADA. Department of Citizenship and Immigration. Indian Affairs Branch.**
1961
CENSUS OF INDIANS IN CANADA, 1959. Ottawa: Queen's Printer. 45 pp.   Also in French.

A census of the Indians of Canada for December 31, 1959, was published. The data are arranged by province, territory, and agency.   JSL

876   **DECORE   ANNE MARIE**
1966
DEMOGRAPHIC CHARACTERISTICS OF CANADIAN INDIANS. Variables 5(1):15-20.

Four tables present birth and mortality rates and age-sex distribution among the Indian population in Canada from 1902 to 1960 (time range varies in tables). Changes through time are explored.   IVY

877   **DUNBAR   MOIRA**
1966
THE ARCTIC SETTING. In The Arctic Frontier. R. St. J. Macdonald, ed. Toronto: University of Toronto Press. pp. 3-25.

The physical environment of the Arctic is outlined in terms of its land masses, seas, climate, vegetation, resources, population, present stage of development, and by comparing the American and Eurasian Arctic. Estimates of population densities of arctic and subarctic Canada are given in comparison to demographic statistics of other northern countries. In 1961, the native population of this region consisted of roughly 11,500 Eskimos and 50,000 Indians.   DGW

878   **GRAHAM-CUMMING   G**
n.d.

REPORT ON VITAL STATISTICS OF REGISTERED CANADIAN INDIANS 1964. Ottawa: Department of National Health and Welfare. 23 pp.

Data on Canadian Indians are discussed under provincial population distribution, residential status, religious status, births in 1964, sex ratios, mortality, infant mortality, average age at death, marriages, fertility, and trends.   CCV

879   **PICHE   VICTOR,   GEORGE   M V**
1969
A NOTE ON THE EVALUATION AND ADJUSTMENT OF REGISTERED DATA ON THE INDIAN POPULATION, 1960-1968. Unpublished paper. Available at Statistics Division, Department of Indian Affairs and Northern Development, Ottawa. 17 pp.

Available data on the registered Indian population, particularly data on births, are subjected to preliminary evaluation.   CCV

880   **QUEBEC. Bureau de la Statistique.**
1965-
ANNUAIRE DU QUEBEC. Vol. 47- .

Beginning with the 47th issue, the Quebec yearbook contains statistics on the Indian and Eskimo population derived from the Canadian censuses and provided by the statistics division of the Indian Affairs Branch. Data are included on Nouveau Quebec by region and by settlement.   CCV

881   **STIBBE   HUGO L P**
1966
THE DISTRIBUTION OF ETHNIC GROUPS IN ALBERTA, CANADA, ACCORDING TO THE 1961 CENSUS. M.S. Thesis. Department of Geography. University of Alberta. 134 pp.

A survey of the distribution of ethnic groups within Alberta reveals that while Alberta's 28,554 Indians are spread evenly over the 15 census divisions, the Index of Areal Segregation is much higher for them than any other group, indicating extreme clustering. TSA

MATERIAL CULTURE

882   **ADNEY   EDWIN RAPPAN,   CHAPELLE   HOWARD I**
1964
THE BARK CANOES AND SKIN BOATS OF NORTH AMERICA. Smithsonian Institution. United States National Museum Bulletin 230. Washington: U.S. Government Printing Office. 242 pp.

Prepared from notes collected by E. T. Adney throughout his lifetime (1868-1950), with additional material provided by Chapelle on the canoes of the Canadian Northwest, this monograph details the design, construction, and decoration of bark canoes including Micmac, Malecite, St. Francis, Beothuk, Cree, Tetes de Boule, Algonkin, Ojibwa,

Chipewyan, Dogrib, Slavey, Kutenai, and Shuswap. Information comes from actual canoes in museum collections, canoes examined by Adney, models of canoes, and descriptions of canoes and their use. In addition to Indian canoes, fur trade canoes and Eskimo water craft are featured.   TSA

883   **ALLODI   MARY**
1970
THE RED RIVER ARTIST: PETER RINDISBACHER 1806-1834. Rotunda 3(4):30-36.

A biographic sketch of the artist is given and 6 of his paintings are reproduced.   IVY

884   **BANERD   D**
1963
HOW MOCCASIN SLIPPERS ARE MADE. Moccasin Telegraph 23(1):12-13.

Mrs. A. B. McIvor of The Pas, Manitoba has described the procedures of processing moose hide and beadwork in making moccasins.   IVY

885   **BARCLAY   ISABEL**
1970
ART OF THE CANADIAN INDIANS AND ESKIMOS. Ottawa: National Museum of Man. 18 pp.

Articles of Indian and Eskimo art exhibited in the National Gallery (November 21, 1969 - January 11, 1970) are presented according to culture area. The culture areas are briefly described and the cultural significance of the artifacts is indicated.   CCV

886   **BELMONT   NICOLE**
1963
AMERIQUE DU NORD. In L'Art et les Societes Primitives a Travers le Monde. Nicole Belmont, Luc de Heusch, et al., eds. Paris: Hachette. pp. 277-313.

An overview of Indian art in North America by region is presented including Northwest Coast, Plains, and Eastern Woodlands. Characteristic motifs and art forms are discussed briefly in relation to materials, utility, and ritual or symbolic character. Selected aspects of social organization are noted.   CCV

887   **BOHANNAN   PAUL**
1965
INTRODUCTION. In Houses and House-Life of the American Aborigines. By Lewis Henry Morgan. Chicago: University of Chicago Press. pp. v-xxi.

This introduction to Houses and House-Life of the American Aborigines reviews the life, work, and influence of its author, Lewis Henry Morgan. Of his many contributions to current anthropology, his greatest are: his analysis of kinship terminology, his theory of the gens, and his holistic theory of domestic groups. In this statement, the author attempts to restate Morgan's theories and evolutionary position in terms of current problems. The publication itself is functional-evolutionary in approach in its attempts to study how man unconsciously orders and arranges the space around him.   DGW

888   **BRONNEUR   FREDERIC**
1967
L'ART INDIEN EXPLIQUE PAR L'INDIEN. Culture 28:386-393.

The relationship between Indian art, particularly that of the Northwest Coast, and mythology is discussed with emphasis on totem poles and argillite sculpture.   CCV

889   **BURNHAM   HAROLD B**
1965
CANADIAN TEXTILES 1750-1900: AN EXHIBITION. Toronto: Royal Ontario Museum, University of Toronto. 30 pp.

The Canadian textiles held by the Royal Ontario Museum are catalogued. Brief discussion of techniques and sources is presented which includes a brief review of Indian textiles reported at contact, their decorative styles, and dyestuffs. Twenty-six of the 95 catalogued articles are of Indian origin. The tribal origin, date, material, and technique are provided for each item.   CCV

890   **BURNHAM   HAROLD B**
1968
CATALOGUE OF ETHNOGRAPHIC TEXTILES OF THE NATIONAL MUSEUM OF MAN: AREA 6. Unpublished paper. Available at National Museum of Man, Ethnology Division, Ottawa, with permission of the author. 235 pp.

One hundred and eighteen utilitarian articles catalogued in the National Museum of Man's ethnographic textile collection are attributed to the Plateau and MacKenzie culture areas. Each item is accompanied by photographs and notation of location, attribution, provenance, name, measurements, condition, description, and technical notes concerning fabrication or provenance. The collection consists largely of beadwork, quillwork, or embroidery on skin or cloth.   CCV

891   **CANADA. Department of Indian Affairs and Northern Development. Indian Affairs Branch.**
1968
CANADIAN INDIAN ART FORMS. Ottawa: Queen's Printer. 7 pp.   Also in French.

An illustrated collection of Indian art and crafts is used to demonstrate available authentic Indian products. A brief text is provided which identifies each item.   CCV

892   **CANADA. Department of Indian Affairs and Northern Development. Indian Affairs Branch.**
1969
INDIAN ARTS AND CRAFTS RETAIL OUTLETS NO. R32-2069. Ottawa: Queen's Printer. 10 pp.

A list of retail outlets for authentic Indian arts and crafts is presented by region. The new symbol indicating authentic Indian arts and crafts is illustrated.   CCV

893   **CANADA. Department of Indian Affairs and Northern Development. Marketing Centre.**
1968

INDIAN ARTS AND CRAFTS. Ottawa: Department of Indian Affairs and Northern Development. 30 pp.   Also in French.

Numerous Indian art forms are presented and described in the catalogue from the Marketing Centre at Ottawa.   CCV

894   **CLARK   IAN CHRISTIE,   DARBOIS   DOMINIQUE**
1970
INDIAN AND ESKIMO ART OF CANADA. Toronto: Ryerson. 120 pp.

The majority of the 120 items illustrated from the 1969-1970 exhibitions in the Museum of Man in Paris and the National Gallery in Ottawa are attributed to British Columbia aboriginal groups. Eskimo art is represented and occasional objects from other culture areas appear. An index names each object and provides size, material, provenance, tribal attribution, date of collection, and a brief description of construction and function.   CCV

895   **CLARKE   GEORGE FREDERICK**
1960
THE BIRCH-BARK CANOE: ITS INFLUENCE ON CANADIAN HISTORY. The Atlantic Advocate 50(11):92-96.

The birch-bark canoe, conceived and fashioned by the North American Indian, played an important part in the fur trade and in the exploration and mapping of the Great Lakes and other waterways. Varying types are described and their use by Indians, voyageurs, and coureurs de bois presented.   IVY

896   **DARBOIS   DOMINIQUE,   CLARK   IAN CHRISTIE**
1970
ART INDIEN ET ESQUIMAU DU CANADA. Barcelona: Ediciones Poligrafa, S. A. 120 pp.

One hundred twenty articles of material culture, largely from Northwest Coast tribes and exhibited in Paris and Ottawa, are illustrated and described briefly. Name, size, materials, tribal source, and use, as well as lending museum, are included for each item. Items represented include both prehistoric and historic (to the end of the 19th century) specimens.   CCV

897   **DOCKSTADER   FREDERICK J**
1968
LATER INDIAN TRIBAL ARTS. In Pre-Columbian Art and Later Indian Tribal Arts, by Ferdinand Anton and Frederick J. Dockstader. New York: Abrams. pp. 213-257.

Material culture from the Northwest Coast, Plains, and Woodlands Indians is illustrated on 15 pages, 8 of which are in color. Each specimen is accompanied by a notation of date, tribal source, materials utilized and cultural significance. A brief introduction summarizes the role of the aboriginal artist and the materials at his disposal in each of the culture areas represented.   CCV

898   **ELLIOTT   JOHN**
1970

THE DEVELOPMENT OF INDIAN HANDICRAFTS. Unpublished paper. Available from Center for Settlement Studies, University of Manitoba. 6 pp.

To develop a viable year-round handicraft industry in the Maritimes, it is recommended that research on Indian culture be initiated to investigate marketable commodities, handicrafts be transformed from common trade articles to works of art that reflect the Indian culture, and markets sought at the national and international levels.   IVY

899   **FATOUROS   A A**
1966
LEGAL PROTECTION OF ESKIMO AND INDIAN ARTS AND CRAFTS: A PRELIMINARY REPORT. Ottawa: Department of Northern Affairs and National Resources. 99 pp.

Under contract with the Department, a study was made of measures to better protect Indian and Eskimo artists and craftsmen against imitations and reproductions. The report includes a comparative study of foreign laws, and an examination of Canadian laws.   The 11 recommendations include both actions possible under existing law and new measures (legislative or non-legislative).   JSL

900   **FEDER   NORMAN**
1964
ART OF THE EASTERN PLAINS INDIANS: THE NATHAN STURGES JARVIS COLLECTION. Brooklyn: Brooklyn Museum. 67 pp.

Clothing and other articles of material culture were collected by Dr. Jarvis near Fort Snelling, Minnesota in the early 1830's.   Feder attributes most articles to the Sioux and Ojibwa as a result of his study of Dr. Jarvis' personal correspondence and paintings by Catlin and Rindisbacher. The 55 illustrations include numerous examples of embroidery and quillwork.   CCV

901   **FEDER   NORMAN**
1965
AMERICAN INDIAN ART BEFORE 1850. Denver Art Museum Quarterly (Indian Leaflet Series) Summer 1965. 28 pp.

The first 9 pages of this booklet prepared for an exhibition devoted to pre-1859 material disucsses early collections and collectors, survival of early collections, and changes in materials and techniques. The scope and diversity of the exhibition is indicated by 43 illustrations of selected objects.   IVY

902   **FEDER   NORMAN**
1967
NORTH AMERICAN INDIAN PAINTING. New York: Museum of Primitive Art. 25 pp.

This illustrated book was prepared to complement an exhibition on the subject. Treatment is accorded to the Northwest Coast and the Plains Indian art types with illustrations of ceremonial coppers, skirt, robes, shield and cover, and drum.   DGW

903   **GRANT   CAMPBELL**
1967
ROCK ART OF THE AMERICAN INDIAN. New York: Crowell. 178 pp.

The results of fieldwork and research begun on rock painting in 1960 is presented with numerous illustrations and photographs. Rock paintings and engravings are discussed on the basis of style, technique, origin, locality, dating, and conservation . In addition, culture areas are considered individually with some attention to ecology, social organization, and cultural context. Canadian examples are featured in the chapters devoted to the Northwest, Plateau, Plains, Eastern Woodlands, and Northern Woodlands.   CCV

904   **GREEN   GORDON HENRY, ed.**
1967
A HERITAGE OF CANADIAN HANDICRAFTS. Toronto: McClelland and Stewart. 222 pp.

A survey of handicrafts in Canada is presented from material gathered by the Federated Women's Institutes in the 1960's. A section in each chapter is devoted to Indian products with attention to modern and traditional activities, materials and techniques, and tribal origin.   CCV

905   **GUNN, S W A**
1970
MEDICINE IN PRIMITIVE INDIAN AND ESKIMO ART. The Canadian Medical Association Journal 102:513-514.

The medicine man was among the best of Canada's early artists. Recent revivals of interest in primitive art have seen an impressive amount of international focus on Canadian Indian art. In the past few years several international artists and art shows have praised Canadian Indian art, especially those items containing themes of a spiritual nature.   ADG

906   **GUY   CAMIL**
1969
L'ART DECORATIF DES INDIENS DE L'EST. Culture Vivante (14):9-18.

A brief description is given of the principal characteristics of color and form in the traditional art among the Algonkin and Huron-Iroquois linquistic groups of Quebec. This type of painting is found on clothing and articles made out of bark. Several hypotheses of Barbeau, Rousseau, Speck, and the author are discussed regarding the origins of this particular art.   DD

907   **HABERLAND   WOLFGANG**
1964
THE ART OF NORTH AMERICA. New York: Crown. 251 pp.

The Indian of North America is discussed and illustrated. Of note are the chapters devoted entirely to Northwest Coast art and the Northeast. Included are discussions of tribal source, legendary or utilitarian significance, age, and medium.   CCV

908   **HAYES   CHARLES F III**
1963

THE LEWIS HENRY MORGAN COLLECTION. Museum Service: Bulletin of the Rochester Museum of Arts and Sciences 36:60-62,65.

Some of the archaeological and ethnolgical items from the Lewis Henry Morgan collection owned by the University of Rochester and housed at the Museum were exhibited there in 1963. Specimens include materials from the Iroquois, Abenaki, Algonkian, Ojibwa, Ottawa, and Cree.   IVY

909   **HEINRICH   THEODORE ALLEN**
1960
FACEMAKERS,   FORMGIVERS. Canadian Art 17:22-33, 47-48.

With examples from around the world, including the Northwest Coast in Canada, masks as a work of art are discussed.   IVY

910   **HOWARD   JAMES H**
1960
THE ROACH HEADDRESS. American Indian Tradition 6:89-94.

References to wearing roach headdresses from the time of Jacques Cartier are mentioned. The 19th century diffusion of the roach onto the Plains is noted. Roaches are grouped into 4 types, 3 of which are worn by Canadian tribes.   TSA

911   **HUNTER   JOHN E**
1967
INVENTORY OF ETHNOLOGICAL COLLECTIONS IN MUSEUMS OF THE UNITED STATES AND CANADA. n.p.: Committee on Anthropological Research in Museums of the American Anthropological Association and Wenner-Gren Foundation for Anthropological Research. 92 pp.

Four Canadian museums and 42 American institutions present inventories of their ethnographic collections. A large majority of these have materials collected from the native peoples of Canada. While the extensiveness of the inventory varies from museum to museum, many list the tribe, extent (number of specimens) of the collection, and date of the collection.   TSA

912   **JOHNSON   MICHAEL G**
1967
FLORAL BEADWORK IN NORTH AMERICA. The W. H. Over South Dakota Museum News 28(9-10):1-7.

Floral beadwork diffused from the East (Iroquois, Abenaki, Micmac, Malecite, and New England groups) northwest to the Great Lakes tribes of the Ojibwa and Cree. The Northern Plains and Plateau were the last major areas to be influenced by floral art. Variations in Ojibwa, Athapaskan, and Northern Athapaskan styles are noted. Examples of realistic floral, stylized floral, and prairie style as shown in the works of Northeastern Algonkian, Iroquois, Ojibwa, Cree, Dakota, Winnebago, Sauk, Northern Athapaskan, and Tlingit are illustrated in 12 plates.   IVY

913   **JOHNSTON   RICHARD B**
1962

ANOTHER DUGOUT CANOE FROM ONTARIO. American Antiquity 28:95-96.

A ,dugout canoe found by Charles Burrison of Cobourg at Rice Lake in 1923 is examined and described.   IVY

914   **KIDD   KENNETH E**
1960
A DUGOUT CANOE FROM ONTARIO. American Antiquity 25:417-418.

A dugout canoe raised from shallow water at Balsam Lake, Ontario, is examined and described.   IVY

915   **LEHMANN   HENRI**
1969
A PROPOS DE L'EXPOSITION "CHEFS-D'OEUVRE DES ARTS INDIENS ET ESQUIMAUX DU CANADA."Objets et Mondes: La Revue du Musee de l'Homme 9:193-214.

An overview of traditional life style and culture history of the Canadian Plains, Eastern Woodlands, and Northwest Coast Indians is presented. Eighteen of 200 objects borrowed from Canadian museums and displayed at the Museum National d'Histoire Naturelle, Paris, in 1969 are illustrated and their cultural significance, tribal derivation, and construction noted.   CCV

916   **LINNE   S**
1960
INDIAN AND ESKIMO ART IN HELSINGFORS (HELSINKI) 1960. Ethnos 25:214-224.

Among the articles displayed at the 1960 Sweden-Finland exhibition were wood carvings and masks from the Northwest Coast; deerskin shirts, Sioux embroideries, bows and arrow, hatchets, and peace-pipes from the Plains area; and Iroquoian dance masks.   IVY

917   **MIKKELSEN   LEATRICE**
1969
THE ANCIENT ART OF QUILLWORK. The Indian Historian 2(2):30-34.

Technical information is provided on the process of quillwork.   IVY

918   **MILES   CHARLES**
1963
INDIAN AND ESKIMO ARTIFACTS OF NORTH AMERICA. Chicago: Regnery. 244 pp.

To complement this collection of photographs of material culture, the author provides introductory statements under functional headings relating to food, homes and housekeeping, manufacturing, pre-Columbian clothing, personal adornment, ceremony and religion, Indian and Eskimo art, pre-Columbian music, toys, games and sports, smoking, travel, and combat. The examples themselves are identified according to cultural area rather than tribe.   DGW

919   **MILES   CHARLES,   BOVIS   PIERRE**
1969
AMERICAN INDIAN AND ESKIMO BASKETRY: A KEY TO IDENTIFICATION.
San Francisco: Pierre Bovis. 144 pp.

Presented is a classification of American Indian basketry types with representative illustrations. Selected Canadian basketry areas consist of Tlingit, Nootka, Kwakiutl, and
Thompson River regions. Included as subjects of discussion are the methods of basketry,
the methods of ornamentation, other specialized forms of basketry, and common utility
baskets.   DGW

920   **MITCHELL   BARRY M,   CROFT   DAVID A**
1968
A DUGOUT CANOE FROM RENFREW COUNTY, ONTARIO. American Antiquity
33:501-502.

A dugout canoe reported from the Ottawa Valley in eastern Ontario is described. Construction was probably before A.D. 1900.   IVY

921   **MOORE   LORENE**
1964
DOLLS OF THE NORTH AMERICAN INDIANS. Lore 15:2-17.

Doll types and their uses are discussed in terms of geographical divisions of North America, including areas referred to as the Eskimo and Canadian Indian Area and the Northwest Coast.   IVY

922   **MUSEE DE L'HOMME PARIS**
1969
CHEFS D'OEUVRES DES ARTS INDIENS ET ESQUIMAUX DU CANADA.
MASTERPIECES OF INDIAN AND ESKIMO ART FROM CANADA. Paris: Societe
des Amis du Musee de l'Homme Paris. 282 pp.

This Canadian material culture collection of 185 specimens is divided into 4 classes: Eskimo, Northwest Coast, Plains, and Eastern Indians. Each section is introduced by a resume of the cultural significance of certain art forms of the area. Each photograph is accompanied by a descriptive text that includes name, size, material, date, tribal source, and
cultural context, in both French and English.   CCV

923   **ONTARIO. Department of Lands and Forests.**
1961
THE BIRCH BARK CANOE. Toronto: Department of Lands and Forests. 8 pp.

This booklet describes the gathering and preparing of materials and their use in building
a birch bark canoe. Illustrations accompany the text.   IVY

924   **PETERSON   HAROLD L**
1965
AMERICAN INDIAN TOMAHAWKS. Museum of the American Indian Heye
Foundation Contributions 19. New York: Museum of the American Indian. 142 pp.

The form and function of metal axes traded to North American Indians is documented, indicating their use both in warfare and ceremony. Types described are the belt axe, the Missouri war hatchet, the spontoon tomahawk, the halbred tomahawk, tomahawks with hammer polls, celtiform tomahawks, and pipe tomahawks. Over 300 specimens are illustrated, including many collected or found in Canada.   TSA

925   **ROGERS   EDWARD S**
1965
AN ATHAPASKAN TYPE OF KNIFE. National Museum of Canada Anthropology Papers 9. Ottawa: Queen's Printer. 16 pp.

Seven knives of unusual shape are examined. It is suggested that the knives come from Indian and Eskimo groups in Alaska and the Northwest Territories. Also discussed are the probable place of manufacture, age, and use of the knives. Athapaskan and Tlingit sources are posited for the Indian knives.   JSL

926   **ROGERS   EDWARD S**
1965
THE DUGOUT CANOE IN ONTARIO. American Antiquity 30:454-459.

Utilizing published and unpublished sources as well as Indian informants and Euro-Americans, it is postulated that the dugout canoe in Ontario was adopted from Euro-Americans or from Indian immigrants from the south.   IVY

927   **SEGUIN   ROBERT LIONEL**
1963
LES TECHNIQUES AGRICOLES EN NOUVELLE-FRANCE. Cahiers des Dix 28:255-288.

Several documents written at the beginning of the 17th century in New France describe the agricultural and horticultural techniques. A portion of the article is concerned with specific Indian techniques: the making of the implements, planting and seeds, and the preservation of the products.   DD

928   **SETON   JULIA M**
1962
AMERICAN INDIAN ARTS: A WAY OF LIFE. New York: Ronald Press. 246 pp.

The author has drawn representative samples from tribes in the United States and Canada to convey the strength and intrinsic value of the Indian crafts and arts. Native arts are presented with sufficient instructions for the reader to recreate dwellings, clothing, woven items, leather work, beadwork, quillwork, jewelry, baskets, pots and pipes, musical instruments, owner sticks, and pictorial arts. The writings and drawings of the author's late husband, Ernest Thompson Seton, assist this reconstruction.   DGW

929   **TRUDEL   MARCEL**
1965
LA RENCONTRE DES CULTURES. Revue d'Histoire de l'Amerique Francaise 18:477-516.

This article describes the impact of the French culture on the Canadian Indian and vice-versa, at the beginning of the 17th century. The second part of the article describes the Indians' admiration for the French material culture: clothing, jewelry, firearms, and recipes for the preparation of food and drinks. It is concluded that beliefs will•meet less ready acceptance by the Indian.   DD

930   **VERMANDER   JOSEPH**
1966
THE USE OF THE BOW BY OUR INDIANS. Historical and Scientific Society of Manitoba Transactions (Series 3) 22:67-85.

The methods and materials used by the Indians of Manitoba in making bows, strings, and arrows are described. Also discussed are the variations on drawing the bow, the release, aiming, and accuracy. Examples of errors made by painters and illustrators of the early 19th century in depicting the bow and arrow are given.   IVY

931   **WEBSTER   DONALD B**
1967
INDIAN TRADE SILVER. Canadian Antiques Collector 2(7):11-13.

Articles made with trade silver are discussed in text and with photographs.   IVY

932   **WINGERT   PAUL S**
1962
PRIMITIVE ART: ITS TRADITIONS AND STYLES. New York: Oxford Univeristy Press. 421 pp.

American Indian material culture is examined from pages 329 to 368 of this discussion of primitive art styles and traditions. Tribal art is considered in pages 339 to 368 and includes brief reviews of the development of traditions in the major culture areas.   CCV

933   **WOOD   KATHLEEN**
1969
PAUL KANE SKETCHES. Rotunda 2(1):4-15.

Twenty field sketches (water-color, pencil) by Paul Kane, which have never before been published, are reproduced. Included are portrait sketches and drawings of canoes and lodges, mainly Ojibwa.   IVY

EDUCATION

934   **1962**
INDIAN YOUTH RECEIVE EDUCATION: "UPGRADING"APPROACH IS SUCCESSFUL. Canadian Home and School 22(1):15-16.

Saskatchewan's up-grading program for Indian youth is described. The program aids youth to qualify for entrance into a trade or vocational school by providing remedial training.   ADG

935   **1963**

VOCATIONAL EDUCATION AT YELLOWKNIFE, N.W.T. Technical and Vocational Education in Canada 2(1):31-32.

Training and employment aspects of Sir John Franklin Vocational High School in Yellowknife, Northwest Territories, are briefly reported.   IVY

936   **1965**

APPENDICES. In The Education of Indian Children in Canada: A Symposium Written by Members of Indian Affairs Education Division with Comments by the Indian Peoples. L. G. P. Waller, ed. The Canadian Superintendent 1965. Toronto: Ryerson Press. pp. 105-129.

Included are: (1) administration chart, Education Division; (2) Indian school legislation - extract from the Indian Act, 1951; (3) Treaty No. 7, 1877; (4) table showing Indian schools by provinces, March, 1964; (5) table showing Indian enrollment, January, 1964; (6) table showing Indian residential schools, January, 1964; (7) table showing Indian enrollment by province, January, 1964; and (8) bibliography.   IVY

937   **1967**

AN ANALYSIS FROM AN INDIAN POINT OF VIEW. In National Conference on Indian and Northern Education Saskatoon 1967. Mary Anne LaVallee, ed. n.p.: Society for Indian and Northern Education and Extension Division, University of Saskatchewan. pp. 111-128.

Native people must become actively involved in education and politics. The major share in the search for equality and self-determination is a responsibility of the native people. Topics discussed in this paper include school dropouts, curriculum, and integrated schooling. Religious teaching for Indian children must be re-evaluated for natives must find spiritual fulfillment. Native people must recognize and accept strong, decisive native leadership - male or female - and support their own academically educated and economically successful people.   IVY

938   **1967**

CITIZENSHIP PROJECTS - CANADIAN INDIAN WORKSHOP. Citizen 13(1):27-29.

The Canadian Indian Workshop was sponsored by the Canadian Indian Youth Council and the University of Manitoba. Designed for young Indians with university status, it was held at the University of Manitoba from July 12 to August 12, 1966. The program included formal lectures, assignments and examinations. Daily work sessions were held which focused on contemporary issues affecting the Indians.   ADG

939   **1967**

INDIANS LEARN FOREST SKILLS AT CHILCOTIN TRAINING CENTRE. Hiballer 18(1):37-42.

Chilcotin Forest Training Centre in British Columbia is designed to train Indians in forestry and other vocational and technical skills. Sponsored by the federal government (Indian Affairs Branch), the Indians run their own logging operation and sawmill and are building the training complex where they will work, live, and learn.   IVY

940   **1968**
MODERN SCHOOL FOR AKIAVIK. School and Society 96:99-100,117.

Plans for a new school for 160 Indian, Eskimo and other children are discussed. At the present time the pupils are attending classes in a portable classroom. It is hoped that school facilities for every child in the North will exist by 1971.   ADG

941   **1970**
ALBERTA STUDENTS TUTOR LOCAL INDIAN CHILDREN. University Affairs 11(2):20.

A free tutoring service for Indian youth is provided by University of Alberta students at the Edmonton campus.   ADG

942   **1970**
CENTRE TO IMPROVE OPPORTUNITY FOR INDIAN STUDENTS. University Affairs 11(9):16.

Plans for an Indian Education Research and Resource Centre in British Columbia are discussed. The center hopes to improve the quality and type of education provided Indian children through special training for Indian teachers, and the provision of current resource materials and aids related to the education of the Indian.   ADG

943   **1970**
HOW MANY NATIVE INDIANS IN CANADIAN UNIVERSITIES? University Affairs 11(7):16.

According to the Department of Indian Affairs and Northern Development, 225, 293, and 337 Indian pupils were enrolled in Canadian universities for the years 1967-68, 1968-69, and 1969-70 respectively.   ADG

944   **1970**
INTEGRATION OR ASSIMILATION. The British Columbia School Trustee 26(2):15-18.

In this interview with Fred Favel, editor of The First Citizen, integrated schooling and differences in Indian and White cultures are discussed.   IVY

945   **1970**
ONTARIO REGION - DEPARTMENT OF INDIAN AFFAIRS. Ontario Education 2(2):18-19.

A learning resource center at Mount Elgin School serves the Chippewa and Oneida Reserves near London, Ontario. Mrs. Leona Hendrick, a Chippewa, works as a lay helper to the librarian.   IVY

946   **1970**
OUR LITTLE BOOK WRITERS OF ONTARIO. Tawow 1(1):32-36.

Reading booklets prepared by primary Indian students are discussed.   IVY

947   **ABU-LABAN   B**
1965
IN-GROUP ORIENTATION AND SELF-CONCEPTIONS OF INDIAN AND NON-INDIAN STUDENTS IN AN INTEGRATED SCHOOL. Alberta Journal of Educational Research 11:118-194.

The inter-ethnic relation patterns and self-attitudes of a group of Indian students were compared with those of a matched group of non-Indian students. Interviews with these students revealed several findings: (1) friendship patterns of both Indian and White students were in-group oriented, (2) White children focused both their likes and dislikes on other White children, but the likes of Indian children were oriented toward the Indians and their dislikes were focused on the Whites, (3) both groups appeared relatively tolerant toward each other; however, only 1 White child indicated he would marry an Indian while 52 percent of the Indians were favorable to marriages with Whites, and (4) it was found that ethnic group identification was a more salient feature of self-concept for Indians than Whites. It was suggested that this is due to being affected by the in-group orientation of the Indian group under study. College attendance and high occupational aspirations were also a significant aspect of the Indian child's identity. It was concluded that (1) if integrated schooling provides feedback that differentiates, it can enhance ethnic identity, (2) intense in-group interaction and voluntary or forced segregation can also increase self-awareness of minority group status, and (3) retention of one's Indian identity is due, in part, to other aspects of integrated high schools such as segregated boarding facilities, high visibility, and specific patterns of selecting one's associations.   ADG

948   **ABU-LABAN   BAHA**
1966
THE IMPACT OF ETHNICITY AND OCCUPATIONAL BACKGROUND ON THE ASPIRATIONS OF CANADIAN YOUTH. Sociological Inquiry 36:116-123.

It was hypothesized that Indians, 7 percent of the population of a coeducational suburban high school in Edmonton, would acquire a set of middle class values which would reflect high aspirations and that they would exhibit a high degree of participation in school activities. In the spring of 1962, interviews were conducted at this school with 47 Indian students (total population) and 48 White students who were selected to match Indian subjects with respect to school class and composition. It was found that (1) the difference in aspirational level between Indian and non-Indian children of manual workers appears negligible, (2) occupational aspirations of Indian and non-Indian were fairly well crystallized before entry into high school, (3) both Indian and non-Indian females whose fathers had manual careers had a high aspirational level, and (4) there was no major difference between Indian and non-Indian membership in school organizations.   IVY

949   **ADAMS   HOWARD**
n.d.
EDUCATION OR BRAINWASHING. Unpublished paper. Available from National Library of Canada. 3 pp.

This account is a review of educational statistics, giving reasons to justify the high dropout rate among the Canadian Indian.   HCV

950   **ADAMS   HOWARD J**
1967
COMMENTS. In National Conference on Indian and Northern Education Saskatoon
1967. Mary Anne LaVallee, ed. n.p.: Society for Indian and Northern Education and
Extension Division, University of Saskatchewan. pp. 40-41.

Comments are expressed on the speeches of Sidney Fineday and Mrs. Hattie Fergusson.
A brief criticism of textbooks is given.   IVY

951   **ADAMS   HOWARD J**
1967
OPENING REMARKS BY CHAIRMAN. In National Conference on Indian and
Northern Education Saskatoon 1967. Mary Anne LaVallee, ed. n.p.: Society for Indian
and Northern Education and Extension Division, University of Saskatchewan. pp. 14-
17.

The conference is focused in the direction of where, how, and why the educational system has failed the native people; the blame lies not with the Indians, Eskimos, and
Metis. Comparing the Indian Act and the Public School Act, it is evident that discriminatory and harsh policies of the past still exist today. Non-native delegates are asked to recognize their cultural bias and listen to the speakers, who are all Indian, Eskimo, and
Metis, with an open mind.   IVY

952   **ADAMS   W A**
1965
NORTH - THE NEW LOOK: A REPORT ON NORTHLAND SCHOOL DIVISION.
Alberta School Trustee 35(5):10-11,20.

Established in 1960, the Northland School Division brought into 1 organization a number of schools including federally operated Indian schools which had accepted Metis and
other children as a courtesy, Metis colony schools, public and separate schools, and both
Catholic and Protestant mission schools. A report on teacher qualifications and recruitment, instructional programs (particularly reading tests for native students), and opportunities for post-elementary education is given.   IVY

953   **ADVISORY COMMITTEE ON EDUCATION FOR PUPILS OF INDIAN
ANCESTRY**
1966
EDUCATION FOR PUPILS OF INDIAN ANCESTRY. Unpublished statement
presented to the Honourable G. J. Trapp, Minister of Education, Government of
Saskatchewan. June 10, 1966. Available from National Library of Canada. 16 pp.

This paper is a series of suggestions to the Saskatchewan government with respect to the
improvement of educational offerings for Indian students.   HCV

954   **AITON   GRACE**
1963
THE HISTORY OF THE INDIAN COLLEGE AND EARLY SCHOOL DAYS IN
SUSSEX VALE. New Brunswick Historical Society Collections 18:159-165.

Under the auspices of The Society for the Propagation of the Gospel, an Indian school
was constructed at Sussex Vale, New Brunswick, in 1787. By 1792 an Indian College had

also been built. The majority of students were White. To gain instruction in trades and farming, Indians were apprenticed out to settlers for part of each year. In 1826 the College closed.   IVY

955   **ANDERSON   FRANCIS GARFIELD**
1969
PERSONAL CONTACT AFFECTING CITY CHILDREN'S KNOWLEDGE OF AND ATTITUDES TOWARD ALBERTA INDIANS. M.Ed. Thesis. Department of Curriculum and Instruction. University of Calgary. 113 pp. Available from National Library of Canada.

From Calgary middle class public schools 133 grade 4 children were studied to determine the extent of change in attitude and knowledge of Indians following personal contact in the school milieu, and the correlation between knowledge and attitude before and after contact. The correlation between city children's knowledge of and attitude towards Indians and reading ability and intelligence was measured as well as alterations in children's attitudes toward the city after an objective study of it. A subjective report of these non-Indian and Indian students' participation in the controlled activities is included.   CCV

956   **ASKELL   ANTHONY**
1968
NO REASON TO SMILE. Monday Morning 2(5):30-31.

A hypothetical case of an idealistic teachers' 1st year at an Indian school and the difficulties she encounters is presented.   IVY

957   **AYOADE   FOLORUNSO**
1970
SOME RELATIONSHIPS BETWEEN THE LEVEL OF NATURALISTIC THINKING AND ACHIEVEMENT OF AN ELEMENTARY SCIENCE DEMONSTRATION LESSON AMONG GRADE SIX PUPILS FROM FOUR CULTURAL BACKGROUNDS. M.A. Thesis. University of Toronto. 150 pp. Available from Ontario Institute for Studies in Education, Toronto.

The standardized elementary science test, standard mental ability test, and the test of animistic-naturalistic thinking were administered in March and April, 1969, to 113 southern Ontario Indian and non-Indian Grade 6 students selected according to their hypothesized positions on Redfield's folk-urban continuum. Observed differences in cognition and achievement are discussed and related to a consideration of integrated schooling and improvement of teaching techniques.   CCV

958   **BAGNELL   K S**
1962
YOUTH AND EDUCATION FOR INDIANS. The United Church Observer N.S. 24(13):38-39.

Educational facilities and opportunities for Indians are improving. The church can play an important role in assisting young migrants to adjust to the city.   IVY

959   **BAKER   MARIE**
1967

THE CULTURAL MEANING OF THE SCHOOL PROGRAM TO THE NATIVE CHILDREN. In National Conference on Indian and Northern Education Saskatoon 1967. Mary Anne LaVallee, ed. n.p.: Society for Indian and Northern Education and Extension Division, University of Saskatchewan. pp.54-59.

Indians learning from Indians about Indians is stressed in this presentation from the point of view of an Indian student.   IVY

960   **BARRIE   J ROSS**
1968
TASK FORCE OPPORTUNITIES FOR PEOPLE OF INDIAN ANCESTRY: TRAINING AND EMPLOYMENT. Unpublished paper delivered to Task Force Opportunities for People of Indian Ancestry, Government of Saskatchewan. Regina, August 9, 1968. Available from Indian and Metis Department, Regina. 5 pp.

To speed up the process of producing skilled tradesmen, on-the-job training is suggested, with possibly government assistance in some form of wage subsidization under certain conditions of in-plant training.   IVY

961   **BENNETT   MICHAEL C,   THELANDER   ANITA**
1967
THE INDIAN CHILD IN SCHOOL: AN EXAMINATION OF SOCIO-CULTURAL FACTORS INFLUENCING THE DEVELOPMENT OF THE OCCUPATIONAL ASPIRATIONS OF CANADIAN INDIAN CHILDREN ATTENDING INDIAN RESIDENTIAL SCHOOLS IN SASKATCHEWAN. M.S.W. Thesis. School of Social Work. McGill University. 143 pp.

Data from the Canadian Welfare Council study on residential schools in Saskatchewan, anthropological and sociological literature, and other publications are utilized in a study of factors relating to occupational aspirations of Indian children. It is suggested that the discontinuity of traditional Indian culture experiences as the child enters residential schools with pressure to conform to the White society's norms reduces the effectiveness of his preparation for active participation in North American society. Proposals are advanced for minimization of conflict by maximization of traditional values.   CCV

962   **BINDER   ALFRED**
1969
INSTRUMENTS TO MEASURE AND COMPARE THE KNOWLEDGE OF AND ATTITUDE TOWARD THE CITY AMONG INDIAN AND NON-INDIAN PUPILS. M.Ed. Thesis. Department of Curriculum and Instruction. University of Calgary. 100 pp. Available from National Library of Canada.

Investigated are the attitudes and levels of knowledge about the city of Indian children living on reserves in comparison with those of urban and rural non-Indian shildren. It is believed that these attitudes govern in many respects the ability of Indians to adapt to the urban environment. Two instruments were constructed to measure conceptual knowledge and attitude toward the city and were administered to Division 2 (Grades 3-6) pupils from 4 different samples. The Indian children interviewed were from bands in southern Alberta.   DGW

963   **BISHOP   RODERICK**
1967
PROBLEMS OF SCHOOL INTEGRATION. In National Conference on Indian and
Northern Education Saskatoon 1967. Mary Anne LaVallee, ed. n.p.: Society for Indian
and Northern Education and Extension Division, University of Saskatchewan. pp. 50-
53.

Speaking from personal experiences, the author describes discrimination in education
and employment.   IVY

964   **BOGLE   DON C**
1970
AN APPROACH TO INDIAN STUDIES. The Canadian Journal of History and Social
Science 5(2):35-41.

Indian history has been poorly treated in Canada and Ontario. For this reason an Indian
Studies program has been developed at Thornlea Secondary School. It covers a 13 week
period and includes reading, discussions and visits to various reserves. The course has
been a success.   ADG

965   **BRADSHAW   THECLA,   RENAUD   ANDRE**
n.d.
THE INDIAN CHILD AND EDUCATION: HERE WE ARE ... WHERE DO WE
GO? Saskatoon: Midwest Litho Ltd. 20 pp.

Pointing out that the general educational objectives of Canada are in direct conflict with
the cultural background of an Indian child, this booklet suggests integration by cooperation and by accepting and building upon what the Indian child knows rather than negat-
ing his beliefs.   IVY

966   **BRITISH COLUMBIA NATIVE INDIAN TEACHERS ASSOCIATION**
1970
PROCEEDINGS. FIRST CONFERENCE: B.C. NATIVE INDIAN TEACHERS.
Unpublished paper. Available from Indian Education Resources Center, University of
British Columbia. 37 pp.

A verbatim report of the proceedings of the British Columbia Native Teachers' first conference held in Vancouver, September 3-4, 1970, is presented. Needs in Indian education were discussed and priorities for consideration established.   IVY

967   **BULLER   JAMES H**
1968
INDIAN AND ESKIMO EDUCATION. Unpublished paper delivered to Indian and
Eskimo Education Convention, sponsored by the Indian-Eskimo Association of Canada.
Toronto, May 23, 1968. Available from Indian-Eskimo Assocation. 10 pp.

At the 1968 convention on Indian and Eskimo education, the author presented this
speech from a layman's point of view on the future of Indian and Eskimo education.   HCV

968   **CALDWELL   GEORGE**
1967
INDIAN RESIDENTIAL SCHOOLS: A RESEARCH STUDY OF THE CHILD
CARE PROGRAMS OF NINE RESIDENTIAL SCHOOLS IN SASKATCHEWAN.
Ottawa: Canadian Welfare Council. 202 pp.

In 1966 354 Indian children from grades 5-12 in 9 Saskatchewan residential schools
were studied. A questionnaire was administered to the children to provide information
concerning their family backgrounds, aspirations and attitudes toward work. The California test of personality was used to establish the adjustment and adaptation levels of
the children. Systematic investigation of legislation concerning education of Indian children, admissions policy, administrative procedures, staff, and the opinions of some senior students, parents, and recent graduates was undertaken. Findings are outlined and
discussed. Numerous recommendations are advanced with the aim of improving the
efficiency and quality of the service and gearing it to the specialized needs of Indian children in the acculturation process.   CCV

969   **CALDWELL   GEORGE**
1967
AN ISLAND BETWEEN TWO CULTURES: THE RESIDENTIAL INDIAN
SCHOOL. Canadian Welfare 43(4):12-17.

This survey of several Saskatchewan residential schools for Indians found the school system itself the principal deterrent to its pupils' adaptation and adjustment. The schools
stress academics rather than meeting the total needs of the children. The school programs lack individualization, maintain poor relations with parents and stifle independence by a high degree of regimentation. Funds at the schools are inadequate in comparison with most progressive institutional care for children. Several recommendations
arose from the study: (1) re-organization of administrative policies and procedures regarding admission, (2) establishment of family and child services for assistance of Indian parents, (3) the withdrawal of the Educational Services Branch of Indian Affairs
from the operation of residential schools as they now exist, and the restriction of its services to the education of Indian children, and (4) establishment of well-supervised Indian
or White foster homes as transition centers for those children who must attend school
away from home. It was proposed that the churches set up urban hostels to facilitate the
urban adjustment of Indian youth.   ADG

970   **CAMERON A,   STORM   T**
1965
ACHIEVEMENT MOTIVATION IN CANADIAN INDIAN, MIDDLE- AND
WORKING-CLASS CHILDREN. Psychological Reports 16:459-463.

This study found that kind of reward (material or non-material) influences learning in
Indian, middle- and working-class boys between 9 and 13 years old. Each subject was
given 50 trials on a concept learning task under conditions of material reward (candy) or
non-material reward (a light flash). Each subject also received parts of the TAT. It was
found that Indian and working-class White children performed better under material
reward conditions. Middle-class children tended more than the other 2 groups to tell stories to projective stimuli containing achievement imagery; they also preferred a larger
delayed reward to a small immediate one.   ADG

971   **CANADA. Department of Citizenship and Immigration. Indian Affairs Branch.**
1961
THE INDIAN IN TRANSITION: YOUR OPPORTUNITY TO SERVE YOUR
PEOPLE: A MESSAGE TO INDIAN STUDENTS IN HIGH SCHOOL. Ottawa:
Queen's Printer. 12 pp.

A brochure was prepared to recruit Indian teachers. Messages from the Minister and
Senator James Gladstone introduce the text.   Discussed are the future of Indian teachers
(employability and salary), financial assistance, and teacher training courses. A list of
school superintendents for each region is included.   JSL

972   **CANADA. Department of Indian Affairs and Northern Development. Education
Branch. Employment and Related Services Division.**
1970
POST SCHOOL PROGRAMS: HIGH LIGHT REPORTS. Ottawa: Department of
Indian Affairs and Northern Development. 20 pp.

A summary of some of the innovative Post School Indian programs for 1969-1970 is
given for the Maritimes, Quebec, Ontario, Manitoba, Saskatchewan, Alberta, and British
Columbia regions. Discussed are programs of interest to both men and women, involving
adult education, vocational training, placement and relocation.   JSL

973   **CANADA. Department of Indian Affairs and Northern Development. Indian Affairs
Branch.**
1968
VOCATIONAL OPPORTUNITY AND THE CANADIAN INDIAN:
EDUCATIONAL ASSISTANCE, SCHOLARSHIPS, JOBS. Revised Edition. Ottawa:
Queen's Printer. 12 pp.

Prepared for the guidance of Indian students, their families, and educators, this booklet
presents figures on the Indian school population in 1966-1967, and discusses the importance of vocational training. The educational assistance program is mentioned, and a list
of scholarships given. There is a listing of the kinds of courses taken by Indians, and an
explanation of counseling and placement services. A list of Indian Affairs Branch education officers for each region is included at the end.   JSL

974   **CANADA. Department of Indian Affairs and Northern Development. Indian Affairs
Branch. Counselling Services.**
n.d.
INDIAN STUDENT'S HANDBOOK. Ottawa: Department of Indian Affairs and
Northern Development. 12 pp.

Advice and regulations for success in urban boarding houses, schools, and employment
are presented in a handbook to familiarize Indian students with an urban milieu.   CCV

975   **CANADA. Department of Northern Affairs and National Resources. Northern
Administration Branch. Education Division.**
n.d.
ANNUAL REPORT OF THE EDUCATION DIVISION CONCERNING
EDUCATION IN THE NORTHWEST TERRITORIES AND ARCTIC QUEBEC
1963-1964. Ottawa: Department of Northern Affairs and National Resources. 57 pp.

The annual report of the Education Division for 1963-1964 outlines activities in the Northwest Territories and Arctic Quebec.   JSL

976   **CANADA. Department of Northern Affairs and National Resources. Northern Administration Branch. Education Division.**
n.d.
EDUCATION IN THE NORTH. Ottawa: Department of Northern Affairs and National Resources. 25 pp.

A booklet discusses education in the Northwest Territories and Arctic Quebec.   JSL

977   **CANADA. Department of Northern Affairs and National Resources. Northern Administration Branch. Education Division.**
n.d.
PROSPECTUS FOR SIR JOHN FRANKLIN SCHOOL AND ITS STUDENT RESIDENCE, AKAITCHO HALL, YELLOWKNIFE, N.W.T. Ottawa: Department of Northern Affairs and National Resources. 84 pp.

A description of Yellowknife's new $3,000,000 integrated vocational and high school and hostel is presented.   JSL

978   **CANADA. Department of Northern Affairs and National Resources. Northern Administration Branch. Education Division.**
1963
EDUCATION IN THE NORTH: SELECTED INFORMATION PREPARED FOR PRESENTATION DURING THE 1963 NORTHERN UNIVERSITY PROGRAM. Ottawa: Department of Northern Affairs and National Resources. 18 pp.

A booklet discusses education in the Northwest Territories and Arctic Quebec.   JSL

979   **CANADA. Department of Northern Affairs and National Resources. Northern Administration Branch. Education Division.**
1966
ANNUAL REVIEW OF EDUCATION IN THE NORTHWEST TERRITORIES AND ARCTIC QUEBEC 1964-1965. Ottawa: Queen's Printer. 53 pp.

Educational activities in the Northwest Territories and Arctic Quebec during the school year 1964-65 are informally described. Discussed are education in the North, school administration, curriculum, adult education, school services, construction, vocational education, and special projects. The Mackenzie district, Fort Smith region, Yellowknife region, Inuvik region, and Arctic district are discussed. A directory of educational personnel concludes the report.   JSL

980   **CANADA. Department of Northern Affairs and National Resources. Northern Administration Branch. Education Division.**
1967
EDUCATION REVIEW 1965-66: NORTHWEST TERRITORIES AND ARCTIC QUEBEC. Ottawa: Department of Northern Affairs and National Resources. 63 pp.

The Education Division reviews educational activities in Arctic Quebec and the Northwest Territories for the school year 1965-1966.   JSL

981   **CANADA. Department of Northern Affairs and National Resources. Northern Administration Branch. Education Division. Vocational Education Section.**
1964
PRACTICAL PROGRAMS IN HOMEMAKING AND RELATED ACTIVITIES. Experimental Edition. Ottawa: Department of Northern Affairs and National Resources. 326 pp.

This is the draft proposal of a unique home economics program, to be used in the 1964-1965 school year. The program is aimed at age-grade retarded pupils of the Northwest Territories. The new curriculum is designed to benefit pupils who will soon enter the wage economy and those who will follow the traditional ways.   JSL

982   **CANADA. Dominion Bureau of Statistics. Education Division.**
1966
THE FEDERAL GOVERNMENT'S ROLE IN EDUCATION. In The Organization and Administration of Public Schools in Canada. Canada, Dominion Bureau of Statistics, Education Division, ed. Ottawa: Queen's Printer. pp. 187-200.

The role of the federal government in education is described. A section is devoted to the educational services provided by the Department of Indian Affairs and Northern Development, including its administrative structure, policy, financing, pupil enrollment, and teaching personnel.   CCV

983   **CANADIAN ASSOCIATION FOR INDIAN AND ESKIMO EDUCATION**
1969
EDUCATION IS PARTICIPATION: PROCEEDINGS OF THE 7th ANNUAL CONFERENCE THE CANADIAN ASSOCIATION FOR INDIAN AND ESKIMO EDUCATION. Ottawa, May 28-30, 1969. Unpublished paper. Available from Library, Department of Indian Affairs and Northern Development, Ottawa. 135 pp.

Parental participation in decision-making; observations on kindergarten in Moosonee; intercultural education programs in Alberta, Manitoba, Northwest Territories, and Saskatchewan; occupational aspirations among Mackenzie Delta students; and difficulties an Indian faces in a White society are among discussion topics.   CCV

984   **CANADIAN TEACHERS' FEDERATION**
1967
A SUBMISSION BY THE CANADIAN TEACHERS' FEDERATION TO THE PRIME MINISTER AND CABINET. Unpublished paper. Available from Library, Ontario Institute for Studies in Education, Toronto, Ont.

The brief is addressed to educational authorities in the Department of Indian Affairs and Northern Development. Special measures are requested to improve the preparation of teachers destined for Indian, Eskimo or Metis communities, to provide facilities to overcome native children's handicaps in learning, to adapt the curricula to the needs of these children, and to encourage and facilitate a greater degree of parental participation in policy making regarding their children's education.   CCV

985   **CARDINAL   DOUGLAS**
1970

EDUCATORS - YOU HAVE FAILED US: ADDRESS TO CEA CONVENTION SEPTEMBER 24, 1970. The Alberta School Trustee 40(5):21-22.

For the Indian, educational systems have failed and their programs are irrelevant. The Indians of Alberta shall teach their children and the immigrant culture to love the land upon which our survival is based.   IVY

986   **CARGILL   ISABEL**
1970
AN INVESTIGATION OF COGNITIVE DEVELOPMENT AMONG INFANTS OF A CANADIAN RESERVATION. M.A. Thesis. University of Toronto. 191 pp.

Fifteen infants from a southern Ontario Indian reserve were administered appropriate sections of the Gesell Developmental Schedules and Uzgiris' and Hunt's Instrument For Assessing Infant Psychological Development. Analysis of results reveals that a differential development of cognitive ability patterns observed in older Indian children may date from infancy. Implications for education programs are discussed. Observations of the home situation, parental attidues, and socialization practices are included in appendices.   CCV

987   **CASTELLANO   MARLENE**
1970
VOCATION OR IDENTITY: THE DILEMMA OF INDIAN YOUTH. In The Only Good Indian: Essays by Canadian Indians. Waubageshig, ed. Toronto: New Press. pp 52-60.

An examination of the struggle of many young Indians in their quest for self-identity and a vocational niche is attempted. In the mind of the Indian, education has negative connotations and therefore is automatically divorced from ethnic identity. By formulating a new definition of what it means to be Indian in this day and age, this gap may be bridged with the aid of an enlightened educational process.   DGW

988   **CHALMERS   J W**
1964
A NEW DEAL IN INDIAN EDUCATION. Quest 2(1):5-7.

Integrated schools may be more successful in bringing Indians from the 19th to 20th century than previous educational attempts.   This is, however, very much dependent upon whether they meet social, economic, and cultural acceptance.   IVY

989   **CHALMERS   J W**
1964
NEW SCHOOLS IN THE FOREST. The Beaver 295(Spring):44-50.

An account of the inspection of 2 federal Indian schools and a mission school in 1958 by 2 Alberta School Superintendents, the Rural Dean, and the School Administrator is given.   IVY

990   **CHALMERS   J W**
1964

VOCATIONAL SCHOOL IN THE FOREST. Technical and Vocational Education in Canada 2(2):6-9.

The educational program at Grovard Vocational School, northern Alberta, is briefly outlined.   IVY

991   **CHALMERS   J W**
1967
INDIANS ALSO GO TO SCHOOL. Alberta School Trustee 37(3):9,25-27.

Enrollment and grade distribution tables show that proportionately only one third as many Indians as other students are in high school. Indian pupil achievement in grade 9 and grade 12 examinations indicate that Indian students do not do as well on examinations as do others and those that go to school off the reserve are more successful than those who attend Indian schools. For Indians to gain more control of schools which operate on their reserves, it is suggested that Indian reserves be established as school districts, and, where appropriate, they be included in divisions or counties. Administrative problems would be complex but not insurmountable.   IVY

992   **CHALMERS   JOHN J**
1969
TEACHERS IN THE FOREST. Monday Morning 3(9):27.

Teaching in Alberta's Northland School Division is briefly discussed.   IVY

993   **CHANCE   NORMAN A**
1969
PREMISES,POLICIES, AND PRACTICE: A CROSS-CULTURAL STUDY OF EDUCATION IN THE CIRCUMPOLAR NORTH. Unpublished paper delivered to Conference on Cross-Cultural Education in the North. Montreal, August 18-21, 1969. Available from National Library of Canada.   8 pp.

This paper compares and contrasts the present educational, political, and economic involvment of the native people of the circumpolar countries (Russia, Canada, United States, Finland, Sweden, Denmark, and Norway) in relation to the importance of initial government policies concerning northern industrialization and native culture preservation.   HCV

994   **CLEMENT   JOSIE**
1968
EDUCATION OF INDIAN CHILDREN IN CANADA. Special Education 42(4):9-18.

Using current literature and interviews, this study attempts to determine why more Indian children leave school earlier than non-Indian children. Factors contributing to dropout rates are: (1) language, (2) attitude of parents, (3) poor housing, (4) cultural differences, (5) poverty, (6) nomadic life style, (7) residential schools, and (8) the curriculum. It is hypothesized that the curriculum is the greatest single cause of early school leaving. Non-Indian society and Indian society are compared to substantiate this. The University of Saskatchewan's research in curriculum development is discussed.   IVY

995   **COLLIOU   ROSE C**
1964
ORAL ENGLISH INSTRUCTION IN INDIAN SCHOOLS. The Northian 1(1):9-12.

Indian children achieve better in written than in oral English because of the stress on
written work. The introduction of mandatory oral instruction by the education division
of Indian Affairs revealed that many teachers felt unprepared for this task and that few
texts on oral English instruction existed. Both a manual and a draft course were developed. The course stressed choral speech, verbal tense, idiomatic expressions and phras-
ing, question and dialogue, vocabulary enrichment and growth in sentence structure. The
program appears successful. However, teachers must receive training in the method of
second language teaching and contact between bilingual Indian youth and English
speaking peers should receive promotion.   ADG

996   **COLLIOU   ROSE C**
1965
SECOND LANGUAGE INSTRUCTION FOR INDIAN CHILDREN AVEC
COMMENTAIRE PAR M. A. GILL. In The Education of Indian Children in Canada:
A Symposium Written by Members of Indian Affairs Education Division with
Comments by the Indian Peoples. L. G. P. Waller, ed.   The Canadian Superintendent
1965. Toronto: Ryerson Press. pp. 75-80.

Lack of English of Indian pupils and the inexperience of personnel in teaching English as
a second language account for much of the discrepancies between pupil achievement and
grade standards. Oral English courses were developed through research and are now part
of the curriculum in Indian schools across Canada. As well, teachers are being trained in
second language instruction, kindergarten classes are expanding, and Indian parents and
youngsters in integrated programs are aware of the advantages to be gained from extended opportunities to speak English. Comments are presented by M. A. Gill of the
Point Bleue Band, Quebec.   IVY

997   **COLLIOU   ROSE C**
1966
GATES READING SURVEY: A STUDY OF STANDARDIZED READING TEST
RESULTS (1965-66) IN THE FEDERAL SCHOOLS OF THE INDIAN AFFAIRS
EDUCATION DIVISION, DEPARTMENT OF INDIAN AFFAIRS AND
NORTHERN DEVELOPMENT. Ottawa: Department of Indian Affairs and Northern
Development, Indian Affairs Branch, Education Division. 29 pp.

Indian pupil scores on standardized reading tests (Gates Reading Tests) are evaluated
providing patterns of reading achievement of pupils in federal schools. Similarities and
differences in achievement by grades and by regions are established, grade difficulty levels are localized, pupil needs in terms of program content are identified, and the relationship between classroom-school learning set and pupil achievement gains are emphasized.   IVY

998   **COLLIOU   ROSE**
1969
A BRIEF STUDY OF AVAILABLE STATISTICAL DATA ON INDIAN PUPIL
ENROLLMENT 1949-69. Ottawa: Department of Indian Affairs and Northern
Development. 17 pp.   Also in French.

Indian pupil enrollment in schools from 1949 to 1969 is summarized and age-grade placement of Indian pupils from 1956-57 to 1966-67 is assessed statistically. Positive trends in Indian education revealed by the data and anticipated patterns are discussed.   CCV

999   **CONNELLY   R M,   CHALMERS   J W**
1965
MISSIONARIES AND INDIAN EDUCATION WITH COMMENT BY JOHN R. MCLEOD. In The Education of Indian Children in Canada: A Symposium Written by Members of Indian Affairs Education Division with Comments by the Indian Peoples. L. G. P. Waller, ed. The Canadian Superintendent 1965. Toronto: Ryerson Press. pp. 11-23.

A review of Roman Catholic and Protestant churches' involvement in the education of Canadian Indian children since 1632 (Catholic) and 1784 (Protestant) is given. John R. McLeod of the James Smith Band, Saskatchewan, comments.   IVY

1000   **COOMBS   W,   ADAMS   HOWARD J**
1967
SUMMATION. In National Conference on Indian and Northern Education Saskatoon 1967. Mary Anne LaVallee, ed. n.p.: Society for Indian and Northern Education and Extension Division, University of Saskatchewan. pp. 90-102.

Points made by speakers at the conference are underlined and elaborated.   IVY

1001   **DANIELS   E R**
1967
ASTA STUDIES POSSIBLE INTEGRATION OF INDIAN STUDENTS INTO PROVINCIAL SYSTEMS. The Alberta School Trustee 37(2):23-24,29.

At the 1966 Alberta School Trustees' Association annual convention the executive was given the responsibility of studying the possibility of bringing Indian people in Alberta under provincial educational jurisdiction. An agreement between the federal government and the government of Alberta similar to those between the British Columbia and Manitoba governments and the federal government should be enacted. Recognized in such an agreement would be that the Indian peoples are residents, citizens, and taxpayers of the province and that they should assume and be accorded more responsibility in the education of their children.   IVY

1002   **DAVIS   BONITA**
1970
AN EVALUATION OF THE RELATIONSHIP BETWEEN SCHOOL EXPERIENCE AND ATTITUDES TOWARDS SCHOOL: INDIAN STUDENTS FROM ONE BRITISH COLUMBIA RESERVE. M.A. Thesis. Department of Anthropology and Sociology. University of Victoria. Available with permission of the author.

The title has been verified, but a copy was not obtained in time to abstract it.   SLP

1003   **DENHOFF   PATRICIA**
1968
INTEGRATION IN THE EYE OF THE STORM. Arbos 4(3):18-23,35-37.

The educational integration program in Prince Albert, Saskatchewan, is discussed. The program and the activities of some of the educational personnel at All Saints Residential School, which purports to be a transition center, are also presented. Comments are expressed on the philosophy of integration by various educational personnel.   HCV

1004   **DILLING   H J**
1965
EDUCATIONAL ACHIEVEMENT AND SOCIAL ACCEPTANCE OF INDIAN
PUPILS INTEGRATED IN NON-INDIAN SCHOOLS OF SOUTHERN ONTARIO.
Ontario Journal of Educational Research 8:45-57.

Indians attending integrated (N = 145) and all-Indian schools (N = 212), along with 1,102 White pupils were administered 3 achievement tests. Data were also obtained on social attraction patterns among the Indian and White youths. Results regarding in- and out-race orientation were inconclusive. Several significant findings were noted regarding the educational status of the Indian pupils: (1) White students performed better than both Indian groups and the integrated-school Indians performed better than those in all-Indian schools in vocabulary and computation, but not comprehension, (2) a positive relationship exists between educational aspiration and achievement for both Indian groups on all tests, (3) those Indian students speaking only English received better scores than those who spoke some Indian language, (4) a positive relationship exists between educational achievement and learning capacity for the Indian subjects, (5) Indian pupils who heard only English spoken by their parents did better on the reading tests than those whose parents spoke some Indian language, and (6) there is an inverse relation between educational achievement and age for Indian groups. The study also found achievement marks biased towards girls, pupils with higher intelligence and non-Indians. No biases were noted in arithmetic marks. Educational and research implications are discussed.   ADG

1005   **DILLING   HAROLD JOHN**
1965
EDUCATIONAL ACHIEVEMENT AND SOCIAL ACCEPTANCE OF INDIAN
PUPILS INTEGRATED IN NON-INDIAN SCHOOLS OF SOUTHERN ONTARIO.
D.Ed. Thesis. Department of Education. University of Toronto. 440 pp.

Two hundred and twelve Indians in Indian schools, 145 integrated Indians and 1102 non-Indians in grade 7 from Southern Ontario Region schools were administered achievement tests in vocabulary and comprehension to determine the relative achievement of integrated Indian pupils in comparison with non-Indian and Indian pupils in Indian schools. A sociometric test was included for the pupils in the integrated schools to evaluate the acceptance of Indians by the non-Indians with whom they are integrated. The numerous findings are reported and the implications for further research and orientation of further integration are discussed.   CCV

1006   **ELLIS   E A**
1967
HOME ECONOMICS EDUCATION IN THE NORTHWEST TERRITORIES.
Canadian Nutrition Notes 23:85-95.

Junior Secondary, Senior Secondary, Pre-Vocational, Vocational, and Special Practical Programs in Home Economics are described with particular reference to courses at Churchill Pre-Vocational Centre and Sir John Franklin Vocational High School.   IVY

1007   **FERGUSSON   HATTIE**
1967
EMPLOYMENT OF NATIVE TEACHERS. In National Conference on Indian and Northern Education Saskatoon 1967. Mary Anne LaVallee, ed.   n.p.: Society for Indian and Northern Education and Extension Division, University of Saskatchewan. pp. 35-39.

Mrs. Hattie Fergusson, a Tsimshian Indian of Vancouver, British Columbia, relates her experiences at a residential school and an integrated high school. As well, as program chairman of the Indian Centre in Vancouver, she presents the aims and objectives of the center. Examples of Indians who have succeeded in various endeavors are used to illustrate the fact that Indians must show initiative.   IVY

1008   **FIALKOW   S**
1965
ACADEMIC PERFORMANCE AND PAST LIFE EXPERIENCES: A COMPARATIVE STUDY OF THE RELATIONSHIP OF PAST LIFE EXPERIENCES TO PRESENT ACADEMIC PERFORMANCE OF INDIAN STUDENTS IN ATTENDANCE AT URBAN TRAINING INSTITUTIONS. M.S.W. Thesis. School of Social Work. University of Manitoba.

The title has been verified, but a copy was not obtained in time to abstract it.   SLP

1009   **FINEDAY   SIDNEY**
1967
NATIVE PEOPLE IN ADMINISTRATION. In National Conference on Indian and Northern Education Saskatoon 1967. Mary Anne LaVallee, ed. n.p.: Society for Indian and Northern Education and Extension Division, University of Saskatchewan. pp. 18-20.

Sidney Fineday of Sweet Grass Reserve, Saskatchewan, discusses the whys and wherefores of integrated schooling in Saskatchewan.   Reserves are destitute of leadership because successfully integrated Indians do not return to reserves. Rather than total integration or total segregation, a flexible program is required to accomodate the Indian people. IVY

1010   **FISHER   ANTHONY D**
1966
EDUCATIONAL AND SOCIAL PROGRESS. Alberta Journal of Educational Research 12:257-267.

Educational attainment among Alberta Indians has not stemmed high unemployment among Indian youth. The reason for the discrepancy between education and good jobs for the Indian is that Anglo-Canadians get Anglo-Canadian jobs. The Indian schools have proven to be inefficient mediators between 2 cultures producing an inferior product.

The government has failed to find suitable employment for the Indian. Of possible alternatives, the more just solution is government intervention on behalf of the Indians in local economies.   ADG

1011   **FISHER   ANTHONY D**
1969
WHITE RITES AND INDIAN RIGHTS. Transaction 7(1):29-33.

Recent studies indicate that the Canadian Indian does not profit from educational opportunities. The schools present an irrelevant set of values and training which conflict with certain moral and cultural values of the student. The schools fail the Indian, not the reverse. To be a good and successful student, the Indian must often be a bad and unsuccessful Indian.   ADG

1012   **FORBES   ROBERT H**
1964
CHILCOTIN FOREST INDIAN TRAINING PROJECT. British Columbia Lumberman 48(7):38-40.

Sponsored by the federal government, the project underway in British Columbia since 1961 is considered in 3 phases: (1) an intensive forest management plan for the one-time Riske Creek Reserve, (2) construction of a forest-industrial school, and (3) a series of short courses related to specific forest skills.   IVY

1013   **FRASER   DON**
1969
MENTAL ABILITIES OF BRITISH COLUMBIA INDIAN CHILDREN. Canadian Counsellor/Conseiller Canadien 3(3):42-48.

The Stanford-Binet Intelligence Scale Forum L-M was administered to 62 Indian school children (27 urban, 35 rural) who were not over 9 years of age. Urban/rural and White/Indian scores were compared. Conclusions give types of remedial help in terms of content and instruction for Indian children.   IVY

1014   **GAGNE   R C**
1966
ENGLISH FOR THE FIRST CANADIANS: ESKIMOS AND INDIANS. Elementary English 43:583-586,595.

Historical information is provided on Canada's educational policies toward Indians and Eskimos from 1763. Concern is focused on the methods of teaching English as a second language to Indians and Eskimos. As yet a well-integrated program does not exist.   IVY

1015   **GALLOWAY   C,   MICKELSON   N**
1968
ORIENTATION, PRE-SCHOOL, AND PRE-KINDERGARTEN SUMMER PROGRAMME FOR INDIAN CHILDREN, JULY 1968. Educational Research Institute of B.C. Studies and Reports 4. Vancouver: Educational Research Institute of B.C. 42 pp.

In the summer of 1968, the University of Victoria sponsored a 4-week pre-kindergarten, pre-school and orientation enrichment program for Indian children living on 4 reserves in the southern region of Vancouver Island. The teaching staff consisted of 2 faculty members of the University of Victoria, 1 visiting lecturer, and 6 teenaged girls who acted as teaching aids. General goals in language development are discussed and the specific behavioral objectives have been programmed in 3 areas: cognitive, affective and psycho-motor. Individual programs for each of the 3 groups are outlined, examples given, and comments follow. An evaluation concludes the report.   IVY

1016   **GALLOWAY   CHARLES,   PHILION   WILLIAM E**
1968
TIME FACTOR IN A STANDARDIZED READING TEST AND THE SCORES OF INDIAN CHILDREN. Unpublished paper. Available from National Library of Canada. 8 pp.

This paper discusses the results of a standardized reading test administered to both Indian and non-Indian children of British Columbia in grades 4 and 5. Explanations are given for the lower reading scores of the Indian children.   HCV

1017   **GEDDES   DONALD W**
1968
INTEGRATION: NORTHERN STYLE. The Educational Courier 38(5):25-26.

Integration of Indian pupils into public schools in Sault Ste. Marie, Ontario, is briefly discussed.   IVY

1018   **GOLDENSON   KAREN**
1970
COGNITIVE DEVELOPMENT OF INDIAN ELEMENTARY SCHOOL CHILDREN ON A SOUTHERN ONTARIO RESERVE. M.A. Thesis. Department of Education. University of Toronto. 80 pp.

Sixty Indian children from a southern Ontario reserve were administered batteries of Piagetian tasks yielding 17 variables for analysis of intellectual development. A subsample consisting of the 45 children attending school were also given Raven's Progressive Matrices and 2 Torrence tests of creativity. Testing was done in May, 1969. The Indians' socio-economic status was found to be below the Canadian national average and little class differentiation was observed. It was concluded that Indian children show a performance detriment compared to White groups but factor patterns suggest a developmental sequence similar to that reported for White subjects.   CCV

1019   **GOODERHAM   G K**
1965
PROSPECT WITH COMMENT BY CLARA TIZYA. In Education of Indian Children in Canada: A Symposium Written by Members of Indian Affairs Education Division with Comments by the Indian Peoples. L. G. P. Waller, ed. The Canadian Superintendent 1965. Toronto: Ryerson Press. pp. 95-104.

This reviewing of the development of Indian education stresses 4 major areas: (1) general education of Indian pupils must be transferred to provincial authorities, (2) it should be made possible for authorities other than federal to develop and carry out programs,

(3) Indian people must assume more responsibility for the education of their children, and (4) a dynamic adult education program is required for every reserve. Clara Tizya of Whitehorse, Yukon, comments.   IVY

1020   **GOODERHAM   KENT**
1969
INDIAN EDUCATION. Unpublished paper delivered to Symposium on Integration. Kamloops, B.C., May, 1969. Available from National Library of Canada. 9 pp.

An overview of the current situation in Indian education is presented. Areas of least effectiveness for Indian children are reviewed. The reasons for this lack of success and improvement in the areas of curriculum, orientation, teacher training, and parent-community participation are outlined.   CCV

1021   **GOUCHER   A C**
1967
THE DROPOUT PROBLEM AMONG INDIAN AND METIS STUDENTS. Calgary, Alta.: Dome Petroleum Limited. 50 pp.

The purpose of this study is to examine the dropout problem among Indian and Metis students with specific reference to Frontier Collegiate Institute, a coeducational residential institute in Manitoba. The study was carried out from April, 1967, to December, 1967. Sources of information were student and teacher questionnaires, a review of the literature, and a study tour of selected educational centers in Canada and the United States. A detailed outline is given on 4 educational institutes: Intermountain School, Brigham City, Utah; the Institute of American Arts, Sante Fe, New Mexico; Haskell Institute, Lawrence, Kansas; and Youth House, New York City, New York. Recommendations for Frontier Collegiate include geographical relocation, curriculum adaptation, a fresh look at basic educational principles, incorporation of a guidance program, and better teacher-parent interaction. The report concludes that the greatest prevention against dropouts is qualified educational personnel.   IVY

1022   **GREEN   RICHARD**
1970
SOME PROBLEMS IN INDIAN EDUCATION. The Northian Newsletter (18):11-13.

Canadian Indian education is examined in the context of 4 problem areas which are derived from Alonjo Spang's analysis of American Indian education: (1) irrelevant curricula, (2) insensitive school personnel, (3) lack of qualified Indians in Indian education, and (4) lack of involvement in and control of educational matters by Indians. The article cites 2 recent studies (1968 and 1970) in which it is revealed that some Saskatchewan teachers are aware of only the language problem which affects school performance, failing to see the underlying value conflicts experienced by the Indian and Metis child, and that only minor curriculum adaptations have been made in Saskatchewan schools. Effective cross-cultural education must involve the parents in the community.   ADG

1023   **GREYEYES   AUDREY**
1966
BETTER EDUCATION FOR INDIANS. The Northian 3(2):13-16.

Originally prepared as a speech for the Bryant Oratory Competition, this article examines the background and present status of Indian education. Until recently Indian education principally focused on agricultural and domestic professions. Although some changes have been made in curriculum, other problems face the Indian student. Parents often fail to adequately support their children's attendance at school. Some show open opposition to schooling. Poverty and low morale on the reserve are also obstacles which confuse the children. Government policies and actions with respect to integrated education have often angered parents, and this too affects the child in school. The author recommends that (1) the government first consult Indian parents to get their views and feelings regarding school administration, (2) home instruction be provided for parents to upgrade their level of learning, and (3) living conditions on the reserve be improved.   ADG

1024   **HAGAN   ALLAN THOMAS**
1965
A STUDY OF THE RELATIONSHIP BETWEEN THE PERFORMANCE OF SELECTED INDIAN STUDENTS ATTENDING COURSES IN METROPOLITAN WINNIPEG AND CERTAIN FACTORS OF SUPPORT IN THEIR PRESENT LIVING SITUATION. Unpublished paper. Department of Social Work, University of Manitoba. Available from Library, University of Manitoba. 76 pp.

Fifty-one Indian students between 18 and 25 years of age attending various Winnipeg educatonal institutions from September, 1964 to April, 1965 were interviewed. The investigation was to determine the relationships between educational achievement and factors viewed as supportive in the boarding homes obtained for them by the Indian Affairs Branch. The findings were termed inconclusive since no discernable pattern emerged to support the hypotheses.   CCV

1025   **HAMILTON   WILLIAM LESLIE**
1966
THE PERCEPTION OF PROBLEMS ASSOCIATED WITH INTER-GROUP RELATIONS IN INTEGRATED SCHOOLS. M.Ed. Thesis. Department of Educational Administration. University of Alberta. 212 pp.

The relationship between several psychological variables and teachers' perception of problems associated with integrated schools was investigated in 4 Alberta public schools in 2 widely separated areas whose Indian pupils belonged to 2 different bands. Questionnaires were completed by 60 teachers, 122 Indian students, and 436 White students. Results revealed agreement among teachers from all schools but student perceptions of conditions were more favorable than were those of teachers. Both teachers and students favored integration. However, some indications of prejudice were found. The hypothesized relationships between teachers' dogmatism and sensitivity to problems of integrated education, ethnocentrism and that sensitivity, and dogmatism and ethnocentrism are confirmed. The implications of these facts for integrated education are explored.   CCV

1026   **HANDLEY   J**
1969
THE TEACHER AND THE COMMUNITY. Unpublished paper. Available from Indian and Northern Curriculum Resources Centre, University of Saskatchewan. 22 pp.

This paper discusses the environment of the Indian child and the necessity of teachers knowing and understanding the community in which they work.   IVY

1027 **HANDLEY   JOE**
1970
TRENDS IN INDIAN EDUCATION. The Northian Newsletter (15):1-2.

There are several outstanding achievements and projects under way in Indian education. Among such developments are (1) the production of films about Indians by Indian producers and cameramen, (2) the introduction of Indian studies programs at Trent University and the University of Western Ontario, and (3) the control of Lebrel Indian Residential School by Indians.   ADG

1028 **HANDLEY   JOSEPH,   KOWALCHUK   MERVIN**
1969
INDIAN AND METIS EDUCATION SERVICES IN SASKATCHEWAN. Reference paper No. 3. Education Committee Workshop, Saskatchewan Task Force on Indian-Metis Employment. Dr. Howard Nixon, Chairman. Saskatoon, May 5-7, 1969. Available from National Library of Canada. 30 pp.

Data relevant to Indian and Metis education services in Saskatchewan are reviewed. Facts concerning enrollment, teachers, finances, programs, vocational training and related services, and education programs for teachers of Indian and Metis children are included in the discussion. Statistical data contained in the report cover the period from 1963 to 1968.   CCV

1029 **HEPBURN   D W**
1963
NORTHERN EDUCATION FACADE FOR FAILURE. Variables 2(1):16-21.

Education provided by the federal government for the natives of the Northwest Territories and Quebec is inadequate. Aims of education as expressed by the department are confused, the curriculum is inappropriate, and many of the current practices (residential schools) of the system are harmful. Reform is urgently needed.   IVY

1030 **HESHIDAHL   GLADYS,   HOFF   FREDA,   et al.**
1970
HOW WELL DO WE TEACH INDIAN CHILDREN? The B.C. Teacher 49:148-153,166.

If we are to integrate rather than assimilate, the Indian must share more fully in the thinking and planning that must be done. Teaching must build around the Indian's concepts and way of thinking and acting. There is a need to focus on the Indian's positive characteristics. The Indian's resentment of the White man must not continue to block progress, and the Indian must learn to stand up for himself. Since language is a basic problem, there is a need for enrichment through the development of nursery and pre-school programs. These programs should focus on the establishment of a positive self-concept and the encouragement of a motivation toward self-expression. Indian teachers might be profitably used at this stage. Given the Indian's make-up, teachers should be subtle in drawing their students into discussions and other classroom activities. Grades should be flexible, and competition de-emphasized. In-service teacher training and the maintenance of home support should also be important facets of the school program.   ADG

1031   **HIRABAYASHI   GORDON K**
1963
SOCIAL DISTANCE AND THE MODERNIZING METIS. In The Metis in Alberta
Society: With Special Reference to Social, Economic and Cultural Factors Associated
with Persistently High Tuberculosis Incidence. B. Y. Card, G. K. Hirabayashi, et al., eds.
University of Alberta Committee for Social Research: A Report of Project A.
Edmonton: University of Alberta. pp. 355-374.

Random samples of university students and northeastern Edmonton youth, aged 13 to
16 years, and Indian, Metis, and White students from 3 schools in the Faust, Alberta,
region were interviewed and analyzed with use of a social distance scale in 1961. The low
status of Metis and Indians is affirmed although they are rated higher by White students
of the Great Slave Lake area than those of Edmonton suggesting that social distance is
lessened through contact. The Metis are rated lower than the Indian, usually near the
bottom of the scale, and tend to rate themselves poorly suggesting an ill-defined self-
image.   CCV

1032   **HOBART   CHARLES**
1966
LOCAL SCHOOLS VERSUS HOSTELS. In People of Light and Dark. Maja van
Steensel, ed. Ottawa: Queen's Printer. pp. 128-131.

The problems associated with providing education for Canada's native peoples in northern areas and deficiencies in the present program are reviewed and compared with policies followed in Alaska and Greenland.   CCV

1033   **HODGKINSON   JEAN**
1970
IS NORTHERN EDUCATION MEANINGFUL? The Western Canadian Journal of
Anthropology 2(1):156-163.

Traditional and historic meanings of education are explored in relation to current conditions. Some of the natives of the Northwest Territories discuss education: past, present,
and future. Attention is focused upon the present curriculum and the complex problem of
whether a part of the traditional native culture can or should be integrated into the formal educational system.   IVY

1034   **HOMEWOOD   E L**
1965
THE INDIAN AND EDUCATION: THIRD OF A SERIES ON THE PLIGHT OF
CANADA'S INDIANS. The United Church Observer 27(3):18-20,32.

Various viewpoints by Indians and Whites concerning integrated and residential schools
as well as the role of the church in education are expressed.   IVY

1035   **HONIGMANN   JOHN J,   HONIGMANN   IRMA**
1969
FAMILY BACKGROUND AND SCHOOL BEHAVIOR IN AN ARCTIC TOWN.

Unpublished paper delivered to 4th Annual Meeting, Southern Anthropological Association. New Orleans, LA, March 14-16, 1969. Available from National Library of Canada. 11 pp.

Household features associated with successful and unsuccessful adaptation to the school situation were analyzed. The sample consisted of 300 native children (Indian, Metis, and Eskimo representing a 100 percent sample) and a small group of White children (a 5 percent sample) at Inuvik, Northwest Territories. Two groups were isolated and compared: high achievers (24 children of whom 7 were Eskimo and none were Indian) and low achievers. Factors considered include: age, sex, neighborhood, employment (of parents) and lawabidingness. It is concluded that degree of conformity to North American middle class values is a function of the success enjoyed at school.   IVY

1036   **HOPKINS   THOMAS R**
1970
SECONDARY EDUCATION OF NATIVE NORTH AMERICANS. The Northian 7(3):5-9.

Secondary education of Indians is characterized by a strong institutional religious influence, a vocational/technical curriculum, residential schooling, profound student problems, and lack of enthusiasm among native parents regarding the education of their children. To be accepted by the adult natives, secondary education must become a part of tribal life through consistent and non-offensive presentation. The heavy vocational and technical emphasis in Indian education should be balanced with a greater stress on academic curricula. Much of the student's problems is due to the necessity of studying away from home. A reduction in residential schooling should aid the mental health of the student.   ADG

1037   **HORN   KAHN-TINETA**
1966
INDIAN EDUCATION CRISIS. Atlantic Advocate 56(9):26-28.

Immediate recommendations include the elimination of religious teaching to Indians, the training of more Indian teachers, and a curriculum harmonious to the cultural background of the child. It is suggested that research be directed to the hypothesis that the White's life style may do something internally to Indians which in turn affects them intellectually.   IVY

1038   **HORN   KAHN-TINETA**
1967
THE ROLE OF CHURCH AND SCHOOL. In National Conference on Indian and Northern Education Saskatoon 1967. Mary Anne LaVallee, ed.   n.p.: Society for Indian and Northern Education and Extension Division, University of Saskatchewan. pp. 60-68.

Aboriginal values and Christian values are compared. Because the Indian's culture is so deeply imbedded within himself, an Indian cannot really be a Christian and an Indian at the same time. Indians must be trained and educated to survive. However, education must not be confused with faith, religion, and belief.   IVY

1039   **HOWES I L**
1968
SCHOOLHOUSE IN THE NORTH. The Educational Courier 38(5):23-25.

Problems in teaching students of a different cultural background in isolated situations are discussed.   IVY

1040   **INDIAN-ESKIMO ASSOCIATION OF CANADA. Northern Regional Committee.**
1965
"EDUCATION FOR WHAT?..."Unpublished paper. Summary of the Reports and Panel Discussion of the 3rd NOREC Conference, Northern Regional Committee, Indian-Eskimo Association of Canada. Toronto, December 1, 1965. Available from Indian-Eskimo Association.   50 pp.

This is a summary of reports and panel discussions of the 3rd Northern Regional Committee of the Indian-Eskimo Association of Canada. Organizations such as the Arctic Institute, the Canadian Handicrafts Guild, the Women's Institutes, Girl Guides, Imperial Order of the Daughters of the Empire, and the Y.W.C.A. gave reports on their present work and future plans in working with Indian people in the North. Discussions pertained to current programs of education for northern people and some plans for improvement.   HCV

1041   **JAENEN C J**
1965
FOUNDATIONS OF DUAL EDUCATION AT RED RIVER 1811-34. Historical and Scientific Society of Manitoba Transactions (Series 3) 21:35-68.

The origins of the dual confessional system of education (Catholic and Protestant) in the Red River Settlement, particularly during the proprietary rule of the Selkirk family from 1811 to 1834, are examined.   IVY

1042   **JAMPOLSKY L**
1965
ADVANCEMENT IN INDIAN EDUCATION WITH COMMENT BY HOWARD E. STAATS. In The Education of Indian Children in Canada: A Symposium Written by Members of Indian Affairs Education Division with Comments by the Indian Peoples. L. G. P. Waller, ed. The Canadian Superintendent 1965. Toronto: Ryerson Press. pp. 49-60.

Eleven tables demonstrate: (1) the increase in the pupil population as compared with the total Indian population, (2) the increasing number of children in day schools and rapid increase of pupils attending public and private schools, (3) the normalization of the distribution of pupils in the various grades, (4) the steady increase of pupils in senior secondary programs, and (5) the numbers attending vocational schools and universities. Comment is made by Howard E. Staats of the Six Nations Band, Ontario.   IVY

1043   **JAMPOLSKY LYMAN,   CUNNINGHAM BERYL**
1966
SURVEY OF INDIAN "SCHOOL-LEAVERS" FROM GRADES 1 TO 12: A STUDY OF THE 1964-65 PUPIL POPULATION. Ottawa: Department of Indian Affairs and Northern Development. 6 pp.

A study in 1965-1966 of Indian pupils who did not return to school after the 1964-1965 school year examines what happens to these pupils, what percentage leaves, and at what grade they leave. Statistical findings are presented. Results of the study suggest pupils entering high school are ill-prepared, are enrolled in unsuitable programs, and require intensive counseling. It is suggested that a minimum objective of grade 10 be sought, that school-leavers be picked up by the Branch, and that accurate records be kept of enrollments in grades 8 to 12.   JSL

1044   **JOHNSTON   BASIL**
1970
BREAD BEFORE BOOKS OR BOOKS BEFORE BREAD. In The Only Good Indian: Essays by Canadian Indians. Waubageshig, ed. Toronto: New Press. pp. 126-141.

The variables and forces which are likely to bring the Canadian Indian out of his suppressed condition are discussed. Distrust in self and in others has been an impeding factor in the regeneration of confidence between races. The recognition of treaties alone would remove much of the suspicion which strains Indian-White relations. Also, by looking to the accomplishments of their ancestors, the Indian people today would renew their strength and make way for an economic, social, and intellectual renaissance.   DGW

1045   **KEE   HERBERT WILLIAM**
1966
REVERSAL AND NONREVERSAL SHIFTS IN INDIAN AND WHITE CHILDREN. M.A. Thesis. Department of Psychology. University of British Columbia. 44 pp.

Sixty-seven Indian and 51 White children aged 7 to 9 were administered tests designed to explore certain aspects of the relationship between language and cognition. Forty-eight from each group attained the first learning criterion and were tested on shift tasks. Each ethnic group contained 24 girls and 24 boys equally distributed among the age groups. The Indian children were attending Alberni and Mission Residential Schools and Southlands Elementary School. The White sample was drawn from Southlands and Lord Kitchener Elementary Schools. No significant differences were observed in original learning, overall performance, or relative difficulty of R and NR shifts for the 2 groups. Supplementary analysis showed consistent learning speed on original discrimination and on shift for White children. The learning speed was inverted for Indian children.   CCV

1046   **KIM   YONG C**
1968
SOCIAL ORIGINS OF SCHOOL RETARDATION AMONG THE INDIAN PUPILS: SUMMARY REPORT. Unpublished paper. Available from National Library of Canada. 14 pp.

Areas visited include the Wallaston Lake, South End, Pelican Narrows, Deschambalt, Stanly Mission, Stony Rapid, Lac La Ronge, and Green Lake Reserves as well as more than 40 others in Saskatchewan from 1966 to 1968. Examined are socio-cultural factors causing retardation among Indian children: (1) language, (2) perception and motivation (parents' indifference to scholastic achievement, inadequate meals for school-age children, disregard for time concepts, and home environment), and (3) interpersonal influence and social structure (influence of family, teachers, and peers, and relation of social class, place of residence, and family composition to educational achievement).   IVY

1047 **KIRMAN   JOSEPH**
1969
THE UNIVERSITY OF ALBERTA'S INTERCULTURAL EDUCATION
PROGRAM. Peabody Journal of Education 47:15-19.

The University of Alberta established an intercultural education program to prepare teachers for their role in culturally different settings. This program is discussed with specific references to tribes in Alberta.   IVY

1048 **KNILL   WILLIAM D**
1963
EDUCATION AND NORTHERN CANADA. The Canadian Administrator 3:9-12.

The history of education in northern Saskatchewan is briefly outlined. A study of pupil failure and retardation shows that failure rates for Indian and Metis students are excessive. A survey of teacher opinions identifies 3 major reasons for lack of pupil achievement: cultural gap, physical health problems, and the need for adult understanding and training. A content analysis of student essays on career interests indicates unrealistic expectations regarding future jobs and that occupational choice and reasons for that choice seem to be closely related to ethnicity. A redefinition of purposes and renewal of effort in northern education is needed.   IVY

1049 **KNILL   WILLIAM D**
1966
EDUCATION - A CULTURAL BRIDGE. The Alberta School Trustee 36(2):10-11,20.

Education is likened to a bridge in which the bridge itself is the curriculum of the instructional program. Using references from schools in northern Alberta, the 3 supports of this educational bridge are discussed: adequate school buildings and equipment, a well-trained teaching and administrative staff, and an effective school board.   IVY

1050 **KNOWLES   DONALD W,   BOERSMA   FREDERIC J**
1968
OPTIONAL SHIFT PERFORMANCE OF CULTURALLY-DIFFERENT
CHILDREN TO CONCRETE AND ABSTRACT STIMULI. Alberta Journal of
Educational Research 14:165-177.

It has been suggested that language mediates in the learning process and that children from culturally disadvantaged backgrounds are thus handicapped in learning involving abstract stimuli. Compared are optional shift performances of 40 8-year olds from suburban middle-class backgrounds and a similar sample from 3 reserves within the Edmonton Agency. Stimuli utilized were both concrete familiar objects and abstract pictorial material. Indian performance was poorer than that of the middle class. However, the Indian sample dealing with concrete stimuli performed no better than the Indian sample dealing with abstract stimuli. Middle-class children exhibited a greater facility to verbalize reasoning behind their responses.   IVY

1051   **LANE   BARBARA S**
1965
THE EDUCATION OF INDIAN CHILDREN. The B.C. School Trustee 21(Winter-Spring):6-10.

To attempt an explanation of the high rate of failure among Indian students, cultural factors must be explored. The first 6 years of an Indian child's life has not prepared him for the conformity required in a grade classroom. Totally different categories of thought and expression are experienced by an Indian child learning English. Verbal virtuosity, a comprehension indicator to teachers, is frequently not characteristic of Indian peoples. Teachers frequently underrate the abilities of an Indian pupil who in turn will soon perform according to the teacher's expectations. Successful educated Indian models are lacking; success in most instances has occurred without formal education. To provide all children with an equal opportunity: (1) the province must recognize the bias of the school system in favor of the urban, middle-class, White Protestant child of English speaking background and assume responsibility for those students encountering special difficulties with the school system, (2) teachers should receive some anthropologically-oriented training, (3) the present curricula and textbooks, particularly in history and social studies, could be improved, and (4) kindergarten classes for Indian children should be mandatory.   IVY

1052   **LANE   BARBARA S**
1970
...FIVE YEARS LATER. British Columbia School Trustee 26(2):13-14.

In this addendum to a 1965 article entitled "The Education of Indian Children"which is reprinted in this issue, the author clarifies her usage of the term "cultural deprivation"and elaborates upon Indian languages.   IVY

1053   **LAVALLEE   ED**
1967
SUITABILITY OF CURRICULUM FOR NATIVE CHILDREN. In National Conference on Indian and Northern Education Saskatoon 1967. Mary Anne LaVallee, ed. n.p.: Society for Indian and Northern Education and Extension Division, University of Saskatchewan. pp. 69-73.

The native school dropout is a victim of inadequate intercultural communication. The Indian child of a different cultural background enters a strange environment with a poor base in the English language and a sensitivity do discrimination. The type of training received in residential schools, emphasizing religious rather than academic studies, is inadequate preparation for students entering university or vocational training. Paternalistic attitudes and methods of guidance counselors do not help students overcome these handicaps.   IVY

1054   **LAVALLEE   MARY ANNE**
1967
END OF AN ERA - WE SPEAK. The Northian 4(2):117-124.

Taken from a speech presented at the Saskatoon Conference, this article reviews the development and failure of the government to educate the Indian. The specific failures of the residential and day schools are discussed. The government's refusal to listen to and act upon the Indian's advice, however, is seen as the chief failure. The Indian's disenchantment with the government, as well as his return to the reserve and excessive drinking, are the results of this failure. What the Indian most needs to learn is how to once again be a man, and this the reserve can teach him better than the government and its trained personnel. The future task of education and its curriculum will be helping the Indian to relearn those things - courage, loyalty, pride, perseverance, character, and a competitive spirit - which characterize a man.   ADG

1055   **LAVALLEE   MARY ANNE**
1967
RESOLUTIONS. In National Conference on Indian and Northern Education Saskatoon 1967. Mary Anne LaVallee, ed. n.p.: Society for Indian and Northern Education and Extension Division, University of Saskatchewan. pp. 87-88.

Resolutions made by the native people who attended this conference are presented. The Indian people of Canada demand their constitutional rights in all aspects of education, equal representation on school boards, the changing of textbooks and media to acknowledge the Indian's contribution, the elimination of the reference "savage"from all textbooks, the establishment of kindergartens on reserves, and the establishment of a provincial central school board composed of Indian representatives.   IVY

1056   **LAVALLEE   MARY ANNE**
1967
SCHOOL INTEGRATION. In National Conference on Indian and Northern Education Saskatoon 1967. Mary Anne LaVallee, ed. n.p.: Society for Indian and Northern Education and Extension Division, University of Saskatchewan. pp. 21-34.

There is no Indian problem but a Canadian one which must be dealt with accordingly. Examined and discussed are social studies courses in Saskatchewan, residential schools and their influence on the family, Indian day schools, integrated schooling, and school committees and their roles on Indian reserves. Progress will have been made when the Indian has been assimilated into the Canadian system of education and is no longer singled out as a cultural curiosity.   IVY

1057   **LAVALLEE   MARY ANNE**
1968
TOO LITTLE AND TOO LATE: INDIAN EDUCATION IN CANADA. Arbos 5(2):26-29,35.

Within the educational system, the Indian must search for his identity and his destiny. Criticisms and recommendations are given on curriculum, residential schools, and school committees.   IVY

1058   **LEE   I A**
1970
THE "CITIZEN MINUS"IN EDUCATION. In The Poor at School in Canada: Observational Studies of Canadian Schools, Classrooms and Pupils. Ottawa: Canadian Teachers' Federation. pp. 106-124.

Discussion of the impediments to academic advancement of Indian school children is presented including a brief survey of Indian education studies. Northern Ontario is the focus of the paper. Although many of the immediate difficulties are associated with poverty it is proposed that White domination of the power structure must be altered with ultimate autonomy for Indians being the objective.   CCV

1059   **LEVAQUE   J E Y**
1968
THE FUTURE OF INDIAN EDUCATION. Kerygma 2(1):37-41.

Three critical areas of human development which must be promoted in Indian education are identity, dignity, and potential. To this end textbooks must be improved, children should be taught to question both Indian and White values, educational facilities and teaching personnel should be the best available, and more and better job prospects should be provided.   IVY

1060   **LOOSELY   ELIZABETH**
1960
EDUCATION IN THE NORTH. Food for Thought 20:258-267.

The problem of education in the North is to get the people to understand what is happening to them and to their land as a result of contact. The early education was not designed to do this; its focus was religious enlightenment and faith. At the present time, both the federal government and churches administer education in the North. Hostels set up near the pupils' homes are presently endorsed because of the nomadic life styles. Education is geared according to the needs and purposes of the educands. Thus full time studies are provided for those who will be in permanent contact with Whites. Schools are being consolidated into 1 federal school to facilitate an effective education program.   ADG

1061   **LOTZ   JIM**
1969
AN INDIAN COMMUNITY COLLEGE IN CANADA: A PROPOSAL. Unpublished paper. Available from Canadian Research Centre for Anthropology, Saint Paul University. 21 pp.

A proposed Indian community college must serve the needs of Indians and Whites, but its primary goal must be to serve Indian students with physical and administrative aspects reflecting the concept of education by and for Indians. It is suggested that a central building be established, together with a traveling component. The college must provide job training which recognizes future employment opportunities.   JSL

1062   **LYON   LOUISE C,   FRIESEN   JOHN W**
1969
CULTURE CHANGE AND EDUCATION: A STUDY OF INDIAN AND NON-INDIAN VIEWS IN SOUTHERN ALBERTA. New York: Associated Educational Services. 160 pp.

This report results from interviews with 60 Indians from 5 bands (Blackfoot, Blood, Piegan, Sarsi, and Stony) and 37 non-Indians. A questionnaire was constructed involving the areas of (1) Indian social system management, (2) changing cultural conditions, (3) socialization of Indian children today, (4) the meaning of the Indian's world view, and (5) the Indian needs. Each chapter interprets and elaborates upon the responses of the questionnaire. In an attempt to discover if some relationships existed which might reveal an Indian way of thinking, the data were subjected to factor analysis. Preliminary analysis involving Indian responses reveals a strong nativistic orientation.   IVY

1063   **MACARTHUR   R S**
1962
ASSESSING THE INTELLECTUAL ABILITY OF INDIAN AND METIS PUPILS AT FORT SIMPSON N.W.T. Ottawa: Department of Northern Affairs and National Resources, Northern Administration Branch, Education Division, Curriculum Section. 23 pp.

In October, 1961, intelligence tests, hypothesized to be "culture-reduced," were administered to 239 Indians and Metis of both sexes attending school in grades 1-9 at Fort Simpson, Northwest Territories. For purposes of this study, the original sample of 239 was reduced to 155. Data are presented in 4 separate groups: (1) grades 7, 8, 9 (32 pupils, mean age of 13.10), (2) grades 5, 6 (58 pupils of mean age 13.11), (3) grades 2, 3 (46 pupils of mean age 10.2), and (4) grade 1 (19 pupils of mean age 7.6). Data of the Faust study are included in this report. It is concluded that the lack of norms appropriate for Indian-Metis are a major drawback of these tests and considerable intellectual potential amongst the Indian-Metis of Fort Simpson and Faust is indicated. Extensive investigation in education methods is required to assist them to realize this potential.   IVY

1064   **MACARTHUR   R S**
1968
ASSESSING INTELLECTUAL POTENTIAL OF NATIVE CANADIAN PUPILS: A SUMMARY. Alberta Journal of Educational Research 14:115-122.

This summary of the intelligence literature pertaining to culture-reduced tests used with the Canadian native finds the Progressive Matrices and SCRIT valid for grades 1 through 8, and the IPAT Cattell and Lorge-Thorndike Non-Verbal acceptable for higher grades. These tests should be included in testing programs aimed at facilitating the interviewer's understanding of the native student, his ability and potential. Further research is suggested by 3 features of such tests as the above: (1) the use of stimulus symbols which are likely to be learned in a variety of cultures, (2) the arrangement of items in a progression which somewhat parallels the development of human cognition, and (3) the arrangement of items in the test such that it provides a crudely programmed sample of learning-on-the-spot.   ADG

1065   **MACARTHUR   R S**
1969
SOME COGNITIVE ABILITIES OF ESKIMO, WHITE AND INDIAN METIS PUPILS AGED 9 TO 12 YEARS. Canadian Journal of Behavioural Science 1:50-59.

Using Indian-Metis, Eskimo and White subjects, this examination of cross-cultural ability tests finds that the amount and nature of verbal material used is very influential in the structuring of certain cognitive abilities. Native pupils performed best on tests highly loaded on the reasoning-from-non-verbal material. The gap existing between native and White pupils on highly verbal tests widened with age. However, the spelling and word memory tests showed little bias against native pupils.   ADG

1066   **MACARTHUR   RUSSELL**
1968

SOME DIFFERENTIAL ABILITIES OF NORTHERN CANADIAN NATIVE
YOUTH. International Journal of Psychology 3:43-51.

Canadian native pupils and a parallel sample of Whites were tested for selected cognitive
abilities to determine which of these was most affected by differences in backgrounds.
Findings indicated that these native peoples have developed abilities in adaptation to
their own environment. Evidence is presented concerning their potential to develop ab-
ilites useful in adaptation to a school-based technological way of life.   IVY

1067   **MACARTHUR   RUSSELL S**
1968
EDUCATIONAL POTENTIAL OF NORTHERN CANADIAN NATIVE PUPILS. In
Proceedings of a Symposium on "Educational Process and Social Change in a Specialized
Environmental Milieu."G. K. Gooderham, chairman. The University of Alberta Boreal
Institute Occasional Publication 4. Edmonton: University of Alberta, Boreal Institute.
pp. 73-81.

Group tests (some using designs, geometric forms, and sometimes numbers as stimuli)
were administered to 3 groups of pupils. Results were tabled and compared. A model of
the nature and development of intellectual abilities is outlined and some evidence is presented of both intellectual potential and differential abilities of Eskimo, Indian-Metis,
and White students. Psychological influences likely to affect development of various cognitive abilities in different cultures are considered.   IVY

1068   **MACDONALD   HUGH A**
1965
PROGRAMMED INSTRUCTION WITH TEACHER PARTICIPATION: AN
EXPERIMENT IN TEACHING FRACTIONS TO PUPILS WHO RESIDE IN THE
NORTHWEST TERRITORIES. Ottawa: Education Division, Northern Administration
Branch, Department of Northern Affairs and National Resources.   75 pp.

Residential schools in Inuvik and Fort Smith and non-residential schools in Yellowknife
and Hay River provided a sample of 203 Metis, Indian, and Eskimo grade 6 pupils for a
study of programed instruction conducted from November 18 to December 21, 1964.
Four matched groups were subjected to different teaching methods - programed instruction with no teacher participation, programed instruction with minimal teacher participation, programed instruction with maximum participation, and conventional teaching
methods. Pupils of White ancestry were found to benefit significantly from programed
instruction while performance of native students did not differ from that achieved with
conventional methods.   CCV

1069   **MACKENZIE   JOHN**
1966
REPORT ON THE OPASQUIA LEADERSHIP COURSE. Unpublished paper.
Available from Indian and Northern Education Resource Center, University of
Saskatchewan. 51 pp.

Upon request by the members of The Pas Reserve, a leadership course was initiated and
held on The Pas Reserve from May 20-23, 1966. The 1st part of this report concerns the
development of the course, and its subsequent evaluation. The remainder is the actual
course content prepared by Professor Walter Lampe.   IVY

1070   **MACLEOD   JOHN MALCOLM**
1964
INDIAN EDUCATION IN CANADA: A STUDY OF INDIAN EDUCATION WITH
SPECIAL REFERENCE TO THE BRIEFS PRESENTED TO THE JOINT
COMMITTEE OF THE SENATE AND HOUSE OF COMMONS ON INDIAN
AFFAIRS, 1959-1961. M.Ed. Thesis. Department of Education. University of New
Brunswick. 224 pp.

Information relating to Indian education in Canada is drawn largely from Minutes of
Proceedings and Evidence of the Joint Committee of the Senate and the House of Commons on Indian Affairs, 1959, 1960, and 1961, supplemented by conversations with native leaders and 10 years of teaching in Indian communities. Contemporary opinions,
criticisms, and needs as expressed by Indian peoples, religious bodies, interested secular
groups, and the Saskatchewan government are discussed. The 1962 results of a survey
of later careers of pupils leaving the 8-grade Bella Bella Indian school and a comparison
of Indian and non-Indian scores on standardized tests are reported. Recommendations
are geared to contemporary thinking on Indian education and aimed to improve the
quality of teaching and teaching personnel and to increase student benefits.   CCV

1071   **MACPHERSON   NORMAN JOHN**
n.d.
PREPARATION OF A TEACHER TRAINING PROGRAM IN ENGLISH AS A
SECOND LANGUAGE FOR INDIAN, ESKIMO AND METIS STUDENTS OF
THE NORTHWEST TERRITORIES. M.Ed. Thesis. University of Alberta.

The title has been verified, but a copy was not obtained in time to abstract it.   SLP

1072   **MANITOBA INDIAN BROTHERHOOD**
n.d.
EDUCATION LIAISON PROGRAM. Unpublished paper. Available from National
Library of Canada. 6 pp.

The education of the Indian child will be most effective when the following principles are
achieved: (1) parental participation, (2) relevancy of education, and (3) the development
of schools as an economic asset to the community. To achieve these objectives, a person
of Indian ancestry must work with educational personnel in the capacity of liaison officer.   IVY

1073   **MANITOBA. Department of Youth and Education. Curriculum Branch.**
1970
RESOURCE MATERIALS PERTAINING TO INDIAN AND ESKIMO
CULTURES. Winnipeg: Curriculum Branch, Department of Youth and Education. 80
pp.

A multi-media resource list pertaining to Indian and Eskimo cultures, both historical and
contemporary, is presented. Grade level is given.   IVY

1074   **MANITOU ARTS FOUNDATION**
1970
PROPOSAL AND PRELIMINARY PLAN FOR DEVELOPMENT AND
OPERATION OF A CULTURAL FINE ARTS PROGRAM FOR PERSONS OF

INDIAN DESCENT IN ONTARIO. Unpublished paper. Available from National
Library of Canada. 20 pp.

Designed to be meaningful to the Indian participants, this arts program will center
around traditional and cultural outputs of Canadian Indians and provide basic
knowledge, skills, and techniques required to continue successfully in arts-related fields.
Included is an outline of procedures, administration, and budget of the program.   IVY

1075   **MARSHALL   LIONEL GEORGE**
1966
THE DEVELOPMENT OF EDUCATION IN NORTHERN SASKATCHEWAN.
M.Ed. Thesis. College of Education. University of Saskatchewan, Saskatoon. 202 pp.

The history of education in northern Saskatchewan is traced from the 1840's. The roles
of the federal, provincial, and imperial governments, the Catholic and Anglican missions, and the Hudson's Bay Company in the establishment and development of a system
of education for the Indian and Metis are described. Day schools, residential schools,
teaching personnel, curriculum, school facilities, and salary are described. The attitudes
of government, traders, and missionaries toward education are discussed as well as Indian attitudes to the signing of treaties.   CCV

1076   **MARSHALL   LIONEL GEORGE**
1967
THE DEVELOPMENT OF EDUCATION IN NORTHERN SASKATCHEWAN. The
Musk-Ox 1:19-25.

Schools in northern Saskatchewan established by the English and Roman Catholic
churches and their respective curricula are described. The responsibilities of the federal
and provincial governments in providing education for the Indian and Metis of northern
Saskatchewan are briefly outlined.   IVY

1077   **MCGANN   DAVID**
1967
MORE IN SORROW: SOCIAL ACTION AND THE INDIAN BOARDING HOME
PROGRAM. Canadian Welfare 43(4):24-29.

This is a brief to the Minister of Indian Affairs describing the establishment, development and failure of a program aimed at providing a home atmosphere for Indian youth
studying away from home. Since 1962 Indian Affairs has sponsored secondary education in Vancouver for Indian youth. Numerous bad experiences have occurred within
the homes where these youth board. In some cases the Indian youths were apparently at
fault, in others, the landlords. The continual breakdown of the placements was having a
detrimental effect on the tolerance and understanding of the Indian. Several failures in
the Boarding Home program were noted: (1) failure to screen students carefully and
match them with boarding homes that have been properly studied, (2) failure to use
properly trained personnel and assign realistic caseloads, and (3) failure to use the practical knowledge which youth-serving agencies have gained through years of research and
experience. Corrective measures are recommended.   ADG

1078   **MCISSAC   J C**
1968

REMARKS. Unpublished paper delivered to Task Force Meeting, Government of Saskatchewan. Regina, August 9, 1968. Available from Indian and Metis Department, Regina. 5 pp.

This summarizes the educational facilities in upgrading and vocational training offered by the Department of Education in Saskatchewan.   IVY

1079   **MCKENZIE   KEITH S**
1969
THE CONFLICT OF VALUES BETWEEN SUB-CULTURAL GROUP: THE INDIAN IN EDUCATION. Unpublished paper. Available from National Library of Canada. 28 pp.

Drawing upon results of programs in the United States, 4 dominant factors emerge as being critical in the education of Indians: culture, language competence, teacher training, and adult involvement. It is suggested that consideration of these factors offers a viable approach to effecting a needed change in Indian education in Canada.   IVY

1080   **MCMANUS   PATRICIA R**
1970
PROBLEMS OF THE ISOLATED AND NON-ISOLATED INDIAN FEMALE STUDENTS IN MANITOBA. M.Ed. Thesis. Faculty of Graduate Studies and Research. University of Manitoba. 66 pp.

During the winter of 1969-70, 64 female Indians residing at home and attending grades 8 or 9 in federal schools and 81 Indian girls boarding away from home and attending grades 9 to 12 in Metropolitan Winnipeg schools were administered the Mooney Problem Check list. Results were examined according to grade, school location, and time period at school and away from home. It is indicated that female Indian students share problems common to non-Indian populations and that isolated students have more problems than non-isolated students. Implications are discussed.   CCV

1081   **MENARIK   ELIJAH**
1967
RESIDENTIAL SCHOOLS. In National Conference on Indian and Northern Education Saskatoon 1967. Mary Anne LaVallee, ed. n.p.: Society for Indian and Northern Education and Extension Division of University of Saskatchewan. pp. 42-45.

Comments are expressed on the following topics: the problem of school integration; the role of education in vocational and practical training for the native children; the attitude and feeling of Indian and Eskimo parents with respect to residential schools; the suitability of the curriculum and textbooks for native children; and the fit of the present school program to the culture of the Metis, Indian, and Eskimo and its real meaning to these children.   IVY

1082   **MICKELSON   NORMA I,   GALLOWAY   CHARLES G**
1969
CUMULATIVE LANGUAGE DEFICIT AMONG INDIAN CHILDREN.
Exceptional Children 36:187-190.

In 1968 a pre-school and orientation enrichment program for reserve children was set up at the University of Victoria. The children, divided into 3 classes (3-4, 5-6, 7-13), received intense training in verbalizing. The objectives were (1) to increase the qualitative and quantitative verbalization patterns of the children, (2) to extend the children's functional knowledge of the structure of the English language, (3) to increase their ability to comprehend and apply information, and (4) to facilitate the children's application, analysis, synthesization and evaluation of issues on the basis of knowledge gained. The study found that language deficiencies tend to remain in the verbal repertoire of disadvantaged children and that such deficiencies cannot be overcome simply as a function of time and undifferentiated school experiences. Success requires the involvement of the child in well-planned and specific language experiences.   ADG

1083   **MICKLEBURGH   BRUCE**
1969
PERSPECTIVE. Monday Morning 3(9):5-6.

Canada's treatment of Indians is briefly reviewed and the challenge issued to educators to recognize each child's tribal culture and identity.   IVY

1084   **MINARD   ANN**
1967
THE INDIAN STUDENT IN VANCOUVER. The Peak (Simon Fraser University) 5(15):13.

Residential schools do not equip Indian youth for the complexities of urban life. However, the work of a few individuals has brought about the enrolment of 750 students in Vancouver and Lower Mainland secondary schools. The boarding parent plays a large part in the success or failure of the student. The author is a boarding parent of 2 Indian boys in high school.   TSA

1085   **MITCHELL   MARJORIE**
1970
TEACHING INDIAN CHILDREN: A DIFFERENT VIEW. The B.C. Teacher 50:66-68.

This reply to a previous article on Indian education (see Heshidahl et al. 1970) stresses several themes related to general attitudes towards and beliefs about the Indian. It is not clear whether most Indians agree that they are at least partially responsible for their experiences with social, economic and political descrimination and its consequences. Indians do speak but we do not listen. Indians are just as intelligent as non-Indians. Perhaps the reason that the Indian ponders before speaking is linguistic or cultural; and he should not be considered slow-witted for this behavioral characteristic. It is a myth held by many teachers that the Indian cannot think in abstract terms and that he is unable to grasp the meaning of some idiomatic expressions.   Perhaps White Canadians should try to learn a few Indian languages and see how well they think abstractly. It has been shown that North American Indian languages are just as rich in abstraction, complexity, figurativeness and structure as any other language. Moreover, all children, including Whites, think in concrete terms. Nor is it fair to disclaim the social experiences of Indian children as inconsequential. And perhaps the Indians' difficulty with certain English sounds should be seen as the result of accent rather than language deficiencies. Teachers have failed with the Indian because of ethnocentric tendencies on their own part. Perhaps the Indian should be paid for the land we took from him, so he can set up his own educational systems and come to terms with White Canada on his own impetus.   ADG

1086   **MOORE   A**
1965
THE TEACHING STAFF IN INDIAN SCHOOLS WITH COMMENT BY SHEILA M. MCGRATH. In The Education of Indian Children in Canada: A Symposium Written by Members of Indian Affairs Education Division with Comments by the Indian Peoples. L. G. P. Waller, ed. The Canadian Superintendent 1965. Toronto: Ryerson Press. pp. 36-48.

An account of teaching and of the teaching staff in Indian schools in Canada is given. Some of the aspects discussed are: terms of employment, salary schedules and regulations, percentage turnover, duties, and fringe benefits. Sheila M. McGrath of the Golden Lake Band, Ontario, comments.   IVY

1087   **MUIR   PEARL,   CHALMERS   JOHN W**
1970
POVERTY AND ALBERTA'S NATIVE PEOPLES. In The Poor at School In Canada: Observational Studies of Canadian Schools, Classrooms and Pupils. Ottawa: Canadian Teachers' Federation. pp. 137-143.

Contributing factors, particularly in the fields of education, employment, and government policies, are discussed in this evaluation of the situation of Alberta's Indians and Metis. The contribution education could make to alleviation of poverty of native peoples is proposed. Recommendations are advanced for adaptation of education to the needs of all peoples, specialized training for educational personnel, involvement of native peoples in decision-making processes, and involvement and adaptation of industry to native needs.   CCV

1088   **NEALE   ELLA**
1966
THE SIOUX NARROWS EXPERIMENT. Continuous Learning 5:177-178.

An adult education program begun in 1966 at Sioux Narrows, Ontario, proved successful.   IVY

1089   **NEUFELD   VICTOR J**
1965
A RESEARCH STUDY RELATING TO THE LEVEL OF SCHOOL FUNCTIONING OF INDIAN STUDENTS TO SELECTED FACTORS OF PAST LIFE EXPERIENCES. M.S.W. Thesis. School of Social Work. University of Manitoba.

The title has been verified, but a copy was not obtained in time to abstract it.   SLP

1090   **NORCROSS   E BLANCHE**
1970
RAY COLLINS' EDUCATION CLUB. Continuous Learning 9:231-232.

Adult education for both Indian and White on a full daytime basis at the elementary school level is offered in Vancouver. The school is geared for 12 to 14 students and the goals are individualistic.   IVY

1091   **ONTARIO. Department of Education.**
1969
SERVICES TO INDIAN PEOPLE PROVIDED BY THE DEPARTMENT OF EDUCATION. Unpublished paper. Available from Library, Ontario Department of Education, Toronto. 7 pp.

Largely financed jointly by the Ontario government and the Department of Indian Affairs and Northern Development and/or the Department of Manpower and Immigration, programs discussed are: representation on school boards, school curriculum, handicapped Indian children, Ontario Manpower Retraining programs in northern Ontario, leadership training courses, and the education program at Moosonee.   IVY

1092   **ORMAN   EDITH**
1963
STUDENTS FOLLOW THROUGH: WITH THE KNOWLEDGE GAINED IN EDUCATION 357. Canadian Home and School 22(3):14-15.

A University of Saskatchewan course for teachers of Indians is described and evaluated by a teacher from an Indian residential school in Kenora, Ontario.   ADG

1093   **O'NEILL   F**
1965
ADULT EDUCATION IN INDIAN COMMUNITIES WITH COMMENT BY AHAB SPENCE. In The Education of Indian Children in Canada: A Symposium Written by Members of Indian Affairs Division with Comments by the Indian Peoples. L. G. P. Waller, ed. The Canadian Superintendent 1965. Toronto: Ryerson Press. pp. 88-94.

A synopsis of accomplishments in federal and provincial programs in adult education for the years 1955-1965 is given. Ahab Spence of The Pas Band, Manitoba, comments.   IVY

1094   **O'NEILL   FLORENCE M**
1963
A PROJECTED PLAN FOR INDIAN COMMUNITIES. Ottawa: Department of Citizenship and Immigration. 40 pp.

The report was prepared when the need to reorganize and expand the Adult Education Services within the Indian Affairs Branch was being examined. The report is concerned with the relevance of adult education programs to community development on Indian reserves. Discussed are the basis for the proposal, the basic philosophy, aims, procedures, organizational structure, staff requirements, staff selection, staff training, program implementation, and evaluation.   JSL

1095   **O'NEILL   FLORENCE M**
1964
BASIC EDUCATION FOR SOCIAL TRANSITION: A PROGRAMME OF ADULT

EDUCATION FOR INDIAN COMMUNITIES. Ottawa: Department of Citizenship and Immigration. 10 pp.

The report is concerned with the role of adult education in socio-economic development. Discussed are the objectives, organization, administration, staff requirements, staff selection, and training aspects of adult education.   JSL

1096   **O'REILLY   ROBERT RICHARD**
1967
NORTHERN STUDENTS ATTENDING POST-SECONDARY INSTITUTIONS IN CANADA, 1966-67: A PRELIMINARY STUDY. Unpublished paper prepared for Education Division, Northern Administration Branch, Department of Indian Affairs and Northern Development. Available from Indian and Northern Education Resource Centre, University of Saskatchewan. 37 pp.

A preliminary examination of the performance and attitudes of students from the Northwest Territories who attended post-secondary institutions in southern Canada in 1966-67 is derived from questionnaires completed by 40 students. The data are analyzed from 4 viewpoints: academic, financial, assistance, and social participation.   IVY

1097   **PARMINTER   ALFRED VYE**
1964
THE DEVELOPMENT OF INTEGRATED SCHOOLING FOR BRITISH COLUMBIA INDIAN CHILDREN. M.A. Thesis. Department of Education. University of British Columbia. 162 pp.

This study of the development of integrated schooling for British Columbia Indian children is comprised of a review of historical aspects of integration and an assessment of the effectiveness of the process based on an examination of opinions and observations provided by teachers, principals, school board members, and Indian Affairs Branch personnel as expressed in response to a questionnaire. Formal educational opportunities historically available to Indians, standards in Indian day and residential schools, and options available to Indian parents in choosing schooling for their children are reviewed. Enrollment, achievement, and integration statistics are presented. A summary of opinions expressed indicates that integration has improved Indian participation and attitudes, many difficulties encountered at the primary level are related to language, reserve environment is detrimental to school progress and encourages dropouts, occurrences of poor achievement depend upon environmental and not hereditary factors, and lack of initiative or perseverance arises from differential cultural values and is perhaps related to the attitudes of the dominant majority.   CCV

1098   **PETER   KARL A**
1970
THE CASE FOR AN INDIAN COMMUNITY COLLEGE. Unpublished paper. Available from National Library of Canada. 9 pp.

Because of cross-cultural social and psychological factors, the Indian student suffers a very high drop-out rate between grades 9 and 12. This paper suggests that an Indian community college should not copy the non-Indian system of education but should be structured around the needs of the Indian.   HCV

1099   **PHILION   WILLIAM L.   GALLOWAY   CHARLES G**
n.d.
INDIAN CHILDREN AND THE READING PROGRAM: A MODEL FOR DIRECT
OBSERVATION AND TEST-ITEM ANALYSIS AS A BASIS FOR GUIDANCE IN
THE FORMULATION FOR INDIAN CHILDREN. Unpublished paper. Available
from Library, University of Victoria. 21 pp.

Form 2 of the Gates Reading Survey was administered to the intermediate grades (4-7)
of an integrated elementary school in British Columbia in which one third of the 225 students are Indian. An item analysis of the test detected specific strengths and deficiencies
of each child. Examination of the data revealed a very limited and narrow concept development for Indian pupils. It was also observed that the Indian child relies to a considerable extent on nonverbal means for communication, that his directional cues tend to be
nonverbal, that he has difficulty with prepositions and conjunctions, and that for him
whole phrases or sounds function like huge words. These results suggest that an effective
language arts program for these pupils must emphasize concept development, word
games, oral reading, and development of listening skills. Clear diction and intonation
should be encouraged.   IVY

1100   **RAMRATTAN   A D,   ENS   E O**
1970
OPERATION RETRIEVAL: THE INTERLAKE ADULT EXPERIMENTAL
GROUP, ST. LAURENT. Unpublished paper. Available from Center for Settlement
Studies, University of Manitoba. 34 pp.

A compilation of reports is given concerning Operation Retrieval which is an inter-departmental project designed to accommodate a feasible academic curriculum relating to
the rural socio-economic environment of the learner. The impact of such a program
in the community is being observed where the Metis of St. Laurent are 1 of the ethnic
groups involved.   IVY

1101   **RATTAN   MONINDAR SINGH**
1966
PREDICTIVE VALIDITY AND STABILITY OF MEASURES OF INTELLECTUAL
POTENTIAL FOR TWO SAMPLES OF INDIAN-METIS AND ESKIMO
CHILDREN. M.Ed. Thesis. Department of Educational Psychology. University of
Alberta. 120 pp.

The identification of culture-reduced tests with long-term predictive validity and stability
is attempted through the examination of 45 Indian-Metis students from Faust, Alberta,
and 99 Eskimo students from Inuvik and Tuktoyaktuk schools. The new data (compiled
in 1965) are analyzed in light of data gathered in 1961-62 by R. S. MacArthur. The culture-reduced tests were found to have long-term predictive validity and stability with
few exceptions for both samples. The type of results obtained with culture-reduced tests
are compared with those yielded by conventional tests and the implications in multicul-
tural situations are discussed.   CCV

1102   **RENAUD   ANDRE**
1962
BLAZING TRAILS IN TEACHER EDUCATION: TEACHERS OF PUPILS WITH

INDIAN BACKGROUND ATTEND SPECIAL CLASS. Canadian Home and School 22(2):24-25.

Stimulated by the absence of a single Indian Education Centre in Canada, the College of Education at the University of Saskatchewan established a center for research and preparation of teachers of Indians.   ADG

1103   **RENAUD   ANDRE**
1963
ACCELERATION OF SOCIO-CULTURAL ADJUSTMENT AND CHANGE IN
NORTHERN COMMUNITIES. Unpublished paper delivered to Canadian
Political Science Association (Anthropology and Sociology Chapter). Quebec City, June 5, 1963. Available from National Library of Canada. 4 pp.

A program for teachers of Indian children at the College of Education, the University of Saskatchewan, is described.   HCV

1104   **RENAUD   ANDRE**
1965
EDUCATION FROM WITHIN; PART ONE: ANTHROPOLOGICAL
DEFINITION OF CURRICULUM DEVELOPMENT WITH CHILDREN OF
INDIAN BACKGROUND. The Northian 2(4):2-10.

Educators will have to combine their understanding of curriculum development and teaching methods with a consideration of the background and life experiences the reserve child brings to school, if he is to learn effectively. He cannot continue to receive his education by the same methods presently used with non-Indian, city-dwelling children, since much of reserve life is the direct opposite of that in urban Canada. In large measure, the Indian's communication continues to be non-verbal, he functions without the use of reading and writing, and older people teach the younger ones, drawing from knowledge gained by experience rather than from recorded material. The reserve also lacks the cultural plurality of the city, as well as the stress on industry and commercialism. The task, as educators in Saskatchewan have defined it, is to prepare teachers who are able to develop a teaching strategy which pays adequate attention to both the differences and assets of each of the communities in which the Indian child must function.   ADG

1105   **RENAUD   ANDRE**
1965
EDUCATION FROM WITHIN; PART TWO: GUIDING PRINCIPLES IN
DEVELOPING CURRICULUM WITH CHILDREN OF INDIAN BACKGROUND.
The Northian 2(5):5-12.

Because the home environment of the Indian child differs so drastically from that of urban Canada, educators must develop their curricula in a manner which does not destroy his natural curiosity. Four guidelines are considered in this regard: (1) the content and specific learning objectives of each lesson or unit must be continually assessed in light of the on-going home activities of the child, (2) the child's own experiences, thoughts and beliefs should be used in all teaching, especially that which is aimed at expanding and enriching the child's understanding of the larger social context, (3) subjects such as math, science, and English must be taught in a manner that assures their applicability in places other than the classroom, and (4) stress should be placed on content which is current and of importance to the adult Indian, whose present level of learning and aids for decision-making are limited.   ADG

1106   **RENAUD   ANDRE**
1969
EDUCATIONAL NEEDS OF THE INDIAN-METIS POPULATION. Reference paper No. 1. Education Committee Workshop, Saskatchewan Task Force on Indian-Metis Employment. Dr. Howard Nixon, Chairman. Saskatoon, May 5-7, 1969. Available from National Library of Canada.   6 pp.

The current situation in Saskatchewan Indian-Metis education is stated briefly. The relationship between the educational system and practices in use and the low levels and lack of formal education persisting among the native population is discussed. Aspects of the educational system which are incomprehensible or frustrating to native students are explained.   CCV

1107   **REVEL   TED**
1968
INTEGRATION - A WAY OF LIFE. The Manitoba Teacher 47(3):7-9.

This article describes the integration of Indian students into the Teulon Collegiate school system. This program, instituted in 1960, is distinguished by its joint community-church-school sponsorship and residences similar to the cottage system. At the present (1968), some 50 Indian pupils are attending the school, and the project has been a success.   ADG

1108   **ROBERTSON   GORDON**
1960
EDUCATION FOR A NORTHERN FUTURE. Speech delivered to Annual Breakfast Meeting of the Canadian Association of School Superintendants and Inspectors. Toronto, September 20, 1960. Available at Information Services, Records and Research, Department of Indian Affairs and Northern Development. 10 pp.

A talk by Gordon Robertson, Deputy Minister of Northern Affairs and National Resources and Commissioner of the Northwest Territories, reviews briefly the school system in the Canadian North, including particular needs in terms of personnel, curriculum, and administration.   CCV

1109   **ROGOW   SALLY,   STEARNS   MARY LEE**
1967
THE INDIAN CHILD IN SCHOOL. The Peak (Simon Fraser University) 5(15):12.

The educational process has failed to recognize the different culture of its Indian students.   TSA

1110   **SAMPSON   GLORIA P**
n.d.
CULTURALLY ATYPICAL CHILDREN AND LANGUAGE CONFLICT.
Unpublished paper. Available from National Library of Canada. 14 pp.

Speakers of Indian languages and non-standard English dialects are not benefiting from current instruction. The same techniques used to teach English as a 2nd language can be used to teach English to speakers of a non-standard dialect. The procedure for initiating a 2nd language program is outlined.   IVY

1111   **SASKATCHEWAN INDIAN SCHOOL TEACHERS ASSOCIATION**
1961
CLASSROOM OBJECTIVES AND ACTIVITIES WITH PUPILS OF INDIAN BACKGROUND. Saskatoon: Saskatchewan Indian School Teachers Association. 93 pp.

A quick-reference outline prepared by the members of Education S-357 at the 1961 summer session of the University of Saskatchewan relates specifically to pupils with a strong Indian cultural background. Of value particularly to new teachers, the report outlines oral language, written language, social studies, scientific training, occupational training, consumer education, health, and visual aids with concrete suggestions and recommendations.   IVY

1112   **SASKATCHEWAN. Department of Education.**
1966
DIVISION II CURRICULUM GUIDE: A SOCIAL STUDIES PROGRAM FOR CHILDREN OF INDIAN ANCESTRY (TENTATIVE). Unpublished paper. Available from National Library of Canada. 54 pp.

This is a tentative outline for a social studies program to be taught to children of Indian ancestry in grades 4 to 6. The program is designed to assist the Indian child to understand and value his own identity through experience and learning about his own people in relation to other Canadians and peoples of the world.   HCV

1113   **SASKATCHEWAN. Task Force on Indian Opportunity. Education Committee.**
1969
RECOMMENDATIONS IN INDIAN AND METIS EDUCATION. Unpublished paper. Education Committee Workshop, Saskatchewan Task Force on Indian Opportunity. Saskatoon, May 5-7, 1969. Available from Indian and Metis Department, Regina. 10 pp.

The education of children of Indian ancestry is recognized to be a specialized and different form of education. Recommendations 1-14 discuss the school program and the training of teachers. Northern schools should be administered from the North. Recommendations 15 and 17 consider this. Indian and Metis people are demanding more control over their affairs, including education. Recommendations 17-27 discuss adult education. Formal systems of communication both within the community and with the outside should be made available. Recommendations 28-38 consider the possibilities.   IVY

1114   **SASKATCHEWAN. Task Force on Indian Opportunity. Education Committee.**
1969
RECOMMENDATIONS OF EDUCATION COMMITTEE, SASKATCHEWAN TASK FORCE ON INDIAN OPPORTUNITY, AND COMMENTS BY DEPARTMENT OF EDUCATION AND NORTHERN SCHOOL BOARD. Unpublished paper. Available from Indian and Metis Department, Regina. 15 pp.

Comments are offered on each recommendation presented by the Education Committee concerning school programs, teacher training, administration, adult education, and communications.   IVY

1115   **SASKATCHEWAN. Task Force on Indian Opportunity. Education Committee.**
1969
SPECIAL PROJECTS RECOMMENDED BY EDUCATION COMMITTEE
SASKATCHEWAN TASK FORCE ON INDIAN OPPORTUNITY. Unpublished
paper. Education Committee Workshop, Saskatchewan Task Force on Indian
Opportunity. Saskatoon, May 5-7, 1969. Available from Indian and Metis Department,
Regina. 2 pp.

Special projects include (1) the establishment of model and/or pilot schools to facilitate the creation of educational relevance, (2) highly flexible secondary schools, and (3) a special teacher training program for people of Indian ancestry. It is strongly recommended that traditional schools become community schools in the fullest sense.   IVY

1116   **SAWADSKY   WALTER,   LANDON   THELMA**
1970
ADMINISTRATIVE PROBLEMS IN INTEGRATION: A SURVEY OF PROBLEM
AREAS CONNECTED WITH INTEGRATING INDIAN STUDENTS INTO THE
BRITISH COLUMBIA PUBLIC SCHOOL SYSTEM. Unpublished paper. Available
from British Columbia School Trustees Association, Vancouver, B.C.   18 pp.

The problems associated with integrating Indian children into the public school system are examined based on information obtained from 2 questionnaires sent to school administrators and staff. A more detailed second questionnaire brought response from 71 of 79 school districts. Results show the major problems are: need for special help in adapting to classroom environment and procedures, irregular attendance, a high dropout rate, need for special teacher training and experience, and difficulty of communicating with parents. Comments which accompanied the questionnaires are summarized and recommendations given.   IVY

1117   **SCHALM   PHILIP**
1968
SCHOOL ADMINISTRATORS' PERCEPTIONS OF PROBLEMS ARISING FROM
THE INTEGRATION OF INDIAN AND NON-INDIAN CHILDREN IN
PUBLICLY SUPPORTED SCHOOLS IN SASKATCHEWAN. M.Ed. Thesis.
Department of Education. University of Saskatchewan. 177 pp.

In order to identify and examine problems arising from the Saskatchewan integrated school program 154 principals and 42 supervisors involved in integrated education were studied by interview and questionnaire. Results of the study indicate that although principals favored integration the program was not viewed as satisfactory. Administrators with the highest percentage of Indian enrollment showed greatest concern for the associated problems. The major areas of difficulty revealed were: communications with the Indian Affairs Branch, irregular attendance and low motivation of Indian pupils, students' inadequate grasp of English, teachers' lack of information concerning the children's background and the implications of a different cultural background, and a lack of interaction between home and school. Recommendations are formulated in reponse to these needs.   CCV

1118   **SEALEY   D B**
1968
INDIAN EDUCATION AND INTER-CULTURAL RELATIONS. Unpublished
paper delivered to Public Meeting, The Pas, Manitoba, February 7, 1968. Available from
Library, Department of Health and Social Development, Winnipeg, Man. 11 pp.

Cultural, economic, biological, motivational, and educational aspects of the intercultural
problem, those people whose cultural habits make it difficult for them to fit into modern
society, are discussed. The focus is upon modifying social studies curricula to assist Indian youth in developing a positive self-concept.   IVY

1119   **SEALEY   D BRUCE**
1968
LO! THE POOR INDIAN! Manitoba Teacher 47(3):4-6.

The few significant educational achievements which have been made with the Indians
cannot outweigh the continued refusal to see the Indians as people and to give control of
their lives and affairs back to them. The government increases the very apathy it wishes
to dispel by its continued form of educational service to which the Manitoba teachers are
not objecting.   ADG

1120   **SHACK   SYBIL**
1969
WHAT THE 'INDIANS' COMING TO OUR URBAN SCHOOLS NEED. Monday
Morning 3(8):8-10.

The experiences of 2 Indian boys are used as an example to illustrate the difficulties native students have in White urban high schools. A solution offered for the high failure
rate of Indian students is the establishment of creches, day nurseries for babies.   IVY

1121   **SHIMPO   MITSURU**
1966
WHAT ARE THE NICEST THINGS ABOUT TEACHING INDIAN CHILDREN?
The Northian 3(2):9-12.

This article is comprised of the edited, but unanalyzed, responses of 41 teachers who
were asked, as part of a sociological study, "What are the nicest things about teaching
Indian children?". The responses vary in perspective and fall into 8 different categories
ranging from the personality of Indian children to the challenge they present to teachers.   ADG

1122   **SIM   R ALEX**
n.d.
THE EDUCATION OF INDIANS IN ONTARIO: A REPORT TO THE
PROVINCIAL COMMITTEE ON AIMS AND OBJECTIVES OF EDUCATION IN
THE SCHOOLS IN ONTARIO. n.p., n.p. 106 pp.

Focus of this report is the necessity of change in schools and their controlling bureaucra-
cies. Eighteen recommendations are made. These include the establishment of an Indian
Council of Ontario (a foundation set up to support projects, sponsor research, and foster
leadership), an Indian college, an Indian cultural and research center at one of Ontario's

major universities, and a Registry of Advancement in Toronto. Teachers should be adequately prepared, textbooks and curriculum improved, the concept of mobile teachers investigated, and teachers' organizations involved. Non-governmental agencies must reexamine their objectives and take the initiative through their organizations to prepare for and facilitate change. Changes in federal and provincial legislation are required to allow elected Indian representatives to sit on school boards.   IVY

1123   **SIM   R ALEX**
1969
INDIAN SCHOOLS FOR INDIAN CHILDREN. Canadian Welfare 45(2):11-13,16.

Arguing that integration, as it has been attempted by the federal and provincial governments, is detrimental to the over-all good of the Indian, this paper offers several recommendations aimed at giving the Indian child and his parents the special treatment they require for equality: (1) an Indian college which will give the Indian people an option to the existing education system, (2) an Indian Culture and Research Institute to serve as repository of rare documents, records and artifacts relating to the Indian's past, and a library and clearing house for information related to contemporary issues, (3) an alternate form of living for the Indian student who cannot fit into conventional high and vocational schools, (4) a private residential school with a small but professional group of teachers for those Indian students who have fallen behind in the conventional school system, and (5) a national interdisciplinary training program for teachers of the Indians.   ADG

1124   **SINCLAIR   WILL R**
1968
THE HIDDEN WORLD OF INTEGRATION. The Northian 5(3):10-11.

The Indian child entering integrated education faces several difficulties: racial rejection, communication and teacher language problems, and adjustment to the goals and values of urban Canadian society. Teachers can help the child face this identity crisis with success if they develop a warm relationship with him. Understanding the child's background should also help the teacher avoid stereotyping him. The requirements for a democratic education are: involvement of all government levels in providing better school facilities, special training for teachers working with the culturally deprived, and involvement of the total community in the various programs.   ADG

1125   **SINDELL   PETER SAMUEL**
1968
THE PSYCHOLOGICAL AND CULTURAL IMPACT OF RESIDENTIAL SCHOOL EXPERIENCE UPON MISTASSINI INDIANS. Ph.D. Thesis. Stanford Univeristy.

The title has been verified, but a copy was not obtained in time to abstract it.   SLP

1126   **SLUMAN   NORMA**
1964
SURVEY OF CANADIAN HISTORY TEXTBOOKS NOW IN USE IN MANITOBA SCHOOLS IN ORDER TO DETERMINE TO WHAT EXTENT THEY TEND TO PROMOTE A PATRONIZING AND DEGRADING ATTITUDE ON THE PART OF THE WHITE PEOPLE TOWARDS INDIANS, ARE HARMFUL TO THE INDIAN CHILD'S SENSE OF RACIAL DIGNITY AND DEAL INACCURATELY

WITH INDIAN LIFE. Unpublished paper submitted by Indian & Metis Conference Committee of the Community Welfare Planning Council to the Curriculum Revision Committee, Department of Education. Winnipeg, Man., November, 1964. Available from Indian-Eskimo Association. 19 pp.

This review was submitted to the Curriculum Revision Committee, established by the Manitoba Department of Education, in November, 1964. Five social studies texts used in Manitoba schools were examined in detail to determine to what extent the Indian and Metis peoples were presented unfairly, inaccurately, or in a manner detrimental to their self-respect. These were: "Canada - Then and Now"by Aileen Garland, "Canada - A Nation"by Chafe and Lower, "Building the Canadian Nation"by G. W. Brown, "Pages from Canada's Story"by Dickie and Palk, and "The Canadian Pageant"by Reeve and MacFarlane. It is shown that the treatment accorded to aboriginal people in history textbooks is still unsatisfactory.   IVY

1127   **SMALL   G W**
1969
THE USEFULNESS OF CANADIAN ARMY SELECTION TESTS IN A CULTURALLY RESTRICTED POPULATION. Canadian Psychologist 10:9-19.

Analysis of scores obtained by Indian/Eskimo/Metis with those of 2 non-native groups indicates the cultural bias of the Canadian Army pre-enlistment screening tests. The experimental sample consisted of 50 permanent male residents of the Northwest Territories between the ages of 15 and 30 with at least 6 years of education in English. The 2 comparison groups were made up of non-native applicants to the army. Two tests were used, one of which - the Select-R - was culture reduced. The experimental group received both tests. One comparison group ($N = 988$) received the Select R, and the other ($N = 7,217$) received the Select-A. Following administration of the tests, each member of the experimental group received a personal, subjective interview in order that tests and interview ratings might be compared. On the Select-R the experimental group performed as well as the comparison group. On the Select-A, which was highly correlated with education and contained much verbal material, the comparison group performed significantly better than the experimental group. The army accepted the researcher's recommendations that (1) the Select-A not be used with culturally isolated groups, and (2) interviews accompany use of the Select-R with such groups.   ADG

1128   **SMITH   LESLIE**
1960
LEARNING FOR EARNING. The Beaver 291(Autumn):39-44.

Integrated schools and placement programs are discussed.   IVY

1129   **SMITHERS   JAMES E**
1969
INDIAN EDUCATION PROGRAM INTERIM REPORT NO. 1. Unpublished paper. Available from Library, Ontario Institute for Studies in Education, Toronto, Ont. 52 pp.

An increase in the number of Indian pupils in the Lakehead area led to the establishment of an Indian education program, sponsored by the Lakehead Board of Education and the Indian Affairs Branch. The development and first year evaluation of this program is reported in this booklet.   ADG

1130   **SMITHERS   JAMES E**
1970
INDIAN EDUCATION PROGRAM INTERIM REPORTS NO. 2. Unpublished
paper. Available from Library, Ontario Institute for Studies in Education, Toronto, Ont.
103 pp.

The "Package Program,"a project of the Lakehead Board of Education and the Indian
Affairs Branch, is described. This program constitutes the first time this school board has
taken jurisdiction over all aspects of its Indian students' lives - clothing, transportation,
personal allowances, and medical services. This report contains a discussion of the success of the various aspects of this board's Indian education program.   ADG

1131   **SOVERAN   M**
1964
SECOND INTER-PROVINCIAL SCHOOLS IN THE FOREST CONFERENCE. The
Northian 1(1):13-14.

Held in Prince Albert, Saskatchewan, this conference focused on curriculum development and federal-provincial government relations relative to educational services for the
Indians. Teachers, superintendents, teacher organizations, curriculum and government
departments each specified their potential areas of aid in the development of a better curriculum for Indians. Participants at the conference agreed that requirements of the pupil
himself have priority over those of the present curriculum and that the entire Indian community should be more deeply involved in the learning process.   ADG

1132   **SOVERAN   MARILYLLE**
1965
I.T.A. AND THE INDIAN CLASSROOM. The Northian 2(5):15-22.

This article describes the use of the Initial Teaching Alphabet in Canadian schools and
includes a summary and some illustrations of the results teachers have obtained with it.
The I.T.A., which was developed by Sir James Pitman in order to make reading easier for
beginners by creating a closer correspondence between the alphabet and spoken language, has been used with Indian children. Its potential value for helping Indian children
learn the English alphabet is a primary concern of the article.   ADG

1133   **SPENCE   AHAB**
1967
REMARKS BY CHAIRMAN. In National Conference on Indian and Northern
Education Saskatoon 1967. Mary Anne LaVallee, ed. n.p.: Society for Indian and
Northern Education and Extension Division, University of Saskatchewan. p. 46.

Indian children should be taught their own treaties. There should be a library of reading
material in each home.   IVY

1134   **SPENCE   AHAB,   HORN   KAHN-TINETA,   et al.**
1967
SYMPOSIUM: IN WHAT RESPECTS IS THE CONTEMPORARY EDUCATION
PROGRAM FAILING THE NATIVE PEOPLE. In National Conference on Indian
and Northern Education Saskatoon 1967. Mary Anne LaVallee, ed. n.p.: Society for

Indian and Northern Education and Extension Division, University of Saskatchewan. pp. 74-86.

Kahn-Tineta Horn is of the opinion that the present education system destroys the Indian's reasoning power. Celestino Makpah of Eskimo Point believes that hunting will become a thing of the past, and that children should get an education before it is too late. Mrs. Mary Anne LaVallee lists 10 reasons why contemporary education is failing. Among these are: the fact that the concept of education is not understood by all, the lack of voice of Indian parents in education, economic instability on reserves, and poor housing conditions with little or no facilities. Wilfred Tootoosis of Poundmaker Reserve, Saskatchewan, feels that the administration has been too domineering, is in favor of integrated schooling, and views the future with optimism.   IVY

1135   **SPINKS   SARAH**
1970
SOME OISE PROJECTS. This Magazine Is About Schools 4(4):28-54.

This article contends that OISE's projects with Indians have been merely a few racist studies and exercises in behavior modification. Analysis of 3 large projects, the Mothercraft Centre, the Blackfoot Kit, and a language and mathematical program for Manitoulin Island students, suggests that OISE staff have not only misused government funds to their own selfish academic and economic ends, but the Indian people have also been used wrongly. OISE is seen as similar to colonial powers and those anthropologists who have long exploited the world's minorities. In short, OISE projects with the Indian are considered detrimental to the Indian culture.   ADG

1136   **STOTT   JIM**
1969
INDIAN EDUCATION: DAWN OF EQUALITY OR DEATH OF A CULTURE.
University of British Columbia Alumni Chronicle 23(Summer):4-9.

Two Indians, Rev. Ernest Willy, an Anglican minister, and Bob Joseph, a reporter, express their opinions on the educational system and residential schools. Professors Frank Hardwick and A. J. More comment on Indian education and the need for well-informed teaching personnel. Dr. Read Campbell discusses her proposed project for a cross-cultural center. Major recommendations of the Hawthorn report are presented.   IVY

1137   **SULLIVAN   MICHAEL**
1960
EDUCATION NORTHERN STYLE. Habitat 3(1):12-14.

A short discourse on the aims of Sir John Franklin School at Yellowknife and the courses provided is given.   IVY

1138   **TAYLOR   T H**
1960
BRIDGING A GAP. Food for Thought 20:268-275.

Specific objectives of northern education are to impart understanding and appreciation of all of the implications of cultural change, to equip Indians and Eskimos with needed skills and knowledge for whatever stage of development they are in and to assist with the provision of community stewardship. Education in the North must, in addition, be flexible and adaptable enough to meet the individual needs of the various northern groups. Finally, adult education in the North must be more active in vocational training than the churches have been.   WRC

1139   **UNIVERSITY OF SASKATCHEWAN. Indian and Northern Curriculum Resources Centre.**
1968
THE INDIAN AND NORTHERN EDUCATION PROGRAM AT THE UNIVERSITY OF SASKATCHEWAN, SASKATOON. Napao 1(2):71-74.

The history and activities of the Indian and Northern Curriculum Resources Centre which was founded in 1968 are given. B.Ed. and M.Ed. programs in Indian and Northern Education are provided.   ADG

1140   **UNIVERSITY OF SASKATCHEWAN. Indian and Northern Curriculum Resources Centre.**
1970
A SYLLABUS ON INDIAN HISTORY AND CULTURE. Saskatoon, Sask.: Indian and Northern Curriculum Resources Centre, University of Saskatchewan. 46 pp.

Each of the 3 sections, The Canadian Indians Prior to the Coming of the Europeans, European Contact to the Signing of the Treaties, and Contemporary Indian and Metis, are organized by topics which provide introduction and objectives, definitions, references, and suggested questions and study projects.   IVY

1141   **VERNON   PHILIP E**
1969
INTELLIGENCE AND CULTURAL ENVIRONMENT. London: Methuen. 264 pp.

Both the content and style of thought characteristic of a given culture are affected by the environment. Explored is the role of the environment and other facilities which hinder the development of cognitive abilities within underdeveloped countries or depressed minority groups. Chapters 26 and 27 pay special attention to the Canadian Indian and Eskimo. Studies have revealed that, gradually over time, motivation is destroyed in the Indian child and his cognitive abilities dwindle. The Eskimo were found to perform better than Indians in many cognitive tasks, and their motivation and enthusiasm in test situations far exceeded that of Indian children studied. It seems that the Eskimo's over-all better adaptation to non-native Canadians accounts for their better performance. Although change is occurring as many Indians wish to assimilate, many are still attached to traditional ways. Despite poverty, lack of cultural stimulation, language difficulties, family instability and lack of purpose, the Indian child does have an affectionate and permissive environment, one in which he is encouraged to cope actively with the physical environment.   ADG

1142   **WALLER   L G P**
1965
THE ENROLMENT OF INDIAN CHILDREN IN PROVINCIAL SCHOOLS WITH COMMENT BY JAMES NAHANEE. In The Education of Indian Children in Canada: A Symposium Written by Members of Indian Affairs Education Division with

Comments by the Indian Peoples. L. G. P. Waller, ed. The Canadian Superintendent 1965. Toronto: Ryerson Press. pp. 61-74.

The integrational program in education is discussed with examples from northern Alberta and Ontario. Legal and administrative implications of a planned transfer of Indian children from federal to provincial schools is briefly examined. Comment is made by James Nahanee of the Squamish Band, North Vancouver.   IVY

1143   **WATSON   JEAN M**
1963
EDUCATION OF INDIAN CHILDREN IN THE PUBLIC SCHOOLS OF ONTARIO. Canadian School Journal 41(6):42-43.

The move of Indian children from reserves to elementary schools of the province marks the beginning of integrated education in Ontario. Administrative arrangements are reviewed.   ADG

1144   **WATSON   JEAN M**
1963
EDUCATION OF INDIAN CHILDREN PART II. Canadian School Journal 41(8):38-39.

This article focuses on some of the reactions of both Indian and White to the trend toward integration. The question is posited: Is integration of Indians into provincial schools for their own good?   ADG

1145   **WATTIE   D K F**
1968
EDUCATION IN THE CANADIAN ARCTIC. Polar Record 14:293-304.

Educational facilities available in the Northwest Territories, Arctic Quebec, and the Yukon are reviewed.   IVY

1146   **WEST   L W, MACARTHUR   R S**
1964
AN EVALUATION OF SELECTED INTELLIGENCE TESTS FOR TWO SAMPLES OF METIS AND INDIAN CHILDREN. Alberta Journal of Educational Research 10:17-27.

This search for the least culture-biased of the available group and sub-tests for Indian and Metis youth found the Progressive Matrices and the SCRIT to be the most useful at all age levels. These had 3 distinctive features which may have contributed to the observed level of culture reduction: (1) a large percentage of items which can be solved in any language or mode of expression, (2) minimal dependence on past specific learning, and (3) content which is probably as novel to 1 culture group as to another.   ADG

1147   **WEST   LLOYD WILBERT**
1962
ASSESSING INTELLECTUAL ABILITY WITH A MINIMUM OF CULTURAL BIAS FOR TWO SAMPLES OF METIS AND INDIAN CHILDREN. M.Ed. Thesis.

Division of Educational Psychology. University of Alberta. 128 pp. Available from Department of Indian Affairs and Northern Development, Ottawa.

Examined are selected intelligence tests with the purpose of identifying instruments which validly measure intelligence with a minimum of cultural bias. Two samples were administered the selection of culture-reduced tests: 126 Metis and Indian children attending the Faust school in Alberta and 155 Indian children attending the Fort Simpson school in the Northwest Territories. Identical tests were administered to both groups at 4 grade levels. The results indicated that some tests show significantly less cultural bias than others, culture-reduced tests show less increase with grade level as a result of selection and school treatment than do traditional educationally loaded tests, and a test which appears to show little culturual bias at 1 level may show greater bias at another.   DGW

1148   **WIEDE   ANTONY**
1965
A STUDY OF THE RELATIONSHIP BETWEEN THE SCHOOL PERFORMANCE OF A GROUP OF INDIAN STUDENTS AND THEIR FORMAL AND INFORMAL ASSOCIATIONS. M.S.W. Thesis. School of Social Work. University of Manitoba.

The title has been verified, but a copy was not obtained in time to abstract it.   SLP

1149   **ZENTNER   HENRY**
1962
PARENTAL BEHAVIOR AND STUDENT ATTITUDES TOWARDS HIGH SCHOOL GRADUATION AMONG INDIAN AND NON-INDIAN STUDENTS IN OREGON AND ALBERTA. Alberta Journal of Educational Research 8:211-219.

Analysis of the questionnaire responses of Indian and White students from Oregon and Alberta revealed that supportive and positive parental behavior influenced student attitude in a parallel direction. White children reported themselves very disappointed at the prospect of failure to graduate from high school more often than did Indian children; they also reported more frequently that their parents would be very upset if they failed to graduate. Although the differences between Indian and non-Indian children's responses were slightly significant, the degree of similarity in their response patterns was impressively consistent and indicates a rapid rate of change in attitudes among Indians favorable to high school graduation. The fact that Oregon Indians reported themselves and their parents likely to be very upset if they should fail more frequently than Alberta Indians did suggests that the Canadian rural and small town culture lags behind that of the United States in the stress which is placed on high school graduation.   ADG

1150   **ZENTNER   HENRY**
1963
PARENTAL BEHAVIOR AND STUDENT ATTITUDES TOWARDS FURTHER TRAINING AMONG INDIAN AND NON-INDIAN STUDENTS IN OREGON AND ALBERTA. Alberta Journal of Educational Research 9:22-30.

The hypothesis that positive and supportive parental behavior will influence student attitudes in a parallel direction was affirmed. Indian students reported themselves very disappointed at the prospect of being unable to go on to further training as frequently as did White students. According to the students, Indian students and their parents were as interested and concerned about post-secondary training as non-Indian pupils and their parents. More Alberta Indians than Alberta Whites reported themselves disappointed at the prospect of being unable to go on to further training after high school. And Alberta subjects, more than Oregon subjects, reported that their parents would be very disappointed if they did not take post-secondary training. This finding suggests that rural areas and small towns in the United States lag behing those in Canada in the amount of stress placed on post-secondary training. The basic similarity between Indian and non-Indian students, within their national culture, as regards the perceptive, affective and cognitive substructures suggests that they should receive similar educational opportunities.   ADG

1151   **ZUK   WILLIAM MICHAEL**
1970
DESCRIPTIVE STUDY OF MOTIVATIONAL THEMES ON THE DRAWINGS OF INDIAN, METIS AND ESKIMO STUDENTS. M.Ed. Thesis. University of Alberta.

The title has been verified, but a copy was not obtained in time to abstract it.   SLP

ECONOMICS

1152   **1960**
CO-OPERATIVES FOR THE INDIANS OF CANADA. Canadian Co-operative Digest 3(3):43-45.

A condensation of the brief presented to the Joint Committee of the Senate and House of Commons on Indian Affairs, June 2, 1960, on behalf of the Co-operative Union of Canada is given. A program of community development and co-operatives for the Indians of Canada is urged.   IVY

1153   **AGRICULTURAL INSTITUTE OF CANADA**
1968
AGRICULTURAL POTENTIAL OF LAND ON INDIAN RESERVATIONS. Unpublished paper. Available from Library, Department of Indian Affairs and Northern Development, Ottawa. 19 pp.

A list of Indian reserves with agricultural potential was compiled as a background to further research and a conference in 1968.   The reserves are listed by name, acreage, and population separately for each province, and in a national summary. There are 582 reserves with agricultural potential. These comprise 3,572,408 acres and involve a population of 91,143.   JSL

1154   **AGRICULTURAL INSTITUTE OF CANADA, CANADA. Department of Indian Affairs and Northern Development.**
1969
THE AGRICULTURAL POTENTIAL OF LAND ON INDIAN RESERVES. In Report of the Indian Act Consultation Meeting. Toronto, Ont. January 20-24, 1969. Ottawa: Department of Indian Affairs and Northern Development. pp. 76-88.

A conference was held October 20-23, 1968, and attended by Indian delegates and representatives of the Indian Affairs Branch and the Agricultural Institute of Canada. The participants found that the 3,000,000 acres of Indian land with agricultural potential could support 4,000 Indian families, 25 percent of the population on these reserves. A total of 24 recommendations were offered to stimulate the development of Indian farm land.   JSL

1155   **ANDERS   G**
1968
NORTHERN INDUSTRIAL DEVELOPMENT AND THE RELEVANCE OF
'KEYNESIAN' POLICIES ON UNEMPLOYMENT. In Proceedings of a Symposium
on the Higher Latitudes of North America: Socio-Economic Studies in Regional
Development. A.D. Hunt, ed. Boreal Institute University of Alberta Occasional
Publication 6. Edmonton: Boreal Institute, University of Alberta. pp. 1-10.

An analysis of "Keynesian"policies on unemployment concludes that they are not applicable in the Northwest Territories.   IVY

1156   **BUCKLEY   HELEN**
1962
TRAPPING AND FISHING IN THE ECONOMY OF NORTHERN
SASKATCHEWAN: ECONOMIC AND SOCIAL SURVEY OF NORTHERN
SASKATCHEWAN. Research Division, Center for Community Studies, University of
Saskatchewan, Economic and Social Survey of Northern Saskatchewan 3. Saskatoon:
Research Division, Center for Community Studies, University of Saskatchewan. 189 pp.

Fieldwork for this report was conducted in the summer and fall of 1962. Tracing revenues received from trapping and fishing from the 1940's, it is shown that the incomes
provided by these traditional industries are inadequate. An increase of population without migration permits many areas to be over-exploited. A household survey was conducted by Center researchers in the summer of 1961 in 4 northern communities: La
Rouge, Ile a la Crosse, Buffalo Narrows, and Pelican Narrows. Results of that survey,
which included questions on employment and earnings, are discussed generally. Twenty-
six tables, 7 maps, and 13 figures accompany the text.   IVY

1157   **BUCKLEY   HELEN**
1962
WORKING PAPER ON MINK RANCHING IN NORTHERN SASKATCHEWAN:
ECONOMIC AND SOCIAL SURVEY OF NORTHERN SASKATCHEWAN.
Research Division, Center for Communitiy Studies, University of Saskatchewan,
Economic and Social Survey of Northern Saskatchewan: Working Paper. Saskatoon:
Research Division, Center for Community Studies, University of Saskatchewan. 57 pp.

Relying almost exclusively on data previously collected, this working paper on the mink
ranching industry is centered on the need to find new employment opportunities for the
Indian and Metis of the northern region. In separate chapters the paper discusses the basis for expansion, conflict with the commercial fishery, costs, prices, profits, and planning
for development.   IVY

1158   **BUCKLEY   HELEN**
1963
RAISING INCOMES IN NORTHERN SASKATCHEWAN. In Research Review 1.
Joan Foulds, ed. Saskatoon: Center for Community Studies, University of
Saskatchewan. pp. 10-12.

This paper arises out of a social and economic survey of Saskatchewan's Northern Affairs Region. Recognizing rapid population growth, the overcrowded traditional industries, and the lack of opportunities, it is recommended that developmental programs and
training and relocation programs be initiated.   IVY

1159   **BUCKLEY   HELEN**
1963
WORKING PAPER ON THE COMMERCIAL FISHING INDUSTRY IN
NORTHERN SASKATCHEWAN (WITH PARTICULAR REFERENCE TO
GOVERNMENT POLICY). Unpublished paper. Available from Indian and Northern
Curriculum Resources Centre, University of Saskatchewan. 23 pp.

An abstract of the fishing industry in northern Saskatchewan shows that inadequate incomes, too many small producers, the excess labor force, and the under-utilization of
some lakes are problems which must be considered in planning future policies. The role
of cooperatives and cooperative marketing in the industry is examined. Recommendations conclude the report.   IVY

1160   **BUCKLEY   HELEN**
1964
THE UNDERDEVELOPED REGION: A SPECIAL PROBLEM IN
DEVELOPMENT. Unpublished paper prepared for Joint Program, American
Sociological Association and Rural Sociological Society. Montreal, August, 1964.
Available from National Library of Canada. 14 pp.

This paper attempts to define a new approach to the poverty of the Indian and Metis people of northern Canada. Starting from certain parallels with an underdeveloped country,
the analysis goes on to explore how the development task will differ between region and
sovereign nation. It finds in the special circumstances of the underdeveloped region located in the wealthy nation some of the key factors which hold back development at the
present time and which, barring basic changes in the attitudes of Canadians and their
governments, will continue to do so.   HCV

1161   **BUCKLEY   HELEN,   KEW   J E**
1963
THE INDIANS AND METIS OF NORTHERN SASKATCHEWAN: A REPORT ON
ECONOMIC AND SOCIAL DEVELOPMENT. Saskatoon: Centre for Community
Studies. 114 pp.

This report is the result of a 3-year study concerning social and economic development of
northern settlements. Data were obtained through interviews and consultations with
people and government employees residing and working in the North. As well, published
and unpublished government reports and documents were utilized. Part I provides an
historical sketch, discusses provincial policy from 1944, and offers predictions for economic and social development in northern Saskatchewan. Part II outlines program recommendations in the area of industrial development, and also in education and local
government. Estimates of costs are also included.   IVY

1162   **CAMPBELL   DAN**
n.d.
FIRST CITIZENS FUND IN BRITISH COLUMBIA. Victoria, B.C.: Queen's Printer. 1
p.

This pamphlet presents the objectives, policy, and procedures through which the Indians
of British Columbia may utilize the Fund for educational, cultural, and economic objectives.   CCV

1163   CAMU   PIERRE,   WEEKS   E P,   et al.
1964
ECONOMIC GEOGRAPHY OF CANADA: WITH AN INTRODUCTION TO A 68-
REGION SYSTEM. Toronto: Macmillan. 393 pp.

Canadian economic geography is presented under the following headings: the individual
and his environment, the natural and historical setting, the general economic geography,
and a system for Canadian regional analysis. The Canadian economic scene from pre-
contact to the present is reviewed on pages 33-51. In addition to aboriginal regional
economy the probable migration paths and territories of native Indian and Eskimo populations are noted. The effects of contact including the fur trade, White exploration, settlement, timber exportation, railway construction, and industrialization are discussed.
Components of Canadian culture areas are described. Pre- and post-Confederation
treaty areas are provided.   CCV

1164   CANADA. Department of Citizenship and Immigration. Economic and Social
Research Division.
1960
THE ROLE OF CRAFTS AND COTTAGE INDUSTRIES IN ECONOMIC
DEVELOPMENT: A PRELIMINARY STUDY OF THE POSSIBILITIES IN
CANADA, WITH SPECIAL REFERENCE TO THE INDIAN POPULATION
(REPORT 1E-1). Available from Library, Department of Indian Affairs and Northern
Development, Ottawa. 43 pp.

A report investigating the role of home arts and crafts industries in the process of economic development describes cottage industries in non-Canadian settings and builds a
model of economic development. This model is applied to Canada with a suggested developmental scheme and proposals.   JSL

1165   CANADA. Department of Citizenship and Immigration. Economic and Social
Research Division.
1960
SOCIAL CORRELATES OF ECONOMIC DEVELOPMENT, WITH SPECIAL
REFERENCE TO THE PROBLEMS OF THE CANADIAN INDIAN: REPORT 1E-2.
Unpublished paper. Available at Library, Department of Indian Affairs and Northern
Development, Ottawa. 21 pp.

This report, prepared in conjunction with report 1E-1 "The Role of Crafts and Cottage
Industries"(1960), explores the wider problem of the relation of social development to
economic development. Some common social and psychological traits of Indian communities are examined. It is stated that economic development must be approached at the
community level. The effects of Indian patterns of thought upon their economic activities
are likewise examined. It is found that Indians have not changed their basic socio-economic thinking in the important directions of self-help. Finally, some basic principle of
social and economic development of Indian communities, and the position of handicrafts in rehabilitation schemes, are discussed. Accepting some social change as inevitable, it is assumed that the most important problem in the development is the creation of a
more favorable Indian identity. Accordingly, a special adult education is necessary.   JSL

1166   **CANADA. Department of Indian Affairs and Northern Development.**
1967
PETROLEUM FROM INDIAN LANDS. Ottawa: Queen's Printer. 25 pp.

A booklet was prepared by the Department to inform Indians about oil and gas on Indian lands. The nature and origin of petroleum, its occurrence, exploration, extraction, and production are outlined. More specifically dealing with Indian reserves is a section on mineral surrenders, prospective oil and gas areas, and a history of the development of petroleum. Finally, a discussion of Indian Affairs policy and management includes information concerning Indian oil and gas regulations, petroleum management, provincial regulations, and Indian participation in management. A map shows oil and gas developments on Alberta Indian reserves.   JSL

1167   **CANADA. Department of Indian Affairs and Northern Development.**
1968
THE AGRICULTURAL POTENTIAL OF LAND ON INDIAN RESERVATIONS: INDIAN RESERVES WITH AGRICULTURAL POTENTIAL. Unpublished paper sent to Agricultural Institute of Canada. Available from Library, Department of Indian Affairs and Northern Development, Ottawa. 19 pp.

Proposals for a conference on the problems of developing the agricultural potential of Indian reserve lands with consideration of economic and social implications are submitted to the Agricultural Institute of Canada. A list of Indian reserves with agricultural potential indicating the number, name, acreage, band, and resident band population is included.   CCV

1168   **CANADA. Department of Indian Affairs and Northern Development.**
1968
DIRECTORY CANADIAN INDIAN TOURIST OUTFITTING FACILITIES INCLUDING OUTDOOR RECREATION, CAMPING AND GUIDE SERVICES. Ottawa: Queen's Printer. 69 pp.   Also in French.

Vacation facilities and services provided by Canadian Indians are catalogued by province. Each entry is accompanied by a brief notation of attractions, facilities, location, access, and source of information.   CCV

1169   **CANADA. Department of Indian Affairs and Northern Development. Manitoba Regional Office.**
1969
T.E.D. COMMISSION REPORT - INDIAN AFFAIRS BRANCH. Unpublished paper. Available at Indian-Eskimo Economic Development Branch, Development Services Division, Department of Indian Affairs and Northern Development, Ottawa. 44 pp.

The human and natural resources at the disposal of Manitoba's Indians are reviewed to provide background material for long-term planning projects. Statistical data on employment fields, demography, and education for 1968 and projections until 1980 are included. Land use, forestry, fishing, and employment are discussed in terms of potential development and expansion.   CCV

1170   **CANADA. Department of Indian Affairs and Northern Development. Resources and Industrial Division.**

1969
FRESHWATER FISH MARKETING CORPORATION. Ottawa: Department of
Indian Affairs and Northern Development. 47 pp.

Information concerning market, processing, prices, handling, storage, transportation,
payments, credit, permits, and methods is prepared for Indian participants in Manitoba,
Saskatchewan, Alberta, the Northwest Territories , and northwestern Ontario by
the Freshwater Fish Marketing Corporation.   CCV

1171   **CARROLL   J B**
1963
PARTNERSHIP IN COMMUNITY DEVELOPMENT. Unpublished address
delivered to 4th National Conference, Indian-Eskimo Association of Canada. Regina,
October 24, 1963. Available from National Library of Canada. 7 pp.

The basic precepts of community development, the problems facing Indian peoples, and
some of the projects developing in Manitoba are outlined by Manitoba's Minister of
Welfare.   CCV

1172   **CHASE   R D**
1967
CO-OPERATIVES AMONG INDIAN AND METIS. Canadian Co-operative Digest
10(2):27-30.

Upon analysis of the operation of co-operatives in Indian and Metis communities in
Manitoba, it is concluded that co-operative techniques improve the economic position of
the Indians and Metis and involve a learning process in business procedures and democratic principles.   IVY

1173   **CHASE   R D**
1970
CO-OPERATIVES AMONG INDIAN & METIS PEOPLE IN MANITOBA.
Unpublished paper. Available from National Library of Canada. 14 pp.

Since 1960, 32 co-operatives - mainly fishing, pulpwood, and merchandising - have been
organized in Indian and Metis communities in Manitoba. A review of the operations of
the co-operatives is given.   IVY

1174   **CURRIE   WALTER**
1970
ADDRESS BY WALTER CURRIE TO MID-CANADA DEVELOPMENT
CORRIDOR CONFERENCE. In Bulletin 201: Recent Statements by the Indians of
Canada, General Synod Action 1969, Some Government Responses, Suggested
Resources. Toronto: Anglican Church of Canada. pp. 35-39.

An appeal to the Canadian people for understanding of and co-operation with native
people, and to industry particularly for employment of native people is tendered to the
Mid-Canada Development Corridor conference by Walter Currie.   CCV

1175   **DEPREZ   P,   EKSTRAND   C,   et al.**
1970

FEASIBILITY OF INDUSTRIAL DEVELOPMENT IN NATIVE COMMUNITIES IN NORTHERN MANITOBA. Unpublished paper delivered to the Conference on Transportation and Regional Development, sponsored by Center for Transportation Studies, University of Manitoba. Winnipeg, May 6-7, 1970. Available from Center for Settlement Studies, University of Manitoba. 31 pp.

Given the premise that the most effective way to gainfully employ the indigenous populations of northern communities is to bring viable industry to them, this paper outlines the critical issues involved in determining the economic feasibility of introducing new industries into a northern setting. In order to evaluate an industrial development project objectively, it is advised that a technical feasibility study, including a detailed estimate of production costs, should be undertaken, and regional economic profitability estimates should be considered. Advantages and disadvantages of industrial development through private enterprise and governmental agencies are discussed and compared.   IVY

1176   **DEPREZ   PAUL,   SIGURDSON   GLENN**
1969
THE ECONOMIC STATUS OF THE CANADIAN INDIAN: A RE-
EXAMINATION. University of Manitoba Center for Settlement Studies Series 2:
Research Reports 1. Winnipeg: University of Manitoba, Center for Settlement Studies.
103 pp.

Differences among reserves according to their degree of isolation and economic self-sufficiency are discussed in this examination of assumptions and attitudes toward Canadian Indians. Exposure to White society through education or day-to-day contact determines his attitude toward the desirability of education and outmigration. Experience may suggest that formal education does not facilitate integration. Migration may be resisted until forced by poverty or unemployment. The degree of paternalism in the attitude of management and the insistence upon formal education serve to impede Indian involvement in non-traditional employment.   Canada Manpower's programs of institutional training and training-in-industry are reviewed in relation to 5 enterprises involving Indians.   CCV

1177   **DEPREZ   PAUL,   SIGURDSON   GLEN**
1969
THE ECONOMIC STATUS OF THE CANADIAN INDIAN: A RE-
EXAMINATION. Center for Settlement Studies, University of Manitoba Series 2:
 Research Reports 1. Winnipeg: Center for Settlement Studies, University of Manitoba.
103 pp.

Five case studies are used to demonstrate truths and fallacies in the 'romantic' and 'imperialistic' positions on Indian economic development. Cases studied include (1) Dominion Bridge-Nelson River Transmission Line, (2) Anglo-Rouyn Mines, (3) Ninna Distributors, (4) Moose Lake Woodlands Training Programme, and (5) Monarch Wear-Pequis Indian Reserve Garment Factory. Diversity between reserves and within a reserve is emphasized. Lack of motivation and discipline by Indian workers is felt to be a myth, and while no reserve can be economically self-sufficient, economic expansion in the surrounding area can lead to viability.   IVY

1178   **F F SLANEY & COMPANY LIMITED**
1970

PROPOSAL FOR MANAGEMENT AND MARKETING ORGANIZATION FOR INDUSTRIES ON RESERVES. Unpublished paper. Available at Indian-Eskimo Economic Development Branch, Economic Development Division, Department of Indian Affairs and Northern Development, Ottawa. 8 pp.

A proposal for combining resources from several reserves to form viable economic units is outlined. Organization of subsidized programs which could develop into self-sufficient councils and companies is suggested.   CCV

1179   **FERGUSON   JOHN,   LIPTON   BARRY**
1969-70
THE SOUR SIDE OF SUGAR. Canadian Dimension 6(6):10-11.

The living and working conditions of Indian workers in the beet fields of southern Alberta are investigated. It is concluded that these agricultural laborers are exploited and receive discriminatory and unfair treatment.   IVY

1180   **FRANK E PRICE AND ASSOCIATES LTD.**
1967
A REPORT ON THE ALEXANDER TRUST & THE ENOCH VEGETABLE PROJECT. Unpublished paper. Available from National Library of Canada. 28 pp.

Examined are the Alexander Indian Band Farm Trust and the Enoch Vegetable Operation at Stony Plain Reserve, Alberta. Concern in the Alexander Trust involves the extent of involvement and participation of Indian people. The Enoch Vegetable Operation, however, is in serious financial difficulties and a temporary solution, that of establishing a trust, is discussed. Also outlined are alternate methods of organizing and developing the vegetable project to assure effective management and involvement and participation by band members.   IVY

1181   **GIMMER   DAVID**
1966
MILADY'S FUR....THE TRAPPER. In People of Light and Dark. Maja van Steensel, ed. Ottawa: Queen's Printer. pp. 25-28.

Some of the problems of trapping encountered by Canada's native peoples are outlined and possible solutions advanced.   CCV

1182   **GORDON   JOHN**
1962
NORTHERN INDIANS - THEIR ECONOMIC FUTURE. North 9(5):28-34.

Various factors affecting the northern Indian's economy are discussed with specific illustrations of relevant commercial developments. Trapping and harvesting of renewable resources are the key factors in contemporary Indian economy. A growing number of Indians is obtaining employment as wage earners.   ADG

1183   **GORDON   JOHN H**
1966
TALK BY MR. JOHN H. GORDON, ASSISTANT DEPUTY MINISTER (NORTHERN AFFAIRS) TO THE WHITEHORSE CHAMBER OF COMMERCE.

Speech delivered to Whitehorse Chamber of Commerce. Whitehorse, January 26, 1966. Available from Information Services, Research and Records, Department of Indian Affairs and Northern Development, Ottawa. 5 pp.

Economic development and expansion in Alaska and the Yukon are compared and areas of potential in the Yukon are underlined by the Assistant Deputy Minister of Northern Affairs and National Resources.   CCV

1184   **HEDLIN-MENZIES AND ASSOCIATES LTD.**
1964
ECONOMIC SURVEY OF THE INTERLAKE REGION OF MANITOBA.
Unpublished paper prepared for Department of Industry and Commerce, Province of Manitoba. Available from Library, Department of Health and Social Development, Winnipeg. 181 pp.

Education, training, and employment of native peoples in the interlake region of Manitoba are discussed in section 6 of this report. To provide employment opportunities for native peoples, serious consideration should be given to the development of a broadly based handicraft industry organized and subsidized mainly by the provincial government.   IVY

1185   **IRWIN   A B**
1968
MANAGEMENT POLICY FOR INDIAN OWNED MINERALS: POSSIBLE APPLICATION TO NORTHERN RESOURCES. In Proceedings of a Symposium on Implications of Northern Mineral Resources Management for Human Development. A. D. Hunt, ed. Boreal Institute University of Alberta Occasional Publication 5. Edmonton: Boreal Institute, University of Alberta. pp. 19-24.

Management policy for Indian-owned minerals is reviewed. This policy should apply to such lands in the Territories which might be set aside for Indians and Eskimos with adjustments made to fit conditions of the Territories. Regardless, provisions should be made for these people to receive benefits from the development of the mineral resources.   IVY

1186   **JAMIESON   STUART M,   HAWTHORN   HARRY B**
1963
ROLE OF NATIVE PEOPLE IN THE NORTH IN INDUSTRIAL DEVELOPMENT.
In Manitoba 1962-1975: Report of the Committee on Manitoba's Economic Future. J. R. McMillan, ed. Winnipeg: Department of Industry and Commerce. Part II. Article 3. pp. 1-18.

One means of approaching the problem of a rapidly expanding Indian population on a restricted land and economic base is out-migration to industrial centers. To prepare native populations for relocation, extensive programs in education and rehabilitation must be directed toward eventual total integration into the industrial labor force of the province.   IVY

1187   **KATES, PEAT, MARWICK & CO.**
1967
A STUDY OF RECREATIONAL DEMAND IN THE VICINITY OF WHITE BEAR

INDIAN RESERVE. Unpublished paper. Available from National Library of Canada. 21 pp.

Existing recreational demand in southeastern Saskatchewan related to the White Bear Indian Reserve is evaluated, the future growth of this demand is forecast, and guidelines for the orientation of future recreational development are given. Sources of information include existing statistics and reports, 2 surveys, and a field trip to the site.   IVY

1188   **KEW   J E**
1963
METIS-INDIAN HOUSING IN NORTHERN SASKATCHEWAN. In Research Review 1. Joan Foulds, ed. Saskatoon: Center for Community Studies, University of Manitoba. pp. 13-16.

This report is based upon the results of a housing survey conducted in 1961 of 5 northern communities - Cumberland House, Ile-a-la Crosse, Buffalo Narrows, La Ronge, and Pelican Narrows - in which Indians and Metis formed the majority of residents. A comparison of the data to Saskatchewan and Canada reflected the inadequacy of northern Metis housing.   IVY

1189   **LASALLE   ROGER**
1967
A WILD CROP MARKETING STUDY. Unpublished paper. Resources and Industrial Division, Indian Affairs Branch, Department of Indian Affairs and Northern Development. Available at Indian-Eskimo Economic Development Branch, Development Services Division, Department of Indian Affairs and Northern Development, Ottawa. 59 pp.

A review of marketing and production methods and problems associated with cranberries, blueberries, saskatoons, fiddleheads, wild rice, and other wild crops is presented as a result of a cross-Canada survey intended to define the marketing opportunities for wild crops and the potential for exploitation by Indians on a regional basis.   CCV

1190   **MACDONALD   A H**
1960
CO-OPERATIVES AND THE PEOPLE OF INDIAN ANCESTRY. Canadian Co-operative Digest 3(1):31-38.

The co-operative movement is proposed as a means to assist the Indians and Metis of Canada in improving their economic condition and managing their own affairs.   IVY

1191   **P S ROSS & PARTNERS**
1967
A STUDY OF DEVELOPMENT OPPORTUNITIES ON INDIAN RESERVES. Unpublished paper. Indian Affairs Branch, Department of Indian Affairs and Northern Development. Available at Indian-Eskimo Economic Development Branch, Development Services Division, Department of Indian Affairs and Northern Development, Ottawa. 7 pp.

A proposed program for systematic evaluation of resources on Indian reserves with a view toward planning for community development is outlined.   CCV

1192   **PHALEN   J T**
1968-1969
CO-OPERATIVE FISHERIES LIMITED. Canadian Co-operative Digest 11(4):16-22.

The formation of co-operatives in northern Saskatchewan is outlined.   IVY

1193   **POPPE   ROGER**
1970
WHERE WILL ALL THE NATIVES GO? The Western Canadian Journal of
Anthropology 2(1):164-175.

In regarding dams and diversionary schemes strictly from the engineering point of view
with an eye to economic benefits, the government has shown poor planning and concomitant lack of foresight. Ecological imbalance and the resulting problems of native peoples
who depend on the natural environment were consequences of the Bennett Dam. These 2
issues must be resolved and considered in future water export schemes.   IVY

1194   **REA   K J**
1968
POLITICAL ECONOMY OF THE CANADIAN NORTH: AN INTERPRETATION
OF THE COURSE OF DEVELOPMENT IN THE NORTHERN TERRITORIES OF
CANADA TO THE EARLY 1960'S. Toronto: University of Toronto Press. 453 pp.

Presented in this essay is a discussion of Canada's economic development in the North.
The study concerns itself solely with the Yukon and the Northwest Territories. A brief
introduction to the native population indicates the demography and sheds light on the
economic dependencies of the Indian and Eskimos. Also discussed is the role of private
and public agencies in the initiation of the northern development process. Trapping,
fishing, tourism, mining, and other industry comprise the privately sponsored activity in
the territories, whereas such things as transportation, electric power installations, public
health, and welfare facilities take up the public sphere of sponsored activity. Problems
which have ensued in northern development sum up the essay.   DGW

1195   **RICH   E E**
1960
TRADE HABITS AND ECONOMIC MOTIVATION AMONG THE INDIANS OF
NORTH AMERICA. Canadian Journal of Economic and Political Science 26:35-53.

This account of the fur trading pattern between Indian and European reveals the North
American Indian to be a shrewd and enthusiastic trader, not subject to European economic motivations. It was the Indian's lack of European sense of property which led
to the Hudson's Bay Company's subsequent monopoly of the fur trade in a time when
England frowned upon the very concept. Only the entrance of the Eskimo, possessor of
a stronger sense of property, as a primary hunter alongside the Indian facilitated the
change in attitude which expanded the fur trade.   ADG

1196   **ROTSTEIN   ABRAHAM**
1967
FUR TRADE AND EMPIRE: AN INSTITUTIONAL ANALYSIS. Ph.D. Thesis.
Department of Political Economy. University of Toronto. 146 pp.

An institutional analysis of the fur trade in Canada, including Indian political institutions, during the historic period is presented. A review of the conduct of the fur trade reveals a close relationship to the intertribal political process. Modes of competition and the economics of the fur trade in terms of the European scene are treated. Outlined are possibilities offered by the institutional approach.   CCV

1197   **SASKATCHEWAN. Task Force on Indian Opportunity. Private Sector Committee.**
1969
REPORT TO SASKATCHEWAN TASK FORCE ON INDIAN OPPORTUNITY.
Regina, December 11, 1969. Unpublished paper. Available from National Library of
Canada. 19 pp.

The general aims of the Private Sector Committee in the area of self-employment programs for Indian and Metis are outlined. Employment, ownership, and control opportunties currently being developed in conjunction with the Interprovincial Steel and Pipe Corporation Limited are reviewed. This project would provide employment and management opportunities in an industrial setting. Control would ideally rest with people of Indian or Metis ancestry and profit-sharing would be possible. An outline of the organization and structure of the operation is included.   CCV

1198   **SOLOMON   DARWIN**
1961
RURAL SOCIOLOGY AND ITS RELATIONSHIP TO RESOURCE
DEVELOPMENT OR "SOME SOCIO-CULTURAL CONSIDERATION IN
NORTHERN RESOURCE DEVELOPMENT."Unpublished paper delivered to 16th
Annual Meeting, Saskatchewan Institute of Agrologists. Waskesiv, Sask., May 26-27,
1961. Available from Indian and Northern Curriculum Resources Centre, University of
Saskatchewan. 8 pp.

Development in the North must take into account the needs of the native peoples.   IVY

1199   **STANFORD RESEARCH INSTITUTE**
1967
CONSIDERATIONS IN A PROGRAM FOR EXPANDING ECONOMIC
OPPORTUNITIES OF THE INDIANS AND METIS OF MANITOBA: SRI
PROJECT 6304. Menlo Park, CA: Stanford Research Institute. 39 pp.

A brief diagnostic survey of the social and economic problems of the Indian and Metis population of northern Manitoba is presented, and possible approaches are suggested that will assist the government of Manitoba in preparing a suitable action program for economic development. This report is based primarily on provincial data (economic surveys and documents) and upon the experience of the SRI staff. Three tenets are explored and discussed, particularly in reference to the native communities of the United States: bringing cottage industries to reserves, training and upgrading of skills required for industries located near Indian and Metis communities, and relocation.   IVY

1200   **TOMASCHUK   HENRY**
1970
INDIAN SUGAR-BEET CUTTERS. Canadian Labour 15(2):20-21,33.

After a 3-week investigation, working and living conditions of Indian and Metis migratory workers from northwest Saskatchewan employed in the sugar beet fields of southern Alberta are reported.   IVY

1201   **TURPEE   ANDREW,   TOSHACK BROS & TURPEE LTD.**
1968
INVESTIGATION, ANALYSIS AND RECOMMENDATIONS WITH RESPECT TO THAT PORTION OF BLOCK E OF INDIAN RESERVE NO. 21 LYING EAST OF P.T.H. NO. 10 AT THE PAS, MANITOBA. Unpublished report prepared for Department of Indian Affairs and Northern Development. Available at Indian-Eskimo Economic Development Branch, Development Services Division, Department of Indian Affairs and Northern Development, Ottawa. 48 pp.

The proposed lease of 400 acres of The Pas Indian Band Reserve lands to Churchill Forest Industries is examined in relation to the development potential of the land and the needs of the band. Recommendations for the modalities of leasing are outlined.   CCV

1202   **VALLEE   FRANK**
1966
THE CO-OPERATIVE MOVEMENT IN THE NORTH. In People of Light and Dark. Maja van Steensel, ed. Ottawa: Queen's Printer. pp. 43-48.

The possibilities offered by development of cooperatives in the North as a means of upgrading living standards and as a vehicle of acculturation for native peoples are discussed.   CCV

1203   **VOGET   FRED**
1961
COMMENTARY. Human Organization 20:243-248.

The articles contained in a special issue of "Human Organization" on American Indians and their economic development are reviewed. Implications from their findings and from primary data on the Six Nations are made for the economic adjustments of Indians to expanding western industrial society. Adaptation of tribal culture and an integrated social organization are viewed as inseparable from economic development. The increasingly active participation of the Indian in the political-legal system and the psychological function of the reserve land are cited as 2 of several vital components of economic development.   WRC

1204   **WESTERN ECONOMIC DEVELOPMENT AND EDUCATION CONFERENCE**
1963
MINUTES OF THE WESTERN ECONOMIC DEVELOPMENT AND EDUCATION CONFERENCE. Banff School of Fine Arts, September 16-19, 1963. Unpublished paper. Available from Library, Department of Indian Affairs and Northern Development, Ottawa. 53 pp.

The minutes of the conference include discussions of community development projects, resource development, encouragement of Indian entrepreneurship, and educational services as they relate to economic development.   CCV

1205   WOODWORTH   DONALD G
1966
FEASIBILITY OF A HANDICRAFTS PRODUCTION AND MARKETING
FACILITY IN NORTHERN MANITOBA: SRI PROJECT M-6304. Menlo Park, CA:
Stanford Research Insitute. 37 pp.

The objective of this study, prepared for the Manitoba Department of Industry and
Commerce, is to determine the feasibility and desirability of establishing, on an experimental basis, a small handicraft production and marketing facility in northern Manitoba
to employ Indian and Metis workers in a semi-factory, semi-rationalized work environment. Sources of information include: federal and provincial data; accounts of other native handicraft enterprises; interviews with people in administrative, technical, marketing, and production capacities. Such a project is considered to be economically viable if
properly located, implemented, financed, and managed. Recommendations to this effect
are presented. Products, markets, and the plant itself are discussed in the report.   IVY

1206   WORSLEY   P M,   BUCKLEY   H L
1961
ECONOMIC AND SOCIAL SURVEY OF NORTHERN SASKATCHEWAN:
INTERIM REPORT NO. 1. Saskatoon: Center for Community Studies, University of
Manitoba. 44 pp.

Presented is a progress report of the research program begun in April, 1960, on the
3-year economic and social survey of northern Saskatchewan. Data on population and
income are presented from an historical perspective. Numerous tables accompany the
text, some which allow comparisons from the 1920's.   IVY

SOCIAL ORGANIZATION

1207   BOCK   PHILIP K
1964
PATTERNS OF ILLEGITIMACY ON A CANADIAN INDIAN RESERVE: 1860-
1960. Journal of Marriage and the Family 26:142-148.

Goode's theory of the norm of legitimacy is used to interpret field data (1961) and ethnographic material on the trend of illegitimate births on a Quebec reserve. Observation has
found the present attitudes and behavior towards illegitimacy on the reserve as matter-
of-fact and tolerant: nearly 20 percent of all live births are illegitimate, ages of the mothers range between 12 and 28, there is little effect of the illegitimacies on marriage opportunities, and adoption of the child into a newly established   marriage is as common as the
establishment of matrifocal families by the unwed mother. Adoption of the child by
non-Indian spouses is also common. Despite the relaxed attitudes regarding illegitimacy,
however, legitimacy is the norm of the subculture and illegitimacy is related to (1) structural factors which weaken the integration of the community and (2) temporary socio-
economic factors which alter the power of the community to maintain conformity. Gos-
sip is 1 form of social pressure used to make the father of the child marry the mother.
Analysis of the fluctuations in the number of illegitimate births over a 100 year period
revealed that structural factors such as political and social unrest, the opening of a lumber mill, and extension of a railroad into the reserve, tend to increase the degree of community integration. During periods of relative prosperity and full local employment, the
illegitimacy rates were low; the depression and the burning of a reserve church saw high

rates of illegitimacy. The norm of legitimacy, the gross physical situation, the family system, and the love of children have all remained constant over the last century.   ADG

1208   **CHALMERS   JOHN W**
1969
SOCIAL STRATIFICATION OF THE FUR TRADE. Alberta Historical Review
17(1):10-20.

The origins and development of an essentially 2-class socio-economic system during the fur trade of the first half of the 19th century, particularly at the Fort Chipewyan post in Alberta, are examined. The environment peculiar to the fur trade and the intermarriage of Indian women with the bourgeois suppressed ethnic differences to a degree which precluded the development of a caste structure.   WRC

1209   **DRIVER   HAROLD**
1966
GEOGRAPHICAL-HISTORICAL VERSUS PSYCHO-FUNCTIONAL
EXPLANATIONS OF KIN AVOIDANCES. Current Anthropology 7:131-148.

The geographical-historical and the psycho-functional approaches to kin avoidance are reviewed in order to delineate methodological problems and oversights in earlier research from Tylor to recent statistical studies. Ethnographic data from 227 native ethnic units of North America are tabulated, mapped, and combined with historical description of major diffusion patterns in a cross-cultural analysis of affinal kin avoidance. Cultural area and language group along with previously examined variables of residence, descent, and kinship terminology are correlated with 4 relationships to yield strong evidence for the geographical-historical explanation of kin avoidances. The incidence of avoidance behavior in societies without pre-existing conditions and the absence of avoidance in some groups which possess them give low credibility to a strict psycho-functional approach. Predictive value of the several correlations is assessed and suggestions for the further development of this cross-cultural method are offered. The article is followed by several comments and a reply by the author.   WRC

1210   **EGGAN   FRED**
1960
LEWIS H. MORGAN IN KINSHIP PERSPECTIVE. In Essays in the Science of Culture in Honor of Leslie A. White. Gertrude E. Dole and Robert L. Carneiro, eds. New York: Crowell. pp. 179-201.

A chronological review of Lewis Henry Morgan's work on kinship systems is presented with a discussion of his findings, inferences, and lacunae. Morgan's most significant discovery regarding kinship is the classificatory system of relationship although he failed to realize the extent and significance of the associated behavior patterns.   CCV

1211   **ELMENDORF   WILLIAM W**
1961
SYSTEM CHANGE IN SALISH KINSHIP TERMINOLOGIES. Southwestern
Journal of Anthropology 17:265-382.

Systemic and linguistic analysis of Salish kinship terminologies reveals that the lineal structure of the Coast Salish developed through socio-cultural change from the original bifurcate collateral structure maintained by the Interior Salish. This shift from a complex to a simpler classification system is considered for a theory of cultural evolution.   WRC

1212   **FRENCH   DAVID**
1962
TYPES OF ORGANIZATION AND CHANGE AMONG NORTH AMERICAN INDIANS. Akten des 34. Internationalen Amerikanistenkongresses. pp. 153-160.

Two contrasting types of social organization, bounded versus unbounded, are defined. From a survey of the forms of organization of Indian populations of the United States and Canada examples of such structuring are presented. As well, the contrasting forms of organization are considered in relation to differing types of change.   IVY

1213   **GROSSMAN   DANIEL**
1965
THE NATURE OF DESCENT GROUPS OF SOME TRIBES IN THE INTERIOR OF NORTHWESTERN NORTH AMERICA. Anthropologica N.S. 7:249-262.

In a review of earlier ethnographic accounts, evidence is cited for the existence of non-unilineal descent groups among the Lower Carrier, Chilcotin, Shuswap, and Lillooet.   WRC

1214   **MCCLELLAN   CATHARINE**
1961
AVOIDANCE BETWEEN SIBLINGS OF THE SAME SEX IN NORTHWESTERN NORTH AMERICA. Southwestern Journal of Anthropology 17:103-123.

Variations in avoidance behavior between same-sex siblings are described for the Teshin Interior Tlingit, Tuchone, and Tagish of the Yukon Territory and for the Atna of Alaska. Fieldwork in 1948, 1949, and 1950-1951 forms the basis for a preliminary examination of social stress as a main condition for the occurrence of same-sex avoidances. It is concluded that more detailed analysis should consider ecological and technological factors and the concept of rank in marginal societies as determinants of particular elements in this interpersonal friction.   WRC

1215   **MURDOCK   GEORGE PETER**
1965
ALGONKIAN SOCIAL ORGANIZATION. In Context and Meaning in Cultural Anthropology. Melford E. Spiro, ed. New York: Free Press.   pp. 24-35.

Surveyed are the social systems of Algonkian speaking tribes. Using ethnographic literature, their social organizations are classified according to specific regions and types. The essential features are analyzed from a structural and historical standpoint. Since the Salish type of social organization is the most widely distributed, it is suspected that it is the prototype from which all others have arisen.   DGW

1216   **PELTIER   W**
n.d.
TRADITIONAL CONCEPTS OF ORGANIZATION. Unpublished paper. Available from National Library of Canada. 3 pp.

The author gives an account of native organizations of today and some of the reasons why they do not function in a manner acceptable to either the Indian or the non-Indian using traditional native organizations as a basis for his argument.   HCV

1217   **SERVICE   ELMAN R**
1962
PRIMITIVE SOCIAL ORGANIZATION: AN EVOLUTIONARY PERSPECTIVE.
New York: Random House. 211 pp.

This theoretical approach to primitive social organization is described from a cultural evolutionary perspective. Divisions into bands, tribes, and chiefdoms provide a structural progression. On pages 84-89 treatment is accorded the contemporary composite bands of the Algonkians and Athabascans. In aboriginal times these groups were more structured in their social organization and supposedly patrilocal.   DGW

1218   **SHAPIRO   ELVIN S**
1962
SOCIAL CONFLICT AND CHANGING VALUES IN THE PROCESS OF ACCULTURATION OF THE INDIAN-CANADIAN: SOME IMPLICATIONS FOR THE PRACTICE OF SOCIAL WORK. M.S.W. Thesis. School of Social Work. McGill University. 36 pp.

A general discussion of Indian social organization, leadership, and cultural values is presented. Comparison is made with pertinent aspects of White culture and areas of conflict are indicated. Implications for social work are indicated.   CCV

1219   **STEARNS   MARY LEE**
1968
CONDITIONS OF SUCCESSFUL COMPETITION BY INDIANS IN A RURAL FISHING COMMUNITY. Unpublished paper. Available from National Museum of Man, Ethnology Division, Ottawa, with permission of the author. 18 pp.

Examined are the circumstances in which Indian political action is likely to be effective and the probable consequences of such action. Using economic and social factors, it is demonstrated how a specific type of political competition evident in this fishing community has been conditioned. The community itself is an economically unified system which includes an Indian reserve village, a frontier town, and a military outpost. Of significance is the fact that even though there has been increasing interdependence between the villages, the political relations between them has gradually worsened.   DGW

1220   **VALETTE   JOSIANE**
1967
LES MINORITES INDIENNES ET L'AMENAGEMENT COMMUNAUTAIRE.
M.A. Thesis. Departement d'Anthropologie. Universite de Montreal. 113 pp.

An up-to-date panorama of the different phases of Indian acculturation is given, starting with the first contacts with the Europeans. Several types of community development are defined and a few Canadian examples are cited. The efficiency of the Canadian method is evaluated. Finally, the author concludes that community development is really possible only when the exact degree of acculturation and the possibility of the group participation are carefully measured.   DD

1221   **WALTERS   C M**
1970
INDIAN CHILDREN'S PERCEPTION OF SEX ROLES. M.Ed. Thesis. University of
Alberta.

The title has been verified, but a copy was not obtained in time to abstract it.   SLP

1222   **ZENTNER   HENRY**
1967
RESERVATION SOCIAL STRUCTURE AND ANOMIE: A CASE STUDY. In A
Northern Dilemma: Reference Papers. A. K. Davis, Vernon C. Serl, et al., eds.
Bellingham, WA: Western Washington State College. Vol. I. pp. 112-123.

The social structure of an isolated northern Saskatchewan Indian reserve is discussed.
North American Indian reservation culture is characterized by borrowed ideology and
federal government control of policy and decision making superimposed on a residual
hunting and gathering social structure. The pre-machine ethic of the traditional society
and the Protestant ethic of industrial society share stressed individualism but diverge in
a focus on the immediate present by the former and on the future by the latter. For
younger Indians an atmosphere of immediate gratification and personalized behavior is
reinforced by a negative outgroup feeling, attachment to reservation lands, and lack of
access to decision-making processes. As long as effective control remains with the dominant society there will be little opportunity for development of an alternative ethic which
will permit a meaningful social participation.   CCV

POLITICS AND LAW

1223   **ANGERS   JEAN-CLAUDE**
1966
COMMENT: INDIANS - FEDERAL AND PROVINCIAL STATUTES - TREATY
RIGHTS - HUNTING AND FISHING. University of New Brunswick Law Journal
15:66-69.

Recent court cases involving Indian hunting rights are discussed. It is submitted that a
conflict exists between certain federal government statutes and various Indian treaties.
Although recent Supreme Court decisions have ruled that treaty rights must be subject to
federal statutes, the Indians may have an "apparent breach of faith"case against the federal government for its failure to abide by treaty obligations.   ADG

1224   **ASSOCIATION DES INDIENS DU QUEBEC**
n.d.
DEUXIEME PROJECT DE MEMOIRE DE L'ASSOCIATION DES INDIENS DU
QUEBEC CONCERNANT LES DROITS DE TAXATION DU GOUVERNEMENT
PROVINCIAL DANS LE TERRITOIRE INDIEN ET DANS LA TERRE DE
RUPERT. Unpublished paper. Available from Bibliotheque Nationale du Quebec. 13
pp.

The meaning and application of several phrases of the Indian Act with respect to Indian
property in Quebec is interpreted by the Association of Quebec Indians. Several para-
graphs of the Indian Act as well as other legal texts are cited regarding indemnities and
taxation of the land.   DD

1225   **ASSOCIATION DES INDIENS DU QUEBEC**
1967
MEMOIRE SUR LE DROIT DE CHASSE ET DE PECHE DES INDIENS DE LA
PROVINCE DE QUEBEC. Unpublished paper. Available from Association des
Indiens du Quebec, Loretteville, Que. 19 pp.

This memoir is a request to the Quebec Government. Its aims are a grant of special hunting and fishing rights to all Quebec Indians, a cessation of all prosecutions against all
supposed infractions of the provincial laws of hunting and fishing, and the establishment
of an agreement between the Ministry of Tourism, Fish, and Game and the Association
of Quebec Indians about the recognition of the Indian rights in this field.   DD

1226   **ASSOCIATION DES INDIENS DU QUEBEC**
1969
MEMOIRE SUR LES DROITS TERRITORIAUX DES INDIENS DE LA
PROVINCE DE QUEBEC. Unpublished paper. Available from Bibliotheque Nationale
de Quebec. 17 pp.

This memoir was addressed to the Quebec government for recognition of the territorial
rights of the Indians of that province. The claim is based on history as well as on existing
laws. Several litigations on territorial rights are cited as further proof of the validity of
the claim. An addendum discusses the 1927 litigation on the Quebec-Labrador
border.   DD

1227   **BOWKER   W F**
1970
THE CANADIAN BILL OF RIGHTS - S. 94(b) INDIAN ACT - IRRECONSILABLE
CONFLICT - EQUALITY BEFORE THE LAW - REGINA V. DRYBONES. Alberta
Law Review 8:409-418.

The case of Regina vs. Drybones focused on whether Section 94 of the Indian Act is discriminatory and if so, does Section 2 of the Bill of Rights render the former legislation
inoperative. This article considers which protective legislation, such as the Indian Act, is
not discriminatory. The legal situation of the Indian cannot be satisfactorily dealt with
by having a court declare sections of the Indian Act inoperative. It is the responsibility of
the legislature to solve the Indian problem. Use of the Bill with respect to the Indian has
revealed its limited scope, and 3 vices emanate from the attempt to gain rights and free-
doms through the power which the Bill accords to the court: (1) it is essentially negative,
(2) it permits Parliament to evade its responsibility, and (3) it creates uncertainty.   ADG

1228   **BUCKNALL   BRIAN**
1967
INDIANS. Osgoode Hall Law Journal 5:113-123.

This article reviews recent court decisions in favor of Indians and Eskimos where the issue has been whether or not the Bill of Rights invalidates previous legislation such as the
Indian Act. Both treaties and the Proclamation of 1763 have often afforded protection
that is more apparent than real. Because they are impotent, moreover, they have often
worked to the disadvantage of the Indian.   ADG

1229   **CAIBAIOSAI   LLOYD ROLAND**
1970
THE POLITICS OF PATIENCE. In The Only Good Indian: Essays by Canadian
Indians. Waubageshig, ed. Toronto: New Press. pp. 143-155.

The intention of this essay is to rouse all Indians into action by working with a national
Indian consciousness. As 1 unified group, Indians will be able to act effectively in their
own interests and for their own betterment.   DGW

1230   **CANADIAN CORRECTIONS ASSOCIATION**
1967
INDIANS AND THE LAW: A SURVEY PREPARED FOR THE HONOURABLE
ARTHUR LAING, DEPARTMENT OF INDIAN AFFAIRS AND NORTHERN
DEVELOPMENT, GOVERNMENT OF CANADA, OTTAWA. Ottawa: Canadian
Welfare Council. 67 pp.

Data collected in a 1965-66 survey of Canadian Indian, Eskimo, and Metis people in relation to the law are assembled by topic with conclusions and recommendations. The
topics treated are: definition and description of the problem, liquor and the Indian act,
police and the courts, probation, institutions, parole and community resources, and preventative services. A final summary indicates that all Indian and Eskimo problems are
based in prejudice and discrimination, and aggravated by a lack of understanding of and
by the members of the White society. Educational programs to increase Indian and Eskimo comprehension of our criminal laws are recommended. Review of the role of the
Indian Affairs Branch to insure legal aid services for all indictable offenses is proposed.
The hiring of Indian and Eskimo personnel and specialized training for others should be
increased where the Indian and Eskimo case loads are heavy.   CCV

1231   **DE MESTRAL A L C**
1965
MICHAEL SIKYEA V. HER MAJESTY THE QUEEN. McGill Law Journal 11:168-
173.

The legal status of the Indian is very uncertain, and his specific rights and privileges, unless soon clarified, are in danger of being lost entirely. While the leading cases involving
Indian rights, such as the Sikyea case, have typically gone in the Indian's favor, judicial
decisions involving Indian law have often revealed the lack of a general philosophy regarding such matters as treaty rights. Thus, such cases have been only a partial victory
for the Indian. Canada might do well to note how the United States has taken a definite
stand regarding Indian treaties. Unless the Canadian Supreme Court and the government of Canada make a definite change in existing policy and action, the Indian's legal
situation will continue to worsen. The present ambivalence in the law governing Canadian Indians must stop. Efforts should be made to either integrate the Indian into Canadian society or present laws and treaties should be reinforced to permit the Indian to live
separately from White society.   ADG

1232   **GREEN   L C**
1970
CANADA'S INDIANS: FEDERAL POLICY,INTERNATIONAL AND
CONSTITUTIONAL LAW. Ottawa Law Review 4(1):101-131.

The government's paper on Indian policy may, in its haste to achieve equality between the Indians and non-Indians, actually promote disregard for the traditionally understood Indian rights and the desires of the Indians as equal members of society. It seems politically unsound for the federal government to refuse to recognize the historical significance of the Indian treaties despite their doubtful legal value, to proceed with any form of alterations of the treaty agreement without full and equal participation by the Indians, and to disengage itself from its responsibilities to the Indians without gaining the consent of the provinces upon whose mercy the Indians will be dependent.   ADG

1233   **JAKEMAN   A H**
1963
INDIAN RIGHTS TO HUNT FOR FOOD. The Canadian Bar Journal 6:223-227,241.

Recent judicial decisions regarding Indian hunting rights have shown that the few hunting privileges given the Indian are lost the moment an important conservation principle is involved. Accordingly, the one practice separating many Indians from starvation is in danger of being lost. If the right to hunt is to be lost, it is fair to ask what compensation is to be made for the loss of this special privilege. The current conflicts between judicial decisions reveal that this is an unresolved issue which needs further study and clarification.   ADG

1234   **LEIGH   L H**
1970
THE INDIAN ACT, THE SUPREMACY OF PARLIAMENT, AND THE EQUAL PROTECTION OF THE LAWS. McGill Law Journal 16:389-398.

The case of the Queen versus Drybones in which an Indian was charged under the Indian Act for being intoxicated off the reserve has resulted in several wider implications for fundamental constitutional importance. One of the questions is whether or not the Bill of Rights is competent to invalidate prior legislation. Another issue concerns the rationale for a decision against Drybones, whose defense had been that the Indian Act, Section 94, is discriminatory.   ADG

1235   **LYSYK   K**
1967
INDIAN HUNTING RIGHTS: CONSTITUTIONAL CONSIDERATIONS AND THE ROLE OF INDIAN TREATIES IN BRITISH COLUMBIA. University of British Columbia Review 2:401-421.

Recent judicial decisions regarding Indian hunting rights and dissenting provincial legislation on conservation have brought several considerations to the surface. One is whether hunting rights granted the Indian by treaty take precedence over provincial legislation conflicting with these rights. Another issue concerns which government, provincial or federal, has legislative competence in the area of Indian hunting rights. This article discusses these 2 issues in light of existing legislation and recent judicial interpretation of this material.   ADG

1236   **LYSYK   KENNETH**
1967
THE UNIQUE CONSTITUTIONAL POSITION OF THE CANADIAN INDIAN.
The Canadian Bar Review 45:513-553.

According to the guidelines set down in the Universal Declaration of Rights, the Canadian Indian's human rights have been severely violated. Effective legal remedies ought to be available so that the law will recognize native claims in the full sense of the word. The proposed Indian Claims legislation will hopefully stimulate research into some of these relatively unexplored areas of direct concern to the Indian. Court action may be significant in removing some of the obstacles to integration. The provinces must take a greater responsibility for creating and implementing legislation for the Indian; there is little justification for the provinces' reluctance to see to the needs of their Indian residents. The constitution has never dictated the withholding of provincial services from reserve Indians and since 1951 a section of the Indian Act has delegated any necessary authority to the provinces.   ADG

1237   **LYSYK   KENNETH**
1968
HUMAN RIGHTS AND THE NATIVE PEOPLES OF CANADA. The Canadian Bar Review 46:695-705.

The legal separation of Indians from the rest of society lacks a constitutional basis and continues to play a role in government response to the needs of Indians. The federal and provincial governments compete over the right to regulate in some areas while disclaiming constitutional and financial responsibility in others. There is an absence of authority, judicially speaking, on the question of the extent to which Parliament may legislate for Indians in areas which would not be open to legislation for non-Indians. Parliament can define Indian status but just how far it can go in determining the consequences of that status has not presently received thorough judicial analysis. Provincial legislation may not relate to Indian lands and Section 87 of the Indian Act does not touch upon the distribution of legislative authority in this respect.   ADG

1238   **MACDONALD   JOHN A**
1967-68
THE CANADIAN BILL OF RIGHTS: CANADIAN INDIANS AND THE COURTS. The Criminal Law Quarterly 10:305-319.

Use of the Canadian Bill of Rights to prevent legal discrimination against Indians has revealed weaknesses in the Bill as an instrument for protecting basic human rights. It is regretted that the Supreme Court has been reluctant to make definitive pronouncements on the meaning of the Bill. Use of the Bill to defend persons charged under sections of the Indian Act has clearly revealed the difficulties in interpreting the Bill. It is necessary to consider the present status of the Bill in the light of conflicting judicial interpretations as to its effect on prior inconsistent legislation.   ADG

1239   **MCEWEN   E R**
1968
RIGHTS OF CANADA'S FIRST CITIZENS - THE INDIAN AND ESKIMO.
Unpublished paper. Available from Indian-Eskimo Association. 13 pp.

The title has been verified, but a copy was not obtained in time to abstract it.   SLP

1240   **MCINNES   R W**
1969

INDIAN TREATIES AND RELATED DISPUTES. University of Toronto Faculty of Law Review 27:52-72.

Treaties do constitute contracts between Indian bands and the Canadian government but have no status at international law. Where the Parliament of Canada has unilaterally and specifically abrogated its promises, the Indian has no legal right to enforce the provisions of a treaty. Indians still, however, retain the power to enforce treaties of unimplemented promises which have not been altered by legislation. A Canadian claims commission is needed to resolve Indian disputes. Studying the American Claims Commission would offer valuable guidelines but its inadequacies as well as the uniqueness of some Canadian cases must be noted. IVY

1241　**MEANS　JOHN E**
1969
HUMAN RIGHTS AND CANADIAN FEDERALISM. Phylon 30:398-412.

Civil rights and equal opportunity do not exist for all of Canada's people. In some respects the provincial governments and the federal government contribute to the present condition of ethnic minorities in Canada. This is especially true since civil rights in Canada are under provincial control and citizens receive differential treatment according to the attitude of the particular province. As Canada's oldest minority group, the Indians receive the most pervasive and widespread maltreatment by the majority. The combined effect of the reserve system, majority group prejudice, and ineffective government policy has created a seriously disorganized, poor, and demoralized people. The reserves can no longer support their people even at a subsistence level. Traditional Indian values along with White prejudice have permitted few Indians to integrate into urban society without great difficulty. ADG

1242　**MORROW　W G**
1969
HUMAN FACTORS AND ENVIRONMENT: LEGAL ASPECTS. Unpublished paper delivered to Mid-Canada Development Corridor Conference. Thunder Bay, August 18-22, 1969. Available from Center for Settlement Studies, University of Manitoba. 11 pp.

The mid-Canada corridor contains 3 kinds of communities: primitive, transitional, and sophisticated. In the primitive communities courts must be flexible and realistic in applying the law, both civil and criminal. The use of circuit courts has proven effective in administering criminal law in the Northwest Territories. The Territorial Court is now experimenting in civil cases by giving free transportation in the Court plane from Yellowknife, the legal center, to whichever community represents the home of the defendant. Transportation covers not only the litigant but his lawyer. IVY

1243　**O'CONNELL　MARTIN**
1969
WHAT DO CANADIAN INDIANS WANT?: INDIANS AND THE PROVINCE. The Canadian Forum 49:58-60.

The provinces' responsibilities for, and power regarding, the Indian remain unclear. Placement of the Indian in a separate, but unequal and discriminatory system is unfounded in constitutional law, and only historical reasons and political pressures on Ottawa to do more have led to this condition. This separation of federal-provincial functions should not be tolerated. While the provinces cannot legislate for Indians, the general laws and policies of the province, can apply to the Indian. It is hoped that changes in the Indian Act will lead to greater power for band governments and a reduction in federal paternalism. Such a change would also facilitate greater interaction between the provincial governments and the Indian. It is vital that the Indian's treaty rights be clarified now. The symbolic relationship between treaties and the Indian's self-identity must be understood and acted upon. There is much provincial involvement that the Indian organizations can demand, but public support will likely be needed to pressure the provinces into recognition of legitimate responsibilities.   ADG

1244   **PATTERSON   E PALMER II**
1967
ARTHUR E. O'MEARA, FRIEND OF THE INDIANS. Pacific Northwest Quarterly 58:90-99.

Arthur Eugene O'Meara, lawyer-missionary, entered British Columbia Indian affairs in 1909. His role as legal advisor to the cause of Indian land claims in British Columbia, particularly the Nishga claims, to 1927 is outlined.   IVY

1245   **SASKATCHEWAN. Department of Welfare. Staff Training Branch.**
1970
INSTITUTIONAL SERVICES FOR FEMALE OFFENDERS IN SASKATCHEWAN: A PROGRAM EVALUATION AND RECOMMENDATIONS FOR FUTURE PLANNING. Unpublished paper. Report No. 15. Available from National Library of Canada. 83 pp.

This report makes recommendations for the future utilization of the facilities at Pine Grove Correctional Centre for female offenders, the higher percentage of whose inmates are women of Indian ancestry.   HCV

1246   **SCHMEISER   DOUGLAS A**
1968
INDIANS, ESKIMOS AND THE LAW. Musk-Ox 3:1-23.

With examples of recent legal decisions, this paper focuses attention on the difficulties and injustices of applying a complex legal system to people living under primitive and harsh circumstances. The manner of appointment and payment of Justices of the Peace in the North is also discussed.   IVY

1247   **SINCLAIR   J GRANT**
1970
THE QUEEN V. DRYBONES: THE SUPREME COURT OF CANADA AND THE CANADIAN BILL OF RIGHTS. Osgoode Hall Law Journal 8:599-619.

In the Queen V. Drybones case, an Indian was charged in the Northwest Territories for being drunk in a public place, by Section 94(b) of the Indian Act. In appeal at the Supreme Court, the case was dismissed, the ruling being that Section 94(b) was inoperative because it is contrary to the Canadian Bill of Rights. This article considers the validity of the conclusion that the Bill is competent to impose restraints on legislation and administrative action which infringes any of its guarantees. It is concluded that there is no reason why the Bill should not prevail over all inconsistent federal legislation which does not contain the notwithstanding clause, until expressly repealed or amended.   ADG

1248   **SISSONS   JACK**
1968
JUDGE OF THE FAR NORTH: THE MEMOIRS OF JACK SISSONS. Toronto: McClelland and Stewart. 190 pp.

Narrated is the story of Judge Jack Sissons, the first judge of the Territorial Court of the Northwest Territories. During his 11 years of service form July 1, 1955, to July 15, 1966, Judge Sissons not only fulfilled his prescribed role on the bench, but acted as public defender for Eskimos and Indians alike. The drive to restore aboriginal and treaty rights often found him pitted against those bureaucratic forces restricting development in the North.   DGW

1249   **STAATS   HOWARD E**
1964
SOME ASPECTS OF THE LEGAL STATUS OF CANADIAN INDIANS. Osgoode Hall Law Journal 3:36-51.

The dislocation and bad social image characterizing the Indian are to some extent due to his legal position. This article examines recent court cases in which the Indian's legal dilemmas are manifest. The Indian is a citizen if he meets the qualifications set out in the Canadian Citizenship Act. The effect of the Bill of Rights on certain sections of the Indian Act is unclear. And the protective and paternalistic features of the Act have rendered it obsolete for most Canadian Indians, if full citizenship is to be achieved. Since the special legal status of the Indian is due essentially to the reserve system, it should be reviewed and perhaps abandoned. The validity of existing treaties should also be established. Some means should be found whereby the provinces can gain power to legislate for the Indian.   ADG

1250   **UNION OF NOVA SCOTIA INDIANS,   UNION OF NEW BRUNSWICK INDIANS,   et al.**
1970
LEGAL STATUS OF INDIANS IN THE MARITIMES. Unpublished paper delivered to seminar sponsored by Indian-Eskimo Association of Canada. Halifax, October 16, 1970. Available from Indian-Eskimo Association. 55 pp.

This paper reports the seminar planned and sponsored by the Indian-Eskimo Association of Canada and requested by the Union of Nova Scotia Indians and the Union of New Brunswick Indians. The seminar's purpose was to clarify the legal status of the Maritime Indians concerning treaty and aboriginal rights, following the announcement in June, 1969, of the government's new Indian Policy.   HCV

1251   **WHITEHEAD   G R B**
1966
INDIAN TREATIES AND THE INDIAN ACT: THE SACREDNESS OF TREATIES? Chitty's Law Journal 14:121-125.

In the recent Supreme Court case (1966) of the Queen vs. George, an Indian was charged with hunting migratory birds out of season. This article discusses the court's analysis of Section 87 of the Indian Act where the major issue is federal legislation overriding Indian treaties. It is argued that the federal government should not be expected to consider early treaties as binding under all circumstances. However, should the government wish to resolve the problem due to the Migratory Birds Convention Act of 1916, it should apply to the United States government for a variation of the Convention.   ADG

MEDICINE

1252   **1961**
INDIAN HEALTH SERVICES. Canadian Medical Association Journal 84:919-921.

Appearing before the Joint Committee of the Senate and House of Commons on Indian Affairs, the Canadian Medical Association outlined several unsatisfactory features of the functioning of the Indian and Northern Health Service. The doctor's inability to distinguish between wards of the government and private patients is 1 reason the Association has asked that the government clarify its responsibility to and policy regarding Indian health services. Several recommendations were offered: (1) the criteria of indigency among Indians be clearly defined, (2) the criteria be accepted and applied by all concerned with care and welfare of Indians, (3) Indian patients be advised of their entitlement, and (4) administration of Indian affairs be placed entirely under the control of a single department of the government.   ADG

1253   **1964**
ALCOHOL AND THE INDIANS OF ONTARIO: PAST AND PRESENT.
Unpublished paper prepared for Drug Addiction Research Foundation. Available from Alcoholism and Drug Addiction Research Foundation, Toronto, Ont. 54 pp.

Based on both library research and field study (1962) conducted on reserves between Kenora and Toronto, this summary of Indian drinking in Ontario argues that the incidence of Indian alcoholism and drinking is likely to increase directly as his economic position improves. Since the Indian's drinking habits are not amenable to current forms of therapy, control must be achieved through education.   ADG

1254   **1965**
NURSES IN THE NORTH: A FASCINATING GLIMPSE OF MODERN MEDICINE AT WORK IN FAR-FLUNG OUTPOSTS OF CANADA. Canada's Health and Welfare 20(1):2-3,8.

Bringing a health program to the people in Canada's Northland has been met by the development of nursing stations and health centers. An outline of the many and diversified duties of nurses who staff these health services is presented.   IVY

1255   **BEST   S C,   GERRARD   J W,   et al.**
1961
THE PINE HOUSE (SASKATCHEWAN) NUTRITION PROJECT. II. Canadian Medical Association Journal 85:412-414.

School children in Pine House, Saskatchewan, suffering from malnutrition, received food supplements. When these food supplements were cut off, the nutritional status of these children decreased but remained adequate. Several recommendations also emerged from the investigation of this isolated Indian community: (1) provisions for better dental care, (2) two-way radios present in all settlements and nursing stations, (3) regular visits by a medical officer, and (4) a nurse-in-residence to provide day to day supervision of personal hygiene.   ADG

1256   **BIBAUD   MYRTLE S,   KEITH   CATHERINE W,**   et al.
1963
GLIMPSES INTO HOSPITAL NURSING. The Canadian Nurse 59:266-267.

In this report of nursing in the Foothills Region (Alberta, Yukon, Northwest Territories) the following hospitals are described: Charles Camsell Hospital, Edmonton (2 children's wards); Whitehorse General Hospital, Yukon Territory; and Inuvik General Hospital, Northwest Territories; as well as several nursing stations in the Arctic.   IVY

1257   **BIRT   ARTHUR R**
1968
PHOTODERMATITIS IN INDIANS OF MANITOBA. The Canadian Medical Association Journal 98:392-397.

A photodermatitis typically found in North American Indians was studied in 64 Manitoba Indians, ranging in age from early childhood to old age. This specific photodermatitis, or light sensitive eruptions, appears to be transmitted as an autosomal dominant trait. It differs from the clinically related polymorphic light eruptions, common to the non-Indian population, in several respects: (1) apparent hereditary nature, (2) early onset and long duration, (3) tendency to persist in minimal form during the winter months, and (4) occasional occurrence as a chronic and recurrent severe cheilitis of the lower lip. Present treatment of the condition is unsatisfactory.   ADG

1258   **BOAG   TOM**
1966
MENTAL HEALTH IN THE NORTH. In People of Light and Dark. Maja van Steensel, ed. Ottawa: Queen's Printer. pp. 137-140.

The implications of the northern habitat and society for the mental health of Indians and Eskimos are reviewed briefly.   CCV

1259   **CAMBON   KENNETH,   GALBRAITH   J D**
1965
MIDDLE-EAR DISEASE IN INDIANS OF THE MOUNT CURRIE RESERVATION, BRITISH COLUMBIA. The Canadian Medical Association Journal 93:1301-1305.

The increasing incidence of chronic aural disease among Indians has given rise to a number of unanswered medical questions. This survey of middle-ear pathology and hearing loss on the Mount Currie reserve found the incidence of ear disease significantly higher (1) in depressed social conditions, (2) where other family members are affected, and (3) among Indians with nasal discharge. No difference was found between the incidence of middle-ear disease among those who had undergone adenotonsillectomy and those who had not. Sensorineural hearing loss, secretory otitis media, and otosclerosis are absent or rare in this population.   ADG

1260   **CAMERON   T W M, CHOQUETTE   L P E**
1963
PARASITOLOGICAL PROBLEMS IN HIGH NORTHERN LATITUDES, WITH
PARTICULAR REFERENCE TO CANADA. Polar Record 11:567-577.

Descriptions of parasitic diseases of man found in the Canadian Arctic are given.   IVY

1261   **CANADA. Department of National Health and Welfare. Indian and Northern
Health Services.**
1964
DISEASES AND DEATH IN INFANTS AND CHILDREN IN THE NORTHWEST
TERRITORIES 1963. Unpublished paper. Available from Library, Department of
Indian Affairs and Northern Development, Ottawa. 10 pp.

Statistics concerning disease and death in infants and children in the Northwest Territories are presented. Contributing factors are reviewed, areas of need are outlined, and
obstacles to meeting these needs are noted.   CCV

1262   **CANADA. Department of National Health and Welfare. Medical Services.**
n.d.
SURVEY OF MATERNAL AND CHILD HEALTH OF CANADIAN REGISTERED
INDIANS 1962. Ottawa: Department of National Health and Welfare. 148 pp.

A survey provides data on Indian births, infant mortality, mortality by region, factors
relevant to birth and infant death, immunization programs, congenital abnormalities,
complicated deliveries, utilization of pre-natal services, and infant growth.   CCV

1263   **CANADA. Department of National Health and Welfare. National Health Service.**
1968
REPORT ON HEALTH CONDITIONS IN THE NORTHWEST TERRITORIES
1967. Ottawa: Department of National Health and Welfare. 14 pp.

Health conditions in the Northwest Territories are reported for 1967. Birth rates, crude
death rate, average age at death, infant mortality rate, major causes of death, hospital
admissions, and incidence of various diseases are presented for Indians and Eskimos.
CCV

1264   **CANADA. Department of National Health and Welfare. Northern Health Service.**
1962
HEALTH SERVICES PLAN, NORTHWEST TERRITORIES, 1962-67, AS
APPROVED BY THE INTERDEPARTMENTAL COMMITTEE OF FEDERAL-
TERRITORIAL FINANCIAL RELATIONS. Ottawa: Department of National Health
and Welfare. 108 pp.

A revised version of the plan prepared for the Committee on Federal-Territorial Financial Relations for submission to the Territorial Council in July, 1961, summarizes present
health services, proposed new health facilities, and a cost-sharing formula and cost estimates. Population distribution by health district and zone, existing proposed facilities,
staffing patterns, and personnel requirements are appended.   CCV

1265   **CANADA. Department of National Health and Welfare. Northern Health Service.**
1963
HEALTH SERVICES FOR SMALL POPULATION GROUPS IN OUTLYING
AREAS OF NORTHERN CANADA. Unpublished paper. Available from Library,
Department of Indian Affairs and Northern Development, Ottawa. 10 pp.

Efforts expended to improve health services to the isolated and scattered population in
the north are described. Facilities and services by zone are estimated. The need to upgrade spending to improve services is emphasized.   CCV

1266   **CARPENTER   C W,   BYRANS   F E**
1965
MATERNAL MORTALITY IN BRITISH COLUMBIA: A STUDY OF 145 DEATHS
FROM 1955 TO 1962. The Canadian Medical Association Journal 92:160-170.

In this study of 145 maternal deaths occurring in British Columbia from 1955 to 1962, it
was found that maternal mortality among Indians is approximately 10 times that of the
general population. Hemorrhage is the principal cause of most Indian maternal deaths.
The failure of Indian women to get satisfactory obstetrical care and routine hospitalization for delivery is due mainly to the geographical isolation of most Indian communities. Geography, moreover, is a difficult problem to eliminate. The co-operation of the
responsible provincial Indian health services is required if the problem is to be dealt with
effectively. Education for Indian women is important, and a greater stress on dietary factors is necessary since anemia is common in antepartum Indian women.   ADG

1267   **CASSELMAN   E**
1967
PUBLIC HEALTH NURSING SERVICES FOR INDIANS. Canadian Journal of
Public Health 58:543-546.

Aims and objectives of public health programs are discussed and accomplishments in the
areas of maternal and infant health, school health, adult health, chronic diseases, and
community health workers are outlined.   IVY

1268   **CORRIGAN   CAMERON,   PENIKETT   E J K,   et al.**
1962
ANTIBODIES TO VIRAL AND OTHER ANTIGENS IN BLOOD SERUM OF
CHILDREN RESIDENT IN THE NORTHWEST TERRITORIES. Canadian Journal
of Public Health 53:284-289.

Serum was collected from 1,142 children (largely Eskimo and Indian) resident in federal
boarding schools in Inuvik, Fort Smith, Fort Simpson, and Fort McPherson and 249 of
these sera were selected for a preliminary survey. Serological tests were performed to
detect antibodies to psittacosis, measles, and syphilis reagin. Results were compared with
sera collected from 65 children in a residential school at Red Deer, Alberta.   IVY

1269   **GALBRAITH   J D,   GRZYBOWSKI S,   et al.**
1969
TUBERCULOSIS IN INDIAN CHILDREN: PRIMARY PULMONARY
TUBERCULOSIS. The Canadian Medical Association Journal 100:497-502.

Two hundred and thirteen patients with an admission diagnosis of primary pulmonary tuberculosis were analyzed. The analysis revealed that this disease was serious in Indian children in the pre-antibiotic era. Of this group, 93 developed post-admission complications and 18 died as a result of the disease. Primary pulmonary tuberculosis in Indian children is a much more serious condition than the same disease in White children, and the risk of development of almost any form of tuberculosis is equally high in all age groups of Indians, while infancy and late childhood are the high risk points for White children. Racial factors, poor nutrition, and heavy exposure to tubercle bacilli may all contribute to high incidences of tuberculosis among Indian children. Regardless of the reasons for high morbidity, however, it is anticipated that Indian children will continue to have higher rates of morbidity than White children since the Indian continues to carry an abundance of the infectious virus.   ADG

1270   **GIROUX   T E**
1967
LA MEDECINE INDIENNE ET LE TRAITEMENT DU CANCER. Laval Medical 38:954-962.

The author compares the efficiency of European medicine to that of the Indian, especially in the cases of inveterate wounds that could be cancer treated by the Micmac shamans. Several contemporary cases of healing have been verified while doctors are still failing to cure these wounds, despite use of the same kind of medicinal plants.   DD

1271   **GRAHAM-CUMMING   G**
1967
HEALTH OF THE ORIGINAL CANADIANS, 1867-1967. Medical Services Journal Canada 23:115-166.

The deterioration of the health of the native peoples of Canada necessitated government intervention. The administrative development of health services is traced. Particularly devastating have been epidemics of tuberculosis, although other infectious diseases have affected the population. Factors, which include living conditions, housing, and diet, facilitated the spread of disease. Educational approaches such as community health workers are now involving the people more directly in present health programs.   IVY

1272   **GRAHAM-CUMMING   G**
1967
PRENATAL CARE AND INFANT MORTALITY AMONG CANADIAN INDIANS. The Canadian Nurse 63(9):29-31.

Based on a study published by the Department of Health and Welfare under the title "Survey of Maternal and Child Health of Canadian Indians, 1961,"evidence seems to indicate that failure to use available prenatal services is a major factor in maintaining the high infant mortality rate and the effect of prenatal services in reducing infant mortality is in direct proportion to the extent and duration of utilization.   IVY

1273   **GRAHAM-CUMMING   G**
1969
NORTHERN HEALTH SERVICES. The Canadian Medical Association Journal 100:526-531.

The history of northern health services is short. It was not until the White man's diseases, particularly tuberculosis, had almost exterminated the Indians and Eskimos that small efforts were made to meet the native Canadians' health needs. The first efforts at medical care for natives were made by the missions and the fur companies. Federal health services for the northern natives did not begin until around the time of the Depression.   ADG

1274   **GROULX   LIONEL**
1962
LE CANADA FRANCAIS MISSIONAIRE: UNE AUTRE AVENTURE. Montreal: Editions Fides. 532 pp.

This review of French Canadian Catholic missionary activities is based on research in archival sources and community records. Missions in the east, west, Arctic, and British Columbia are noted with brief references to the type of projects undertaken, difficulties encountered, and the congregations concerned.   CCV

1275   **GRZYBOWSKI   STEFAN**
1965
ONTARIO STUDIES ON TUBERCULIN SENSITIVITY: SECTION I: TUBERCULIN TESTING OF VARIOUS GROUPS. Canadian Journal of Public Health 56:181-185.

Tuberculin sensitivity is high among Indians, as revealed in a tuberculin-testing survey of 3 groups of Ontario residents.   IVY

1276   **HAWORTH   J C,   FORD   J D,   et al.**
1967
FAMILIAL CHRONIC ACIDOSIS DUE TO AN ERROR LACTATE AND PYROVATE METABOLISM. The Canadian Medical Association Journal 97:773-779.

Chronic metabolic acidosis is a rare disease caused by elevated blood levels of lactate and pyruvate. The recent discovery of this rare disease in 2 Indian children resulted in an attempt to glean additional information regarding chronic metabolic acidosis through a thorough study of the patients' family histories.   ADG

1277   **HELLON   C P**
1969
LEGAL AND PSYCHIATRIC IMPLICATION OF EROSION OF CANADIAN ABORIGINAL CULTURE. University of Toronto Law Journal 19:76-79.

Traditional aboriginal life has eroded and the aboriginal is a person in transition. Assimilation, however, has not been achieved for the traditional values, rewards, control systems, and thinking processes of the aboriginal stand in great contrast to, and are inappropriate for, western society. As a result, much of his behavior is seen as sociopathic. He is a person unable to conform to cultural milieu, to profit from punishment, and to control his hedonistic, aggressive behavior. Moreover, he is a transgressor of both traditional aboriginal and contemporary western law. If the transference of this sociopathic personality syndrome to native offspring, and aggression at mass level are to be avoided, several changes must occur: (1) socioeconomic planning with assurance of attainable training, employment and satisfaction, and intensive prenatal care, (2) quick cultural transition, if any at all, (3) early identification and treatment of deviant behavior, and (4) integration of rehabilitation work with employment opportunities and facilities for geographic relocation when necessary.   ADG

1278   **HELLON   C P**
1970
MENTAL ILLNESS AND ACCULTURATION IN THE CANADIAN ABORIGINAL. Canadian Psychiatric Association Journal 15:135-139.

The range of mental illness and its relation to acculturation were studied for a group of Indians, Eskimos, and Metis in an Alberta hospital. Results showed the aboriginal group to be similar to the control group in most illness categories, with the most significant difference in the personality disorder category. Violence toward others and promiscuity were more common in aboriginals than in non-aboriginals, but the incidence of criminality was only over-present in specific aboriginal groups. Diagnosis of personality disorder and the promiscuity factors all correlated with at least 1 of the acculturation measures used. The presence of folklore within delusional systems does not protect significantly against the expression of violence to others. The findings are discussed in relation to the earlier report which found that mal-adaptive social behavior in aboriginals was due to the eroding of traditional cultural patterns and the invalidation of cultural controls.   ADG

1279   **HERBERT   F A,   MAHON   W A**
1967
PNEUMONIA IN INDIAN AND ESKIMO INFANTS AND CHILDREN: PART I. A CLINICAL STUDY. The Canadian Medical Association Journal 96:257-265.

Pneumonia is a very serious illness in Indian and Eskimo infants and youth. To gain a better insight into the nature, symptoms, and development of the disease in this population, 97 Indians and Eskimos were studied and treated under control conditions during the summer of 1963 and August, 1964. Bacterial, viral and rickettsial were the principal kinds of pneumonia found in this group. Recurrent pneumonia and anemia were common to all 97 cases. It was found that pulmonary tuberculosis might be a problem in the differential diagnosis of pneumonia patients. It is noted that the Indian's poor physical environment and infrequent medical care are likely contributory factors in the contraction and recurrence of this disease.   ADG

1280   **HILDES   J A,   PARKER   W L,   et al.**
1965
THE ELUSIVE SOURCE OF PSITTACOSIS IN THE ARCTIC. The Canadian Medical Association Journal 93:1154-1155.

The unexpected occurrence of a high incidence of psittacosis antibodies in Arctic Indians and Eskimos led to a search for their origin. Although examination of several kinds of migratory birds did reveal the migrating geese as having psittacosis, the virus did not appear to come from the birds. Thus, the problem remains unanswered.   ADG

1281   **HILDES   J A,   WILT   J C,   et al.**
1965

SURVEYS OF RESPIRATORY VIRUS ANTIBODIES IN AN ARCTIC INDIAN POPULATION. The Canadian Medical Association Journal 93:1015-1018.

During 1958 and 1960 several epidemics occurred in the small Indian village of Old Crow, located in the northern Yukon. The occurrence of influenza, mumps, and whooping cough within the community is discussed.   ADG

1282   **HILL   ROBERT H,   ROBINSON   H S**
1969
RHEUMATOID ARTHRITIS AND ANKYLOSING SPONDYLITIS IN BRITISH COLUMBIA INDIANS: THEIR PREVALENCE AND THE CHALLENGE OF MANAGEMENT.   The Canadiañ Medical Association Journal 100:509-511.

While it would appear that rheumatoid arthritis is as common in the Indian population as in other populations investigated, there is some indication that juvenile rheumatoid arthritis occurs more commonly in Indians of British Columbia. The incidence of ankylosing spondylitis in the Haida of the Queen Charlotte Islands is very high. The absence of sufficient medical facilities on the remote reserves on which these diseases often exist threatens the physician's provision of optimal medical management which will have a lasting impact. At the present time, the best form of management may be the resettlement of the patient in communities with adequate medical and rehabilitative facilities. Caution must be exercised in removing the patient from his family and home environment.   ADG

1283   **HILL   ROBERT H,   WALTERS   K**
1969
JUVENILE RHEUMATOID ARTHRITIS: A MEDICAL AND SOCIAL PROFILE OF NON-INDIAN AND INDIAN CHILDREN. The Canadian Medical Association Journal 100:458-464.

Thirteen Indian and 57 non-Indian youth who had been referred to a juvenile arthritis clinic in British Columbia were studied to reveal the relationship between their clinical and social characteristics. It was found that social pathology was more prevalent in those families with severely affected children. The relatively worse social position of the Indian families as well as the higher incidences of juvenile arthritis suggest that juvenile rheumatoid arthritis may be more common and serious in British Columbia Indian children than White children.   ADG

1284   **LANG   M G**
1960
NUTRITION IN INDIAN AND NORTHERN HEALTH SERVICES. Canadian Nutrition Notes 16:49-52.

Indian and Northern Health Services, a Directorate of the Department of National Health and Welfare, is responsible for the health program for Indians and Eskimos. The average diet of Indians and Eskimos replacing their traditional diet is not considered nutritionally adequate. The progress in attempting to improve food habits is briefly described.   IVY

1285   **LEACH   F**
1966

INDIAN MEDICINE MEN AND THEIR REMEDIES. Moccasin Telegraph 26(1):1-3.

Information is provided on some medicinal roots and herbs.   IVY

1286   **MAHON   W A,   HERBERT   F A**
1967
PNEUMONIA IN INDIAN AND ESKIMO INFANTS AND CHILDREN: PART II. A CONTROLLED CLINICAL TRIAL OF ANTIBIOTICS. The Canadian Medical Association Journal 96:265-268.

Administration of 3 different antibiotics, phenethicillin, ampicillin and tetracyclene, under controlled conditions failed to yield a differential effect on 97 Indian and Eskimo children. The antibiotics also failed to show any specific advantages in terms of side effects.   ADG

1287   **MANITOBA INDIAN BROTHERHOOD**
n.d.
FAMILY HEALTH EDUCATION PROGRAM. Unpublished paper. Available from National Library of Canada. 7 pp.

To provide women in Indian communities needed information on family planning, alcoholism, venereal disease, and cultural and social life, it is suggested that 2 teams of Indian people (preferably women) be trained in the technique of communication termed social animation and work in each community in Manitoba for 2 weeks each year.   IVY

1288   **MARTENS   ETHEL G**
1962
CANADA: A PILOT PROJECT. International Journal of Health Education 5:172-175.

A training course for native community health workers conducted by the Medical Services personnel of the Department of National Health and Welfare, and jointly sponsored by the Indian Affairs Branch of the Department of Citizenship and Immigration, is described.   IVY

1289   **MARTENS   ETHEL G**
1963
COMMUNITY HEALTH WORKER TRAINING PROGRAM. Canadian Nutrition Notes 19:61-66.

A training program for native Community Health Workers was conducted from November, 1961, to April, 1962, by Medical Services, Department of National Health and Welfare. The project was jointly sponsored by the Indian Affairs Branch of the Department of Citizenship and Immigration. Thirteen candidates were selected (11 by the chiefs and councilors for their leadership abilities) for training which was conducted in 3 parts: (1) field orientation (2 months), (2) formal training (2 1/2 months), and (3) probation or continued on-the-job training. An informal evaluation of the program concludes that the results are encouraging.   IVY

1290   **MARTENS   ETHEL G**
1966

CULTURE AND COMMUNICATIONS - TRAINING INDIANS AND ESKIMOS
AS COMMUNITY HEALTH WORKERS. Canadian Journal of Public Health 57:495-
503.

In an attempt to bridge the cultural gap between medical service personnel and Indians
and Eskimos, a program of training native peoples as community health workers was
initiated. Observations of the 5-month training course (2-month orientation in the home
community, 3 months in a central location, and continued on-the-job training) are recorded.   IVY

1291   **NATIVE BROTHERHOOD OF BRITISH COLUMBIA**
1961
BRIEF. In Minutes of Proceedings and Evidence. No. 5. March 22, 1961. Joint
Committee of the Senate and the House of Commons on Indian Affairs. Canada. 24
Parliament, 4 Session. Ottawa: Queen's Printer. pp. 108-109.

The Brotherhood outlines the bases for their claim for free medical services to Indians in
the province.   JSL

1292   **NEMETZ   EMMI**
1968
INDIAN MEDICINE. The Northian 5(2):14-15.

Many aspects of aboriginal medicine still continue to impress contemporary public health
personnel. This article contains a discussion of the use by Indians of roots and herbs as
abortives. A description of an aboriginal birth is also included.   ADG

1293   **NEMETZ   EMMI**
1968
PLANT LIFE AND INDIAN MEDICINE. The Northian 5(1):6-8.

This article describes the Indian's use of plants and herbs to cure diseases. Many of the
medical practices performed by the Indians during pre-historic times were similar to
those used in Europe and by ancient civilizations.   ADG

1294   **PARTINGTON   M W,   ROBERTS   NORMA**
1969
THE HEIGHTS AND WEIGHTS OF INDIAN AND ESKIMO SCHOOL
CHILDREN ON JAMES BAY AND HUDSON BAY. The Canadian Medical
Association Journal 100:502-509.

A comparative analysis of the heights and weights of 3 groups of Indians and Eskimos
suggests that Indians and Eskimos might be racially different. Specifically, comparison of
754 Cree, 119 Mohawk, and 263 Eskimo children found the Mohawk children taller and
heavier than the Cree who were typically taller and heavier than the Eskimos.   ADG

1295   **PORTH   F J**
1968
TUBERCULOSIS CONTROL AMONG INDIANS IN SASKATCHEWAN.
Canadian Journal of Public Health 59:111-114.

The tuberculosis control program among Treaty Indians as of 1966, with comparisons with the program of 1962, is discussed. At present, the BCG vaccination of primarily preschool and teenage populations is one of the main methods of approach.   IVY

1296   **RATH   OTTO J S**
1965
PUBLIC HEALTH PRACTICE AMONG THE INDIAN POPULATION. Manitoba Medical Review 45:644-649.

Outlined are the historical development from 1755, present organization, and objectives of the Medical Services Directorate of the Department of National Health and Welfare. Public health programs such as maternal, child, and school health, control of various diseases, and dental and eye services in Manitoba are described.   IVY

1297   **RYMER   SHEILA**
1969
NEW APPROACHES TO HEALTH PROBLEMS OF THE INDIAN PEOPLE. The Canadian Medical Association Journal 101:614-615.

Community health workers have recently been employed in the attempt to solve Indian and Eskimo health problems. This article describes the Department of National Health and Welfare's development of a project whereby delegates from various Indian communities were trained and returned to their respective communities to awaken the community to its health problems and ways of solving them. The role of Indians in the administration of their own health services is also considered in the article.   ADG

1298   **SASKATCHEWAN. Department of Public Health. Saskatchewan Hospital Services Plan.**
1963-1966
INDIAN HOSPITAL CARE IN SASKATCHEWAN (1962,1963,1964,1965). 4 vols. Regina: Queen's Printer.

Since July 1, 1958, Indians living on reserves and those living off reserves for less than 12 months have been insured under the Saskatchewan Hospital Services Plan by the Government of Canada. These reviews of Indian hospital care concern only this portion of the Indian population. Their hospitalization experience is compared with that of the Plan's total covered population, and, in certain aspects, with the experience of non-Indians. A comparison of the previous years' hospitalization experience of the 9 Indian agencies in the province is also included (exception, 1962).   IVY

1299   **SASKATCHEWAN. Department of Social Welfare and Rehabilitation. Bureau on Alcoholism.**
1963
ALCOHOLISM AND THE INDIAN: PROCEEDINGS OF A CONFERENCE HELD AT THE FEDERAL GOVERNMENT HOSPITAL FOR INDIANS. Unpublished paper. Available from Public Health Library, Department of Public Health, Regina, Sask. 35 pp.

Medical and counseling approaches to alcoholism are given in 4 of the 5 papers presented. General references to Indians are given in the paper by J.F.A. Calder which discusses the problem of alcoholism, the history of alcohol, and Alcoholics Anonymous.

Also included are 2 talks by Indian members of Alcoholics Anonymous. A 2-page summary of the discussion and recommendations of 4 workshop groups by F.R. Fraser deals specifically with Indians. The topics discussed were patterns of drinking and causes of alcoholism. It was recommended that community helpers help form Alcoholics Anonymous groups, treatment facilities be located on or near reserves, an intensive education program be initiated, Friendship Centers be established in urban centers near Indian reserves, and liquor legislation be reviewed. The conference was held November 8, 1953, at Fort Qu'Appelle, Saskatchewan.   IVY

1300   **SCHAEFER   O**
1962
ALCOHOL WITHDRAWAL SYNDROME IN A NEWBORN INFANT OF A YUKON INDIAN MOTHER. The Canadian Medical Association Journal 87:1333-1334.

This case study reports the birth of an Indian infant who was not only intoxicated at birth, but who developed withdrawal symptoms 12 to 18 hours after birth.   ADG

1301   **SCHMITT   N, HOLE   L W, et al.**
1966
ACCIDENTAL DEATHS AMONG BRITISH COLUMBIA INDIANS. The Canadian Medical Association Journal 94:228-234.

Review of the British Columbia Division of Vital Statistics files concerning Indian and non-Indian mortality reveals that accidents were the leading cause of death among Indians and only fourth among non-Indians for the period 1959-1963. Among the causal factors noted in the article are the following: (1) substandard living conditions containing hazards which expose the Indian to greater possibility of accidental death than the non-Indian, (2) a possible association of the prevalence of accidents among Indians with social change from traditional aboriginal to urban Canadian culture, and (3) psychological factors and alcohol. Moreover, young Indian males, more than their non-Indian peers, suffer from an undue amount of repressed hostility and frustration and the extremely high fatality rate in this age group might be partially an expression of emotional instability and unconscious revolt. Viable preventive measures should be taken immediately.   ADG

1302   **SMITH   ALICE K**
1963
NURSING WITH INDIAN AND NORTHERN HEALTH SERVICES. The Canadian Nurse 59:130-131.

Indian and Northern Health Services, a division of the Medical Services Directorate, Department of National Health and Welfare, is responsible for the administration of health and treatment services. These include 18 hospitals (with a total of 2,100 beds and bassinets), 35 nursing stations, 80 health centers, and 31 clinics which collectively employ a staff of approximately 2,500.   IVY

1303   **SMITH   NICHOLAS N**
1964
INDIAN MEDICINE: FACT OR FICTION? Massachusetts Archaeological Society Bulletin 26:13-16.

Acceptance of the colonial concepts of herb medicine changed the role of a shaman to that of an herbalist. A glossary of approximately 105 plants with the diseases they are thought to cure, as used by either the Malecite, Passamaquoddy, or Penobscot Indians, concludes the report.   IVY

1304   **TERMANSEN   P E,   SIMPSON   C A,   et al.**
1968
INDIAN HEALTH COMMITTEE. British Columbia Medical Journal 10:264-266.

The Committee on Indian Health reports on current health problems of the British Columbia Indian population and existing medical services available to deal with these problems. Discussed are Indian health problems and attitudes, provision of medical and health care, physician services, hospital care, drugs, and public health care. It is recommended that the provincial and federal governments increase funds available for health care of Indians, that these governments develop a comprehensive health plan in negotiation with each band of the province, and that they clarify their respective responsibilities for the provision of health services.   IVY

1305   **THOMAS   W D**
1968
MATERNAL MORTALITY IN NATIVE BRITISH COLUMBIA INDIANS, A HIGH RISK GROUP. The Canadian Medical Association Journal 99:64-67.

Investigation of the 26 maternal deaths of British Columbia Indians during 1955 and 1965 reveals that Indians account for a disproportionate part of the total provincial maternal mortalities. Among the 26 cases, hemorrhages and infections accounted for the largest percentages of deaths. Twenty-five of the 26 cases were classified as preventable and in most cases (19) the patient was ruled responsible for the death. Several factors seem to influence Indian maternal mortality in British Columbia: (1) age and parity, (2) lack of prenatal care, (3) residence in isolated areas, and (4) medical economics, that is, the lower pay doctors receive from the federal government for Indian patients and the absence of sufficient doctors in isolated areas. Reduction of the high rate of maternal mortality among Indians should be facilitated by government provision of medical care to Indian patients on a basis equal to that of White patients. Medical referral centers for high risk patients, health education for expectant mothers, sterilization, and birth control are other possible remedial measures.   ADG

1306   **VOGEL   VIRGIL J**
1970
AMERICAN INDIAN MEDICINE. Norman: University of Oklahoma Press. 583 pp.

Focus is directed toward the cure of disease and the healing of injuries. Indigenous botanical drugs receive major attention. Tribes include Iroquois, Huron, Kwakiutl, Montagnais, and Ojibwa. In the appendix (pages 267-414), American Indian contributions to pharmacology are listed alphabetically by common name.   IVY

1307   **WHITEFORD   JEAN L**
1963
NURSING WITH INHS IN THE SASKATCHEWAN REGION. The Canadian Nurse 59:365-368.

In this description of nursing in the Saskatchewan region (administering to 23,000 Indians scattered over approximately 240,000 square miles), maternal care, child care, tuberculosis, and health education are discussed.   IVY

1308   **WIEBE   J H,   MCDONALD   HEATHER P**
1963
WORK AMONG THE INDIAN AND ESKIMO PEOPLE OF EASTERN CANADA.
The Canadian Nurse 59:539-544.

In the Eastern Region, the Indian Northern Health Service administers 34 health centers, 9 nursing stations, and 3 hospitals. An annual health survey conducted from the Canadian Government Ship C. D. Howe as well as other less extensive patrols by air and land provide X-rays, medical examinations, dental work, innoculations, and, if necessary, evacuation. These facilities serve 55,000 Indians and 5,570 Eskimos.   IVY

1309   **WILLIS   JOHN S,   MARTIN   MORGAN**
1962
MENTAL HEALTH IN CANADA'S NORTH. Unpublished paper. Available from Public Health Library, Department of Public Health, Regina, Sask. 11 pp.

This paper deals with the external environment of Canada's North and its psychological effect on 3 ethnic groups - Indian, Eskimo, and White.   IVY

RELIGION

1310   **ANGLICAN CHURCH OF CANADA**
n.d.
A NATIVE MINISTRY. Anglican House (Toronto) Mission Capsules 10. Toronto: Anglican Church of Canada. 1 p.

This pamphlet reviews the training of Eli Spence, a Cree Indian from York Factory, for the Anglican ministry.   IVY

1311   **ANGLICAN CHURCH OF CANADA**
n.d.
STEWARDSHIP AMONG KEEWATIN'S INDIANS. Anglican House (Toronto) Mission Capsules 16. Toronto: Anglican Church of Canada. 1 p.

This pamphlet reports the development of native assumption of responsibility for supporting their church.   IVY

1312   **ANGLICAN CHURCH OF CANADA**
1962
THE MINISTRY OF THE ANGLICAN CHURCH OF CANADA WITH CANADIAN INDIANS: AN INTERDEPARTMENTAL REPORT PREPARED BY REPRESENTATIVES OF THE DEPARTMENTS OF MISSIONS, RELIGIOUS EDUCATION, CHRISTIAN SOCIAL SERVICE, INFORMATION AND STEWARDSHIP. Toronto: Anglican Church of Canada. 10 pp.

A report prepared by representatives of several departments is presented to the general synod of the Anglican Church of Canada. The report concerns the ministry of the Anglican Church among Canadian Indians and consists of a review of Indian-White relations, a review of Anglican Church activity among Indian people, and an evaluation of the present situation and needs. Recommendations are advanced for greater church commitment and Indian participation, measures to insure increased co-operation and involvement, and the initiation of 1 or more pilot projects in the area of community development.   CCV

1313   **CHAMBERLAND   CHARLES**
1968
LE SERVICE MISSIONAIRE DES JEUNES AU SECOURS DE NOS MISSIONS.
Kerygma 2(1):12-17.

The religious situation in an Oblate Mission in northern Saskatchewan is reviewed. Religious affiliation and participation of Indian, Metis, and White population are presented. Intermarriage, poor examples set by White Catholics, alcohol, reduced conviction in the church, and distractions have led to a decline in religious fervor.   CCV

1314   **CRONIN   KAY**
1960
CROSS IN THE WILDERNESS. Vancouver: Mitchell. 255 pp.

The 19th and early 20th century story of the Oblates' difficulties in establishing and maintaining missions among the British Columbia Indians is recounted from published and archival sources. Details of health and medical problems experienced by the Indians as well as their attitudes toward Christianity are revealed by the narrative of which the main focus is the Oblate Fathers.   CCV

1315   **DEITER   WALTER,   CARDINAL   HAROLD**
1970
WHAT DO INDIAN LEADERS ASK OF THE CHURCH NOW? In Bulletin 201:
Recent Statements by the Indians of Canada, General Synod Action 1969, Some
Government Responses, Suggested Resources. Toronto: Anglican Church of Canada. p.
40.

Proposals advanced by Indian leaders representing the National Indian Brotherhood and the provincial organizations of Indians of Nova Scotia, New Brunswick, Ontario, Manitoba, Saskatchewan, Alberta, and British Columbia are presented to the Anglican Church. Priorities include funding for consultations with the federal government, liaison workers, communications equipment and personnel, consultants with expertise in economic development, and establishment of a committee to ensure greater relevance of church activity to native needs.   CCV

1316   **DOZIER   EDWARD**
1962
DIFFERING REACTIONS TO RELIGIOUS CONTACTS AMONG NORTH
AMERICAN INDIAN SOCIETIES. Akten Des 34. Internationalen
Amerikanistenkongresses. pp. 161-171.

In a survey of North American Indian contact with Christian religions, 6 general types of adjustment are suggested: (1) rejection, (2) assimilation, (3) compartmentalization, (4) fusion, (5) reactive adaptation, and (6) stabilized pluralism. These are described and illustrations offered. Possible causes of such reactions or accomodations are summarized.   IVY

1317   **ELIADE   MIRCEA**
1967
FROM PRIMITIVES TO ZEN: A THEMATIC SOURCEBOOK OF THE HISTORY
OF RELIGIONS. New York: Harper and Row. 644 pp.

Religious beliefs, conceptions, rituals, and institutions are illustrated in this anthology of religious texts representing various religious and cultural-geographical areas. Specific Canadian examples include: the Dakota, Lenape, and Naskapi in a discussion of supernatural beings; the road to the nether world and the creation myth of the Thompson Indians of British Columbia; becoming a shaman among the Kwakiutl; the Ghost dance movement; and pre-existence and incarnation among North American Indians in general.   CCV

1318   **HENDRY   CHARLES E**
1969
BEYOND TRAPLINES. Toronto: Ryerson Press. 102 pp.

This action-oriented study attempts to analyze the role of the church in its work with the native people of Canada. It is assumed that the church in active collaboration with other Christian churches can make a significant contribution to the development of the economic and human needs of Indians, Eskimos, and Metis. Discussed are the forces which have shaped the present status of the native people, the contributions and the failures of the church in its work with the Indians, and some recommendations for individual and cooperative action in this effort. Appended are specific steps which should be followed for participatory democracy of community redevelopment, a statement on the breakdown of tribal culture from 1760-1820, and a position paper concerning the stance of the Anglican Church with respect to Indian work.   DGW

1319   **HOMEWOOD   E L**
1965
THE INDIAN AND THE CHURCH: LAST OF A SERIES ON THE PLIGHT OF
CANADA'S INDIANS. The United Church Observer N.S. 27(4):21-23,32.

The church's past and present role in Indian affairs is critically examined by both Indians and Whites.   IVY

1320   **HULTKRANTZ   AKE**
1965
THE STUDY OF NORTH AMERICAN INDIAN RELIGION: RETROSPECT,
PRESENT TRENDS AND FUTURE TASKS. Temenos 1:87-121.

Modern works dealing with North American Indian religion are grouped in the following categories: (1) recordings of Indian tribal religions in the field; (2) comparative analyses of religious materials; (3) structural studies; (4) acculturation studies; (5) ethnohistory; and (6) personality studies. Two major forms of interpretation, phenomenology
and history, are discussed. Included is a bibliography, pages 108-121.   IVY

1321   **HULTKRANTZ   AKE**
1967
NORTH AMERICAN INDIAN RELIGION IN THE HISTORY OF RESEARCH: A
GENERAL SURVEY: PART III. History of Religions 7:13-34.

The contributions and the achievements of the Boasian school in the field of religion are
outlined.   IVY

1322   **HULTKRANTZ   AKE**
1967
NORTH AMERICAN INDIAN RELIGION IN THE HISTORY OF RESEARCH: A
GENERAL SURVEY: PART IV. History of Religions 7:112-148.

Major anthropological works since 1925 in the field of American Indian religion are surveyed.   IVY

1323   **JAENEN   CORNELIUS J**
1968
FRANCISATION ET EVANGELISATION DES AMERINDIENS DE LA
NOUVELLE-FRANCE AU XVIIe SIECLE. La Societe Canadienne d'Histoire de
l'Eglise Catholique, Sessions d'Etude 35:33-46.

The acculturation and evangelization of the Amerindian in New France during the 17th
century are examined. The development of interest in the mission field represented by
New France and attitudes toward the native peoples are reviewed. It is noted that evangelism had limited success and that the French, a widely dispersed minority group,
tended to be assimilated into Amerindian society.   CCV

1324   **JOBLIN   E E M**
1970
INDIAN WORK IN LONDON CONFERENCE, THE UNITED CHURCH OF
CANADA; CO-ORDINATOR: THE REV. F. E. KEMPLING. Unpublished paper.
Available from National Library of Canada. 4 pp.

Group ministry, an approach using both ordained and lay personnel, was proposed for
Indian communities in the London Conference.   The role of Reverend F. E. Kempling in
this area is examined.   IVY

1325   **KEHOE   ALICE B**
1963
SASKATCHEWAN INDIAN RELIGIOUS BELIEFS. Saskatchewan Museum of
Natural History Popular Series 7. Regina, Sask.: Department of Natural Resources. 15
pp.

General information is provided on the aboriginal religious beliefs of the natives of Saskatchewan including shamanism and the Sun Dance. Modern beliefs such as the Ghost Dance, the Native American Church, and the Baha'i faith are briefly mentioned. IVY

1326 **KOWAPINA TOKA**
1970
THE ANCIENT PIPE CEREMONY. Tawow 1(1):23.

The meaning of the ceremony is given. IVY

1327 **LABARRE WESTON**
1970
THE GHOST DANCE: ORIGINS OF RELIGION. Garden City: Doubleday. 677 pp.

The development of religion and revitalization movements are considered in an anthropological and psychological study. Examples are drawn from a variety of cultures. The role of Handsome Lake in the development of the Longhouse religion and that of other Canadian tribal heroes are included in the discussion of culture heroes in Chapter 6. Chapter 7 is devoted to a review of the Ghost Dance and parallels in other societies. CCV

1328 **LABARRE WESTON**
1970
THE PEYOTE CULT. Enlarged edition. New York: The Shoe String Press. 259 pp.

The Peyote cult among North American Indian groups is examined with emphasis on psychological and historical aspects of its use, tribal differences and similarities, ritual and non-ritual use, and diffusion. Progress in Peyote studies from 1938 to 1963 is reviewed. Canadian tribes are mentioned briefly. Peyotism as opposed to the use of hallucinatory drugs by other groups is discussed in the preface. CCV

1329 **MELLING JOHN**
1967
RIGHT TO A FUTURE: THE NATIVE PEOPLES OF CANADA. Don Mills, Ont.: Anglican Church of Canada and United Church of Canada. 150 pp.

This statement concerning the human rights of the native peoples of Canada is supported by a co-operative denominational front. Outlined in the study is the development of missions among the natives of Canada from the mid-19th century onwards. Of immediate concern, however, is the question of the church's role in current Indian affairs. The church is viewed as being in an influential position in bringing social justice to bear on the reserve community. Through the processes of education and effective community development programs, a challenging community life could be created in the best interests and total well being of the natives concerned. Education and community development are viewed as interdependent - community development is one of the processes of education - while education affects and conditions the development of the community. Also discussed are the conditions of Indians migrating to the urban setting and the role of Friendship Centres in community development programs. DGW

1330 **MONTOUR ENOS**
1961

A NEW DEAL FOR PRAIRIE INDIANS. The United Church Observer N.S. 23(2):8-9,20.

The Good Samaritan Plan initiated by Rev. Earl Stotesbury recommends that congregations and organizations befriend at least 1 Indian family over an extended period of time.   IVY

1331   **MULLER   WERNER**
1962
LES RELIGIONS DES INDIENS D'AMERIQUE DU NORD. In Les Religions Amerindiennes. Walter Krickeberg, Werner Muller, et al., eds. Paris: Christel-Matthias Schroder. pp. 215-326.

Aboriginal religious beliefs of Canadian Indian groups are summarized in Chapters 1 to 5 and 7 of this section which is devoted to North American Indian religions. A general discussion of the Athabaskans and Algonkians in terms of shared traits is followed by an overview of certain aspects of aboriginal beliefs as reflected in folklore and religious practices among the Algonkians of the Atlantic coast and the Great Lakes, the Ontario Iroquois, and Northwest Coast tribes.   CCV

1332   **MULLER   WERNER**
1968
NORTH AMERICA. In Pre-Columbian American Religions. Walter Krickberg and Hermann Trimborn, eds. New York: Holt, Rinehart, Winston. pp. 147-229.

The nature of the alien consciousness which underlies all forms of religious beliefs and practices are studied in this analysis of pre-Columbian religions in the Americas. The chapter discusses drums and the acquiring of a guardian spirit among the Canadian Algonkians and Athapascans, the dreams and visions of the Algonkian of the Great Lakes region, the twin gods and dual nature of the Longhouse religion among the Iroquois, and the death and rebirth symbolism inherent in the initiation ceremonies of the Kwakiutl.   DGW

1333   **NEWELL   WILLIAM J**
1967
CANADA'S OTHER SHEEP. The Alliance Witness 102(13):7-8.

It is the intention of the Alliance to proclaim the gospel to Canada's neglected peoples, the Eskimos, Indians, and French-speaking citizens.   IVY

1334   **NIX   JAMES ERNEST**
1960
MISSION AMONG THE BUFFALO: THE LABOURS OF THE REVERENDS GEORGE M. AND JOHN C. MCDOUGALL IN THE CANADIAN NORTHWEST, 1860-1876. Toronto: Ryerson Press. 123 pp.

This historical account of the life and work of the McDougall family reveals their contribution as prophets and promoters of Western Canada. It explains the Methodist branch of the development of the Christian Church among the Indians spanning the years 1850-1916. Besides opening the doors for future missionary work, the combined efforts of this family is as well marked in their initiation of educational services for the Indians. To effectively continue this work, the author proposes the establishment of a central training school for workers among the Indians with special considerations given to the specific needs of the community being served.   DGW

1335   **OBLATE SERVICES INC.**
1960
GAZETTEER OF INDIAN AND ESKIMO STATIONS OF THE OBLATE FATHERS IN CANADA. Ottawa: Oblate Services. 119 pp.

The gazetteer records every Indian or Eskimo community in Canada visited on a regular basis by an Oblate Father. If the area is cited as a mission, the Oblate Father resides there and conducts services on a permanent basis. Communities visited intermittently by an Oblate Father are listed as chapels. Each provincial and vicariate listing indicates the rank of the establishment (mission or chapel), name-patronage of the church or chapel, date of establishment, name of the diocese, number of priests, number of brothers and sisters, number of parishioners (with a breakdown of those from Indian or Eskimo descent), the Indian Affairs Branch agency in the area, and details concerning local school attendance.   DGW

1336   **RIEGEL   MARY BYER**
1963
SOCIAL INTERACTION IN THE ESCHATOLOGY OF SELECTED EASTERN AMERICAN INDIAN TRIBES. M.A. Thesis. Department of Anthropology. Catholic University of America. 80 pp.

The eschatologies of the Abenaki, Algonkin, Cree, Delaware, Fox, Huron, Iroquois, Malecite, Menominee, Micmac, Montagnais-Naskapi, Neutral, Ojibwa-Chippewa-Saulteaux, Ottawa, Shawnee, and Winnebago are reviewed and patterns of social interaction of the souls of the dead among themselves or with the living are compared. Functional patterns of interaction were revealed by analysis.   Insufficient data are available to term the selected eschatologies dynamic, although they are considered to be more developed than indicated in the literature by Lowie and Benedict.   CCV

1337   **SCOTT   EDWARD W**
1966
A POSITION PAPER CONCERNING THE STANCE OF THE ANGLICAN CHURCH TO INDIAN WORK PREPARED FOR DISCUSSION PURPOSES. Unpublished paper. Available from National Library of Canada. 3 pp.

Since the situation relating to the Indian people in Canada has changed so drastically, it is necessary for the Anglican Church to re-think its approach to Indian work in terms of its goals, methods of work, and general attitudes.   IVY

1338   **SETON   ERNEST THOMPSON, SETON   JULIA M, comps.**
1966
THE GOSPEL OF THE REDMAN: A WAY OF LIFE. Sante Fe: Seton Village. 108 pp.

This publication of the Indian creed was compiled and presented with the intention of helping the White man realize the character of the Indian aboriginal past. The spiritual nature which governed every facet of Indian life - motives, thoughts, and behavior - is revealed. The message of the Indian closely parallels dogma espoused by modern world religions. Included in this compiled edition are prayers, teachings, and laws of the Indian as well as White expressions of Indian thought.   DGW

1339   **UNITED CHURCH OF CANADA. Board of Home Missions.**
n.d.
MAPS: INDIAN COMMUNITIES SERVED BY THE UNITED CHURCH OF CANADA. Available from National Library of Canada. 5 pp.

Indian communities served by The United Church of Canada are designated on maps of Ontario and Quebec, Manitoba, Saskatchewan, Alberta, and British Columbia.   IVY

1340   **VACHON   ANDRE**
1960
L'EAU-DE-VIE DANS LA SOCIETE INDIENNE. Canadian Historical Association Annual Report 1960. pp. 22-32.

The role of alcohol in Indian life is analyzed with emphasis on the contact period when the Indian need to recreate his cultural climate was satisfied only in inebriation. The abrupt introduction to Christianity without a corresponding acculturation process which resulted in deterioration of Indian culture is seen as a factor in the Indian's attitude toward drinking.   CCV

1341   **WALKER   DEWARD E**
1969
NEW LIGHT ON THE PROPHET DANCE CONTROVERSY. Ethnohistory 16:245-255.

Ethnographic, documentary, and recent archaeological sources pertaining to the Prophet Dance among Indians of the Plateau and Northwest Coast are reviewed. It is suggested that the Prophet Dance was not a purely "aboriginal"innovation but was inspired by indirect, protohistoric influences stemming from Euro-Americans.   IVY

1342   **WILKINSON   FLORENCE G**
1963
THE INDIANS OF ALBERTA HEAR THE GOSPEL: THE STORY OF THE DEVELOPMENT OF INDIAN MISSIONS IN ALBERTA UNDER THE CHURCHES WHICH ENTERED UNION 1840-1925. Th.M. Thesis. Victoria College. University of Toronto. 185 pp.

Methodist mission activities in Alberta are traced from their beginnings in 1840 when the Hudson's Bay Company allowed them to enter the area. These missions received a new challenge with the transfer of their control to the Canada Conference in 1854. After enduring the trials of epidemics and rebellion, the missions emerged into an era for establishing permanent work (1885-1925). For this last period both evangelistic and educational activities are outlined. A concluding chapter praises Canadian Indian policy and missionary labor.   IVY

1343   **WILLOYA   WILLIAM,   BROWN   VINSON**
1962
WARRIORS OF THE RAINBOW. Healdsburg, CA: Naturegraph. 94 pp.

A collection of Indian dreams, prophecies, and folklore is presented including accounts of Iroquois and Plains visions.   CCV

ORAL TRADITION AND FOLKLORE

1344   **1970**
STORIES OF THE INDIAN AND ESKIMO: A NEW CBC RADIO PROGRAM. Tawow 1(2):36-37.

Stories collected by James McNeill are broadcast by CBC Northern Service. An Interior Salish tale, "The Marriage of the North Wind and South Wind,"is presented.   IVY

1345   **BURLAND   COTTIE**
1965
NORTH AMERICAN INDIAN MYTHOLOGY. London: Hamlyn. 153 pp.

Relying chiefly on publications by Marius Barbeau, some Eskimo and Canadian Indian legends are presented in the first 99 pages of this book. Mythology is related to the ecological niche and artistic productions of various tribes. Oral tradition and objects of material culture are illustrated by numerous color photographs.   CCV

1346   **CLARK   ELLA ELIZABETH**
1960
INDIAN LEGENDS OF CANADA. Toronto: McClelland and Stewart. 177 pp.

Myths, legends, historical traditions and personal narratives from archives, personal collections, and Indian informants (1950's) are presented in this anthology representative of Canadian Indian oral literature. Narratives are chosen in an effort to present interesting examples of each type and to provide information about the everyday life, belief systems, and ceremonies of the first Canadians.   CCV

1347   **CLARK   ELLA ELIZABETH**
1966
INDIAN LEGENDS FROM THE NORTHERN ROCKIES. Norman, OK: University of Oklahoma Press. 350 pp.

Stories from archives and personal collections as well as some recorded directly from Indian informants in the 1950's are presented according to linguistic group. The Canadian Flathead, Kutenai, Gros Ventre, Blackfoot, Sioux, Assiniboine, and Blood Indians are represented. Accounts are chosen to promote understanding of Indian beliefs and customs and to demonstrate the origin of tribal ceremonies and sacred objects. Numerous origin myths are included. The traditional life style, ecology, and general social organization of the Plains and Plateau Indians are summarized in an introductory chapter.   CCV

1348   **DARIOS   LOUISE**
1965
STRANGE TALES OF CANADA. Translated by P.C. Gerry. Toronto: Ryerson Press. 162 pp.

In this collection of unusual Canadian tales each province is represented by a story reflecting folkways and the cultural background of the inhabitants. From British Columbia comes a Northwest Coast tale of the sea serpent's vertebra, an Indian talisman. Another Indian legend of the south wind represents Manitoba. Tribal sources are not specified.   CCV

1349   **DUNDES   ALAN**
1962
THE MORPHOLOGY OF NORTH AMERICAN INDIAN FOLKTALES. Ph.D. Thesis. Department of Folklore. Indiana University. 219 pp. Available from University Microfilms.

Subscribing to the thesis that a definite structure underlies North American Indian folktales, a morphological model is constructed and tested. Each model is considered a motifeme pattern whose properties are compared with those of the actual folktales. Treatment and analysis is accorded to individual folktales such as Earth-Diver, Eye-Juggler, and Orpheus. It is considered that such a structural analysis may prove invaluable in such areas as typology, prediction, acculturation, content analysis, cross-genre comparison, function, and etiology.   DGW

1350   **DUNDES   ALAN**
1963
STRUCTURAL TYPOLOGY IN AMERICAN INDIAN FOLKTALES. Southwestern Journal of Anthropology 19:121-130.

Contrary to earlier assertions, North American Indian tales are considered in terms of definite patterns, or motifemes. This morphological analysis of tales is considered essential in establishing typolgies and subsequently in making cross-cultural comparisons to examine the cultural determination of content.   WRC

1351   **EGOFF   SHEILA**
1967
CANADIAN FOLKLORE. Canadian Library Association Centennial Series 55. Ottawa: Canadian Library Association. 11 pp.

The style, sources, and several noteworthy examples and collections of Indian folklore are mentioned in this discussion of Canadian folklore.   CCV

1352   **GOODERHAM   KENT, ed.**
1969
I AM AN INDIAN. Toronto: Dent. 196 pp.

An anthology consisting of 66 Canadian Indian works including folklore, songs, history, poetry, and narratives is presented. Each selection is accompanied by a brief introduction to the author, and where relevant, discussion of the cultural context of the subject matter. Much of the material has been published elsewhere. Illustrations and photographs are by Indians or of Indians or their material culture.   CCV

1353   **HANSEN   L TAYLOR**
1963
HE WALKED THE AMERICAS. Amherst, WI: Amherst Press. 256 pp.

A collection of legends of the Healer, the Prophet or Kate-Zahl includes a legend of a sacred city in Canada.   CCV

1354   **HAYS   H R**
1963
IN THE BEGINNINGS: EARLY MAN AND HIS GODS. New York: Putnam. 575 pp.

Aboriginal and traditional beliefs for culture areas around the world are described from archaeological, historical, and ethnographic sources. Social stratification, the roles of sha-man, mythology, dreams, secret societies, and the potlatch in Northwest Coast society are discussed in Chapter 37. The guardian spirit quest, mythology, folklore, and secret societies in Plains and Woodlands cultures are described in Chapter 38.   CCV

1355   **LERMAN   NORMAN H,   CARKIN   HELEN S**
1968
ONCE UPON AN INDIAN TALE: AUTHENTIC FOLK TALES. New York: Carleton. 54 pp.

Nine folktales collected from Indian women of the British Columbia coast and Fraser River Valley are presented.   CCV

1356   **MCCLELLAN   CATHARINE**
1970
INDIAN STORIES ABOUT THE FIRST WHITES IN NORTHWESTERN AMERICA. In Ethnohistory in Southwestern Alaska and the Southern Yukon: Method and Content. Margaret Lantis, ed. Studies in Anthropology 7. Lexington, KY: University Press of Kentucky. pp. 103-133.

The ethnohistoric value of oral testimonies from northern and southern Tutchone Ath-abascans, the Tlingit-speaking Tagish, the inland Tlingit of the Yukon, and Indian groups in Alaska is assessed and the method of classification, function, style, and content of this group of stories (about the first Whites) is analyzed in relation to the total bodies of literature in which they appear. Native traditions relating to a specific historical figure, Robert Campbell of the Hudson's Bay Company, show much variability in the versions given by different informants. Taken in the total literary context, it appears that the Coastal Tlingit value standardization and formality in their tales about the first Whites, while the interior groups employ free variation.   IVY

1357   **MCKAY   FORTESCUE**
n.d.
AN INDIAN TALE OF BIRCH BARK, MUSK-RAT TAILS & RABBITS EARS. North 13(6):14-17.

In this tale of Old Naynapuss, father of all Indians, we learn why the grain of the birch trees runs horizontally, the muskrat has an odd-shaped tail, and the rabbit long ears.   IVY

1358   **MELANCON   CLAUDE**
1967
LEGENDES INDIENNES DU CANADA. Montreal: Editions du Jour. 160 pp.

Thirty-three Indian legends from the Atlantic Coast and Woodlands, Plains, and North-west Coast are compiled.   CCV

1359   **RICKETTS   MAC LINSCOTT**
1964
THE STRUCTURE AND RELIGIOUS SIGNIFICANCE OF THE TRICKSTER-TRANSFORMER-CULTURE HERO IN THE MYTHOLOGY OF THE NORTH AMERICAN INDIANS. Ph.D. Thesis. Divinty School. University of Chicago. 653 pp.

The "Trickster-Transformer-Culture Hero"is the most prominent mythical person throughout non-agricultural North America. His acts (including bringing fire and death) do much to place the world in its present condition, but he is also a very worldly being. The variations of his representation are discussed region by region including the North-western Coast (Central and Southern Zones being in Canada), the Athabascans, the Algonkians, the Great Plains, the Plateau, the Strait of Georgia, and the Iroquois.   TSA

1360   **ROTHENBERG   JEROME**
1968
TECHNICIANS OF THE SACRED: A RANGE OF POETRIES FROM AFRICA, AMERICA, ASIA & OCEANIA. New York: Doubleday. 520 pp.

Eight songs or poems from Canadian Indians are represented in this collection of chants and poems from Africa, America, Asia, and Oceania.   CCV

1361   **SAVARD   REMI**
1970
STRUCTURES SEMANTIQUES ET MYTHOLOGIE: LE PERSONNAGE DE DECEPTEUR DANS LA LITTERATURE ORALE AMERINDIENNE. Upublished paper delivered to Symposium sur les Structures et les Genres de la Litterature Ethnique, sponsored by Associazione per le Conservazione delle Tradizioni Popolari and Instituto di Storia della Tradizioni Popolari. Palerme, April 5-10, 1970. Available from Bibliotheque Nationale du Quebec. 15 pp.

In a discussion of semantic structures and mythology the tale of the trickster from North American oral tradition is analyzed. The degree to which it varies according to the narra-tor is noted.   DD

1362   **SPENCE   AHAB**
1970
THE LITTLE BIRD'S ARROW. Tawow 1(3):19.

A little bird shows We-sa-kay-chak the accuracy of an arrow.   IVY

1363   **TOWEGISHIG   LARRY (HAWK)**
1970
THE WOLF CRY, THE GREAT BEAR. Tawow 1(3):20-22.

In the first of 2 folk tales, the wolf cries in sorrow, for long ago he lost a race to a dog, thereby losing the great prize, to become man's best friend. The legend of The Great Bear relates why the bear is referred to as "Grandfather"and respected.   IVY

1364   **WILSON   EDDIE W**
1965
THE MOON AND THE AMERICAN INDIAN. Western Folklore 24:87-100.

In the American Indian's concepts of deity, ritual, and creation stories, the moon figured prominently. Using a wide scope of examples, including the Nootka, Haida, Athabaskan, Cree, Micmac, and Iroquois, these aspects are discussed.   IVY

1365   **YOUNG   FRANK C**
1970
A FIFTH ANALYSIS OF THE STAR HUSBAND TALE. Ethnology 9:389-413.

Based on 24 ethnographies and 86 versions, a structural-symbolic analysis of the Star Husband tale prevalent among North American Indians is made to discern the diverse patterning of social symbols. Application of Pearsonian correlations to various dramatic contrasts in the data reveals that the solidarity expressed in the tale by such highly differentiated tribes as those of the Plains may be a response to the marginal condition to which they have been relegated by the larger social order. A methodological comparison is made among the technique employed and 4 earlier ones in analyzing this tale of the life cycle of 2 girls and their ascent to the skyworld in pursuit of a husband.   WRC

MUSIC AND DANCE   .

1366   **1967**
EVENING PROGRAM OF NATIVE ENTERTAINMENT. In National Conference on Indian and Northern Education Saskatoon 1967. Mary Anne LaVallee, ed. n.p.: Society for Indian and Northern Education and Extension Division, University of Saskatchewan. pp. 103-110.

Wilf Tootoosis and his people from Cutknife, Saskatchewan, dressed in full regalia, presented several authentic Indian dances. Mr. Harry Bird of the File-Hills Indian Agency sang folk songs, some his own compositions. Mr. Wilfred Pelletier of Toronto and Mr. Isaac Beaulieu of Manitoba performed a skit. The Indian Youth of Saskatoon also presented a skit.   IVY

1367   **1970**
CANADIAN PRAIRIE INDIAN DANCE TROUPE. Tawow 1(1):8-13.

A Canadian Prairie Dance Troupe consisting of 23 members performed in Holland and Paris. Their tour and repertoire is recapitulated through text and photographs.   IVY

1368   **CRAWFORD   DAVID E**
1967
THE JESUIT RELATIONS AND ALLIED DOCUMENTS: EARLY SOURCES FOR AN ETHNOGRAPHY OF MUSIC AMONG AMERICAN INDIANS.
Ethnomusicology 11:199-206.

The role of music in Huron, Iroquois, and Abnaki culture as described by Jesuit missionaries is presented in 2 categories: the medicine man and his music, and music by groups and other individuals.   IVY

1369   **HOWARD   JOSEPH H**
1967
DRUMS IN THE AMERICAS. New York: Oak Publications. 319 pp.

The major drums found and used in the Americas are named, localized, and described. Classification and construction of drums as well as rhythm and drumming are dealt with in separate chapters. Amerindian music is discussed briefly in Chapter 4. Amerindian drums of North America are described by culture area in Chapter 5. Details of construction and relationship of drum use and dancing or singing to the culture complex are included.   CCV

1370   **JENKINS   CHARLES**
1969
THE DANCE-DRAMA OF THE AMERICAN INDIAN & ITS RELATIONS TO THE FOLK NARRATIVE. Lamda Alpha 1(2):23-29.

The American Indian dance-drama (1 of the 3 classifications of American Indian dance along with entertainment dance and ritual dance) is subdivided into 4 categories: the imitative pantomime, the dramatic episode, the dramatic narrative, and the dramatic cycle. To illustrate the dramatic narrative (the dramatization of legends) the structure and relationships of the False-Face ceremonies of the Iroquois are examined.   IVY

1371   **KALLMANN   HELMUT**
1960
A HISTORY OF MUSIC IN CANADA 1534-1914. Toronto: University of Toronto Press. 311 pp.

Included in the historical review of Canadian music are brief references, particularly in Chapter 1, to the music of Canada's native peoples as observed by explorers and missionaries. Indian use of European songs is also discussed.   CCV

1372   **KURATH   GERTRUDE P**
1961
AMERICAN INDIAN DANCE IN RITUAL AND LIFE: DANCES OF FRENZY. Folklorist 6:446-449.

Ceremonial clowns connected with shamanistic and visionary dances are discussed including those of the Iroquois winter rites and   False Face Society rituals.   IVY

1373   **KURATH   GERTRUDE P**
1961
AMERICAN INDIAN DANCE IN RITUAL AND LIFE: DANCES OF FRENZY. Folklorist 6:479-482.

Shamanistic and vision dances are described with reference to the Midewiwin and Iroquois Society of Shamans and Mystic Animals.   IVY

1374   **KURATH   GERTRUDE P**
1961
AMERICAN INDIAN DANCES IN RITUAL AND LIFE. Folklorist 6:428-435.

Content, theme, and style of American Indian dances are discussed in choreographic areas which approximate cultural areas.   IVY

1375   **KURATH   GERTRUDE P**
1961-62
AMERICAN INDIAN DANCES: RITUALS FOR SUSTENANCE. Folklorist 7:8-11.

The Iroquois Bear Dance which has former hunting associations and is linked to a clan origin legend and a curative society is 1 of the North American Indian animal dances described.   IVY

1376   **KURATH   GERTRUDE P**
1962
AMERICAN INDIAN RITUAL DANCES FOR SUSTENANCE. Folklorist 7:41-47.

Iroquois and Chippewa Fish Dances, the Iroquois Eagle Dance, and the Ottawa Swan Dance are among the dances described.   IVY

1377   **KURATH   GERTRUDE P**
1962
AMERICAN INDIAN RITUAL DANCES FOR SUSTENANCE. Folklorist 7:70-78.

Iroquois ritual is included in this description of the harvest rites of Woodland agriculturalists.   IVY

1378   **KURATH   GERTRUDE P**
1963
AMERICAN INDIAN DANCE PROGRAMS IN THE UNITED STATES, 1962.
Ethnomusicology 7:42-43.

Locations of Indian dance programs (powwows) performed in the Michigan and Ontario area in 1962 are given.   IVY

1379   **KURATH   GERTRUDE P**
1966
WOODLAND INDIAN PROGRAMS, 1965. Ethnomusicology 10:202-204.

Brief comments are given on the location, sponsorship, participation, contents, and motivation of Indian programs east of the Mississippi River (Canada and the United States).   IVY

1380   **OBOMSAWIN   ALANIS**
1970
COMMENTARY BY ALANIS OBOMSAWIN WHICH ACCOMPANIED THE SONGS SHE SANG TO GENERAL SYNOD, 1969. In Bulletin 201: Recent Statements by the Indians of Canada, General Synod Action 1969, Some Government Responses, Suggested Resources. Toronto: Anglican Church of Canada. pp. 15-17.

The traditional meaning of the syllable songs are discussed. They have a purpose in that they transmit Indian legends, history, and culture which have never been recorded.   DGW

1381   **POWERS   WILLIAM**
1960
AMERICAN INDIAN MUSIC: PART ONE: AN INTRODUCTION. American
Indian Hobbyist 7:5-9.

The characteristics of Indian singing are presented so the untrained person may appreciate and duplicate the styles. While the bulk of the article concerns Indians resident in
Oklahoma, some attention is paid to other regions, including Canada.   TSA

URBAN

1382   **1960**
CITIZENSHIP PROJECTS: INDIAN AND METIS FRIENDSHIP CENTRE,
WINNIPEG. Citizen 6(1):25-28.

A survey of the situation of Winnipeg's natives resulted in the establishment of a center
aimed at helping the newcomer through the provision of a counseling service, a recreational program, and a referral service.   ADG

1383   **1960**
INDIAN AND METIS FRIENDSHIP CENTRE, WINNIPEG. Citizen 6(1):25-28.

The organization and the functions of the center, which was established to meet the
needs of Indian and Metis newcomers to the city, are discussed.   IVY

1384   **1960**
INDIAN AND METIS SERVICE COUNCIL OF PRINCE ALBERT. Citizen 6(4):26-
28.

Briefly presented are the objectives of the Service Council and its organization.   IVY

1385   **1962**
NATIVE LEAGUE SPONSORS INDIAN YOUTH CONFERENCE. Citizen 8(3):9-
11.

This article describes the Native League of Saskatoon, a group of young Indians, and its
role in the presentation of the 1st Prairie Indian Youth Conference. Delegates from several urban centers in Saskatchewan and Manitoba met for 2 days to discuss the problems
confronting the urban Indian. Senator James Gladstone was the guest speaker.   ADG

1386   **1963**
INDIAN YOUTH CLUB, VANCOUVER. Citizen 9(5):34-36.

Conceived by Indian young people, the Indian Youth Club in Vancouver and its activities
are described.   IVY

1387   **1963**
THE PAS INDIAN-METIS FRIENDSHIP CENTRE. Citizen 9(1):22-25.

The Pas in northern Manitoba has established a center for Indians and Metis which provides counseling and referral services and recreational activities. Community response
and support are discussed.   ADG

1388 **1964**
URBAN SERVICES FOR PEOPLE OF INDIAN ANCESTRY. Citizen 10(1):18-25.

A report is provided of the various kinds of friendship centers and programs that have been established in different Canadian cities.   ADG

1389 **1969**
"DARBY LODGE"SYMBOLIZES ONE OF THE SPECIAL MINISTRIES OF HOME MISSIONS. The United Church Observer N.S. 31(4):24-25.

Established in 1967 by the Board of Home Missions, Darby Lodge primarily offers short-term accomodations to Indians in Vancouver. The resident superintendent, Rev. Wm. Robinson, is himself an Indian.   IVY

1390 **ASIMI   A D**
1967
THE URBAN SETTING. In Kenora 1967: Resolving Conflicts - A Cross-Cultural Approach. Winnipeg: University of Manitoba, Department of Extension and Adult Education. pp. 88-96.

If the Indians of Canada are to survive they must move into urban centers. Problems of adjustment, admittedly difficult, are discussed.   IVY

1391 **ATWELL   PHYLLIS HARRYETTE**
1969
KINSHIP AND MIGRATION AMONG CALGARIAN RESIDENTS OF INDIAN ORIGIN. M.A. Thesis. Department of Sociology and Anthropology. University of Calgary. 85 pp. Available from National Library of Canada.

The relationship between kinship and migration among Calgary residents is explored. In 1966-1967, 65 people of Indian origin and 13 non-Indians were interviewed. Family relations did not stimulate migration. Kinship relations did not serve as an agency of socialization for the migrant in the new milieu. Education and employment were the most common reasons for migration. Anticipatory socialization in residential schools, emphasizing the formal aspects, was not successful. Considerable conflict was involved in the choice to move to the city. Social agencies were utilized when necessary for urban adjustment. The importance of a non-exploitative contact situation in the process of socialization in the urban setting was observed. Migrants exhibited considerable and frequent ethnic social interaction. Successful migrants tended to be enfranchised.   JSL

1392 **BARRIER   MARC**
1968
LE MILIEU INDIEN DE LA VILLE D'EDMONTON. Kerygma 2(4):141-149.

Aspects of the urban environment experienced by Indians in Edmonton are noted. Motivation for coming to the city, social problems encountered, and voluntary associations sought out are reviewed. The origins and development of the Edmonton Native Brotherhood Society aimed at alleviating problems encountered by Indians in Edmonton are described.   CCV

1393   **BEAR ROBE ANDREW**
1970
INDIAN URBANIZATION. Tawow 1(1):2-5,28,31.

Three factors are considered in the Indian migration to urban centers: the population growth on reserves, limited economic opportunities on reserves, and desire for higher education. The difficulties in relocating to an urban environment are discussed and the function of social service agencies and friendship centers in rendering assistance is presented.   IVY

1394   **BEAULIEU   ISAAC**
1964
URBANIZING THE INDIAN. Ontario Housing 10(1):16,22.

Cultural differences impede the urbanization of the Indian.   IVY

1395   **BRODY   HUGH**
1970
INDIANS ON SKID ROW: THE ROLE OF ALCOHOL AND COMMUNITY IN THE ADAPTIVE PROCESS OF INDIAN URBAN MIGRANTS. Department of Indian Affairs and Northern Development, Northern Science Research Group, No. 70-2. Ottawa: Information Canada. 86 pp.

The results of fieldwork carried out in the summer and autumn of 1969 on skid row of a prairie town are reported. Observations on the life style of Indians and Metis migrants to the city are reported with attention to their income sources, socio-economic status, drinking practices, interaction with Whites, and recourse to violence.   CCV

1396   **CANADA. Department of Citizenship and Immigration. Citizenship Branch.**
1964-65
WORKING PAPER ON FRIENDSHIP CENTRES. Ottawa: Department of Citizenship and Immigration. 28 pp.

The facilities, services, personnel, and orientation of Canadian Indian friendship centers are reviewed. Recommendations are advanced to develop greater communication between centers, and between Indian and non-Indian citizens.   CCV

1397   **COULTER   E J**
1966
INDIANS ON THE MOVE. The Beaver 297(Summer):49-53.

The personnel of many friendship centers across Canada discuss their facilities, aims, and purposes.   IVY

1398   **DAVIS   ARTHUR K**
1967
EDGING INTO MAINSTREAM: URBAN INDIANS IN SASKATCHEWAN. In A Northern Dilemma: Reference Papers. Arthur K. Davis, Vernon C. Serl, et al., eds. Bellingham, WA: Western Washington State College. Vol. 2. pp. 339-585.

The living and working conditions of Indian-Metis of Prince Albert, North Battleford, and Meadow Lake, Saskatchewan, were studied during the period from 1960 until 1962 by means of interviews (159), participant observation, and comparative analysis. Discussion of the data and comparison with census data on White populations are presented within the following categories: migration patterns, social characteristics of households, labor force, income, housing, social participation, and the problems, aspirations, and needs created by a rural-urban movement. The viability of cultural pluralism and local self-development is contested on the basis of the findings. It is proposed that urban migration is the most effective means of integration of the Indian-Metis. Statistical support for the discussion is provided.   CCV

1399   **DAVIS   ARTHUR K**
1968
URBAN INDIANS IN WESTERN CANADA: IMPLICATIONS FOR SOCIAL THEORY AND SOCIAL POLICY. The Royal Society of Canada Transactions (Series 4) 6:217-228.

The areas of housing, employment, leisure activities, and the use of mass media, as well as other aspects of urban life, were explored in a study of 160 Metis and Indian households in Prince Albert, North Battleford, and Meadow Lake, Saskatchewan. Research was conducted in the early 1960's. It is suggested that social policy should (1) foster migration to the cities; (2) aim general programs at housing, low incomes, unemployment, underemployment, and undereducation; and (3) modify the structure of Canadian society. The doctrine of cultural relativism is dead as is a unique Indian way of life in Canada.   IVY

1400   **DENTON   TREVOR**
1970
STRANGERS IN THEIR LAND: A STUDY OF MIGRATION FROM A CANADIAN INDIAN RESERVE. Ph.D. Thesis. Department of Anthropology. University of Toronto. 460 pp.

Fieldwork done with Indians from an acculturated reserve in southern Ontario from June, 1967, to August, 1968, is reported in detail. Ten months were spent on the reserve and 5 among migrants residing in a nearby large city. Data were compiled relative to migration, including the predisposing factors, the attitudes of those who migrated and those who did not, the problems encountered in the urban milieu, mechanisms developed to cope in a White community, attitudes toward migration, and the role of an Indian in contemporary urban society. In addition information is presented relative to the life on the reserve including census data, historic background, and reviews of social, economic, and political organization. Although migration fluctuates, the reasons for migration remain the same. It is felt that ethnicity is a crucial factor in off-reserve adjustment. Pan-Indian identity minus pan-Indian interaction is observed. When migrants return to the reserve it is because they never intended to stay away. Those who do not return remain in the city because of strong kinship, economic, or friendship ties.   CCV

1401   **EVANS   MARJORIE GERTRUDE**
1961
FELLOWSHIP CENTRES FOR URBAN CANADIAN INDIANS: A COMPARATIVE ASSESSMENT OF THE COQUALEETZA MOVEMENT IN VANCOUVER, AND OTHER COMPARABLE DEVELOPMENTS IN EIGHT CANADIAN CITIES. M.S.W. Thesis. School of Social Work. University of British Columbia. 64 pp.

The special needs of Indians in an urban milieu and efforts to provide for them are examined with particular attention to the Koqualeetza Fellowship in Vancouver. The history of Indian-White relations in Canada is reviewed and the contemporary tendency to stereotype the Indian is described. Information provided by questionnaire responses from Canadian native associations is reported according to association objectives, sponsored activities, and problems solved.   CCV

1402   **FAMILY SERVICE ASSOCIATION OF EDMONTON**
n.d.
ADJUSTMENT FACTORS IN THE INDIAN MOVING TO THE URBAN
COMMUNITY: A DESCRIPTIVE STUDY. Unpublished paper. Available from
National Library of Canada. 18 pp.

Questionnaires were administered in 1965 to 34 urban Indians, clients of the Family Service Association, and its Project Counsellors to elicit an assesment of the Association's service program, an evaluation of the role of Project Counsellor, patterns of adjustment of Indians to the city, and differences between those Indian persons who remain in the city and those who return to the reserve. The importance of social services to these migrants in their new urban environment is indicated. Suggestions are presented to lead to better adjustment to the city. The questionnaire administered to the Project Counsellor indicated his view of his role and performance, and his view of his clients.   TSA

1403   **FRANSEN   J J**
1964
EMPLOYMENT EXPERIENCES AND ECONOMIC POSITION OF A SELECTED
GROUP OF INDIANS IN METROPOLITAN TORONTO. M.S.W. Thesis. School of
Social Work. University of Toronto. 195 pp.

Interviewed were 21 male and 9 female Indians from southern Ontario reserves assisted in coming to Toronto for employment by the Placement Program of the Indian Affairs Branch. Problems encountered in employment and attitudes toward employment, co-workers, and placement are discussed.   CCV

1404   **HIRABAYASHI   GORDON K,   CORMIER   A J,   et al., eds.**
1962
THE CHALLENGE OF ASSISTING THE CANADIAN ABORIGINAL PEOPLE TO
ADJUST TO URBAN ENVIRONMENTS: REPORT OF THE FIRST WESTERN
CANADA INDIAN-METIS SEMINAR. Unpublished paper. Available from National
Library of Canada. 49 pp.

Primarily concerned with the urban situation, the conference focused essentially on the establishment and operation of friendship centers in urban areas to assist Indian newcomers to the city. Jean Lagasse discussed the cultural implications in leaving the reserve to migrate to the cities. Bert Marcuse reported findings of a research study completed May, 1961, "The Canadian Indian in an Urban Community."R. A. Sim examined migration, technological change, race and minority questions, the trusteeship problem, and poverty, and discussed 4 points of emphasis in planning and sustaining a friendship center. Evaluations of the seminar were presented by John Melling and Gordon Hirabayashi.   IVY

1405   **HONIGMANN   JOHN J**
1970
HOUSING FOR NEW ARCTIC TOWNS. Unpublished paper delivered to 69th
Annual Meeting, American Anthropological Association. San Diego, November 19-22,
1970. Available from National Library of Canada. 8 pp.

Based on fieldwork, housing in Frobisher Bay and Inuvik is examined as it is related to
the social organization accompanying its acquisition and to social stratification, hostility,
and the regulation of behavior. Housing figures prominently in the motivational system
of many members of the native communities and influences a broad range of personal
and social behavior.   IVY

1406   **HONIGMANN   JOHN J,   EGLOFF   MARGARET STEPHENS,   et al.**
1968
ETHNOGRAPHIC SURVEY OF CHURCHILL: URBANIZATION IN THE
ARCTIC AND SUBARCTIC. University of North Carolina at Chapel Hill, Institute for
Research in Social Science Working Paper 3. Chapel Hill, NC: University of North
Carolina, Institute for Research in Social Science. 145 pp.

The living conditions, hygiene, child care, family life, patterns of drinking, residence,
and employment among the Chipewyan and Metis populations are discussed in Chapters 4 and 5 of this ethnographic survey carried out in Churchill during the summer of
1966.   CCV

1407   **HUNTER   BOB**
1969
THERE IS NO BOUNTY ON INDIANS ANY MORE...OR IS THERE? The United
Church Observer N.S. 31(13):25-26,40.

A reporter joined an Indian patrol formed by the Native Alliance for Red Power for a
night on Vancouver's Skid Row. The function of the patrol is to protect natives from
anyone who might obstruct or abuse them. This article condenses 4 columns
originally published in the Vancouver Sun.   IVY

1408   **INDIAN-ESKIMO ASSOCIATION OF CANADA**
1967
AN ACTION RESEARCH PROJECT ON "INDIANS IN THE CITY"FOR
PRESENTATION TO THE HONOURABLE ARTHUR LAING MINISTER
INDIAN AFFAIRS AND NORTHERN DEVELOPMENT, SEPTEMBER, 1967.
Unpublished paper. Available from Indian-Eskimo Association of Canada. 13 pp.

An action-research project is proposed by the Indian-Eskimo Association to clarify the
role of Native Friendship Centres in relation to other urban agencies. Five selected communities would be involved over a 3 year period at an estimated cost of $150,000,000
and would assist Indians migrating to the cities with housing, employment, job training,
and social problems.   DGW

1409   **MARCUSE   B**
1961
REPORT TO THE COMMUNITY CHEST AND COUNCILS OF THE GREATER
VANCOUVER AREA COMMITTEE ON THE CANADIAN INDIAN IN AN

URBAN COMMUNITY (VANCOUVER). Unpublished paper. Available from
Library, University of British Columbia. 100 pp.

This exploratory study is concerned with the needs of urban Canadian Indians residing
in the Vancouver area. Data and information was gathered in 1960 through the use of
basically similar questionnaires distributed to students, inmates of the Oakalla gaol, and
various agencies. Employment, urban housing (location of Indians in Vancouver), and
the function of key agencies specifically related to the findings are presented. Recom-
mending that an Indian Center be located in Vancouver, material relevant to such an objective is investigated. Sixty pages include the nature of the questionnaire, statistical data
relating to Canadian Indian inmates of Oakalla gaol, taped interviews with Jean Lagasse
and Pearl Warren, and a bibliography.   IVY

1410   **MCCASKILL   DONALD N**
1970
MIGRATION, ADJUSTMENT AND INTEGRATION OF THE INDIAN INTO
THE URBAN ENVIRONMENT. M.A. Thesis. Department of Sociology and
Anthropology. Carleton University. 277 pp.

A study of reserve to urban migration is based on data gathered by interview of 46 Indian and 25 Metis family heads in Winnipeg during late 1968. An attempt is made to
report events or factors leading to the decision to move, through initial adjustment experiences, to possible integration. Largely negative motivations for migration were observed, which, coupled with a low degree of adjustment success and integration, project
an image of poverty and social disorganization. It is also noted that even if the Winnipeg
urban Indians develop a group consciousness, successful integration into the urban milieu
will depend at least partially on attitudes of the White population.   CCV

1411   **NAGLER   MARK**
1970
INDIANS IN THE CITY: A STUDY OF URBANIZATION OF INDIANS IN
TORONTO. Ottawa: Canadian Research Centre for Anthropology, St. Paul University.
107 pp.

Between May, 1964, and September, 1966, data were gathered from 150 Indians, mainly
in Toronto, in order to throw light upon the processes of Indian urban adjustment. Government programs, mass media, incentives to urbanization, group identity, kinship obligations, and adjustment problems are included in discussion. The results indicate that
processes leading to adjustment are varied and closely related to the initial and diverse
reasons for migration to the city. The data also suggest an association between successful
urban adjustment and proximity to urban influence.   CCV

1412   **NAGLER   MARK**
1970
STATUS AND IDENTIFICATION GROUPING AMONGST URBAN INDIANS.
The Northian 7(2):23-25.

Indians living within, or having contact with, Toronto, Ottawa, and Montreal reveal 6
adjustment patterns: (1) the white collars who bear similarity to most other white collar
workers economically, (2) the blue collars, (3) the transitionals who attempt to become
permanent urban residents, (4) urban users who come to seek supplies, (5) seasonal
workers, and (6) vagabonds. Among those who live in the city, there are 3 subgroups: (a)

those who identify positively as Indians, (b) those who are apathetic about identity, and (c) those who pass. At present, urban Indians lack group unity especially with regards to leadership. Emerging Indian groups have typically failed to unite the urban Indian. A common link, poverty, may still unite them. Both a link with the past and pan-Indianism may aid the quest for stability and continuity in urban society.   ADG

1413   **NICHOLSON   JOHN R**
1965
ADDRESS BY THE HONOURABLE JOHN R. NICHOLSON, P.C., O.B.E., Q.C., M.P., MINISTER OF CITIZENSHIP AND IMMIGRATION, M.P. VANCOUVER CENTRE. Unpublished paper delivered to Indian Friendship Centre. Vancouver, June 12, 1965. Available from Indian-Eskimo Bureau, Department of Indian Affairs and Northern Development, Ottawa. 9 pp.

In an address by John Nicholson, Minister of Citizenship and Immigration, the Vancouver Indian Friendship Centre is commended for its community contribution. The possibility of forming a federation of friendship centers is advanced and the willingness of the federal government to assist and cooperate is stated.   CCV

1414   **THE PRINCE ALBERT INDIAN AND METIS SERVICE COUNCIL**
n.d.
A BRIEF: PRINCE ALBERT'S NEED FOR AN INDIAN AND METIS SERVICE CENTRE. Unpublished paper. Available from Library, Department of Health and Social Development, Winnipeg, Man. 7 pp.

The need for a referral center in Prince Albert for the Indian and Metis people is examined. The establishment of the Winnipeg Indian and Metis Friendship Centre provided background information for this brief. Appendices include discussions on employment, native crafts, and the provincial gaol for women.   IVY

1415   **SHACKLETON   DORIS**
1969
THE INDIAN AS NEWCOMER. Canadian Welfare 45(4):7-9,16.

Survival in Winnipeg is easier for the European immigrant than it is for the Manitoba Indian. For this reason the Indian-Metis Friendship Centre has been established. The center provides services ranging from pre-school programs to an Alcoholics Anonymous chapter. Following a description of the programs and personnel at the center, the Harvey Report presented to the Winnipeg Welfare Department is discussed. According to the report provincially sponsored educational material on alcoholism has not been directed at many Indians who need it, disproportionate variations in welfare payment rates have adverse implications for the Indians' decision regarding residence, employers take unfair advantage of both the Indian and government because of the too low minimum wage, Winnipeg should alleviate the housing shortage by buying up and improving existing houses, and urban adaptation programs should be placed on the reserve to prepare the Indian for his move to the city. The article also notes that Manitoba reserves cannot sufficiently provide for existing population. Both large scale enterprises and restrictive conservation laws have curtailed the Indian's ability to earn a livelihood in the traditional manner. The overflooding of the cities has awakened some to the need for economic measures in the home locality to provide Indians with a real alternative to this type of exodus.   ADG

1416   **TRUDEAU   JEAN**
1969
THE INDIAN IN THE CITY. Kerygma 3:118-123.

Many Indians unable to adapt to the city return to reserves dissatisfied, while those who do remain often live in slums and on welfare. A need for counseling and guidance for Indians living in urban environments is evident. Oblates could fill that need.   IVY

1417   **UNIVERSITY OF SASKATCHEWAN. Extension Division., INDIAN-ESKIMO ASSOCIATION OF CANADA**
1967
SUMMARY REPORT OF THE INDIAN-METIS FRIENDSHIP CENTRE SHORT COURSE. Saskatoon, November 3, 1967. Unpublished paper. Available from National Library of Canada. 7 pp.

The Indian-Metis Friendship Centre Short Course is summarized including discussion of the role of friendship centers, the type of programs most appropriate to immediate needs, the social responsibility of the center, and the best means of achieving desired ends.   CCV

CASE LAW DIGEST

1418   **ALBERTA DISTRICT COURT. JUDGE: BUCHANAN.**
1954
IN RE WILSON. 12 W.W.R. 676.

FACTS: This was an appeal under Section 9(3) and (4) of the Indian Act protesting the deletion of Wilson from a band list. HELD: Wilson had been on the original annuity pay list of 1900 for the band. He comes, therefore, within Section 11(1)(b) of the Indian Act. Since it was impossible to determine that he was the illegitimate child of a non-Indian, he falls within Section 11(1)(e). He was, therefore, entitled to be on the band list.   DES/ PCT

1419   **ALBERTA DISTRICT COURT. JUDGE: BUCHANAN.**
1957
RE SAMSON INDIAN BAND. 21 W.W.R. 455, 7 D.L.R. (2d) 745.

FACTS: The registrar ruled that 27 people were not entitled to be registered as Indians as their forebearers had taken half-breed scrip. That decision is appealed under Section 9 of the Indian Act. HELD: Section 9 refers to both future and past registrations. If the Act states that descendants of scrip takers who have lived all their lives on a reserve are to be deleted from the list, this must be upheld even if inhumane. The protest was not properly brought and the proceedings protesting the registrar's ruling were a nullity.   DES/ PCT

1420   **ALBERTA DISTRICT COURT. JUDGE: FEIR.**
1951
R. v. SHADE. 4 W.W.R. 430, 102 C.C.C. 316, 14 C.R. 56.

FACTS: Shade, an Indian, was intoxicated in a private motor vehicle on the main street of Pincher Creek, Alberta. He is charged with being intoxicated in a public place contrary to the Government Liquor Control Act of the Province of Alberta. HELD: Shade was intoxicated in a public place, but the offence of intoxication when committed by an Indian, whether on or off the reserve, is completely dealt with by the Indian Act, Sections 94 and 96 (now 95 and 97). By Section 87 of the Indian Act (now 88) and Section 91(24) of the British North America Act, an Indian cannot be convicted under provincial legislation for such an offence.   DES/PCT

1421   **ALBERTA DISTRICT COURT. JUDGE: LEES.**
1933
R. v. GULLBERG. 3 W.W.R. 639, 62 C.C.C. 281.

FACTS: Gullberg, a non-Indian, sold food on a reserve to Indians and non-Indians during a stampede held on the reserve. He had the permission of the Indian Agent. He was convicted under the Restaurant Act of Alberta for not having a licence. HELD: The conviction was upheld. A White man while on an Indian reserve is subject to the general laws of the province.   DES/PCT

1422   **ALBERTA DISTRICT COURT. JUDGE: LEGG.**
1966-67
R. v. EAR. 49 C.R. 42.

FACTS: Moses Ear was an Indian and a member of the R.C.M.P. He purchased beer on the instructions of 2 other members of the R.C.M.P. and immediately delivered the beer to them. He is charged with possession of beer off a reserve contrary to S. 94(a) (now 95(a)) of the Indian Act. HELD: Statutory protection of a peace officer under the Police Act of Alberta from criminal responsibility cannot extend to excuse offences under federal law, as here. Because Moses Ear only had possession as a public duty, he should not be convicted.   DES/PCT

1423   **ALBERTA DISTRICT COURT. JUDGE: TAYLOR.**
1907-08
R. v. PICKARD. 7 W.L.R. 797, 14 C.C.C. 33.

FACTS: Pickard, a non-Indian, sold liquor to 2 Indians. The circumstances were sufficient that he should have suspected that the purchasers were Indians. The Indian Act prohibition of sale of liquor to Indians is an absolute prohibition and the usual requirement of mens rea (guilty mind) does not apply. The conviction was upheld.   DES/PCT

1424   **ALBERTA DISTRICT COURT. JUDGE: TURCOTTE.**
1963
R. v. SPEAR CHIEF. 45 W.W.R. 161, 42 C.R. 78.

FACTS: Spear Chief, an Indian, was charged under the Criminal Code for driving while his licence was suspended. He had been driving on a reserve. HELD: Spear Chief could only be convicted if he were driving in a place where provincial law required him to have a driver's licence. The Vehicles and Highway Traffic Act of Alberta only required a person to have a licence if he was driving on a highway. The road in question was a highway as defined in the legislation as the public were ordinarily entitled to use it. The conviction was upheld.   DES/PCT

1425   **ALBERTA MAGISTRATES COURT. JUDGE: HUDSON.**
1968

R. v. RIDER. 70 D.L.R. (2d) 77, (1969) 1 C.C.C. 193.

FACTS: Rider, an Indian, was charged under the National Parks Act, a federal statute, for hunting. He was hunting for food within the area of Treaty 7 for food. The treaty protected hunting rights except on tracts taken up for settlement or other purposes. HELD: The park is land within the exception in the treaty. Even if it were not, the federal government can take away such rights. The accused was convicted.   DES/PCT

1426   **ALBERTA SUPREME COURT (CHAMBERS). JUDGE: BECK.**
1912
R. v. FITZGERALD. 19 W.L.R. 462, 1 W.W.R. 109.

FACTS: A procedural case arising out of a charge of selling liquor to an Indian.   DES/PCT

1427   **ALBERTA SUPREME COURT (CHAMBERS). JUDGE: BECK.**
1912-13
R. v. TROTTIER. 6 ALTA. L. R. 451.

FACTS: A procedural case arising out of a charge of selling liquor to an Indian.   DES/PCT

1428   **ALBERTA SUPREME COURT (CHAMBERS). JUDGE: HYNDMAN.**
1920
R. v. HONG. 3 W.W.R. 21, 33 C.C.C. 153.

FACTS: A case dealing with procedure and evidence arising out of a charge of selling liquor to an Indian.   DES/PCT

1429   **ALBERTA SUPREME COURT (CHAMBERS). JUDGE: SIMMONS.**
1912
IN RE BAPTISTE PAUL. 2 W.W.R. 892, 927.

FACTS: A procedural case arising out of a charge of selling liquor to an Indian.   DES/PCT

1430   **ALBERTA SUPREME COURT APPELLATE DIVISION. JUDGES: CLEMENT ALLEN CAIRNS.**
1971
R. v. CARDINAL. 22 D.L.R. (3d) 716, 1 W.W.R. 536.

FACTS: Cardinal, an Indian, sold moose meat to a non-Indian on the reserve. He is charged with trafficking in big game contrary to the Wildlife Act of Alberta. HELD: The Natural Resources Transfer Agreement makes provincial game laws apply to Indians with specified exceptions which do not include sale to non-Indians. The rights under that agreement extend to lands to which the Indians have a right of access, which includes reserve lands. The powers under the Indian Act to make regulations (S. 73(1)(a)) or by-laws (S. 81(o)) have not been exercised and therefore do not prevent the application of provincial law to Indians by Section 88 of the Indian Act. Those sections could only be invoked within the framework of paragraph 12 of the Natural Resources Transfer Agreement (This case has been appealed to the Supreme Court of Canada).   DES/PCT

1431 ALBERTA SUPREME COURT APPELLATE DIVISION. JUDGES: FORD MACDONALD MCBRIDE PORTER JOHNSON.
1958
R. v. LITTLE BEAR. (1958) 26 W.W.R. 335, 122 C.C.C. 173: APPEALED FROM 25 W.W.R. 580, 28 C.R. 333.

FACTS: Little Bear, an Indian, was convicted under the Game Act of Alberta for killing a deer during a closed season. He was hunting for food over land covered by treaty, but owned by a non-Indian. The non-Indian had given Little Bear permission to hunt on the land. HELD: Treaty Seven did not give Little Bear the right to hunt as he did because the treaty exempted lands from hunting which had been taken up for settlement. Right of access, in the Natural Resources Transfer Agreement, includes a right to enter privately owned land by consent of the owner. Section 87 of the Indian Act (now 88) does not make the Game Act apply to Indians as that section only applies subject to federal legislation and the Natural Resources Transfer Agreement was passed by the Parliament of Canada. DES/PCT

1432 ALBERTA SUPREME COURT APPELLATE DIVISION. JUDGES: LUNNEY MCGILLIVRAY CLARKE MITCHELL.
1932
R. v. WESLEY. 26 Alta. L.R. 433, 2 W.W.R. 337, 58 C.C.C. 269, (1932) 14 D.L.R. 774.

FACTS: Wesley, an Indian, was charged under the Gaming Act of Alberta with hunting a deer with dogs and without a licence. He was hunting for food on unoccupied Crown lands. HELD: The Royal Proclamation of 1763 did not apply to this area since it was Hudson's Bay Company lands. The Indians in question have hunting rights under Treaty Seven. Though government regulations about hunting are contemplated in the treaty the makers of the treaty could not have contemplated a day when the Indians would be deprived of an unfettered right to hunt game of all kinds for food on unoccupied Crown lands. The Natural Resources Transfer Agreement protects the hunting from provinical laws. DES/PCT

1433 ALBERTA SUPREME COURT APPELLATE DIVISION. JUDGE: FORD.
1959
R. v. GINGRICH. 29 W.W.R. 471, 31 C.R. 306, 122 C.C.C. 279.

FACTS: A non-Indian missionary was on a reserve at the invitation of certain members of the band after having been refused a permit to visit the reserve by the band council. He was arrested and charged with trespass. HELD: Trespass means entering the land of another person without lawful justification. Section 87 (now 88) of the Indian Act means that Indians have all the rights of a citizen of the province, except where curtailed by treaty or act of Parliament. One such right is freedom of religion, provided for in the 1851 "freedom of religion" act of the Province of Canada which has been incorporated into the law of Canada and Alberta by Section 129 of the British North America Act. That law gives the right to one who preaches or teaches religion to accept an invitiation to enter upon land occupied by individuals in order to preach or teach the gospel. Gingrich, therefore, had lawful justification to enter the reserve and was not a trespasser. Similarly a band council could not prevent the entry onto the reserve of teachers, inspectors, or other school officials. DES/PCT

1434   **ALBERTA SUPREME COURT APPELLATE DIVISION. JUDGE: STUART.**
1925
R. v. MYERS. 21 ALTA: L. R. 352.

FACTS: A procedural case arising out of a charge of selling liquor to an Indian.   DES/ PCT

1435   **BRITISH COLUMBIA COUNTY COURT (CARIBOO). JUDGE: MORROW.**
1961
ATTORNEY-GENERAL OF BRITISH COLUMBIA v. MCDONALD. 131 C.C.C. 126.

FACTS: McDonald, an Indian, was charged with possession of liquor off a reserve contrary to Section 94(a) (now 95(a)) of the Indian Act. He argues that the section of the Act is inconsistent with the Bill of Rights. HELD: McDonald has the right to equality with other Indians before the law. The Bill of Rights was never intended to repeal laws without expressly saying so.   DES/PCT

1436   **BRITISH COLUMBIA COUNTY COURT (NANAIMO). JUDGE: MCKAY.**
1971
R. v. SPORT. Unreported. ·

FACTS: Sport, an Indian, was charged with driving without a driver's licence. He was driving on a reserve. The road was used by the general public for recreational purposes. HELD: The road had been gazetted as a highway under the Highway Act of British Columbia. Furthermore, when reserves were transferred to the federal government by British Columbia, highways were exempted from the transfer. Furthermore, the road was used by the general public and therefore was a highway under the provincial motor vehicle legislation. Sport was convicted.   DES/PCT

1437   **BRITISH COLUMBIA COUNTY COURT (VANCOUVER). JUDGE: SCHULTZ.**
1968
R. v. DISCON AND BAKER. 67 D.L.R. (2d) 619, 63 W.W.R. 485.

FACTS: Discon and Baker, 2 Indians, were convicted under the Wildlife Act of British Columbia for hunting deer during closed season. They were hunting for food off a reserve but within the traditional tribal territory of their band. There was no treaty for the area. HELD: The accused Indians have no aboriginal right to hunt in the absence of treaty or statutory recognition of such rights. The Royal Proclamation of 1763 did not apply to British Columbia. In the absence of treaty or federal statutory provisions Section 87 (now 88) of the Indian Act makes the Wildlife Act applicable to Indians, since it is a law of general application.   DES/PCT

1438   **BRITISH COLUMBIA COUNTY COURT (VANCOUVER). JUDGE: SWENCISKY.**
1966
R. v. SUPERIOR CONCRETE PRODUCTS LTD. Unreported.

FACTS: Does a noise abatement by-law of a local government apply to the activities of a non-Indian on lands surrendered by a reserve for lease? HELD: The by-law would be invalid if it legislated about noises made by Indians on reserve lands. The appellant company is not an Indian so the fact that it happens to be a tenant on Indian lands has no bearing on the issue. The power of the band council to enact by-laws concerning nuisance is of no consequence here, in that the appellant is not an Indian. The conviction is upheld.   DES/PCT

1439   **BRITISH COLUMBIA COUNTY COURT (WESTMINISTER). JUDGE: BOLE.**
1901
R. v. MICHAEL GEE. 5 C.C.C. 148.

FACTS: Two Indians purchased liquor from a cook in a hotel. The owner of the house is charged under Section 4 of the Indian Act, which then provided that an employer was responsible if any "clerk, servant or agent"sold liquor to an Indian. HELD: It was not the intention of Section 94 to make the employer responsible when a servant sold liquor to an Indian without knowledge or connivance on the part of the employer. The conviction of Gee was set aside.   DES/PCT

1440   **BRITISH COLUMBIA COUNTY COURT (WESTMINISTER). JUDGE: BOLE.**
1906
R. v. HUGHES. 4 W.L.R. 431, 12 B.C.R. 290.

FACTS: Hughes, a non-Indian, was convicted of selling liquor to an Indian. The Indian was a quarter-breed. The Indian Act defines "Indian"to include any person who is reputed to belong to a particular band or who follows the Indian mode of life. It was alleged that the purchaser followed the Indian mode of life and lived on a reserve. HELD: The evidence was not sufficient to prove that the purchaser was an Indian as defined by the Indian Act. Additionally, Hughes would have to know that the purchaser was an Indian before he could be convicted, and that knowledge had not been proven.   DES/PCT

1441   **BRITISH COLUMBIA COUNTY COURT (YALE). JUDGE: SWANSON.**
1920
R. v. TAPE. 33 C.C.C. 113.

FACTS: A case examining evidence in an appeal arising out of a charge of selling liquor to Indians.   DES/PCT

1442   **BRITISH COLUMBIA COUNTY COURT. JUDGE: ELLIS.**
1937
POPE v. PAUL. (1937) 2 W.W.R. 449.

FACTS: Paul, an Indian, used a boat to travel from one part of the reserve to another and to fish in the area. Paul defaulted on payments on the boat and Pope seized it under a warrant of execution. HELD: The boat was bought off the reserve and remained off the reserve except when hauled up on the beach. It is not situated on the reserve and therefore is subject to seizure in execution of a judgment.   DES/PCT

1443   **BRITISH COLUMBIA COUNTY COURT. JUDGE: LINDSAY.**
1959

R. v. WILLIAMS. Unreported.

FACTS: Williams, an Indian, was charged under the Fisheries Act of Canada for fishing with a spear. He argues that Clause 13 of the Terms of Union of British Columbia and Canada prevents such a restriction on his right to fish. HELD: Assuming Clause 13 gives Williams certain rights, there was no evidence presented as to the treatment of Indian fishing rights prior to the 1871 Union. Further, regulation of the manner of fishing cannot be termed illiberal. Section 87 (now 88) of the Indian Act does not apply to federal legislation.   DES/PCT

1444   **BRITISH COLUMBIA COUNTY COURT. JUDGE: SWANSON.**
1930
R. v. MCLEOD. 2 W.W.R. 37, 54 C.C.C. 107.

FACTS: McLeod, a non-Indian agent, shot a pheasant on an Indian reserve and was convicted under the Game Act of British Columbia for shooting during a closed season. HELD: In the absence of federal legislation the provincial legislation applies.   DES/PCT

1445   **BRITISH COLUMBIA COUNTY COURT. JUDGE: SWANSON.**
1932
R. v. TRONSON. (1932) 1 W.W.R. 537, 57 C.C.C. 383.

FACTS: Tronson was a half-breed whose mother was Indian and father non-Indian. He had originally lived off the reserve on Crown land which had been granted to him (an Indian was forbidden to take such a grant). He was registered as a provincial voter. He was charged with residing on a reserve contrary to Section 115 of the Indian Act (the residency not being with the authorization of the Superintendent-General, the equivalent section being Section 28). HELD: Tronson was not an Indian of the particular band and was therefore a trespasser. The conviction was upheld.   DES/PCT

1446   **BRITISH COLUMBIA COUNTY COURT. JUDGE: SWENCISKY.**
1958
GEOFFRIES v. WILLIAMS. (1958) 26 W.W.R. (N.S.) 323, 16 D.L.R. (2d) 157.

FACTS: Williams, an Indian, cut a quantity of timber on a reserve and sold it to a company off the reserve. A creditor of Williams garnisheed the payment owing to Williams. HELD: The debt was situated where the debtor (the company) resided and therefore was located off the reserve. Section 87 (now 88) of the Indian Act makes the British Columbia Attachment of Debts Act apply in the absence of any exemption in the Indian Act. The provisions in the Indian Act could not be challenged constitutionally as being less liberal than the pre-Confederation policies of British Columbia and therefore in violation of the Terms of Union of British Columiba because no notice had been given under the Constitutional Questions Determination Act of British Columbia. The garnishee was upheld.   DES/PCT

1447   **BRITISH COLUMBIA COURT OF APPEAL. JUDGES: DAVEY BULL BRANCA.**
1969
R. v. JOE. Unreported.

FACTS: Joe, an Indian, was charged for driving without current licence plates. He was driving on a reserve. HELD: The term "highway"in the provincial motor vehicle legislation was defined to mean a road "used by the general public..."That means that the road must be used by the general public for their own purposes and not for the purposes connected with the reserve, such as making deliveries. The road upon which Joe was driving was not a highway and therefore the law did not require his vehicle to have licence plates.   DES/PCT

1448   **BRITISH COLUMBIA COURT OF APPEAL. JUDGES: DAVEY BULL MCFARLANE.**
1971
SAMMARTINO v. ATTORNEY GENERAL OF BRITISH COLUMBIA. (1972) 1 W.W.R. 24.

FACTS: Sammartino, a non-Indian, occupied land on a reserve. The land had not been surrendered nor had the Minister approved of the occupancy. Can he be taxed as occupier of the land under provincial legislation? HELD: The Public Schools Act of British Columbia imposes a tax on land and cannot apply to reserve lands. The Taxation Act of British Columbia imposes a tax on the occupier of land and can apply to Sammartino as the occupant of reserve land.   DES/PCT

1449   **BRITISH COLUMBIA COURT OF APPEAL. JUDGES: DAVEY TYSOE BIRD.**
1962
R. v. GONZALES. 37 W.W.R. 257, 37 C.R. 56: APPEALED FROM 35 W.W.R. 703, 130 C.C.C. 400, 35 C.R. 320: APPEALED FROM 34 W.W.R. 622, 130 C.C.C. 206, 35 C.R. 155.

FACTS: Gonzales, an Indian, was convicted of possession of liquor off a reserve, contrary to Section 94(a) (now 95(a)) of the Indian Act. The section of the Indian Act is challenged as being inconsistent with the Bill of Rights. HELD: The Bill of Rights does not have the effect of repealing legislation inconsistent with it. Per Tysoe - The concept of equality before the law is not offended as everyone to whom the section applies is being treated in the same way.   DES/PCT

1450   **BRITISH COLUMBIA COURT OF APPEAL. JUDGES: DAVEY TYSOE MACLEAN.**
1970
CALDER v. ATTORNEY GENERAL FOR BRITISH COLUMBIA. 13 D.L.R. (3d) 64, (1970) 74 W.W.R. 481.

FACTS: Calder, an Indian, seeks on behalf of the Nishga tribe a declaration that their aboriginal title to their traditional tribal territory has never been extinguished. HELD: There was no treaty or statute or prerogative act which conferred or recognized the Indians' title to the land in question. The Royal Proclamation of 1763 did not apply to British Columbia. Without a recognition by the state of Indian land rights, such rights did not have legal force (This case has been appealed to the Supreme Court of Canada).   DES/ PCT

1451   **BRITISH COLUMBIA COURT OF APPEAL. JUDGES: LORD MACLEAN BULL.**

1966
R. v. GINGER. Unreported.

FACTS: Ginger, an Indian, was convicted of murder. The county in which the trial was held had a population which included 8,000 Indians. No Indians had ever been selected to serve on juries in the county. It was alleged that this violated the Bill of Rights. HELD: There was no evidence before the court that any Indians had made application and become registered as voters so as to qualify for jury duty. The sherrif of the county testified that the officials selecting the jury list had never given consideration to the question of race. The lists they had contained no information beyond name, occupation, and address.   DES/PCT

1452   **BRITISH COLUMBIA COURT OF APPEAL. JUDGES: MACDONALD GALLIHER.**
1921
IN RE WATER ACT. (1921) 2 W.W.R. 834.

FACTS: The Department of Indian Affairs applied to a board constituted under the Water Act of British Columbia for a licence to divert water for the use of an Indian reserve. HELD: The Indians did not have any claim to the water based on any former Act or Ordinance and, therefore, by the provisions of the Water Act, the board could not settle conflicting claims to water in their favor.   DES/PCT

1453   **BRITISH COLUMBIA COURT OF APPEAL. JUDGES: MACDONALD MARTIN GALLIHER**
1923
R. v. COOPER. 35 B.C.R. 457, 44 C.C.C. 314.

FACTS: Cooper, a non-Indian, was charged under the Government Liquor Act of British Columbia of selling liquor to an Indian. HELD: The federal government having prohibited the sale of liquor to Indians, and provided for its punishment as a crime, no matter where whether on a reserve or off a reserve, they have occupied the field or part of the field so as to exclude provincial legislation. There is no question of the jurisdiction of the federal government to pass Section 135 (now S. 94) of the Indian Act, under its powers in respect to the peace, order, and good government of Canada. The province may, in the absence of federal legislation, pass a prohibitory law under its powers with respect to matters of a merely local or private nature in the province. But when the 2 jurisdictions come in conflict the federal legislation excludes the operation of the provincial laws. The action of 2 legislative bodies making the same act an offence and subjecting the offender to a double penalty is contrary to the B.N.A. Act. The conviction was set aside.   DES/PCT

1454   **BRITISH COLUMBIA COURT OF APPEAL. JUDGES: MACDONALD MARTIN GALLIHER MACDONALD MCPHILLIPS.**
1925
THE DEPARTMENT OF INDIAN AFFAIRS v. BOARD OF INVESTIGATION UNDER THE WATER ACT AND CROSINA. 36 B.C.R. 62.

FACTS: Persuant to British Columbia legislation the Department of Indian Affairs was granted a licence to divert certain water for the benefit of an Indian reserve. The licence was not approved by an order-in-council as required by the legislation until after 2 licences had been issued to a non-Indian, Crosina. HELD: Crosina's licence prevailed over the licence granted for the Indian reserve.   DES/PCT

1455   **BRITISH COLUMBIA COURT OF APPEAL. JUDGES: MACDONALD MARTIN.**
1924
ARMSTRONG v. HARRIS. (1924) 1 W.W.R. 729, 33 B.C.R. 285, (1924) 1 D.L.R. 1043.

FACTS: An Indian sold grain to Harris, a non-Indian, the sale taking place on an Indian reserve. Armstrong seeks to garnishee the money owing by Harris to the Indian. HELD: The grain, while on the reserve, was not subject to execution nor should the proceeds be subject to execution. Harris was obliged to pay the Indian at the Indian's home, which was on the reserve. The garnishee was disallowed. The Indians are wards of the federal government and the provision dealt with here was for their protection since they lack business experience and knowledge of world affairs.   DES/PCT

1456   **BRITISH COLUMBIA COURT OF APPEAL. JUDGES: MARTIN GALLIHER MCPHILLIPS MACDONALD MACDONALD**
1932
R. v. MORLEY. 46 B.C.R. 28, 58 C.C.C. 166, 2 W.W.R. 193, 4 D.L.R. 483.

FACTS: Morley, a non-Indian, shot a pheasant on an Indian reserve and was convicted under the Game Act of British Columbia for shooting during a closed season. HELD: Two Judges (Martin and Galliher) held that provincial game laws could apply to on-reserve hunting by a non-Indian at least when no authorization for the particular hunting had been granted to the non-Indian. The matter of on-reserve hunting by a non-Indian was a double aspect area in which the province could legislate to the degree that it did not conflict with federal legislation. One Judge (McPhillips) held that even an Indian shooting on a reserve would not be entitled to disobey provincial law. Two Judges (Macdonald and MacDonald) dissented.   DES/PCT

1457   **BRITISH COLUMBIA COURT OF APPEAL. JUDGES: O'HALLORAN SLOAN ROBERTSON SYDNEY SMITH BIRD.**
1945
R. v. PRINCE. 85 C.C.C. 97.

FACTS: Prince, an Indian, was convicted of murder. He was illiterate and had a poor understanding of English. Although an interpreter was present at the trial, Prince gave his evidence without interpretation. He now states that he was prejudiced by not using an interpreter. HELD: The translator was dispensed with at the request of counsel for Prince and the trial judge agreed with the request. Prince appears to have substantially understood the evidence given and therefore suffered no prejudice.   DES/PCT

1458   **BRITISH COLUMBIA COURT OF APPEAL. JUDGES: SLOAN O'HALLORAN MACDONALD.**
1942
CITY OF VANCOUVER v. CHOW CHEE. 1 W.W.R. 72, 57 B.C.R. 104.

FACTS: Chow Chee, a non-Indian, occupied land on an Indian reserve, renting it from a band member. The City of Vancouver attempted to tax the land. The Vancouver Incorporation Act exempts from taxation land held in trust by the Crown for a band of Indians and occupied officially or unoccupied. HELD: The Act does not exempt from taxation the interest of a person who rented land from an Indian. The occupier in this case may be assessed and taxed, although the land itself would not be subject to tax nor to any lien.   DES/PCT

1459   **BRITISH COLUMBIA COURT OF APPEAL. JUDGE: MACDONALD.**
1922
MERRIMAN v. PACIFIC GREAT EASTERN RAILWAY. (1922) 1 W.W.R. 935.

FACTS: Merriman, a non-Indian, rented certain reserve land from an Indian, on which he pastured a cow. The cow went through a hole in a railway fence and was killed by a train. Merriman sued the railway for the death of the cow. HELD: The rental was illegal and therefore the cow was a trespasser and the railway company was not bound to fence to protect it.   DES/PCT

1460   **BRITISH COLUMBIA COURT OF APPEAL. JUDGE: MACLEAN.**
1970
SURREY v. PEACE ARCH ENTERPRISES. 74 W.W.R. 380.

FACTS: A band surrendered certain reserve land to the Crown on trust to be leased. The defendants leased the land and were constructing an amusement park on the land. The question arose whether they were subject to municipal by-laws enacted under the Health Act of British Columbia. HELD: The surrender of the lands to the Crown by the Indian band was not final and complete, but merely conditional. The lands therefore did not cease to be lands set aside by Her Majesty for the use and benefit of Indians.   The lands continued to be lands reserved for Indians and the Parliament of Canada, accordingly, had exclusive jurisdiction over them. The appellants, as developers, were therefore not subject to municipal by-laws or regulations made under the provincial Health Act.   DES/PCT

1461   **BRITISH COLUMBIA COURT OF APPEAL. JUDGE: SHEPPARD.**
1957
R. v. POINT. (1957) 22 W.W.R. 527, 119 C.C.C. 117.

FACTS: Point, an Indian, failed to file an income tax return. HELD: Point was a "person" and so was required to file an income tax return. His rights are determined not by the Terms of Union of British Columbia but by common law and statute.   DES/PCT

1462   **BRITISH COLUMBIA DISTRICT COURT (NEW WESTMINISTER). JUDGE: MARTIN.**
1901
RE SING KEE. 8 B.C.R. 20.

FACTS: A procedural case arising out of a charge of selling liquor to an Indian.   DES/PCT

1463   **BRITISH COLUMBIA DISTRICT COURT (VICTORIA). JUDGE: GREGORY.**
1913

R. v. CHEW DEB. 18 B.C.R. 23.

FACTS: A procedural case arising out of a charge of selling liquor to an Indian.   DES/PCT

1464   **BRITISH COLUMBIA PROVINCIAL COURT (PENTICTON)**
1971
R. v. DERRIKSAN. Unreported.

FACTS: Derriksan, an Indian, was charged under the Fisheries Act, a federal statute, for catching salmon. He was fishing off a reserve for food. He claims aboriginal rights to fish in the area, rights guaranteed by the Royal Proclamation of 1763. HELD: Aboriginal rights do not exist without some recognition by the state. The Royal Proclamation of 1763 did not apply in British Columbia. Because of that the argument that Section 88 of the Indian Act does not operate to make the Fisheries Act apply to the accused cannot be maintained. Derricksan was convicted.   DES/PCT

1465   **BRITISH COLUMBIA SUPREME COURT (CHAMBERS). JUDGE: BOLE.**
1906
R. v. GOW. 3. W.L.R. 308, 11 C.C.C. 88.

FACTS: A procedural case arising out of a charge of selling liquor to an Indian.   DES/PCT

1466   **BRITISH COLUMBIA SUPREME COURT (CHAMBERS). JUDGE: HUNTER.**
1907-08
REX v. MCHUGH. 7 W.L.R. 252, 13 B.C.R. 224, 13 C.C.C. 104.

FACTS: A procedural case arising out of a charge of selling liquor to an Indian.   DES/PCT

1467   **BRITISH COLUMBIA SUPREME COURT (CHAMBERS). JUDGE: MCDONALD.**
1924
R. v. TOY. (1924) 3 W.W.R. 196, 34 B.C.R. 194.

FACTS: Toy, a non-Indian, sold liquor in violation of the Liquor Act of British Columbia. The conviction is challenged on the basis that the purchaser was an Indian and only the Indian Act should apply. HELD: The objection was rejected on the authority of R. v. Martin (1917) 39 D.L.R. 635.   DES/PCT

1468   **BRITISH COLUMBIA SUPREME COURT. JUDGE: BROWN.**
1969
R. v. COOPER, GEORGE AND GEORGE. 1 D.L.R. (3d) 113.

FACTS: The appellants, all Indians, were convicted for unlawful possession of salmon contrary to the Fisheries Act of Canada. They claim treaty protected rights to fish. HELD: There is no onus on the accused to show that the fish were taken as formerly in order to employ the treaty as a defence. Any ambiguity in a treaty must be interpreted in favor of the Indians. The Fisheries Act, however, has taken away the rights claimed. The conviction was upheld.   DES/PCT

1469   **BRITISH COLUMBIA SUPREME COURT. JUDGE: DRAKE.**
1902
R. v. SING. 6 C.C.C. 156.

FACTS: A procedural case arising out of a charge of selling liquor to an Indian.   DES/
PCT

1470   **BRITISH COLUMBIA SUPREME COURT. JUDGE: GREGORY.**
1921
R. v. WILLIAMS. 30 B.C.R. 303.

FACTS: In a murder trial the question arose whether a woman was the wife of the accused and therefore unable to give evidence against him. The accused had been married
by native custom to 2 other women who were still living but who had purchased their release from marriage in a manner permitted by native custom. After that had occurred the
accused married the woman in question and she too had purchased her release from the
marriage and left her husband. HELD: The evidence was not admissable. The court did
not decide on the validity of the divorce and advised the Crown to apply by stated case to
a higher court to determine the question. DES/PCT

1471   **BRITISH COLUMBIA SUPREME COURT. JUDGE: HUNTER.**
1915
R. v. JIM. 22 B.C.R. 106, 26 C.C.C. 236.

FACTS: Jim, an Indian, shot a deer on a reserve for food. He was convicted of hunting
without a permit contrary to provincial law. HELD: The federal government has exclusive jurisdiction in relation to such matters as shooting, hunting, and fishing upon reserves or the bringing of intoxicants onto reserves. The conviction was set aside.   PCT

1472   **BRITISH COLUMBIA SUPREME COURT. JUDGE: LORD.**
1960
RE WILLIAMS ESTATE. (1960) 32 W.W.R. 686.

FACTS: The widow of an Indian had been living in adultery. There was a son of the
marriage and a daughter by the adulterous relationship. The Administration Act of Brit-
ish Columbia provided that a wife living in adultery would not share in the estate and
therefore the entire estate would pass to the son. The widow and daughter argue that
Sections 48, 49, and 50 of the Indian Act are the complete and exclusive provisions for
Indian estates. They argue that Section 48(3)(a) includes illegitimate children. HELD: By
Section 87 (now 88) of the Indian Act all provincial laws of general application apply to
Indians unless provisions of the Indian Act are inconsistent with the provincial legisla-
tion. There is no inconsistency between the relevant sections here. Section 48(3)(a) of the
Indian Act does not include illegitmate children. The entire estate passes to the
son. DES/PCT

1473   **BRITISH COLUMBIA SUPREME COURT. JUDGE: MACDONALD.**
1929
R. v. THOMPSON. 3 W.W.R. 333, 42 B.C.R. 77, 52 C.C.C. 278.

FACTS: Thompson, a non-Indian, was convicted under Section 126(c) (now S. 97(a)) of
the Indian Act for possession of liquor in the home of an Indian. HELD: The conviction

was set aside. The Indian home was not on a reserve and therefore, there was no offence under the Section.   DES/PCT

1474   **BRITISH COLUMIBA COURT OF APPEAL. JUDGES: MARTIN GALLIHER.**
1923
DOUGLAS v. MILL CREEK. (1923) 1 W.W.R. 529, (1923) 1 D.L.R. 805, 32 B.C.R. 13.

FACTS: Certain Indians were employed by the defandant lumber company to take out timber. The Indians brought proceedings under the Woodmans Lien for Wages Act of British Columbia to obtain a lien against the logs cut. HELD: By Section 103 (there is no equivalent in the present Act) of the Indian Act, an Indian can sue for debts or to compel the performance of obligations contracted with him. Indians can claim a lien under the provincial legislation.   DES/PCT

1475   **EXCHEQUER COURT OF CANADA. JUDGE: ANGERS.**
1935
DREAVER v. THE KING. Unreported.

FACTS: Chief Dreaver and 2 councilors, on behalf of the Indians of the band, seek an accounting of government handling of band funds and rulings on other matters related to the reserve. HELD: (1) The Statute of Limitations did not bar the claims as the petitions were seeking to recover trust property or the proceeds retained by the trustee (the Crown). (2) The evidence did not warrant the conclusion that the Department of Indian Affairs overpaid $2,000.00 on the horses it bought for the band and therefore that claim failed. (3) The Department had no right to charge $25.00 for the jailing of 2 Indians against the band fund and the band was to be reimbursed. (4) All medicines, drugs, or medical supplies which might be required by the Indians of the band were to be supplied to them free of charge under the Medicine Chest provision of Treaty 6. (5) The salary of the farm instructor should not have been charged against the band funds and therefore the claim of $7,720.00 was well founded. (6) The Superintendent-General was not allowed to charge the tuition and care of a blind child to the band funds. (7) The interest money paid to 2 women was rightly paid since the Indian Agent believed that they were members of the band. (8) Permission to have a garden and pasture horses and a cow did not entitle the Indian Agent to farm 80 acres of the reserve.   DES/PCT

1476   **EXCHEQUER COURT OF CANADA. JUDGE: AUDETTE.**
1916
L'HIRONDELLE (ANTOINE) v. THE KING. 16 Ex. C. R. 193.

FACTS: L'Hirondelle, a half-breed, was granted a scrip certificate by the federal government in 1900 entitling him to 240 acres of land in compensation for the extinguishment of Indian title. While a minor he gave the certificate to his father, the father having requested it to pay a debt. The federal government came into possession of the certificate and L'Hirondelle seeks to recover it. HELD: The gift of the scrip certificate to the father was legally valid. Even if he had retained a legal interest in the scrip, he lost any rights by his delay in reclaiming the scrip.   DES/PCT

1477   **EXCHEQUER COURT OF CANADA. JUDGE: AUDETTE.**
1916

L'HIRONDELLE (JOSEPH) v. THE KING. 16 Ex. C. R. 196.

FACTS: This case is identical to the case of Antoine L'Hirondelle. Joseph L'Hirondelle was 18 years old when he gave his scrip certificate to his father. HELD: L'Hirondelle could have repudiated the gift within a reasonable time after he reached the age of 21 years. He delayed for 10 years and cannot now repudiate the gift.   DES/PCT

1478   **EXCHEQUER COURT OF CANADA. JUDGE: AUDETTE.**
1918
RE INDIAN RESERVE, SYDNEY, NOVA SCOTIA. 17 Ex. C. R. 517, 42 D.L.R. 314.

FACTS: Section 49(a) of the Indian Act (there is no equivalent current section) permitted the relocation of an Indian reserve if the Exchequer Court recommended the removal as being in the interest of the public and the welfare of the Indians. The Court was instructed to hold a hearing on the relocation of a reserve located in the downtown area of a city. The majority of the Indians opposed relocation. HELD: Relocation was recommended. The court fixed compensation for the buildings and improvements on the reserve.   DES/PCT

1479   **EXCHEQUER COURT OF CANADA. JUDGE: AUDETTE.**
1920
THE KING v. ONTARIO AND MINNESOTA POWER COMPANY. 20 Ex. C. R. 279.

FACTS: In 1873, Treaty 3 effected the surrender of land and title to the land passed to the Province of Ontario by Section 109 of the British North America Act. In 1915 and 1916 certain lands were set aside by the province as Indian reserves and title transferred to the federal government. Between 1873 and 1915 Ontario granted the defendant company the right to flood certain lands up to a bench mark of 497. In 1917 flooding above that level took place as a result of the defendant company's dam and certain reserve lands were flooded. The federal government sues for damages resulting from that flooding. HELD: The reserves were created subject to any rights which the province had given the defendant company. The claim was upheld. Damages were found to be minimal.   DES/PCT

1480   **EXCHEQUER COURT OF CANADA. JUDGE: BURBIDGE.**
1905
HENRY v. THE KING. 9 Ex. C. R. 417.

FACTS: A band sued the federal government for a declaration in relation to obligations arising out of a surrender and other dealings. HELD: The Exchequer Court has jurisdiction in any case in which the claim arises out of a contract entered into by the Crown and therefore the Court has jurisdiction here to the extent that the claim is supported by the agreement or treaty or by the surrender. The Crown, in respect of Indian lands and monies, is not in the position of an ordinary trustee. Subject to the terms and conditions of the several agreements or treaties with the Indians, or of the surrenders from them and to the provisions of the statutes from time to time in force respecting Indians and Indian lands, the Superintendent-General of Indian Affairs has the management and control of Indian lands, property, and funds. The Superintendent-General and the government are responsible to Parliament and Parliament alone has the authority to review the decision or action taken. The court has no jurisdiction. The Crown's obligation under Treaty to pay the band a fixed annuity of $2,090.00 per year is not as a trustee but as a debtor.

The Court ordered deficiencies in payment of that debt to be made up and made a declaration that the band is entitled to be paid the full amount of the annuity each year.   DES/PCT

1481   **EXCHEQUER COURT OF CANADA. JUDGE: BURBRIDGE.**
1891
THE QUEEN v. THOMAS. 1 Western Law Times Reports 222, 2 Western Law Times Reports 159, 2 Ex. C. R. 246.

FACTS: Thomas, a half-breed, owned land in Manitoba prior to the creation of the province and prior to the Treaty of 1871. Having been assured by a federal official that it would not affect his right to hold private property, he participated in the Treaty and received annuity payments in the years 1871 to 1874. In 1874 he learned that his acceptance of the annuities deprived him of his rights as a half-breed. He returned the annuity for 1874 and did not take annuity payments after that time. The Crown recognized his rights as a half-breed by issuing him half-breed scrip in 1876. The Crown seeks to annul the letters patent to the land owned by Thomas on the basis that by participating in the treaty he forfeited his right to the land. HELD: In the circumstances, Thomas never intended to end his status of half-breed and acquire that of an Indian. Even if his status became that of an Indian, the only provision which would end his rights to his land was a provision of the Indian Act enacted in 1876 whereby land of an Indian included in or surrounded by a reserve became part of the reserve. That provision cannot deprive Thomas of rights to property earlier acquired, seeing that at the time of the enactment there was no pretence that he was an Indian.   DES/PCT

1482   **EXCHEQUER COURT OF CANADA. JUDGE: CATTANACH.**
1964
BRICK CARTAGE v. THE QUEEN. (1965) 1 Ex. C.R. 102.

FACTS: Brick Cartage sued the federal government for damages caused to a vehicle by the collapse of a bridge on an Indian reserve. HELD: The federal government was not responsible because any negligence was not that of a servant of the federal government and the federal government had no responsibility in relation to the bridge. The provincial government has a bare legal title to the reserve land and the band has a possessory right. The band has the same day to day control of the land as a person holding title in fee simple. The federal government does not have any right or status to interfere with possession of the land by the band.   DES/PCT

1483   **EXCHEQUER COURT OF CANADA. JUDGE: MACLEAN.**
1926
THE KING v. MCMASTER. (1926) Ex. C. R. 68.

FACTS: In 1817 certain chiefs of a band leased land for 99 years with an option for renewal. McMaster became assignee of the lease with the approval of the Department of Indian Affairs and now seeks a renewal of the lease. HELD: By the Royal Proclamation of 1763 and later by the provisions of the Indian Act no band could sell or lease reserve land on their own. The lease was, therefore, void.   DES/PCT

1484   **EXCHEQUER COURT OF CANADA. JUDGE: O'CONNOR.**
1948
CHISHOLM v. THE KING. (1948) Ex. C.R. 370, (1948) 3 D.L.R. 797.

FACTS: Chisholm, a lawyer, rendered legal services to an Indian band. The executrix of his estate petitions the Crown for payment of legal fees. HELD: The Indians are wards of the Crown and the Crown is trustee for the Indians. The Crown is under no liability for legal services rendered to a band of Indians at their request in connection with a claim by them against the Crown. The fact that the Crown is trustee for the Indians' trust fund places no obligation on the Crown. Further, where the Minister of Indian Affairs did not instruct the solicitor to act, no liability rests on the Crown.   DES/PCT

1485   **EXCHEQUER COURT OF CANADA. JUDGE: ROBSON.**
1943
R. v. WEREMY. (1943) 1 D.L.R. 9.

This was an action under Section 39 (now 31) of the Indian Act by the Attorney General for recovery of land forming part of an Indian reserve. Weremy was held to be a trespasser and the Indian Act section was held to be within the legislative juridsiction of the federal government.   DES/PCT

1486   **EXCHEQUER COURT OF CANADA. JUDGE: THORSON.**
1951
THE KING v. COWICHAN AGRICULTURAL SOCIETY. (1951) 1 D.L.R. 96, (1950) Ex. C.R. 448.

FACTS: In 1888 a portion of an Indian reserve was surrendered "to lease and surrender the same"to the Cowichan Agricultural Society. Section 51 of the Indian Act (the predecessor to the present Section 53) provided that surrendered reserve lands "shall be managed, leased and sold as the Governor in Council directs..."The 1st lease was authorized by an order-in-council in 1888. The Deputy Superintendent General of Indian Affairs extended the 1st lease in 1909 and executed a new lease of the same lands in 1913 for 99 years. Neither the extension in 1909 nor the new lease of 1913 were authorized or confirmed by an order-in-council. The Crown seeks a declaration that the 99-year lease is null and void. HELD: As was decided in "St. Anns Island Hunting and Fishing Club Ltd. v. The King,"the Governor in Council cannot delegate its authority under Section 51. An order-in-council is a necessary preliminary to the validity of any lease. Therefore the lease of 1913 was void. The fact that the Crown stood by and let the Society make improvements on the land does not prevent the Crown from asserting the invalidity of the lease. The concept of estoppel cannot be used to defeat the express requirements of a statute, particularly when they are designed for the protection of the interests of special classes of person (note that the present Section 53 permits "The Minister or a person appointed by him"to manage, sell, and lease surrendered lands).   DES/PCT

1487   **FEDERAL COURT OF APPEAL. JUDGE: THURLOW.**
1971
RE LAVELL AND ATTORNEY GENERAL OF CANADA. (1971) F.C. 347, 22 D.L.R. (3d) 188: APPEALED FROM (1972) 1 O.R. 390, 22 D.L.R. (3d) 182.

Lavell, an Indian woman, married a non-Indian and as a result her name was removed from the band list persuant to Section 12 (1)(b) of the Indian Act. She argues that the section is discriminatory on the basis of sex and inoperative because inconsistent with the Bill of Rights. HELD: The section is discriminatory on the basis of sex in that an Indian man who marries a non-Indian does not thereby lose Indian status. The section is inoperative and Lavell is entitled to retain Indian status (This case has been appealed to the Supreme Court of Canada). DES/PCT

1488   **JUDICIAL COMMITTEE OF THE PRIVY COUNCIL. JUDGE: DUFF.**
1921
ATTORNEY GENERAL FOR QUEBEC v. ATTORNEY GENERAL FOR
CANADA. (1921) 1 A.C. 401, 56 D.L.R. 373.

FACTS: A band surrendered a portion of their reserve in 1882. The federal government sold the surrendered lands. The province of Quebec challenges the power of the federal government to sell the land. HELD: When the reserve was established under the legislation of 1850 the Indians acquired a usufructuary right only or a personal right to the benefits of the land. This right was not full title to the land. In fact they could only surrender it to the Crown. The Act tried to prevent encroachment upon the lands set out for use by the Indians but such provisions did not intend to grant to the Indians any absolute title. The federal government has full power to accept the surrender of Indian lands. The title to the lands affected by the surrender passes to the Crown in the right of the province. The sale by the federal government was, therefore, invalid. DES/PCT

1489   **JUDICIAL COMMITTEE OF THE PRIVY COUNCIL. JUDGE: LORD LOREBURN.**
1910
DOMINION OF CANADA v. PROVINCE OF ONTARIO. (1910) A.C. 637.

FACTS: As held in the St. Catherines Milling case, the effect of Treaty 3 was to give the province of Ontario full title to the lands covered by the treaty. The federal government, who negotiated the treaty, now seeks a declaration that the Province of Ontario is obliged to compensate the federal government for all monies that the federal government is required to pay by the treaty. HELD: When the federal government signed the treaty they did so under the mistaken belief that the lands were not within the province of Ontario. They did not purport to act of behalf of the province; they acted as guardians of the Indian interest. The federal government was not entitled to be repaid by the province. DES/PCT

1490   **JUDICIAL COMMITTEE OF THE PRIVY COUNCIL. JUDGE: LORD WATSON.**
1888
ST. CATHERINES MILLING v. THE QUEEN. 14 A.C. 46: APPEALED FROM 13
S.C.R. 577: APPEALED FROM 10 O.R. 196.

FACTS: In 1873, Treaty 3 was signed whereby the Indians surrendered certain land to the Crown. In 1883 the federal government issued a timber licence to the St. Catherines Milling Company. The Province of Ontario claims that the licence is invalid. HELD: The Indians' right to the land was a personal and usufructuary right dependant upon the good will of the sovereign. Prior to the surrender the Crown in the right of the province had the underlying title to the land. When the Indian right was surrendered the entire beneficial interest in the land was in the Province of Ontario. Under Section 109 of the British North America Act, the province had the beneficial interest in all lands, subject to exceptions which did not apply here. The fact that the federal government had legislative jurisdiction over "lands reserved for the Indians"was not inconsistent with the province having the ownership of the land.   DES/PCT

1491   **JUDICIAL COMMITTEE OF THE PRIVY COUNCIL. JUDGE: LORD WATSON.**
1896
ATTORNEY GENERAL FOR CANADA v. ATTORNEY GENERAL FOR ONTARIO. (1897) A.C. 199.

FACTS: The Robinson Treaties of 1850 provided for an increase of annuities when the revenue from the sale of the surrendered land reached a certain amount. Was the province or the federal government liable for the increase? HELD: The annuity was not a charge on the surrendered land which was held by the province. It was properly owing by the federal government and was a personal obligation of the Governor General.   DES/PCT

1492   **JUDICIAL COMMITTEE OF THE PRIVY COUNCIL. JUDGE: VISCOUNT HALDANE.**
1912
CORINTHE v. SEMINARY OF ST. SULPICE. (1912) A.C. 872, 5 D.L.R. 263.

FACTS: A band of Indians claims title to land which was granted to a religious order by the King of France and by legislation in 1841. They claim the land on the basis of unextinguished Indian title, prescription, or as beneficiaries of a trust of which the religious order was trustee. HELD: The legislation of 1841 settles that the title is in the religious order. The appeal did not decide whether there was a charitable trust governing the ownership which could be enforced in some way.   DES/PCT

1493   **JUDICIAL COMMITTTEE OF THE PRIVY COUNCIL. JUDGE: LORD DAVEY.**
1903
ONTARIO MINING COMPANY v. SEYBOLD. (1903) A.C. 73.

FACTS: The land in question was surrendered under Treaty 3 in 1873. The federal government subsequently established it as part of an Indian reserve. The band surrendered the land in trust to the federal government. HELD: The treaty resulted in full beneficial interest in the land being in the Crown in the right of the province of Ontario. The federal government acted beyond its powers in purporting to establish the land as an Indian reserve.   DES/PCT

1494   **MANITOBA COURT OF APPEAL. JUDGES: FREEDMAN GUY DICKSON.**
1971
R. v. MCPHERSON. (1971) 2 W.W.R. 640: APPEALED FROM (1971) 1 W.W.R. 299.

FACTS: McPherson, an Indian, was convicted under the Wildlife Act of Manitoba for shooting a moose with metal cased hard-point shells. He was hunting on a reserve for food. HELD: Following the decision in R. v. Prince the conviction must be set aside.   DES/PCT

1495   **MANITOBA COURT OF APPEAL. JUDGES: MCPHERSON COYNE DYSART ADAMSON MONTAGUE.**
1952
CHILDREN'S AID SOCIETY OF EASTERN MANITOBA v. ST. CLEMENTS. 6 W.W.R. (N.S.) 39, 60 Man. R. 229.

FACTS: The issue was whether a municipality was liable under the provincial law for maintenance payments for an Indian child normally resident on an Indian reserve. HELD: The municipality was not liable.   DES/PCT

1496   **MANITOBA COURT OF APPEAL. JUDGES: PERDUE FULLERTON DENNISTOUN PRENDERGAST.**
1923
R. v. RODGERS. 2 W.W.R. 353, (1923) 3 D.L.R. 414, 40 C.C.C. 51, 33 M.L.R. 139.

FACTS: Rodgers, a non-Indian, purchased a pelt from an Indian off a reserve. He is charged under provincial law for failing to record the name and permit number of the trapper. The Indian trapped the animal on his reserve. HELD: The provincial government had no jurisdiction to pass laws interfering with the rights of an Indian to hunt or trap on a reserve. The Indians have the right to do what they wish with what they catch on the reserve.   DES/PCT

1497   **MANITOBA COURT OF KINGS BENCH. JUDGE: MATHERS.**
1909
SANDERSON v. HEAP. 11 W.L.R. 238, 19 M.L.R. 122.

FACTS: A band surrendered reserve land in return for each band member receiving 16 acres of the land surrendered. Sanderson, a band member who had not yet received his Crown Patent, entered into an agreement of sale of the land. He now seeks to set aside that agreement. HELD: There is no restriction on an Indian's right to sell his individual property. The Estoppel Act of Manitoba applies to Sanderson as Indians are subject to all provincial laws.   DES/PCT

1498   **MANITOBA COURT OF KING'S BENCH (CHAMBERS). JUDGE: MACDONALD.**
1914
R. v. ATKINSON. 28 W.L.R. 412, 6 W.W.R. 1055, 23 C.C.C. 149, 18 D.L.R. 462, 24 M.L.R. 308.

HELD: The conviction by an Indian Agent of a non-Indian for being drunk on a reserve contrary to the Indian Act was upheld.   DES/PCT

1499   **MANITOBA COURT OF KING'S BENCH. JUDGE: MCPHERSON.**
1938
R. v. BEYAK. 2 W.W.R. 153, (1938) 2 D.L.R. 723.

FACTS: A procedural case arising out of a charge of selling liquor to an Indian.   DES/PCT

1500   **MANITOBA COURT OF KING'S BENCH. JUDGE: PRENDERGAST.**
1913
PRINCE v. TRACEY. 25 W.L.R. 412, 13 D.L.R. 818.

FACTS: The plaintiff, an Indian, sought to set aside a mortgage upon land executed by the defendant under a power of attorney from the plaintiff. The plaintiff claimed that the power of attorney had been procured by fraud and false representations. HELD: The plaintiff owed the defendant $35.00 for hay. The document which he signed was altogether different from the security he was led to believe he was signing. The mortgage was declared null and void. The court further decided that subject to special statutory limitations, Indians are British subjects, enjoying full civil rights as such. Further the words "grain, root, crops, or other produce" in Sections 38 and 39 of the Indian Act (the predecessors of the present Section 93) should not be taken to cover wild hay.   DES/PCT

1501   **MANITOBA COURT OF QUEENS BENCH. JUDGES: DUBUC TAYLOR KILLAM BAIN.**
1890
RE MATHERS. 1 Western Law Times Reports 235.

FACTS: Certain land was allocated to Mathers, a half-breed. The Crown patent was not issued until 1886. In 1887 the land was sold for taxes for the years 1884 and 1885. HELD: Mathers had a beneficial interest in the land from the time of the allotment to the time of the issuance of the Crown patent and that interest could be taxed by the province of Manitoba.   DES/PCT

1502   **MANITOBA COURT OF QUEENS BENCH. JUDGES: TAYLOR KILLAM DUBUC.**
1893
HARDY v. DESJARDAIS, KERR v. DESJARDAIS. 4 Western Law Times Reports 26.

FACTS: Desjardais, a half-breed, while a minor, applied through his father for a grant of land under the Manitoba Act. The grant was made and the land ordered sold, the proceeds to be applied to the maintenance and education of Desjardais. Desjardais seeks to obtain the land on the basis of non-compliance with the order of sale. HELD: The order of sale had not been sufficiently complied with: the court had never sanctioned a sale which had already been made, nor a sale for which the purchase money was not to be paid for 10 months after nor until the purchaser succeeded in reselling the land at a large advance.   DES/PCT

1503   **MANITOBA COURT OF QUEENS BENCH. JUDGE: BAIN.** ·
1893
ROBINSON v. SUTHERLAND. 4 Western Law Times Reports 111.

FACTS: Marie Cardinal, an illegitimate child of a half-breed head of a family was allotted the land in question. When she was 18 years old and married, she executed an assignment of her land to the defendent without the consent of her husband. At the age of 21 she executed a deed of the land to the plaintiff. The plaintiff refused to pay the balance of the purchase money until he obtained possession of the land. HELD: By Section 3 of the Half-Breeds Lands Act, a child of 18 years or over could make a valid conveyance, but if married, she must obtain the consent of her husband. Since the 1st conveyance was not made with the consent of her husband, the conveyance was voidable at her option upon reaching 21 years of age. When she made the 2nd conveyance she automatically made inoperative the 1st conveyance. Accordingly the plaintiff was entitled to the land.   DES/PCT

1504   **MANITOBA COURT OF QUEENS BENCH. JUDGE: WILSON.**
1969
RE MANITOBA HOSPITAL COMMISSION AND KLEIN AND SPENCE. (1970) 9
D.L.R. (3d) 423: APPEALED FROM 67 W.W.R. 440.

FACTS: Spence, an Indian, was injured by a motor vehicle on a reserve and hospitalized. She recovered damages in a civil action and the Manitoba Hospital Commission seeks to recover the costs of hospital services provided to her. HELD: The Manitoba Hospital Services Commission Act applies to residents including Indians by Section 7 of that act and Section 87 (now 88) of the Indian Act. A federal order-in-council authorized the Minister of National Health and Welfare to pay premiums on behalf of Indians so they could be eligible for health care. This indicated that Indians were to be subject to the provincial scheme. If Mrs. Spence worked she would pay premiums through her employer. The Manitoba Court of Queens Bench in the judgment appealed from had held that the "medicine chest" treaty promise referred exclusively to medicines, drugs, and medical supplies, and did not include hospitalization.   DES/PCT

1505   **MANITOBA COURT OF QUEENS BENCH. JUDGE: WILSON.**
1971
PROVINCIAL MUNICIPAL ASSESSOR v. RURAL MUNICIPALITY OF
HARRISON. (1971) 3 W.W.R. 735.

FACTS: Tenants of leased Indian reserve land challenge the ability of a municipal government to tax them. HELD: The tax immunity given by Section 125 of the British North America Act to "lands or property belonging to Canada" does not confer immunity upon private persons who have some interest in such land. The interest of the lessee is subject to assessment and taxation.   DES/PCT

1506   **MANITOBA COURT OF QUEEN'S BENCH. JUDGE: KILLAM.**
1894
R. v. KENNEDY. 5 W.L.T. 168.

FACTS: A procedural case arising out of a charge of selling liquor to an Indian.   DES/PCT

1507   **NEW BRUNSWICK COURT OF APPEAL. JUDGES: ALLAN FRASER TUCK WETMORE.**
1890
BURK v. CORMIER. 30 N.B.R. 142.

FACTS: In 1878 Cormier, an Indian, mortgaged land on an Indian reserve to Burk, a non-Indian. The mortgage provided that in case of a default in payments the land could be sold. After default, the land was sold to a 3rd party and subsequently resold to Burk. In 1882 Burk obtained a grant of land under the great seal of Canada granted with all the formalities required by the Indian Act. Burk seeks possession of the land. HELD: Two judges held that even if the province of New Brunswick received beneficial interest in this land by Section 109 of the British North America Act, Cormier is estopped from alleging that title is in another after himself having granted a mortgage to Burk. They held that Burk obtained good title to the land. Two other judges held that upon the surrender the lands passed to the province under the holding in the St. Catherines Milling case. The grant to Burk conveyed no title. The court being evenly divided, the judgement below upholding Burk's rights to the land was sustained.   DES/PCT

1508   NEW BRUNSWICK COURT OF APPEAL. JUDGES: PALMER KING FRASER TUCK.
1891
EX PARTE HILL. 31 N.B.R. 84.

FACTS: A procedural case arising out of a charge of selling liquor to an Indian.   DES/PCT

1509   NEW BRUNSWICK SUPREME COURT APPEAL DIVISION. JUDGES: BRIDGES LIMERICK HUGHES.
1970
R. v. FRANCIS. 10 D.L.R. (3d) 189, 9 C.R.N.S. 249.

FACTS: Francis, an Indian, was convicted under the Fisheries Act, a federal statute, for fishing without a licence. He claims treaty-protected fishing rights. HELD: The treaty of 1779 did not give a perpetual right to hunt and fish. Even if it did, such rights can be taken away by federal legislation since Section 87 of the Indian Act (now 88) only refers to provincial laws. The conviction was upheld.   DES/PCT

1510   NEW BRUNSWICK SUPREME COURT APPEAL DIVISION. JUDGES: MCNAIR BRIDGES RITCHIE.
1958
R. v. SIMON. 124 C.C.C. 110, 43 M.P.R. 101.

FACTS: Simon, an Indian, was convicted under the Fisheries Act, a federal statute, for fishing. He claims treaty protected fishing rights. HELD: Simon had not established any connection with the 1752 treaty. No treaty rights having been established, Simon cannot invoke Section 87 of the Indian Act (now 88). Conviction was upheld.   DES/PCT

1511   NEW BRUNSWICK SUPREME COURT APPELLATE DIVISION. JUDGE: GRIMMER.
1931
EX PARTE TENASSE. (1931) 1 D.L.R. 806, (1931) 2 M.P.R. 523.

FACTS: Tenasse, an Indian, questions the ability of the courts in New Brunswick to issue a judgment against him in debt. HELD: Real or personal property of Indians off the reserve is to be treated on the same basis as property of non-Indians and is subject to execution under a judgment. Therefore a court can issue judgment against an Indian. Whether the judgment will be of any use is a separate question.   DES/PCT

1512   NEW BRUNSWICK SUPREME COURT QUEENS BENCH DIVISION. JUDGE: ANGLIN.
1960
WARMAN v. FRANCIS. (1960) 20 D.L.R. (2d) 627, 43 M.P.R. 197.

FACTS: Certain Indians assert rights to cut timber on certain lands which are not reserve lands and belong to a non-Indian. HELD: The non-Indian's title was based on a valid pre-Confederation grant. The Indians had not had title to New Brunswick, but only a usufructuary or personal right dependant upon the good will of the sovereign, a right granted by the Royal Proclamation of 1763. DES/PCT

1513   NEW BRUNSWICK SUPREME COURT. JUDGE: ALLEN.
1885
EX PARTE GOODINE. 25 N.B.R. 151.

FACTS: Goodine was convicted of selling liquor to an Indian and fined $50.00, or in lieu of payment of the fine, 2 months imprisonment. Imprisonment in lieu of payment could not be ordered. The magistrate had exceeded his jurisdiction and the conviction was set aside.   DES/PCT

1514   NORTHWEST TERRITORIES SUPREME COURT (CHAMBERS). JUDGE: SCOTT.
1906
R. v. GRAY. 3 W.L.R. 564.

FACTS: A procedural case arising out of a charge of selling liquor to an Indian.   DES/PCT

1515   NORTHWEST TERRITORIES SUPREME COURT. JUDGES: SCOTT ROULEAU RICHARDSON WETMORE
1897
R. v. MONAGHAN. 2 N.W.T.R. 186 and 298.

FACTS: Monaghan was charged with "giving and selling"liquor to an Indian. He argued that these were 2 charges and were improperly considered as 1. A single judge of the Supreme Court of the Northwest Territories ruled it was 1 charge. No review of that decision could now be made by the full court.   DES/PCT

1516   NORTHWEST TERRITORIES SUPREME COURT. JUDGE: HARVEY.
1906
R. v. GEHRKE. 11 C.C.C. 109.

FACTS: A procedural case arising out of a charge of selling liquor to an Indian.   DES/PCT

1517   NORTHWEST TERRITORIES SUPREME COURT. JUDGE: ROULEAU.
1899
R. v. BEAR'S SHIN BONE. 4 Terr. L. R. 173.

FACTS: Bear's Shin Bone, an Indian, was charged with polygamy for marrying 2 women in accordance with the customs of the Blood tribe. HELD: The Criminal Code barred polygamy even though it was a practice, custom, or ceremony of a denomination or society. The marriage customs of the Blood Indian tribe came within that provision and Bear's Shin Bone was convicted.   DES/PCT

1518   NORTHWEST TERRITORIES SUPREME COURT. JUDGE: ROULEAU.
1900
R. v. MELLON. 7 C.C.C. 179, 5 Terr. L.R. 301.

FACTS: Mellon, a non-Indian, was convicted of selling liquor to an Indian contrary to the Indian Act. HELD: The defendant, to have committed an offence under the Act, must have known that the half-breed (who by reason of having taken treaty was an Indian within the Indian Act) was an Indian. Since the defendant was not aware of this, and he acted in good faith, the conviction was set aside.   DES/PCT

1519   **NORTHWEST TERRITORIES SUPREME COURT. JUDGE: SCOTT.**
1899
RE SHERAN. 4 Terr. L. R. 83.

FACTS: Sheran, a non-Indian, co-habited with an Indian woman by whom he had 2 children. They had agreed to live together for the rest of their lives but did not go through a marriage ceremony by Indian custom or Roman Catholic practice (Sheran being a Roman Catholic). No Catholic priests passed through the area (now southern Alberta). Sheran's sister claims the estate on the basis that there was no marriage to the Indian woman and the children are illegitimate. HELD: The marriage was not valid because the Northwest Territories of 1875 was a civilized, not a barbarous country, and therefore a religious ceremony was required for a valid marriage.   DES/PCT

1520   **NORTHWEST TERRITORIES SUPREME COURT. JUDGE: WETMORE.**
1889
R. v. NAN-E-GUIS-A-KA. 1 Terr. L. R. 211.

FACTS: The 2 polygamous Indian wives of an Indian charged with assault testified at his trial. HELD: Marriages by native custom are recognized, even when 1 partner is non-Indian. The situation in the Territories made it impracticable to require marriage by English laws. The Indian Act by implication recognizes Indian marriages. However, no polygamous marriage will be recognized. Therefore the testimony of the 1st wife of the accused cannot be permitted (the marriage being valid) but the testimony of the 2nd woman is admissible.   DES/PCT

1521   **NORTHWEST TERRITORIES SUPREME COURT. JUDGE: WETMORE.**
1890
R. V. FARRAR. 1 N.W.T.R. 13.

FACTS: A procedural case arising out of a charge of selling liquor to an Indian.   DES/PCT

1522   **NORTHWEST TERRITORIES SUPREME COURT. JUDGE: WETMORE.**
1894
R. v. HOWSON. 1 Terr. L.R. 492, 1 N.W.T.R. 44.

FACTS: Howson, a non-Indian, was convicted of selling liquor to an Indian. The purchaser was a half-breed, his father being French and his mother Indian. He lived on a reserve and was a member of the band. HELD: The Indian Act defines Indian as "any male person of Indian blood reputed to belong to a particular band." The purchaser had Indian blood and belonged to a band. It is not required that the person have full Indian blood. There are many persons who are not full-blooded Indians whose associations, habits, modes of life, and surroundings generally are essentially Indian and it was the intention of Parliament to bring such persons within the provisions and objects of the Indian Act. Since the purchaser was an Indian the conviction was upheld.   DES/PCT

1523   NORTHWEST TERRITORIES SUPREME COURT. JUDGE: WETMORE.
1897
R. v. PAH-CAH-PAH-NE-CAPI. 4 C.C.C. 93, 3 Terr. L. R. 7, 2 N.W.T.R. 126.

FACTS: The accused, an Indian, made an admission of murder to the Indian Agent. Admissions made to a person in authority cannot be admitted in evidence unless they are proven to have been voluntary. The agent was not prepared to say he did not hold out any threats or inducements. HELD: The Indian Agent was a person in authority. He was ex officio a Justice of the Peace, appointed to carry out the Indian Act and was legal adviser on the reserve. The admission could not be admitted in evidence. The murder conviction was set aside.   DES/PCT

1524   NORTHWEST TERRITORIES TERRITORIAL COURT. JUDGE: MADDISON.

1970
R. v. TOOTALIK E4-321. 74 W.W.R. (N.S.) 740: APPEALED FROM 9 C.R.N.S. 92.

FACTS: Tootalik, an Eskimo, was convicted under the Game Ordinance of the Northwest Territories for hunting a female polar bear with young. HELD: There was reasonable doubt whether the cubs in question were of an age at which they could not survive without their mother to bring the situation within the ambit of the section. The defence abandoned the ground of appeal that the activity took place outside the jurisdiction of the trial court in that it took place on off-shore sea ice. The conviction was set aside.   DES/PCT

1525   NORTHWEST TERRITORIES TERRITORIAL COURT. JUDGE: MORROW.
1969
RE INDIAN CUSTOM ADOPTIONS: RE BEAULIEU'S PETITION. 67 W.W.R. 669.

FACTS: An Indian couple seek to have an adoption made by Indian custom confirmed by the Court. HELD: Indian customary adoptions, like Eskimo customary adoptions, are legally effective. Customary adoption is recognized by Section 48(16) of the Indian Act which states that the term child in the section includes a child adopted in accordance with Indian customs.   DES/PCT

1526   NORTHWEST TERRITORIES TERRITORIAL COURT. JUDGE: MORROW.
1972
IN RE DEBORAH E4-789. Unreported.

FACTS: The natural parents of an Eskimo child permitted another Eskimo family to adopt the child in accordance with Eskimo custom. The natural parents repossessed the child and the adoptive parents seek an order confirming the validity of the customary adoption. HELD: The customary adoption was valid.   DES/PCT

1527   NORTHWEST TERRITORIES TERRITORIAL COURT. JUDGE: SISSONS.
1959
R. v. KOGOGOLAK. 28 W.W.R. 376, 31 C.R. 12.

FACTS: Kogogolak, an Eskimo, was charged under the Game Ordinance for shooting a musk-ox. HELD: The Royal Proclamation of 1763 applies to the Eskimos. The Eskimos have the right of hunting, trapping, and fishing game and fish of all kinds at all times on all unoccupied Crown lands in the Arctic. Those rights can only be extinguished or abridged by legislation of the Parliament of Canada. The Game Ordinance does not apply to Eskimos.   DES/PCT

1528   **NORTHWEST TERRITORIES TERRITORIAL COURT. JUDGE: SISSONS.**
1959
R. v. OTOKIAK. 28 W.W.R., 30 C. R. 401.

FACTS: Otokiak, an Eskimo, was charged under the Liquor Ordinance of the Northwest Territories for unlawful consumption of liquor. The Ordinance provides that no Eskimo shall possess or consume liquor unless he holds a class A permit. Eskimos with class C permits may possess or consume beer on licensed premises. HELD: Eskimos are within the exclusive legislative jurisdiction of the federal government. General legislation of a province or territory may affect Indians and Eskimos, but this legislation deals specifically with Eskimos. Only the federal government can enact such legislation. DES/PCT

1529   **NORTHWEST TERRITORIES TERRITORIAL COURT. JUDGE: SISSONS.**
1960
R. v. MODESTE. 31 W.W.R. 84, 127 C.C.C. 197, 33 C.R. 39.

FACTS: A case dealing with evidence in a charge of intoxication off a reserve.   DES/PCT

1530   **NORTHWEST TERRITORIES TERRITORIAL COURT. JUDGE: SISSONS.**
1961
RE NOAH ESTATE. 36 W.W.R. 577, 32 D.L.R. (2d) 185.

FACTS: Noah and his wife lived together for a trial period in 1957 according to Eskimo custom. Some time in 1958 the Eskimo community recognized the marriage and that it was monogamous. There was no certificate of marriage. HELD: Eskimo customary marriage is a consensual union for life of 1 man and 1 woman to the exclusion of all others and is a legal marriage. The Marriage Ordinance of the Northwest Territories does not affect or abolish Eskimo customary marriage. The wife and children are entitled to share the estate.   DES/PCT

1531   **NORTHWEST TERRITORIES TERRITORIAL COURT. JUDGE: SISSONS.**
1961
RE KATIE'S ADOPTION. 38 W.W.R. 100, 32 D.L.R. (2d) 686.

FACTS: An Eskimo couple had obtained custody of an Eskimo child from its natural parents. They seek an adoption order. The provisions of the Child Welfare Ordinance of the Northwest Territories requiring notice to the Superintendent within 30 days of the placement of the child had not been complied with. HELD: There was an adoption in compliance with native custom and that was as effective as an adoption made in compliance with the Child Welfare Ordinance.   DES/PCT

1532   **NORTHWEST TERRITORIES TERRITORIAL COURT. JUDGE: SISSONS.**
1963
R. v. KOONUNGNAK. 45 W.W.R. 282, 42 C.R. 143.

FACTS: Koonungnak, an Eskimo, was convicted under the Game Ordinance of the Northwest Territories for shooting a musk-ox. HELD: The proceedings, for various reasons, were not in compliance with the Bill of Rights; the shooting was in self-defence of an Eskimo camp. The Game Ordinance does not apply to Eskimos. The Royal Proclamation of 1763 applies to the Eskimos. Vested rights, such as Eskimo hunting rights, cannot be taken away without express federal legislation. The law is discriminatory on the basis of race in that the restrictions on Indian and Eskimo hunting are different than those on White men. The conviction was set aside.   DES/PCT

1533 **NORTHWEST TERRITORIES TERRITORIAL COURT. JUDGE: SISSONS.**
1964
R. v. KALLOOAR. 50 W.W.R. (N.S.) 602.

FACTS: Kallooar, an Eskimo, was convicted under the Game Ordinance of the Northwest Territories for killing and abandoning game. HELD: Kallooar had not abandoned the game as he intended to return for it. Additionally, the Royal Proclamation of 1763 applies to the area and the Eskimos have the right to hunt for food on all unoccupied Crown lands in the Arctic. Such a vested right cannot be taken away without express language to that effect.   DES/PCT

1534 **NORTHWEST TERRITORIES TRIAL COURT. JUDGE: NEWLANDS.**
1906
R. v. RUSSELL. 4 W.L.R. 16.

FACTS: Conviction for sale of liquor to Indians was set aside on the basis that the evidence was insufficient and contradictory.   DES/PCT

1535 **NOVA SCOTIA COUNTY COURT (HALIFAX). JUDGE: WALLACE.**
1914
R. v. VERDI. 23 C.C.C. 47.

FACTS: Verdi, a non-Indian, was charged with selling liquor to an Indian (the actual sale being made by an employee). The purchaser testified that he was a half-breed, did not live on the reserve, received no bounty, belonged to the Micmac tribe, and had voted the previous August in band elections. HELD: The evidence satisfied the court that the purchaser was an Indian. Verdi's instructions to his employees not to sell liquor to Indians was no defence as the prohibition of sale in the Indian Act was an absolute prohibition.   DES/PCT

1536 **NOVA SCOTIA COUNTY COURT (INVERNESS). JUDGE: PATTERSON.**
1928
R. v. SYLIBOY. 50 C.C.C. 389.

FACTS: Syliboy, an Indian, was convicted under the Lands and Forests Act of Nova Scotia for having 15 green pelts of muskrat and fox in his possession. He claims treaty protected hunting rights. HELD: The treaty of 1752 did not apply to Cape Breton where this activity took place. It applied only to a small body of Nova Scotia proper. The Royal Proclamation of 1763 does not apply to Nova Scotia. The treaty was not ended by the outbreak of war between the Indians and England, but only suspended for its duration. The treaty may have lost validity by not being ratified by the Parliament of Nova Scotia. Even if valid it would be superceded by game legislation of the colony. The document was not a treaty in any case as the Indians did not have the status to enter into a treaty and Governor Hopson had no authority to enter into a treaty.   DES/PCT

1537   **NOVA SCOTIA COUNTY COURT. JUDGE: MCARTHUR.**
1940
RE KANE. (1940) 1 D.L.R. 390.

FACTS: Eleven Indians, residents of a reserve in Quebec, were employed in Sydney, Nova Scotia, and had resided there for several months. All their real and personal property remained on the reserve. Under provincial law the City of Sydney assessed them for a poll tax. The Indians refused to pay and were imprisoned. HELD: By Sections 102, 103, and 104 of the Indian Act (now Sections 87, 89, and 90) the federal government has completely exhausted the field of taxation in regards to Indians and thereby has excluded any provincial legislation. Therefore the City of Sydney cannot tax an Indian whether living on or off a reserve.   DES/PCT

1538   **NOVA SCOTIA SUPREME COURT. JUDGES: MCDONALD SMITH WEATHERBE RIGBY THOMPSON.**
1885
MCLEAN v. MCISAAC. 18 N.S.R. 304.

FACTS: McLean, a non-Indian, had squatted upon a part of an Indian reserve for 20 to 25 years. McIsaac, an Indian Agent, ordered him to leave the reserve but McLean refused. McIsaac, with some Indians, entered the land occupied by McLean and took some hay. McLean was convicted of trespass contrary to the Indian Act. McLean now sues McIsaac for damages resulting from trespass and assault by McIsaac. HELD: McLean, as a trespasser, had no legal standing to bring an action against McIsaac for trespass.   DES/PCT

1539   **NOVA SCOTIA SUPREME COURT. JUDGES: MEAGHER RUSSELL DRYSDALE LAWRENCE TOWNSEND.**
1908
JOHNSTON v. ROBERTSON. 13 C.C.C. 452, 42 N.S.R. 84.

FACTS: A procedural case arising out of a charge of selling liquor to an Indian.   DES/PCT

1540   **NOVA SCOTIA SUPREME COURT. JUDGES: WEATHERBE GRAHAM MEAGHER RUSSELL.**
1906
R. v. JOHNSTON. 41 N.S.R. 105, 1 E.L.R. 163.

FACTS: A procedural case arising out of a charge of selling liquor to an Indian.   DES/PCT

1541   **ONTARIO CHAMBERS**
1885
BRYCE v. SALT. 11 P.R. 112.

FACTS: Salt, an Indian, who gave evidence he owned no property off the reserve, sought to prevent a judgment being made against him for a debt. HELD: A judgment could be obtained even though it could not be enforced against property on the reserve.   DES/ PCT

1542   ONTARIO CHAMBERS. JUDGE: DALTON.
1870
R. EX REL GIBB v. WHITE. 5 P.R. 315.

FACTS: The election of an Indian as Reeve of a Township was challenged. HELD: Indians are subjects, not aliens, and are able to be elected to public office if they meet the regular statutory requirements such as in this case owning property. The election was upheld.   DES/PCT

1543   ONTARIO CHAMBERS. JUDGE: GALT.
1870
MCKINNON v. VAN EVERY. 5 P.R. 284.

FACTS: A debt was contracted by Indians during the period that federal legislation prohibited any judgment being obtained against an Indian. HELD: The debt cannot now be sued on although the prohibition against any judgment against an Indian is no longer part of the law.   DES/PCT

1544   ONTARIO CHANCERY DIVISION. JUDGE: BOYD.
1888
TOTTEN v. TRUAX. 16 O.R. 490.

FACTS: A band surrendered reserve land to the Crown in trust to sell for the benefit of the band. A piece of the land was sold and upon failure of the owner to pay property taxes, the land was sold for tax arrears. HELD: The tax sale was valid by Section 3 of the Indian Act (there is no equivalent section in the present act; Section 87 would have the same effect).   DES/PCT

1545   ONTARIO CHANCERY DIVISION. JUDGE: BOYD.
1889
RE METCALFE. 17 O.R. 357.

FACTS: The court ruled that Indians residing on an Indian Reserve were not entitled to vote in a referendum to repeal prohibition, under the Canada Temperance Act. The Indian Act is more stringent than the Canada Temperance Act on liquor and it must, therefore, be concluded that the Canada Temperance Act does not apply to Indians.   DES/ PCT

1546   ONTARIO CHANCERY DIVISION. JUDGE: MOWAT.
1871
ATTORNEY GENERAL FOR CANADA v. FOWLDS. 18 Gr. 433.

FACTS: The Superintendent-General of Indian Affairs granted a timber licence over certain reserve lands to Fowlds. The validity of the licence was challenged. HELD: The Timber Act had been made to apply to Indian lands by an order in council and therefore the licence was valid until revoked.   DES/PCT

1547   **ONTARIO CHANCERY DIVISION. JUDGE: ROSE.**
1895
JOHSNON v. JONES. 26 O.R. 109.

FACTS: An Indian woman died with a will. The next of kin challenge her ability to make a will. HELD: Section 20 of the Indian Act (the predecessor to Sections 45 and 46) empower the Superintendent-General of Indian Affairs to make the "final"decision as to the disposition of personal and real property of an Indian. This may interfere with a will being carried out but does not prevent an Indian from making a will. Because of the power of the Superintendent-General, the court held that it had no power to decide whether the bequest under the will was a valid one.   DES/PCT

1548   **ONTARIO COUNTY COURT (HALDIMAND). JUDGE: KINNEAR.**
1956
CAMPBELL v. SANDY. (1956) 4 D.L.R. (2d) 754, (1956) O.W.N. 441.

FACTS: Campbell, a non-Indian, obtained a judgment in debt against Sandy, an Indian living on a reserve. Sandy failed to appear under a judgment summons to be examined as to what assets he had. HELD: For the contempt involved in failing to appear in response to the judgment summons, Sandy was sentenced to jail for 10 days, persuant to the Division Courts Act of Ontario. Section 87 (now 88) of the Indian Act provides that all laws of general application in the province apply to Indians.   DES/PCT

1549   **ONTARIO COUNTY COURT (HASTINGS). JUDGE: LANE.**
1951
R. v. HILL. 101 C.C.C. 343, 14 C.R. 266, (1951) O.W.N. 824.

FACTS: Hill, an Indian, was in possession of 2 seine nets on a reserve, without a licence required by provincial law. HELD: The Parliament of Canada is the only competent legislative authority which can regulate the situation. Conviction was set aside.   DES/PCT

1550   **ONTARIO COUNTY COURT (YORK). JUDGE: DENTON.**
1930
R. v. BENNETT. 55 C.C.C. 27.

FACTS: The accused sold liquor to Jack Post, an Indian, and was convicted for doing so contrary to Section 126(a) (now 94(a)) of the Indian Act. He gave evidence that he did not know, believe, or suspect the purchaser to be an Indian. The accused thought he was a Japanese. HELD: The hearing of the appeal was adjourned in order for the Indian to be brought before the Judge. The Judge found the purchaser to be typically Indian in appearance. His appearance would have at least caused the accused to suspect him to be an Indian. The appeal was therefore dismissed.   DES/PCT

1551   **ONTARIO COURT OF APPEAL. JUDGES: KELLY JESSUP BROOKE.**
1971
R. v. FIREMAN. (1971) 3 O.R. 380.

FACTS: Fireman, an Indian, was living in a remote Indian settlement. He shot his cousin while highly intoxicated. He was convicted of manslaughter and sentenced to imprisonment for 10 years. Fireman appeals the sentence imposed. HELD: Rejection by his community for his action, unfamiliarity with anything outside his community, and a stable background made a shorter sentence desirable. The sentence was reduced to 2 years. The

court discussed the nature of the community and the background of Fireman.   DES/
PCT

1552 **ONTARIO COURT OF APPEAL. JUDGES: OSLER MEREDITH.**
1908
R. v. BEBONING. 17 O.L.R. 23, 12 O.W.R., 13 C.C.C. 405.

FACTS: Beboning, an Indian, was convicted under the criminal code of theft for removing hay from a reserve. He argues that the conviction was improper because the facts as
found by the court had indicated an offence of trespass under the Indian Act. He argues
that he could only be charged under the Indian Act. HELD: The conviction under the
criminal law was proper.   DES/PCT

1553 **ONTARIO COURT OF APPEAL. JUDGE: MOSS.**
1905
JONES v. GRAND TRUNK. 5 O.W.R. 611: APPEALED FROM 3 O.W.R. 370.

FACTS: Jones, an Indian, held an Indian railway ticket. She was refused a seat in the 1st
class coach and was requested to travel in the only other car, a smoking car. HELD: Providing a smoking car was not sufficient: therefore she was entitled to sit in the 1st class
coach. The railway was in breach of its contract with her.   DES/PCT

1554 **ONTARIO COURT OF APPEAL. JUDGE: OSLER.**
1900
R. v. MURDOCK. 4 C.C.C. 82, 27 O.A.R. 443.

FACTS: A procedural case arising out of a charge of selling liquor to an Indian.   DES/
PCT

1555 **ONTARIO COURT OF APPEAL. JUDGE: OSLER.**
1907
R. v. HILL. 15 O.L.R., 11 O.W.R. 20.

FACTS: Hill, an Indian living on a reserve, was convicted for practicing medicine off the
reserve without being registered under the Ontario Medical Act. HELD: The Indian Act
does not profess to deal with all the rights and obligations of an Indian. Parliament may
remove Indians from the scope of provincial laws in their dealings outside the reserve but
to the extent to which Parliament has not done so, they must be governed by the general
laws of the province. Hill was properly convicted.   DES/PCT

1556 **ONTARIO COURT OF COMMON PLEAS. JUDGE: GWYNNE.**
1878
CHURCH v. FENTON. 28 U.C.C.P. 384.

FACTS: Land was surrendered by a band of Indians to the Crown in 1854. In 1857 the
land was sold and the plaintiff is the successor in title. In 1869 the Crown Patent was issued by the federal government. In 1870 the land was sold for taxes for the years 1864 to
1869. The plaintiff maintains that the tax sale was invalid because the lands remained
Indian lands until 1869 when the Crown Patent was issued, and so not subject to taxation. HELD: The Crown never leased or granted title to land until the Indian title was
extinguished by treaty or surrender. In following this policy the Crown was waiving the

rights it had by conquest and imposing upon itself certain restrictions in its rights to deal with the land. Prior to Confederation Upper Canada treated Indian lands as subject to taxation when they were sold. After Confederation Section 91(24) of the British North America Act applied only to unsurrendered Indian lands. The taxation of the land was therefore valid both before and after Confederation and the tax sale of 1870 was valid.   DES/PCT

1557 **ONTARIO COURT OF COMMON PLEAS. JUDGE: MACMAHON.**
1892
R. v. FEARMAN. 22 O.R. 456.

FACTS: Fearman, a non-Indian, was convicted of unlawfully keeping liquor for the purposes of sale, contrary to the Liquor License Act of Ontario. On appeal it is argued that the conviction should be set aside as the offence was committed on the Six Nations Indian Reserve. HELD: There was no evidence to show that the offence actually occurred on the reserve. If it had been shown that the offence was committed on the reserve there could have been no conviction under the provincial Liquor Licence Act, as the offence would have been punishable under the Indian Act. The conviction was upheld.   DES/PCT

1558 **ONTARIO COURT OF COMMON PLEAS. JUDGE: ROSE.**
1884
R. v. MACKENZIE. 6 O.R. 165.

FACTS: A procedural case arising out of a charge of selling liquor to an Indian.   DES/PCT

1559 **ONTARIO COURT OF COMMON PLEAS. JUDGE: ROSE.**
1889
R. v. GOOD. 17 O.R. 725.

FACTS: Good, a non-Indian, was married to an Indian woman and resided on a reserve. He was convicted under Section 26 of the Indian Act (the predecessor to Section 93) for removing hay from the reserve without permission. HELD: "Hay"in the section means either natural or cultivated hay. The conviction was quashed because the costs of commitment and transportation to jail were improperly included in the conviction.   DES/PCT

1560 **ONTARIO COURT OF COMMON PLEAS. JUDGE: WILSON.**
1887
R. v. MCAULEY. 14 O.R. 643.

FACTS: A procedural case arising out of a charge of selling liquor to an Indian.   DES/PCT

1561 **ONTARIO COURT OF QUEENS BENCH. JUDGES: ARMOUR O'CONNOR WILSON.**
1886
R. v. FEARMAN. 10 O.R. 660.

FACTS: Fearman, a non-Indian, was charged under Sections 64 and 66 of the Indian Act (the predecessors to Section 93) for taking cut wood off a reserve without the authorization of the Superintendent-General of the Indian Department. The Indian in possession of the lot on the reserve from which the wood had been taken consented to the removal. HELD: The consent of the Indian did not justify the removal in the absence of approval of the Superintendent-General.   DES/PCT

1562   **ONTARIO COURT OF QUEENS BENCH. JUDGES: ARMOUR WILSON O'CONNOR.**
1885
HUNTER v. GILKISON. 7 O.R. 735.

A malicious imprisonment case arising out of a trial on a charge of trespass conducted by the visiting superintendant and commissioner of Indian Affairs.   DES/PCT

1563   **ONTARIO COURT OF QUEENS BENCH. JUDGES: MORRISON HARRISON.**
1877
REGINA v. GUTHERIE. 41 U.C.Q.B. 148.

FACTS: In 1843 Robinson transferred certain land to the Crown in trust for a band of Indians. The land was sold in 1861 by a sheriff for arrears of taxes assessed in the years after 1843. Gutherie claims title from the person who purchased the land from the sheriff. The Crown seeks to eject Gutherie from the land. HELD: By the provisions of the Assessment Act of 1850, lands vested in the Crown in trust for the Indians were not liable to taxation and therefore the tax sale was invalid. Gutherie was ordered ejected from the land.   DES/PCT

1564   **ONTARIO COURT OF QUEENS BENCH. JUDGES: WILSON MORRISON RICHARDS.**
1869
FEGAN v. MCLEAN. 29 U.C.Q.B. 202.

FACTS: An Indian cut cordwood on his land on a reserve and sold it to Fegan. McLean, a commissioner and forest warden seized the wood before Fegan could take possession of it, on the instructions of the Indian Department. Fegan brings an action in trespass against McLean for seizing the wood. HELD: The sale to Fegan was valid. McLean had no right to seize the wood.   DES/PCT

1565   **ONTARIO COURT OF QUEEN'S BENCH. JUDGE: OSLER.**
1884
R. v. YOUNG. 7 O.R. 88.

FACTS: Young sold liquor to an Indian and was convicted both under the Indian Act and the Liquor License Act of Ontario. On appeal it was held that both convictions were proper.   DES/PCT

1566   **ONTARIO COURT OF QUEEN'S BENCH. JUDGE: STREET.**
1888
R. v. GREEN. 12 P.R. 373.

FACTS: A procedural case arising out of a charge of selling liquor to an Indian.   DES/PCT

1567   **ONTARIO COURT OF QUEEN'S BENCH. JUDGE: WILSON.**
1886
R. v. SHAVELEAR. 11 O.R. 727.

FACTS: Shavelear, a non-Indian, was convicted for having sold liquor on the day on which the vote for accepting the Canada Temperance Act in the county of Brant was taken. He challenges the validity of the proceedings under the Canada Temperance Act in that the geographical area involved includes reserve land and therefore there is a conflict with the Indian Act, and secondly, no arrangements were made for the Indians to vote. HELD: There was no conflict between the Temperance Act and the Indian Act as both prohibit liquor. As for the other objection, there was no evidence before the court that the electors on the Indian lands had not voted, or that there were electors on the Indian lands.   DES/PCT

1568   **ONTARIO DISTRICT COURT (PERRY SOUND). JUDGE: LITTLE.**
1969
R. v. MOSES. 13 D.L.R. (3d) 50, (1970) 3 O.R. 314.

FACTS: Moses, an Indian, was convicted under the Game and Fish Act of Ontario for hunting moose during a closed season. He was hunting off the reserve for food, within the area of the Robinson-Huron treaty. HELD: Moses has treaty protected hunting rights which only the federal government can take away. Section 87 (now 88) of the Indian Act was referred to. The conviction was set aside.   DES/PCT

1569   **ONTARIO DIVISIONAL COURT. JUDGE: RIDDELL.**
1912
RICHARDS v. COLLINS. 4 O.W.N. 375, 9 D.L.R. 249, 27 O.L.R. 395, APPEALED FROM 3 O.W.N. 1479, 27 O.L.R. 390.

FACTS: The Indian Act provided that when surrendered reserve lands were being sold for taxes the Superintendent General of Indian Affairs could approve the conveyance of title and issue a patent to the new grantee when the original conditions of sale were completed (there are no equivalent provisions in the present act). HELD: The trial court held that where approval of the Superintendent General had not been obtained there was no limit of time for attacking the tax sale and deed of title resulting from it. The Divisional Court dismissed an appeal from that holding.   DES/PCT

1570   **ONTARIO DIVISIONAL COURT (THUNDER BAY). JUDGE: MCKAY.**
1930
R. v. PADJENA AND QUASAWA. Unreported.

FACTS: Padjena and Quasawa, 2 Indians, were convicted under the Game and Fisheries Act of Ontario for possession of 30 raw beaver pelts without a licence. They were hunting within the area of the Robinson-Superior Treaty. HELD: Only the federal government has jurisdiction to legislate in relation to Indians. The conviction was set aside. Treaties are to be construed liberally in favor of the Indians.   PCT

1571   ONTARIO DIVISIONAL COURT. JUDGES: ARMOUR FALCONBRIDGE
STREET.
1898
R. v. MACHEKEQUONABE. 28 O.R. 309.

FACTS: The accused, an Indian, was a member of a tribe who believed in the existence
of Wendigos, evil spirits that took human form and which would eat human beings. In
the belief that there was a Wendigo in the area, sentries were posted around the camp.
The accused, a sentry, called out to a running figure to identify itself, which the figure did
not. Believing the figure was that of a Wendigo, he shot it. The person killed was the
accused's foster father. HELD: Conviction for manslaughter upheld.   DES/PCT

1572   ONTARIO DIVISIONAL COURT. JUDGE: BOYD.
1908
RE HILL v. TELFORD. 12 O.W.R. 1090.

FACTS: The plaintiff, an Indian, sued a police magistrate for false imprisonment. An
order requiring the plaintiff to post security for costs was made and the plaintiff seeks to
have that order set aside. HELD: By Section 103 of the Indian Act (there is no equivalent
Section in the present act) an Indian can sue. That section does not give him any special
privileges. The order for costs was authorized under provincial law and such an order
could be made against an Indian plaintiff.   DES/PCT

1573   ONTARIO DIVISIONAL COURT. JUDGE: MEREDITH.
1904
BRIDGE v. JOHNSTON. 8 O.L.R., 4 O.W.R. 36.

HELD: The purchaser of surrendered Indian lands even prior to completion of payment
of the purchase price is, except as against the Crown, in the same position as if the land
had been granted to him by letters patent. He can assign his interest in the land or in timber.   DES/PCT

1574   ONTARIO DIVISIONAL COURT. JUDGE: RIDDELL.
1910
SIMKEVITZ v. THOMPSON. 16 O.W.R. 865.

FACTS: An Indian sent milk from the reserve to a cheese factory. A creditor of the Indian attempted to garnishee the money owing to the Indian from the factory for the
milk. HELD: The money held by the factory for the Indian was not personal property
outside the reserve and was therefore not subject to garnishment.   DES/PCT

1575   ONTARIO HIGH COURT (CHAMBERS). JUDGE: MIDDLETON.
1918
RE CALEDONIA MILLING v. JOHNS. 42 O.L.R. 338, 14 O.W.N. 1.

FACTS: A court made an order committing Johns, an Indian, to 40 days in jail for debt
on the basis that he had sufficient property and money to pay the debt. Johns appeals on
the basis that all his property is on his reserve and exempt from seizure by Section 102
(now 89) of the Indian Act. HELD: This was an attempt to do indirectly what could not
be done directly and the order was improper. An Indian is a ward of the dominion government and could not be taken under the laws of the province. The provisions of the

Ontario Division Court Act which gave the court power to jail a debtor did not apply to Indians.   DES/PCT

1576   ONTARIO HIGH COURT OF JUSTICE (CHAMBERS). JUDGE: MCTAGUE.
1935
RE NELSON. O.W.N. 562, 1936 O.R. 31.

FACTS: An order was made pursuant to Section 132 of the Indian Act (the predecessor to Section 103 of the present Act) confiscating a car used to convey liquor to Indians. HELD: Such an order could only be made after a trial established that an offence had been committed. There had been no trial here so the order was set aside.   DES/PCT

1577   ONTARIO HIGH COURT. JUDGE: KING.
1960
LOGAN v. STYRES. 20 D.L.R. (2d) 416, (1959) O.W.N. 361.

FACTS: Logan, an Indian, seeks to prevent the surrender of certain land forming part of the Six Nations Indian Reserve on the basis that the Six Nations are allies, not subjects of the Crown. HELD: The Six Nations Indians, by accepting the protection of the Crown when they entered Canada became subjects of the Crown and subject to the laws in force. The Court examined the Haldimand and Simcoe deeds.   DES/PCT

1578   ONTARIO HIGH COURT. JUDGE: OSLER.
1971
BEDARD v. ISAAC. (1972) 2 O.R. 391.

FACTS: Bedard, an Indian, married a non-Indian. After separating from her husband she returned to live on the reserve. The Band Council passed a resolution to expel her from the reserve. She seeks an injunction to prevent her expulsion. HELD: Section 12 (1)(b) of the Indian Act is discriminatory on the basis of sex and inoperative because inconsistent with the Bill of Rights.   Therefore Mrs. Bedard did not lose Indian status upon her marriage. The injunction was granted.   DES/PCT

1579   ONTARIO MAGISTRATES COURT (SIMCOE). JUDGE: JASPERSON.
1958
R. v. WILLIAMS. 120 C.C.C. 34.

FACTS: Williams, an Indian, drove his car at an excessive speed on a provincial highway and was followed onto the reserve by 2 police constables. He refused to produce his driver's licence and ran inside his house. He was charged with obstructing police in the execution of their duty, an offence under the Criminal Code of Canada. Williams argues that the police were trespassers on the reserve. HELD: Section 87 (now 88) of the Indian Act makes the Ontario Highway Traffic Act apply to Indians. For police to carry out their duties under the provincial act they will be required to go on reserves. The officers were not trespassers.   DES/PCT

1580   ONTARIO POLICE COURT (TORONTO). JUDGE: JONES.
1930
R. v. BROWN. 55 C.C.C. 29.

FACTS: A clerk was charged under the Indian Act for selling liquor to an Indian. HELD: The clerk was convicted since the purchaser was obviously an Indian by appearance and the clerk did not question him about his "nationality."   DES/PCT

1581   **ONTARIO PROVINCIAL COURT (COBURG). JUDGE: BASTER.**
1972
R. v. MARSDEN. Unreported.

FACTS: Marsden, an Indian, was charged with possession of an unregistered firearm contrary to the Criminal Code, a federal statute. He possessed the gun for the sole purpose of trapping on the reserve, something protected by treaty. HELD: The accused is subject to the Criminal Code. He was convicted.   DES/PCT

1582   **ONTARIO PROVINCIAL COURT (NIPPISSING). JUDGE: LUNNEY.**
1971
R. v. PENASSE AND MCLEOD. (1971) 8 C.C.C. (2d) 569.

FACTS: Penasse and McLeod, 2 Indians, sold fish caught on the reserve to a non-Indian. They were charged under the Game and Fish Act of Ontario for failing to have a commercial fishing licence. HELD: By the Robinson Treaty the Indians were granted the rights to hunt and fish "as they have heretofore been in the habit of doing" prior to 1850. The Crown did not put forth any evidence to show that the defendants were acting outside the scope of their rights under the treaty. Further, since the treaty preceded the provincial statute (The Game and Fish Act), the defendants' rights under the treaty were superior to the Act unless they were acting outside their rights under the treaty. The charge was dismissed.   DES/PCT

1583   **ONTARIO PROVINCIAL COURT. JUDGE: DUNLAP.**
1972
R. v. ISAAC. Unreported.

FACTS: Isaac, an Indian, was charged with driving without current licence plates. He was driving on a reserve. HELD: The road was used by the general public and was therefore a highway. Section 88 of the Indian Act was referred to as making the provincial legislation apply. Isaac was convicted.   DES/PCT

1584   **ONTARIO SUPREME COURT APPELLATE DIVISION. JUDGE: MEREDITH.**

1913
AVERY v. CAYUGA. (1913) 13 D.L.R. 275, 28 O.L.R. 517, 4 O.W.N. 1164: and see 5 O.W.N. 471.

FACTS: By farming on a reserve, Avery, an Indian, earned money which he deposited in a bank off the reserve. A creditor seeks to garnishee the bank account. HELD: The bank deposit is property situated off the reserve and therefore the money deposited there can be garnisheed. DES/PCT

1585   **ONTARIO SUPREME COURT. JUDGES: MEREDITH RIDDELL.**
1917
R. v. MARTIN. 29 C.C.C. 189, 39 D.L.R. 635, 41 O.L.R. 79: APPEALED FROM 12 O.W.N. 396, 40 O.L.R. 270.

FACTS: Martin, an Indian, was convicted of possession of liquor in the City of Hamilton contrary to the Ontario Temperance Act.   HELD: An Indian is subject to provincial laws off a reserve just as all other persons. The legislation is not legislation concerning Indians however much Indians may be affected in common with other persons.   DES/PCT

1586   **ONTARIO SUPREME COURT. JUDGE: ARMOUR.**
1934
POINT v. DIBBLEE CONSTRUCTION COMPANY. 2 D.L.R. 785, (1934) O.W.N. 88, (1934) O.R. 142.

FACTS: A band council approved the use of certain reserve land for a highway on certain conditions, including the condition that the title to the roadway was to remain in the Indians and the individual Indians whose improvements or land were taken were to be compensated. The Superintendent General of Indian Affairs granted the Bridge Corporation a licence of occupation for the purpose of constructing the highway across the reserve. The plaintiff, an Indian resident on the reserve, refused compensation for the required portion of the land on which he resided and sued for an order prohibiting the defendants from trespassing on his land, damages for illegal trespass, and an order that the defendants restore his land to its prior condition. He argued that there was no authorization in the Indian Act for the licence of occupation granted by the Superintendent General, that the compensation offered him was inadequate, and that the band council was improperly constituted. HELD: The compensation offered was adequate. The plaintiff's delay in bringing the action when he knew of the plans to build the highway was grounds for denying an injuction. The council was properly constituted in accordance with the elective system which, by law, displaced the system of life chiefs. The licence of occupation was not a lease; therefore Section 50 and 51 of the Indian Act did not apply (they are the predecessors to Sections 37 and 28 of the present Act). The prerogative rights of the Crown to deal with its own property had not been limited by the Indian Act. Sections 34 and 35 of the Act contemplate that non-Indians may occupy or use reserve land with the authority or licence of the Superintendent General (the present Act has no equivalent sections). The plaintiff is not in lawful possession of the land in that he has never been located on the land under Section 21 (now Section 20(1)) nor has a location ticket been issued under Section 22 (now Section 20(2)). His possession has been recognized and approved by the government, but that creates no estoppel against the Crown preventing it from disputing the plaintiff's right to occupy the land. As a result, the plaintiff had no right to maintain the action, whether it was an action for ejectment or trespass. Additionally, Sections 34, 35, 115, and 116 provided a method of dealing with persons who trespass on or occupy or use reserve land (the equivalent current sections are Section 30 and 31). Action is to be taken by the Superintendent General and not by the Indians of the band. These provisions necessarily exclude any action by an Indian for the same purpose. Finally, any action of the plaintiff could only have been brought in the Exchequer Court.   DES/PCT

1587   **ONTARIO SUPREME COURT. JUDGE: GREEN.**
1939
R. v. COMMANDA. 72 C.C.C. 246, (1939) O.W.N. 466, (1939) 3 D.L.R. 635.

FACTS: Commanda, an Indian, was charged with possession of game during a closed season, contrary to the Game and Fisheries Act of Ontario. He was in possession of the game off a reserve but within the area covered by the Robinson-Huron treaty. HELD:

The privilege to hunt granted by the treaty was not a trust or interest in land other than that of the province of Ontario within the meaning of Section 109 of the British North America Act. The Game and Fisheries Act is valid provincial legislation which affects Indians only incidentally. The conviction was upheld.   DES/PCT

1588   **ONTARIO SUPREME COURT. JUDGE: MEREDITH.**
1917
ATKINS v. DAVIS. (1917) 34 D.L.R. 69, 38 O.L.R. 548, 11 O.W.N. 377.

Atkins, an Indian, seeks to enforce a judgment against Davis, an Indian, by seizure and sale of goods belonging to Davis which are located on a reserve. The judgment being enforced was obtained by a non-Indian. HELD: The Indian Act prohibited any person obtaining a judgment on property of an Indian located on a reserve. The prohibition applied to both Indians and non-Indians.   DES/PCT

1589   **ONTARIO SUPREME COURT. JUDGE: ORDE.**
1922
FISHER v. ALBERT. 64 D.L.R. 153, 50 O.L.R. 68, 20 O.W.N.

FACTS: The defendant, an Indian, claims a right to possession of property on a reserve as a result of a gift made by the former owner. The right of the defendant to possess the land is challenged by the heirs of the former owner. The Superintendent-General of Indian Affairs ruled that the defendant had a right to possession of the land. The heirs ask a declaration by the Supreme Court of Ontario as to who has the rights to the land. HELD: The Supreme Court has jurisdiction to hear and adjudicate the dispute. In this case the rights of each party were not clearly enough set out and so the dispute should not be set down for trial.   DES/PCT

1590   **ONTARIO SUPREME COURT. JUDGE: RIDDELL.**
1921
SERO v. GAULT. 20 O.W.N. 16, 50 O.L.R. 27.

FACTS: Sero, an Indian, seeks the return of the value of seine nets seized on the reserve. HELD: Federal and provincial legislation in parallel terms justify the seizure, so the seizure was valid unless general laws of the country do not apply to Indians. General laws of the country do apply to Indians. The reserve was established by the Simcoe Deed of 1793 which granted the land "according to the several customs and usages" of the Indians. These were words of tenure, not indicative of the manner in which the land was to be used. Moreover there was no evidence that fishing with a seine was one of the customs of the Indians in 1793. The grant does not exclude Indians from the ordinary laws of the land.   DES/PCT

1591   **ONTARIO SUPREME COURT. JUDGE: ROSE.**
1921
R. v. GODIN. 36 C.C.C. 191, 20 O.W.N. 343.

FACTS: A case concerning evidence in a charge of selling liquor to an Indian.   DES/PCT

1592   **QUEBEC CIRCUIT COURT (MONTREAL). JUDGE: PURCELL.**
1906

CHARBONNEAU v. DE LORIMIER. 8 Que. P. R. 115.

HELD: The status of an Indian, as such, may be proved by his certificate of birth, his general reputation, his residence in the reserve, or his election as municipal councillor.   DES/PCT

1593   **QUEBEC CIRCUIT COURT. JUDGE: ANDREWS.**
1900
BUSSIERES v. BASTIEN. (1900) 17 Que. C. S. 189.   French.

FACTS: The plaintiffs, non-Indians, took out a writ of execution against Bastien, an Indian living on a reserve, intending to seize property of Bastien's located on the reserve. HELD: The Indian Act exempted movable and immovable property of an Indian situated on a reserve from seizure.   DES/PCT

1594   **QUEBEC COURT OF KINGS BENCH. JUDGES: TELLIER RIVARD GALIPEAULT ST. GERMAIN BARCLAY.**
1937
DELORIMIER v. CROSS. 62 Que. K. B. 98: APPEALED FROM 73 Que. C.S. 377.

FACTS: Two Indians claim possession of the same property on the reserve. HELD: By the Indian Act no Indian has rightful possession of the land on a reserve unless he has been located on the land by the band with the approval of the Superintendent-General. The approval of the Superintendent is not reviewable by any Court in Quebec. The plaintiff's action was dismissed.   DES/PCT

1595   **QUEBEC COURT OF QUEENS BENCH APPEAL SIDE. JUDGES: CASEY OWEN BROSSARD.**
1968
WHITFIELD v. CANADIAN MARCONI. 68 D.L.R. (2d) 251.

FACTS: Whitfield was dismissed from his job because he associated with an Eskimo, something prohibited by his contract of employment. HELD: The term in the contract of employment did not infringe Whitfield's rights under the Bill of Rights nor did it contravene any laws of public order or good morals (as provided in the Quebec Civil Code). The dismissal was valid.   DES/PCT

1596   **QUEBEC COURT OF QUEENS BENCH. JUDGES: DORION TESSIER CROW CHURCH BOSSE.**
1889
CHERRIER v. TERIHONKOW. 5 Montreal L.R. (Q.B.) 33.

A procedural case on the exemption from seizure of property of an Indian located on a reserve.   DES/PCT

1597   **QUEBEC COURT OF QUEENS BENCH. JUDGES: LACOSTE BOSSE BLANCHET HALL WURTELE.**
n.d.
MOWAT v. CASGRAIN. 6 Que. Q. B. 12.

FACTS: The dispute related to rent owing for the use of reserve lands on a reserve established by the Jesuits during the period of New France. The Jesuits had given the land to the Indians. The federal government attempted to collect the back rent owing. The government of the province of Quebec asserts that it is the proper government to collect the rent on behalf of the Indians since it owns the land. HELD: The reserve was owned by the Crown in the right of the province of Quebec subject to the enjoyment or usufruct of the Indians. The federal government had legislative jurisdiction over the land and was the proper government to collect the rent.   DES/PCT

1598   **QUEBEC COURT OF SESSIONS OF THE PEACE. JUDGE: GUERIN.**
1944
R. v. WILLIAMS. (1944) 2 D.L.R. 488, 82 C.C.C. 166.

FACTS: Williams, an Indian, residing on a reserve, refused to pay $1.00 as required by the Retail Sales Tax Act of Quebec for a licence to sell tobacco at his shop on the reserve. Williams argued that he was not subject to the Quebec Act because the Indian Act exempts property held on the reserve from taxation. HELD: The $1.00 only represented the cost of acquiring the licence and did not constitute a tax. Further, Indians are subject to all laws of general application in the province unless the province has specifically legislated about Indians or lands reserved for Indians or unless they are in conflict with the Indian Act. The Quebec Retail Sales Tax Act did neither and validly applied to Indians.   DES/PCT

1599   **QUEBEC COURT OF SESSIONS OF THE PEACE. JUDGE: PETTIGREW.**
1943
R. v. GROSLOUIS. 81 C.C.C. 167, (1944) R.L. 12 (French).

FACTS: Groslouis, an Indian, operated a retail store on a reserve. He did not have a permit under the Retail Sales Tax Act of Quebec. He sold goods to a non-Indian who did not reside on the reserve and did not collect any sales tax. HELD: The transaction is like a sale to a person off the reserve and is therefore subject to the provincial sales tax. A sale to an Indian would not be subject to that tax.   DES/PCT

1600   **QUEBEC DISTRICT COURT (ABITIBI). JUDGE: BEAULIEU.**
1965
R. v. POLSON. Unreported.

FACTS: The accused, an Indian, killed a moose on the Temiskaming Indian Reserve in Quebec without a licence and out of season, contrary to the Quebec Game Act. HELD: Since the Governor in Council had not legislated in this area as provided by Section 72(a) of the Indian Act and the band had not enacted a by-law as provided in Section 80(o) of the Indian Act there was no necessity for protective legislation. Consequently, the accused was not guilty of an offence under the Quebec Game Act.   PCT

1601   **QUEBEC DISTRICT COURT (HULL). JUDGE: BOUCHER.**
1965
R. v. GROULX. Unreported.

FACTS: The accused, an Indian, killed a moose on the Maniwaki Indian Reserve in Quebec without a licence and out of season, contrary to the Quebec Game Act. HELD: Since the Governor in Council had not legislated as provided in Section 72(a) of the Indian Act and the band had not enacted a by-law as provided in Section 80(o) of the Indian Act, the Quebec Game Act applies. Consequently, the accused was found guilty under the Game Act.   DES/PCT

1602   **QUEBEC SUPERIOR COURT. JUDGE: ARCHAMBAULT.**
1940
DIABO v. RICE. (1942) Que. S.C. 418.

FACTS: In satisfaction of a judgment obtained by 1 Indian against another, immovable property located on a reserve was seized by a sheriff. HELD: Section 23 (now 24 and 29) of the Indian Act prevents land on a reserve from being seized. Land on a reserve is only transferable to an Indian of the same band and such a transfer must be with the consent of the Superintendent General. The seizure and order for sale were both improper.   DES/PCT

1603   **QUEBEC SUPERIOR COURT. JUDGE: BOULANGER.**
1955
JOHN MURDOCK v. LA COMMISSION DES RELATIONS OUVRIERES. (1956) Que. C. S. 30, (1956) R.L. 257.   French.

FACTS: A question arose in certification proceedings of a trade union as bargaining agent for a unit of employees under provincial law whether Indian employees should be considered part of the unit. The provincial labor commission ruled they should not be included. HELD: The provincial legislation made no distinction between Indians and non-Indians. The commission had no right to ignore the Indian salaried employees under the pretext that they were wards of the state. They should properly have been included in the unit.   DES/PCT

1604   **QUEBEC SUPERIOR COURT. JUDGE: BRUNEAU.**
1927
JACOBS v. UNITED POWER COMPANY LIMITED. 65 Que. C. S. 133.   French.

FACTS: Jacobs, an Indian residing on a reserve, sued the defendant company. The Code of Civil Procedure of Quebec required foreigners bringing an action in Quebec to post security for costs. The defendant seeks an order requiring Jacobs to post security for costs. HELD: Indians have the right to commence legal actions and cannot be considered strangers with respect to the law of Quebec. The requirement that foreigners post security does not apply to Canadian Indians.   DES/PCT

1605   **QUEBEC SUPERIOR COURT. JUDGE: DAVIDSON.**
1887
EX PARTE LEFORT. 3 M.L.R. 298.

FACTS: A case dealing with evidence in a charge of selling liquor to an Indian.   DES/PCT

1606   **QUEBEC SUPERIOR COURT. JUDGE: DEMERS.**
1924
PATTON v. HERITIERS. 30 R.L. 300, 15 U.C.R. 392.   French.

FACTS: The plaintiff, an Indian, claimed possession of land on a reserve as his father's heir. The father had sold the land in 1890 but without the consent of the Superintendent-General of Indian Affairs. For that reason the sale was of no effect. The Department of Indian Affairs ruled that the defendant was in rightful possession. HELD: An Indian is not lawful heir to a piece of land on a reserve until he has received title from the Superintendent-General. The plaintiff, not being a party to the sale by the father, cannot challenge that sale. The court cannot interfere with the decision of the Superintendent-General. The plaintiff's claim was dismissed.   DES/PCT

1607   **QUEBEC SUPERIOR COURT. JUDGE: DEMERS.**
1929
CREPIN v. DELORIMIER. 68 Que. C. J. 36.   French.

FACTS: An Indian, resident on a reserve, had a deposit in a bank located off the reserve. Crepin, a judgment creditor, seeks to distain (garnishee) the money contained in the account. HELD: The bank deposit was a debt, an incorporal right, and did not have a situs or location of its own but was located where the person who owned it was located. Therefore the bank deposit was personal property situated on the reserve and exempt from seizure.   DES/PCT

1608   **QUEBEC SUPERIOR COURT. JUDGE: DEMERS.**
1941
DELISLE v. SHAWINIGAN WATER. (1941) 4 D.L.R. 556, 79 Que. S.C. 353.

FACTS: Delisle, an Indian resident on a reserve, purchased electricity from the defendant company. An 8 percent sales tax was imposed on the sales of the company by the Government of Canada and the company accordingly raised its rates to its customers by 8 percent. Delisle claims the rate increase is a tax on personal property on the reserve contrary to the Indian Act. HELD: Indirect taxes levied upon commodities become part of the purchase price to the consumer and are not taxes. The essential characteristic of taxation, that it is an enforced contribution, is not present here as Delisle is not obligated to purchase electricity.   DES/PCT

1609   **QUEBEC SUPERIOR COURT. JUDGE: DEMERS.**
1956
LAZARE v. ST LAWRENCE SEAWAY AUTHORITY. (1957) Que. C.S. 5.   French.

FACTS: The plaintiffs seek a declaration that the lands within their reserve are not subject to expropriation. HELD: The right of the Caughnawaga Indians to their reserve is the same as that of other Canadian Indians, namely a right of occupation and possession. The right of title to the land remains with the Crown. The Indian Act permits reserve land to be expropriated.   DES/PCT

1610   **QUEBEC SUPERIOR COURT. JUDGE: GREENSHIELDS.**
1935
FELDMAN v. JOCKES. 74 Que. S.C. 56.

FACTS: An Indian, living on a reserve, drove his car into a nearby city to have it repaired. While it was in the city it was seized by a judgment creditor. HELD: Under Section 105 of the Indian Act (the predecessor to Section 89(1)), no one can obtain a lien, charge by mortgage, or judgment on real or personal property of an Indian unless the property is subject to taxation. Section 102 (the predecessor to Section 87) provides that no real or personal property of an Indian located on a reserve is subject to be taxed. The fee paid for the registration of the car and for the licence to drive it are not taxes within the meaning of that term in the Indian Act. An automobile of an Indian which is outside the reserve merely for the purpose of some temporary repairs is not personal property held outside the reserve and is not subject to seizure by a judgment creditor.   DES/PCT

1611   **QUEBEC SUPERIOR COURT. JUDGE: LANGELIER.**
1901
BOUCHER v. MONTOUR. 20 Que. C.S. 291.

FACTS: Montour, an Indian, refused to pay Boucher, a non-Indian money owing on the basis that Boucher owed him rental payments on a lease of reserve land. Boucher claims the lease is a nullity as it had not been authorized by the Commissioner for Indian Affairs as required by the Indian Act. HELD: The requirement of authorization by the Commissioner is part of the general intent of the Indian Act to treat Indians as minors with the Commissioner of Indian Affairs as their tutor (guardian). Since the nullity of the lease was a protection for Indians it could only be invoked by Indians.   DES/PCT

1612   **QUEBEC SUPERIOR COURT. JUDGE: MACKINNON.**
1940
PETERSON v. CREE. 79 Que. S.C. 1.

FACTS: Cree, an Indian, was employed off the reserve. A judgment creditor garnisheed his wages. HELD: Cree was domiciled on his reserve but his wages were personal property earned and payable off the reserve and therefore subject to seizure.   DES/PCT

1613   **QUEBEC SUPERIOR COURT. JUDGE: MERCIER.**
1935
DELORIMIER v. DELORIMIER. 74 Que. C. S. 101.   French.

FACTS: The plaintiff, an Indian, obtained a judgment with costs against the defendant, also an Indian. He now seeks to recover the award of costs. HELD: To grant the right to an Indian to sue another in court under Section 106 of the Indian Act (there is no equivalent Section in the present act) and to employ for this purpose lawyers and then to refuse him the means to pay the costs is to misconstrue the intention of the Indian Act. If this were the intention Indians would be deprived of legal services and advice. The purpose of the Act is to protect the Indians.   DES/PCT

1614   **QUEBEC SUPERIOR COURT. JUDGE: MONK.**
1867
CONNOLLY v. WOOLRICH. 11 Lower Canada Jurist 197.

FACTS: Connolly, a non-Indian, married a Cree Indian woman in the Northwest Territories in 1803. A son of the marriage seeks to establish the legal validity of the marriage for succession purposes. HELD: The court examined the nature of civil and religious authority in the Northwest in 1803 and concluded that the marriage was valid.   DES/PCT

1615   **QUEBEC SUPERIOR COURT. JUDGE: TASCHEREAU.**
1891

TIORAHIATA v. TORIWAIERI. 7 M.L.R. 304.   French.

FACTS: Tiorahiata, an Indian, brought an action as tutor (guardian) for a minor to recover damages against another Indian for malicious prosecution. HELD: The appointment of Tiorahiata as tutor was made by a court and not by the Superintendent General
of Indian Affairs, as required by Section 20(8) of the Indian Act (the predecessor to Section 52). The appointment was therefore invalid.   DES/PCT

1616   **SASKATCHEWAN COURT OF APPEAL. JUDGES: CULLITON MAGUIRE
HALL.**
1966
R. v. BALDHEAD. (1966) 4 C.C.C. 183.

FACTS: Baldhead, an Indian, killed his wife while highly intoxicated. He was convicted
of manslaughter and was sentenced to imprisonment for 10 years. He appeals the sentence imposed. HELD: There had been a substantial number of similar convictions
of Indians. Almost without exception liquor had been a dominant factor in the activity.
The sentences imposed have varied from 1 year to 5 years. The sentence here was reduced to 3 years to bring it into reasonable equality with other sentences imposed for
similar offences.   DES/PCT

1617   **SASKATCHEWAN COURT OF APPEAL. JUDGES: CULLITON WOODS
BROWNRIDGE MACGUIRE HALL.**
1966
R. v. JOHNSTON. 56 D.L.R. (2d) 749, 49 C.R. 203.

FACTS: Johnston, an Indian resident on a reserve, was charged for failure to pay a tax
required by the Saskatchewan Hospitalization Act. He argues that he is not liable as the
federal promise to supply a "medicine chest" written into Treaty 6 should be interpreted
to include the supplying of hospitalization. HELD: The obligation to supply a medicine
chest is to have a supply of medicine on the reserve for the use and benefit of the Indians
under the supervision of the agent.   DES/PCT

1618   **SASKATCHEWAN COURT OF APPEAL. JUDGES: GORDON PROCTOR
MCNIVEN CULLITON.**
1953
R. v. STRONGQUILL. (1953) 2 D.L.R. 264, 8 W.W.R. (N.S.) 247, 105 C.C.C. 262, 16
C.R. 194.

FACTS: Strongquill, an Indian, was convicted under the Game Act of Saskatchewan for
hunting a moose during a closed season. He was hunting for food within a forest reserve.
HELD: Non-Indians could hunt in the reserve with a licence. The reserve was land to
which the Indian had a right of access and therefore his right to hunt there for food was
protected by the Natural Resources Transfer Agreement from provincial laws. A section
in the Game Act defining forest reserves as lands to which Indians did not have a right of
access was invalid (a) since it was not a law of general application it did not come within
Section 87 (now 88) of the Indian Act, (b) since it was ineffective because in conflict with
the Saskatchewan Bill of Rights, (c) since it purported to define terms in the Natural Resources Transfer Agreement, something beyond the power of the province.

1619   **SASKATCHEWAN COURT OF APPEAL. JUDGES: TURGEON MARTIN.**
1935
R. v. SMITH. 2 W.W.R. 433, 64 C.C.C. 131, (1935) 3 D.L.R. 703.

FACTS: Smith, an Indian, was charged under the Game Act of Saskatchewan with carrying a firearm on a provincial game preserve. HELD: The treaty only bears on the case to the extent that it may throw some light upon the interpretations of words in the Natural Resources Transfer Agreement, which now governs the relations of Indians with the game laws of Saskatchewan. A provincial game preserve is not unoccupied Crown lands and Indians have only a limited right of access to the preserve. Therefore provincial laws apply. Smith was convicted.   DES/PCT

1620   **SASKATCHEWAN COURT OF APPEAL. JUDGE: CULLITON.**
1971
R. v. SWIMMER. (1971) 1 W.W.R. 756, 17 D.L.R. (3d) 476.

FACTS: Swimmer, an Indian not residing on a reserve, refused to pay Saskatchewan hospitalization and medical care premiums. He argues that he is not liable as the federal promise to supply a "medicine chest" written into Treaty 6 should be interpreted to include the supplying of hospitalization and medical services. HELD: The obligation to supply a medicine chest did not create an obligation to supply medical and hospital services. The Indian Act Section 72(1)(g) (now 73(1)(g)) enables the federal government to make regulations to provide medical treatment and health services for Indians. The federal government pays the hospitalization tax and provides medical care for Indians residing on a reserve and for those residing off a reserve for less than 12 months. These provisions are recognized in regulations under the provincial legislation. The provincial laws apply by Section 87 (now 88) of the Indian Act.   DES/PCT

1621   **SASKATCHEWAN COURT OF KINGS BENCH. JUDGE: BIGELOW.**
1922
KAMSACK v. CANADIAN NORTHERN TOWN PROPERTIES. (1922) 3 W.W.R. 1, 68 D.L.R. 660.

FACTS: A one-half interest in surrendered reserve lands was sold to the defendant's predecessors. The land was to be developed as a townsite. After the defendant's initial advance was recouped, the defendant and the Indians were to share equally in the profits. The Town of Kamsack seeks to tax the land. The defendant maintains that they acted solely as a sales agent and thereby were not owners and were not taxable. HELD: They were owners of the land under provincial legislation and their one-half interest in the land was taxable.   DES/PCT

1622   **SASKATCHEWAN COURT OF KINGS BENCH. JUDGE: MACLEAN.**
1933
PAP-WEE-IN v. BEAUDRY. (1933) 1 W.W.R. 138.

FACTS: The defendants, upon the invitation of a number of Indians and with the consent of the Superintendent-General of Indian Affairs, entered the reserve and erected a church. No permission had been obtained from the band council. HELD: By Section 51 (now Sections 28 and 37) of the Indian Act, no portion of an Indian reserve can be alienated, leased, surrendered, or released to anyone outside the band without the concurrent consent of the band and the Superintendent General. As the defendants did not have the consent of the band they were trespassers. An injuction was granted restraining the defendants from using and occupying the building.   DES/PCT

1623   **SASKATCHEWAN COURT OF KING'S BENCH. JUDGE: BIGELOW.**
1943
R. v. WEBB. 2 W.W.R. 239, 80 C.C.C. 151.

FACTS: A case dealing with evidence and holding that the offence of selling liquor to an Indian is not an absolute liability offence.   DES/PCT

1624   **SASKATCHEWAN COURT OF QUEEN'S BENCH. JUDGE: BROWNRIDER.**
1961
R. v. BENJOE. 34 W.W.R. 463, 130 C.C.C. 238, 35 C.R. 157.

FACTS: The accused, an Indian, had intoxicating liquor in his possession on the Muscowpetung Reserve, Saskatchewan, contrary to Section 96(a) of the Indian Act (now 97(a)). The Accused had taken possession of the liquor when exercising his authority as a Councilor of his tribe, by requiring an Indian youth to give the liquor to him. He did this to prevent the harmful effects that would ensue if the Indian youth consumed the intoxicants. HELD: Section 96(a) (now 97(a)) is not an absolute prohibition against possession of intoxicants on a reserve especially as the Act provides for certain exceptions. Mens rea (wilful intent) is an essential ingredient in any charge under the Section. As the accused was trying to preserve the law on the reserve and did not have any wilful intent in taking possession of the liquor he has not committed an offence under the Act.   DES/PCT

1625   **SASKATCHEWAN DISTRICT COURT (BATTLEFORD). JUDGE: MACLEAN.**
1910
R. v. EDELSTON. 15 W.L.R. 279, 17 C.C.C. 155.

FACTS: A procedural case arising out of a charge of selling liquor to an Indian.   DES/PCT

1626   **SASKATCHEWAN DISTRICT COURT (PRINCE ALBERT). JUDGE: NELSON.**
1968
SCHAURTE v. PAUL. Unreported.

FACTS: Paul, an Indian, was charged with hunting on privately owned land out of season for food, contrary to the Game Act of Saskatchewan. There were no signs posted on the land prohibiting hunting as required by the Act. HELD: There being no signs prohibiting hunting, the land was land to which Paul had "a right of access" even though the owner had not consented to his being on the land. By the Natural Resources Transfer Agreement he could not be convicted under provincial law for such hunting.   DES/PCT

1627   **SASKATCHEWAN DISTRICT COURT. JUDGE: BENDAS.**
1968
R. v. BEAR. 63 W.W.R. 754.

FACTS: Bear, an Indian, was charged with possession of liquor contrary to the Liquor Act of Saskatchewan. He was on the reserve at the time. HELD: The provincial Act prohibits any person having liquor on his possession except in a dwelling house of the land appurtenant to a dwelling house. That would mean, on a reserve, land allotted to the individual Indian. Bear was not on land allotted to him, therefore, had committed the offence and was found guilty.   DES/PCT

1628   **SASKATCHEWAN DISTRICT COURT. JUDGE: FORBES.**
1963
R. v. JOHNS (NO. 2). (1963-64) 45 W.W.R. 65, 41 C.R. 380: APPEALED FROM 41 W.W.R. 385: APPEALED FROM 39 W.W.R. 49: APPEALED FROM 36 W.W.R. 403.

FACTS: Johns, an Indian, was charged under the Vehicles Act of Saskatchewan for driving without a licence on a road on an Indian reserve. HELD: The road was not a public "highway"as defined in the Vehicles Act because it was built and maintained by the Indians and access by the general public could be refused. Even if the road was a public highway Johns could not be convicted for he had a right to use lands over which he was passing.   DES/PCT

1629   **SASKATCHEWAN DISTRICT COURT. JUDGE: HOGARTH.**
1956
RE JOSEPH POITRAS. 20 W.W.R. 545.

FACTS: A protest was lodged challenging the band membership of Joseph Poitras who had resided on the reserve for 36 years. HELD: The absence of proof of proper posting of the band list in compliance with Section 8 of the Indian Act precludes any protest being entertained. Section 9(1)(a) requires the Council of the Band to protest and it is not sufficient, as here, that the Chief and 2 councilors protest. The protest alleged that Joseph Poitras received half-breed scrip, but the registrar upheld the protest on the basis that his father took half-breed scrip. There was no evidence before the court to show that any ancestor of Joseph Poitras took scrip. The registrar erred in basing his decision on grounds not stated in the protest. In the alternative he failed to properly weigh the evidence. Section 12 of the Indian Act was not intended to have retrospective effect. The words "to be registered"in that section should be interpreted to refer only to future registrations, the alternative interpretation causing a gross and intolerable injustice.   DES/PCT

1630   **SASKATCHEWAN DISTRICT COURT. JUDGE: MCLELLAND.**
1971
R. v. WHITEMAN (NO. 1). 2 W.W.R. 316.

FACTS: Whiteman, an Indian, was charged with being drunk on a reserve, contrary to Section 96(b) (now 97(b)) of the Indian Act.   He was in his home at the time. HELD: Section 96(b) does not discriminate on the basis of race in that it applies to Indians or non-Indians. It is therefore not in conflict with the Bill of Rights. The conviction was upheld.   DES/PCT

1631   **SASKATCHEWAN DISTRICT COURT. JUDGE: MAHER.**
1969
R. v. NIPPI. 70 W.W.R. 390.

FACTS: Nippi, an Indian, shot a moose for food within the boundaries of an area designated as a game preserve under the Game Act of Saskatchewan. He was charged with hunting in a game preserve contrary to the Saskatchewan Game Act. HELD: A game preserve is occupied Crown land within the meaning of paragraph 12 of the Natural Resources Transfer Agreement and therefore provincial laws can prohibit Indians hunting in the area.   DES/PCT

1632   **SASKATCHEWAN DISTRICT COURT. JUDGE: MCFADDEN.**
1962
RICHARDS v. COTE. 39 C.R. 204, 40 W.W.R. 340.

FACTS: Cote, an Indian, was charged with being intoxicated off a reserve contrary to Section 94(b) (now 95(b)) of the Indian Act. HELD: Section 94(b) treated Indians differently than non-Indians and was therefore in conflict with the Bill of Rights and of no effect. Alternatively for there to be a conviction it was required that the Indian cause a disturbance, which had not been proven.   DES/PCT

1633   **SASKATCHEWAN DISTRICT COURT. JUDGE: MCLELLAND.**
1970
R. v. WHITEMAN (No. 2). 13 C.R. N.S. 356.

FACTS: Whiteman, an Indian, was convicted under the Liquor Act of Saskatchewan for being intoxicated in a public place. He was off a reserve. He argues that he could only be charged under Section 94(b) of the Indian Act. HELD: The provincial legislation applies to the whole of the province with the exception of Indian reserves and is valid legislation under the province's power to legislate in relation to property and civil rights. It may be open to question whether Parliament has jurisdiction to legislate on a subject matter relating to property and civil rights. However, Section 94(b) of the Indian Act, as held in R. v. Drybones, is inoperative because it is in conflict with the Bill of Rights. Therefore the Liquor Act of Saskatchewan applies to Whiteman and he was properly convicted.   DES/PCT

1634   **SASKATCHEWAN MAGISTRATES COURT (PRINCE ALBERT). JUDGE: ELDER.**
1954
R. v. CONNOLLY. 109 C.C.C. 378.

FACTS: A bartender was charged under the Indian Act for selling liquor to Indians. HELD: The use of the word "knowingly" in Section 93 (now 94) of the Indian Act requires that the person realize he is selling intoxicants to Indians, and this must be proved affirmatively by the prosecution. Where the evidence is as consistent with no knowledge as with knowledge the accused must be acquitted. Furthermore, where the only evidence against the accused is supplied by the Indians as purchasers themselves, it should be accepted with great reservation as they also are guilty of an offence under the Act. For these reasons the charge was dismissed.   DES/PCT

1635   **SASKATCHEWAN MAGISTRATES COURT. JUDGE: BENCE.**
1958
R. v. WATSON. Unreported.

FACTS: Watson, an Indian, was charged under the Fisheries Act, a federal statute, with possession of a snare while fishing for food from a position on a dam. HELD: He was fishing for food on unoccupied Crown lands and is protected by the Natural Resources Transfer Agreement.   DES/PCT

1636   **SASKATCHEWAN POLICE COURT. JUDGE: LUSSIER.**
1942
R. v. MIRASTY. 1 W.W.R. 343.

FACTS: Mirasty, an Indian, was charged under the Fur Act of Saskatchewan for possession of the unprime pelt of a beaver without a permit. He had shot the beaver within a provincial forest preserve. HELD: The Natural Resources Transfer Agreement is now the instrument which governs the relations of the Indians to provincial game laws. The treaty can only have bearing on a case if it throws light upon the interpretation of certain words in the Agreement. The forest preserve is not unoccupied Crown lands and is an area to which the accused's right of access is limited by law. Therefore the provincial law applies to the hunting and the accused was convicted.   DES/PCT

1637   **SASKATCHEWAN SUPREME COURT. JUDGE: LAMONT.**
1911
CARTER v. NICHOL. 1 W.W.R. 392.

FACTS: Carter, a non-Indian farmer, sued Nichol, a non-Indian Indian Agent, for damages to his farm resulting from a prairie fire caused by a threshing machine operating on a reserve under Nichol's control. The thresher did not comply with provisions of the Prairie Fires Ordinance of Saskatchewan. HELD: Nichol was in breach of his duty to comply with the Prairie Fires Ordinance and therefore was liable for damages caused to Carter's farm.   DES/PCT

1638   **SUPREME COURT OF CANADA. JUDGES: CARTWRIGHT FAUTEUX ABBOTT MARTLAND JUDSON RITCHIE HALL**
1966
R. v. GEORGE. 55 D.L.R. (2d) 386, (1966) S.C.R. 267: APPEALED FROM 45 D.L.R. (2d) 706, (1965) 2 C.C.C. 148, (1964) 2 O.R. 429:   Appealed from 41 D.L.R. (2d) 31, (1963) 3 C.C.C. 109, (1964) 1 O.R. 24.

FACTS: George, an Indian, shot 2 ducks on a reserve for food and was charged under the Migratory Birds Convention Act, a federal statute. He argues that a treaty protects his rights to hunt off the reserve. HELD: Section 87 of the Indian Act (now 88) provides that "all laws of general application in a province" apply to Indians subject to any treaty. That section applies to provincial laws only. The Migratory Birds Convention Act is a federal law and applies to Indians irrespective of any treaty.   DES/PCT

1639   **SUPREME COURT OF CANADA. JUDGES: CARTWRIGHT FAUTEUX ABBOTT MARTLAND JUDSON RITCHIE HALL.**
1965
R. v. WHITE AND BOB. 52 D.L.R. (2d) 481: APPEALED FROM 52 W.W.R. (N.S.) 193, 50 D.L.R. (2d) 613.

FACTS: White and Bob, 2 Indians, were charged under the Game Act of British Columbia for hunting deer during a closed season. They were hunting for food on unoccupied

Crown lands and claimed treaty protected hunting rights under a document of 1854. HELD: The document of 1854 was a treaty. Therefore, by Section 87 (now 88) of the Indian Act, the Game Act did not apply to the accused Indians.   DES/PCT

1640   **SUPREME COURT OF CANADA. JUDGES: CARTWRIGHT RITCHIE FAUTEUX MARTLAND JUDSON ABBOTT PIGEON**
1970
R. v. DRYBONES. 71 W.W.R. 161, (1970) 9 D.L.R. (3d) 473, 10 C.R. (2d) 334: APPEALED FROM (1968) 61 W.W.R. 370, (1968) 2 C.C.C. 69: APPEALED FROM (1967) 60 W.W.R. 321.

FACTS: Drybones, an Indian, was charged with being intoxicated off a reserve, contrary to Section 94(b) of the Indian Act (now 95(b)). HELD: The fact that there are no reserves in the Northwest Territories is not a bar to conviction under the section. The section is harsher than the territorial laws on intoxication in that unlike the territorial laws it (a) makes it an offence to be intoxicated in a private place and (b) establishes a minimum fine of $10.00. Therefore the section denies Indians equality before the law by reason of race and is inoperative because it is in conflict with the Canadian Bill of Rights.   DES/PCT

1641   **SUPREME COURT OF CANADA. JUDGES: DUFF CANNON CROCKET DAVIS KERWIN HUDSON.**
1939
IN RE ESKIMOS. (1939) S.C.R. 104, 2 D.L.R 417.

FACTS: The question whether the term "Indians"in Section 91(24) of the British North America Act included Eskimo inhabitants in the province of Quebec was referred to the court for determination. HELD: Documents of the Hudson's Bay Company, a Committee of the Imperial House of Commons, and various colonial administrators referred to the Eskimo as an Indian tribe. For this reason, the term "Indians"in the British North America Act was meant to include Eskimos.   DES/PCT

1642   **SUPREME COURT OF CANADA. JUDGES: FITZPATRICK DAVIES IDINGTON ANGLIN BRODEUR.**
1918
KING v. BONHOMME. 59 S.C.R. 679: APPEALED FROM 16 Ex. C. R. 437, 38 D.L.R. 647.

FACTS: The federal government claimed that the island of St. Nicholas was part of the Caughnawaga Indian Reserve. The Province of Quebec had sold the island to Bonhomme. HELD: The land was not part of the reserve.   DES/PCT

1643   **SUPREME COURT OF CANADA. JUDGES: FITZPATRICK DAVIES IDINGTON MACLENNAN DUFF.**
1907
ARMOUR v. ONONDAGA. 42 S.C.R. 218: APPEALED FORM 14 O.L.R. 606, 9 O.W.R. 833.

A procedural case dealing with the application of a municipal by-law to an Indian reservation.   DES/PCT

1644   **SUPREME COURT OF CANADA. JUDGES: FITZPATRICK IDINGTON DUFF ANGLIN BRODEUR.**
1916
ATTORNEY GENERAL FOR CANADA v. GIROUX. 53 S.C.R. 172, 30 D.L.R. 123.

FACTS: In 1869 the land in question was surrendered to the Crown by an Indian band for sale. In 1878 a portion of the land was sold to an Indian. In 1889 the Indian's land was sold by the sheriff in satisfaction of a debt and was purchased by the defendant. The issue was the validity of the sheriff's sale. If the land was still land reserved for Indians it was not subject to seizure and sale. HELD: The land owned by the Indian was not reserve land. An Indian can acquire title to land as an individual person.   DES/PCT

1645   **SUPREME COURT OF CANADA. JUDGES: IDINGTON DUFF ANGLIN BRODEUR.**
1915
BOOTH v. THE KING. 51 S.C.R. 20: APPEALED FROM 14 Ex. C. R. 115.

FACTS: The Superintendent-General of Indian Affairs granted a timber licence to Booth. The Indian Act provided that no licence could be granted for a longer period than 12 months (such licences are now handled by regulations under Section 57(c)). Regulations under the Indian Act provided that licence holders who had complied with all existing regulations shall be entitled to renewal on application. Booth asserts a right to have the licence renewed. HELD: A licence holder who has complied with the regulations has no absolute right to a renewal.   DES/PCT

1646   **SUPREME COURT OF CANADA. JUDGES: JUDSON FAUTEUX ABBOTT MARTLAND CARTWRIGHT HALL RITCHIE**
1968
R. v. DANIELS. (1968) S.C.R. 517, (1969) 1 C.C.C. 299.

FACTS: Daniels, an Indian, was convicted under the Migratory Birds Convention Act, a federal statute, for possession of 2 wild ducks. He had shot the birds on a reserve for food. HELD: The Natural Resources Transfer Agreement guarantee of Indian hunting rights only limits provincial legislation. The federal government can make laws restricting hunting on reserves. The conviction was upheld.   DES/PCT

1647   **SUPREME COURT OF CANADA. JUDGES: KERWIN TASCHEREAU RAND ESTEY LOCKE.**
1950
ST ANN'S ISLAND SHOOTING AND FISHING CLUB v. THE KING. (1950) S.C.R. 211, (1950) 2 D.L.R. 225.

FACTS: The Club leased reserve land. Although the original lease had been entered into by the Superintendent General of Indian Affairs persuant to the decision of an order in council, subsequent renewals of the lease were not made persuant to any order in council. HELD: The Indian Act required action of the Governor in Council before any lease could be made. The current lease was held to be invalid.   DES/PCT

1648   **SUPREME COURT OF CANADA. JUDGES: KERWIN TASCHEREAU RAND KELLOCK CARTWRIGHT.**
1956

R. v. FRANCIS. (1956) S.C.R. 618, 3 D.L.R. (2d) 641.

FACTS: Francis, an Indian, imported certain appliances from the United States to his home on the St. Regis Indian Reserve without clearing the goods with Canadian Customs officials. He claims he is exempt from any duty or tax by virtue of the Jay Treaty of 1794. HELD: The Jay Treaty has not been implemented by legislation in Canada. Implementing legislation is necessary before a treaty alters the law applying within Canada. The Jay Treaty was not a peace treaty (which could be self-implementing) and was terminated by the War of 1812 (since war ends the terms in any treaty which are not permanent in nature).   DES/PCT

1649   **SUPREME COURT OF CANADA. JUDGES: RITCHIE STRONG HENRY TASCHEREAU FOURNIER GWYNNE.**
1886
JONES v. FRASER. 12 Q.L.R. 327.

FACTS: Fraser, a non-Indian, lived with the Indian woman in the Northwest Territories by whom he had children. Later he returned to Quebec and began to live with a non-Indian woman, by whom he had children. HELD: The lower court ruled on the validity of the marriage to the Indian woman. Evidence of long cohabitation of a non-Indian and an Indian woman where the woman has never received the title of wife is not sufficient to establish a valid marriage. The question of the validity of the marriage was not dealt with by the Supreme Court of Canada.   DES/PCT

1650   **SUPREME COURT OF CANADA. JUDGES: STRONG TASCHEREAU SEDGEWICK KING GIROUARD.**
1898
PROVINCE OF QUEBEC v. DOMINION OF CANADA: IN RE INDIAN CLAIMS 30 S.C.R. 151.

FACTS: As a result of the decision of the Judicial Committee of the Privy Council in 1897 (Attorney General for Canada v. Attorney General for Ontario) the federal government was responsible for the annuities for the Robinson treaties. Arbitrators determined that under the Britsh North America Act the amounts were owing conjointly by Quebec and Ontario. HELD: The determination of the arbitrators was upheld.   DES/PCT

1651   **SUPREME COURT OF CANADA. JUDGES: TASCHEREAU CARTWRIGHT FAUTEUX ABBOTT MARTLAND JUDSON RITCHIE HALL SPENCE.**
1963
R. v. PRINCE AND MYRON. (1964) S.C.R. 81, 46 W.W.R. (N.S.) 121, (1964) 3 C.C.C. 2, 41 C.R. 403: APPEALED FROM (1963) 1 C.C.C. 129, 39 C.R. 43.

FACTS: Prince and Myron, 2 Indians, were charged under the Game and Fisheries Act of Manitoba with hunting deer by means of a night light. They were hunting for food off a reserve on land that was cultivated. There were no signs prohibiting hunting on the land. HELD: The Natural Resources Transfer Agreement means that Indians hunting for food are not subject to provincial laws. They were hunting on lands to which they had a right of access. They were acquitted.   DES/PCT

1652   **SUPREME COURT OF CANADA. JUDGES: TASCHEREAU CARTWRIGHT FAUTEUX ABBOTT MARTLAND JUDSON RITCHIE HALL SPENCE.**
1966
R. v. SIGEAREAK E1-53. 56 W.W.R. 478, (1966) 4 C.C.C. 393, (1966) 57 D.L.R. (2d) 536, 49 C.R. 271, (1966) S.C.R. 645: APPEALED FROM (1966) 55 W.W.R. 1, 55 D.L.R. (2d) 29.

FACTS: Sigeareak, an Eskimo, was charged under the Game Ordinance of the Northwest Territories for killing and abandoning game. HELD: The Royal Proclamation of 1753 does not apply to territory granted to the Hudson's Bay Company and therefore does not apply to the area here in question. The Game Ordinance applies to Eskimos. The cases R. v. Kallooar and R. v. Kogogolak are overruled. The accused is convicted.   PCT

1653   **SUPREME COURT OF CANADA. JUDGES: TASCHEREAU CARTWRIGHT FAUTEUX ABBOTT MARTLAND RITCHIE HALL**
1964
R. v. SIKYEA. (1964) S.C.R. 642, 50 D.L.R. (2d) 80, 49 W.W.R. (N.S.) 306, 44 C.R. 266: APPEALED FROM 43 D.L.R. (2d) 150, 46 W.W.R. (N.S.) 65, 43 C.R. 83: APPEALED FROM 40 W.W.R. (N.S.) 494.

FACTS: Sikyea, an Indian, was convicted under the Migratory Birds Convention Act, a federal statute, for shooting a duck. He was hunting for food in an area covered by Treaty 11. HELD: The judgment of Johnson, J.A. in the Northwest Territories Court of Appeal was approved. The Hudson's Bay Company lands were excluded from the Royal Proclamation of 1753. Sikyea's treaty protected hunting rights had been taken away in relation to ducks, apparently inadvertently, by the federal government's enactment of the Migratory Birds Convention Act. That Act was within the legislative competence of the federal government. Sikyea was convicted.   DES/PCT

1654   **SUPREME COURT OF CANADA. JUDGES: TASCHEREAU MARTLAND JUDSON HALL CARTWRIGHT.**
1965
R. v. DEVEREAUX. (1965) S.C.R. 567, 51 D.L.R. (2d) 546.

FACTS: Devereaux, a non-Indian, was in possession of land on a reserve. He had held a lease from the Crown (void by Section 28(1) of the Indian Act) and 2 subsequent permits under Section 28(2) of the Indian Act. He sought to remain in possession as a divisee of the land under the will of an Indian who had held the land. The Exchequer Court held that as the right to possession of the farm was held by a particular band member, the band did not have an interest in the land which permitted it to exclude a person from possession, even if that possession was wrongful. HELD: Devereaux had no right to possession of the land and was ordered to give up possession to the band.   DES/PCT

1655   **SUPREME COURT OF CANADA. JUDGE: KERWIN TASCHEREAU RAND KELLOCK LOCKE.**
1950
MILLER v. THE KING. (1950) 1 D.L.R. 513: APPEALED FROM (1948) Ex. C.R. 372.

FACTS: This was an action against the Crown on behalf of the Six Nations Indian Reserve seeking compensation for 3 separate matters: (1) flooding of 1,800 acres of land on the reserve in 1824 as a result of government works relating to the Welland Canal, (2)

the taking without compensation of 368 acres by Upper Canada in 1836 for the Grand River Navigation Company, and (3) the use of band funds by the government for the purchase of shares in the Grand River Navigation Company. HELD: Claims against the federal government on matters arising before the Act of Union of 1840 cannot be sustained. Section 111 of the British North America Act made the federal government responsible for the debts and liabilities of each province but it is not suggested that the Act of Union of 1840 made the Province of Canada liable for the liabilities of the Province of Upper Canada. Therefore the 1st 2 claims fail. The 3rd claim, alleging breaches of trust obligations on the part of the Government of Canada after 1840 discloses a possible claim and is referred back to the Exchequer Court.   DES/PCT

1656   **SUPREME COURT OF CANADA. JUDGE: NEWCOMBE.**
1931
EASTERBROOK v. THE KING. (1931) S.C.R. 210, (1931) 1 D.L.R. 628.

FACTS: In 1821, a band leased 200 acres of reserve land to a non-Indian for a period of 99 years, renewable to a total term of 999 years. The lease was never approved by the Indian Department of Upper Canada. In 1920 the Indians, through the Crown, refused to renew the lease. HELD: By the Royal Proclamation of 1763 colonialists were prohibited from negotiating leases or purchasing Indian land from Indians. The lease was void.   DES/PCT

1657   **YUKON POLICE MAGISTRATES COURT. JUDGE: TRAINOR.**
1966
R. v. CARLICK. 3 C.C.C. 323, 47 C.R. 302.

FACTS: Carlick, an Indian, was charged with being intoxicated off a reserve contrary to Section 94(b) (now 95(b)) of the Indian Act. The question arose whether he should have been charged under the Liquor Ordinance of the Yukon Territory. HELD: Section 87 (now 88) of the Indian Act provides that all laws of general application in a province apply to Indians except to the extent inconsistent with the Indian Act. The Liquor Ordinance is a law of general application but does not apply to Indians because the Indian Act deals with the offence of public intoxication. The fact that there are no reserves in the Yukon Territory does not affect Section 94(b) (now 95(b)) of the Indian Act. (Note: In R. v. George the Supreme Court of Canada held that Section 88 did not refer to federal law. Here the territorial ordinance is being considered a provincial law not a federal law).   DES/PCT

1658   **YUKON TERRITORY COURT OF APPEAL. JUDGE: MCFARLANE.**
1966
R. v. PETERS. 57 W.W.R. 727, (1967) 2 C.C.C. 19, 50 C.R. 68.

FACTS: Peters, an Indian, was charged with drinking under age contrary to the Liquor Ordinance of the Yukon Territory. HELD: Since the Indian Act has clearly made provision for the use and possession of liquor by Indians, Section 87 (now 88) of the Indian Act does not make the provision of the Yukon Territorial Ordinance apply to Indians.   DES/PCT

1659   **YUKON TERRITORY TERRITORIAL COURT. JUDGE: MORROW.**
1969

R. v. SMITH. 71 W.W.R. 66, (1970) 10 D.L.R. (3d) 759, (1970) 3 C.C.C. 83, 9 C.R. (2d) 117.

FACTS: Smith, an Indian, was convicted under the Game Ordinance of the Yukon Territory for shooting a moose in a game sanctuary. He was hunting for food within the traditional hunting grounds of his band. The Yukon Act provides that the Territorial Council cannot prohibit Indians or Eskimos hunting for food on unoccupied Crown lands. HELD: The prohibition of hunting in a game sanctuary nullifies the protection of Indian and Eskimo rights to hunt on unoccupied Crown lands and is beyond the power of the Territorial council. Conviction was set aside.   DES/PCT

SUB-ARCTIC

1660   **ALBRECHT   EARL C**
1965
OBSERVATIONS ON ARCTIC AND SUBARCTIC HEALTH. Arctic 18:151-157.

Health hazards resulting from waste disposal and sewage problems characteristic of extensive permafrost regions in the Arctic and Sub-Arctic of Canada and Alaska are considred. Data on serious diseases, such as tuberculosis, affecting Indian and Eskimo populations are presented. Remedial programs of the past and future are outlined.   WRC

1661   **ALLEN   VICTOR**
1967
THE ESKIMO AND THE INDIAN TODAY. In Proceedings: Fourth National Northern Development Conference: Theme: Man and the North.   Sponsored jointly by Alberta and Northwest Chamber of Mines and Resources and Edmonton Chamber of Commerce. Edmonton: National Northern Development Conference. pp. 41-45.

The position of the Indian and Eskimo in Canadian society today is discussed. Education is seen by the native community as a necessary requirement in adjusting to rapid cultural change, provided it is not introduced at the expense of traditional language and customs. Of major concern is the job situation in the North. Many Eskimos and Indians who have the experience but not the requisite education should have the opportunity to exchange experience for grades. Trappers are also in need of assistance in the form of northern allowances and short term loans.   DGW

1662   **ANDERSON   J W**
1961
FUR TRADER'S STORY. Toronto: Ryerson Press. 245 pp.

A Hudson's Bay Company trader's experiences from 1910-1947 in posts of the James Bay area are recounted. Incidents and difficulties encountered by the fur traders reveal their impressions of the Indians and the hardships of life in the northern habitat. Included are Indian survival techniques adopted by the traders as well as general descriptions of Indian clothing, dwellings, diet, hygiene, and family hunting territory.   CCV

1663   **AVERKIEVA   IU P**
1962
THE PROBLEM OF PROPERTY IN CONTEMPORARY AMERICAN ETHNOGRAPHY. Soviet Anthropology and Archaeology 1(1):50-63.

Analyzing works of scholars who have studied hunters and gatherers, mainly the Algonkian and Athabaskans of northern Canada, it is concluded that the concept of private ownership of hunting territories arises only as they undergo transition from a subsistence economy (hunting collectively) to a trapping economy.   IVY

1664   **BAERGEN   WILLIAM PETER**
1967
THE FUR TRADE AT LESSER SLAVE LAKE, 1815-1831. M.A. Thesis. Department of History. University of Alberta. 209 pp.

The competition for furs, the use of liquor in trade, the society composed of Indians, freemen, and traders at Lesser Slave Lake, and the significance of the trade in this area for Hudson's Bay Company operations are examined. Liquor is not considered to have been the chief article of trade. The extent of its use and the results, as well as the life style at Fort Waterloo and the relationship between Indians and traders are discussed in Chapters 3 and 5.   CCV

1665   **BAKER   W B**
n.d.
SOME OBSERVATIONS ON THE APPLICATION OF COMMUNITY DEVELOPMENT TO THE SETTLEMENTS OF NORTHERN SASKATCHEWAN. Unpublished paper. Available from National Library of Canada. 14 pp.

Each of 6 urban-industrial features are examined: (1) a permanent residence pattern, (2) material accomplishment as a central value, (3) an expandable community base, (4) effective informal organization, (5) effective formal organization, and (6) adaptive social control. Restraining and facilitating factors of Metis/Indian culture to the direction of the urban-industrial features are analyzed. The interdependence of these factors are then evaluated from a community development viewpoint. Planned change involving a deliberate effort to generate forces which will contribute to minimal disruption by acculturative processes is emphasized. Sources of information for this study include the studies of V. F. Valentine, visits to 14 of Saskatchewan's northern settlements, and observation of India's national program of community development.   IVY

1666   **BEAN   RAYMOND E**
1966
AN EXPLORATORY COMPARISON OF INDIAN AND NON-INDIAN SECONDARY SCHOOL STUDENTS' ATTITUDES. M.Ed. Thesis. Department of Education Administration. University of Alberta. 171 pp.

From May 10 until May 13, 1964, 329 non-Indian and 127 Indian students from schools in the Sault Ste. Marie area were administered questionnaires to determine differences in attitude. Significant group differences were revealed in various areas. Indian students were found to hold conflicting attitudes. While shown to be more family-, collectively-, and present-oriented, Indians were also willing to work hard and showed concern for the future, suggesting acquisition of new attitudes through education.   CCV

1667   **BERRY   J W**
1970
PSYCHOLOGICAL RESEARCH IN THE NORTH. Unpublished paper. Available from National Library of Canada. 22 pp.

This paper is a summary of the psychological work that has been done in the North by psychologists, psychiatrists, and psychologically oriented anthropologists.   HCV

1668   **BISHOP   CHARLES A**
1969
DEMOGRAPHY,ECOLOGY AND TRADE IN NORTHERN ONTARIO DURING THE 19TH CENTURY. Unpublished paper delivered to 68th Annual Meeting, American Anthropological Association. New Orleans, LA, November 20-23, 1969. Available from National Library of Canada. 10 pp.

The primary source of information for this study was the Hudson's Bay Archives. Focusing upon microhistorical and microecological changes for the James Bay Cree and northern Ojibwa of Ontario during the 18th and 19th centuries, it is demonstrated that a functional relationship existed between subsistence persuits, population density, hunting group size and area exploited, property concepts, and dependence on the trading post.   IVY

1669   **BLACK   W A**
1961
FUR TRAPPING IN THE MACKENZIE RIVER DELTA. Department of Mines and Technical Surveys Geographic Bulletin 16:62-85.

Growth of fur trapping in the Mackenzie Delta from 1840 is outlined. Mink and muskrat, the 2 major fur-bearing animals trapped in the Delta, and the methods of grading and marketing these furs are discussed in detail. Eleven tables of statistics are incorporated in the text. While fur trapping has been declining in importance since 1952, it is felt that the establishment of a sound, stable economy is feasible and necessary for the local populations. Needs which must be recognized however are (1) rehabilitation of trapping areas, (2) renewed production of high quality pelts, (3) adequate utilization of subsistence resources, and (4) development of local specialties.   IVY

1670   **BOEK   WALTER E,   BOEK   JEAN K**
1960
A REPORT OF FIELDWORK IN AKLAVIK AND INUVIK, N.W.T. Unpublished report for Northern Co-ordination and Research Centre, Department of Northern Affairs and National Resources. Available at Northern Science Research Group, Department of Indian Affairs and Northern Development, Ottawa. 174 pp.

Results of study and fieldwork in Aklavik and Inuvik during the summer of 1959 are reported. The establishment and organization of Aklavik, the background for the decision to move the settlement to Inuvik, and the lay-out of the new town are reviewed. The native and White populations are discussed in terms of subsistence activities, life style, dwellings, and employment. The advantages and disadvantages of the move to Inuvik and its implications for the population are considered.   CCV

1671   **BONNEAU   L**
1969
ALCOHOLICS ANONYMOUS AND THE COMMUNITY DEVELOPMENT APPROACH TO SOCIAL CHANGE. Unpublished paper delivered to 11th Annual Conference, Western Association of Sociology and Anthropology. Banff, Alta.,

December, 1969. Available from Indian and Northern Curriculum Resources Centre, University of Saskatchewan. 22 pp.

By combining the program of Alcoholics Anonymous with the community development approach, social change was accomplished in the Indian and Metis settlement of Sandy Bay, Saskatchewan.   IVY

1672   **BOOTH   W G**
1965
THE CENTRALIZED SCHOOL. In Education North of 60: A Report Prepared by Members of the Canadian Association of School Superintendents and Inspectors in the Department of Northern Affairs and National Resources. B. Thorsteinsson, ed. The Canadian Superintendent 1964. Toronto: Ryerson Press. pp. 96-103.

To provide the best possible education for Indian and Eskimo children in sparsely settled areas, centralized schools, operated in conjunction with pupil residences, furnish the best solution. The establishment and operation of pupil residences at Inuvik, Fort McPherson, Fort Simpson, Yellowknife, and Fort Smith and the transportation of pupils to and from the hostels are discussed.   IVY

1673   **BURNFORD   SHEILA**
1969
WITHOUT RESERVE. London: Hodder and Stoughton. 252 pp.

Impressions of encounters with northwestern Ontario Ojibwa and Cree Indians, particularly the Lake Nipigon rice harvesting tribes and those from Sandy Lake, Big Trout, and Fort Severn are recounted. Some observations of living conditions, medical services, and attitudes found in these isolated Indian communities in the 1950's and 1960's are included.   CCV

1674   **BUTLER   G C**
1965
INCIDENCE OF SUICIDE AMONG THE ETHNIC GROUPS OF THE NORTHWEST TERRITORIES AND YUKON TERRITORY. Medical Services Journal Canada 21:252-256.

Incidence of suicide among Indians, Eskimos, and Whites of the Yukon and Northwest Territories for 1959-1964 is investigated. Data obtained from the Royal Canadian Mounted Police, "G" Division, was checked with the record of the Registrar of Deaths, Northwest Territories. Compared are ethnicity, sex, age, and method in both suicides and attempted suicides. Over the period 1959-1964, suicide rates in both the territories are higher than the avacrage Canadian rate.   IVY

1675   **CANADA. Department of Citizenship and Immigration. Indian Affairs Branch.**
1965
INDIANS OF THE YUKON AND THE NORTHWEST TERRITORIES. Ottawa: Department of Citizenship and Immigration. 29 pp.

An introduction to the Indians living in the Yukon and the Northwest Territories was prepared. Discussed are the Chipewyan, Yellowknife, Slave, Dogrib, Hare, Nahane, and Kutchin cultures. Also included are their prehistory, the explorers and traders, and the history of the region. Accounts of the activities of missions, and description of the contemporary scene and population conclude the work.   JSL

1676   **CANADA. Department of Indian Affairs and Northern Development. Education Branch. Employment and Related Services Division.**
1970
AN EVALUATION STUDY OF A PILOT RELOCATION PROJECT FOR INDIANS AT ELLIOT LAKE ONTARIO. Ottawa: Department of Indian Affairs and   Northern Development. 37 pp.

The Elliot Lake pilot relocation project for Cree and Ojibwa Indians is evaluated and recommendations are made for future projects. Described are the criteria for selection of families from Trout Lake, Sandy Lake, Deer Lake, and Pikangikum. The government departments and their roles in the project, the 21 participating families, the programs and assistance offered, difficulties encountered, and cultural implications of relocation are provided.   CCV

1677   **CANADA. Department of Indian Affairs and Northern Development. Indian Affairs Branch.**
1967
INDIANS OF YUKON AND NORTHWEST TERRITORIES. Ottawa: Queen's Printer. 20 pp.

A minor revision of the 1965 edition.   JSL

1678   **CANADA. Department of Indian Affairs and Northern Development. Indian Affairs Branch.**
1967
THE NORTHWEST TERRITORIES CANADA. Ottawa: Department of Indian Affairs and Northern Development. 17 pp.

A brief description of government administration in the Northwest Territories is presented including resource development, fishing, trapping, co-operatives, tourism, transportation, communication, education, housing, welfare, and health services.   CCV

1679   **CANADA. Department of Indian Affairs and Northern Development. Mackenzie Delta Task Force.**
1970
REPORT OF THE MACKENZIE DELTA TASK FORCE. PART 2. Ottawa: Department of Indian Affairs and Northern Development. 88 pp.

A task force investigating environmental problems associated with resource development operations in the Mackenzie Delta Region submits its observations and recommendations. Brief summaries of encounters with native groups are included with allegations of detrimental effects on hunting, trapping, and fishing activities.   CCV

1680   **CANADA. Department of Indian Affairs and Northern Development. Northern Administration Branch. Education Division. Economic Staff Group of the Resource and Economic Development Group.**
1968
A BRIEF ANALYSIS OF THE HUMAN AND ECONOMIC RESOURCES OF THE

GREAT SLAVE LAKE AREA NORTHWEST TERRITORIES. Unpublished paper. Available from Resource and Economic Development Group, Department of Indian Affairs and Northern Development, Ottawa. 20 pp.

Data derived from a 1967 Department of Indian Affairs and Northern Development and Dominion Bureau of Statistics manpower test survey and other economic studies are utilized in this analysis of the economic and human potential of the Great Slave Lake area. Limited employment prospects for indigenous people in the North are indicated in a review of income, employment, education, training, job experience, mobility, and health. Industries in which expansion is possible are listed.   CCV

1681   **CANADA. Department of Indian Affairs and Northern Development. Northern Economic Development Branch.**
1969
NORTH OF SIXTY PROSPECTUS: A PROSPECTUS FOR RESOURCE AND ECONOMIC DEVELOPMENT IN THE YUKON AND THE NORTHWEST TERRITORIES. Ottawa: Department of Indian Affairs and Northern Development. 360 pp.   Also in French.

Data on incentive programs, oil and gas, mines and minerals, water, forestry, land, tourism and recreation, and transportation are included in this prospectus of economic and resource development north of the 60th parallel. Information on northern peoples, education and employment, housing, social problems, background history, population characteristics, and labour force are provided.   CCV

1682   **CANADA. Department of Northern Affairs and National Resources. Northern Administration Branch. Industrial Division.**
1961
THE SQUATTERS OF WHITEHORSE YUKON TERRITORIES. A.E.S.R. No. 60/1. Ottawa: Department of Northern Affairs and National Resources. 82 pp.

The results of fieldwork in Whitehorse in November, 1960 are reported in this study of squatters. Dwelling units, availability of land, and services in particular areas of Whitehorse are described. A breakdown by ethnic origin, income, family makeup, and employment is contained in the discussion of squatters as a social group. It was found that 11.8 percent of the squatter household heads were Indians of Indian or White status, and 21.2 percent of households had at least 1 person of Indian ancestry.   CCV

1683   **CARRIERE   GASTON**
1957-1961
HISTOIRE DOCUMENTAIRE DE LA CONGREGATION DES MISSIONAIRES OBLATS DE MARIE-IMMACULEE DANS L'EST DU CANADA (1ere PARTIE): DE L'ARRIVEE AU CANADA A LA MORT DU FONDATEUR (1841-1861). Ottawa: Editions de l'Universite d'Ottawa. 3 vols.

The development of Oblate missionary services in Canada is reviewed in detail. Volume 1 is devoted to a summary of the historic context of the Oblates, their beginnings in Canada, and initial works in Ottawa and the Montreal area. The review of works in Ottawa and at Bytown College is continued in Volume 2. Efforts are extended to the Ottawa Valley, the lumber camps, and to the Quebec Diocese and the Saguenay. In Volume 3 continuing works in the Saguenay and areas north of Montreal are described. Beginning with Chapter 22 discussion is focused on the Indian and Eskimo missions providing a detailed account of their establishment, particular circumstances, and problems, development, and success. Occasional references to Indians occur throughout Volume 2 and in the early chapters of Volume 3.   CCV

1684   **CAVERHILL   WILMA**
1969
NEW HOUSING FOR NORTHERN INDIANS. North 16(6):8-12.

The Northern Rental Program, a federal housing project, is designed to provide Northern Indians and Eskimos with suitable low-cost housing. The project covers the Great Slave Lake region, the Eastern Arctic, and the Mackenzie District.   ADG

1685   **CHRISTIAN   JOHN D**
1967
NORTHERN MANPOWER NEEDS: BRAWN AND BRAINS. In Proceedings: Fourth National Northern Development Conference. Theme: Man and the North. Sponsored jointly by Alberta and Northwest Chamber of Mines and Resources and Edmonton Chamber of Commerce. Edmonton: National Northern Development Conference. pp. 57-61.

The North is not attracting skilled laborers in the numbers and types that are required. Proposed is an extensive on the job training program in which men interested in self-improvement would be able to work their way up to better positions as they become more qualified. Experience with less integrated Indians has shown their inability to stay on the job. In time however, trained Eskimos and Indians who have become acculturated to the rigid discipline of shift work on the production line, will prove to be a valuable asset to northern industry.   DGW

1686   **CLARKE   GEORGE FREDERICK**
1968
SOMEONE BEFORE US: OUR MARITIME INDIANS. Fredericton: Brunswick Press. 240 pp.

Archaeological discoveries and material culture of the Micmac and Malecite of New Brunswick are described. Confirmations and repudiations of certain early historical sources are made through comparisons with this evidence. Indian rights, and attitudes towards Indians in New Brunswick are discussed briefly in the last chapter. Another chapter is devoted to the construction of birchbark canoes. Excerpts from the journals of Nicholas Denys and Marc Lescarbot are commented on in the appendix.   CCV

1687   **COHEN   RONALD**
1962
AN ANTHROPOLOGICAL SURVEY OF COMMUNITIES IN THE MACKENZIE-SLAVE LAKE REGION OF CANADA. Department of Northern Affairs and National Resources, Northern Co-ordination and Research Centre Reports No. NCRC-62-3. Ottawa: Department of Northern Affairs and National Resources. 119 pp.

Observations recorded during visits to Fort Providence, Fort Simpson, Fort Norman, Fort Good Hope, Fort McPherson, and the urban centers of Yellowknife, Hay River, Aklavik, and Inuvik from June 15 through September, 1960, are reported. An overview of natural setting, population and settlement pattern, economy, social organization, and acculturation is provided for each center. Analysis and comparison, based on these data, include interaction patterns, social mobility, community organization, and White and non-White intermediaries.   CCV

1688   **COHEN   RONALD**
1963
THREE ARCTIC TOWNS. Unpublished report for Northern Co-ordination and Research Centre, Department of Northern Affairs and National Resources. Available at Northern Science Research Group, Department of Indian Affairs and Northern Development, Ottawa. 63 pp.

A comparative study of Snowdrift, Fort Good Hope, and Fort McPherson, Northwest Territories is produced from secondary analysis. The historical development of these communities is reviewed briefly. The contemporary life style of the Chipewyan, Hare, and Kutchin is discussed in relation to the regional resource potential and government policy. Community development proposals are included.   CCV

1689   **COHEN   RONALD**
1966
MODERNISM AND THE HINTERLAND: THE CANADIAN EXAMPLE.
International Journal of Comparative Sociology 7:52-75.

The history of the Mackenzie Slave Lake Region and its aboriginal culture is summarized. Attitudes and policies of the industrial society to its hinterland area are briefly discussed. The examination of 3 towns, Snowdrift, Fort Good Hope, and Fort McPherson, which vary in size and degree of modernization, provides a basis for uncovering variations and constancies that result from socio-economic change.   IVY

1690   **COLBORNE   G L**
1965
REPORT ON TRIP TO THOMPSON MANITOBA TO INVESTIGATE INDIAN AND METIS IN THE MINING INDUSTRY, FEBRUARY 9, 1965 TO FEBRUARY 12, 1965. Unpublished paper. Available from Center for Settlement Studies, University of Manitoba. 9 pp.

The background of the Thompson mine, mill, and smelter as well as the community is presented. A decline in the number of casual jobs reduced the number of Indian workmen employed. This led the Indians to picket in 1963. The Placement Program in Thompson with federal aid assists Indian and Metis families to relocate emphasizing the placement of Indians from Nelson House. Candidates were selected to ensure success both with the employer and the community. Observation in 1965 of 19 relocated families indicates integration within the community without apparent conflict.   IVY

1691   **COLPRON   LUCETTE**
1967
FORT ALBANY. In Problemes Nordiques des Facades de la Baie James: Recueil de Documents Rediges en Collaboration a la Suite d'une Rencontre de Nordistes a Moosonee en Ontario. Centre d'Etudes Nordiques Travaux Divers 18. Quebec: Centre d'Etudes Nordiques, Universite Laval. pp. 104-111.

This is a brief presentation of aboriginal life at Fort Albany. The author explains the little change in the community as a product of inadequate federal assistance. Suggestions are made to build a road, to direct a better distribution of subsidies, and to consider the family and the maternal language of children in educational programs.　DD

1692　**COTE　E A**
1967
REMARKS BY MR. E. A. COTE: DEPUTY MINISTER OF INDIAN AFFAIRS AND NORTHERN DEVELOPMENT AT THE FOURTH NATIONAL NORTHERN DEVELOPMENT CONFERENCE, ON PANEL 2. In Proceedings: Fourth National Northern Development Conference: Theme: Man and the North. Sponsored jointly by Alberta and Northwest Chamber of Mines and Resources and Edmonton Chamber of Commerce. Edmonton: National Northern Development Conference. pp. 71-73.

Discussed is the potential for indigenous peoples filling qualified and trained positions in the Sub-Arctic. In the Yukon, the Indian people constitute 16 percent of the population, whereas in the Northwest Territories they constitute 60 percent of the population. Since most of the people are underemployed and undertrained, more adult education is needed. The objective of the government is to have 75 percent of the government and crown agency jobs filled by native people in 1977. Government apprenticeship programs are now underway as are programs in occupational up-grading and vocational training. The crucial question, however, seems to be one of job placement. The Indian and Eskimo workers and their families must feel socially accepted and secure in positions into which they are placed.　DGW

1693　**COX　BRUCE**
n.d.
LAND RIGHTS OF THE SLAVEY INDIANS AT HAY RIVER, N.W.T. Unpublished paper. Available from National Library of Canada. 9 pp.

Provisions of Treaties 8 and 11 for the Athabaskan people of the Mackenzie River Basin are discussed. The practical consequences of the unfulfilled treaty provisions are considered for Mackenzie peoples, especially the Slavey Indians of the lower Hay River and the southern shore of the Great Slave Lake.　HCV

1694　**CRUIKSHANK　JULIA MARGARET**
1969
THE ROLE OF NORTHERN CANADIAN INDIAN WOMEN IN SOCIAL CHANGE. M.A. Thesis. Department of Anthropology and Sociology. University of British Columbia. 139 pp. Available from Library, Department of Indian Affairs and Northern Development, Ottawa.

The effects of changing life styles of Canadian Indian women, particularly in northern communities, is considered with attention to the changing opportunities available to women, limitations on their choices, and adaptations to cultural stress. Supporting data are derived from research conducted from October 1967 to September 1968 including 9 weeks spent in the Yukon. The traditional role of women in several Canadian Indian societies and some current attitudes expressed by Indian women are reviewed briefly. More extensive discussion on the difficulties specific to the northern milieu is included.　CCV

1695   **CZUBOKA   MICHAEL PETER**
1960
ST. PETER'S: A HISTORICAL STUDY WITH ANTHROPOLOGICAL
OBSERVATIONS ON THE CHRISTIAN ABORIGINES OF RED RIVER (1811-
1876). M.A. Thesis. Department of History. University of Manitoba. 144 pp.

The history of the Christian Indians of the Red River area is traced from the establishment of the Red River Colony in 1811 through to 1876 when formal division of the St.
Peter's reserve between the Saulteaux and the Cree marked the end of Canada's first primarily Indian settlement. Cree-Saulteaux conflict, Anglican missionary efforts to educate
and make the Indians self-sufficient through agriculture, resistance to these efforts offered by the Hudson's Bay Company and the Indians themselves, and the political
manoeuvers involved in obtaining control over Indian lands are discussed.   CCV

1696   **D W CARR AND ASSOCIATES**
1968
THE YUKON ECONOMY: ITS POTENTIAL FOR GROWTH AND
CONTINUITY. Ottawa: Queen's Printer. 8 vols.

A report of the potential growth and viability of the Yukon economy contains some specific references to the native population.   Volume I contains the final report. Remaining
volumes pertain to more specific topics: statistical data, a model simulation of the Yukon
economy, social services and resource industries, minerals, hydro-electric power, transportation, and forest resources.   JSL

1697   **DAVIES   K G, ed.**
1963
NORTHERN QUEBEC AND LABRADOR JOURNALS AND
CORRESPONDENCE, 1819-35. London: Hudson's Bay Record Society. 383 pp.

The Hudson's Bay Company's early 19th century attempts to establish and develop trade
from Hudson's Bay to Labrador are described from the employees' letters, records, accounts, and journals of the Company's archives. References to Indians are frequent but
limited to mentions of survival techniques, guiding, hunting, fishing, and trading activities.   CCV

1698   **DENTON   TREVOR**
1970
THE PRESENTATION OF SELF IN HOUSEHOLD SETTINGS. Anthropologica
12:221-240.

Ten months' fieldwork at a Canadian Indian reserve forms the basis for a dramaturgical
approach to social relations within the setting of a house. With emphasis on architectural
design, the preparation of, access to, and appropriate behavior for the setting are considered in relation to the presentation of the self.   WRC

1699   **DEVITT   W G**
1965
HISTORY OF EDUCATION IN THE NORTHWEST TERRITORIES. In Education
North of 60: A Report Prepared by Members of the Canadian Association of School
Superintendents and Inspectors in the Department of Northern Affairs and National

Resources. B. Thorsteinsson, ed. The Canadian Superintendent 1964. Toronto: Ryerson Press. pp. 61-71.

Three eras in the history of education in northern Canada are discussed. These are (1) missions, (2) transition, and (3) federal and territorial administration. It is the last, with the expansion of educational facilities from the time the federal and territorial governments became active in northern education, which is the concern of this paper. Discussed are in-service training programs and workshops for teachers, expansion of vocational training programs, and adult education.   IVY

1700   **DUMONT-JOHNSON   MICHELINE**
1964
INTRODUCTION A UNE ETUDE DE LA DEPORTATION DES ACADIENS: LE ROLE POLITIQUE DES MISSIONAIRES AUPRES DES SAUVAGES. D.E.S. Thesis. Departement d'Histoire. Universite Laval. 206 pp.

The missionary's role with the Indians after 1713 and preceeding the deportation of the Acadians in 1755 is examined. Historical sources on the subject are reviewed. It is suggested that the Catholic missionaries knew their converts well and kept them loyal to the church but in so doing maintained them in a state of relative ignorance in terms of language and life style. Allegiance to France became closely related to faith and the missionaries became important figures who occasionally used the faith as an instrument of propaganda. The important role of the missionaries may have prevented France from assessing adequately the political situation in Acadia.   CCV

1701   **DUNFIELD   J D**
1970
AIR PHOTO RECONNAISSANCE RECORD MAJOR LAND USE AREAS INDIAN RESERVES IN ONTARIO: INDIAN RESERVE FOREST SURVEY REPORT NO. 30. Unpublished report prepared for Forest Management Institute, Department of Fisheries and Forestry. Available at Indian-Eskimo Economic Development Branch, Development Services Division, Department of Indian Affairs and Northern Development, Ottawa. 6 pp.

An air photo inventory of reserve lands in Ontario presents data concerning productive forest lands, the nature of the stands, their accessibility, and their development potential for each area.   CCV

1702   **EGGAN   FRED**
1967
NORTHERN WOODLAND ETHNOLOGY. In The Philadelphia Anthropological Society: Papers Presented On Its Golden Anniversary. Jacob W. Gruber, ed. Philadelphia: Temple University Publications. pp. 107-124.

Ethnographic literature concerned with the Algonkian-speaking populations north of the Great Lakes - St. Lawrence region is surveyed.   IVY

1703   **ERWIN   A M**
1968
NEW NORTHERN TOWNSMEN IN INUVIK. Mackenzie Delta Research Project 5.

Ottawa: Department of Indian Affairs and Northern Development, Northern Science Research Group. 25 pp.

Adaptation of the native peoples of the Mackenzie Delta to the Inuvik urban environment is assessed through consideration of ethnicity, life style, social stratification, and social interaction as observed from June 21 through October 5, 1966 at Inuvik. Emergence of a northern identity among people from all ethnic groups in response to a feeling of southern domination is observed. Obstacles to the acculturation of this population arising from the pre-urban life style and lack of adequate economic, educational, and employment opportunities are identified. Proposals are directed to these needs and to increasing northern leadership and autonomy.   CCV

1704   **FIELDS   GLENN**
1970
MANITOBA NEWSTART INCORPORATED REPORT (Nos.
3,4,5,6,9,10,11,12,14,15,16, and 17). Unpublished papers. Available from Center for Settlement Studies, University of Manitoba.

Data for this study were obtained from the Human Resources Survey done by David Jackson and Associates under contract with Manitoba Newstart in 1969. These are community reports, and only through family statistics, provided in the forward, are Indian and Metis distinguished. A preliminary analysis collates data consisting of (1) educational levels, (2) vocational training and upgrading, (3) labor force data, and (4) income data. Communities examined are The Pas and Big Eddy Indian Reserve (Report No. 3), Cross Lake (No. 4), Wabowden-Ponton (No. 5), Camperville (No. 6), Moose Lake (No. 9), Duck Bay and Good Harbour (No. 10), Easterville (No. 11), Grand Rapids and Grand Rapids Indian Reserve (No. 12), Norway House (No. 14), Nelson House (No. 15), Pelican Rapids (No. 16), and Pukatawagan (No. 17).   IVY

1705   **FOGELSON   RAYMOND D**
1965
PSYCHOLOGICAL THEORIES OF WINDIGO "PSYCHOSIS" AND A PRELIMINARY APPLICATION OF A MODELS APPROACH. In Context and Meaning of Cultural Anthropology. Melford E. Spiro, ed. New York: Free Press. pp. 74-99.

A psychological interpretation of the Windigo disorder among the Northern Algonkian linguistic group is attempted. The first part of the study reviews and synthesizes the theories propounded by travelers, missionaries, and anthropologists about the behavior and ideology of the phenomenon. In the second part, a theoretical model, "Normality-Upset-Psychosis", is applied to selected case materials in delineating the 5 basic types of Windigo disorders. It is hoped that this theoretical approach to the study of an ethno-specific type of mental derangement will be the initial step to a transcultural psychiatry.   DGW

1706   **FRASER   FIL R**
1964
A REFLECTIVE VIEW OF INDIAN DRINKING PROBLEMS IN SASKATCHEWAN. Unpublished paper. Available from National Library of Canada. 6 pp.

At a leadership training seminar at Fort Qu'Appelle in November of 1964 the problems of excessive drinking of alcohol were discussed. Participating in this seminar were between 25 and 30 people of native descent who were chosen to attend this seminar by the people of their reserves because of their leadership and decision-making abilities. It concludes that Saskatchewan Indians have problems with beverage alcohol, although very few Indians are alcoholics.   HCV

1707   **FRASER   SIMON**
1960
THE LETTERS AND JOURNALS OF SIMON FRASER, 1806-1808. W. Kaye Lamb, ed. Toronto: MacMillan. 292 pp.

The journals of Simon Fraser's early 19th century explorations in interior British Columbia are presented along with miscellaneous family documents. The explorer's impressions of the Indian are recorded in brief references particularly in respect to survival techniques, weapons, dwellings, slaves, and hospitality and honesty.   CCV

1708   **FREDERICKSON   C J**
1965
THE CURRICULUM FOR THE NORTHERN SCHOOLS. In Education North of 60: A Report Prepared by Members of the Canadian Association of School Superintendents and Inspectors in the Department of Northern Affairs and National Resources. B. Thorsteinsson, ed. The Canadian Superintendent 1964. Toronto: Ryerson Press. pp. 40-54.

Curriculum development is discussed concerning: programs relevant to Indian and Eskimo children, the teaching of English as a second language, a distinctive science program for the Mackenzie region, and in-service education for personnel. Excerpts from Richard Fyfe's "Anderson River Summer Field Programme"make up the Appendix (pages 50-54). This diary account of a field trip from May 15 to July 16, 1964, was designed to provide background information and materials necessary for the development of a meaningful science program for northern schools.   IVY

1709   **FRIED   J**
1963
SETTLEMENT TYPES AND COMMUNITY ORGANIZATION IN NORTHERN CANADA. Arctic 16:93-100.

As part of the research on northern communities conducted by the Northern Coordination and Research Centre from June 1961 to June 1962, several types of settlements emerging in the Northwest Territories since World War II are summarized. Social organization, function, and the degree of planning are the 3 criteria by which 7 types are distinguished. The difficulties involved in the absorption of the marginal Indian, Metis, and Eskimo peoples, culturally different from but economically tied to the fabric of White society, are considered.   WRC

1710   **FRIED   JACOB**
1963
WHITE-DOMINANT SETTLEMENTS IN THE CANADIAN NORTHWEST TERRITORIES. Anthropologica N.S. 5:57-67.

A brief sketch based on fieldwork from June, 1961, to May, 1962, describes the type of settlements emerging in the Northwest Territories as a result of the government's northern development policies. The Indian, Metis, and White population components are considered and a schema of social distance between the components is illustrated. The article is part of a special issue on community organization and pattern change in the Canadian North.   WRC

1711   **FRIED   JACOB**
1964
URBANIZATION AND ECOLOGY IN THE CANADIAN NORTHWEST
TERRITORIES. Arctic Anthropology 2(2):56-60.

A contribution to a symposium on the consequences of culture contact in the Arctic and Sub-Arctic considers the implications of northern development programs begun on a large scale in 1953. Based on 7-months fieldwork in 1961-1962 at Frobisher Bay, Inuvik, Yellowknife, and Hay River, an analysis is made of the emerging urban townships as obstacles upsetting the traditional ecological balance between Indians and Eskimos and the natural environment. Three adaptive responses of the native peoples to the shift in the mode of production and to their low status assigned by the White society are noted.   WRC

1712   **FRISCH   JACK A**
1964
COGNATIC KINSHIP ORGANIZATION AMONG THE NORTHEAST
ALGONKIANS. M.A. Thesis. Department of Anthropology. Indiana University. 58 pp.

The literature concerning Abnaki, Malecite, Micmac, and Montagnais-Naskapi kinship organization is reviewed. Cognatic kinship ties rather than unilinear descent are felt to be the basis of kinship organization. It is suggested that the residence pattern for the entire area is ambilocal rather than patrilocal. The need for re-evaluation of former descriptions in terms of recent analytical concepts is stressed.   CCV

1713   **FRISCH   JACK A**
1965
THE SOCIAL ORGANIZATION OF THE NORTHEASTERN ALGONKIANS.
Indiana Academy of Science Proceedings 74:112-113.

Evidence is presented supporting the use of the deme as the unit of social organization among the Northeastern Algonkians.   IVY

1714   **GABER   ARCHIE**
1966
SUMMARY REPORT: COMMUNITY DEVELOPMENT SERVICES IN THE
INTERLAKE. Unpublished paper. Available from Library, Department of Health and Social Development, Winnipeg, Man. 19 pp.

A background of the area and its Indian and Metis residents is provided with specific profiles of the Peguis, Fisher River, Lake St. Martin, and Lake Manitoba Reserves, and the communities of Pine Dock, Matheson Island, and Vogar.   IVY

1715   **GILLESPIE   BERYL C**
n.d.
ATHABASKANS WHO HAVE CREE FOR NEIGHBORS. Unpublished paper.
Available from National Museum of Man, Ethnology Division, Ottawa, with
permission of the author. 51 pp.

Hudson's Bay Company records and other historical materials are analyzed to give a
more accurate interpretation of the location of northern Athabascan groups at the beginning of the historical period, their movement prior to the fur trade, and the changes
which have occurred in native technology and economy. The area of the study comprises
the region from the West Coast of Hudson's Bay to the Rocky Mountains and north to
the Mackenzie River. The study covers the years between 1700 and 1830. Early maps relating to Athabascan locations and the regional ecology are appended.   DGW

1716   **GILLESPIE   BERYL C**
1970
NOTES ON SOME OF THE ATHABASKANS OF THE MACKENZIE RIVER AND
THE ROCKY MOUNTAINS. Unpublished paper. Delivered to Athabaskan
Conference. Available at National Museum of Man, Ethnology Division, Ottawa, with
permission of the author. 7 pp.

Excerpts from early historical documents of the fur trade era are presented to illustrate
the geographical distribution of several Mackenzie Basin tribes. In the early 19th century,
the Slave were not as far north as later in the century. Similarly, the Dogrib were not as
far west. In the 1820's, Fort Simpson was a center for the Dogrib and Slave, and a few
Dahotinne and Nahane. Fort Norman was a center for Dogrib and Dahotinne Indians,
and later a few Slave and Hare.   JSL

1717   **GILLESPIE   BERYL C**
1970
YELLOWKNIVES: QUO IVERUNT? American Ethnological Society Proceedings of
the 1970 Annual Spring Meeting. pp. 61-71.

From fieldwork in the summers of 1968 and 1969 at Great Slave Lake, oral tradition,
particularly Dogrib accounts of the enemy chief Akaitcho, is employed to examine the
amalgamation of the Yellowknife Indians by the Dogrib and Chipewyan prior to 1920.
Appended is a map of the territory exploited by the Yellowknife.   WRC

1718   **GILLESPIE   P J**
1964
THE ALCOHOL PROBLEM IN NORTHERN CANADA. Unpublished paper.
Available from Library, Department of Indian Affairs and Northern Development,
Ottawa. 16 pp.

The nature of the problem presented by the consumption of alcohol by native peoples in
Northern Canada is reviewed. The history of the problem, infractions involving use of
liquor, homebrew, drinking habits, the situation in other countries, and drinking in primitive societies are examined.   CCV

1719   **GILLIE   B C**
1965

THE FLYING SUPERINTENDENT. In Education North of 60: A Report Prepared by Members of the Canadian Association of School Superintendents and Inspectors in the Department of Northern Affairs and National Resources. B. Thorsteinsson, ed. The Canadian Superintendent 1964. Toronto: Ryerson Press. pp. 72-83.

The District Superintendent of the Mackenzie relates the details of a visit to the southwestern part of his territory.   IVY

1720   **GODIN   CLAUDE**
1969
INTERMEDIAIRES ET ACCULTURATION A FORT-SMITH ET HAY RIVER, T.N.O. M.A. Thesis. Departement d'Anthropologie. Universite de Montreal. 249 pp.

This study follows a 5-month stay (May-October, 1968) at Fort Smith and Hay River where the author was employed by the Indian Affairs Branch. The principal interest is the part played by the White intermediaries towards the Indian population of the 2 cities. After a short theoretical introduction on the identity of these agents and their influence on the Indian groups, the author describes the environment of the whole area and summarizes the history of Indian-White contacts. The 2 cities are then separately described in terms of ethnic composition, settlement pattern, and the ability for each individual to participate directly in his social environment, without the help of intermediaries. Afterwards, the author enumerates several points of contact between the 2 cultures, putting into light the work of intermediaries. Finally, the importance of intermediaries is summarized for each city.   DD

1721   **GOLD   DOLORES**
1967
PSYCHOLOGICAL CHANGES ASSOCIATED WITH ACCULTURATION OF SASKATCHEWAN INDIANS. Journal of Social Psychology 71:177-184.

It was hypothesized and demonstrated that the urban, acculturated Indians were more similar to White urbanites in following a predominantly deferred gratification pattern than they were to unacculturated reserve Indians who followed a predominantly immediate gratification pattern. A positive correlation was reported between degree of acculturation and socio-economic status. Regional differences as well as socio-economic status had an impact on the particular goal pattern of the reserve Indian.   ADG

1722   **GOUDREAULT   REJEAN**
1968
MON TRAVAIL DE MONITEUR DANS UNE RESIDENCE INDIENNE. Kerygma 2(3):97-101.

Observations from a year as monitor in an Indian residence in the Mackenzie area are reported by an Oblate father. The advantages offered by residential schools, some characteristics of Indian boys, and some difficulties presented by integration are noted.   CCV

1723   **GUY   CAMIL**
1966
LES STRUCTURES DE GROUPE DANS L'EST SUBARCTIQUE DU CANADA. Unpublished paper. Available from Bibliotheque Nationale du Quebec. 32 pp.

Ecology and acculturation stand out as the determinants of the social organization of Sub-Arctic groups. The importance of these factors are examined, taking into consideration several typologies of hunting groups and bands.   DD

1724   **HABRICH   WULF**
1964-1965
THE WINTER FISHING INDUSTRY OF GREAT SLAVE LAKE. The Albertan Geographer 1:23-25.

Investigations made during a visit to Hay River in January, 1965, provide the basis for a description of the winter fishing industry carried on by Metis, Whites, Cree, and Slave.   IVY

1725   **HAMILTON   WALTER R**
1964
THE YUKON STORY: A SOURDOUGH'S RECORD OF GOLDRUSH DAYS AND YUKON PROGRESS FROM THE EARLIEST TIMES TO THE PRESENT DAY. Vancouver: Mitchell. 261 pp.

A sourdough's recollection of the Yukon, particularly the period 1898-1980, includes a chapter devoted to a description of the Yukon natives, which touches briefly on social organization, religion, the agency, Indian-White relations, and the Eskimo.   CCV

1726   **HARVEY   JAMES B**
1965
SCOUTING AMONGST THE ESKIMOS AND NORTHERN INDIANS. North 12(3):18-23.

The history and development of scouting in the North is recalled at a recent scouting conference. It is felt that scouting will help prepare young Eskimos and Indians for leadership in the development of the North.   ADG

1727   **HATT   JUDITH**
1968
CULTURAL TRANSMISSION AMONG THE NORTHERN ALGONKIANS: A STRUCTURAL ANALYSIS. Alberta Anthropologist 2(2):24-47.

The effects of social structure and physical environment on patterns of socialization among Northern Algonkians are considered. Based on ethnographic accounts, the distribution of power in kin and non-kin relations, the sexual division of labor, and differentials in male and female socialization are examined.   WRC

1728   **HEDLIN MENZIES AND ASSOCIATES LTD.**
1969
AN EVALUATION OF THE OPPORTUNITIES FOR ECONOMIC DEVELOPMENT ON PEGUIS INDIAN RESERVE. Unpublished paper prepared for Chief and Band Council of Peguis Indian Reserve. Available from Center for Settlement Studies, University of Manitoba. 83 pp.

Sources of information for this study include the Dominion Bureau of Statistics, Indian Affairs Branch, Manitoba's Department of Agriculture, the University of Manitoba, and the reserve residents. Chapter 2 describes the northern Interlake in which the reserve is located, and the various resources present on the reserve. In Chapter 3 the opportunities and obstacles for development on the reserve are examined, and some guidelines and recommendations are presented. The report concludes that economic development on Peguis Indian Reserve is feasible because of its population size (1,985) and its potential in agriculture, fishing, and forestry, provided that the band members want it and are willing to work for it, and provided that the Department accepts that goal and is willing to give the program its moral backing and full technical, managerial, and financial support.   IVY

1729   **HEINRICH   ALBERT C,   ANDERSON   RUSSELL**
1968
CO-AFFINAL SIBLINGSHIP AS A STRUCTURAL FEATURE AMONG SOME
NORTHERN NORTH AMERICAN PEOPLES. Ethnology 7:290-295.

Based on fieldwork conducted periodically from 1955 to 1967, kinship terms of 2 Athapaskan groups at Fort Laird (Northwest Territories), and the Upper Tanana River drainage, and 2 Eskimo groups are examined. As an isolated aspect of these kinship systems co-affinal siblingship is defined as an enduring bond of moral obligations uniting 2 persons of the same sex who are the spouses of siblings. This relationship is noted as a development common to these widely separate groups. Structural and functional explanations of this phenomenon are considered. For future study it is suggested that the functional aspects of co-affinal kinship are important in relation to both ecology and culture in the process of natural selection.   WRC

1730   **HELLABY   HILDA**
1961
THE INDIAN IN SOCIAL ADJUSTMENT. North 8(5):22-23.

The religious, educational, and social status of the Yukon Indian is discussed. Because he is not a reserve Indian, he lacks many of the special privileges of the Prairie Indians. The Yukon Indian's liabilities are just as bad, however. His survival is dependent upon adjustment to the changing times.   ADG

1731   **HELM   JUNE**
1960
KIN TERMS OF ARCTIC DRAINAGE DENE: HARE, SLAVEY, CHIPEWYAN.
American Anthropologist 62:279-295.

Kinship terminology of the Hare, Slave, and Chipewyan Indians are compared to determine the incidence of cross-cousin marriage among the aboriginal Arctic Drainage Dene. Based on earlier reports and the author's own fieldwork a reconstruction of terms is presented in tables. Scant and conflicting data from modern informants prevent a complete analysis. Despite these historical problems initial evidence is given for an aboriginal social organization based on bifurcate-merging terminology and cross-cousin marriage, similar to that of the Northern Algonkians.   WRC

1732   **HELM   JUNE**
1965
BILATERALITY IN THE SOCIO-TERRITORIAL ORGANIZATION OF THE
ARCTIC DRAINAGE DENE. Ethnology 4:361-385.

Based on genealogical, demographic, and historical data from the Dene of the Mackenzie Drainage, units of socio-territorial organization are reconsidered from pre-contact to
the present. Inferences from fieldwork among the Hare, Slave, and Dogrib are
made about a continuum of task group, local band, regional band, and tribe. Degree of
primary consanguineal ties, number of conjugal pairs, and the duration of delimited settlement are the criteria employed for the identification of specific units. It is argued that
the criteria of the presence or absence of unilineal organization alone are insufficient for
analysis of the development of band composition and the building of structural models.
It is concluded that flexible bilateral kin affiliations were characteristic of all social units
in this area and provided ready integration of surviving members in view of environmental fluctuations and recurrent disasters. Kinship charts and tables are included.   WRC

1733   **HELM   JUNE**
1965
PATTERNS OF ALLOCATION AMONG THE ARCTIC DRAINAGE DENE.
American Ethnological Society Proceedings of the 1965 Annual Spring Meeting. pp. 33-
45.

In a symposium on economic anthropology, fieldwork among the Slave Indians at Lynx
Point, Northwest Territories, and the Dogrib at Marten Lake and Fort Rae, Northwest
Territories, yields a description of the adventitious nature of economic distribution at the
community level. Delineated are the prestations between nuclear families, communal
sharing of resources, and the functions of the trading chiefs in the integration of the
economy.   WRC

1734   **HELM   JUNE**
1966
CHANGES IN INDIAN COMMUNITIES. In People of Light and Dark. Maja van
Steensel, ed. Ottawa: Queen's Printer. pp. 106-109.

The social solidarity manifested by Dene Indian bush communities as well as their contemporary subsistence activities are described relative to changes to be anticipated with
acculturation.   CCV

1735   **HELM   JUNE**
1969
A METHOD OF STATISTICAL ANALYSIS OF PRIMARY RELATIVE BONDS IN
COMMUNITY COMPOSITION. In Contributions to Anthropology: Band Societies:
Proceedings of the Conference on Band Organization, Ottawa, August 30 to September
2, 1965. David Damas, ed. National Museums of Canada Bulletin 228. Ottawa: Queen's
Printer. pp. 218-239.

This is essentially a methodological work, but Northern Athapaskan (and some Eskimo)
data are used for illustration. Tables and diagrams show the kin composition of Northern Athapaskan bands. Discussed are 2 quantifying procedures to describe band structure. The first of these measures the significance of primary kin bonds between co-resi-
dent conjugal pairs in the community. A second method was discussed, with the intent of
scoring male and female statuses in the primary consanguineal bonds among these pairs.
It is suggested that the latter method might assess the extent to which residence behavior
conforms to conscious cultural norms.   JSL

1736 **HELM JUNE, DAMAS DAVID**
1963
THE CONTACT-TRADITIONAL ALL-NATIVE COMMUNITY OF THE
CANADIAN NORTH: THE UPPER MACKENZIE "BUSH"ATHAPASKANS AND
THE IGLULIGMIUT. Anthropologica N.S. 5:9-21.

Ten years of field research among the Slave and Dogrib of the Upper Mackenzie Drainage and 12 months among the Igluligmiut of Melville Peninsula and Baffin Island by the
respective ethnographers yields a description of settlement patterns stabilized by Euro-
Canadian technological and economic factors in the contact-traditional horizon of acculturation. WRC

1737 **HICKERSON HAROLD**
1967
SOME IMPLICATIONS OF THE THEORY OF THE PARTICULARITY, OR
"ATOMISM,"OF NORTHERN ALGONKIANS. Current Anthropology 8:313-328.

The facts presented by contrasting theories on the aboriginal social organization and personality types of the northern Algonkians, especially the Ojibwa, are re-examined and
their implications for a more general theory of social relations are considered. Ethnohistorical evidence is cited for co-operation and communal production in aboriginal times
whereas none is found for particularity and individual family ownership. The characterization of atomism as the basic personality structure of the Algonkians and Indians in
general is questioned as ethnocentric. Analysis of change in the economic basis of social
organization is viewed as necessary in accounting for the shift from aboriginal commu-
nality to post-contact individuality. Following the article are the comments of several
scholars and a reply by the author. WRC

1738 **HONIGMANN JOHN J**
1960
CIRCUMPOLAR FOREST NORTH AMERICA AS A MODERN CULTURE AREA.
In Men and Cultures: Selected Papers of the Fifth International Congress of
Anthropological and Ethnological Sciences. Anthony F. C. Wallace, ed. Philadelphia:
University of Pennsylvania Press. pp. 447-451.

Two types of culture are distinguished: the indigenous Indians and the largely immigrant
Whites. Some aspects of contemporary cultural configurations in the circumpolar forest
of North America are discussed including occupation, social organization, and behavior.
IVY

1739 **HONIGMANN JOHN J**
1963
COMMUNITY ORGANIZATION AND PATTERNS OF CHANGE AMONG
NORTH CANADIAN AND ALASKAN INDIANS AND ESKIMOS. Anthropologica
N.S. 5:3-8.

As guest editor of a special issue on community organization and pattern change in the
Canadian North, the author reviews the general scope of the articles and discusses theory
and method of comparative study of specific communities in the process of
change. WRC

1740   **HONIGMANN   JOHN J**
1965
SOCIAL DISINTEGRATION IN FIVE NORTHERN COMMUNITIES. Canadian
Review of Sociology and Anthropology 2:199-214.

Based on fieldwork from 1944 to 1963 among the Kaska at Lower Post, British Columbia, the Cree at Attawapiskat, Ontario, the Eskimos and Algonkian Indians at Great
Whale River, Quebec, the Eskimos at Frobisher Bay, and on an ethnography of the
Kutchin at Old Crow, Yukon Territory, the 5 settlements are surveyed in an attempt to
discern the relationship of social disintegration to other variables, such as poverty, social
relations, and cultural and ethnic pluralism. Within the scope of the larger social order
disintegration is measured in terms of deviance from Euro-Canadian norms.   WRC

1741   **HONIGMANN   JOHN J**
1968
THE FUR-TRADE PERIOD AS A DEVELOPMENTAL STAGE IN NORTHERN
ALGONKIAN CULTURE HISTORY. Unpublished paper delivered to 1st Conference
on Algonquian Studies. St-Pierre de Wakefield, Que., September 13-15, 1968. Available
from National Library of Canada. 7 pp.

Northeastern Algonkians, the Ojbiwa, Cree, and related groups of Ontario and northern
Quebec are the concern of this paper. From an aboriginal base, the development of
Northeastern Algonkian culture history is presented in 3 historical periods: Formative,
Florescent, and Modern. The Formative, the early-contact period in which European cultural materials were introduced, upset cultural stability and undermined cultural integration. In the Florescent period, the fur trade period, the Indians had achieved a meaningful new culture including a system of social organization that integrated them around the
trading post settlement and an emotionally satisfying belief system. During the 3rd period, the modern period of planned social development, cultural organization achieved
during the fur trade period began to dissolve.   IVY

1742   **HONIGMANN   JOHN J**
1969
DECULTURATION AND PROLETARIZATION OF CANADA'S FAR
NORTHERN NATIVE PEOPLE. Unpublished paper delivered to Annual Meeting of
the Canadian Sociological and Anthropological Association. Toronto, June 5-7, 1967.
Available from National Library of Canada. 20 pp.

This paper defines and reviews deculturation and proletarization and then applies these
concepts to modern North American communities in the Arctic and Sub-Arctic.   HCV

1743   **HONIGMANN   JOHN J**
1969
INTEGRATION OF CANADIAN ESKIMO, INDIAN AND OTHER PERSONS OF
NATIVE ANCESTRY IN MODERN, ECONOMIC AND PUBLIC LIFE:
EVIDENCE FROM INUVIK. Unpublished paper delivered to Symposium on
Circumpolar Problems, Nordic Council for Anthropological Research. Stockholm,
Sweden, March 2-7, 1969. Available from National Library of Canada. 24 pp.

Having done fieldwork at Inuvik, Northwest Territories, the author describes the composition of the native population in the Canadian Arctic and Sub-Arctic, then analyses the

extent to which the diverse ethnic groups are participating in available economic and educational opportunities.   HCV

1744   **HONIGMANN   JOHN J**
1970
FORMATION OF MACKENZIE DELTA FRONTIER CULTURE. Unpublished paper delivered to Northeastern Anthropological Society. Ottawa, May 7-9, 1970. Available from National Library of Canada. 10 pp.

Using the town of Inuvik as an example, the author gives a history of formation and an explanation of the frontier culture. At the west end of Inuvik the population of 1,100 people is made up primarily of native people while at the east end the population of 1,300 is primarily non-native. Although both ends of the town appear to live by the same economic standard, close examination reveals a different life style practiced by the people of native background.   HCV

1745   **HONIGMANN   JOHN J,   HONIGMANN   IRMA**
1968
ALCOHOL IN A CANADIAN NORTHERN TOWN. Unpublished paper delivered to 1968 Meeting, Canadian Sociology and Anthropology Association. Available from National Library of Canada. 81 pp.

Three ethnic categories of native people in a far-northern Canadian town called Fort Mackenzie were studies for visits to the government liquor store, liquor expenditures, and convictions under the liquor ordinance. Results were compared to those of a Frobisher Bay study. More extensive and heavier drinking in Fort Mackenzie is indicated and a profile of the drinking population is presented with regard to sex, age, ethnic group, and employment. The diversity in handling of alcohol is explained by the concept of a stake in society manifested in regular employment and commitment to the dominant society's values as opposed to its repudiation and subscription to a frontier ethic.   CCV

1746   **HONIGMANN   JOHN J,   HONIGMANN   IRMA**
1970
ARCTIC TOWNSMEN: ETHNIC BACKGROUNDS AND MODERNIZATION. Ottawa: Canadian Research Centre for Anthropology, Saint Paul University. 303 pp.

Fieldwork carried out from February until August of 1967 studied child behavior, socialization, social organization, and adaptation processes of native peoples in Inuvik. Social participation, interviews, and census data provide information, and numerous comparisons between Indian and Eskimo life styles are offered.   CCV

1747   **HURLEY   DANIEL M**
1962
REPORT ON INDIAN LAND RIGHTS IN THE ATLANTIC PROVINCES. Unpublished paper. Available from National Museum of Man, Ethnology Division, Ottawa, with permission of the author. 34 pp.

Prepared jointly for the National Museum and Indian Affairs Branch, currently existing land rights are examined in the Maritimes. Complications arise from jurisdictional division between provincial and federal governments, and the absence of legally recognized treaties. Complicated situations exist in Labrador, New Brunswick, Nova Scotia, and Prince Edward Island. Both subjective and objective analyses explore the moral and legal bases of Indian claims to hunting, fishing, and land rights. It is concluded that existing treaties or agreements do not substantiate these claims in the eyes of the courts. A lengthy appendix reproduces the relevant treaties, agreements, and court decisions.   JSL

1748   **JENNESS   R A**
1963
GREAT SLAVE FISHING INDUSTRY. Department of Northern Affairs and National Resources, Northern Co-ordination and Research Centre Reports No. NCRC-63-10. Ottawa: Department of Northern Affairs and National Resources. 41 pp.

The fishing industry in Great Slave Lake is reviewed with discussion of methods, financing, markets, potential for expansion, and government policies. Occasional brief mention of local Indian and Metis fishermen occurs.   IVY

1749   **KEW   M**
1961
BACKGROUND TO CUMBERLAND HOUSE. Unpublished paper. Available from Northern Curriculum Resources Centre, University of Saskatchewan. 3 pp.

The community of Cumberland House is briefly described noting its history, its population, its resources, its services and organizations, and the incomes of Metis and Indian residents.   IVY

1750   **KING   ALFRED RICHARD**
1964
A CASE STUDY OF AN INDIAN RESIDENTIAL SCHOOL. Ph.D. Thesis. School of Education. Stanford University. 280 pp. Available from University Microfilms.

The total operation of the Carcross Indian residential school is studied with emphasis placed on the existing communication and interaction patterns within that school. Fieldwork at the school was carried out in the months spanning August, 1962, to July, 1963. It is assumed that the initial school experiences of children are a determining factor for societal adaptation. The results of the study revealed the operation of a self-reinforcing cyclical pattern in the history of the Yukon Indian experience. This involves a willingness on the part of the Indian to adapt to the White man's verbalized belief system, resulting in a trend towards disintegration.   DGW

1751   **KING   ALFRED RICHARD**
1967
THE SCHOOL AT MOPASS: A PROBLEM OF IDENTITY. New York: Holt, Rinehart and Winston. 96 pp.

The educational processes operative in the Mopass Indian residential school in the Yukon are described from a study executed during the 1962-1963 school year. The subculture which the school represents for Indians, the resulting roles, personnel relations, and communication difficulties are described revealing obstacles to full Indian participation and acculturation.   CCV

1752   **KNIGHT   ROLF**
1965

A RE-EXAMINATION OF HUNTING, TRAPPING, AND TERRITORIALITY AMONG THE NORTHEASTERN ALGONKIAN INDIANS. In Man, Culture, and Animals: The Role of Animals in Human Ecological Adjustments. Anthony Leeds and Andrew P. Vayda, eds. American Association for the Advancement of Science Publication 78. Washington: American Association for the Advancement of Science. pp. 27-42.

From fieldwork at Rupert House and Nemiscau, Quebec, in the summers of 1961 and 1962, it is argued that compartmentalized, family hunting territories were not characteristic of the pre-fur trade northeastern Algonkians, and in fact, did not develop in response to the fur trade. An analysis of the geophysical environment, human and animal demography and behavior, and the use of firearms as aspects of 1 ecological system yields non-cultural limitations which maintained communal subsistence activities and initiated family territoriality in the brief instances of its occurrence.   WRC

1753   **KNILL   WILLIAM D,   DAVIS   ARTHUR K**
1967
PROVINCIAL EDUCATION IN NORTHERN SASKATCHEWAN: PROGRESS AND BOG-DOWN, 1944-1962. In A Northern Dilemma: Reference Papers. A. K. Davis, Vernon C. Serl, et al., eds. Bellingham, WA: Western Washington State College. Vol. 1. pp. 170-337.

A comprehensive study of provincial education in northern Saskatchewan is reported. Detailed sections are devoted to the history of education in Saskatchewan's North until 1944; a review of the organization and administration of the Northern Areas Branch of the Department of Education; the yields of the present system; a discussion of teachers, their qualifications and views; occupational aspirations of White, Indian, and Metis children; and recommendations, innovations, and proposals for a combined operations approach to education in the North. Discussion is supported by data, largely applying to the 1960-62 period.   CCV

1754   **LEVESQUE   GERARD R**
1962
THE NORTH. Edmonton: Gerard R. Levesque. 127 pp.

Brief reference to the Athabaskan residents of the Yukon and Northwest Territories is included in this survey of the North.   CCV

1755   **LOTZ   JIM R**
1962
INUVIK, N.W.T.: A STUDY OF COMMUNITY PLANNING IN A NEW NORTHERN TOWN. Unpublished paper. Northern Affairs and National Resources, Northern Administration Branch, Industrial Division. Available from Library, Department of Indian Affairs and Northern Development, Ottawa. 45 pp.

Discussion of planning problems in Inuvik based on 3 weeks of fieldwork in September and October, 1966 reveals living conditions and attitudes of Indian, Eskimo, and Metis residents. Recommendations are based on an evaluation of the present town layout and housing, services and utilities, employment and commercial facilities, community institutions and associations, recreation and social problems.   CCV

1756   **LOTZ   JIM R**
1965
THE DAWSON AREA: A REGIONAL MONOGRAPH. Northern Co-ordination and
Research Centre, Yukon Research Project Series No. 2. Ottawa: Department of
Northern Affairs and National Resources. 209 pp.

Settlement pattern and social and economic conditions in Dawson are reported in a study
arising from brief visits to the area in 1961, 1962, and 6 weeks during the summer of
1963. Indians and their interaction with other citizens as well as household composition,
living conditions, attitudes, educational and employment opportunities, and income resources are discussed in Chapters 18 and 19.   CCV

1757   **LOTZ   JIM R**
1965
THE SQUATTERS OF WHITEHORSE: A STUDY OF THE PROBLEMS OF NEW
NORTHERN SETTLEMENTS. Arctic 18:173-188.

Based on a survey conducted in 1960 and recurrent visits to Whitehorse from 1960-1965,
the social and economic problems of squatters, inhabitants of unplanned settlements peripheral to the townsite, are delineated. Indians, who comprised 12 percent of the squatter population, Metis, and some White settlers were faced with a rapidly increasing standard of living and the high cost of land in a community not yet integrated into the urban
tone of the northern development program. Relevant data on dwelling types, income levels, seasonal unemployment, employment, duration of residence, and government investment in the Yukon from 1954 to 1962 are tabulated.   WRC

1758   **LOTZ   JIM R**
1966
MAN-POWER AND SOCIO-ECONOMIC DEVELOPMENT IN THE YUKON
TERRITORY: A PRELIMINARY STUDY. Unpublished report prepared for
Minister of Citizenship and Immigration. Available from Library, Department of
Indian Affairs and Northern Development, Ottawa. 129 pp.

An overview is presented of manpower mobility and economic development problems in
Yukon terrritory as observed during a study undertaken from July 17 to August 6, 1966.
Brief references to Indian and Metis citizens occur in relation to settlement pattern, hous-
ing, and employment problems.   CCV

1759   **LOTZ   JIM R**
1969
SOCIAL SCIENCE RESEARCH IN THE CANADIAN NORTH. Ottawa: Canadian
Research Centre for Anthropology, St. Paul's University. 88 pp.

A list of research centers, bibliographies, and current research projects in the North is
compiled.   CCV

1760   **LOTZ   JIM R**
1970
NORTHERN REALITIES: THE FUTURE OF NORTHERN DEVELOPMENT IN
CANADA. Toronto: New Press. 307 pp.

Discussed is the development of the Yukon Territory as 1 segment of Canadian northern development. It is admitted that Canada must accept its northern nature as the key to national fulfillment. Problems and solutions to culture change are explored with cognizance of the human factor - for it is the indigenous people who will have to learn to adapt to emerging changes. It is the southern Canadian, however, who must realize that old solutions cannot be used for northern problems. Appended is a statement on the redevelopment of Dawson City.   DGW

1761   **MANITOBA. Department of Welfare. Community Development Services.**
1963
A SOCIO-ECONOMIC SURVEY OF THE LAKE WINNIPEG CHANNEL AND NARROWS AREA. Winnipeg: Community Development Services, Department of Welfare. 23 pp.

This socio-economic survey investigates commercial fishing and trapping, timber resources, agricultural potential, and industrial development. The specific area under study includes the following communities: Loon Straits, Bloodvein, Berens River, Poplar River, Matheson Island, Pine Dock, Jackhead Harbor, Fisher River, Koostatak, and Anama Bay.   IVY

1762   **MANSELL   R L**
1970
A SOCIO-ECONOMIC SURVEY OF ISOLATED COMMUNITIES IN NORTHERN ALBERTA. Edmonton: Human Resources Development Authority. 120 pp.

The Lesser Slave Lake area, designated as a "Special Area"by the federal government, is the focal point of this study. This abridged research document examines the quality and quantity of the natural resources of the following isolated areas: Little Buffalo Lake, Peerless Lake, Chipewyan Lake, Utikuma, and East Prairie. The report seeks to identify or establish which of the isolated communities or areas have the greatest growth potential and which can maximize the services provided.   IVY

1763   **MARTENS   ETHEL G**
1966
MEXICO AND CANADA: A COMPARISON OF TWO PROGRAMS WHERE INDIANS ARE TRAINED IN COMMUNITY DEVELOPMENT. Ottawa: Department of National Health and Welfare. 48 pp.

Community development programs in Canada and Mexico emphasizing training of the village level Indian worker are compared. The history of the indigenous groups and government activities on their behalf are reviewed to provide background information. Program aims, affected population, organization, and success of the training programs are described.   CCV

1764   **MCFEAT   TOM F S**
1962
MUSEUM ETHNOLOGY AND THE ALGONKIAN PROJECT. National Museum of Canada Anthropology Papers 2. Ottawa: Queen's Printer. 80 pp.

It is concluded that the museum, with its predilection to collect, is best suited for cumulative, diachronic research. A report of the Algonkian Project which includes the Micmac,

Malecite, Naskapi, Montagnais, Cree, and Ojibwa, discusses the Montagnais - a territorial group - and contrasting stabilized reserve groups, such as the Micmac and Malecite. Appendices include an early prospectus for study of the Montagnais, and a list of the National Museum's recent work in ethnology.   JSL

1765   **MCGUIRE   MAUREEN**
1966
INTER-ETHNIC RELATIONS IN THE CANADIAN BOREAL FOREST: A STUDY OF POLITICAL CONTROL, PREPARED FOR THE ADVISORY COMMISSION ON POLITICAL DEVELOPMENT IN THE NORTHWEST TERRITORIES.
Available from Library, Department of Indian Affairs and Northern Development.   108 pp.

Leadership in the boreal forest is discussed in historical perspective. The contents are organized into 4 parts - indigenous political system, effects of the fur trade, Indian administration to 1945, and contemporary status. The author concludes that leadership is generally weak.   JSL

1766   **MCKAY   F I**
1965
ADULT EDUCATION. In Education North of 60: A Report Prepared by Members of the Canadian Association of School Superintendents and Inspectors in the Department of Northern Affairs and National Resources. B. Thorsteinsson, ed. The Canadian Superintendent 1964. Toronto: Ryerson Press. pp. 55-60.

An adult education program was established by the Education Division of the Northern Administration Branch of the Department of Northern Affairs and National Resources in late 1960 to provide fundamental or functional education for adults. In addition, it is to prepare the people for the rapidly occurring changes in the region. Types of programs (formal and informal), attendance, and texts used in the program are discussed.   IVY

1767   **MICHEA   JEAN**
1967
ESQUIMAUX ET INDIENS DU GRAND NORD. Paris: Societte Continentale d'Editions Modernes Illustrees. 348 pp.

An overview of Indian and Eskimo life in the North is presented. Physical geography, climate, and fauna are outlined. Indian origins and language groups are treated and the life style of Sub-Arctic Indian groups is outlined. Tribes are situated geographically and selected aspects of clothing, transportation, hunting, fishing, cooking, warfare, recreation, division of labor, life cycle, disease, and religious beliefs are reported. A brief review of exploration, fur trade, and the contemporary scene make up the final chapters. CCV

1768   **MONTURE   G C**
1959-1960
THE INDIANS OF THE NORTH. Queen's Quarterly 66:556-563.

A general description of contemporary Indians outside the agricultural areas of Canada is given.   IVY

1769   **MOODIE   D W,   KAYE   BARRY**
1969
THE NORTHERN LIMIT OF INDIAN AGRICULTURE IN NORTH AMERICA.
The Geographical Review 59:513-529.

The occurrence of Indian agriculture (other than wild rice) north of the Upper Missouri in the southern Manitoba lowlands and in adjacent areas of Ontario and Minnesota is documented.   IVY

1770   **MORROW   W G**
1968
INQUIRY RE ADMINISTRATION OF JUSTICE IN THE HAY RIVER AREA OF THE NORTHWEST TERRITORIES. Unpublished paper. Available from Library, Department of Indian Affairs and Northern Development, Ottawa. 112 pp.

An investigation into the administration of justice in the Hay River area in response to criticisms appearing in March and April, 1967, issues of "Tapwe" is reported by Commissioner W.G. Morrow. The charges that courts proceedings are not open, that the press has been hampered, and that all individuals do not receive fair treatment are discussed, evidence and conclusions are summarized, and recommendations are advanced. General complaints voiced in editorials or during the hearing are discussed briefly. Although the commission does not support the accusations as such, recommendations are geared to improve the administration of justice and ensure a greater impartiality. A general discussion of the problems inherent in the administration of justice in northern areas and strong recommendations for improved facilities and increased personnel are included.   CCV

1771   **NEEDHAM   G H**
1965
NORTHERN SCHOOL PROFILE. In Education North of 60: A Report Prepared by Members of the Canadian Association of School Superintendents and Inspectors in the Department of Northern Affairs and National Resources. B. Thorsteinsson, ed. The Canadian Superintendent 1964. Toronto: Ryerson Press. pp. 84-95.

A brief overall view of northern schools, the pupil population, and the teaching personnel is given.   IVY

1772   **NICHOLAS   ANDREW**
1970
INTRODUCTION. In Land of the Four Directions. By Frederick John Pratson. Old Greenwich, CT: Chatham Press. pp. 11-12.

The Executive Director of the Union of New Brunswick Indians attributes a lack of respect for and understanding of Canadian Indians to Prime Minister P. E. Trudeau, Jean Chretien, and the Canadian government as manifested in policy statements and administrative policies. A plea for understanding and co-operation is advanced in this brief introduction to Pratson's "Land of the Four Directions."   CCV

1773   **ONTARIO HOUSING CORPORATION**
1968

HOUSING SURVEY OF MOOSONEE. Unpublished paper. Available from National Library of Canada. 28 pp.

Between 30 and 40 interviews and discussions with both Indians and non-Indians were used to assess local housing needs and preferences. Since water and sewer services are now available, the Ontario Housing Corporation will now commence a housing program. Discussed are the size and location of the project, the type of dwelling and its construction, rents and services, administration, maintenance, homemaker services, and operating losses. Photographs, maps and plans accompany the text.   IVY

1774   **ONTARIO HOUSING CORPORATION**
1969
REPORT ON THE NEED AND DEMAND FOR RENT-GEARED-TO-INCOME HOUSING: MANITOULIN ISLAND INDIAN RESERVE. Unpublished paper. Available from National Library of Canada. 14 pp.

Housing analysts visited the reserve and interviewed persons in 31 households in Wikwemikong whose present housing was considered inadequate according to a survey conducted. It was concluded that programs administered by Ontario Housing Corporation would not meet local requirements.   IVY

1775   **ONTARIO HOUSING CORPORATION**
1970
REPORT ON THE NEED AND DEMAND FOR ONTARIO HOUSING FOR FAMILIES: TOWNSHIP OF RED LAKE. Unpublished paper. Available from National Library of Canada. 20 pp.

Of 18 respondents to a questionnaire, 13 were considered to be very interested in and in need of low-rental housing. From an analysis of this questionnaire and of the economic base of the township of Red Lake, the report recommends the construction of 13 family units for which the rent is to be geared to income.   IVY

1776   **ONTARIO. Department of Education. Youth Branch.**
1967
A STUDY OF THE WALPOLE INDIAN RESERVE. Toronto: Department of Education. 35 pp.

This study presents statistical data on education, employment, social conditions, crime, and delinquency.   IVY

1777   **ORVIS   BRIAN N**
1970
AMY GREETS THE QUEEN. Tawow 1(3):30-31.

A biographic sketch of Amy Clemens, descendent of Chief Peguis, is given.   IVY

1778   **PARSONS   GEORGE F**
1970
ARCTIC SUBURB: A LOOK AT THE NORTH'S NEWCOMERS. Northern Science Research Group, Mackenzie Delta Research Project No. 8. Ottawa: Queen's Printer. 94 pp.

Interviews were obtained from a stratified sample of 53 government employees at Inuvik during 2 months of 1967. Social characteristics, opinions, and attitudes of the subjects are examined and their impressions of northern life, community activities, and contacts with Indians and Eskimos are discussed.   CCV

1779   **PETITOT   EMILE**
1970
INDIAN LEGENDS OF NORTH-WESTERN CANADA. The Western Canadian Journal of Anthropology 2(1):94-129.

A selection of origin myths of the Hare, Loucheux, Dogrib, Chipewyan, and Slave have been translated from French by Thelma Habgood.   IVY

1780   **PRATSON   FREDERICK JOHN**
1970
LAND OF THE FOUR DIRECTIONS. Old Greenwich, CT: Chatham Press. 131 pp.

Some aspects of contemporary culture and life of the Micmac and Malecite of New Brunswick and the Passamaquoddy of Maine are presented accompanied by numerous photographs. A desire to inform and enlighten White citizens is expressed.   CCV

1781   **PRESTON   RICHARD J**
n.d.
FACING NEW TASKS: CREE AND OJIBWA CHILDREN'S ADAPTATION TO RESIDENTIAL SCHOOL. Unpublished paper. Available from National Library of Canada. 30 pp.

The purpose of this study is to assess changing psychological patterns by comparing the traditional style of life with the data from psychological tests, dormitory supervisors' evaluations, and other notes from Indian children. The test research was undertaken at Horden Hall, Moose Factory. This paper is part of a long-term research project begun in 1963.   HCV

1782   **PUXLEY   PETER H L**
1969
CANADA'S NORTHERN INDIANS IN POST-INDUSTRIAL SOCIETY: A CASE OF INTER-CULTURAL PLANNING. M.S. Thesis. Department of Urban and Regional Planning. University of Toronto. 95 pp.

The problem of inter-cultural planning is discussed with attention to the Canadian North and specifically the needs of the Indian population. Regional co-operative programs integrating traditional values and giving priority to Indian participation and independence are proposed. An educational orientation, co-ordinated with the co-operative programs, which would provide a link with day-to-day realities and de-emphasizes acculturation, is suggested. Development of the North and its integration with the rest of the country is seen to be dependent on these factors rather than development of natural resources by White immigrants. The university's role as a center of research, innovation, and cultural exchange is outlined.   CCV

1783   **RADOJICIC   D**
1969

GREAT SLAVE LAKE - SOUTH SHORE: AN AREA ECONOMIC SURVEY
(A.E.S.R. No. 67/3). Ottawa: Queen's Printer. 128 pp.

Discussion of ecology, subsistence activities, economic development, resource potentials, communication and transportation, life style, and community services are included in the economic survey of the Great Slave Lake South Shore settlements. A high degree of integration and acculturation of the native population is reported. Recommendations are directed to accelerating economic development both on a regional and a segmental basis.   CCV

1784   **RAE   GEORGE RAMSEY**
1963
THE SETTLEMENT OF THE GREAT SLAVE LAKE FRONTIER NORTHWEST
TERRITORIES, CANADA: FROM THE EIGHTEENTH TO THE TWENTIETH
CENTURY. Ph.D. Thesis. Department of Geography. University of Michigan. 356 pp.
Available from National Library of Canada.

The Great Slave Lake frontier and the significance of fur trading, fishing, and mining in its development from Indian times to the present is described using the techniques of historical geography. The development of the fur trade is reconstructed with attention to details of Indians at contact, hunting and game conditions, transportation methods, trade items, and middlemen, and intertribal relations. Of note is the indication of an Indian fur-iron trade operative previous to the arrival of the first English and Canadian explorers and traders.   CCV

1785   **RANCIER   G J**
1965
VOCATIONAL EDUCATION NOW AND IN THE FUTURE. In Education North of
60: A Report Prepared by Members of the Canadian Association of School
Superintendents and Inspectors in the Department of Northern Affairs and National
Resources. B. Thorsteinsson, ed. The Canadian Superintendent 1964. Toronto: Ryerson
Press. pp. 32-39.

Training northern residents for gainful employment in the north or south is the focus of this paper. Discussed are curricula, short courses inside and outside the Territories, and on-the-job training.   IVY

1786   **RICHMOND   SARA**
1970
COGNITIVE AND STRUCTURAL BASES FOR GROUP IDENTITY: THE CASE
OF THE SOUTHERN ARCTIC DRAINAGE DENE. The Western Canadian
Journal of Anthropology 2(1):140-149.

Field research was conducted among the Beaver and Slave of northern Alberta and the Slave, Chipewyan, and Dogrib of the Northwest Territories during 4 separate trips totaling approximately 3-1/2 months. Concerned with larger groupings (tribes) among the Southern Arctic Drainage Dene, research has been directed to the problem of whether there is any cognitive reality in such group designations as Slavey, Beaver, Dogrib, and Chipewyan to the people for whom such names are used.   IVY

1787   **ROBERTSON   GORDON**
1961
NORTHERN PEOPLE IN TRANSITION. Speech delivered to Annual Banquet of the
National Council of Women of Canada. Windsor, June 8, 1961. Available from
Information Services, Records and Research, Department of Indian Affairs and
Northern Development, Ottawa. 13 pp.

A speech delivered by Gordon Robertson, Deputy Minister of Northern Affairs and National Resources and Commissioner of the Northwest Territories, presents implications
of northern development for Canadian Indians and Eskimos. Also reviewed are their
needs in the areas of education, employment, and housing.   CCV

1788   **ROBERTSON   GORDON**
1962
ADDRESS. Speech delivered to Annual Meetings of the Canadian Public Health
Association and the Ontario Public Health Association. Toronto, May 30, 1962.
Available from Information Services, Records and Research, Department of Indian
Affairs and Northern Development, Ottawa. 8 pp.

Changing conditions in Canada's North including the cultural transition for Indians and
Eskimos and the problem areas of education, health, and employment are reviewed.   CCV

1789   **ROGERS   EDWARD S**
1964
THE FUR TRADE, THE GOVERNMENT AND THE CENTRAL CANADIAN
INDIAN. Arctic Anthropology 2(2):37-40.

The emergence of the nuclear family and sedentary villages, and the concomitant social
fragmentation and decline of traditional leadership are summarized as trends among the
Cree-Ojibwa of interior northern Ontario in a symposium on the consequences of culture
contact in the Arctic and Sub-Arctic. The fur trade and the federal government are considered as primary agents of acculturation from 1890 to the present. It is concluded that
the influence of Euro-Canadian contact is inevitable, but that the direction can be altered
through change in policy and public opinion.   WRC

1790   **ROGERS   EDWARD S**
1965
LEADERSHIP AMONG THE INDIANS OF EASTERN SUBARCTIC CANADA.
Anthropologica N.S. 7:263-284.

Based on fieldwork among the Mistassini Cree of south-central Quebec, the Round Lake
Ojibwa of northern Ontario, and on published materials, the transition in forms of leadership in the Eastern Sub-Arctic is examined. It is concluded that the band-elective chiefs
of the present era (1940-1965) have less authority than the eldest male of the hunting
band of the contact era (1600-1800) and the acculturated leaders of the fur trade era
(1800-1940).   WRC

1791   **ROGERS   EDWARD S**
1966
A CURSORY EXAMINATION OF THE FUR RETURNS FROM THREE INDIAN

BANDS OF NORTHERN ONTARIO: 1950-1964. Ontario Department of Lands and Forests Research Branch Technical Series 75. Toronto: Department of Lands and Forests. 61 pp.

Fur returns from 3 bands (Moose Factory, Round Lake, and Fort Severn) for the period 1950-1964 are examined based on data secured from the Ontario Department of Lands and Forests, discussions with administrators, and a year's residence (1958-1959) among the Round Lake Ojibwa. The yield of furbearers (mink, muskrat, otter, bear) varied between (1) the Hudson Bay Lowland versus the Laurentian Uplands, (2) Moose Factory versus Fort Severn, (3) the Coastal Tundra versus Open Boreal Forest at Fort Severn, and (4) the Coastal versus the Peripheral area at Round Lake. Annual trend in fur production is viewed both in gross figures and the yield of pelts per trapper. A decrease is noted. Considering social aspects it is observed that (1) there are fewer trappers, particularly teenage ones; (2) the size and composition of trapping groups have altered; (3) age has a direct bearing on yield; and (4) density of trappers varied. Six maps and 19 graphs are included.   IVY

1792   **ROGERS   EDWARD S**
1967
INDIANS OF PARRY ISLAND: THE RISE AND FALL OF ALGONKIAN FARMING. Varsity Graduate 13(4):104-106.

The development of farming by the Indians of Parry Island, Ontario (Ojibwa, Ottawa, Potawatomi), and the factors leading to its demise are discussed.   IVY

1793   **ROGERS   EDWARD S**
1967
SUBSISTENCE AREAS OF THE CREE-OJIBWA OF THE EASTERN SUBARCTIC: A PRELIMINARY STUDY. In Contributions to Ethnology V. National Museum of Canada Bulletin 204. Ottawa: Queen's Printer. pp. 59-90.

The food economy of eastern sub-arctic Indians was examined for evidence of basic subsistence patterns. An approximate mapping of these Cree-Ojibwa areas was attempted. Fieldwork among the Mistassini Cree (1953-54) and Round Lake Ojibwa (1958-59) was supplemented with contemporary and historical accounts. Three time periods are suggested, 20th century, 19th century, and the 17th-18th century. It is concluded that a caribou-fish pattern was once widespread. This pattern was displaced by a moose-fish pattern where caribou became scarce. The once uninhabited Hudson Bay lowland became a waterfowl-fish area. In the 20th century a moose-fish pattern is evident in southern Quebec and central Ontario. In the Labrador peninsula, a caribou-fish pattern remained.   JSL

1794   **ROGERS   EDWARD S**
1969
BAND ORGANIZATION AMONG THE INDIANS OF EASTERN SUBARCTIC CANADA. In Contributions to Anthropology: Band Societies: Proceedings of the Conference on Band Organization, Ottawa, August 30 to September 2, 1965. David Damas, ed. National Museums of Canada Bulletin 228. Ottawa: Queen's Printer. pp. 21-55.

Band structure and organization among the Cree-Ojibwa of the eastern Sub-Arctic is discussed. Fieldwork among the Round Lake Ojibwa and Mistassini Cree was conducted in

1958-1959 and 1953-1954 respectively. Three types of bands are discerned historically: the aboriginal local group, the trading post band, and the government band. The author's primary concern is with the aboriginal band, and a definition and description is attempted. The aboriginal band was a loosely structured group, often patrilineal, composed of 75-125 people and inhabiting a drainage basin alone or in conjunction with other groups. Groups united in the summer on lake shores, and dispersed in winter into groups to hunting areas. The groups were often bilateral extended families led by a head man. The structure was an adaptation to a severe environment by a hunting-fishing economy. A discussion follows.   JSL

1795   **ROGERS   EDWARD S**
1969
NATURAL ENVIRONMENT - SOCIAL ORGANIZATION - WITCHCRAFT:
CREE VERSUS OJIBWA - A TEST CASE. In Contributions to Anthropology:
Ecological Essays: Proceedings of the Conference on Cultural Ecology, Ottawa, August 3-6, 1966. David Damas, ed. National Museum of Canada Bulletin 230. Ottawa: Queen's Printer. pp. 24-39.

A survey of Cree and Ojibwa social organization in relation to the natural environment and witchcraft practices was undertaken.   Fieldwork in the Eastern Sub-Arctic communities of Mistassini (1953-1954), Round Lake (1958-1959), and Parry Island (1963-1966) was supplemented by excursions and relevant literature. It is concluded that a strictly environmental explanation cannot account for social organization in the Eastern Sub-Arctic. Population density rapidly increases to the west, but the size of the small hunting group-band remains constant. In the Laurentian Uplands of Ontario the Cree hunting group-band is an adjustment to the harsh environment. In the Laurentian Uplands of Quebec and the Hudson Bay Lowlands the Ojibwa hunting group-band is the result of a preoccupation with, and highly developed concepts of, witchcraft in interpersonal relations.   JSL

1796   **ROGERS   EDWARD S**
1970
ALGONKIANS OF THE EASTERN WOODLANDS. Toronto: Royal Ontario
Museum. 16 pp.

Aspects of culture discussed in this introductory booklet of the Algonkians of the Upper Great Lakes include material culture, subsistence activities, social organization, warfare, ritual, and religion. Photographs and drawings accompany text.   IVY

1797   **ROGERS   EDWARD S**
1970
INDIANS OF THE SUBARCTIC. Toronto: Royal Ontario Museum. 16 pp.

This introductory booklet discusses material culture, subsistence activities, social organization, trade, warfare, and religion.   Photographs and drawings accompany the text.   IVY

1798   **ROHRL   VIVIAN J**
1970
A NUTRITIONAL FACTOR IN WINDIGO PSYCHOSIS. American Anthropologist
72:97-101.

Nutritional deficiencies are viewed as extracultural factors in the etiology of the Windigo psychosis among Northern Algonkian peoples. As seen in a review of case studies, the persistent native ritual of ingesting animal fat, particularly of the bear, and more recent biological discoveries on the relationship between psychological disorders and vitamins B and C provide strong evidence for an effective traditional cure which has received empirical verification through time by such tribes as the Cree and Ojibwa.   WRC

1799   **ROY   CHUNILAL,   CHOUDHURI   ADJIT**
1970
THE PREVALENCE OF MENTAL DISORDERS AMONG SASKATCHEWAN INDIANS. Journal of Cross-Cultural Psychology 1:383-392.

This report covers a retrospective study of 1st admission statistics at North Battleford psychiatric institution for the period 1961 to 1966 (51 treaty Indians, 2,607 non-Indians) and a comprehensive case-finding survey in a region northwest of North Battleford which contained 18 rural municipalities (non-Indian, population 28,096) and 10 Indian reserves (9 Cree and 1 Saulteaux, population 4,723). Results of the study showed that Indians were the younger of the 2 groups and that a significantly higher percentage of Indians than non-Indians received the diagnosis of epilepsy, schizophrenia, and organic psychosis. Among observations recorded in the survey were that there is a higher prevalence rate for psychiatric disorders and severe mental deficiency among the Indians and that a large number of Indian school children are suffering from a severe form of emotional disturbance.   IVY

1800   **SALZER   ROBERT**
1960
WOODLAND BUSTLE. American Indian Tradition 6:62-64.

While always rare, woodland bustles were most popular in the 1920's. Two examples, one a single panel and the other a double panel bustle, collected from unspecified sources early in the 20th century, are described.   TSA

1801   **SALZER   ROBERT**
1961
CENTRAL ALGONKIAN BEADWORK. American Indian Tradition 7:166-178.

Central Algonkian beadwork is distinguished from that of other tribes. Some geographical and cultural differences and similarities are seen within the central Algonkian area. Techniques (loom weaving, "double warp"method, edge-beading, applique beading), design, color, and placement of decoration are described. Numerous photographs illustrate the text.   IVY

1802   **SASKATCHEWAN. Department of Welfare. Research Planning Branch.**
1968
THE BROADVIEW RURAL DEVELOPMENT AREA STUDY: AN EXTENSION UNDER GENERAL RURAL DEVELOPMENT ARDA PROJECT, NO. 8067.
Unpublished paper. Available from National Library of Canada. 136 pp.

The Broadview rural development area is located in the southeastern part of Saskatchewan, 97 miles west of Regina. The resident population of,3,703 contains 1,900 people of Indian ancestry. The Agricultural and Rural Development Administration (ARDA)

identified area problems such as low income, poor communication and transportation, lack of skilled manpower, lack of leadership, social and cultural factors that prevent social change, and public health problems. To implement a successful, comprehensive development ARDA carried out several proposals: a specialized staff to implement the plan, an integration administrator, an all-weather north and south road, multi-purpose education facilities, land clearing and farm management, recreational development, and development of tourism.   HCV

1803   **SAVARD   REMI**
1965
LA DIFFERENCIATION DES ACTIVITES SEXUELLES ET ALIMENTAIRES: REPRESENTATIONS MYTHIQUES ESQUIMAUDES ET INDIENNES. Anthropologica N.S. 7(1):39-58.

This attempts an interpretation of a myth which occurs in at least 12 variants among Sub-Arctic Indians and Eskimos. Certain narrative elements of those variants (4 of them are Indian) have parallels in South America as well as in Polynesia and in the Eastern Mediterranean. This recurrence suggests that the so-called famous metamorphoses, consistently dear to scholarly commentators, could indeed logically derive from the very structure of the mythic vision.   DD

1804   **SAVOIE   DONAT**
1970
LES AMERINDIENS DU NORD-OUEST CANADIEN AU 19e SIECLE SELON EMILE PETITOT. VOLUME 1: LES ESQUIMAUX TCHIGLIT. VOLUME 2: LES INDIENS LOUCHEUX. Department of Indian Affairs and Northern Development, Northern Science Research Group, Mackenzie Delta Research Projects Nos. 9-10. Ottawa: Information Canada. 2 vols.

Extracts from the writings of Emile Petitot are compiled providing ethnographic information on the Indian and Eskimo population of the Mackenzie Delta region during the early contact period. Relations between the Eskimo and the Hare, Loucheux, and Dene are described in the volume. Volume 2 includes a general account of the Dene including the tribal classification of Petitot, demography, geographic description, material culture, social organization, religion and world view, and inter-ethnic relations. Material relating to the Loucheux is organized in the same manner.   CCV

1805   **SEGUIN   ROBERT-LIONEL**
1969
LES JOUETS ANCIENS DU QUEBEC. Ottawa: Lemeac. 107 pp.

Indian games for adults and children, toys, and children's play are described on pages 31-43 of this study of old toys of Quebec.   CCV

1806   **SERVICE   ELMAN R**
1966
THE HUNTERS. Englewood Cliffs, NJ: Prentice-Hall. 118 pp.

Presented is an analytical and theoretical interpretation of the structure and organization of primitive band societies. Treatment is accorded to the Algonkian and Athabascan hunters in the Canadian Sub-Arctic. The technology, economy and society, polity, and ideology of these hunters and gatherers are discussed on pages 89-93.   DGW

1807   **SIEMANS   L B**
1968
CENTER FOR SETTLEMENT STUDIES: PROCEEDINGS OF THE SYMPOSIUM ON RESOURCE FRONTIER COMMUNITIES. Winnipeg: University of Manitoba. 86 pp.

Discussion of Indians as employees and of the possibilities for increasing their employment in northern industry is included in the proceedings of this symposium on resource frontier communities.   CCV

1808   **SIM   R ALEX**
1965
A RADIO FORUM PROJECT FOR THE CANADIAN NORTH. Unpublished paper. Available from Indian-Eskimo Association. 63 pp.

This is a report to the Indian-Eskimo Association of Canada on the feasibility of initiating a radio listening group project in the Canadian North in co-operation with the Canadian Broadcasting Corporation and other governmental agencies. The study resulted in several recommendations, one of which is that of an adult education program in the north using the radio as the main vehicle of communication.   HCV

1809   **SIMPSON   D W**
1965
ACCOMODATION FOR LEARNING AND LIVING. In Education North of 60: A Report Prepared by Members of the Canadian Association of School Superintendents and Inspectors in the Department of Northern Affairs and National Resources. B. Thorsteinsson, ed. The Canadian Superintendent 1964. Toronto: Ryerson Press. pp. 22-31.

Northern conditions, such as climate and permafrost, pose unique problems in the construction and operation of schools. These problems are discussed as well as the staffing of schools and the funding of higher education.   IVY

1810   **SLOBODIN   RICHARD**
n.d.
NORTHERN ATHAPASKAN ACCULTURATION. Unpublished paper. Available from Library, Department of Indian Affairs and Northern Development. 22 pp.

The traditional culture of the Northern Athabaskan-speaking peoples, the agents of contact, and acculturation processes are reviewed. Alterations in material culture, seasonal cycle, and social organization arising from acculturation are discussed.   CCV

1811   **SURTEES   ROBERT J**
1966
INDIAN RESERVE POLICY IN UPPER CANADA, 1830-1845. M.A. Thesis. Department of History. Carleton University. 184 pp. Available from National Library of Canada.

The period 1830 to 1845 is discussed with reference to Indian reserve policy in Upper Canada. No longer were the Indians regarded as allies, but rather as savages to be civilized and Christianized. The nomadic Ottawa, Chippewas, and Missisaugas were to be induced to settle on special lots of land and become civilized farmers. However, experimental farms at Coldwater and Manitoulin Island failed. The Indian Affairs branch had insufficient staff and resources, there was no consensus on how best to civilize the Indian, and the Indians were unwilling to cooperate.   IVY

1812   **SYMINGTON   FRASER**
1965
TUKTU: THE CARIBOU OF THE NORTHERN MAINLAND. Ottawa: Queen's Printer. 92 pp.   Also in French.

The caribou is viewed from the viewpoint of wildlife management and discussed are the significance of the caribou to the aboriginal population, the effects of the arrival of the White man, and the importance of the caribou in the North today. It is suggested that the caribou retains a cultural and economic significance for natives of the North which cannot be abruptly replaced.   CCV

1813   **TANNER   ADRIAN**
1965
TRAPPERS, HUNTERS AND FISHERMEN: WILD LIFE UTILIZATION IN THE YUKON TERRITORY. Department of Northern Affairs and National Resources, Northern Co-ordination and Research Centre, Yukon Research Project Series No. 5. Ottawa: Department of Northern Affairs and National Resources. 79 pp.

Fieldwork in Yukon territory in 1964 indicated that most of the Indians, Metis, and Whites involved in subsistence hunting, fishing, and trapping pursue all 3 activities and require some form of welfare assistance. Proposals intended to increase the economic feasibility of these pursuits are advanced.   CCV

1814   **TARASOFF   KOOZMA J,   SCHULTZ   HERB,**   et al.
1970
A SOCIO-ECONOMIC REVIEW OF THE GARMENT PLANT - FISHER RIVER AND PEGUIS COMMUNITIES: A FRED PROJECT IN MÅNITOBA. Winnipeg: Department of Regional Economic Expansion. 95 pp. 2 vols.

The satellite garment plant of Monarch Wear Limited on Peguis Indian Reserve was financed as an experimental project by the Canada Department of Manpower and Immigration with technical assistance provided by the provincial government. Established in February 1969, the plant was primarily conceived as an industrial training facility for disadvantaged peoples. In volume 2 the stated objective is to try to determine if the plant has made a significant difference to the community in terms of increased industrial life skills, social awareness, and potential for mobility. Sources of information include: data derived from questionnaires distributed to present workers, former workers, and a control group; a review of documents; meetings with chiefs and councilors; discussions with local government officials; perusal of a photographic documentary; and participant observation. It is generally concluded that the effects of the plant on the community in social and economic terms has been good, and the expressed desire to see it remain open is unanimous. Forty-one statistical tables are included in the report.   IVY

1815   **TEICHER   MORTON**
1960
WINDIGO PSYCHOSIS: A STUDY OF A RELATIONSHIP BETWEEN BELIEF
AND BEHAVIOR AMONG THE INDIANS OF NORTHEASTERN CANADA.
American Ethnological Society, Proceedings of the 1960 Annual Spring Meeting. 129 pp.

Examination of the concept and psychosis of the Windigo monster prevalent among Algonkian tribes of northeastern Canada yields evidence for belief structure as a major determinant of behavior. Reproduced are 31 folktales and 70 known cases of the psychosis from the 17th to the 20th centuries to indicate the dominant position of the belief among the Ojibwa, Cree, and Montagnais-Naskapi. The cultural and geographical settings in which the belief and the cannibalistic psychosis developed are also considered. Appended are a geographical list of Windigo place names, an index of folktale titles, and an index, location list, and distribution map of the cases.   WRC

1816   **TENOR   J S**
1965
WILDLIFE AND NATIVE PEOPLES. In Twenty-Ninth Federal-Provincial Wildlife
Conference, Winnipeg, June 18-19, 1965. Ottawa: Canadian Wildlife Service. pp. 92-95.

A Canadian wildlife staff specialist in mammalogy suggests a parallel between the Canadian North and Uganda in the relationship of wildlife resources to native populations. Referring to the success of wildlife management programs in Uganda, Canadian possibilities are briefly discussed.   CCV

1817   **THOMAS   ROBERT K,   MACKENZIE   JOHN A**
1970
SURVEY REPORT TO THE ANGLICAN CHURCH OF THE WESTERN REGION
OF THE NORTHWEST TERRITORIES. Unpublished paper. Available from National
Library of Canada. 21 pp.

Fieldwork was conducted the month of July using the participant observation method in the western region of the Northwest Territories. For purposes of analysis this region was divided into the 3 areas of (1) Mackenzie River Proper (from Fort Providence to Fort Good Hope), (2) the northern region around Inuvik, and (3) Yellowknife-Fort Rae. Each area is described separately, with the main concern being social organization/disorganization. Varying intensities of a caste system that exists in all regions are discussed. It is suggested that established churches either withdraw from some communities or begin a program directly related to the needs of the people. Other recommendations for the churches include re-evaluating their models for ministry in Indian communities, educating clergy about recent nativistic movements, using remaining power to protect the rights of Indians against the rapid encroachment of secular power, working willingly with each other, and exploring ways of developing social cohesiveness internally within these communities.   IVY

1818   **THORMAN   GEORGE**
1969
THE MAMATOWASSINI. The Beaver 300(Summer):60-62.

Discussed is a large greenstone lava boulder which is located about 35 miles up the Albany River from Fort Albany in the James Bay lowland and is considered sacred or magical by the Cree and Ojibwa. A legend entitled "The Origin of the Muskegon Cree"concludes the article.   IVY

1819   **THORSTEINSSON   B**
1965
BEYOND THE THRESHOLD. In Education North of 60: A Report Prepared by Members of the Canadian Association of School Superintendents and Inspectors in the Department of Northern Affairs and National Resources. B. Thorsteinsson, ed. The Canadian Superintendent 1964. Toronto: Ryerson Press. pp. 104-112.

Educational opportunities for 3 age groups are discussed: adolescents and young adults, older adults, and those who form the younger generation.   IVY

1820   **THORSTEINSSON   B**
1965
EDUCATION AT THE TOP OF THE WORLD - AN OVERVIEW. In Education North of 60: A Report Prepared by Members of the Canadian Association of School Superintendents and Inspectors in the Department of Northern Affairs and National Resources. B. Thorsteinsson, ed. The Canadian Superintendent 1964. Toronto: Ryerson Press. pp. 1-10.

Reviewing the educational system north of the 60th parallel, the following aspects are discussed: the country and the people, the school system, unique features, school organization on religious bases, administration of the school system, and educational objectives.   IVY

1821   **TOMPKINS   ROBERT G**
1969
RECENT ECONOMIC DEVELOPMENT AND SOCIAL CHANGE IN THE NORTHWEST TERRITORIES. In Perspectives on Regions and Regionalism and Other Papers. B. Y. Card, ed. Proceedings of the Tenth Annual Meeting of the Western Association of Sociology and Anthropology, Held at Banff, Alberta, December 28, 29 and 30, 1968. Edmonton: University of Alberta Printing Service. pp. 121-125.

The influx of Whites into the Northwest Territories makes it necessary that the native peoples adapt to the new technology. The failure of the government to provide adult education contributes to the high rate of native unemployment. It is recommended that persons destined to work with native peoples serve an apprenticeship with them, that formal education not be required for employment, that native language and culture be taught in the schools, and that the school system serve the needs of Indians and Eskimos.   TSA

1822   **TRUDEL   MARCEL**
1960
L'ESCLAVAGE AU CANADA FRANCAIS: HISTOIRE ET CONDITIONS DE L'ESCLAVAGE. Quebec: Presses de l'Universite Laval. 432 pp.

Slavery in French Canada is discussed. It is impossible to date exactly the beginning or the end of this practice except that an isolated case is recorded at Quebec in 1629. Slaves were either Negroes or Indian captives and their offspring. It is clear that in some cases slaves were treated as freemen or servants and in others more stringent restrictions were applied. Legalization of slavery, origin of the slaves, the Canadian slave market, living conditions for slaves, religion for slaves, crime and punishment, legal status, liaisons and marriage, descendants of slaves in Canada, and disappearance of slavery are discussed in turn.   CCV

1823   **TRUDEL   MARCEL, ed.**
1968
JACQUES CARTIER. Montreal: Editions Fides. 95 pp.

Texts describing Jacques Cartier's 3 voyages are compiled from archival sources. The Indians encountered by Cartier and his crew are mentioned frequently. Clothing, diet, subsistence dwellings, and relations with the White explorers are described. The groups being discussed are those of the northern New Brunswick coast, Gaspe, Saguenay, Quebec, and the general St. Lawrence area.   CCV

1824   **UNION OF NOVA SCOTIA INDIANS**
1970
BRIEF PRESENTED BY THE UNION OF NOVA SCOTIA INDIANS TO THE COMMITTEE FOR THE STUDY OF LEGAL AID IN NOVA SCOTIA. THIS COMMITTEE APPOINTED BY THE HONOURABLE RICHARD A. DONAHOE, Q.C. ATTORNEY GENERAL OF THE PROVINCE OF NOVA SCOTIA, SEPTEMBER 30, 1970. Unpublished paper delivered to Committee for the Study of Legal Aid in Nova Scotia. Available from National Library of Canada. 8 pp.

This brief was presented to the Legal Aid Committee of Nova Scotia to draw attention to the paradoxical legal situation of the Canadian Indian. It outlines the federal-provincial division of responsibility to the Indians in relation to the Indian Act, the Department of Indian Affairs, legal policy, and provincial taxation.   HCV

1825   **VOKES   V**
1965
INDIAN ARTS AND CRAFTS. Unpublished paper in Norec Conference: The Development of Indian and Eskimo Art and Crafts in the Far North. Northern Regional Committee, Indian-Eskimo Association of Canada. Toronto, May 3, 1965. Available from Indian-Eskimo Association. pp. 4-6.

This report from the Indian Affairs Branch discusses financial assistance, training, marketing, and promotion. Specific reference is made to the 330 craftsmen of the Yukon and Mackenzie District.   IVY

1826   **WEIR   DOUGLAS ALLAN**
1967
A STUDY OF THREE NORTHERN SETTLEMENTS: FORT NORMAN, FORT FRANKLYN, AND NORMAN WELLS, N.W.T. M.A. Thesis. Department of Geography. University of Alberta. 156 pp.

Fort Norman, Fort Franklyn, and Norman Wells are examined in a geographical perspective by means of library research and a month of fieldwork in each settlement during the summer of 1966. Discussion is devoted to locations and physical environment, historical background, and subsistence economy and seasonal activity. Services, demography, employment, housing, land use, community organization, and regional significance are treated for each settlement. Fundamental differences between the 3 settlements were observed and they are classified according to historical development and current function. Fort Norman is labeled as a local service and administrative center, Fort Franklyn a satellite settlement, and Norman Wells a company town.   CCV

1827   **WELCH   ROBERT**
n.d.
STATEMENT TO THE LEGISLATURE: EXPERIMENTAL HOUSING IN NORTHERN ONTARIO. Available from National Library of Canada. 3 pp.

Proposed experimental housing projects at Armstrong, Macdiarmid, Minaki, and Dinorwic are explained. Upon completion of construction, the ownership of the houses will be transferred to community development corporations which will assume responsibility for allocating the homes, as well as for maintenance and management of the project.   IVY

1828   **WHITBY   BARBARA**
1967
THE BEOTHUCKS AND OTHER PRIMITIVE PEOPLES OF NEWFOUNDLAND: A REVIEW. Anthropological Journal of Canada 5(4):2-19.

Archaeological and ethnohistoric evidence sheds light upon prehistoric and historic tribal movements of the aboriginals of Newfoundland. The ways of life of the Micmac, Beothuck, Montagnais, and Naskapi, as well as 7 others, are described.   IVY

1829   **WILLIS   JOHN S**
1962
DISEASE AND DEATH IN CANADA'S NORTH. Arctic Conference, Document No. 20. Unpublished paper delivered to Conference on Medicine and Public Health in the Arctic and Subarctic. World Health Organization. Geneva, August 28-September 1, 1962. Available from Library, Department of Indian Affairs and Northern Development, Ottawa. 30 pp.

Disease and health services in the Arctic are reviewed. Causes of death, mortality rates, and incidence of disease are tabulated separately for Indian, White, and Metis. The current trends in disease and health services are discussed.   CCV

1830   **WILLIS   JOHN S,   MARTIN   MORGAN**
1962
MENTAL HEALTH IN CANADA'S NORTH. Arctic Conference, Document No. 26. Unpublished paper delivered to Conference on Medicine and Public Health in the Arctic and Subarctic. World Health Organization. Geneva, August 28-September 1, 1962. Available from Library, Department of Indian Affairs and Northern Development, Ottawa. 26 pp.

Mental illness among persons of White, Indian, and Eskimo ancestry in Canada's North is discussed. Behavioral problems are reviewed briefly in relation to traditional culture, physical environment, alcohol, and acculturation.   CCV

1831 **WILSON   AMY V**
1966
A NURSE IN THE YUKON. New York: Dodd, Mead. 209 pp.

Narrated are the experiences of Amy Wilson who was employed as Alaska Highway nurse for Indian Health Services. Her medical tour of duty brought her into contact with Indians along the thousands of miles which separate Dawson Creek, British Columbia, from Whitehorse in the Yukon. This is a reprint of the 1965 publication entitled "No Man Stands Alone."   DGW

1832 **WILSON   CLIFFORD**
1970
CAMPBELL OF THE YUKON. Toronto: Macmillan. 185 pp.

Drawing from archival sources and his autobiography an account of Robert Campbell's experiences from 1830 through 1871 is presented. Explorations and trade with Indians of northern Manitoba, Northwest Territories, and the Yukon are described.   CCV

1833 **WOLFORTH   JOHN**
1966
THE MACKENZIE DELTA - ITS ECONOMIC BASE AND DEVELOPMENT: A PRELIMINARY STUDY. Mackenzie Delta Research Project 1. Ottawa: Department of Indian Affairs and Northern Development, Northern Science Research Group. 85 pp.

The significance of trapping, reindeer herding, forestry, and fishing for the Mackenzie Delta economy is evaluated with consideration of current trends and expansion potential as the result of fieldwork during July and August, 1965. The demography and economies of Delta settlements are described including employment and income and their distribution among White, Indian, Metis, and Eskimo. Recommendations for further research and comments on viable economic prospects are made.   CCV

1834 **WOODLEY   GEORGE WILLIAM**
1965
ADMINISTRATION FOR DEVELOPMENT: THE CO-ORDINATION OF FEDERAL AND TERRITORIAL GOVERNMENT ACTIVITIES IN THE NORTHWEST TERRITORIES. M.A. Thesis. Department of Political Studies. Queen's University. 229 pp.

The development of administration in the North is examined and the structure of federal agencies and the territorial government are discussed. The problems of co-ordination, particularly of development, arising from fragmentation of responsibility are outlined with improvements being suggested.   CCV

1835 **YARNELL   RICHARD ASA**
1964
ABORIGINAL RELATIONSHIPS BETWEEN CULTURE AND PLANT LIFE IN THE UPPER GREAT LAKES REGION. University of Michigan Museum of Anthropology Anthropological Papers 23. Ann Arbor, MI: University of Michigan. 218 pp.

While this Ph.D. thesis (University of Michigan, 1963) relies primarily on archaeological data, the examination of the interrelationship between aboriginal culture and plant life in the Upper Great Lakes also utilizes data from ethnographic and ethnohistoric sources. Plant resources, aboriginal agriculture, and the effect of subsistence activities on the flora of the region are evaluated. CCV

1836 ZENTNER HENRY
1967
THE PRE-MACHINE ETHIC OF THE ATHABASKAN-SPEAKING INDIANS: AVENUE OR BARRIER TO ASSIMILATION. In A Northern Dilemma: Reference Papers. Arthur K. Davis, Vernon C. Serl, et al., eds. Bellingham, WA: Western Washington State College. pp. 69-89.

The pre-machine ethic which characterizes native cultures is described and related to underlying beliefs and values with particular focus on the native concept of the relationship between the natural and supernatural. Comparison of the pre-machine ethic and the post-industrial ethic of the dominant Canadian society demonstrates a degree of conflict between them which impedes integration. It is proposed that policy makers orient programs of integration to reinforce native held values which have parallels in modern society. Native leadership lacks reinforcement but training programs could be developed with special attention to the native value system. Special consideration of native mythology and religious beliefs and particularly notions of time and space is merited. At the same time economic opportunities must be made available for trained native personnel. CCV

ABNAKI

1837 BECK HORACE P
1966
GLUSKAP THE LIAR AND OTHER INDIAN TALES. Freeport, ME: Bond, Wheelwright. 182 pp.

Material presented in this collection of eastern Maine and New Brunswick Indian legends derives from fieldwork (n.d.) mainly at Indian Island, Maine. The archaeology, early history, warfare on land and sea, and the present life of the Pennobscot and Passamaquoddy Indians are sketched briefly in 3 introductory chapters. The origin of folktales of Nourumbec, the fabled cities of the North, is discussed. Legends are chosen representatively with a view to illustrating different aspects of Eastern Woodlands culture. CCV

1838 CHARLAND THOMAS
1961
UN VILLAGE D'ABENAKIS SUR LA RIVIERE MISSISQUOI. Revue d'Histoire de l'Amerique Francaise 15:319-332.

Observations concerning the establishment in 1732 of a group of Abnaki from Becancour and St.-Francois in the area of Missisquoi Bay of Lake Champlain are based on archival sources. The settlement was probably prompted by better hunting and better access to the English traders. The nature of the settlement is described. CCV

1839 CHARLAND THOMAS M
1964

HISTOIRE DES ABENAKIS D'ODONAK (1765-1937). Montreal: Editions du
Levrier. 368 pp.

The history of the Abenakis at Odonak is traced from 1675 to 1937. Archival and historical sources are used to document the beginnings of Abenaki settlements near Sorel and
the nature of their contacts with the European settlers and traders. The establishment of
Abenakis at Missiquoi Bay on Lake Champlain, Jesuit activities among the Abenakis, the
role of the Abenakis in the fur trade competition between French and English, Abenaki
participation in the American Revolution, introduction of Western education, and the
question of land title are discussed.   CCV

1840   **CONKLING   ROBERT**
1970
SOCIAL AND CULTURAL CHANGE AMONG THE WABANAKI IN FRENCH
COLONIAL TIMES, 1600-1750. Unpublished paper. Available from National Library
of Canada. 68 pp.

This preliminary draft based on historical data, describes and analyzes culture contact
processes of the Algonkian Indians of Maine, New Brunswick, Nova Scotia, and the
Gaspe Peninsula. Concerned with the relationship between social and cutural changes,
attention is focused upon the social changes brought about largely by the fur trade and
cultural changes that took place under the charismatic missionaries. The change from a
nomadic to a sedentary way of life made Christian values and norms relevant. The conversion to Christianity established a significantly different authority structure.   IVY

1841   **DAY   GORDON M**
1963
THE TREE NOMENCLATURE OF THE SAINT FRANCIS INDIANS. In
Contributions to Anthropology, 1960. Part II. National Museum of Canada Bulletin
190. Ottawa: Queen's Printer. pp. 37-48.

The Abnakis of Odanak Reserve, Quebec, are a highly acculturated group. To test their
plant nomenclature, 5 informants were chosen: 4 were retired woodsmen and guides,
and 1 was a herbalist's son. This report discusses only the tree nomenclature. It was
found that the aboriginal taxonomy was retained by men who maintained life-long contact with the woods despite acculturation.   JSL

1842   **DAY   GORDON M**
1964
THE TREE NOMENCLATURE OF THE SAINT FRANCIS INDIANS. New
Hampshire Archaeologist 13:6-10.

Five informants and published materials provide Abnaki names for 64 species of trees.
Native classification is compared to scientific taxonomy.   TSA

1843   **GREENING   W E**
1966
HISTORIC ODANAK AND THE ABENAKI NATION. Canadian Geographical
Journal 73:92-97.

The Abnaki figured prominently in the history of New England and New France in the 17th and 18th centuries. A general description of their role in the warfare between the French and English is outlined.   IVY

1844   **JOSEPH   MARY ANNA**
1962
FRENCH AND ENGLISH PRESSURES ON THE INDIANS OF ACADIA AND EASTERN NEW ENGLAND. M.A. Thesis. Department of History and Anthropology. University of New Brunswick. 187 pp.

The English-French struggle for supremacy in North America is studied for its effects on the peoples native to Acadia and Maine.   The native tribes, settlement patterns, and the differences in French and English attitudes toward colonization and thus toward the Indians are described. Salient events in warfare are analyzed to further the comparison between French and English treatment of the Indians.   CCV

1845   **SMITH   NICHOLAS N**
1962
ST. FRANCIS INDIAN DANCES - 1960. Ethnomusicology 6:15-18.

A 300th anniversary celebration held at St. Francis Wabanaki village of Odanak, Quebec, featured the following tribal dances: Snake Dance, Eagle Dance, Blanket Dance, Friendly Dance, War Dance, Tomahawk Dance, and Calumet Dance. Information is provided on each of these.   IVY

1846   **SNOW   DEAN R**
1968
WABANAKI "FAMILY HUNTING TERRITORIES."American Anthropologist 70:1143-1151.

From a review of literature on the Northern and Eastern Algonkians implications are drawn for Wabanaki territoriality in the Maritime provinces and Maine. Difficulties are noted in postulating a uniform social organization for the many tribes of this cultural area in view of the different environmental and historical conditions. It is argued that the accordance of hunting group and hunting property around the nucleus of a river provided a definitive notion of territory among the Wabanaki. Boundary definition is cited as the main factor differentiating the Eastern from the Northern groups, for which the introduction of the fur trade was the cause of explicit territorial organization.   WRC

ALGONKIN

1847   **BECHMANN-KHERA   SIGRID**
1964
LAC BARRIERE INDIANS: FIELD REPORT. Unpublished paper. Available from National Museum of Man, Ethnology Division, Ottawa, with permission of the author. 91 pp.

Fieldwork among the Lac Barriere Band in 1964 forms the basis of a discussion of most aspects of life to their historical antecedents. Short histories of trapping-line ownership are included.   DGW

1848   **CARRIERE   GASTON**
1963
MISSIONNAIRE SANS TOIT: LE P. JEAN-NICOLAS LAVERLOCHERE, O.M.I.,
1811-1884. Montreal: Rayonnement. 146 pp.

The missionary life of Father Laverlochere is recounted. Brief references to the Algonkins of Maniwaki and Temiskaming, particularly their relations with the missions, are
included.   CCV

1849   **COTE   REMI**
1967
SOMMES-NOUS DES IMPOSTEURS? Kerygma 1(2):69-71.

Distrust shown by Indians at Maniwaki, Quebec, for the Whites in general and the priest
in particular is described by an Oblate.   Some manifestations of this distrust are described and explained and Father Cote wonders how the image of the church can be improved in this respect.   CCV

1850   **GILBERT   LOUIS**
1967
ORGANISATION ECONOMIQUE ET RELOCATION A WEYMONTACHINGUE.
Unpublished paper. Available from Bibliotheque Nationale du Quebec. 127 pp.

From fieldwork in 1966, the Algonkin of Weymontachie Reserve are discussed in terms
of demography, history, economic instability, consumption, and political organization.
Each chapter is concluded by recommendations to the federal government.   DD

1851   **GUY   CAMIL**
1967
LES INDIENS DU QUEBEC: DESAGREGATION CULTURELLE ET
PROLETARISATION. Parti Pris 4(9-12):165-181.

This proposes that Indians are losing their traditional culture and at the same time, are
being assimilated by the occidental working class. The author cites the case of the Weymontaching group to argue his point. He analyzes their progressive "deculturation"as a
direct result of the usurpation of their territory by large enterprises. There is continual
conflict between the Indian traditional life and the modern system. On one hand, the stability attached to a job goes against the Indian day-by-day living, while on the other,
most Indians still live in tents which are the best housing for a nomadic group, but which
goes against all hygienic principles of the federal agents. According to the author, the
Indian has little choice as he is already partly integrated into the western culture and into
a specific group - the working class.   DD

1852   **HIRBOUR   RENE**
1969
ETUDE DE TROIS NIVEAUX D'INTEGRATION SOCIALE D'UNE SOCIETE DE
CHASSEURS-CUEILLEURS: KITCHEZAGIK ANICHENABE. M.A. Thesis.
Departement d'Anthropologie. Universite de Montreal. 80 pp.

The data used in this thesis were collected during 2 summers plus an additional 3 days a
month for a whole year. The main topic is the social organization of an Algonkin band
of Grand Lake Victoria, Quebec. The theoretical framework is June Helm's typology of

hunting and gathering bands. The author adds a new element to the typology which is the acculturation level of a band and its complement, sedentary life. The original Helm typology is then transformed by the author who now introduces his own, considering 3 levels of social integration.   DD

1853   **JAY   ROGER**
1970
A NEW PEOPLE, A PREVAILING OLD TRADE. Tawow 1(3):26-29.

In an interview Dan Sarazin of the Golden Lake Reserve discusses trapping.   IVY

1854   **LEE-WHITING   BRENDA B**
1966
DANIEL SARAZIN STILL MAKES BIRCHBARK CANOES. Canadian Geographical Journal 72:124-129.

Detailed text and photographs describe the making of a birchbark canoe by a master craftsman from Golden Lake Reserve in Ontario.   IVY

BEAVER

1855   **CHIPESIA   JOHNNY**
1966
BEAVER TALES. Toni Ridington and Robin Ridington, eds. Unpublished paper. Available from Provincial Archives, Victoria, B.C.   84 pp.

A translation of Beaver Indian tales told mainly by Johnny Chipesia.   IVY

1856   **RIDINGTON   ROBIN**
1968
THE MEDICINE FIGHT: AN INSTRUMENT OF POLITICAL PROCESS AMONG THE BEAVER INDIANS. American Anthropologist 70:1152-1160.

An analysis of interpersonal relations cites continual competition for supernatural power (the medicine fight) as the means of channeling authority in the absence of institutionalized political structures and hierarchies. Fieldwork among the Beaver Indians in 1965 and 1966 reveals that the control of supernatural power was a function of success in hunting. In view of the scarcity and variability of game this interpersonal struggle resulted in the continual alternation in the positions of dominance and authority. The accordance of a Beaver story with field observations provides evidence of this institution which maintains social control through attempts to control nature.   WRC

1857   **RIDINGTON   ROBIN**
1969
KIN CATEGORIES VERSUS KIN GROUPS: A TWO-SECTION SYSTEM WITHOUT SECTIONS. Ethnology 8:460-467.

Based on field research (1964-1969) Beaver kinship is analyzed to indicate that the conceptual dichotomy between cross and parallel relations does not necessarily extend to corporate groups. This dichotomy along with sex and generation was the main criterion by which a Beaver accounted for all persons in his social network and distinguished marriageable individuals in his own, the ascending, and the descending generations. Since this delineation was not made for kin groups, he had considerable flexibility in choice of spouse, affiliating group, and location of postmarital residence. It is hypothesized that the nomadic behavior of the Beaver in which women did not have vital subsistence roles was more congenial to an egocentric and diffuse kinship system. This form stands in contrast to sociocentric and concentrated groups formed according to the cross/parallel dichotomy to exchange women due to their primary role in subsistence. WRC

1858 **RIDINGTON ROBIN, RIDINGTON TONIA**
1970
THE INNER EYE OF SHAMANISM AND TOTEMISM. History of Religions 10:49-61.

It is argued that the symbols of totemic thought are also those of shamanic cosmology. The Beaver Indians illustrate this point. Three topics are presented: Beaver cosmic structure (based on Beaver myths, shamanic texts, and unpublished field notes compiled between 1964 and 1968), the vision quest, and Beaver shamanism. IVY

1859 **RIDINGTON WILLIAM ROBIN**
1968
THE ENVIRONMENTAL CONTEXT OF BEAVER INDIAN BEHAVIOR. Ph.D. Thesis. Department of Anthropology. Harvard University.

The title has been verified, but a copy was not obtained in time to abstract it. SLP

BEOTHUK

1860 **CUFF HARRY**
1966
I INTERVIEWED THE GREAT-GRANDCHILD OF A BEOTHUCK. The New Newfoundland Quarterly 65(2):25.

Mrs. Richard White states her great-grandfather was a Beothuck, who married a full-blooded Micmac girl. IVY

1861 **DEVEREUX E J**
1970
THE BEOTHUK INDIANS OF NEWFOUNDLAND IN FACT AND FICTION. Dalhousie Review 50:350-362.

Reviewed are the only depictions in English literature of the Beothuks: a romantic novel entitled "Ottawah: Last Chief of the Red Indians of Newfoundland"published in anonymous parts in London, 1848, and in later editions attributed to Sir Charles Augustus Murray, and George Webber's "The Last of the Aborigines: A Poem Founded on Facts"published in St. John's in 1851. IVY

1862 **ENGLISH LEO E F**
1960
SOME ASPECTS OF BEOTHUK CULTURE. The Newfoundland Quarterly 59(2):11-13,37.

The problems of the origin, language, and race affinities of the Beothuks are explored. It is noted that some Celtic words bear resemblance to certain Beothuk terms. Evidence points to emigration of the Norse Irish southward, first to Labrador, then to Newfoundland. Population, relics, and certain customs of the Beothuk are also discussed.   IVY

1863   **FRASER   ALLAN M**
1962
THE BEOTHUKS OF NEWFOUNDLAND. Canadian Geographical Journal 65:156-159.

The physical characteristics of the Beothuks and their costume, subsistence pattern, material culture, and religious beliefs are briefly described. The series of events leading to their extinction are outlined.   IVY

1864   **FRASER   ALLAN M**
1965
SHANAWDITHIT: LAST OF THE BEOTHUKS. Atlantic Advocate 56(3):34-35,37,39.

From 1823 when she was 24 until her death in 1829, Shanawdithit lived in White households. In 1827 the Beothuk Institution was founded in St. John's to make friends with the Indians and civilize them. Shanawdithit was viewed as the last hope of establishing contact with her people. William Epps Cormack worked with her to compile a limited Beothuk vocabulary and record historical events and manners and customs. Some pictures drawn by Shanawdithit appear in this article.   IVY

1865   **KRISTJANSON   W**
1963
WERE THE BEOTHUKS PART ICELANDIC? The Icelandic Canadian 21(3):26-29.

Evidence demonstrates that there could have been only slight admixture of Icelandic blood in the Beothuks.   IVY

1866   **ROUSSEAU   JACQUES**
1962
LE DERNIER DES PEAUX-ROUGES. Cahiers des Dix 27:47-76.

Events that led to the extinction of the Beothuk starting with the arrival of the first Europeans are chronicled. The author presents materials which contradict the Henness-Howley thesis. After a brief ethnographic description of the Beothuk material culture, the author tries to establish the persistant aggression of the Newfoundland coast fishermen towards the Beothuk, the reluctance on the part of the Anglican missionaries, the non-intervention of the provincial government, and its clumsy Indian policy until the death of the last survivor of the Beothuk in 1829. The article also includes as an appendix an account of the trip of 2 Europeans to Newfoundland when most of the tribe was still living.   DD

1867   **WHITBY   BARBARA**
1963
THE BEOTHUCKS: A PORTRAYAL OF THEIR BACKGROUND FROM TRADITIONAL SOURCES. The Newfoundland Quarterly 62(2):3-6,24-25,34-35.

From oral and written sources and archaeological data the Beothuck way of life is outlined. Presented are material culture, subsistence activities, and religious beliefs. A number of Beothuck sites and artifacts are also discussed in some detail.   IVY

CARRIER

1868   **MACDONALD   JOSEPH LORNE**
1967
A STUDY OF STRESS IN THE SOCIAL STRUCTURE OF THE MORICETOWN
INDIANS AS A FACTOR IN RESERVE HOUSING DEVELOPMENT. Ph.D. Thesis.
Department of Sociology. Brandeis University. 301 pp. Available from University
Microfilms.

Attitudes and opportunities available to River Babine Indians of Moricetown, British
Columbia, are examined in terms of significance for reserve housing development and
stress on the social structure. Data are derived from fieldwork conducted at Moricetown
between June and September, 1964, and research into government, missionary, and anthropological documents. Analysis of data on marriage practices, residence patterns,
work attitudes, social mobility, child-rearing, and other aspects of social organization
indicates that Indian responses to planned programs are a function of the traditional
value system. Stress is created by a failure to consider aspirations and values historically
associated with Indian identity. Communication between Indians and non-Indians
around areas of real need is stressed for effective planning.   CCV

1869   **STEWARD   JULIAN H**
1960
CARRIER ACCULTURATION: THE DIRECT HISTORICAL APPROACH. In
Culture in History: Essays in Honor of Paul Radin. Stanley Diamond, ed. New York:
Columbia University Press. pp. 732-744.

Carrier culture change is discussed from an historical viewpoint and compared to similar
processes in Labrador and the Amazon. The wealth and prominence of local chiefs created by the introduction of the fur trade was influenced by contacts with Coastal Indians.
This nobility-potlatch pattern was in turn supplanted by the family-held trapping territory as contact with and access to Europeans and their goods increased.   CCV

CHILCOTIN

1870   **VON TIESENHAUSEN H D**
1966
CHILKO FISHING CAMP. The Beaver 297(Autumn):28-31.

Photographs and text describes a summer fishing camp on the Chilko River.   IVY

CHIPEWYAN

1871   **COHEN   RONALD,   VANSTONE   JAMES W**
1964
DEPENDENCY AND SELF-SUFFICIENCY IN CHIPEWYAN STORIES. In
Contributions to Anthropology, 1961-62. Part II. National Museum of Canada Bulletin
194. Ottawa: Queen's Printer. pp. 29-55.

The culture and personality literature for the Sub-Arctic is reviewed. Three hypotheses are put forth. First, it is suggested that manifestations of both self-sufficiency and dependency are present. Second, it is suggested that both motivations are durable, and persist despite acculturation. Third, it is hypothesized that government welfare stimulates dependency motivations. These hypotheses are tested by an analysis of early 20th century Chipewyan folklore, and an analysis of contemporary Chipewyan children's stories. All 3 hypotheses are supported, although the authors admit to methodological weaknesses. Appended are the categories used for content analysis, a sample story, and the criteria used for judging motivational components.   JSL

1872   **DICKMAN   PHIL**
1969
THOUGHTS ON RELOCATION. The Musk-Ox 6:21-31.

A Community Development Officer comments on the relocation program of the federal government for the Churchill band of Chipewyan Indians to Dene Village, Churchill, from Duck Lake. Though there are many tangible benefits resulting from the move such as better housing, free fuel, and free medical service, in less than a decade their old way of life has been totally destroyed and they have not adapted to the urban life at Churchill. Houses located in close proximity are large but without adequate furniture and sufficient heat. Alienation between Chipewyan youths and their parents as well as the town people is evident. Truancy, juvenile delinquency, theft, vandalism, child neglect, and alcoholism underline the social disorganization which has taken place. In order to halt this social and psychological deterioration it is suggested: (1) adults be given the opportunity of returning to the fishing, hunting, and trapping for which they were trained; (2) the special needs of Indian children be met by an adjusted curriculum, specialists on Indian culture, and extra staffing; (3) various government departments coordinate their purposes, goals, and services; (4) adult education be initiated; and (5) native leadership be encouraged.   IVY

1873   **HLADY   WALTER M**
1960
A COMMUNITY DEVELOPMENT PROJECT AMONGST THE CHURCHILL
BAND AT CHURCHILL, MANITOBA, SEPTEMBER 1959-MARCH 1960.
Unpublished paper. Available from Legislative Library, Winnipeg. 38 pp.

Described as an action project rather than a study, community development principles were applied to the problems of the Churchill Band by the author for a period of 6 months. The stated purposes were (1) to see what could be effected among a primitive group in a short period of time and (2) to determine what the climate for community development would be in a longer project. Observations of the economic and social projects (i.e., hide tanning project, dogteam service, Christmas tree project, weekly film program, and boy scouts) begun as a result of the community development program are detailed. It is concluded that the results are beneficial and that the Chipewyan respond to this type of program. A community development officer for the community is recommended.   IVY

1874   **IRVING   W N**
1968
THE BARREN GROUNDS. In Science, History and Hudson Bay: Volume I. C. S. Beals, ed. Ottawa: Queen's Printer. pp. 26-54.

The 18th century life of the Eskimo in the coastal plain south of Baker Lake as far as Fort Churchill is compared with that of the Chipewyan Indians of the adjacent boreal forest. The Chipewyan inhabited larger villages and were more mobile. The Eskimo had greater access to the caribou while the Chipewyan had more variety in their game foods. Transportation, hunting, dwellings, and ecology are described. Description and dating of archaeological finds for the area are included.   CCV

1875   **KEW   J E**
1962
CUMBERLAND HOUSE IN 1960: ECONOMIC AND SOCIAL SURVEY OF NORTHERN SASKATCHEWAN REPORT NO. 2. Saskatoon: Center for Community Studies. 136 pp.

This report is based on a full year's participant observation in 1960 at Cumberland House, Saskatchewan. The report focuses upon the economy and social organization of the settlement. Income derived from trapping, fishing, wage labor, entrepreneurial activities, and welfare payments is discussed. Power roles in the community, those who control the local economy, are described. The social organization of the community of 450, including Indians, Metis, and Whites, is analyzed in 3 parts: (1) basic social groups - family, informal groups, and formal organizations; (2) outside agents - store managers, and missionaries; and (3) class and status-class divisions and status within classes. A discussion of some factors which limit planned change concludes the report.   IVY

1876   **LAL   RAVINDRA**
1969
FROM DUCK LAKE TO CAMP 10: OLD FASHIONED RELOCATION. The Musk-Ox 6:5-13.

An historical outline of the settlement of Duck Lake, including the moving of the Hudson's Bay post which precipitated the relocation of about 300 Chipewyans during 1957-1958, is presented. Changes in living conditions experienced by the Chipewyans since the move to Camp 10, Churchill, are discussed.   IVY

1877   **LAL   RAVINDRA**
1969
SOME OBSERVATIONS ON THE SOCIAL LIFE OF THE CHIPEWYANS OF CAMP 10, CHURCHILL, AND THEIR IMPLICATIONS FOR COMMUNITY DEVELOPMENT. The Musk-Ox 6:14-20.

In 1957, approximately 200 Chipewyan people who had lived a semi-nomadic life at Duck Lake were relocated to Camp 10 in Churchill. The rapid social disorganization of this Chipewyan community is discussed and a community development program is recommended.   IVY

1878   **MELLOR   A H**
1968
ORIGIN OF THE CHIPEWYAN. The Beaver 299(Summer):51.

This legend was recorded in 1913 by a Royal North West Mounted Police officer.   IVY

1879   **OSWALT   WENDELL H,   VANSTONE   JAMES W**
1963
PARTIALLY ACCULTURATED COMMUNITIES: CANADIAN ATHAPASKANS
AND WEST ALASKAN ESKIMOS. Anthropologica N.S. 5:23-31.

Fieldwork at the Chipewyan settlement of Snowdrift, Northwest Territories, and the
Eskimo community of Napaskiak, Alaska, led to a consideration of forms of village
leadership, changing settlement patterns, and policies of Canada and the United States
as differential factors underlying the higher level of formal community organization
among the Eskimos.   WRC

1880   **PARKER   JAMES MCPHERSON**
1967
THE FUR TRADE OF FORT CHIPEWYAN ON LAKE ATHABASKA, 1778-1835.
M.A. Thesis. Department of History. University of Alberta. 214 pp.

The problems encountered during the establishment of the fur trade centred at Fort
Chipewyan are recounted from archival sources. Chapter 5 is devoted to discussion of
the Cree and Chipewyan who traded and worked at Fort Chipewyan. The manner in
which trade was carried out, Indian-White relations, and the effect of White activity and
trade on traditional Indian life style are described. Throughout the remainder of the text
occasional references reveal the role of the Indian in the fur trade and details of his life
style and social organization.   CCV

1881   **ROGERS   EDWARD S,   UPDIKE   LEE**
1970
THE CHIPEWYAN. The Beaver 301(Winter):56-59.

The aboriginal way of life of the Chipewyan including their material culture and their
subsistence pattern adapted to the yearly cycle of the caribou is described and illustrated.   IVY

1882   **SMITH   DAVID M**
1970
EKONZE: MAGICO-MEDICAL BELIEFS OF CONTACT-TRADITIONAL
TRADING AT FORT RESOLUTION, NWT, CANADA. Unpublished paper.
Available at National Museum of Man, Ethnology Division, Ottawa, with permission of
the author. 31 pp.

Four Chipewyan informants provided information during the summers of 1968 and
1969 on magico-medical beliefs and practices in the contact-traditional community of
Fort Resolution, Northwest Territories, for the period 1900-1945. The present decline in
the number of shamans is attributed not only to the presence of priests and Euro-Canadian medical personnel but also to the limited possibilities presented by the life style of
the town-dwelling Indian. Dependence upon White personnel and institutions likewise
undermine other native institutions of leadership and reciprocity.   CCV

1883   **SMITH   JAMES G E**
n.d.

THE DECLINE AND FALL OF THE CONTACT-TRADITIONAL COMMUNITY IN THE NORTHERN CANADIAN "BUSH."Unpublished paper. Available from National Library of Canada. 27 pp.

The introduction of the fur trade to the Athabaskan-speaking peoples of the northwestern boreal forest resulted in a stable cultural adaptation characterized by all-native log cabin bush communities oriented to the trading post. The extension of government educational, medical, and welfare services within the last generation resulted in concentration of the local bands in large villages with urban characteristics. The consequences of micro-urban village life on traditional kin groupings and political organization are noted as they appeared in the initial years of adjustment of one band of Cariboo Eater Chipewyans.   HCV

1884   **SMITH   JAMES G E**
1970
THE CHIPEWYAN HUNTING GROUP IN A VILLAGE CONTEXT. The Western Canadian Journal of Anthropology 2(1):60-66.

Field research was conducted from August, 1967, to August, 1968 and from September, 1969, to January, 1970. A description of how the northeastern Chipewyan (Caribou-Eaters) have adjusted to a more or less sedentary life at Brochet is given. Four phases of post-contact adjustment are outlined and changes in traditional social units discussed.   IVY

1885   **SPECK   G**
1963
SAMUEL HEARNE AND THE NORTHWEST PASSAGE. Caldwell, ID: Caxton. 337 pp.

Presented is an interpretation of the significance of Samuel Hearne's explorations. An enumeration of some of the major steps in the search for the North West Passage, a chronological ordering of these events, and a delineation of Hearne's work at the culmination of this search are attempted. Hearne, who entrusted his life completely to the natives, described the Chipewyan Indians in colorful and sympathetic terms. In Chapter 5, the world view of the Chipewyans is expressed in relation to the rival Cree or Home Guards. Chapter 11 describes the personality of Matonabbee, the Chipewyan leader who rescued Hearne from near death and acted as a guide for his third attempt up the Coppermine River.   DGW

1886   **THOMPSON   H PAUL**
1966
ESTIMATING ABORIGINAL AMERICAN POPULATION: A TECHNIQUE USING ANTHROPOLOGICAL AND BIOLOGICAL DATA. Current Anthropology 7:417-424.

As 1 of 2 special articles on the estimation of aboriginal American populations, this paper establishes maximal (10,652) and minimal (4,670) limits of the pre-contact (1770) Chipewyan. By discerning the effects of human exploitation of the biomass, a method of estimation is developed based on the interaction of biological-physical habitat, technology, and available resources. A review of ethnohistorical and zoological reports provides data for the derivation of an equation indicating the ecological population equilibrium of barren-ground caribou. From this equation inferences are drawn placing the maximum estimate of Chipewyan population at 6,426. Further application of the technique is suggested. The section is followed by comments from other scholars and an extensive bibliography.   WRC

1887   **VANSTONE   JAMES W**
1961
THE ECONOMY OF A FRONTIER COMMUNITY: A PRELIMINARY
STATEMENT. Department of Northern Affairs and National Resources, Northern Coordination and Research Centre Reports No. NCRC-61-4. Ottawa: Department of Northern Affairs and National Resources. 33 pp.

The background for this study of an isolated trading-trapping community was provided by fieldwork among the Chipewyan at Snowdrift on Great Slave Lake during 13 weeks of the summer of 1960. The setting, historical background, and yearly cycle are reviewed briefly. Trapping, fishing, source and use of income, and village economics are described in greater detail.   CCV

1888   **VANSTONE   JAMES W**
1963
THE SNOWDRIFT CHIPEWYAN. Department of Northern Affairs and National Resources, Northern Co-ordination and Research Centre Reports No. NCRC-63-4. Ottawa: Department of Northern Affairs and National Resources. 115 pp.

Subsistence activities, life cycle, social structure and community life, the individual in Chipewyan culture, religious institutions and beliefs, and Chipewyan acculturation are discussed based on fieldwork conducted during the summers of 1960 and 1961 and a month in the winter of 1961-62.   CCV

1889   **VANSTONE   JAMES W**
1964
SOME ASPECTS OF RELIGIOUS CHANGE AMONG NATIVE INHABITANTS
IN WEST ALASKA AND THE NORTHWEST TERRITORIES. Arctic Anthropology 2(2):21-24.

In a symposium on the effects of contact situations in the Arctic and Sub-Arctic, the methods, attitudes, and consequences of the missionary activities of 5 Christian denominations during the 19th century are compared. From fieldwork and historical documents it is asserted that the Roman Catholic mission at the Chipewyan Snowdrift Settlement in the Great Slave Lake region, Northwest Territories, was more removed from the native people. It concludes that despite this detachment it had lasting effects similar to those of the Russian Orthodox, Moravian, Presbyterian, and Episcopal churches in Alaska during the subsequent period of increasing contact.   WRC

1890   **VANSTONE   JAMES W**
1965
THE CHANGING CULTURE OF THE SNOWDRIFT CHIPEWYAN. National Museum of Canada Bulletin 209. Ottawa: Queen's Printer. 133 pp.

Twenty-eight weeks were spent among the Chipewyan residents of Snowdrift, a typical bush community, during 1960-1961. The author concludes that directed culture change has resulted in a deculturated community, approximating a poor-White subculture. Very little remains of Chipewyan culture, especially in the economic sphere. Trapping income is low, and people are dependent on the Husdon's Bay Company. Atomization of social relationships has accompanied the adoption of an individualistic economy. The author concludes with some random thoughts on the economic future of Snowdrift. Appended are 8 plates and a summary of the author's field notes of a trapping expedition. JSL

CREE

1891 **1962**
THE PAS INDIAN BAND. In The Pas 50th Anniversary 1912-1962: Golden Jubilee Celebrations August 24-25-26. Harry Dunn, ed. n.p., n.p. pp. 22-23.

A brief general history of The Pas Indian Band from 1871 to 1962 is given. IVY

1892 **1963**
BITE A BIRCH BARK PATTERN. Canadian Geographical Journal 66:130-131.

Photographs illustrate the creation of a design on birch bark by biting with the incisors, eyeteeth, and molars. IVY

1893 **ADAMS HOWARD**
1969
THE CREE AS A COLONIAL PEOPLE. The Western Canadian Journal of Anthropology 1(1):120-124.

Decolonization must take place before the natives will be liberated and before Canada will be rid of its colonialism and racism. This will entail political and psychological struggles for the Indians and extensive structural changes in the socio-economic order of Canada. IVY

1894 **AHENAKEW EDWARD**
1960
AN OPINION OF THE FROG LAKE MASSACRE. Alberta Historical Review 8(3):9-15.

In an address originally presented in June, 1931, at the commemoration of the Frog Lake Massacre, the causes of this incident in the Riel Rebellion of 1885 are enumerated. Basing his conclusions on missionary work among his native Cree people, the author cited Indian discontent and resentment with increasing control by the government as factors underlying the event. Four photographs are included. WRC

1895 **BAICH B V**
1962
OXFORD HOUSE INDIAN RESERVE: ECONOMIC DEVELOPMENT SURVEY. Unpublished paper. Available at Indian-Eskimo Economic Development Branch, Development Services Division, Department of Indian Affairs and Northern Development, Ottawa. 25 pp.

Socio-economic conditions and human and natural resources of Oxford House Indians are reviewed as a result of a study in March, 1962. An 8-page discussion of current conditions, acculturation processes, and community development potential is appended to the study. CCV

1896   **BAUER   GEORGE W**
1966
CHIKAPASH ACQUIRES WIVES: A CREE STORY TOLD BY THOMAS RUPERT
AND RECORDED AT FORT GEORGE BY GEORGE W. BAUER. The Beaver
297(Summer):35.

By tricking and killing the mother of 2 young girls, Chikapash acquires wives.   IVY

1897   **BAUER   GEORGE W**
1966
TALES OF CHIKAPASH: TOLD BY THOMAS RUPERT TO GEORGE W. BAUER.
The Beaver 296(Spring):53-54.

Two Cree stories told by Thomas Rupert are translated into English by Robert Kanate-
wat. The first relates how Chikapash avenges the death of his parents by killing the
monster, Kotchichikosk. The sun in the second story is captured in a snare set by
Chikapash and finally released, thus accounting for darkness and light.   IVY

1898   **BENNETT   JOHN W**
1969
NORTHERN PLAINSMEN: ADAPTIVE STRATEGY AND AGRARIAN LIFE.
Chicago: Aldine. 352 pp.

The use of social and natural resources in the adaptation of 4 groups to the northern
great plains environment is studied in a southern Saskatchewan town. The Plains Cree
population is examined in Chapter 5. The history of the evolution from Woodlands
to migratory Plains culture is reviewed and the effects of White contact including fur
trade, smallpox epidemics, whiskey, and the depletion of the buffalo herds are demonstrated. The marginal status of the contemporary Indian in the community is discussed.
Brief mention of the Indians reappears in the chapters devoted to the region, culture, and
economy.   CCV

1899   **BERESKIN   A I**
1966
CREE INDIAN PLACE NAMES. Saskatchewan Archaeology Newletter 4:15-17.

A number of geographical names of Cree origin in Saskatchewan are presented.   IVY

1900   **BOON   T C B**
1964
THE CENTENARY OF THE SYLLABIC CREE BIBLE, 1862-1962. United Church of
Canada Committee on Archives Bulletin 17:27-34.

The first edition of the complete Cree Bible bears the date 1861 and was revised in 1908.
Its history from inception to completion is outlined.   IVY

1901   **BRADY   J P**
1967
FIELD REPORT ON A SURVEY OF METIS AND INDIAN HOUSEHOLDS IN
PRINCE ALBERT, SASKATCHEWAN, 1960-61 WITH SOME GENERAL
OBSERVATIONS. In A Northern Dilemma: Reference Papers: Volume 2. Arthur K.

Davis, Vernon C. Serl, et al., eds. Bellingham, WA: Western Washington State College. pp. 555-577.

A resume of field methods, impressions, and interpretations of over 100 interviews conducted in Prince Albert, Saskatchewan, in 1960-1961 is presented by a Metis researcher. Insights into sexual problems, economic difficulties, Indian-Metis passivity, educational aspirations, and voting behavior are included.   CCV

1902   **BRAROE   NIELS WINTHER**
1965
RECIPROCAL EXPLOITATION IN AN INDIAN-WHITE COMMUNITY. Southwestern Journal of Anthropology 21:166-178.

Field research (summer, 1963) in a small western Saskatchewan prairie town and a nearby Indian settlement yields information for a social-psychological analysis of the different perceptions which Indians and Whites had of each other. The contradiction on the part of both between the view of the self and its presentation in daily interactions provided a self-validating pattern of behavior in which conflict was regulated and its overt expression minimized.   WRC

1903   **BROCHU   MICHEL**
1964
FORT-SAINTE-FOY AU SERVICE DU NOUVEAU-QUEBEC INDIEN ET ESQUIMAU. Relations 285:267-269.

The services offered to the Indians of Fort-Ste-Foy on James Bay by the Catholic mission are enumerated and described. Discussed is the importance to the community of the residential school, the hospital, employment opportunities, agricultural produce, and the sawmill. The value of these services in the event of assumption of responsibility by the Quebec government is underlined.   CCV

1904   **BROCHU   MICHEL**
1967
ETUDE COMPARATIVE DE L'EVOLUTION DE LA VIE ECONOMIQUE ET SOCIALE AU NOUVEAU-QUEBEC ESQUIMAU ET INDIEN: LE NOUVEAU-QUEBEC INDIEN. L'Actualite Economique 42:805-834.

This is a description of the traditional culture of the Cree of Northern Quebec and a mention of all the changes brought by the Europeans: hunting techniques, traditional and modern transportation, clothing, nutrition, housing, time perception and chronology, leisure, Indian and White names, and the influence of school and politics. The origin of each change is given and is related to an ecological explanation.   DD

1905   **BROCHU   MICHEL**
1970
ETUDE PRELIMINAIRE SUR L'ETABLISSEMENT D'UN PRIX DE PEREQUATION DES PEAUX D'ANIMAUX A FOURRURE AU NOUVEAU-QUEBEC. L'Actualite Economique 46:287-315.

The instability of income of the fur-trapping northern Quebec Indian and Eskimo is analyzed. The 2 major factors of the fur market instability affecting Indians are thought to be the number of animals trapped and the variation of the sale price. Figures from 1940 to 1970 are provided. Several propositions for establishing a 5-year standardization of prices are discussed in the conclusion.   DD

1906   **BROCHU   MICHEL**
1970
LES GRANDES PHASES DE L'HISTOIRE ECONOMIQUE DU NOUVEAU-QUEBEC INDIEN ET ESQUIMAU. L'Action Nationale 60:27-41.

A review of the factors that influenced the economic development of northern Quebec is presented. Three periods are distinguished: the pre-historical period from the arrival of the first Indians and Eskimos up to the establishment of the first European trading posts; the second period, beginning in 1668, characterized by the opposition between 2 fur-trading companies; and the contemporary period, marked by the progressive diversification of the economy. "New Quebec"is now faced with the problem of planning the future exploitation of its mines and the actual working conditions of Indian miners.   DD

1907   **BROWN   C H**
n.d.
FOLK-TALES WITH EPISODES FREQUENTLY RELATED INDEPENDENTLY. Unpublished paper. Available from National Museum of Man, Ethnology Division, Ottawa, with permission of the author. 99 pp.

The contents of this report consist of 30 folk-tales and 12 folk histories of the Swampy Cree. Different versions of the same tale are included.   DGW

1908   **BRYAN   ALAN L**
1969
LATE PROTOHISTORIC CREE EXPANSION INTO NORTH CENTRAL ALBERTA. The Western Canadian Journal of Anthropology 1(1):32-38.

Drawing upon local informants and historic records, an attempt is made to identify the Indian inhabitants of Lesser Slave Lake region and the area to the north before the arrival of the Cree.   IVY

1909   **BUCK   RUTH MATHESON, ed.**
1965
LITTLE PINE: AN INDIAN DAY SCHOOL. Saskatchewan History 18:55-62.

The notes and unfinished manuscript of the late Reverend Canon Edward Attenakew are used to describe the events and persons responsible for the development of an Indian day school among the Cree.   ADG

1910   **BUCKLEY   HELEN,   CAMPBELL   SHERIDAN**
1966
THE FARM POTENTIAL ON TWO SASKATCHEWAN INDIAN RESERVES AND A PROPOSAL FOR ARDA PROGRAM. Saskatoon: Center for Community Studies. 53 pp.

An economic analysis of 2 Saskatchewan reserves, Muskeg Lake and Mistawasis, undertaken for a possible agricultural rehabilitation program, is presented.   IVY

1911   **BUCKSAR   RICHARD G**
1968
MOOSONEE AND THE SQUATTERS. Canadian Welfare 44(5):15-16.

The squatters of Moosonee, principally of Cree descent, number nearly 1000. Attracted to Moosonee by offers of high wages, these squatters have remained even though housing is inadequate and the dietary levels are extremely low. The squatters' discontent relates to their feelings of maltreatment and inequality due to their Indianness. Some of these persons have been asking for the establishment of a reserve, a mechanism which would render them eligible for Indian Affairs funds.   ADG

1912   **CANADA. Department of Citizenship and Immigration. Economic and Social Research Division.**
1964
BIG TROUT LAKE: A PILOT STUDY OF AN INDIAN COMMUNITY IN RELATION TO ITS RESOURCE BASE: REPORT 1G-3. Unpublished paper. Available at Library, Department of Indian Affairs and Northern Development. 147 pp.

A study of Big Trout Lake Reserve, Ontario, was conducted by the Research Division of the Indian Affairs Branch. Fieldwork was conducted over a total of 8 months in 1961 and 1962. The study is organized into 3 parts. Part 1 is an anthropological study of the community. Part 2 is a detailed analysis of the income and expenditure patterns of the community. Part 3 contains a summary, and conclusions in which economic development and out-migration of individuals are foreseen for the area.   JSL

1913   **CANADA. Department of Citizenship and Immigration. Economic and Social Research Division.**
1964
A PILOT STUDY OF AN INDIAN COMMUNITY IN RELATION TO ITS RESOURCE BASE - REPORT IG-3. Unpublished report prepared for Economic Development Division, Department of Northern Affairs and National Resources. Available at Indian-Eskimo Economic Development Branch, Development Services Division, Department of Indian Affairs and Northern Development, Ottawa. 138 pp.

A social anthropological study was conducted in the Big Trout Lake settlement in April, May, and June, 1961, and January and February, 1962, simultaneously with a resources survey and analysis of the fish and fur markets. Material from a 1962 summer study of Big Beaver house and Wunnummin is included. Historic setting, population, community organization, social organization, acculturation, income, employment, resource use, and recommendations for project planning are discussed.   CCV

1914   **CANADA. Department of Fisheries and Forestry. Forest Management Institute.**
1969
AIR PHOTO RECONNAISSANCE RECORD MAJOR LAND USE AREAS INDIAN RESERVES IN MANITOBA 1967: INDIAN RESERVE FOREST SURVEY REPORT NO. 22. Unpublished paper. Available at Indian-Eskimo Economic Development Branch, Development Services Division, Department of Indian Affairs and Northern Development, Ottawa. 75 pp.

A 1967 air photo survey of Manitoba's 102 Indian reserves is presented. An attempt is made to assess major land uses and to evaluate forest cover and its potential.   CCV

1915   **CARRIERE   GASTON**
1961
LE VOYAGEUR DU BON DIEU: LE PERE JEAN-MARIE NEDELEC, O.M.I.
(1834-1896). Montreal: Rayonnement. 158 pp.

Included in this account of the missionary life of Father Nedelec are some details of the
missions to the Indians in Temiskaming and Abitibi.   CCV

1916   **CARRIERE   GASTON**
1962
LE PERE DU KEEWATIN: MGR OVIDE CHARLEBOIS, O.M.I. 1862-1933.
Montreal: Rayonnement. 239 pp.

The missionary life of Monseigneur Ovide Charlebois among the Indians of northern
Manitoba and Saskatchewan is recounted. Mgr. Charlebois' role in construction of
schools and missions and in the development of medical services in Keewatin is emphasized.   CCV

1917   **CASS   ELIZABETH**
1964
THE STORY OF EY-ASH-CHIS. The Beaver 295(Summer):50-52.

After many adventures, Ey-ash-chis returns home and takes revenge on his wicked father.   IVY

1918   **CHANCE   NORMAN A,   TRUDEAU   JOHN**
1963
SOCIAL ORGANIZATION, ACCULTURATION, AND INTEGRATION AMONG
THE ESKIMO AND THE CREE: A COMPARATIVE STUDY. Anthropologica N.S.
5:47-56.

Research in the summer of 1958 among the Alaskan Eskimos at Kaktovik and the Cree
at Winisk, Ontario, yields a comparative analysis of the responses of traditional forms of
social organization to the type and extent of culture contact initiated by radar installations in the 1950's. Traditional intra- rather than inter-family resolution of conflict, the
termination of wage labor in 1957, and inter-generational factionalism are 3 factors
which precluded community decision-making and cohesiveness among the Cree at
Winisk and thereby differentiated them from the Eskimos.   WRC

1919   **DUSSION   J B**
1969
THE DELTA OUTFITTERS MUTUAL LIMITED: CUMBERLAND HOUSE, SASK.
Unpublished paper. Available from National Library of Canada. 4 pp.

The activities and development of the Delta Outfitters Mutual Limited of Cumberland
House, Saskatchewan, are outlined from its beginning in autumn, 1968. Future plans are
mentioned briefly.   CCV

1920   **ELLIS   C DOUGLAS**
1964

THE MISSIONARY AND THE INDIAN IN CENTRAL AND EASTERN
CANADA. Arctic Anthropology 2(2):25-31.

As part of a symposium on the consequence of culture contact in the Arctic and Sub-Arctic, this paper considers the missionary activities of the Anglican Church of Canada as
examples of religious innovations which result in cultural modifications in native people.
Fieldwork among the Cree at Moose Factory, Ontario (summer, 1947), Mistassiny, Quebec (summer, 1948), and Albany Post, Ontario (August, 1955, to spring, 1958) cites a
sedentary life style, ascribed leadership, elimination of cross-cousin marriage, Euro-Canadian patterns of child-rearing, the academic and urban aspirations of the young, and
the introduction of syllabics and English as specific changes.   WRC

1921   **EVANS   DOUGLAS**
1969
SOME OBSERVATIONS ON THE USE OF WILLOW BARK BY THE CREE.
Manitoba Archaeological Newsletter 6(1-2):7.

Preparation of bark is briefly described. Cree bark articles collected in 1968 now in the
collection of the Manitoba Museum of Man are noted. There seems to be sufficient evidence to indicate a tradition of willow bark use among the Cree.   IVY

1922   **FISHER   ANTHONY D**
1967
THE CREE OF CANADA: SOME ECOLOGICAL AND EVOLUTIONARY
CONSIDERATIONS. The Western Canadian Journal of Anthropology 1(1):7-19.

The Cree reside in Canada's 5 central provinces: Quebec, Ontario, Manitoba, Saskatchewan, and Alberta. Cree social organization reflects the varied ecological niches which
they occupy.   IVY

1923   **FLANNERY   REGINA**
1962
INFANCY AND CHILDHOOD AMONG THE INDIANS OF THE EAST COAST
OF JAMES BAY. Anthropos 57:474-482.

The recollections of middle-aged and older informants obtained in fieldwork among the
Algonkian-speakers in Quebec during the summers of 1937 and 1938 provide initial data
for a future reassessment of the change in beliefs and practices associated with the early
part of the life cycle. A strong emphasis on subsistence skills in the rearing of children
from infancy to adolescence is noted.   WRC

1924   **FRANK E PRICE AND ASSOCIATES LTD.**
1968
AN EVALUATION OF THE RESOURCES OF THE LITTLE RED RIVER INDIAN
BAND: JOHN D'OR PRAIRIE RESERVE NO. 215, FOX LAKE RESERVE NO. 162.
Unpublished paper. Available from National Library of Canada. 114 pp.

The reserves and communities of John d'Or Prairie and Fox Lake, Alberta, are described
and an inventory of human and physical resources are assessed for possible development.
An agricultural program and off-reserve employment are emphasized. Requirements in
land, equipment, and livestock are outlined. A major appraisal of the economy of Census

District 15 was undertaken to define the areas which will be useful to Indian people in the future.   IVY

1925   **FRANK E PRICE AND ASSOCIATES LTD.**
1968
AN EVALUATION OF THE RESOURCES OF THE SUCKER CREEK RESERVE.
Unpublished paper. Available from National Library of Canada. 68 pp.

This land use survey of Sucker Cree Reserve, Alberta, describes the community and its economy. The total population of the Band in July, 1967, was 423 of whom 282 lived on the reserve and 141 made their homes off the reserve. Human and physical resources are evaluated for possible development. An assessment shows that agricultural resources are substantial and development has been limited. However, they are not sufficient to provide livelihood for all residents now or in the future. Off-reserve employment and farming and relocation should be considered. A program of agricultural development is outlined and present and anticipated effects of periodic flooding explored.   IVY

1926   **FRANK E PRICE AND ASSOCIATES LTD.**
1968
AN EVALUATION OF THE RESOURCES OF THE TALLCREE BAND: BEAVER
RANCH INDIAN RESERVE NO. 163, TALLCREE INDIAN RESERVE NO. 173
AND 173A. Unpublished paper. Available from National Library of Canada. 114 pp.

Included in this report are general descriptions of the reserves and communities, inventories of the physical and human resources of the reserves, and an evaluation of the economy of the Tallcree Band with its relationship to the economy of the district. Programs for the development and utilization of band resources emphasizing agricultural programs and the establishment of economic farm units are outlined.   IVY

1927   **FRASER   WILLIAM B**
1966
BIG BEAR, INDIAN PATRIOT. Alberta Historical Review 14(2):1-13.

An historical account of the Plains Cree chief, Big Bear (ca. 1825-1888), is presented. His resistance to unilateral treaty proposals and complete subjugation of his people was considered a major threat to the government's combined policy of westward expansion and control and the relegation of Indians to reserves. A 3-year prison sentence caused by White prejudice and misconception of the authority invested in an Indian chief marked an annihilation of Big Bear's efforts to unify passive Indian resistance.   Three photographs and 1 sketch of the chief are included.   WRC

1928   **FRENCH   CECIL L**
1967
SOCIAL CLASS AND MOTIVATION AMONG METIS, INDIANS AND WHITES
IN ALBERTA. In A Northern Dilemma: Reference Papers. A. K. Davis, Vernon C.
Serl, et al., eds. Bellingham, WA: Western Washington State College. Vol. 1. pp. 124-169.

Tests administered to White, Metis, and Indian children in Alberta urban and rural schools in 1960 and 1961 are described. The results are related to Metis failure to embrace the values of the dominant Canadian society and the lack of success suffered by agencies seeking to upgrade Metis life style. It is hypothesized that the Metis reflect the cultural values of the lower social classes with which they are in contact. The results of the "Name Occupations," the "Achievement Orientation," and the "Twenty Statements" tests support this notion. Indians having little contact with White society score about as well as Whites and significantly higher than Metis.   CCV

1929   **FRIEDMAN   HARRIET U**
1970
EXCHANGE OF CHILDREN: A SUPPORTIVE SYSTEM. Unpublished paper delivered to 69th Annual Meeting, American Anthropological Association. San Diego, CA, November 19-22, 1970. Available from National Library of Canada. 13 pp.

This paper considers the circumstances under which children are lent, adopted, or exchanged in an Eastern Cree reserve community. Data were derived from fieldwork in 1969 and 1970, and from published materials. The author considers the child inovlved, the child's parents, and the person or family with whom the exchange takes place. Children's services are resources to be exchanged in transactions through which the families are able to procure their own aims.   HCV

1930   **GERRITSEN   WILLIAM D**
1970
ROCKY CREE FISHING AT SOUTHEND, REINDEER LAKE, SASKATCHEWAN. Unpublished paper. Available from National Museum of Man, Ethnology Division, Ottawa, with permission of the author. 35 pp.

The commercial fishing enterprise of the Rocky Cree is discussed. Of significance is the outfit, the so-called unit of production which normally consists of the family. Whereas in the aboriginal past fishing was of relative unimportance, commercial fishing now provides most of Southend's cash income. Of the 400 Indian inhabitants of Southend, there are 10 fishing camps for 35 outfits. Also discussed in the paper is the ethnoecology of fish, referring especially to the ethnotaxonomy and ethnocognition of species.   DGW

1931   **GIBBON   MARY**
1962
TRAPPER'S WIFE. The Beaver 292(Spring):38-42.

This article presents the life and activities of a Cree woman in Moose Factory who, when winter comes, moves her household into the bush where her husband will trap beaver.   IVY

1932   **GOLD   DOLORES**
1966
PSYCHOLOGICAL CHANGES ASSOCIATED WITH ACCULTURATION. Ph.D. Thesis. Department of Psychology. University of Saskatchewan. 304 pp. Available from National Library of Canada.

Explored are the changes in psychological functions which accompany the acculturation of Saskatchewan Indians to industrialized North American society. Acculturated and unacculturated subjects from 6 reserves in southeastern Saskatchewan were taken as well as volunteers from the Indian-Metis Friendship Centre in Regina. The reserve Indians were from the Kahkewistahaw, White Bear, Picipot, Cowessess, Starblanket, and

Keeseekoose reserves. Using objective and standardized techniques, the study illustrates that values and motivations of acculturated Indians are more similar to those of White subjects than to those of unacculturated Indians. The view that Indians with a lower socio-economic and educational level who live on reserves share the immediate gratification pattern to a greater extent than Indians who have left the reserves, was supported by the majority of the data collected.   DGW

1933   **GUE   LESLIE R**
1966
NEW INSIGHTS. The Northian 3(2):4-8.

The author provides a sketch of a typical isolated Indian community in northern Alberta, through his description of 2 weeks spent among this group while collecting data (1966) for his doctoral dissertation.   ADG

1934   **GUY   CAMIL**
1970
LE CANOT D'ECORCE A WEYMONTACHING. Musee National de l'Homme
Etudes Anthropologiques 20. Ottawa: Imprimeur de la Reine. 55 pp.

A birch bark canoe constructed for the National Museum of Man is described in detail. The canoe was constructed by Albert Birote, a Tete de Boule of the Weymontaching Band, Upper Mauricie. The 1st part of the monograph discusses the distribution and variations of the canoe among the Tete de Boule and their neighbors. Details of the construction are presented, illustrated by photographs and diagrams.   CCV

1935   **HANSON   HAROLD C,   GAGNON   ANDREW**
1964
THE HUNTING AND UTILIZATION OF WILD GEESE BY THE INDIANS OF
THE HUDSON BAY LOWLANDS OF NORTHERN ONTARIO. Ontario Fish and
Wildlife Review 3(2):2-11.

Information for this report was gathered in the springs of 1959, 1962, and 1963. Methods of hunting and efficient, total utilization of the fowl are described in text and photographs.   IVY

1936   **HASSE   F R**
1969
SUN DANCE. RCMP Quarterly 34(4):54-55.

A brief item relates the halting of a Sun Dance at Red Pheasant Reserve in 1922 by Constable Kem.   IVY

1937   **HETLAND   G L**
1969
SOCIO-ECONOMIC CHANGE IN THE GRANDE CACHE REGION OF
ALBERTA. M.S. Thesis. Department of Agricultural Economics and Rural Sociology.
University of Alberta. 139 pp.

Results of personal interviews conducted in the Metis community of Grand Cache, Alberta, are compared with those derived from surveys of the more modern communities of Brule and Entrance in order to assess the community's capacity to adapt to and benefit from social change anticipated with development of coal reserves in the area. Twenty-four individuals or families in Grand Cache, 18 in Brule, and 16 at Entrance were interviewed concerning their land, homes, utilities, employment, income, expenditures, aspirations, recreation, and attitudes toward employment, education, industrial development, and urbanization. The low socio-economic status observed at Grand Cache was related to unstable employment and extremely limited educational opportunities. Vertical mobility is minimal due to lack of opportunities and to attitudes toward education and industrialization. The role of socialization, attitudes toward development, and the predicted alienation of adults are discussed and an effort is made to indicate the sources of influence and opinion leaders. The absence of agents of change is noted. Recommendations are geared to these observations.   CCV

1938   **HICKS   JOSEPH**
1970
WITH HATTON'S SCOUTS IN PURSUIT OF BIG BEAR. Alberta Historical Review 18(3):14-23.

In pursuit of Big Bear and the Crees following the Frog Lake massacre in 1885, the army march from Calgary, which was climaxed by the battle at Loon Lake, Saskatchewan, is recounted by a recruit in Sergeant Hatton's scout troop. Included are 2 photographs of troops, a sketch of the 65th Battalion's Fort Edmonton, and a map of the expedition.   WRC

1939   **HLADY   WALTER M**
1969
THE CUMBERLAND HOUSE FUR PROJECT: THE FIRST YEARS. The Western Canadian Journal of Anthropology 1(1):124-139.

In 1960 the Saskatchewan government decided to take over the lease which the Hudson's Bay Company relinquished on a large area south of the Saskatchewan River and Cumberland House with the view that the trappers of the region would gradually assume control. The developments from 1960-1962 in this regard are discussed.   IVY

1940   **HLADY   WALTER M,   FRANK E PRICE AND ASSOCIATES LTD.**
1967
A SOCIOLOGICAL STUDY OF THE SASKATCHEWAN RIVER DELTA: A STUDY OF INDIAN AND METIS ATTITUDES TO POTENTIAL DEVELOPMENT IN THE CUMBERLAND HOUSE AREA. Unpublished paper. Available from National Library of Canada. 90 pp.

Based on results of a questionnaire (38 of the 47 completed were by persons of Indian ancestry), attitudes of the population of Cumberland House, Saskatchewan, to possible plans of development of the Saskatchewan River Delta are presented. The study looked at the attitudes toward present natural resource use, and expanded use of these natural resouces as well as the development of recreation, the development of agriculture, and a combination of these possibilities. Further, 2 years experience and research in the community, 1960-1962, by the author, and information and statistics gained from interviews permitted the development of a framework through which the ideas and opinions expressed in the questionnaire could be incorporated where possible into the development which occurs.   IVY

1941   **HOFFMAN   HANS**
1961
CULTURE CHANGE AND PERSONALITY MODIFICATION AMONG THE
JAMES BAY CREE. University of Alaska Anthropological Papers 9:81-91.

The hypothesis tested is that wider cultural experiences are associated with idiosyncratic emotional reactions whereas more restricted experiences are associated with homogeneous reactions to a stranger. Evaluation of the hypothesis is carried out with data from Attawapiskat, a Cree community. Data were elicited from 40 subjects using the Thematic Apperception Test in the summer of 1955. People camping in larger enclaves differed significantly from those camping with nuclear families in the strength of their tendency to exhibit idiosyncratic responses and the number of years of mission schooling experienced.   IVY

1942   **HONIGMANN   JOHN J**
1961
FOODWAYS IN A MUSKEG COMMUNITY: AN ANTHROPOLOGICAL
REPORT ON THE ATTAWAPISKAT INDIANS. Department of Northern Affairs and National Resources, Northern Co-ordination and Research Centre Reports No. NCRC-62-1. Ottawa: Department of Northern Affairs and National Resources. 216 pp.

Fieldwork from July 27, 1947, to June 6, 1948, among the Attawapiskat Indians of the west coast of James Bay is reported. Various aspects of community and family life are described but the focus lies with the economy and activities, food stuffs and their sources, and the life style as it related to the diminishing resources in the area.   CCV

1943   **HONIGMANN   JOHN J**
1961
THE INTERPRETATION OF DREAMS IN ANTHROPOLOGICAL FIELD
WORK: A CASE STUDY. In Studying Personality Cross-Culturally. Bert Kaplan, ed. New York: Harper and Row. pp. 579-585.

The dream of an Attawapiskat Cree is presented and analyzed revealing details of Cree life syle and methodology in dream interpretation.   CCV

1944   **HOOD   ROBERT**
1967
SOME ACCOUNT OF THE CREE AND OTHER INDIANS, 1819. Alberta Historical Review 14(1):6-17.

An excerpt from the journal of a member of Sir John Franklin's first exploring expedition in 1819-1821 provides an early ethnography of Woodland Cree culture. Physical characteristics, clothing, child rearing practices, and subsistence activities are described, and impressions of Cree ethics are given.   WRC

1945   **INDIAN-ESKIMO ASSOCIATION OF CANADA**
1966
AHAB SPENCE, L.Th., B.A., LL.D. Canadian Indians and Eskimos of Today No. 5. 2 pp.

A biographic sketch of Ahab Spence, a Swampy Cree from Manitoba, is given. Anglican priest and teacher, recipient of an honorary degree of doctor of laws, he is now on the staff of the Indian Affairs Branch.   IVY

1946   **JOHNSON   MICHAEL G**
1965
IDENTITY AND DEMOGRAPHY OF THE CREE INDIANS. Abhandlungen der Voelkerkundlichen Arbeitsgemeinschaft 12. 11 pp.

The various names used to designate divisions of the Cree are defined. The distribution of the 56,000 modern Cree is presented, based on the 1959 census, grouping the Indians by agency, reserve, and Cree division.   TSA

1947   **JOHNSON   WILLIAM D**
1962
AN EXPLORATORY STUDY OF ETHNIC RELATIONS AT GREAT WHALE RIVER. Department of Northern Affairs and National Resources, Northern Co-ordination and Research Centre Reports No. NCRC-62-7. Ottawa: Department of Northern Affairs and National Resources. 21 pp.

From fieldwork during July and August, 1960, at Great Whale River, Quebec, an over-view of relations between the Crees, Eskimos, and Whites is provided. More detailed information is included concerning differences in administration of Indians and Eskimos and differential employment possibilities, attitudes toward acculturation, and life style.   CCV

1948   **KEHOE   ALICE BECK**
1964
THE GHOST DANCE RELIGION IN SASKATCHEWAN: A FUNCTIONAL ANALYSIS. Ph.D. Thesis. Department of Anthropology. Harvard University. 134 pp.

An examination and comparison of the Plains Cree and Ghost Dance religions is based on a review of the literature, a week of research in 1961, and 2 weeks in 1962 at Round Plains as well as brief visits to Moose Woods and Standing Buffalo and numerous interviews with other Plains, Cree, Dakota, and White informants in southern and central Saskatchewan. Although remnants of the Dakota Ghost Dance congregation hold prayer meetings at Round Plains, this movement is being replaced by modified Plains Cree religion among younger generations of mixed Cree-Dakota. Modification of traditional Plains Cree religion is considered to be adaptive in that it offers a basis for identity on an individual and a group level as well as sustaining physical and emotional well-being through curing practices. A Dakota curer from Standing Buffalo Reserve combines traditional Indian curing concepts and ceremonies with pseudo-Christian terms. The success of these therapeutic religions as opposed to the Ghost Dance is attributed to the function of relieving stress created by inability to achieve satisfactory status either in terms of the traditional or the dominant society.   CCV

1949   **KING   GILLIAN MARY**
1968
A GEOGRAPHIC ANALYSIS OF THE SETTLEMENT OF LA RONGE, SASKATCHEWAN. M.S. Thesis. Department of Geography. University of Saskatchewan, Saskatoon. 133 pp.

Data were collected in a 5-week survey of La Ronge, Saskatchewan, for an urban renewal study by Underwood, McLellan and Associates. Population, employment and
mobility characteristics, and details of household, community, and business facilities are
reported for the White, Metis, and Indian population. Distinct physical entities were observed in terms of housing and living standards which were associated with certain social
groups. The major distinction observed was between Whites and the Indian-Metis population. Mobility and education characteristics were found to follow patterns consistent
with the White and Indian-Metis distinctions. Procedures for urban renewal are suggested but it is noted that sufficient local employment cannot be created for the growing
native population and outmigration will be necessary.   CCV

1950   **KING   GILLIAN MARY**
1969
A CONSIDERATION OF FACTORS AFFECTING THE DEVELOPMENT OF LA
RONGE, SASKATCHEWAN. The Musk-Ox 5:26-36.

La Ronge, Saskatchewan, consists of 2 Indian reserves (156B-Kitsaki and 156), the incorporated village of La Ronge, and the unincorporated community of Air Ronge. Of
1650 inhabitants in 1966, 45 percent are Treaty Indians, 11 percent are Metis, and 44
percent are non-Indian. A geographical analysis of La Ronge carried out in 1966 studied
the settlement within its regional context with particular reference to the availablility of
natural resources. Analyzed as well were physical environment, historical growth, areal
differentiation of the townscape, and the socio-economic characterstics of the inhabitants. La Ronge suffers from low standards of living and associated phenomena (outlined in tables 1-6) which applies particularly to the Indian-Metis population. A plan for
physical redevelopment and controlled urban expansion must recognize the close interrelationship between physical, social, and economic factors.   IVY

1951   **KIOKEE   GEORGE**
1967
ATTAWAPISKAT. In Problemes Nordiques des Facades de la Baie de James: Recueil
de Documents Rediges en Collaboration a la Suite d'une Rencontre de Nordistes a
Moosonee en Ontario. Centre d'Etudes Nordiques Travaux Divers 18. Quebec: Centre
d'Etudes Nordiques, Universite Laval. ppp. 112-113.

The Indian chief of Attawapiskat speaks for the people of his community at a meeting on
the James Bay area in 1967 when he asks for heated houses, appropriate medical treatment, residential schools for children, and special allowances for poor families. The paper is followed by a Cree translation.   DD

1952   **KNIGHT   ROLF**
1961
RUPERT HOUSE REPORT. Unpublished paper. Available from National Museum of
Man, Ethnology Division, Ottawa, with permission of the author. 33 pp.

A report on fieldwork from June 13 to August 29, 1961, among the Rupert House Cree of
Quebec discusses the present community and its environment, changes in the community since 1900, and the question of family hunting territories. The author demonstrates
drastic fluctuations in the numbers of fur animals because of over-hunting and over-trap-
ping in the historic period, fluctuating fur prices, and alternate opening and closing of
posts. It is concluded that the introduction of more efficient goods and techniques, and

extensive welfare payments and services have removed the pressing need for community aid to incapacitated consumption groups. The independent nuclear family has become the important co-residential and commensal group. This has resulted in the establishment of band endogamy and solidarity.   JSL

1953   **KNIGHT   ROLF**
1962
CHANGING SOCIAL AND ECONOMIC ORGANIZATION AMONG THE RUPERT HOUSE CREE. M.A. Thesis. Department of Anthropology and Sociology. University of British Columbia. 212 pp.

Fieldwork conducted among the Cree at Rupert House, Quebec, during the summer of 1961 is reported. Change in the composition and activities of production and consumption groups is described and related to environmental change over the last 60 years. The importance of country foods and the persistence of certain aspects of a trapping society are underlined. Social groups are found to be characterized by small consumption groups and relatively fluid trapping groups. Ecological exigencies are differentially reflected in life style and social organization. The latter has been simplified markedly by new productive techniques and economic trends. Important differences in income and living standards are noted between commensal groups as well as a clear distinction between White administrators and Indian trappers.   CCV

1954   **KNIGHT   ROLF**
1968
ECOLOGICAL FACTORS IN CHANGING ECONOMY AND SOCIAL ORGANIZATION AMONG THE RUPERT HOUSE CREE. National Museum of Canada Anthropology Papers 15. Ottawa: Queen's Printer. 112 pp.

Fieldwork was conducted in 1961 and 1962 among the Cree of Rupert House, Quebec. Discussed are the habitat and ecology, past European agents of acculturation, local White agencies today, demography and residence patterns, and economic and productive organization. In the past 40 years the Cree social organization has been simplified, and the smaller hunting-trapping groups have emerged. An appendix compares the community with other Woodland areas. Rural poverty is forecast for Rupert House.   JSL

1955   **KNOWLES   DONALD W**
1968
A COMPARATIVE STUDY OF MEDIATIONAL-TASK PERFORMANCE OF INDIAN AND MIDDLE CLASS CHILDREN. Ph.D. Thesis. Department of Educational Psychology. University of Alberta. 107 pp.

Ninety Indian students were chosen randomly from the 8-year olds of Ermineskin, Hobbema, and Gooderham reserve schools. Thirty 8-years olds were chosen randomly from Meadowlark School which serves children whose parents enjoy higher-than-average income, educational, and occupational levels. No significant differences were revealed by comparison of Indian and middle-class performance on 2 mediational tasks - optional reversal shifts and transportation. Linguistic performance of Indian 8-year olds was significantly poorer than that of middle-class age mates. In addition, due to slower development of mediational responses, the Indian student appears to be handicapped in problems not requiring verbal comprehension or expression.   CCV

1956   **KOWALISHEN   ANGELINE**
1968
PLAINS CREE WE.SAKE.CHAK STORIES. Na'Pao 1(1):24-39.

Many stories have been told about the Cree culture-hero We.Sake.Chak. According to legend, he made the earth, the animals, and man. He had human, animal, and god-like qualities, and was known for both his trickery and buffoonery. Although the stories told about him helped instill moral values in the children and place the Cree nearer to the supernatural, their purpose was to provide enjoyment.   ADG

1957   **KUPFERER   HARRIET J**
1966
IMPOTENCY AND POWER: A CROSS-CULTURAL COMPARISON OF THE EFFECT OF ALIEN RULE. In Political Anthropology. Marc J. Swartz, Victor W. Turner and Arthur Tuden, eds. Chicago: Aldine. pp. 61-71.

An analysis of the leadership and authority status and role performance of a "band chief"at Rupert House is presented. The authority of the elected chief is manifested in limited social spheres and precludes control in major areas of concern to Indians, economy, health, and education. The chief is expected to please both his fellow band members and the Euro-Canadians. This results in a "modal role"behavior largely ineffectual from the Indians' standpoint and in frustration of the chief himself. Contrasted with this situation is a case study in New Guinea where the status of achieved authority does not result in impotence of power nor does it become conflict-inducing. A number of variables which may be operative in the role behavior of native officials are suggested.   DGW

1958   **LAFORCE   MARGUERITE MARIE**
1967
MORAL JUDGEMENTS AMONG INDIAN AND WHITE CHILDREN. M.Ed. Thesis. Department of Educational Psychology. University of Alberta.   102 pp.

One hundred and eighty-two Indian children aged 6 to 12 from Saddle Lake Reserve attending the reserve elementary school and Blue Quills residential school and 182 White children aged 6 to 10 of Vital Grandin Public School were examined for information relating to moral judgments. Information concerning beliefs in imminent and retributive justice was elicited using story situations adapted from Piaget. Moral traits of 11 and 12 year olds were evaluated by the teachers and their own age groups. Similar judgments were manifested by Indian and White subjects in their evaluation of moral traits. Results indicate differences in beliefs in imminent and retributive justice of Indian and White children of the lower and middle class particularly at 6 to 7 years of age.   CCV

1959   **LANDA   MICHAEL J**
1969
EASTERVILLE: A CASE STUDY IN THE RELOCATION OF A MANITOBA NATIVE COMMUNITY. M.A. Thesis. Department of Anthropology. University of Manitoba. 131 pp.

Fieldwork conducted during summer, 1968, and winter, 1969, provides the basis of this examination of the co-operative at Easterville, a community relocated from Chemuhowan. The relocation of the community, and the creation of the reservoir which necessitated that relocation, led to a shift from a broad economic base to one dependant upon a single resource, fish. The result was a poorer economic condition and a more atomistic community. The imposed co-operative failed to alter this situation.   TSA

1960   **LANEGRAFF   T G**
1961
PIONEERING AMONG THE INDIANS. Utica, NY: Lewis. 20 pp.

Migrating to Saskatchewan in 1906, T. G. Lanegraff - hunter, fisherman, guide, trader, dog-sled driver, and missionary - reminisces about his experiences with the Cree Indians of the Battleford, Meadow Lake, and Loon Lake regions. A list of Cree words with English equivalents is included.   IVY

1961   **LAPOINTE   GERTRUDE**
1969
L'INDIEN...CE QUIDAM. Bien-etre Social Canadien 21(4):103-109.

During 1968-1969, 691 Cree men over 15 and 650 women over 14 from Moosonee, Moose Factory, Fort Albany, Attawapiskat, Rupert House, and Fort George were interviewed by 8 students from the University of Ottawa. Impressions arising from these interviews are summarized.   CCV

1962   **LEGUERRIER   JULES**
1967
ALLONS-NOUS ABANDONNER LA LANGUE INDIENNE. Kerygma 1(2):51-55.

The problem of the use of syllabics in preparation of texts for Indians is reviewed briefly. Since most Indian people themselves are now familiar with and using roman letters this practice should be adopted by the church. Publication in Indian using roman symbols poses problems of standardization according to whether the second language is English or French. Several points requiring attention are listed which would permit uniformity in presentation of texts.   CCV

1963   **LEGUERRIER   JULES**
1967
LES PROBLEMES SOCIAUX DANS LE TERRITOIRE DE LA BAIE JAMES. Kerygma 1(2):83-87.

The social and economic problems found among the Indian population of James Bay are reviewed briefly.   CCV

1964   **LEITCH   ADELAIDE**
1961
PATTERN OF PROGRESS AT LAC LA RONGE. Canadian Geographical Journal 62:88-93.

The opening of a handicrafts co-operative at Lac La Ronge, Saskatchewan, and the beadwork of the 119 Cree worker-owners are discussed.   IVY

1965   **LEMIRE   FRANCOIS**
1967
UN APERCU DU POSTE DE NOUVEAU-COMPTOIR. In Problemes Nordiques des

Facades de la Baie de James: Recueil de Documents Rediges en Collaboration a la Suite
d'une Rencontre de Nordistes a Moosonee en Ontario. Centre d'Etudes Nordiques
Travaux Divers 18. Quebec: Centre d'Etudes Nordiques, Universite Laval. pp. 80-86.

A history of this new Cree community is given with an explanation of the purposes for
relocation and the subsequent social and economic organization which arose. The final
section is devoted to a discussion of the educational problems, and means of transportation and communication.   DD

1966   **LESSARD   JOHN L**
1965
THE FORT SEVERN GOOSE HUNT. Ontario Fish and Wildlife Review 4(4):14-17.

A brief description of the Fort Severn Goose Camp is given.   IVY

1967   **LEVASSEUR   LEON**
1960
THE CULTURAL DIFFERENCES BETWEEN CANADA'S EARLY AND RECENT
SETTLERS. Unpublished paper. Available from Legislative Library, Regina, Sask. 25
pp.

Part I of this paper is concerned with the traditional system of Central Northern Canada's Indians which were organized around the sharing concept. The 2nd part compares
their culture to that of recent settlers. Attitudes resulting from Indian-White contact are
examined from both points of view. To those involved with planned change it is suggested that the Indian culture be understood in its own terms and community development programs emulate from the needs and desires expressed by the peoples concerned.
IVY

1968   **LONGMUIR   GORDON**
1965
SUMMER ATHLETIC PROGRAM AT THE PAS RESERVE, JUNE 1 TO
SEPTEMBER 1, 1964. Unpublished paper. Available from Library, Department of
Health and Social Development, Winnipeg, Man. 5 pp.

Sports activities at The Pas Reserve in the summer of 1964 are outlined.   IVY

1969   **MACFIE `JOHN**
1967
THE COAST CREES. The Beaver 298(Winter):13-21.

Photographs, with captions, taken mainly in the Fort Severn and Winisk area portray the
contemporary Coast Cree.   IVY

1970   **MANDELBAUM   DAVID G**
1967
ANTHROPOLOGY AND THE PEOPLE: THE WORLD OF THE PLAINS CREE.
University of Saskatchewan, University Lectures, No. 12. Available from National
Library of Canada. 14 pp.

This lecture discusses the world of the Plains Cree as it has changed from aboriginal to modern times, and the world of the anthropologist as it was in the 1930's and as it is today in relation to the Plains Cree. HCV

1971 **MASON LEONARD**
1967
THE SWAMPY CREE: A STUDY IN ACCULTURATION. National Museum of Canada Anthropology Papers 13. Ottawa: Queen's Printer. 75 pp.

This monograph based on fieldwork among the Swampy Cree of Oxford House, Manitoba, in 1938 and 1940 was originally written in 1941. Discussed are the tribe and its environment, and the 3 stages of Cree-European contact are seen following first contact in 1611. Emphasized are the effects of the fur trade upon material culture, changes in leadership and religion, and the position of youth. Ecological adaptations in the fur trade era ultimately resulted in dependence on government and mission aid following the decline of a fur market. Many traditional values remain, although much of the culture was replaced. Fur farming and limited agriculture may provide avenues to self-sufficiency. JSL

1972 **MCKIM ELEANOR**
1965
THE CHANGES IN SANDY FLETT'S CREE RESERVE. The United Church Observer N.S. 26(19):18.

Sandy Flett, a Cree Indian from Red Sucker Lake, Manitoba, informally outlines the economic and educational changes on his reserve in the last 20 years. IVY

1973 **MITCHELL ROSS**
1968
ACORUS CALAMUS. The Beaver 298(Spring):24-26.

Guttormur J. Guttormsson, the Icelandic poet, in a letter and interview discusses Indian root and other medicinal plants used by the Cree in Manitoba. IVY

1974 **MONK CARL E**
1965
THAR'S GOLD IN THEM THAR HILLS. Ontario Fish and Wildlife Review 4(4):9-13.

Commercial fishing for goldeye at Sandy and Finger Lakes, Ontario, by the Deer Lake Band is described. IVY

1975 **MORIN LEOPOLD**
1967
MOOSE FACTORY. In Problemes Nordiques des Facades de la Baie de James: Recueil de Documents Rediges en Collaboration a la Suite d'une Rencontre de Nordistes a Moosonee en Ontario. Centre d'Etudes Nordiques Travaux Divers 18. Quebec: Centre d'Etudes Nordiques, Universite Laval. pp. 101-103.

This paper, read at a meeting on the James Bay area in 1967, is a brief presentation of the unique status of the Moose Factory community which is built on an island that belongs exclusively to the Hudson's Bay Company.   DD

1976   **MORIN   LEOPOLD**
1968
INTEGRATION DES INDIENS DE MOOSONEE. Kerygma 2(4):160-164.

The Indian community at Moosonee is discussed briefly. It is proposed that although integration is a desirable eventuality the Indians of Moosonee are not yet ready.   CCV

1977   **NEWMAN   MORTON**
1967
INDIANS OF THE SADDLE LAKE RESERVE. In Community Opportunity Assessment. Edmonton: Alberta, Human Resources Research and Development Executive Council. 109 pp.

Four sources of information were utilized for this study: an 8-week residence in the settlement, informal conversations, formal interviews (3 interviewers, 2 female Indians and 1 White male), and federal and provincial statistical data. Interviewed were 102 families. Explored were religion, age, welfare status, and size of family. Part of the study was conducted in the Lethbridge sugar beet area and in the Fort Saskatchewan Gaol. The study contains a description of the physical conditions of the reserve, an analysis of the social organization and economy, an exploration of attitudes of the population concerning reserve life and the non-reserve world, particularly in education and law, and recommendations for change in the reserve structure.   IVY

1978   **OMAND   D N**
1961
A TOUR OF THE PATRICIAS. Sylva 17(1):37-41.

This photo story records a visit by J. W. Spooner, Minister of the Department of Lands and Forests, to some of the Indian bands of the Patricias.   IVY

1979   **O'BRODOVICH   LLOYD**
1968
PLAINS CREE ACCULTURATION IN THE NINETEENTH CENTURY: A STUDY OF INJUSTICE. Na'Pao 2(1):2-23.

Although they were able to successfully adapt to Plains culture, the Plains Cree have been unable to adapt to White Canadian society. In fact, the present eroded state of Cree culture has been due to contact with European culture including the destruction of the buffalo, the treaties of the 1870's, the 1885 rebellion, and the establishment of the Indian Act and the reserve system.   ADG

1980   **O'BRODOVICH   LLOYD**
1969
THE PLAINS CREE OF LITTLE PINE: CHANGE AND PERSISTENCE IN CULTURE CONTACT. M.A. Thesis. Department of Anthropology and Archaeology. University of Saskatchewan, Saskatoon. 124 pp.

Acculturation of ?ree to Plains Indian neighbors and Whites is examined in this survey of the historical development of Plains Cree culture and the contemporary Little Pine Reserve. Fieldwork conducted from May 1, 1968, to September 15, 1968, yields a summary of the demography and economy of Little Pine plus a detailed analysis of the Sun Dance conducted that year.   TSA

1981   **O'BRODOVICH   LLOYD**
1969
PLAINS CREE SUN DANCE - 1968. The Western Canadian Journal of Anthropology 1(1):71-87.

A Sun Dance at Sweet Grass Reserve, Saskatchewan, is reported in detail including both preliminary ceremonies and observances as well as the main ceremony. Acculturation as evidenced in the Sun Dance is also recorded.   IVY

1982   **P S ROSS AND PARTNERS**
1970
OPPORTUNITIES FOR INDIAN PEOPLE IN MANITOBA'S VEGETABLE INDUSTRY. Unpublished report prepared for Manitoba Regional Office, Department of Indian Affairs and Northern Development. Available at Indian-Eskimo Economic Development Branch, Development Services Division, Department of Indian Affairs and Northern Development, Ottawa. 117 pp.

The Manitoba Roseau River, Sandy Bay, Long Plain and Long Plain Sioux, Swan Lake, Birdtail Sioux, Oak River, Oak Lake, Keeseekoowenin, Lizard Point, and Rolling River Reserves were examined early in 1970 in relation to opportunities in the vegetable production industry. Opportunities are summarized for each reserve according to soils and climate, experience and interest, recommended programs, market, organization, capital investment required, on-reserve processing, and off-reserve employment. Strategy for implementation of vegetable farming as a supplement to other income sources is presented on a priority basis for each reserve according to evaluation of the natural and human resource potential.   CCV

1983   **THE PAS MANITOBA COMMUNITY CONFERENCE THE PAS MANITOBA**
1961
RECOMMENDATIONS OF THE GROUP DISCUSSION OF THE COMMUNITY CONFERENCE. Unpublished paper. Available from Center for Settlement Studies, University of Manitoba. 3 pp.

Housing, employment, recreation, and education are included in 21 recommendations of a conference held at The Pas, January 29-30, 1961.   IVY

1984   **PEEL   BRUCE**
1966
THE LAST BATTLE. The Beaver 297(Winter):12-14.

An American war-party of 50 Mandan and their allies, the Gros Ventre, crossed into Canada in September, 1880, to avenge the death of a Mandan killed by 1 of Chief Pasqua's men. Suspecting an Assiniboine hunting camp (9 warriors, their wives, and children) of sheltering the enemy, since 2 hunters were Saulteaux, the war-party attacked.

The survivors walked 150 miles to Fort Ellice. This was the last battle between Indian tribes on Canadian soil.   IVY

1985   **PETERS   GEORGE A**
1970
PROBLEMS OF ISOLATED AND NON-ISOLATED MALE INDIAN STUDENTS. M.Ed. Thesis. University of Manitoba. 83 pp.

Fifty-one Indian boys in grades 8 or 9 of federal day schools and 86 Indian boys in high schools of Metropolitan Winnipeg were administered the Mooney Problem Check List during the period from November 1, 1969, to February 15, 1970. Comparisons were drawn between the isolated and non-isolated students on the basis of grade, school location, and time away from home. Similar problems were indicated for isolated and non-isolated students. Adjustment to school work was found to be a primary concern as well as concern for the future, financial independence, and church attendance.   CCV

1986   **PETERS   MARY JANE**
1970
ALLEN SAPP. Tawow 1(3):10-11.

A biographic sketch of a Cree artist from the Red Pheasant Reserve is presented. A list of his exhibitions is included.   IVY

1987   **POHORECKY   ZENON S**
1965
SASKATCHEWAN STONEHENGE. Saskatchewan Archaeology Newsletter 12:5-12.

Historical documentation supplemented by statements of local Indian informants reveals that the massive 400-ton boulder near Elbow, Saskatchewan, is a Plains Cree shrine. This impressive object of Indian veneration is in immediate danger of destruction unless it can be moved to higher ground.   IVY

1988   **POHORECKY   ZENON S**
1966
THE GREAT CREE STONE. Canadian Geographical Journal 73:88-91.

The legend and the sacred ceremony of Mistaseni (Cree for Great Stone) are briefly described.   IVY

1989   **PRESTON   RICHARD J**
n.d.
GOING SOUTH TO GET A LIVING: A SUMMARY REPORT TO THE ONTARIO DEPARTMENT OF LANDS AND FORESTS ON THE RESPONSE OF THE RUPERT'S HOUSE CREE INDIANS TO TRAPPING IN THE SOUTH. Unpublished paper. Available from National Library of Canada. 9 pp.

The Lands and Forests program provides competent Indians with a bush living where fur-bearing animals are relatively plentiful - in the south. Specific attitudes of individual Indians to the project are examined. It is concluded that the Indians feel positively towards the program and the risks involved in making a living in the south are surmountable. IVY

1990   **PRESTON   RICHARD J**
1964
RITUAL HANGINGS: AN ABORIGINAL 'SURVIVAL' IN A NORTHERN
NORTH AMERICAN TRAPPING COMMUNITY. Man 64:142-144.

A 3 month field trip in the summer of 1963 to the Rupert House settlement of the
Swampy Cree in Quebec yields a description of the ritual practice of hanging animal
remains outdoors or in a residence immediately after a successful hunt. The necessity for
further study of this practice surviving 295 years of contact is noted. Included are 8 photographs illustrating the various types of hangings.   WRC

1991   **PRESTON   RICHARD J**
1966
PEER GROUP VS. TRAP LINE: SHIFTING DIRECTIONS IN CREE
SOCIALIZATION. Unpublished paper delivered to Annual Meeting, Pennsylvania
Sociological Society. Haverford, Pa, October 14, 1966. Available from National Library
of Canada. 11 pp.

Patterns of traditional and contemporary socialization among the Eastern Cree are compared. Placed on a continuum, bush-orientation to community-orientation, sample families show differential adaptation in a process of culture change.   IVY

1992   **PRESTON   RICHARD J**
1967
RETICENCE AND SELF-EXPRESSION IN A CREE COMMUNITY: A STUDY OF
STYLE IN SOCIAL RELATIONSHIPS. Unpublished paper. Available from National
Museum of Man, Ethnology Division, Ottawa, with permission of the author. 22 pp.

The modal personality of the Cree is discussed, based upon fieldwork at Rupert's House,
Quebec. The concept of reserve or stoicism is given more precision by an analysis of variation. Quiet behavior or reticence in self-expression is shown to be a relatively strong
norm. Relaxation of the norm, however, illustrates its varying situational compul-
siveness. Further variation derives from inter-individual differences and intra-individual
variation throughout the life cycle.   JSL

1993   **PRESTON   RICHARD J**
1968
FUNCTIONAL POLITICS IN A NORTHERN INDIAN COMMUNITY.
Unpublished paper delivered to 38th International Congress of Americanists. Stuttgart-
Muenchen, August, 1968. Available from National Library of Canada. Available from
National Library of Canada. 19 pp.

The contemporary status of political patterns both in and relating to the Cree community
of Rupert's House, Quebec, are described. The chief and councilor system begun in 1946
is discussed in terms of conflicting concepts of leadership and authority expected by
Euro-Canadians and Indians.   IVY

1994   **PRESTON   RICHARD J**
1968
HUNTING, TRAVELLING, AND CONJURING SONGS OF THE EASTERN
CREE. Unpublished paper delivered to 1st Conference on Algonquian Studies. St.-Pierre

de Wakefield, Que., Sept. 12-15, 1968. Available from National Library of Canada. 9 pp.

This paper describes and discusses 6 songs and 1 conjuring ceremony recorded at the 3 Eastern Cree settlements of Rupert's House, Fort George, and Eastmain.   HCV

1995   **PRESTON   RICHARD J**
1969
EASTERN CREE ATTITUDES TOWARDS HARDSHIP: EMOTIONAL
RESPONSES TO THE CONTINGENCIES OF BUSH LIFE. Unpublished paper
delivered to 2nd Conference on Algonkian Studies. St. John's, Nfld., August 23-24,
1969. Available from National Library of Canada. 12 pp.

Using short stories about hardship in the Cree environment, the author attempts to explain the pattern of thinking and mental competence of the eastern bush Cree.   HCV

1996   **PRESTON   RICHARD J**
1969
EASTERN CREE MAN AND NATURE: A HUNTER'S VIEW OF GETTING A
LIVING IN THE BUSH. Unpublished paper delivered to 68th Annual Meeting,
American Anthropological Association. New Orleans, LA, November 20-23, 1969.
Available from National Library of Canada. 8 pp.

The Eastern Cree hunters' perception of, and response to, their environment, the Eastern Subarctic boreal forest area, is the concern of this paper. Speck's image of a threatening environment is criticized. Discussed are the Cree other-than-human persons that inhabit the hunter's world: human-distorted persons, alien human persons, animal-distorted persons, ambiguous animal persons, attending spirit persons, human-animal persons, and food persons. Data strongly suggest that fear plays a secondary role.   The Cree hunter enjoys hunting, a passion believed to be reciprocally shared by the animals they hunt. Hardship narratives regularly express attitudes of fortitude, regret, and grief. The deep emotional bases that define and motivate much of Cree culture are both complex and obscure.   IVY

1997   **PRESTON   RICHARD J**
1969
EASTERN CREE SONGS AND TEXTS. Unpublished paper. Available from National
Library of Canada. 30 pp.

This paper contains a transcribed collection of over 50 eastern Cree ceremonial songs and texts sung by 4 older men from Fort George, Quebec. Because the report contains very few verbatim translations of the songs, the author uses explanatory notes and analytical comments.   HCV

1998   **PRESTON   RICHARD J**
1969
EASTERN CREE SONGS: THE EXPRESSION OF PERSONAL SYMBOLISMS IN
THE USE OF CULTURE PATTERNS. Unpublished paper delivered to 9th Annual
Meeting, Northeastern Anthropological Association. Providence, RI, April 25-27, 1969.
Available from National Library of Canada. 14 pp.

The 13 Eastern Cree songs in this collection were recorded at the Fort George Indian settlement, Quebec. The songs were translated in an attempt to analyze words, concepts, values, and sentiments.   HCV

1999   **PRESTON   RICHARD J**
1970
THE DEVELOPMENT OF SELF-CONTROL IN THE EASTERN CREE LIFE
CYCLE. Unpublished paper delivered to 10th Annual Meeting, Northeastern Anthropological Association. Ottawa, May 7-9, 1970. Available from National Library of Canada. 9 pp.

Traditional child rearing practices and socialization processes among the Cree communities on the eastern coast of James Bay form a basis for an analysis of the development of self-control.   HCV

2000   **PRESTON   RICHARD J**
1970
ON THE RELATIONSHIPS BETWEEN HUMAN PERSONS AND FOOD-
ANIMAL PERSONS. Unpublished paper delivered to 3rd Conference on Algonquian Studies. Peterborough, Ont., August 29-30, 1970. Available from National Library of Canada. 12 pp.

Analyzing narratives involving such food-animal persons as the caribou, beaver, and bear, it is argued that a love relationship exists between the human hunter and the animal he kills.   IVY

2001   **PROVENCHER   MAURICE**
1967
SCHEMA DE PROBLEMES A FORT-RUPERT ET DANS LA BAIE JAMES,
SECTION QUEBECOISE, 1967. In Problemes Nordiques des Facades de la Baie de James: Recueil de Documents Rediges en Collaboration a la Suite d'une Rencontre de Nordistes a Moosonee en Ontario. Centre d'Etudes Nordiques Travaux Divers 18. Quebec: Centre d'Etudes Nordiques, Universite Laval. pp. 95-100.

This paper tells of the social and economic situation of the Indians of the James Bay region and suggests changes by intensifying communication among the 4 communities of James Bay on the Quebec side.   DD

2002   **RACHLIN   CAROL KING**
1960
THE HISTORIC POSITION OF THE PROTO-CREE TEXTILES IN THE EASTERN
FABRIC COMPLEX, AN ETHNOLOGICAL-ARCHAEOLOGICAL
CORRELATION. In Contributions to Anthropology, 1958. National Museum of Canada Bulletin 167. Ottawa: Queen's Printer. pp. 80-89.

A comparison of protohistoric Cree textiles from Manitoba with historic and archaeological materials was undertaken. It was concluded that the protohistoric complex had a long history in eastern North America. The complex may have diffused from the river valley cultures to the south. The proto-Cree material does not represent a decline of high culture, but an enduring subsistence culture.   JSL

2003   **REDEKOPP   HAROLD I**
1968
AN ANALYSIS OF THE SOCIAL AND ECONOMIC PROBLEMS OF FOUR
SMALL COMMUNITIES IN NORTHERN MANITOBA: WABOWDEN, THICKET
PORTAGE, NORWAY HOUSE AND OXFORD HOUSE. M.A. Thesis. Department
of Anthropology and Geography. University of Manitoba. 214 pp. Available from
National Library of Canada.

The results of a 1967 summer survey and study of the housing and utilities, education,
employment, residential mobility, and cultural background of the residents of 2 Indian
communities and 2 Indian reserves in northern Manitoba are reported. Rapidly expanding populations, diminishing resources for the trapping and fishing industry, and lack of
industrial development are common problems. Proposals are advanced for further study
and a co-ordinated development program in the areas of trapping and fishing, agriculture, mink ranching, tourism, housing, education, and recreation in view of encouraging
greater involvement of the Indian-Metis population in economic development.   CCV

2004   **ROBBINS   RICHARD H**
1967
THE OUT: SOCIAL SURVIVAL IN A SMALL SCALE COMMUNITY. Unpublished
paper delivered to 66th Annual Meeting, American Anthropological Association.
Washington, DC, November 30-December 3, 1967. Available from National Library of
Canada. 7 pp.

Fieldwork was conducted in Great Whale River, Quebec, from July to August, 1965.
The social mechanism which minimizes risks in decision-making is called "the out."This
functions to enable a decision to be reached without risking any one person's self image
or social standing should the decision be wrong. The Cree Indians inhabiting the eastern
coast of Hudson Bay are used to illustrate the mechanism.   IVY

2005   **ROBBINS   RICHARD H**
1967
THE TWO CHIEFS: CHANGING LEADERSHIP PATTERNS AMONG THE
GREAT WHALE RIVER CREE. Unpublished paper delivered to 7th Annual Meeting,
Northeastern Anthropological Association. Montreal, April 2, 1967. Available from
National Library of Canada. 11 pp.

This account of the 1965 elections for chief councilor at Great Whale River, Quebec,
describes the 2 separate elections held at the settlement. The first was organized by the
Indians while the second, nullifying the first, was organized by the Indian agent.   HCV

2006   **ROGERS   EDWARD S**
1965
THE NEMISCAU INDIANS. The Beaver 296(Summer):30-35.

The Nemiscau Indians, who speak a dialect of Cree, are located at Lake Nemiscau, Quebec. Fieldwork of a few days duration was conducted in June, 1964. Discussed are the
economy (hunting, trapping, and fishing), material culture, and the retention of native
social customs.   IVY

2007 **ROGERS EDWARD S, UPDIKE LEE**
1969
PLAINS CREE. The Beaver 300(Autumn):56-59.

A pictorial article depicting 19th century tribal life including customs, dress, tools, subsistence, and dwellings. IVY

2008 **RORDAM VITA**
1967
THE WOMAN WHO SPOKE TO A DOG: A STORY OF THE COAST CREES TOLD
BY A MAN OF WINISK TO VITA RORDAM. The Beaver 298(Winter):54.

A folk tale of the Coast Cree explains why it is unwise to speak to a dog in the same way
you speak to a human being. IVY

2009 **RUE LEONARD LEE III**
1961
BARRIERE INDIANS. The Beaver 292(Autumn):27-32.

Text and photographs describe the physical characteristics of the Barriere, or Tete-de-
Boule, their present material culture, and their subsistence pattern. IVY

2010 **SHIPLEY NAN**
1962
PROGRESS AND THE PEOPLE OF GRAND RAPIDS. Canadian Geographical
Journal 65:182-191.

A brief history of Grand Rapids is presented. The building of the Grand Rapids Dam
and its ramifications for the native populace are discussed. IVY

2011 **SHIPLEY NAN**
1967
ALMIGHTY VOICE AND THE RED COATS. Don Mills, Ont.: Burns and
MacEachern. 19 pp.

This tragic story of a 21-year old Cree recounts his confrontation with the North West
Mounted Police in the spring of 1897. As a result of a misunderstanding - that Indians
are hanged for stealing deer - Almighty Voice became a fugitive and was later shot to
death by the forces of the Mounted Police. Based on North West Mounted Police reports
and the eye-witness accounts of Indians, the incident tells of the last bloodshed between
the White man and Canadian Indians. DGW

2012 **SIGURDSON S E**
1963
A REPORT ON THE ECONOMY OF CEDAR LAKE AND MOOSE LAKE.
Unpublished report prepared for Grand Rapids Forebay Economic Committee.
Available at Indian-Eskimo Economic Development Branch, Development Services
Division, Department of Indian Affairs and Northern Development, Ottawa. 49 pp.

Economic conditions at Cedar Lake and Moose Lake, Manitoba, are discussed for a 10-
year period on the basis of 2 months research and visits to the Grand Rapids Forebay
area. Recommendations for stimulation of the economy and the role of the Forebay
Committee in the area are outlined for a 10-year span. CCV

2013   **SLUMAN   NORMA**
1967
POUNDMAKER. Toronto: Ryerson Press. 301 pp.

Narrated is the story of Poundmaker from the time of his adoption by Crowfoot, the Blackfoot chief, until his death at the age of 44. Spanning the years 1872-1886, we see Poundmaker as a liaison agent attempting a truce between his native Cree and the Blackfoot and as a chief faced with the problems of culture change. Information for this study was taken from the reports, correspondence, and speeches of the policemen, settlers, officials, clergymen, Metis, and Indians involved.   DGW

2014   **SMALLBOY   ROBERT**
1969
DECISION TO LEAVE HOBBEMA. The Western Canadian Journal of Anthropology 1(1):112-118.

In 1968 Robert Smallboy, a 71-year old leader from the Ermineskin Band in Hobbema, along with 150 men, women, and children, decided to leave Hobbema and relocate in the Kootenay Plains area of Alberta. His comments for the public have been translated and edited by Eugene Steinhauer.   IVY

2015   **SMALLBOY   ROBERT**
1970
A NARRATIVE TOLD BY ROBERT SMALLBOY. The Northian 7(3):25-27.

In 1968 an Ermineskin chief and 150 of his tribesmen settled in the Kootenay Plains, after abandoning the Hobbema Reserve. The transition, however, was difficult. The government's refusal to assist the group was especially disappointing. In addition to describing this experiment, the narrative also contains a native's reflections on White civilization and those Indian leaders who appease it.   ADG

2016   **SMITH   JAMES G E**
1968
PRELIMINARY NOTES ON THE ROCKY CREE OF REINDEER LAKE.
Unpublished paper. Available from National Library of Canada. 24 pp.

The limits of the western Woods Cree distribution in the northern portion of the prairie provinces are noted. The Cree of Reindeer Lake, who moved north within the last century, exhibit both continuity and change in social organizations as they have moved from a traditional fur trade economy to one in which Euro-Canadian institutions are dominant. History, economics, and social organization are briefly reviewed.   HCV

2017   **SPAULDING   PHILIP**
1967
THE SOCIAL INTEGRATION OF A NORTHERN COMMUNITY: WHITE MYTHOLOGY AND METIS REALITY. In A Northern Dilemma: Reference Papers. Arthur K. Davis, Vernon C. Serl, et al., eds. Bellingham, WA: Western Washington State College. Vol. 1. pp. 90-111.

The social organization of the Swampy Cree population of a northern Saskatchewan community is discussed on the basis of fieldwork done in the summers of 1961, 1962, and

1965. The relationship between the White and Indian community is described and attention directed to the so-called deviant behavior which characterizes the Indian-Metis. It is maintained that this behavior is not evidence of social disintegration but an expression of "Indianness" and a manifestation of their inferior social role. The kinship-based internal organization and residence pattern combined with lack of opportunity for social mobility function to perpetuate the sense of Indian identity and associated behavior patterns.   CCV

2018   **STEINHAUER   EUGENE**
1969
INTRODUCTION TO CHIEF SMALLBOY'S NARRATIVE. The Western Canadian Journal of Anthropology 1(1):111-112.

In 1968 Robert Smallboy along with 150 followers decided to relocate in the Kootenay Plains area of Alberta. Their life is briefly described.   IVY

2019   **STOBIE   MARGARET**
1967-68
BACKGROUNDS OF THE DIALECT CALLED BUNGI. Historical and Scientific Society of Manitoba Papers (Series 3) 24:65-75.

Three different levels of usage for the word Bungi are examined: (1) a synonym for Saulteaux; (2) an uncomplimentary nickname connotating begging or beggars; and (3) a designation to those of Scotch-Indian, specifically Scotch-Cree, parentage and their speech. The article focuses upon the third usage, an English dialect called Bungi.   IVY

2020   **TRUDEAU   JEAN**
1966
CULTURE CHANGE AMONG THE SWAMPY CREE INDIANS OF WINISK, ONTARIO. Ph.D. Thesis. Department of Anthropology. Catholic University of America. 182 pp. Available from University Microfilms.

Thirteen months during the summer of 1958 and from August, 1959, to June, 1960, were spent studying social and cultural transformation among the Swampy Cree at Winisk, Ontario. The subsistence economy and life style are traced from pre-contact to the present. Before contact the subsistence economy was primarily based on hunting of large game. The minimal contact period extending from 1670 to 1901 was marked by a shift to a trapping emphasis but the Indians continued to live in small isolated groups. In 1901 the sustained contact phase began with construction of a Roman Catholic church and a trading post at the mouth of the river where the Indians gathered every summer. The maximal contact phase was initiated in 1955 with the construction of a radar base near the post. This had the effect of shifting the economic emphasis from hunting and trapping to wage earning and, instead of isolated family groups, year-round residence at the post was adopted. Analysis of the cultural system shows it to be "open," having a propensity toward change which, however, was not uniform over the 3 contact phases. Variations in processes and factors during the 3 phases are described and examined.   CCV

2021   **TRUDEAU   JEAN**
1968
THE PEOPLE OF HUDSON BAY. In Science, History and Hudson Bay: Volume I. C. S. Beals, ed. Ottawa: Queen's Printer. pp. 127-140.

The traditional culture of the Indian population of the Hudson and James Bay coastal areas is summarized. Sustained contacts with White men in fur trading, socialization at trading posts, and religious activities have altered the traditional Indian culture. These influences and the effects of changing health and educational facilities on Indian life are described briefly.   CCV

2022   **VAILLANCOURT   LOUIS PHILIPPE**
1967
PROBLEMES D'EASTMAIN. In Problemes Nordiques des Facades de la Baie de James: Recueil de Documents Rediges en Collaboration a la Suite d'une Rencontre de Nordistes a Moosonee en Ontario. Centre d'Etudes Nordiques Travaux Divers 18. Quebec: Centre d'Etudes Nordiques, Universite Laval. pp. 90-94.

A brief contemporary presentation of the Eastmain community is given which focuses on the social and economic problems of the Indians of the James Bay region. The author suggests a few solutions for economic problems.   DD

2023   **VANDERSTEENE   ROGER**
1960
WABASCA: DIX ANS DE VIE INDIENNE. Gemmenlich, Belgique: Editions O.M.I. 223 pp.

Highlights of 10 years among the Cree at Wabaska, Alberta, are described by an Oblate Father. Details of life style, subsistence activities, and attitudes toward religion are included.   CCV

2024   **VANDERSTEENE   ROGER**
1969
SOME WOODLAND CREE TRADITIONS AND LEGENDS. The Western Canadian Journal of Anthropology 1(1):40-65.

An excerpt from Vandersteene's book Wabasca is translated by Thelma Habgood. This section includes: the birth of the world; 3 legends of Wesakitchak; anecdotes involving the appearance of Witigo (a cannibal-spirit) and the devil Mantchimanitou; and concept of soul, burial customs, Kisemanitou, and other beliefs. Also described is the ceremony of the cult of the dead, Wikkokkewin. The religious customs of the Indians are interpreted from the viewpoint of the Christian missionary.   IVY

2025   **WATSON   G**
1967
POUNDMAKER'S MEDICINE BUNDLE. Saskatchewan Archaeology Newsletter 17:14-15.

The ceremony at Sweetgrass Indian Reserve, Saskatchewan, accompanying the opening of Poundmaker's medicine bundle in 1965 is briefly described.   IVY

2026   **WELSH   M A**
1968
A CREE REMEDY FOR CHEST PAINS AND FEVER. Na'Pao 1(1):23.

The Cree used Chimaphila umbellata for the reduction of pain or fever induced by heart diseases. Europeans have also discovered and used this plant for medicinal purposes. ADG

2027   **WHITFORD   JAMES R**
1962
THE GRAND RAPIDS FISHERMEN'S CO-OP: A REPORT ON THE ORGANIZATION OF A FISHERMEN'S CO-OP. Unpublished paper. Available from National Library of Canada. 9 pp.

A detailed account of the steps followed by a group of fishermen in Grand Rapids, Manitoba, organizing a co-operative is given.   Described are method of fishing (trap nets), construction of a plant, fish harvests, and marketing.   IVY

2028   **WILTSHIRE   E BEVAN,   GRAY   JOHN E**
1969
DRAW-A-MAN AND RAVEN'S PROGRESSIVE MATRICES (1938) INTELLIGENCE TEST PERFORMANCE OF RESERVE INDIAN CHILDREN. Canadian Journal of Behavioural Science 1:119-122.

The conclusion that the Draw-a-Man and Raven tests are not culture-free is the result of this study in which the scores of 54 girls and 32 boys from 2 Cree reserves were analyzed for cross-cultural effects. On the Draw-a-Man test the Indian children equalled or surpassed the standardization group, with no sex differences being found significant. On the Raven, however, the experimental group averaged 20 points below the standardization group. In addition, older children scored lower than did younger ones.   ADG

2029   **WOOD   W J,   SWAIL   ANNA M**
1963
OUTPOST NURSING STATION. The Canadian Nurse 59:445-447.

A nurse relates her experiences at God's Lake Nursing Station, Manitoba, which in 1947 consisted of 3 small log shacks (sick bay, living quarters, and storage and laundry) serving 477 Indian people. In 1954 a modern nursing station was opened at God's Lake Narrows, 12 miles from the previous site.   IVY

2030   **WOODWARD   JOHN A**
1969
PLAINS CREE BEADWORK. The Masterkey 43:144-150.

Based on observations among Alberta Plains Cree in 1969, this article reviews the style and technique of contemporary beadwork.   Very little beadwork is done for commercial purposes.   ADG

2031   **WOODWARD J A,   WOODWARD V C**
1970
A LEISURE TIME ACTIVITY OF THE PLAINS CREE. Anthropological Journal of Canada 8(4):29-31.

The women's dice game (Chekawawin) of the Plains Cree was observed and recorded during the summer of 1969. This contemporary version is a revival from memory of a traditional game that was played at the Hobbema Reserve, Alberta, during the 19th and early 20th centuries. An explanation of the game is given and innovations are noted.   IVY

2032   **WUTTUNEE   WILLIAM I**
1962
THIRST DANCE OF THE CREES. The Beaver 293(Winter):20-23.

The ceremonies of the Thirst Dance, also known as the Sun Dance or Rain Dance, are described, particularly the construction of the ceremonial lodge.   IVY

2033   **WUTTUNEE   WILLIAM I**
1968
PEYOTE CEREMONY. The Beaver 299(Summer):22-25.

A Peyote ceremony at the Red Pheasant Indian Reserve in Saskatchewan in July, 1964, is described.   IVY

2034   **YELLOWBIRD   LYDIA**
1970
TO BE YOUNG AND INDIAN. In The Only Good Indian: Essays by Canadian Indians. Waubageshig, ed. Toronto: New Press. pp. 104-109.

Commented on is the dilemma of Canadian Indian youth today. They are searching for their identity in a society which suppresses traditional native values and beliefs.   DGW

DOGRIB

2035   **ANDERS   G**
1969
RAE - LAC LA MARTRE: AN AREA OF ECONOMIC SURVEY 1966 (A.E.S.R) No. 66/2. Ottawa: Queen's Printer. 113 pp.

The Dogrib communities of Fort Rae and Lac La Martre were surveyed during the summer of 1966 to evaluate human and natural resources and to determine the development potential in maximizing Dogrib participation. The historical background, subsistence patterns, population groupings, communication and transporation networks, and current economic activity including the importance of hunting, fishing, and trapping are reviewed. Comments and recommendations are submitted concerning the contemplated relocation of the townsite of Rae, development pattern of other Dogrib settlements, tourism and fisheries development, and possibilities for improving living standards. CCV

2036   **HELM   JUNE**
1968
THE NATURE OF DOGRIB SOCIOTERRITORIAL GROUPS. In Man the Hunter. Richard B. Lee and Irven De Vore, eds. Chicago: Aldine. pp. 118-125.

From analysis of post-contact data 3 kinds of socio-territorial groups are revealed among the Dogrib and Arctic Drainage Athapaskans. Territorial range, resources, and kinship networks are seen as determining factors in the creation and structuring of regional bands, local bands, and task groups. The determination of actual patterns of post-marital residence in order to understand and compare cross-culturally hunting societies is indicated. CCV

2037   **HELM   JUNE**
1969
REMARKS ON THE METHODOLOGY OF BAND COMPOSITION ANALYSIS. In Contributions to Anthropology: Band Societies: Proceedings of the Conference on Band Organization, Ottawa, August 30 to September 2, 1965. David Damas, ed. National Museum of Canada Bulletin 228. Ottawa: Queen's Printer. pp. 212-217.

Based on fieldwork among the Martin Lake Dogrib the author discusses the nature of social organization of Northeastern Athapaskan bands. A distinction between settlement pattern and community pattern is suggested. The former refers to the exploitative pattern; the latter refers to social relationships. An analysis of community patterns of the Dogrib demonstrates that there is no married adult in the group who does not have a primary affinal or consanguineal tie to at least one other member of the group. Thus any ego has a wide range of choice among alternative band residences. This method of analyzing community pattern proved useful in perceiving and quantifying the fluctuating socio-territorial membership of Northern Athapaskan bands. JSL

2038   **HELM   JUNE,   LURIE   NANCY O**
1961
THE SUBSISTENCE ECONOMY OF THE DOGRIB INDIANS OF LAC LA MARTRE IN THE MACKENZIE DISTRICT OF THE NORTHWEST TERRITORIES. Department of Northern Affairs and National Resources, Northern Co-ordination and Research Centre Reports No. NCRC-61-3. Ottawa: Department of Northern Affairs and National Resources. 119 pp.

Fieldwork among the Dogrib at Lac La Martre from August to December, 1959, yields a description of community social and economic interaction and features of life style. Attention is focused on the subsistence economy with a review of exploitation of local flora and fauna revealing sources of food and clothing and techniques of acquisition, processing, and distribution. CCV

2039   **HELM   JUNE,   LURIE   NANCY OESTREICH**
1966
THE DOGRIB HAND GAME. National Museum of Canada Bulletin 205. Ottawa: Queen's Printer. 101 pp.

The Dogrib hand game with its unique complexities is described based on fieldwork conducted in 1962 at Rae, N.W.T. The annual summer payment of treaty was also observed. Eighteen plates and 22 figures accompany the text. Tape recordings were analyzed by Gertrude Kurath, who in a chapter discusses the choreography and music. Helm and Lurie discuss the general background of the game, the hand game itself, the position of the game in Dogrib culture, and comparison with other games. JSL

2040   **HELM   JUNE,   THOMAS   VITAL**
1966
TALES FROM THE DOGRIBS. The Beaver 297(Autumn):16-20.

The following 3 stories related how things came to be: Zhamonzha and His Beaver Wife, The Origin of the Dogribs, and How the Barrens Came to be and Went-Inside-Mountain Got Its Name. The next 3 stories recount critical times in tribal history: The Captive Woman, When the First Pale Men Came, and How the Medicine Man Got the Hudson's Bay Man's Mind.   IVY

2041   **HELM   JUNE,   THOMAS   VITAL**
1966
TALES FROM THE DOGRIBS. The Beaver 297(Winter):52-54.

Tales demonstrate proper Dogrib manners and morals by relating how things are; the nature of animals, man, and magic medicine; and how things should be. These are titled: A Fish Story, The Boy with Thunder Medicine in the Land of the Icebergs, and The Young Man Who Did Not Shame Himself Before Strangers.   IVY

2042   **LAWTON   ERNEST PETER**
1970
A STUDY OF THE ATTITUDES OF INDIAN PARENTS TOWARD EDUCATION IN FORT RAE. M.Ed. Thesis. College of Education. University of Saskatchewan, Saskatoon. 150 pp.

Parents in a random sample consisting of 18 Dogrib families were interviewed to determine their attitudes toward a proposed innovative Edzo school. Problems recognized by these parents proved to be those recognized in the literature - a need for Indian content and participation in the educational process. Euro-Canadians at Fort Rae were also interviewed and their approval of local control of schools varied with the permanence of the residence in the area.   TSA

2043   **LURIE   NANCY OESTREICH**
1961
THE DOGRIB INDIANS OF CANADA. Lore 11:60-67.

A brief report on fieldwork of 4-months duration (August to November) conducted at Lac la Martre, Northwest Territories, focuses upon the economic activities of the Dogrib Indians.   IVY

HAN

2044   **SLOBODIN   RICHARD**
1963
NOTES ON THE HAN. Unpublished paper prepared for Northern Co-ordination and Research Centre, Department of Northern Affairs and National Resources. Available at Northern Science Research Group, Department of Indian Affairs and Northern Development. 28 pp.

A reconstruction of the traditional life style of the Han is derived from notes compiled as a by-product of research on the Kutchin at Dawson during the summers of 1961 and 1962. Information on subsistence activities including aboriginal hunting and fishing techniques, kinship, life cycle, socialization patterns, and leadership is provided.   CCV

HARE

2045   **ANDERSON   R J**
1969
INDIAN JUSTICES. The RCMP Quarterly 34(4):32.

Edward Cook and Noel Kaktwi, 2 Indians form Fort Good Hope, are sworn in as Justices of the Peace in and for the Northwest Territories.   IVY

2046   **BALIKCI   ASEN,   COHEN   RONALD**
1963
COMMUNITY PATTERNING IN TWO NORTHERN TRADING POSTS.
Anthropologica N.S. 5:33-45.

A comparison between the organization of the Povungnitak Eskimos of northeastern Hudson Bay and that of the Hare Indians at Fort Good Hope on the Mackenzie River, N.W.T., indicates common trends through the 1930's. However, Fort Good Hope lacks the form of community cohesiveness characteristic of the Eskimos.   WRC

2047   **HURLBERT   JANICE**
1962
AGE AS A FACTOR IN THE SOCIAL ORGANIZATION OF THE HARE INDIAN OF FORT GOOD HOPE, N.W.T. Department of Northern Affairs and National Resources, Northern Co-ordination and Research Centre Reports No. NCRC-62-5. Ottawa: Department of Northern Affairs and National Resources. 79 pp.

The community, social organization, and acculturation are discussed in this report based upon 14 weeks of fieldwork during the summer of 1961. Age groups are described individually with attention to groupings occasioned by sex and emphasis on socialization processes functioning to prepare individuals for successive roles.   CCV

2048   **SAVISHINSKY   JOEL S**
1970
ANTHROPOLOGY'S ETERNAL TRIANGLE: THE MISSIONARY, THE FUR TRADE AND THE ETHNOGRAPHER. Unpublished paper delivered to 69th Annual Meeting, American Anthropological Association. San Diego, CA, November 19-22, 1970. Available from National Library of Canada. 33 pp.

The ethnographer relates a feud between the 2 non-Indians in the Hare Indian settlement of Colville, N.W.T.: the fur trader and the priest. The independent fur trader opened an outpost which attracted the Indians to settle and this in turn attracted a priest who established a church. Both non-Indian men, realizing that they were the focus of the community, decided that they would have a "gentlemen's agreement", the priest encouraging the Indians to sell their furs at the trader's outpost and the trader attending church regularly. A misunderstanding between the 2 led to a continuing struggle that eventually involved everyone in the community.   HCV

2049   **SAVISHINSKY   JOEL S**
1970
KINSHIP AND THE EXPRESSION OF VALUES IN AN ATHABASKAN BUSH COMMUNITY. The Western Canadian Journal of Anthropology 2(1):31-59.

A year of fieldwork (August, 1967, to August, 1968) was carried out among the members of the Colville Lake band in the Northwest Territories. Drawn from material presented in the author's unpublished thesis (1970) this essay focuses on kinship as a basic social dimension and examines how kinship attitudes and behavior exhibit the complementary themes of generosity, emotional restraint, and flexibility.   IVY

2050   **SAVISHINSKY   JOEL STEPHEN**
1970
STRESS AND MOBILITY IN AN ARCTIC COMMUNITY: THE HARE INDIANS OF COLVILLE LAKE, NORTHWEST TERRITORIES. Ph.D. Thesis. Department of Anthropology. Cornell University. 646 pp. Available from University Microfilms.

In the Hare Indian village of Colville Lake scarcity of fur and food resources and shelter are sources of physical stress. Acculturative processes, in-group conflict, prolonged periods of isolation, population concentration, and conflicting values are related to social stress. Population mobility is seen to be closely related to stress. The annual cycle of subsistence activities sees each phase relieving stresses arising in the former and in turn creating new stresses. Population mobility is high in each phase but accomodation to stress was found to be related to factors such as age, sex, acculturation, and local ties. Other socially acceptable responses to stress were observed.

2051   **SUE   HIROKO**
1962
REPORT ON ETHNOLOGICAL FIELDWORK AT FORT GOOD HOPE, N.W.T., CANADA, SUMMER, 1961. Unpublished paper. Available from Library, American Philosophical Society, Philadelphia, PA, with permission of the author. 59 pp.

Special emphasis is placed on the interrelationship of the social organization, yearly cycle, and the subsistance economy in this summary of fieldwork conducted from June to September, 1961.   HCV

2052   **SUE   HIROKO**
1964
HARE INDIANS AND THEIR WORLD. Ph.D. Thesis. Bryn Mawr College. 504 pp. Available from University Microfilms.

Presented is an ethnographic report on the Hare Indians of the northern Mackenzie River who reside and hunt in the Fort Good Hope Game Area. Fieldwork for the study was carried out between June and September, 1961, and between June, 1962, and January, 1963. The thesis is intended to clarify the world view of the Hare Indians and what it is to be a Hare person. From a historical perspective, treatment is given to their social structure, religion, acculturation, methods of utilizing their environment, pastime activities, and life processes. Seven maps, 58 figures, and 15 plates supplement the study.   DGW

2053   **SUE   HIROKO**
1965
PRE-SCHOOL CHILDREN OF THE HARE INDIANS. Department of Northern Affairs and National Resources, Northern Co-ordination and Research Centre Reports No. NCRC-65-1. Ottawa: Department of Northern Affairs and National Resources. 49 pp.

Hare child-rearing practices observed in the Fort Good Hope area during the summer of 1961 and the winter of 1962 are reported. Pregnancy, adoption, socialization, and parental attitudes are discussed. CCV

2054   **VILLIERS   D**
1968
THE CENTRAL MACKENZIE: AN AREA ECONOMIC SURVEY (A.E.S.R. No. 67/4). Ottawa: Department of Indian Affairs and Northern Development, Resources and Industrial Division. 157 pp.

Fieldwork in 1967 followed by library research is reported in this survey of the economies of the Norman Wells, Fort Norman, Fort Franklyn, Fort Good Hope, and Colville Lake settlements. The physical environment, communication and transportation systems, natural resources, and the economy are examined and yield proposals for community development, co-operatives, tourism, training and education, and economic development projects. CCV

2055   **VOUDRACH   PAUL,   COHEN   RONALD,   et al.**
1967
GOOD HOPE TALES. In Contributions to Ethnology V. National Museum of Canada Bulletin 204. Ottawa: Queen's Printer. pp. 1-58.

The manuscript of Mr. Voudrach, a Kutchin of Fort Good Hope, Northwest Territories, was analyzed by Cohen and Helgi Osterreich. An introduction and outline of the cultural context precede the tales. Thirteen Kutchin-Hare tales, including 65 episodes, were isolated. Summaries of the tales are given in standard English. Cohen and Osterreich test further the self-sufficiency and dependency hypothesis. Results are compared with Chipewyan materials and are found similar. Contact with Canadian society, especially government welfare programs, has encouraged dependency. This increasing dependency, and decreasing self-sufficiency are manifested at the psychological level.   JSL

KASKA

2056   **DARNELL   REGNA**
1970
THE KASKA AESTHETIC OF SPEECH USE. The Western Canadian Journal of Anthropology 2(10):130-139.

If amount of speech and valuation upon it vary cross-culturally, the minimal case of speech elaboration should be described. The Kaska provide such a minimal case. Re-examining Honigmann's studies, Kaska speech behavior is described and a correlation between ecology and speech use can be drawn.   IVY

2057   **HONIGMANN   JOHN J**
1970
FIELDWORK IN TWO NORTHERN COMMUNITIES. In Marginal Natives: Anthropologists at Work. Morris Freilich, ed. New York: Harper and Row. pp. 39-72.

Honigmann's fieldwork among the Kaska in 1944-45 reveals practical problems in a subarctic setting. Particular attention is devoted to the ethnographer's participation in community activities, his living conditions, and his data collection techniques. Fieldwork among the Frobisher Bay Eskimos is described and compared with the Kaska experience.   CCV

KUTCHIN

2058   **ALFORD   M E**
1964
OLD CROW. Alaska Sportsman 30(2):22-24,41.

The Kutchin natives of Old Crow, Yukon, have distinguished themselves at cross-country skiing.   IVY

2059   **BALIKCI   ASEN**
1963
FAMILY ORGANIZATION OF THE VUNTA KUTCHIN. Arctic Anthropology
1(2):62-69.

Based on fieldwork in the summer of 1961, the emergence of the matrifocal family among the Vunta Kutchin at the Old Crow Settlement during the past few decades following the decline of communal subsistence activities is examined. Interpersonal hostility and extra-marital relations are viewed as forces initiating this form of family organization. The economic independence of women occasioned by welfare benefits and the confusion of male and female subsistence roles are viewed as factors sustaining it.   WRC

2060   **BALIKCI   ASEN**
1963
VUNTA KUTCHIN SOCIAL CHANGE: A STUDY OF THE PEOPLE OF OLD
CROW, YUKON TERRITORY. Department of Northern Affairs and National
Resources, Northern Co-ordination and Research Centre Reports No. 63/3. Ottawa:
Department of Northern Affairs and National Resources. 161 pp.

Ethnographic material is based on a 9 week field trip to Old Crow, Yukon Territory during the summer of 1961. The ecological niche, geographic setting, traditional culture, the period of contact and subsequent change, and the contemporary culture of the Vunta Kutchin are described.   CCV

2061   **BALIKCI   ASEN**
1968
BAD FRIENDS. Human Organization 27:191-199.

The negative aspects of social relations are emphasized to describe the behavioral complex of the Vunta Kutchin Indians on the Old Crow settlement. Fieldwork conducted in the summer of 1961 yields informants' statements on various interpersonal relations. Since their introduction in the 19th century, Euro-Canadian authority and technology are postulated as causes for the disappearance of a cohesive aboriginal political organization and kinship collaboration. An unstable nuclear family and individualistic subsistence activities are the contemporary results characteristic of marked social atomism. It is concluded that in the absence of ritualized expression of ambivalence and hostility and an integrated social structure covert verbal hostility serves a cohesive function in an isolated, face-to-face community.   WRC

2062   **BISSETT   DON**
1967
THE LOWER MACKENZIE REGION (A.E.S.R. No. 66/1). Ottawa: Department of
Indian Affairs and Northern Development, Industrial Division. 520 pp.

The settlements of Inuvik, Aklavik, Fort McPherson, Arctic Red River, Reindeer Station,
and Tuktoyaktuk and their resource areas are considered in this 1966 economic survey
of the Lower Mackenzie Region. Data on population, employment and income, trade
and commerce, welfare, housing, and community services are provided for each settlement. Additional chapters are devoted to transportation, subsistence economy, trapping,
domestic fisheries, forestry, mink ranching, tourism, commercial dog foods, reindeer,
handicrafts, and fur garment industries.   CCV

2063   **CLAIRMONT   DONALD HAYDEN**
1962
NOTES ON THE DRINKING BEHAVIOR OF THE ESKIMOS AND INDIANS IN
THE AKLAVIK AREA: A PRELIMINARY REPORT. Department of Northern
Affairs and National Resources, Northern Co-ordination Research Centre Reports No.
62-4. Ottawa: Department of Northern Affairs and National Resources. 13 pp.

Drinking patterns, attitudes toward drinking, police and law enforcement, and the relationship between drinking and deviance in the Aklavik area are described from material
collected during the summer of 1961. Internalization of some of the dominant society's
values is observed. Deviant behavior is in part attributed to the lack of means to attain
new cultural goals and is felt to be related to the development of gangs whose members
usually have been visiting Yellowknife for education training.   CCV

2064   **CLAIRMONT   DONALD HAYDEN**
1963
DEVIANCE AMONG INDIANS AND ESKIMOS IN AKLAVIK. M.A. Thesis.
Department of Sociology. McMaster University. 158 pp.

The demographic patterns, traditional and modern economic activities, family composition, socialization practices, ethnic relations, and deviance among the Indians and Eskimos of the Aklavik area were studied in the summer of 1961. Value orientations, possibilities for realization of goals, and deviance were examined and groups formed by an
over or under 30 years of age classification were compared. Most of the area's deviant
behavior is attributed to the young settlement natives. Observed growth of gangs among
these youth is considered to be an adaptive phenomenon related to discontinuity between
goals and attainment possibilities and lack of acceptable models.   CCV

2065   **CLAIRMONT   DONALD HAYDEN**
1963
DEVIANCE AMONG INDIANS AND ESKIMOS IN AKLAVIK, N.W.T.
Department of Northern Affairs and National Resources, Northern Co-ordination and
Research Centre Reports No. 63-9. Ottawa: Department of Northern Affairs and
National Resources. 84 pp.

Deviant behavior observed among Aklavik area Indians and Eskimos during the 3 summer months of 1961 is described and analyzed. Pursuit of traditional as opposed to
White society's goals is associated with less deviance attributed to those young natives
having greater contact with White society and lacking means of attaining the associated

goals. Other factors considered relevant to the response to ambivalent pressures are marital status, family ties, religious and political involvement, and attitudes manifested by the White community.   CCV

2066   DREWERY   ELLEN M
1964
INDIANS OF THE ARCTIC. North 11(1):31-33.

The contemporary life-style of the Loucheux of Fort MacPherson is presented and opinions of the problems relating to culture contact are expressed.   IVY

2067   HADLEIGH-WEST   FREDERICK
1963
THE NETSI KUTCHIN: AN ESSAY IN HUMAN ECOLOGY. Ph.D. Thesis.
Department of Anthropology. Louisiana State University. 450 pp.   Available from
University Microfilms.

Fieldwork among the Netsi Kutchin in the southeastern Brooks range is reported. Aspects of traditional life style are described focusing on the relationship between subsistence activities and the ecological niche. Changes due to acculturation are noted.   Similarities with other northern peoples in both Siberia and America are found to be ecological in nature due to the limited possibilities offered by similar environments to people on similar technical levels.   CCV

2068   HARRINGTON   LYN
1961
OLD CROW: YUKON'S ARCTIC VILLAGE. The Beaver 292(Winter):4-10.

A brief visit is reported and illustrated with photographs.   IVY

2069   HENOCH   W E S
1961
FORT MCPHERSON, N.W.T. Department of Mines and Technical Surveys
Geographic Bulletin 16:86-103.

Situated on the Peel River, Fort McPherson has a population of 453, the majority of whom are Loucheux Indians whose livelihood depends on hunting, fishing, and trapping, In this geographical analysis of Fort McPherson, information is provided on population changes, settlement patterns, food, and income of the natives. As well a map of the settlement (1958) is included with photographs of various dwellings.   IVY

2070   HONIGMANN   JOHN J.   HONIGMANN   IRMA
1969
SUCCESS IN SCHOOL: ADAPTATION IN A NEW, CANADIAN ARCTIC TOWN.
Unpublished paper. Available from National Museum of Man, Ethnology Division, with permission of the authors. 170 pp.

Eskimo and Indian young people between the ages of 6 years and 20 years are studied according to the degree of their adaptation to school. It was hypothesized that children from Eskimo backgrounds would be better adapted to school than children from Indian backgrounds. Four different criteria were administered in measuring the students as well as 5 empirical indicators to guage the influence of household characteristics. The criteria were geared to measure relative ethnic and behavioral characteristics.   All the facts supported the view that adaptation to school is directly related to the norms, values, and cultural traits of the home. It was suggested, however, that it would be more practical for the school to accomodate in order to change the experience of youngsters, than to try to alter the attitudes and cultural features of adults.   DGW

2071   **JOSIE   EDITH**
1964
OLD CROW NEWS: THE BEST OF EDITH JOSIE 1963. Whitehorse: Whitehorse Star. 24 pp.

News reported periodically by Miss Edith Josie, Loucheux Indian, from the isolated 200-inhabitant village of Old Crow, Northwest Territories, is presented for the period December, 1962, until October 9, 1963. Details of social life and customs are revealed.   CCV

2072   **JOSIE   EDITH**
1966
HERE ARE THE NEWS BY EDITH JOSIE. Toronto: Clarke, Irwin. 135 pp.

Columns written from December 5, 1962, to June 22, 1966, by Miss Edith Josie, Old Crow correspondent of the Whitehorse Star, are presented. Social and subsistence activities of the 200 inhabitants of the isolated Loucheux Indian village are reported by Miss Josie.   CCV

2073   **KEIM   CHARLES J**
1964
KUTCHIN LEGENDS FROM OLD CROW, YUKON TERRITORY. University of Alaska Anthropological Papers 11(2):97-108.

Mrs. Effie Linklater of Old Crow was engaged by Dean Keim to collect these stories. The 11 tales are diversified including 2 which recount White contact.   IVY

2074   **MAILHOT   JOSE**
1968
INUVIK COMMUNITY STRUCTURE - SUMMER 1965. Department of Indian Affairs and Northern Development, Northern Science Research Group, Mackenzie Delta Research Project No. 4. Ottawa: Information Canada. 38 pp.

Analysis of community organization and associations in Inuvik based on material collected during the summer of 1965 is presented. Existence of a permanent and a transient group and dominance of community organization by the latter group, predominantly White, was observed. Recommendations are directed to increasing native participation and facilitating leadership training.   CCV

2075   **PURITT   PAUL**
1962
SOCIAL AND CULTURAL INTEGRATION IN A NORTHERN CANADIAN COMMUNITY. Unpublished report for Northern Co-ordination and Research Centre,

Department of Northern Affairs and National Resources. Available at Northern Science Research Group, Department of Indian Affairs and Northern Development. 67 pp.

Three months of fieldwork in the Fort McPherson area during the summer of 1961 are reported in this discussion of social and cultural change among the Kutchin. Contemporary life style is described and areas of change are noted with reference to the traditional culture as described by Slobodin.   CCV

2076   **SLOBODIN   RICHARD**
1960
EASTERN KUTCHIN WARFARE. Anthropologica N.S. 2:76-94.

Based on fieldwork among the Kutchin at Peel River, Arctic Red River, Crow River, and Yukon Flats in 1938-1939 and 1946-1947, the forms of conflict between the Kutchin and Eskimos are considered. Predominantly in the form of vengeance raids to restore social balance, warfare between these 2 people is viewed as having been initiated and stimulated by the introduction of trading goods.   WRC

2077   **SLOBODIN   RICHARD**
1960
SOME SOCIAL FUNCTIONS OF KUTCHIN ANXIETY. American Anthropologist 62:122-133.

Four case studies are reviewed to illustrate anxiety projection among the Peel River Kutchin toward isolation resulting from natural hazards. Field research conducted in 1938-1939 and again in 1946-1947 revealed that social distance was equated with physical distance in the presence of this fear. It is postulated that ambivalence toward the separated individual produced centripetal social forces and community cohesion in contrast to the extreme individualism and centrifugal tendencies documented for other northern Woodland Indians.   WRC

2078   **SLOBODIN   RICHARD**
1962
BAND ORGANIZATION OF THE PEEL RIVER KUTCHIN. National Museum of Canada Bulletin 179. Ottawa: Queen's Printer. 97 pp.

This is a revision of the author's Ph.D. thesis (1959) based on fieldwork among the Peel River Kutchin in 1938-39 and 1946-47. Focus is on supra-family groupings, set in their ecological and historical setting. Four types of grouping are discerned - mobile trapping party, meat camp, fish camp, and obsolete trading party. These types are defined in terms of ecological adaptations which have proven to be successful throughout the 20th century.   JSL

2079   **SLOBODIN   RICHARD**
1963
KUTCHIN POLYANDRY AND THE CULTURE OF POVERTY. Unpublished paper delivered to 62nd Annual Meeting, American Anthropological Association. San Francisco, CA, November 22, 1963. Available from National Library of Canada. 15 pp.

Attention is focused upon the Eastern Kutchin of the Mackenzie River drainage, concentrated in 4 settlements, Fort McPherson, Arctic Red River, Aklavik, and Inuvik. On the basis of genealogies collected and parish records studied in 1946-1947, informants' statements in 1938-1939 and 1946-1947, there were 8 instances of polyandrous unions in the 1860's. Polyandry has recently reappeared in the class stratified towns of Aklavik and Inuvik rather than the more traditional settlements of Fort McPherson and Arctic Red River. In 1962-1963, out of a total of 60 Kutchin households, 6 were polyandrous. Describing and comparing traditional and modern polyandry in Kutchin culture, both may be seen as one of several types of adjustment to economic uncertainty and lengthy separation of the spouses.   IVY

2080   **SLOBODIN   RICHARD**
1963
'THE DAWSON BOYS' - PEEL RIVER INDIANS AND THE KLONDIKE GOLD RUSH. Polar Notes 5:24-36.

The Tetlet Kutchin or Peel River Indians, numbering approximately 300, survived the experience of the Klondike gold rush of 1897-1898 as a stable community with a distinct way of life. During 1900-1915, Peel River people oriented toward the Yukon for trading, employment, and social life. By 1917 the Kutchin were back on the Peel, strongly affected but not demoralized by the experience. Those youths and young men who had actively participated in the boom-town social life of Dawson were known as the "Dawson Boys."Approaching the Kutchin ideal of manhood, they continued to be hunters and "tough travelers"and provided much of the social and economic leadership of the band in the 1930's and 1940's.   IVY

2081   **SLOBODIN   RICHARD**
1966
INDIAN LIVING - OLD STYLE. In People of Light and Dark. Maja van Steensel, ed. Ottawa: Queen's Printer. pp. 100-105.

An overview of traditional Kutchin life style and social organization is presented.   CCV

2082   **SLOBODIN   RICHARD**
1969
LEADERSHIP AND PARTICIPATION IN A KUTCHIN TRAPPING PARTY. In Contributions to Anthropology: Band Societies: Proceedings of the Conference on Band Organization, Ottawa, August 30 to September 2, 1965. David Damas, ed. National Museums of Canada Bulletin 228. Ottawa: Queen's Printer. pp. 56-92.

A number of extra-familial groupings are present among the Kutchin: the local group, fish camp, band assembly, meat camp, paired family, and the trapping party. The last of these is examined, based on observations in 1947. Discussed are the formation of the group consisting of 5 nuclear families, its itinerary, structure of the group, joking and humor, leadership, and non-economic functions.   JSL

2083   **SLOBODIN   RICHARD**
1970
KUTCHIN CONCEPTS OF REINCARNATION. The Western Canadian Journal of Anthropology 2(1):67-79.

Discussed are the nature of reincarnation, the relationship between original incarnation and reincarnation, repetitive dreaming, Christianity and reincarnation, and survival of the concept.   IVY

2084   **SMITH   DEREK G**
n.d.
THE MACKENZIE DELTA - DOMESTIC ECONOMY OF THE NATIVE PEOPLES: A PRELIMINARY STUDY. Department of Indian Affairs and Northern Development, Northern Science Research Group, Mackenzie Delta Research Project No. 3. Ottawa: Department of Indian Affairs and Northern Development. 59 pp.

Eskimo, Indian, and Metis subsistence patterns observed during fieldwork in the Mackenzie Delta from June to August of 1965 are reported. According to their goals and utilization of resources people are classified as (1) people on the land, (2) irregularly employed settlement dwellers, and (3) continuously employed settlement dwellers. Problems associated with each group are reviewed.   CCV

2085   **SPENCE   IAN**
1961
HUMAN ADAPTATION IN THE MACKENZIE DELTA: A STUDY IN FACILITATING THE ADJUSTMENT OF THE NORTHERN INDIAN AND ESKIMO TO RAPID SOCIAL CHANGE. M.S.W. Thesis. Department of Social Work. McGill University. 262 pp. Available from Library, Department of Indian Affairs and Northern Development, Ottawa.

Relying on notes from experience as a student welfare officer in Aklavik during the summer of 1960 and supplementary data compiled from library resources and the files of the Department of Northern Affairs and Natural Resources, a preliminary plan is presented for a research project to determine methods of improving and assisting the processes of acculturation in the Mackenzie Delta. The study includes chapters devoted to the Loucheux, Eskimo, Aklavik, and Inuvik in culture, social structure, and change. Proposals for an experimental project, a control project, and a survey to determine comparative success are outlined including questionnaires and interview schedules.   CCV

2086   **TANNER   ADRIAN**
1965
THE STRUCTURE OF FUR TRADE RELATIONS. M.A. Thesis. Department of Anthropology. University of British Columbia. 96 pp. Available from National Museum of Man, Ethnology Division, with permission of the author.

Presented is an analysis of the cross-cultural trade institutions of the Northern Athapaskans of the Upper Yukon River drainage system. Using historical data pertaining to the changes in trade institutions, 4 stages are recognized and described: inter-tribal trade, trading chief trade, monopoly trade, and market trade. In each type of trade institution, an examination is made of the roles through which exchanges were made. Generally, the study approaches trade institutions from a structural point of view. An analysis of changes in value patterns as well as the study of emerging power structures is considered an important area for further research in this subject.   DGW

2087   **WELSH   ANN**
1970

COMMUNITY PATTERN AND SETTLEMENT PATTERN IN THE DEVELOPMENT OF OLD CROW VILLAGE, YUKON TERRITORY. The Western Canadian Journal of Anthropology 2(1):17-30.

Historical and ecological approaches are utilized in an analytic discussion of the changing nature of settlement (spatial) and community (social) patterns at Old Crow. Discussed are: aboriginal social groupings, settlement patterns, and housing patterns; the effects of White contact on settlement and community patterns; and the present communities (White, native) of Old Crow. This report is based on 8 months of field research from June, 1968, to January, 1969. IVY

2088 **WOOTEN D T F**
1966-67
THE COMING OF CHRISTIANITY TO THE KUTCHIN. Unpublished paper. Available at Northern Science Research Group, Department of Indian Affairs and Northern Development, Ottawa. 76 pp.

The introduction and spread of Christianity among the Kutchin during the latter half of the 19th century is revealed in this account of the establishment of Anglican missions. The Indian reaction to Christianity and some brief observations of their traditional life style are included. CCV

MALECITE

2089 **1960**
ST. MARY'S HOME AND SCHOOL, INDIAN RESERVE, FREDERICTON. Citizen 6(3):33-35.

The development of the Home and School Association and its projects are briefly presented. IVY

2090 **BRADDOCK JOHN**
1965
INDIAN RESERVES: HOW LONG WILL THEY LAST? Atlantic Advocate 56(4):50-54.

Interviews with various members of 6 bands in New Brunswick (Edmundston, Tobique, Woodstock, Kingsclear, Devon (Fredericton), and Oromocto) led to the conclusion that if the Malecites with higher education return to the reserves and set up industries of their own, reserves may not disappear. IVY

2091 **DUNFIELD J D**
1967
REPORT ON THE FORESTRY SURVEY OF THE TOBIQUE INDIAN RESERVE NO. 20 IN THE PROVINCE OF NEW BRUNSWICK 1962. Unpublished paper. Available at Indian-Eskimo Economic Development Branch, Department of Indian Affairs and Northern Development, Ottawa. 24 pp.

The results of a forest survey on the Tobique Indian Reserve Number 20 are reported with forestry management and supplementary resource possibilities outlined. CCV

2092   **IVES   EDWARD D, ed.**
1964
MALECITE AND PASSAMAQUADDY TALES. Northeast Folklore 6. Orono, ME:
Northeast Folklore Society. 81 pp.

Presented are a collection of 17 Malecite tales gathered by G. Hegeman, D. Daigle, and
M. Daigle in 1962. Tales were collected both in English and in Malecite with English
translation (only English versions are presented in the article). Also included are a Malecite and 10 Passamaquoddy tales collected by E. Tappen Adney and a short (pp. 13-16)
paper by Adney on stories and story-telling.   TSA

2093   **MCFEAT   TOM F S**
1962
TWO MALECITE FAMILY INDUSTRIES: A CASE STUDY. Anthropologica N.S.
4:233-271.

The development of cottage industry among the 5 Malecite reserves in New Brunswick is
considered, and 2 main types, basket and barrel making, with reference to 2 families are
contrasted in order to indicate the function of each in a changing Indian identity. Models
based on the temporal and spatial relations of nuclear and peripheral social regions are
developed and indicate that the basket industry has been more successful in maintaining
the concept of Indian work within the domestic unit as well as in external relations with
the Canadian community.   WRC

2094   **MCFEAT   TOM F S**
1967
THE OBJECT OF RESEARCH IN MUSEUMS. In Contributions to Ethnology V.
National Museums of Canada Bulletin 204. Ottawa: Queen's Printer. pp. 91-99.

Six propositions outlining the author's philosophy of museology, and the relationship
between ethnology and museum research are presented. The Malecite basket industry of
New Brunswick is discussed. The form, principle, use-function, and meaning-value
of the baskets are explored.   JSL

2095   **RESOURCES MANAGEMENT CONSULTANTS**
1970
A FEASIBILITY STUDY OF THE INDIAN HERITAGE CENTER PREPARED
FOR THE UNION OF NEW BRUNSWICK INDIANS. Unpublished paper. Available
at Indian-Eskimo Economic Development Branch, Economic Development Division,
Department of Indian Affairs and Northern Development, Ottawa. 94 pp.

The feasibility of the proposed Indian Heritage Centre at Meductic is examined in relation to marketing, human resources, operations, and cost/benefit. It is felt that this project will foster and preserve aspects of traditional Indian culture in addition to having
economic advantages.   CCV

2096   **RESOURCES MANAGEMENT CONSULTANTS**
1970
OUR APPROACH TO THE DEVELOPMENT AND MANAGEMENT OF
RESOURCES: AN ASSESSMENT OF THE DEVELOPMENT POTENTIAL OF
THE ST. BASILE INDIAN RESERVE. Unpublished paper. Available at Indian-Eskimo

Economic Development Branch, Development Services Division, Department of Indian Affairs and Northern Development, Ottawa. 55 pp.

The development potential of the St. Basile Reserve near Edmunston, New Brunswick, are reviewed. A 10-year outline of organization and financing for development is proposed to include: lease of land to Fraser Company for a sewage treatment facility, construction of a townsite and relocation, lease of land to the city for an industrial park, construction of a mobile home park, and a residential development.   CCV

2097   **SQUIRES   AUSTIN**
1968
THE GREAT SAGAMORE OF THE MALISEETS. The Atlantic Advocate 59(3):49,51-52.

A biographic sketch is provided of Gabriel Acquin (1810-1901), Malecite Indian of St. Mary's Band in New Brunswick, renowned hunter, trapper, guide, philosopher, and story-teller.   IVY

2098   **TRUEMAN   STUART**
1966
THE ORDEAL OF JOHN GYLES: BEING AN ACCOUNT OF HIS ODD ADVENTURES, STRANGE DELIVERANCES ETC. AS A SLAVE OF THE MALISEETS. Toronto: McClelland and Stewart. 155 pp.

An account of John Gyles' capture in August, 1689, and his enslavement among the Malecite, his sale to the French, and finally his gaining freedom in 1698 is presented with excerpts from Gyles' own diary. His observations include details of subsistence activities, folk medicine, religious beliefs, and mores among the 17th century Malecite and Penobscot as well as information concerning missionary activity, French-English competition in New France, treatment of captives, and manipulation of the Indians by competing White factions.   CCV

MICMAC

2099   **ATLANTIC AREA CONSULTANTS LTD (FREDERICTON)**
1967
PROJECT FOR ANDREW NICHOLAS, B.SC. (CIVIL), P.ENG. AND GEORGE FRANCIS. Unpublished report for Department of Indian Affairs and Northern Development, Resources and Industrial Division, Indian Affairs Branch. Available at Indian-Eskimo Economic Development Branch, Department of Indian Affairs and Northern Development, Ottawa. 34 pp.

Evaluation of a proposed specialized contracting company for Andrew Nicholas and George Francis is submitted to Indian Affairs Branch along with recommendations and guidelines for financing and organization.   CCV

2100   **BERNARD   ANGEL B**
1970
INDIAN PLACE NAMES OF CAPE BRETON ISLAND. Tawow 1(1):16-17.

Explanations are given for 18 place names.   IVY

2101   **BOCK   PHILIP K**
1963
THE SOCIAL STRUCTURE OF A CANADIAN INDIAN RESERVE. Ph.D. Thesis.
Department of Social Relations. Harvard University. 277 pp.

See P. Bock, 1964 and 1966.   SMW

2102   **BOCK   PHILIP K**
1964
SOCIAL STRUCTURE AND LANGUAGE STRUCTURE. Southwestern Journal of
Anthropology 20:393-403.

A technique for describing the social structure of a group, analogous to that of language
structure, is illustrated using cultural forms of time, space, and roles as analytical units.
From fieldwork at the Restigouche Micmac Reserve in 1961, an Indian wake is cited for
the application of this technique and the development of a situational matrix.   WRC

2103   **BOCK   PHILIP K**
1966
THE MICMAC INDIANS OF RESTIGOUCHE: HISTORY AND
CONTEMPORARY DESCRIPTION. National Museum of Canada Bulletin 213.
Ottawa: Queen's Printer. 95 pp.

This monograph, part of the author's Ph.D. dissertation, describes the contemporary culture of the Restigouche Micmac Reserve based on 7 months fieldwork in 1961, including
a brief survey of other Micmac reserves. Part 1 discusses the history of the area, the aboriginal culture, and successive post-contact periods. Part 2 discusses the contemporary
Restigouche Reserve. The author concludes that there is no group identity higher than
the tribe. The Micmac are a powerless ethnic group, legally and socially hindered. The
role of the Canadian government and the churches are discussed. Drastic changes since
1900 have nearly erased any cultural continuity. For the individual, personal identity is
problematic. Appended is some local folklore.   JSL

2104   **BOCK   PHILIP K**
1966
SOCIAL TIME AND INSTITUTIONAL CONFLICT. Human Organization 25:96-12.

A structural analysis of time reckoning is made based upon fieldwork at the Restigouche
Micmac Reserve, 1961. Social time is divided into diffuse and compact periods in accord-
ance with the dispersal and concentration of population in the annual subsistence cycle.
This temporal pattern of pre-contact times has continued in the acculturation process re-
sulting in conflicts between scheduled activities of the Band and those of the Roman
Catholic Church and civil government. The incongruity of the potato harvest activity in
Maine and the Quebec school year is cited as a central example.   WRC

2105   **BUYS   A A**
1963
PRELIMINARY REPORT ON THE FOREST SURVEY OF THE SHUBENACADIE
(GRAND LAKE) INDIAN RESERVE NO. 13, HALIFAX COUNTY, NOVA

SCOTIA. Unpublished paper. Available at Indian-Eskimo Economic Development Branch, Development Services Division, Department of Indian Affairs and Northern Development, Ottawa. 45 pp.

Logging and pulping potential as surveyed in August, 1962, and recommendations for forestry management on the Shubenacadie Indian Reserve Number 13 are presented. CCV

2106   **CANADA. Department of Fisheries and Forestry. Canadian Forestry Services. Forestry Management Institute.**
1969
REPORT ON THE FOREST SURVEY OF SIX INDIAN RESERVES IN THE MIRIMICHI AREA OF NEW BRUNSWICK 1962: INDIAN RESERVE FOREST SURVEY REPORT #16. Unpublished paper. Available from Department of Indian Affairs and Northern Development, Indian-Eskimo Economic Development Branch, Development Services Division, Ottawa. 21 pp.

A forest survey of the Eel Ground, Tabusintac, Red Bank Number 4, Red Bank Number 7, Big Hole Tract, and Burnt Church Reserves executed in 1962 is reported with guidelines for beneficial forest management programs. General physical and demographic conditions relevant to land use management in the Mirimichi district and land and forest conditions particular to each reserve are discussed. CCV

2107   **CHARLES A CAMPBELL & ASSOCIATES**
1967
REPORT ON A FEASIBILITY STUDY FOR A COMMUNITY PLAN OF DEVELOPMENT FOR ESKASONI INDIAN RESERVE. Unpublished paper. Available from Department of Indian Affairs and Northern Development, Development Services Division, Indian-Eskimo Economic Development Branch, Ottawa. 79 pp.

Proposals for economic ameliorations of water and sewage disposal facilities of the Eskasoni Indian Reserve are presented. Existing facilities and housing conditions are reviewed and changes in community structure necessary to the project are outlined. CCV

2108   **CLARK   ANDREW HILL**
1968
ACADIA: THE GEOGRAPHY OF EARLY NOVA SCOTIA TO 1760. Madison: University of Wisconsin Press. 450 pp.

The geography of Nova Scotia, New Brunswick, and Prince Edward Island is given with special emphasis on the Acadians. The natural habitat, climate, vegetation, and soils are described. Chapter 3 is devoted to the Micmac at contact, with information derived from archaeological and historical sources. Material culture, economy, subsistence activities, travel, and social organization are summarized. Throughout the balance of the text, which traces the origin, development, and expansion of Acadian settlements until 1760, the Micmac receive frequent but brief mention in relation to fur trading and missions. CCV

2109   **CORSETTI   M**
1963
MICMAC LEGENDS FROM BIG COVE, N.B. Unpublished paper. Available from

National Museum of Man, Ethnology Division, Ottawa, with permission of the author. 13 pp.

Three legends told by a Micmac Indian from Big Cove reserve, New Brunswick, were recorded and translated in 1963. Each legend concerns a great chief, war with the Mohawks, near starvation, and a struggle with witches or evil spirits. The chief, through his supernatural powers as a kinap, is able to defeat the enemy, secure game, and overcome the witches.   JSL

2110   **CREVEL   JACQUES**
1967
L'ALCOOL, PREMIER ET TENACE HERITAGE DES BLANCS AUX MICMACS DE LA GASPESIE. Revue d'Histoire de la Gaspesie 5:186-189.

This contains testimonies of settlers in the 2nd half of the 17th century about the damage done to the Micmac by alcohol which was easily obtained from the Europeans for furs.   DD

2111   **CREVEL   JACQUES**
1967
QUI ETAIENT CES GASPESIENS OU MICMACS DU NORD? Revue d'Histoire de la Gaspesie 5:93-96.

This article presents a brief overview of the social and political organization of the Micmac of the 17th century as described by the French who came to Canada at that time.   DD

2112   **CREVEL   JACQUES,   CREVEL   MARYVONNE**
1970
HONGUEDO OU L'HISTOIRE DES PREMIERS GASPESIENS. Quebec: Editions Garneau. 211 pp.

Excerpts from historical and archival sources form the basis of discussion of the Micmac at the time of contact. Subsistence activities are described and Micmac reaction to the missionaries sent to convert them is discussed.   CCV

2113   **DAYE   VERA L**
1964
MICMAC INDIAN CRAFTSMEN. Atlantic Advocate 54(11):29-32.

The construction and operation of the Micmac Indian Craftsmen Centre at Big Cove Reservation are described. Also included are personal sketches of 2 artists, Stephen Dedam and Michael Francis.   IVY

2114   **DUMONT-JOHNSON   MICHELINE**
1970
APOTRES OU AGITATEURS: LA FRANCE MISSIONNAIRE EN ACADIE. Trois-Rivieres: Boreal Express. 150 pp.

Historic sources are analyzed to reinterpret the relationship of missionaries to the Indians of Acadia during the 18th century. France's Indian policy, Indians and religion, missionary techniques, missionaries as political instruments, and religion as a political tool are examined in turn. In proximity to competitive English colonists, the missionaries associated allegiance to France with adherance to the Catholic faith. The French government was able to take advantage of this association and the missionaries became, by virtue of their position, involved in political manipulation of their flocks.   CCV

2115   **ELLIOTT   JOHN**
1970
ATTITUDES TOWARDS THE BAND COUNCIL AND THE SOURCES AND FLOW OF INFORMATION ON A SMALL INDIAN RESERVE. Unpublished paper. Available from National Library of Canada. 34 pp.

Two surveys at Pictou Landing Reserve, Nova Scotia, in 1967 and 1969 investigated attitudes toward the band council. The 1969 study solicited data on the mass media and interpersonal relationships as sources of information. Appendix A (4 pages) discusses the findings of the 1967 study and Appendix B (14 pages) reproduces the 1969 questionnaire. Six areas are investigated: (1) influence with school authorities, (2) support of band council, (3) equal treatment, (4) informed public, (5) strength of band council, and (6) band influence with the Indian Affairs Branch. Sociograms of interpersonal communication concerning problems in housing, welfare, employment, and of Indians in general are presented. It is concluded that the Indian problem may be described as a lack of community organization.   IVY

2116   **ELLIOTT   JOHN G**
1968
RESOURCE DEVELOPMENT ON INDIAN RESERVES. Unpublished paper. Available from National Library of Canada. 14 pp.

This paper examines the need for, and potential value of, recreational programs and facilities for the Whycocomagh Reserve. As economic changes continue to influence social life on the reserve, recreational development will also gain in importance.   ADG

2117   **ELLIOTT   JOHN G**
1970
EDUCATIONAL AND OCCUPATIONAL ASPIRATIONS AND EXPECTATIONS: A COMPARATIVE STUDY OF INDIAN AND NON-INDIAN YOUTH. Antigonish, N.S.: Extension Department, St. Francis Xavier University. 142 pp.

A questionnaire was administered in November, 1968, to 225 Indian students from 5 Cape Breton reserves plus Afton and Pictou Landing, and 818 non-Indian students. Educational and occupational expectations and aspirations were examined. Non-Indians exhibited higher aspirations and expectations in both categories and tended, unlike Indians, to aspire to higher education than that of their parents. Factors related to these attitudes and aspirations are examined, particularly the cultural milieu and the role of parents and others. The implications of findings are discussed.   CCV

2118   **ELLIOTT   JOHN G**
1970
A STUDY OF THE CHANGES WITHIN FOUR INDIAN COMMUNITIES OVER A THREE YEAR PERIOD: STUDY II. Bound with Community Resources, Dimensions of Alienation, and Social Change on Indian Reserves by A. A. MacDonald (1967). Antigonish, N.S.: Extension Department, St. Francis Xavier University. 50 pp.

This study is a follow-up of the study done by A. A. MacDonald, "Community Resources and Dimensions of Alienation on Indian Reserves"of May, 1967. Interviewing was carried out in 1969 among a sample of Micmacs from Eskasoni, Sydney, Afton, and Pictou Landing, Nova Scotia. One main observation which stood out over the 3-year period was the greater reliance on the government since 1967. The respondents changed from placing the responsibility on themselves for doing things to placing the responsibility on other agencies. Data for age, education, alienation, and government involvement were studied to determine the rate and direction of change over the period. Social change was measured in rates of social mobility, government responsibility in the community, individual needs and government support, and changes in alienation.   HCV

2119   **HOWARD   JAMES H**
1965
THE ST. ANNE'S DAY CELEBRATION OF THE MICMAC INDIANS, 1962. South Dakota Museum News 26(3-4):5-13.

St. Anne's festival fuses the summer council - an aboriginal Micmac institution - and a saint's festival. Two days of observation are informally recorded depicting activities at "Chapel Island"or "Indian Island"(an island in Lake Bras d'Or), Nova Scotia. Interest is focused upon activities of Roman Catholic origin, those of traditional Indian culture, and the various forms of syncretism which had occurred.   IVY

2120   **HOWARD   JAMES H,   GLUCKMAN   STEPHEN J**
1962
THE MICMAC BOWL GAME. American Indian Tradition 8:206-209.

This description of Waltes, the bowl game, was secured in June, 1962. The 2 principal informants were Mr. Levi Poulette and Mrs. Mary Anne Sylliboy, both of Eskasoni Reserve, Cape Breton Island, Nova Scotia. Described are (1) the occasions for playing, (2) implements, (3) method of play, (4) the court, and (5) scoring the game. Photographs illustrate the text.   IVY

2121   **HOWARD   JAMES H,   GLUCKMAN   STEPHEN J**
1965
PHOTO FEATURE: MICMAC INDIANS OF NOVA SCOTIA. South Dakota Museum News 26(3-4):14-20.

Eleven photographs of Micmacs taken on Cape Breton Island, Nova Scotia, 1962, or copied from Micmac heirloom photographs are accompanied by descriptive captions.   IVY

2122   **HUTTON   ELIZABETH ANN**
1961
THE MICMAC INDIANS OF NOVA SCOTIA TO 1834. M.A. Thesis. Dalhousie University. 239 pp.

With reference to archival and historical sources, the history of the Micmac Indians of Nova Scotia is traced from the primitive civilization existing before European contact to the establishment of reserves early in the 19th century. Indian-White contact, influences of European culture on Indian life style and economy, the Indians' role in the Anglo-French struggle for North American supremacy, Anglo-Micmac treaties, English efforts to cope with the Indians' growing dependency relationship, and problems arising as settlement encroached on Indian lands are described.   CCV

2123   **MACDONALD   A A**
1967
COMMUNITY RESOURCES AND DIMENSIONS OF ALIENATION ON INDIAN RESERVES: STUDY I. Bound with A Study of the Changes Within Four Indian Communities Over a Three Year Period, by J. G. Elliott (1970). Antigonish, N.S.: Extension Department, St. Francis Xavier University. 81 pp.

Four Micmac reserves in eastern Nova Scotia (Membertou, Pictou Landing, Afton, and Eskasoni) provided the sample for this research on community development undertaken by the Extension Department of St. Francis Xavier University. The major objective was to determine the relationship between alienation from political, economic, and leadership aspects of the communities and such other variables as level of income, expectations of government support, perception of government support, age, and education. Evidence indicated that alienation in the economic and political realms was related to expectations and perception of government performance, and to earned income level. Unrealistically high levels of expectation should not be fostered among Indians unless these can be realized.   HCV

2124   **NOWLAN   ALDEN**
1967
THE CAPTIVE: AN AUTHENTIC MICMAC LEGEND. Atlantic Advocate 57(12):54-55.

A young boy desires to seek the land of his ancestors. After killing many warriors in his village including his foster-father, he escapes. Upon reaching his mother's tribe, he is taken for a spy and killed.   IVY

2125   **NOWLAN   ALDEN**
1967
THE INVISIBLE BOY: AN AUTHENTIC MICMAC LEGEND. Atlantic Advocate 57(8):50-51.

A mistreated young girl is able to see the invisible boy and is made his bride.   IVY

2126   **NOWLAN   ALDEN**
1967
THE MAN WHO WANTED TO LIVE FOREVER. Atlantic Advocate 57(5):46-47.

A man fearful of death begs Glooskap to lengthen his life. He is changed into an old cedar tree.   IVY

2127   **NOWLAN   ALDEN**
1967
THE SNOW VAMPIRE: AN AUTHENTIC MICMAC LEGEND. Atlantic Advocate 57(6):52-53.

A rejected suitor changes a lovely maiden into a snow vampire. She dies by 7 arrows; he dies simultaneously.   IVY

2128   NOWLAN   ALDEN
1969
THE CHIEF WHO REFUSED TO DIE: AN AUTHENTIC MICMAC LEGEND. The
Atlantic Advocate 59(5):36-37.

This adaptation tells of an immortal chief who continuously protected and provided for
his people until the time came when they deserted him.   IVY

2129   **RESOURCES MANAGEMENT CONSULTANTS**
1969
OUR APPROACH TO MANAGEMENT CONSULTING: AN OPPORTUNITY
INVENTORY AND A PRELIMINARY DEVELOPMENT PLAN FOR THE
DEVON AND ST. MARY'S RESERVES. Unpublished paper. Available at Indian-
Eskimo Economic Development Branch, Development Services Division, Department of
Indian Affairs and Northern Development, Ottawa. 46 pp.

The economic development potential of the Devon and St. Mary's Reserves is evaluated.
Brief outlines of the opportunities afforded by a motel/office-retail complex, residential/
shopping mall/offices complex, car clinic and carwash, medical arts and restaurant complex, and sand and gravel exploitation are included.   CCV

2130   **RESOURCES MANAGEMENT CONSULTANTS**
1969
OUR APPROACH TO THE DEVELOPMENT AND MANAGEMENT OF
RESOURCES: A LAND-USE STUDY FOR THE EEL RIVER INDIAN RESERVE.
Unpublished paper. Available at Indian-Eskimo Economic Development Branch,
Development Services Division, Department of Indian Affairs and Northern
Development, Ottawa. 50 pp.

Tourist and recreation potential of Eel River Reserve is evaluated in relation to the regional potential and facilities. With consideration for the reserve population and labor
force a 5-year land use plan for organization and administration of a motel, park, and
recreational development, and leasing of lake-front lots is proposed.   CCV

2131   **RESOURCES MANAGEMENT CONSULTANTS**
1969
OUR APPROACH TO THE DEVELOPMENT AND MANAGEMENT OF
RESOURCES: AN ASSESSMENT OF THE ECONOMIC POTENTIAL OF THE
ESKASONI RESERVE. Unpublished paper. Available at Indian-Eskimo Economic
Development Branch, Development Services Division, Department of Indian Affairs and
Northern Development, Ottawa. 81 pp.

Human and natural resources on the Eskasoni Reserve are evaluated in relation to the
local economy to assess development opportunities. Recommendations for planning of
projects include beach and park development, oyster farming, forestry development, car-
pentry and woodworking, handicrafts, a hennery, laundromat, and a private club.
CCV

2132   **RESOURCES MANAGEMENT CONSULTANTS**
1969
OUR APPROACH TO THE DEVELOPMENT AND MANAGEMENT OF

RESOURCES: PHASE II: DETAILED PLANNING FOR THE PROPOSED
DEVELOPMENT AT EEL RIVER RESERVE. Unpublished paper. Available at
Indian-Eskimo Economic Development Branch, Development Services Division,
Department of Indian Affairs and Northern Development, Ottawa. 39 pp.

Detailed planning procedures for initiation of a recreational park followed by development of a tent and trailer park on the Eel River are presented.   CCV

2133   **RESOURCES MANAGEMENT CONSULTANTS**
1970
A CONCEPT OF THE ESKASONI DEVELOPMENT CORPORATION.
Unpublished report delivered to Regional Superintendent of Community Affairs.
Amherst, N.S., April, 1970. Available at Indian-Eskimo Economic Development Branch,
Development Services Division, Department of Indian Affairs and Northern
Development, Ottawa. 57 pp.

Legal and administrative steps necessary for the creation of a private company with
share capital registered in the province of Nova Scotia and located on the Eskasoni Reserve are presented.   CCV

2134   **ROBERTSON   MARION**
1969
RED EARTH: TALES OF THE MICMACS WITH AN INTRODUCTION TO THE
CUSTOMS AND BELIEFS OF THE MICMAC INDIANS. Halifax: Nova Scotia
Museum. 97 pp.

Twenty-six Micmac folk tales and traditions are compiled from the literature and Nova
Scotia Micmac informants. Tracings from the Lake Kedjimkoojik petroglyphs, Queens
County, Nova Scotia, serve as illustration.   CCV

2135   **WALLIS   WILSON D**
1961
HISTORICAL BACKGROUND OF THE MICMAC INDIANS OF CANADA. In
Contributions to Anthropology, 1959. National Museum of Canada Bulletin 173.
Ottawa: Queen's Printer. pp. 42-63.

An historical description of the Micmac from first contact with Europeans in the 16th
century is presented. Analysis of early records provides insight into Micmac reactions to
contact with the French, Micmac personality, Micmac military impact on French-Iroquois relations, the American revolution, the Wabanaki confederacy, Micmac religious
changes, material culture, and economic activities.   JSL

MONTAGNAIS

2136   **ANDERSON   WILLIAM ASHLEY**
1961
ANGEL OF HUDSON BAY: THE TRUE STORY OF MAUD WATT. Toronto:
Clarke, Irwin. 177 pp.

Maud Watt's experiences as wife of a Hudson's Bay factor in the early 20th century in
Quebec are recounted. An unprecedented overland trip from Fort Chimo to Sept Isles
with an Indian family and their subsequent posting at Rupert House are described.

When declining beaver and game populations threatened the Indians with starvation, Mrs. Watt persuaded the Quebec government to establish a game preserve.   CCV

2137   **BELANGER   RENE**
1962
LA FAMILLE ASSINI (OU ASHINI). Saguenayensia 4:51-55.

A genealogy is presented of the Ashini family (Montagnais), several members of which played an important role in the political and social background of Quebec's north coast.   DD

2138   **BIRD   CHRISTOPHER**
1962
THE FUR AND FISH FRONTIER. Explorers Journal 1962(December):2-12.

A party canoing through the Rupert River system encountered a band of Mistassini Cree also traveling. The mode of life of the Indians while on the move is described.   TSA

2139   **BROCHU   MICHEL**
1964
LE NOUVEAU QUEBEC INDIEN: PAYS D'OCCUPATION. Relations 278:44-46.

The contemporary situation among the Indians of Nouveau-Quebec is reviewed briefly, particularly with regard to organization of education and medical services. Proposals for the assumption of administration in these areas by the Quebec government and improvement of services are presented.   CCV

2140   **BROCHU   MICHEL**
1964
SUGGESTIONS POUR UN REAMENAGEMENT DE L'ADMINISTRATION DU NOUVEAU-QUEBEC. L'Actualite Economique 40:306-422.

Existing administration of Nouveau-Quebec, shared by the federal and Quebec governments, is analyzed in terms of jurisdiction, administrative efficiency, and impact on territories and people. Proposals are outlined for reorganization of administration geared to eventual takeover of entire responsibility by the province. Included are law enforcement, taxation, municipal affairs, federal-provincial agreements, agriculture, natural resources, tourism, hunting and fishing, industry, transportation and communication, public works, education, labor, health, and welfare. Programs for improved education, vocational training, health services, employment, and community development for Indians and Eskimos are included.   CCV

2141   **BROCHU   MICHEL**
1965
PRESENTATION ET COMMENTAIRES DE CARTES SUR LE NOUVEAU-QUEBEC. L'Actualite Economique 40:691-759.

A series of maps of Nouveau Quebec and accompanying text provide data on use and potential of the physical environment. Administrative organization, judicial and police organization, features of physical geography, forestry and agriculture, hunting and fishing, economic organization, transportation, telecommunication, population, public services for native peoples, educational organization, health, and missions are documented.   CCV

2142   **BROCHU   MICHEL**
1967
LES ILES LITTORALES ET DU LARGE DU NOUVEAU-QUEBEC:
DESCRIPTION ET VALEUR ECONOMIQUE. Montreal: Conseil de la Vie Francaise et Societe Saint-Jean Baptiste de Montreal. 120 pp.

The coastal and off-shore islands of Nouveau-Quebec are discussed in terms of physical characteristics and economic value as part of a larger study aimed at confirming Quebec's jurisdiction over these areas. The subsistence activities of the Montagnais, Naskapi, and Cree Indians as well as the Eskimo of Nouveau-Quebec are reviewed briefly and each island or group of islands is discussed in its relevance to a particular group in relation to hunting, fishing, and gathering activities, residence, or hunting territory. Appendix 2, pages 53-55, consists of a statement by Maurice Provencher, O.M.I., at Fort Rupert, reporting the results of interrogation of the Jolly family on the traditional hunting territory on Charlton and Strutton Islands held by Fort Rupert Indians. It is noted in conclusion that most of the islands in James Bay and Northward and all of those in the Ungava Bay are on the Quebec side. In addition these islands are economically linked with Quebec both in the commerical and the traditional sense being extensions of traditional Indian and Eskimo hunting territories.   CCV

2143   **BROCHU   MICHEL**
1969
DOSSIERS CHRONOLOGIQUE COMMENTE DES FAITS RELATIFS A LA CHASSE (ORNITHOLOGIE) AU NOUVEAU-QUEBEC INDIEN ET AU SUD-OUEST DU TERRITOIRE DE MISTASSINI. Revue d'Histoire de l'Amerique Francaise 23:92-109.

A journal (kept from October 3, 1944, to August 25, 1968) records the arrival of birds important in the economy of the Cree of Fort-Rupert, Eastmain, and Fort-Georges. The importance of various species is noted and their earliest and latest arrival dates recorded. CCV

2144   **BROCHU   MICHEL**
1969
DOSSIERS SOCIO-ECONOMIQUES SUR LE NOUVEAU-QUEBEC - DOSSIER CHRONOLOGIQUE COMMENTE DES FAITS RELATIFS A L'AGRICULTURE AU NOUVEAU-QUEBEC ET AU SUD-OUEST DU TERRITOIRE DE MISTASSINI. Revue d'Histoire de l'Amerique Francaise 23:425-461.

A record of sowing and harvesting at Fort Rupert, Eastmain, and Fort-Georges from 1922 to 1968 is presented. Obstacles to agriculture are discussed. Agricultural expansion is dependant upon an agreement with the Cree.   CCV

2145   **BROCHU   MICHEL**
1969
DOSSIERS SOCIO-ECONOMIQUES SUR LE NOUVEAU-QUEBEC: DOSSIER

CHRONOLOGIQUE COMMENTE DES FAITS RELATIFS A LA CHASSE EN GENERAL (ANIMAUX A FOURRURE) AU NOUVEAU-QUEBEC INDIEN ET AU SUD-OUEST DE MISTASSINI. Revue d'Histoire de l'Amerique Francaise 23:429-440.

The seasonal cycle of the Indian hunters of Northern Quebec and those southwest of Mistassini territory is presented through chronological documents pertaining to Fort Rupert and Eastmain from 1946 to 1967. DD

2146 **BROCKMAN MAC**
1969
NEW EXPERIENCES WITH OLD CANADIANS. Monday Morning 3(9):18-21.

A principal relates his experiences at Knob Lake Protestant School, Shefferville, Quebec, which is attended by many Naskapi children. IVY

2147 **BURNHAM HAROLD B**
1969
A NASKAPI PAINTED SHIRT. In Material Culture Notes. Revised Edition. Denver: Denver Art Museum. pp. 53-59.

Revised from the Denver Art Museum Material Culture Notes (Number 10, June, 1939) by the late Frederic H. Douglas, this paper discusses the techniques of manufacture, decoration, and design style of the painted skin coats of Labrador. The hypothesis that the coats are the result of European contact is considered. IVY

2148 **CANADA. Department of Indian Affairs and Northern Development. Indian Affairs Branch. Quebec Region.**
1969
THE SHEFFERVILLE PROJECT. Ottawa: Queen's Printer. 15 pp.   Also in French.

The Shefferville housing project for the Montagnais from Sept-Isles and Fort Chimo regions who have moved to Shefferville is explained in a pamphlet by the Indian Affairs Branch. The reasons for the project, the conditions and services as well as the answers to citizens' questions are reviewed briefly. CCV

2149 **CARON ANDRIEN**
1963
LA MISSION DU PERE PAUL LE JEUNE, S.J. SUR LA COTE-DU-SUD 1633-1634. Revue d'Histoire de l'Amerique Francaise 17:371-395.

Experiences derived from missionary work among the Montagnais-Naskapi in the region between L'Isle d'Orleans and Riviere du Loup, particularly on the south shore, are recounted from the journal of Pere Le Jeune. The winter of 1633-34 is reconstructed in detail revealing subsistence activities, supernatural beliefs, and reactions to Catholicism. An attempt is made to identify the course of Le Jeune's travels. CCV

2150 **CARRIERE GASTON**
1960
UN APOTRE A QUEBEC: LE PERE FLAVIEN DUROCHER, O.M.I. (1800-1876) PREMIER CURE DE SAINT-SAUVEUR. Montreal: Rayonnement. 191 pp.

The missionary life of Father Durocher, O.M.I., is reviewed. His activities among the Montagnais of the Saguenay from 1844 to 1853 are discussed in the 1st 7 chapters. CCV

2151   **CARRIERE   GASTON**
1962
EXPLORATEUR POUR LE CHRIST: LOUIS BABEL, O.M.I., 1826-1912. Montreal: Rayonnement. 150 pp.

Oblate missionary Father Babel's works among the Montagnais-Naskapi of Quebec's north shore from 1851 to 1911 are described. Occasional references to the Indians are usually comments on their religious attitudes. Four trips into Labrador to evangelize the Naskapi are discussed as well. CCV

2152   **CARRIERE   GASTON**
1964
L'OEUVRE DES OBLATS DE MARIE-IMMACULEE DANS LE NORD CANADIEN ORIENTAL. In Le Nouveau Quebec: Contributions a l'Etude de l'Occupation Humaine. Jean Malaurie and Jacques Rousseau, eds. Ecole Pratique des Hautes Etudes - Sorbonne, France. Sixieme Section: Sciences Economiques et Sociales. Centre d'Etude Arctiques et Finno-Scandinaves. Bibliotheque Arctique et Antarctique 2. Paris: Mouton. pp. 395-425.

The establishment of Oblate missions to administer to the Montagnais-Naskapi of Nouveau Quebec is reviewed historically. Demographic notes are appended for certain settlements in the late 19th and early 20th centuies. CCV

2153   **CHANCE   NORMAN A**
1967
THE CHANGING WORLD OF THE CREE. Natural History 76(5):16-23.

The construction of major industries near the Mistassini and Waswanipi Reserves has had profound impact on Cree Indian life. Photographs by Paul Conklin complement the text. IVY

2154   **CHANCE   NORMAN A**
1968
THE CREE DEVELOPMENTAL CHANGE PROJECT: AN INTRODUCTION. In Conflict in Culture: Problems of Developmental Change Among the Cree: Working Papers of the Cree Developmental Change Project. Norman A. Chance, ed. Ottawa: Canadian Research Centre for Anthropology, Saint Paul University. pp. 1-9.

The Cree Developmental Change Project is discussed briefly in terms of background, setting, and aims. Attention is devoted to explanation of the points of reference and research model for this study. CCV

2155   **CHANCE   NORMAN A**
1968
ECONOMIC OPPORTUNITY AND CULTURAL VIABILITY AMONG THE CANADIAN CREE: A STRATEGY FOR DEVELOPMENTAL CHANGE. Unpublished paper delivered to 67th Annual Meeting, American Anthropological

Association. Seattle, WA, November 21, 1968. Available from National Library of Canada. 17 pp.

By reviewing Waswanipi Cree history, adaptation, and government policy, the article develops a strategy aimed at removing dependency feelings and disparaging attitudes characteristic of Indian-White relations.   HCV

2156   **CHANCE   NORMAN A**
1968
IMPLICATIONS OF ENVIRONMENTAL STRESS FOR STRATEGIES OF DEVELOPMENTAL CHANGE AMONG THE CREE. In Conflict in Culture: Problems of Developmental Change Among the Cree: Working Papers of the Cree Developmental Change Project. Norman A. Chance, ed. Ottawa: Canadian Research Centre for Anthropology, Saint Paul University. pp. 11-32.

Factors influencing developmental change and theories of environmental stress and stress-management are discussed and related to the Cree Indians of North Central Quebec. It is hypothesized that certain ecological, social, and cultural features of Cree life style are distinctly different from those of the White culture. Programs not recognizing these differences often elicit adaptive responses which frustrate program goals. Physical environmental stresses to which these Cree were exposed are being replaced by severe social and cultural stresses. Successful adaptation will be facilitated by policy based on adequate understanding of the mechanisms of developmental change.   CCV

2157   **CHANCE   NORMAN A**
1970
DEVELOPMENTAL CHANGE AMONG THE CREE INDIANS OF QUEBEC (SUMMARY REPORT). Ottawa: Queen's Printer. 288 pp.   Also in French.

Pages 1 to 39 contain the summary report of the McGill Cree Project (ARDA Project No. 34002) among the Cree Indians of north central Quebec. Fieldwork was conducted among the Mistassini, Waswanipi, and Nemiscau bands in 1966-1968. The report establishes that the Indian population is underdeveloped, and proceeds to examine how economic-social-political achievements could be attained without sacrificing cultural differences. The history of Indian-White relations, Indian responses and adaptions, and the values underlying government policy are explored. Recommendations are made: (1) establishment of economically viable reserves, (2) establishment of a regional economic corporation directed by Indians, (3) revamping the educational system, and (4) establishing an Indian social development program. Appended to the summary report are 3 reports by D. E. W. Holden, I. E. La Rusic, and R. M. Wintrob and P. S. Sindell (separately abstracted).   JSL

2158   **CHANCE   NORMAN A,   POTHIER   ROGER**
1967
UNE ETUDE DU DEVELOPPEMENT CHEZ LES INDIENS CRIS. In Problemes Nordiques des Facades de la Baie de James: Recueil de Documents Rediges en Collaboration a la Suite d'une Rencontre de Nordistes a Moosonee en Ontario. Louis-Edmond Hamelin and Hugues Morrissette, eds. Centre d'Etudes Nordiques Travaux Divers 18. Quebec: Centre d'Etudes Nordiques, Universite Laval. pp. 49-68.

This is a presentation of the McGill Cree Project according to 4 topics that are closely re-lated to developmental change: economic development, the influence of schooling, cultural change, and political development. From this study, problems arise which should stimulate research in the fields of ethnology, sociology, and psychology.   DD

2159   **COTE   ERNEST A**
1967
NOTES FROM SPEECH BY MR. E. A. COTE, DEPUTY MINISTER AT THE INAUGURATION OF THE SEPT-ISLES HOUSING PROJECT. Speech delivered at the Inauguration of the Sept-Isles housing project. Sept-Isles, P.Q., 1967. Available from Information Services, Records and Research, Department of Indian Affairs and Northern Development, Ottawa (Speech #3-6715). 4 pp.

The successful teamwork resulting in the Sept-Isles housing project and projected programs in education and employment are discussed by Deputy Minister E. A. Cote at the inauguration ceremony.   CCV

2160   **COX   BRUCE**
1970
MODERNIZATION AMONG THE MISTASSINI-WASWANIPI CREE: A COMMENT. Canadian Review of Sociology and Anthropology 7:212-215.

Despite the high subjective utility of wage work, as shown by David Holden's study, "Modernization Among Town and Bush Cree in Quebec,"the majority of adult men trap in the winter. It is argued that the risk of abandoning trap-lines for year-round wage labor is presently too high for most local men.   IVY

2161   **DAGENAIS   BERNARD,   POTHIER   ROGER**
1963
DESCRIPTION ETHNOGRAPHIQUE DE LA CULTURE CONTEMPORAINE DES INDIENS DE MISTASSINI: RAPPORT PRELIMINAIRE. Unpublished paper. Available from Bibliotheque Nationale du Quebec. 226 pp.

This is a preliminary report of the 2 authors' fieldwork in the summer of 1962. The ethnographic description of the Montagnais concentrates on their economy and social organization. The 1st part is divided into chapters on demography, trapping, hunting and fishing, transportation and communication, summer work, and hunting groups and territories. The 2nd part is devoted to social aspects: the nuclear family, marriage, rules of residence, life-cycle, the band, the government, and external agents.   DD

2162   **DESBARATS   PETER, ed.**
1969
WHAT THEY USED TO TELL ABOUT: INDIAN LEGENDS FROM LABRADOR. Toronto: McClelland and Stewart. 92 pp.

Twenty-seven legends collected from Montagnais-Naskapi informants of Labrador and northern Quebec during the summer of 1967 are presented. The collection is accompanied by a brief commentary on the Montagnais-Naskapi subsistence techniques, and their neighbors.   CCV

2163 **DESY PIERRETTE**
1963
ACCULTURATION ET SOCIO-ECONOMIE CHEZ LES MONTAGNAIS ET LES
NASKAPI DU LAC JOHN PRES DE SCHEFFERVILLE. M.A. Thesis. L'Institut de
Geographie. Universite Laval. 171 pp.

This thesis is divided into 3 parts, and after a brief presentation of the surrounding area,
the author presents the general characteristics of both the Montagnais and Naskapi and
their geographical distribution in the region. The 2nd part deals with the Lake John community (near Schefferville, Quebec), its population movements, education and settlement
patterns, sedentary life, and economic activities. The 3rd part is devoted to the traditions
of the community and Indian-White relations. The acculturation problems are discussed
in the conclusion where the author suggests a possible solution in terms of integration. DD

2164 **DESY PIERRETTE**
1968
FORT-GEORGE OU TSEPA-SIPPA: CONTRIBUTION A UNE ETUDE SUR LA
DESINTEGRATION CULTURELLE D'UNE COMMUNAUTE INDIENNE DE LA
BAIE JAMES. Ph.D. Thesis. Universite de Paris. 325 pp. Available from Centre
d'Etudes Nordiques, Universite Laval.

Fieldwork between 1963 and 1966, supplemented with library research, provides data
for this work which aims at exploring and explaining the causes of cultural evolution and
disintegration of the Indian community at Fort George. The contemporary problems are
analyzed from an ecological perspective with less emphasis placed on historical analysis.
Photographs accompany the text. DD

2165 **DORION HENRI**
1970
LES NOMS DES LIEUX MONTAGNAIS DES ENVIRONS DE MINGAN:
CONTRIBUTION A LA CONNAISSANCE DE LA CHORONYMIE ABORIGENE
DE LA COTE-NORD. Centre d'Etudes Nordiques, Groupe d'Etudes de Choronymie et
de Terminologie Geographique (GECET) 2. Quebec: Presses de l'Universite Laval. 214
pp.

This is a detailed inventory of all the names that the Montagnais from the Mingan Reserve (Quebec) give to their surroundings. To build this Montagnais dictionary of to-
ponymes, the author collected his data in the summer of 1966. All the words (in alpha-
betical order) are given the same treatment. First, the Montagnais expression is situated
geographically, then it is followed by the term which figures on the topographic map.
The official noun is then mentioned when possible and followed by a translation and an
explanation of the word and its origin. For each expression, several ethnographic details
are noted by the author. DD

2166 **DYKE A P**
1966
TRANSHUMANCE STUDIES ON THE LABRADOR COAST
NEWFOUNDLAND: A PRELIMINARY REPORT. In Field Research In Labrador -
Ungava. McGill Sub-Arctic Research Paper 21. Montreal: Department of Geography,
McGill University. pp. 54-77.

Collecting census data and surveying settlements in northern Labrador in the summer of 1965 included a visit to Davis Inlet, an Indian settlement (of which 148 of 160 people are Naskapi). The life-style of these natives is briefly described (pages 67-69).   IVY

2167   **DYKE   A P**
1970
MONTAGNAIS-NASKAPI OR MONTAGNAIS AND NASCAUPI? AN EXAMINATION OF SOME TRIBAL DIFFERENCES. Ethnohistory 17:43-48.

Genetic and ethnographic data are offered to support the argument that the Montagnais and Nascaupi of the Labrador-Ungava peninsula represent 2 distinct groups. Montagnais-Naskapi should refer only to the offspring of mixed marriages between the Montagnais and Nascaupi.   IVY

2168   **GENDRON   JEAN-LOUIS,   GOURGUES   JULES-HENRI**
1968
POINTE-BLEUE: ETUDE D'UNE POPULATION INDIENNE DE SES LEADERS ET DE SES MARGINAUX. M.A. Thesis. Ecole de Service Social. Universite Laval. 387 pp.

Leaders and marginals among the population of Pointe Bleue were identified and factors in these roles were clarified through the use of questionnaires. Population characteristics are outlined. Conflict between Indian and White culture is ever apparent. The inadaptation of marginals is cultural rather than social. Leaders face a discontinuity between Indian culture and the bureaucratic system with which they relate.   CCV

2169   **GILBERT   LOUIS**
1966
LA POPULATION ET L'ORGANISATION ECONOMIQUE DE MINGAN.
Unpublished paper. Available from Bibliotheque Nationale du Quebec. 159 pp.

This is an ethnographic report on the Montagnais of the Mingan Reserve, Quebec. Subsistence activities in the forest, the preparation of hides, and the seasonal cycle are described, with comment on transportation and relations with the outside world. Montagnais income is carefully analyzed. Chapter 2 is devoted to social organization: the importance of the extended family, the characteristics of the kinship system, and Indian-White relations. Chapter 3 discusses political organization: the structure of authority and relations with the government. The last chapter analyzes religious beliefs. The disappearance of many traditional aspects of Montagnais culture is noted.   DD

2170   **GRABURN   NELSON**
1966
MIXED COMMUNITIES. In People of Light and Dark. Maja van Steensel, ed. Ottawa: Queen's Printer. pp. 120-127.

Some of the characteristics of the mixed communities occurring when both Indians and Eskimos settle near a White group are described. Indians and Eskimos did not mix before they were both drawn toward White trading centers. In addition stratification is noted as is differential reaction to the dominant culture.   CCV

2171 **GUNN HUBERT**
1970
HOW RABBIT BROUGHT FIRE. Tawow 1(2):21-23.

A Naskapi tale relates how a young rabbit outwitted a woman and her children and brought home fire to cook fish that he had caught earler.

2172 **GUNN HUBERT**
1970
THE WOLVERINE AND THE ROCK. Tawow 1(2):21-22.

A Naskapi tale relates how the wolverine got her shape and coloring.   IVY

2173 **HAMELIN LOUIS-EDMOND, DUMONT BENOIT**
1964
LA COLLINE BLANCHE AU NORD-EST DE MISTASSINI: GEOMORPHOLOGIE ET SCIENCE HUMAINES. Centre d'Etudes Nordiques Travaux Divers 6.   Quebec: Institut de Geographie, Universite Laval. 27 pp.

Historical, ethnological, and geographic sources are examined in this investigation of a cave in the Mistassini area. A summary of geographic and geological data is presented as is speculation on the ethnographic significance. At present the caverns and quarries appear to be abandoned.   CCV

2174 **HARPER FRANCIS**
1964
THE FRIENDLY MONTAGNAIS AND THEIR NEIGHBORS IN THE UNGAVA PENINSULA. University of Kansas Miscellaneous Publications 37. Lawrence, KS: University of Kansas. 121 pp.

The Montagnais, Naskapi, and Mistassini Cree of the Ungava Peninsula are described from 1953 fieldwork and a review of the literature. Special attention is accorded the distinction between the 3 tribes advanced in the literature. Also discussed are tribal characteristics, subsistence activities, life style, some observations of social characteristics, and personal experiences with informants during research for Montagnais names for plant and animal specimens.   CCV

2175 **HARTWEG RAOUL**
1965
LES MALPOSITIONS DENTAIRES DES INDIENS WABEMAKUSTEWATSH DE LA COTE ORIENTALE DE LA BAIE D'HUDSON (COMPARISONS AVEC LES ESQUIMAUX DE L'UNGAVA). Societe des Americanistes Journal 54(1):123-126.

Dental positions of 24 Indian men and 36 women from Great Whale River, Quebec, were examined during the winter of 1963-64 for comparison with Ungava Eskimo. While the dental implantation is similar for both groups, as is the rest of the dental structure, the Indians examined are in a more favorable condition comparable to that of the Eskimo of earlier generations.   CCV

2176 **HOLDEN DAVID E W**
1968
FRIENDSHIP CHOICE AND LEADER CONSTITUENCY AMONG THE

MISTASSINI-WASWANIPI CREE. In Conflict in Culture: Problems of Developmental Change Among the Cree: Working Papers of the Cree Developmental Change Project. Norman A. Chance, ed. Ottawa: Canadian Research Centre for Anthropology, Saint Paul University. pp. 69-81.

Using sociometric techniques, friendship choice and leadership were studied for the Mistassini-Waswanipi Cree in the 1960's. The results for the 8 groups observed are analyzed and discussed in relation to the community type. The conclusion is that since there traditionally has been little need for a decision-making hierarchy the structure is weak. Projections are advanced concerning the development of such a hierarchy as acculturation continues.   CCV

2177   **HOLDEN   DAVID E W**
1969
MODERNIZATION AMONG TOWN AND BUSH CREE IN QUEBEC. Canadian Review of Sociology and Anthropology 6:237-248.

Based on a sample of 327 Cree over the age of 15 obtained in fieldwork in the Mistassini-Waswanipi areas of Quebec in the summers of 1965 and 1966, a modernization scale is developed and statistical methods applied to indicate the changes associated with the adjustment of traditional groups to industrialized society. Educational, residential, occupational, attitudinal, and orientation differences are noted between town and bush groups, with a more complex role structure for the former. Impermanence of occupation for nearly all persons interviewed was the most outstanding finding.   WRC

2178   **HOLDEN   DAVID E W**
1970
MODERNIZATION AMONG TOWN AND BUSH CREE. In Developmental Change Among the Cree Indians of Quebec: Summary Report. Norman A. Chance, ed. Department of Regional Economic Expansion ARDA Project 34002. Ottawa: Department of Regional Economic Expansion. pp. A-1 - A-25.

Three hundred twenty-seven Cree urban and non-urban Indians from Chapais, Chibougamau, Matagami, Mistassini Post, Dore Lake, Waswanipi River, Miquelon, Bachelor Lake, and Nemiscau were rated on modernization according to a Likert scale. Differences between urban and non-urban Indians were related to age; education; occupation; and attitudes toward job training, urban living, and traditional religion. A tendency for in-town Indians, when employed for wages, to participate less in jobs resembling traditional activities and more in situations with Whites was revealed.   CCV

2179   **HOLDEN   DAVID E W**
1970
REJOINDER. Canadian Review of Sociology and Anthropology 7:215-217.

In this rejoinder to Bruce Cox's comment on "Modernization Among Town and Bush Cree in Quebec," it is emphasized that the original paper discussed adaptation of Cree to White society and not economic growth. The risk-taking model suggested by Cox offers nothing to the basic understanding of the problems faced by the people making the change from a hunting and trapping economy to wage labor.   IVY

2180 **HONIGMANN   JOHN J**
1962
SOCIAL NETWORKS IN GREAT WHALE RIVER: NOTES ON AN ESKIMO,
MONTAGNAIS-NASKAPI, AND EURO-CANADIAN COMMUNITY. National
Museum of Canada Bulletin 178. Ottawa: Queen's Printer. 110 pp.

Fieldwork was conducted in 1949-1950 in the tri-ethnic community of Great Whale
River, Quebec. Discussed are the habitat, prehistory, demography, morbidity, and the
social networks linking the Eskimo, Montagnais-Naskapi, and Euro-Canadian residents.
Social organization, religion, recreation, and world view are presented. An appendix by
Frances N. Ferguson discusses Eskimo personality as deduced from Rorschach
tests.   JSL

2181 **HONIGMANN   JOHN J**
1964
INDIANS OF NOUVEAU-QUEBEC. In Le Nouveau Quebec: Contribution a l'Etude
de l'Occupation Humaine. Jean Malaurie and Jacques Rousseau, eds. Ecole Pratique des
Hautes Etudes - Sorbonne, France. Sixieme Section: Sciences Economiques et Sociales,
Centre d'Etudes Arctiques et Finno-Scandinaves. Bibliotheque Arctique et Antarctique
2. Paris: Mouton. pp. 315-373.

The literature related to the Naskapi-Montagnais and Swampy Cree of Quebec is reviewed. Included are: subsistence activities, social life, folklore and personality of the
traditional culture and on the contemporary scene, contact, land tenure, seasonal cycle,
hunting, trapping, the trading economy, social organization, residence, marriage and
family, and value and belief systems.   CCV

2182 **HORWOOD   HAROLD**
1967
TALES OF THE LABRADOR INDIANS: PART 1. The New Newfoundland
Quarterly 66(1):17-20.

These Montagnais-Naskapi folk tales, some of which had never been collected before,
were translated from Naskapi by bilingual senior students at Northwest River. The stories are entitled: "The Sun in the Snare,""Why Indians are Good to Their Children,""The
Rabbit and the Toad,""The Dancing Geese,"and "How the Robins Were Made."   IVY

2183 **HORWOOD   HAROLD**
1968
TALES OF THE LABRADOR INDIANS. The New Newfoundland Quarterly
66(2):16-18.

The Montagnais-Naskapi folk tales translated from the Naskapi are: "Caribou Man,"
"The Eaters of Human Flesh," and "Legend of the Winter."   IVY

2184 **HORWOOD   HAROLD**
1968
TALES OF THE LABRADOR INDIANS: PART 3. The New Newfoundland
Quarterly 66(3):17-19.

"Why the Ice Booms in Winter"and "Biography of the Man in the Moon"are the Montagnais-Naskapi folk tales presented in Part 3.   IVY

2185 **INGSTAD HELGE**
1969
WESTWARD TO VINLAND: THE DISCOVERY OF PRE-COLUMBIAN NORSE
HOUSE-SITES IN NORTH AMERICA. London: Cape. 250 pp.

Chapter 18 of this account of archaeological exploration along the north coast of the
Gulf of St. Lawrence reports a visit to a band of Nascapi Indians at Davis Inlet. Details
of the Indians' fall camp and a few notes comparing Nascapi and Eskimo are included.
CCV

2186 **LA RUSIC IGNATIUS EDWIN**
1968
THE NEW AUCHIMAU: A STUDY OF PATRON-CLIENT RELATIONS AMONG
THE WASWANIPI CREE. M.A. Thesis. Department of Sociology and Anthropology.
McGill University. 63 pp. Available from National Library of Canada.

Discussed are the recent geographical and occupational shifts of the Waswanipi Cree
band. Abandonment of Waswanipi Post, the locus of the band for over 200 years, was
due to the development of mining and forestry industries in the territory of Abitibi-East
in central Quebec, and the decline in traditional hunting and trapping. Patron-client theory is suggested as an explanation of why the band members chose particular occupational categories and settlements when they deserted Waswanipi Post and splin-
tered into 5 groups. DGW

2187 **LA RUSIC IGNATIUS EDWIN**
1970
FROM HUNTER TO PROLETARIAN: THE INVOLVEMENT OF CREE INDIANS
IN THE WHITE WAGE ECONOMY OF CENTRAL QUEBEC. In Developmental
Change Among the Cree Indians of Quebec: Summary Report. Norman A. Chance, ed.
Department of Regional Economic Expansion ARDA Report 34002. Ottawa:
Department of Regional Economic Expansion. pp. B-1 - B-59.

The history of the Mistassini, Nemiscau, and Waswanipi initiation into White wage
economy is traced briefly. The role of the Indian worker, his economic benefits, and the
potentials offered him in lumbering, mining, commercial fishing, guiding, sawmill operations, and odd jobs are reviewed. The employment opportunities available to Indians of
the Waswanipi-Mistassini-Nemiscau region, while neutralizing his chances to continue
traditional hunting activities, do not provide an adequate income. In addition to the deni-
gration of the traditional life style current contexts of employment do not permit or facilitate social interaction with Whites. It is recommended that projects intended to provde
employment for Indians be tied strongly with the regional economy to ensure their lon-
gevity and thus employment security. CCV

2188 **LACHANCE DENIS**
1967
LE REAMENAGEMENT DE LA RESERVE INDIENNE DE SEPT-ILES.
Unpublished paper. Available from Bibliotheque Nationale du Quebec. 93 pp.

This aims at a presentation of the refitting project of the old Sept-Iles Reserve and the
reactions of the Montagnais band involved. The Maliotenam group is also involved in
this project, though indirectly, and after a few demographic and economic details, the
author reports its reaction to the project. DD

2189   **LACHANCE   DENIS**
1968
L'ACCULTURATION DES INDIENS DE SEPT-ILES ET MALIOTENAM. M.A.
Thesis. Departement de Sociologie et Anthropologie. Universite Laval. 197 pp. .

The author spent the summers of 1966 and 1967 among the Montagnais bands of Sept-Iles and Maliotenam, where he studied acculturation. The first part of his thesis is a theoretical review of several acculturation concepts. The second part of the thesis is divided into 3 chapters that represent a different phase in the acculturation process of this particular band. Each chronological phase is studied in the context of the Indian group and the non-Indian group in contact.   DD

2190   **LEACOCK   ELEANOR**
1969
THE MONTAGNAIS-NASKAPI BAND. In Contributions to Anthropology: Band Societies: Proceedings of the Conference on Band Organization, Ottawa, August 30 to September 2, 1965. David Damas, ed. National Museums of Canada Bulletin 228. Ottawa: Queen's Printer. pp. 1-20.

Ethnohistorical sources show matrilocality to be an organizing factor among the Quebec Montagnais-Naskapi. The loosely organized composite band is a recent adaptation to the fur trade. In the 17th century, 4 types of grouping were discerned: multi-family lodge group, winter band, band, and band gatherings. It is not clear which was the exogamous unit. Generalized reciprocity and wide individual latitude in choice of movement and group affiliation ensured effective co-operative units. In-group cohesion and out-group ties were fortified by exogamy and cross-cousin marriage. A discussion follows.   JSL

2191   **LEE   THOMAS E**
1966
THE NASKAPI. Anthropological Journal of Canada 4(3):12-14.

A brief description of traditional Naskapi material culture and customs is given.   IVY

2192   **LEFEBVRE   MADELEINE**
1970
"TSHAKABESH": UN RECIT MONTAGNAIS-NASKAPI. M.A. Thesis. Departement d'Anthropologie. Universite de Montreal. 254 pp.

Versions of a Montagnais-Naskapi myth provided by 4 different narrators are presented and analyzed. These narrations were recorded in Northwest River, 3 during the summer of 1967, the other in 1963. One informant is now a resident of Davis Inlet; the other 3 reside in Northwest River. The 4 versions are compared and discussed in terms of Montagnais mythology and the order of components is examined to throw light on the signs and symbols utilized. While a striking difference in style is observed, little variation is noted between narratives. The most important difference seems to be the varying order of episodes.   CCV

2193   **LEGUERRIER   JULES**
1967
LES PROBLEMES SOCIAUX DANS LE TERRITOIRE DE LA BAIE JAMES. In Problemes Nordiques des Facades de la Baie de James: Recueil de Documents Rediges

en Collaboration a la Suite d'une Rencontre de Nordistes a Moosonee en Ontario. Centre d'Etudes Nordiques Travaux Divers 18. Quebec: Centre d'Etudes Nordiques, Universite Laval. pp. 33-38.

This is a brief presentation of the contemporary social problems of the Indians of James Bay. This paper was presented at a meeting of specialists on the Canadian North in Moosonee and is divided into 3 parts: economic problems, social problems, and suggestions for change. The paper is followed by a Cree translation. DD

2194 **LESAGE SYLVIO**
1968
LA CULTURE INDIENNE A BETSIAMITES. Kerygma 2(4):149-156.

Aspects of Montagnais culture and contemporary life style at Betsiamites are examined briefly. It is proposed that a gradual assimilation and integration of the community are inevitable. The use of the language of the dominant culture is considered important to a successful adaptation and measures to hasten these processes are desirable if an equitable life style is to be attained by the Indians of Betsiamites. CCV

2195 **LESAGE SYLVIO**
1968
LA LANGUE INDIENNE A BETSIAMITES. Kerygma 2(1):29-36.

The use of Montagnais in daily life at Betsiamites (Bersimis) is discussed. The advantages and disadvantages of conducting Mass and school in Montagnais are weighed against the eventuality of its replacement by French in response to practical needs. CCV

2196 **LIEBOW ELLIOT, TRUDEAU JOHN**
1962
A PRELIMINARY STUDY OF ACCULTURATION AMONG THE CREE INDIANS OF WINISK, ONTARIO. Arctic 15:191-204.

Based on fieldwork in the summer of 1958, the effects of intensified contact on the Mistassini Cree at Winisk from 1901 to 1958 are examined. Changes in the social unit of production, leadership, and social relations occasioned by the Roman Catholic mission, the trading post, and the Indian agent are considered not nearly as radical as the shift in the mode of production from semi-sedentary hunting and trapping to wage-labor and village life caused by the construction of a radar base from 1955 to 1958. WRC

2197 **MAILHOT JOSE, MICHAUD ANDREE**
1965
NORTH WEST RIVER: ETUDE ETHNOGRAPHIQUE. Centre d'Etudes Nordiques Travaux Divers 7. Quebec: Centre d'Etudes Nordiques, Universite Laval. 120 pp.

This monograph is the result of the 2 authors' fieldwork in the summer of 1963. It is divided into 3 sections. The first describes the environment, the origins, and characteristics of the non-Indian population, and its relationships with the federal government. The 2nd is devoted exclusively to the traditional Montagnais-Naskapi technology and economy. The 3rd part deals with the social and political organization of the Montagnais-Naskapi. DD

2198   **MALAURIE   JEAN**
1964
PREFACE. In Le Nouveau Quebec: Contribution a l'Etude de l'Occupation Humaine.
Jean Malaurie and Jacques Rousseau, eds. Ecole Pratique des Hautes Etudes - Sorbonne,
France. Sixieme Section: Sciences Economiques et Sociales, Centre d'Etudes Arctiques et
Finno-Scandinaves. Bibliotheque Arctique et Antarctique 2. Paris: Mouton. pp. 9-28.
In both English and French.

The accumulated knowledge in the human sciences arising from research on the New
Quebec region is reviewed.   CCV

2199   **MARSH   D B**
1964
HISTORY OF THE ANGLICAN CHURCH IN NORTHERN QUEBEC AND
UNGAVA. In Le Nouveau Quebec: Contributions a l'Etude de l'Occupation Humaine.
Jean Malaurie and Jacques Rouuseau, eds. Ecole Pratique des Hautes Etudes - Sorbonne,
France. Sixieme Section: Sciences Economiques et Sociales. Centre d'Etudes Arctiques et
Finno-Scandinaves. Bibliotheque Arctique et Antarctique 2. Paris: Mouton. pp. 427-437.

A brief history is provided of the establishment and development of Anglican missions
among the Montagnais-Naskapi and Eskimo of northern Quebec and Ungava.   CCV

2200   **MARTEL   JULES**
1968
MISSION DE LA ROMAINE, SUR LA COTE-NORD: LOINTAINS ECHOS DE LA
BASSE-COTE-NORD. La Federation des Freres Educateurs Bulletin 1968(Mai):9-15.

Life in the mission of La Romaine on the Quebec north shore is described revealing details of Indian living conditions. A marriage is described and a letter written by Judith
Mestokosho, student at Sept-Isles, clarifying the Indian position is included.   CCV

2201   **MARTIJN   CHARLES A,   ROGERS   EDWARD S**
1969
MISTASSINI-ALBANEL: CONTRIBUTIONS TO THE PREHISTORY OF
QUEBEC. Centre d'Etudes Nordiques Travaux Divers 25. Quebec: Universite Laval 440
pp.

An ethnohistory of the Mistassini Indians is presented in Chapter 3 of this book which
traces the history and ecology from contact to the present day. Attention is focused on
the nature of contact, material culture, exploitation of the environment, social and religious orientation, and the contribution of exterior forces to changes in the life style and
culture patterns.   CCV

2202   **MCGEE   JOHN T**
1961
CULTURAL STABILITY AND CHANGE AMONG THE MONTAGNAIS
INDIANS OF THE LAKE MELVILLE REGION OF LABRADOR. The Catholic
University of America Anthropological Series 19. Washington, DC: Catholic University
of America Press. 159 pp.

Based on more than 3 years residence in the Lake Melville area of Labrador, 1942-1943 and 1951-1953, this dissertation attempts to discover what factors contributed most to the stability of the Montagnais hunting-fishing-gathering economy. Discussing social and political organization, seasonal subsistence pattern, material culture, and ecological adaptation, it is concluded that conservatism and catholicism are factors in stabilizing them in their culture. It is hypothesized that compulsory school attendance may become a chief factor conducive to a change of Montagnais outlook and culture.   IVY

2203 **MCGEE   JOHN T**
1964
CARIBOU INDIANS OF THE QUEBEC LABRADOR PENINSULA. Massachusetts Archeological Society Bulletin 25:38-44.

Economic activities felt to have great time depth provide the focus of this study of the Montagnais-Naskapi. Both the mode of hunting caribou and the uses thereof are described. Fish and berries are staples during the summer while in other months a variety of animals are hunted for both food and trade.   IVY

2204 **NEWFOUNDLAND. Department of Public Welfare. Northern Labrador Division.**
1961
BRIEF. In Minutes of Proceedings and Evidence. No. 4. March 21, 1961. Joint Committee of the Senate and the House of Commons on Indian Affairs. Canada. 24 Parliament, 4 Session. Ottawa: Queen's Printer. pp. 81-87.

Discussed are the administration, and social and economic conditions of the Montagnais and Naskapi of Labrador.   JSL

2205 **POTHIER   ROGER**
1964
RELATIONS INTER-ETHNIQUES ET ACCULTURATION A MISTASSINI. M.A. Thesis. Departement d'Anthropologie. Universite de Montreal. 162 pp.

Fieldwork conducted at Mistassini during the summers of 1962 and 1963 is reported. The population characteristics, subsistence activities, inter-ethnic relations, and acculturation are described. A reduction in the time spent on the traplines is anticipated. As big game, notably caribou, moose, and bear decreased, a corresponding rise in individualized trapping was observed in spite of the sustained cultural significance of big game. The inefficiency of transportation also served to decrease the accessible hunting territories and reduce the time in the bush. The hunters questionned stated a unanimous preference for winter employment at the post.   CCV

2206 **POTHIER   ROGER**
1965
RELATIONS INTER-ETHNIQUES ET ACCULTURATION A MISTASSINI. Centre d'Etudes Nordiques Travaux Divers 9. Quebec: Centre d'Etudes Nordiques, Universite Laval. 154 pp.

This describes the process of acculturation among the Indians of the Mistassini Reserve, Quebec. The data taken from an earlier report (1963) describe the subsistence activities, the annual seasonal cycle, sources of income, and consumption patterns. Some causes of

change are analyzed according to their influence on the social and economic organization
of the population.   DD

2207   **POTHIER   ROGER**
1968
COMMUNITY COMPLEXITY AND INDIAN ISOLATION. In Conflict in Culture:
Problems of Developmental Change Among the Cree: Working Papers of the Cree
Developmental Change Project. Norman A. Chance, ed. Ottawa: Canadian Research
Centre for Anthropology, Saint Paul University. pp. 33-45.

The 6 communities studied by the Cree Developmental Change Project are defined and
evaluated for their degree of complexity. Seven factors are used to estimate complexity:
communication systems, community services and organizations, commercial organizations, religious organizations, educational system, medical services, and recreational
services and organizations. Indian communities differed greatly in degree of complexity
from White-dominated communities. At the same time as community complexity increases Indian participation diminishes. Some of the difficulties encountered by Indians
as members of a minority groups vis-a-vis the more complex White culture are discussed.   CCV

2208   **PRESTON   RICHARD J**
n.d.
THE CONJURING HOUSE OF THE EASTERN CREE. Unpublished paper. Available
from National Museum of Man, Ethnology Division, Ottawa, with permission of the
author. 76 pp.

A discussion of the conjuring tent ritual of the Montagnais-Naskapi is based on fieldwork in the summers of 1963, 1964, and 1966, and in January of 1966. The paper has 3
parts, a transcription of a conjuring tent performance, a series of narratives illustrating
various aspects of conjuring from the native view-point, and a discussion of the ritual. It
is concluded that the latter is properly subsumed under the more inclusive Mistabeo (attending spirit) concept, although the ritual is more conspicuous and more observable.
The author makes a plea for more long-term fieldworkers, and more attention to the inside view or psychological reality of Eastern Cree culture.   JSL

2209   **QUEBEC. Royal Commission of Enquiry on Education in the Province of Quebec.**
1966
REPORT OF THE ROYAL COMMISSION OF ENQUIRY ON EDUCATION IN
THE PROVINCE OF QUEBEC. Alphonse-Marie Parent, chairman. Quebec:
Imprimeur de la Reine.   Also in French.

Conclusions of the Parent commission on education are reported to the Quebec government. The current situation in education is reviewed briefly under discussion of organization, administration and finance, curriculum, religion and language, teacher training,
adult education, and over-all cultural policy. Recommendations geared to making education readily accessible to Indians and Eskimos and to permit them to adapt to the requirements of modern society are found in volume 3, part 1, pages 117-132.   CCV

2210   **QUIMBY   GEORGE I**
1960

HABITAT, CULTURE AND ARCHAEOLOGY. In Essays in the Science of Culture. Gertrude E. Dole and Robert L. Carneiro, eds. New York: Crowell. pp. 380-389.

The possibility of analyzing correlations between cultural and environmental factors as a means of reconstructing culture history in areas of stable habitat, such as the Great Lakes Region, is discussed. The Naskapi of Quebec and Labrador are described to demonstrate a hunting culture which has reached equilibrium in its articulation with its environment.   CCV

2211   **RICHARDSON   R ALAN**
1961
ACCULUTRATION AMONG THE SEVEN ISLANDS MONTAGNAIS. M.A. Thesis. Department of Sociology and Anthropology. McGill University. 176 pp. Available from National Museum of Man, Ethnology Division, Ottawa, with permission of the author.

Three historical-functional phases of acculturation are described for the Seven Islands Montagnais of Quebec. The 3 phases, defined on the basis of degree of cultural autonomy, are deduced from analysis of scholarly literature plus 12 weeks of fieldwork in 1960. A traditional phase of cultural autonomy preceded a semi-traditional phase (1650-1940) of partial autonomy which was followed by a non-traditional phase of restricted autonomy and intensive acculturation. Most of the fieldwork was done in the community of Maliotenam, and a portion of the thesis is devoted to analysis of this community. Five significant vectors of culture change are noted: (1) from local group to band, (2) from autonomous land use to welfare and limited wage labor, (3) from male dominance to increasing female equality, (4) from family cultural homogeneity to heterogeneity, and (5) from loose political organization to more structured forms. Environmental mastery and interpersonal relations are discussed in the context of cultural maintenance. Appended is a list of Montagnais place names.   JSL

2212   **ROBBINS   RICHARD H**
1968
ROLE REINFORCEMENT AND RITUAL DEPRIVATION: DRINKING BEHAVIOR IN A NASKAPI VILLAGE. Unpublished paper delivered to 8th Annual Meeting, Northeastern Anthropological Association. Hanover, NH, April 6, 1968. Available from National Library of Canada. 11 pp.

This paper attempts to account for the actions and negative reactions of the Naskapi Indians under the influence of alcohol rather than their initial reasons for drinking.   HCV

2213   **ROBBINS   RICHARD H**
1969
RESOURCE ALLOCATION AND ECONOMIC CHANGE. Unpublished paper delivered to Southern Anthropological Society and American Ethnological Society. New Orleans, LA, March 13-15, 1969. Available from National Library of Canada. 8 pp.

Fieldwork was conducted in Schefferville, Quebec, in 1968. Commencing in 1956, the Naskapi migrated to Schefferville and now number 300 in 36 households. This move introduced the Naskapi to a fairly steady wage labor and access to a variety of goods and urban services. Goods available are categorized in terms of their economic and social function: (1) basic subsistence items, (2) household items, (3) hunting and fishing equipment, (4) luxury items, and (5) consumable luxury items. An analysis of income allocated to these categories indicates a preference for goods which increase prestige, which serve to promote social interaction, or which serve to satisfy individual whim. There now appears to be a trend away from the status-luxury pattern toward new types of capital investment. IVY

2214 **ROGERS EDWARD S**
1963
THE HUNTING GROUP - HUNTING TERRITORY COMPLEX AMONG THE
MISTASSINI INDIANS. National Museum of Canada Bulletin 195. Ottawa: Queen's
Printer. 95 pp.

This modified version of the author's Ph.D. dissertation (1958) has 3 objectives: to isolate factors responsible for the limited variability in size of hunting groups, to trace the history of hunting territories, and to examine previous theories of the genesis of the hunting group and hunting territory. One year was spent living with the Mistassini Cree of Quebec. Discussed are the environment, history, social organization, subsistence, annual cycle, hunting group, and hunting territory. The author concludes that hunting group and hunting territory are independent variables. The hunting group of 6-25 persons is a balance between factors which inhibit or promote expansion of the group. This hunting group has maintained a constant size since contact. An aboriginal hunting area system was transformed by the fur trade to a hunting territory system with concepts of trespass, conservation, property rights, and punishment for trespass. By mid-20th century this system was beginning to collapse. Recently introduced individual trapping territories are expected to induce further change. JSL

2215 **ROGERS EDWARD S**
1963
NOTES ON LODGE PLANS IN THE LAKE INDICATOR AREA OF SOUTH-
CENTRAL QUEBEC. Arctic 16:219-227.

Fieldwork among the Mistassini Cree from July 1953 to July 1954 yields a description of the remains of traditional dwellings used for hunting and trapping activities in the early winter period of the seasonal cycle. Noted is the change from excavated, earth-covered conical lodges (1915-1920) to log cabins (1953-1954) under Euro-Canadian influence. Diagrams are included. WRC

2216 **ROGERS EDWARD S**
1964
THE ESKIMO AND INDIAN IN THE QUEBEC-LABRADOR PENINSULA. In Le
Nouveau Quebec: Contribution a l'Etude de l'Occupation Humaine. Jean Malaurie and
Jacques Rousseau, eds. Ecole Pratique des Hautes Etudes - Sorbonne, France. Sixieme
Section: Sciences Economiques et Sociales, Centre d'Etudes Arctiques et Finno-
Scandinaves. Bibliotheque Arctique et Aanarctique 2. Paris: Mouton. pp. 211-249.

In an attempt to evaluate contacts the distribution of the Eskimo and Montagnais-
Naskapi of the Labrador Peninsula for the past and ethnographic present are presented.
Similarities in culture traits and results of contact are reviewed. Many common traits are
attributed to an ancient cultural stratum said to be possessed by both groups before their
arrival in the Labrador Peninsula. Contacts are found to have been minimal, restricted to

the coastal trading area, and recent, primarily arising from Euro-American contacts. It is observed that actual borrowings are few and tend to be of a utilitarian nature.   CCV

2217   **ROGERS   EDWARD S**
1967
THE MATERIAL CULTURE OF THE MISTASSINI. National Museum of Canada Bulletin 218. Ottawa: Queen's Printer. 156 pp.

One year's residence with the Mistassini Indians of Quebec in 1953-1954 formed the basis of the monograph. The study had 2 objectives, to record observations, and to examine changes in material culture. A hunting group was accompanied on its winter migration. Despite 300 years of European influence, much of the native material culture has been retained. Changes that occurred in material items are analyzed as losses, substitutions, innovations, additions, and copies. Eighteen plates and 71 figures illustrate the text.   JSL

2218   **ROGERS   EDWARD S**
1968
THE QUEST FOR FOOD AND FURS: THE MISTASSINI-CREE 1953-54.
Unpublished paper. Available from the National Museum of Man, Ethnology Division, Ottawa, with permission of the author. 138 pp.

One year was spent among the Mistassini Cree of Quebec studying techniques employed in their search for and preparation of food and furs. A hunting group of 13 members was accompanied in 1953-1954. Following a brief resume of the environmental setting and a short description of Mistassini Cree culture, information on the seasonal activities, technology, social organization, economics, and religion of this group is presented. The focus is on production. Details on the poundage taken are analyzed to compile weekly and seasonal frequencies. Figures are given for income from sale of furs, and relief payments. Two purposes are said to be fulfilled by the study. First, a hunting-fishing people's adaptation to the sub-arctic and Europeans is described for the final phase of the fur trade era. Secondly, archaeologists are provided with information on the disposal of faunal remains.   JSL

2219   **ROGERS   EDWARD S,   ROGERS   JEAN H**
1963
THE INDIVIDUAL IN MISTASSINI SOCIETY FROM BIRTH TO DEATH. In Contributions to Anthropology, 1960. Part II. National Museum of Canada Bulletin 190. Ottawa: Queen's Printer. pp. 14-36.

Twelve months were spent with the Mistassini Cree in 1953-1954. The life cycle of the individual, and the socialization process are described. There is a gradual and continuous transition through 4 stages - infancy, unmarried, adulthood, and old age. Discussed are pregnancy, birth, rites of passage, marriage, death, and the division of labor.   JSL

2220   **ROGERS   EDWARD S,   UPDIKE   LEE**
1969
THE NASKAPI. The Beaver 300(Winter):40-43.

A pictorial article depicting 19th century tribal life including customs, dress, tools, subsistence, and dwellings.   IVY

2221   **ROGERS   EDWARD S,   UPDIKE   LEE**
1970
MISTASSINI CREE. The Beaver 301(Summer):22-25.

The material culture, subsistence pattern, and social organization of the Mistassini Cree are described in text and illustrations.   IVY

2222   **ROUSSEAU   JACQUES**
1964
COUPE BIOGEOGRAPHIQUE ET ETHNOBIOLOGIQUE DE LA PENINSULE QUEBEC-LABRADOR. In Le Nouveau-Quebec: Contribution a l'Etude de l'Occupation Humaine. Jean Malaurie and Jacques Rousseau, eds. Ecole Pratique des Hautes Etudes - Sorbonne, France. Sixieme Section: Sciences Economiques et Sociales, Centre d'Etudes Arctiques et Finno-Scandinaves. Bibliotheque Arctique et Antarctique 2. Paris: Mouton. pp. 29-94.

The temperate, subarctic, mid-Arctic, and Arctic zones of New Quebec are discussed in terms of animal and plant life and native peoples including features of subsistence activities, dwellings, clothing, transportation, and intellectual, religious, and social life. CCV

2223   **ROUSSEAU   JACQUES**
1967
APERCU BIOGEOGRAPHIQUE DES REGIONS NORDIQUES DU QUEBEC. 2nd Revised Edition. Quebec: Centre d'Etudes Nordiques, Universite Laval. 90 pp.

A biogeographical review of the Quebec-Labrador peninsula is reproduced from the text of a series on the North prepared by the Centre d'Etudes Nordiques and the Departement d'Extension de l'Universite Laval for the French network of Radio-Canada in 1964-1965. Flora, fauna, and human occupants of the area are discussed for the Superior temperate, sub-arctic, mid-arctic, and arctic biogeographical zones. Details of the environmental equilibrium are reported and certain aspects of life style such as clothing, subsistence activities, transportation, religion, social organization, social groups, and acculturation are included. These data are drawn from travel and study among the Montagnais-Naskapi between 1944 and 1951.   CCV

2224   **ROUSSEAU   JACQUES**
1968
L'AVENIR DES AMERINDIENS DE LA TOUNDRA ET DE LA TAIGA QUEBECOISES. Cahiers des Dix 33:55-77.

The first part of this article is a brief description of the traditional subsistence activities of the Indians (and Eskimos) of northern Quebec. The contemporary situation of these people, divided politically and socially between the provincial and federal government administrations, is presented. Most of the traditional culture of the Indian is now a thing of the past and little has come to fill up the emptiness. The author suggests several urgent solutions, at the 2 government levels, to the problems.   DD

2225   **ROUSSEAU   JACQUES,   VALLEE   FRANK,   et al.**
1963
HUMAN PROBLEMS: FOURTH PANEL DISCUSSION TUESDAY, SEPTEMBER

17TH, 1963 MORNING SESSION. In The Canadian Arctic: A Symposium: Extracts from the Verbatim Record of the Panel Discussions. Dean F. K. Hare, chairman. Montreal: Arctic Institute of North America. pp. 72 -112.

Included in the discussions are Jacques Rousseau's comments on language and curriculum in education, employment for Indians and Eskimos, and the pitfalls of acculturation.   CCV

2226   **SAVARD   REMI**
n.d.
MYTH COLLECTION FROM THE LABRADOR COAST (PRIMARILY FROM THE NORTH WEST RIVER). Unpublished paper. Available at National Museum of Man, Ethnology Division, with permission of the author. 116 pp.

Myths collected from Labrador Coast informants are recorded, 26 in English and 1 in French.   CCV

2227   **SAVARD   REMI,   LACHAPELLE   CLAUDE**
1970
L'ANALYSE DES MYTHES ET LES ORDINATEURS. Unpublished paper delivered to Annual Meeting of the Canadian Society of Sociology and   Anthropology Association. Winnipeg, May 29-31, 1970. Available from Bibliotheque Nationale du Quebec. 14 pp.

Several types of interpretation of a myth are presented. The authors begin by systematizing a Montagnais-Naskapi myth with the help of semantic axes and values and then proceed to a general classification of all aboriginal myths of North America. The conclusion suggests several possibilities of computer research in the field of mythology.   DD

2228   **SINDELL   PETER S**
1968
SOME DISCONTINUITIES IN THE ENCULTURATION OF MISTASSINI CREE CHILDREN. In Conflict in Culture: Problems of Developmental Change Among the Cree: Working Papers of the Cree Developmental Change Project. Norman A. Chance, ed. Ottawa: Canadian Research Centre for Anthropology, Saint Paul University. pp. 83-92.

Research at the La Tuque Indian residential school in 1966 gives rise to this discussion of the lack of continuity in the nature of the behavior expected from Mistassini Cree children. The traditional socialization processes and cultural expectations of the Mistassini Cree are discussed and it is demonstrated that the child's residential school experiences stress values and behavior patterns which are in direct opposition to his enculturation experiences. Many of these new behavior patterns are highly inappropriate in the Mistassini cultural setting and conflicts in identity and in values arise.   CCV

2229   **SINDELL   PETER S,   WINTROB   RONALD M**
1969
CROSS CULTURAL EDUCATION IN THE NORTH AND ITS IMPLICATIONS FOR PERSONAL IDENTITY: THE CANADIAN CASE. Unpublished paper delivered to "Cross-Cultural Education in the North", University of Alaska and Arctic

Institute of North America. Montreal, August, 1969. Available from National Library
of Canada. 18 pp.

Psychiatric and ethnographic data were collected on all 109 Cree adolescents of the Mistassini and Waswanipi Bands attending elementary and high schools in 1967-68. Forty-
two percent of these students showed clear evidence of identity conflict. Symptoms indicative of identity confusion were apparent in 14 percent. These findings indicate that the
philosophy governing education in northern Canada should change. Two essential principles for the reduction of identity conflict among Indian and Eskimo youth are (1) the
validation of the student's self-image and the strengthening of his self-esteem as an Indian or Eskimo and (2) the effective involvement of parents in the formulation of educational policy for their children.   IVY

2230   **SMITH   SHIRLEY S**
1965
THE NASCAPI INDIANS OF DAVIS INLET. Among the Deep Sea Fishers 63:20-23.

Based on a conversation with Antoon van der Schot, a lay brother with the Rev. Father
Peters in 1963-1964, a description of 130 Naskapi Indians of Davis Inlet, Labrador, is
presented. Changes occuring since 1952, the year Rev. Father Peters settled in Davis Inlet, are recounted.   IVY

2231   **TANNER   ADRIAN**
1968
OCCUPATION AND LIFE STYLE IN TWO MINORITY COMMUNITIES. In
Conflict in Culture: Problems of Developmental Change Among the Cree: Working
Papers of the Cree Developmental Change Project. Norman A. Chance, ed. Ottawa:
Canadian Research Centre for Anthropology, Saint Paul University. pp. 47-67.

Three types of communities were identified in 1967 for the Indian population of the
Waswanipi-Mistassini region: the Indian majority or bush community type; the Indian
minority community, satellite to a White town, type; and the urban minority type. A relationship between community type and culture structure type is proposed and discussed
for the minority communities of Matagami "Reserve"and Dore Lake, and for Indian
communities satellite to the White towns of Matagami and Chibougamau. Occupational
patterns and minority community isolation in terms of Indian-White exchange, recreation, and services are described. It is demonstrated that the tendency to casual employment found in minority communities is part of an adaptive pattern of social relations.   CCV

2232   **THERIAULT   YVES**
1969
TEXTES ET DOCUMENTS. Montreal: Lemeac. 133 pp.

The life and works of Yves Theriault, who is of Indian descent, are summarized. A portrait of Yves Theriault as individual and as writer is presented by Renald Berube. Yves
Theriault discusses himself, his works, and literary criticism.   CCV

2233   **TREMBLAY   MARC-ADELARD,   et al.**
1966
L'ORGANISATION ECONOMIQUE ET SOCIALE DE LA RESERVE DE

MINGAN. Unpublished paper. Available at Centre d'Etudes Nordiques, Universite Laval. 102 pp.

The data contained in this preliminary report were collected by anthropology students at Laval University in 1965-66. The informant, a Montagnais from Mingan, a reserve on the north shore of the St. Lawrence River, was at the time working as a research assistant at Laval. The general topic, economic organization of the reserve, was divided into the traditional categories: occupation, the seasonal cycle, property, income, government assistance, consumption, and credit. There are 4 complementary sections to this main chapter: relations with White people, task division, political organization, and world view. A 2nd part of this report, entitled "Social Organization", describes the family, education, and leadership.   DD

2234   **TREMBLAY   VICTOR**
1964
CHAMPLAIN ET LES INDIENS DU SAGUENAY: PREMIERS CONTACTS.
Saguenayensia 6:122-124.

Samuel de Champlain's account of the first Montagnais Indians he met along the St. Lawrence River is provided. Montagnais physical appearance, houses, clothing, beliefs, and several ceremonial rites are described.   DD

2235   **TREMBLAY   VICTOR**
1964
LE MARTYRE BLANC DES MISSIONNAIRES DU SAGUENAY. La Societe Canadienne d'Histoire de l'Eglise Catholique Rapport 31:45-53.

Details of the hardships endured by missionaries among the Montagnais of the Saguenay area in the 17th and 18th centuries are reported from historical sources. The discussion gives some insight into the life style of the Indians at that time.   CCV

2236   **TREMBLAY   VICTOR**
1968
HISTOIRE DU SAGUENAY DEPUIS LES ORIGINES JUSQU'A 1870. La Societe Historique du Saguenay Publications 21. Chicoutimi: Librairie Regionale. 465 pp.

The history of the Saguenay is recounted. Chapter 4 contains a description of the Montagnais-Naskapi, original inhabitants of the area. Impressions of their stature, life style, religious practices, and subsistence activities at contact are reported. Chapter 5 includes details of exploration, missionary activity, fur trade, and intrusions by the Iroquois. Chapter 14 is devoted to discussion of the effects of 19th century colonization on the Indians of Saguenay.   CCV

2237   **TREMBLAY   VICTOR**
1968
UNE DELEGATION DES MONTAGNAIS AUPRES DE LORD ELGIN.
Saguenayensia 10:38-40.

A delegation of Montagnais was sent in 1848 to seek help from the authorities in Montreal. One of the tribe's ambassadors describes the journey and the petition presented to the Governor.   DD

2238   **TYMAN   JOHN L**
1961
MAN AND THE NORTH SHORE: A STUDY IN ENVIRONMENTAL RESPONSE.
M.A. Thesis. Department of Geography. McGill University. 195 pp.

Historic materials pertaining to Quebec's North Shore are reviewed selectively to describe man's interaction with this rugged environment and to note his failure to appreciate its potential until the industrial age. Brief references to the Montagnais inhabitants are included in the first 3 chapters which are concerned with exploration, early trade, and missions.   CCV

2239   **VINCENT   PIERRE**
1969
A MENTAL HEALTH CONSULTATION TO A NORTHERN COMMUNITY:
SCHEFFERVILLE MARCH 31, APRIL 1, 1969. Unpublished paper. Available from Center for Settlement Studies, University of Manitoba. 16 pp.

Dealing mainly with the White population of Schefferville, the paper notes, however, special problems resulting from the integration of the Indian children from the nearby reserve into the Schefferville school system.   IVY

2240   **WEBBER   ALIKA PODOLINSKY**
1964
DIVINATION RITES. The Beaver 295(Summer):40-41.

Chief Joe Rich of the Davis Inlet Band of Naskapi demonstrates the use of a caribou shoulder blade for divining the location of game.   IVY

2241   **WEBBER   ALIKA PODOLINSKY,   WEBBER   RAY**
1963
THE NASKAPI CHILD. The Beaver 294(Winter):14-17.

The socialization of the Naskapi child of Labrador is briefly described.   IVY

2242   **WILLS   RICHARD H**
1965
PERCEPTIONS AND ATTITUDES OF THE MONTAGNAIS-NASKAPI OF
GREAT WHALE RIVER CONCERNING THE WESTERN WORLD. M.A. Thesis.
University of North Carolina. 135 pp.

Data were compiled from participant observation and informal interviews with 33 Montagnais-Naskapi at Great Whale River, Quebec, from June 9 to September 2, 1964. Attitudes toward government, employment, community development, religion, and Whites in general were solicited. The general life style and socio-economic status of the Montagnais-Naskapi is also reviewed. Lack of understanding of White value systems and motives, generally poorly developed communication networks, and serious misconceptions or ignorance of the outside world or the "south"were observed.   CCV

2243   **WINTROB   RONALD M**
1968
ACCULTURATION, IDENTIFICATION, AND PSYCHOPATHOLOGY AMONG

CREE INDIAN YOUTH. In Conflict in Culture: Problems of Developmental Change Among the Cree: Working Papers of the Cree Developmental Change Project. Norman A. Chance, ed. Ottawa: Canadian Research Centre for Anthropology, Saint Paul University. pp. 93-104.

Four of the several interviews conducted among Mistassini-Waswanipi Cree young adults and students in 1966 are reported. Material on normal, neurotic, and psychotic informants is included. Attention is directed to the conflict between socialization into the traditional life patterns and socialization into that of the White culture to which the young people are exposed during extended periods at residential school or in White homes. Mechanisms by which individuals attempt to deal with their anxiety are noted. It is expected that as participation in the economic development of the region increases, the sharp differentiation between the traditional and White identity models will decrease.   CCV

2244   **WINTROB   RONALD M**
1969
RAPID SOCIO-CULTURAL CHANGE AND STUDENT MENTAL HEALTH: PART 1. McGill Journal of Education 4:174-183.

The effects of rapid socio-cultural change on the role identity of Liberian (West African) and Cree (north-central Quebec) adolescent students are compared. Evidence of socio-cultural change in both environments is witnessed in rapid economic development, and inter-generational conflict of values and attitudes toward education.   IVY

2245   **WINTROB   RONALD M**
1970
RAPID SOCIO-CULTURAL CHANGE AND STUDENT MENTAL HEALTH: PART 2 - A COMPARISON OF FINDINGS. McGill Journal of Education 5:56-64.

Data on inter-generational and identity conflicts of Cree and Liberian adolescent students are compared along 3 parameters: (1) attitudes toward education, (2) the influence of beliefs in witchcraft and spirit possession, and (3) defense mechanisms employed to cope with role conflict. Resolution of identity conflict is considered and hypotheses formulated for further study.   IVY

2246   **WINTROB   RONALD M,   SINDELL   PETER S**
1969
CULTURE CHANGE AND PSYCHOPATHOLOGY: THE CASE OF CREE ADOLESCENT STUDENTS IN QUEBEC. Unpublished paper delivered to Annual Meeting, Canadian Psychiatric Association. Toronto, June, 1969. Available from National Library of Canada. 20 pp.

The psychological consequences which result from students living alternately in the traditional milieu of family and hunting groups, and in the urban school setting is examined. Psychiatric and ethnographic data were collected on all 109 Cree adolescents of the Mistassini and Waswanipi Bands attending elementary and high schools in 1967-68. Identity conflict was evident in 42 percent of these students. Symptoms indicative of identity confusion were apparent in 14 percent which were predominantly female.   Case material is included to illustrate these findings. The etiology and pathogenesis of identity confusion among Cree adolescent students are discussed.   IVY

2247   **WINTROB   RONALD M,   SINDELL   PETER S**
1969
EDUCATION AND IDENTITY CONFLICT AMONG CREE INDIANS.
Unpublished paper delivered to Annual Meeting, American Psychiatric Association. Bal
Harbour, FL, May, 1969. Available fron National Library of Canada. 28 pp.

Cree students live alternately in 2 very different environments: traditional, represented
primarily by kin, and the White middle or working class. It is hypothesized that the identity conflict experienced during adolescence reflects their attempt to resolve incompatibil-
ities between 2 major models for identification. Data has been collected (Adolescent Adjustment Interview Schedule, fieldwork, and interviews with adults and non-student adolescents) on all 109 teen-aged members of the Mistassini and Waswanipi bands, Quebec,
attending elementary and high schools during 1967 and 1968. One case is presented
which is representative of Cree students experiencing identity conflict who attempt to
resolve their conflict through polarization toward the White middle class identity
model.   IVY

2248   **WINTROB   RONALD M,   SINDELL   PETER S**
1970
EDUCATION AND IDENTITY CONFLICT AMONG CREE YOUTH. In
Developmental Change Among the Cree Indians of Quebec: Summary Report. Norman
A. Chance, ed. Department of Regional Economic Expansion ARDA Report 34002.
Ottawa: Department of Regional Economic Expansion. pp. C-1 - C-113.

Interviews with 109 Mistassini and Waswanipi students attending elementary and high
schools in LaTuque, Brantford, and Sault Ste. Marie provide information on the relationships between identity conflict and education. Areas of conflict between parental and
student values are related to a polarization toward the traditional or the dominant White
life style. Four case studies are included and areas of conflict, educational aspirations,
and attempts at resolution are discussed. Recommendations are centered around the
minimization of the enculturative discontinuity experienced by these students, the opportunities for more positive relationships with White adults and peers, and the validation
of the Cree cultural heritage in the school curricula.   CCV

MOUNTAIN

2249   **MICHEA   JEAN**
1963
LES CHITRA-GOTTINEKE: ESSAI DE MONOGRAPHIE D'UN GROUPE
ATHAPASCAN DES MONTAGNES ROCHEUSES. National Museum of Canada
Bulletin 190. Ottawa: Queen's Printer. pp. 49-93.

The life style of approximately 40 Mountain Indians as observed in the Fort Norman
area in 1957-1958 is reviewed. The bio-geographical milieu and seasonal cycle, life style,
daily activities, attitudes, social organization, and activities and relations at the trading
post are discussed in turn. The Mountain Indians are characterized by a technology
evolved in response to their ecological niche. In spite of this their sense of identity as
Mountain is giving way to identification with the general Mackenzie Valley population.
Christianity, education, and emancipation of the women and youth are important contemporary facts. The Chitra-gottineke are at a turning point, distinguishable today.
Tomorrow they will form part of the indigenous group identified with the Mackenzie,
less a group than a social class.   CCV

OJIBWA

2250   **1964**
EXPERIMENT IN HOUSING FOR INDIANS: RED LAKE. Ontario Housing
10(1):11-15.

The development of government-sponsored housing for the town of Red Lake and that
development's impact on the lives of the people are described.   ADG

2251   **1965-66**
ONTARIO INDIANS BENEFIT FROM PROGRAM FIVE. Technical and Vocational
Education in Canada 7:38-39.

A brief report on the Cape Furniture Factory at Cape Croker Reserve, Ontario, is
given.   IVY

2252   **1969**
PAT KERWIN AND THE OJIBWAYS. Canadian Labour 14(1):21-23.

A biographic sketch of a community development worker is given. His work in the
Kenora region is described.   IVY

2253   **1970**
NORVAL MORRISSEAU. Tawow 1(1):14-15.

A biographic sketch of the artist, Norval Morrisseau, is given.   IVY

2254   **1970**
WHAT'S HAPPENING ON THE HOME FRONT: MANITOBA - ROSEAU RIVER
RESERVE. In Love is Caring. Toronto: United Church of Canada. p. 8.

Community service and activities of the United and Roman Catholic churches are briefly
mentioned.   IVY

2255   **AIRPHOTO ANALYSIS ASSOCIATES**
1970
LAND USE STUDY HENLEY INLET INDIAN RESERVE NO. 2, LOWER
FRENCH RIVER INDIAN RESERVE NO. 13. Unpublished paper. Available at
Indian-Eskimo Economic Development Branch, Development Services Division,
Department of Indian Affairs and Northern Development, Ottawa. 30 pp.

Factors affecting development of the total areas of the Henley Inlet Reserve No. 2 and
Lower French River Reserve No. 13 are investigated and discussed. Marinas, gravel de-
posits, hunting, forestry, shoreline development, and other land uses are considered in
relation to the available resources. Recommendations involving tourism and recreation
are geared to resource potentials and development costs.   CCV

2256   **BARNOUW   VICTOR**
1961
CHIPPEWA SOCIAL ATOMISM. American Anthropologist 63:1006-1013.

Earlier assertions by Bernard James and Harold Hickerson in regard to the development of Chippewa social order are disputed. From ethnohistorical data it is argued that the more recent individualism and decentralization were not subsequent to an earlier period of social integration and cohesion. Chippewa society is considered traditionally atomistic, given the ecological setting of dispersed subsistence activity during most of the year. A definition of social atomism is offered.   WRC

2257   **BISHOP   CHARLES A**
1969
CHANGES IN THE SOCIAL ORGANIZATION OF THE NORTHERN OJIBWA DURING THE FIRST HALF OF THE 19TH CENTURY. Unpublished paper delivered to Southern Anthropological Society. New Orleans, LA, May, 1969. Available from National Library of Canada. 14 pp.

Changes in the social organization among the northern Ojibwa during the 1st half of the 19th century are examined. The primary source was the Hudson's Bay archival materials, especially those relating to the Osnaburgh House and Lac Seul posts in Ontario. It is concluded that the individualism of the northern Ojibwa was a product of increasing dependence on trade materials, the correlated increasing significance of trapping, and the subsistence change from large to small game.   IVY

2258   **BISHOP   CHARLES A**
1969
THE NORTHERN OJIBWA: AN ETHNOHISTORICAL STUDY. Ph.D. Thesis. State University of New York at Buffalo. 387 pp. Available from National Museum of Man, Ethnology Division, Ottawa, with permission of the author.

Social and economic change from the mid-18th century to the present day among the Northern Ojibwa who inhabit the region drained by the Upper Albany River, its tributaries, and the region above Lake Saint Joseph is studied. Using ethnohistorical methods, 8 eras of social and economic change are discerned for the Northern Ojibwa. These are: Late Prehistoric - Earliest Contact Era (? to 1660's), Era of Population Concentration (+ 1640 to ca. 1680), Era of Dispersal and Relocation (1680-1736), Era of Interior Expansion and Settlement (1736-1782), Era of Large Game Hunting Under Conditions of Competition Among Traders (1782-1821), Era of Small Game Hunting and Dependency Upon the Trading Post (1821-1890), Era of Early Government Influence (1890-1945), and Present Era of Village Ojibwa (1945-1967). Fieldwork among the Northern Ojibwa at Osnaburgh House was done in 1965 and 1966.   DGW

2259   **BISHOP   CHARLES A**
1970
THE EFFECTS OF FORMAL EDUCATION ON TWO NORTHERN OJIBWA COMMUNITIES. Unpublished paper delivered to Algonquian and Iroquoian Conference. Peterborough, Ont., August 29-30, 1970. Available from National Library of Canada. 11 pp.

This paper focuses on the effect of formal education at 2 northern Ojibwa communities in Ontario: Osnaburgh House and Ogoki (Martin Falls Band). Osnaburgh House has had a permanent day school since 1962, while Ogoki parents have sent their children to residential schools since 1963. The establishment of the school at Osnaburgh House has disrupted the economic cycle involving trapping activities which some parents resent.

Though the parents at Ogoki trap in the fall and winter they are reluctant to send their children away for 10 months. Ambivalent feelings toward education compounded by poorly qualified and uninterested (socially aloof) educational personnel have resulted in widening the gap between the Indian community and White society.   IVY

2260   **BISHOP   CHARLES A**
1970
THE EMERGENCE OF HUNTING TERRITORIES AMONG THE NORTHERN OJIBWA. Ethnology 9:1-15.

From ethnohistorical reports, it is argued that the establishment of trading posts was not the only variable accounting for the emergence of delimited family hunting territories among the Northern Ojibwa during the mid-19th century. Type and amount of game resources and demographic factors are combined with the effects of the fur trade in examining the shift from mobile and communal subsistence activities to sedentary, individualistic territories circa 1810, before the notable effects of the trading post itself.   WRC

2261   **BLACK   MARY**
1967
AN ETHNOSCIENCE INVESTIGATION OF OJIBWA ONTOLOGY AND WORLD VIEW. Ph.D. Thesis. Department of Anthropology. Stanford University. 269 pp. Available from University Microfilms.

Fieldwork accomplished with 8 Ojibwa informants of the Red Lake Indian Reservation, Minnesota, from January 1 until November 12, 1965 is reported. A question-response procedure was found useful in producing an ethnographic statement of Ojibwa ontology and world view. The power and control hierarchy involved in the Ojibwa belief system is shown to have greater effects on higher levels. Results are compared and found to be essentially in agreement with Hallowell's finding on the Saulteaux.   CCV

2262   **BLACK   MARY**
1970
LEGENDS AND ACCOUNTS OF WEAGAMOW LAKE. Rotunda 3(3):4-13.

A selection of legends and accounts from over 100 recorded by the author in a 2-year ethnological study of the northern Ojibwa community of Round Lake is given. Illustrations are by Saul Williams (Ojibwa artist) and stories were translated from Ojibwa by Greta Kakekayash, Janosa Quequish, David Ogemawene, Saul Williams, and Gary Quequish, all of Weagamow Lake.   IVY

2263   **BOND   J JAMESON**
1968
A REPORT ON THE PILOT RELOCATION PROJECT AT ELLIOT LAKE, ONTARIO. Ottawa: Department of Indian Affairs and Northern Development, Indian Affairs Branch. 46 pp.

The pilot relocation project at Elliot Lake is evaluated with a view to providing guidelines for further projects of this nature. Discussed in this respect are: Indian-White relations, administrative arrangements, influences of cultural adaptation on the internal relationships of Indian families, the role of alcohol, the training program, and recruitment policies. Recommendations stress greater consideration of social and cultural values in the orientation of such programs, choice of personnel, choice of participants, choice of location, and determination of curriculum.   CCV

2264   BURCH   JOHN C
1962
REPORT ON PULPWOOD OPERATION: BERENS RIVER, 1961-1962.
Unpublished paper. Available from National Library of Canada. 19 pp.

The formation of the Berens River Pulpwood Co-op. Ltd. is discussed and a detailed description of the pulpwood operation is presented.   IVY

2265   CANADA. Department of Forestry and Rural Development.
1963
REPORT ON THE FOREST SURVEY OF THE CHRISTIAN ISLAND INDIAN
RESERVE NO. 30. ONTARIO 1961. Unpublished paper. Available at Indian-Eskimo
Economic Development Branch, Development Services Division, Department of Indian
Affairs and Northern Development, Ottawa. 50 pp.

A forest inventory of Christian Island Indian Reserve No. 30 which includes Christian,
Beckwith, and Hope Islands in Lake Huron is reported. A brief resume of socio-economic
conditions is included as well as recommendations for forest management.   CCV

2266   CANADA. Department of Forestry and Rural Development.
1964
REPORT ON THE FOREST SURVEY OF THE CAPE CROKER INDIAN
RESERVE NO. 27, BRUCE COUNTY, ONTARIO, 1961. Unpublished paper.
Available at Indian-Eskimo Economic Development Branch, Development Services
Division, Department of Indian Affairs and Northern Development, Ottawa. 51 pp.

Results of a 1961 forest survey of the Cape Croker Reserve are reported. Socio-economic
conditions on the reserve and aspects of community development operating and planned
are included.   CCV

**2267   CANADA. Department of Forestry and Rural Development. Forest Management
Institute. Services Section.**
1968
REPORT ON THE FOREST SURVEY OF THE DOKIS INDIAN RESERVE NO. 9,
ONTARIO, 1966: INDIAN RESERVE FOREST SURVEY REPORT NO. 8.
Unpublished paper. Available at Indian-Eskimo Economic Development Branch,
Development Services Division, Department of Indian Affairs and Northern
Development, Ottawa. 31 pp.

A forest survey of the Dokis Indian Reserve conducted in July and August, 1966, is reported including an inventory of forest resources and condition, recommendations for
management, and a review of local conditions.   CCV

**2268   CANADA. Department of Forestry and Rural Development. Forest Management
Institute. Services Section.**
1968
REPORT ON THE FOREST SURVEY OF THE WHITEFISH LAKE INDIAN
RESERVE NO. 6 ONTARIO, 1967: INDIAN RESERVE FOREST SURVEY

REPORT NO. 21. Unpublished paper. Available at Indian-Eskimo Economic
Development Branch, Development Services Division, Department of Indian Affairs and
Northern Development, Ottawa. 65 pp.

A 1967 forest survey of Whitefish Lake Indian Reserve No. 6 is reported. Data concerning the topography, forest, logging operations, and wildlife are presented. Forest management and recommendations for planned cutting, reforestation, and cottage development are discussed with consideration of the labor force and economic development of
the reserve. The results of a survey of sulphur fume damage are included.   CCV

2269   **CANADA. Department of Forestry. Administration Branch.**
        1963
        REPORT ON THE FOREST SURVEY OF THE CHRISTIAN ISLAND INDIAN
        RESERVE NO. 30, GEORGIAN BAY, ONTARIO. Unpublished report made in co-
        operation with the Indian Affairs Branch of the Department of Citizenship and
        Immigration, May 24-June 8, 1961. Available at Indian-Eskimo Economic Development
        Branch, Development Services Division, Department of Indian Affairs and Northern
        Development, Ottawa. 33 pp.

        A forestry survey conducted from May 24 to June 8, 1961, on Christian Island Indian
        Reserve No. 30 reviews forestry resources and present land use and makes recommenda-
        tions for maximization of resources through development and management, including
        recreational and wildlife use.   CCV

2270   **CANADA. Department of Forestry. Administration Branch. Forest Management
        Section.**
        1961
        REPORT ON THE FOREST SURVEY OF THE MOUNTBATTEN INDIAN
        RESERVE NO. 76A, SUDBURY DISTRICT, ONTARIO. Unpublished paper.
        Available at Indian-Eskimo Economic Development Branch, Development Services
        Division, Department of Indian Affairs and Northern Development, Ottawa. 70 pp.

        The results of a 1961 forest survey on Mountbatten Indian Reserve No. 76A are pre-
        sented including distribution of existing resources and recommendations for forest man-
        agement.   CCV

2271   **CANADA. Department of Forestry. Administration Branch. Forest Management
        Section.**
        1964
        PRELIMINARY REPORT ON THE FOREST SURVEY ON THE OSNABURGH
        INDIAN RESERVES NO. 63A AND NO. 63B, PATRICIA AND THUNDER BAY
        DISTRICTS, ONTARIO. Unpublished paper. Available at Indian-Eskimo Economic
        Development Branch, Development Services Division, Department of Indian Affairs and
        Northern Development, Ottawa. 60 pp.

        A 1961 forest survey carried out on the Osnaburgh Indian Reserves Nos. 63A and 63B is
        reported. The land and distribution, age, and condition of the stand is described. Rec-
        ommendations for forest management are outlined and related to the employment po-
        tential for the reserve labor force.   CCV

2272   **CANADIAN MITCHELL ASSOCIATES LIMITED**
1970
CHIPPEWAS OF RAMA INDIAN BAND: BLACK RIVER PARK REPORT AND
PLAN. Unpublished paper. Available at Indian-Eskimo Economic Development
Branch, Development Services Division, Department of Indian Affairs and Northern
Development, Ottawa. 16 pp.

A report and plan for development of a park at the Black River site was prepared for the
Rama Band Council. Details for camping, picnic, and recreation use are outlined with
attention to site improvements, costs, and organization.   CCV

2273   **CANADIAN MITCHELL ASSOCIATES LTD.**
1965
CAPE CROKER INDIAN BAND: REPORT AND MASTER PLAN FOR THE
DEVELOPMENT OF CAPE CROKER INDIAN PARK. Unpublished report prepared
for Cape Croker Chief and Band Council. Available at Indian-Eskimo Economic
Development Branch, Development Services Division, Department of Indian Affairs and
Northern Development, Ottawa. 29 pp.

A master development plan for Cape Croker Indian Park is presented. Details are outlined for a camping, picnic, and recreation site in terms of facilities, management, and
finance.   CCV

2274   **CARROLL   JOY**
1964
THE STRANGE SUCCESS - AND FAILURE OF NORVAL MOSSISEAU. Canadian
Art 21:348-350, 395.

The possible reasons of the success of the artist's 1st exhibition in 1952 and the failure of
the 2nd in 1963 are examined. An interview given in 1964 is also presented.   IVY

2275   **CASS   ELIZABETH E**
1963
OJIBWA TALES. The Beaver 294(Winter):58.

These stories about Nanabush or Nanabozho were related to Dr. Elizabeth E. Cass by
Indian friends on Manitoulin Island in Lake Huron.   IVY

2276   **CASS   ELIZABETH E**
1968
WHY DOGS HATE CATS. The Beaver 299(Summer):51.

The president cat outwits the sled dogs.   IVY

2277   **CHAMPAGNE   ANTOINE**
1963
JOURNAL DE MARIN, FILS. Quebec Rapport des Archives 41(1):236-308.

A journal kept from August 17, 1753, to June 20, 1754, by Joseph de la Margue charged
with exploration in the Upper Mississippi and maintenance of trade alliances with local
tribes is published for the first time. Marin's encounter with LaVerendrye is mentioned

and Marin's dealings with the Sioux, Saulteaux, and Illinois are reported in detail with emphasis on his ability to suppress intertribal warfare and raiding.   CCV

2278   **CHARLES   K J**
1968
A SOCIO-ECONOMIC SURVEY OF THE KENORA-KEEWATIN REGION.
Unpublished paper. Available from National Library of Canada..123 pp.

Since the 2,000 Indians of the Kenora region constitute 20 percent of the population, references to them are contained throughout the report. Pages 62-76 are concerned solely with their economic and social conditions. While contributing substantially to the economy of Kenora, Indians are excluded from the mainstream of life in the community. Tables include (1) income and expenditure of Indians in the District of Kenora, (2) crime rate in the District of Kenora, and (3) the different charges laid against treaty Indians in the District of Kenora. Appendix G (pages 118-123) is the Memorandum of Agreement Respecting Community Development Programs for Indians made in 1965 between the federal government and the government of Ontario.   IVY

2279   **CLIFFORD   JOHN**
1970
REPORT ON THE MOUNT MCKAY SKI RESORT. Clarkson Gordon & Co.
Unpublished report prepared for Department of Indian Affairs and Northern Development on behalf of the Fort William Indian Band. B.C.R. No. 19. Available at Indian-Eskimo Economic Development Branch, Development Services Division, Department of Indian Affairs and Northern Development, Ottawa. 38 pp.

The operations and expansion potential of the Mount McKay ski resort on the Fort William Reserve No. 52 are reviewed. Considerations for purchase of this enterprise by the Fort William band council and an estimate of the employment opportunities and revenue it could provide are submitted.   CCV

2280   **COLEMAN   SISTER BERNARD,   FROGNER   ELLEN,   et al.**
1962
OJIBWA MYTHS AND LEGENDS. Minneapolis: Ross and Haines. 135 pp.

Indian myths and legends are given as recorded in the late 1950's among the Ojibwa of Leech Lake, Fond du Lac, Nett Lake, White Earth, and Grand Portage. Included are: tales showing European cultural influence, stories used in socialization of children, accounts of the creation of the earth and how the Indian reached the continent, as well as tales of Nanabozho, central figure in Ojibwa mythology. A brief description of the Grand Medicine society is appended to the collection.   CCV

2281   **COMMUNITY DEVELOPMENT SERVICES**
1963
COMMUNITY DEVELOPMENT SERVICES IN MACGREGOR. Unpublished paper. Available from Library, Department of Health and Social Development, Winnipeg, Man. 6 pp.

Initiated with a survey in 1959, the results of a program whose cost was shared by the municipal, provincial, and federal governments are presented. Five areas are discussed: food and clothing, education, housing, human relations, and employment.   IVY

2282   **COMMUNITY DEVELOPMENT SERVICES**
1963
INDIAN RE-SETTLEMENT AT MACGREGOR. Ontario Housing 9(11):6-8.

A 1959 survey of the Indian and Metis community of MacGregor concluded with a recommendation for a 5-point program designed to guarantee adequate food and clothing,
housing, education, human relations, and employment. A brief progress report (1963) of
each of these aspects is given.   IVY

2283   **CROCKETT   GARTH C**
1964
PRIMO LABORARE. Unpublished paper. Available from Library, Department of
Health and Social Development, Winnipeg, Man. 3 pp.

The organization of a pulpwood operation and incorporation of a cooperative at Fort
Alexander, Manitoba, are discussed.   IVY

2284   **DANIELS   SHIRLEY**
1968
OJIBWA SONGS, NARRATIVES AND OTHER TRADITIONS FROM LAKE OF
THE WOODS. Unpublished paper. Available from National Museum of Man,
Ethnology Division, Ottawa, with permission of the author. 35 pp.

Songs, narratives, and other traditional beliefs and practices reflecting the traditional
Ojibwa religion were collected in the Lake of the Woods area in 1968. Focus is on the Big
Island band, but some information of Sabaskong was obtained. The former band pos-
sesses a religious council, the latter does not. Information is provided on drums, dances,
and the ceremonial Big Island Round House. The participants in the ceremonies are described.   JSL

2285   **DAVIS   EDWARD W**
1961
SEEGWIN: A LEGEND OF THE FUR TRADE. Minnesota History 37:235-254.

Joe Blackjack's tale of Seegwin, daughter of LaVerendrye and an Indian mother, who
aided and married an English fur trader in the summer of 1766, is translated.   IVY

2286   **DEWDNEY   SELWYN,   KIDD   KENNETH E**
1962
INDIAN ROCK PAINTINGS OF THE GREAT LAKES. Toronto: University of
Toronto Press. 127 pp.

The locating and recording of the Indian rock paintings of the Great Lakes area during
the summers of 1957-1960 are reported. The motifs from each site and from Ojibwa
birch bark scrolls are described and compared with many being illustrated. Content
and style, significance, sources, and dating difficulties are included for discussion. An
age of 400-500 years and an interest in content exceeding interest in form is indicated by
these paintings.   CCV

2287   **DEWDNEY   SELWYN,   OTTO   EBERHARD**
1970

ECOLOGICAL NOTES ON THE OJIBWAY SHAMAN-ARTIST. Artscanada 27(4):17-28.

Various aspects of Ojibwa customs and traditions are discussed including the significance of dreams, the vision quest, and shamanism. Photographs of pictographs illustrate the text. IVY

2288 **DILLING HAROLD JOHN**
1961
INTEGRATION OF THE INDIAN CANADIAN IN AND THROUGH SCHOOLS, WITH EMPHASIS ON THE ST. CLAIR RESERVE IN SARNIA. M.Ed. Thesis. Department of Education. University of Toronto. 168 pp.

Background material was derived from teaching experience in the Sarnia system during negotiations between the Indian Affairs Branch and the Sarnia Board of Education resulting in integration of St. Clair Indian Day School pupils into the Bluewater Public School in 1954. Additional data are drawn from school records, interviews, library research, and administration of standardized tests to Indian and non-Indian students. Some features of education in the St. Clair Day School are reported and compared with aspects of Bluewater Public School Education. Achievement, attendance, and other factors are examined for Indians and non-Indians before and after integration. Some comparisons are made with national figures. While attitudes in Indian pupils, enrollment, attendance, and achievement have improved, suggestions are outlined to further the success of integrated schooling. CCV

2289 **DRIBEN PAUL**
1969
OJIBWA AND JEWISH CHILDREN: A COMPARATIVE STUDY OF N-ACHIEVEMENT. M.A. Thesis. University of Manitoba. 129 pp. Available from National Library of Canada.

Examined are the psycho-social variables which influence the development of N-achievement among Ojibwa and Jewish children of Manitoba. Projective tests were administered to the 2 groups to determine whether statistically there would be a significant difference between the 2 groups with Jewish children attaining a higher level. Since N-achievement is considered a psychological prerequisite for economic development, the results of this study could be of value for applied anthropology. Fieldwork among the Ojibwa was carried out in July and August of 1968. DGW

2290 **DUNNING R W**
1960
DIFFERENTIATION OF STATUS IN SUSBSISTENCE LEVEL SOCIETIES. The Royal Society of Canada Transactions (Series 3) 54:25-32.

Fieldwork among the northern Ojibwa in Pekangekum, Ontario, was conducted during 1954 and 1955. By examining the concept of status and status differential in a near-subsistence level society, it is shown that there is a considerable area for high status positions. High status, for example, was accorded a person with a number of dependents and the ability to control the supernatural world. IVY

2291 **DUNNING   ROBERT   WILLIAM**
1964
SOME PROBLEMS OF RESERVE INDIAN COMMUNITIES: A CASE STUDY.
Anthropologica N.S. 6:3-38.

Based on fieldwork in the summer of 1958, an Ojibwa reserve in Ontario is briefly described as a sample of acculturative adjustment of the southern type of community with the large degree of detachment from traditional Ojibwa cultural traits. A functional analysis of social relations, sanctions, and organization is preferred to a treatment of culture as such, and indicates that the particular aggregate under study is not a cultural isolate but rather positioned in the lower class as part of the larger Canadian socio-economic system. Thus it is hypothesized that the recognition of Indian status persons and control by the government, rather than elements inherent in Ojibwa culture, form the basis of a community.   WRC

2292 **EGGAN   FRED**
1966
THE AMERICAN INDIAN: PERSPECTIVES FOR THE STUDY OF SOCIAL
CHANGE. Chicago: Aldine. 193 pp.

Cross-cousin marriage, kinship behavior, and kinship terminology of the Ojibwa and other Great Lakes Indians are revealed to be indicators of acculturation processes. The series of steps or stages through which kinship behavior passes and its significance in the modification of terminology is noted. The comparison is extended to other more distant groups in a brief review of analagous observations.   CCV

2293 **ELLIOT LAKE CENTRE FOR CONTINUING EDUCATION**
1969
BLIND RIVER PROGRAM: AN EXPERIMENTAL UPGRADING
ORIENTATION COURSE. Unpublished paper. Available from Center for Settlement
Studies, University of Manitoba. 29 pp.

An outline of an 8 week academic orientation course is given with stated emphasis on establishing and reaching goals.   IVY

2294 **ENGLAND   R E**
1968
COMMERCIAL RECREATION DEVELOPMENTS ON INDIAN LANDS.
Unpublished paper prepared for Department of Indian Affairs and Northern
Development, Resources and Industrial Division, 1968. Available from Center for
Settlement Studies, University of Manitoba. 98 pp.

This research investigates the commercial recreational developments on the following 4 Ontario reserves: Saugeen, Kettle Point, Cape Croker, and Moose Deer Point. Examining these enterprises from the standpoint of providing guidelines for future development projects, attention was focused on 5 factors: (1) potential market area and demand, (2) development alternatives and socio-economic benefits, (3) the zoning of reserve lands, (4) native involvement in the planning process, and (5) administrative frameworks. Throughout the report native involvement in the planning, developing, and operating processes are stressed.   IVY

2295   **ENGLAND   RAYMOND EDWARD**
1969
THE PLANNING AND DEVELOPMENT PROCESS IN INDIAN RESERVE
COMMUNITIES. Ph.D. Thesis. Department of Geography and Planning. University of
Waterloo. 272 pp. Available from National Library of Canada.

Five commercial recreation developments on the Cape Croker, Moose Point, Kettle
Point, and Saugeen reserves of Ontario were examined in light of planning and development processes from fieldwork executed in 1967. Shortcomings revealed were: absence
of consideration of the natural resource base in selection of type of development, inadequate information input particularly concerning market possibilities and regional context, and a lack of involvement of reserve residents in decision-making. Proposals are
advanced concerning the type of information input desirable and the possibilities of encouraging resident participation. This includes an organizational framework at the reserve level. This framework was subjected to evaluation by a cross-section of the population of the Cape Croker Reserve which was intensively interviewed during the summer
of 1968.   CCV

2296   **FISHER   MARSHALL**
1968
WORLD VIEW AS SOCIAL ORGANIZATION: AN EXAMINATION OF THE
TRANSMISSION OF AUTHORITY PATTERNS AND LEADERSHIP ROLES IN
OJIBWA SOCIETY. Alberta Anthropologist 2(2):23-34.

Assuming the inseparability of concepts of the supernatural order and subsistence activities, it is argued that leadership among the Ojibwa is based on the strongly socialized
ability to dream. Thus world view is considered a determinant of social organization
through the distribution of power and authority.   WRC

2297   **FOERSTER   JOHN W**
1964
AN INDIAN SUMMER. Canadian Geographical Journal 68:156-163.

A summer spent at Lansdowne House, Ontario, a settlement of 170 Ojibwa Indians of
the Fort Hope band, is described by a worker of the Department of Lands and
Forests.   IVY

2298   **FORTIER   SYLVIA**
1963
A STUDY OF VALUED BEHAVIORS IN OJIBWA MYTHOLOGY. M.A. Thesis.
Department of Anthropology. Catholic University of America. 33 pp.

A collection of 141 Ojibwa tales recorded by William Jones and published by the American Ethnological Society, 1917-19, are analyzed for information concerning valued
behavior patterns in traditional Ojibwa society.   CCV

2299   **FOSTER   JOHN E**
1966
THE ANGLICAN CLERGY IN THE RED RIVER SETTLEMENT: 1820-1826. M.A.
Thesis. Department of History. University of Alberta. 151 pp.

The development of Anglicanism in the Red River Settlement between 1820 and 1826 is recounted. The early 1820's were marked by a struggle between the Hudson's Bay Company and the settlers for control of the fur trade. Prior to 1823 the right of the Church to criticize immoral behavior was established, but only at the expense of alienating many important people. In the following years workable relations were developed between the inhabitants and organizations in the community. The church was firmly established and enjoying success in the Day and Sunday schools established for the Indian-Metis population. Indian-White relations are described, as are Indian attitudes toward education, the missionaries' concept of the Indian, and competition between the Anglican and Catholic clergy.   CCV

2300   **FRANK E PRICE AND ASSOCIATES LTD.**
n.d.
AGRICULTURAL EVALUATION OF COTE INDIAN RESERVE. Unpublished
paper. Available from National Library of Canada. 41 pp.

This feasibility study examines 4 alternate methods of farm production: band farm, cooperative farms, corporate farming, and individual farm enterprises.   IVY

2301   **FRANK E PRICE AND ASSOCIATES LTD.**
n.d.
AGRICULTURAL REPORT OF ROSEAU RIVER INDIAN RESERVE.
Unpublished paper. Available from National Library of Canada. 11 pp.

From an inventory and evaluation of the agricultural resources of the Roseau River Reserve, Manitoba, utilization of these resources is projected. Cost of the development is considered as is the revenue that could be derived from that development, both to the band and the individuals involved. A high capability for growing field crops is evident and approximately 320 acres show potential for vegetable and small fruit production.   IVY

2302   **FRANK E PRICE AND ASSOCIATES LTD.**
n.d.
AGRICULTURAL STUDY OF THE BROKENHEAD INDIAN RESERVE.
Unpublished paper. Available from National Library of Canada. 14 pp.

From an inventory and evaluation of the agricultural resources of the Brokenhead Reserve, Manitoba, utilization of these resources is projected. Cost of the development and the revenue that could be derived from that development, both to the band and individuals involved, are considered. It is concluded that the growing of field crops has good potential.   IVY

2303   **FRANK E PRICE AND ASSOCIATES LTD.**
n.d.
ROSEAU RAPIDS INDIAN RESERVE. Unpublished paper. Available from National
Library of Canada. 7 pp.

Roseau Rapids Reserve occupies an area of approximately 2,080 acres in the eastern edge of the Red River Valley. In view of the factors detrimental to arable culture, it is recommended that 1,280 acres of sandy loam soil be fenced off and used for pasture. This

should have a carrying capacity of one animal unit for each 5-7 acres. Land already cultivated should be used for growing forage.   IVY

2304   **FRANK E PRICE AND ASSOCIATES LTD.**
1967
AN ECONOMIC EVALUATION OF THE BROKENHEAD INDIAN RESERVE:
PREPARED FOR THE CHIEF AND BAND OF THE BROKENHEAD INDIAN
RESERVE. SEPTEMBER 1967. Unpublished paper. Available from Center for
Settlement Studies, University of Manitoba. 79 pp.

This study consists of an inventory of all social and economic resources on the reserve,
and an evaluation of these resources and those of the surrounding area to determine the
economic potential of the members of Brokenhead Reserve (population 408). The report
recommends: development of agricultural resources, tourist and handicraft facilities, incentives in the form of loans and services to entice industry to the reserve, an organized
community on the reserve to serve as a focal point for residents, the examination of development at Selkirk, and the search for participation in future industrial development of
the area as a whole. The report focuses on the methods of maximizing agricultural potential.   IVY

2305   **FRANK E PRICE AND ASSOCIATES LTD.**
1968
ECONOMIC SURVEY OF ROSEAU RIVER INDIAN RESERVE. Unpublished
paper. Available from National Library of Canada. 69 pp.

This study investigates and evaluates the economic development potential of the Roseau
River and Roseau Rapids Indian Reserves.   Both social and economic resources of the
reserves and their surrounding areas are evaluated.   IVY

2306   **FRANK E PRICE AND ASSOCIATES LTD.**
1969
BROKENHEAD FARM CORPORATION. Unpublished paper. Available from
National Library of Canada. 14 pp.

This report sets out a proposed farming program, capital requirements for equipment,
and operating capital requirements for the 1st year of operation at Brokenhead Reserve,
Manitoba.   IVY

2307   **FRANK E PRICE AND ASSOCIATES LTD.**
1969
AN ECONOMIC EVALUATION OF THE LIZARD POINT INDIAN RESERVE.
Unpublished paper. Available from National Library of Canada. 56 pp.

This is an inventory of all social and economic resources on the Lizard Point Reserve and
an evaluation of these resources and those of the surrounding area to determine the economic potential of the members of the reserve (population 681). Agricultural resources
are limited, hence education and training should be provided to aid in relocation and job
placement. Community facilities and services should be improved and contacts with surrounding centers encouraged. A Community Development Board, which would add continuity and consistency to long range planning and development, should be established.   IVY

2308   **FRANK E PRICE AND ASSOCIATES LTD.**
1969
AN ECONOMIC SURVEY OF THE VALLEY RIVER INDIAN RESERVE.
Unpublished paper prepared for The Department of Indian Affairs and Northern
Development, Manitoba Region. Available from National Library of Canada. 49 pp.

This economic study consists of an evaluation of the physical, social, and human resources of the Valley River Reserve. Comments are also expressed on the relationship of
the reserve to the area in which it is located. Considered an underdeveloped rural area,
the reserve consists of 332 members of whom 252 live on the reserve. The main recommendation of the study is the exploitation of agricultural potential. Two types of farms
are considered, corporate and individual. Organizing and operating costs are estimated
for both and compared. Other recommendations include a possible commercial gravel
operation, educational training and relocation, the raising of housing standards, an adequate water supply, the establishment of community development organizations, and a
social orientation program.   IVY

2309   **FRANK E PRICE AND ASSOCIATES LTD.**
1969
EVALUATION OF COMMERCIAL POTENTIAL: FORT ALEXANDER INDIAN
RESERVE. Unpublished paper. Available from National Library of Canada. 96 pp.

This study was undertaken to determine whether there was economic justification for the
establishment of retail stores and service operations on the reserve, based on available
purchasing power. A survey (questionnaire) of reserve residents examined retail expenditure patterns and amounts spent, present purchasing patterns, shopping preference, commercial and service requirements, and employment and income. Based on results of the
research, types of enterprises and commercial facilities which could be established are
outlined in a 3-phase plan.   IVY

2310   **FRANK E PRICE AND ASSOCIATES LTD.**
1970
RESORT DEVELOPMENT STUDY OF BUFFALO POINT INDIAN RESERVE.
Unpublished paper. Available from National Library of Canada. 96 pp.

A detailed analysis of the reserve's potential for recreational development and the capital
cost of a tourist development are given. With large scale surveys presenting an overview,
a survey of tourists throughout Lake-of-the-Woods provided the data on which the proposed development has been based. The text is supplemented by 34 tables.   IVY

2311   **G V KLEINFELDT & ASSOCIATES LTD.**
1968
PRELIMINARY GEORGINA ISLAND REPORT. Unpublished paper. Available at
Indian-Eskimo Economic Development Branch, Development Services Division,
Department of Indian Affairs and Northern Development, Ottawa. 14 pp.

Plans for development of an urban center on Georgina Island to be leased from Georgina Island Band are outlined. Conditions of the lease are noted including mention of
utilities to be developed for the band on land reserved for its use.   CCV

2312   **GAUTHIER   RENE**
1968
MOUVEMENT COMMUNAUTAIRE CHEZ LES INDIENS DU LAC DES BOIS:
UNE ENTREVUE AVEC LE PERE RICHARD FERRON. Kerygma 2(2):67-71.

Community development and improvement in socioeonomic conditions achieved over
the past 10 years in the Indian community at Lake of the Woods, Ontario, are described.
The role of the Oblates in the co-operative enterprise Amik and other community projects are outlined.   CCV

2313   **GLEASON   AILEEN MAY**
1970
A STUDY OF THE RELATIONSHIPS THAT EXIST BETWEEN THE
DECELERATION IN ACADEMIC ACHIEVEMENT OF THE INDIAN
CHILDREN INTEGRATED IN THE SEPARATE SCHOOLS OF FORT FRANCIS,
ONTARIO AND THEIR SOCIAL ACCEPTANCE AND PERSONALITY
STRUCTURE. M.Ed. Thesis. Faculty of Graduate Studies and Research. University of
Manitoba. 131 pp. Available from National Library of Canada.

Indian and non-Indian children from grades 1 to 8 in Fort Francis integrated schools
were tested for intelligence, personality traits, and social acceptance from September,
1966 until June, 1968 in order to explore the attitude changes accompanying decelerating
academic achievement of Indian children. Testing indicated that standard intelligence
tests measure ability to function in a particular cultural setting. Neither Indian nor non-
Indian children achieve according to measured ability and Indian children achieve less
than non-Indian children. Social acceptance of Indians by non-Indians declines with increasing age. Correlation exists between personality traits and academic achievement.
The achieving Indian child demonstrates the opposite temperament to that characterizing the Indian group as a whole.   CCV

2314   **GREEN BLANKSTEIN RUSSELL ASSOCIATES**
1967
FAIRFORD INDIAN RESERVE, MANITOBA: COMMUNITY STUDY.
Unpublished paper. Available from Center for Settlement Studies, University of
Manitoba. 42 pp.

A regional and land use survey was requested by the Fairford Indian Reserve Council in
1966 to investigate the most desirable location for a townsite, collect topographical and
soil information, and provide a layout for the townsite. Due to uncertainty in water control works and the proposed location of the consolidation school site for the area, it was
decided in 1967 to omit the layout from the study. Sources of information include a
physical survey of the reserve and its subregion, discussions with various local leaders
and senior government officials, and an analysis of all relevant and published reports and
statistics. Surveying the physical, economic, and social conditions of the region and the
reserve, this report concludes that the development of a new townsite on Fairford Reserve is not advisable, the dominant urban community should be at Gypsumville, and
reserve people should be encouraged to relocate in better agricultural regions around
Gypsumville and surrounding urban towns. Specific recommendations to this effect conclude the report.   IVY

2315   **GRISDALE   ALEX**
1968

BLACK STONE'S WIFE: A SAULTEAUX INDIAN TALE. Queen's Quarterly 75:592-595.

An Indian tale about cowardice, deceit, and poetic justice is related.   ADG

2316   **HALL   FRANK**
1960
MEDICINE ON THE ROCKS...THE STRANGE TALE OF THE OJIBWA MOSAICS. Bison 1960(June):14-16.

Geometric and zoomorphic patterns of boulders are found in Manitoba's Whiteshell Forest Reserve. While the age of these boulder mosaics is unknown, a Saulteaux informant suggests their sacred character to historic Ojibwa.   TSA

2317   **HALLOWELL   A IRVING**
1960
OJIBWA ONTOLOGY, BEHAVIOR AND WORLD VIEW. In Culture in History: Essays in Honor of Paul Radin. Stanley Diamond, ed. New York: Columbia University Press. pp. 19-52.

Evidence derived from fieldwork among northern Ojibwa is presented in support of the hypothesis that their world view is based on individual actions. A different perspective is indicated in the notion of social interaction between human and other beings.   This is reflected in the mythology, in the kinship terminology utilized in reference to the elements and inanimate objects, the role of dreams, the concept of metamorphosis, of self, and of power. Harmony is realized between the concepts of nature and of individual roles and operative social sanctions.   CCV

2318   **HALLOWELL   A IRVING**
1963
OJBIWA WORLD VIEW AND DISEASE. In Man's Image in Medicine and Anthropology. Iago Galdston, ed. The New York Academy of Medicine Institute of Social and Historical Medicine Monograph 5. New York: International Universities Press. pp. 258-315.

Serious illness is explained in Ojibwa culture as a consequence of deviation from expected patterns of behavior. Causes of disease are sought within the web of interpersonal relations which include other-than-human persons. Hence the disease sanction effectively reinforces the basic values of Ojibwa culture by discouraging deviations or innovations which would disrupt their social organization. Several cases are discussed to illustrate this.   IVY

2319   **HALLOWELL   A IRVING**
1966
THE ROLE OF DREAMS IN OJIBWA CULTURE. In The Dreams and Human Societies. G. E. Von Grunebaum and Roger Caillois, eds. Berkely: University of California Press. pp. 267-292.

The dream experience of the Ojibwa is analyzed as being a positive factor in the maintenance of their aboriginal socio-cultural system. Since no sharp dichotomy exists between fantasy and reality in the cognitive orientation of the Ojibwa, dreams and their interpretations bring meaning to their lives and play an important role in psychocultural adaptation. Discussed are dreams and dream fasts in the light of individual motivation and the functioning of the Ojibwa socio-cultural system.   DGW

2320   **HANNIN   DANIEL**
1967
SELECTED FACTORS ASSOCIATED WITH THE PARTICIPATION OF ADULT OJIBWAY INDIANS IN FORMAL VOLUNTARY ORGANIZATIONS. Ph.D. Thesis. Department of Extension Education. University of Wisconsin. 184 pp. Available from University Microfilms.

A random sample of 170 adults from 3 Ojibwa communities in northern Ontario was studied in 1966 to provide information on adult participation in formal voluntary organizations. Analysis of results of an interview schedule reveals levels of participation and characteristics of participants providing a basis for recommendations for increasing participation and gearing voluntary associations to meet local needs in future problem-solving.   CCV

2321   **HAY   THOMAS HAMILTON**
1968
OJIBWA EMOTIONAL RESTRAINT AND THE SOCIALIZATION PROCESS. Ph.D. Thesis. Department of Anthropology. Michigan State University. 245 pp. Available from University Microfilms.

Observations of adult and child interaction in 9 Ojibwa households at Lac du Flambeau, Wisconsin, and 4 Ojibwa households at Berens River, Manitoba, were used to test hypotheses concerning the motivation of restraint in adult Ojibwa. Observations on 29 adults and 32 children were tested on motivation and learning hypotheses respectively. The theory that Ojibwa restraint is motivated by fear of retaliation and that fear of retaliation is learned through punishment in childhood is not supported by the data.   The theory attributing fear of restraint to fear of doing injury to others can be neither supported nor rejected. Parental acquiescence in a child's behavior giving rise to fear of injuring others is unsupported for only 2 of 32 children.   CCV

2322   **HEDLIN MENZIES AND ASSOCIATES LTD.**
1969
AN EVALUATION OF THE OPPORTUNITIES FOR ECONOMIC DEVELOPMENT ON EBB AND FLOW INDIAN RESERVE. Unpublished paper prepared for Chief and Band Council of Ebb and Flow Indian Reserve. Available from Center for Settlement Studies, University of Manitoba. 59 pp.

Sources of information for this study include the Dominion Bureau of Statistics, Indian Affairs Branch, Manitoba's Department of Agriculture, the University of Manitoba, and the residents of the reserve. Chapter 2 describes the West Lake area in which the reserve is located and the various resources present on the reserve. In Chapter 3 the opportunities and obstacles for development on the reserve are examined, and some guidelines and recommendations are presented. Since natural resources are minimal and agriculture has a very limited potential, this report focuses upon schooling for adults. A set of economic criteria has been developed to judge the soundness of investment in adult education over an extended period of time. It is recommended that a school for adults be established on the reserve.   IVY

2323   **HEDLIN MENZIES AND ASSOCIATES LTD.**
1969
AN EVALUATION OF THE OPPORTUNITIES FOR ECONOMIC DEVELOPMENT ON FISHER RIVER INDIAN RESERVE. Unpublished paper prepared for Chief and Band Council of Fisher River Indian Reserve. Available from Center for Settlement Studies, University of Manitoba. 86 pp.

Sources of information for this study include the Dominion Bureau of Statistics, Indian Affairs Branch, Manitoba's Department of Agriculture, the University of Manitoba, and the residents of the reserve. Chapter 2 describes the northern Interlake region in which the reserve is located and the various resources present on the reserve. In Chapter 3 the opportunities and obstacles for development on the reserve are examined, and some guidelines and recommendations are presented. The report concludes that the Peguis-Fisher River Reserve complex has the potential in agriculture, fishing, and forestry to become an economically viable community and suggests cooperation between the chiefs and band councils of the 2 reserves with specific reference to commercial development, forestry, and high school education.   IVY

2324   **HEDLIN MENZIES AND ASSOCIATES LTD.**
1969
AN EVALUATION OF THE OPPORTUNITIES FOR ECONOMIC DEVELOPMENT ON JACKHEAD INDIAN RESERVE. Unpublished paper prepared for Chief and Band Council of Jackhead Indian Reserve. Available from Center for Settlement Studies, University of Manitoba. 42 pp.

Data for this study were obtained from the Dominion Bureau of Statistics, Indian Affairs Branch, Manitoba's Department of Agriculture, the University of Manitoba, and the residents of the Reserve. This economic study of Jackhead Indian Reserve, resident population of 201, provides a description of the northern Interlake region where the reserve is located, a description of resources on the reserve, an analysis of opportunities and obstacles for development, and recommendations based on the findings. The reserve is isolated, the level of education low, and natural resources upon which economic development can be based meager. Recommendations include relocation in cities, the need for the members of the community to be better organized in order to exploit fishing and logging more efficiently, and the establishment of adult education courses on the reserve. IVY

2325   **HEDLIN MENZIES & ASSOCIATES**
1969
AN EVALUATION OF THE OPPORTUNITIES FOR ECONOMIC DEVELOPMENT ON LAKE MANITOBA INDIAN RESERVE. Unpublished report prepared for Chief and Band Council of Lake Manitoba Indian Reserve. Available at Indian-Eskimo Economic Development Branch, Development Services Division, Department of Indian Affairs and Northern Development, Ottawa. 41 pp.

Limited development potential of the Lake Manitoba Reserve leads to the recommendation that off-reserve employment opportunities be provided for young people.   CCV

2326   **HICKERSON   HAROLD**
1960
THE FEAST OF THE DEAD AMONG THE SEVENTEENTH CENTURY
ALGONKIANS OF THE UPPER GREAT LAKES. American Anthropologist 62:81-107.

A review of ethnohistorical data cites increased participation in the fur trade as the main factor in the flourish and decline of the Feast of the Dead among the Saulteaux during the mid-17th century. By means of periodic gatherings and exchanges associated with the Feast socio-economic alliances were established between the Saulteaux and the neighboring tribes with whom they had increased contact due to trade. It was through intensifying economic dependence on Europeans and the depletion of game resources that Indian alliances and hegemony began to fragment. It is argued that the social atomism of the post-contact Ojibwa stands in contrast to the social cohesion of their aboriginal ancestors, the Saulteaux.   WRC

2327   **HICKERSON   HAROLD**
1962
THE SOUTHWESTERN CHIPPEWA: AN ETHNOHISTORICAL STUDY.
American Anthropological Association Memoir 92. 110 pp.

The social, political, and economic organization of the southwestern Chippewa of Minnesota, Wisconsin, and the southern extreme of Ontario during the early 19th century is reconstructed. The segmentation and dispersal of the Ojibwa from the trade center of Sault Sainte-Marie is traced and the displacement of the Dakota by the southwestern Chippewa through continuous warfare is described. The integration of villages, bands, and households into a community among these people is contrasted throughout with the less organized existence of the northern Ojibwa of Ontario. The ecological and historical factors underlying this difference and the subsequent deterioration of collective institutions during the reservation period are examined.   WRC

2328   **HICKERSON   HAROLD**
1963
THE SOCIOHISTORICAL SIGNIFICANCE OF TWO CHIPPEWA
CEREMONIALS. American Anthropologist 65:67-85.

An examination of earlier reports outlines the functions of the Feast of the Dead and the Midewiwin ceremonies in the development of Chippewa social and political organization from the 17th to the early 19th century. Corresponding to the change from an alliance to a confederated tribal structure among the various Saulteur (proto-Chippewa) gentes, the Midewiwin replaced the Feast of the Dead as a mechanism of social cohesion. An organized priesthood and extensive village participation made the Midewiwin a strong political institution. It is concluded that the origin and development of these ceremonials were not nativistic reactions to European pressures, but rather were responses in the form of social bondage to various historical processes.   WRC

2329   **HICKERSON   HAROLD**
1967
LAND TENURE OF THE RAINY LAKE CHIPPEWA AT THE BEGINNING OF
THE 19TH CENTURY. Smithsonian Contributions to Anthropology 2:41-63.

Land tenure among the Chippewa at Rainy Lake from 1793-1826 is discussed in relationship to subsistence and social organization.   It is concluded that the Chippewa at Rainy Lake had advanced halfway to individual or small-family usufruct in the trapping grounds in the late 18th and early 19th centuries.   IVY

2330   **HICKERSON   HAROLD**
1970
THE CHIPPEWA AND THEIR NEIGHBOURS: A STUDY IN ETHNOHISTORY.
New York: Holt, Rinehart and Winston. 133 pp.

The Ojibwa are discussed in terms of several problems of historical and anthropological interest in order to demonstrate the ethnohistorical method. Comparative analysis of primary sources leads to the conclusion that the clan was an important element of pre-contact Ojibwa social organization which broke down under the weight of contact. By means of re-evaluation of early sources and some later authorities, the Midewiwin is concluded to have been a nativistic movement, a reaction to European contact. Relying on primary sources and publications from natural historians Hickerson focuses on the historical and ecological background of the warfare between the Ojibwa and the Dakota in the 18th and 19th centuries. Discussion of what is called the debatable zone between the 2 warring tribes, the habitat and importance of the Virginia deer, and the role of the trading companies indicates that the sustained warfare may have had value as a survival mechanism.   CCV

2331   **HLADY   WALTER**
1960
STARTING A BOY SCOUT TROOP IN SANDY BAY: WORKING PAPER FOR
WORKSHOPS. Unpublished paper. Available from Center for Settlement Studies,
University of Manitoba. 4 pp.

This report (written in September, 1959) is a detailed outline of the necessary organization required to begin a Boy Scout troop. The postscript (1960) provides additional information of the developments that have occurred in Sandy Bay since 1959.   IVY

2332   **HOWARD   JAMES H**
1961
THE IDENTITY AND DEMOGRAPHY OF THE PLAINS-OJIBWA. Plains
Anthropologist 6:171-178.

An examination of such features as language, social organization, art, ceremonies, and costume demonstrates that the Plains-Ojibwa, or Bungi, who descended from Woodland groups 150 years ago, are a distinct ethnic group. Due largely to semantic confusion in their identification by writers and official agencies, they go unmentioned in most histories despite their importance in the historic period.   IVY

2333   **HOWARD   JAMES H**
1962
TWO WAR BUNDLES FROM THE BUNGI OR PLAINS OJIBWA. American Indian
Tradition 8:77-79.

Two war bundles purchased from John Daniels, an elderly medicine man of the Long Plains band, are illustrated and described. The significance of this protective regalia for the Plains Ojibwa is discussed. Component elements of each bundle are examined.   CCV

2334   HOWARD   JAMES H
1963
THE PLAINS-OJIBWA OR BUNGI: HUNTERS AND WARRIORS OF THE NORTHERN PRAIRIES WITH SPECIAL REFERENCE TO THE TURTLE MOUNTAIN BAND. South Dakota Museum News 24(11-12):1-18 (1-17).

In this issue, the preface and the first 2 chapters of the study examining the Plains-Ojibwa (and the Metis who make up part of this distinct ethnic group) trace the expansion and migration from their parent group, the Woodland Ojibwa, which resulted in their transformation from Woodland hunters to bison-hunting equestrians.   IVY

2335   HOWARD   JAMES H
1964
THE PLAINS-OJIBWA OR BUNGI: HUNTERS AND WARRIORS OF THE NORTHERN PRAIRIES WITH SPECIAL REFERENCE TO THE TURTLE MOUNTAIN BAND. South Dakota Museum News 25(1-2):3-24 (18-39).

In Chapters 3, 4, and 5 subsistence activities are presented including methods of hunting and fishing, utilization of wild vegetal foods, and methods of butchering and storing meat. Various aspects of material culture such as snowshoes, tumplines, pipes, tobacco boards and pouches, woodcarving, and flutes are also described.   IVY

2336   HOWARD   JAMES H
1964
THE PLAINS-OJIBWA OR BUNGI: HUNTERS AND WARRIORS OF THE NORTHERN PRAIRIES WITH SPECIAL REFERENCE TO THE TURTLE MOUNTAIN BAND. South Dakota Museum News 25(3-4):2-28 (41-66).

Descriptions of land and water transport and male and female costumes (including Metis), both traditional and contemporary, are given. Organization and functions of clans, chiefs, councils, tribal police, and dancing societies are presented.   IVY

2337   HOWARD   JAMES H
1964
THE PLAINS-OJIBWA OR BUNGI: HUNTERS AND WARRIORS OF THE NORTHERN PRAIRIES WITH SPECIAL REFERENCE TO THE TURTLE MOUNTAIN BAND. South Dakota Museum News 25(5-6):2-24 (67-89).

Some principles of kinship terminology and such customs as kinship taboos, cross-cousin marriage, and adoption are presented in Chapter 9. In Chapter 10, aboriginal games no longer common among the Bungi have been reconstructed in the following categories: men's games, games played by both men and women, women's games, boy's games, and girl's games. War parties, taboos, divination ceremonies, the war honor system, individual war bundles, and weapons are described in Chapter 11.   IVY

2338   HOWARD   JAMES H
1964
THE PLAINS-OJIBWA OR BUNGI: HUNTERS AND WARRIORS OF THE

NORTHERN PRAIRIES WITH SPECIAL REFERENCE TO THE TURTLE
MOUNTAIN BAND. South Dakota Museum News 25(7-8):2-15 (90-103).

Cosmology and beliefs are explored including myths of creation, concepts of the supernatural, animal spirits, and spirits of the dead.   IVY

2339   **HOWARD   JAMES H**
1964
THE PLAINS-OJIBWA OR BUNGI: HUNTERS AND WARRIORS OF THE
NORTHERN PRAIRIES WITH SPECIAL REFERENCE TO THE TURTLE
MOUNTAIN BAND. South Dakota Museum News 25(9-10):2-15 (104-107).

Plains-Ojibwa have retained a great amount of their aboriginal ceremonial life. Observations of a Sun Dance are recounted in some detail. Also described are the Smoking
Tipi, Trade Dance, Sawanogan, Bear Dance, Elk Dance, Horse Dance, and Windi-
gokanek.   IVY

2340   **HOWARD   JAMES H**
1964
THE PLAINS-OJIBWA OR BUNGI: HUNTERS AND WARRIORS OF THE
NORTHERN PRAIRIES WITH SPECIAL REFERENCE TO THE TURTLE
MOUNTAIN BAND. South Dakota Museum News 25(11-12):1-22 (118-139).

A typical initiation ceremony into the Midewiwin, a religious society, is fully described in
Chapter 14. Also included are the Wabano ceremony and secular dances.   IVY

2341   **HOWARD   JAMES H**
1965
THE PLAINS-OJIBWA OR BUNGI: HUNTERS AND WARRIORS OF THE
NORTHERN PRAIRIES WITH SPECIAL REFERENCE TO THE TURTLE
MOUNTAIN BAND. South Dakota Museum News 26(1-2):1-26 (140-165).

In Chapter 16, the life cycle of the Bungi is presented. Curing methods such as bloodlet-
ting, pricking, and sucking cures are briefly described as are forms of burial practices.   IVY

2342   **HYDE   MARTIN JAMES**
1963
INDIAN COMMERCIAL FISHERIES IN THE PATRICIA DISTRICT OF
ONTARIO: AN ECONOMIC ANALYSIS. Ph.D. Thesis. Department of Economic and
Political Science. McGill University. 360 pp.

An economic analysis of Indian commercial fisheries of the Central Patricia District of
Ontario is based on data collected during 1961 and 1962 while the author was employed
with the Ontario Resources Development Advisory Committee. Inland fish markets; fish
production and marketing in part of the Patricia district; and marketing costs, policies,
and agencies are examined and analyzed. Estimates of fishermen's net earnings and of
the value of the assistance provided by the Indian Affairs Branch are based on these data.
Characteristics of a fish marketing agency to deal with the area's marketing problems
and policy alternatives destined to improve the efficiency of fish resource utilization while
increasing fishermen's incomes are outlined.   CCV

2343   **JAMES   BERNARD J**
1970
CONTINUITY AND EMERGENCE IN INDIAN POVERTY CULTURE. Current
Anthropology 11:435-443.

The regressive, involuted, and atomistic personality structure presented in previous
studies of the Ojibwa of Canada and the United States is viewed not as a persisting aboriginal trait but as response to western society. Reservation culture and the marginality
of the Indian are examined as situations common to minorities living in poor economic
conditions. The application of role theory to the observed behavior in the modern situation of rapid change is thought to yield a more substantial understanding of the relation
between the culture of poverty and personality. The implications of this approach for the
elimination of socio-economic differences as well as the methodological problems arising
from the cultural biases of social scientists are noted. The article is followed by comments from several scholars and a reply by the author.   WRC

2344   **JOHNSTON   PATRONELLA**
1970
TALES OF NOKOMIS. Toronto: Musson. 65 pp.

Originally told to the author by an elderly Ojibwa woman, these tales relate how Nokomis explains to her grandchildren, Badahin and Tawa, traditional beliefs and customs.
Illustrations by Francis Kagige complement the text.   IVY

2345   **K   M E**
1964
RED LAKE - EXPERIMENT IN HOUSING FOR INDIANS. Ontario Housing
10(1):11-15.

Comments are presented on a re-housing and rehabilitation program in an Indian community at Red Lake, Ontario.   IVY

2346   **KERWIN   PAT**
1970
THE KENORA PROJECT. Canadian Labour 15(2):24-25,36.

A report on the Kenora project, January, 1969, identified 4 stages of involvement: aid to
the individual, aid to individual bands in obtaining aid for a particular project, the development of initiative within individual bands, and the development of joint action by
bands to obtain a common end. Events occurring in Ojibwa communities in the Kenora
regions are recorded by a Canadian Labour Congress representative and evaluated in
terms of these stages.   IVY

2347   **KNUDSEN   JOYCE**
1964
BUCKSKIN BOOSTER: THE STORY OF A REMARKABLE INDIAN WOMAN.
The United Church Observer N.S. 26(12):30-31.

A biographic sketch of Mary Jane Simpson, a Mississauga, is given.   IVY

2348   **LAL   RAVINDRA**
1965
MACGREGOR. Unpublished paper. Available from Library, Department of Health
and Social Development, Winnipeg, Man. 7 pp.

A social and cultural profile of the Indian settlement of MacGregor, consisting of approximately 100 persons, is presented. Problem areas such as lack of social contact
between the town and the Indians, hostility toward workers from the government services, and unemployment are discussed.   IVY

2349   **LANDES   RUTH**
1968
OJIBWA RELIGION AND THE MIDEWIWIN. Madison, WI: University of
Wisconsin Press. 250 pp.

Fieldwork done in Western Ontario and Northwestern Minnesota during the summer of
1932, 1933, and the fall of 1935 as well as correspondence from informants are used in
this study of Ojibwa religion and the Midewiwin. The significance of religion in Ojibwa
society, the role of a shaman, acquisition of supernatural powers, curing, ceremonial activities, taboos, dreams, and oral tradition are discussed.   CCV

2350   **LEACH   F**
1968
TRAPPING IN THE OLDEN DAYS. Moccasin Telegraph 28(1):4.

This account of aboriginal trapping was told by Mr. Willie Frog Ross of the Berens River
Reserve.   IVY

2351   **LEITCH   ADELAIDE**
1961
ROCK SERPENTS OF THE WHITESHELL. Canadian Geographical Journal 63:182-
183.

Text and photographs describe figures such as the snake and turtle which are outlined
with rocks at the Whiteshell Forest Reserve on the Manitoba-Ontario border.   IVY

2352   **LITTLEJOHN   BRUCE M**
1965
QUETICO COUNTRY: PART I. Canadian Geographical Journal 71:40-55.

Recounting the history of Quetico Country in Ontario, some information is given on the
Ojibwa Indians and the pictographs found in that region.   IVY

2353   **LOCKWOOD SURVEY CORPORATION**
1970
SAUGEEN AND CHIEF'S POINT INDIAN RESERVES LAND CAPABILITY
STUDY. Unpublished paper. Available at Indian-Eskimo Economic Development
Branch, Development Services Division, Department of Indian Affairs and Northern
Development, Ottawa. 53 pp.

The Saugeen and Chief's Point Reserves are evaluated for present use and potential for agricultural, forestry, and recreational development. Recommendations are based on the economic context of location, natural resources, and land ownership. The limitations occasioned by soils and location necessitate regional consideration of development in agriculture, forestry, recreation, and urbanization.   CCV

2354 **LOWER   ARTHUR R M**
1968
THREE OJIBWAY FOLK TALES AS TOLD BY PAUL MICHEL OF THE LAKE NIPIGON OJIBWAYS. Queen's Quarterly 75:584-591.

Presented are "How the Fisher Lost His Tale,""Waydoasaun Whaseegany,"and "The Boy and the Little Black Fox"(possibly of French origin).   IVY

2355 **LYON   NOEL ADVERSE**
1966
THE ECONOMIC DEVELOPMENT OF THE CAPE CROKER INDIAN RESERVE. M.S. Thesis. University of Guelph. 109 pp.

The natural resources of the Cape Croker Reserve, Ontario, are examined in relation to their present use and economic development potential. Recreational, lumbering, cedar furniture construction, and souvenir making projects are suggested and plans for financing are outlined. Proposed plans would increase employment, per capita income, and band funds, but off-reserve employment would still be necessary if all resident Indians were to be employed full-time.   CCV

2356 **MAJERUS   YVETTE**
1967
LE JOURNAL DU PERE DOMINIQUE DU RANQUET, S.J. La Societe Historique du Nouvel-Ontario Documents Historiques 49-50. Sudbury: Universite de Sudbury. 57 pp.

Extracts from accounts of missionary travels north and south of Lake Superior between 1853 and 1877 are compiled. Details of subsistence activities and traditional religious beliefs among the Saulteaux are included.   CCV

2357 **MAKALE HOLLOWAY & ASSOCIATES LTD.**
1966
DEVELOPMENT PLAN: PART 1 - PLANNING SECTION: TURNER LAKE RESERVE SASKATCHEWAN. Unpublished paper. Available from Legislative Library, Regina, Sask. 7 pp.

The objective of this study was to investigate the potential of the site and to prepare a development plan with provision for housing the present population and an additional 12 families transferring from Claire Lake. Since an adequate economic base is non-existant and the population is small, it is recommended that the development plan providing for 30 home sites be considered temporary until conditions are created in Dillon to encourage direct population transfer from Claire Lake and Turner Lake. A map of the development plan for Turner Lake concludes the report.   IVY

2358   **MAKALE HOLLOWAY & ASSOCIATES LTD.**
1966
DEVELOPMENT PLAN: PART 1 - SURVEYS & STUDIES: PETER POND
INDIAN RESERVE DILLON SASKATCHEWAN. Unpublished paper. Available
from Legislative Library, Regina, Sask. 23 pp.

The purpose of the report is to prepare a plan dealing with the physical aspects of development of the Dillon Indian Reserve. After surveying the physical, social, and economic conditions of the community of 361 persons, improvements and future requirements are proposed in the areas of housing, school and community facilities, gardens, dog control, and utilities. A map of the Dillon development plan concludes the report.   IVY

2359   **MALLORY   ENID SWERDFEGER**
1964
THE AGAWA PICTOGRAPHS. Canadian Geographical Journal 59:126-129.

The Agawa site which is possibly Ojibwa is located along Lake Superior's east shore. Text and photographs describe the pictographs.   IVY

2360   **MALLORY   GORDON,   MALLORY   ENID SWERDFEGER**
1961
THE PETERBOROUGH PETROGLYPHS. Canadian Geographical Journal 62:130-135.

The petroglyphs are located in the Blue Mountain area around Stoney Lake, Ontario. One hypothesis suggests a relatively recent date of 300-400 years ago. Photographs accompany text.   IVY

2361   **MANITOWABI   EDNA**
1970
AN OJIBWA GIRL IN THE CITY. This Magazine Is About Schools 4(4):8-24.

Life in the city can be a most painful, confusing, and destructive experience for an Indian girl. In this article, a young Ojibwa reveals how her childhood on the reserve, with its admixture of permissiveness, boarding schools, and dogmatic Catholicism, affected her life in the city, where personal strength, integrity and happiness could only be attained after she had gone from job to job, through several pregnancies, 1 illegal abortion, 2 psychiatric hospitals, and 1 attempted suicide.   ADG

2362   **MARSH   WILLIAM H C**
1967
INDIAN EMPLOYMENT IN THE SIOUX NARROWS AREA: AN APPRAISAL
OF JOB OPPORTUNITIES AVAILABLE TO THE INDIANS OF THE SIOUX
NARROWS-NESTOR FALLS REGION IN THE DISTRICT OF KENORA,
ONTARIO. Unpublished paper delivered to Ontario Economic Council, Resources and Industrial Division. Available from Ontario Economic Council, Toronto. 58 pp.

Forty Indians and non-Indians of Sioux Narrows, Kenora, McIntosh, Dryden, and Toronto were interviewed early in 1967 to permit evaluation of employment opportunities for Indians and problems associated with employment in the Kenora area. Details of participation in tourist camps, Department of Lands and Forests, trapping, wild rice harvesting, commercial fishing, Ontario Junior Forest Ranger Program, adult education, high school, paper companies, and Ontario Provincial Police are outlined as well as management attitudes and employment potential in each case. The Indian co-operative venture at McIntosh, activities of the corporations at Whitefish Bay and Sabaskong Reserves, and suggestions for small business enterprises to increase employment opportunities are discussed.   CCV

2363   **MICKLEBURGH   BRUCE**
1970
BY THE BAY OF THE BEAVER ON THE ISLAND OF GOD. Educational Courrier
40(4):4-5.

Describing his methods and philosophy in working with Indian children, Robert Aller, who has taught Indian children since 1958, discusses art of Ojibwa children.   IVY

2364   **MORRISEAU   NORVAL**
1965
LEGENDS OF MY PEOPLE THE GREAT OJIBWAY. Toronto: Ryerson Press. 130
pp.

Presented are a group of legends and illustrations by the Indian author-artist. It is his belief that the folklore represented here is correct and has been revealed to him in their proper form through his medicine dreams. The topics themselves are grouped between those that echo the oral tradition and those that more clearly reflect European influence.   DGW

2365   **MORRISSEAU   NORVAL**
1963
MISSHIPESHOO & OTHER WATER MONSTERS. Alphabet 7:4-6.

These 3 legends were taken from a notebook of Mr. Morrisseau's entitled "Ojibwa Legends Beliefs etc, of Lake Nipigon Ojbiwa Indians."Two legends demonstrate the benevolent and malevolent aspects of Misshipeshoo and the 3rd speaks of the mermen who lived in the waters and were powerful dream guardians.   IVY

2366   **MURRAY   FLORENCE B, ed.**
1963
MUSKOKA AND HALIBURTON 1615-1875: A COLLECTION OF DOCUMENTS.
Champlain Society Publications (Ontario Series) 6. Toronto: Champlain Society. 445 pp.

The chapter entitled "The Indian in the Muskoka and Haliburton Region"(pages 97-132) presents documents from 1785-1865 relating to the Chippewa and Mississauga concerning Indian treaties and surrenders underlining the government policy towards the aboriginal tribes.   IVY

2367   **NARVEY   MARGERY**
1970
JOHNNY YESNO. Tawow 1(3):12-13.

The career of Johnny Yesno, actor in motion pictures, radio, television, and theatre, is outlined.   IVY

2368   **ONTARIO. Department of Lands and Forests.**
1969
REPORT ON THE FOREST SURVEY OF THE HENLEY INLET INDIAN
RESERVE NO. 2 AND THE LOWER FRENCH INDIAN RESERVE NO. 13,
PARRY ISLAND NO. 16, SHAWANAGA NO. 17 AND GIBSON INDIAN
RESERVE NO. 13 PARRY SOUND FOREST. Unpublished reports prepared as a
project under the Federal Provincial Resources Development. Available at Indian-
Eskimo Economic Development Branch, Development Services Division, Department of
Indian Affairs and Northern Development, Ottawa. 32 pp.

Forest surveys of 5 Indian reserves in the Parry Sound Forest District carried out in 1965
are reported. Forest resources are described and recommendations for land use are included.   CCV

2369   **P S ROSS AND PARTNERS**
1969
A RESOURCES DEVELOPMENT STUDY OF THE CHRISTIAN, BECKWITH
AND HOPE ISLANDS OF THE BEAUSOLEIL INDIAN BAND. Unpublished paper.
Available at Indian-Eskimo Economic Development Branch, Development Services
Division, Department of Indian Affairs and Northern Development, Ottawa. 89 pp.

An in-depth study of the natural and environmental resources of the Christian, Beckwith, and Hope Islands is reported. Recommendations are outlined for programs to expand existing enterprises and to introduce new industry including details of financing
and revenue as well as employment potential. An appendix comprises maps showing topography, existing development, land use, development projects, tourist attractions, and
a hydrographic chart of the area.   CCV

2370   **P S ROSS & PARTNERS**
1967
AN OPPORTUNITY INVENTORY OF THE RED ROCK, ROCKY BAY AND
GULL BAY BANDS. Unpublished report prepared for Ontario Regional Director,
Indian Affairs Branch, Department of Indian Affairs and Northern Development.
Available at Indian-Eskimo Economic Development Branch, Development Services
Division, Department of Indian Affairs and Northern Development, Ottawa. 50 pp.

The natural and human resources of the Red Rock, Rocky Bay, and Gull Bay bands are
reviewed and a number of feasible proposals for development are advanced. Feasibility
studies of a camp and trailer park, handicrafts operation, and a band farm are recommended for the Red Rock Band residing at Lake Helen Settlement and the Red Rock
Indian Reserve No. 53 at Parmachene. Consideration and study of a community commercial fishing and band coarse fish processing plant, a band farm, and a band tourist
camp are suggested for the Rocky Bay Band including Macdiarmid Settlement, McIntyre
Bay Indian Reserve No. 57, and Sand Point Indian Reserve No. 80. Feasibility studies
relating to commercial fishing, trapping, mink farming, agricultural opportunities, and
professional guiding services are proposed for the Gull Bay Band of Gull River and Jack-
fish Indian Reserves. The appointment and training of full-time band managers for each
band prior to initiation of projects is recommended.   CCV

2371   **P S ROSS & PARTNERS**
1967

A SELECTIVE RESOURCE DEVELOPMENT STUDY OF THE MT. MCKAY
PROPERTY. Unpublished report prepared for Fort William Indian Reserve No. 52 and
Indian Affairs Branch. Available at Indian-Eskimo Economic Development Branch,
Development Services Division, Department of Indian Affairs and Northern
Development, Ottawa. 80 pp.

The potentials for development on the Mt. McKay property of Fort William Reserve No.
52 are reviewed. Preliminary plans for construction of a village and initiation of a ceremonial powwow, operation of a trailer camp, exploitation of potentials of waterfront
property, and introduction of commercial enterprise are outlined as means by which to
benefit from local and tourist trade.   CCV

2372   **P S ROSS & PARTNERS**
1968
A LONG RANGE DEVELOPMENT PLAN FOR THE LITTLE SASKATCHEWAN,
LAKE ST. MARTIN, AND FAIRFORD INDIAN RESERVES. Unpublished paper.
Available from Center for Settlement Studies, University of Manitoba. 63 pp.

Outlining information on the human and natural resources, a plan of development for
attainment of the maximun resource development compatible with the current and projected resources of the reserves is presented. A restricted economic base, complicated
by the flooding of Lake St. Martin from time to time, necessitates the acquisition of additional land adjacent to the reserves to allow expansion of an agricultural base. The existence of fishing, forestry, minerals, game, and a labor force leads to other economic possibilities including developments in industry, manufacturing, and tourism. That some
enterprises be developed jointly by the reserves is recommended.   IVY

2373   **P S ROSS & PARTNERS**
1970
THE EVALUATION OF THE RECREATIONAL POTENTIAL OF THE GARDEN
RIVER RESERVE. Unpublished paper delivered to Regional Superintendent of
Economic Development, Ontario. Available at Indian-Eskimo Economic Development
Branch, Development Services Division, Department of Indian Affairs and Northern
Development, Ottawa. 77 pp.

Development potential particularly in relation to tourist trade on the Garden River Reserve near Sault Ste. Marie, Ontario, is evaluated. Consideration is given to arena, ma-
rina, campgrounds, cottage, recreation center, airstrip, and other commercial development projects. Formation of an economic planning committee for the band is recommended to organize and co-ordinate projects in a long-term perspective.   CCV

2374   **PARKER   SEYMOUR**
1960
THE WIITIKO PSYCHOSIS IN THE CONTEXT OF OJIBWA PERSONALITY
AND CULTURE. American Anthropologist 62:603-623.

A psychodynamic approach to the Windigo psychosis is taken based on earlier studies of
the Ojibwa. The modal personality structure of the Ojibwa is outlined in reference to the
socialization process, social institutions, religion, and mythology. The psychosis and its
associated cannibalistic tendencies are viewed as pathological extensions of the normal

anxiety and dependency frustrations of the earlier stages of life. This continual deprivation and the resultant ambivalence toward dependency objects provided a predisposi-
tion in adult life for this bizarre mental disorder in extreme social and physical environmental conditions.   WRC

2375   **PARKER   SEYMOUR**
1962
MOTIVES IN ESKIMO AND OJIBWA MYTHOLOGY. Ethnology 1:516-523.

Content of Ojibwa and Eskimo myths are examined to test the assumption that myths are
projections of conscious rather than unconscious social motives. Based on earlier indications of Ojibwa individualism and early independence training, in contrast to Eskimo
communalism and relatively mild socialization, it is predicted that in the 3 categories
measured, the Ojibwa myths will rank higher in achievement and power motives, but
lower in affiliation. Results verified the assumption. It is concluded that this survey
method may offer insight into culture and personality through designs dealing with the
complex levels of myth analysis.   WRC

2376   **PARSONS   GEORGE FRANKLIN**
1968
RETREATISTS AND INNOVATORS IN AN INDIAN COMMUNITY. M.A. Thesis.
Department of Sociology and Anthropology. McMaster University. 188 pp.

Community development on a western Canadian Saulteaux Indian reserve was studied
during the summer of 1964 focusing on decision-making by Indian leaders. Eighteen
members of a political-economic elite, members of the band council or officers of one of
the 3 co-operatives, were identified. Formal interviews were conducted with 15 of the
elite group and 24 other band members. Attitudes and value orientations in relations to
social change, co-operatives, self-determination, government, work, and leadership are
explored extensively. Evidence of severe and continued disparagement of this Indian
group by local Whites and a perception, widely shared by the Indians themselves, of the
Indians as inferior and incapable of managing their own affairs is noted. Widespread
retreatist orientation tending to inhibit autonomous action and decision-making, interpersonal and intergroup hostility, and lack of commitment to group goals are observed.
Retreatist tendencies were found in the leadership group to a lesser extent with leaders
manifesting less dependency, less alienation, and tending less to perceive themselves as
powerless. More active members of the elite were future and achievement oriented, ener-
getic, independent, and self-confident, perceiving the environment as manageable to
some extent and recognizing their own capacity in this regard.   CCV

2377   **PASKELL   ANTHONY**
1969
A LITTLE BIT OF MO GOES A LONG WAY: ANTHONY PASKELL DESCRIBES
A DAY IN HIS OJIBWA CLASSROOM. Monday Morning 3(9):22-23.

An elementary teacher humorously describes a day's activities in his primary classroom.   IVY

2378   **PETERSEN   KAREN DANIELS**
1963
CHIPPEWA MAT-WEAVING TECHNIQUES. Smithsonian Institution. Bureau of

American Ethnology Bulletin 186:217-285. Washington, DC: U.S. Government Printing Office.

This presentation of mat-weaving techniques is based on fieldwork conducted in 1957, 1961, and 1962 on Minnesota reservations. References to Canadian Ojibwa are included, particularly to the mat-makers on Parry Island. The method of construction including the gathering of materials and the use of the completed product is described for cedar-bark mats, rush rectangular mats, cattail rectangular mats, reed mats, oval cattail and rush mats, and sweetgrass mats. The article is illustrated by 17 plates and numerous figures.   TSA

2379   **PRICE BALCHEN AND ASSOCIATES LIMITED**
1967
BROKENHEAD INDIAN RESERVE NO. 4: DEVELOPMENT PLAN. Unpublished paper. Available from National Library of Canada. 26 pp.

A plan to develop the proposed townsite of 80 acres on the north-west corner of the Brokenhead Reserve, Manitoba, is presented.   Engineering aspects such as a sewage system, water distribution system, and electrical power distribution are discussed in detail.   IVY

2380   **PRICE BALCHEN AND ASSOCIATES LIMITED**
1968
ROSEAU RIVER INDIAN RESERVE DEVELOPMENT PLAN. Unpublished paper. Available from National Library of Canada. 25 pp.

In this proposed townsite development plan for the Roseau River Reserve, Manitoba, a planned community containing all the essential features of a small village, including an earth dike to protect against flooding is considered. Engineering aspects such as sewer and water systems, electrical power distribution, and roadways are discussed.   IVY

2381   **REID   DOROTHY M**
1961
NANABOZHO AND THE SONG: A NEW NORTHERN "LEGEND."Ontario Library Review 45:227.

Moved by a brown sparrow's faith in the Great Spirit, Nanabozho changes its coloration to become the first white-throated sparrow.   IVY

2382   **REID   DOROTHY M**
1963
TALES OF NANABOZHO. New York: Walck. 128 pp.

In this publication, the author draws on many incidents from the mythology of the Ojibwa and other tribes of the Algonkian language group to present as accurately as possible the true spirit, humor, and adventure of the tale of Nanabozho - the creator-magician of the Ojibwa. Many of the tales told about Nanabozho's trickery and exploits were originally recorded by Henry R. Schoolcraft.   DGW

2383   **RIDDIOUGH   NORMAN**
1962
TREATY TIME. The Beaver 293(Summer): 10-13.

Paying treaty, taking X-rays, and making nominations for band council at Lac Seul Reserve are activities described (with photographs) in this article.   IVY

2384   **ROGERS   EDWARD S**
1962
THE ROUND LAKE OJIBWA. Royal Ontario Museum, Art and Archaeology Division Occasional Paper 5. Toronto: Royal Ontario Museum; University of Toronto. 299 pp.

Fieldwork was undertaken at Weaganow Lake, Ontario, from July, 1958, to July, 1959. Aims of this report are to provide a description of the contemporary Round Lake Ojibwa; to chronicle alterations that have occured in traditional Ojibwa culture; to show the degree to which social organization, economics, and religion are interrelated; and to examine the degree of integration of the Round Lake Community. The study is presented in 4 parts: background (environmental and historical); social organization (kinship, family, community); economics (economic organization and activities); and religion (discussed as an amalgam of aboriginal and Christian teachings). A glossary (16 pages) and plates (9 pages) conclude the report.   IVY

2385   **ROGERS   EDWARD S**
1963
CHANGING SETTLEMENT PATTERNS OF THE CREE-OJIBWA OF NORTHERN ONTARIO. Southwestern Journal of Anthropology 19:64-88.

The change in settlement pattern of the Round Lake Ojibwa from temporary encampments to semi-permanent villages during the 20th century is examined. Field research from July, 1958, to July, 1959, among one of the last native peoples to face Euro-American contact indicated that the primary forces in this shift were the initial institutions of traders and missionaries followed by those of government intervention. These forces, combined with the Indian desire to emulate White society in terms of customs and material goods, have resulted in what might be termed a dependency complex.   WRC

2386   **ROGERS   EDWARD S**
1967
OJIBWA CULTURE: THE TRADITIONAL CULTURE HISTORY. In Kenora 1967: Resolving Conflicts - A Cross-Cultural Approach. Winnipeg: University of Manitoba, Department of University Extension and Adult Education. pp. 32-44.

Discussed are: subsistence activities, material culture, social and political organization, and religion. Major changes that have occurred in Ojibwa culture since the 1700's are briefly summarized.   IVY

2387   **ROGERS   EDWARD S,   UPDIKE   LEE**
1969
THE OJIBWA. The Beaver 300(Summer):46-49.

A pictorial article depicts 19th century tribal life including customs, dress, tools, subsistence, and dwellings.   IVY

2388   **ROLLING RIVER RESERVE. Editorial Committee.**
1970
OTITEPINESEPI ISHKONIGAN (ROLLING RIVER RESERVE). Unpublished

paper presented to Her Majesty, Elizabeth II at the Time of the Royal Tour of Manitoba. Available from Legislature Library, Winnipeg, Man. 24 pp.

Saulteaux Indian students of Erickson College discuss the past and present of Rolling River Reserve providing personal sketches of some of the chiefs.   IVY

2389   **SCHWARTZ   HERBERT T**
1969
WINDIGO AND OTHER TALES OF THE OJIBWAYS. Toronto: McClelland and Stewart. 40 pp.

Nine Ojibwa folk tales recounted and illustrated by Norval Morrisseau are presented.   CCV

2390   **SHIMPO   MISTURU,   WILLIAMSON   ROBERT**
1965
SOCIO-CULTURAL DISINTEGRATION AMONG THE FRINGE SAULTEAUX. Saskatoon: Extension Division, University of Saskatchewan. 291 pp.

The Cote, Keeseekoose, and Key Indian reserves, and the community of Kamsack are the setting of this study. Data were obtained from intensive and unstructured interviews from October, 1963, to July, 1964, and secondary sources. This report provides a reconstruction of the traditional culture and the social organization of the Fringe Saulteaux, a detailed analysis of the historical processes which influenced the Indian culture of the reserve, the nature of current problems, and an attempt to explain the development of the patterns of living now established.   IVY

2391   **SHIPLEY   NAN**
1968
BLACK STONE'S WIFE: A SAULTEAUX INDIAN TALE. Queen's Quarterly 75: 592-595.

Alex Grisdale of the Brokenhead Reserve relates the tale of how Black Stone's deceit and cowardice causes him to lose his pretty young wife.   IVY

2392   **SMITH   JUNE ELIZABETH**
1963
ANOMIE: A DEFINITION OF THE CONCEPT AND AN APPLICATION TO THE CANADIAN INDIAN RESERVATION. M.A. Thesis. McMaster University. 131 pp.

The concept of anomie is defined and explored through library research and fieldwork conducted on Manitoulin Island Reserve, June to September, 1961, and 3 further weeks during the summer of 1962. Using participant observation, interviews, and census data the reserve social system is examined in terms of status positions, reservation activities, role definitions, and role performance. The conflicting expectations impeding fulfillment of expectations according to traditional criteria and lack of means for performance according to Western standards are reviewed with emphasis on the role of the male Ojibwa.   CCV

2393   **STEINBRING   J**
1965

SAULTEAUX PERSONALITY, ALCOHOL, NATIVISTIC REVIVAL. Mandala: United College Creative Quarterly 1965 (January):8-10.

Saulteaux experience a reversal in behavior when under the influence of alcohol. Among these people Alcoholics Anonymous constitutes a kind of nativistic revival.   TSA

2394   **STEINBRING   J**
1967
OJIBWA CULTURE: THE MODERN SITUATION AND PROBLEMS. In Kenora 1967: Resolving Conflicts - A Cross-Cultural Approach. Winnipeg: University of Manitoba, Department of University Extension and Adult Education. pp. 46-71.

The processes of assimilation (de-culturation) among the Ojibwa are analyzed. Since education can be considered the central and most forceful vehicle in assimilation theory, attention is focused upon educational programs and personnel. Based on field-work experiences the effects of the relocation of the Little Black River Band in Manitoba and the integration of Alcoholics Anonymous among some Ojibwa communities in Manitoba are discussed.   IVY

2395   **STEINBRING   JACK**
1964
RECENT STUDIES AMONG THE NORTHERN OJIBWA. Manitoba Archaeological Newsletter 1(4):9-12.

Two student field assistants collected ethnological data from several bands along the east shores of Lake Winnipeg, Manitoba, selecting a small, homogeneous, and conservative band for a more intensive study. Briefly discussed are magic and sorcery, technical crafts and arts, and the institution of Alcoholics Anonymous as a form of nativistic revival.   IVY

2396   **STEINBRING   JACK**
1965
CULTURE CHANGE AMONG THE NORTHERN OJIBWA. Historical and Scientific Society of Manitoba Transactions (Series 3) 21:13-24.

The adoption of Alcoholics Anonymous by the Little Black River Band of Manitoba and other southern Lake Winnipeg bands is examined. Alcoholics Anonymous tends to fulfill some basic prerequisites to a reformative movement and it is predicted that it will continue to spread north as the road system is extended.   IVY

2397   **STEINBRING   JACK**
1965
THE STURGEON SKIN "JAR."Manitoba Archaeological Newsletter 2(3):3-6.

Data were collected from the Little Black River Reserve, and confirmed through field-work at the Fort Alexander and Hollow Water River (Wanipigow) Indian Reserves in the summer of 1964. The informant was a 65-year old Ojibwa man, a senior councilor of Black River Band. Steps in the manufacture of the sturgeon jar (with a diagram) are given and the use of the vessel to store oil and food described.   IVY

2398   **STEVENSON & KELOGG LTD.**
1966
MARKETING EVALUATION AND PLANNING FOR THE CAPE CROKER
INDIAN FURNITURE PROJECT. Unpublished paper. Available at Indian-Eskimo
Economic Development Branch, Development Services Division, Department of Indian
Affairs and Northern Development, Ottawa. 81 pp.

A proposed rustic-furniture production on Cape Croker Indian Reserve is evaluated in
terms of market, competition, consumer needs, retailers, and market reaction to the proposed furniture. Recommendations to initiate the project in a line of outdoor furniture
which would entail less risk economically are outlined. It is suggested that production of
rustic indoor furniture be delayed until the line has been restyled or existence of a good
market can be ascertained.   CCV

2399   **STEWARD   OMER C**
1960
CART-USING INDIANS OF THE AMERICAN PLAINS. In Men and Cultures:
Selected Papers of the Fifth International Congress of Anthropological and Ethnological
Sciences. Anthony F. C. Wallace, ed. Philadelphia: University of Pennsylvania Press. pp.
351-355.

Plains Ojibwa of North Dakota and Manitoba from about 1815 to 1865 employed
2-wheeled wooden carts for their spring and fall buffalo hunts. To designate the Plains
Ojibwa as the cart-using Indians of the American Great Plains is deemed proper since the
Metis of the Red River were usually half-breeds and were then and are today Ojibwa
Indians. IVY

2400   **SUTTON   RICHARD W**
1965
THE WHITESHELL BOULDER MOSAICS. Manitoba Archaeolgoical Newsletter
2(1):3-10.

Four sites of boulder mosaics (snake and turtle) located in Manitoba are described with
accompanying diagrams. It is believed that they are of Ojibwa origin constructed not
more than 250 years ago and are religious symbols.   IVY

2401   **TAYLOR   J GARTH**
n.d.
ECONOMIC DEVELOPMENT IN TWO OJIBWA COMMUNITIES IN
NORTHERN ONTARIO: 1949-1969. Unpublished paper. Available from National
Library of Canada. 15 pp.

Economic development in 2 Ojibwa communities situated in the central Patricia district
of Northern Ontario, Lansdowne House and Webiquie, during the period 1949-1969 is
summarized. Fieldwork was carried out at Lansdowne House from May 13 to September 8, 1969, and at Webiquie from July 8 to August 22, 1970. Income derived from commercial fishing, tourism, fur trapping, and seasonal wage labor is examined and trends
noted. The only economic pursuit which has not displayed a marked development is fur
trapping. This trend is reflected both in the number of men who take part in trapping and
the efforts of those who do take part. Since the marked increase in seasonal employment
has not had any significant effect on the trapping of furs, the decline of trapping must be
due to other factors.   IVY

2402   **TAYLOR   J GARTH**
1969
AN ASSESSMENT OF THE EFFECT OF THE TREE PLANTING PROGRAMME
ON THE COMMUNITY AT LANSDOWNE HOUSE, LAKE ATTAWAPISCAT: A
REPORT BASED ON THE RESEARCH CARRIED OUT WITH THE SUPPORT OF
THE ONTARIO DEPARTMENT OF LANDS AND FORESTS AND WITH THE
CO-OPERATION OF THE ROYAL ONTARIO MUSEUM. Unpublished paper.
Available from Center for Settlement Studies, University of Manitoba. 5 pp.

The purpose of the report is to assess the effect that the hiring of tree planters from Lansdowne House has on the social and economic life of the community. Lansdowne House,
a community of 328 Ojibwa and 13 Whites, was studied from May 13 to September 8,
1969. The comparison of incomes derived from trapping, commerical fishing, and tree
planting indicates the importance of tree planting as a major source of earned income.
Attitudes seem favorable to the program, and although disruptive forces appear operative at the present time, it is unlikely that these can be attributed to attitudes acquired
during the tree planting program. IVY

2403   **TENNENHOUSE   PENNY**
1970
WHEN A NURSING STATION CAME TO NEW OSNABURGH. Canada's Health
and Welfare 25(2):20-22.

Celebrations to officially open the new nursing station at New Osnaburgh, Ontario, included speeches, refreshments, and a ceremonial dance.   IVY

2404   **TODGHAM AND CASE LIMITED**
1969
ROAD NEEDS STUDY FOR CARADOC INDIAN RESERVE 1969. Unpublished
paper. Available from National Library of Canada. 17 pp.

The road system at the Caradoc Indian Reserve has been examined and evaluated and an
inventory of physical needs, of the monies required, and of the timing of recommended
works, is provided. Relative priorities have been assigned and a financial basis for pro-
jecting the expenditures required is provided. Plans, tables, and appraisal sheets are also
included. IVY

2405   **TRITES   STEWART D**
1970
POVERTY IN AN INDIAN-METIS COMMUNITY (SWAN RIVER AREA,
MANITOBA). In This Is Tomorrow: A Sequel to the Home Missions Digest. C. Alvin
Armstrong, ed. Montreal: Baptist Federation of Canada. pp. 52-61.

Poverty in Swan Lake, Manitoba, and surrounding communities is described with its
causes and its effect on the family and community life. Measures which the church can
take to alleviate this problem are discussed.   IVY

2406   **UNIVERSITY OF WESTERN ONTARIO. History Club.**
1970
THE KETTLE POINT QUESTION. Unpublished paper. Available from National
Library of Canada. 10 pp.

In 1942, under the provisions of the War Measures Act, Stoney Point Indian Reserve, established under Treaty 27, 1829, was appropriated for use by the Department of National Defense. Conditions of compensation are disputed. Although the emergency need no longer exists, the ownership of Stoney Point has not been renegotiated.   IVY

2407   **VIPOND   DOROTHY**
1966
EVERYTHING'S LILY WHITE IN DOMINION CITY. The United Church Observer
N.S. 28(16):20-23,28,40.

In May, 1966, the school board at Dominion City, Manitoba (population 534), resolved to bar Indian children - specifically the children from Roseau River Reserve. Provincial grants figured in this administrative decision. Reasons for the decision were investigated. Reactions to the decision by various Indians and Whites are reported. The effect of this closure upon White students is also discussed.   IVY

2408   **WAGMAN   BARBARA**
1970
PRESCHOOL AND CHILDHOOD COGNITIVE DEVELOPMENT OF INDIANS
AT CURVE LAKE RESERVE. M.A. Thesis. Department of Education. University of
Toronto. 85 pp.

The cognitive development of 60 Indian band status children aged 4 to 11 was investigated during May, 1969, at Curve Lake Reserve, Ontario. Data were collected on age, occupation, and 17 Piagetian tasks for the entire sample and a subsample, those between 4 and 8 years of age. In addition the Stanford-Binet Intelligence Scale and the Goodenough-Harris Drawing Test were administered to the preschoolers. Factor analysis was employed on the data for the 3 samples and results and implications are discussed. In comparison to the national average a homogeneously depressed socio-economic status was observed. A decrement in expected performance on cognition development tasks was shown for grade 1 and 2 subjects, a delayed pattern of cognitive development was found, and a correlation between flexibility in hindsight and foresight and conservation factors is reported.   CCV

2409   **WAY   REUBEN**
1970
FORFEIT THE EARTH: MAN AND ENVIRONMENT IN MANITOBA. Queen's
Quarterly 77:231-235.

A project to flood Southern Indian Lake in Manitoba was re-examined by the government and Manitoba Hydro when an informed public protested the social and ecological consequences of the proposal.   ADG

2410   **WILDE   C J R**
1970
REPORT ON DAMAGES OCCURRING ON THE WHITEFISH INDIAN
RESERVE NO. 6 FROM SULPHUR DIOXIDE CAUSES. Forest Resources
Consultants Limited. Unpublished report prepared for Department of Fisheries and
Forestry, Forest Management Institute. Available at Indian-Eskimo Economic
Development Branch, Development Services Division, Department of Indian Affairs and
Northern Development, Ottawa. 13 pp.

Whitefish Indian Reserve No. 6 was surveyed from July 27 through August 6, 1970, to assess damages caused to the environment by sulphur fumes. In addition to an estimated monetary loss in terms of damaged wood, anticipated losses related to cottage leasing, hunting, fishing, recreation, and employment in tourist and logging industries, as well as cost of regenerating the reserve, are reviewed. CCV

2411 **WYLLIE & UFNAL LIMITED**
1968
TRANSPORTATION STUDY FOR THE CHRISTIAN CHANNEL CROSSING.
Unpublished paper. Available at Indian-Eskimo Economic Development Branch,
Development Services Division, Department of Indian Affairs and Northern
Development, Ottawa. 33 pp.

Results of a study focusing on the feasibility of different forms of transportation from the mainland to Christian Island Indian Reserve No. 30, Ontario, are presented. The history and development of Christian Island and beneficial effects of improved transportation are outlined. CCV

OTTAWA

2412 **BAUMAN   ROBERT F**
1960-1961
OTTAWA FLEETS AND IROQUOIS FRUSTRATION. Northwest Ohio Quarterly
33:6-40.

Ottawa supremacy in the Upper Great Lakes region in the 17th century is the concern of this paper. Ottawa-Iroquois-Huron intertribal and territorial relations are discussed. Ottawa intratribal relations and characteristics are examined coupled with a study of that nation's region of occupancy and activity during the first half of the 17th century. IVY

2413 **BAUMAN   ROBERT F**
1963
THE OTTAWAS OF THE LAKES 1615-1766 PART 2: THE HEYDAY OF THE
OTTAWA SUPREMACY OVER THE GREAT LAKES FUR TRADE, 1660-1701.
Northwest Ohio Quarterly 35:69-100.

Ottawa power was strengthened by their alliance with Huron survivors resulting in a successful trading system. Ottawa-Huron and Sioux conflicts are discussed. IVY

2414 **BAUMAN   ROBERT F**
1964
THE OTTAWA TRADING SYSTEM (PART 1). Northwest Ohio Quarterly 36:60-78.

In the 2nd half of the 17th century in the Great Lakes region, the Ottawa dominated the fur trade. The Ottawa system of trade centering at Michilimackinac is analyzed and the effects of beaver price disparity at Montreal and Albany are discussed. IVY

2415 **BAUMAN   ROBERT F**
1964
THE OTTAWA TRADING SYSTEM (PART 2): KEYSTONE OF THE GREAT
LAKES BEAVER TRADE. Northwest Ohio Quarterly 36:146-167.

Examining the extent of beaver and fur production by the Five Nations after 1650 and the efforts and methods of the Iroquois to gain the beaver skins of the Ottawa trading system, it is concluded that the Iroquois gained nothing by their aggressions upon the Huron nations other than a new and more potent trading rival.   IVY

2416   **GREENMAN   E F**
1962
THREE MICHIGAN WAMPUM BELTS. Michigan Archaeologist 8:16-19.

A discussion of 3 wampum belts includes a drawing of a wampum belt made in 1852 by Reverend George Hallen from an original lent him by Assiginack, Ottawa chief at Manitowaning on Manitoulin Island, Ontario.   IVY

2417   **KURATH   GERTRUDE P**
1964
OTTAWA INDIAN CATHOLIC HYMNS. Folklorist 8:105-107.

Special hymns in the Ottawa language sung at certain festivals show the European folk song style of melodies. This is explained by the fact that many of the 19th century missionaries, Jesuits and Fransiscans, were German or Austrian. Transcriptions of 2 hymns are included.   IVY

2418   **WILLIAM L SEARS AND ASSOCIATES LIMITED**
1967
ROAD PROGRAMMING STUDY FOR THE MANITOULIN UNCEDED INDIAN RESERVE. Unpublished paper. Available from National Library of Canada. 68 pp.

The road system of the Manitoulin Island Unceded Indian Reserve has been examined and evaluated to determine what improvements are necessary to bring the roadway system to adequate condition and serviceabilty. Listed in detail are the procedures followed, the conditions observed, and the financial considerations made. Also included are plans, charts, graphs, and tables.   IVY

2419   **WOLFF   ELDON G**
1965
STARING HAIRS. Lore 15:107-109.

Seventeenth century sources are utilized to discover the aboriginal costumes, method of ornamentation, and hairstyles of the Ottawa of the Great Lakes Region.   IVY

SARSI

2420   **FRANK E PRICE AND ASSOCIATES LTD.**
1969
TSO-TINA FARM AND RANCH PROPOSAL. Unpublished paper. Available from National Library of Canada. 38 pp.

It is proposed that Mr. Harley Crowchild, Mr. Amos Many Wounds, and Mr. Rupert Crowchild of the Sarcee Indian Reserve, Alberta, form a limited corporation. Leases have been approved by the Sarcee band council to rent areas of land to these individuals for development (agriculture and ranching). Long term feasibility of the project based on long term projections of land use is analyzed.   IVY

2421   **HUBERT   KENNETH W**
1969
A STUDY OF THE ATTITUDES OF NON-INDIAN CHILDREN TOWARD
INDIAN CHILDREN IN AN INTEGRATED URBAN ELEMENTARY SCHOOL.
M.Ed. Thesis. Department of Curriculum and Instruction. University of Calgary. 73 pp.
Available from National Library of Canada.

Attitudes of non-Indian children in an integrated urban elementary school toward Indian children are examined. Using a sample of 455 grade 4, 5 and 6 pupils from the integrated experimental school and 569 pupils in grades 4, 5, and 6 from 3 comparison
schools, semantic differential tests were administered as well as a knowledge test constructed to reveal the relationshiop between knowledge and attitude. For the attitude
test, the children were asked to rate 6 concepts - "friend," "Negro," "Indian," "White
Man," "Eskimo," and "Savage," according to a 7 point bipolar scale. Twenty-four multi-
ple choice questions about Indians and Sarcee Indians in particular made up the
knowledge test. The major findings of the study indicated that contact with Indian children in an urban integrated elementary school increased non-Indian children's
knowledge about Indians. There was not, however, any significant change in non-Indian
children's attitudes toward Indians as a result of the contact experience. DGW

2422   **STANLEY ASSOCIATES ENGINEERING LTD.**
1970
A SOCIO-ECONOMIC AND RESOURCE EVALUATION STUDY OF THE
SARCEE INDIAN RESERVE. Unpublished paper. Available at Indian-Eskimo
Economic Development Branch, Development Services Division, Department of Indian
Affairs and Northern Development, Ottawa. 84 pp.

Social, educational, and existing economic and physical conditions on the Sarcee Indian
Reserve are reviewed. Evaluation of these data and consultation with the Indian citizens
are the bases for recommendations of agricultural, recreational, industrial, and urban
development. Projects proposed for immediate initiation include a mobile home park, an
overnight tent and trailer park, and a secondary homes development. CCV

SLAVE

2423   **COX   BRUCE**
1970
LAND RIGHTS OF THE SLAVEY INDIANS AT HAY RIVER, N.W.T. The Western
Canadian Journal of Anthropology 2(1):150-155.

The provisions of Treaties 8 and 11 for the Athabascan peoples of the Mackenzie River
drainage basin are discussed. Assessing unfulfilled treaty provisions and the current land
situation, the Hay River Slavey advocate reserves for Northwest Territories Indians.
IVY

2424   **DE VOS GEORGE**
1961
SYMBOLIC ANALYSIS IN THE CROSS-CULTURAL STUDY OF PERSONALITY.
In Studying Personality Cross-Culturally. Bert Kaplan, ed. New York: Harper and Row.
pp. 599-634.

A Slavey Indian family is included in a series of case studies whose Rorschach responses were analyzed. The Slavey material was derived from a paper being prepared by McNeish, De Vos, and Carterette and includes a brief review of family behavior and interaction patterns as well as interpretations of individual Rorschachs.   CCV

2425   **FOWLER   H L,   PHALEN   J T**
1963
THE GREAT SLAVE LAKE AREA: ITS POTENTIAL FOR THE DEVELOPMENT OF CO-OPERATIVES: A REPORT FOR THE NORTHWEST TERRITORIES COUNCIL.   Ottawa: Co-operative Union of Canada. 20 pp.

Results of a 12-day preliminary survey in the Great Slave Lake area by a 2-man team in 1963 are reported. Settlements visited were Fort Smith, Fort Resolution, Snowdrift, Yellowknife, Fort Simpson, Jean Marie River, Fort Providence, and Hay River. Present economic activities, needs, and potential for development are reviewed briefly for each settlement. Planned exploitation of the human and natural resources of the area would provide a reasonable life style for the inhabitants. This would necessitate guided community development, co-operative projects, and government aid in the form of capital resources, technical assistance, and training programs.   CCV

2426   **HELM   JUNE**
1961
THE LYNX POINT PEOPLE: THE DYNAMICS OF A NORTHERN ATHAPASKAN BAND. National Museum of Canada Bulletin 176. Ottawa: Queen's Printer. 193 pp.

Fieldwork among the Slave Indians of Lynx Point, near Fort Simpson, was conducted in 1951-1952, and visits in 1954 and 1955. The first 3 chapters are a modified Ph.D. thesis. Chapter 4 is new material . The ecology, economics, social organization, and religion of the Lynx Point people are discussed. The author stresses that the world of Lynx Point is a true community. Chapter 4 deals with cooperative economic ventures, atypical of Slave Indians. These activities are explained by the traditional society and culture, community motives, historical factors, and individual personalities. The author leaves unanswered her questions of future development.   JSL

2427   **HELM   JUNE,   DE VOS G A,   et al.**
1963
VARIATIONS IN PERSONALITY AND EGO IDENTIFICATION WITHIN A SLAVE INDIAN KIN-COMMUNITY. In Contributions to Anthropology, 1960. Part II. National Museum of Canada Bulletin 190. Ottawa: Queen's Printer. pp. 94-138.

Projective tests administered to 16 subjects representing 3 families, and data from observation of the Lynx Point Slave provide the moded personality configuration and variations from the mode.   JSL

2428   **HIGGINS   G**
1969
THE LOWER LIARD REGION: A.E.S.R. No. 68/3. Ottawa: Queen's Printer. 275 pp.

An economic survey is produced from fieldwork done in the Lower Liard River area from June through August of 1968. An overview of the physical environment, communications, and natural resources is presented. In addition, data on living conditions, income, and employment opportunities for native populations are included in the chapters on populations, current economic activities, and potential for economic growth.   CCV

2429   **MACAULAY   ALEXANDER JAMES**
1968
WATERFOWL UTILIZATION BY A GROUP OF SLAVE INDIANS: A PREDATOR-PREY RELATIONSHIP. M.S. Thesis. Department of Zoology. University of Alberta. 73 pp.

An investigation was conducted during the summers of 1966 and 1967 into natural resource utilization by the Slave of Habay, Alberta. Waterfowl was revealed as the primary prey species during the open water period. Documented are hunting methods, the magnitude of the kill, species selectivity, age and sex selectivity, hunting efficiency, and utilization of the kill. A decline in the prey population coupled with a greater availability of jobs led to a decline in hunting in 1967. Slave utilization of other resources (both animal and plant) is discussed.   TSA

2430   **TETSO   JOHN**
1964
TRAPPING IS MY LIFE. Fort Simpson, N.W.T.: Sacred Heart Mission. 84 pp.

Diary entries covering approximately 2 years describe the life of a Slavey Indian working his trapline in the Mackenzie area.   IVY

2431   **TETSO   JOHN**
1970
TRAPPING IS MY LIFE. Toronto: Martin. 116 pp.

In addition to materials published previously (1964), this edition contains letters from John Tetso to Claire V. Molson (pages 99-116).   IVY

TUTCHONE

2432   **ARCAND   BERNARD**
1966
ETHNOGRAPHIE DES TUTCHONE: ORGANISATION SOCIO-ECONOMIQUE ET PROCESSUS ACCULTURATIF. M.A. Thesis. Departement d'Anthropologie. Universite de Montreal. 156 pp.

The data for this thesis were collected in the summer of 1965. The study is directed toward the economy of a group of hunters and fishermen and its relation to the environment, and in addition examines the structure and the leadership of large social units. After a short introduction on the environment, the traditional life of the Carmacks groups around 1840 is described. A characterization of the period of transition is followed by an analysis of the contemporary social situation. In his conclusion, the author builds a theoretical framework to gather all the aspects of the acculturation process.   DD

NORTHWEST COAST

2433   **n.d.**
THE COURTENAY CENTENNIAL POLE. Unpublished paper. Available from Provincial Museum, Victoria, B.C. 2 pp.

This report relates the stories of the mythical figures of the totem pole erected in front of the Tourist Bureau building in Courtenay, one of a series carved specifically for the "Route of the Haidas"which stretches from Victoria to Prince Rupert.   IVY

2434   **1968**
DEATH AT AN EARLY AGE. The Labour Gazette 68:190-194.

In December, 1967, the Southern Vancouver Island Tribal Federation of British Columbia presented a brief to the federal government. It stressed the large percentage of Indians who die before 34 years of age because they have tired of living. Drawing heavily from the recommendations and observations of the Hawthorn Report, this brief calls upon Canada to right its wrongs against the Indian people.   ADG

2435   **ANDREWS   RALPH W**
1960
INDIAN PRIMITIVE. Seattle: Superior. 175 pp.

Illustrated by photographs taken by pioneers, an attempt is made to reconstruct the life style of several Northwest Coast tribes as it was before White contact. Warfare, mythology, ecology, and material culture are described for different tribal groups. The correlation between particular tribal manufacturing activities and intertribal economic relationships is discussed.   CCV

2436   **AVERKIEVA   U P**
1966
SLAVERY AMONG THE INDIANS OF NORTH AMERICA. Translated by G. R. Elliott. Victoria, B.C.: Victoria College. 138 pp.

Slavery among the Indians of British Columbia's Northwest Coast tribes is discussed from a review of literature and analysis of folklore. In addition to the subsistence activities and life style on the Northwest Coast attention is devoted to the concept of property, division of labor, the economic significance of slavery, the social position of slaves, and the ideology involving slavery.   CCV

2437   **AYRE   ROBERT HUGH**
1961
SKETCO THE RAVEN. Toronto: MacMillan. 183 pp.

The Raven legends common to the Indians of the Northwest Coast inspire this narrative. The Raven, a hero of Northwest Coast mythology, is credited with having given the Indians the sun, moon, stars, and fire. The alternation of the tides, game migrations, and birds' colorful plumage are also attributed to the Raven.   CCV

2438   **B.C. INDIAN ARTS & WELFARE SOCIETY. Totem Committee.**
n.d.

BRIEF ON INDIAN ART PRESERVATION. Unpublished paper. Available from
National Library of Canada. 3 pp.

The need for an extended program of preservation of Indian totemic art in British Columbia is indicated.   IVY

2439   **BADNER   MINO**
1966
THE PROTRUDING TONGUE AND RELATED MOTIFS IN THE ART STYLES
OF THE AMERICAN NORTHWEST COAST, NEW ZEALAND AND CHINA. In
Two Studies of Art in the Pacific Area. By Mino Badner and Robert Heine-Geldern.
Horn-Wien: Verlag Ferdinand Berger & Sohne. pp. 7-44.

The cultural context of the various combinations in which the long tongue appears in
Northwest Coast art is investigated. Parallels in New Zealand art permit speculation of
late Chou influence in both. The discussion is illustrated by 25 pages of photographs.
CCV

2440   **BANFILL   B J**
1966
WITH THE INDIANS OF THE PACIFIC. Toronto: Ryerson Press. 176 pp.

The impressions of a year at an isolated British Columbia coastal reserve are recounted
by a nurse. Besides the health of the children in the residential school her responsibilities
included midwifery, preliminary diagnosis, and care of disease among residents of the
Indian village. Tuberculosis was frequently encountered. Her experiences and difficulties
reveal details of diet, housing, schooling, and general hygiene. Observations of socialization and burial practices, Indian crafts, use of medicinal barks and herbs as well as
folklore are reported.   CCV

2441   **BARBEAU   MARIUS**
1961
TSIMSYAN MYTHS - ILLUSTRATED. National Museum of Canada Bulletin 174.
Ottawa: Queen's Printer. 97 pp.

One Haida myth and 15 Tsimshian myths and tales were collected by William Beynon in
the 1950's. Only English translations are presented. Twenty-one pictures of Haida and
Bella Coola art are interspersed with the myths. Five of the Haida illustrations are described at the end of the book.   JSL

2442   **BARROW   SUSAN H L,   GRABERT   GARLAND F**
1968
ARTS OF A VANISHED ERA: AN EXHIBITION OF THE WHATCOM MUSEUM
OF HISTORY AND ART, BELLINGHAM, WASHINGTON. Bellingham, WA:
Whatcom Museum. 63 pp.

A collection of Northwest Coast ceremonial and utilitarian objects in contemporary and
traditional style is displayed and catalogued by the Whatcom Museum. Artistic and
crafted works are presented from the Haida, Kwakiutl, Nootka, Tsimshian, Tlingit, and
Coast Salish tribes. Each article is named and the material, size, owner, and often tribal
source are noted. Background information is provided concerning the general ecology,

the competitive nature of Northwest Coast society, form and media of artistic expression, and the influences of contact and trade on the life style and art. A discussion of the pre-contact artist and craftsman is included.   CCV

2443   **BIRKET-SMITH   KAJ**
1964
AN ANALYSIS OF THE POTLATCH INSTITUTION OF NORTH AMERICA. Folk 6(2):5-13.

Analyzing the potlatch among different Northwest Coast groups, similarities and differences are compared. Varying explanations of the institution are given.   IVY

2444   **BIRKET-SMITH   KAJ**
1967
STUDIES IN CIRCUMPACIFIC CULTURE RELATIONS: POTLATCH AND FEASTS OF MERIT. Royal Danish Academy of Sciences and Letters Studies in Circumpacific Culture Relations 1. Copenhagen: Munksgaard. 98 pp.

The potlatch is examined to investigate the parallels drawn by many writers between it and feasts of merit in East Asia and Oceania. The background and function of potlatching, the importance of wealth, and the significance of life crises are reviewed for Northwest Coast society. Tribal variations are noted. It is concluded that a misconception of the basic ideas of the potlatch has led to parallels being made with other institutions in distant parts of the world.   CCV

2445   **BRONNEUR   FREDERIC**
1962
INDIAN LEGENDS OF THE WEST COAST AND THEIR RELATION TO THE FRENCH LANGUAGE. Culture 28:44-50.

The importance of salvaging Indian folklore is emphasized with particular reference to the Northwest Coast. The literary potential of Indian folktales is discussed.   CCV

2446   **BUDIC   CAROLINE MARY**
1964
WOLF RITUAL DANCES.OF THE NORTHWEST COAST INDIANS. M.S. Thesis. Department of Physical Education. University of Washington. 121 pp. Available from Library, York University.

The wolf ritual dances of the Northwest Coast Indians are reconstructed from a survey of historic materials and literature. In order to study steps, gestures, components, and concepts the dances were divided into 4 categories: animal, bird, marine life, and miscellaneous objects and supernaturals. Details of costuming and tribal variations are included. Analysis suggests that the wolf ritual dances were misconstrued by early observers and that most dances are based on the concept of the Warrior Spirit, Lightning Serpent, and Thunderbird.   CCV

2447   **BURNHAM   HAROLD B**
1967
TSHMISHIAN AND TLINGIT. Canadian Antiques Collector 2(7):16-18.

The origin, motifs, and the weaving technique of the pattern blankets of the Tsimshian and Tlingit are discussed.   IVY

2448   **BURNHAM   HAROLD B**
1968
CATALOGUE OF ETHNOGRAPHIC TEXTILES OF THE NATIONAL MUSEUM OF MAN: AREA 4. Unpublished paper. Available at National Museum of Man, Ethnology Division, Ottawa, with permission of the author. 150 pp.

Sixty-nine items from the National Museum of Man's ethnographic textiles collection, most of them blankets, woven bands, or dance aprons, are presented in a catalog of Northwest Coast materials. Each item is accompanied by a photograph and a notation of location, attribution, provenance, name, condition, measurements, description, and technical notes concerning fabrication or provenance.   CCV

2449   **BUTTERWORTH   PAUL**
1969
THE EFFECTS OF MATERIAL AND NONMATERIAL REINFORCEMENT ON THE PERSEVERANCE BEHAVIOR OF INDIAN CHILDREN. M.A. Thesis. Department of Education. University of Victoria. 60 pp.

Sixty Indian children, aged 6 to 8 years, from the Tsartlip and Duncan reserves at Brentwood Bay and Duncan, British Columbia respectively, were tested to discover the effectiveness of material and non-material reinforcement in increasing perseverance behavior. The children were divided into 2 groups according to the degree of parental participation in school activities. In the low parental participation group perseverance was longer with material than non-material reinforcement. In the high parental participation group no significant difference in perseverance scores appeared.   CCV

2450   **CARL   G CLIFFORD**
1969
TREASURES FROM THE NORTHWEST COAST. Canadian Antiques Collector 4(11):56-57.

A general discussion of Indian material collected by the Provincial Museum in British Columbia is presented.   IVY

2451   **CHAPMAN   ANNE**
1965
MATS TOTEMIQUES: AMERIQUES: AMERIQUE DU NORD, COTE NORD-OUEST. Objets et Mondes: La Revue du Musee de l'Homme 5:175-196.

Totem poles in the Museum National d'Histoire Naturelle, Paris, are described, illustrated, and explained. The significance of the totems is examined as are their sources in mythology.   CCV

2452   **CHOWNING   ANN**
1962
RAVEN MYTHS IN NORTHWESTERN NORTH AMERICA AND NORTHEASTERN ASIA. Arctic Anthropology 1(1):1-5.

The origin, distribution, and diffusion of the Raven myths are reconsidered. From earlier ethnographic reports it is concluded that the myth spread from Northwest North America to Siberia through the Eskimos.   WRC

2453   **CLEMSON   DONOVAN**
1966
SCENES ALONG THE SKEENA. Canadian Geographical Journal 72:154-159.

Totem poles are one of the attractions for a traveler traversing the Skeena River.   IVY

2454   **COLLINS   BARBARA ROSE,   DOUHANIUK   WILLIAM,   et al.**
1966
INDIANS IN VANCOUVER: AN EXPLORATIVE OVERVIEW OF THE PROCESS OF SOCIAL ADAPTATION AND IMPLICATIONS FOR RESEARCH. M.S.W. Thesis. School of Social Work. University of British Columbia. 155 pp.

Unstructured interviews conducted in 1966 elicited opinions on the process of Indian social adaptation, the means of facilitating this process, and the feasibility of research in this area. Of the 16 experts interviewed, 5 were Indians in administrative positions, 6 were non-Indians highly involved with Indian people, and 5 were Indian Affairs employees. Interviews conducted with 20 Indians encountered largely on a casual basis in Vancouver were centered generally on education, language, reserves, employment, urban milieu, integration, and assimilation.   CCV

2455   **COUTURE   A,   EDWARDS   J O**
1964
ORIGIN OF COPPER USED BY CANADIAN WEST COAST INDIANS IN THE MANUFACTURE OF ORNAMENTAL PLAQUES. In Contributions to Anthropology, 1961-62. Part II. National Museum of Canada Bulletin 194. Ottawa: Queen's Printer. pp. 199-220.

This is a condensed version of the authors' 1962 report. Nine coppers, chosen from 65 coppers in the National Museum, were examined to determine if the copper was native or European. The sample included Bella Coola, Kwakiutl, and Haida forms. It is concluded that the original sheet copper was of European manufacture with subsequent fabrication by Indians, perhaps with Europeans' assistance.   JSL

2456   **DOCKSTADER   FREDERICK J**
1962
INDIAN ART IN AMERICA. Greenwich, CT: New York Graphic Society. 224 pp.

A collection demonstrating North American Indian artistic qualities and everyday craftmanship is presented to include important regions, pre-eminent tribes and major artistic techniques. The material is divided into pre- and post-contact (historic) periods. From the historic period items 80-144 are almost exclusively attributed to Canadian Northwest Coast tribes: Haida, Tlingit, Kwakiutl, Niska, Tsimshian, and Gitksan. Each specimen is named and accompanied by ethnographic information concerning source, use, size, and material. The Indian artist, media, artistic forms, and regional variations in art are presented as is a discussion on the methods employed in dating Indian art.   CCV

2457   **DRUCKER   PHILIP**
1965
CULTURES OF THE NORTH PACIFIC COAST. San Francisco: Chandler. 243 pp.

Major established findings and theories as well as over 30 years of fieldwork are represented in a comprehensive study of the Northwest Coast culture area. The material is presented under general chapter headings: habitat, economy and technology, social and political organization, religion and ritual, and population and cultural subdivisions. The Tsimshian, Nootka, Yurok, and Chinook are individually described in greater detail and the final chapter is devoted to a discussion of culture change and modernization in Alaska and British Columbia. Numerous illustrations and photographs of fishing gear and techniques as well as of objects of material culture accompany the text.   CCV

2458   **DUFF   WILSON**
1963
THUNDERBIRD PARK. Victoria, B.C.: Queen's Printer. 30 pp.

Following a brief historical sketch of the Northwest Coast Indians and their art style, totem poles are classified according to their function. Information on interpreting totem poles, their age, and their construction is given. An illustrated guide to the exhibits in Thunderbird Park concludes the booklet.   IVY

2459   **DUFF   WILSON**
1964
CONTRIBUTIONS OF MARIUS BARBEAU TO WEST COAST ETHNOLOGY.
Anthropologica N.S. 6:63-96.

Briefly discussed is the wealth of ethnographic data collected by Marius Barbeau and his field associate, William Beynon, relating to Tsimshian narratives (semi-mythical histories) and social organization. More intensively, Barbeau's interpretation of persistent Asiatic migration to the Northwest Coast by way of the Aleutian Islands and his belief that the crest system, totem poles, exogamy, and secret societies are recent innovations brought by the Siberian nomads or contact with Europeans are critically analyzed. Not accepting Barbeau's hypotheses, and using essentially the same evidence, the author presents the highly distinctive culture of the Northwest tribes as an indigenous and aboriginal accomplishment.   IVY

2460   **DUFF   WILSON,   HOLM   BILL,   et al.**
1967
ARTS OF THE RAVEN: MASTERWORKS BY THE NORTHWEST COAST
INDIAN. Vancouver: Vancouver Art Gallery. 110 pp.

A catalog is presented of the Vancouver Gallery's 1967 exhibition of Northwest Coast Indian art from the Haida, Kwakiutl, Tsimshian, Tlingit, and Bella Coola tribes. Each item is listed with its name, tribal source, size, owner, and component materials. Photographs of 54 of these articles are included in the catalog. Background information is provided concerning the people and the ecology of the Northwest Coast as well as discussion of the significance, media, and form of their art. An analysis of the Northwest Coast art forms and symbolism is treated in an additional article. An appreciation of Northwest Coast art is presented by a Haida art authority and craftsman.   CCV

2461   **FRASER   DOUGLAS**
1962
PRIMITIVE ART. London: Thames and Hudson. 320 pp.

A general discussion of primitive art is followed by chapters devoted specifically to Africa, Asia-Oceania, and America. Pages 275-312 contain a brief survey of Iroquois (mostly wooden masks) and Plains art as well as a more detailed discussion of Northwest Coast art. Individual examination of Coast Salish, Nootka, Kwakiutl, Bella Coola, Tsimshian, Haida, and Tlingit art, particularly the use of masks, is included. Speculation concerning East Asian influence on North American Indian culture and art concludes the text which is accompanied by illustrations.   CCV

2462   **FRASER   DOUGLAS**
1966
THE HERALDING WOMAN: A STUDY IN DIFFUSION. In The Many Faces of Primitive Art: A Critical Anthology. Douglas Fraser, ed. Englewood Cliffs, NJ: Prentice-Hall. pp. 36-99.

The cultural contexts and stylistic variations in which is displayed the female figure, symmetrically flanked by 2 other beings, is reviewed. This theme in Northwest Coast art and mythology is explored on pages 57-60 and accompanied by photographs.   CCV

2463   **FRASER   WILLIAM DONALD**
1969
MENTAL ABILITIES OF BRITISH COLUMBIA INDIAN CHILDREN. M.A. Thesis. Faculty of Education. University of British Columbia. 65 pp.

Indian pupils aged 6 to 9, including 27 children from Vancouver School District and 35 rural children from Merritt School District, were administered the Stanford-Binet Intelligence Scale Forum L-M. Results were examined for differences between urban and rural Indian groups. It is concluded that Indian children rate lower (but not uniformly so) than White children on abilities requisite to successful performance in school. Further research to determine remedial programs is proposed and it is suggested that such programs would be equally suitable for rural and urban Indian pupils.   CCV

2464   **GADDES   W R,   MCKENZIE   AUDREY,   et al.**
1968
PSYCHOMETRIC INTELLIGENCE AND SPATIAL IMAGERY IN TWO NORTHWEST INDIAN AND TWO WHITE GROUPS OF CHILDREN. Journal of Social Psychology 75:35-52.

One hundred and twenty-four Salish, Kwakiutl, and White children between 6 and 14 were administered 4 culture-reduced tests. Statistical analysis revealed no superiority or inferiority of spatial imagery for the groups, although it had been hypothesized that the Indian pupils would be superior in spatial ability because of their distinctive cultural art forms. The non-significance of the findings was discussed in terms of both the possible cultural bias of the tests used and the apparent sociological advantage the rural and urban White children had over even the urban-dwelling Salish subjects. The article concludes that the hypothesis might have been supported had genuinely culture-free intelligence tests been available.   ADG

2465 **GRUNFELD FREDERIC V**
1969
INDIAN GIVING: BEING A TREATISE ON THE CURIOUS BUT EXEMPLARY
CUSTOM OF THE POTLATCH: OR HOW TO KILL YOUR ENEMY WITH
KINDNESS, BANKRUPT YOUR COMPETITOR WITH GENEROSITY, BURY
YOUR MOTHER-IN-LAW WITH USELESS PRESENTS, AND BECOME POORER
BUT RICHER BY GETTING RID OF EVERYTHING. Horizon 11(1):46-47.

A tongue-in-cheek commentary on the potlatch is given. Potlatching was essentially a
primitive, pre-literate form of investment banking. IVY

2466 **GUNN SISVAN WILLIAM**
1965
THE TOTEM POLES IN STANLEY PARK, VANCOUVER B.C. Totem Poles of
British Columbia Series I. 2nd Edition (B.C. Centenary Issue). Vancouver: W. E. G.
Macdonald. 24 pp.

Following a general introduction of the nature and function of totem poles, the following are specifically discussed: Skedans mortuary pole, Nhe-is-bik salmon pole, thunderbird houseposts, Wakias pole, Sis-kiulas pole, pole of the Yakdzi myth, thunderbird dynasty totem. Illustrations accompany text. IVY

2467 **GUNN SISVAN WILLIAM**
1966
TOTEMIC MEDICINE AND SHAMANISM AMONG THE NORTHWEST
AMERICAN INDIANS. The American Medical Association Journal 196:700-706.

Supernatural spirits and totems played an important role in the lives of Indians of the
Northwest Coast with respect to disease. Shamans were the primitive psychotherapists,
tending the psychosomatic needs of the natives by interceding with the supernatural
world on the patient's behalf. Many of the Indian's needs were met by lay practitioners
and there were some forms of non-shamanistic medicine. Today few shamen exist. ADG

2468 **GUNTHER ERNA**
1961
INDIAN CRAFT ENTERPRISE IN THE NORTHWEST. Human Organization
20:216-218.

The present absence of aboriginal arts and crafts among Northwest Coast Indians in
Canada and the United States is analyzed. Decline in traditional purpose, modern marketing techniques, and the import of foreign replicas are viewed as reasons for the disappearance of traditional crafts from the regional native economy. Suggested are methods
of reintroducing these activities for modern ends. WRC

2469 **GUNTHER ERNA**
1962
NORTHWEST COAST INDIAN ART: AN EXHIBIT AT THE SEATTLE WORLD'S
FAIR FINE ARTS PAVILION. Seattle: University of Washington Press. 101 pp.

The Seattle World's Fair exhibit of Northwest Coast Indian Art is catalogued. Northwest Coast ecology and life style; artistic styles, forms, and materials; the utilitarian roles

of art forms; and the historical perspective of exhibited articles are described in the accompanying text. The text is supplemented by photographs of 104 of these items. Their description, material, size, and often tribal attribution and cultural significance are provided in the catalogue notation.   CCV

2470   **GUNTHER   ERNA**
1963
WEST COAST INDIAN ART GOES TO THE FAIR. The Beaver 292(Spring):4-13.

Northwest Coast Indian Art was part of the Fine Arts Exhibition at the Seattle World's Fair in 1962. The choice of pieces and their collection is the concern of this article.   IVY

2471   **GUNTHER   ERNA**
1966
ART IN THE LIFE OF THE NORTH WEST COAST INDIANS WITH A CATALOGUE OF NORTHWEST INDIAN ART AT PORTLAND ART MUSEUM. Seattle: Superior.

Northwest Coast Indian art is reviewed with emphasis on ethnographic information detailing its relationship with folklore and cultural setting. Included are the characteristic features of Northwest Coast art, the role of art in daily life, occupations and dress, the function of art in ceremonial life, the relationship with the supernatural, art forms intended for trade, and the Rasmussen collection of the Portland Art Museum. Numerous photographs of this collection accompany the text with source, age, materials, size, function, and interpretation of motif.   CCV

2472   **HARNER   MICHAEL J,   ELSASSER   ALBERT B**
1965
ART OF THE NORTHWEST COAST: AN EXHIBITION AT THE ROBERT H. LOWIE MUSEUM OF ANTHROPOLOGY OF THE UNIVERSITY OF CALIFORNIA, BERKELEY MARCH 26-OCTOBER 17, 1965. Berkeley: Lowie Museum of Anthropology, University of California. 112 pp.

Photographs of 88 articles, including masks and articles used in ritualistic productions, are presented in the catalogue of an exhibition held in 1965 at the Robert H. Lowie Museum. The introduction provides background information to the collection. Each photograph is accompanied by notation of name, size, materials, date, provenience, and use.   CCV

2473   **HARRIS   CHRISTIE**
1963
ONCE UPON A TOTEM. New York: Atheneum. 148 pp.

Five folktales illustrating the significance of totems and potlatch on the Northwest Coast are recounted. The origin of names and clan or family emblems is a dominant theme.   CCV

2474   **HASSRICK   ROYAL B,   BACH   CILE M**
1960
INDIAN ART OF THE AMERICAS. Denver Art Museum Quarterly (Indian Leaflet Series), Winter 1960. 108 pp.

A survey of North American Indian art includes and illustrates works of the Pacific Northwest (pages 76-95). IVY

2475 **HAWTHORN HARRY B**
1961
THE ARTIST IN TRIBAL SOCIETY: THE NORTHWEST COAST. In The Artist in Tribal Society: Proceedings of a Symposium held at the Royal Anthropological Institute. Marian W. Smith, ed. London: Routledge and Kegan Paul. pp. 59-70.

The role of the carver in Northwest Coast societies is presented regarding recruitment, social response, motivation, and rewards. Mungo Martin, a master carver from Fort Rupert, was the source of much of the data. In commissioning a carver for a special project, it was required that he come from the individual's paternal group. The carver's task was then to communicate in wood the main meaning of the work for which he had been hired. Individuality and originality in style was considerable, consequently the authorship of a carving was recognizable. There was a balance, however, between the expected traditional style and the aesthetic and individual goals of the craftsman. DGW

2476 **HOLM BILL**
1965
NORTHWEST COAST INDIAN ART: AN ANALYSIS OF FORM. Seattle: University of Washington Press. 115 pp.

An analysis of the form of Northwest Coast art is presented with numerous graphic and photographic illustrations. Examination and discussion of 392 specimens reveals a highly developed system operative in the organization of form and space in 2-dimensional design allowing for a wide range of application. The concept of a continuous primary formline pattern elaborated with secondary complexes and tertiary elements is important as are the prescribed usage of the colors black, red, and blue-green and the use of a set series of design units variable in arrangement and proportion according to needs of space and design. A relationship between Northwest Coast 2-dimensional art and dance movement is suggested. CCV

2477 **HYMES DELL**
1965
SOME NORTH PACIFIC COAST POEMS: A PROBLEM IN ANTHROPOLOGICAL PHILOLOGY. American Anthropologist 67:316-341.

The discrepancies between literal and aesthetic translations of Amerindian folklore materials are discussed. With reference to 6 Kwakiutl and Haida poems the importance of linguistics in developing an anthropological philology is emphasized for the re-analysis and re-evaluation of Indian poetry. This effort is viewed as a cultural index which can provide a deeper appreciation of the original texts. WRC

2478 **INGLIS GORDON B**
1970
NORTHWEST AMERICAN MATRILINY: THE PROBLEM OF ORIGINS. Ethnology 9:149-159.

Origin theories of matrilineage among Northwest Coast tribes are reconsidered and an alternative approach is offered. Based on the assumption that ecologically limited residence patterns affect social structures, the rise of matrilocality on the Coast and its diffusion to the interior Athapascans are examined historically. Male and female subsistence activities are viewed as interrelated variables and localization of newly acquired activities is postulated as a major criterion in determining the shift from matrilocal to avunculocal residence. It is concluded that the matrilineal structures of northwest North America are neither anomalous nor remnants of earlier Asiatic forms, but arose and are maintained as advantageous to environmental exploitation.   WRC

2479   **JACOBS   MELVILLE**
1960
HUMOR AND SOCIAL STRUCTURE IN AN ORAL LITERATURE. In Culture in History: Essays in Honor of Paul Radin. Stanley Diamond, ed.   New York: Columbia University Press. pp. 181-189.

The classification of humor resulting from analysis of Chinook oral literature is presented. Types of humor are related to specific areas of social stress, and discussion is extended briefly to parallels with other Northwest Coast tribes.   CCV

2480   **JAMIESON   STUART**
1961
NATIVE INDIANS AND THE TRADE UNION MOVEMENT IN BRITISH COLUMBIA. Human Organization 20:219-225.

Following a brief history of industrial trends in British Columbia the relationship of Indians and trade unionism is described from 1893 to the present. As examples of the variability of Indian involvement 3 major industries are considered: fishing, forest products, and longshoring. Estimates of membership are made, though difficulty is noted in this regard due to seasonal and casual participation in these occupations. The consolidation of certain industries has presented conditions contrary to traditional Indian life. Decasualization of occupations and technological change are hypothesized as major factors in the decrease of employment opportunities. To the extent that Indians have been involved it is concluded that trade unions are less marked by prejudice and discrimination than other occupations.   WRC

2481   **JONES   JOAN MEGAN**
1968
NORTHWEST COAST BASKETRY AND CULTURE CHANGE. The Thomas Burke Memorial Washington State Museum Research Report 1. Seattle: Thomas Burke Memorial Washington State Museum. 60 pp.

In essentially the same format as the author's thesis, the purpose of this study is to identify basket attributes useful for studying change in baskets. Attributes selected for this study are: construction techniques of basket bottom, body, and rim; decoration style and technique; and shape. Baskets with a known chronology used in this research are from the collections of the Thomas Burke Memorial Washington State Museum in Seattle and Field Museum of Natural History in Chicago. Tribes of the Northwest Coast are grouped into 3 sub-areas, Wakashan group, Coast Salish, and the Northern group (Tlingit, Haida, Tsimshian) and are treated as single geographical units. The method used in this study resembles the method of frequency seriation. Basket attributes are coded and sorted, and these data are used to construct graphs (10-year time intervals) which show the change through time of the frequency of occurence of the basketry modes and thus, changes in the popularity of these modes through time.   IVY

2482   **JORGENSEN   GRACE MAIRI MCINTYRE**
1970
A COMPARATIVE EXAMINATION OF NORTHWEST COAST SHAMANISM.
M.A. Thesis. Department of Anthropology and Sociology. University of British Columbia. 220 pp.

Ethnographic sources have been examined and myths searched for evidence on Northwest Coast shamanism. Data are reviewed presenting shamanism from the perspective of form and structure. Successive chapters discuss shamanism among the Coast Salish, Nootka, Southern Kwakiutl, Bella Coola, Coast Tsimshian, Haida, and Tlingit. Differences in the practice of shamanism are expressed in the public initiation of novice shamans.   TSA

2483   **KEITHAHN   E L**
1964
ORIGIN OF THE "CHIEF'S COPPER"OR "TINNEH". University of Alaska Anthropological Papers 12:59-78.

Evidence is presented to demonstrate that the chief's copper was never made of native copper and appeared after 1774 when commercial copper became available. Its prototype was the treasured copper arrowhead from the interior. The first coppers were made by native craftsmen with European tools and techniques or custom-made by ship's armorers and imported craftsmen. Later, completed chief's coppers manufactured elsewhere flooded the coast, destroying its value as a prestige piece. Twelve plates of coppers accompany the text.   IVY

2484   **KEITHAHN   EDWARD L**
1963
MONUMENTS IN CEDAR. Seattle: Superior. 160 pp.

Numerous photographs of totem poles, house posts, mortuary poles, and other objects of Northwest Coast material culture are presented to illustrate discussion of the totem poles, their origin, interpretation, carving and erection, and relationship to social organization and folklore.   CCV

2485   **KLAVINS   MARTA**
1961
AN EXPLORATORY STUDY OF THE ADJUSTMENT TO HOSPITALIZATION OF TUBERCULOUS INDIANS. M.A. Thesis. Department of Psychology. University of British Columbia. 83 pp.

A summer's study and employment at Miller Bay Indian hospital near Prince Rupert were directed at providing insight into the adjustment tubercular Indians make to hospital environment. In addition to participant observation, semi-structured interviews were conducted with 15 staff members and 15 patients. Focus is on the patient's attitudes toward life, illness, staff, staff-planned social activities, hospital routine, and hospitalization, as well as his reactions to the diagnosis, visitors, alcohol, his treatment by staff, and irregular leaves and discharges. A considerable indication of prejudice among White staff members was found and a wide range of adjustments were observed among patients. It is suggested that reduction of prejudice would be instrumental in facilitating adjustment and a re-evaluation of other aspects of nursing routine whose rigidity impedes adjustment might be useful.   CCV

2486   **LAVIOLETTE   FORREST E**
1961
THE STRUGGLE FOR SURVIVAL: INDIAN CULTURES AND THE PROTESTANT ETHIC IN BRITISH COLUMBIA. Toronto: University of Toronto Press. 201 pp.

Ethnographic and historical sources supported by fieldwork done in 1946 document the British Columbia Indian's struggle against the White man's intrusion into his culture and territory. Attention is given to the conflict surrounding potlatches and land rights and to the eventual development of the Native Brotherhood of British Columbia.   CCV

2487   **LEVI-STRAUSS   CLAUDE**
1963
STRUCTURAL ANTHROPOLOGY. New York: Basic Books. 410 pp.

Seventeen papers representative of Levi-Strauss' application of the structural method of anthropology are compiled. Among the particular interpretations of data, Canadian groups appear briefly, often with reference to Franz Boas' work. The acquisition of supernatural powers, the basis of their effectiveness, and the role of the shaman and his social group in Northwest Coast society (Kwakitul) are examined in the discussion of the nature of the shamanistic complex, Chapter 9. Art forms, in particular split representation, in Asian and Northwest Coast art are compared in Chapter 13.   CCV

2488   **MALIN   EDWARD,   FEDER   NORMAN**
1962
INDIAN ART OF THE NORTHWEST COAST. Denver Art Museum Quarterly (Indian Leaflet Series) Winter, 1962. 90 pp.

The cultural background of the art, including the land and the people, the artist and his materials, and design and symbolism in the art are discussed in Part 1. In Part 2 notes accompany 47 illustrations of selected pieces from the Denver Art Museum collection. IVY

2489   **MCKERVILL   HUGH W**
1967
THE SALMON PEOPLE: THE STORY OF CANADA'S WEST COAST SALMON FISHING INDUSTRY. Sidney, B.C.: Gray's. 187 pp.

From the time of the Tsimshian and the Kwakiutl to the present day, people on the Northwest Coast have depended on salmon for their livelihood. It is their story which is retold - the story of aboriginal Indians who speared for salmon and celebrated special ceremonies during the spawning season, to the canners and commercial fishermen in business today.   DGW

2490   **MURRAY   KEITH A**
1961
THE ROLE OF THE HUDSON'S BAY COMPANY IN PACIFIC NORTHWEST
HISTORY. Pacific Northwest Quarterly 52:24-31.

Hudson's Bay Company policy towards Indians of the Northwest Coast is briefly
stated.   IVY

2491   **MYRON   ROBERT**
1966
MOUNDS, TOWNS AND TOTEMS: INDIANS OF NORTH AMERICA. Cleveland:
World. 127 pp.

Material culture, subsistence activities, warfare activities, potlatch, masks, and totem
poles are described.   IVY

2492   **NELSON   MARY FRANCES**
1968
VOICE OF THE MYTHICAL BEING. M.A. Thesis. Department of Art and
Architecture. University of Idaho. 57 pp.

Mythical beings are often portrayed in the art work of the Haida and Tsimshian. These 2
groups were selected because of the richness of their mythology and their art. The style
of the art and techniques utilized to produce it are described. Myths concerning Raven,
the Bear Mother, Skookum-Oolala, the Wild Woman of the Woods, the Frog, and the
Water Monster are paraphrased and artistic representations of these beings illustrate the
work.   TSA

2493   **PIDDOCKE   STUART MICHAEL**
1960
WERGILD AMONG NORTHWEST COAST INDIANS. M.A. Thesis. Department of
Anthropology. University of British Columbia. 216 pp.

Ethnographic materials pertaining to Northwest Coast societies are reviewed in order to
explain the existence of feud-indemnities or wergild in some and its absence in others.
Social organization, particularly aspects relating to primitive law, chieftanship, legal system, warfare, and feuding are discussed. The presence of wergild is examined in relation
to the presence or absence of conflicting alliances created by divergent marriage rules and
kinship affiliation. Where there are feud indemnities conflicting alliances exist but not
exclusively. It is demonstrated that the Kwakiutl, Nootka, Bella Coola, and Upper Stalo
who had high individual geographic mobility lacked feud-indemnities and the Tlingit,
Haida, Tsimshian, Northwestern Californians, Chinook, and the remainder of the Salish
had low to moderate geographic mobility and feud-indemnities.   CCV

2494   **PRINCETON UNIVERSITY. Art Museum.**
1969
ART OF THE NORTHWEST COAST. Princeton, NJ: Princeton University Art
Museum. 46 pp.

One hundred and nineteen items of Northwest Coast material culture exhibited at the
Princeton University Art Museum from January 22 through March 2, 1969, are cata-
loged. Twelve are illustrated. The name, material, tribal source, and size are noted for

each article. The natural and social settings, materials and techniques, and motifs characteristic of Northwest Coast sculpture are reviewed in the introduction.   CCV

2495   **PYM   HAROLD,   PYM   IRENE,   eds.**
1967
PORT HARDY AND DISTRICT: THE HISTORICAL STORY OF
NORTHERNMOST VANCOUVER ISLAND. n.p.: n.p. 64 pp.

Scattered references are made throughout the booklet to Indians of Vancouver Island and the Northwest Coast. One chapter entitled Indian Notes gives general information on the Kwakiutl Indians. Photographs accompany the text.   IVY

2496   **ROGERS   EDWARD S**
1967
NORTH PACIFIC COAST INDIANS. Canadian Antiques Collector 2(7):19-21.

The elaborate material culture of the Indians of the North Pacific Coast is described.   IVY

2497   **ROGERS   EDWARD S**
1970
INDIANS OF THE NORTH PACIFIC COAST. Toronto: Royal Ontario Museum. 18 pp.

Outlined in brief is the culture type characteristic of the North Pacific Coast culture area. The publication is 1 in a series of 6 introductory guides to the Indians of Canada. Discussed are settlement pattern, social organization, subsistence, trade, technology, clothing, transportation, utensils, warfare, ritual, and present cultural status.   DGW

2498   **SCARGILL   M H**
1968
CANADIANISMS FROM WESTERN CANADA, WITH SPECIAL REFERENCE
TO BRITISH COLUMBIA. The Royal Society of Canada Transactions (Series 4) 6:181-185.

An examination of regional expressions of British Columbia shows that a number of words are of Indian origin, the majority coming from the Chinook Jargon.   IVY

2499   **SHEPHERD   HARVEY L**
1967
INDIANS IN THE CITY: WILL HELP BE TOO LITTLE AND TOO LATE? The United Church Observer N.S. 29(3):19-22.

Robert Sullivan and Pearl Willows, the only full-time workers of the United Church with Indians in Vancouver, report on their work providing assistance and counseling. Urgent needs are better preparation of native Indians for urban life, improved educational facilities, improved job placement facilities, hostels, and improved housing.   IVY

2500   **SHEPHERD   HARVEY L**
1967

THE NEW DOCTORS OF THE INDIAN FRONTIER (FIRST OF THREE PARTS).
The United Church Observer N.S. 29(1):12-15,40.

A visit to 2 church-affiliated hospitals (United Church) at Bella Coola and Bella Bella,
British Columbia, underlines the changes which have occurred in the role of the mission
hospital and its personnel. Provincial and federal contributions provide for hospital operating costs. Excluding doctors, salaries are on a par with the rest of the province. Not
all personnel are United Church people and mission doctors are primarily concerned with
healing and seldom regard themselves as missionaries.   IVY

2501   **SHEPHERD   HARVEY L**
1967
WHAT'S HOLDING BACK THESE MISSION CHURCHES? (SECOND OF A
SERIES). The United Church Observer N.S. 29(2):16-19,45.

The redefined role of the United Church missionaries in British Columbia emphasizing
self-help and local control has resulted in frustration among ministers, conflict among
the hospital staff of mission hospitals, and confusion to Indians who view the role of hospital personnel and teachers as missionaries. Since the Pentecostal Church is attracting
many members, a return to old-style evangelism may be indicated.   IVY

2502   **SIEBERT   ERNA**
1967
NORTH AMERICAN INDIAN ART: MASKS, AMULETS, WOOD CARVINGS
AND CEREMONIAL DRESS FROM THE NORTHWEST COAST. London:
Hamlyn. 204 pp.

With a brief report on the culture and art style of the Indians of the Northwest Coast, the
author introduces the collections of the Museum of Anthropology and Ethnography of
the Academy of Sciences, Leningrad, and the Anthropological Museum of the Lomono-
sov State University in Moscow. The objects include such things as masks, ceremonial
dress, armor, rattles, dishes, wood carvings, shamanistic amulets, household objects, costumes, and head-dresses. The major portion of the objects illustrated were collected prior
to 1830.   DGW

2503   **SIEBERT   ERNA,   FORMAN   WERNER**
1967
L'ART DES INDIENS D'AMERIQUE. Paris: Editions Cercle d'Art. 211 pp.

A collection of Northwest Coast Indian art and material culture in the Leningrad Museum of Anthropology and Ethnography is catalogued. Most of this material was collected by Russian explorers and navigators during the 18th and 19th centuries. Some details of these exploratory voyages are included followed by a review of the physical environment, social organization, life style, subsistence activities in the area, as well as art
forms, tools, media, and use of symbols and color. The collection is composed largely of
wood and stone carved masks, dishes, tools, ceremonial headdresses, rattles, amulets or
charms, and articles of hand-woven clothing.   CCV

2504   **STEWART   JOSEPH L**
1960

THE PROBLEM OF STUTTERING IN CERTAIN NORTH AMERICAN INDIAN SOCIETIES. Journal of Speech and Hearing Disorders No. 6. 87 pp.

Indians of British Columbia were compared with the Ute regarding child rearing methods which may accompany the presence of stuttering. It was found that the Ute, non-stutterers, were generally less demanding and more supportive of their children, permitting them to develop and mature at their own rates, than were the Salish who are known to stutter.   ADG

2505   **SUTTLES   WAYNE**
1960
AFFINAL TIES, SUBSISTENCE, AND PRESTIGE AMONG THE COAST SALISH. American Anthropologist 62:296-305.

Based on field research conducted periodically from 1948 to 1960 an analysis of social organization of several Coast Salish tribes is offered. Intercommunity marital ties and exchange patterns were characteristic of a social network which maintained a high level of food production and equalization of food consumption. Contrary to earlier reports of a dichotomy between susbistence and prestige economies in this region, food, wealth, and status are considered to interact in an adapted socio-economic system.   The potlatch itself is termed a regulatory mechanism whose primary function was to redistribute wealth in view of variable environmental resources.   WRC

2506   **SUTTLES   WAYNE**
1962
VARIATION IN HABITAT AND CULTURE ON THE NORTHWEST COAST. Akten des 34. Internationalen Amerikanistenkongresses. pp. 552-537.

Comparing the environment and culture of the Coast Salish to the Wakashan (Nootka, Kwakiutl) and Northern peoples (Tsimshian, Haida, Tlingit), it was found that there are fewer types but greater concentration of resources in the environments of the Wakashan and Northern peoples. Concerned with the extent of spatial and temporal variations in resources and their implication for social organization, it is suggested that some of the differences in culture along the coast may be related to differences in the environment.   IVY

2507   **SUTTLES   WAYNE**
1963
THE PERSISTENCE OF INTERVILLAGE TIES AMONG THE COAST SALISH. Ethnology 2:512-525.

Field research conducted periodically from 1948 to 1962 provides the basis for a re-examination of community among the Coast Salish in view of the persistance of intervillage social relations. It is postulated that these ties, established aboriginally through intermarriage and potlatch exchange, have continued to comprise the primary social unit. It is argued that the concept of community in earlier reports as the isolated village or reserve is erroneous. Despite the destruction of aboriginal wealth and occupation systems by contact, the intervillage community continues to express itself in winter dances, summer sports events, and the Shaker Church. These institutions are viewed as mechanisms which maintain social relations and status, although Indian identity and nativistic themes now replace traditional economic and professional roles.   WRC

2508 **SUTTLES   WAYNE**
1964
SPIRIT DANCING AND THE PERSISTENCE OF NATIVE CULTURE AMONG
THE COAST SALISH. In VIe Congres International des Sciences Anthropologiques et
Ethnologiques: Paris - 30 Juillet - 6 Aout 1960. Tome II, Ethnologie (deuxieme volume).
Andre Leroi-Gourhan, Pierre Champion, et al., eds. Paris: Musee de l'Homme. pp. 485-
486.

The Coast Salish, in contrast to other native peoples in the area, have retained a vigorous
native ceremonialism. The individualistic and loosely organized nature of spirit dancing
is felt to be a better vehicle for cultural persistence than the more organized ceremonies
of the neighbors of the Salish.   TSA

2509 **SUTTLES   WAYNE**
1968
COPING WITH ABUNDANCE: SUBSISTENCE ON THE NORTHWEST COAST.
In Man the Hunter. Richard B. Lee and Irven De Vore, eds. Chicago: Aldine. pp. 56-68.

Subsistence patterns of the Northwest Coast are discussed. Described are the habitat,
food-getting methods, food storing methods, values, and social organization. It is concluded that where considerable variation in food resources exists, success in exploitation
depends not only on technology but also on some means of organization of labor, some
means of distributing the population and/or goods, and some motivating value.   CCV

2510 **TAYLOR   HERBERT C**
1963
ABORIGINAL POPULATIONS OF THE LOWER NORTHWEST COAST. Pacific
Northwest Quarterly 54:158-165.

Mooney's estimates of aboriginal populations in the lower Northwest Coast are critically
examined in light of unpublished Hudson's Bay historical documents and archaeological
surveys. More reliable population estimates are suggested.   IVY

2511 **TAYLOR   HERBERT C JR**
1960
THE FORT NISQUALLY CENSUS OF 1838-1839. Ethnohistory 7:399-409.

An evaluation of a census listing not only location and numbers of Indian tribes of Puget
Sound but also a breakdown of the population into men, women, boys, girls, and slaves
is presented. An enumeration of horses, guns, and canoes is included. A copy of the census appears in the report (pages 402-403).   IVY

2512 **TAYLOR   HERBERT C JR**
1961
THE UTILIZATION OF ARCHEOLOGICAL AND ETHNOHISTORICAL DATA
IN ESTIMATING ABORIGINAL POPULATION. Texas Archeological Society
Bulletin 32:121-140.

The area under discussion includes Vancouver Island but not the mainland coast of British Columbia above the Strait of Georgia.   Utilizing available archaeological and ethnohistorical data, a critique of Mooney's population estimates (felt to be too low) for the
southern Northwest Coast is presented.   IVY

2513 **TERMANSEN PAUL E.   RYAN JOAN**
1970
HEALTH AND DISEASE IN A BRITISH COLUMBIAN INDIAN COMMUNITY.
Canadian Psychiatric Association Journal 15:121-127.

Indians have a large number of severe health problems which receive very unbalanced
medical attention, and even then, often only in the more acute stages of disease, thereby
resulting in high rates of morbidity and mortality. A study is described which sought to
compare the standards of health and health care of Indians with those of non-Indians in
a selected area and to determine the factors relating to any differences found. It was
found that Indian mental hospital inmates did not differ significantly from the other patients and that Indian patients did not exhibit any unique patterns of illness.   ADG

2514 **THORNTON MILDRED VALLEY**
1966
INDIAN LIVES AND LEGENDS. Vancouver: Mitchell. 301 pp.

Experiences while painting portraits of prominent British Columbia Indians over 2 decades (beginning ca. 1935) are related. Included are anecdotes concerning the subjects and
their own personal recollections. Twelve of the author's paintings, including portraits of
Kwakiutl chiefs Herbert Johnson, William (Billy) Assu, and Hemos Johnson, Tsimshian
chief Billy Williams, and the following Squamish - Mary Capilano, Mathias Joe Capilano, Siamelaht (Aunt Polly), Mary Ann, Chief George, and Madelaine - illustrate the
volume. An appendix updates information on the subjects to 1966.   IVY

2515 **THORNTON MILDRED VALLEY**
1967
COAST INDIANS PRODUCED MATCHLESS NATIVE ART. Canadian Antiques
Collector 2(7):24-25.

General information is given on native art in British Columbia.   IVY

2516 **TOLMIE WILLIAM FRASER**
1963
THE JOURNALS OF WILLIAM FRASER TOLMIE - PHYSICIAN AND FUR
TRADER. Vancouver: Mitchell. 413 pp.

Diary entries of Dr. Tolmie (1812-1886), botanist, ethnologist, and trader with the Hudson's Bay Company record his experiences at Fort McLoughlin and Fort Simpson, British
Columbia, during the years 1883-1835.   IVY

2517 **VASTOKAS JOAN MARIE**
1966
ARCHITECTURE OF THE NORTHWEST COAST INDIANS OF AMERICA. Ph.D.
Thesis. Department of Fine Arts. Columbia University. 369 pp.   Available from
University Microfilms.

The traditional architecture of the Northwest Coast Indians is analyzed and described.
Two structural types are distinguished.   The ridge-pole structure with a 2-pitched gable
roof is characteristic of the Hadia; the single-pitched shed-roof is found among the
Coast Salish. Both types appear to have co-existed among the Bella Coola, Kwakiutl, and
Nootka.   CCV

2518 **VERNER   COOLIE, director**
1968
A SOCIO-ECONOMIC SURVEY OF THE PEMBERTON VALLEY: REPORT #3.
ARDA-CANADA LAND INVENTORY PROJECT #49009. Vancouver: Faculty
of Education, University of British Columbia. 137 pp.

Pages 86-91 of the survey deal explicitly with the Mount Currie Indian Reserve, British
Columbia. Indians comprise half the population of Pemberton Valley. A random sample
of 32 Indians was interviewed. It is concluded that the natives are living under deprivation relative to local Whites. Indian residents lag in education, occupation, and income.
Although over 6,000 acres of rural land are owned by natives, little land is utilized. It is
suggested that the Indians are improving to some extent, but will cease to be marginal
only when higher levels of education and job training are achieved.   JSL

2519 **WALHOUSE   FREDA**
1961
THE INFLUENCE OF MINORITY ETHNIC GROUPS ON THE CULTURAL
GEOGRAPHY OF VANCOUVER. M.A. Thesis. Department of Geography.
University of British Columbia. 379 pp.

The various minority groups found in Vancouver are studied to provide an indication of
the relationships between these groups and the city's appearance and spatial differentiation. Chapter 20 is devoted to discussion of the Musqueam and the Squamish Indian citizens of Vancouver including a review of historical background, settlement pattern, land
use and tenure, population characteristics, religious affiliations, employment, life style,
and impact on the general atmosphere of Vancouver. Of minority groups, the Indian
group accomodates least successfully to the urban milieu.   CCV

2520 **WARD   PHILIP R**
1967
SOME NOTES ON THE PRESERVATION OF TOTEM POLES IN BRITISH
COLUMBIA. Unpublished paper delivered to 2nd Conference on Southeast Alaska
Native Artifacts and Monuments, Alaska State Council on the Arts. Anchorage,
November 17, 1967. Available from National Library of Canada. 17 pp.

In this review of preservation projects in British Columbia - Kitwanga, 1925; Kitsegukla,
1930's; Kitanmaks (Hazelton), 1960; Kispiox, 1966; and Kitwancool, 1967 - the actual
techniques of preservation are described and illustrated. Another method is the restoration program of the Provincial Museum in which original poles are purchased and placed
in the museum and copies are erected in the community and Thunderbird Park. It is
stressed that only the finest artists be selected to reproduce the poles.   IVY

2521 **WARDWELL   ALLEN**
1964
YAKUTAT SOUTH INDIAN ART OF THE NORTHWEST COAST. Chicago:
Chicago Art Institute. 82 pp.

An exhibition of Northwest Coast art at the Chicago Art Institute from March 13 to
April 26, 1964, is described. Plates accompany the text.   IVY

2522   **WARDWELL   ALLEN**
1965
NORTHWEST COAST MINIATURES. Lore 16:23-27.

Eight Northwest Coast carved specimens from the Milwaukee Public Museum are described and illustrated. These include a rattle (Haida), shaman's charms (Tlingit), pipe bowl (Tlingit), soul-catcher, whistle (Kwakiutl), and knife (Tlingit).   IVY

2523   **WATERTON   ERIC CLAUDE**
1969
GAMBLING GAMES OF THE NORTHWEST COAST. M.A. Thesis. Department of Anthropology and Sociology. University of British Columbia.   131 pp.

Material for this study of gambling in traditional Northwest Coast society is derived from museum records and holdings in material culture, the ethnographic literature, and an analysis of published myths. Gambling, a very popular activity, exhibited a high degree of homogeniety in the areas considered, and areal differences in the games of chance were quantitative rather than qualitative. Gambling themes expressed in myths revealed that gambling usually involved very high stakes, losing was considered shameful particularly when the property of others was involved, serious gambling for high stakes was considered strictly a man's activity, cheating was common and accepted as long as it remained undiscovered, and luck was associated with the supernatural.   CCV

2524   **WELLS   OLIVER NELSON**
1969
SALISH WEAVING PRIMITIVE AND MODERN AS PRACTISED BY THE SALISH INDIANS OF SOUTHWEST BRITISH COLUMBIA. Revised Edition. Sardis, B.C.: Oliver N. Wells. 28 pp.

The publication is intended for the interest and use of native people of Salish origin who may wish to undertake the production of articles woven in the traditional methods. The technical aspects of weaving, the preparation of material, and production of color, both primitive and modern, are discussed. Illustrations and photographs accompany the text. Four pages of Salish design elements taken from the Bureau of American Ethnology's 41st Report and a bibliography are included in the revised edition.   IVY

2525   **WHERRY   JOSEPH H**
1964
THE TOTEM POLE INDIANS. New York: Funk & Wagnalls. 152 pp.

Various aspects of Northwest culture discussed include legends of migration, homes, crafts, social organization, religion, mythology, totem poles (their construction and purposes), and the potlatch.   IVY

2526   **WHERRY   JOSEPH H**
1969
INDIAN MASKS AND MYTHS OF THE WEST. New York: Funk & Wagnalls. 273 pp.

Scattered references are found to Tsimshian, Haida, Tlingit, and Kwakiutl concerning creation myths, migration myths, mythical and spiritual deities, legends of giants and monsters, and masks and their use in religious ceremonies.   IVY

2527   **WILSON   RENATE,   DICKMAN   THELMA**
1964
THEY'RE GIVING THE CULTURE BACK TO THE INDIANS. Imperial Oil Review
48(2):14-18.

A general commentary on contemporary British Columbia native artists and their works
is given. Photographs accompany the text.   IVY

BELLA COOLA

2528   **KOPAS   CLIFF**
1970
BELLA COOLA. Vancouver: Mitchell. 296 pp.

The folk history of the Bella Coola is traced from contact to the present relying on historical and contemporary sources.   CCV

2529   **MCILWRAITH   T F**
1964
FACTS AND THEIR RECOGNITION AMONG THE BELLA COOLA. In Fact and
Theory in Social Science. Earl W. Count and Gordon T. Bowles, eds. Syracuse: Syracuse
University Press. pp. 183-200.

Relying on fieldwork data published in 1948 the recognition of fact among the Bella
Coola is discussed. In our society there are 4 kinds of facts according to the type of evidence: those dependent upon the senses or experience, those dependent on hearsay,
those dependent upon experiment, and those dependent on belief. Bella Coola society
shares these kinds of facts with the exception of those dependent upon deliberate experi-
mentation. The tendency to "see"objects or events according to culture patterns without
regard for possible lapse of memory or error in perception is felt to be important to the
Bella Coola secret society rituals.   CCV

2530   **PATTERSON   E PALMER II**
1962
ANDREW PAULL AND CANADIAN INDIAN RESURGENCE. Ph.D. Thesis.
Department of History. University of Washington. 405 pp. Available from National
Library of Canada.

The biography of Andrew Paull and his involvement in the Indian resurgence movement
is discussed. As spokesman for his fellow Indians, Paull sought to secure legal recognition of the aboriginal land titles. In June, 1943, he founded the North American Indian
Brotherhood.   DGW

2531   **STOTT   MARGARET A**
1968
BELLA COOLA CEREMONY AND ART. Unpublished paper submitted to Wenner-
Gren Foundation for Anthropological Research. Available from National Museum of
Man, Ethnology Division, Ottawa, with permission of the author. 118 pp.

The nature and significance of Bella Coola ceremonialism and art as well as an analytical
summary of the art style itself is given. Stylistic analysis of the art form concentrates primarily on techniques employed in masks. Specifically studied is the collection held by the

National Museum of Canada - material which was originally collected by Harlan I. Smith and T. F. McIlwraith in 1922. The author herself spent 2 months in that community with members of the tribe in her attempt to reveal the significance of material culture in relation to other aspects of society. Sixteen color plates as well as 10 figures complement the study.   DGW

COMOX

2532   **BAND   RICHARD W**
1969
DECISION MAKING AND LEADERSHIP AMONG THE SQUAMISH. M.A.
Thesis. Department of Political Science, Sociology, and Anthropology.   Simon Fraser University. 212 pp. Available from National Library of Canada.

Fieldwork from November 1968 to May 1968 and personal experience as a member of the Squamish community provide material for a discussion of the community, the band council, and leadership concepts. It is demonstrated that perpetuation of kinship obligations has obstructed the development of a status system based on unequal access to economic, political, and social opportunities. This tendency blocks the development of leadership and of organization of a bureaucratic nature.   CCV

2533   **BRITISH COLUMBIA. Planning and Property Department.**
1964
INDIAN RESERVES. Victoria, B.C.: Planning and Property Department. 32 pp.

The past, present, and future of 3 Squamish reserves (Seymour Indian Reserve, Squamish Band; Squamish - Burrard Inlet Band; and Squamish - Kapilano Band), is presented from the viewpoint of the community and the overall development plan, Plan '64. Background information, both historical and current, is provided, and a series of policy recommendations and development proposals is outlined. Each reserve is treated in the following manner: general, existing land use, adjacent land use, development principles (and goals), and recommended development with accompanying maps.   IVY

2534   **BUCKLEY   PATRICIA LORRAINE**
1968
A CROSS CULTURAL STUDY OF DRINKING PATTERNS IN THREE ETHNIC GROUPS, COAST SALISH INDIANS OF THE MISSIONS RESERVE, IMMIGRANT ITALIANS AND ANGLOSAXONS OF EAST VANCOUVER. M.A.
Thesis. Department of Anthropology and Sociology. University of British Columbia. 115 pp.

In 1967-68 Coast Salish from Mission Reserve, and immigrant Italians and Anglo-Saxons of East Vancouver were studied to determine the relationship, if any, between ethnic background and drinking patterns. Data were supplied by questionnaires administered to 30 members of each group, obeservation, and documentation. A high degree of similarity was found between Indian and Anglo-Saxon drinking patterns while Italian and Anglo-Saxon drinking patterns were shown to differ.   IVY

2535   **CLUTESI   GEORGE**
1967

SON OF RAVEN SON OF DEER: FABLES OF THE TSE-SHAHT PEOPLE. Sidney, B.C.: Gray's. 126 pp.

As told to him by his parents, deer and raven legends are retold by a Tse-Shaht Indian. Nursery rhymes are contrasted with Indian fables which reveal the Indian way of admonishing children.   CCV

2536   **CLUTESI   GEORGE**
1969
POTLATCH. Sidney, B.C.: Gray's. 188 pp.

Drawing from personal experience and oral tradition, a Tse-Shaht Indian recounts the story of a potlatch. Ceremonial activity is described as it appeared to an observer. Considerable detail is furnished in description of dramatic presentations, dances, costumes, and masks. Occasional Indian legends and numerous chants are included.   CCV

2537   **KHAHTSAHLANO   AUGUST JACK,   CHARLIE   DOMANIC**
1966
SQUAMISH LEGENDS. Oliver N. Wells, ed. British Columbia: Charles Chamberlain & Frank T. Coan. 32 pp.

These legends were tape-recorded by the editor and set down in the words of Jack Khahtsahlano and Domanic Charlie in 1965. An exception is the 1st legend which is an interpretation. Illustrations accompany the text.   IVY

2538   **MATTHEWS   J S**
1967
CONVERSATIONS WITH KHAHTSAHLANO 1932-1954: CONVERSATIONS WITH AUGUST JACK KHAHTSAHLANO, BORN AT ANAUQ, FALSE CREEK INDIAN RESERVE, CIRCA 1877, SON OF KHAYTULK AND GRANDSON OF CHIEF KHAHTSAHLANOGH. Vancouver: Webber. 443 pp.

Conversations with August Jack Khahtsahlano from 1932 to 1954 are recorded verbatim. Details of genealogies, traditional subsistence activities, oral tradition, ceremonial practices, techniques used to construct dwellings and canoes, preparation of food and clothing, and early European contact are included. The text is supplemented with conversations with other Indians and knowledgeable persons from the area.   CCV

2539   **PHILPOTT   STUART BOWMAN**
1963
TRADE UNIONISM AND ACCULTURATION: A COMPARATIVE STUDY OF URBAN INDIANS AND IMMIGRANT ITALIANS. M.A. Thesis. Department of Anthropology and Sociology. University of British Columbia. 152 pp.

Trade unionism as a factor in acculturation and social change is examined in relation to the Squamish Indians on North Vancouver reserves and Italians living in the Queensborough district of New Westminister. Data were gathered from both groups by means of participant observation and interviews during the summer of 1962 and supplemented by library research. Comparative analysis revealed greater union activity among the Squamish than among the Italians. This is attributed to union structure, aspirations and values of the ethnic groups themselves, length of contact with the union, and other historical and cultural factors. It was observed that union activity tends to further other aspects of acculturation in the Indian community and acts as a liaison between Squamish unionists and an equivalent sector of White society.   CCV

HAIDA

2540   **1966**
HAIDA ARGILLITE CARVING. B.C. Credit Unionist 26(6):6-9.

The history of argillite carving by the Indians of the Queen Charlotte Islands, British Columbia, is sketched. Photographs show a detailed view of a carving by Robert Davidson, Sr., and Claude Davidson carving and polishing a totem pole.   IVY

2541   **APPLETON   FRANK M**
1970
THE LIFE AND ART OF CHARLIE EDENSAW. Canadian Geographical Journal 81:20-25.

The life and times of the Haida artist, Charlie Edensaw (1839-1924), are described. Works in various media are illustrated.   IVY

2542   **BARKER   ROY D**
1967
THE HAIDA. B.C. Outdoors 23(6):54-59.

Focusing upon warfare in Haida society, descriptions of socialization of infants and children, construction of canoes, tactics, captives, armor, weapons, and taboos are presented.   IVY

2543   **CARTER   ANTHONY L**
1968
THIS IS HAIDA. Vancouver: Anthony Carter. 137 pp.

A record of the vanishing culture of the Haida of the Queen Charlotte Islands is provided in 94 pages of color photographs and brief commentary. The selection includes scenic views, local Indian citizens, crafts, and craftsmen. The past is represented by photos of abandoned longhouses, decaying totem and mortuary poles, and specimens of material culture.   CCV

2544   **CLASS   LORETTA**
1968
IN-GROUP ATTITUDES AS EXPRESSED IN HAIDA FOLKTALES. M.A. Thesis. Department of Anthropology. University of Washington.

The title has been verified, but a copy was not obtained in time to abstract it.   SLP

2545   **DOCKSTADER   FREDERICK J**
1962
KWAWHLHAL CARVINGS FROM SKIDEGATE: AN UNTRADITIONAL HAIDA ART. Natural History 71(9):30-39.

A photographic presentation of 19th century Haida argillite carvings is given.   IVY

2546   **DUFF   WILSON**
1960
MORTUARY POLES OF THE NINSTINTS. Victoria Naturalist 16:65.

A brief historical sketch of the long-deserted Haida Indian village of Ninstints, Queen Charlotte Islands, British Columbia, is given.   IVY

2547   **FRASER   DOUGLAS**
1968
VILLAGE PLANNING IN THE PRIMITIVE WORLD. New York: George Braziller. 128 pp.

The village plans of several traditional societies are discussed from a structural-functional approach. The Haida are examined on pages 23-26 with particular attention to the Ninstints townsite on Anthony Island. Social and aesthetic cohesion as well as the maritime orientation and the underlying religious beliefs of the Haida are said to be reflected in their village plan.   CCV

2548   **GLATTHAAR   TRISHA CORLISS**
1970
TOM PRICE (c. 1860-1927): THE ART AND STYLE OF A HAIDA ARTIST. M.A. Thesis. Department of Fine Arts. University of British Columbia. 160 pp.

Haida art is the product of a small number of brilliant artists. The life and works of one of these, Tom Price, are examined. Interviews with contemporary Haida and documentary evidence provide information on the artist. Works of art attributed to Price are used to establish his style and, on the basis of style, undocumented works are attributed to him. Numerous photographs of the work of Price and other Haida artists illustrate the thesis.   TSA

2549   **GUNN   SISVAN WILLIAM**
1967
HAIDA ART IN ARGILLITE. Canadian Antiques Collector 2(7):9-10.

A brief history of Haida argillite carving is given.   IVY

2550   **GUNN   SISVAN WILLIAM**
1967
HAIDA TOTEMS IN WOOD AND ARGILITE. Totem Poles of British Columbia and Alaska Series III. n.p.: Whiterocks Publications. 24 pp.

An historic sketch of the Haida and their totem poles is given. Specific discussion of Chief Skedans' memorial, the Flower Totem of Yan, the Kaigani Totem, and Chief Weha's Totem and house is presented.   IVY

2551   **HARRIS   CHRISTIE**
1966
RAVEN'S CRY. New York: Atheneum. 193 pp.

Narrated is the story of culture contact among the Haida of the Queen Charlotte Islands. Special treatment is accorded to the lineage of Chief Edinsa, the last of the great Haida Eagle chiefs. The story, which is presented from the standpoint of the Haida themselves, reveals a changing world view resulting from the breakdown of traditional culture.   DGW

2552   **HAWTHORN   AUDREY**
1963
A LIVING HAIDA CRAFT: SOME TRADITIONAL CARVINGS FOR OUR TIMES. The Beaver 294(Summer):4-12.

A Haida house, its family crest poles, and an adjacent mortuary house have been permanently installed in the University of British Columbia's Totem Pole Park section. Conceived, designed, and carved by Haida artist Bill Reid and his Kwakiutl assistant Doug Cranmer, the 3-year project is described in text and photographs.   IVY

2553   **HAYNES   BESSIE DOAK**
1966
GOLD ON THE QUEEN CHARLOTTE'S ISLAND. The Beaver 297(Winter):4-11.

News reached Fort Simpson in 1850 that gold had been discovered on Queen Charlotte Islands. Described are the various American attempts during 1851-1853 to prospect among the hostile Haida.   IVY

2554   **HOBSON   ROBERT W**
1967
ARGILLITE. The Beaver 298(Summer):46-51.

Argillite as a medium for carving is described and a trip to the quarry presented.   IVY

2555   **KAUFMANN   CAROLE NATALIE**
1969
CHANGES IN HAIDA INDIAN ARGILLITE CARVINGS 1820 TO 1910. Ph.D. Thesis. Department of Anthropology. University of California, Los Angeles. 236 pp. Available from University Microfilms.

Data gathered on 450 artifacts were analyzed in this study of changes in Haida argillite carvings. Since argillite carvings were produced for sale and distribution the collection dates are felt to be fairly reliable indices of date of manufacture. Morphic and iconic features exhibiting change over time were recorded. The most consistent and changeable indicator was the anthropomorphic eye marker. It is felt that social change resulted in change in material objects and this is demonstrated by the articles reviewed.   CCV

2556   **MORLEY   ALAN**
1967
ROAR OF THE BREAKERS: A BIOGRAPHY OF PETER KELLY. Toronto: Ryerson Press. 164 pp.

The life of Peter Kelly, a Haida noble (1885 to 1966), who was ordained a Methodist minister is recounted. Family life, education, the ministry, and the political context of the 1st half of the 20th century are described revealing details of traditional Northwest

Coast life, difficulties encountered in the acculturation process, his personal achievements and leadership qualities, and his role in organizing and representing Northwest Coast Indians in claims for land and other aboriginal rights.   CCV

2557   **STEARNS   MARY LEE**
n.d.
MECHANISMS OF ROLE DEFINITION IN AN INTERCULTURAL SITUATION. Unpublished paper. Available from National Museum of Man, Ethnology Division, Ottawa, with permission of the author. 17 pp.

Three social units are considered - Indian Affairs, the Masset Band of British Columbia, and local Whites. Focus is on the expectations of behavior attached to the role of the Indian, plus the Indian's expectations of non-Indians. A set of prescriptions and expectations was imposed on the subordinate Indian population. Following an Indian fishing strike, and political competition, the behavior expected of Indians is being redefined through conflict. Traditional Haida ideology, oral history, and social relations are being adjusted to the contemporary situation, and provide a source of community solidarity in the face of intercultural conflict. It is concluded that all mechanisms of role definition are securely vested in the dominant non-Indian sector. Ambivalent responses by the Haida result from the imposition of ambivalent role definitions.   JSL

2558   **STEARNS   MARY LEE**
1968
LIFE CYCLE RITUALS OF THE MODERN HAIDA. Unpublished paper delivered to 21st Annual Meeting, Northwest Anthropological Conference. Portland, OR, April 13, 1968. Available from National Library of Canada. 39 pp.

Fieldwork was conducted at Masset, Queen Charlotte Islands, British Columbia, during the periods June 15 to September 1, 1962; September 1, 1965, to September 1, 1966; and June 15 to September 1, 1967. The content and functions of the life cycle rituals in the modern Haida system are analyzed. Marriage and death rituals are discussed in detail focusing upon such elements as donations of money, speeches, payment for ritual services, gift distribution, food, and sponsorship. Modifications of traditional practices in feast complex of which the life cycle rituals are the most important reflect a conscious adaptation to changed social conditions.   IVY

2559   **WILLETT   FRANK**
1961
A SET OF GAMBLING PEGS FROM THE NORTH-WEST COAST OF AMERICA. Man 61:8-10.

A Haida set of 28 carved pegs from a gambling game is described and illustrated. The work probably dates from 1850 to 1875. An identification of animal motifs is made.   WRC

HALKOMELEM

2560   **ATAMANENKO   GEORGE THEODORE**
1962
LAND USE PLANNING OPPORTUNITIES AND LIMITATIONS FOR INDIAN RESERVES: SELECTED CASE STUDIES IN THE GREATER VANCOUVER

AREA. M.S. Thesis. Department of Community and Regional Planning. University of British Columbia. 106 pp.

Musqueam Reserve and the Squamish Capilano, Burrard, Mission, and Seymour Creek Reserves of the Greater Vancouver area are studied in terms of land use and planning. Indian Affairs authorities and personnel, planners in adjacent municipalities and on regional and provincial levels, and Indian chiefs and councilors were interviewed during 1960-1962 concerning land use planning attitudes, practices, and proposals. It is concluded that reserves in an urban environment are in transition and that some degree of co-operation with municipal planning departments exists. The scope of on-reserve land-use planning is severely limited despite a high level of interest. This may be related to insufficient understanding of planning or a lack of communication between Indian Affairs authorities and appropriate planning agencies.   CCV

2561   **BAXTER   KENNETH WAYNE**
1967
THE SEARCH FOR STATUS IN A SALISH INDIAN COMMUNITY. M.A. Thesis. Department of Anthropology and Sociology. University of British Columbia. 47 pp.

An attempt is made to relate the search for status and active participation in winter dancing to aspirations toward an Indian or non-Indian cultural value set on the basis of 34 interviews collected over a period of 12 weeks on the Cowishan reserve at Duncan, British Columbia. The range of institutions in which Cowichan band members participate and the status sets maintained by individuals are described. It is concluded that perception of non-ethnic threat was greatest among those who negatively evaluate ethnic institutions but could not acquire non-ethnic status.   CCV

2562   **BROTHERS   RYAN**
1965
COWICHAN KNITTERS. The Beaver 296(Summer):42-46.

The process of producing the Cowichan sweaters from raw wool to finished product is described. A Victoria merchant supplies the raw wool, then buys and distributes the sweaters.   IVY

2563   **CAMERON   CATHERINE ANN**
1964
ETHNIC DIFFERENCES IN THE RELATIVE EFFECTIVENESS OF INCENTIVES. M.A. Thesis. Department of Psychology. University of British Columbia. 31 pp.

Sixty-six boys aged 6 to 13 were administered trials on a discrimination task and TAT stories scored for achievement and delayed-reward choice. The group tested was divided equally among Indian boys from Musqueam Reserve attending Southlands Elementary or Immaculate Conception Schools, sons of blue-collar workers, and sons of white-collar workers. Results for the 3 groups were compared and supported the hypothesis that Indian children's performance for non-material incentives would be inferior to performance for material rewards. White-collar children were significantly superior to blue-collar and Indian students under conditions of non-material reward. This superiority was not found, however, under conditions of material reward. No significant differences were found between Indians and working-class Whites. The middle-class children showed greater achievement imagery and chose larger, delayed rewards on the TAT test stories, thus differentiating themselves from Indian and working-class children.   CCV

2564   **KARGBO   MARIAN JUDITH TANNER**
1965
MUSQUEAM INDIAN RESERVE: A CASE STUDY FOR COMMUNITY
DEVELOPMENT PURPOSES. M.S.W. Thesis. School of Social Work. University of
British Columbia. 150 pp.

Data gathered during employment in community development on Musqueam Indian
Reserve during 1964 and 1965 were analyzed according to Warren's community study
model focusing on the systematic relationships between the local people and organizations and the extra-community. The social systems felt to have endured over time and
the communication process were selected for description and analysis. Communication is
found inadequate and extra-community control of most of the intra-community's social
system is related to weakness in horizontal patterns and is obstructive to community development.   CCV

2565   **KEW   JOHN EDWARD MICHAEL**
1970
COAST SALISH CEREMONIAL LIFE: STATUS AND IDENTITY IN A MODERN
VILLAGE. Ph.D. Thesis. Department of Anthropology. University of Washington. 359
pp.

A description of demography, life style, and social organization are provided as background to description of Musqueam Indian ceremonies identified and studied during
fieldwork in 1967 to 1968. The Spirit dance, Shaker Church, funeral services, and canoe
races are described. Ritual is shown to be responsive to needs for self-esteem and social
status which are accentuated by acculturation processes thus reducing the necessity for
the development of alternatives.   CCV

2566   **MORTON   JAMES W**
1970
CAPILANO: THE STORY OF A RIVER. Toronto: McClelland and Stewart. 184 pp.

The traditional life style of the Musqueam and Squamish is reviewed briefly in Chapter 2
of this history of the Capilano River.   Some consideration is given to the history of Indian-White relations and traditional and contemporary Indian leaders of the
area.   CCV

2567   **RAWSON AND WILES LIMITED**
1966
A PLAN OF RESIDENTIAL SUBDIVISION FOR NANAIMO INDIAN RESERVE
NO. 4. Unpublished paper. Available from Library, University of British Columbia. 12
pp.

The stated purpose of this study was to prepare a residential subdivision plan for Nanaimo Indian Reserve Number 4 and to supply estimates of servicing costs for various
stages of development. Discussed in the report and in the 3 page appendix are the replacement of the Nanaimo River bridge and the realignment of approaches to it proposed by the provincial Department of Highways. Maps accompany text.   IVY

2568   **ROBINSON   SARAH ANNE**
1963
SPIRIT DANCING AMONG THE SALISH INDIANS, VANCOUVER ISLAND,
BRITISH COLUMBIA. Ph.D. Thesis. Department of Anthropology. University of
Chicago. 163 pp.

Participant observation, interviews, and library research provide data for examination of
spirit dancing among the Nanaimo of Vancouver Island. Fieldwork was conducted from
November 1, 1957, to October 15, 1959. Traditional Salish social organization, the contact period and the following transition, the contemporary social organization and structural discontinuity, and the supernatural are reviewed. The modern role of spirit dancing
is discussed. It is proposed that a long-standing dissatisfaction in the status quo has resulted in a nativistic movement. Continued use of old rites such as spirit dancing serves to
reduce tension and inhibits the search for alternative courses of action.   CCV

2569   **SCHMIDBAUER   ERIC**
1969
LEARNING THEIR OWN LANGUAGE. Monday Morning 3(9):27.

At Chehalis Indian Reserve school, Stalo children are being taught Salish by Ed Leon, a
member of the band.   IVY

2570   **SEPASS   CHIEF**
1963
SEPASS POEMS: THE SONGS OF Y-AIL-MIHTH. Recorded by Eloise Street. New
York: Vantage. 110 pp.

Fifteen poems provided by hereditary Chilliwack chief Sepass are presented. These
poems or songs were Chief Sepass' personal inheritance through his mother, daughter of
a Thompson River chieftain.   CCV

2571   **VOLLMANN   WERNER**
1962
WEST COAST CANOE RACE PREPARATIONS. Canadian Geographical Journal
65:160-161.

Constructed similarly to the traditional war canoes, 3 50-year old canoes on the
Musqueam Indian Reserve are prepared for racing.   IVY

2572   **WELLS   OLIVER N**
1966
RETURN OF THE SALISH LOOM. The Beaver 296(Spring):40-45.

The revival of the art of loom weaving among Stalo Indian women is discussed. A technical presentation of the looms and method of weaving is given.   IVY

2573   **WELLS   OLIVER NELSON**
1969
SALISH WEAVING: RETURN OF AN ANCIENT ART. Beautiful British Columbia
1969 (Summer):35-39.

Traditional and modern techniques of weaving used by the Stalo tribes of the lower Fraser River are discussed. IVY

KWAKIUTL

2574 **BARRETT SAMUEL A**
1966
INTRODUCTION: TAPE-RECORDED INTERVIEW WITH SAMUEL A. BARRETT, AUGUST 1962. In Masks of the Northwest Coast. Robert Ritzenthaler and Lee A. Parsons, eds. Milwaukee Public Museum Publications in Primitive Art 2. Milwaukee: Milwaukee Public Museum. pp. 17-22.

Samuel A. Barrett discusses his collecting expedition to Vancouver Island and the adjacent mainland in British Columbia in 1915, including a description of a potlatch. IVY

2575 **BARRETT SAMUEL A**
1966
MASKS AND FIELD NOTES. In Masks of the Northwest Coast. Robert Ritzenthaler and Lee A. Parsons, eds. Milwaukee Public Museum Publications in Primitive Art 2. Milwaukee: Milwaukee Public Museum. pp. 49-99.

Seventy-one masks (57 Kwakiutl ceremonial masks, 1 Bella Bella, 13 Bella Coola) are illustrated and documented by Barrett's 1915 field notes. IVY

2576 **BELSHAW CYRIL S**
1965
TRADITIONAL EXCHANGE AND MODERN MARKETS. Englewood Cliffs, NJ: Prentice-Hall. 149 pp.

Different economics from primitive to modern are discussed and compared. Pages 20-29 are an analysis of Kwakiutl potlatch referring primarily to Boas' and Codere's ethnographic and historical material. The numaym was a patrilineal descent group whose defined functions were the basis of corporate action in Kwakiutl society. The potlatch ceremony stressed the co-operative, competitive relationship with an affinally linked group. As observed in the 19th century the potlatch economy was the result of inflation induced by depopulation and the introduction of monetary trading. CCV

2577 **BOAS FRANZ**
1966
KWAKIUTL ETHNOGRAPHY. Helen Codere, ed. Chicago: University of Chicago Press. 439 pp.

Unpublished data gathered by Boas among the Kwakiutl between 1885 and 1930 is combined with some Boas publications by Helen Codere. Potlatch, warfare, winter ceremonial, mythology, and material culture are described extensively. An analysis of Kwakiutl art and a discussion of its symbolism is included. Accounts of ceremonialism and ritual are particularly detailed. CCV

2578 **CODERE HELEN**
1961

KWAKIUTL. In Perspectives in American Indian Culture Change. Edward H. Spicer, ed. Chicago: University of Chicago Press. pp. 431-516.

Presented is a cultural historical analysis of culture change among the Southern Kwakiutl. Fieldwork was undertaken in 1941 and 1955. Kwakiutl history is divided into 3 periods: the Pre-Potlatch Period, 1792-1849; the Potlatch Period, 1849-mid-1920's; and the Post Potlatch Period, from the mid-1920's to the present. In each case, treatment is accorded the community organization, external relations, economic and social organization, potlatch, ceremonialism and supernaturalism, curing and non-supernatural knowledge, and arts of that period. Summarized are cultural persistences and changes over the 150 years of Kwakiutl cultural history in relation to the contact condition. It is concluded that European and Kwakiutl cultures were profoundly alike, and that reports of the death of Kwakiutl culture are greatly exaggerated.   DGW

2579   **CODERE   HELEN**
1968
MONEY-EXCHANGE SYSTEMS AND A THEORY OF MONEY. Man N.S. 3:557-577.

In a theoretical discussion of the concept of money the historical development of the Kwakiutl potlatch is traced from pre-contact to the 1920's, when it was finally repressed by the Canadian government. The transition from barter and fur blankets to the symbolic money-stuff of woolen blankets introduced by White traders and finally to the incorporation of Canadian money fits well the developmental model of money as a symbolic system of exchange. Coppers are considered analogous to checks in western monetary transactions.   WRC

2580   **DONG   ALICE,   FEENEY   MOIRA C**
1968
THE NUTRIENT INTAKE OF INDIAN AND NON-INDIAN SCHOOL CHILDREN. Canadian Journal of Public Health 59:115-118.

Research dietary histories were obtained from 61 Indian and non-Indian children from the logging and fishing community of Alert Bay, British Columbia. The 14 nutrients as analyzed in the Home and Garden Bulletin No. 72(4) served as a basis for the comparison. Deficiencies in both diets are noted.   IVY

2581   **DRUCKER   PHILIP,   HEIZER   ROBERT F**
1967
TO MAKE MY NAME GOOD: A REEXAMINATION OF THE SOUTHERN KWAKIUTL POTLATCH. Berkeley: University of California Press. 160 pp.

Conclusions drawn from fieldwork during 1937 and 1953 among the Southern Kwakiutl are presented along with other material and theories concerning the Kwakiutl potlatch. It is proposed that warfare was more significant among the Kwakiutl than the literature allows and that, in fact, the Kwakiutl differed little from their neighbors. The ideas that the potlatch had an economic origin or was a survival mechanism or means of circulating wealth items are rejected. It is maintained that the potlatch complex developed gradually from simple elements sharing functional value.   CCV

2582   DUFF   WILSON
1961
THE KILLER WHALE COPPER (A CHIEF'S MEMORIAL TO HIS SON). British
Columbia, Provincial Museum of Natural History and Anthropology Report for the
Year 1960:32-36.

In December, 1960, Chief Mungo Martin put into the permanent care of the Provincial
Museum of Victoria his valued copper, Ma-haynootsi, Great Killer Whale. The history
of the copper is recorded on tape. This article puts the story into print with certain sections given verbatim from the tape.   IVY

2583   GRIGSBY   JEFFERSON EUGENE
1963
AFRICAN AND INDIAN MASKS: A COMPARATIVE STUDY OF MASKS
PRODUCED BY THE BA KUBA TRIBE OF THE CONGO AND MASKS
PRODUCED BY THE KWAKIUTL INDIANS OF THE NORTHWEST PACIFIC
COAST OF AMERICA. Ph.D. Thesis. School of Education. New York University. 299
pp. Available from National Library of Canada.

A comparative study of Kwakiutl and Ba Kuba masks is presented. The cultural context
in which the masks were employed and the material, form, design, and functions in each
case were analyzed and compared. Evidence is presented to indicate that the role of the
masks differed greatly. Among the Kwakiutl the masks served to dramatize tribal origin,
social structure, ritual activities, and marking of stages in individual development. It is
noted that the Kwakiutl masks are part of a total costume, and that extensive variation in
form exists although curving movement dominates the design. From comparison on the
basis of aesthetic factors, Kwakiutl masks are classified as expressionistic and the Ba
Kuba as impressionistic.   CCV

2584   GUNN   SISVAN WILLIAM
1966
KWAKIUTL HOUSE AND TOTEM POLES AT ALERT BAY, B.C. Totem Poles of
British Columbia, Series II. West Vancouver, B.C.: Whiterocks Publications. 24 pp.

A brief history of the Kwakiutl Indians is presented. The Kwakiutl motifs of the Sisiutl,
Thunderbird, Tsonoqua, Qolus, Grizzly, and Kelp are discussed.   IVY

2585   HARRIS   GRACE
1963
HEALTH CARE FOR WEST COAST INDIANS. The Canadian Nurse 59:132-134.

The British Columbia Department of Health in cooperation with Indian Health Services
provides specialized services such as the Registry for Handicapped Children. Voluntary
agencies also include care of Indians in their plans. Public health nurses employed by the
province provide nursing services to approximately 6,000 Indians on reserves. Twenty
nurses employed by the federal government maintain health centers and clinics. Health
services at Alert Bay, British Columbia, include a health center and a small general hospital staffed by 2 physicians.   IVY

2586   HAWTHORN   AUDREY
1964
MUNGO MARTIN: ARTIST AND CRAFTSMAN. The Beaver 295(Summer):18-23.

Mungo Martin's paintings which appear on 4 pages in this article depict the supernatural beings of clan and family crests.   IVY

2587   **HAWTHORN   AUDREY**
1967
ART OF THE KWAKIUTL INDIANS AND OTHER NORTHWEST COAST TRIBES. Vancouver: University of British Columbia. 410 pp.

A collection of Kwakiutl art from the Museum of Anthropology of the University of British Columbia is presented with emphasis on items intended for ceremonial use. The text concerns the setting, characteristics of Northwest Coast art, religion and mythology, the potlatch, ceremonial calendar, dancing and dancing societies, and ritual. Photographs of the collection are accompanied by notation of size, tribal attribution, name, material, and source. Articles from some other Northwest coast tribes appear occasionally.   CCV

2588   **HOLM   BILL**
1961
CARVING A KWAKIUTL CANOE. The Beaver 292(Summer):28-35.

In 1908 George Hunt recorded a detailed description of the making of a canoe by a Nakoaktoq Indian of Blunden Harbour. The step-by-step construction is presented by photographs and captions.   IVY

2589   **INGLIS   JOY**
1964
THE INTERACTION OF MYTH AND SOCIAL CONTEXT IN THE VILLAGE OF CAPE MUDGE: THE MYTHS OF A PEOPLE ARE BOUND INTO THE TOTAL SYSTEM OF SOCIAL RELATIONS. M.A. Thesis. Department of Anthropology and Sociology. University of British Columbia. 163 pp.

The relationship between mythology and social organization is explored in relation to the Kwakiutl village of Cape Mudge, British Columbia. Data are derived from prolonged personal contact with the village, 1 month of intensive fieldwork during the summer of 1963, and ethnohistorical sources. Several aspects of social organization are considered in discussion focusing on the contemporary village, the historical background, mythology, social control, and values. The contemporary scene is outlined in detail in terms of rank, social status, marriage practices, authority, desirable behavior, social aspirations, and relations with the nearby White community. It is concluded that myth is not lost with a society's moving from a tribal organization to a modern one but rather adapts to changing needs.   CCV

2590   **KEMP   SAMUEL JAMES**
1967
SOME RELATIONSHIPS BETWEEN STYLE AND TOOL FORM IN KWAKIUTL AND AFRIKPO CARVED MASKS. M.A. Thesis. Department of Anthropology. University of Washington.

Tools and the 3-dimensional forms they produce in Kwakiutl and Nigerian Afrikpo masks are compared. Appropriate tools were used by the author to carve masks in each tradition and an attempt to carve the forms of 1 culture with the tools of the other was made. It was determined that the concave ellipsoids characteristic of Kwakiutl carvings can be carved only with a Kwakiutl curved knife and Afrikpo forms were easier to carve with Afrikpo tools. The relationship between tools used and forms created is indicated to hold cross-culturally.   CCV

2591   **KENYON   WALTER A**
1961
KWAKIUTL MASKS. World Theatre 10(Spring):41-45.   Also in French.

Aspects of the carving and dramatic use of Kwakiutl Masks are touched upon. Illustrations depict 6 masks from the Royal Ontario Museum, the National Museum of Canada, and private collections.   TSA

2592   **LARGE   R GEDDES**
1968
DRUMS AND SCALPEL: FROM NATIVE HEALERS TO PHYSICIANS ON THE NORTH PACIFIC COAST. Vancouver: Mitchell. 145 pp.

An account of life among the Bella Bella from the end of the 19th century is presented from a doctor's experiences in the 1920's and his memories and records of his doctor-missionary father's services from 1898 until 1910. Some observations of Indian medicinal beliefs and practices as well as their interaction with White men are included.   CCV

2593   **MEADE   E F**
1962
THE MUTE GHOSTS OF CAPE MUDGE. The Beaver 293(Autumn):34-39.

Territorial expansion of the Lekwiltok, a branch of the Kwakiutl, from Jackson Bay into Discovery Passage between 1792 and 1850 is reviewed. By 1850 the Comox Salish had vanished from the area and the Lekwiltok commanded Discovery Passage from Cape Mudge and Ucle-Tah.   IVY

2594   **MEADE   E F**
1965
A EUCLATAW CHIEF. The Beaver 296(Winter):48-53.

A historical background of the Wiwekae Band is provided. Born around 1867, Billy Assu was chosen as a boy to undergo instruction in leadership. In his mid-twenties he became chief of the Wiwekae. He began a school; encouraged employment in canning industries and commercial fishing; negotiated for better wages, better prices, and better equipment; attempted to curtail drinking; and put an end to potlatching.   IVY

2595   **MOCHON   MARION JOHNSON**
1966
KWAKIUTL DANCE DRAMAS. In Masks of the Northwest Coast. Robert Ritzenthaler and Lee A. Parsons, eds. Milwaukee Public Museum Publications in Primitive Art 2. Milwaukee: Milwaukee Public Museum. pp. 23-48.

The masks of the Barrett collection are discussed in their cultural context.   IVY

2596   **NORCROSS   ELIZABETH**
1969
HEAD START AT ALERT BAY. Monday Morning 3(9):24-25.

The conception and growth of a nursery school in Alert Bay, attended and taught by Indians and non-Indians, is described.   IVY

2597   **PARKER   SEYMOUR**
1964
THE KWAKIUTL INDIANS: "AMIABLE"AND "ATROCIOUS."Anthropologica
N.S. 6:131-158.

Examination of Kwakiutl economic activity, socialization, myths, and ceremonies yields an interpretation of the apparently contradictory cooperative and competitive elements of Kwakiutl society as integrate outgrowths of the dynamic relation between personality and culture.   WRC

2598   **PIDDOCKE   STUART**
1965
THE POTLATCH SYSTEM OF THE SOUTHERN KWAKIUTL: A NEW
PERSPECTIVE. Southwestern Journal of Anthropology 21:244-264.

An analysis of the literature on the Southern Kwakiutl suggests that food sources were of variable productivity. The aboriginal potlatch is seen as a mechanism for trading food for prestige.   TSA

2599   **POSTAL   SUSAN KOESSLER**
1965
BODY-IMAGE AND IDENTITY: A COMPARISON OF KWAKIUTL AND HOPI.
American Anthropologist 67:455-462.

Kwakiutl and Hopi legends provide the basis for formulating body-image as a concept in the study of culture. In contrast to the Hopi concern with internal fitness, the Kwakiutl notions of body boundaries and self identity are characterized as externally directed. Clothing, nomenclature, and wealth were considered extensions of the individual. It is concluded that on the cultural level the review of oral tradition gives some understanding of how the self is viewed within a cultural context.   WRC

2600   **ROGERS   EDWARD S,   UPDIKE   LEE**
1969
THE KWAKIUTL. The Beaver 299(Spring):24-27.

A pictorial article depicts 19th century tribal life including customs, dress, tools, subsistence, and dwellings.   IVY

2601   **ROHNER   RONALD P**
1964
ETHNOGRAPHY OF A CONTEMPORARY KWAKIUTL VILLAGE: GILFORD

ISLAND BAND. Ph.D. Thesis. Department of Anthropology. Stanford University. 345 pp. Available from University Microfilms.

A report is presented on research conducted among the Gilford Island Kwakiutl from June, 1962, through August, 1963. Traditional Kwakiutl life is reveiwed and areas of social change are noted. Conflict and behavior patterns are traced through the description of various aspects of contemporary life including subsistence and economic activities, education, marriage and family, social organization, social interaction, religion, and death. Some corrections and clarifications are noted in reference to various publications concerning the Kwakiutl.   CCV

2602   **ROHNER   RONALD P**
1965
FACTORS INFLUENCING THE ACADEMIC PERFORMANCE OF KWAKIUTL CHILDREN IN CANADA. Comparative Education Review 9:331-340.

Fieldwork undertaken during 1962 and 1964 has shown that the depressed academic performance of Kwakiutl children is influenced by the demands and assumptions of the Canadian-American education system which are inconsistent with the values of Kwakiutl society, and by the teachers' attitudes toward and relationships with members of the community which are non-facilitative.   ADG

2603   **ROHNER   RONALD P**
1967
THE PEOPLE OF GILFORD: A CONTEMPORARY KWAKIUTL VILLAGE.
National Museum of Canada Bulletin 225. Ottawa: Queen's Printer. 179 pp.

The 2 major aims of the author were to present a holistic description of Kwakiutl life, and to develop a source book. A general ethnographic description of the Gilford Island Band, British Columbia, follows. Fieldwork was conducted in 1962-1963 and in 1964. Discussed are the cultural, ecological, and historical setting, demography, economics, social organization, the family, life cycle, education, intoxicants, political organization, death, and religion. The epilogue provides insights into the field situation. Conflict and valued behavior were emphasized. Among the appendices is a suggestion for future research problems.   JSL

2604   **ROHNER   RONALD P,   ROHNER   EVELYN C**
1970
THE KWAKIUTL: INDIANS OF BRITISH COLUMBIA. New York: Holt, Rinehart and Winston. 111 pp.

Life style at the Gilford Island Kwakiutl village is described from fieldwork conducted from September, 1962, until August, 1963, and during June and July, 1964. Traditional Kwakiutl social organization - particularly social stratification, potlatching, and the winter ceremonial - are also discussed.   CCV

2605   **SEWID   JAMES**
1969
GUESTS NEVER LEAVE HUNGRY: THE AUTOBIOGRAPHY OF JAMES SEWID, A KWAKIUTL INDIAN. James P. Spradley, ed. New Haven: Yale University Press. 310 pp.

This autobiography of James Sewid, a Kwakiutl Indian, demonstrates how he adapted successfully to a bicultural environment. Sewid is not only a respected leader in his own community, but a successful entrepreneur by western standards. Sewid's behavior was observed by Spradley over a 2 year period, during which he was administered various psychological tests. This research allows examination of the complex relationship between such an individual and culture change per se.   DGW

2606   **SISMEY   ERIC D**
1961
H'KUSAM A KWAKIUTL VILLAGE. The Beaver 292(Winter):24-27.

An historical presentation of the village of H'Kusam from 1880 to 1953 is given utilizing photographs.   IVY

2607   **SPECK   HENRY**
1964
KWAKIUTL ART. Vancouver: B.C. Indian Designs. 16 pp.

This is an illustrated booklet of paintings by Chief Henry Speck. A background of Kwakiutl art and its traditions is presented.   IVY

2608   **SPICER   EDWARD H**
1961
TYPES OF CONTACT AND PROCESSES OF CHANGE. In Perspectives in American Indian Culture. Edward H. Spicer, ed. Chicago: University of Chicago Press. pp. 517-544.

The intention of this cross-cultural analysis of case materials was to reveal recurrent regularities in the association of processes of change with types of contact. Incorporation, replacement, fusion, and compartmentalization were delineated as the processes of alteration of a culture under contact conditions. Incorporation was considered the dominant process among the Kwakiutl during the pre-potlatch and early potlatch period. Five specific contact communities were distinguished: the Spanish mission, fur trade, United States reservation, Canadian reservation, and urban segment. These types differed in relation to systemic linkage, role and sanction patterns, and structural stability. A distinction was made between directed and non-directed contact situations. The view of differential change set forth recognizes the importance of discovering regularities in the sequence of change within a contact community.   DGW

2609   **SPRADLEY   JAMES P**
1966
PERSONALITY AND INNOVATION: A KWAKIUTL CASE STUDY. Unpublished paper delivered to 65th Annual Meeting, American Anthropological Association. Pittsburgh, November 17-20, 1966. Available from National Library of Canada. 20 pp.

Selecting a highly innovative individual of the Mamalilikulla tribe of the Southern Kwakiutl, data were collected to test the hypotheses that the innovative personality type results from: (1) a large number of different identity models during childhood, (2) an early perception of extraordinary respect and esteem from significant adults, (3) an exposure to and internalization of the values of the Protestant ethic, (4) the presence of a strong mother and a weak or absent father, (5) socialization into 2 contrasting cultures, and (6) early freedom and geographical mobility. Methods of obtaining information include an extensive life history of the subject, structured interviews, participant observation, projective tests, secondary records (council minutes), and interviews with Indians and Whites who have played important roles in relation to the subject. From this data, the subject's experiences supported the hypotheses.   IVY

2610   **SPRADLEY   JAMES P**
1969
GUESTS NEVER LEAVE HUNGRY: THE AUTOBIOGRAPHY OF JAMES
SEWID, A KWAKIUTL INDIAN. See James Sewid.

2611   **SPRADLEY   JAMES PHILLIP**
1963
THE KWAKIUTL GUARDIAN SPIRIT QUEST: AN HISTORICAL,
FUNCTIONAL, AND COMPARATIVE ANALYSIS. M.A. Thesis. Department of
Anthropology. University of Washington. 128 pp.

The guardian spirit quest in Kwakiutl society is subjected to analysis by the historical, functional, and comparative methods. The relationship between the general ritual and the Kwakiutl variation is shown. Explored are the principal manifest and latent functions of the secret society ceremonial as it developed among the Kwakiutl. The ceremonial organization and secret elements in it served to reinforce the concepts of rank and prestige related to wealth thus supporting Kwakiutl norms and values and contributing to social solidarity.   CCV

2612   **SPRADLEY   JAMES PHILLIP**
1967
JAMES SEWID: A SOCIAL, CULTURAL AND PSYCHOLOGICAL ANALYSIS OF
A BICULTURAL INNOVATOR. Ph.D. Thesis. Department of Anthropology.
University of Washington. 530 pp. Available from University Microfilms.

A high-ranking Kwakiutl's responses to culture conflict and culture change are examined in this study of James Sewid's successful participation in both Indian and Western cultures. James Sewid's autobiography as recorded on tape and edited is presented and followed by an analysis of his personality and sociocultural environment. Bicultural adaptation and innovative activity are emphasized. His innovations are examined to determine where his ideas originated, how he combined elements from both cultures, and how his personality permitted this. Seven features in his early socialization are examined and compared to those associated with creative individuals in Western society.   CCV

2613   **WAITE   DEBORAH**
1966
KWAKIUTL TRANSFORMATION MASKS. In The Many Faces of Primitive Art: A
Critical Anthology. Douglas Fraser, ed. Englewood Cliffs, NJ: Prentice-Hall. pp. 266-
300.

Aspects of Northwest Coast religion, ceremony, and mythology, particularly that of the Kwakiutl, are investigated to throw light on the character, origin, and meaning of the Kwakiutl transformation mask. Guardian spirit, shamanism, and seasonal ceremonial cycle are discussed and related to mask construction. Siberian and Kwakiutl shamanism as well as the Kwakiutl and Eskimo transformation masks are compared. The influence of Siberian shamanism especially in naturalistic bird or animal masks encompassing a human head is suggested. Similarity with true Eskimo transformation masks is likewise indicated. Mythological characters portrayed by certain of the masks are clearly of local origin although other influences may be present. Numerous illustrations accompany the text.   CCV

2614   **WEINBERG   DANIELA**
1965
MODELS OF SOUTHERN KWAKIUTL SOCIAL ORGANIZATION. General
Systems: Yearbook of the Society for General Systems Research 10:169-181.

Kwakiutl social organization is examined and explanations of the potlatch scrutinized. An ecological model incorporating 2 subsystems, culture and environment, is diagramed. Fluctuation between scarcity and surplus in the environment necessitates the position of chief (in times of scarcity) and his use of the potlatch (in times of surplus).   IVY

2615   **WILHELMSEN   FINN**
1969
SALMON, STATUS, ETIQUETTE AND WORLD RENEWAL AMONG THE
KWAKIUTL. M.A. Thesis. Department of Anthropology. Tulane University. 91 pp.

The significance of salmon recipes in Kwakiutl society is analyzed with reference to the Kwakiutl concept of annual rejuvenation of the world. Exploitation of the ecological niche; property rights; rank and status; religion; salmon fishing techniques; preservation, storing, and preparation methods; and the protocol associated with meal preparation and eating are discussed.   CCV

2616   **WOLCOTT   HARRY F**
1964
A KWAKIUTL VILLAGE AND ITS SCHOOL: CULTURAL BARRIERS TO
CLASSROOM PERFORMANCE. Ph.D. Thesis. Department of Anthropology.
Stanford University. 519 pp. Available from University Microfilms.

Participant observation was employed during a year's fieldwork (1962-1963) in a Kwakiutl village. Data were gathered while teaching during the school year and sharing community activities in the summer. Contemporary village life is described including social and economic organization. Attention is focused on the school and education, attitudes toward education, aspirations, acculturation influences on scholastic success, village influences on learning, barriers to classroom achievement, and the notion of the value of education.   CCV

2617   **WOLCOTT   HARRY F**
1967
A KWAKIUTL VILLAGE AND SCHOOL. New York: Holt, Rinehart and Winston.
132 pp.

The 1962 fieldwork on which this study is based was reported in the author's doctoral dissertation. The study by the ethnographer and teacher is presented in 2 major parts: (1) village life and the social environment of the children and (2) teachers, the village school, the classroom program, and attitudes. Part 1 incorporates a description of every-day life, the annual economic cycle (in which clam digging, logging, and fishing domi-nate the cash economy of the village), and the social activities of the villagers. Part 2 traces the educational history of the village, deals with attitudes toward education of both Indian parents and White teachers as well as the interaction between parents and teachers, and describes the attitudes and performance of the pupils in the 1-room school.   IVY

2618   **WOLCOTT   HARRY F**
1969
THE TEACHER AS AN ENEMY. Unpublished paper. Available from National
Library of Canada. 23 pp.

Based upon his teaching experience (1962-63) at a 1-room elementary school (ages 6 to 16) at Blackfish Village, British Columbia, the role of the teacher is analyzed. Accultura-tion not infrequently breeds antagonism on the part of the dominated group. A descrip-tion of the behavior of Blackfish pupils, both collectively and individually, which mani-fests this hostility is given. The student's perception of school and the role of teacher and student is presented first from the teacher's impression and secondly from written com-ments of the older pupils. In a cross-cultural setting in which a teacher encounters antag-onistic behavior rooted in cultural rather than classroom origins, it is believed that a teacher would be able to cope more successfully with conflict situations if he were to rec-ognize and analyze his ascribed role as "enemy."By examining his own culture as the alien one, a teacher would become more effective, gain a perspective for understanding, and recognize cherished differences.   IVY

NOOTKA

2619   **BAIRD   RON**
1962
MAN WITH A VISION. The Beaver 292(Spring):4-10.

A biography of Nootka artist George Clutesi is presented. Two paintings, "The Spirit of the Yellow Cedar Tree"and "Pookmiss,"are also described.   IVY

2620   **BRITISH COLUMBIA. Provincial Museum.**
1968
NOOTKA WHALING: MAN AND NATURE IN BRITISH COLUMBIA. Victoria,
B.C.: Queen's Printer. 1 p.

A technical analysis of the traditional whaling technique employed by the Nootka of Vancouver Island's west coast is given.   IVY

2621   **DUFF   WILSON**
1965
THOUGHTS ON THE NOOTKA CANOE. Victoria, B.C.: Queen's Printer. 8 pp.

The concern of this paper is the remote ancestry of the Nootka canoe. The thesis of the author is that the canoe reveals its ancestry in its form. Through a comparison of the fea-tures of construction and details of ornamentation of the Nootka canoe and the Eskimo umiak, the author suggests that the umiak might be a direct ancestor of the Nootka craft. Sketches and photographs accompany the text.   IVY

2622   **FOLAN   WILLIAM J,   DEWHIRST   JOHN T**
1970
YUQUOT: WHERE THE WIND BLOWS FROM ALL DIRECTIONS. Archaeology
23:276-286.

Documents from the Cook expedition serve as sources for a description of the Nootka of
Yuquot of 1778. An archaeological excavation of a midden at Yuquot is also described.   IVY

2623   **GUNTHER   ERNA**
1960
A RE-EVALUATION OF THE CULTURAL POSITION OF THE NOOTKA. In Men
and Culture: Selected Papers of the Fifth International Congress of Anthropological and
Ethnological Sciences. Anthony F. D. Wallace, ed. Philadelphia: University of
Pennsylvania Press. pp. 270-276.

Examining pieces of Nootka art in some early European collections and utilizing historical documents and ethnographic materials, it is shown that the Nootka, after reaching a
similar cultural level to other Northwest Coast tribes, suffered a period of cultural regres-
sion and stagnation.   IVY

2624   **MOZINO   JOSE MARIANO**
1970
NOTICIAS DE NUTKA: AN ACCOUNT OF NOOTKA SOUND IN 1792.
Translated and edited by Iris Higbie Wilson. American Ethnological Society Monograph
50. Seattle: University of Washington Press. 142 pp.

This is an account by a botanist-naturalist following his visit to Nootka Sound, Vancouver Island, from April 29 to September 21, 1792. Mazino discusses the natives themselves, their material culture, subsistence activities, religion, language, music, poetry, and
system of government. A Nootkan-Spanish dictionary, drawings by Atanasio Eshever-
ria, and a catalog of plants and animals supplement the text.   IVY

2625   **SERVICE   ELMAN R**
1963
PROFILES IN ETHNOLOGY. New York: Harper and Row. pp. 207-228.

One chapter presents an ethnological study of the Nootka chiefdomship using data from
the period 1870 to circa 1900. It's priesthood, attitudes towards individual status, and
social organization are more inclined towards the chiefdomship patterns in Polynesia
and Asia than to the social organization of aboriginal America.   DGW

STRAITS SALISH

2626   **AZIZ   SALIM AKHTAR**
1970
SELECTED ASPECTS OF CULTURAL CHANGE AMONG AMERINDIANS: A
CASE STUDY OF SOUTHEAST VANCOUVER ISLAND. M.A. Thesis. Department
of Geography. University of Victoria. 92 pp.

The variables of population, occupation and income, housing, and formal education are
examined for 1880 and 1969 to demonstrate economic changes in the Sanetch, Sooke,

and Songish communities in southeast Vancouver Island. Historic documents, government records, and a field survey of 8 reserves provide data. An occidental form of economy has strongly influenced life style but traditional kinship and family patterns persist.   CCV

2627   **BRITISH COLUMBIA. Capital Region Planning Board.**
1968
THE INDIAN ACT AND PUBLIC POLICY STATEMENTS: RELEVANCE TO
LAND USE PLANNING FOR INDIAN COMMUNITIES: (INDIAN
COMMUNITIES AND LAND USE PLANNING). Victoria, B.C.: Capital Region
Planning Board. 30 pp.

This report endeavours to relate the Indian Act to land use planning and community development. Sections of the Indian Act are quoted and discussed within the framework of the following 5 headings: administration, government of the band, social-cultural-community development, land tenure-natural resource development, financial status. The appendix (8 pages) gives comparative statistical information on the Indian communities of Beecher Bay, Esquimalt, Pauquachin, Tsartlip, Tsawout, Tseycum, Songhees, and Sooke.   IVY

2628   **BRITISH COLUMBIA. Capital Region Planning Board.**
1968
PAUQUACHIN INDIAN COMMUNITY: PLANNING STUDY 1968. Victoria,
B.C.: Capital Region Planning Board. 35 pp.

This report was prepared for the Pauquachin Indian Council and the federal Department of Indian Affairs and Northern Development. The stated objective is to prepare a land use planning study showing the present and future land use requirements as they are related to the human development of the Pauquachin Indian Community in the setting of the Capital Region of British Columbia. Plans and diagrams accompany the text.   IVY

2629   **BRITISH COLUMBIA. Capital Region Planning Board.**
1969
BEECHER BAY INDIAN COMMUNITY: PLANNING STUDY 1969. Victoria, B.C.:
Capital Region Planning Board. 50 pp.

This report was prepared for the Beecher Bay Indian Community. The objective is to prepare a planning study showing the present and future land use requirements as they are related to the human development of the Beecher Bay Indian Reserve community in the setting of the Capital Region of British Columbia. Plans and diagrams accompany the text.   IVY

2630   **DUFF   WILSON**
1969
THE FORT VICTORIA TREATIES. BC Studies 3:3-57.

Between 1850 and 1854, James Douglas concluded 14 agreements, purchasing land from the Indians of Vancouver Island. The manner in which the treaties describe the territories of the various "tribes"or "families"is examined to test their accuracy as ethnographic documents. Together with the treaties and information from informants and historic materials, Songish place names and their history are recounted.   IVY

2631   **FLOYD   PATRICK   DONALD**
1963
THE HUMAN GEOGRAPHY OF SOUTHEASTERN VANCOUVER ISLAND,
1842-1891. M.A. Thesis. Department of Geography. University of Victoria. 215 pp.

While the Straits Salish shared with other Northwest Coast tribes a reliance on marine
resources, they to a greater extent utilized land flora and fauna. The writings of explorers
and early settlers and later anthropologists are utilized to provide a description of the
environment and human use of it at the time Whites moved into southern Vancouver Island (1842). The impact of the fur trade upon the establishment of the Hudson's Bay
post is described. The examination of the area at other points in time (1863, 1880-81, and
1890-91) includes references to the native population.   TSA

2632   **LEWIS   CLAUDIA**
1970
INDIAN FAMILIES OF THE NORTHWEST COAST. Chicago: University of
Chicago Press. 224 pp.

Fieldwork among the "Camas"Indians of Vancouver Island - an unidentified Indian tribe
- was done during the summers of 1954 and 1957. In the summer of 1968, the author
recorded the social and structural changes which occurred in the community over a 10
year interval. Problems of the Indian family in adjusting to the dominant culture are examined in the relief of traditional values and practices. Recommended programs to help
increase the self-respect of the Indians as well as predictions for the future condition of
"Camas"families are also made.   DGW

2633   **MICKELSON   NORMA I,   GALLOWAY   CHARLES G**
1968
IMPROVING LANGUAGE PATTERNS: A STUDY OF LANGUAGE
DEVELOPMENT OF INDIAN CHILDREN. Unpublished paper delivered to
Conference on Grass Root Developments in Education (Co-ordinated by L.E.A.R.N.).
Duncan, B.C., October 19, 1968. Available from National Library of Canada. 8 pp.

A 4-week pre-kindergarten, pre-school, and orientation enrichment program for Indian
children living on 4 reserves in the southern region of Vancouver Island (Tsartlip, Patricia Bay, Cole Bay, and East Saanich) was conducted at the University of Victoria during
the 1968 Summer School Session. A major area of concern was the methodology employed to increase the quality and quantity of the children's verbalizations. Tests were
administered to the children to measure improvement. Goal-directed teaching elicited
significant improvement.   IVY

2634   **THE OPTIMIST**
1961
TSAWWASSEN LEGENDS. Ladner, B.C.: Dunning Press. 59 pp.

Eleven legends unique to the Tsawwassen Indian Band of the Delta Municipality, originally collected in 1946 and 1947 by Geraldine McGeer Appleby, are presented. A history of the band provides an introductory note for the publication.   DGW

TLINGIT

2635 **BULLEN   EDWARD LESTER**
1968
AN HISTORICAL STUDY OF THE EDUCATION OF THE INDIANS OF TESLIN,
YUKON TERRITORY. M.Ed. Thesis. Department of Educational Foundations.
University of Alberta. 252 pp.

From ethnographic sources, teaching experiences in the Yukon from 1961 to 1966, and
fieldwork done in August and September of 1967 the Teslin Indians are considered from
pre-contact times to the present. Changes introduced by White contact before and after
the Alaska highway are described with special attention to mission and residential
schools and native acculturation.   CCV

2636 **KEITHAHN   E L**
1962
HERALDIC SCREENS OF THE TLINGIT. Alaska Sportsman 28(2):16-19,45.

Origins of heraldic screens and of their designs in Alaska and British Columbia are discussed. Photographs accompany text.   IVY

2637 **KEITHAHN   E L**
1962
HUMAN HAIR IN TLINGIT ART. Alaska Sportsman 28(5):22-23,39-40.

Ideas of contagious magic associated with human hair suggest that hair used in art was
obtained from slaves. Since, however, slaves were kept shorn to indicate their status this
hypothesis is false. The use of hair in art is related to the concept of hair as a sacred em-
blem or magical tie with deceased relatives. The method of applying hair to embellish
heads of masks and human figurines is briefly described.   IVY

2638 **KEITHAHN   E L**
1963
BURIAL CUSTOMS OF THE TLINGIT. Alaska Sportsman 29(4):18-19,33-36.

Aboriginal mortuary practices are described and the transition from the dead house to
grave fence to headstone in Alaska is outlined.   IVY

2639 **MCCLELLAN   CATHARINE**
1963
WEALTH WOMAN AND FROGS AMONG THE TAGISH INDIANS. Anthropos
58:121-128.

Fieldwork among the Tagish Indians in 1948, 1949, and 1950-51 revealed informants'
attitudes toward individual success or failure in attaining material wealth. The development of the Wealth Woman story following the cataclysmic Klondyke gold rush of 1898
provided 1 example of how the Tagish incorporated recent, dissonant events into their
balanced world view.   WRC

TSIMSHIAN

2640   **ADAMS   ALICE K**
1968
STATISTICAL METHODS FOR THE STUDY OF MARRIAGE PREFERENCES.
Unpublished paper delivered to 67th Annual Meeting, American Anthropological
Association. Seattle, WA, November 21-24, 1968. Available from National Library of
Canada. 14 pp.

This paper discusses and compares 2 methods of marriage patterns evaluating their usefulness for the Gitksan, a group of interior Tsimshian in British Columbia. The 2 methods are useful in bringing to light significant patterns that are not apparent from the raw
frequencies. They both reveal the fact that one cannot conclude from raw frequencies
alone how important a marriage pattern is or its true nature.   HCV

2641   **ADAMS   ALICE K**
1969
POLITICAL ASPECTS OF GITKSAN COUSIN MARRIAGE. Unpublished paper
delivered to 68th Annual Meeting, American Anthropological Association. New
Orleans, LA, November 20-23, 1969. Available from National Library of Canada. 10
pp.

This paper argues that marriage with a cross-cousin among the Gitksan has more relevance for internal politics of the descent group than for the relationships outside it, sig-
naling the fact that inheritance is switching from one line to another within the descent
group.   HCV

2642   **ADAMS   ALICE KASAKOFF**
1970
EXPLICIT AND IMPLICIT MARRIAGE RULES AMONG THE GITSKAN. Ph.D.
Thesis. Department of Social Relations. Harvard University. 262 pp.

Marriage practices in the Gitskan villages of Gitsegueklas, Kitwanga, Cedarvale, and
Kitwankool are examined using marriage records and genealogies to supplement 16
months fieldwork during 1966-67. Although certain marriage preferences were mentioned inconsistently by informants, no generally accepted rules could be articulated.
Detailed analysis of data was undertaken to examine the influence, if any, of kinship,
corporate group membership, and residence on marriage choice. It was found that individuals avoided marriage with others who were in the same phratry or first cousins.
Marriage was also avoided between those people whose fathers resided in the same
house and those whose fathers called each other cousin. Preferences were either very
general, applicable only in particular cases, or involved those not normally considered relatives. Marriages were used to create new ties rather than to reinforce those existing.
Definite preferences for marriage between a variety of corporate groups were revealed.
The 4 villages studied form an endogamous unit. It is concluded that the basic system of
marriage preference remains implicit or unexpressed because it is obvious or an accomodation to conflict. Explicit or stated preferences are qualifications or modifications of the
basic system.   CCV

2643   **ADAMS   JOHN W**
1969

THE EFFECT OF THE GITKSAN POTLATCH ON THE REDISTRIBUTION OF PEOPLE TO RESOURCES. Unpublished paper delivered to 68th Annual Meeting, American Anthropological Association. New Orleans, LA, November 20-23, 1969. Available from National Library of Canada. 5 pp.

This paper describes some of the mechanisms of the Gitksan potlatch and discusses its functions as a redistribution mechanism for cash and goods. It is concluded that the redistributional processes of these feasts serve to allocate people to resources rather than to redistribute wealth.   HCV

2644   **ADAMS   JOHN WINTHROP**
1970
THE POLITICS OF FEASTING AMONG THE GITKSAN. Ph.D. Thesis. Harvard University.

The title has been verified, but a copy was not obtained in time to abstract it.   SLP

2645   **BARBEAU   MARIUS**
1962
BUDDHIST DIRGES ON THE NORTH PACIFIC COAST. International Folk Music Council Journal 14:16-21.

Funeral songs (dirges) of the Kitwinlkul (Kitwancool) and Kitwanga tribes of northern British Columbia are compared in terms of content, style, and melody to Buddhist chants. As well, similarities in mortuary rituals and musical instruments are noted. It now seems practically certain that an early derivation of Buddhism long prevailed in the mortuary rituals of the Northwest Coast Indians.   IVY

2646   **DOCKSTADER   FREDERICK J**
1964
TOTEM POLES: FAMILY TREES. Natural History 73(8):62-63.

Four Kitsan totem poles are briefly discussed: the Skaimsem Pole at Gitwanlkul; the Kaohdihgyet Pole; the Tsemelih Pole at Gitsegyukla; and a pole at Kitwanga. Photographs showing portions of the poles accompany the text.   IVY

2647   **DREW   LESLIE**
1964
FOREST OF THE TOTEMS. The Beaver 297(Winter):49-55.

The restoration of the totem poles found in the villages of Kitwancool, Kitwanga, Kitseguecla, Gitanmaks (now Hazelton), and Kispiox is discussed.   IVY

2648   **HANNA   MARION WOODSIDE**
1963
KISPIOUX LEGEND. The Beaver 294(Autumn):40-41.

A Gitksan legend explains the unusual totem pole at Kispioux on the Skeena River.   IVY

2649   **INDIAN-ESKIMO ASSOCIATION OF CANADA**
1965
FRANK ARTHUR CALDER, L.Th. M.L.A. Canadian Indians of Today No. 2. 2 pp.

A biographic sketch of Frank Arthur Calder, born at Nass Harbour, British Columbia, is given. A former member of Parliament who has held numerous positions in native organizations, he is concerned with the settlement of the British Columbia Indian land question and advocates the gradual elimination of the Indian reserve system.   IVY

2650   **ISSUTH-GWEKS**
1967
AN EXCERPT FROM MY MEMOIRS. The Peak (Simon Fraser University) 5(15):11.

A member of the Kispioux band recalls the atmosphere of the potlatch in her youth and laments the problems faced by Indians today.   TSA

2651   **LEVI-STRAUSS   CLAUDE**
1967
THE STORY OF ASDIWAL. In The Structural Study of Myth and Totemism. Edmund Leach, ed. Association of Social Anthropologists of the Commonwealth Monographs 5. London: Tavistock. pp. 1-47.

The geographic, economic, social, and cosmological levels in the structure of the Tsimshian Asdiwal myth are examined. This analysis of 2 major versions indicates the inversion of and the weakening of oppositions in the myth in its passage from the Skeena to the Nass River peoples.   WRC

2652   **MOELLER   BEVERLEY B**
1966
CAPTAIN JAMES COLNETT AND THE TSIMSHIAN INDIANS, 1787. Pacific Northwest Quarterly 57:13-17.

Excerpts with commentary from Colnett's journal describe various encounters with the Tsimshian, both friendly and otherwise.   IVY

2653   **NISHGA TRIBAL COUNCIL**
1960
IN THE MATTER OF COMPENSATION FOR THE LAND AND NATURAL RESOURCES, AND THE DESTRUCTION OF TRAPLINES IN THE NASS RIVER AREA. In Minutes of Proceedings and Evidence. No. 7. May 26-27, 1960. Joint Committee of the Senate and the House of Commons on Indian Affairs. Canada. 24 Parliament, 3 Session. Ottawa: Queen's Printer. pp. 580-583.

Aboriginal rights to the Nass River country are claimed. Compensation for the loss of land and timber resources, and for the destruction of traplines is demanded.   JSL

2654   **ROUGH   STAN**
1965
CASE FOR TOPPLING TOTEMS. Alaska Sportsman 31(1):28-29.

A volunteer fact-finding survey of poles has been conducted in the villages of the Upper Skeena River of British Columbia with the ultimate objective of preserving these poles. IVY

2655   **USHER   JEAN**
1969
WILLIAM DUNCAN OF METLAKATLA: A VICTORIAN MISSIONARY IN BRITISH COLUMBIA. Ph.D. Thesis. Department of History. University of British Columbia. 373 pp. Available from National Library of Canada.

Analyzed is the model Christian Indian utopia of Metlakatla in British Columbia. Established for the Tsimshian nation in 1862, it was the dream of the Victorian missionary William Duncan. As a result of an ensuing conflict between Duncan and the Anglican Church Missionary Society, there was an eventual breakdown in the unity of Metlakatla. It is the purpose of this study to examine the role of the missionary in a situation of rapid social change such as was evident in this Tsimshian community. DGW

2656   **WRIGHT   WALTER**
1962
MEN OF MEDEEK. By Will Robinson as told by Walter Wright. 2nd Edition. Kitimat: Northern Sentinel Press. 93 pp.

This history of Medeek was told by Chief Walter Wright of the Kitselas Band to Will Robinson in 1935-1936. The story goes back several centuries. Details concerning the legendary city of Tum-L.-Hama and the migration westward to the Kitselas Canyon are given. DGW

PLATEAU

2657   **BRUNTON   BILL B**
1968
CEREMONIAL INTEGRATION IN THE PLATEAU OF NORTHWESTERN NORTH AMERICA. Northwest Anthropological Research Notes 2(1):1-28.

Taking a diachronic, structural-functional approach based on ethnographic materials from both the aboriginal and contemporary periods, it is shown that 2 linguistically based ceremonial congregations (Interior Salish, Sahaptian) are tied together by dyadic and polyadic relations. This ceremonial integration persisting into the present binds Plateau groups into larger social entities, independent of Euroamerican society. IVY

2658   **BURNS   ROBERT IGNATIUS**
1966
THE JESUITS AND THE INDIAN WARS OF THE NORTHWEST. New Haven: Yale University Press. 493 pp.

The history of the Indian wars of the American Northwest is reviewed and expanded with material from unpublished Jesuit records and the archives of the American War Department and Indian Bureau in addition to those of the Hudson's Bay Company. The focus is the role of the Catholic missions, particularly the Jesuits, in the exploration and evangelization of the Northwest as well as in negotiation of peace and treaties with the Indians. Allusions to the effects and influences of colonization and fur trade are included.

Reference to and descriptions of Canadian Plateau tribes of the border are frequent.   CCV

2659   **CONN   RICHARD G**
1967
THE RAREST TYPE OF BLUE JAY. The Blue Jay 25:2-5.

The Salishan shamans of the Plateau region who are known as Bluejays are discussed.   IVY

2660   **CORNER   JOHN**
1968
PICTOGRAPHS (INDIAN ROCK PAINTINGS) IN THE INTERIOR OF BRITISH COLUMBIA. Vernon, B.C.: Wayside Press. 131 pp.

Pictographic sites in the interior of British Columbia are discussed. Illustrations accompany the text. The author has recorded and studied pictographs in the central and southern interior of British Columbia for 8 years.   IVY

2661   **GEORGE   GRAHAM**
1962
SONGS OF THE SALISH INDIANS OF BRITISH COLUMBIA. International Folk Music Council Journal 14:22-29.

Fifteen of some 60 songs of the Salish tribe of British Columbia, living on the Upper Thompson and Lillooet Rivers, recorded under the direction of Marius Barbeau in 1912 are used to demonstrate some of the characteristics of Salish songs. Included are phrase-structure, scale-structure, interval-structure, percussion, and exclamations. Transcriptions illustrating these aspects accompany the text.   IVY

2662   **JOHNSON   OLGA WEYDEMEYER**
1969
FLATHEAD AND KOOTENAY: THE RIVERS, THE TRIBES AND THE REGION'S TRADERS. Glendale, CA: Clark. 392 pp.

From historical and archival sources and interviews an account of numerous aspects of Flathead and Kutenai social organization and history are described before and after contact. Included are: aboriginal and contemporary subsistence activities, migrations, intertribal relations, folklore and oral tradition, aboriginal religious belief, Indian-White relations, intermarriage, missions, and acculturation.   CCV

2663   **MITCHELL   DONALD HECTOR**
1963
ESILAO: A PIT HOUSE VILLAGE IN THE FRASER CANYON, BRITISH COLUMIBA. M.A. Thesis. Department of Anthropology and Sociology. University of British Columbia. 156 pp.

The Tait and Thompson Indians of the Fraser River Canyon are compared on the basis of ethnographic data and archaeological results of excavation of a recent Tait pit houses

near Yale, British Columbia, in 1961 and 1962. Uniformity of Canyon culture and align-
ment with the interior culture complex are revealed by the ethnographic survey. Overlap-
ping areas of archaeological data support the ethnographic conclusions.   CCV

2664   **SANGER   DAVID**
1969
DEVELOPMENT OF THE PACIFIC NORTHWEST PLATEAU CULTURE AREA:
HISTORICAL AND ENVIRONMENTAL CONSIDERATIONS. In Contributions to
Anthropology: Ecological Essays: Proceedings of the Conference on Cultural Ecology,
Ottawa, August 3-6, 1966. David Damas, ed.   National Museums of Canada Bulletin
230. Ottawa: Queen's Printer. pp. 15-23.

Environmental and historical factors associated with the development of the Plateau culture area are examined. The Plateau's prehistory reveals that there was a long separation
of northern and southern portions of the area. The southern Columbia Plateau was af-
filiated with Desert cultures while the northern Interior Plateau of British Columbia was
more closely related to the Canadian Prairies and Sub-Arctic. About 1000 A.D. an influx
of Interior Plateau traits (including housepits, woodworking, and an intensive riverine
orientation) into the Columbia Plateau coincided with the reintroduction of salmon into
the latter area. The result, in historic times, was an observed similarity throughout the
Plateau.   JSL

2665   **SPRAGUE   RODERICK**
1967
ABORIGINAL BURIAL PRACTICES IN THE PLATEAU REGION OF NORTH
AMERICA. Ph.D. Thesis. Department of Anthropology. University of Arizona. 258 pp.
Available from University Microfilms.

An historic burial site in eastern Washington is described and analyzed. Also included is
a review of burial practices in the Plateau with Canadian Plateau discussed on pages 119-
122. An overview of ethnographic burial practices in the Plateau area is presented in
Chapter 5 including brief summaries for the Flathead, Sinkaietk, Thompson, Lillooet,
Shuswap, Kutenai, Chilcotin, Carrier, and Sekani.   CCV

KUTENAI

2666   **DEMPSEY   HUGH A, ed.**
1965
THOMPSON'S JOURNEY TO THE RED DEER RIVER. Alberta Historical Review
13(1):1-8.

An excerpt is presented from the journal of David Thompson, in charge of the North
West Company's Rocky Mountain House. The account from October 5 to October 23,
1800, is of the first probable meeting and negotiations between White traders and the
Kutenai across the Rocky Mountains, a preliminary to the westward expansion of the
fur trade. Included are 2 photographs and a map of the probable route taken by
Thompson and his Indian guides.   WRC

2667   **GRAHAM   CLARA**
1963
THIS WAS THE KOOTENAY. Vancouver: Evergreen Press. 270 pp.

The history of the Kootenay district of British Columbia is described. One chapter is devoted to a reconstruction of the aboriginal life of the Kutenai. Folktales and legends, mostly of Indian origin, are reported in another chapter. The balance of the book treats the arrival of settlers, traders, prospectors, and the railway. References to Indians are frequent and include accounts of clashes between Indian and White, Kutenai and Lake, and Kutenai and Blackfoot. Prominent Indian figures and culture heroes are discussed as are the effects of acculturation.   CCV

2668   **LEECHMAN   DOUGLAS**
1962
THE KOOTENAY CANOE. The Beaver 292(Spring):11-15.

This article describes the Kutenai canoe and discusses its form, construction, and distribution.   IVY

2669   **SCHAEFFER   CLAUDE E**
1965
THE KUTENAI FEMALE BERDACHE: COURIER, GUIDE, PROPHETESS, AND WARRIOR. Ethnohistory 12:193-236.

Utilizing documentary and traditional sources, supplemented by information collected from Kutenai Indians, the life history of a Kutenai berdache named Qanqon is outlined. Her role is analyzed and compared to similar deviants of the Blackfoot, Cheyenne, and Crow among others.   IVY

2670   **SCHAEFFER   CLAUDE E**
1966
LE BLANC AND LA GASSE: PREDECESSORS OF DAVID THOMPSON IN THE COLUMBIAN PLATEAU. Museum of the Plains Indian Studies in Plains Anthropology and History 3. Browning, MT. 13 pp.

An account is given of the earliest Whites to venture into the interior and of their relations with the Kutenai.   IVY

LILLOOET

2671   **DICKINSON   JAMES GARY**
1968
AN ANALYTICAL SURVEY OF THE PEMBERTON VALLEY IN BRITISH COLUMBIA WITH SPECIAL REFERENCE TO ADULT EDUCATION. Ed.D. Thesis. Faculty of Education. University of British Columbia. 302 pp. Available from National Library of Canada.

Examined in detail is the rural community of the Pemberton Valley with the intent of determining relevant factors which influence participation in adult education. Subjected to analysis were 158 non-Indian household heads as well as 32 Indian respondents from the Mount Currie Indian Reserve in British Columbia. Nine socio-economic characteristics were studied to see whether differences between groups related to participation in adult education. These included age, number of children at home, birthplace, number of years resident in the area, number of related families living in Pemberton, farm or non-farm resident, father's education, perceived adequacy of skills, and desire for further education or training.   DGW

2672   MURPHY   JAMES
n.d.
REPORT ON REMEDIAL READING. Unpublished paper. Available from National
Library of Canada. 2 pp.

This article, written by a school teacher of Cayoosh Elementary School, Lillooet, explains
some problems Indian pupils have in reading and writing English.   HCV

2673   WILSON   RENATE
1964
BASKET MAKERS OF MOUNT CURRIE. The Beaver 295(Autumn):26-33.

The methods used to weave baskets are illustrated by text and photographs.   IVY

OKANAGON

2674   BRENT   MARIE HOUGHTON
1966
INDIAN LORE. Mrs. Harold Cochrane, comp. Okanagan Historical Society Report
30:105-114.

Mary Houghton Brent was chosen as a child to remember the story of her family and her
ancestors. Here she recounts the events which occurred during the lives of Chief Pelka-
Mu-Lox, Chief N'Kwala (her great grandfather), Young Chief N'Kwalia (her mother's
father), and Chief Joseph Tonasket.   IVY

2675   GRAY   ALAN S
1965
TEETH AND THE INDIAN CHILD. Canada's Health and Welfare 20(9):2-3,7.

Problems which arise in providing dental care for Canada's Indian population are: (1)
the small numbers seeking conservative dental care on their own, (2) not keeping ap-
pointments, and (3) not recognizing a new need caused by the adoption of a cariogenic
diet. At Penticton Reserve, British Columbia, out of a total of 64 children between the
ages of 3 and 17 living on the reserve, 59 registered in a dental health program developed in co-operation with the Canadian Department of National Health and Welfare
and the Health Branch of the Province of British Columbia. Complete treatment was received by 37 children, 14 received partial treatment, and 5 would not keep any appoint-
ments. A follow-up program is intended in 1965. Education in dental hygiene must accompany this effort.   IVY

2676   LOUIS   MRS BEN,   ROSS   D A
1969
PIERRE LOUIS, OKANAGAN CHIEF. Okanagan Historical Society Report 33:23.

Pierre Louis (1882-1968) was Chief of Okanagan Indian Reserve Number 1, of Number
2 (Westbank), and also of Duck Lake at Winfield, British Columbia, for 29 years.   IVY

2677   MCGLASHING   GREG
1970
THE SIMILKAMEEN INDIANS. Okanagan Historical Society Report 34:23-24.

A grade 8 essay winner gives a general description of the aboriginal Indians from the area of Similkameen, British Columbia.   IVY

2678   **RATCLIFF   RICHARD U**
1967
ANALYSIS OF DEVELOPMENT PROPOSAL FOR TSINSTIKEPTUM INDIAN RESERVE NO. 10, WESTBANK, B.C. Unpublished report prepared for J. V. Bays, Indian Commissioner for British Columbia. Available at Indian-Eskimo Economic Development Branch, Development Services Division, Department of Indian Affairs and Northern Development. 22 pp.

A contract with Grosvenor-Laing for development of Indian Reserve No. 10 at Westbank, British Columbia, is examined for practicality, financial impact, alternatives, and recommendations. The report is based on impressions arising from a field visit to Kelowna on November 10-11, 1967, and a meeting with 10 band members at that time. It is concluded that the contract terms could be improved upon and recommendations are advanced to this end.   CCV

2679   **SISMEY   ERIC D**
1966
QUIL'-STEN: OKANAGAN STEAM BATH. The Beaver 297(Summer):41-43.

The construction, significance, and method of use of a sweat lodge on the Pentiction Reserve is described in text and photographs.   IVY

2680   **SISMEY   ERIC D**
1969
CHIEF JACK ALEC. Okanagan Historical Society Report 33:20-21.

Chief Jack Alec (1901-1969) of the Penticton Band, British Columbia, guided the band for 17 years.   IVY

2681   **STEFFENS   SOPHIA**
1961
THE LAND OF CHIEF NICOLA: POEMS, VERSES AND HISTORICAL REMINISCENCES OF THE NICOLA VALLEY. Unpublished paper. Available from National Library of Canada. 28 pp.

This paper contains poems, verses, legends, and historical reflections of the late Chief Nicola and the valley bearing his name.   ADG

2682   **WATKINS   DONALD**
1970
THE PRACTICE OF MEDICINE AMONG THE INDIANS. Okanagan Historical Society Report 34:30-32.

When special healing skills were required, Okanagans went to their shaman. For less serious illnesses herbal remedies were applied. Fourteen plants of the Okanagan Valley and their use in curing are lsted.   IVY

2683 **WHITE   HESTER EMILY**
1962
STENWYKEN. Okanagan Historical Society Report 26:130-131.

Susap relates the story of the kidnapping of 2 Indian maidens by Stenwyken, the Hairy Giant of the Okanagan.   IVY

2684 **WHITE   HESTER EMILY**
1969
NOTES ON THE OKANAGANS. Okanagan Historical Society Report 33:100-101.

Activities within an aboriginal Okanagan camp have been recreated.   IVY

SHUSWAP

2685 **AKRIGG   HELEN BROWN**
1964
HISTORY AND ECONOMIC DEVELOPMENT OF THE SHUSWAP AREA. M.A. Thesis. Department of History. University of British Columbia. 140 pp.

As the history and economic development of the Shuswap area is outlined, brief reference is made to Indian-White relations as prospectors and settlers entered the area in the 19th century.   CCV

2686 **BROW   CATHERINE J**
1968
A SOCIO-CULTURAL HISTORY OF THE ALKALI LAKE SHUSWAP. M.A. Thesis. Department of Anthropology. University of Washington.

The title has been verified, but a copy was not obtained in time to abstract it.   SLP

2687 **RAWSON AND WILES LIMITED**
1966
STUDY OF BOUNDARY EXTENSION: KAMLOOPS, B.C. Unpublished paper. Available from Library, University of British Columbia. 41 pp.

This report was prepared for the Kamloops city council and the council of the Kamloops Indian Band. The purpose is to describe the probable consequences of extending the city boundaries to include part of Kamloops Indian Reserve No. 1 known as the Industrial Subdivision, particularly what costs and/or benefits will accrue to the band and to the city through boundary extension. Maps and illustrations accompany the text.   IVY

2688 **ROGERS   EDWARD S,   UPDIKE   LEE**
1970
THE SHUSWAP. The Beaver 300(Spring):56-59.

The aboriginal way of life of the Shuswap of British Columbia is depicted with illustrations. Described are the material culture, habitat, houses, subsistence pattern (hunting and fishing), and trade.   IVY

THOMPSON

2689   **ACRES WESTERN LIMITED**
1970
THE UPPER NICOLA INDIAN BAND DEVELOPMENT PLAN. Unpublished
paper. Available at Indian-Eskimo Economic Development Branch, Economic
Development Division, Department of Indian Affairs and Northern Development,
Ottawa. 53 pp.

Resource evaluation of the Nicola Lake, Hamilton Creek, Douglas Lake, Spahomin
Creek No. 4, Chapperon Lake, Chapperon Creek, Salmon Lake, and Spahomin Cree No.
8 Reserves occupied by the Upper Nicola Band is presented. With consideration of the
band's long-term needs and wants and predictable social and economic factors, recommendations are prepared for development, particularly in agriculture.   CCV

2690   **KITPOU**
n.d.
THE TRIBAL LAWS OF THE CHILDREN OF LIGHT. Unpublished paper. Available
from National Library of Canada. 13 pp.

Compiled and translated by Shaman Chief Kitpou, the 190 tribal laws of the Children of
Light are given.   IVY

2691   **MCDONNELL   ROGER FRANCIS**
1965
LAND TENURE AMONG THE UPPER THOMPSON INDIAN. M.A. Thesis.
Department of Anthropology and Sociology. University of British Columbia. 106 pp.

Fieldwork was conducted among the Upper Thompson Indians in the vicinity of Lytton,
British Columbia, during the summers of 1963 and 1964 to examine the contemporary
land tenure system. Data obtained from participant observation, interviews, Indian
Office files, and discussion with administrators report lack of conflict between official
policy as expressed in the Indian Act and the indigenous system of land tenure. This is
attributed to the fact that official administration is focused on land, largely unoccupied,
held for common band use or benefit. At the individual level little interference has occurred so that the considerable variations observed are related to other, generally non-ad-
ministrative, factors.   CCV

2692   **RAWSON AND WILES LIMITED**
1967
A PRELIMINARY STUDY OF RECREATIONAL POTENTIAL AND
RECREATION DEMAND IN BOTAHNIE VALLEY. Unpublished paper. Available
from Library, University of British Columbia. 27 pp.

A preliminary land use study of the Botahnie Reserve prepared for the Indian Commissioner for British Columbia and the Lytton Band assesses recreation potential and recreation demand. Part 1 of the report describes the physical features of the site and its attributes and discusses land use conflicts which have arisen. General development possibilities are presented in Part 2, focusing upon recreation. Part 3 examines and evaluates
Botahnie's recreation capabilities and limitations individually and to related competitive

recreation areas. Recommendations for immediate action by the Branch and the band are outlined in Part 4. Three maps accompany the text.   IVY

PLAINS

2693   **1963**
SMALLPOX EPIDEMIC OF 1869-70. Alberta Historical Review 11(2):13-19.

Three news articles printed in the Manitoban in 1871 are reproduced and reveal the rapid spread of smallpox, morbidity rates, and preventative measures among the Plains tribes in 1869-1870.   WRC

2694   **1964**
PEMMICAN AND HOW TO MAKE IT. The Beaver 295(Summer):53-55.

Discussed are the preparation, use, and methods of eating pemmican. Included are photographs of a contemporary Cree woman making pemmican.   IVY

2695   **1967**
NORTH-WEST MOUNTED POLICE: A BRIEF HISTORY. Alberta Historical Review 15(3):1-7.

Based on a report prepared by the Royal Canadian Mounted Police, a history of the Northwest Mounted Police from its establishment in 1873 to 1920 includes an account of law enforcement during the Riel Rebellion and the advent of the Sioux after Little Big Horn.   WRC

2696   **ALBERS   PATRICIA CAROL**
1969
THE VISION EXPERIENCE: A NEO-EVOLUTIONARY STUDY. M.S. Thesis. Department of Anthropology. Michigan State University. 206 pp. Available from National Library of Canada.

The vision experience was an important cultural phenomenon among the Plains Indians during the 17th through the 19th centuries. Using ethnographic literature on the vision experience of the Great Plains and of peripheral areas, this thesis demonstrates that variations in the meaning and function of the vision experience are systematically related to differences in selected social features. It tries to show that the vision experience was a form of rationale which served to justify a society's manner of distributing power and explains how variations in the vision experience are associated with changes between 3 ecological types of Plains societies. The findings suggest that the vision experience can be viewed as an adaptive mechanism whose meaning and manner of functional integration change in response to overall modification in social structure and ultimately, ecology.   HCV

2697   **BAPTIE   SUE**
1968
EDGAR DEWDNEY. Alberta Historical Review 16(4):1-10.

The career of Edgar Dewdney (1835-1916) is reviewed. With his joint appointment as Indian Commissioner (1879) and Lieutenant-Governor of the old Northwest Territories (1881), Indian affairs became the major concern of the Canadian government's policy of westward expansion. Indian grievances of starvation and impoverishment, the establishment of reserves, and the 2nd Riel Rebellion were the foci of Dewdney's administration. Two photographs and 1 sketch are included.   WRC

2698   **BINDING   FREDERICK RICHARD STADELMAN**
1963
A SOCIOMETRIC STUDY OF RACIAL CLEAVAGE IN INDIAN-WHITE GROUPS. M.A. Thesis. Faculty of Graduate Studies and Research. University of Manitoba. 148 pp.

Sociometric tests were administered to 682 public school students in the Portage la Prairie, Rossburn, Elphinstone, and Erickson districts of Manitoba and to 139 unskilled, semi-skilled, and skilled male workers in 4 Manitoba construction and lumber camps in 1962. The results are analyzed to determine the effects of age and degree of minority concentration on measures of racial cleavage in Indian-White groups. Both groups showed a preference to associate within their racial group although the White tendency was stronger with White girls being strongest and Indian girls weakest. Differences in the patterns of racial cleavage as age increases are observed between Indian and White groups and in adult groups.   CCV

2699   **BIRKET-SMITH   KAJ**
1960
PRIMITIVE MAN AND HIS WAYS: PATTERNS OF LIFE IN SOME NATIVE SOCIETIES. Translated by Roy Duffell. Cleveland: World. 247 pp.

The life styles of a variety of native societies are described. Chapter 3 is devoted to the Plains Indians as an advanced hunting culture. The importance of the horse, bison, and warfare is discussed. Tribal divergencies from the Plains culture are examined and the Blackfoot are mentioned for their age-graded brotherhoods. Dwelling units, clothing, subsistence activities, supernatural beliefs, revitalistic movements, Sun Dance, and Ghost Dance are treated and some north-south comparisons are drawn. References to northern groups are included in Chapter 6, devoted to southern Algonkian speaking tribes.   CCV

2700   **BRETON   PAUL EMILE**
1962
HOBBEMA: UNE FLORISSANTE MISSION INDIENNE DE L'OUEST. Edmonton: L'Ermitage. 62 pp.

The history of the Indian mission at Hobbema, Alberta, is traced from its founding in 1881 to 1962. Brief references to epidemics among the Blackfoot and Plains Cree, government policy, practical problems encountered in construction of the mission, repercussions of the Northwest Rebellion, the residential school, and activities organized for pupils are included.   CCV

2701   **BURNHAM   HAROLD B**
1968
CATALOGUE OF ETHNOGRAPHIC TEXTILES OF THE NATIONAL MUSEUM OF MAN: AREA 5; PLAINS. Unpublished paper. Available at National Museum of Man, Ethnology Division, Ottawa, with permission of the author. 200 pp.

Ninety items from the National Museum of Man's Plains collection of ethnographic textiles are presented in this catalog. Each article is photographed and accompanied by a notation of its location, attribution, provenance, name, measurements, condition, description, and technical notes.   CCV

2702   **CANADA. Department of Northern Affairs and National Resources.**
1965
PRESS RELEASES. No. 1-6585, 1-65118. Available from Information Services, Records and Research, Department of Indian Affairs and Northern Development, Ottawa.   Also in French.

Two of the Department of Northern Affairs and National Resources' communiques in 1965 refer to sites commemorating respectively the last major skirmish between Indians and Canadian troops and establishment of missions in Alberta.   CCV

2703   **CANADA. Twenty-Fifth Federal-Provincial Wildlife Conference.**
1961
MINUTES OF THE TWENTY-FIFTH FEDERAL-PROVINCIAL WILDLIFE CONFERENCE. W. Winston Mair, chairman. Ottawa, June 14-16, 1961. Ottawa: Department of Northern Affairs and National Resources, National Parks Branch. pp. 38-39.

The possibility of releasing buffalo to Indian reserves is discussed by representatives from Manitoba, Saskatchewan, Alberta, and Indian Affairs. The implications of the release of buffalo are discussed. No motions were made.   CCV

2704   **CARRIERE   GASTON**
1967
L'APOTRE DES PRAIRIES: JOSEPH HUGONNARD, O.M.I., 1848-1917. Montreal: Rayonnement. 170 pp.

The life and works of Joseph Hugonnard, O.M.I., are reviewed. Details of his missionary work at Qu'Appelle, Saskatchewan, from 1874 to 1917 include much of the history of the Qu'Appelle residential and industrial school. Both the curriculum of the school and the Indian-Metis attitude toward religion are treated.   CCV

2705   **CORRIGAN   SAMUEL W**
1970
THE PLAINS INDIAN POWWOW: CULTURAL INTEGRATION IN MANITOBA AND SASKATCHEWAN. Anthropologica N.S. 12:253-277.

Based on fieldwork in Manitoba (1964 and 1965) and Saskatchewan (1966, 1967, and 1968), a description of the annual summer powwow as a recent ceremonial institution among the Plains Indians is presented. The functions of dancing, singing, and gift exchange are examined as cutting across tribal lines promoting regional and pan-Indian identification.   WRC

2706   **DEMPSEY   HUGH A, ed.**
1967
THE LAST LETTERS OF REV. GEORGE MCDOUGALL. Alberta Historical Review 15(2):20-30.

Collected are 3 letters written by George McDougall in 1875 shortly before his death, and 2 letters by his wife and a Northwest Mounted Police official concerning his death. A brief description of 15 years among the Plains Indians as a Wesleyan Methodist missionary is presented in McDougall's communications.   WRC

2707   **DENIG   EDWIN THOMPSON**
1961
FIVE INDIAN TRIBES OF THE UPPER MISSOURI: SIOUX, ARICKARAS, ASSINIBOINES, CREES, CROWS. John C. Ewers, ed. Norman: University of Oklahoma Press. 217 pp.

Previously published material by Edwin Denig is assembled and presented with updating of certain footnotes. The editor's revised introduction includes details derived from journals and personal correspondence. Denig describes the Sioux, Arickara, Assiniboine, Cree, and Crow tribal history, location, customs, and makes comparisons as observed in the middle 19th century during his employment with the American Fur Company on the Upper Missouri.   CCV

2708   **DEWDNEY   SELWYN**
1964
WRITINGS ON STONE ALONG THE MILK RIVER. The Beaver 295(Winter):22-29.

Prehistoric and historic petroglyphs along the Milk River in southern Alberta are analyzed. Based on subject matter and style, a tentative chronology is drawn.   IVY

2709   **EWERS   JOHN C**
1967
WAS THERE A NORTHWESTERN PLAINS SUB-CULTURE? AN ETHNOGRAPHICAL APPRAISAL. Plains Anthropologist 12:167-174.

Examining such features as economy, political organization, intertribal warfare, and the religious life of the resident tribes of the Northwestern Plains, it is evident that these tribes shared too many significant traits with other Plains Indians to be regarded as a distinct division of the Plains Indians Culture Area.   IVY

2710   **EWERS   JOHN C**
1968
INDIAN LIFE ON THE UPPER MISSOURI. Norman: University of Oklahoma Press. 222 pp.

Several aspects of Plains Indian culture are described using ethnohistorical data. Most of the material dates to the middle and late 18th century but later references occur including fieldwork done in the 1940's and 1950's. A section is devoted to the evolution of the existing Indian stereotype. With reference to Canadian groups, the reported Blood Indian's concept of life in Dog Days, examination of the fur trade, introduction of the gun, intermarriage, and description of traditional religious beliefs including ritual and ceremonial activities are of note. All of this material, published previously, has been revised for this book.   CCV

2711   **FAIRFIELD   DAVID J**
1970
CHESTERFIELD HOUSE AND THE BOW RIVER EXPEDITION. M.A. Thesis.
Department of History. University of Alberta. 177 pp.

Early attempts (1800-1802) to establish a fur trading post (Chesterfield House) in the
South Saskatchewan drainage and the later (1822-23) Bow River expedition into the
same area are recounted based on published materials and documents in the Hudson's
Bay Archives. Both actions met with great hostility from the Indian population of the
area. Appendices present documents and accounts of the Bow River Expedition.   TSA

2712   **FISHER   ANTHONY D**
1968
THE ALGONQUIAN PLAINS? Anthropologica N.S. 10:219-234.

From ethnohistorical evidence the exploitative efforts of the fur trade among the Northern and Central Algonkian tribes since the 16th century are reconstructed to indicate the
role of these efforts in the adaptational transition from a tribal to a family form of social
organization among the Plains Indians.   WRC

2713   **FISHER   ANTHONY D**
1968
CULTURE CONFLICT ON THE PRAIRIES: INDIAN AND WHITE. Alberta
Historical Review 16(3):22-29.

The origins of Plains Indian culture in Canada and the United States are traced historically, and the geographical and ecological settings in which the band gave way to a tribal
structure at the time of first contact during White westward expansion are examined. The
form of this contact which was characterized by culture conflict and warfare is considered a result of adaptations to Plains life.   WRC

2714   **FRANK E PRICE AND ASSOCIATES LTD.**
1969
AN ECONOMIC EVALUATION OF THE LONG PLAIN AND LONG PLAIN
SIOUX INDIAN RESERVES. Unpublished paper. Available from National Library of
Canada. 64 pp.

This economic study consists of an evaluation of the physical, social, and human resources of the Long Plain and Long Plain Sioux Reserves. Also considered is the relationship of the reserves to the area in which they are located. Specific developmental opportunities are identified and recommendations to achieve these are made. The Long Plain
Reserve (population 742 of whom 496 reside on the reserve) and Long Plain Sioux Reserve (population 40) are located adjacent to each other and a history of conflict between
the 2 bands exists. Potential for agricultural development exists, particularly in the area
of livestock production, and would best include the resources of both reserves. Since the
reserves are located in an industrial area of the province, it is suggested that training programs be designed to enable them to participate in the commercial and industrial activities of the area. Fourteen appendices provide organizing and operating costs of different types of farms.   IVY

2715   **FRASER   FRANCES**
1968
THE WIND ALONG THE RIVER. Toronto: Macmillan. 83 pp.

Seventeen Plains Indian legends and folk tales are presented, most with indication of
tribal source.   CCV

2716   **FRECHKOP   SERGE**
1968
QUELQUES REMARQUES AU SUJET DES PEAUX-ROUGES ET DE LEUR
CHEVAUX. Societe Royale Belge d'Anthropologie et de Prehistoire Bulletin 79:21-29.

The preference for spotted (appaloosa) and colored (pinto) horses among the North
American Indians of the Plains is discussed. The implications of this preference for horse
breeding and the occurrence of these markings, particularly the spotted variety, in other
parts of the world are noted.   CCV

2717   **GENTY   ROBERT**
1968-69
CONTRIBUTION A L'ETUDE DE L'ORIGINE DE L'HOMME AMERICAIN.
L'Ethnographie 62-63:119-141.

Hypotheses concerning the origins of human inhabitants of North America are reviewed. Parallels are drawn between Canadian and some American place names of Indian origin, particularly Algonkian, and Japanese sources. It is speculated that this may
be an indication of Asiatic origins.   CCV

2718   **GILLES   GEORGE**
1967
THREE INDIAN TALES. Alberta Historical Review 15(1):25-28.

Three Indian tales concerning horse theft, marriage relations, and war parties, originally
transcribed by the Metis author in the late 1890's, are reproduced.   WRC

2719   **HARDING   DAVID JAMES**
1964
AM EMPIRICAL CLARIFICATION OF MOTIVATIONAL VARIABLES AMONG
SASKATCHEWAN PEOPLE OF INDIAN ANCESTRY. M.A. Thesis. Department of
Psychology. University of Saskatchewan, Saskatoon. 130 pp.

A modified TAT and a specially developed attitude questionnaire were administered to
295 Indian, White, and Metis subjects from Saskatoon Vocational School, the provincial
jail in Prince Albert, and students and non-students from Beauval, Ile a la Crosse, and
Buffalo Narrows in 1963-64. Data were analyzed comparing all subjects from northern
schools with an out-of-school sample; comparing subjects from the 3 communities; comparing White, Indian, and Metis subjects from the jail and an out-of-jail male Metis sample; and comparing all tested individuals from northern communities and the jail according to ethnic categories. It is concluded that people of Indian ancestry have developed
educational motivation and this is independent of school setting. Different acculturation
levels existed in the 3 northern communities and these differences are related to Indian
motivation. Greater marginality occurs in Metis personalities. Indian low achievement is
associated with social and economic discrimination rather than low aspiration.   CCV

2720   **HOLDER   PRESTON**
1970
THE HOE AND THE HORSE ON THE PLAINS: A STUDY OF CULTURAL
DEVELOPMENT AMONG NORTH AMERICAN INDIANS. Lincoln, NE:
University of Nebraska Press. 176 pp.

The socio-cultural development among North American Plains Indians is reviewed from
archaeological, ethnographic, and historical sources. Special attention is directed toward
social organization, the influences of European contact, and contrasts between those societies dependent upon horticulture and the horse.   CCV

2721   **HOWARD   JAMES H**
1960
NORTHERN STYLE GRASS DANCE COSTUME. American Indian Hobbyist 7:18-
27.

Elements of the Northern Costume, worn by the young, active dancers in the area, include a roach headdress, a fringed shirt, beaded necklaces, armbands, gauntlets, fringed
trousers, a variety of belts, bells, ankle bands, Plains or Ojbiwa moccasins, and a breech-
cloth.   TSA

2722   **IRWIN   JOAN MARIE**
1969
AN ANALYSIS OF THE MISCUES IN THE ORAL READING OF INDIAN
CHILDREN IN SELECTED GRADES. M.Ed. Thesis. Department of Curriculum and
Instruction. University of Calgary. 218 pp. Available from National Library of Canada.

An analysis is presented of miscues in oral reading of 25 randomly selected children from
each of grades 2, 4, and 6 from 4 schools operated by the Department of Indian Affairs
and Northern Development in southern Alberta. The miscues were examined at
the phoneme-morpheme and grammatical levels of linguistic structure from taped readings of science content tests. The data and findings as well as comparisons within each
level of analysis are discussed. Some difficult aspects of reading in English for Indian
children are revealed.   CCV

2723   **JOHNSTON   ALEXANDER**
1966
THE BATTLE AT BELLY RIVER: STORIES OF THE LAST GREAT INDIAN
BATTLE. Lethbridge: Historical Society of Alberta, Lethbridge Branch. 28 pp.

The 1870 battle between Plains Cree and tribes of the Blackfoot Confederacy is reconstructed from information received from survivors and observers.   CCV

2724   **KEHOE   ALICE B**
1970
THE FUNCTION OF CEREMONIAL SEXUAL INTERCOURSE AMONG THE
NORTHERN PLAINS INDIANS. Plains Anthropologist 15:99-103.

As part of the military society structure, 3 Algonkian Plains tribes used sexual intimacy as
a means of transferring spiritual power. The difference between nomadic and village
Plainsmen's use of this ritual reflects the differences in the 3 tribes' kinship structure.   ADG

2725   **MALLORY   ENID SWERDFEGER**
1965
LUXTON MUSEUM AT BANFF. Canadian Geographical Journal 71:64-67.

Plains Indian exhibits, life-size figures grouped to depict various events, are described.   IVY

2726   **MOORE   P E**
1961
NO LONGER CAPTAIN: A HISTORY OF TUBERCULOSIS AND ITS CONTROL AMONGST CANADIAN INDIANS. Canadian Medical Association Journal 84:1012-1016.

This article draws extensively from Dr. Robert Ferguson's material on tuberculosis among the Plains Indians. Analysis of this material revealed that (1) the depressed conditions of the reserves along with those of the boarding schools were principal factors in the wide spread of tuberculosis after the 1880's, and (2) the Indian race survived because it was able to resist the infection through elimination of susceptible strains in the tribes and families. Only after 1920 did White Canada become concerned enough to take preventive measures in the control and elimination of tuberculosis as a principal threat to Indian health.   ADG

2727   **OLIVER   SYMMES C**
1962
ECOLOGY AND CULTURAL CONTINUITY AS CONTRIBUTING FACTORS IN THE SOCIAL ORGANIZATION OF THE PLAINS INDIANS. University of California Publications in American Archaeology and Ethnology 48(1):1-90.

A dynamic, evolutionary view of the social organization of True Plains tribes (including the Blackfoot, Sarsi, Plains Cree, Assiniboine, and Gros Ventre) is presented. Emphasized is the common adaptation involving horse and buffalo and differing backgrounds (as hunters and gatherers or as horticulturists). Brief mention is given groups on the periphery including the Kutenai and Sub-Arctic hunters and gatherers. The ecological situation on the Plains with the introduction of the horse and its use to hunt bison fragmented bands in winter months and concentrated tribal units in the summer. This led to basic changes in the social organization of these tribes. While differing origin has led to the presence or absence of specific traits, the similarities in social organization among the True Plains tribes are remarkable.   TSA

2728   **PEARCE   WILLIAM**
1968
CAUSES OF THE RIEL REBELLION: A PERSONAL VIEW. Alberta Historical Review 16(4):19-26.

From a first-hand account presented to the Alberta Land Surveyor's Association annual meeting in 1921, the conflict between claims to free land by Metis and Indians and the interests of White settlers and the government is considered along with other events (1870-1885) surrounding the 2nd Riel Rebellion. A description of the trial and conviction of Louis Riel in 1885 is given. Two sketches and a photograph are included.   WRC

2729 **POWERS   WILLIAM K**
1969
INDIANS OF THE NORTHERN PLAINS. New York: Putnam. 256 pp.

The ethnographic literature coupled with field experience (primarily on U.S. Sioux reservations) among Northern Plains tribes provides the basis for this introduction to the life style and history of these Indians. Numerous photographs spanning a century illustrate the work.   TSA

2730 **ROGERS   EDWARD S**
1970
INDIANS OF THE PLAINS. Toronto: Royal Ontario Museum. 16 pp.

A brief outline of the Plains Indians' traditional life-style is presented with a note on the Indian today.   CCV

2731 **SACHER   JERRY L**
1968
A STUDY OF THE EFFECTS OF ENVIRONMENT ON INDIAN STUDENT'S ATTITUDES. M.Ed. Thesis. Department of Industrial and Vocational Education. University of Alberta. 116 pp.

One hundred and thirty-five Indian pupils in grades 9 to 12 and 38 White pupils from Drumheller Composite High School were administered attitude tests between March 5 and May 3, 1968. The Indian sample came from 4 environments: 33 lived on a reserve and attended reserve school, 36 lived on a reserve but commuted to provincial schools, 32 boarded in Lethbridge and attended city schools, and 34 lived in a student residence in Drumheller and attended school there. The results suggest that boarding in non-Indian homes or living in residence with Indian and non-Indian students while attending integrated schools maximize acculturation attributes. Indian self-concept most closely resembled that of the non-Indian when both non-Indian and Indian peers were a part of his environment.   CCV

2732 **SANDERSON   JAMES FRANCIS**
1965
INDIAN TALES OF THE CANADIAN PRAIRIES. Alberta Historical Review 13(3):7-21.

Originally transcribed in 1894 by a White trader, 13 legends of Indian valor in intertribal conflicts on the Plains are reproduced. Illustrating the tales are 8 sketches.   WRC

2733 **SPRY   IRENE M**
1968
THE TRANSITION FROM A NOMADIC TO A SETTLED ECONOMY IN WESTERN CANADA, 1856-96. The Royal Society of Canada Transactions (Series 4) 6:187-201.

The events and personalities which opened up and transformed Rupert's Land and Indian Territory are chronicled.   IVY

2734 **STEWART   DAVID**
1967

PLANNING USE OF AVAILABLE RESOURCES IN UPGRADING THE HEALTH OF REGISTERED INDIANS IN ALBERTA. M.S. Thesis. Department of Public Health. University of Toronto. 226 pp.

The role of planning and an activity-oriented program in improving National Health and Welfare medical services to registered Indians in Alberta is explored. The history of health services, current services, and federal government policies are reviewed and the health status of Alberta Indians and medical problem areas are related to available services and staff. The co-ordination of goals and objectives with resources is discussed and it is proposed that a planned program would maximize benefits and result in an improved level of health for Indians.   CCV

2735   **VERNON   PHILIP E**
1966
EDUCATIONAL AND INTELLECTUAL DEVELOPMENT AMONG CANADIAN INDIANS AND ESKIMOS: PART I. Educational Review 18:79-91.

As part of a series of cross-cultural studies of environmental influence on educational and intellectual growth, 40 11 year old Blackfoot and Stoney Indians and 50 Eskimo youth were interviewed and tested. Part I of this study contains a brief review of the history and present condition of Canada's aboriginal peoples, and a discussion of the pertinent characteristics of the samples.   ADG

2736   **VERNON   PHILIP E**
1966
EDUCATIONAL AND INTELLECTUAL DEVELOPMENT AMONG CANADIAN INDIANS AND ESKIMOS: PART II. Educational Review 18:186-195.

Both Indian and Eskimo youth were very backward in arithmetic and it seems that much of the handicap was due to the high verbal content of the new math. Results of the reading comprehension and vocabulary test suggest that both groups can make fair progress with classroom English and can cope with the conventional group tests of attainment provided they are adequately explained and demonstrated. Test scores in concept formation, creativity, and inductive reasoning indicated a great variation according to the different tests used.   ADG

ASSINIBOINE

2737   **ANDERSON   RAOUL R**
1968
AN INQUIRY INTO THE POLITICAL AND ECONOMIC STRUCTURES OF THE ALEXIS BAND OF WOOD STONEY INDIANS, 1880-1964. Ph.D. Thesis.
Department of Anthropology. University of Missouri. 285 pp. Available from University Microfilms.

Fieldwork observations among the modern Alexis Stoney band are combined with data derived from historical and anthropological sources to reconstruct the Wood Stoney culture during the historic period. Specific cultural ecological adaptations attributed to the Wood Stoney groups resulted in a fishing, hunting, and trapping life style and a continued involvement in the fur trade altered little by the introduction of the horse and the depletion of the Plains buffalo herds. The nature of contact, the changes in economic and political structures, and the modern distribution of authority are reviewed.   CCV

2738   **ANDERSON   RAOUL R**
1970
ALBERTA STONEY (ASSINIBOIN) ORIGINS AND ADAPTATIONS: A CASE
FOR REAPPRAISAL. Ethnohistory 17:49-61.

Reviewing historical and ethnographic data, an attempt is made to discern the origins of
the modern Alberta Stoney. Attention is focused on those bands which since the late 18th
century exploited the area drained by the Athabasca and North Saskatchewan rivers
west of Edmonton, and those bands located about the Bow River valley west of Calgary
since about the 1840's. The histories of these bands and their particular cultural adaptations are examined.   IVY

2739   **BISHOP   CHARLES A,   SMITH   M ESTELLIE**
1970
EARLY HISTORIC POPULATIONS IN NORTHWEST ONTARIO:
ARCHAEOLOGICAL AND ETHNOHISTORICAL INTERPRETATIONS.
Unpublished paper delivered to Society for American Archaeology Meetings. Mexico
City, 1970. Available from National Library of Canada. 16 pp.

Archaeological and historic evidence is presented to support the view that the Assiniboine were located in northern Minnesota and southwestern northern Ontario at contact (circa A.D. 1620).   IVY

2740   **BUCSIS   WILLIAM**
1968
NOTES ON SOME ASSINIBOINE INDIAN RELIGIOUS BELIEFS AND
CEREMONIES. Na'Pao 1(1):17-22.

The author's sojourn at the Assiniboine reserve in Saskatchewan during 1956 gave him
an opportunity to learn about some of the traditional Assiniboine religious
ceremonies.   ADG

2741   **DUSENBERRY   VERNE**
1960
NOTES ON THE MATERIAL CULTURE OF THE ASSINIBOINE INDIANS.
Ethnos 25:44-62.

This paper is based on material supplied by Rex Flying, an Assiniboine who, beginning
in 1940, attempted to preserve some of the stories of the old people. The bow and arrow
is discussed in detail considering such aspects as type of wood used, feathers, points, and
method of preparation. Also included are knives, glue, spears, war clubs, pipe manufacture, and horn spoons.   IVY

2742   **KENNEDY   MICHAEL STEPHEN, ed.**
1961
THE ASSINABOINES: FROM THE ACCOUNTS OF THE OLD ONES TOLD TO
FIRST BOY (JAMES LARPENTEUR LONG). Norman, OK: University of Oklahoma
Press. 207 pp.

Accounts of Assiniboine history and life style as recorded by a Montana Assiniboine, James Larpenteur Long, in the early 20th century are presented. Two of Long's aged informants were Canadian-born. Tribal legends, social activities, subsistence activities, ceremonial practices, and contact with the White men are described.   CCV

2743   **MACEWAN   JOHN WALTER GRANT**
1969
TATANGA MANI: WALKING BUFFALO OF THE STONIES. Edmonton: Hurtig.
208 pp.

The life of Walking Buffalo, a Stoney from Alberta who served as tribal councilor, minor chief, chief, and medicine man, bridged the old and new in western Canadian history. This biography recounts his experiences from the coming of missionaries, mounties, and the iron horse to the confrontation with Calgary Power and Transmission regarding hydroelectric construction at Stoney Reserve. Speaking for peace, he went on world tours totaling 150,000 miles.   IVY

2744   **MCDOUGALL   MRS JOHN**
1966
INCIDENTS OF MISSION LIFE, 1874. Alberta Historical Review 14(1):26-29.

An original account is presented of a missionary family of the Wesleyan Methodist Church and their Stoney protectors in the wilderness of the Bow River Valley, Alberta.   WRC

2745   **MCNUTT   C S**
1960
LIFE ON AN INDIAN RESERVATION. The United Church Observer N.S.
22(12):12-13,24.

A United Church missionary at McDougall Indian Mission, Morley, Alberta, discusses his work with the Stoney Indians.   IVY

2746   **MEDICINE   BEATRICE**
1970
THE USE OF MAGIC AMONG THE STONEY INDIANS. Verhandlungen des
XXXVIII. Internationalen Amerikanistenkongresses. Vol. 2. pp. 283-292.

Based on 1966 fieldwork and ethnographic literature, the use of love magic among the Stoney of Alberta is documented. Description of the ritual includes the preparation, the administrative act, manufacturing the amulet, the "depression-dispensing" packet, the prescriptions, and the reimbursement. This isolated case observed in 1966 illustrates how the precise traditional pattern continues in the contemporary native belief system.   IVY

2747   **MORANT   NICHOLAS,   MORANT   W**
1963
INDIAN DAYS. The Beaver 294(Summer):30-37.

Each July, Cree, Kutenais, Sarcee, Blood, and Blackfoot join the Stoney at Banff, Alberta, to hold a week-long exhibition and celebration. A pictorial presentation of this event is given.   IVY

2748   **MUNROE   SCOTT   WILLIAM**
1969
WARRIORS OF THE ROCK: BASIC SOCIAL STRUCTURE OF THE MOUNTAIN
BANDS OF STONEY INDIANS AT MORLEY, ALBERTA. M.A. Thesis. Department
of Sociology and Anthropology. University of Calgary. 92 pp. Available from National
Library of Canada.

Analyzed is the degree of support which Stoney Indians in Western Alberta are willing to
extend to their traditional band affiliations. Using 9 sociometric questions and participant observation, 100 Stoney Indians were studied in the summer of 1966 at their main
reserve 40 miles west of Calgary. It was found that band distinctions do exist which also
influence certain behavior activities. The study revealed a major division between north-
erly and southerly Stoney Bands with the northern bands being more traditional and isolated than the acculturated southern bands.   DGW

2749   **POCATERRA   GEORGE W**
1963
AMONG THE NOMADIC STONEYS. Alberta Historical Review 11(3):12-19.

Having lived with Stoney Indians from 6 weeks to several months each year (1905 to
1925, approximately), the author describes a hunting and trapping way of life.   IVY

2750   **UNDERWOOD MCLELLAN & ASSOCIATES**
1969
REPORT ON THE RESIDENTIAL DEVELOPMENT OF THE STONY PLAIN
INDIAN RESERVE NO. 135. Unpublished report prepared for Chief Cardinal and
Members of Council, Enoch Indian Band. Available at Indian-Eskimo Economic
Development Branch, Development Services Division, Department of Indian Affairs and
Northern Development, Ottawa. 33 pp.

Proposed expansion of a recreational area and development of a mobile home park for
use by non-Indians on the Stony Indian Reserve is evaluated.   CCV

2751   **WENZEL   JOHANNA**
1968
WALKING BUFFALO: WISE MAN OF THE WEST. The Beaver 298(Spring):19-23.

A biography of Walking Buffalo, also known as George Maclean or Tatunga Mani by his
people, the Assiniboines, is presented.   IVY

BLACKFOOT

2752   **BRYAN   ALAN L**
1970
AN ALTERNATE HYPOTHESIS FOR THE ORIGIN OF THE NAME
BLACKFOOT. Plains Archaeologist 15:305-308.

Animal hooves, not artificially blackened feet or moccasins, appear to be what the original Cree term for "Blackfoot"signified.   ADG

2753   **CARR   KEVIN JAMES**
1968

A HISTORICAL SURVEY OF EDUCATION IN EARLY BLACKFOOT INDIAN CULTURE AND ITS IMPLICATIONS FOR INDIAN SCHOOLS. M.A. Thesis. Department of Educational Foundations. University of Alberta. 254 pp.

An attempt is made to explore aspects of Blackfoot culture history which have relevance for planning and organization of educational programs for contemporary Blackfoot children. The components of the cultural education received by these Blackfoot children which are common language, common knowledge of the supernatural and the group, group norms, and shared values are discussed in relation to the education offered by the dominant society. It is estimated that education to date has attempted to substitute for the cultural inheritance already acquired by Blackfoot children. It is likewise suggested that many aspects of Blackfoot culture serve as barriers to acculturation and that progress could be achieved by teaching in the Blackfoot languge and attempting to reduce cultural differences.   CCV

2754   **CONN   RICHARD**
1960
NORTHERN PLAINS BUSTLES. American Indian Hobbyist 7:12-17.

Bustles spread onto the Northern Plains with the spread of the Grass Dance in the 1880's. The first 2 types of bustle (both known as Crow Belts) are described. The modern bustle superseded these in the 1930's. Two bustles from the Denver Art Museum and a possible Blackfoot specimen from the Museum of the Plains Indian are illustrated.   TSA

2755   **CONN   RICHARD**
1961
BLACKFEET WOMEN'S CLOTHING. American Indian Tradition 7:113-127.

The classic dress, other skin dresses, cloth dresses, moccasins, and leggings are described in detail. Numerous photographs and patterns are included.   IVY

2756   **DEMPSEY   HUGH A**
1963
RELIGIOUS SIGNIFICANCE OF BLACKFOOT QUILLWORK. Plains Anthropologist 8:52-53.

Interviews with the primary informant, Mrs. Victoria McHugh, were conducted at Blackfoot Reserve, Alberta, October 17 and November 16, 1960. Inquiry among other Blackfoot tribes revealed additional information. Quillwork was restricted to a few women who owned their designs. Quilling embodied features of religious significance such as specific prayers, face and hand painting, and the wearing of specific ornaments while quilling. Quillwork was done in return for gifts and could not be sold.   IVY

2757   **DEMPSEY   HUGH A**
1965
A BLACKFOOT WINTER COUNT. Glenbow-Alberta Institute Occasional Paper No. 1. 20 pp.

Commentary is presented on a calendar of events for the period of 1810-1883 kept by Bad Head, a Blood Indian. Sources of information include: the winter counts of Robert

N. Wilson, Father Emile Legal, and Jim White Bull; fur trade journals; Indian Department reports; published works; and a number of Blood informants.

2758   **DEMPSEY   HUGH A**
1968
BLACKFOOT GHOST DANCE. Glenbow-Alberta Institute Occasional Paper No. 3. Calgary: Glenbow-Alberta Institute. 19 pp.

A modern version of the ghost dance was recorded in 1963 by members of the Glenbow Foundation in Calgary. An analysis shows a series of adjustments have been made to accomodate reserve life and the influence of the Crees. The ghost dance has become a kind of good luck dance.   IVY

2759   **DEMPSEY   HUGH A, ed.**
1961
ROBERTSON-ROSS' DIARY: FORT EDMONTON TO WILDHORSE, B.C., 1872. Alberta Historical Review 9(3):5-22.

Population figures, mortality rates, inventory data on armaments, and the results of the last yearly hunt of the Blackfoot Nation are reported by Colonel P. Robertson-Ross. Included is a map of the journey, made in 1872, the purpose of which was to recommend government procedure in dealing with the lawlessness and smuggling operations which characterized the interim period between Hudson's Bay Company control and that of the newly formed Dominion.   WRC

2760   **DEMPSEY   HUGH A, ed.**
1962
FINAL TREATY OF PEACE. Alberta Historical Review 10(1):8-16.

Statements of Indian chiefs and correspondence between officials in the administration of Indian affairs indicate the nature of an intertribal peace conference between the Blood of southern Alberta and the Gros Ventre and Assiniboine of Montana in 1887.   WRC

2761   **DOTY   JAMES**
1966
A VISIT TO A BLACKFOOT CAMP. Hugh A. Dempsey, ed. Alberta Historical Review 14(3):17-26.

A diary account of a journey to the Blackfoot Nation of southern Alberta from September 1 to September 23, 1855, was kept by an assistant negotiator of the United States government. He was instructed to make the trip from Montana to inform the chiefs of bands that were hunting or trading on United States territory of a treaty conference aimed at establishing peaceful relations. A map of the probable route, a sketch, and a pictograph from Writing-on-Stone are included.   WRC

2762   **EWERS   JOHN C**
1960
A BLOOD INDIAN'S CONCEPTION OF TRIBAL LIFE IN DOG DAYS. The Blue Jay 18:44-48.

Reminiscences of a Blood Indian, Weasel Tail, born in 1859, describing some aspects of Blood Indian life in pre-horse times, are presented.   IVY

2763   **EWERS   JOHN C**
1963
BLACKFOOT INDIAN PIPES AND PIPEMAKING. Smithsonian Institution. Bureau of American Ethnology Bulletin 186:29-60. Washington: U.S. Government Printing Office.

Based on ethnohistoric and ethnographic data, a detailed discussion on pipes and techniques of pipe making among the Blackfoot is given. Also discussed is the possible origin of the modified Micmac pipe bowl.   IVY

2764   **FISHER   ANTHONY D**
1964
INDEPENDENT DEPENDENCY. Unpublished paper delivered to 63rd Annual Meeting, American Anthropological Association. Detroit, MI, November 20, 1964. Available from National Library of Canada. 14 pp.

Instrumental Activities Inventory, a picture interview technique, was administered in 1963 to 40 Blood young men, who reside within a semi-isolated environment of the reserve community, and are employed in casual or temporary occupations. In an analysis of favored and rejected occupations, it was found that almost all of those favored are outside occupations. Reasons for this selection in order of importance are (1) previous knowledge and experience, (2) excitement and activity, and (3) good wages or other economic benefits. Interpreted in a larger context, the young Blood pursues his goals within the Blood community (a traditionally Plains Indian culture) and according to the suppositions of that community.   IVY

2765   **FISHER   ANTHONY D**
1965
CONTEMPORARY BLOOD INDIAN SOCIAL ORGANIZATION: A CONFLICT AMELIORATING STRUCTURE? Unpublished paper delivered to Annual Meeting, South Western Anthropological Association. Available from National Library of Canada. 8 pp.

This paper presents Blood kinship terminology, political and ritual authority, and religious status before the signing of Treaty Number Seven in 1877. Also discussed are marriage forms, population, and types of households.   HCV

2766   **FISHER   ANTHONY DWIGHT**
1966
THE PERCEPTION OF INSTRUMENTAL VALUES AMONG YOUNG BLOOD INDIANS OF ALBERTA. Ph.D. Thesis. Stanford University. 223 pp. Available from University Microfilms.

Forty Blackfoot males of Cardston, Alberta were interviewed with the Instrumental Activities Inventory in 1963 in order to note occupational evaluations. Two attitudinal orientations were revealed by the data: manifest success and practicality relevant to the

Blood Reserve. Success is perceived as relating to money, achievement, and financial security but is conditioned by the activity whereby it is achieved. Examination of 3 ethnohistoric texts reveals a consistency of conditioning factors in early and mid-19th century value orientation. It is concluded that the young Blood is predisposed to retention of traditional values by the nature of the face-to-face, primary group-oriented interaction of the Blood community.   CCV

2767   **FRANK E PRICE AND ASSOCIATES LTD.**
n.d.
BLACKFOOT DEVELOPMENT CORPORATION. Unpublished paper. Available from National Library of Canada. 54 pp.

It is proposed that the Blackfoot Development Corporation act as trustee on behalf of the tribe to exercise control of land in agricultural use, provide security of tenure for Indian operators, and provide financial and other assistance for members of the tribe. Legal and financial mechanisms for achieving these ends are outlined. Series of tables indicate future operations in terms of loans, leases, and acquisition of capital equipment for both the entire tribe and individual tribal members.   IVY

2768   **FRANK E PRICE AND ASSOCIATES LTD.**
n.d.
LAND USE HANDBOOK FOR BLOOD INDIAN RESERVE. Unpublished paper. Available from National Library of Canada. 101 pp.

Information pertaining to the settlement and resources of the Blood Indian Reserve, Alberta, is provided. Major subjects considered are: (1) identification of land holders and land held, (2) location of cultivated land, (3) distribution of settlement, (4) soil classification, (5) soil productivity, (6) topography, and (7) transportation systems. Maps are used extensively.   IVY

2769   **FRANK E PRICE AND ASSOCIATES LTD.**
1967
DEVELOPING AGRICULTURE ON THE BLOOD INDIAN RESERVE.
Unpublished paper. Available from National Library of Canada. 45 pp.

This report outlines the requirements of the development of an agricultural program leading to full utilization of the agricultural resources of the Blood Reserve, Alberta. Development has been projected over a period of 18 years to full development. Establishment of capital requirements is indicated. It is recommended that a land use authority be established.   IVY

2770   **FRANK E PRICE AND ASSOCIATES LTD.**
1967
AN EVALUATION OF THE AGRICULTURAL RESOURCES OF THE BLOOD RESERVE. Unpublished paper. Available from National Library of Canada. 81 pp.

Land use on the reserve is examined. It is concluded that much of the land is not being used for any purpose. Full development of the agricultural resources of the Blood Reserve is dependent on 5 primary factors: climate for development, land control, people, financial requirements, and adequate technical assistance.   IVY

2771   **FRANK E PRICE AND ASSOCIATES LTD.**
1968
ECONOMIC SURVEY OF THE BLACKFOOT INDIAN RESERVE. Unpublished
paper. Available from National Library of Canada. 92 pp.

Investigating the economic potential of the Blackfoot Reserve in Alberta, this study consists of an inventory of all the social and economic resources of the reserve, an evaluation
of these resources and those of the surrounding area, and an outline of specific primary
and secondary commerical undertakings that might be developed for the benefit of
members of the band.   IVY

2772   **FRANK E PRICE AND ASSOCIATES LTD.**
1968
INTERIM REPORT OF THE EVALUATION OF IRRIGATION POTENTIALS OF
THE BLOOD INDIAN RESERVE. Unpublished paper. Available from National
Library of Canada. 61 pp.

This study is confined to an evaluation of the irrigation potential of 17,000 acres on the
eastern side of the reserve. Primary functions of this evaluation are to determine the economics of production, to determine the potential returns to the Blood Reserve from this
development, and to make specific recommendations respecting the type and operation
of irrigation program that should be developed.   IVY

2773   **FRANK E PRICE AND ASSOCIATES LTD,   BLACKFOOT LAND USE
COMMITTEE**
1969
BLACKFOOT DEVELOPMENT CORPORATION. Unpublished paper. Available
from National Library of Canada. 39 pp.

The projected Development Corporation will act as a leasing and financial agent on
behalf of the band. Agricultural resources of the reserve would be the primary economic
base upon which commercial and service industry would be built. Legal and
financial mechanisms for achieving these ends are outlined.   IVY

2774   **GERSHAW   F W**
n.d.
THE BLACKFEET CONFEDERACY. Medicine Hat, Alta.: Modern Press. 10 pp.

A brief description of the Blackfoot includes a discussion of Treaty No. 7 and the role of
Crowfoot as leader.   CCV

2775   **GLADSTONE   JAMES**
1967
INDIAN SCHOOL DAYS. Alberta Historical Review 15(1):18-24.

Boyhood experiences from 1894 to 1905 at Saint Paul's Anglican mission school, near
Blood Reserve, and the Calgary Industrial School are described by the first Indian appointed to the Senate.   WRC

2776   **GRINNELL   GEORGE BIRD**
1962

BLACKFOOT LODGE TALES: THE STORY OF A PRAIRIE PEOPLE. Lincoln: University of Nebraska Press. 310 pp.

Thirty tales and legends recorded from Blackfoot and Metis informants in the 1880's and 90's are reported. Adventure, history, and Old Man stories are included in the collection. Pages 177 to 287 are devoted to a description of the Blackfoot, Blood, and Piegan life style, subsistence techniques, warfare, religion, medicine, and details of social organization. This book is prepared from an earlier edition.   CCV

2777   **HUBENIG   A A**
1968
THE NATIVES ARE INDEED RESTLESS. Canadian Co-operative Digest 11(3):2-8.

The formation of Blackfoot Co-operative Enterprises Limited on the Blackfoot Reserve, Alberta, is related by an Oblate priest.   IVY

2778   **JOHNSTON   ALEX**
1960
USES OF NATIVE PLANTS BY THE BLACKFOOT INDIANS. Alberta Historical Review 8(4):8-13.

Species of plants and their traditional uses in war, hunting, medicine, and household activities among the Blackfoot are outlined. A photograph and 2 sketches are included.   WRC

2779   **JOHNSTON   ALEX**
1969
THE OLD INDIAN'S MEDICINE. Saskatchewan Archaeology Newsletter 26:1-4.

The Blackfoot Indians utilized the diverse vegetation of southern Alberta in a variety of ways. These include 76 plant species used for medicine, 58 species used for food, 35 used in miscellaneous ways, 12 species used as horse medicine, 10 for dyes, 8 for perfumes, and 8 for smoking.   IVY

2780   **JOHNSTON   ALEX**
1970
BLACKFOOT INDIAN UTILIZATION OF THE FLORA OF THE NORTHWESTERN GREAT PLAINS. Economic Botany 24(3):301-324.

The Blackfoot utilized 185 species of plants for food, medicine, the production of dyes and perfumes, the manufacture of weapons, and as construction materials.   IVY

2781   **KEHOE   THOMAS F**
1960
STONE TIPI RINGS IN NORTH-CENTRAL MONTANA AND THE ADJACENT PORTION OF ALBERTA, CANADA: THEIR HISTORICAL, ETHNOLOGICAL, AND ARCHAEOLOGICAL ASPECTS. Smithsonian Institution. Bureau of American Ethnology Bulletin 173:417-474. Washington: U. S. Government Printing Office.

Historical and ethnographic evidence from Alberta and Montana and archaeological evidence from the Blackfoot Reservation, Montana, support the conclusion that the stone circles known as tipi rings were used to hold down lodge covers.   IVY

2782   **LEWIS   MAURICE H**
1966
THE ANGLICAN CHURCH AND ITS MISSION SCHOOLS DISPUTE. Alberta
Historical Review 14(4):7-13.

The state of mission schools of the Church of England in Canada at the turn of the 20th
century is reviewed. The conflict between layman Samuel Hume Blake and missionary
John W. Tims in regard to conditions at a residential school on the Blackfoot Reserve is
examined. The key issue was the per capita government grant extended to schools. After
prolonged delay by the government, the school as a boarding institution was closed in
May, 1909, but allowed to continue day operations. A photograph of the Old Sun mission school is included.   WRC

2783   **MACLEAN   JOHN**
1961
BLACKFOOT MEDICAL PRIESTHOOD. Alberta Historical Review 9(2):1-7.

Based on missionary work in the Methodist Church at the Blood Reserve from 1880 to
1889 this address to the British Association for the Advancement of Science in Winnipeg
in 1909 describes the therapeutic methods and beliefs of Blackfoot medical fraternities.
The effectiveness and persistence of the combined functions of religion and medicine
despite the introduction of Western diseases and cures were noted.   IVY

2784   **MCGUSTY   H A**
1966
AN ENGLISHMAN IN ALBERTA. Alberta Historical Review 14(1):11-21.

Included in this excerpt from a journal reporting travels through Alberta and Manitoba
from 1889 to 1891 are impressions of the attitudes, life style, clothing, and dwellings of
the Blackfoot.   WRC

2785   **NETTL   BRUNO**
1967
STUDIES IN BLACKFOOT INDIAN MUSICAL CULTURE, PART I:
TRADITIONAL USES AND FUNCTIONS. Ethnomusicology 11:141-160.

Based on an analysis of ethnographic writings, 19th century Blackfoot musical culture is
described with respect to: (1) the single, basic function of music in Blackfoot culture; (2)
attitudes about song ownership, origin, and value; (3) basic problems in performance;
(4) musical biography; (5) the Blackfoot classification of music compared to an investiga-
tor's classification; and (6) music in Blackfoot mythology. The function and use of music
in the Sun Dance, bundle ceremonies, and man's societies are briefly described. Information on musical instruments is also included.   IVY

2786   **POTVIN   ANNETTE**
1966
THE SUN DANCE LITURGY OF THE BLACKFOOT INDIANS. M.A. Thesis.
Department of Religious Sciences. University of Ottawa. 171 pp.

The Sun Dance ceremony as traditionally practiced among the Blackfoot is described and its significance in relation to their life style and subsistence activities is discussed. Parallels are drawn between the Blackfoot liturgy and religious values shared with Christianity. It is suggested that this provided an excellent basis for transfer to the Christian religion.   CCV

2787   **ROWAND   JOHN**
1963
A LETTER FROM FORT EDMONTON. Alberta Historical Review 11(1):1-6.

In a circular, the common method of disseminating information among distant fellow traders, the Chief Factor at the Fort Edmonton post in 1840 gives his impressions of the Blackfoot obtained in trade relations and of the problems and prospects of future trade. IVY

2788   **SCHAEFFER   CLAUDE E**
1969
BLACKFOOT SHAKING TENT. Glenbow-Alberta Institute Occasional Paper No. 5. Calgary: Glenbow-Alberta Institute. 38 pp.

Utilizing existing literature and field data obtained on the Blackfoot Reservation in Montana in 1953-1954, certain elements in the Blackfoot Shaking Tent ritual are compared with those of the Northern Plains, Woodlands, and the Plateau. The physical structure of the tent, binding techniques of participants, types of spirits, and attitudes towards spirits are examined.   IVY

2789   **SPINDLER   GEORGE D**
1968
PSYCHOCULTURAL ADAPTATION. In The Study of Personality: An Interdisciplinary Appraisal. Edward Norbeck, Douglass Price Williams, et al., eds. New York: Holt, Rinehart and Winston. pp. 326-347.

Analyzed are the processes of psychological adaptation which are concomitant with manifest cultural change. In the comparison between the Menomini and Blood Indians, the thesis is propounded that the Blood Indians of Alberta are able to adapt overtly to the cultural system of Whites without a corresponding psychological reformulation. This is explained by the similarity in certain psychological features between Blood Indians and Whites. The consequences which develop from the confrontation of divergent psychocultural systems provide the basic framework of the study. It is the ability of groups to retain cognitive control of their environment which is considered the central adaptive process.   DGW

2790   **SPINDLER   GEORGE, SPINDLER   LOUISE**
1965
THE INSTRUMENTAL ACTIVITIES INVENTORY: A TECHNIQUE FOR THE STUDY OF THE PSYCHOLOGY OF ACCULTURATION. Southwestern Journal of Anthropology 21:1-23.

A preliminary report is presented from on-going research (since 1958) in cultural change at the Blood Indian Reserve in Alberta. As a projective technique for discerning Blood cognitive orientations to certain types of work, the Instrumental Activities Inventory provided an index of concrete behavior in the process of acculturation. The combined results of the IAI and the Rorschach indicated that the Blood were economically differentiated but culturally homogeneous in such traits as pragmatism and the maintenance of Indian identity. It is concluded that the present-orientation of the Blood and the future-orientation of White society are the main differences to be accounted for in the future of economic development. Comparison with similar research conducted among the Menomini is made.   WRC

2791   **WATT   ELLEN**
1967
TRANSFERRAL OF A BUNDLE. The Beaver 298(Summer):22-25.

The sacred ritual transferring ownership of the Medicine Pipe Bundle from Lewis Running Rabbit, Blackfoot Indian, to John Hellson, assistant curator, is described. The Bundle is to be placed in the Provincial Museum and Archives in Edmonton.   IVY

2792   **ZENTNER   HENRY**
1963
CULTURAL ASSIMILATION BETWEEN INDIANS AND NON-INDIANS IN SOUTHERN ALBERTA. Alberta Journal of Educational Research 9:79-86.

This study used a series of statements and questions bearing upon attitudes toward the issues of equality, association, and personal conduct to survey feelings regarding native-White assimilation. The study revealed that Indian students view their acceptance as equals more optimistically than do the White students. However, substantially less than half of the students in either group favored the Indians' abandonment of the reserve and competition with the White man on equal terms. A clear majority of students in each population were against full and unrestricted contact between Indians and Whites. The less advanced and younger Indian pupils were significantly more inclined to agree with the proposition that Indians ought to leave the reserve than were older and more advanced Indian students. It is not clear, moreover, why Indian boys more than Indian girls endorsed this proposition. Another difficult finding to interpret was the older and more advanced boys' significantly greater acceptance of the proposition that Indians should try to be like Whites. This survey concludes that (1) the rate of Indian assimilation is increasing remarkably, (2) Indian parents of all socio-economic strata recognize to some extent the necessity and desirability of adopting more of the non-Indian ways of behavior, and (3) Indian youth believe that it is now time for them to stop being traditional Indians and simply be citizens and persons.   ADG

2793   **ZENTNER   HENRY**
1963
VALUE CONGRUENCE AMONG INDIAN AND NON-INDIAN HIGH SCHOOL STUDENTS IN SOUTHERN ALBERTA. Alberta Journal of Educational Research 9:168-178.

Young Indians living on the Blood and Blackfoot reserves are rapidly adopting certain values which are dominant in urban Canadian society. This study found, contrary to its predictions, that the positive urban values of rationality, calculation, and reserve are endorsed more commonly and uniformly by Indians than by their non-Indian peers. Negative urban values such as isolation, withdrawal, and resignation were very faint among this particular group of minority students. The younger generation of Indians exude a remarkable optimism, self-confidence, and self-assurance. This study concludes that, on the whole, these Indians are prepared for entrance into Canadian society. Failure to change public policy and school practices in line with these developments may well result in a future shift in Indian status from a depressed cultural minority to a militant and agressive racial minority hardly different from the Negro minority in the United States.   ADG

2794   **ZENTNER   HENRY**
1964
REFERENCE GROUP BEHAVIOR AMONG HIGH SCHOOL STUDENTS. Alberta Journal of Educational Research 10:142-152.

Re-analyzing data collected and reported previously (see Zentner 1963), this article finds that these high school students respond selectively and situationally to the values of the environments in which they live and function. The students seem to feel that certain categories of important people, such as parents and acquaintances, are more concerned with some kinds of behavior than they are with other kinds. Their influence on the student is therefore varied.   ADG

SIOUX

2795   **BEVERIDGE   DANIEL MURRAY**
1964
THE SOCIO-ECOLOGICAL CORRELATES OF ECONOMIC DEPENDENCE IN FOUR DAKOTA (SIOUX) COMMUNITIES IN SASKATCHEWAN. M.A. Thesis. Department of Sociology. University of Saskatchewan. 194 pp.

Four rural Dakota communities in Saskatchewan are studied in a socio-ecological framework to explain variation in dependence upon public assistance. Extensive statistical analysis of data gathered from household interviews, fieldwork (1961-1963), and government census reports is effected to test the hypothesis of a relationship between economic dependence and social disorganization resulting from increased contacts. A lower degree of economic dependence was found for Moose Woods and Wood Mountain than for Round Plain and Standing Buffalo. Moose Woods and Wood Mountain are farther from urban centers and report a higher proportion of farm residents in their populations. The statistical analysis shows a significant strength of correlation between degree of economic dependence and degree of non-farm residence and the population distance factor. A review of the literature indicates studies with parallel findings.   IVY

2796   **FRANK E PRICE AND ASSOCIATES LTD.**
n.d.
AGRICULTURAL STUDY OF THE OAK LAKE RESERVE. Unpublished paper. Available from National Library of Canada. 12 pp.

From an inventory and evaluation of the agricultural resources of the Oak Lake Reserve, Manitoba, utilization of these resources is projected. Cost of the development is considered as is the revenue that could be derived from that development, both to the band and the individuals involved. Agricultural resources are limited. About half of the land on the reserve (1,157 acres) is adaptable to the production of grain crops and could support at least 2 family units.   IVY

2797   **FRANK E PRICE AND ASSOCIATES LTD.**
1967
AN ECONOMIC STUDY OF THE OAK LAKE SIOUX INDIAN RESERVE.
Unpublished paper. Available from National Library of Canada. 45 pp.

This is an inventory of all social and economic resources on the Oak Lake Reserve and an evaluation of these resources and those of the surrounding area to determine the economic potential for the members of the reserve (population 230). Because of the lack of economic opportunity and the limited agricultural resources, it is recommended that a Farm Advisory Committee be established to organize a more intensive land exploitation, and that a sociological survey be undertaken to examine attitudes to relocation.   IVY

2798   **FRANK E PRICE AND ASSOCIATES LTD.**
1967
AN ECONOMIC SURVEY OF THE BIRDTAIL SIOUX INDIAN RESERVE.
Unpublished paper. Available from National Library of Canada. 40 pp.

This is an inventory of all social and economic resources on the Birdtail Reserve and an evaluation of these resources and those of the surrounding area to determine the economic potential for the members of the band (population 196, of which 184 reside on the reserve). Because of lack of economic opportunity and limited agricultural resources, it is recommended that a Farm Advisory Committee be established to exploit the land more intensively, and a sociological survey be undertaken to examine attitudes to relocation. It is noted that not until the industrial and economic growth of the Brandon-Mindeosa-Carberry area is substantial will the reserve itself be affected.   IVY

2799   **HOWARD   JAMES H**
1960
THE CULTURAL POSITION OF THE DAKOTA: A REASSESSMENT. In Essays in the Science of Culture in Honor of Leslie A. White. Gertrude E. Dole and Robert L. Carneiro, eds. New York: Crowell. pp. 249-268.

A synopsis of Dakota culture patterns reveals 3 distinct divisions, each of which is an adaptation to a different environment. The necessity of recognizing these patterns as regional rather than tribal variations is stressed. The thesis that associates a settled life style with government by kinship and nomadic living with selection of leaders on the basis of personal qualities is supported by the data.   CCV

2800   **KEHOE   ALICE B**
1970
THE DAKOTAS IN SASKATCHEWAN. In The Modern Sioux: Social Systems and Reservation Culture. Ethel Nurge, ed. Lincoln: University of Nebraska Press. pp. 148-172.

The history of the Dakotas in Saskatchewan is traced from the first migration to Canada in 1862 to the 1960's. They now number approximately 650 on 4 reserves. Canadian government policies towards physical welfare, education, employment, and economic development are reviewed. Aspects of reservation culture are indicated generally, and more specifically in the comparison of 2 reserves, Round Plains and Standing Buffalo. Tribal identity shown in resistence to Cree domination is unique to the Standing Buffalo Reserve. Indian identity is reaffirmed at a powwow sponsored by Standing Buffalo and a pan-Indian movement.   IVY

2801 **KEHOE ALICE B**
1968
THE GHOST DANCE IN SASKATCHEWAN, CANADA. Plains Anthropologist
13:296-304.

Fieldwork was conducted during the summers of 1961 and 1962. Of the 4 Dakota Reserves in Saskatchewan, only Sioux Wahpaton near Prince Albert practised the Ghost Dance religion. It was brought there by Fred Robinson, an Assiniboine. Surviving members of this congregation, a handful of middle-aged and elderly Dakota, profess a creed that closely follows Wilson's (Wovoka) later teachings. Tangible and intangible traits of traditional Dakota have been integrated into the Saskatchewan congregation's Ghost Dance. It is suggested that the Saskatchewan creed was a viable accomodation to early reserve period conditions. IVY

2802 **LANDES RUTH**
1968
THE MYSTIC LAKE SIOUX: SOCIOLOGY OF THE MDEWAKANTONWAN
SANTEE. Madison, WI: University of Wisconsin Press. 224 pp.

Fieldwork done in the summer and fall of 1935 among the Mystic Lake Sioux is reported in the study of their traditional culture. Information is provided on political and social organization including leadership, religious and civil conformity, kinship terms, marriage, widowhood, and mourning. Traditional division of labor, war, and subsistence activities are also described. CCV

2803 **MEYER ROY W**
1968
THE CANADIAN SIOUX: REFUGEES FROM MINNESOTA. Minnesota History
41:13-28.

Canadian Indian policy is reflected in this history of the Sioux, from their entry into Canada to the contemporary situation. IVY

2804 **MULLER WERNER**
1969
THE "PASSIVITY OF LANGUAGE AND THE EXPERIENCE OF NATURE": A
STUDY IN THE STRUCTURE OF THE PRIMITIVE MIND. In Myths and Symbols:
Studies in Honor of Mircea Eliade. Joseph M. Kitagawa and Charles H. Long, eds.
Chicago: University of Chicago Press. pp. 227-239.

The Dakota language is examined to contribute to an understanding of Dakota thought and perception. Fundamental attitudes expressed in language reveal the Indians' concept of integration and relatedness of the natural order - the mythical value system. The cultural distance between Dakota and Euro-American thought is indicated. CCV

2805 **PENNANEN GARY**
1970
SITTING BULL: INDIAN WITHOUT A COUNTRY. The Canadian Historical
Review 51:123-140.

Since fleeing to Canada in the winter and spring of 1867-1868, Sitting Bull had become a key figure in an international dispute involving Great Britain, the United States, and

Canada. The legalities of the situation and the attitudes of the nations involved are discussed. Neither Canada nor the United States wanted Sitting Bull, neither acknowledged responsibility for his behavior, and each waited for her neighbor to solve the problem.   IVY

EASTERN WOODLANDS

2806   **ABLER   THOMAS S**
1969
THE DEFEAT OF THE HURON. Courier (Ontario Model Soldier Society) 5(2):1-4.

An outline of the Huron-Iroquois war of 1649 is followed by a reconstruction of the dress of the participants based on documentary evidence, early illustrative material, archaeological evidence, and material culture found in museums.   TSA

2807   **ABLER   THOMAS S**
1970
LONGHOUSE AND PALISADE: NORTHEASTERN IROQUOIAN VILLAGES OF THE SEVENTEENTH CENTURY. Ontario History 62:17-41.

A description of the Iroquoian villages during the 17th century is provided through the analysis of writings of the Jesuits, Champlain, and others in contact with these tribes.   ADG

2808   **BARBEAU   MARIUS**
1962
DIALECTES HURONS-IROQUOIS. Revue d'Histoire de l'Amerique Francaise 16:178-183.

This is a brief chronological inventory of all the studies of Huro-Iroquois dialects since the discovery of Canada. In a 2nd part of the article, the author describes the leading grammatical characteristics of this linguistic family.   DD

2809   **BARBEAU   MARIUS**
1965
PEAUX-ROUGES D'AMERIQUE: LEURS MOEURS, LEUR COUTUMES. Montreal: Librairie Beauchemin. 125 pp.

A general discussion of American Indian mores and customs is presented touching on the Huron-Iroquois and other groups.   CCV

2810   **BLAU   HAROLD**
1963
DREAM GUESSING: A COMPARATIVE ANALYSIS. Ethnohistory 10:233-249.

The Iroquois Dream Ceremony among the Onondaga and a similar practice of the Hurons during the Midwinter Rites are compared. Seven major components of the ritual are analyzed: going from cabin to cabin, riddles, generosity, food symbolism, rejoicing, charms and tokens, and tally. Similarities and differences in the ceremony among the Iroquois at the Six Nations Reserve in Ontario, the Coldspring Seneca, and the Tonawanda Seneca are noted.   IVY

2811   **BURNHAM   HAROLD B**
1968
CATALOGUE OF ETHNOGRAPHIC TEXTILES OF THE NATIONAL MUSEUM
OF MAN: AREA 3. Unpublished paper. Available at National Museum of Man,
Ethnology Division, Ottawa, with permission of the author. 276 pp.

One hundred and thirty-eight articles of material culture demonstrating quillwork, beadwork, embroidery, and plaiting are attributed to the Eastern Woodlands culture area in
the National Museum of Man's ethnographic textile collection. Each item is accompanied by photographs and notation of location, attribution, provenance, name, measurements, condition, description, and technical notes concerning fabrication or provenance.   CCV

2812   **CAMPBELL   DOROTHY L**
1963
INDIAN AND PIONEER USES OF NATIVE PLANTS GROWING AT DOON
PIONEER VILLAGE. Waterloo Historical Society Annual Volume 51:36-40.

The uses of 14 trees (wood, bark, fruit, roots, leaves) native to Waterloo County, Ontario, are listed.   IVY

2813   **DOUVILLE   R,   CASANOVA   J D**
1967
LA VIE QUOTIDIENNE DES INDIENS DU CANADA: A L'EPOQUE DE LA
COLONISATION FRANCAISE. Paris: Hachette. 317 pp.

A general description of the Indians of eastern Canada at the time of contact examines
their physical appearance, morality, language, political and social organization, intertribal relations, religious beliefs, dreams, family life, tribal life, technology, relations
with Europeans, the confrontation of religious beliefs, the fur trade, and the Indian
wars.   CCV

2814   **GABOR   BOB**
1960
TUTELOES. American Indian Hobbyist 7:10-11.

The Tutelo of the Appalachian highlands found a home among the Cayuga of the Six
Nations Reserve where the Tutelo Spirit Adoption Ceremony is preserved among the
upwards of 50 descendents of this tribe.   TSA

2815   **HYDE   GEORGE E**
1962
INDIANS OF THE WOODLANDS: FROM PREHISTORIC TIMES TO 1725.
Norman, OK: University of Oklahoma Press. 295 pp.

Historical, archaeological, ethnolgical, and traditional materials are used for this version
of the story of the Indian tribes between the Ohio and the Great Lakes during the prehistoric and early historic periods.   CCV

2816   **JOHNSTON   STAFFORD**
1967

THE INDIAN HUNTING GROUNDS OF PERTH COUNTY. Western Ontario Historical Notes 23(1):1-8.

White settlers entering Perth County found no Indian occupants; Indian residents in the vicinity were all recent migrants from the United States.   IVY

2817   **LACOMBE   LILIANE**
1967
LE POINT DE VUE D'HALDIMAND SUR LES PROBLEMES CANADIENS DE 1781 A 1784. M.A. Thesis. Departement d'Histoire. Universite d'Ottawa. 250 pp.

The activities of Governor Haldimand during the 2nd part of his administration are discussed in this examination of the Haldimand documents and other historical materials. Pages 65 to 100 describe Haldimand's relationships with the Indians. The important role of Indians in defense and warfare, the difficulty of retaining their loyalty, the expenses of gift-giving, and details of administration of the Indians are included.   CCV

2818   **LAJEUNESSE   ERNEST J**
1960
THE WINDSOR BORDER REGION: CANADA'S SOUTHERNMOST FRONTIER. The Champlain Society Ontario Series 4. Toronto: Champlain Society. 375 pp.

A collection of early documents relating to the Windsor Border Region on the Canadian side of the Detroit River is compiled with editorial comment tracing the development of the area from the 16th through the 18th century. Mention is made of the Indian inhabitants of the area, their intertribal relations, and their dealings with missions, settlers, and traders.   CCV

2819   **MARIE DE L'INCARNATION**
1967
WORD FROM NEW FRANCE: THE SELECTED LETTERS OF MARIE DE L'INCARNATION. Joyce Marshall, ed. Toronto: Oxford University Press.   433 pp.

Letters written by Marie de l'Incarnation are compiled yielding considerable data concerning the establishment of the Ursuline hospital and monastery at Quebec in the mid-17th century. Details of the life style of the converts and their devotion to Catholicism as well as accounts of events during the Iroquois wars including Iroquois attacks and treatment of prisoners are included.   CCV

2820   **NOBLE   WILLIAM C**
1968
IROQUOIS ARCHAEOLOGY AND THE DEVELOPMENT OF IROQUOIS SOCIAL ORGANIZATION (1000-1650 A.D.): A STUDY IN CULTURE CHANGE BASED ON ARCHAEOLOGY, ETHNOHISTORY AND ETHNOLOGY. Ph.D. Thesis. Department of Archaeology. University of Calgary. 335 pp. Available from National Library of Canada.

A general review of relevant aspects of Iroquois culture as they pertain to archaeological reconstructions is given on pages 40-83. The early historic northeastern Iroquoian religion, burial, warfare, politics, kinship, material culture, subsistence, division of labor, property, settlement pattern, and population density are discussed. Using the baseline provided by the years 1615-1680, archaeologists may attempt to reconstruct prehistoric Iroquois social organization.   JSL

2821   **PELLETIER   WILFRED**
1969
CHILDHOOD IN AN INDIAN VILLAGE. This Magazine is About Schools 3(2):6-22.

Life on the reserve was very different from that in White society. Religion, for example, was centered entirely on man. Listening, observing, and feeling were the core of all learning, which was, itself, holistic - a way of life. Work, too, was a way of life. Power and leadership were situational and temporary. Outsiders who come into the Indian's community and tell him to have order, system, and organization disrupt existing community patterns. In this way the White man has made the Indian dependent; but the Indian has withdrawn from society, rejecting it. Unlike some minorities Indians cannot and will not fight on the White man's terms since they lack both the inclination and sufficient numbers of people.   ADG

2822   **POULIOT   ADRIEN,   DUMAS   SILVIO**
1960
L'EXPLOIT DU LONG-SAULT: LES TEMOIGNAGES DES CONTEMPORAINS. La Societe Historique de Quebec Cahiers d'Histoire 12. Quebec: Universite Laval. 138 pp.

Archival sources related to Dollard des Ormeaux and the Long-Sault episode are examined and re-evaluated. The reports of contemporary observers are emphasized in an attempt to clarify the circumstances surrounding preparation for the undertaking, its purpose, the role of the Indians who accompanied the French, and the fate of Indian and French captives. Testimony of 2 Hurons who escaped captivity is the principal source.   CCV

2823   **POULIOT   ADRIEN,   DUMAS   SYLVIO**
1960-61
L'EXPLOIT DU LONG-SAULT. Vie Francaise 14-15.

A series of 7 articles present an examination of the engagement of the Iroquois at Long-Sault by 17 Frenchmen and around 40 Huron in 1660. The basic documents relating to the event are evaluated, the prolonged battle is reconstructed in detail, the role of the Hurons discussed, and the fate of the captives described.   CCV

2824   **RICHARDS   CARA E**
1967
HURON AND IROQUOIS RESIDENCE PATTERNS 1600-1650. In Iroquois Culture, History, and Prehistory: Proceedings of the 1965 Conference on Iroquois Research. Elisabeth Tooker, ed. Albany: New York State Museum and Science Service. pp. 51-56.

Reviewing historical documents on actual household composition, 19 cases which indicate that residence among the Huron and Iroquois was not matrilocal, as well as 5 ambiguous ones, are examined. It is suggested that the most customary residence pattern followed by the Huron and probably most Iroquois before their culture was seriously disturbed by European contact was virilocal with frequent village exogamy.   IVY

2825   **ROUSTANG   FRANCOIS**
1960
JESUITES DE LA NOUVELLE-FRANCE. Paris: Desclee de Brouwer. 346 pp.

A selection of excerpts from the Jesuit Relations are compiled depicting experiences in New France. Many of the accounts include details of torture by the Iroquois.   CCV

2826   **TOOKER   ELISABETH**
1960
THREE ASPECTS OF NORTHERN IROQUOIAN CULTURE CHANGE.
Pennsylvania Archaeologist 30(2):65-71.

A comparison of the Jesuit materials on the Huron with recent anthropological findings on the Iroquois reveals significant cultural changes during the past 3 centuries. Examples include fewer curing ceremonies and less dependence upon the dream.   ADG

2827   **TOOKER   ELISABETH**
1963
THE IROQUOIS DEFEAT OF THE HURON. Pennsylvania Archaeologist 33:115-123.

A review of various theories of the Huron-Iroquois war reveals that both Leagues were equal in strength, similar in political structure, cultural organization, and response to European trade. The Iroquois who were victorious enjoyed a geographical advantage which could not be matched by the Hurons.   ADG

2828   **TOOKER   ELISABETH**
1970
NORTHERN IROQUOIAN SOCIOPOLITICAL ORGANIZATION. American Anthropologist 72:90-97.

A review of 17th century documents reveals that the confederacy of tribes, clan structure (tabulated), and chieftanship characteristic of the Iroquois were also traits of Huron aboriginal sociopolitical organization. It is asserted that the defeat and dispersal of the Huron by the Iroquois (1649-1650) resulted in the termination of this type of government among the former.   WRC

2829   **TRIGGER   BRUCE GRAHAM**
1963
SETTLEMENT AS AN ASPECT OF IROQUOIAN ADAPTATION AT THE TIME OF CONTACT. American Anthropologist 65:86-101.

Historical data from 4 Iroquoian societies reveal variation in settlement pattern in precontact times. The Huron, Neutral, Five Nations, and Laurentian Iroquois are chosen as representing a continuum of adaptation types in a relatively homogeneous geographic region. Climate, topography, trade, warfare, disease, and subsistence activity are considered interacting variables accounting for a particular distribution in each of the societies. These factors are viewed as limitations rather than strict determinants of certain patterns, such as the sedentary village. It is concluded that adaptation can only be explained by the specific interaction of such factors within a given society.   WRC

2830   **VACHON   ANDRE**
1968
ELOQUENCE INDIENNE. Montreal: Editions Fides. 95 pp.

Thirty speeches delivered by Indians and recorded in the mid-17th century are reproduced. The significance of oratory among the Indians is discussed in the introduction. It is noted that a chief's authority was traditionally proportional to his ability to influence his followers. Speeches are classified as traditional, political, or situational according to the circumstances of their delivery and certain identifiable characteristics.   CCV

2831   **ZELLER   A G**
1962
THE CHAMPLAIN-IROQUOIS BATTLE OF 1615. Oneida, NY: Madison County Historical Society. 40 pp.

The successful Oneida defense of their village on Nicholas Pond against a French-Huron-Algonkin expedition is seen as a turning point in Iroquois history. Prior to the battle the Five Nations were on the defensive; following their victory they took an agressive role which led to their dominant position in North America.   TSA

DELAWARE

2832   **BRUEMMER   FRED**
1964
THE DELAWARES OF MORAVIANTOWN. Canadian Geographical Journal 68:94-97.

A brief history of the Delaware Indians and their association with the Moravians is presented. Three hundred and seventy-five Delaware now live at Moraviantown in Ontario.   IVY

HURON

2833   **BARBEAU   MARIUS**
1960
HURON-WYANDOT TRADITIONAL NARRATIVES IN TRANSLATIONS AND NATIVE TEXTS. National Museum of Canada Bulletin 165. Ottawa: Queen's Printer. 338 pp.

Forty Huron-Wyandot texts and their translations are presented. They were collected by Barbeau from among the last 10 or 15 survivors of this linguistic groups. Free translations are followed by phonetic transcriptions and literal translations. Although the Huron proper dialect is extinct, Wyandot speakers were found in Oklahoma and on the Detroit River. The recordings were made in 1911-1912.   JSL

2834   **DESJARDINS   PAUL**
1966
LA RESIDENCE DE SAINTE-MARIE-AUX-HURONS. La Societe Historique du Nouvel Ontario Documents Historiques 48. Sudbury: Universite de Sudbury. 46 pp.

The residence constructed at Ste. Marie by the Jesuits, background details, organization of the mission, and missionary activity among the Hurons for the period 1639-1649 are described. The physical organization of the mission is discussed in detail relying on the Jesuit Relations and the archaeological evidence.   CCV

2835   **FORTIN   BERTHE**
1960
REALISATIONS D'ORGANISATION COMMUNAUTAIRE CHEZ LES INDIENS. Bien-etre Social Canadien 12(5):161-162.

Leadership courses held annually by the Indian Affairs Division to provide specialized training for Indian leaders in Quebec are discussed. The orientation of the courses, the participation, and results are reviewed.   CCV

2836   **GREENING   W E**
1962
LORETTEVILLE AND THE TREASURE OF THE JESUITS. Canadian Geographical Journal 65:90-93.

Fleeing the Iroquois, the Huron, under the supervision of the Jesuits, settled at Loretteville, Quebec. The artistic treasures and relics of the chapel at Loretteville are described including some which may have been executed by Indians.   IVY

2837   **HAYES   JOHN F**
1969
WILDERNESS MISSION: THE STORY OF SAINTE-MARIE-AMONG-THE-HURONS. Toronto: Ryerson Press. 118pp.

Details of the reconstruction on the site of Ste.-Marie-among the-Hurons is accompanied by an account of early 17th century Jesuit missions in Huronia. Also reported is the closely related story of the Hurons including a resume of details of life style, subsistence techniques, social and political organization, trade networks, and the Huron-Iroquois wars.   CCV

2838   **HEIDENREICH   CONRAD E**
1966
MAPS RELATING TO THE FIRST HALF OF THE 17TH CENTURY AND THEIR USE IN DETERMINING THE LOCATION OF JESUIT MISSIONS IN HURONIA. The Cartographer 3:103-126.

Following a discussion of all known maps relevant to Southern Ontario and specifically to Huronia in northern Simcoe County, these and other primary source material are used to reconstruct the distribution of Indian villages and Catholic missions in Huronia during the first half of the 17th century.   IVY

2839   **HEIDENREICH   CONRAD E**
1967
THE INDIAN OCCUPANCE OF HURONIA, 1600-1650. In Canada's Changing Geography: A Selection of Readings. R. Louis Gentilcore, ed.   Scarborough: Prentice-Hall. pp. 15-29.

A synopsis of information concerning Huron population, geographical distribution, dwellings, migration, land use, subsistence techniques, and economy is derived from historical sources and archaeological data.   CCV

2840   **HEIDENREICH   CONRAD E**
1968
A NEW LOCATION FOR CARHAGOUHA, RECOLLET MISSION IN HURONIA. Ontario Archaeology No. 11:39-46.

In locating the Huron village of Carhagouha, the limitations of A. E. Jones' reconstruction of Huronia are demonstrated. Three maps unavailable to Jones and a reinterpretation of historic sources places Carhagouha on Midland Bay. As well, the locations of Quieunonascaran, Cahiague, and Tequenonquiaye (the earlier Ossossane) are also examined.   IVY

2841   **HEIDENREICH   CONRAD E**
1970
THE HISTORICAL GEOGRAPHY OF HURONIA IN THE FIRST HALF OF THE 17TH CENTURY. Ph.D. Thesis. Department of Geography. McMaster University. 570 pp.

Early 17th century geography of Huronia is reconstructed from historic, archival, geographic, and archaeological sources. Trade and politics, subsistence economy, settlement pattern, and interaction between occupation and physical environment are described.   CCV

2842   **JOLICOEUR   H R**
1965
LES INDIENS DE LA PROVINCE DE QUEBEC AVEC COMMENTAIRE PAR EDITH DUMONT-BLAIS. In The Education of Indian Children in Canada: A Symposium Written by Members of Indian Affairs Education Division with Comments by the Indian Peoples. L. G. P. Waller, ed. The Canadian Superintendent 1965. Toronto: Ryerson Press. pp. 81-87.

Discussion of education among Quebec Indians is commented on by Edith Dumont-Blais of Lorette on pages 86-87. An educational system planned as a function of the Indians' socio-economic status and in the context of today's society will necessarily facilitate retention of Indian identity, traditions, and cultural values. The sense of a particular identity, acquired at a young age, in relation to a larger network is the foundation for personal realization and contribution in the larger sphere of relations.   CCV

2843   **JURY   ELSIE MCLEOD**
1963
INDIAN VILLAGE AND MISSION SITES OF HURONIA. Canadian Geographical
Journal 67:94-103.

Jesuit writings and archaeological evidence provide a description of Indian villages and
Jesuit missions in 17th century Huronia.   IVY

2844   **JURY   ELSIE MCLEOD**
1967
TOANCHE. Canadian Geographical Journal 74:40-45.

In the early 17th century, Toanche was the western terminus of the trade that first
brought substance to the tiny post at Quebec. A brief history of Toanche is given outlining the activities of the Catholic missionaries, traders, and explorers.   IVY

2845   **LE BLANC PETER G**
1968
INDIAN-MISSIONARY CONTACT IN HURONIA, 1619-1649. Ontario History
60:133-146.

Although the Hurons developed some degree of trust and affection for the missionaries,
early 17th century French attempts to establish a mission base in Huronia failed, with
resentment and fear being the ultimate outcome. The failure was due to many factors.
During this period the Iroquois and famine plagued the Hurons, and the missionaries
only complicated the issue with their European diseases and their systematic questioning
of Huron beliefs. The Hurons' inability to fully understand the Jesuits' role in terms of
their own role structure also affected the conflict.   ADG

2846   **LEITCH   ADELAIDE**
1963
LAND OF THE WENDATS. The Beaver 294(Autumn):14-19.

General information on Huron history and culture is provided and some archaeological
sites in Ontario are mentioned.   IVY

2847   **LEITCH   ADELAIDE**
1965
THE SNOWSHOE MAKERS OF LORETTEVILLE. Canadian Geographical Journal
70:62-63.

Text and photographs describe the craft of snowshoe making by Huron Indians at Loretteville, Quebec.   IVY

2848   **MORISSONNEAU   CHRISTIAN**
1970
DEVELOPPEMENT ET POPULATION DE LA RESERVE INDIENNE DU
VILLAGE-HURON, LORRETTEVILLE. Cahiers de Geographie de Quebec 14:337-
357.

The history of the Huron population at Lorette Reserve is traced from contact to the present. The population characteristics at Lorette, typical of a White population, reveal the

high degree of acculturation when compared to Mistassini and Pointe Bleue. A crucial problem facing the reserve is a need for space for expansion. Numerous small shops maintain successful production and sale of outdoor sporting goods and handicrafts. Administration of the reserve is increasingly controlled by the Huron and this is felt to be an important factor of positive integration.   CCV

2849   **MORISSONNEAU   OLIVIER CHRISTIAN**
1968
POPULATION ET DEVELOPPEMENT DU VILLAGE-HURON (RESERVE INDIENNE, LORETTEVILLE). M.A. Thesis. Institut de Geographie. Universite Laval. 70 pp.

This is an analysis of the economic development of the Huron of Loretteville, Quebec. In the past these Huron exploited a large territory in the Laurentians, but today this land cannot support the population. The community is growing into a small suburb of Quebec city with handicraft and the making of sporting goods being the only economic activities. Canoe building and snowshoe making earn the most profits. The author approves of the growing participation of the Indians in the administration of their reserve.   DD

2850   **SAGARD   GABRIEL (FRERE THEODAT)**
1964
GABRIEL SAGARD, THEODAT. Jean de la Rioux, ed. Montreal: Editions Fides. 94 pp.

Excerpts from the works of the Recollet Brother Theodat (Gabriel Sagard) resulting from his stay in Canada among the Hurons from 1623-1624 are compiled. Detailed descriptions of dwellings, food processing, subsistence activities, marriage practices, morality, recreation, medical practices, warfare, religion, and burial practices are included in Sagard's observations. A resume of the Recollet missionary's works is found on pages 83 to 94.   CCV

2851   **SMITH   WALLIS M**
1970
A RE-APPRAISAL OF THE HURON KINSHIP SYSTEM. Anthropologica N.S. 12:191-206.

Based on ethnohistoric sources, the presence of matrilineality and matrilocality among the Huron from 1609-1640 is questioned and evidence is cited for a shift to virilocality and village-level government as an adaptive measure to contact with the fur trade. It is concluded that a complete change from matrilineal to patrilineal organization did not occur.   WRC

2852   **TOOKER   ELISABETH**
1964
AN ETHNOGRAPHY OF THE HURON INDIANS, 1615-1649. Smithsonian Institution. Bureau of American Ethnology Bulletin 190. Washington: U.S. Government Printing Office. 183 pp.

The writings of Champlain, Sagard, and the Jesuits (principally Brebeuf) are utilized to give a description of the Huron culture for the period 1600-1649.   ADG

2853   **TRIGGER   BRUCE GRAHAM**
1960
THE DESTRUCTION OF HURONIA: A STUDY IN ECONOMIC AND
CULTURAL CHANGE, 1609-1650. Royal Canadian Institute Transactions 33:14-45.

An explanation of the collapse of Huron society must depend on a full examination of
both pre-contact Huron culture and the changes that occurred within it during the contact period. Using the historical approach, various aspects of the native culture are described: subsistence economy, religion and rituals, political organization, warfare, and
trade. The importance of war and trade in the aboriginal culture is stressed. Five contact
periods are discussed: 1609-1629, 1629-1632, and the Jesuit periods of 1634-1640, 1640-
1647, and 1647-1650. Differences in the post-contact development of the Iroquois and
Huron societies may be attributed to differences in ecology and the contact situation. The
initial Iroquois responce to a simple economic challenge appears to have been less socially
disruptive, and to have exposed their society to less damage from external competition,
than did the Huron responce to a new ideology.   IVY

2854   **TRIGGER   BRUCE GRAHAM**
1962
THE HISTORICAL LOCATION OF THE HURONS. Ontario History 54:137-148.

In historic times the Huron, although numbering nearly 30,000, lived in an area of 800
square miles. This population concentration in such a small area is given 2 explanations:
soil type and attacks from the Iroquois. Analysis of the Jesuit Relations and archaeological findings reveal that the Huron likely settled in Huronia because of a combination of
good soil which could be easily worked, a location close to fish resources, and a proximity
to northern tribes which was favorable to the development of intertribal trade.   ADG

2855   **TRIGGER   BRUCE GRAHAM**
1963
ORDER AND FREEDOM IN HURON SOCIETY. Anthropolgica N.S. 5:151-169.

The various levels of social control among the 17th century Huron are examined. Despite
individual autonomy and the predominance of kin groups in the regulation of conflict,
fear of witchcraft functioned to maintain a degree of central authority in the chiefs in a
society without organic integration.   WRC

2856   **TRIGGER   BRUCE GRAHAM**
1965
THE JESUITS AND THE FUR TRADE. Ethnohistory 12:30-53.

The history of the tripartite relationship between priests, fur traders, and Indians which
constituted the foundation for Huron missions has been examined. It is concluded that
the Jesuits were neither political agents nor agents of the fur trade. Religious motives
combined with a sense of responsibility for the welfare of a primitive people were the
considerations uppermost in their minds.   IVY

2857   **TRIGGER   BRUCE GRAHAM**
1968

THE FRENCH PRESENCE IN HURONIA: THE STRUCTURE OF FRANCO-HURON RELATIONS IN THE FIRST HALF OF THE SEVENTEENTH CENTURY. The Canadian Historical Review 49:107-141.

The history of Huronia is outlined. Discussed are the developments in Huronia prior to the fur trade, early Franco-Huron relations, control by the Jesuits, the epidemics of 1635 to 1640, the development of a Christian faction, and the pagan reaction and destruction of Huronia.   IVY

2858   **TRIGGER   BRUCE GRAHAM**
1969
THE HURON: FARMERS OF THE NORTH. New York: Holt, Rinehart, Winston. 130 pp.

An historical ethnography of Huron life and social organization in the 1st half of the 17th century discusses ecology, economy, warfare, kinship and family life, government and law, power, institutions, and the dead. The study relies primarily on the writings of Champlain, the Jesuits, and the Recollets as well as archaeological and ethnographic reports.   CCV

2859   **VACHON   ANDRE**
1964
VALEUR DE LA SOURCE HURONNE: L'AFFAIRE DU LONG SAULT. Revue de l'Universite Laval 18:495-515.

The only survivors of the French allies of the famous Long Sault battle were a few Hurons who managed to escape the Iroquois in 1660. The reports of the authorities of the time are based only on the testimony of these few Indians. The author insists therefore on the importance for today's historian of verifying the reliability of these sources. The 5 texts that relate the events are cited and the origin of the information is analyzed before the author concludes that those rare testimonies are precious and unquestionable.   DD

2860   **WRIGHT   GARY A**
1968
A FURTHER NOTE ON TRADE FRIENDSHIP AND GIFT GIVING IN THE WESTERN GREAT LAKES. Michigan Archaeologist 14:165-166.

Additional data concerning gift exchanges among the Huron are given.   IVY

IROQUOIS

2861   **1961**
CENTENNIAL OF AN INDIAN POET. Citizen 7(3):23-25.

The life of the Mohawk poetess, Pauline Johnson, is reviewed. Mention is made of several of the events such as speeches, displays of her work, and reserve entertainment to take place in her honor.   ADG

2862   **1961**
ONTARIO LEGISLATURE PAYS TRIBUTE TO MEMORY OF PAULINE JOHNSON. Human Relations (Ontario Human Rights Commission) 1(3):1.

On March 10, 1961, Premier Frost and Former Premier Nixon and the Ontario Legislature paid tribute to Pauline Johnson for her great leadership of the Indian people and her efforts to unite Indians and non-Indians. Mr. Nixon also noted great strides toward Indian-controlled and province-sponsored education.   ADG

2863   **1965**
THE INTRODUCTION OF ALCOHOL INTO IROQUOIS SOCIETY. SUBSTUDY 1. Unpublished paper. Available from Alcohol and Drug Addiction Research Foundation, Toronto. 37 pp.

Indians of the Northeast had no alcoholic beverages of their own and did not seem familiar with alcohol until the introduction of wine, brandy, and rum in the 17th century. For the Iroquois alcohol was an intoxicant and they drank it to feel the full effect of intoxication. European society did not look favorably upon the Iroquois' use of alcohol as a drug to cure diseases and enhance visions, and eventually imposed strong negative sanctions upon the Indians' form of drinking. The Indians themselves had also asked for stoppage of the liquor traffic. The introduction of alcohol into Indian society was disastrous, since it led to murders, injuries, the release of hostility, and the disruption of hunting and agriculture.   ADG

2864   **1970**
BELTS OF "SACRED SIGNIFICANCE." The Indian Historian 3(2):5-9,50.

A review of information concerning wampum is given including description and manufacture, its civil and religious uses, and its origins.   IVY

2865   **ADAMS   DARIAN**
1967
Canadian Antiques Collector 2(7):5,26.

A brief history and description of the 6 pieces of Queen Anne Communion plate owned by the Mohawks of Brantford, Ontario, and Deseronto, Ontario, are given.   IVY

2866   **BAUMAN   ROBERT F**
1960
CLAIMS VS REALITIES: THE ANGLO-IROQUOIS PARTNERSHIP. Northwest Ohio Quarterly 32:87-101.

The Iroquois invasion of Huronia is examined and their claim to control over the Great Lakes analyzed. It is shown that elimination of the Huron did not result in trade and a new supply of beaver for the Iroquois, for the Ottawa and Algonkins stepped into the position vacated by the Huron, and for a time assumed command of the French-Indian trading empire.   IVY

2867   **BAUMAN   ROBERT F**
1960
IROQUOIS "EMPIRE": IROQUOIS MAKE ALL-OUT EFFORT TO DESTROY THE HURONS AND GAIN CONTROL OF THE GREAT LAKES FUR TRADE.
Northwest Ohio Quarterly 32:138-172.

Four factors accounting for the Iroquois upheaval of Huronia are discussed: (1) superiority of armament, (2) plague and famine, (3) vulnerability of Huronia, and (4) mental attitude of the foe. It is concluded that the Iroquois failed to gain their objective, the Algonkian beaver supply, and it was the Ottawa, not the Iroquois, who assumed the middleman position after the fall of Huronia.   IVY

2868   **BENEDICT   ERNEST**
1970
INDIANS AND A TREATY. In The Only Good Indian: Essays by Canadian Indians. Waubageshig, ed. Toronto: New Press. pp. 147-160.

A Mohawk Indian from the St. Regis Reserve expresses his sentiments on the Jay Treaty of 1795, claiming exemption from payment of duties on goods imported into Canada from the United States. The government's non-recognition of these treaty rights was the target of a 1968 bridge blockade on the international road at St. Regis.   JSL

2869   **BLUMENFELD   RUTH**
1961
THE CAUGHNAWAGA MOHAWK IN BROOKLYN: A CASE STUDY OF
INDIAN URBANIZATION. M.A. Thesis. Department of Anthropology.
University of Pennsylvania. 129 pp. Available from Library, Department of Indian
Affairs and Northern Development, Ottawa.

The development of a Caughnawaga colony in Brooklyn is presented including an historical review of the Iroquois from early periods of contact through establishment of Caughnawaga to the present. Fieldwork was done in Brooklyn from February until June and in Caughnawaga during September and December, 1956. In addition to the social and political organization in Caughnawaga the occupational pursuits, ritual belief and tradition, and Brooklyn-Caughnawaga ties are discussed.   CCV

2870   **BONVILLAIN   NANCY**
1969
GENERAL DESCRIPTION OF FIELDWORK CARRIED OUT AT ST. REGIS
RESERVE. Unpublished paper. Available from Library, American Philosophical
Society, Philadelphia, with permission of the author. 5 pp.

This paper is a report of the descriptive linguistic research done during the summer of 1969. Bilingualism (Mohawk-English) among most of the St. Regis population is noted, as is factionalism along political and religious cleavages.   HCV

2871   **BROWN   JUDITH K**
1970
ECONOMIC ORGANIZATION AND THE POSITION OF WOMEN AMONG THE
IROQUOIS. Ethnohistory 17:151-167.

The position of Iroquois and Bemba women and their role in the economic organization of their matrilineal and matrilocal tribes are compared. Examining the role of Iroquois women in politics, religion, and domestic life, it is concluded that the high status of Iroquois women was the result of their control of the economic organization of their tribe.   IVY

2872   **BRUEMMER   FRED**
1965
THE CAUGHNAWAGAS. The Beaver 296(Winter):4-11.

The history of the Caughnawagas since 1667 to 1964 is briefly outlined including their role in the French-English conflicts; their skills in handling canoes and boats in Canada, the United States, and Egypt; and their work on high steel.   IVY

2873   **CANADA. Department of Indian Affairs and Northern Development. Resources and Industrial Division.**
1969
RESERVE INVENTORY PROGRAM: PILOT PROJECT TYENDINAGA RESERVE - ONTARIO REGION. Unpublished paper. Available at Indian-Eskimo Economic Development Branch, Development Services Division, Department of Indian Affairs and Northern Development, Ottawa. 45 pp.

A pilot study to evaluate the economic potential of the Tyendinaga Reserve in the regional context is presented. The physical setting, population characteristics, housing and utilities, land use and holdings, reserve economic activity, and possibilities for development are outlined.   CCV

2874   **CANADIAN MITCHELL ASSOCIATES**
1970
CHIEFSWOOD INDIAN PARK DEVELOPMENT PLAN AND REPORT.
Unpublished report prepared for Ontario Government Conservation Branch. Available at Indian-Eskimo Economic Development Branch, Development Services Division, Department of Indian Affairs and Northern Development, Ottawa. 17 pp.

The Chiefswood Indian Park owned by the Six Nations Indians is evaluated in terms of expansion and development. Provision of additional recreational facilities is discussed in terms of management, cost, and rentability.   CCV

2875   **CHAFE   WALLACE L**
1964
LINGUISTIC EVIDENCE FOR THE RELATIVE AGE OF IROQUOIS RELIGIOUS PRACTICES. Southwestern Journal of Anthropology 20:278-285.

By examination of the chronological order of linguistic forms in the Seneca language, a corresponding stratification of meaning is established which indicates that shamanistic rituals may have preceded agricultural ceremonies in Iroquois cultural history.   WRC

2876   **CHARLTON   THOMAS H**
1968
ON IROQUOIS INCEST. Anthropologica N.S. 10:29-41.

A review of previous studies of Iroquois kinship reveals 4 distinct interpretations of the incest taboo. It is concluded that the application of the taboo has always been bilateral and that the emergence of clans and moieties throughout Iroquois culture history has given the false impression of matrilineal application.   WRC

2877   **COLWELL   ELEANOR J**
1968
THE OKA LAND QUESTION: HISTORICAL FACTORS IN A COMMUNITY
STRUCTURE. M.S.W. Thesis. School of Social Work. McGill University. 65 pp.

The land controversy at Oka beginning with the establishment of the Sulpician mission
at Mount Royal and transfer to the seigniory at the Lake of Two Mountains through to
the present day is reviewed. The contention over the title to the seigniory land is described and these events are related to patterns of political organization among the Six
Nations Iroquois, British, and Canadian administration, and attitudes prevalent among
the Oka Iroquois today. CCV

2878   **CORK   ELLA**
1962
THE WORST OF THE BARGAIN: CONCERNING THE DILEMMAS INHERITED
FROM THEIR FOREFATHERS ALONG WITH THEIR LANDS BY THE
IROQUOIS NATION OF THE CANADIAN GRAND RIVER RESERVE. San
Jacinto, CA: Foundation for Social Research. 196 pp.

The status of Canadian Indians, particularly the Iroquois of the Grand River, from contact to the present is reviewed by a political scientist. Current difficulties encountered by
Iroquois efforts at self-determination are related to federal government legislation and
policy which derive in turn from the historical context of Indian-White relations. Incon-
sistencies between Indian and White interpretations are reported as an attempt is made
to present the Indian point of view. Recommendations are advanced for improved local
government at Grand River, lucrative Indian exploitation of Grand River lands, and
provision of a trained advisory body to guide Indian Affairs in policy making. CCV

2879   **CORLEY   NORA T**
1964-65
THE MOHAWKS OF CAUGHNAWAGA. CIBA Journal 32:36-42.

The military and economic history of the settlement of Caughnawaga is traced from its
founding in 1667-68 to Mohawk participation in the construction of the Unisphere at the
New York World's Fair. TSA

2880   **DAY   GORDON M**
1967
IROQUOIS: AN ETYMOLOGY. In Iroquois Culture, History, and Prehistory:
Proceedings of the 1965 Conference on Iroquois Research. Elisabeth Tooker, ed.
Albany: New York State Museum and Science Service. pp. 57-61.

Five possibilities of the derivation of the name Iroquois are discussed including a reference to a Montagnais etymology which suggests that some Montagnais group adopted,
with appropriate phonetic changes, a name heard from Iroquoian speakers. IVY

2881   **DESROSIERS   LEO-PAUL**
1962
REVERS ET SUCCES (1662-1663). Cahiers des Dix 27:77-95.

The peace proposals of an Onondaga, Cayuga, and Seneca embassy in 1662 presented by
Garakonthie to the French of Montreal were answered suspiciously. The 3 tribes were

still fighting with the Mohawk and Oneida who explicitly declined any alliance with the French. Based primarily on "Les Relations"of the Jesuits, the solicitations of the French colony concerning its protection against the Iroquois and addressed to the King of France are enumerated.   DD

2882   **DESROSIERS   LEO-PAUL**
1963
FRONTENAC: L'ARTISAN DE LA VICTOIRE. Cahiers des Dix 28:93-145.

This is an analysis of the political and military events that affected the English and the French colonies and the Iroquois at the beginning of Frontenac's 2nd term as Governor of New France (1690-1694). The Americans had established a solid alliance with the Iroquois and wanted to force them into an open war against New France. Worn out by the repeated attacks, New France attempted to sign a lasting peace treaty with the Iroquois. As for the Iroquois, they committed themselves at times to the Americans, at times to the French. Considerably weakened by heavy losses in human life over the years, the Iroquois tried to satisfy both parties to avoid any further fighting.   DD

2883   **DOCKSTADER   JOHN**
1969
REPORT: AN INDUSTRIAL DESIGN STUDY BASED ON TRADITIONAL IROQUOIAN ART AND FORMS: A PRELIMINARY STUDY OF THE ARTS AND CRAFTS OF HISTORIC AND PRE-HISTORIC IROQUOIAN CULTURE AND ITS PRACTICAL APPLICATION TO CONTEMPORARY CRAFTS. Ottawa: Department of Indian Affairs and Northern Development. 23 pp.

Research into historical and museum sources from December 1, 1967, until February 28, 1968, provides a discussion of traditional Iroquoian art and form. Proposals are advanced for initiating a program on the Six Nations Reserve which would revive interest in traditional craftmanship and provide training and materials for production of traditional and adapted items for the consumer market.   CCV

2884   **DRUMM   JUDITH**
1962
IROQUOIS CULTURE. New York State Museum and Science Service Educational Leaflet 5. Albany, NY: New York State Museum and Science Service. 14 pp.

Prepared mainly for teachers, a general description of Iroquois culture is given including subsistence economy, religion, social structure, and warfare. The discussion is related to the exhibits in the Clark Hall of the State Museum in the State Education Building at Albany.   IVY

2885   **ECCLES   W J**
1960
DENONVILLE ET LES GALERIENS IROQUOIS. Revue d'Histoire de l'Amerique Francaise 14:408-429.

The belief that Denonville captured over 200 Iroquois during the summer of 1687 with the purpose of sending them as galley slaves to France is questioned. Examination of historical sources shows that the Iroquois were captured in the course of military operations. The subterfuge of which Denonville is accused was actually practiced by Champigny.

Finally indications are that only 40 Iroquois were sent to France. Thirteen survived and returned.   CCV

2886   **ECKERT   ALLAN W**
1969
WILDERNESS EMPIRE: A NARRATIVE. Boston: Little, Brown. 653 pp.

This interpretation of the struggle between England and France for control of Eastern North America during the first half of the 18th century is derived from original documents. Emphasis is on Indian-White alliances and the role of leaders, particularly William Johnson, among the Iroquois. Frequent descriptive passages of warfare and torture appear.   CCV

2887   **EINHORN   ARTHUR**
1961
A NOTE ON: SNAPPING TURTLE SHELL RATTLES. American Indian Tradition 7:136-137.

The method of constructing a turtle shell rattle from capturing the snapping turtle to coating the shell with shellac is presented.   TSA

2888   **EWERS   JOHN C**
1963
IROQUOIS INDIANS IN THE FAR WEST. Montana: The Magazine of Western History 13(2):2-10.

Extensive Iroquois participation as paddlers and trappers in the fur trade as far west as the Columbia, as well as activities of some of these individuals who settled among western Indians, is documented. This activity began as early as 1784 and continued through the first half of the 19th century.   TSA

2889   **EYMAN   FRANCES**
1964
LACROSSE AND THE CAYUGA THUNDER RITE. Expedition 6(4):14-19.

The game of lacrosse played both as a sport and as a ritual is discussed. Changes in the crosses are outlined referring specifically to 3 sticks from the Cayuga of the Six Nations Reserve which span a century in the history of the game (pre-1845, pre-1910, and 1932).   IVY

2890   **FENTON   WILLIAM N**
1960
THE HIAWATHA WAMPUM BELT OF THE IROQUOIS LEAGUE FOR PEACE: A SYMBOL FOR THE INTERNATIONAL CONGRESS OF ANTHROPOLOGY. In Men and Cultures: Selected Papers of the Fifth International Congress of Anthropological and Ethnological Sciences. Anthony F. C. Wallace, ed. Philadelphia: University of Pennsylvania Press. pp. 3-7.

A description of the belt, dated between 1755 and 1774, and its meaning is given.   IVY

2891   **FENTON   WILLIAM N**
1961
IROQUOIAN CULTURE HISTORY: A GENERAL EVALUATION. In Symposium
on Cherokee and Iroquois Culture. William N. Fenton and John Gulick, eds.
Smithsonian Institution. Bureau of American Ethnology Bulletin 180. Washington, DC:
U.S. Government Printing Office. pp. 253-277.

Drawing together the papers presented at the symposium, the cultural history of the Iroquois is outlined and the methodological problems in comparing the Iroquois and Cherokee discussed.   IVY

2892   **FENTON   WILLIAM N**
1962
INTRODUCTION: LEWIS HENRY MORGAN (1818-1881) PIONEER
ETHNOLOGIST. In League of the Iroquois. By Lewis Henry Morgan. New York:
Corinth Books. pp. v-xviii.

Discussed in this introductory statement are the methodology and approach used by
Lewis Henry Morgan in his study of Iroquoian culture. Dubbed as the first scientific ac-
count of an Indian tribe, the work is an attempt at describing the tribe in their own terms.
DGW

2893   **FENTON   WILLIAM N**
1962
"THIS ISLAND, THE WORLD ON THE TURTLE'S BACK."Journal of American
Folklore 75:283-300.

The story of the Earth-Grasper is examined historically as the first of 3 epics in the Iroquois cosmological myth. The persistence of its cultural themes throughout Iroquois history
is noted.   WRC

2894   **FENTON   WILLIAM N**
1963
HORATIO HALE: M.A. (HARVARD), F.R.S.C. (1817-1896). In The Iroquois Book of
Rites. William N. Fenton, ed. Toronto: University of Toronto Press. pp. 7-27.

Horatio Hale's 1883 publication is reprinted with an introduction by William Fenton.
Hale's work is discussed including his methods, informants, contacts, contributions, and
oversights. Of note are the examination of Hale's estimates of the dating of the Iroquois
confederation, and expansion upon Hale's explanation of the rituals involved in the con-
dolence council.   CCV

2895   **FENTON   WILLIAM N**
1965
THE IROQUOIS CONFEDERACY IN THE TWENTIETH CENTURY: A CASE
STUDY OF THE THEORY OF LEWIS H. MORGAN IN "ANCIENT
SOCIETY."Ethnology 4:251-265.

Observations and analysis of Iroquois society and government presented by Lewis Henry Morgan in his Ancient Society are examined. Subsequent ethnohistorical and ethnological materials are employed in assessment of Morgan's theory of cultural evolution with specific reference to the Iroquois of Six Nations, Grand River, Ontario, and the Seneca Nation of New York. Reasonable accuracy is attributed to Morgan's developmental scheme of Barbarism to Civilization. It is concluded that its strict classification did not account for the persistence of aboriginal values which has had a strong effect on the process of acculturation, as evidenced in the actual historical development of Iroquois political systems.   WRC

2896   **FENTON   WILLIAM N**
1968
INTRODUCTION. In Parker on the Iroquois. William N. Fenton, ed. Syracuse, NY: Syracuse University Press. pp. 1-47.

Arthur C. Parker's 3 famous monographs on the Iroquois are reprinted in this volume. Originally they were published as New York State Museum Bulletins. Various roles which Parker assumed were folklorist, ethnologist, archaeologist, museologist, defender of Indian rights, writer of children's books, historian, and museum director. As far as contributing to the field, Parker was a pioneer in describing the subsistence patterns and food resources of the Iroquois - the major strength of "Iroquois Uses of Maize and Other Food Plants."His recovery of the Code of Handsome Lake was a beginning in the understanding of native revitalization movements. And in "The Constitution of the Five Nations,"we have a representative effort of native scribes to codify custom, law, and usage in the face of external and internal pressures. Most of the data for these studies were obtained from reservations in New York and the Six Nations Reserve in Canada.   DGW

2897   **FENTON   WILLIAM N**
1969
J.-F. LAFITAU (1681-1746), PRECURSOR OF SCIENTIFIC ANTHROPOLOGY.
Southwestern Journal of Anthropology 25:173-187.

The method of cross-checking ancient customs with field observations is considered the main contribution of the Jesuit missionary, Joseph-Francois Lafitau, to the development of scientific ethnology. His theories of psychic unity, unitary human origin, primitive monotheism, and cultural relativism, and the attempt at empirical verification while working among the Mohawk at Saint-Louis du Sault (Caughnawaga) led to several notable discoveries, acknowledged only after long delay by the history of anthropological thought.   WRC

2898   **FORBES   ALLAN JR**
1970
TWO AND A HALF CENTURIES OF CONFLICT: THE IROQUOIS AND LAURENTIAN WARS. Pennsylvania Archaeologist 40(3-4):1-20.

Utilizing the same ethnohistoric sources as earlier writers - Champlain, Sagard, and the Jesuits - it is hypothesized that the League of the Iroquois was in a position of political and military supremacy from 1580 to 1640 rather than, as is widely believed, a defeated people on the defensive. Factors responsible for the misinterpretation of the Iroquois position are discussed. The struggle for the St. Lawrence Valley (the Laurentian Wars) is seen in 2 phases. By 1580 the Hochelagans had been driven out of the valley by the Iroquois who consolidated their hold by the turn of the century. The second, the European-cum-Indian phase, ended with the defeat of the French at Quebec (1759) and Montreal (1760). The Iroquois were a decisive factor in this defeat.   IVY

2899   **FREILICH   MORRIS**
1963
SCIENTIFIC POSSIBILITIES IN IROQUOIAN STUDIES: AN EXAMPLE OF
MOHAWKS PAST AND PRESENT. Anthropologica N.S. 5:171-186.

Based on fieldwork in Brooklyn and Caughnawaga, aboriginal and modern Mohawk cultural adaptations are compared to test whether changes in cultural ecological adaptations parallel changes in Mohawk culture. Due to (1) cultural persistence and (2) culture change unrelated to changed ecology, this hypothesis is rejected. Also it is noted that a more precise terminology is required to use the experimental method.   IVY

2900   **FREILICH   MORRIS**
1970
MOHAWK HEROES AND TRINIDADIAN PEASANTS. In Marginal Natives:
Anthropologists at Work. Morris Freilich, ed. New York: Harper and Row. pp. 185-206.

Some experiences, problems, methods, and yields of fieldwork among Mohawk steel workers in Brooklyn are described by an anthropologist. Particular attention is devoted to Indian socialization in a bar, Indian steel workers' attitudes toward their work and toward danger, and their trips to Caughnawaga. Freilich suggests that steel working presents an opportunity for the Mohawk to assert his maleness and conceives the steel workers as the modern Mohawk warriors.   CCV

2901   **FRISCH   JACK A**
n.d.
THE MIDWINTER RITES OF THE ST. REGIS LONGHOUSE. Unpublished paper.
Available from National Museum of Man, Ethnology Division, Ottawa, with permission of the author. 19 pp.

Focus is on the 1968 Midwinter ceremony held on the St. Regis Reserve. The 4 days of activities, including attendance, costume, songs, dance, and ceremonies, are described. Also described is the public False Face dance held 4 days after the end of Midwinter. The latter is a thanksgiving ritual, the former a curing rite. Some comparisons are made with similar ceremonies on other Iroquois reserves. It is concluded that local peculiarities at St. Regis must be interpreted as being due to the interaction of ceremonial conservatism and the dual pressures of acculturation and compromises.   JSL

2902   **FRISCH   JACK A**
1970
REVITALIZATION, NATIVISM AND TRIBALISM AMONG THE ST. REGIS
MOHAWKS. Ph.D. Thesis. Department of Anthropology. Indiana University. 217 pp.
Available from University Microfilms.

The growth and development of the Longhouse religion among the St. Regis Mohawks of New York, Ontario, and Quebec is reviewed. The development of the St. Regis community is traced to 1888 when the Indian Act abolished tribal government. This event is considered a direct cause of the nativistic movement which, in the years that followed, developed a unique St. Regis composition in response to the pressures of acculturation and culture change.   CCV

2903   **FRISCH   JACK A**
1970
TRIBALISM AMONG THE ST. REGIS MOHAWKS: A SEARCH FOR SELF-IDENTITY. Anthropologica N.S. 12:207-219.

Fieldwork at the St. Regis Reserve at the division of Quebec, Ontario, and New York State leads to a brief history of the conflicts in the political jurisdiction of the settlement from its founding in 1755 to the present. The development of tribalism among the Mohawks as a response to international infringements on Indian rights is traced and the recently increased pressures of acculturation are viewed as intensifying, not hindering, Indian identity.   WRC

2904   **GAMBILL   JERRY**
1968
CONTROVERSY: HUNTING AND FISHING RIGHTS OF INDIANS OF ONTARIO: HOW OUR POLITICAL CONSIDERATIONS DENY JUSTICE. Unpublished paper. Available from Public Archives of Canada, Manuscript Division. 11 pp.

The efforts of Ontario Indians to obtain recognition of hunting and fishing rights as outlined in the 1850 Robinson treaty are demonstrated in this review of correspondence among Indians, the Indian Affairs Branch, and the Department of Justice, 1892-1918. Following the 1888 provincial amendment to the "Act for the Protection of Game and Fur-Bearing Animals", Indian hunting privileges were restricted.   CCV

2905   **GAMBILL   JERRY**
1968
HOW DEMOCRACY CAME TO ST. REGIS. Unpublished paper. Available at Public Archives of Canada, Manuscript Division. 16 pp.

Referring to records, correspondence, and newspaper reports, a reconstruction is presented of some of the events occurring between the 1884 Indian Advancement Act and the 1890 trial of 15 St. Regis life chiefs. The St. Regis, Oka, and Caughnawaga Indians' reaction to federal government attempts to impose a system of municipal government is described by means of numerous quotations from petitions and letters.   CCV

2906   **GHOBASHY   OMAR Z**
1961
THE CAUGHNAWAGA INDIANS AND THE ST. LAWRENCE SEAWAY. New York: Devin-Adair. 137 pp.

Legal aspects of relations between the Caughnawaga Indians and the St. Lawrence Seaway Authority are discussed with reference to original documents and correspondence.

The history of the Caughnawaga Indians, their land rights, and their legal status are examined relative to the legal status of Indian nations, the St. Lawrence Seaway Act, and the British North America Act. Correspondence between the Band Council and the Seaway Authority is noted with attention to compensation and expropriation. The Six Nations appeal for support from the League of Nations and the United Nations is reported and the legal status of the Caughnawaga Band before these groups is evaluated.   CCV

2907   **GOLDSTEIN   ROBERT A**
1969
FRENCH-IROQUOIS DIPLOMATIC AND MILITARY RELATIONS 1609-1701.
The Hague: Mouton. 208 pp.

The nature of French-Iroquois diplomatic and military relations, 1609-1701, is examined; the importance of the conflict over the fur trade in these relations is demonstrated; and the relationship of the French-Iroquois conflict to the larger issue of Anglo-French rivalry is shown.   IVY

2908   **HAMILTON   S R**
1960
INDIAN VILLAGE. Sylva 16(6):12-14.

An Indian village, a commercial venture depicting how Indians of the Niagara Falls area lived in the past, was built near Niagara Falls, Ontario. A brief account of its construction is given.   IVY

2909   **HARRINGTON   MARK RAYMOND**
1961
QUAINT QUILL-WORK. Masterkey 35:116-117.

A little birchbark box with quill decoration, probably of Mohawk-Iroquois origin, in the Southwest Museum is described.   IVY

2910   **HILL   BRUCE EMERSON**
1964
THE GRAND RIVER NAVIGATION COMPANY. M.A. Thesis. Department of History. University of Western Ontario. 157 pp.

Events leading to the incorporation in 1832 of the Grand River Navigation Company whose development was important in opening up the Grand River Valley to settlement and trade are traced to June, 1861, when financial failure led to foreclosure of its mortgages. Of note is the financial support for the company which was derived largely from Six Nations' funds (albeit without their knowledge or consent). Details of the construction, use, and management of the canal and its inability to compete with other means of transport once it had served to open up the Grand River Valley are derived largely from archival sources and records of the Indian Department.   CCV

2911   **HILL   MELVILLE**
1962
ADDRESS. Unpublished paper delivered to 8th Annual Indian and Metis Conference, sponsored by the Community Welfare Planning Council of Greater Winnipeg. Winnipeg, February 7, 1962. Available from Legislative Library, Winnipeg. 9 pp.

The elective band council of the Tyendinaga Reserve in Desoronto, Ontario, provides the background for this address by its chief, Melville Hill. Using direct examples, he discusses the development of band leadership, elections, policy-making, public relations with other agencies, the duties of the chief and council, and the Indian Act.   IVY

2912   **HOULE   ROBERT**
1970
FALSE FACE SOCIETY. Tawow 1(3):2-9.

Masks, a significant part of Iroquois culture for almost 300 years, are discussed including origin, style, technical process, and the religious aspects of masking.   IVY

2913   **INDIAN-ESKIMO ASSOCIATION OF CANADA**
1965
DR. GILBERT C. MONTURE, O.B.E., D.Sc. Canadian Indians of Today No. 1. 2 pp.

The distinguished career of Dr. Monture, a member of the Mohawk tribe, and his outstanding service to Canada and the world in the field of mining and mineral resources, both in war and peace, are recapitulated.   IVY

2914   **JOHNSON   DAVID**
1969
JOSEPH BRANT - THAYENDANAGEA. The Indian Historian 2(2):35-36.

A biographic sketch of Joseph Brant is given.   IVY

2915   **JOHNSON   ROY F**
1967
THE TUSCARORAS: MYTHOLOGY - MEDICINE - CULTURE. Murfreesboro, NC: Johnson. 264 pp. Volume 1 of 2 vols.

A collection of tales on Tuscarora mythology and medicine is compiled from informants and archival sources revealing traditional beliefs, philosophy, crafts, customs, and laws.   CCV

2916   **JOHNSON   ROY F**
1968
THE TUSCARORAS: HISTORY - TRADITIONS - CULTURE. Murfreesboro, NC: Johnson. 284 pp. Volume 2 of 2 vols.

Tuscarora history from the time of contact to modern times is reconstructed from historical sources. Traditions and cultural modifications are discussed as well as conflict with White settlers and migrations.   CCV

2917   **JOHNSTON   CHARLES M**
1963
JOSEPH BRANT, THE GRAND RIVER LANDS AND THE NORTHWEST CRISIS. Ontario History 55:267-282.

Joseph Brant's coercion of the Upper Canada administration with respect to the sale of Indian lands on the Grand River is analyzed.   IVY

2918   **JOHNSTON   CHARLES M**
1964
THE VALLEY OF THE SIX NATIONS: A COLLECTION OF DOCUMENTS ON
THE INDIAN LANDS OF THE GRAND RIVER. The Champlain Society
Ontario Series 7. Toronto: University of Toronto Press. 344 pp.

A collection of documents written by missionaries, travellers, army officers, government
officials, settlers, and Indians reveals the history of the Six Nations from their arrival in
Canada to the middle of the 19th century.   IVY

2919   **JOHNSTON   CHARLES M**
1965
WILLIAM CLAUS AND JOHN NORTON: A STRUGGLE FOR POWER IN
ONTARIO. Ontario History 57:101-108.

Bitter competition grew between 2 forceful personalitites. William Claus and John Nor-
ton. Claus, as Deputy Superintendent-General of Indian Affairs (appointed in 1800), and
Norton, an adopted Mohawk chief, clashed over the administration and control of the
Six Nations of the Grand River.   IVY

2920   **JOHNSTON   CHARLES MURRAY**
1967
BRANT COUNTY: A HISTORY 1784-1945. Toronto: Oxford University Press.

Based on historical and archival materials, the history of Brant County is recounted from
the 1784 land grant to the Six Nations through the establishment of Brantford and development of the area until 1945. Discussed are land transactions, settlement, warfare,
local politics, and expansion.   CCV

2921   **JOSEPHY   ALVIN M**
1962
THE PATRIOT CHIEFS: STUDIES OF NINE GREAT LEADERS OF THE
AMERICAN INDIANS. London: Eyre and Spottiswoode. 364 pp.

Chapter 1 is devoted to the teachings of Deganawidah and Hiawatha, the founders of
the Iroquois confederacy.   CCV

2922   **KLINCK   CARL F**
1966
NEW LIGHT ON JOHN NORTON. The Royal Society of Canada Transactions (Series
4) 4:167-177.

A biograhic study of John Norton, known among the Mohawks as Teyoninhokarawen,
in relation to his manuscript (written in 1816) is presented. Norton was the adopted
nephew of and deputy to Joseph Brant.   IVY

2923   **KURATH   GERTRUDE P**
1961
EFFECTS OF ENVIRONMENT ON CHEROKEE-IROQUOIS CEREMONIALISM,
MUSIC, AND DANCE. In Symposium on Cherokee and Iroquois Culture. William N.

Fenton and John Gulick, eds. Smithsonian Institution. Bureau of American Ethnology Bulletin 180. Washington, DC: U.S. Government Printing Office. pp. 173-195.

Parallel ceremonial practices of the Iroquois and Cherokee indicate they shared a substratum of northern winter rites in addition to southern influences on summer rites. Iroquois divergence from Cherokee is due to acceptance of Algonkian, Plains, and Boreal traits. Adjustment to European intrusion led to more conspicuous divergence. Transcriptions of Iroquois and Cherokee music are presented to support conclusions.   IVY

2924   **KURATH   GERTRUDE P**
1962
THE IROQUOIS BEAR SOCIETY: RITUAL DRAMA. American Indian Tradition 8:84-85.

A description of the Bear Society dance of the Longhouse Iroquois is given including transcriptions of music and diagrams showing the spatial arrangements of the actors in the ritual.   IVY

2925   **KURATH   GERTRUDE PROKOSCH**
1968
DANCE AND SONG RITUALS OF SIX NATIONS RESERVE, ONTARIO. National Museum of Canada Bulletin 220. Ottawa: Queen's Printer. 205 pp.

Musical and choreographic information on Canadian Longhouse ceremonies and the art of costuming are presented. Observations at Six Nations Reserve, Ontario, extended from 1948 to 1964. Discussed are the ceremonial calendars, Longhouse activity, choreography, dance and song, traditional style and variations, costumes, and modernization.   JSL

2926   **LECLERC   JEAN**
1961
DENONVILLE ET SES CAPTIFS IROQUOIS. Revue d'Histoire de l'Amerique Francaise 14:545-558.

The motives and actions of Denonville in his capture of 219 Iroquois in 1687 and his subsequent shipment of 39 to France where they served as galley slaves is defended.   CCV

2927   **LECLERC   JEAN**
1961
DENONVILLE ET SES CAPTIFS IROQUOIS: JEAN DE LAMBERVILLE ET LES QUARANTE DELEGUES IROQUOIS. Revue d'Histoire de l'Amerique Francaise 15:41-58.

The observations of Pere de Lamberville concerning the capture of Iroquois prisoners during the summer of 1687 are re-examined.   Comparison with other sources necessitates rejection of several of de Lamberville's assertions. It is felt that de Lamberville did not understand Denonville's strategy, underestimated Iroquois guile, overestimated their fidelity, and generally resented the interruption of missionary efforts. His conciliatory role is noted.   CCV

2928   **LINGARD   BIL**
1969
LACROSSE - THE FASTEST GAME ON TWO FEET. The Beaver 300(Autumn): 12-
16.

The history of the Chisholm Lacrosse Factory founded on the St. Regis Reserve in 1930
is traced.   IVY

2929   **MARCHAND   LEONARD S**
1968
NOTES FOR A SPEECH BY LEONARD S. MARCHAND, M.P. AT THE OPENING
OF THE LACROSSE STICK FACTORY ST. REGIS RESERVE. Speech delivered at
the opening of the lacrosse stick factory. St. Regis Reserve, October 25, 1968. Available
from Information Services, Records and Research, Department of Indian Affairs and
Northern Development, Ottawa (Speech #3-6810). 4 pp.

The successful co-operation between Indians and the Department of Indian Affairs and
the role of Indians in determining their own destiny is commented on by Leonard S.
Marchand, M.P.   CCV

2930   **MARCOUX   J**
1961
MEMOIRE POUR LA DEFENSE DE LA NEUTRALITE DES SAUVAGES DE ST.
REGIS DANS LA DERNIERE GUERRE AVEC LES AMERICAINS. Bulletin des
Recherches Historiques 67:20-30.

A manuscript prepared in 1818 by a missionary attesting to the neutrality of the St. Regis
Indians during the War of 1812-14 is published. The behavior of the Indians during this
period is explained, their political position is defended, and pressures exerted upon them
by American officers are described. The factions created in the village by arrival of Indians from New York who assumed leadership positions are discussed. Appended to the
paper are lists of early chiefs and their descendants, chiefs from "across the border,"and
those who took up arms and did not use them.   CCV

2931   **MATHUR   MARY E FLEMING**
1969
THE IROQUOIS IN ETHNOGRAPHY ... A TIME SPACE CONCEPT. The Indian
Historian 2(3):12-18.

Identification of membership in the group termed Iroquois through time and space involves not only the Iroquois themselves but also the milieu of the ethnographers and how
they see the Iroquois, or have seen them. Examining the writings of lawyer-politician
Morgan (1851 and 1877), and the Jesuit missionary Lafitau (1724), shows each was a
product of his own cultural environment and thus handicapped by this and by his expectations and prejudices in his own particular area of interest.   IVY

2932   **MATHUR   MARY E FLEMING**
1970
THE JAY TREATY AND CONFRONTATION AT ST. REGIS BOUNDARY. The
Indian Historian 3(1):37-40.

The issue of duty-free border crossing for Indians is examined from the constitutional point of view of Canada and the United States.   IVY

2933   **MATHUR   MARY E FLEMING**
1970
THE TALE OF THE LAZY INDIAN. The Indian Historian 3(3):14-18.

The ethnocentrism evident in the writings of Joseph Francis Lafitau, a Jesuit priest from the mission now termed the Caughnawaga   Reservation, is examined and the lazy Indian stereotype challenged.   IVY

2934   **MITCHELL   JOSEPH**
1960
THE MOHAWKS IN HIGH STEEL. In Apologies To The Iroquois. By Edmund Wilson. London: Allen. pp. 1-36.

A brief history of the Mohawk high steel workers of the Caughnawaga Reserve, Quebec, is presented.   IVY

2935   **MOESER   ANTHONY G**
1963
THE IROQUOIS WATER DRUM. American Indian Tradition 9:24-26.

Method of construction of an Iroquois water drum is given. The tuning of the drum is also described.   IVY

2936   **MONTGOMERY   MALCOLM**
1965
THE SIX NATIONS AND THE MACDONALD FRANCHISE. Ontario History 57:13-25.

The Grand River Iroquois, along with other bands in Canada, received the federal franchise in 1885. For various historic reasons the Iroquois voted for the Liberal member for South Brant. It is suggested that because of their Liberal preference the franchise was withdrawn from all Indians in 1898. In 1960, the federal franchise was again granted the Canadian Indians.   ADG

2937   **MURPHY   H BRIAN M**
1963
PSYCHOLOGICAL TEST PERFORMANCE OF CHILDREN ON THE CAUGHNAWAGA RESERVE: A PILOT STUDY. Unpublished paper. Available from Library, Department of Indian Affairs and Northern Development, Ottawa. 18 pp.

The validity of psychological tests and the presence of social or personal problems among Caughnawaga school children are investigated in the study executed in 1961 and 1962. One hundred and thirty-two 9, 10, and 11 year-olds from grades 4 and 5 of the Kateri Tekakawitha School were administered the Thurstone Primary Mental Abilities group test and 25 were given an individual battery of tests followed up by a home visit by an anthropologist and the addition of background information. Results indicated that the Caughnawaga life experiences approximate sufficiently that of North American society to permit the use of the W.I.S.C. subtest. Relative immaturity, symptoms of mental disturbance, and a corresponding decline in intelligence quotient in older children was observed and supported by testing. Results are compared with those of American studies. CCV

2938   **MUSEE DE RENNES**
1964
ART ET ARTISANAT DES INDIENS IROQUOIS. Rennes, France: Musee de Rennes. 31 pp.

A catalog documents the exhibit of Iroquois art at the Musee de Rennes from December 5, 1964, to January 25, 1965.   CCV

2939   **MYERS   MERLIN G**
1963
HOUSEHOLD STRUCTURE AMONG THE LONGHOUSE IROQUOIS. Ph.D. Thesis. Cambridge University, Cambridge, England. 315 pp. Available from Cambridge University, with permission of the author.

The results of fieldwork carried out on the Six Nations Reserve during 1956-58 are reported in this study of Longhouse household structure and its development in time. Elements derived from the traditional matrilineal descent system and from Canadian society are considered in analysis of roles in relation to Meyer Fortes' structural theories. A polarization of interests between the nuclear family and the matrilineal sub-lineage group is observed with economic exigencies contributing to the solidarity of the former and ceremonial activities reinforcing the latter. The role of sanctions in controlling the economic activity and impeding acculturation thus perpetuating itself is noted.   CCV

2940   **NAROLL   RAOUL**
1969
THE CAUSES OF THE FOURTH IROQUOIS WAR. Ethnohistory 16:51-81.

Cultural factors are more important than economic factors in understanding the Iroquois and French wars of the 17th century. The dominant motives of the Iroquois in 1657-58 were blood revenge and the desire of individual warriors to obtain prestige by feats of arms. French hostility was a result of their viewing the Iroquois as being untrustworthy. The French felt they were insulted and mocked by the Iroquois.   IVY

2941   **NEWELL   WILLIAM B**
1965
CRIME AND JUSTICE AMONG THE IROQUOIS NATIONS. Caughnawaga Historical Society 1. Montreal: Caughnawaga Historical Society. 92 pp.

Presented is a description of Iroquois society as it is presumed to have been with reference to the position of crime in the fabric of that society. Specific crimes such as witchcraft, murder, theft, adultery, rape, prostitution, seduction, and incest are analyzed according to Iroquois laws, customs, and means of punishment. Some possible factors for the retardation of crime in Iroquois society are given.   DGW

2942   **OTTERBEIN   KEITH F**
1964

WHY THE IROQUOIS WON: AN ANALYSIS OF IROQUOIS MILITARY TACTICS. Ethnohistory 11:56-63.

An analysis of Iroquois tactics as compared with those of their enemies has indicated 3 periods in time - 1630's, 1640's, and 1660's - when the discrepancy between weapons and tactics gave an advantage to the Iroquois.   IVY

2943   **PETERS   MARY JANE**
1970
CHIEF LOUIS JACKSON: A FORGOTTEN INDIAN HISTORIAN. Tawow 1(3):24-25.

Chief Louis Jackson, a Mohawk from Caughnawaga, and his book, "Our Caughnawagas in Egypt,"are briefly discussed.   IVY

2944   **PILANT   RICHARD**
1969
ADDRESS TO THE 1969 INSTITUTE OF IROQUOIAN STUDIES SEMINAR. Unpublished paper delivered to Institute of Iroquoian Studies. Hamilton, Ont., April 6, 1969. Available from National Library of Canada. 3 pp.

An address given to the 1969 Institute of Iroquoian Studies Seminar is a plea to the Ontario government to recognize the great contribution of the Six Nations to the birth and growth of the province.   HCV

2945   **POSTAL   SUSAN KOESSLER**
1965
HOAX NATIVISM AT CAUGHNAWAGA: A CONTROL CASE FOR THE THEORY OF REVITALIZATION. Ethnology 4:266-281.

Field research at Caughnawaga Mohawk Reserve near Montreal in the summer of 1963 and earlier reports indicate that analysis of community factors rather than of the prophet and the content of his doctrine may have more import for the functional theory of revitalization. A nativistic movement led by a non-Indian resident (Chief Thunderwater), and based upon pseudo-Indian themes during the period 1915-1920, provides a control case for this analysis. The contradiction between persisting traits of traditional Mohawk social organization and the absence of native institutions in support of them are postulated as the primary reasons for adherence to the Council of Tribes and subsequent nativistic affirmation. Appended are the preamble to the constitution and the membership certificate of Thunderwater's organization.   WRC

2946   **POULIOT   ADRIEN**
1961
LA MENACE IROQUOISE, DE 1657 A 1660. Revue de l'Universite Laval 15:430-440.

Events from 1657-1660 are related from archival sources in an attempt to demonstrate the state of anxiety in which the Iroquois kept settlements of New France. Negotiations, repeated and unexpected attacks, and the taking and torturing of prisoners are described. CCV

2947   **QUILLIAN BOYCHUK & ASSOCIATES**
1969
EVALUATION REPORT ON THE PRODUCING AND DISTRIBUTION
OPERATIONS SIX NATIONS INDIAN RESERVE, BRANT AND HALDIMAND
COUNTIES, ONTARIO, OCTOBER 9, 1969. Unpublished report prepared for Dr. A.
B. Irwin, Head, Indian Minerals Section, Department of Indian Affairs and Northern
Development. Available at Indian-Eskimo Economic Development Branch,
Development Services Division, Department of Indian Affairs and Northern
Development, Ottawa. 20 pp.

A petroleum and natural gas lease on Six Nations Indian Reserve in Tuscarora and Onondaga Townships of Brant County and Oneida Township of Haldimand County is examined in terms of future production potential, associated economic conditions, and pos-
sibilties of additional reserves. The limitations of the potential and the costs of extending
distribution are reviewed.   CCV

2948   **READ   JOHN H,   STRICK   FRANCES L**
1969
MEDICAL EDUCATION AND THE NATIVE CANADIAN: AN EXAMPLE OF
MUTUAL SYMBOSIS. The Canadian Medical Association Journal 100:515-520.

A school health program for Mohawk children on the Tyendinaga Reserve was initiated
in 1964 to provide practical experience for medical students at Queen's University and
needed medical services for native children. Counseling, immunization, and tuberculin-
testing programs were among the services provided.   ADG

2949   **REAMAN   G ELMORE**
1967
THE TRAIL OF THE IROQUOIS INDIANS. London: Muller. 138 pp.

The author's purpose is to correct the stereotype of the Iroquois as cruel, bloodthirsty,
lazy, and nomadic. By tracing their history from prehistoric times it is hoped that their
culture will speak for itself and illustrate the debt Canadians owe them. Specifically the
study focuses on the Iroquois who settled along the Grand River near Brantford. The
present reluctance to take on responsibility of more self-government is due to the past 2
centuries of government denegration of their stature and rights. It is recommended that
the Six Nations receive unique status since their historical and political past has differed
from other tribes. Biographies of certain Six Nations people, past and present, are appended.   DGW

2950   **RICCIARDELLI   ALEX FRANK**
1961
FACTIONALISM AT ONEIDA, AN IROQUOIS INDIAN COMMUNITY. Ph.D.
Thesis. Department of Anthropology. University of Pennsylvania. 287 pp. Available
from University Microfilms.

Results of a year of fieldwork begun in June, 1956 and theoretical analysis are united in
this study of factionalism at Oneida, Ontario. The period studied, 1900-1960, is believed
to cover the factions arising since the migration of the Oneida from New York in 1840.
In analysis of political organization and decision-making processes the role of leader is
emphasized and internal strains are seen as contributing to the formations of factions.
CCV

2951   **RICCIARDELLI   ALEX FRANK**
1963
THE ADOPTION OF WHITE AGRICULTURE BY THE ONEIDA INDIANS.
Ethnohistory 10:309-328.

A successful transition from hunting and war activities to farming as the principal and
ideal role for men took place among the Oneida who settled near Delaware, Ontario,
during the 19th century. Five factors are considered significant: (1) end of the warrior-
hunter role, (2) a carry-over from the aboriginal culture of an ideal conception of the
male, (3) a horticultural tradition among women similar to that within the White farming complex, (4) an operating model of the White pattern of agriculture presented by
Whites and acculturated Indian neighbors, and (5) relocation of the community.   IVY

2952   **RICCIARDELLI   CATHERINE HINCKLE**
1966
KINSHIP SYSTEMS OF THE ONEIDA INDIANS. Ph.D. Thesis. Department of
Anthropology. University of Pennsylvania. 415 pp. Available from University
Microfilms.

The changing kinship structure of the Oneida of the Thames is analyzed. Discussion and
analysis is with reference to kinship terminology, social relationships, and kinship groupings. Comparison is made with the Oneida of Green Bay and the Mohawks of
Caughnawaga. Fieldwork among the Oneida of the Thames in 1956-1957 and historical
materials provide the basis for componential analysis of kinship terms. All 3 reserves
show a change from bifurcate, merging to an Eskimo type. Differences between Oneida
groups are due to specific acculturative variables. A change in basic subsistence pattern
and a change to bilocal or neolocal residence explain the increased importance of the
male economic role, a narrowed range of relatives, bilateral descent, increased emphasis
on the nuclear family, and a shift to lineality. Close contact with western culture, by way
of adopting English and exposure to the western kinship system, explain the rapidity of
recent changes and the form of certain kinship system alterations.   JSL

2953   **RITCHIE   WILLIAM A**
1963
THE IROQUOIAN TRIBES: PART 2 OF THE INDIAN HISTORY OF NEW YORK
STATE. New York State Museum and Science Service Educational Leaflet 7. Albany,
NY: New York State Museum and Science Service. 20 pp.

A general cultural description of the original Five Nations of New York is given including material culture, social and political organization, warfare, and ceremonialism. Much
of the data is also pertinent to the northern Iroquoian tribes. Indian artifacts reproduced
in this leaflet are from the New York State Museum collections.   IVY

2954   **RITZENTHALER   ROBERT**
1969
IROQUOIS FALSE-FACE MASKS. Milwaukee Public Museum Publications in
Primitive Art 3. Milwaukee: Milwaukee Public Museum. 71 pp.

Illustrations and descriptive data are presented on all masks in the Milwaukee Public
Museum Collection. An overview regarding the general construction, function, and
meaning of Iroquois False-Face masks is given. There are 56 illustrations, some in
color.   IVY

2955   **ROGERS   EDWARD S**
1966
THE FALSE FACE SOCIETY OF THE IROQUOIS: WHAT? HOW? WHY?
WHERE? WHEN? WHO? Royal Ontario Museum Series 10. Toronto: Royal Ontario
Museum; University of Toronto Press. 16 pp.

The False Face Society of the Iroquois performed curing rituals to deal with physical as
well as psychosomatic illnesses. The Faces were believed to be a supernatural race of evil
spirits, the origin of disease and destruction. Through the proper ritual, the supernatural
power could be appeased and conferred upon the masked men of the False Face society.
As early as the late 17th century Europeans visiting the Iroquois found the Society flour-
ishing. Information is presented relating to society membership, ritual performance, and
mask making.   DGW

2956   **ROGERS   EDWARD S**
1970
IROQUOIANS OF THE EASTERN WOODLANDS. Toronto: Royal Ontario
Museum. 16 pp.

Apsects of Iroquoian culture discussed in this introductory booklet include material culture, subsistence activities, social and political organization, trade, warfare, ritual, and
religion. Photographs and drawings accompany the text.   IVY

2957   **SAMPLE   KATHERINE ANN**
1968
CHANGES IN AGRICULTURE ON THE SIX NATIONS INDIAN RESERVE. M.A.
Thesis. McMaster University. 131 pp.

The history of settlement and land use of the Six Nations Reserve at Brantford are reviewed from the end of the 18th century to determine its relationship to present-day poverty. Soil conditions and agricultural trends and practices on the reserve and in neighboring townships are examined and compared. It is demonstrated that the semi-agricultural
economy practiced by Six Nations broke down after contact and restriction of hunting
movements. Also, traditional land use concepts impeded agricultural success. The reserve
poverty is found to be related to long-standing aspects of Indian-White relations and not
soil conditions.   CCV

2958   **SEIBERT   EMILY**
1963
JOSEPH BRANT. Waterloo Historical Society Annual Volume 50:96-98.

A biographic sketch of Joseph Brant is presented.   IVY

2959   **SELDON   SHERMAN   WARD**
1965
THE LEGEND, MYTH AND CODE OF DEGANAWEDA AND THEIR
SIGNIFICANCE TO IROQUOIS CULTURE HISTORY. Ph.D. Thesis. Folklore
Program. Indiana University. 241 pp. Available from University Microfilms.

Differing published versions, along with versions collected by the author, of the oral tradition of the founding of the Iroquois Confederacy are examined. The legend of Deganawidah is found to change to myth and the roles of Deganawidah and Hiawatha

change through time dependant upon social and psychological pressures on the Iroquois. Included are several versions collected in English during visits in 1963, 1964, and 1965 to several Iroquois reserves and reservations including Tyendinaga, Six Nations, and St. Regis.   TSA

2960   **SHIMONY   ANNEMARIE ANROD**
1961
CONSERVATISM AMONG THE IROQUOIS AT THE SIX NATIONS RESERVE. Yale University Publications in Anthropology 65. New Haven: Department of Anthropology, Yale University. 302 pp.

A revision of a doctoral thesis is based on fieldwork among the 7,000 Indians residing at Six Nations Reserve, Oshweken, Ontario, in periods of 3 days to 3 months from the summer of 1953 to the spring of 1958, and later the summer of 1960. In spite of intense acculturation, much of the Iroquois culture is preserved. To understand this persistence, this study describes the conservative culture and examines the devices of the society for maintaining its membership and continuing its practices as well as the motivations of its practitioners.   IVY

2961   **SHIMONY   ANNEMARIE ANROD**
1961
THE IROQUOIS FORTUNETELLERS AND THEIR CONSERVATIVE INFLUENCE. In Symposium on Cherokee and Iroquois Culture. William N. Fenton and John Gulick, eds. Smithsonian Institution. Bureau of American Ethnology Bulletin 180. Washington, DC: U.S. Government Printing Office. pp. 205-211.

Because health is a central tenet of the life view of the modern Longhouse member, fortunetellers (male or female), who are consulted in the diagnosis and cure of disease, are believed indispensable and are highly respected. Their supernatural gift or highly specialized knowledge, as well as frequent contacts with malevolent forces, puts them in a position of authority in which they are able to direct a large segment of the community. Since their prescriptions are almost always in terms of elements taken from the Longhouse culture, the overall influence of fortunetellers is highly conservative.   IVY

2962   **SIX NATIONS CONFEDERACY**
1960
THE STATUS OF THE SIX NATIONS IN CANADA: THEIR STATUS BASED ON HISTORY. In Minutes of Proceedings and Evidence. No. 13. June 22, 1960. Joint Committee of the Senate and the House of Commons on Indian Affairs. Canada. 24 Parliament, 3 Session. Ottawa: Queen's Printer. pp. 1197-1316.

A legal document was submitted. Discussed are the treaty relations and legal status of the Six Nations from 1664 to 1797. The status of sovereignty for the Six Nations is claimed. Appended is the judgment of Mr. Justice King in the case of Logan vs. Styres, Stallwood, and the Attorney General of Canada; the Haldimand Deed of 1784; and the Simcoe Deed of 1793.   JSL

2963   **SNYDERMAN   GEORGE S**
1961
THE FUNCTION OF WAMPUM IN IROQUOIS RELIGION. American Philosophical Society Proceedings 105:571-608.

This paper relates how wampum was and is used in religious ceremonials. Religious beliefs and practices prior to Handsome Lake which are still held are included. The history of Handsome Lake and his religion is presented. Found in Handsome Lake's Code is the religious basis for present-day use of wampum. One type of wampum includes the short strings which are used to summon believers to religious meetings; the longer strings (sometimes bunches) are used in the repentence confession rites.   IVY

2964   **SPITTAL   WILLIAM GUY**
1961
A BRIEF NOTE ON: IROQUOIS MUSICAL INSTRUMENTS. American Indian Tradition 7:137.

Different usage leads False Faces to carry large turtle shell rattles while smaller instruments are used to accompany the Great Feather Dance.   TSA

2965   **SPITTAL   WILLIAM GUY**
1961
CONTEMPORARY IROQUOIS FOODS. American Indian Tradition 8:34-40.

Recipes for traditional foods that are still prepared by the Iroquois on the Six Nations Reserve, Ontario, are given. Photographs accompany the text.   IVY

2966   **STANLEY   G F G**
1964
THE SIX NATIONS AND THE AMERICAN REVOLUTION. Ontario History 56:217-232.

The unity of the Iroquois Confederacy was shattered by the effect of the American Revolution. It is questionable, however, whether the League would have survived if the British or Americans had permitted neutrality.   ADG

2967   **STURTEVANT   WILLIAM C**
1961
COMMENT ON GERTRUDE P. KURATH'S "EFFECT OF ENVIRONMENT ON CHEROKEE - IROQUOIS CEREMONIALISM, MUSIC, AND DANCE."In Symposium on Cherokee and Iroquois Culture. William N. Fenton and John Gulick, eds. Smithsonian Institution. Bureau of American Ethnology Bulletin 180. Washington, DC: U.S. Government Printing Office. pp. 197-204.

Objections are raised to Gertrude Kurath's decision as to whether identified homologies in Iroquois and Cherokee ceremonialism and music are due to diffusion or common inheritance, and if diffused, to the direction assumed.   IVY

2968   **TOOKER   ELISABETH**
1965
THE IROQUOIS WHITE DOG SACRIFICE IN THE LATTER PART OF THE EIGHTEENTH CENTURY. Ethnohistory 12:129-140.

The White Dog Sacrifice of the 19th century in which 1 or more white dogs were ritually strangled, decorated, hung up on a long pole, and then later burned, was part of the Iroquois Midwinter ceremonial. Analyzing documents of the latter part of the 18th century indicates, according to Samuel Kirkland's description, that the ceremony had lapsed among the Mohawks and Oneidas and was revived as a result of a vision experienced by a Mohawk at Grand River. Also, the ceremony had strong war connotations.   IVY

2969   **TOOKER   ELISABETH**
1968
ON THE NEW RELIGION OF HANDSOME LAKE. Anthropological Quarterly 41:187-200.

The interpretation that the introduction of the New Religion of Handsome Lake was due to gross disorganization of Iroquois society is inadequate. It is suggested rather that changes advocated by Handsome Lake in the value systems were needed by the Iroquois to support the economic changes in their way of life.   IVY

2970   **TOOKER   ELISABETH**
1970
THE IROQUOIS CEREMONIAL OF MIDWINTER. Syracuse, NY: Syracuse University Press. 189 pp.

Though the fieldwork which formed the basis of this study was done principally on the Tonawanda Reservation, New York, comparisons are made to the Midwinter ceremonial at 6 Iroquois longhouses including the Six Nations' Onondaga and Sour Springs.   IVY

2971   **TOROK   CHARLES H**
1965
THE TYENDINAGA MOHAWKS: THE VILLAGE AS A BASIC FACTOR IN MOHAWK SOCIAL STRUCTURE. Ontario History 57:69-77.

The Tyendinaga Mohawks have little in common with the Grand River Mohawks. Examination of several historic developments reveals that the village was a basic unit in Iroquois social structure, and that the League's structure had always been unstable.   ADG

2972   **TOROK   CHARLES HAMORI**
1966
THE ACCULTURATION OF THE MOHAWKS OF THE BAY OF QUINTE. Ph.D. Thesis. Department of Anthropology. University of Toronto. 183 pp. Available from National Library of Canada.

Fieldwork conducted in 1963-1965 examined the acculturation of the Mohawks of the Bay of Quinte (Tyendinaga Reserve). Acculturation did not result in traumatic disorganization despite radical change. It is suggested that socio-cultural losses were balanced by innovations. All residents of the reserve are acculturated, either to lower middle class or rural lower class behavior patterns. No aboriginal structural features remain. Members are fully involved in the Canadian economy. However, sustained patterns of interaction between residents are seen as 1 factor maintaining a Mohawk identity.   JSL

2973   **TOROK   CHARLES HAMORI**
1967
TYENDINAGA ACCULTURATION. In Iroquois Culture, History, and Prehistory:

Proceedings of the 1965 Conference on Iroquois Research. Elisabeth Tooker, ed. Albany: New York State Museum and Science Service. pp. 31-33.

Aspects of conservatism found on most Iroquois reserves - identification with the Longhouse religion, use of the native language, acceptance of the principle of hereditary leadership, and retention of clans - do not exist at the Tyendinaga Indian Reserve, Ontario. The Tyendinaga Mohawks (approximately 900) are more highly acculturated than the Iroquois of the Six Nations, Caughnawaga, and New York reserves.   IVY

2974   **TOROK   CHARLES HAMORI**
1968
THE CANADIAN INDIAN RESERVES. The Indian Historian 1(4):15-16,23.

The majority of highly acculturated and economically successful Mohawks of Caughnawaga and Tyendinaga depend psychologically, culturally, and socially upon their home communities. As long as this continues and satisfactory employment can be had relatively close to these communities, these reserves will not disappear.   IVY

2975   **TRELEASE   ALLEN**
1962
THE IROQUOIS AND THE WESTERN FUR TRADE: A PROBLEM IN INTERPRETATION. The Mississippi Valley Historical Review 49:32-51.

The thesis that the middlemen role accounted for the Iroquois wealth and power is questioned. Their economic mainstay was their own hunting and the robbing of other tribesmen on their way to the fur mart at Montreal during the intertribal wars of the 17th century. Iroquois power or success is attributed to several factors: intertribal warfare motivated by desire for revenge and prestige; the strategic importance economically (furs and arms) of access to 1 of the few passes in the Appalachian mountain chain; a superior political organization; and acquisition of firearms from the English which was further intensified by the increasing rivalry with France after 1680.   IVY

2976   **TRITON ENGINEERING SERVICES LIMITED**
1969
ROAD PROGRAMMING STUDY FOR THE ONEIDA INDIAN RESERVE. Unpublished paper. Available from National Library of Canada. 43 pp.

The road system of the Oneida Indian Reserve has been examined and evaluated to determine what improvements are necessary to bring the roadway system to adequate condition and serviceability. A 10-year program is outlined. Appendices include 24 township road appraisal sheets and 6 township bridge and culvert appraisal sheets. Drawings, charts, and tables are also provided.   IVY

2977   **VACHON   ANDRE**
1961
MGR DE LAVAL ET LA MENACE IROQUOISE. Bulletin des Recherches Historiques 67:36-46.

The situation in New France in 1659 which led Mgr. Laval, soon after his arrival, to agree that annihilation of the Iroquois was the only means of safeguarding the colony is discussed. After the destruction of Huronia the Iroquois were unable to reconcile themselves with the neighboring tribes or the French. Widespread and persistent Iroquois attacks brought the fur trade, colonization, and evangelization to a standstill. Increasing competition in the fur trade created the danger that those tribes allied with the French might turn to the English to trade. The Iroquois, however, prevented them from passing through their territory. Thus the presence of the Iroquois became a necessity for the French.   CCV

2978   **VAN STEEN MARCUS**
1965
PAULINE JOHNSON: HER LIFE AND WORK. Toronto: Musson. 279 pp.

Presented is a biography of Pauline Johnson (1861-1913), the Canadian poetess born on the Six Nations Reserve in Brantford, Ontario. A generous selection of her prose and poetry supplements this edition.   DGW

2979   **VOGET   FRED**
1969
A SIX NATIONS' DIARY, 1891-1894. Ethnohistory 16:345-360.

Portions of the ledger-diary outlining the activities in 1891-1892 of an elite acculturated farmer on the Six Nations Reserve are analyzed indicating the seasonal round of activities, the division of labor within the family, reciprocity in labor between farmers, and the extent of cash transactions between the farmer and his neighbors, both Indian and non-Indian.   IVY

2980   **WALLACE   ANTHONY F C**
1966
RELIGION: AN ANTHROPOLOGICAL VIEW. New York: Random House. 300 pp.

A psychological and cultural approach to religion is developed including traditional anthropological theories, classification of religious institutions and culture areas, goals of religious ritual, functions of religion, and consideration of longterm change. Theory is illustrated with examples from various societies including the Naskapi and the Plains tribes, but with frequent reference to the Iroquois. Of note are discussions of revitalization movements among the Iroquois on pages 31 to 34, and Iroquois ritual, belief, and cultural institutions, described and compared to religious practices in a small Pennsylvania town, on pages 66 to 82.   CCV

2981   **WALLACE   ANTHONY F C**
1970
THE DEATH AND REBIRTH OF THE SENECA. New York: Knopf. 384 pp.

Discussed is the religion of Handsome Lake, its origin, and its adoption by the Iroquois. The story of the Seneca Indians during the late colonial and early reservation period is told with emphasis accorded to its cultural renaissance at the hands of the prophet Handsome Lake. Field research for the study began in 1951 and was largely completed by 1956.   DGW

2982   **WEAVER   SALLY MAE**
1967

HEALTH, CULTURE AND DILEMA: A STUDY OF THE NON-CONSERVATIVE IROQUOIS, SIX NATIONS RESERVE, ONTARIO. Ph.D. Thesis. Department of Anthropology. University of Toronto. 435 pp. Available from National Library of Canada.

Based on 14 months fieldwork between 1963 and 1967 at Grand River Reserve, Ontario, an analysis of medical acculturation among the non-conservative (i.e. Christian) Iroquois is presented. Historical analysis from 1850 to 1967 revealed a slow adaptation to Western medical technology. The contemporary non-conservatives' knowledge of Iroquois herbal remedies was found to be meager, and the dependence and demands on hospital facilities high. Three status categories of the non-conservative population were found to exist, and the health practices and ideology of each are discussed. Recent crises involving the closing down of the reserve hospital are analyzed in terms of community sanitation innovations, doctor-patient relationships, and band council involvement.   SMW

2983   **WEAVER   SALLY MAE,   COOPER   VIRGINIA**
1970
AN EARLY HISTORY OF THE DEHORNERS, 1904-1910 (A WORKING PAPER). Unpublished paper. Available from National Museum of Man, Ethnology Division, Ottawa, with permission of the authors. 26 pp.

Derived from fieldwork and ethnohistorical sources, an analysis is made of materials relating to a social-political movement known as the Dehorners. Focus is on the period 1904-1910. Documentation is provided for correspondence, petitions, and counter-petitions. During this time, a resurgence of Six Nations activity in promoting an elective system while concurrently complaining of the traditional, hereditary system becomes manifested. Although an elective system was not instituted until 1924, and then by Order-in-Council, the original impetus for change was the Six Nations people themselves.   JSL

2984   **WEAVER   SALLY MAE,   COOPER   VIRGINIA**
1970
AN EARLY HISTORY OF THE MOVEMENT FOR AN ELECTIVE FORM OF LOCAL GOVERNMENT AMONG THE SIX NATIONS OF GRAND RIVER, 1861-1903 (A WORKING PAPER). Unpublished paper. Available from National Museum of Man, Ethnology Division, Ottawa, with permission of the authors. 36 pp.

Documents are utilized to trace the movement for an elective system of local government among the Six Nations for the period 1861-1903. Increasing federal powers over Indians generated much local discussion and debate. The traditional chiefs were also pressured by the actions of some Six Nations people who desired an elective local government as the reserve became a growing farming community. The chiefs failed to adopt these decision-making processes. The pro-election movement continued in the 20th century.   JSL

2985   **WILSON   EDMUND**
1960
APOLOGIES TO THE IROQUOIS. London: Allen. 253 pp.

Focusing upon the confrontation of 2 cultures, particularly over land rights and religion, an historical presentation of the Iroquois is given with specific reference to the St. Regis and Six Nations Reserves. The nationalist movement among the Iroquois is discussed.   IVY

NEUTRAL

2986   **WHITE   MARIAN E**
1961
IROQUOIS CULTURE HISTORY IN THE NIAGARA FRONTIER AREA OF NEW
YORK STATE. University of Michigan Museum of Anthropology Anthropological
Papers 16. Ann Arbor: University of Michigan. 155 pp.

Ethnohistorical and cartographic evidence suggest the historic location of the Neutral in
southwestern Ontario and western New York. Also discussed is the disposition of the
Wenro and Erie. Archaeological investigations in New York State, with comparisons to
Canadian data, are presented in relation to the above problem.   IVY

2987   **WRIGHT   GORDON K**
1963
THE NEUTRAL INDIANS: A SOURCE BOOK. New York State Archaeological
Association Occasional Papers 3. Rochester, NY: New York State Archaeological
Association. 95 pp.

References from the writings of missionaries and travelers are used to reconstruct the
culture of the Neutral prior to their dispersal by the Iroquois.   TSA

LAURENTIAN IROQUOIS

2988   **TRIGGER   BRUCE GRAHAM**
1962
TRADE AND TRIBAL WARFARE ON THE ST. LAWRENCE IN THE
SIXTEENTH CENTURY. Ethnohistory 9:240-256.

In the latter half of the 16th century groups competed for access to a single market on the
lower St. Lawrence. It is hypothesized that in the resulting conflict the Laurentian Iroquois disappeared, the survivors absorbed by surrounding tribes. European diseases may
have been an additional factor in their decline.   IVY

2989   **TRIGGER   BRUCE GRAHAM**
1966
WHO WERE THE "LAURENTIAN IROQUOIS"? Canadian Review of Sociology and
Anthropology 3:201-213.

This paper outlines the controversy with respect to the identity of the 16th century inhabitants of the St. Lawrence Valley. Based on research of the historical and ethnohistorical
problems of Hochelaga, a critique of the main positions taken is provided.   IVY

2990   **TRIGGER   BRUCE GRAHAM**
1967
CARTIER'S HOCHELAGA AND THE DAWSON SITE. In Iroquois Culture, History,
and Prehistory: Proceedings of the 1965 Conference on Iroquois Research. Elisabeth
Tooker, ed. Albany: New York State Museum and Science Service. pp. 63-66.

Examining historical and ethnohistorical literature dealing with Hochelaga, the hypothesis that the Dawson site on McGill campus is the Hochelaga visited by Cartier is highly

unlikely. Various theories that have been proposed concerning the ethnic identity of the Hochelagans are briefly discussed.   IVY

2991   **TRIGGER   BRUCE GRAHAM**
1968
ARCHAEOLOGICAL AND OTHER EVIDENCE: A FRESH LOOK AT THE "LAURENTIAN IROQUOIS."American Antiquity 33:429-440.

Alternate hypotheses based on archaeological and linguistic evidence of the ethnic iden-tity of the Laurentian Iroquois who inhabited the St. Lawrence Valley in the 16th cen-tury are presented.   IVY

2992   **TRIGGER   BRUCE GRAHAM**
1969
CRITERIA FOR IDENTIFYING THE LOCATIONS OF HISTORIC INDIAN SITES: A CASE STUDY FROM MONTREAL. Ethnohistory 16:303-316.

The Dawson site and the Iroquoian village of Hochelaga visited by Jacques Cartier an 1535 are compared in terms of their age, location, and layout. Results suggest that the archaeological site is not the village of Hochelaga, although it is close to it in time and probably in cultural affinities as well.   IVY

METIS

2993   **ALLAN   IRIS**
1964
A RIEL REBELLION DIARY. Alberta Historical Review 12(3):15-25.

Excerpts from the diary of Robert K. Allan (March 26 to July 13, 1885) who fought with the C Company, 90th Battalion, have been edited. Daily activities are sketched.   IVY

2994   **AVERY   IBBS**
1965
THE SAGA OF WILLIAM PIERCE. The United Church Observer N.S. 27(6):16-17.

Of Tsimshian and Scottish ancestry, William Pierce pioneered mission work along the British Columbia coast in the 19th century.   IVY

2995   **BARTLETT   FRED E**
1966
THE FALL OF FORT GARRY. The Beaver 296(Spring):48-52.

Riel's capture of Fort Garry in 1869 sustained the Red River insurrection. Reasons for the fort's easy fall are outlined.   IVY

2996   **BOISSONNAULT   CHARLES MARIE**
1970
L'EXPEDITION DU NORD-OUEST: LE RAPPORT WOLSELEY. The Royal Society of Canada Transactions (Series 4) 8:123-131.

Two Canadian battalions were led by Colonel Wolseley to Fort Garry to protect the Metis of the newly formed province from Canadian immigrants. Some aspects of this voyage during the late summer of 1870 and details of the political background and context are reviewed. The report Wolseley made of his activities is reexamined and a reinterpretation is offered. It is pointed out that if Wolseley arrived safely at Fort Garry in spite of difficult conditions it was because Riel restrained Indian and Metis partisans. Also, Riel abandoned Fort Garry due to a desire to avoid warfare, not because of an inability to defend it.   CCV

2997   **BRADSHAW   THECLA**
1966
PROUD TO BE A METIS. Arbos 3(2):10-11.

A biographic sketch is given of Dr. Howard Adams, a Metis recently appointed to the University of Saskatchewan.   IVY

2998   **CARD   B Y**
1963
IMPROVEMENT DISTRICT 124: A CASE STUDY. In The Metis in Alberta Society: With Special Reference to Social, Economic and Cultural Factors Associated with Persistently High Tuberculosis Incidence. B. Y. Card, G. K. Hirabayashi, et al., eds. University of Alberta Committee for Social Research: A Report on Project A. Edmonton: University of Alberta. pp. 65-294.

Improvement district 124 of the Athabaska Health Unit in the Southern Lesser Slave Lake area is reviewed in terms of the local geography; ecology and history; economics; ethnic relations; housing and households; organization and recreation; and social, economic, and cultural factors related to tuberculosis as of June, 1960. The area is described as marginal to Alberta society in many respects. It is economically depressed and economic factors are closely related to other social and cultural patterns observed in the area. It is felt that a successful plan of tuberculosis control in the area would have to alter statuses, particularly of the Metis, and would require national consideration of the present status networks and residence patterns. Certain aspects of community organization and recreation could be exploited to advantage.   CCV

2999   **CARD   B Y**
1963
TUBERCULOSIS AND THE METIS: TUBERCULOSIS AMONG ALBERTA METIS: HISTORICAL AND ECOLOGICAL. In The Metis in Alberta Society: With Special Reference to Social, Economic and Cultural Factors Associated with Persistently High Tuberculosis Incidence. B. Y. Card, G. K. Hirabayashi, et al., eds. University of Alberta Committee for Social Research: A Report on Project A. Edmonton: University of Alberta. pp. 16-61.

An historical and ecological review of the incidence of tuberculosis among Alberta Metis is supported by statistical data for the years 1934 to 1961. The proportions of patients of selected ethnic background discharged from Alberta sanitoria in 1941 and 1951 are included. Communities in improvement district 124 of the Athabaska Health Unit, which has a high Metis population, are objects of a 1960 survey. Incidence of tuberculosis is highest for reserve Indians followed by Metis and lowest for Whites. It is suggested that race, contact with tubercular persons, and socio-cultural factors operate to create these differences, with social and cultural factors assuming the greatest importance.   CCV

3000   **CLUBB   SALLY**
1965
RED RIVER EXODUS. Arbos 1(3):17-28.

After the Red River uprising of 1870, many Metis migrated to Saskatchewan founding colonies along the South Saskatchewan River. Here they briefly prospered. A provisional government at the St. Laurent colony was set up in 1873 with Gabriel Dumont as president. By the 1880's, however, there were no buffalo, farming was not profitable, little cash was available, and the federal government ignored constant petitions for land rights. In 1885, again under the leadership of Louis Riel, the Metis rebelled. costing the Canadian government $5,000,000 and the Metis their identity as a separate people. IVY

3001   **COMMUNITY DEVELOPMENT SERVICES**
n.d.
METIS STUDY TOUR BRIEF. Unpublished paper. Available from National Library of Canada. 56 pp.

Beginning on November 29, 1968, 10 Metis fieldworkers spent 9 days visiting all of the principal Metis centers in Alberta (in 2 groups of 5) and 4 days meeting in Edmonton for interviews with government and private agencies to obtain a minimum of information for purposes of policy making. This document presents the written observations recorded at meetings with community residents, government officials, and personnel of private agencies. Examined were land problems, employment, housing, education, law, welfare, recreation, health, and various organizations. Recommendations of the Tour Group conclude the report.   IVY

3002   **DEMPSEY   HUGH A**
1966
JERRY POTTS: PLAINSMAN. Glenbow Foundation Occasional Papers 2. Calgary: Glenbow Foundation. 23 pp.

The life and exploits of Jerry Potts (1840-1896), Metis scout and interpreter for the Northwest Mounted Police and the American Fur Company, are reconstructed from interview data, archival records, and publications. His role as warrior and plainsman which made Potts a legendary figure among his mother's people, the Blood Indians, and a valued employee of the Whites is reviewed.   CCV

3003   **DROUIN   EMERIC O**
1962
LA COLONIE SAINT-PAUL-DES-METIS, ALBERTA: 1896-1909. Ph.D. Thesis. Departement d'Histoire. Universite d'Ottawa. 808 pp.

The establishment and history of the colony, St. Paul-des-Metis, in northern Alberta is reconstructed from archival materials, historic sources, and numerous interviews. The efforts and eventual failure of the Oblate fathers Lacombe and Therrieu to demonstrate and create interest in agriculture as well as their participation in other religious, educational, and economic spheres is included.   CCV

3004   **DROVIN   EMERIC O**
1963

ST. PAUL DES METIS. Alberta Historical Review 11(4):12-14.

The founding of a Metis colony, Saint Paul des Metis, by 2 Oblate Fathers in 1896 and its subsequent failure are described.   IVY

3005 **DUNFIELD   H C**
1960
GREEN LAKE METIS SETTLEMENT AND CENTRAL FARM. Unpublished paper. Available from National Library of Canada. 4 pp.

A brief economic report deals mainly with the agricultural aspects of the Green Lake Metis Settlement and Central Farm which is owned and operated by the government of Saskatchewan.   IVY

3006 **FRENCH   CECIL L**
1962
SOCIAL CLASS LEVEL AND MOTIVATION AMONG THE METIS INDIANS AND WHITES IN THE PROVINCE OF ALBERTA. Unpublished paper. Available from Legislative Library, Regina, Sask. 44 pp.

To test the hypothesis that the Metis have adopted the values of the lower classes of North America, tests were given to the pupils of 6 schools including urban and rural, segregated, and mixed. The 3 tests administered were a name occupations test, an achievement orientation test, and an unstructured test which consists of asking the subject to make 20 statements about himself. Nineteen tables compare results. The hypothesis is adequately supported.   IVY

3007 **FRENCH   CECIL L**
1963
SOCIAL CLASS AND MOTIVATION. In The Metis in Alberta Society: With Special Reference to Social, Economic and Cultural Factors Associated with Persistently High Tuberculosis Incidence. B. Y. Card, G. K. Hirabayashi, et al., eds. University of Alberta Committee for Social Research: A Report on Project A. Edmonton: University of Alberta. pp. 313-354.

Reasons for lack of adequate motivation and aspiration for successful Metis integration into White society are examined with particular reference to conditions near Faust, Alberta. Attitudes and occupational aspirations of urban White students in Edmonton and rural White, Metis, and reservation Indian pupils attending high schools in or near Faust, Alberta are compared. The hypothesis that Metis life style is related to a frequency of contacts with lower class persons and that relations between the Metis and those White people who could provide desirable role models are few and discourage identification is supported by the data.   CCV

3008 **GREENHILL   STANLEY,   RUETHER B A**
1963
HEALTH AND EMPLOYABILITY. In The Metis in Alberta Society: With Special Reference to Social, Economic and Cultural Factors Associated with Persistently High Tuberculosis. B. Y. Card, G. K. Hirabayashi, et al., eds. University of Alberta Committee for Social Research: A Report on Project A. Edmonton: University of Alberta. pp. 297-304.

Eighty-one adult male Metis of working age in the Lesser Slave Lake area were surveyed and examined for duration of employment, work habits, living standards, nutrition, and physical defects. Work and earning characteristics were observed to be more closely related to socio-economic status and psycho-anthropological background than to physical well-being.   CCV

3009   **HAFTER   RUTH**
1965-66
THE RIEL REBELLION AND MANIFEST DESTINY. Dalhousie Review 45:447-456.

Religion, race, and language governed Riel's action in not seeking to join the United States during the period the Metis controlled Rupert's Land. The United States was not willing to fight Great Britain. The lure of northern land in the 1870's was not a decisive factor in the history of America.   IVY

3010   **HARRINGTON   LYN**
1963
PRAIRIE BATTLEFIELD. Canadian Geographical Journal 66:28-37.

Photographs and description of the 1962 visit of the Royal Regiment of Canada to the battlefield of Batoche complement a brief history of the North West Rebellion of 1885.   IVY

3011   **HATT   FRED K**
1967
METIS OF THE LAC LA BICHE AREA. In Community Opportunity Assessment. Edmonton: Alberta, Human Resources Research and Development, Executive Council. Appendix A. 231 pp.

This report is based on a 10-week study of 4 different settlements of Metis: Lac la Biche, a small urban setting; Kikino, a provincial Metis colony setting; Mission, a rural fishing district; and Owl River, a rural fishing-trapping district. Interviews were conducted in 124 out of 149 households. This report provides: (1) a description of the physical characteristics of the area of study, (2) a description of the current setting of the area including population, housing, diet, health, and water, (3) an analysis of the forms of social organization and economic conditions of the Metis, (4) a discussion of the relationships of the Metis with the larger society including channels of contact, discrimination, and education, and (5) recommendations for change.   Tables are used extensively, particularly in the comparison of the 4 communities.   IVY

3012   **HATT   FRED K**
1969
THE METIS AND COMMUNITY DEVELOPMENT IN NORTHEASTERN ALBERTA. In Perspectives on Regions and Regionalism and Other Papers. B. Y. Card, ed. Proceedings of the Tenth Annual Meeting of the Western Association of Sociology and Anthropology, Held at Banff, Alberta, December 28, 29 and 30, 1968. Edmonton: University of Alberta Printing Services. pp. 111-110.

The historical position of the Metis in western social structure is summarized. A recent development is the entrance of a new mediator between the Metis and the rest of society

- the community development worker. The goals of these workers are discussed as are their techniques of information control and tension management.   TSA

3013   HATT   FRED KENNETH
1969
THE RESPONSE TO DIRECTED SOCIAL CHANGE ON AN ALBERTA METIS
COLONY. Ph.D. Thesis. Department of Sociology. University of Alberta. 290 pp.
Available from National Library of Canada.

It is believed that organizations are formed to implement the goals of superordinate groups upon subordinate groups, thus becoming institutionalized mediators. This approximate form of directed social change is examined as 1 form of ethnic group relations. A structural-interactional approach was employed in the case study of relations between the Metis of Alberta and the provincial government. Fieldwork carried out between 1966 and 1968 was done in 1 of Alberta's 8 Metis colonies in northeastern Alberta.   DGW

3014   HATT   JUDITH KEEVER
1969
RIGHTS AND DUTIES OF A METIS PRESCHOOL CHILD. M.A. Thesis. University
of Alberta.

The title has been verified, but a copy was not obtained in time to abstract it.   SLP

3015   HATT   JUDY K
1969
HISTORY, SOCIAL STRUCTURE, AND LIFE CYCLE OF BEAVER METIS
COLONY. The Western Canadian Journal of Anthropology 1(1):19-32.

In the role of participant-observer, data were collected during the summers of 1966, 1967, and 1968. Discussed are the background, history, and social structure of the colony and the life cycle of its inhabitants.   IVY

3016   HLADY   WALTER M
1960
POWER STRUCTURE IN A METIS COMMUNITY. Unpublished paper. Available
from National Library of Canada. 7 pp.

The community of Cedar Lake, Saskatchewan, serves as basis for a discussion of the power structure in a Metis community. The White influence in the community, the Half-breed Council, and the family are evaluated in terms of distribution of power.   CCV

3017   KEW   J E
1961
AGRICULTURAL DEVELOPMENT AT CUMBERLAND HOUSE. Unpublished
paper delivered to 3rd Annual Short Course for Northern Personnel. Saskatoon, Sask.,
April 11, 1961. Available from Indian and Northern Curriculum Resources Centre,
University of Saskatchewan, Saskatoon. 11 pp.

Background information and a critical resume of the Department of Natural Resources'
farm program at Cumberland House since 1946 is provided.   IVY

3018   **LAGASSE   JEAN**
1960
THE METIS IN MANITOBA. Historical and Scientific Society of Manitoba Papers
(Series 3) 15:39-57.

Discussed are the birth and growth of the Metis; an explanation of the word Metis as
used in Manitoba; and the economic, cultural, and social problems facing the Metis.
Community development programs are proposed as possible solutions to these problems.
Also included is a listing of Metis population in Manitoba by community.   IVY

3019   **LAL   RAVINDRA**
1964
DUCK BAY, MANITOBA: ECONOMIC AND SOCIAL ASPECTS: FALL 1964.
Unpublished paper. Available from Library, Department of Health and Social
Development, Winnipeg, Man. 51 pp.

This study is the result of a 22-day residence in Duck Bay, August, 1964. Methods used in
the investigation were visits, inquiry, and participation in some local activities and home
life. The historical background and economic and social life of the community are discussed. Needs of the community are considered from the perspective of residents and
non-residents.   IVY

3020   **MACARTHUR   R S**
1963
THE INTELLECTUAL ABILITY OF METIS PUPILS AT FAUST, ALBERTA. In The
Metis in Alberta Society: With Special Reference to Social, Economic and Cultural
Factors Associated with Persistently High Tuberculosis Incidence. B. Y. Card, G. K.
Hirabayashi, et al., eds. University of Alberta Committee for Social Research: A Report
on Project A. Edmonton: University of Alberta. pp. 305-310.

In May and June of 1961, 147 male and female Metis students attending school in grades
1 to 8 at Faust, Alberta, were administered conventional and culture-reduced intelligence
tests in order to evaluate their validity for this sample. Despite some residual cultural
bias, the proposed tests are observed to measure more adequately intellectual potential
for subjects at Faust and Fort Simpson and are recommended for use for such
samples.   CCV

3021   **MACDONALD   R H**
1963
FORT BATTLEFORD, SASKATCHEWAN. Canadian Geographical Journal 67:54-
61.

In outlining the history of Fort Battleford, Saskatchewan, its part in the Riel rebellion of
1885 is presented.   IVY

3022   **MALLORY   ENID SWERDFEGER**
1963
THE LIFE OF LOWER FORT GARRY. Canadian Geographical Journal 66:116-123.

In outlining the history of Lower Fort Garry, mention is made of its part in the Riel rebellion of 1869.   IVY

3023   **MANITOBA METIS FEDERATION**
1969
MINUTES OF THE MANITOBA METIS FEDERATION 2nd ANNUAL
CONFERENCE. Unpublished paper. Manitoba Metis Federation 2nd Annual
Conference. Winnipeg, March 22-24, 1969. Available from National Library of
Canada. 37 pp.

Questions of organization and unity and needs in the areas of housing, education, and
medical services are discussed. Problems of several settlements are brought to the attention of the Federation by local delegates.   CCV

3024   **MARTIN   JOSEPH E**
1966
THE 150TH ANNIVERSARY OF SEVEN OAKS. Historical and Scientific Society of
Manitoba Transactions (Series 3) 22:99-111.

The Nor'Westers saw the main purpose of Lord Selkirk's settlement on the Red River,
on lands granted in 1811 by the Hudson's Bay Company, as an attempt to cut across the
supply line and destroy the North West Company. Their goal of driving the settlers out
was accomplished with the aid of half-breeds. In 1815 at Seven Oaks, 21 settlers were
killed and 1 wounded with 7 escaping in an attack by a party of half-breeds on the way
with supplies to join the Nor'Westers.   IVY

3025   **MASSEY   PARTICIA GRAHAM**
1962
FOSTER HOME PLANNING FOR THE INDIAN CHILD: A CASEWORK STUDY
OF FOSTER CHILDREN, PARENTS, FOSTER PARENTS, AND AGENCY
SERVICE: CHILDREN'S AID SOCIETY OF VANCOUVER, 1959-61. M.S.W.
Thesis. University of British Columbia. 92 pp.

Research material drawn from the Vancouver Children's Aid Society files, returns from
24 questionnaires mailed to foster parents in 1961, consultations with social workers,
and personal experience as a social worker in this area are reported. Indian foster children, natural parents, foster parents, and services provided for each by the Children's
Aid Society are described. The needs of these groups are contrasted with existing services
and proposals are outlined for planning of foster placement of Indian children and improvement of services for child, parents, and foster parents alike.   CCV

3026   **MCKEE   SANDRA LYNN**
n.d.
GABRIEL DUMONT: INDIAN FIGHTER. Calgary: Frontiers Unlimited. 51 pp.

Gabriel Dumont's life story is compiled with description of his rise to fame as hunter,
fighter, sharpshooter, and leader, his role in the Riel rebellion, his career with the Wild
West Show, his pardon from the Canadian government, and subsequent return to Canada.   CCV

3027   **MORTON   W L**
1970
THE 1870 OUTFIT AT RED RIVER. The Beaver 300(Spring):4-11.

The history of the Red River settlement is outlined including the Riel Rebellion of 1869. IVY

3028 **MORTON   WILLIAM**
1961
THE BATTLE AT THE GRAND COTEAU: JULY 13 AND 14, 1851. Historical and Scientific Society of Manitoba Papers (Series 3) 16:37-49.

A narration of the defeat of some hundreds of Sioux by a small band of Metis buffalo hunters from Saint Francois-Xavier is given.   IVY

3029 **OSLER   E B**
1961
THE MAN WHO HAD TO HANG: LOUIS RIEL. Toronto: Longmans Green. 320 pp.

Presented is a biographical account of Louis Riel, prophet and charismatic leader of his Metis people. The mental struggle which harassed Riel in the fulfilling of his role is emphasized. DGW

3030 **RATTAN   M S,   MACARTHUR   R S**
1968
LONGITUDINAL PREDICTION OF SCHOOL ACHIEVEMENT FOR METIS AND ESKIMO PUPILS. The Alberta Journal of Educational Research 14:37-41.

In 1961 a number of ability tests (some culture-reduced tests) were administered to 74 Metis pupils (grades 1 to 3) at Faust, Alberta. In 1965, 45 of the 74 were tested again. Results show that such tests have substantial validity in predicting school achievement. Of importance is that the predictive validities of 2 culture-reduced tests, in the Metis sample, did not differ significantly from those of conventional intelligence tests.   IVY

3031 **SILVER   ARTHUR ISAAC**
1966
FRENCH-CANADIAN ATTITUDES TOWARD THE NORTH-WEST AND NORTH-WEST SETTLEMENT, 1870-1890: FRENCH CANADIANS AND PRAIRIE SETTLEMENT, 1870-1890. M.A. Thesis. Department of History. McGill University. 323 pp. ,

Frequent references to Metis occur in this study of French-Canadian attitudes toward the settlement of Manitoba.   CCV

3032 **SLOBODIN   RICHARD**
1964
EXTERNAL RELATIONS OF THE MACKENZIE METIS. Unpublished paper delivered to 63rd Annual Meeting, American Anthropological Association. November, 1964. Available from National Library of Canada. 13 pp.

Emphasis in this paper is placed on the Mackenzie Metis and the fact that there has been no social transition from 1 generation to the next. The author suggests that the Mackenzie Metis as a whole exist between native and White worlds, and also between bush and urban worlds.   HCV

3033   **SLOBODIN   RICHARD**
1966
METIS OF THE MACKENZIE DISTRCIT. Ottawa: Canadian Research Centre for
Anthropology. St. Paul University. 175 pp.

Discussion of the Northern Metis is based on research done in 1962 and 1963 at Fort
Smith, Fort Resolution, Hay River, Fort Providence, Fort McPherson, Inuvik, Arctic
Red River, and Aklavik supplemented by observations during visits to the area in 1938-
39 and 1961. Family composition and relationships, kinship, occupation, education, and
life style are described.   CCV

3034   **SPAULDING   PHILIP TAFT**
1970
THE METIS OF ILE-A-LA-CROSSE. Ph.D. Thesis. Department of Anthropology.
University of Washington. 153 pp. Available from University Microfilms.

Observations derived from 9 months of fieldwork in Ile-a-la-Crosse, Saskatchewan, were
supplemented by statistical data procured from the Department of Natural Resources
local and branch offices and St. Joseph's Roman Catholic Mission, Ile-a-la-Crosse. Focus
is on the social organization of the community and White-Metis relations with employment, social interaction, cultural values, prestige-seeking activities, and deviance being
discussed.   CCV

3035   **STANLEY   GEORGE FRANCES GILMAN**
1963
LOUIS RIEL. Toronto: Ryerson Press. 219 pp.

Louis Riel's family life, religious beliefs, and political aspirations are accented in this
biography which also presents a history of the Metis cause in the Red River colony.   CCV

3036   **VALENTINE   V F**
1968
SOME PROBLEMS OF THE METIS OF NORTHERN SASKATCHEWAN. In
Canada: A Sociological Profile. W. E. Mann, ed. Toronto: Copp Clark. pp. 207-212.

Problems incumbent on the Metis community resulting from the C.C.F.'s implementation of the Saskatchewan Fur Marketing Service and the Block Conservation System are
analyzed. The former is a system of collective marketing, and the latter, a system for allocating land for trapping in the interest of wildlife conservation. The nearly doubling of
relief money paid to Metis, the loss of prestige on the part of Metis men by Metis
women, and the new generation of poorly trained and inefficient trappers, has forced
administrators to ask of themselves, (1) what are we as administrators really doing when
we define other people's problems, and (2) what are we really trying to do when we pre-
sume to be helping people?   DGW

3037   **VALENTINE   VICTOR F**
1966
THE FORGOTTEN PEOPLE. In People of Light and Dark. Maja van Steensel, ed.
Ottawa: Queen's Printer. pp. 110-114.

The history of the Canadian Metis is reviewed briefly and their status and associated problems in contemporary society are described with focus on northern Saskatchewan communities.   CCV

3038   **WOODCOCK   GEORGE**
1960
LOUIS RIEL: DEFENDER OF THE PAST. The Beaver 290(Spring):24-29.

This article is concerned mainly with the final phase of Riel's life, leading up to the last rising of the Metis along the North Saskatchewan River in 1884-1885. A brief consideration of the roots and results of the Red River insurrection of 1869-70 also led by Riel is presented.   IVY

Index to Bibliography

2597, 2598, 2600, 2601, 2602, 2603, 2604, 2605,
2606, 2607, 2608, 2609, 2611, 2613, 2614, 2615,
2616, 2617, 2618, 2619, 2620, 2621, 2622, 2624,
2625, 2626, 2627, 2628, 2629, 2630, 2631, 2632,
2634, 2636, 2637, 2638, 2640, 2641, 2642, 2643,
2645, 2646, 2647, 2648, 2649, 2650, 2651, 2652,
2653, 2654, 2655, 2656, 2657, 2658, 2659, 2660,
2661, 2662, 2663, 2664, 2665, 2667, 2668, 2669,
2670, 2671, 2672, 2673, 2674, 2675, 2676, 2677,
2678, 2679, 2680, 2681, 2682, 2683, 2684, 2685,
2687, 2688, 2689, 2690, 2691, 2692, 2936, 2994,
3025
BRITISH COLUMBIA ASSOCIATION OF
NON STATUS INDIANS
85
BRITISH COLUMBIA INDIAN ARTS AND
WELFARE SOCIETY
478
BRITISH NORTH AMERICA ACT
1234, 1237
BRULE
775
BUFFALO
70, 149, 665, 772, 778, 800, 828, 832, 834, 835,
844, 845, 1944, 1970, 2335, 2662, 2699, 2703,
2707, 2710, 2720, 2727, 2730, 2742, 2802
BUNGI
1215, 2019, 2332, 2333, 2335, 2336, 2337, 2338,
2339, 2340, 2341
BUNGI DIALECT
2019
CALDER-FRANK
185
CALUMET
1196
CANADIAN CATHOLIC CONFERENCE
610, 635
CANADIAN FRIENDS (QUAKERS)
638
CANADIAN FRIENDS (QUAKERS)
SERVICE COMMITTEE
606
CANADIAN INDIAN YOUTH COUNCIL
938
CANADIAN METIS SOCIETY
257
CANNIBALISM
806, 1354, 1705, 1798, 1815, 2374, 2577, 2815
CANOE-BARK
1934

CANOES
835
CANOES-BARK
900, 918, 1686, 1854, 2234, 2849
CANOES-BIRCH BARK
829, 882, 895, 2009
CANOES-DUGOUT
900, 2435, 2457, 2497, 2587, 2588
CAPILANO-JOE
2566
CAPTIVES-WAR
151, 789, 791, 815, 816, 817, 836, 1822, 2542,
2858, 2885, 2886, 2926, 2927
CARDINAL-HAROLD
137, 185, 328
CARIBOU
70, 1697, 1723, 1752, 1793, 1812, 1833, 1874,
1881, 1885, 1886, 1995, 1998, 2000, 2035, 2044,
2060, 2067, 2071, 2162, 2169, 2185, 2197, 2202,
2203, 2260
CARRIER
77, 92, 96, 104, 110, 249, 774, 824, 826, 854,
890, 1213, 1707, 2665
CARROTHERS COMMISSION
87, 88, 89, 90
CARTIER-JACQUES
2990
CARTOGRAPHY
122, 314, 802, 811, 846, 1885, 2838, 2840, 2986
CARVING
581, 918, 928, 2468, 2559
CARVING-ARGILLITE
2492, 2545, 2548
CARVING-BONE
922, 2435, 2460, 2469, 2471, 2502, 2522, 2541,
2543
CARVING-IVORY
897, 2522
CARVING-OTHER
2460, 2522, 2541
CARVING-ROCK
2554
CARVING-STONE
891, 903, 907, 922, 1345, 2435, 2442, 2456,
2460, 2469, 2471, 2502, 2540, 2541, 2543, 2545,
2549, 2550, 2555, 2623
CARVING-WOOD
557, 886, 888, 891, 893, 894, 896, 900, 904, 907,
915, 922, 1345, 2435, 2442, 2451, 2457, 2460,
2461, 2469, 2471, 2472, 2475, 2476, 2484, 2492,
2494, 2497, 2502, 2503, 2522, 2531, 2541, 2543,

Index to Case Law Digest

ABORIGINAL RIGHTS
1437, 1450, 1464, 1488, 1490, 1492, 1512, 1556, 1597

ADOPTION
1525, 1526, 1531

ANNUITIES
1481, 1489, 1491, 1650

BAND COUNCIL
1482, 1586, 1624

BAND FUNDS
1475, 1480, 1484, 1655

BILL OF RIGHTS
1435, 1449, 1451, 1487, 1532, 1578, 1595, 1618, 1630, 1632, 1640

BRITISH NORTH AMERICA ACT S. 109
1479, 1490, 1491, 1493, 1507, 1587, 1597, 1650

BRITISH NORTH AMERICA ACT S. 125
1505

BRITISH NORTH AMERICA ACT S. 129
1433

CANADA TEMPERANCE ACT
1545

CAUGHNAWAGA RESERVE
1642

CHILD WELFARE
1495

CIVIL RIGHTS OF INDIANS
1474, 1497, 1500, 1542, 1572, 1590, 1604, 1613

COMMERICAL TRANSACTION-ON RESERVE
1564

CRIMINAL LAW
1451, 1457, 1470, 1517, 1520, 1523, 1551, 1552, 1571, 1616

CROSS-CULTURAL PROBLEMS
1571

CUSTOMARY NATIVE PRACTICES
1470, 1517, 1520, 1525, 1526, 1530, 1531, 1614, 1649

CUSTOMS DUTIES
1648

DEBT
1442, 1446, 1455, 1511, 1541, 1543, 1548, 1574, 1575, 1584, 1588, 1593, 1596, 1602, 1607, 1610, 1612

DIVORCE-BY NATIVE CUSTOM
1470

ESKIMO
1524, 1527, 1528, 1532, 1533, 1641, 1652

ESTATES AND SUCCESSION
1472, 1547, 1589, 1594

EXPROPRIATION
1609

FREEDOM OF RELIGION
1433, 1622

GRAND RIVER NAVIGATION COMPANY
1655

GUARDIAN
1615

HALDIMAND DEED
1577

HALF-BREED
1419, 1440, 1445, 1476, 1477, 1481, 1518, 1522, 1535, 1629

HALF-BREED LANDS
1419, 1481, 1501, 1502, 1503, 1629

HUNTING AND FISHING-BY ESKIMO
1524, 1527, 1532, 1533, 1652

HUNTING AND FISHING-COLONIAL LAWS
1536

HUNTING AND FISHING-FEDERAL LAWS
1425, 1443, 1464, 1468, 1509, 1510, 1581, 1590, 1635, 1638, 1646, 1653

HUNTING AND FISHING-NATURAL RESOURCES TRANSFER AGREEMENT
1430, 1431, 1432, 1494, 1618, 1619, 1626, 1631, 1635, 1636, 1646, 1651

HUNTING AND FISHING-NO TREATY PROVISIONS
1437, 1443, 1464, 1468, 1471, 1510, 1549, 1590, 1600, 1601, 1652, 1659

HUNTING AND FISHING-OFF RESERVE
1425, 1431, 1432, 1437, 1464, 1509, 1510, 1536,

INDIAN ACT S. 89
1442, 1446, 1455, 1511, 1537, 1541, 1548, 1574,
1575, 1584, 1588, 1593, 1596, 1607, 1610, 1612

INDIAN ACT S. 90
1537

INDIAN ACT S. 93
1500, 1559, 1561

INDIAN ACT S. 94
1423, 1426, 1427, 1428, 1429, 1434, 1439, 1440,
1441, 1453, 1462, 1463, 1465, 1466, 1467, 1469,
1499, 1508, 1513, 1514, 1515, 516, 1518, 1521,
1522, 1534, 1535, 1539, 1540, 1550, 1554, 1558,
1560, 1565, 1566, 1580, 1591, 1605, 1623, 1625,
1634

INDIAN ACT S. 95
1420, 1422, 1435, 1449, 1529, 1632, 1640, 1657

INDIAN ACT S. 95(b)
1633

INDIAN ACT S. 97
1473, 1498, 1557, 1624, 1630

INDIAN ACT S. 103
1576

INDIAN AGENT
1506, 1523

INDIAN RAILWAY TICKET
1553

INDIAN RESERVE-INDIAN RIGHTS TO
1479, 1482, 1488, 1492, 1597

INDIAN RESERVE-RELOCATION OF
1478

INDIAN RESERVE-SURRENDER OF
1438, 1459, 1460, 1483, 1486, 1488, 1505, 1507,
1544, 1546, 1556, 1569, 1573, 1586, 1611, 1621,
1644, 1645, 1647, 1656

INDIAN STATUS
1418, 1419, 1440, 1445, 1481, 1487, 1522, 1535,
1550, 1578, 1592, 1629, 1641

INDIANS-OFF RESERVE
1435

JAY TREATY
1648

LABOR LAWS
1603

LIMITATIONS OF ACTIONS
1475

LIQUOR
1420, 1422, 1423, 1426, 1427, 1428, 1429, 1434,
1435, 1439, 1440, 1441, 1449, 1453, 1462, 1463,
1465, 1466, 1467, 1469, 1473, 498, 1499, 1506,
1508, 1513, 1514, 1515, 1516, 1518, 1521, 1522,
1528, 1529, 1534, 1535, 1539, 1540, 1545, 1550,
1554, 1557, 1 58, 1560, 1565, 1566, 1567, 1576,
1580, 1585, 1591, 1605, 1623, 1624, 1625, 1627,
1630, 1632, 1633, 1634, 1640, 1657, 1658

MARRIAGE-BY COMMON LAW
1519, 1614

MARRIAGE-BY NATIVE CUSTOM
1470, 1520, 1530, 1614, 1649

MEDICINE CHEST
1475, 1504, 1617, 1620

MIGRATORY BIRDS CONVENTION ACT
1638, 1646, 1653

NON-INDIANS AND LIQUOR
1423, 1426, 1427, 1428, 1429, 1434, 1439, 1440,
1441, 1453, 1462, 1463, 1465, 1466, 1469, 1473,
1499, 1506, 1508, 1513, 1514, 515, 1516, 1521,
1522, 1534, 1535, 1539, 1540, 1558, 1560, 1565,
1566, 1591, 1605, 1623, 1625

NON-INDIANS-ON RESERVE
1421, 1433, 1438, 1448, 1458, 1459, 1498, 1538,
1559, 1586, 1599, 1622, 1637

OKA RESERVE
1492

POLYGAMY
1517, 1520

PROPERTY-OFF RESERVE
1446, 1497, 1511, 1574, 1584, 1607, 1610, 1612

PROPERTY-ON RESERVE
1442, 1455, 1541, 1548, 1561, 1564, 1574, 1575,
1586, 1588, 1589, 1593, 1594, 1596, 1602, 1606,
1607, 1627, 1654

PROVINCIAL LAWS-OFF RESERVE
1420, 1422, 1432, 1437, 1438, 1453, 1467, 1474,
1496, 1497, 1504, 1528, 1536, 1537, 1555, 1565,
1568, 1570, 1572, 1575, 1585, 587, 1603, 1617,
1618, 1619, 1620, 1633, 1636, 1639, 1651, 1658

PROVINCIAL LAWS-ON RESERVE
1421, 1424, 1430, 1438, 1444, 1447, 1448, 1452,

1454, 1456, 1458, 1460, 1471, 1495, 1496, 1548, 1549, 1557, 1582, 1583, 1590, 598, 1599, 1627, 1628, 1637, 1643

PROVINCIAL MOTOR VEHICLE LEGISLATION
1424, 1436, 1447, 1579, 1583, 1628

REMOVAL OF MATERIAL FROM A RESERVE
1561, 1564

ROADS-ON RESERVE
1424, 1436, 1447, 1583, 1628

ROYAL PROCLAMATION OF 1763
1437, 1450, 1464, 1483, 1507, 1512, 1527, 1532, 1533, 1536, 1652, 1653, 1656

SCRIP
1476, 1477

SENTENCING OF INDIANS
1551, 1616

SIMCOE DEED
1577, 1590

SOVEREIGNTY OF INDIANS
1577

TAXATION
1448, 1458, 1461, 1501, 1505, 1537, 1544, 1556, 1563, 1569, 1598, 1599, 1608, 1610, 1621, 1648

TERMS OF UNION OF BRITISH COLUMBIA
1443, 1446, 1461

TERRITORIAL ORDINANCES
1657

TREATIES-EFFECT OF
1479, 1489, 1490, 1493

TREATIES-INTERPRETATION OF
1468, 1475, 1504, 1509, 1510, 1570, 1617, 1620

TREATIES-LEGAL FORCE OF
1475, 1480, 1491, 1536

TRESPASS
1433, 1445, 1459, 1485, 1538, 1562, 1579, 1586, 1622, 1654

TRUST OBLIGATION OF GOVERNMENT
1475, 1480, 1484, 1655

UNOCCUPIED CROWN LANDS
1619

UTILITIES
1608

WARD-INDIAN AS
1455, 1484, 1575, 1603, 1611, 1655

WATER-RIGHTS
1452, 1454

WINDIGO
1571